P9-DMT-588

# EAST AND SOUTHEAST ASIA

JAMES E. HOARE

# THE WORLD TODAY SERIES®

2022-2023

54TH EDITION

**James E. Hoare**

Dr. Hoare served in the British Diplomatic Service from 1969 until his retirement in January 2003. He holds a BA in history and a PhD in Oriental history from the University of London. He served in the British embassies in Seoul (1981–1985) and Beijing (1988–1991) and was in charge of opening the embassy in Pyongyang in the Democratic People's Republic of Korea (2001–2002). Since his retirement, he has become a regular broadcaster, mainly on things Korean, and has taught regularly at the School of Oriental and African Studies University of London, of which he is an Honorary Research Associate, and an Associate Fellow of the Asia Program of the Royal Institute of International Affairs in London (Chatham House). A former president of the Royal Asiatic Society Korea Branch, he was for several years chair of the British Association for Korean Studies.

He is the editor/author of a number of works, including *Japan's Treaty Ports and Foreign Settlements 1859–1899: Uninvited Guests in Meiji Japan* (1994); *Korea* (ABC-CLIO Bibliographies, vol. 204, 1997); *Embassies in the East: The Story of the British and Their Embassies in China, Japan and Korea from 1859 to the Present* (1999); *Historical Dictionary of the Democratic People's Republic of Korea* (2012); and *Critical Readings on North and South Korea* (3 vols., 2013). With his wife, Susan Pares, he has produced *Korea: An Introduction* (1988), *Conflict in Korea: An Encyclopedia* (1999); *Beijing* (ABC-CLIO Bibliographies, vol. 226, 2000); *A Political and Economic Dictionary of East Asia* (2005); *North Korea in the 21st Century: An Interpretive Guide* (2005); and *Korea: The Past and the Present* (2 vols., 2008). He lives in London.

In December 2021, he was awarded the Woodang Prize 2021 by the Seoul-based Woodang Foundation for Education and Culture.

First appearing as a book entitled
*The Far East and Southwest Pacific 1968*,
revised annually and published in succeeding years by

**Rowman & Littlefield**
An imprint of The Rowman & Littlefield Publishing Group, Inc.
4501 Forbes Blvd., Suite 200, Lanham, MD 20706
www.rowman.com

Copyright © 2022 by The Rowman & Littlefield Publishing Group, Inc.

Library of Congress Control Number Available

ISBN 978-1-5381-6588-1 (pbk. : alk. paper)
ISBN 978-1-5381-6589-8 (electronic)

Cover design by Sarah Marizan

Cartographer: William L. Nelson

Typography by Barton Matheson Willse & Worthington
Baltimore, MD 21244

The World Today Series has thousands of subscribers across the U.S. and Canada. A sample list of users who annually rely on this most up-to-date material includes:

Public library systems
Universities and colleges
High schools
Federal and state agencies
All branches of the armed forces & war colleges
National Geographic Society
National Democratic Institute
Agricultural Education Foundation
ExxonMobil Corporation
Chevron Corporation
CNN

# CONTENTS

**Mongolia's increasingly globalized capital city of Ulaanbaatar**  **Courtesy of Steven A. Leibo**

**Downtown Jakarta**

# ACKNOWLEDGMENTS

I took over the role of editor in 2020, responsible for the 53rd edition, dated 2020–2022. Although I have never met him, I am grateful for the work done by my precessor, Professor Stephen Leibo and his collegues, as listed in the last edition. I am in a somewhat different position, since I am a retired British diplomat and not a professional academic—although after retirement from the British Diplomatic Service in 2003, I did do some teaching on Korea, both North and South, at the School of Oriental and African Studies University of London (SOAS). I have had to rely much more on my own resources and so take full responsibilities for any inaccuaracies or errors in the current text.

Of course, I have many debts both to those who taught me at Queen Mary College, Univeristy of London from 1961 (now Queen Mary University of London, where I took my batchelor's degree in history, and then at SOAS, where I carried out research for my PhD in Japanese history under the late Professor W. G. Beasley. While I had hoped to become an academic, I failed to find a post and instead became a Research Office in the Foreign and Commonwealth Office in London. Curiously enough, most of my diplomatic career was spent working on things Chinese. These developments broadened my knowledge and, I hope, understanding, of East Asia as did my postings to Seoul, Beijing, and Pyongyang, as well as a three-year period when I headed the research section dealing with South and South East Asian affairs. I remain grateful to all my former colleagues, who guided me into the paths of government research and the ways of the Foreign Office, as well as to all those whom I met or worked with overseas, many of whom I am still in contact with. As well as teaching at SOAS in retirement, I enoyed a a ten or so year period as a radio and television commentator, mainly on North Korea, which also added to my knowledge and understanding.

Finally, I must thank the staff at Rowman & Littlefield, first on the Historical Dictionary series and, since 2020 on the World Today. They have been helpful and supportive and amazingly tolerant of my problems with American spelling and the wonders of modern technology.

J E Hoare jh3@soas.ac.uk
London, UK, February 21, 2022

Mongolia's international airport

Courtesy of Steven A. Leibo

UNIFORMS . . . lifesize clay warriors, 4,000 strong, somberly guard Chinese emperor Qin Shihuang Di's tomb near Xian, while Japanese baseball ("Yah-kyu") players thrill their fans in Tokyo

# East and Southeast Asia Today

The election of Joe Biden as United States' president has seen a steady move away from President Trump's hints of an American withdrawal from our region, following his "America First" isolationist tendencies of Donald Trump's administration were. Te administration's withdrawal from the Trans-Pacific Trade Partnership which subsequently reorganized itself without American participation was a particularly good example of that retreat.

Recent years have seen a dramatic transformation of the international circumstances of all the nations of the region as Chinese influence continues to grow. Indeed, China has dramatically gone from merely recovering from more than a century of stagnation to a nation increasingly asserting a formidable international footprint. From the growth of its increasingly ambitious Belt and Road Project, that has long sought to recreate and expand upon the ancient Silk Road, to Beijing's growing commitment in South America and Africa the weakened China of the last century is fast moving into the realm of history.

Moreover, China has made it clear that it is quite willing to engage in a "tit for tat" escalating tariff-based trade war with the United States. Unfortunately, given how economically linked the two nations are, the battle has had a negative impact on both their economies that perhaps will continue for decades to come. In this case, at least, the Biden administration seems content to continue the confrontation with China.

Even more dramatically, regional relationships appear to be transforming themselves as Moscow and Beijing continue to form closer diplomatic and military ties even as Japan and Russia have opened talks about finally resolving their World War II–era territorial disputes.

Meanwhile, North Korea, having finally accomplished its generation-long effort to develop its own nuclear and missile deterrence system, (despite the world's best efforts) has managed to carve out a new international role for itself, " as Kim Jong-un managed high profile meetings with leaders from America's Donald Trump to Singapore's Lee Hsien Loong and South Korea's Moon Jae-in. With the departure of Donald Trump from power, and the likely end of South Korea's engagement policy under a new administration after the March 2022 presidential election, coupled with the North's closure to outside contacts to prevent COVID, this phase has passed for the present.

Clearly, every day brings news of developments important for an understanding of the entire region. With that in mind, for more than four decades the annual publication of *East and Southeast Asia* has allowed readers to keep abreast of developments. True, with the arrival of the Internet and its plethora of online newspapers, materials never before available have become so at the click of a computer mouse. Thus, at least in theory, it is extraordinarily easy to "keep up."

Unfortunately, the availability of materials on day-to-day developments is still meaningless without the broader context necessary to understand those events. Thus, the goal of *East and Southeast Asia*, remains that of offering enough of the political, social, environmental, and economic background needed to understand those events.

**Tokyo by night**

Courtesy of Joel Z. Leibo

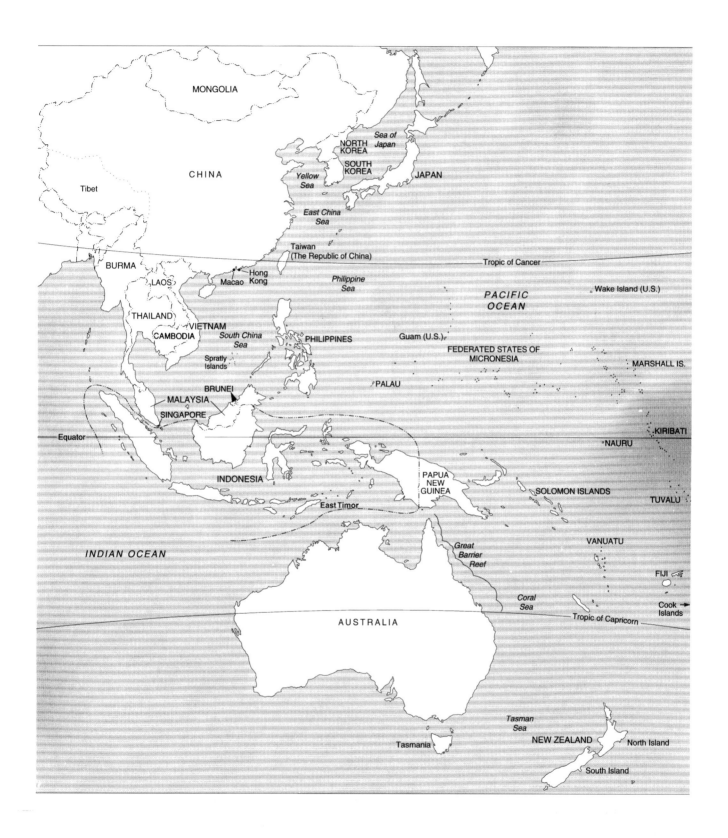

## A Diversity of People

The region discussed in this volume covers an enormous range of different ethnic and linguistic groups—from the Mongoloid communities of East Asia and the Caucasian immigrant communities of Australia and New Zealand to the heavily pigmented peoples of Micronesia who most closely resemble the aborigines of Australia. With the exception of a few countries like North Korea, almost every nation in the area includes many different ethnic and linguistic groups. While East Asians, Chinese, Japanese, and Korean are largely made up of people from the "Mongoloid" racial community they are sharply divided by their linguistic heritage.

Chinese, for example, is part of a Sino-Tibetan language group that looks somewhat similar in its written appearance, but is totally different from the languages spoken in Japan and Korea. Southeast Asia is even more diverse and has at times been called an "anthropologist's delight" in recognition of the extraordinary diversity of ethnic communities found there. Although most nations in Southeast Asia have a "dominant majority" ethnic community, almost all of them include both indigenous minority communities like the Montagnards of Vietnam and more recent ethnic communities, often made up of Chinese and South Asians, who immigrated to places other than their region of origin during the colonial era. The island communities of the Western Pacific themselves include a wide variety of peoples most notably divided into three groups, Polynesian, Melanesian, and Micronesian. More than a thousand different languages are spoken among them.

Although not often discussed in the West, many of these countries from East Asia to the Western Pacific have experienced considerable tensions between the majority and minority communities. In some parts of the region, people of Indian origin are regularly treated as second-class citizens, and the Chinese in places like Indonesia have had similar treatment. In Burma, now known as Myanmar, the efforts by the Burman majority to dominate the political life of the nation have led to decades of tensions and struggle with non-Burman peoples.

1

# Historical Background

**Lhasa, Tibet**

Courtesy of Steven A. Leibo

## Religious Beliefs

### Confucianism

The original Confucianism of early Chinese civilization was more a social philosophy than a religion—perhaps more like the Hellenic thoughts of Aristotle and Plato than the divine musings of the Hebrews across the Mediterranean. In fact, Confucius himself was not particularly interested in issues of the supernatural. For Confucius and his followers, what mattered was the world of human, and how they could best govern themselves.

Originating from a feudal elite society of blood nobility, Confucius nevertheless developed a new theory of nobility based on merit, rather than birth. How was that merit defined; by a single-minded commitment to nurturing the truly "noble heart."

Traditional Confucianism's core emphasis was on the family and hierarchy. This was reinforced by the belief that true stability was attained when everyone within a society understood the appropriate relations among people. How was that stability to be maintained? The traditional Chinese answer of course; by an extraordinary emphasis on the ability of education to elevate the soul of humanity.

Later Confucian thinkers, especially people like Mencius, further emphasized the necessity of the development of "virtue" specifically through the study of various writings from antiquity known eventually as the Five Classics. Over time, mastery of the material came to be the key to a successful career through the developing Chinese Civil Service Examinations that dominated the selection of elites during the last 1,000 years of traditional China's existence. As time went on, however, Confucianism was challenged by other more spiritual philosophical and religious traditions—like Daoism and Buddhism—and began to assimilate aspects of their more metaphysical orientation. Thus was born the Neo-Confucianism of later traditional history.

Although it has been generations since millions of Chinese males spent their lives preparing to pass the Confucian civil service exams, Confucian influence as a social philosophy remains tremendously strong in China. In fact, Confucianism, both as a religious and intellectual tradition and as an ongoing theory of social behavior, continues to be very influential. From China to Korea, from Taiwan to Japan, Confucianism remains influential not only among the millions of ethnic Chinese who live in the People's Republic, Singapore, and Taiwan, but also among those millions of others who live as Chinese minorities from the Philippines to Malaysia and Indonesia. Moreover, it remains important among many other societies whose people if not ethnically Chinese were nevertheless fundamentally influenced by Confucianism, even as they developed their own unique cultures. These include not only the Vietnamese and Koreans but also other more distant neighbors, like the Japanese, who did not share a common border with China.

Obvious examples of Confucian influence are easy to note. Despite the assaults on Confucianism under Mao Zedong, the Confucian priority given to education and the family remain strong in East Asia. Moreover, the strong sense of the group over the needs of the individual, while perhaps diminishing somewhat at the beginning of the 21st century, still figures prominently as a clear contrast to the Western preoccupation with the individual. Interestingly, Confucianism has been undergoing something of a more official revival in China in recent years. Confucian ceremonies are also performed in South Korea, while the devotion to education and the respect for those with education remains high throughout East Asia

### Buddhism

Buddhism remains one of the strongest religious traditions throughout East and

Southeast Asia. From Thailand to Vietnam, from Myanmar to China, Buddhism is present if not in the lives of everyone in the region, then as part of their cultural and architectural heritage. Even within the People's Republic, which saw so much energy directed against traditions like Buddhism in the 1960s, a revival has been going on. Emerging about the same time that Confucius lived, Buddhism was founded in Nepal by Gautama. It eventually became an extraordinarily influential tradition through much of Eastern Asia.

Given the vast differences between the traditions of South Asia and East Asia, it often required considerable modification of the originally rather pessimistic Buddhist message to assimilate into the generally optimistic Chinese environment. It actually was, in some ways, a protest against the teachings of Brahmanism, or Hinduism, which was then dominant in India. The Buddha, as Gautama is called, preached the message that beings moved through a series of lives in this world which was largely an experience of pain and suffering. Within Buddhism there is a deep belief that fate can be influenced by human efforts through the force of "Karma." A good person moves upward through successive existence to an ultimate reward. The greatest reward possible, according to this belief, was the attainment of Nirvana, a philosophically complicated concept that essentially postulated that a person who had attained "Nirvana" reached a state of individual nonexistence, that is often compared to the snuffing out of a flame which as a "practical" matter ended the process of constantly being reborn into a series of burdensome lives.

These teachings, which urged withdrawal from the world for meditation, created monastic communities in the ensuing centuries. The stress on personal and universal religious experience made this much more of a missionary religion than Hinduism and was thus more similar to Islam and Christianity in its core belief in the universality of its message.

The form in which Buddhism migrated to Southeast Asia is known as Hinayana ("the Lesser Vehicle"), or more recently, Theravada ("the Way of the Teachers") or simply, the Southern School of Buddhism. This school, which is closest to original Buddhism in its early years, had its major home on the island of Sri Lanka (Ceylon) which converted to Buddhism in the 3rd century B.C.

Theravada countries in Southeast Asia—Vietnam, Laos, Cambodia, Thailand and Burma—all have large communities of monks devoted to the daily practice of Buddhism. In recent times, these communities have been influential and increasingly active in national and political affairs. Although the Theravada Buddhists share the same central beliefs, there is no overarching system of central authority comparable to Vatican Catholicism that attempts to regulate the entire community. Almost every country has its own individual Buddhist sects.

Buddhism also spread north and northeast from India in the first centuries of the Christian era in the form known as Mahayana ("Greater Vehicle"), which entered Tibet, China, Korea, and Japan. This form of the religion places less emphasis on good works and monastic withdrawal for contemplation, and greater weight on elaborate scriptures and faith. The canon (authorized texts) was printed in China in the 10th and 11th centuries, using some 130,000 wooden blocks on which characters had been carved. It was widely

**Inside the Liu Rong Buddhist temple (built in 479 A.D.) in Guangzhou, China**

Courtesy of Miller B. Spangler

# Historical Background

followed in central Asia until almost eliminated by the growing influence of Islam.

Mahayana Buddhism became widespread in China in the first centuries of the modern era, during a period of considerable social disruption associated with the collapse of the Han (206–222 B.C.). It continued to grow in influence until it reached its height under the Tang dynasty (618–907). Thereafter, its official influence began to wane although it continued to be profoundly influential in the lives of ordinary Chinese.

Although at times Buddhists have suffered persecution in both Japan and Korea, the religion survived and is now flourishing in Japan and South Korea. Even in North Korea, there are a number of Buddhist temples, and supposedly attract worshippers.

A form of Buddhism developed in Tibet known as Tantrism, which was heavily influenced by a type of Hinduism that engaged in demon worship and varieties of magical practices. It still exists today, particularly in eastern Tibet, but has been largely replaced by another form known as Lamaism, or "The Yellow Sect" to distinguish it from Tantrism. This is a combination of a purer form of Buddhism similar to Mahayana with an elaborate monastic organization common to Theravada, but even more highly formalized. Lamaism, of which the Dalai Lama is the leading figure, spread to Inner and Outer Mongolia in the 16th century (see Tibet section for more details).

The teachings of Buddhism have changed over the centuries and have been modified by many varied external influences. It does not contain a formal universal hierarchy, as does Catholicism. It is in general more administratively decentralized in the fashion of traditions such as Protestantism, Judaism, Hinduism, and Islam.

### Naturalism

Long before the formal development of the major schools of Chinese thought, Confucianism, Taoism, and Buddhism, the Chinese had already developed an elaborate intellectual system. It covered ideas of governance (see Mandate of Heaven in the China section) to metaphysical ideas associated with the stability of the entire cosmic order—from the universe to each person's physical body. Chief among those ideas were the concepts of yin, yang, and qi.

Yin and yang are often difficult for Westerners to understand because they superficially resemble aspects of the Western idea of duality, of the idea of "good" and "evil." The resemblance, though, is

**Panda Research Center, Chengdu**    

purely superficial. In the West, this ancient idea, originally derived from the Persian religion of Zoroastrianism, involves a duality of forces in the universe, one evil, one good, that struggle over the fate of the universe and humanity.

Yin and yang are quite different. This Eastern version of duality is one of complementary opposites that need each other. Some things are associated with yin more than yang, but both are always present and vital for cosmic and personal stability. This distinction may appear minor but it has had a significant impact on how the two civilizations have viewed the world around them. An understanding of yin and yang are critical to an understanding of things Chinese, from philosophy to medicine. In the same vein, qi is another important aspect of this naturalist worldview.

According to Chinese tradition, every living thing possesses a sort of "vital element" that, in the case of humans, is drawn both from our parents and our environment. This qi, which is said to flow through the body, is considered to be absolutely vital to good health. It is the flow of qi that Chinese traditional physicians still attempt to manipulate with techniques like acupuncture and acupressure to heal patients. Thus, an understanding of issues like naturalism, yin and yang, and qi remain even today a vital part of the tools necessary to understand the enormous civilization that has so influenced most of the rest of East Asia.

### Daoism (Taoism)

Daoism (Taoism) is in many ways a complementary parallel to China's long Confucian tradition. Daoism, which was formalized at about the same time as Confucianism, is often portrayed as a clear contrast to Confucianism's obsession with how human beings in society should behave. Daoism is less social in its orientation and more interested in the individual's relationship with the natural and metaphysical world. A flavor of this tone is captured in the famous Daoist dictum for government that what was really important was keeping people's heads empty and their stomachs full. Overall Daoism is more personal and self-consciously contemplative than the social activism of Confucian practice. Daoism varies enormously from an association with a popular religion of magic and spirits to a very philosophical discussion of the relationship of beings to the universe. On a practical level, the early Daoism's interest in the search for elixirs of life brought to Chinese civilization an acute interest in nature, which continues to have a strong influence on contemporary Chinese food and medicine.

### Christianity

Although Christian missionaries have been active in Asia for centuries few people in the region have been influenced by any of its various sects. In China, for example, Christianity was often seen simply as an element of Western imperialism and rejected out of hand. Today, although Christianity is a vigorous tradition within the People's Republic, the actual numbers, given China's enormous size, are relatively insignificant. On the other hand, some of the countries covered by this text have been tremendously influenced by Christianity. The Philippines and Vietnam both developed large Catholic communities during the colonial eras. The Philippines today is almost exclusively Christian with the exception of the southernmost island of Mindanao where Islam remains dominant.

Among the East Asian nations, Korea is the most influenced by Christianity. Koreans first came into contact with Christians among the Japanese forces that invaded the country during the Imjin Wars between 1592 and 1598, but it was contacts with Christian missionaries in Beijing that led to the development of an indigenous Catholic coomunity in the late 18th century. Later, at the Vatican's insistence, French missionaries went to Korea. Because Christian beliefs clashed with Confucianism's principles, especially over the question of honoring one's ancestors, there were a series of savage persecutions that produced a large number of martyrs, including several French priests, and which continued until the "opening of Korea" from the 1870s onward. By that time, Protestant missonaries had also begun to arrive. During the 19th and early 20th centuries, Christian missionaries in Korea

often sided with the Koreans against the colonizing Japanese, thus linking Christianity to the emerging Korean nationalism. In South Korea, Christianity is a very influential tradition with millions of followers. While in theory, it is allowed in North Korea, the North Korean churches are widely viewed as a sham.

The Pacific Islands people are largely committed to the various Christian traditions. Christians are found widely throughout the region among those whose families were originally converted by the earliest Protestant and Catholic missionaries and, more recently, to new denominations ranging from Jehovah's Witnesses in Tahiti-Polynesia, Fiji and New Caledonia, and the Solomon Islands, to Mormons in Tonga and Western Samoa. The Anglo communities of New Zealand and Australia, made up as they are largely by immigrants from England, are, of course, largely Christian as well.

### Shinto

Shinto emerged in the earliest period of Japanese history, and originally was an animistic religion that gave human form to the various gods that rule the forces of nature. Although indigenous to the Japanese home islands, this religious tradition is in many ways similar to the animistic beliefs found among Southeast Asian and African groups. As in many traditional Native American beliefs, it embraces the sense that a "divinity" of sorts exists among many natural objects in nature

from beautiful trees to waterfalls. Shinto, a tradition that refers to the "Way of the Kami," puts emphasis on what might be called entities of "awe," the Kami that include myriad objects from ancestors to legendary heroic figures and natural phenomena. Especially important within the tradition is the belief that the Sun Goddess, Amaterasu, sent her descendants to earth to create the Japanese home islands. It was the association of the Yamato clan line with that tradition that became the basis of its claim to imperial power.

Unlike religions such as Buddhism and Christianity that developed very elaborate traditions of religious ritual and sacred texts, Shinto tended to be very much more loosely organized and was overshadowed in Japan by the arrival of Buddhism in the 6th century. As Mahayana Buddhism entered the islands, the two beliefs tended to influence each other. Thus, it was possible to profess the ideologies of both without feeling inconsistent.

Buddhism in Japan eventually split into numerous sects, and for several centuries Shinto beliefs were somewhat dormant, although not forgotten. In the late 19th and early 20th century, the Shinto heritage became the state religion; it was reemphasized that the emperor was a descendant of the Sun Goddess and possessed her divine powers. Although the imperial house had long been respected in Japan, the late 19th century development of a cult-like imagery around it was not a product of Japanese tradition, but rather part of the modernizing effort. It

Courtesy of Steven A. Leibo

# Historical Background

was believed by 19th century thinkers that Japan needed a "unifying element" to fully join the nation. Enhancing the symbolism of the emperor was thought the most appropriate way to do so. Thus, the imperial house was far more celebrated in the late 19th and early 20th century than it had been for centuries. In many ways it is helpful to think of this revival of Shinto as "State Shinto" in contrast to the more decentralized tradition of Japan's earlier history.

This revival corresponded with a rise of militarism in Japan, culminating with World War II. After defeat by the allies, Japan renounced the idea of the "divinity" of the Emperor. Shinto lost its official status. Ironically the supposed "imperial divinity" which Westerners found offensive about the Japanese system was only remarkable when viewed from the outside by Westerners bred in the traditions of monotheism. In Japan the spiritual aspects of the emperor had operated in a very different context for the Japanese.

### Islam

Although there is a mid-spread tendency to associate Islam with the Arab communities of the Middle East, the reality is that the largest communities of Muslims in the world are found in Asia and among a very wide variety of ethnic groups. Especially large communities of Muslims are found in South Asia, but they are also a very important religious community in East and Southeast Asia as well. From western China to the southern Philippines, from Malaysia to Indonesia (the largest Muslim nation in the world) Islam is very important to this region.

Islam, which emerged in the 7th century, is part of the enormously rich Middle Eastern monotheistic religious tradition that had earlier seen the development of Judaism and Christianity. Muhammad, a poor merchant from the Arabian Peninsula, developed the religion after experiencing what he called a revelation from the angel Gabriel regarding the Unity of God. As a tradition, Islam is a militantly monotheistic creed that requires giving charity to the poor and a life of regular daily prayer as well as, if at all possible, a pilgrimage to the holy places at Mecca in today's Saudi Arabia.

Although Islam is a growing movement within the United States, few Americans know much about it and would probably be surprised at how much of its theology is shared with both Christianity and Judaism. The tradition includes the idea of a heaven and resurrection and a system of predestination. Seeing itself as a clear continuation of the line of revelation that had begun with the Patriarch Abraham,

Muhammad revealed himself to be the "final prophet" in a long tradition that extended back through both the Old and New Testaments. Basically, Muhammad taught that the Judeo-Christian biblical texts are not complete. Thus, the Islamic movement embraced a new document, one, said to have been dictated by God. That text is known as the Qur'an (Koran). This new sacred document, which makes regular reference to biblical personalities and events, is distinctly influenced by the Judeo-Christian traditions which had preceded it.

Sometimes stories are derived from the bible texts and modified with startling results. For example, the story of the fall from Eden is also found in the Qur'an, yet in the Islamic version, the female, Eve, is not blamed for the transgression against God, a very thought-provoking modification, especially for those who think Islam can be easily categorized on issues of gender. The text of the Qur'an itself includes 114 chapters that Muslims

believe confirms and clarifies the revelation received earlier by the Christians and Jews.

Like many religions, Islam spread through a complicated series of developments that ranged from militant conquest to merchant activities and mystical religious missionaries. Today it is found widely in parts of Southeast Asia and western China. Small Muslim communities exist in Japan and South Korea, and theoretically, in North Korea. In both Japan and South Korea, there are estimated to be around 100,000 Muslims, but the majority are foreigners. Historically, there were links because of trade with Japan and Korea, but today's Muslim communities are of recent origin. Tokyo had the first Japanese mosque, completed in 1938. In South Korea, it was contact with Turkish forces during the Korean War (1950–53) that led to the first converts. Later, some South Korean workers in the Middle East converted in the 1970s and early 1980s. The first mosque opened in Seoul in 1976

**Woman with bound feet**

and there are now mosques in many major cities. The only mosque in North Korea is in the Iranian embassy.

The resurgence of militant Islam in the Middle East and northern Africa has had its effect in such Southeast Asian countries as Indonesia and Malaysia. Here, it has taken the form of increased wearing of the traditional dress, stricter dietary rules, and the establishment of Muslim banking operations. Though Islam is more strictly adhered to in Malaysia, religious resurgence in that country or in any other part of Southeast Asia does not usually approach the fervor which is found today in the Middle East. Until recently few of the Muslim states in the region—Brunei, Indonesia, Malaysia, or the Philippines (the latter has only a small Muslim minority) had seen the extensive level of Islamic militancy experienced elsewhere. Nevertheless, such tendencies have grown considerably in recent years and have become a significant factor in public affairs from Thailand to Indonesia.

## Women in Traditional Asia

Although until recently women have lived in few societies that have afforded them even a semblance of equality with men, the women of Asia have often been particularly challenged by the limitations of their own unequal status. Nevertheless, our region is large and it is difficult to make generalizations. In some traditional societies and especially hierarchical societies like those dominated by Confucianism, which has had such an important influence throughout much of the region, women are regarded as decidedly inferior to men. As elsewhere, they were commonly less valued both as infants and as adults. Female babies were less likely to be nurtured when young and more frequently experienced infanticide than males. They were raised to serve as a wife for a male chosen by others (if they were lucky). Too often, in times of financial distress, daughters found themselves sold into virtual sexual slavery by their parents.

The specific nature of their unequal status has varied widely from region to region and from period to period. In China, for example, it appears that women were more influential early on and that their status deteriorated around the 8th century A.D. By about the 11th century the horrendously painful practice of foot binding, that is, of forcing the female child's foot into an artificially tiny shape, had emerged, a practice that would cause immense suffering among Chinese women

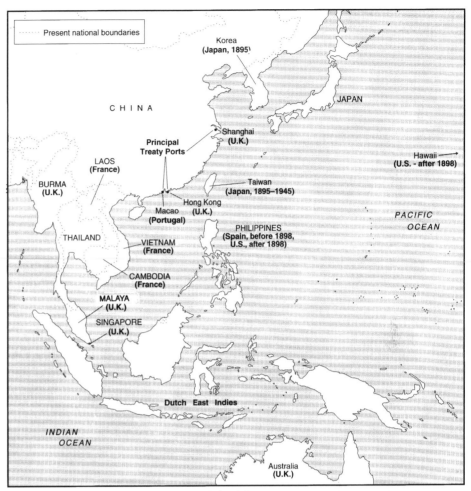

Colonial era

until the 20th century. Elsewhere though, the status and circumstances were quite different. In early Japan, women appear to have been much more important than their latter status suggests and imperial women of the court, individuals like Lady Murasaki, are credited with creating the modern form of the novel, most notably in works like the *Tale of Genji* written around 1000 A.D. In Korea, women seem to have enjoyed a relatively free life before the beginning of the Yi dynasty in 1392 and the adoption of strict Neo-Confucian principles. From that time, women lost their earlier right to a measure of independence, which persisted into the 20th century.

In Southeast Asia, peasant women remained much more important than their peers in either East Asia or South Asia and played an important role in the local economies. In places like Vietnam, whose elite was especially influenced by Confucianism, the peasant women's lives remained much less constricted than the elite women of the Confucian aristocracy. And among the latter, women played a more significant and respected role than they did in Vietnam's giant neighbor to the north.

## The Impact of the West

One of the most dramatic aspects of modern world history was the enormous movement of colonialism and imperialism that saw the various Western nations spread their influence and direct administrative control over a large percentage of the globe. From a period running from approximately 1500 through the early 20th century, the various Western powers, and eventually Japan, gained control over much of the world. Only a few nations remained outside of their control. In Africa the ages-old empire of Abyssinia, today's Ethiopia, managed to resist an Italian effort at conquest in 1896 and in Southeast Asia the kingdom of Siam, today's Thailand, survived albeit hemmed in by English and French colonies on either side.

It was that world of colonial and imperial control that brought the globe into the 20th century, and much of the 1900s, dealt with the reversal of that process as individual national communities eventually found their way to national freedom from colonial administrations. East and Southeast Asia were not exempt from this global

# Historical Background

A Chinese "opium den" in 1898

phenomenon and in fact, they were part of the region whose products had originally attracted the 15th-century Europeans at the dawn of the modern colonial age.

The countries of early modern Western Europe, especially Spain, Portugal and the Netherlands, tried to reach East Asia and the Western Pacific in order to acquire the profits from the extraordinarily lucrative spice trade, to gain converts to Christianity, and to acquire new territories for their respective governments. Especially significant in those early years were the Iberians, adventurers from Spain and Portugal, who had also led the efforts in the Western Hemisphere.

Ferdinand Magellan, a Portuguese in the service of Spain, was the first to lead Europeans to the region. He was killed in the Philippines in 1521. Half a century later Spain, operating from its bases in the New World, began to colonize the Philippines, which it eventually held for three centuries. In the 16th century, Portuguese explorers, traders, and missionaries spread similarly from the Indian Ocean to Southeast Asia and the coast of southern China. They were not strong enough however to make much of an impact on the region, and most of their holdings soon fell to the Dutch.

The Dutch East India Company was the strongest European influence in East Asia and the Western Pacific in the 17th

century. Its main theater of operations was the Dutch (or Netherlands) East Indies (now Indonesia), the richest in the region in the resources then in most demand in Europe (spices, coffee, etc.). Although the Dutch government eventually took direct control of the East Indies from the Dutch East India Company in the early 19th century, its rule was distinctly paternalistic and did little to develop the islands from either an economic or a political point of view.

The British impact on the region was less than they had in the Indian Ocean and South Asia, where they built up their enormous empire in India, but it was still significant. In Southeast Asia, the British colonial presence began first in Burma. For the British, expanding control was usually a response to growing commercial interests. In Burma, territorial disputes and issues of sovereignty arose in the late 18th century. Anglo-Burmese relations deteriorated until 1823, when British forces captured Rangoon. By the end of the 1860s, the British had integrated all of the Burmese provinces into British Burma and into the Indian empire.

By 1826, they had established what was known as the Straits Settlements along the coast of Malaya (today, Malaysia). These settlements consisted of the island of Penang, just off Malaya's north coast, Malacca, formerly a Dutch possession on the

central coast, and Singapore at the southern tip of the Malay Peninsula. Over the next 50 years their control extended over all of Malaya. They obtained vast quantities of tin from the interior and commerce from the Straits Settlements. An Anglo-Dutch Treaty of 1824 recognized British dominance along the Malay coast and also acknowledged Dutch interests to the south. This resulted in the effective splitting up of the old Malay world. The Dutch eventually established their control over all of Sumatra and Java, and became the colonial masters of the future Indonesia. The British controlled Malaya and Singapore until their independence.

In the 19th century the British East India Company had also become a major commercial force along the South China coast, its main interest being Chinese tea, silk, and porcelain. Merchants brought opium, usually bought from the Company in India, to the South China coast and sold it in defiance of an official ban. Machine-made British textiles eventually became a major Chinese import in the 19th century, especially after the British East India Company lost its legal monopoly of its share of the China trade early in the century.

The British government used armed force at intervals to compel China to lower its barriers to expanded foreign trade (including opium imports) and residence (including missionary activity). These pressures eventually culminated in the famous "Opium Wars" of the early 19th century and resulted in a series of unequal treaties with the Chinese that saw Westerners establish themselves along the China coast in a series of "treaty ports" which were outside of formal Chinese control.

Although the United States had been late to enter the competition for empire in the Pacific, it eventually became very involved there. By the mid-19th century, the United States had established itself on the American West Coast and had begun the effort to extend its influence into the Pacific. The Hawaiian Islands came under American control in 1898.

Meanwhile, by the late 19th century, a number of educated Filipinos were moved by modern nationalist ideals to declare independence from Spain and cooperate briefly with the United States in expelling the Spanish during the Spanish-American War of 1898. Unfortunately for them, after the defeat of Spain, the United States proceeded to take over the Philippines for itself. After crushing a spirited Filipino resistance, the U.S. set up a reasonably efficient colonial regime and did a good deal to prepare the Filipinos for self-government, but like the other colonial powers in the region it did not qualitatively develop the economy, which remained essentially an extractive (mining) and plantation one.

Earlier, the U.S. had, beginning in the mid-19th century, spearheaded the western entry into Japan. In contrast to many other communities in what became the colonial world, the Japanese, were much better able to control the process, and Japan never became a colony of the West. In effect, in attempting to avoid the fate of so many other Asian peoples, Japan decided to dramatically transform its society. Thus, it borrowed from the West (mostly technology and organization) and combined it with the essentials of its own culture. In the process, Japan became a military and imperial power strong enough to defeat China (in 1894) and Russia (in 1905) and itself emerge as a major colonial power with control over the Chinese island of Taiwan and the Korean peninsula.

Certainly not content to be left behind by their colonial rivals, France was involved in Southeast Asian colonialism. The Treaty of Saigon of 1862 established the French colony of Cochin China in southern Vietnam. The conflict leading to this treaty was in response to several decades of tension as a result of inroads into Vietnamese society by French Catholicism. The French seemed to be as much interested in the spread of their religion as the potential for economic gain. Especially important, in the minds of the French, was the necessity of keeping up with their British rivals. French control of Cambodia and Laos followed and, with Vietnam, became French Indochina. The Laotians and Cambodians were more favorably disposed toward the French, having been under the authority of both Siam and Vietnam previously. For Vietnam, the period of French domination was culturally much more difficult.

Remarkably, even though it was sandwiched between the British colonies of Burma and Malaya and the French in Indochina, Siam (now Thailand) was able to survive under its own monarchy without being colonized by any European power. This was partly because the British and French were more interested in penetrating Southwest China from their bases in Southeast Asia than in colonizing Siam and because they both saw the benefit of Siam as a buffer between their respective territories. Siam also benefited from a highly talented monarchy that earlier saw the need to learn about western institutions and governing methods. When the British did come, the Siamese showed considerable diplomatic skill in meeting the challenge.

An important product of western colonial rule in Southeast Asia was the influx (from about 1850 to 1920) of large numbers of Chinese immigrants, driven by poverty and chaos at home and drawn by the economic opportunities created by colonialism. These "overseas" Chinese have tended to be resented by the indigenous peoples and have never been allowed a share of real political power (except in Singapore, where they are the majority), but their economic activity and influence have been very great.

Major political and military trends of the 20th century, culminating in Japan's launching of World War II in the Pacific (see Japan), were to sweep away Western colonial rule in Southeast Asia, and make its restoration after the war a practical impossibility. As we shall see, during the postwar era, colony after colony emerged from Western control although some anti-colonial struggles, like that of Vietnam, were to become particularly bloody as anti-colonialist momentum became entwined with the struggles of the Cold War.

The islands of the Western Pacific were no exception to this process. Even as they were among the first communities absorbed into the Western colonial empires, many of them have only recently gained their autonomy. A few, like New Caledonia, still remain as colonies.

## Nationalism, Communism, and Revolution

One of the most predictable results of Western colonialism was the emergence of an organized resistance to that control. Not surprisingly the effort to reject imperialism eventually became a fundamental part of the struggle for Asia's modern identity. But initially Western political control over colonial Asia seemed unshakable, and there was thus little basis for the emergence of such nationalism. When Japan defeated Russia in 1905, however, the myth that the Western powers were invincible was shattered.

Japan also showed by its example that it was possible, however difficult, for an Asian country to modernize itself along the lines of Western nations. During the brief period that it controlled substantial portions of Southeast Asia, Japan weakened the prestige of the colonial powers to the point where it would be all the more difficult for them to reestablish themselves in the region after the war.

Next to the influence of the West itself and that of Japan's successes, the third great external influence on the emergence of modern Asian nationalism was the example of Soviet Russia. Before 1917 Marxism had almost no following in the area, but many Asian leaders became impressed with the seemingly rapid success of Lenin's Bolsheviks in seizing power within Russia in 1917. Of even greater importance was the loudly declared determination to modernize Russia along socialist lines, and to help the people of the non-Western world to throw off alien influence. The communism of Marx, prescribed for industrial nations of Europe and America, was billed as the medicine that would allegedly cure the ills of the poor, non-Western countries of Asia.

Lenin attracted great attention with his theory that the main obstacle to progress in the non-Western world was Western "imperialism"; he urged that local nationalists, supported by Soviet Russia, could make progress toward expelling this imperialism. This would be, according to Lenin, a preparation for the day when "proletarian" parties, in other words, communist parties, could emerge and seize power. The combination of the concept of imperialism, the exploitation of existing nationalism, and the triumph in Russia

# Historical Background

of a communist party had an enormous influence in Asia as well as elsewhere in the world. These ideas became part of the mental equipment of many, although by no means all, Asian nationalists, whether or not they consider themselves communists. Stated otherwise, many Asian nationalists adopted some communist ideas and techniques without becoming communists—or for a time found it politically useful to act as though they had.

The result was often a complex alignment of nationalist and communist elements, in which it is often difficult to see where the nationalistic spirit ends and the communist aims begin. Ho Chi Minh was a member of the Communist International and the founder of the Vietnamese Communist Party but he was also a committed Vietnamese nationalist. Unlike the situation in Eastern Europe where communists and nationalists were often bitter enemies for most of the 20th century, the dynamics of anti-colonial struggles in much of the world often saw the two groups not only closely aligned but united in the personalities of many of the anti-colonial leaders. Unfortunately this reality was often misunderstood by Western leaders and analysts, who were often far better trained in the politics of Europe than Asia.

Anti-colonial movements began to assume importance in the colonies of Asia about 1920. The spread of Western education and political ideas, the limited measure of self-government granted by the colonial powers, the influence of Woodrow Wilson's doctrine of self-determination—the idea that every people has the right to choose the form of government under which it will live—and the Bolshevik Revolution in Russia, all played parts in the spread of nationalism.

The Chinese communities living in Asian countries other than their homeland (the "overseas Chinese") were stimulated to nationalist activity by the revolutionary forces then at work within China, but usually preferred a continuation of Western political rule to the possibly oppressive rule of the native majorities where they lived. Non-Chinese nationalists usually resented the Chinese for their hard-earned wealth and economic influence, to the same degree that they also opposed the political control of the Western powers. As a result, their agitation was usually directed against both groups of outsiders.

Prior to World War II, there were no nationalist movements in Southeast Asia able to challenge the well-armed colonial governments. Nationalists were unable to gather sufficient support for the independence cause until the outbreak of the war changed the dynamics of the entire region. As will be seen in the individual national state sections, the combination of the Japanese temporary occupation of the region and the weakening of the colonial powers made a complete reestablishment of the former Western colonial world in East and Southeast Asia simply impossible. Certainly in some areas, like Indonesia and Vietnam, the colonial powers attempted to reestablish their power but each in turn was eventually stymied in the face of the worldwide anti-colonial momentum. The age of formal colonies had passed. Only the rise of the Cold War in the late 1940s made this trend somewhat less certain as many nationalist and economic struggles became entwined with the politics of Soviet/American rivalries.

Communist challenges arose in the Philippines, in the form of the Huk rebellion in the early 1950s; in Malaya, under the "emergency" declared from 1948 to 1960; and in Indochina and Indonesia. Burma, Thailand, and even Singapore also experienced communist activities. In Indonesia, the movement was strongest in Central Java. The Indonesian Communist Party met its bloody demise in 1965 when it was destroyed by the Indonesian military under Suharto whose regime continued to maintain stability under an authoritarian government until 1998.

Presently, Vietnam is the only surviving nominally communist regime in Southeast Asia, and that will be increasingly debatable as reforms move ahead. Laos no longer qualifies as a genuine Marxist state. In Laos, as in other nations of the region, the military has emerged particularly important.

Nevertheless, communism was often an essential ingredient in the emerging nationalism of the region. In some cases, it forced colonial and then newly independent governments to address social problems that they might have otherwise ignored. In contrast to Eastern Europe, communism still remains a vital if evolving force. The tensions of the old Cold War have dimmed in East Asia much more slowly than they have in Europe.

## Women in Modern East and Southeast Asia

Along with many women of the Western World, the women of the East, Southeast Asia, and the Western Pacific have often made enormous strides during the 20th century. Although the dominant figure as the century began was a woman, the famous Cixi, the dowager empress, most women in China labored under both the physical pain of foot binding and the limitations of their educational and career possibilities. Yet within the first quarter century not only was foot binding outlawed and eventually suppressed, but those years saw women in large numbers begin to gain higher education and to take part in political activism as shown in their role in the famous May Fourth Movement. When the communists came to power in 1949 one of their first moves was to legislate improvements in the lives of women that, if not creating a society of equality, have much improved the lives of millions of Chinese women.

In Japan, the century began with a few women striving to establish their own political and literary activities and more often ending up in trouble with the conservative governments of the time. Nevertheless, Japanese women gained the vote as a result of the changes brought about during the American Occupation of Japan and the end of the century even saw a woman emerge for a time as the head of one of the major Japanese parties, the Japanese Socialist Party.

Throughout the world the development of better contraceptive devices and the growing perception that women need to be educated in order to contribute to the economic lives of their families has also spurred improvements in many areas of East and Southeast Asia. Not surprisingly the women of the more urban classes have gained the most from these changes while poorer women are less likely either to have the finances, access, or education necessary to take advantage of the new technologies available for family planning. In some areas, like the Philippines, where the Catholic Church is influential, there is considerable opposition to birth control.

Politically the single most important element to affect the lives of women of the region was probably the emergence of nationalism as a driving force. In many regions, especially in places like Vietnam, women played important roles in the anti-colonial struggles of the postwar era. Moreover, in recent years, women activists have been especially involved in encouraging democratic growth in the region. Corazon Aquino emerged triumphant in the struggle that saw the end of the Marcos dictatorship in the Philippines and elsewhere in the region, most notably in Burma, where Aung San Suu Kyi has led the democratic opposition. During 1996 Megawati Sukarnoputri the daughter of the late Indonesian ruler Sukarno, attempted (unsuccessfully) to challenge the continuing dictatorship of Suharto. By mid-1999 she had become vice president and eventually emerged as Indonesia's first female president. Meanwhile, the Philippines have had their second female president, Gloria Macapagal Arroyo, while in both Taiwan and South Korea women have held the office of president.

Of course, the success of these women, as often elsewhere, has also been tied to their relations with previous generations of successful male family members who were themselves political leaders. That trend continues to the present. For example, in South Korea, the daughter of the former leader, Park Chung-hee, was elected the nation's first female president. In Thailand, Yingluck Shinawatra, the sister of the controversial former Prime Minister Thaksin, served as prime minister.

Despite these changes, real improvements in the lives of women have never been even or routine across the region. In some areas like China where recent economic liberalization has at times given more discretionary power to families and individual factory managers, we have seen the emergence of more traditional values regarding the worth of daughters than was experienced under the height of socialist control. These new freedoms have sometimes actually worked against women's rights. Elsewhere a religious backlash against Western secularism has also challenged those gains.

## From Postcolonialism to Globalization

As the new states of East and Southeast Asia began to emerge after the demise of colonialism, hopes were high, especially in the West that economically vibrant western style capitalist democracies would emerge. In fact, many new states began their existence as free countries using models borrowed from the Western liberal democracies that had originally colonized them.

Today Singapore and Malaysia—the latter to a diminishing extent—survive as single-party-dominated systems while Thailand, after years of military domination, appeared for a time to be evolving toward a much more open democracy. Recently that evolution seemed to backslide toward the sort of one-party "guided democracy," common elsewhere, at least until the Thai military once again intervened. It remains unclear how real a blow to Thailand's democratic momentum recent events will be as the situation remains fluid. On the other hand, the Philippines, and even more recently Indonesia, have returned to the democratic fold after decades under dictatorship.

In what became known as the East Asian Newly Industrialized Countries (NICs), such as Taiwan and South Korea, extended periods of strongman government lasted until the late 1980s. Although the American occupation authorities re-established Japan's 1920s-era parliamentary

system, it was until quite recently largely governed by the combination of a single party (The Liberal Democratic Party) and an especially powerful bureaucracy. Only in recent years has it moved toward becoming a more established two-party political system.

Economically, after the Second World War, the hope was to see the region smoothly recover from the devastation of the war. Sadly, that was not the case. Their economies were weakened by the anti-communist struggles of the era, wars in Korea and Vietnam, and related struggles like those in the southern Philippines. The region's natural economic structure was also undermined by the turmoil that engulfed China during the first decades after the People's Republic emerged in 1949.

Of course, the communist states initially embraced a system of single-party domination over their countries' economic and political life. Nevertheless, by the late-1970s in China and the mid-1980s in Vietnam, political decisions were made that led their peoples farther and farther from

the communist command economies that had once dominated their lives.

In fact, by the late-20th century, China in particular had largely traded the central planning of communist economic systems for a vibrant and more mixed economy that included very significant levels of private capitalist activity. However, the rejection of communist economics was not paralleled by an equally impressive move toward more open political systems. Nevertheless, as people found themselves less economically dependent on the state, their lives were often increasingly freer.

If the immediate postwar years were not very successful in establishing more democratic governments and economically open capitalist systems, the region's more recent record is much more promising. As we enter more deeply into the 21st century, East and Southeast Asia, so recently an area in constant turmoil, has emerged as an extremely dynamic part of the world. The Industrial Revolution that transformed Western Europe a century ago and has now dramatically hit East and Southeast Asia has not only radically

**Street food vendor, Tien Shui, China**

# Historical Background

changed the economic life of its citizens but raised their educational and political aspirations.

Most important has been the role East and Southeast Asia have played in the phenomenon of globalization that was so obviously transforming the planet by the early 21st century. In fact, it has probably impacted Asia more than almost anywhere else—in both positive ways and negative ways.

"Globalization" is the term that refers to the increasing integration of the world, particularly economically. It has been a phenomenon particularly nurtured by the combination of lowered legal barriers to international trade, the acceleration of international communication through such vehicles as the Internet, and dramatically faster and lowered cost for international transport of manufactured goods.

The combination of the above made it possible for many of the region's less developed countries to transform themselves economically by placing their primary emphasis on exports while attracting foreign investors who, in the 1990s, poured huge amounts of money into the region in search of lower production costs and higher financial returns. At least initially, East and Southeast Asia's movement into the global marketplace seemed mostly without great costs.

In the ensuing years national and personal incomes often rose substantially while their cities began increasingly to resemble the ultramodern skylines of many long developed nations. If Japan had initially led the way during the 1960s and 1970s, by late century nations from Thailand to South Korea and Indonesia where experiencing similarly impressive growth rates and the emergence of new and urbanized middle classes. Unfortunately, the price of such growth became more obvious when the combination of over-heated construction markets and poorly timed liberalization of their economic markets (encouraged by the International Monetary Fund) caused many to fall into a deep economic slump as the Asia's economic crash set in during late-1997.

For a time East and Southeast Asia's recession seemed to destroy the momentum of decades of growth. For many it would take years to recover. Nevertheless, by 2007 most of the region from Malaysia to South Korea was back on track. For the largest economy of the area, China, the decision to reject communism for a major role in the newly globalized world economy was transforming the nation faster than any other in world history. More importantly, that decision helped China develop the necessary economic resources to confront successfully the challenges of the more recent economic downturn that hit in late 2008.

Not surprisingly, given all the economic changes, authoritarian regimes have been more and more challenged in their efforts to dominate national political life. From South Korea to Taiwan and Indonesia new leadership has been elected democratically with the support of more politically involved middle classes, the very middle classes required and nurtured by economic changes. Even the seemingly all-powerful Communist Party of China has seen its authority challenged in ways unimaginable only a few years ago, although under Xi Jinping, who has been China's leader since 2012, there has been a growing reassertion of state and party control.

How these economic and political changes will ultimately transform the entire region is only just beginning to become clear. What is certain is that the entire region will play a much more significant role in the global arena in the 21st century than it did during the 20th and that the global challenge caused by humanity's prolific burning of fossil fuels will be a major aspect of that future.

# Asia and the Climate Crisis

*By Steven A. Leibo*

An earlier version of this article appeared in the Journal, *Education about Asia*, reprinted with permission of the Association for Asian Studies (footnotes are available online at Leibo's World Watch and in hard copy with the January 2011 of *Education about Asia*). For more specific information on the individual nations see the specific chapters devoted to each country.

If life were fair, Asia would not have to deal with the climate crisis at all. After all, its population per capita emits significantly less greenhouse enhancing gases like $CO_2$ than the Western countries. Moreover, despite recent growth, it has not been industrialized nearly as long as Western Europe and the United States. That reality is especially significant considering that what really matters with the longer lasting atmospheric gases is the cumulative impact of decades of industrialization ($CO_2$ can last over 100 years in the atmosphere).

Japan is the only Asian country with a relatively lengthy history of pumping $CO_2$ into the atmosphere. The United States, in contrast to most Asian countries, itself long industrialized and physically enormous is and remains the cumulative winner of humanity's unknowing and accidental disruption of the earth's heat balance and the subsequent dramatic build-up of planet-warming greenhouse gases.

The original approach to international climate negotiations overtly recognized the historical differences in emissions by

**Great Buddha at Kamakura, Japan (built in 1252)**

12

exempting developing nations like China and India from the effort. At that time, the approach certainly seemed to make sense. Then as now, the average Asian used significantly fewer fossil fuel based energy sources and their nations were still trying to catch up with the living standards of the West. It would not have been fair nor were they likely to agree to retard their own development simply because the West had already messed up the global atmospheric heat balance.

## A Growing Sophistication of Knowledge

That initial approach came before a more sophisticated science of climate change had emerged. Since then one thing has become obvious. Asia had already become an important source of the problem long before China passed the United States as the largest annual emitter of greenhouse gases, and even more recently according to the International Energy Agency, emerged as the largest single national energy user on the planet.

Moreover, due to the massive amounts of carbon dioxide released when forests are destroyed, Indonesia's long burning of their tropical forests had made them among the top three national emitters of greenhouse gases. The cumulative effect of the rising smoke of small cooking fires and the other fossil fuel based exhausts throughout South Asia has deposited massive amounts of what is known as black soot aerosols on the Tibetan glaciers. Often called "black carbon" many scientists believe this very dark material is facilitating Himalayan glacial melt by augmenting the mountains' heat absorbing properties rather than reflecting sunlight as ice usually does.

Even more recently, as China and India opened their national economies successfully enough to enter the new technology-driven era of economic globalization, it has become abundantly clear that what happens in Asia is an essential factor in confronting climate change. Today an increasingly developed Asia represents one third of the global emissions of greenhouse gases. Still, no one seriously expects Asia to hold back its own economic development to confront a problem largely caused by Westerners. It has become obvious to regional national leaders that Asia's economic growth must be decoupled from future increases of greenhouse gas emissions. It is not just a question of Asia's growing responsibility for the problem. Asia's own development goals cannot be accomplished, if the different nations of the region find themselves not advancing

economically but simply trying to respond to a changing global climatic circumstance that will find them particularly vulnerable.

## Asia's Special Vulnerability to Climate Change

Humanity may be upsetting the earth's heat balance and changing long familiar climate patterns globally. Nevertheless, that does not mean each region will be impacted equally. Some communities will probably experience relatively positive impacts while others a much more dire fate. Russia's vast and terribly cold northern Siberian plains would most likely be improved by a more general warming while at the other end of the spectrum many South Pacific nations like Tuvalu will see their very existence threatened.

Unfortunately, much of Asia is likely to fit into the category of the especially stressed regions as dramatic climate change continues to unfold. The most immediate impacts of climate change have already begun in Asia; from the increasingly powerful storms hitting Southern China, South and Southeast Asia to the drying out of north central China. The vast Mongolian Gobi Desert's rapid expansion is significantly challenging the lives of farmers in both Mongolia and China. Within Indonesia over the last several years, farmers have been challenged by the nation's increasingly unpredictable weather patterns that make it especially difficult to plan annual plantings.

At the core of the climate crisis is that essential commodity, water. Some areas, like North Central China have experienced droughts while other parts of China are flooding. Overall, China has experienced periods of extreme rainfall at rates that have increased by a factor of seven since 1950. As we shall see later, Beijing itself experienced historic flooding during the summer of 2012.

An especially dramatic and existential threat is the impact of rising waters on low-lying coastal regions. The plight of nations like the Maldives has received significant international attention, especially since the former President Mohamed Nasheed's dramatic 2009 underwater cabinet session publicizing his nations' plight. Bangladesh is not quite as mortally threatened, but given how close to sea level much of the country is it could lose an enormous percentage of its national territory. Meanwhile to Bangladesh's Southeast, Vietnam has estimated that rising waters seriously threaten the Mekong Delta.

Less dramatic is the impact of increasing salinization that is polluting the fresh waters that feed Vietnam's economically

important coastal mangroves. The northern migration of largely incurable tropical diseases like Denge fever is becoming an increasingly big concern for some Southeast Asian populations that have not heretofore had to deal with the challenge.

The heart of the climate crisis and the real root of the problem is the rising heat. There, the numbers are especially dramatic. Pakistan for example just broke the long-standing Pakistani record by measuring a temperature of 54°C (129°F) in May of 2010. In the following months Pakistan then experienced a series of horrendous rainfalls that inundated somewhere between one quarter and one fifth of the country and created millions of refugees.

For teachers of Asian civilization, the impact of climate change on China's famous Yellow River is particularly helpful pedagogically. Previous generations of teachers have told students of the massive floods that so often inundated the Chinese. In contrast, today's Yellow River, deeply impacted by human activities from the draining of regional ground water to the impact of global warming on the permafrost of the Tibetan plateau of its origins, often does not even reach the ocean to disgorge its once mighty flow. Meanwhile in South Asia as well, climate refugees have already emerged as glacial melt has forced some farmers to relocate as their traditional glacial based water supplies have diminished.

## Long-Term Impact

The long-term impact of the climate crisis is much more problematic and potentially explosive. The core of the challenge for many mainland Asians is that the glaciers of the Tibetan plateau supply the water for 40% of the people of the world. As is well known, a controversy developed last year over an erroneous quote buried in some of the non peer-reviewed media reports that carelessly ended up in one of the Intergovernmental Panel on Climate Change documents about those glaciers melting by 2035. It was an error that turned out to be more about the IPCC's final proofing processes than anything significant to the actual findings. Nevertheless, the controversy, like so many of the assaults against climate science masked the reality of the threat; something very dramatic is happening in the Himalayan glacial area. In fact, India's minister of the environment, Jairam Ramesh, has made it very clear that he and his government are "very concerned" about the apparent retreat of the majority of the Himalayan glaciers. Ramesh also explains that that his government is taking proactive steps to understand more about the impact

# Historical Background

of global warming on the Himalayan glaciers.

For reasons that are not altogether clear, the temperatures in the Himalayan glacial region are heating faster than the world's average. Such melting will initially release significantly more water and then trickle away. Or As Zheng Guoguang, head of the China Meteorological Bureau, recently put it, "If the warming continues, millions of people in western China will face floods in the short term and drought in the long run."

Under such circumstances long-term geopolitical tensions are likely. The world's military leaders began long ago to game plan the geopolitical implications of climate change. It is particularly significant that, India, Pakistan's long-term rival, controls the headwaters of the rivers necessary to Pakistan's survival. China of course could potentially divert water from the Tibetan plateau for its own needs. The nations of the lower Mekong of Southeast Asia are currently working together to deal with the river's resources. However, China, which is not involved controls the headwaters of the Mekong and given their recent dam-building is increasingly able to control those vital water resources needed by its Southeast Asian neighbors.

## Asia Confronts the Climate Crisis

It is certainly easy enough to find those in Asia who, as in the West, deny the findings of climate scientists, but Asia was not generally subjected to the paid lobbying effort by fossil fuels industries to confuse the public about the threat of climate change. However, residents of the region have had their own reasons to resist the changes that dealing with this challenge requires. Regionally based resistance has been more likely to focus on the equally familiar arguments about the short-term economic costs of confronting the challenge, or the mini-tempest over whether the Indian government should rely on western scientists or their own experts to judge developments in the Himalayan glacial region.

## What Is Being Done?

Not surprisingly, most commentators focus on China's terrible environmental record and its prolific $CO_2$ emissions. The fact that China continues enthusiastically to open new coal burning plants is of course regularly cited in the media. The reality is that for decades, Chinese leaders tended to dismiss the issue of anthropogenic climate

change almost entirely. And, even if they understood the science of the climate crisis, it was assumed to be a problem of the West's making. The central government's priority was growth and if lip service needed to be paid to the growing pollution danger, the assumption was that China would clean up its environmental act, just as the West did: after its core development had been accomplished. Moreover, the reticence of the world's supreme greenhouse gas producer, the United States, to accomplish something truly trans-formative gave China "cover" to do less than it might otherwise have done.

Those days though are fast ending. In the last several years, China has shut down more than a thousand older-style coal plants and is increasingly forcing regional authorities to shutter inefficient factories. Impressively, even as the United States continues to fight over the imposition of some sort of carbon trading system to facilitate a move toward a greener energy infrastructure, Beijing's leaders announced in the summer of 2010 that such a plan, focused on the coal industry, would be included in its upcoming 12th five-year plan. There is even talk of extending the carbon trading plan to work cooperatively with California. In early 2013 another important agreement on climate change cooperation was signed between the United States and China during the new American secretary of state's first official visit.

Moreover, China, the nation that once largely ignored environmental issues has issued dramatically enhanced vehicle emissions standards and become a major player in the world's production of wind and other types of green energy. Indeed China's wind energy capacity increased from 760 megawatts in 2004 to over 20,000 in 2009 as the nation became the third largest wind power market in the world.

What is happening in China is what some have hoped for in the United States, the linking of environmental and economic concerns into the goal of invigorating the economy and generating new jobs through a massive green energy

revolution of the sort that once stimulated the fossil fuel–driven Industrial Revolution of another age. Unfortunately, faced with the major economic turndown as a result of the COVID-19 pandemic that began in China in late 2019, China has had to turn again to coal usage to help its economic recovery.

It is not just the giant Asian nations that have played significant roles. The Maldives, for example, saw their former president, Mohamed Nasheed, emerge as a world leader when his government announced the goal of making the nation carbon neutral by 2020.

Leaders of larger Asian countries have also stepped forward. Japan's new Democratic Party of Japan, which came into power In 2009, proclaimed an especially ambitious agenda to reduce carbon emissions while Susilo Bambang Yudhoyono, president of Indonesia, personally took part in the symbolic planting of a million new trees, an effort he referred to as a gift to the international community on the eve of the 2007 Bali Conference. Under his leadership, Indonesia has been especially involved in this struggle. Sadly though, it is also true that the growing global demand for palm oil, which has prompted enormous amounts of deforestation within Indonesia, continues to make the nation a major contributor to the global atmospheric instability which is at the heart of climate change.

## Popular Activism

It is not just Asian national governments that are slowly coming around to the threat of climate change. Increasingly Asian communities are taking up the matter for themselves. These activities have included indigenous movements and as part of Asia's global integration deepening links to Western international organizations. Within China, for example, the China Youth Climate Action Network was formed in August of 2007 with the goal of taking on global warming. Meanwhile,

---

Although global climate change is an extraordinarily multifaceted and complicated topic, the basic premise of "global warming" is fairly simple. earth's energy comes from the sun in the form of electromagnetic radiation and exits the earth in the form of infrared radiation, or heat energy. Apart from the greenhouse effect, this heat energy is not enough to maintain a temperature which is conducive to life on earth as we know it. If the immediate flow of the sun's energy were the only source of heat, our planet would on average be around 0°F (–18°C). The greenhouse effect, powered by the earth's greenhouse gases, slows the rate of heat loss, thereby making earth warmer than it would be otherwise. These gases, discovered almost two centuries ago, developed naturally over the eons but are now being augmented by humanity's burning of fossil fuels. The vast majority of scientists believe that this enhanced greenhouse effect is contributing to global warming and global climate change.

Internet café in Chengdu, China

Courtesy of Steven A. Leibo

# Historical Background

former U.S. Vice President Al Gore, America's domestically controversial but internationally acclaimed and respected Nobel laureate climate activist has trained hundreds of Asians, from China to India, from Indonesia to the Philippines, to give updated versions of the presentation he gave in the Academy Award winning documentary *The Inconvenient Truth*. Additionally, on October 24, 2009, Bill McKibben and the 350.org organization (dedicated to getting the amount of CO2 parts per million down to a safer 350 ppm in the atmosphere) put on what CNN called the most widespread day of political action in history, including hundreds of separate events in India and China. That effort was then followed up throughout Asia by a similar series of climate actions organized by 350.org on October 10, 2010.

Indeed several prominent Asians have become world leaders in the effort to deal with the challenge. Examples include India's Dr. Rajendra K. Pachauri who, for years, chaired the UN's IPCC as well as Ban Ki-moon, the former South Korean foreign minister and later United Nations secretary general.

Probably the most optimistic development, despite some initial disappointment, was the progress made over the last year in the evolution of the international commitment to confront the climate crisis by putting international regulations in place to facilitate the movement toward a greener global energy fuel infrastructure. Most importantly has been the movement away from the Kyoto Protocol's system, which made a major distinction between developed countries that bore the greatest burden and the developing countries that, as discussed above, were largely exempt.

In the decades since Kyoto, the belief has spread that regardless of which countries have historically contributed the most to the climate crisis, the entire international community, regardless of how developed individual countries are, need to contribute to the solution. That belief culminated as we have seen in the historical Paris Climate talks of 2015 which saw the successful negotiations of a binding international agreement on curbing fossil fuel emissions.

Ironically, as the new American administration came into power under Donald Trump a wave of climate change denial appeared likely to dominate the American federal government to the extent that some speculated that the People's Republic might soon emerge as the global leader in the conversion to green energy. This has all changed since the advent of COVID and the replacement of Trump as president by Joe Biden, who has reversed a number of the former's energy policies.

# The People's Republic of China

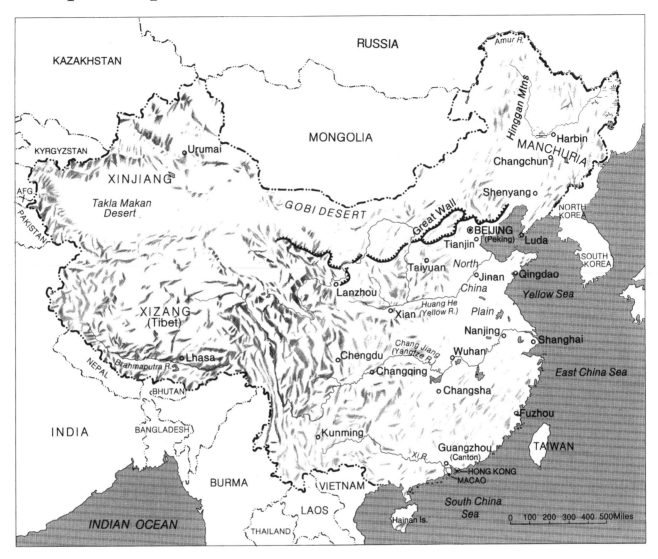

**Area:** Approximately 3.7 million sq. mi., including Inner Mongolia and Tibet (95,829,560 sq. km.)

**Population:** 1,411,780,000 (2020 census)

**Capital City:** Beijing, Pop. 20,897,000 (2021 est.)

**Climate:** Dry, cold with bitter winters in the mountainous West and North, temperate in the East, subtropical with rainy monsoons in the South

**Neighboring Countries:** Russia (Northeast, sharing a tiny border on the Northwest); Mongolia (North); Kazakhstan, Kyrgyzstan (Northwest); Afghanistan, Pakistan (East); India, Nepal, Bhutan (Southwest); Burma, Laos, Vietnam (South); Korea (Northeast) and Taiwan (not considered a separate country by the PRC)

**Official Language:** Mandarin Chinese, the dialect of the Chinese language spoken in Central and Northern China

**Other Principal Tongues:** South and West Chinese dialects, including Cantonese, Hakka, Fukienese, and Wu, the Tibetan language. Tribesmen of remote Xinjiang, Inner Mongolia, and the Northeast are expected to know Mandarin but also have their own languages and dialects. Koreans in the Yanbian Autonomous region on the border with North Korea speak Korean as well as Mandarin.

**Ethnic Background:** Chinese, or Han (about 91.9%). Relatively small minorities of Mongol, Turkic, Tibetan, Thai, and Korean ethnicity

**Principal Religions:** Confucianism, Taoism, Buddhism, Islam, and Christianity

**Main Exports:** Electrical and other machinery, including computers and telecommunications equipment, apparel, furniture, and textiles

**Main Imports:** Machinery and equipment, oil and mineral fuels, plastics, optical and medical equipment, organic chemicals, iron and steel, automobiles, and gold

**Currency:** Renminbi (people's currency) expressed in units called Yuan

**Former Colonial Status:** China as a whole was never colonized, but Portugal occupied Macao from the 1550s and Britain occupied Hong Kong from the 1840s. Both have reverted to China since the late 1990s. During the nineteenth century, Western powers and Japan established quasi-colonial enclaves in a variety of Chinese ports and inland cities. The largest of these, Shanghai, enjoyed a high degree of autonomy but was never actually a colony.

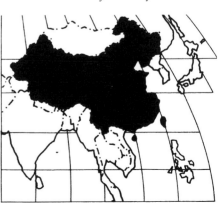

# China

National Day: October 1, anniversary of the founding of the People's Republic in 1949
Chief of State: Xi Jinping, president (since March 2013)
Head of Government: Li Keqiang, premier (since March 2013)
General Secretary, Communist Party: Xi Jinping (since November 2012)
National Flag: Red, with one large and four small five-pointed stars at upper left
Per Capita GDP Income: $18,260 (2022 est.) (purchasing power parity)

(Note: At the beginning of 1979, the People's Republic of China officially adopted an already-existing system known as Pinyin for writing out Chinese names and terms in the Western alphabet. That system is now increasingly used in both the West and even on Taiwan. Thus the capital of China, once known commonly as "Peking" is now more often rendered "Beijing." The Pinyin system is used in the following text except where possible confusion might occur with terms already quite familiar, thus "Daoism," will also be followed by the less correct but more familiar "Taoism.")

Occupying a land area larger than that of the 50 United States, China stretches for a distance of 3,400 miles from its Northeastern region adjacent to remote Russian Siberia to the mountainous regions of Tibet bordering on Nepal and India. As for temperature, altitude and roughness of terrain, fertility of the soil, and rainfall, there are two distinct regions. The invisible line that divides the two starts in the distant north at the Amur River and runs southward through the crest of the Great Khingan Mountains. It follows the contours of the Huang He, or Yellow River,

turning northwest and then west to accommodate that part of the river that arches toward Mongolia. Turning again southward, it searches out the upper part of the river, passing through the region around Lanzhou and Chengdu and finally becomes obscure in the hilly southern area of Kunming near the Vietnamese border.

In the West, on the left-hand side of the rough demarcation line, the land is a combination of closely crowded mountains with rough surfaces possessing little greenery even in the warmer regions of the lower altitudes. The towering peaks are occasionally interrupted by expanses of flat territory that is also desolate and dry, being surrounded by a natural barrier that withstands the invasion of rain clouds. The mountains in the North on the edge of the "line" give way to the Gobi Desert, filled with shifting earth, harsh rock formations, and severe extremes in temperature, all of which combine to exclude more than occasional visits of man and beast. The mountains envelop this desert which extends from Manchuria into southern Mongolia.

These areas of outer China are largely unmapped by Western standards. The thinly scattered people of Tibet, Xinjiang, and the North East (known in the West as Manchuria, although the Chinese do not use the term), have traditionally relied on herds of animals as their principal resource, although great treasures of mineral wealth may lie buried below the surface of the earth. A short growing season

provides the small amount of greenery available. The air is dry in both summer and winter, blowing out of Asiatic Russia (Siberia). The great distance the wind has traveled prior to its arrival in China has taken almost all moisture from the air. The lack of significant bodies of water in the endless expanses also makes the dry winds cold—bitterly so, almost beyond belief, in the winter.

In the spring enough warmth arrives to melt the snow in the lower altitudes of the mountains. This is sufficient to support limited agriculture at the lower edges of the mountains bordering the Gobi Desert of western Manchuria and Mongolia in the area between the mountains and the Takla Makan Desert in Xinjiang and the valleys of Tibet, but only during the brief summer season.

To the south and east of the "line" the land changes into temperate farmland; it is relatively flat and somewhat drier in parts of northern China, notably in the North China Plain. The hillier and more mountainous areas found in southern China have more moisture and warmer temperatures, producing thick growths of forest on the land not under cultivation.

The three main rivers, the Huang He (Yellow), the Yangzi, and the Xijiang (West River) have their origins deep within the remote territory west of the mountains, but flow through the more level eastern regions in a sluggish manner. Refreshed by the cool water of melting snow, they are quickly swollen in the spring by rains

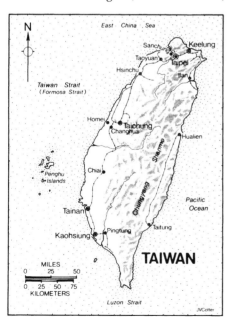

18

brought by the southeastern monsoon, and overflow their banks, spreading rich silt over the surrounding land. Rivers overflowing their banks continue to be a major problem. They also are a traditional source of communication and transportation in the region, but this is being replaced by railroads.

The lower valley of the Huang He is temperate and is the area in which the major aspects of Chinese civilization were born. The river itself is unpredictable. It left its old course south of the Shandong peninsula in which it had flowed for more than 800 years, and assumed its present course north of the peninsula in 1853, a shift of more than 500 miles. The immense quantities of silt it carries in its waters gave it the name "Yellow River" and also have built up a riverbed so much so over the years that is higher than the surrounding land. When it enters flood stage, the results have been catastrophic.

The growing season increases in the central and eastern region of China that is drained by the Yangzi River; it becomes almost continuous throughout the year in the southeastern area through which the Xijiang (Sikiang) River flows. If the rainfall in these regions were uniform from year to year, both would produce great quantities of food to feed the huge number of Chinese. The variations in rain, however, cause periodic loss of crops by either drought or flood. During a prolonged drought, even the violent summer rains are not of much help, since they run quickly into the rivers and flow into the sea rather than watering the land, which then dries out, unless there is further, preferably steady, rainfall.

The island of Taiwan has an elongated oval shape and its entire length is dominated by a chain of mountains rising with regularity to heights of 6,000 to 11,000 feet. These peaks lie close to the eastern side of the island and drop steeply at the coastline into the warm waters of the Pacific. The western slopes descend gently to a fertile plain that occupies almost one-half of the island's surface. The climate varies from tropical to temperate, depending upon altitude. As is true on the Chinese mainland 100 miles across the Taiwan Strait, the summer winds bring abundant rain, which supports intense agriculture. The smaller rivers do not cause the catastrophic floods of the three mighty rivers of continental China, so that bountiful harvests of a variety of produce, principally rice, are regularly gathered.

## History

### The Formative Era

China is the world's oldest continuous civilization in the sense that contemporary Chinese civilization recognizably resembles its earliest origins. Today's Arabic and Islamic Egypt, for example, is far more different from the civilization of the Pharaohs than China is from its early years. Still China is actually of much more recent vintage than the major early civilizations of Southwest Asia and North Africa.

Archeological evidence from north China, where its drier climate better preserves artifacts, reveals Neolithic communities based in several parts of the region dating from around 5000 B.C. These communities cultivated dogs and pigs and, even at that early date, silk worms.

By the period 1800–1000 B.C., the Chinese had begun to develop into a highly stylized, complex pattern. Advanced and very artistic techniques of casting bronze developed. The system of ideographic writing was refined and became the method of communicating and recording of ideas. But it did not and it does not now have an alphabet; it consists of a collection of thousands of symbols, each of which represents a word. Somewhat similar to Egyptian hieroglyphics, these characters have evolved far beyond their original graphic origins. Today, merely looking at a character provides few clues to its meaning. For many hundreds of years this system of writing was known only to scribes and intellectuals and has only recently become more widely known among the general population.

Nevertheless, using this tremendously demanding writing system, the Chinese developed quite early a society more dependent on a wide dispersal of learning than almost any other major civilization. The 20th century saw many modifications to both the format and structure of the characters to make them more accessible to the average person.

### The Early Dynasties

From around 1800 B.C. the Chinese were ruled by kings of the Shang, an apparently feudal and aristocratic dynasty. The Shang rulers were replaced by the Zhou (Chou) dynasty, which formally governed from about 1100 to 800 B.C., after which their power rapidly diminished until it was destroyed centuries later. Although the details of the fall of the Shang need hardly concern us here, what is astonishing is that from that collapse emerged one of the most significant Chinese contributions to political philosophy ever devised, The concept of the "Mandate of Heaven."

In originally justifying their conquest of the Shang, the Zhou leaders explained that the Shang, due to their degeneracy, had forfeited the "Mandate." According to their reasoning, which would dominate Chinese political thought down through

**Shanghai's skyline . . .**                    Courtesy of Steven A. Leibo

# China

... to the parched wastes of the Gobi Desert

Courtesy of AP Images

the ages, "Heaven" was not viewed as a spiritual place of post-life salvation. It was a conscious entity that insisted that governments on earth must rule for the benefit of the masses. And leaders maintained the right to do so only as long as they continued to behave well toward the people. In a world where too often political power has derived more from the sword or inheritance, this provisional nature of power has been an important idea first developed in ancient China and eventually complementary to many modern democratic theories of government. Some early Chinese thinkers even went so far as to claim that the "Mandate" actually justified the right of the masses to revolt!

The real power of the Zhou dynasty lasted only a few centuries before North China then disintegrated into a number of feudal states led by "princes" who occupied their time and that of their subjects in a variety of wars against each other. The use of iron tools in agriculture during this period produced a high yield from the earth, which, together with irrigation and (after 1,000 A.D.) the widespread cultivation of rice permitted a correspondingly high rate of population growth. As the people pressed outward, they came into greater conflict with non-Chinese people who inhabited central China around the Yangzi River. The stronger rulers subdued the weaker and smaller states, and the number of feudal princedoms became fewer, gradually falling under the control of two major states: Qin, which ultimately triumphed in the 3rd century B.C., was in the west central and northwestern part of China and Chu in the central Yangzi valley. Graphically, this period is known as the "Warring States Period."

## The Hundred Schools

Though China was divided during the later Zhou period, this diversity of political power proved to be a major benefit for its cultural development. In fact, one of the most interesting features of Chinese civilization is that, given its usual tendency toward centralization and successive government enthusiasm for promoting an orthodoxy of thought, it is most often during periods of relative weakness that Chinese intellectual life most dramatically has flourished.

Several points in modern history, the 1920s and most recently in the era before the clashes at Tiananmen Square in 1989, serve as good examples. The later Zhou was just such an era, a time when in the 5th and 4th centuries B.C. China enjoyed an intellectual blossoming comparable to that of Greece during the same period. Literature and the arts flourished, and the desire for knowledge and social order led to the creation and formalization of the two intellectual systems which originated in China: Confucianism and Taoism, the latter a mystical and contemplative system of belief and magical imagery (see Historical Background).

Confucianism, in contrast, is largely a system of social philosophy, and became a very influential source of satisfaction for the learned Chinese as well as providing a sense of imperial legitimacy and the security arising out of its emphasis on hierarchy and deference to authority, a feature many in East Asia today claim still plays an important role in their recent economic successes.

## The First Empires

By 221 B.C. the Qin ruler, who led a highly organized and militarily strong state, conquered his rivals and established control over all of north and central China as well as part of the southern region. For China this was one of the darkest periods in its history. The Qin dynasty unified the empire in more ways than military conquest; the Great Wall of China was constructed laboriously over a period of years to ward off the periodic raids by the nomadic central Asians from the North. Roads and other public works were built and the system of writing and weights were standardized. Obsessed with the needs of state power, the Qin leadership ignored the precepts of Confucianism, even killed many of its adherents, rejecting totally the idea that the state existed to serve the masses. Not surprisingly the rule of the Qin was extremely oppressive and produced much discontent among the Chinese people. It was soon overthrown by a new dynasty that took the name Han.

These new rulers, successfully avoiding the arrogance which had brought down the Qin, eventually governed for almost 400 years (2nd century B.C.–2nd century A.D.) before and after the beginning of the Western Christian era. The people of China today are sometimes referred to as Han to differentiate them from the minorities that live in the outer part of what is modern China. In spite of a brief collapse at the halfway point of its reign, the Han dynasty succeeded in making China into an empire of power, wealth, and cultural brilliance comparable to the other great civilization of the same period, the Roman Empire.

Technologically, it was in fact far more advanced than its Roman counterpart on the other side of Eurasia. Its boundaries were pushed well into central Asia, where local leaders were awed by the brilliance of Chinese advances in learning and military prowess. Even if not directly supervised by the Chinese, rulers of the outlying states of Asia were often willing to acknowledge themselves tributary and vassal states of the mighty empire.

When the Han dynasty collapsed, the following four centuries were marked by frequent nomadic invasions from the North which resulted in a series of states in northern China ruled by non-Chinese. A few Chinese, or Han states, did survive in the South, however, under a series of weak dynasties. During this time of uncertainty, Mahayana Buddhism, sometimes referred to as northern Buddhism (see Historical Background), spread quickly following its arrival from northern India by way of Central Asia at the beginning of the Christian era.

### The Middle Dynasties

China was reunited by the Sui and Tang dynasties after 581 A.D., and under an energetic succession of emperors it once more extended the area of its power far into Central Asia. For the first time in world history, a written examination was developed for civil servants, appointment of whom was based more and more on ability rather than family ties. Ironically, aspects of this movement away from aristocracy and toward a more individually based system of merit had begun earlier under the generally hated Qin dynasty.

Although the officials of the Tang dynasty were largely Confucian in outlook, it was in this period that Buddhism reached the height of its influence in Chinese civilization. Nevertheless, that influence was not long lasting and the later Tang era saw many cruel persecutions of Buddhists. Though losing its hold on official Chinese thought to Confucian scholars and Daoists (Taoists), this South Asian belief system would nevertheless remain influential on the popular level into the modern period.

There was a short period of disunity following the decline and fall of the Tang dynasty in the 10th century A.D. The brilliant cultural advances of the ensuing three-century period centered chiefly on painting and the discipline of philosophy. Under the influence of Buddhist theology, official Confucianism was modified by about 1200 into Neo-Confucianism which concerned itself more with abstract philosophy than had the original form of this belief.

The country was ruled by emperors of the Song (Sung) dynasty, and was continually threatened by a succession of powerful non-Chinese states that emerged along the northern border. The end of this era came with defeat by the most powerful northern force, the Mongols, who were able to succeed in their conquest only after a long and bitter campaign. The Song had withstood the Mongols longer than any of the other civilizations of the world into which the conquerors intruded, but ultimately became a part of a vast empire stretching from the Pacific to what is now the Middle East.

The Mongols finally unified all China in 1279 and ruled for a century, taking the name Yuan dynasty. Already disliked by the Chinese in a number of ways, the Mongols had but slight respect for Confucianism and the civil service examinations. These factors led to even greater opposition by the Chinese, particularly the upper classes. The rulers were religiously tolerant and permitted small communities of Franciscan missionaries to introduce Christianity into several parts of coastal China.

The Mongols were expelled from China in 1368 in a great upheaval with strong anti-foreign tendencies. This new, ethnically Chinese dynasty that came to power, the Ming (1368–1644), at first ruled firmly and energetically and created a powerful empire.

Following the momentum of the outward-looking Yuan dynasty, the Ming Emperor even sent out huge overseas flotillas toward the west to explore and demonstrate the might of the Chinese Empire. Starting in 1405 the Ming Emperor Yong Le sent out an extraordinary series of naval expeditions which over the years eventually traveled throughout Southeast Asia and parts of India and ranged as far away as Aden in Arabia and Mogadishu in East Africa. The final expedition in 1431 even sent some ships as far as Jedda on the Red Sea. The efforts, whose motives are not exactly clear, certainly had its impact. The Chinese flotilla intervened in a number of local disputes and worked to further the prestige of the Chinese emperors.

However, they lacked the ongoing significance of the voyages Westerners mounted in the opposite direction several generations later in the 15th century. By the time the Europeans attempted similar voyages, memory of the early Chinese flotillas had been all but forgotten.

Within China, a period of decline began about 1500. Japanese pirates began to increase their activities along the coast. Internal weakness became an increasing problem which was transformed into an even greater liability by the rise in power of the Manchu rulers to the north. In 1644, a combination of domestic rebellion and Manchu might was sufficient to overthrow the Ming dynasty; within a few decades, the Manchus had subdued all of China.

### The Manchus

The new rulers took the name Qing (Ch'ing) dynasty, but are more commonly referred to in the West as the Manchus. Although Chinese culture was by this time static to a degree that made basic changes difficult, under them the country was once again united and became rapidly powerful. In an effort to consolidate their positions, they ruled through existing Chinese institutions, including the very formal civil service examination system with its Confucian orientation. For this reason, and others, they were accepted rapidly by their Chinese subjects.

Interestingly, they devised a system whereby major offices and responsibilities were shared by matched sets of Manchu and Chinese officials. After an initial period of wise and successful rule, the Manchus indulged themselves in a period of energetic, but arbitrary and costly, warfare in the late 18th century that undermined the dynasty and coupled with internal corruption and a number of

**The 1,400-mile-long Great Wall of China**

Courtesy of Bruce Terry Howe

# China

internal revolts combined to make China less able to deal with the challenges the 19th century would bring.

## The Western Arrival

Although Westerners from the Roman era on had periodically visited China, the modern period of Sino-Western relations begins in the 16th century, with the arrival of traders and, above all, missionaries. It was at this time that the Portuguese established themselves at Macao, although it would not be until the 1880s that the Chinese government would recognize Portuguese sovereignty over the enclave. The real takeoff came in the 18th century when Europeans, principally the British, started to seek Chinese silk and tea. Unfortunately for these early merchants they had, at first, little to offer, save silver bullion in exchange for the coveted Chinese goods. The Chinese seemed quite disinterested in Western products. In fact, the famous emperor Qian Long even explained to a Western visiting dignitary in 1793 that China had "all things" in abundance and was simply not interested in Western goods. Nevertheless, the trade did develop and at the insistence of the Beijing government it was confined to the southern port of Guangzhou known to foreigners as Canton.

For the English though, this "Canton System" although lucrative enough, did cause problems. They were interested in trading further north in China where there might be a better market for their goods and in having direct contact with Chinese officials when various problems, legal and commercial, arose.

None of these things was possible, given the prevailing Chinese disinterest in any Western-style foreign relations or commercial exchanges beyond those considered important to maintaining the dignity and universal legitimacy of Chinese

imperial claims. For the Chinese, foreign relations as understood in the West did not exist.

The Chinese emperor was considered the "son of heaven" and people interested in having relations with China were expected to take part in the Chinese "Tributary System," largely a symbolic system whereby other communities recognized the supreme symbolic authority of the Emperor. On a technical level, that required a physical prostration before the emperor known as the kowtow and an exchange of various presents. In fact, the presents the Chinese gave away were not uncommonly more valuable than those they received. For the Chinese emperors, it was the symbolism of the relationship that mattered, not the cash transaction. Britain, the country that some disparaged as the nation of shopkeepers, had met an empire completely uninterested in commerce. It was a bad match.

But by the late 18th and early 19th centuries, two developments occurred which led to dramatic changes in China's relations with the Western powers. The British discovered that opium, grown in their possessions in India, could be sold at a handsome profit in China. Over the next decades the amount of opium imported into China by the British and other Westerners, including Americans, grew enormously until by the first quarter of the 19th century the drug was devastating Chinese society, especially in the south.

After first undergoing an internal debate in the late 1830s about how best to deal with the crises, the imperial government decided to force the foreign traders to give up their trade. To that end, an imperial commissioner, Lin Zexu, was sent to Guangzhou in 1839 to attempt to suppress the trade. Although the imperial commissioner managed to confiscate the traders' opium stocks and destroy them, the British government, by then

especially committed to the drug trade, declared war. Over the next generation and during two successive "Opium Wars" one of which culminated in the capture of Beijing itself in 1860, the British, and eventually their French allies, managed to impose a series of "unequal treaties" on the Chinese. Other countries were swift to follow where the British had led. Those treaties would dominate Sino-Western relations until the middle of the 20th century.

What had gone wrong for China? For most of world history Chinese technology had far outshone the skills of the Westerners, but by the 18th century, the Industrial Revolution, especially centered in England, gave the British enormous advantages over the once self-sufficient Chinese empire. That advantage would last for more than the next hundred years with profound implications for our own century.

## The Diplomacy of Imperialism

Under the series of "unequal treaties" signed under pressure in the first half of the 19th century, China lost a large part of its sovereignty. The Westerners gained the right to dominate a series of ports, soon known as Treaty Ports along the coast. Hong Kong and Shanghai are the best known of them. The treaties also gave the foreigners immunity to Chinese law and control over China's tariffs. Additionally foreigners gained the legal right to preach Christianity in the interior of the country. Moreover, due to the concept of "most favored nation," the rights won by the English and French guns applied to all other foreigners in China including the Americans who had hardly taken part.

## Cutting the Melon

The culmination of this era of imperialist greed occurred just as the 19th century was coming to a close. Known as the "Cutting of the Melon," one European power after another began demanding further spheres of influence in China. The British demanded an expansion of their influence in the region west of Shanghai and north of Hong Kong while the French pushed into southern China from their base in Vietnam. To the north the Russians and Germans made their demands while the Japanese insisted on gaining further rights in the Chinese coastal areas opposite Taiwan. In each of these, a particular Western power (with the exception of the United States) was granted sweeping and exclusive economic rights in its area, coupled with a great degree of political influence.

Russian domination was established in Manchuria, but the fertile southern

---

### The Chinese Exam System

The Chinese examination system, which existed in various forms until the early 20th century, was truly remarkable for a traditional society. Rather than relying on birthright to choose the bulk of their elites, as was so common among the Europeans and even their East Asian neighbors, the Japanese, the Chinese eventually developed a massive system of offering Confucian-based exams to thousands upon thousands of males annually. Those who advanced beyond the first demanding tests went on to even more rigorous exams at the provincial and eventually imperial level. Although few became great government officials, the system created an enormous pool of educated people who served the needs of society as local leaders and, for the lucky few, officially within the imperial bureaucracy.

Not surprisingly those who came from educated and reasonably well-off households had a major advantage in the competition. Nevertheless, the record of graduates shows that it was a true system of social mobility that allowed many people year after year to rise beyond their families' earlier accomplishments.

**Marble sculpture of a Ming soldier at the Imperial Tombs**

portion of that region went to the Japanese in 1905 after their victory in the Russo-Japanese War. The Germans established themselves in the province of Shandong (Shantung); the British became the major power in the Yangzi valley region; the Japanese controlled Fujian (Fukien) Province; and the French asserted their dominance over Southwest China.

Interestingly for students of modern Chinese history, the new demands were often made in the form of forced 99-year leases. Although most of these arrangements were long ago terminated, the lease on the New Territories of Hong Kong ran its full course.

That imperialistic high point known as the "Melon Cutting" did not stop at the century's end. Outside what had been China, places like Korea and Okinawa, which had paid tribute to the Manchu emperors, also became colonies or spheres of influence of Britain, France, Russia, and Japan. Russian influence became paramount in Outer Mongolia, and penetrated into Xinjiang (Sinkiang) in the 1930s. The British became a powerful influence in Tibet.

These losses of territory and authority were dramatic demonstrations of China's basic weakness by the standards of the 20th century Western powers and were an insult to the sense of national pride of the Chinese. The economy of the coastal regions, traditionally more wealthy than the interior areas, was almost totally dominated by foreign trade and investment.

Although many among the Chinese tended toward an inwardness that made effective response to these pressures difficult, there were other more far-sighted individuals within the Chinese leadership. They foresaw crises developing and began as early as the 1860s to adapt to the various Western military techniques needed to maintain the country's sovereignty in that imperialistic age. Led by perceptive individuals at both the imperial and military level, most notably the Manchu Prince Gong, a period known as "Self Strengthening" was begun. He was aided at the provincial level by leaders like Li Hongzhang and Zuo Zongtang. Under this program, during an energetic era dating from the late 1860s through the 1890s, several military arsenals and dockyards were founded and scores of students sent abroad—to America and Europe—to learn Western military and engineering techniques. Sadly, though considerable effort was put out and significant gains made, they were overall too little to stem the flow of China's diminishing strength nor to equal similar but more energetic efforts like those of their neighbors, the Japanese, who were simply far more successful.

As seen below, in the first test of their respective efforts at mastering Western military techniques during the Sino-Japanese War of 1894, the Chinese accomplishments proved sorely lacking and the country experienced yet another massive humiliation. The significance of these humiliations and the various unequal treaties cannot be underestimated. It is important to understand that even today many of China's oldest citizens grew up when these special Western and Japanese privileges were still in effect.

## The Heavenly Kingdom of Great Peace

Although the long-term implications of the Western pressures on China were enormous, the larger issue at the time for the Chinese themselves was the outbreak in 1851 of an enormous rebellion which eventually devastated much of the country over the next 15 years. The origins of the Taiping Heavenly Kingdom, as the rebels called themselves, lay in the startling increases in population which had added enormous pressures on the land. Moreover, the Opium Wars themselves had disrupted economic life in southern China. It was in that disrupted environment that one of the more curious dramas of world history arose.

The story began in the early 19th century when a frustrated Confucian scholar, who had for years been unable to pass the demanding Confucian civil service exams, decided that he was the younger brother of Jesus Christ. He developed a new "trinity" that included "God, the Father," "God, the Son" and in this new theology, himself, the "little brother."

For fifteen years, dating from the original revolt in 1851, China was divided between two governments, the ethnically Manchu, but Confucian-oriented Qing dynasty, and the unique Chinese Taiping Rebels with their semi-Chinese semi-Christian orientation. Following ideas found both in the Old Testament and drawn from mythic memories of early China, the Taipings established a theocracy with a communal economic structure. Life was organized, especially at their capital at Nanjing, around a religious military structure which at least on the surface seemed quite puritanical. Women, in sharp contrast to traditional Confucian practice, were far freer. Foot binding was not practiced and the women also took part in battle. But the assault on traditional practice had been too great and by 1864 the Heavenly Kingdom of Great Peace collapsed under pressures from Qing Militia leaders aroused by the struggle to preserve Confucianism (and assisted by Western military soldiers and advisers).

Following the death of the Emperor in 1861, his widow, referred to as the Empress Dowager Cixi, became co-regent during the reign of her son and wielded considerable influence. When he died in 1874 the throne then passed to Cixi's own young nephew and her power continued as before. Probably the most powerful woman in world history, Cixi dominated China, the largest population under a single government in the world, from the early 1860s through 1908. Her influence cannot be underestimated. Traditionally seen as ruthless, able, and extremely conservative, she embodied the traditions cherished by the Manchu court officials who clung to the security of the past. More recent research has suggested that a somewhat different interpretation of her role might be in order. What is clear, though, is that under her reign, the first efforts to deal with the Western challenge in the form of the various industrial efforts known as the "Self-Strengthening Projects" were begun.

Cixi's power was so great that when she felt threatened by the Emperor Guang Xu's dramatic effort during the summer of 1898 to drastically reorganize the Chinese government and educational system, the better to make it able to withstand imperialistic pressures, she had him arrested.

# China

**Visiting the "Army" of the First Emperor**

Courtesy of Steven A. Leibo

But if the Empress Dowager Cixi had intensely disliked the Emperor's response to the weakening of China, that did not mean that she failed to recognize the peril the dynasty faced. It is probably with that reason in mind that she soon pinned her hopes on yet another approach to the question of saving China. And in that case, one that arose from the popular masses' anger with the disruptions in their lives said to be caused by the foreigners. The results came to be known as the Boxer Rebellion.

At the popular level, there were many anti-foreign and anti-Christian outbreaks of violence in the years following 1870. Both sentiments joined to provide discontent resulting in the famous 1900 Boxer Rebellion a dramatic effort by thousands of Chinese to literally drive the Westerners out of China. In fact, the "Boxers" as the foreigners called them because of their ritualized style of physical and mental exercise, were encouraged by influential members of the Manchu court. For months, especially in north China, the Boxers terrorized Westerners and their Chinese converts.

Eventually, a joint military expedition sent by the Western powers crushed the Boxers. American and other foreign troops stormed Beijing in August 1900. Less than 50 years after the 1860 capture of Beijing by the Westerners, it was again under their control.

The Empress Dowager, who had fled the city as a young woman in 1860 was understandably shaken by the defeat and granted her reluctant assent to certain innovations in the imperial government. But it was too late. She died in 1908. The Manchu Qing dynasty had only a few more years to survive.

## Trying to Save China

In the years after the 1839–1842 Opium War several important officials and thinkers had come forward with theories and projects for reforming the Chinese empire. Some among them, as influential provincial leaders, put into place the various projects of the "Self-Strengthening Movement." More radical reformers later in the century played an important role in the Emperor's dramatic and failed reform effort of 1898, the so called "100 Day Reform." Nevertheless, as China moved into the 20th century its problems worsened and the ability of the imperial Manchu government to respond to the crises became less and less significant. These early reformers were not unified and their disunity prevented them from achieving any real influence on the Manchu court until it was too late.

As the situation deteriorated, the influences of these reformers became increasingly irrelevant, and leadership passed to those calling for more radical actions. It was in that context that a new generation of leaders arose, men not interested in reforming the Manchu Qing Empire but in replacing it with a republic more along the lines of Western models.

The most important of these radicals was Sun Yat-sen, who dedicated himself to the overthrow of the Manchus and to the modernization of China along semi-Western lines. Although he was eventually able to attract a relatively large following, Sun was not very effective in organizing his followers. Nevertheless due to the drama of Sun having been unsuccessfully kidnapped by Chinese agents in London in 1896, he became very well known in the West and eventually personified, in the minds of many Westerners, the goal of a Chinese republican revolution.

When the Empress Dowager died in 1908, the Manchu court installed the two-year-old Pu-Yi as child emperor. He reigned through regents appointed by the court until 1912. Later he was to serve as the "Emperor" of Manchukuo (Manchuria) when the Japanese attempted in the 1930s to colonize northern China.

### The Revolution of 1911

In the fall of 1911, the ability of the Court to maintain the 250-year-old Qing dynasty finally failed. A rebellion broke out in the city of Wuhan which, given prevailing frustrations with the Manchu leadership, spread rapidly across the country. One after another, various provinces declared themselves for the revolution. Sun Yat-sen, although at the time visiting the United States, emerged by December as the provisional president of a new Chinese republic. It appeared at first that China was about to take its place among the democracies of the modern world. But that was not to be. If the forces of the old regime had been unable to maintain themselves, portions of their strength remained potent enough to direct the course of events over the next several years.

To avoid a civil war, Sun turned over power to Yuan Shikai, a former Qing general who still held considerable loyalty among many government soldiers. There was actually little choice. A civil war between the new revolutionary forces and those of Yuan Shikai would have only weakened China further. The compromise seemed necessary to save what had been already won. But sadly, Yuan was more interested in establishing a new dynasty than serving as a true democratic president, and within a few years China literally collapsed from the stress.

By 1916, when Yuan died, China had disintegrated into a score of petty states run by individual military governors, usually referred to as "warlords." They had little governing ability and their rule was almost uniformly oppressive. The legal government of China in Beijing continued to be recognized diplomatically by the foreign powers. In reality, this "government" was an ever-shifting combination of one or more warlords, sometimes under the influence of foreign nations. Communications were extremely poor and there was a thin scattering of modern arms in the outlying regions, making it almost impossible to achieve any genuine national unity.

Sun Yat-sen, the "Father of the Revolution," embittered by his experiences in these developments, established himself in the south and tried in various ways, without success, to overthrow the shadow government at Beijing and to reunite the country. During those years he devoted himself to the building up the Guomindang (Kuomintang, KMT)—"National People's Party," or "GMD." But far to the north, an intellectual energy and nationalist momentum was growing that would go far beyond even Dr. Sun's revolutionary plans.

### The May Fourth Movement

The May Fourth Movement of the years 1915 to 1921 was a multi-dimensional era which embraced few central themes save a general disregard for China's traditional Confucian culture. On an individual level many of those involved loudly advocated a reorientation of cultural values. The young were told to become more independent, less tied to the more tradition-bound older generation. Confucianism, it was said, simply did not allow China the vitality necessary to withstand the aggressive modern world.

In addition to the trend toward economic modernization in the cities and coastal regions and cultural speculation during the 1920s, there was a marked growth of nationalism among the Chinese, who sought an end to foreign influence in their country. The "central" government was in the hands of a group under Japanese influence who cooperated with the latter's efforts to have their control over the Chinese province of Shantung formalized by the treaties that ended World War I. An outburst of patriotism, led by students, which became known as the May Fourth Movement, prevented the actual signing of the treaty and sparked an era of intense popular political activity.

On the national level the people of China, particularly the youth, desired the end of imperialism and internal disunity and came to believe that these goals could only be achieved through a major political and social revolution. Some chose the Guomindang, while a smaller number joined the infant communist movement.

### Communism

The Chinese Communist Party (CCP) was founded in 1921 mostly by young Chinese intellectuals. The movement quickly came under the control of the Third International, more familiarly known as the Comintern of Russia under its energetic revolutionary leader, Lenin. The picture became even more complicated when the Comintern decided to enter into an alliance with Sun Yat-sen's Guomindang and ordered the local Chinese communists to do the same. This unstable union was produced by a common, overwhelming desire to expel Western and Japanese influence from China and to eliminate the power of the warlords.

To accomplish these aims, the Comintern reorganized and greatly strengthened the Guomindang through money and military aid, but it also hoped that communists could gradually acquire control over it by infiltrating top positions, and by putting pressure on the party through communist-dominated labor and peasant unions. Although there was considerable uncertainty about the collaboration of the Guomindang's nationalists and the communists, what mattered above all was that their cooperation help unify the country once more. In 1926 that great effort, known as the "Northern Expedition," began. For the next several years, sometimes by fighting, sometimes by negotiation, the nationalists marched north enthusiastically attempting to build a new, stronger, and now unified China. The march was to prove ultimately successful, although tensions inherent in the nationalist/communist alliance eventually broke out.

While Sun Yat-sen had been alive, the effort to both unify China and to maintain the coalition of nationalists and communists continued fairly well. But after his death in 1925 he was eventually succeeded by General Chiang Kai-shek, who had become increasingly alarmed at the threat of Soviet domination of China and

**Kunmings Shopkeeper, 1945**
**Courtesy of Gregg Millett**

the more immediate threat of potential communist revolution.

Chiang determined to head off these threats by military force and in 1927 sent his forces into the newly liberated Shanghai to slaughter his communist allies. The alliance between the Chinese nationalists and the communists was thus broken. For the moment the nationalists—the Guomindang forces, under Chiang—seemed triumphant.

Chiang captured Beijing in 1928, and proclaimed the renewed Republic of China with its new capital at Nanjing, a city which has often served as an alternative capital in Chinese history. Actually the GMD controlled only the eastern provinces of China and was faced with tremendous problems: a large army that had to be fed and clothed, floods, famine, and political apathy. After a generation of struggle the Guomindang had finally come fully to power. But its ability to attempt a rebirth of China was soon to be severely curtailed when, in 1931, the Japanese began their effort to dominate the country.

### The Japanese Invasion

Japanese efforts to establish an East Asian empire began in the late 19th century. By the early 1920s, their influence had grown considerably. Korea and Taiwan were already colonies and Japanese influence in Manchuria was considerable. China's weakness during the era of the "Warlords," 1916–1928, had given them even greater leeway to assert themselves. Moreover, the worldwide depression, which struck at the end of the 1920s, convinced many Japanese nationalists that Japan's future lay in furthering their hold on northern China. That commitment led to the Japanese Manchurian army's (see Japan) decision to provoke an incident which would allow them to take over Manchuria.

The Japanese seized it in 1931–1932; the territory was renamed Manchukuo (Manzhouguo in pinyin) and the former Manchu emperor of the Chinese Empire, the youthful Henry Pu-Yi, took the throne as "Emperor of Manchukuo." This interesting character had been tutored in the Western classics by an Englishman after the ouster of the Manchus, who suggested that he take an English name. Having been enthroned as emperor and deposed while still a child, the possibility of once again becoming an emperor must have been exhilarating for the young man. Nevertheless, during his years as emperor over Manchuria, he would prove as powerless under the Japanese control as he had been as a child under the direction of the adults around him in the Chinese

大清國當今慈禧端佑康頤昭豫莊誠壽恭欽獻崇熙聖母皇太后

The Empress Dowager Cixi

imperial court. His story is a fascinating one, and it eventually became well known to millions of filmgoers through the movie "The Last Emperor".

To Chiang Kai-shek, the Japanese assault, while dangerous, was still not his most immediate concern. The Generalissimo was more concerned about what he saw as a disease of the "heart," the Chinese communists, who, while weakened by his assault in 1927, had remained a potent force. While Chiang had managed to weaken the city-based Shanghai communists, many others, most notably Mao Zedong in southeastern China, had managed to establish communist strongholds far beyond GMD control.

Chiang Kai-shek then made the poorest of choices. He decided to concentrate his energies on dealing with the Chinese communists rather than the Japanese invaders. That decision would eventually put into question whether the GMD really had any right to call itself the "Nationalists." His primary opponent, Mao Zedong, himself both a nationalist and committed communist, was often alienated from the leadership of the Chinese communist party; it often saw him as less orthodox in his ideological outlook. But these differences were hardly significant to the Guomindang which set out in the early 1930s to destroy the Chinese communist base known as the Jiangxi Soviet.

After long and difficult campaigns—the communist resistance was initially very effective—the communists were forced by overwhelming Guomindang military pressures to evacuate their base areas in Central and South China. Eventually, after a long dramatic trek of thousands of miles and extraordinary hardships later known as the "Long March," the temporarily defeated Chinese communists took refuge in the remote and desolate regions of Northwest China. During the march, after a crucial meeting at Zhunyi, Mao Zedong at last emerged as the leader of the Chinese communists, a position he would not relinquish until his death in 1976. While Chiang Kai-shek may have felt some satisfaction with the weakening of the communists, he had more pressing pressures to the north.

## World War II

By late 1936 in the midst of yet another effort to completely destroy the Chinese communists, Chiang was kidnapped by his own troops who were angry about his preoccupation with the communists in the midst of the imminent Japanese threat. After a dramatic episode that came close to bringing China to civil war, the Guomindang and Chinese communists made yet another alliance. From

**General Chiang Kai-shek**

Mao's perspective and that of many patriotic Chinese, it was absurd for Chinese to fight in the interior while Japan pressed forward in the northeastern part of the country. Moreover, Russia's Stalin had been urging the communists to enter into another alliance with the Guomindang in order to resist the invaders. Mao probably saw an opportunity not only to resist the Japanese, but to ultimately overthrow the Nationalists after they had been weakened by the enemy.

The new alliance came none too soon, for Japanese forces invaded eastern China in 1937 and started an assault of extraordinary brutality that at times foreshadowed later Nazi acts in Eastern Europe. The Japanese conquered the prosperous coastal regions of China, depriving the Guomindang of its major economic and political bases. Driven into the hills and mountains of southwest China, it became even more conservative and subject to corruption than before. Under Japanese control, cities like Nanjing, the Nationalist's capital, experienced a horror of mass murder and rape that went on for weeks. To the north, Japanese doctors would eventually establish a medical experimentation center that carried out live vivisections on hapless Chinese captives. Though less well known than the Nazi brutalities, they left a legacy of bitterness between China and Japan that still exists.

The expansion of the communists from that time forth was actually at the expense not only of the Japanese but also of the Guomindang. Inflation and weakness also sapped the strength of the Nationalists, enabling the Japanese to inflict further heavy defeats on it as late as 1944. Nevertheless, the Japanese were unable to prevent the communists, more skilled in the art of guerrilla warfare than the Nationalists, from infiltrating and setting up base areas within territory that was supposed to be Japanese. Partly in retaliation for this resistance, the Japanese committed more atrocities against the Chinese people in the occupied areas, driving many into sympathy with the communists and thus assisting them to seize political control on an anti-Japanese, more than an anti-Guomindang, platform.

## The Struggle for Power: Nationalists and Communists

Increasing numbers of Japanese soldiers were withdrawn from China starting in 1943 because of the defeats that were being suffered in the Pacific war. This permitted the communists to expand

**Dr. Sun Yat-sen addresses a crowd before departing with his troops on the campaign against Beijing**

# China

**Japanese troops in China, 1937**

rapidly, so that by the end of the war they controlled 19 base areas, in various parts of China, principally in the North and Northwest.

The elimination of Japanese troops from China at the end of the war brought a frantic flurry of political and military activity by both the Guomindang and the communists. In the immediate period after the war the U.S. was the major political power in the Pacific area and it attempted to bring about some sort of settlement between these two competing Chinese parties. The talks conducted under the encouragement of U.S. General George C. Marshall, special envoy of President Truman, completely broke down in 1946 because neither side had any real desire for an agreement. Each preferred a trial of armed strength. Neither political party had any interest in sharing China's future with the other.

Unfortunately f, the Nationalists, nominally more powerful, were plagued by their inability to deal with China's most serious problems: inflation, corruption, and loss of political unity. The military leadership also employed very poor tactics against the communists, especially in the battle over Manchuria, and soon found itself losing control over the mainland.

By the end of 1949 the Guomindang was driven to the island of Taiwan. The Chinese communists under Mao then controlled all of mainland China except for Tibet, which had been outside Beijing's control since the collapse of the Qing. They proclaimed the People's Republic of China and reestablished the Chinese capital at Beijing.

The next year the soldiers of the People's Liberation Army invaded Tibet. Although there was some initial resistance, the "roof the world" was brought under Chinese control again; the Dalai Lama, spiritual leader of the Tibetans who also was vested with rather wide governing powers, was soon made a figurehead. He eventually fled Tibet in 1959 after an unsuccessful uprising against the Chinese in the eastern part of the region.

The "People's Liberation Army" brought the new regime to power, and it remained important as a defense against possible enemies, both internal and external. The Chinese Communist Party, however, was the real instrument behind Mao and his regime; its members held and now hold all important public offices. It has proven to be the only political force since the Manchus that has demonstrated itself able to hold China together. For the first quarter century of the People's Republic's existence, Mao Zedong played an overpowering role. He made himself into a cult-like father figure whom all Chinese, especially the youth, were taught to worship to a degree that would have created envy in the hearts of previous emperors.

## Building a New China

The team of Mao, the Chinese Communist Party (CCP) and the army, held together quite successfully through the late 1950s and achieved results which were quite impressive considering how devastated the country was after generations of invasion and civil war. The majority of the people regarded the regime as the only hope of escape from the

long nightmare of civil and foreign war, chaos, and abject poverty, and gave it overwhelming support. Initially following the Soviet model of development, China's new leaders restored the defunct economy and launched an impressive program of heavy industrialization with Russian technical assistance and equipment. After igniting a frequently violent purge against the rural landowning classes, small plots of farmland were distributed to the peasants and then as the years went on collectivized. The lives of women were improved with the passage in 1950 of a new marriage and divorce law that gave women more marital and property rights.

In short, China progressed from war-inflicted chaos toward a centralized, autocratic, and rationally administered state. Traditional Chinese culture and society were forcibly changed in directions desired by the communists with widespread, fundamental, and seemingly impossible effects. By 1956 the regime apparently felt confident enough to encourage the masses to voice their opinions on the many changes the CCP had brought about. "Let a hundred Flowers Bloom," Mao, the supreme leader, proclaimed although apparently what the CCP's leadership heard was not to their liking. By 1957 a cruel repression known as the "Anti-rightist Campaign" had commenced which was to destroy the careers of millions of Chinese intellectuals and others who had been naive enough actually to speak out.

In foreign relations, the Chinese regime initially established a close alliance with the Soviet Union, still led by the aging Stalin. Doing so was not without its difficulties. The Soviet dictator would clearly

**Mao Zedong (Mao Tse-tung) in 1945**

have preferred a Chinese leadership more servile to Moscow and had even made Mao wait three days in Moscow before receiving him in November of 1949. Nevertheless the tie was formalized into a 30-year treaty of friendship. China also entered into diplomatic relations with all communist countries and with a number of neutral and Western nations. The United States, which had become protector of the Nationalists on Taiwan, refused to recognize Mao's government. With only slight success, the Chinese communists initially tried to promote revolutions elsewhere in Asia. Eventually they retreated from this policy somewhat in order to be in a better position to cultivate the friendship of the neutral Asian nations.

### The Korean War

Although the Chinese leadership may have wished to concentrate on solidifying their control over China in their first years of power, and especially to take-over Taiwan, international developments became impossible to ignore. In June of 1950, the North Koreans, apparently with Soviet support, invaded South Korea with the goal of unifying the entire peninsula under their leadership.

Although the immediate Chinese reaction was somewhat restrained, the American decision to intervene through the United Nations aroused their ire, as did President Truman's decision to send the US Seventh Fleet to patrol the Taiwan Straits to preempt a conflict between China and Taiwan. More to the point, after the UN troops (mainly American) successfully drove the North Koreans back across the 38th Parallel line, they decided to invade North Korea with little thought to the consequences of moving toward the Chinese border (see the Korea section).

From the Chinese perspective, the American troops (the apparent allies of their enemies the Chinese Nationalists) were pushing toward their borders and ignoring Beijing's warning that they would intervene if the Americans continued north. Unfortunately, the American forces did continue north and the Chinese, urged on and with the support of the Soviets, committed massive numbers of "volunteers" to stop the UN forces and to the aid the besieged North Korean communist government. Whatever possibilities might have existed for a successful relationship between Washington and Beijing was destroyed in the explosion that followed and killed so many Americans, Chinese, and Koreans over the next few years. By July of 1953 an armistice was signed dividing the peninsula between the North Koreans and their communist allies in the north and the South Koreans

**Silk tapestry**     Courtesy of B. R. Graham

and the UN force to the south. U.S. forces have remained in South Korea ever since.

### The "Great Leap Forward"

By the mid-1950s, the Chinese leadership had at last successfully stabilized the economy and begun the long effort to recover from so many decades of war and civil war. The Soviet model of a command economy with its five-year planning models was being used and significant progress was made.

But Mao wanted more; he wanted China to literally leap forward toward a more industrialized and socialized future, not at some distant point in the future but immediately with one giant effort of the Chinese people united in the endeavor. By 1958, new and far more ambitious plans were announced for the country. Mao declared that China should catch up with industrialized Britain within 15 years.

**Wenhang Hall**     Courtesy of Steven A. Leibo

The "Great Leap Forward" as it was known was to have two fundamental aspects; one industrial, one social. Toward the first, enormous industrial goals were announced. Each work unit was, among other things, expected to create "back-yard furnaces" to boost iron production. Every industry was expected to dramatically increase its output of goods using an emphasis less on industrial know-how than the cumulative willpower of the energized population.

On the "communitarian/socialist" side Mao's planners herded people into what would become known as "People's Communes," which would dominate almost every aspect of their lives from child care to the use of their labor. Moving far past the Soviet model of state farms and limited private plots, the peasants were now told to live in completely egalitarian communities where there was literally no room for individual family initiative (or privacy). Even such mundane activities as growing a pig and raising it for market were branded "capitalist" and made impossible to carry out.

Most of these programs were terrible failures. Industrial production collapsed. The famous "backyard furnaces" often produced completely useless materials. The harvest revenues plummeted horrendously. Amidst the propagandistic circus of claims and boasts, a very real food disaster developed which turned into an enormous famine. Millions of people died in the following years due to this man-made disaster.

Late in the decade, policy differences and political tensions began to appear between the aging Mao and some of his colleagues who were more pragmatic than he and obviously worried about the suffering brought on by the failures of the Great Leap Forward. Few though were

# China

willing to challenge the Great Leader openly. Moreover, problems with their enormous socialist neighbor were as well beginning to develop.

### Relations with the Soviets

By the late 1950s, relations with the Soviet Union, the principal source of economic and military aid, were becoming severely strained. In 1956, Soviet leader Nikita Khrushchev criticized the cult of Stalin in a secret speech, which the Chinese believed was also a criticism of other communist leaders, including Mao. The Soviet Union was also concerned at the internal developments in China described above. Soviet technicians and experts were withdrawn from China and Khruschev cut off all aid in 1960. Actually a clash between Mao and Nikita Khrushchev was probably inevitable—the former regarded the younger Khrushchev as an upstart and at the same time Khrushchev, blessed with an over abundance of ego, considered Mao a fanatic and an adventurer. China's enthusiasm for considering itself, rather than Moscow, the leader of their world revolutionary movements hardly endeared it to the Soviet Union either.

Soon growing Chinese political pressures on the Soviet Union, calculated to prove the correctness of Mao's brand of communism and the error of the Soviet "deviation," produced serious and fundamental tensions not only between the Soviets and the Chinese, but within the entire communist world. Over these years relations with the Soviets, never close, would continue to deteriorate until by 1956 they seemed in competition for leadership of the communist world.

In the summer of 1958, Mao engaged in another unsuccessful gesture—the shelling of the islands of Quemoy and Matsu, controlled by the Nationalists, close to mainland China in the Taiwan straits. Whatever his original intentions had been, nothing more than an artillery and air-power duel occurred, notwithstanding the alarm of other nations because of the possibility of a Chinese-U.S. confrontation. The Soviet Union's unwillingness to be supportive during the crises and later when tensions developed with India further alienated Beijing's leadership from Moscow.

The Soviet Union was accused of being as great if not greater political enemy than the United States. The task of struggling against the supposed imperialistic designs of the U.S. was in effect assigned to other revolutionary movements in Asia, Africa, and Latin America.

The revolutionary zeal of the Chinese, and their tendency to urge radical and nationalistic movements to greater tasks than were possible, with endless quantities of advice and of Mao's "thoughts," coupled with quantities of arms, did not produce the desired results. A number of nationalist and socialist leaders of Asia and Africa became rapidly aware of the not yet serious threat, and took steps to expel Chinese agents. There were especially serious setbacks in Indonesia and in sub-Saharan Africa, which had seemed promising to the Chinese in the years 1963–1965. After the fall in 1964 of Khrushchev, who had handled the revolutionary impatience of the Chinese rather clumsily, his more practical successors offered China a limited agreement, which was spurned by Mao. With this refusal, Mao worsened his relations with some of his critics at home and abroad who wanted a less antagonistic attitude toward Russia.

By the early 1960s, tensions within China's leadership had become more obvious. Mao had withstood the direct criticism of former allies like Peng Dehuai regarding the disasters caused by the Great Leap Forward. But his influence over events within China was being lost to the more pragmatic bureaucratic leadership of the Chinese Communist Party, most notably individuals like Liu Shaoqi and Deng Xiaoping. For the aging leader Mao Zedong, this development was completely unacceptable.

### The Great Proletarian Cultural Revolution

By the last half of 1965, Mao became convinced that the time had come to silence his critics within the party. The first public sign of the split in the leadership was an attack on the writer Yan Wenyuan for his play "Hai Rui Dismissed from Office." (Hai Rui was a Ming dynasty official, famed for being upright and honest.) This was taken to be an attack on Mao. Thus began another mass campaign: the "Great Proletarian Cultural Revolution." His first obstacle, the reluctant municipal boss of Beijing, Peng Zhen, was soon overthrown by a combination of political pressures and military threats. Mao then proceeded to call on the revolutionary young people, organized into "Red Guards" to root out his enemies. Moreover, in his struggle with the leadership of the Chinese Communist Party, Mao also had the support of Lin Biao, the commander of the People's Liberation Army. Mao's wife, the former actress, Jiang Qing, led an attack on traditional culture and the arts. The youthful Red Guards attacked and terrorized Mao's real and imagined opponents in the universities, in the party structure, and anywhere else they were thought to be found.

The victims ranged from party officials to teachers and other professionals in almost all fields from medicine to religion. Almost anyone the young enthusiasts could accuse of being insufficiently Maoist was in danger. The students created their own kangaroo courts to punish their victims and broke into homes looking for anything considered counter-revolutionary. Those found with materials ranging from books by Confucius to Western writings, even possession of materials written by the now-purged former leadership of the Communist Party, could cause an individual serious problems.

Throughout the country, former officials and others who had held authority previously were beaten and humiliated as they were marched through the streets wearing banners proclaiming their supposed guilt. The lives of countless millions were affected by the malicious chaos of the era.

The struggle was as much an assault on the full heritage of Chinese tradition as it was against Mao's enemies. Throughout the country the "Red Guards," aroused as they were against almost any object connected to China's imperial past, destroyed or defaced materials of enormous beauty. Practitioners of traditional arts, from Buddhist monks to magicians and fortune tellers, were hounded from their professions.

Eventually even central power began to break down in many parts of the country as Mao's "Cultural Revolution" went far beyond what even he had envisioned. By early 1967, it was necessary for Mao to urge the army to intervene in order to prevent chaos and yet to keep the Cultural Revolution moving. The army quickly discovered that these

**Kaifeng shoe repair**

30

two tasks were inconsistent and increasingly began to emphasize the restoration of order in place of the disorder created by the unruly Red Guards. In 1967, Mao was brought, willingly or unwillingly, to endorse a turn toward a more conservative line. After that time, the impact of the Cultural Revolution on everyday life lessened. During 1968 the army acquired more and more local power, and with Beijing's consent, it forcibly suppressed the Red Guard movement. The young Red Guards were banished to the countryside to "educate" themselves among the peasants.

How much they actually "learned" is less certain; being inexperienced at farming, many were shunted into "song and dance troops" to entertain the peasants. What is clear is that a huge percentage of the young people of that era lost their opportunity for higher education and a better life. Many of their older contemporaries whom they had been persecuting were able to resume their former lives once calm was restored. That was less true for many of these youth, who were in many ways the real victims of the Cultural Revolution. Not only were they as individuals to lose, but China itself ultimately lost out on the professional skills they would have potentially made available to build a new, more modern China.

### The Vietnam Wars

While China itself was going through the chaos of the Cultural Revolution, just to the south one of the longest struggles of the 20th century, the Vietnam War, was entering an especially critical stage (see the Vietnam section). For China, despite the eons of tension and ambivalence that separated the Chinese and Vietnamese, there was no question but that Beijing would support North Vietnam in its struggles against the Americans during the Vietnam War (approximately 1965–1975 for the American stage). But here, unlike in Korea, China did not play a major role.

China did, though, send some arms and personnel to North Vietnam cooperated for a time in shipping Soviet weapons by rail. Additionally, Beijing sent railway engineering units to help keep the main Vietnamese railway lines open in spite of American bombardment. After the American withdrawal in 1973, China stepped up its flow of arms to Hanoi and in this way contributed significantly to the rapid fall of South Vietnam in the spring of 1975.

By that time, however, Hanoi had already begun to show signs of abandoning its neutrality in the Sino-Soviet disputes. It was "tilting" toward Moscow. By 1977 Vietnam was involved in a border war

**Mao Zedong in 1966**    Courtesy of AP Images

with Cambodia, where the pro-Chinese rather than the pro-Vietnamese wing of the Khmer Rouge (the Cambodian communist movement) had come to power in 1975. When China began in 1978 to put pressure on Vietnam in support of Cambodia, Hanoi expelled several hundred thousand "boat people," many of them of Chinese ancestry, and moved still closer to Moscow. At the end of 1978, Vietnam invaded Cambodia and installed a puppet government in Phnom Penh. Accordingly, China then experienced its own Vietnam War for a time by invading Vietnam briefly in February–March 1979 with the announced purpose of teaching Hanoi a lesson.

The lesson did not take. Vietnamese forces did far better than expected against those of their giant neighbor, and relations were tense for decades. Not surprisingly, despite the alliances of the war, the animosity that had existed between China and Vietnam for centuries was revived.

Tensions have continued for years in the vicinity of their common border, as well as in the South China Sea, where there are conflicting territorial claims and naval rivalry. . Nevertheless, the collapse of the Soviet Union eventually led to a slight warming of relations between China and Vietnam.

### A Fundamental Shift

The military clash along the Sino-Soviet border in early 1969, which turned out badly for the Chinese, eventually led to some astonishing shifts in East Asian politics. Given the reality that China was finding itself "squeezed" between two different antagonists, the jealous Soviets to the north, and the Americans struggling against communism in Vietnam,

many in China felt it was time to rethink China's international position. A moderate coalition, led by Premier Zhou Enlai and some of the military, tried to restore a greater degree of domestic stability and more workable foreign relations.

Zhou felt it advisable, after several months of Soviet threats, to enter into negotiations on border problems and related matters, and to downgrade disputes concerning communist theory. Nevertheless, by the end of 1970, it appeared that the negotiations had resulted in a deadlock.

Internal politics also played a role in bringing about the new international alignment when Lin Biao, the longtime leader of the contentious PLA, who had supported improved Sino-Soviet relations, conspired against Mao. He was eventually killed in a 1971 abortive plan to flee the country. The way was clear to open relations with the United States, a relationship many in the Chinese leadership hoped would serve as a balance to the potential threats posed by the Soviet Union.

To the surprise of the Americans, China extended in 1971 an invitation to an American table tennis team to visit. This "ping-pong diplomacy" was quickly followed by a visit by Dr. Henry Kissinger, then US National Security Advisor, in July 1971 and later by President Richard Nixon in 1972. For the Americans, of course, better relations with Beijing offered the possibility of finding a new tool to end their frustrating involvement in Vietnam. Beijing's help did eventually prove significant in developing the treaties that allowed for the United States to withdraw, even though that aid hardly affected the ultimate outcome of the Vietnam War itself.

Nevertheless, American ties to China continued to improve, and by 1978 President Carter of the United States formalized diplomatic relations with Beijing. At the same time, the United States terminated its formal diplomatic relations and defense treaty with the Republic of China on Taiwan. Other important ties, however, remained intact and the U.S. continued to sell arms to Taiwan and to offer considerable "moral support." Once Beijing and Washington began to improve their relations Taiwan's international position began to deteriorate. In a humiliating move, Nationalist China lost the "China seat" at the United Nations in 1972 and the People's Republic of China became the official representative of China at that organization.

### The Emergence of Deng Xiaoping

In the mid-1970s an upsurge of political ferment reflected radical dissatisfaction,

# China

**Shanghai Bund**

Courtesy of Steven A. Leibo

especially from the individuals eventually known as the "Gang of Four" which included Madame Mao, Jiang Qing, as its most prominent representative. They were clearly dissatisfied with Premier Zhou Enlai's more moderate policies, desiring another dose of Mao's sloganeering agitation. In spite of this, Zhou, a highly skilled and educated person, and a notable survivor, though suffering from cancer, remained in power until his death, counterbalancing the influence of the waning Mao, who though physically frail was still perceived as supporting, or at least protecting, the more radical Maoists.

Zhou Enlai was still effectively in charge, though in a hospital, possibly hoping that an early demise on his own part would not give the radicals an opening to resume their initiatives. Whatever his goals, Zhou died in January 1976, more than 10 months before Mao Zedong passed away. The timing appeared to allow Madame Mao and her radical allies their opportunity to come to full power at last.

The death of Zhou Enlai deprived the world of one of its most astute statesmen and placed the future of the moderates in Beijing in jeopardy for a time. Vice Premier Deng Xiaoping, Zhou's main assistant since 1973, had badly antagonized the Maoist radicals and did not remain in office long; he was forced out by April, presumably with Mao's approval. The new premier announced at that time, however, was not formally a radical, but a compromise choice, Hua

Guofeng, whose record suggested a closer affinity with the moderates than the radicals.

A major earthquake in July 1976 tightened the political ties between Hua and the army, which handled most of the relief work. Given the trauma and demands required to recover, it was apparent that China needed a breathing spell away from the political bickering of the communist era.

Frail, senile, and moribund, Mao died in September 1976. His death removed the main shield of the leading radicals, including his widow, Jiang Qing. They were purged by Hua a month later. The so-called "Gang of Four" soon came to be seen as central symbols of the suffering experienced by so many during the previous decade's Cultural Revolution. After their purge, propaganda against them continued unabated.

Deng Xiaoping, the leader of the more pragmatic communist officials was "rehabilitated" and soon became the most powerful man in the country. His general approach could not be more in contrast to Mao Zedong, his longtime leader. Mao had been committed to an ideological approach to governing that often excluded basic realities, thus making possible movements like the "Great Leap Forward." In dramatic contrast, Deng was more concerned about emphasizing a pragmatic approach to issues, preferably devoid of ideology. And it was with that approach that he set about, in what in hindsight turned out to be an incredibly successful effort, to build a new China.

## Opening to the World

Under Deng Xiaoping's leadership China underwent an extraordinary series of changes almost unprecedented in Chinese history. Famous for his comment that "it did not matter if a cat were black or white, as long as it caught mice," Deng, while committed to the political power of the Chinese Communist Party was first and foremost a pragmatist. Early on he forced the retirement of Premier Hua Guofeng. Ultimately he was replaced by Hu Yaobang. Deng then successfully went forward with the trial of the "Gang of Four," thus neutralizing radical opposition, some of which was within the army, making it easier to move against the ideas and policies they and Mao had represented.

The purge of radicals continued in both the party and the bureaucracy during the early 1980s. In 1985, 64 members of the Central Committee "resigned" under pressure from Deng. Zhao Ziyang was named General Secretary of the party in 1987, replacing Hu Yaobang. Eventually, he in turn, after the crises of Tiananmen Square, was replaced by Jiang Zemin, in 1989.

Deng was also the driving force behind significant agricultural reforms during the 1980s, which led to partial de-collectivization. In 1984, control over industry was eased, giving local managers more authority. Prices were set at the local instead of the national level (at least in theory), and food and housing subsidies were reduced for urban dwellers. In 1985, the economy grew by 15%. That astounding leap in GNP would begin a pattern of growth that continued for decades.

Unfortunately, inflation and corruption also exploded. Attempts by more conservative forces to rein in the freer economic environment were not as successful as they would have liked. Deng also took a more "open" approach toward the outside world. Relations with the U.S. improved after the issue of American arms sales to Taiwan was aired in 1982. From Deng's perspective, that was particularly important given his assumption that China could not accomplish its modernizing goals without good relations with the United States. A cautious move to improve relations with the Soviet Union was also undertaken, but in the aftermath of the Soviet invasion of Afghanistan that became more difficult.

## 1989—Tiananmen Square

The death of Hu Yaobang, once considered the likely successor to Deng, in April 1989, ignited demonstrations by students who had long idolized him as a true reformer. By early May, they had turned out by the hundreds of thousands in the larger cities, particularly Beijing, waving banners with statements unheard of in China: "Down with Corruption! . . . Long Live Democracy! . . . Press Freedom!" . . . "Down with Rule by Men, Long Live the Rule of Law!" A level of student and public activism emerged that had not been seen since the most dramatic days of the 1919 May Fourth Movement 70 years before.

Tiananmen Square was literally taken over by a huge encampment of protesting students some of whom gained even more support by going on a hunger strike to demonstrate their commitment. Not only students but workers in cities throughout China became involved and their demands ranged from moderate calls for further democratization in China to protests against political and economic corruption. A shaken Communist Party leader, Zhao Ziyang, mingled with the student demonstrators and made some vague concessions, but was swept aside by Deng Xiao-ping and the more conservative Premier Li Peng.

There were clearly conflicting opinions among the leadership on just how to deal with the protesters. Moreover, the leadership itself appeared divided on larger issues of policy regarding the economy. Should it continue its rapid growth or rein in the increasingly open economy toward a more party-dominated one? Who would win in the leadership struggle thus had clear ramifications for China's entire economic future as well. But the more immediate crisis was in the streets and for the moment, the hardliners both political and economic were in the ascendance. For weeks, during a period of leadership indecision complicated by the visit of the Soviet leader Mikhail Gorbachev, the crisis grew and the humiliation of the government leaders along with it.

**President Xi Jinping**

Suddenly on June 4, tens of thousands of well-armed troops smashed their way through Beijing to the heart of the city, Tiananmen Square. The tanks crushed many in their path; estimates of those killed and wounded varied, from several hundred to the thousands. There were reports of soldiers firing indiscriminately into the crowds, invading hospitals to yank out life-support systems of the wounded, attacking doctors and engaging in other violent acts. The hardliners had won, at least for the time being.

The massacre in Beijing was followed by a massive nationwide campaign of political repression involving many arrests. This evoked outrage abroad and some limited, largely temporary, sanctions on the part of China's major trading partners, which had little effect on the hardliners dominant in Beijing. Clearly China's Communist leaders had weathered the storm, but the events of June 1989 would continue to haunt them for decades to come. The CCP had come very close to losing control of the country. The fall of eastern European communism over the next few years only reinforced that sense of vulnerability.

Parallel with this political crackdown, Deng Xiaoping's economic reform program went into reverse. In fact, some have surmised that the economic conservatives among the leadership had used the confrontation for their own ends, to return to a more Soviet-style command economy at almost the same time that the Soviet Union was unraveling. Central control over the economy was strengthened, prices were more closely controlled, and there was even talk of the "voluntary" recollectivization of agriculture.

Whatever senior leader Deng's commitment to stopping the political challenge and chaos of the streets in 1989 had been, he himself clearly remained convinced that China needed more, not fewer, economic freedoms. But for a time after the clashes on Tiananmen Square, Deng's pro-economic reformers were clearly in the minority among China's leading decision makers.

Eventually, though, by 1992, Deng Xiaoping and his supporters once again prevailed over the economic conservatives to reinvigorate the reforms. The private sector received encouragement, and in 1993 the free market concept was legitimized in the constitution. The "open" policy toward the outside world remained in effect, and foreign investment continued to flow in from the United States as well as from other sources.

Although opposition continued to be sternly repressed, China in the early 1990s experienced one change with important political possibilities. The provinces were gaining in autonomy and authority at the expense of the center. This was especially true of the comparatively prosperous and dynamic provinces along the coast.

### The Death of Deng Xiaoping

After years of waiting, the world heard of the news of Deng Xiaoping's death in February 1997. While he had not been influential in decision-making for years, many had waited for word of his death with trepidation. After all, more than once before, the death of a senior leader had set off dramatic developments in the People's Republic. In 1976, both the early death of Zhou Enlai in January and Mao's death in October had set off dramatic changes in the leadership of the country. Indeed, it was only with Mao's death that the forces were released that brought Deng Xiaoping to supreme power. And more recently the death of the former party Chairman Hu Yaobang, had set off the chain of events that eventually brought on the Tiananmen Crisis of June 1989. But in the first weeks after Deng's death it appeared that nothing of the sort was likely to occur this time around.

Chief among the differences was the very success Deng had brought about. When Deng first emerged in real power in the late 1970s he led a weak China with a military that would soon embarrass itself in the expedition against Vietnam, one that hardly made a dent on the international, political, or economic scene. A generation later the China of Deng has been drastically transformed.

In 1978 when Deng's authority began to be significant, Chinese exports to the world were U.S. $9.8 billion, but by 1995 they were U.S. $149 billion. By 2021, they reached U.S $340.5 billion. Steel production soared and urban Chinese lived increasingly in cities that often resembled huge construction sites that were the product of a building boom. More than a decade of double-digit growth rates had transformed China. Even the World Bank estimated that the number of people living in poverty had been cut by two thirds.

Thus by the time Deng died, an enormous percentage of Chinese felt invested in the new changes. While there were clear differences between some of the top leaders, the sort of issues that had divided the leadership in 1976 and for a time in 1989 seemed much milder. With even the conservative military making billions from their role in the surging economy there was clearly no turning back from the world that Deng had built. China would be an involved player in the world community. Only the details needed to be worked out. The dramatic and sometimes deadly struggle between the Maoists and

# China

**Deng Xiaoping**

the Pragmatists that had characterized aspects of the earlier Mao years seemed to have passed. There was far more general agreement on the new China that Deng had set in motion.

By Deng's death, Jiang Zemin was already well positioned to establish himself as the new dominant figure. His prominent role during the July 1997 Hong Kong transition and later his leadership at that fall's 15th congress of the Chinese Communist Party only confirmed his power through late 2002 when another smooth transition of power occurred.

### New Generations Emerge

In the fall of 2002 the long awaited 16th National Party Congress took place, and yet another generation of leaders emerged from the shadows. Most importantly, Hu Jintao, 59, the vice president and previous party boss of Tibet was chosen to head the 65-million-member Chinese Communist Party while a host of older leaders, men long known to the outside world retired. They included Zhu Rongji, the longtime premier, and Li Peng, who became infamous during the Tiananmen Crisis of 1989. Even as President Jiang was leaving office, his influence remained obvious, not only in the makeup of the new politburo, which was still packed with his supporters, but the apparently forced retirement as well of Li Ruihuan, one of Jiang's principal rivals.

Still, China's then new leader in 2003, Hu Jintao, steadily expanded his influence after coming to power. In fact, by the fall of 2004 ex-President Jiang formally surrendered his last official position of significance, as leader of the party's military commission. Hu Jintao added this to his other titles as president and head of the party. Jiang continued to remain influential behind the scenes.

Both leaders, Jiang and his immediate successor Hu Jintao, were clearly committed to continuing the general lines of reform begun by Deng Xiaoping, but they have faced a China much different from the one Deng had led. China has become far more integrated into the world system, its military and economy are far stronger, and the challenges its leaders face are different from those with which Deng dealt. That integration had become particularly important over the last year. Not only did the world watch as Chinese leaders found themselves increasingly involved in discussions of whether China would play a financial role in helping address the European debt crisis. But it took note of the care the United States took in establishing a strong relationship with the even newer leadership in China, which by mid-2011 was starting to assume authority.

That was especially important by 2014 because whatever the ambiguity of China's role during the earlier years of the 21st century, by 2014 China had clearly accomplished one of the nation's long-term goals. It had become a superpower along the lines people had once thought of the Soviet Union and of course the United States. Moreover, it was a superpower that was clearly looking forward to a day when the influence of the United States would become less paramount in world affairs and would be replaced by a system within which global issues would be decided by a larger group of the world's more influential countries including China and perhaps a newly reinvigorated Russia.

Unlike his predecessor, Mr. Hu, Mr. Xi is much more a member of the generation that came of age after the earliest years of the People's Republic. Indeed he came of age during the drama of the Cultural Revolution. Especially poignant is that the people who are now starting to take power are, unlike their predecessors, the first generation that did not arrive in power under Deng Xiaoping's more immediate sponsorship. Xi Jinping himself has traveled extensively abroad and even sent his daughter to study at Harvard. Perhaps of even greater significance regarding Xi Jinping is where and what he studied in college: chemical engineering at Tsinghua University, often known as China's MIT. Given the nature of 21st-century challenges from climate change to energy conversion, that background allows him the sort of perspective shared by the late British Conservative leader Margaret Thatcher, who was a chemist by education, or German Chancellor Angela Merkel, a physicist by training. That background is decidedly different from the legal training most American's leaders bring to the technical and scientific challenges of today's world.

**May 21, 1989: A People's Liberation Army convoy is engulfed by demonstrators in Tiananmen Square, Beijing**    Courtesy of AP Images

But as with any American president, China's current president does not completely dominate his own nation's political decision making. He shares power with a premier and a range of other institutions influential within the country.

The NPC or National People's Congress is no longer the rubber stamp it had once been. Over the years it has become more and more effective in occasionally challenging the Communist Party and in pushing for an enhancement of the rule of law. In 1995, it had successfully opposed changes in the education system and banking reform sponsored by party leaders. The body had also become the locus for increasingly popular expressions of opposition to government policies. Congress members are free to introduce their own legislative bills and members have even been willing to publicly oppose the government on matters as sensitive as politburo nominations. Public polling in recent years has shown that more and more citizens view the NPC as an important institution to which they can address their complaints. But it is not just public polling that shows a growing respect for institutions like the NPC. Until the mid 2010s, the Chinese Communist Party appeared to be increasingly interested in knowing what people are thinking and ever more concerned about being responsive to those opinions. Under Xi Jinping, however, the NPC has once again become something of a rubber stamping body.

At the local level it is still possible for non-party members to hold important positions of influence, something that would have been practically impossible in the past. Even more interesting has been the decision to allow local elections. Still, the Chinese Communist Party has made it clear that it intends to remain in ultimate control. It has worked vigorously to reinvigorate and train its more than 80 million members with precisely that goal in mind.

The government has continued to battle economic corruption especially that associated with the families of the senior leaders. This has been fundamentally weakening the Communist Party's ability to lead. The government has charged and convicted of corruption people holding positions of great political and economic responsibility. That effort has expanded dramatically since Xi Jinping came to power with reports in late 2013 that over 17,000 officials had been disciplined for corruption and financial extravagance. In early 2014 there were even reports of suicides by such officials.

### Xi's Bid for Power

Over the years since Xi first became head of state, his power has grown enormously, as has that of the government and party, reimposing tight control over the lives of ordinary Chinese in a fashion not seen in decades. This control includes the widespread use of surveillance devices in cities. In addition, under a plan introduced in 2014, a "social credit system" can be and is used to penalize deviant behavior—jaywalk, eat smelly food on a train, or play music too loudly and you can be penalized. Developments in 2020 as a reaction to COVID-19 (see below) have led to a further increase in state and party power, tolerated because of the successful containment of the virus after initial fumbling. Under the 2021-2025 Five Year Plan, the system is due to become more embedded. As for Xi, he has no obvious rival or successor. The lifting of the two term limit on the state presidency in 2018 cleared the way for Xi to go on indefinitely if he wants. The signs are that he does indeed intend to do so.

### Looking Forward: Thematic Issues for the 21st Century

In the 21st century, the People's Republic is not simply going to proceed on the path Deng laid out a generation ago. Deng Xiaoping was trying to "jumpstart" an economy that had been artificially wounded by impractical economic leadership. His goal was to reinvigorate that economy through internal reforms and an external opening to the world. But those initial goals were accomplished. His heirs, especially Jiang Zemin and Hu Jintao, were committed to refining the economic and social message that dominated Deng's years. With a few possible ideological exceptions, such as the recently disgraced Bo Xilai, most of China's emerging leaders have continued the commitment to China's growing role in the globalized world economy

Given the weakness of communism as an important unifying message, Jiang embarked upon several efforts to revitalize the party's rule starting with a call for a new "spiritual civilization" that combined elements of economic growth with both communitarian and nationalist elements.

More specifically, Jiang moved to revitalize the Chinese Communist Party by successfully opening up party membership to practicing capitalists. In short, China's leading party may still formally call itself "communist," but it has evolved far beyond the purely working class orientation of early communist theorists. But opening the doors of the party to members who are clearly not "communists" in any real sense of the word is hardly the same thing as opening up the political system. In short, is there any chance of a parallel opening toward democracy on the national level? At this point it seems not at all probable. Nevertheless, as discussed in the human rights section below, real changes are occurring at the grassroots level.

Overall, day-to-day developments will have to be understood in the context of an evolving China that is quite unevenly moving toward a more open future. For example, throughout the last few years the government continued to give mixed signals on its attitude toward reform. On the one hand, a new more open attitude evolved for a time that allowed for the publication and discussion of quite radical political ideas. Moreover the government has allowed village level elections and expanded those elections to the regions in China's far west. China's former leader, President Hu, had at times spoken

# China

very positively of expanding what he called democratic participation and democratic scrutiny of government activities. But that has not always been the case in reality.

Those who have challenged the ultimate authority of the Chinese Communist Party—however subtly—have over the years felt its wrath. This was well demonstrated by the harsh sentences handed down in late 1998 to several dissidents for attempting to organize a new party called the China Democracy Party.

Even more dramatically, the government moved in 1999 against those who had involved themselves in spiritual activities that seemed beyond official control. Most prominent was the official banning and at times brutal persecution of members of the Falun Gong, a quasi-religious movement that practices physical and meditative activities and had become enormously popular. In fact, the movement was so popular that the authorities, nervous that a mass movement able to attract such support and mindful of how dangerous such movements had been in earlier eras, set out to suppress Falun Gong. In the years since, thousands of Falun Gong followers have been arrested. Many of its leaders were given long prison sentences for having played a role, not in an organization that had formally challenged the authority of the state, but apparently for having taken part in a movement that might potentially do so.

Partly as an offshoot of China's growing economic transformation and the stresses that is putting on rural communities, China has been experiencing a regular series of violent local protests. Tens of thousands of these have been suppressed by local authorities. One incident that received much publicity was a confrontation in a village near Guangzhou in 2004. Over 20 people were killed by police officials attempting to quell demonstrations against land seizures.

Of more immediate interest is the fact that, unlike Deng Xiaoping or Jiang Zemin, whose emphasis was largely on economic growth, China's next leadership team, President Hu Jintao and Premier Wen Jiabao, seemed much more concerned about dealing with the more negative consequences of China's spectacular recent growth, from environmental degradation to social inequality. Indeed, as his last public speech departing President Hu especially focused on these issues as an important challenge for the future.

On the other hand, Xi Jinping, who took over during the spring of 2013, has led the CCP into an era when the momentum of political liberalization seems to be fast retreating into distant memory as the

**Former President Hu Jintao**

party has moved to reassert its dominant role in society.

As a practical matter, though, it has not been domestic democratic activists or even religious or spiritual movements like the Falun Gong that have really challenged the party. Rather, it was the drastic economic downturn that began in the United States in late 2008 that started to undermine the economic strength that has long been one of the most important features of the CCP's retention of power in China. All of these are probably the primary reasons the government moved quickly in the aftermath of the crisis of 2008 to implement a massive stimulus program to jump-start the economy while dramatically slowing down movement toward a more open Chinese society. Apparently greater openness in a time of economic crisis was not seen by

the leadership as a particularly helpful development.

Moreover, Xi himself has been quoted as saying that the most important issues he faces on a daily basis are, not surprisingly, corruption and environmental degradation. Both are undermining not only the country but the party's credibility.

### Economic Trends: From Communism to State Capitalism?

As the Chinese moved into the new millennium there was plenty of reason to feel both confidence and some concern. On one hand, the economies of many of her neighbors had been terribly hurt by the economic meltdown of the late 1990s and were only just beginning to recover. This was a meltdown that China itself had initially managed largely to avoid. In fact, despite her neighbors' problems the PRC maintained a very positive growth rate after 2008.

It was, of course, not the first time that China had missed the bullet of a major global economic meltdown. While not quite as planetary in scope as 2008, the Asian economic crises in 1997 had been very dangerous and had seen the economic collapse or near collapse of a great many of China's neighbors.

For Beijing, moving decisively was of fundamental importance. After all, the economy, which had boasted double-digit growth rates in the previous decade, had slowed to 9.7% in 1996 and dipped to an official 7.8% in 1998. Much of that growth was simply a result of government infrastructure spending. The numbers continued to dip for a time. But by 2000 they had started climbing again. GDP for 2002 came in at 8%, that for 2003 at 9.1%. By 2007 the figure had grown to over 11%. But that growth streak came to an abrupt

**Campus life in China, students walking on campus of Tian Shui Normal Teacher's College**

halt in late 2008 as another world economic crisis set in.

Unlike in 1997, China was far more impacted, especially as exports to the United States slowed dramatically. In fact, as the crisis set in, it began to look like China's growth rates were likely to dip to under 8%. However, while China did take a dramatic economic hit in the 2008 global economic downturn, decisive leadership by the central government was able to avert much of the damage. They did so by instituting a massive economic stimulus plan of over $586 billion coupled with directions to the nation's bankers to loosen credit restrictions to spur growth. The effort worked and China ended 2009 with a growth rate again over 8%. The following year came in a much healthier 10.4% while the next dropped to only a bit over 9%. It has not been an encouraging trend. Growth in 2012 of 7.8% was still enviable by the standards of many countries, but it was under the 8% figure the nation's leaders have often said was the minimum growth rate China required. Relatively strong growth or not, there have for years been plenty of reasons for long-term economic concern.

The entire economy continues as it has for years to be handicapped by the inefficient state-owned enterprises (SOEs). China has hundreds of thousands of SOEs, many of which operate at a financial loss. The total cost of propping them up over the years has been enormous. Chinese leaders have long been aware of the problem, but doing something about it has been quite another matter. After all, Beijing's leadership has understood that hundreds of millions of workers are still employed in the state sector. Fearing social unrest, the government until recently was very hesitant to begin the reorganization, especially given the subsequent growth in unemployment that reforming that sector would require.

With Deng's departure and Jiang Zemin's solidification of power, the leadership was finally ready to bite the bullet and begin in earnest the transformation of the state enterprises. At the 1997 fall party Congress, Jiang announced that a major effort would commence—despite the perhaps necessary massive layoffs—to reform that lagging part of the economy. The program called for a range of actions from complete shutdowns to mergers and reorganizations to deal with the problem. Recognizing by the spring of 1998 the dangers of further economic dislocation given the regional economic slowdown and the anticipated problems associated with reforming the state enterprises, Beijing decided to move even more dramatically. It committed itself to further reforms and a massive economic stimulus effort,

especially aimed at the agricultural and the housing sector, to spur the economy.

However, China's leadership has been interested in far more than merely reforming the state enterprises. More recent years have seen a very committed effort to move dramatically away from the entire system of a communist-based command economy. Building on the momentum begun during Deng Xiaoping's tenure in office, the last decades have seen an incredible array of changes that in their totality fundamentally represent an almost complete repudiation of communism as China's governing economic principle.

Thus during the late spring of 1999 the Chinese Parliament finally decided officially to recognize capitalism as an important part of China's new socialist market economy. A few months later Beijing announced that henceforth private enterprises would be placed on an "equal footing with state-owned enterprises." Capitalists have officially been invited to join the Communist Party, and China's national legislature moved to amend the constitution to protect private property. By 2004, while the state-owned enterprises were still undergoing massive changes, more than three million private companies had emerged that were themselves employing close to 50 million workers. Perhaps most interesting was the decision to strengthen the laws on private property. This was another clear sign of Beijing's fundamental rejection of formal communism as a guiding economic principle. Of special interest

in this regard was the adoption of the new Property Law in 2007, which finally passed after years of controversy. It dealt with issues ranging from transferring property to ownership. While not overturning the core socialist assumption that the state owned all land, it did provide important new safeguards for individual citizens and businesses. That momentum continued into 2008 as moves were underway to give rural Chinese the right to buy and sell long-term land rights.

China's entrance into the World Trade Organization has also forced many new challenges on the once relatively isolated Chinese environment. The gradual opening of markets forces enormous changes. They range from continuing efforts to transform the Chinese legal system so that they conform to international norms to putting even more pressure on her still important state enterprises to become more financially efficient.

Aside from the years of obvious growth, other signs indicate the changing international economic environment. That the People's Republic of China emerged a few years ago as an even bigger market for Volkswagens than the United States is a fact that highlights the growing interest by Chinese consumers in purchasing their own automobiles. This is a development that was unimaginable only a few years ago. China's trading patterns are also evolving. In recent years Southeast Asia has become a particularly important market for Chinese goods and might one

**Chengdu's famous panda park**

# China

day soon even pass the United States as a market.

Of particular interest for outside commercial interests is the reality that after generations of frustrated foreign entrepreneurs who mistakenly embraced the famous image of China as a vast untapped market, the situation is finally starting to change for the better. For more than a hundred years the idea of the endless "China Market" was one that had seduced foreign businessmen. They embraced the dream of seeing hundreds of millions of Chinese becoming a vast heretofore untapped market for foreign sales. Alas, for most of China's recent history, that rarely turned out to be true. But soon after the dawn of the new century, a majority of American firms reported that their Chinese efforts have finally become profitable. Even the Chinese government has gotten involved in China's new consumer market. Concerned that the nation is too dependent on foreign export markets, Beijing has been encouraging the growth of its own consumer markets to insulate the nation's economy from the sort of economic shocks that were arriving by early 2009. Still, research suggests that, despite the popular impression that encouraging more consumerism will help, that may not be the case. Apparently Chinese consumers already play such a role and are not likely to do more than they already do.

China's economy has been struggling to coordinate successfully the new green renewable energy sources that are quickly coming on line. The problem is that China's impressive ability to ramp up production facilities and lower prices has seen the over production, for example, of solar energy materials. Moreover there is also a parallel effort going on to wean the economy from more energy intensive industries like steel and cement production to less environmentally demanding economic activities.

Still, the fact that China entered 2015 as, by some calculations, the world's largest economy, a position that has been maintained, finally passing the United States (when adjusted for the purchasing power of their currencies) marked a major milestone in the evolution of the global economy. Another important milestone came early in 2021, when President Xi Jinping announced that the country had reached the goal that he had set on coming to power in 2012 of eradicating extreme poverty by the time of the 100th anniversary of the CCP. Clearly great progress had been made, but critics have pointed out that the bar was set rather low, with extreme poverty being defined as under $600. There had also been human costs, with people compelled to move to new apartments, sometimes with few work opportunities. Massive construction expenditure had also provided new opportunities for corruption. Nevertheless, a major target had been met within its planned timeframe, further strengthening Xi's position.

## Foreign Relations of the People's Republic

After riding out the international tensions created by the events of 1989, China has begun to play a much more significant international role than it did in the early years of its existence. Beijing was the site for the 1995 UN-sponsored Fourth World Conference on Women. In 2008, it hosted the successful Summer Olympics, and in September 2016, the G-20 Summit took place for the first time in China. In 2022, it hosted the Winter Olympics. This event was somewhat overshadowed by tight security designed to prevent protests over Xi Jinping's increasingly autocratic rule and then by the Russian invasion of Ukraine. In the end, the games were deemed a qualified success, not the

least because the Ukrainian athletes came second in the tally of medals. China's role in the world has become more like that of a traditional superpower, in a fashion it has not exhibited during the last two centuries of world history. In short, China is back.

It is also true that China has entered a more assertive period in its foreign relations. Its economic progress has certainly created conditions where the country's leaders apparently feel it appropriate and necessary for China to assume a higher profile internationally. In effect, after more than a century of weakness, Beijing is clearly ready to resume its former place of significance in the world.

As mentioned, with the relative weakening of communist ideology, Han Chinese nationalism has become the best means of drumming up support for the Central Government and the CCP. This works both domestically and internationally. Domestically, it has led to the rallying of the Han Chinese behind the government's policies towards unrest in Tibet in 2008 and 2013 and its steadily harsher policies towards the Uighur of Xinjiang since 2013. This insistence that China is, at heart, a Han country, has spread to other areas. It is one of the factors that have led to a tough approach to perceived dissidence in Hong Kong, and there is increasing evidence of its application in other minority areas such as the Yanbian Korean Autonomous Prefecture in Jilin Province.

Internationally, nationalism has supported a more robust policy over China's claims in the East China Sea. Claims and counter-claims over the island group that are known as the Daiyu-tai in China and as the Senkaku Islands in Japan have led to tensions with Japan and the United States. The United States also opposes the Chinese claims in the South China Sea, which are challenged to a greater or lesser degree by Vietnam, the Philippines, Malaysia, Brunei and Taiwan. But because the area has become a major international trade route, Chinese claims are also challenged by the United States and other countries that believe the area constitutes international waters. So far, while there are regular confrontations between Chinese and US warships in the area, more serious conflict has been avoided. The change of president in the US may help, since Joe Biden is unlikely to follow the brinkmanship apparently favored by Donald Trump, even if he seems to share many of the latter's suspicions of Chinese economic and foreign policy aims.

The attempts by Japanese extremists to assert their control over the islands known in China as the Diaoyus have long been a good example of the complexities of nationalism in this new era. Chinese

**Morning exercises in Shanghai**

Courtesy of Steven A. Leibo

**Carved Buddha in Tibet**

Courtesy of Steven A. Leibo

Especially important has been Beijing's support for a sanctions regime declared by the United Nations against North Korea since 2013. Soon after that, Beijing made another important announcement regarding a reduction in the number of military related materials it was willing to export to North Korea.

But while Beijing is clearly concerned about the significance of North Korean nuclear activities, there is also a growing concern that Washington's unwillingness to recognize North Korea's genuine security concerns only adds to the problems. While North Korean leaders were probably heartened by Beijing's comments about Washington's supposed lack of sympathy for their security concerns, they were not likely to be pleased by other reports that influential Chinese figures were openly discussing the idea of regime change and the advantages such a change might bring to China. That loss of confidence was no doubt reinforced in 2013 when North Korea's young leader abruptly executed his uncle, who had been thought to have strong ties to Chinese officials.

There are other examples of China's more assertive stance with its more immediate neighbors. Most notably in that regard has been its recent successful effort to pressure its South East Asian neighbors to prohibit the outlawed Falun Gong from using their territories for broadcasting what Beijing sees as anti-government Chinese-language programming back into the People's Republic. Not surprisingly there has also been a bit of a backlash as China's neighbors have l shown more receptivity to stronger ties to the United States than they had for years. Most obvious in the deterioration of relations with Southeast Asia are the growing tensions with Vietnam. A regular series of clashes in the waters that separate the two nations is inflaming nationalist tensions in both countries and has prompted Beijing to evacuate some of its citizens from Vietnam.

On a different front, relations with India have became much more complicated after India's government not only officially announced its new status as a nuclear power by setting off a series of underground nuclear tests in 1998, but it did so while citing tensions with China as one of the reasons to do so. Not surprisingly, that outraged Beijing and played a role in its willingness to work with Washington to try to avoid a nuclear arms race in South Asia. Nevertheless, by the spring of 2003 relations between Beijing and New Delhi were improving and eventually culminated in the visit by India's ex-Prime Minister Vajpayee. In 2014, Xi Jinping visited India, and the following year,

of all stripes, from Hong Kong to Taiwan and the People's Republic, can be united in anger against these Japanese efforts.

This evolution has also been especially obvious in China's efforts to challenge more vigorously both Japan and its more powerful ally, the United States, in the Western Pacific. For example, in November 2013 China announced that all aircraft entering a significant percentage of the East China Sea would henceforth be expected to register with Chinese authorities and submit their flight plans. Predictably neither the United States nor Japan was willing to comply with Beijing's not-so-subtle attempt to claim greater authority over the area. Sadly, the tensions and frequency of incidents and the potential for even more dramatic clashes have gone up. Some even speculate on the possibility of a genuine military clash of the sort not seen between Japan and China in more than a half century.

But such tension cannot be exclusively associated with Beijing's desire to justify its leadership as the defender of the nationalist honor in the vacuum left by the weakening of communism. The sentiments are quite genuine among the Chinese population. In part, they are caused by the postwar unwillingness of Japan, unlike the Germans have in Europe, to confront fully the reality of the horrors Tokyo inflicted on so many peoples of the region during the Second World War. The

issue was obvious during the spring of 2005 when thousands of Chinese demonstrated against the Japanese government's continuing effort to downplay the violence of its World War II assault on China as portrayed in its school textbooks. It also plays a role in popular Chinese sentiment against Japan's gaining a permanent position in the United Nations' Security Council. The fact that Japan itself is clearly moving past its postwar pacifism as well is only likely to exacerbate these developments.

Relations with North Korea's remain very important to Beijing. In fact, Beijing's new international role has been especially obvious when one looks at the growing involvement in the issue of North Korea's ongoing and controversial efforts to develop not only a nuclear weapon's program but the complementary missile systems necessary to deliver such weapons. Over the years though not only have Beijing leaders made it quite clear that they oppose their old ally's efforts to develop such weapons but became the host and sponsor of a new set of multilateral talks between the regional powers and the United States on the problem. Unfortunately, those "Six Party Talks" petered out in 2009, without achieving their objective.

Beijing has in many ways emerged as an important player in the effort to confront North Korea's nuclear ambitions.

# China

**Lake side in Kaifeng**

Courtesy of Steven A. Leibo

the Indian prime minister, Narendra Modie, made a return visit. Still Sino-Indian relations have remained quite volatile, with regular border clashes, and clearly lack the ongoing and improving relations Beijing has long maintained with India's archrival, Pakistan.

The future of Sino-Indian relations are likely to be even more complicated as modern technology and the two Asian giants' growing interests in areas from Southeast Asia, especially Myanmar, to South and Southwest Asia brings their interests more and more frequently into potential conflict. It should also be assumed that Chinese influence in Pakistan and Afghanistan, especially as the American role in the region diminishes, is likely to grow thus adding to the areas of potential tension with India.

The fact that India joined with the United States, Japan, and Australia to form The Quad (originally formed in 2004 but dormant from 2007–2017) with the aim of countering Chinese influence in Asia indicates that a major improvement in relations is not likely for some time to come.

Within the United Nations China has also played an increasingly important role. In 1999 China opposed NATO's violent intervention in Kosovo. On the other hand Beijing has not always been absolutely against intervention in the internal affairs of other nations. When the United Nations decided in mid-1999, with the permission of Indonesia, to send a force

to East Timor, China cooperated by sending a team of Chinese policemen to help. That continuing commitment to the work of the United Nations has continued. By 2004 Beijing had even dispatched a contingent of Chinese security people to help out in Haiti, China's first contribution to such a force in the Western Hemisphere.

China was also been involved in the controversy that arose early in the century over the question of whether Saddam Hussein's Iraq was sufficiently complying with its international obligations to end the most dangerous of its weapons programs. Within that context the PRC often worked closely with other Security Council members like France and Russia to resolve the issues. When the United States chose to overthrow Saddam Hussein's government in Iraq, China, along with many nations including France to Russia, made it clear that it would have preferred a less violent and diplomatic resolution to the crisis than what eventually transpired. China's more recent role vis-à-vis recent international efforts to deal constructively with the uprising in Syria has been equally complicated, as have her relatively good relations with Iran, another internationally problematic nation in the Middle East.

One of the newer dimensions of China's international role has been a newly developed relationship with the nations of Central Asia that emerged out of the collapse of the Soviet Union. Not only have Chinese goods become especially common in the central markets of those

nations, but Beijing has offered significant levels of support to help the region build up its infrastructure. Relations with Russia have become closer over the years. Russian President Vladimer Putin was one of the few world leaders to attend the opening ceremony of the 2022 Winter Olympics in Beijing. China has responded cautiously to the Russian invasion of Ukraine, and there were some reports that Putin agreed to postpone the beginning of the attack so that the games could open successfully. Chinese commentators take a consistently pro-Russian line, which must have the tolerance at least of the country's leadership.

Particularly interesting has been China's growing economic and diplomatic relationships with the countries of Latin America and Africa. President Hu visited both continents and was well received. While Beijing's ties to South America are currently dwarfed by the relationship the region has with its northern neighbor, the United States, they are likely to grow significantly over the next several decades.

In the case of Africa, both China and the United States have been showing renewed interest because of the available oil resources. For its part, China has promised enormous loans to various African nations as well as debt cancellation. Both efforts complement the large sums China is investing in the continent. Especially significant is the fact that from 2001 to 2007 Chinese trade with Africa went up over seven times and has continued to grow at an impressive rate. Moreover, China's role in the Darfur crisis also evolved significantly in recent years from what was early perceived as support for the Sudan's government to one more in line with other major United Nation powers' efforts to confront one of the world's most human-rights challenged regions.

### Sino-American Relations

A significant part of China's foreign policy has centered on resolving issues with the United States. Unfortunately, relations continue to be very complicated, at times quite tense. Those tensions were exacerbated in 2005 by one of China's leading energy firm's offer to purchase the relatively unknown American oil company, Unocal. This company has been especially involved in efforts to develop central Asian oil fields. Although the company itself was a minor player, and American companies, particularly banks, have of late been buying into the Chinese banking industry, the Unocal offer set off a dramatic set of concerns in Washington that ultimately resulted in the cancellation of the offer and a new round of anti-Chinese rhetoric in the United States. The revelation in

Courtesy of Steven A. Leibo

early 2013 that a very specific unit of the Chinese military based near Shanghai has been behind the long-term series of cyber attacks against Western governmental and corporate interests has been particularly inflammable. None of the charges were particularly new, but they did represent a growing American anxiety about China's emerging world influence and economic power. Even more recently, tensions related to conflicting claims in the East China Sea have added to the problems. Overall, though, these differed little from the earlier moments of tension that have been so common a feature of the complicated relationship that exists between the two world giants.

During the early Clinton administration, the United States government's policy was geared toward exacting human rights concessions from China before economic relations could progress. This included holding up "most favored nations" status for China. In May 1994, however, the policy was modified. Despite his early campaign statements, President Clinton changed his approach to one of "comprehensive engagement," assuming the same approach to China as the administration of George H. W. Bush. The change was not surprising. Clinton had come to understand that the People's Republic was simply too large and too important economically and diplomatically to ignore. Far too many economic and geopolitical issues required Beijing's cooperation. China was critical for dealing with issues ranging from North Korea's nuclear aspirations to progress on nuclear

non-proliferation to working within the United Nation's Security Council where China holds a permanent veto. But that change hardly resolved all the problems.

The 1994 decision again to allow high-tech exports to China had by 1999 become very controversial. At that time charges surfaced that sophisticated missile technology had "accidentally" been transferred to the PRC by American companies as well as claims that the Chinese had gained valuable nuclear technology by spying. These charges, which put the Clinton administration on the defensive, eventually forced a cutback in nuclear cooperation.

Moreover, the American-led military campaign in Yugoslavia also added to the tensions when the People's Republic sided with those nations which found the NATO bombing campaign unacceptable. Concerns over the NATO campaign in Yugoslavia and most probably the accumulated tensions that had developed over the years were dramatically revealed when in May 1999 the United States accidentally bombed the Chinese embassy in Belgrade, Serbia. The resulting explosion of Chinese anger clearly highlighted how potentially divisive the relationship can become.

Ironically, given the fact that former President Clinton had largely adopted the China policy of his predecessor, George Herbert Walker Bush, his own successor, George W. Bush began his administration with a China policy considerably more critical than either of his two predecessors. In fact, from the new American

president's plans to build a missile defense system (which the Chinese feared would negate their own limited nuclear missile program) to the mid-air crash in early 2001 between an American surveillance plane and a Chinese jet, a host of tensions emerged.

Thus, it is not surprising that the Chinese side too has plenty of its own criticism of America. Especially important was the sense by many in China that the Americans were frequently unwilling to treat them with the respect and equality their size and accomplishments have earned them. The Chinese were also particularly aware that many American groups, from environmentalists and human rights activists to religious fundamentalists and many politicians, had "adopted" China as their "favorite whipping boy." America's continuing support of the Tibetan exile community and Taiwan remain long-term irritants given the Chinese perspective that the U.S. has too often intervened in what are seen as domestic issues.

Fortunately, after the drama of September 11, 2001, as Americans began to focus on the War on Terrorism and the ways China might help in that struggle, the more immediate tensions between the two nations started to wane and a level of cooperation not seen for years began to prevail. It was unfortunately that smoother relationship that again began to unravel later in the decade as more Americans once again started vocalizing their anxiety about the eventual impact on the United States of China's extraordinary recent growth.

Today, many Americans openly talk of the People's Republic with considerable antagonism and argue that China's growth fundamentally threatens the United States. Under the circumstances, it is not at all surprising that it is commonplace among many groups in China to believe that the United States is committed to limiting its emergence as a major world power. But perhaps even more to the point, many have come to see the United States as a declining power in a world that will see China ever more dominant.

Many issues, from Xinjiang, to Hong Kong, to environmental concerns, have added fuel to the frequently open tensions between the two nations. On an even more fundamental level, there is a very good chance that Sino-American relations will become dominated in the near future by tensions stemming from their respective need to find new sources of oil. As an especially poignant reminder of evolving world realities, it was reported in late 2012 that China had finally surpassed the United States as the largest national importer of petroleum.

# China

One should not forget the simple reality that irresponsible financial policies in the United States have left it increasingly dependent on Beijing's good will to maintain the flow of Chinese money invested in American treasury bills. They are, of course, needed to keep America's precarious financial house in relative health.

During President Obama's first official visit to China in late 2009, he was, to the irritation of some of his political opponents much more conciliatory toward China's leadership than visiting presidents have usually been. Eschewing the long-term American enthusiasm for confrontations over human rights and trade imbalances for a more positive and respectful tone, Obama was willing to recognize Beijing's significant accomplishments. Still he forged ahead in areas that the PRC's leadership still finds especially irritating: the official reception of Tibet's long-exiled Dalai Lama and support for Taiwan. These policies were even more to the fore during the presidency of Donald Trump, who gave strong vocal support to those who feared the "rise of China." While the rhetoric has been somewhat toned down since 2021 under President Biden, the latter, too, is concerned about China's policies both towards its neighbors and its growing economic might. Biden has repeatedly asserted that the United States will not abandon Taiwan,

especially since the Russian invasion of Ukraine in February 2022.

For some, the relationship between the United States and China has taken on new significance as more and more people have come to understand that only successful cooperation between the world's two largest carbon polluters and economies can enable humanity to seriously arrest the dangers of an increasingly destabilized global climate system.

One of the most prominent issues to emerge in Sino-American relations has centered on China's assertive role in claiming sovereignty over the South China Sea and more specifically literally building small atols into formally occupied islands using land fill as a tool to assert their claims. This has aroused tensions with most of China's neighbors and seen the United States in support of those nations asserting the international status of the region by flying over and sailing through the region with military patrols.

Another important reality behind Sino-American relations is that the two powers have entered an almost unprecedented period in their relationship. There is almost no global issue, from energy to terrorism, from global warming to North Korea that does not require a cooperative relationship between Washington and Beijing. That level of unprecedented global international cooperation was not part of the earlier Anglo-American, Russo-American, or

even Japanese-American relationship. But it certainly is central to today's contemporary international reality.

Over the decades, though, another much more limited issue tended to dominate U.S.-China relations. The fate of a relatively small island, Taiwan, once known as Formosa, has long remained at the core of American-Chinese relations and an issue that emerged again on the world scene in the aftermath of the election of Donald Trump in the U.S. who initially appeared willing to challenge long-term understandings about Taiwan.

### The U.S./PRC/Taiwan Triangle

From Beijing's perspective, Taiwan remains a very important issue in Sino-American relations. That is not surprising. The PRC's leaders and much of the Chinese population continue to see the island as a fundamental part of the Chinese homeland and remain deeply committed to seeing Taiwan become part of the People's Republic one day. Perhaps of even more immediate concern is the general impression among China's leadership that an official loss of the island might ultimately signal its own downfall. After all, communism no longer commands much allegiance in the People's Republic, and the party has had to define itself in much more nationalist terms. This new legitimacy requires the CCP to do everything

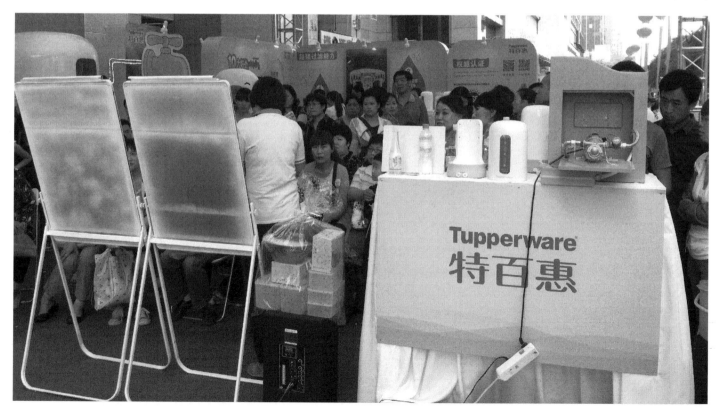

Courtesy of Steven A. Leibo

42

it can to keep the hope alive of Taiwan eventually reuniting with the mainland.

Thus it is from that ongoing aspiration that Beijing constantly works to negate Taiwan's efforts to join the international community officially. In fact, Beijing has long applied pressure to any country that cooperated with Taiwan's efforts to integrate itself more formally into the world community. In that context, relations with the United States have been particularly problematic due to Beijing's constantly frustrated hope that the United States would lessen its long-term support of Taiwan. From Beijing's perspective the hope is that the island's leaders might be more willing to resolve their differences with the mainland if America were not so openly supportive.

During 1996, U.S.-China relations were especially tense as Taiwan's first presidential election campaign was going on. In fact, concerned that voters would support a pro-independence party, Chinese naval forces initiated very provocative military maneuvers off the coast of the Republic, actually firing live shells vaguely in the direction of Taiwan's leading port. As the election decision drew near, Beijing kept up the threatening stance, clearly hoping to weaken the popularity of those who were calling for Taiwan's independence from the mainland.

For its part, Washington responded by sending two carriers into the waters off Taiwan. When the election finally took place, the result was an impressive victory for then Taiwan's President Lee, who

had maneuvered his campaign brilliantly between those on the island who emphasized independence and those who wanted reunification with the mainland. China had not succeeded with its scare tactics. Sadly, tensions over this issue are easily aroused. During 1999 Taiwan President Lee started another firestorm of new tensions by announcing that henceforth discussions between Taiwan and the People's Republic should be carried out as equal "state-to-state" relations. But that was nothing compared to the reaction when, in the 2000 elections, the Democratic Progressive candidate, Chen Shuibian, long an advocate of formal Taiwanese independence from China, was quite unexpectedly elected the new president.

It is true that Beijing's reaction to Chen's election was reasonably restrained. Nevertheless, Taiwan's slow yet obviously committed efforts to keep distancing itself from the mainland continued to be a constant irritation. Sometimes the efforts were quite subtle, as when Taipei decided to print the word "Taiwan" on its citizens' passport—a move that was done, it was said simply to make things easier during international travel. Sometimes the efforts have been much less subtle: during the run-up to the 2004 presidential elections on Taiwan, President Chen's government backed plans for a referendum on the question of Beijing's military threat toward the island. In that particular case the administration of George W. Bush, putting aside its usually strong commitment to Taiwan, publicly argued

against holding the referendum, a move that gained Beijing's public gratitude.

As we have seen elsewhere the American balancing act on relations with China and Taiwan have been relatively stable though that bi-partisan approach was challenged as a result of the American election of 2016.

It is important, though, not to overemphasize the tensions that are often at the heart of the Taiwan–People's Republic relationship. Over the years, the two have become closer and closer in economic areas, and the days when it was impossible to travel or communicate directly from Taiwan to the mainland are long over. In fact, in 2007 an extraordinarily new development occurred. After years of discussion, both governments officially agreed to begin direct flights. Finally, at very long last, travelers were not required to go first to some alternate destination such as Hong Kong before moving on to their final Taiwan destination. The first official and regularly scheduled direct flights began in the summer of 2008.

For a time the most important development in Taiwanese-Chinese relations was the Nationalists' return to power through the Presidency of Taiwan. Taiwan's then president, Ma Ying-jeou, specifically ran on a platform of lessening tensions with Beijing with the hope of using those improved relations to help Taiwan's weakening economy. Ma carried out that pledge despite significant criticism from some quarters in Taiwan which of course also played a role in his party's most recent loss of the presidency.

Since the return of the Taiwan's more independence minded DPP to power the situation has of course changed. Changed because Beijing knows they have no interest in ever reuniting with the mainland and more importantly the simply fact that the People's Republic's growing strength makes Taiwan's formally becoming independent from the mainland an impossible dream.

Overall, Americans need to understand that when dealing with Beijing on issues related to Taiwan, the fate of the latter is viewed through mainland Chinese lenses as primarily a domestic issue and more specifically tied to the long-term viability of China's Communist Party. The reality of that issue's complications became especially obvious in late 2016 when America's president elect Donald Trump began suggesting that he was open to a reevaluation of the question of the United States' relationship with Taiwan despite Beijing's long-term insistence that Taiwan must ultimately retake its place within a unified China. Chinese worries about a possible U.S. change of policy grow stronger once Trump was in the White House.

**Downtown Chengdu**     Courtesy of Steven A. Leibo

# China

These concerns proved to have some foundation. From the very beginning of his presidency, when he took a congratulatory call from Taiwan's President Tsai In-wen, Trump adopted a conciliatory approach to Taiwan. He allowed the export of $15 billion worth of arms, including F-16 fighters that had been blocked by the Obama administration. And just before he left office in 2021, he lifted the rules that had banned U.S. senior administration offficials from having contact with their Taiwan counterparts. The change of president in 2021 at first reduced the Chinese concern somewhat; after all Joe Biden had been Obama's vice president.

But as Biden settled into office, he showed himself just as willing as former President Trump to indicate support for Taiwan. In an unprecdented move, he invited the Taiwan representative in Washington to attend his inauguration. Later, he also approved further arms sales to Taiwan. In October 2021, he said that the U.S. would defend Taiwan if it was attacked, although officials said that there was no change in official policy. It was reported in April 2022 that Nancy Pelosi, the Democratic Party speaker of the house of representatives, would visit Taiwan. In the meantime, she caught COVID and was unable to go.

The Russian invasion of Ukraine in February 2022—an attack by a large neighboring country on a smaller entity that it claimed had no right to exist—raised alarm bells in Taiwan and elsewhere. But the Western response and aid to Ukraine proved reassuring. And in Japan in May 2022, on his first presidential visist to Asia, Biden drew an explicit linkage between events in Ukraine and Taiwan, and warned China that if it attacked the island, the U.S. would intervene militarily.

The official Chinese response was that there were no parallels between Ukraine and Taiwan and the U.S. should abide by the "one China" principle.

### U.S.-China Economic Relations

The Sino-American economic relationship has taken on a new and potentially burdensome dimension in recent years. There are very serious arguments about differing methods of registering trade and whether such measurements are meaningful in a world where products are often assembled from parts made in many regions of the world. These complicate discussions. But it is still clear that frustrations associated with the trade imbalance between the United States and China have come to resemble the sort of economic tensions that once dominated the American-Japanese relationship.

That trade imbalance is enormous; according to one estimate, it has been usually around the $350 billion annually, although it dropped to just over $310 billion in 2020, as a result of the Covid pandemic. It is also true that the numbers can vary considerably, depending on who is consulted and how the figures are calculated. The Chinese estimates of the imbalances are generally lower than those the U.S. claims. Of course, it is usually forgotten that most of the so-called Chinese "sales" are not really Chinese goods per se. They are outside goods produced by Western—often American—companies that arrange for the manufacture within China of goods they plan to sell in the United States. Perhaps most revealing is the example of the very familiar American product, the Barbie doll. Such a doll might sell for $20 in an American store, but the Chinese themselves only pocket around 35 cents from its production. Even more importantly, much of the imbalance really reflects the centralization of Asian manufacturing in China from other Asian countries, something very few commentators have apparently noticed. It is worth noting as well that recent talks have focused on the various trade restrictions that the United States has imposed on its own trade with China. This is a significant burden that Chinese officials cite when explaining why the gap is so great. From their perspective, expanding the range of goods China can buy from the United States would have a significant impact on the trade balance.

Regardless of the different interpretations, the Clinton, Bush, Obama, Trump and Biden administrations have all been committed to basing these economic ties on a more equal footing than had evolved over the years with Japan. Unfortunately, the success of the agreements too often relied on success in other areas of the complex relationship. Progress in other areas, such as weapons sales and nuclear technology, seemed likely to impact positively on the trade imbalance if politics did not intervene.

One of the most important early economic issues in Sino-American relations over the years was the question of whether the United States would support China's entry into the World Trade Organization (WTO). The principal problem was whether China would be admitted as a developing nation or as an already developed one. The definitional issue was important in that each carried with it different requirements concerning a country's economic obligations to the rest of the world. The Chinese wanted to be admitted as a developing nation. The West insisted it adhere to the standards set for the developed world. Obviously, given its enormous size and diversity, China represents aspects of both. After years of negotiations, real progress was made in 1999 when the U.S. and China finally signed and ratified an agreement on China's bid to enter the WTO. The deal itself obliged China to cut tariffs an average of 23% and offer greater access for U.S. firms.

By 2001 China finally did enter the WTO. It was accomplished with the support of the United States although that hardly made their economic relations any less complicated. By 2005, an entirely new

**Chengdu**

By early 2009, even as the United States was going deeper and deeper into debt to jump-start its dramatically weakening economy, China itself was not only starting to spend billions of dollars on its own infrastructure-building stimulus programs. It was also reportedly more wary of becoming even more deeply linked to America's financial problems than it already was. Dramatically, the governor of the People's Bank of China even suggested during 2010 that the world consider ending its reliance on the dollar as the most important international currency.

Perhaps most important was the reality that as the global economic recession of 2008–2009 emerged, it was increasingly obvious that the United States and China were linked at the hip economically. The deep linkages between the two societies had created a situation that made the economic health of each nation of vital interest to the other. This was becoming more apparent with each passing day and one made especially graphic by the fact that America has over the years become the world's biggest debtor nation while China has emerged as the world's creditor nation. China itself had replaced Japan as the nation to which America owes the most. Despite periodic political tensions, that remains the case in 2022.

While not yet as significant an issue as it is likely to become in future years, China's increasing need for more imported oil to fuel its growing economy is certainly going to add to the tensions with the United States. Indeed China has become the world's largest importer, and the U.S. also continues to demand more of the world's limited oil resources for its own needs. Sadly, some have already predicted a future "resource war" between Washington and Beijing. Events in 2022, that have seen a massive rise in oil prices worldwide, have once again highlighted the issue.

More to the point, though, is the simple reality that China is has caught up to the United States as an economic power. Demonstrating that especially graphically was the news in 2013 that China had finally surpassed America as the largest trading nation in the world.

On a more positive note, the American administration under Barack Obama offered to work with Beijing more creatively and cooperatively with regard to energy. This would not only reduce the likelihood of a clash over diminishing energy based on fossil fuels. It would affect their mutual impact on the global climate as well.

Of course, of late even that has become more complicated as China seems to have committed itself even more to a green energy future while America under the Trump administration appears intent on

**Catholic church in Shanghai**

Courtesy of Steven A. Leibo

dimension had been added to their relationship as American coat hanger manufacturers began using China's new status as a WTO member to attack their Chinese competitors. China fought back with a combination of American law firms and their own anti-dumping legal charges. Concerns about trade could often go far beyond that of coat hangers. Chinese purchases of Boeing airplanes have been among the most important products the Americans have been able to sell to the Chinese.

But Boeing's future in China is not certain. During 2005, Chinese officials signed a very lucrative deal with Boeing's principal competitor, the European firm Airbus, for the eventual purchase and cooperative assembly of 150 planes. There were, no doubt, many reasons for the Chinese decision. Boeing's chances were not helped by the discovery that a new Boeing aircraft that had been ordered by the Chinese leadership was "somehow" built with dozens of spying devices included.

Boeing continued to operate in China but has not had any new orders since 2017—aircraft are still being delivered from earlier contracts. But there have been other problems. Like other coutries, China grounded the 737 Max after two fatal crashes were attributed to design

faults. And in March 2022, a Boeing 737-800 belonging to China Eastern Airlines that crashed in Guangxi Province, killing all 132 people aboard.

Another dramatic issue was the American decision in 2005 to put limits on the growth of Chinese textile exports to the United States. In response, hoping to avoid an escalation of tensions, China raised its own export tariffs, while slightly revaluing its currency around 2.5%. This was, in some measure, a response to its critics. Still, as mentioned above, the majority of American companies are now reporting that their Chinese-based operations have become profitable.

Although rarely discussed publicly, one aspect of enormous significance to the Sino-American economic relationship is that the United States has been running extraordinarily large budget deficits that have been kept largely manageable only because the PRC, with its growing economy, has been making huge purchases of dollar-based goods, including American treasury notes. In fact, the amounts are so large that they have helped keep American interest rates low and the American economy vital. However, China's willingness to continue to "subsidize" the American economy with its purchase of treasury notes has started to come into question.

# China

reviving the climate busting fossil fuel industry particularly coal.

## Defense Issues for the People's Republic

The Chinese military has long enjoyed the fruits of economic expansion and has also been deeply involved in commercial ventures. In fact, at one point it was estimated that about one fifth of all domestically produced consumer goods were produced in factories owned by the military. The military had a role in most economic spheres from hotels and restaurants to road and air transport.

Regardless of whether the entrepreneurial army was hurting its military orientation, its activities were getting in the way of the leadership's desire to remove the government from the economy. Thus as part of Beijing's effort to lessen the importance of the state-owned enterprises it also ordered the military to withdraw from business. Officially at least, the military did so in 1999 although the People's Liberation Army was allowed to keep control of those industries that directly served its needs. Still, because of this new wealth, China has purchased billions in military hardware from Russia.

Given how close the CCP came to losing control of China in 1989, it is not at all surprising that the party leadership has been particularly generous with the military.

China's military spending—which is now second only to that of the United States—has begun to worry her neighbors. They are concerned about the possibility of military expansionism. This has been most prominent with regard to Beijing's willingness to assert itself in disputes regarding many islands in the region. It has become public enough for very high officials, upward to the Japanese Foreign Ministry, to have commented about them publicly. These disputes have ranged from the Diaoyu Islands in the East China Sea to the Spratly Islands.

One issue that has already raised international concern is the growth of China's naval forces. That is probably not surprising given the fact that it is now importing close to 50% of its petroleum needs through relatively narrow and vulnerable water lanes in Southeast Asia. Nevertheless, China's decision to give itself more power to protect those vital shipping lanes has raised international "interest" in some quarters.

For the Chinese this associated problem has become known as the "Malacca Challenge." On the one hand, they understandably have wanted to develop a naval presence in that particularly narrow strait through which so much of their energy needs to pass.

By 2019 that goal had been accomplished symbolically complimented by the launch of the first domestically made Chinese aircraft carrier. Indeed, China's navy has in recent years developed the ability to challenge the generations long American domination of the waters of the Eastern Pacific.

Clearly the growing Chinese economy is giving the People's Republic the ability to strengthen its forces although for the immediate future their effectiveness remains limited. But China does have ambitious goals. Most obviously, it has again moved to downsize the military. During 2003 it began efforts to demobilize another 200,000 troops while making it clear that its goal is to have a smaller but more technologically sophisticated force ready to serve the nation's military needs. As the 20th century passed into history, the commander of China's air force announced major plans to build a stronger air force with greater capabilities beyond China proper. Still, while some might be concerned about the increasing sophistication of the Chinese military, defense spending by the People's Republic is still only around 10% of the figure spent by the American military. In short, compared to the ability of, say, the United States to move troops quickly by air around the world, the Chinese army is still very limited despite its significant interest in expanding its international capabilities.

Perhaps an even more significant sign of China's arrival as a major player on the international scene was its late-2008 decision to commit its navy to a long-term effort to help suppress the Somali pirates that have plagued international shipping in the Gulf of Aden. This was the first such long-distance effort since 1949 for China's navy. But that was not the only new development. During 2008 the Chinese navy has become less willing to tolerate American surveillance ships in nearby waters. Those changing attitudes were particularly obvious in 2009, when Chinese naval vessels approached and apparently harassed an American ship operating about 75 miles off the coast of China's Hainan Island.

The growing reach of China's navy has become a concern for more than just the United States. India has become increasingly watchful regarding its giant East Asian neighbor's ambitious move into those South Asian waters that surround India. Moreover it is not just the presence of the Chinese fleet in India's nearby waters that concerns New Delhi. Beijing's efforts to establish port facilities from Southeast Asia to Pakistan also do. China's expanding

**Billboard encouraging family planning**

Courtesy of Miller B. Spangler

## The Chinese Health Care Systems

The practice of medicine in China is easily one of the oldest and most continuous systems in world history. Indeed, its traditional practices from the utilization of ideas associated with balancing forces from yin and yang to the idea of an essential life force known as qi continue to play an important role alongside the more recent growth of western medical practices. But despite that continuity, systems of health care delivery have changed dramatically over the last half century.

During the first decades after the Communist Revolution of 1949, Beijing implemented a government funded and operated health care system, the famous barefoot doctors being the most well-known element, that managed to provided basic health care and significantly reduced, for example, the nation's infant mortality rates.

In the aftermath of the economic reforms implemented by Deng Xiaoping, the government's role in health care, as in so many areas, was dramatically reduced and the system in significant measure privatized as both institutions and individuals increasingly worked in a profit-based system that saw patients expected to personally finance their health care costs. Unfortunately, those administrative changes occurred in the context of a society within which neither government nor private health insurance care existed leaving large numbers, especially in the rural areas, without access to affordable health care. That was especially true for medications which were not, as were the fees of physicians and nurses, regulated. Recognizing the problem and the significant public anger the new and largely market-based system had caused, the early years of the 21st century saw the government working to implement a more substantial health care insurance system and to reject the model of a health care system largely based on a capitalist market.

In 2009 about the same time that the United States was working to implement a new health insurance system to facilitate medical care access to larger numbers of Americans, the Chinese government was going about the same task. The goals were of course as different as the two societies. In China's case the goal was to establish a system of basic health care available for everyone while strengthening health care at the local level. As in the United States, the system was based on various sorts of health insurance programs for urban and rural workers, as well as a scheme, introduced in 2007, that provided basic cover for the non-regularly employed, such as children, the elderly, and self-employed people. By 2011 the system was said to cover 95% of the population. One element that would surprise many in the west is the practice of insisting that a specified number of medications, deemed "essential medicines" be set at fixed prices said to contain no "mark up." Still, despite the more recent accomplishments, there remains considerable discrepancy between the health care options of those in rural and more wealthy urban regions of the country. There is also private health insurance, provided by for-profit organizations, which by 2015 accounted for just under 6% of total health expenditures. Drawing on traditional practices, wider care is seen as mainly a responsibility for familes. Under the one-child policy, this has become more difficult but families are still expected to provide such care

As with so many other countries, China continues to search for ways to supply universal health care at a price society and individual patients can afford. Yet with the onset of COVID-19, which seems to have begun in the Chinese city of Wuhan in the late autumn of 2019, the state stepped in and, through a drastic system of control, seemed on top of the disease. However, periodic outbreaks have continued and as late as March 2022, the whole of Jilin Province n the north-east was again under a lockdown.

naval reach, while growing, still remains well behind that of the United States but that situation is changing fast.

In short, Chinese economic power is growing steadily which not surprisingly has also added resources for the impressive growth of its military power as well.

### China's Space Program

Particularly fascinating has been China's decision to enter that rare club of nations that have been able to put manned spaceships into orbit. To carry out this task, there emerged the China National Space Administration in 1993, and the goal was realized in the fall of 2003 when Beijing successfully sent its first astronaut into a orbital flight. Once that was accomplished, China set out to prepare for its first lunar launch, a goal that was realized in the fall of 2007 as the People's Republic's first unmanned lunar rocket settled into orbit around the moon. By 2013 China put a robotic module on the moon's surface and in January 2019, China became the first country to put a lander on dark side of the moon. China's ambitions in space have not stopped with the moon. It is actively pursuing the establishment of its own space station. It is also the third

nation to have developed a program for exploring Mars. This was successful in landing on the "Red Planet" in 2021,

when it was the first nation to carry out an orbiting, landing and recovery operation there. Like other explorations, much

**Mall shopping in Shanghai**

Courtesy of Steven A. Leibo

# China

valuable data was sent back from this mission, despite a temporary interruption of all such communications in autumn 2021.

### China and the World of Globalization

If making the transformation from a communist command economy to a more capitalist market economy was the biggest economic challenge the People's Republic faced in the last decades of the 20th century; the opening years of the 21st century have been dominated by her entrance into the new globalized world economy. In doing so China has done particularly well. The combination of a very industrious workforce, particularly low wages, and a government deeply interested in economic matters has increasingly made China the official workshop for much of the world. In fact, by 2004 China overtook Japan to become the third-largest exporter of goods. Its goods were valued then at over $600 billion. By 2014, China had even passed the United States.

In keeping with the general evolution of industrial globalization, that is from outsourcing manufacturing to that of service activities, China's Dailin region has become filled with "call centers" where Japanese-speaking Chinese handle technical service calls for Japanese customers. In fact, China has become so involved in the manufacture of goods by outside companies that the term "China Price" has come to refer to the power of China to offer the best possible manufacturing base for corporations all around the world. It is the price other nations and industries have to compete with to be competitive.

The downside, of course, was that China, in its role as the world's workshop, had become so deeply tied to the global economy that its own long-term economic growth was deeply threatened by the slowdown in the purchase of its exported consumer goods. This was especially obvious by early 2009. Nevertheless, the decades of strong growth have given the nation's leaders the hundreds of billions of dollars necessary to stimulate the economy with thousands of basic infrastructure projects China needed anyway. Of course, they had also created the enormous numbers of new jobs required to survive the loss of so many international export markets.

### Culture and Society in China

The 20th century has seen extraordinary changes in culture and society in China. Ironically, Chinese communities in Hong Kong, the PRC, and Taiwan spent much of the 20th century moving farther apart while more recently their societies have started to appear more similar again. Keeping up with these changes is breathtaking for the outside observer; actually living them would be astounding.

In 1900, most Chinese were rural peasants living very simple lives as farmers. The fundamental and lasting institutions of family life and farming completely dominated Chinese culture for thousands of years. This was certainly true throughout most of Asia, but these two foundations were developed to a higher level within China. Agriculture combined the careful cultivation of cereal grains, skillful efforts to control water by the construction of levees and irrigation ditches, and the return of all available fertilizer, including human waste, to the soil. This permitted high nutritional content of the harvests, which in turn permitted a rapid rate of population growth. The family was the basic social unit—above it stood the village, governed usually by the heads of the leading families.

Society was dominated by an intellectual elite known as the scholar gentry who were very influential on the local level and supplied most of the personnel for the imperial bureaucracy that ran the empire. The traditional upper class culture was also based on the family and on the group of related families that together formed a clan. Ancestor worship, involving sacrifices to dead forebears, who were not considered to be actually divine, had begun among the upper classes and spread to the lower classes. The wealthy avoided manual labor and regarded literacy and education—especially in the Confucian tradition—ownership of land and public service, as the highest social goals and symbols of status. This upper crust, dominating education, government service, and land ownership, was not so exclusive that the lower classes were entirely excluded from it. Unlike India, China never had a caste system as part of its culture, but in reality, it was highly unusual for a person of peasant origin to acquire enough education, wealth, or influence to move to the top of the social scale.

In spite of tendencies toward conservatism and anti-foreignism, traditional Chinese culture was the richest, and certainly the longest lived and most continuous of the great civilizations, ancient, and modern. It was relatively free from the religious bigotry and intolerance that was evident in much of Western history.

**Mahjong players in Kaifeng**

Courtesy of Steven A. Leibo

In contrast to the principles of decaying despotism of France under the Bourbon kings, China's traditional philosophy and culture greatly impressed well-educated Jesuit missionaries who came to China in the 17th century.

Sadly, the decline of the traditional Chinese political system in the late 19th and early 20th centuries brought a loss of confidence in many aspects of traditional Chinese cultural values. Education was increasingly altered to conform to Western ideals; literature began to be written in the vernacular, or conversational language, rather than in the old, more difficult and formal literary language.

By early years of the 20th century new groups of elites and workers became significant. On the elite level, new types of soldiers, business people, and intellectuals emerged as well as the formation of a new industrial working class that lived in the Western ports. China was starting its extraordinary century-long transformation.

During the 1920s, the new ideas and values including Marxism were gaining ground among intellectuals. At the level of the uneducated, the solidarity of the family was greatly weakened by the beginnings of economic progress toward industrialization, which created jobs for women, drawing them away from their families to the factories in the cities. The Japanese invasion in 1937 and the ensuing chaos uprooted millions of people and heavily contributed to the further breakdown of the traditional social and cultural order.

In the first generation after the Second World War, society in the several parts of China began to diverge. Both Taiwan and Hong Kong were aligned with the Western capitalist economies and each saw tremendous economic changes in their respective communities over the years. Economic growth was significant and people's lives were dramatically altered by the changing circumstances.

Within the People's Republic in contrast, while economic growth remained the principal goal, Mao Zedong's ideologically driven approach as demonstrated in the Great Leap Forward and the Cultural Revolution, failed to economically raise people's living standards; indeed at times the situation simply deteriorated dramatically. Even a casual visitor to the area in the late 1970s and early 1980s could see great differences in the lifestyle of these different parts of the Chinese community.

But again, the revolutionary cycle has changed and since the late 1970s under the direction of Deng Xiaoping, the People's Republic has itself chosen to enter and compete in the world market. It has done so with enormous success. Real gains have been made in people's economic possibilities. Individual citizens can now purchase their own apartments. In Shanghai, which has been allowed to experiment with private housing more than 90% of the homes are privately owned but of course such changes are also required an ongoing effort to make the laws of the People's Republic more compatible with such private ownership.

These dramatic changes go far beyond property issues. Professionals like lawyers are now free to privately organize themselves to develop clients. Chinese citizens can now travel within their own country and abroad far more often then they ever did before. And the luxury practically unimaginable only a few years ago, that of owning a private automobile has become very real for a growing number of Chinese as a galnce at the roads in any major Chinese city will show! The West hears much about the harsh repression of individual dissidents who have chosen to challenge the state, the reality of a general improvement in human rights was also true until quite recently.

Urban life has become increasingly the norm in China as well. Today China has over 174 cities with more than a million people, and more than 50% of the population lives in those cities. By 2020, the expectation was that 55%–60% of the population would be city dwellers.

Other changes are underway as well. For generations the leadership encouraged the famous "one-child policy." Designed to allow the PRC to get its long-term growth under control, the program was a complicated combination of propaganda, financial incentives and disincentives, and social pressure brought against families wishing to have more than one child. As is well known, the policy brought China under considerable outside criticism for the excesses of the program, which critics charged included forced abortions.

In recent years the policy has modified. Indeed by the fall of 2015 the Chinese Central Committee, concerned about the changing demographics of the society discussed below, officially decided to modify the famous one-child policy into one that will in the future allow couples to have a second child if they so chose. By mid-2021, the one-child policy was firmly dead, with an announcement that families would be allowed to have upto three children.

Even more recently, concerned about a growing "demographic time bomb" the authorities are reported investigating the possibility of not only expanding the number of allowed children a family can have but literally reversing decades of pressure to have only one child for a policy that actually encourages more children!

As mentioned above, one of the primary drivers of China's recent move away from the understandable but draconian policies known as the one-child policy is the long-term impact the program had on the nation's demographic balance. While a generation ago China's primary challenge was limiting its population growth so it could maintain its population at a reasonable living standard and even to advance. The the first years of the 21st century began to illuminate a new and very different challenge. After decades of lowering the fertility rates and improving people's

**Shanghai's high-speed Maglev train**　　　　Courtesy of Steven A. Leibo

# China

lives with better health care, China's population is now becoming increasingly older. Moreover, the number of working adults is declining as the population of aging citizens grows. This trend is creating a very problematic demographic imbalance between retired and working adults. For example, in 1975 China had 7.7 working adults available to support each citizen over 60. By the middle of the 21st century, that number was projected to drop to only 1.6. In short, while still largely a developing country, China is experiencing the same sort of demographic problems that more economically mature societies have long faced.

Other changes are also impacting Chinese society. The chasm between China's wealthier citizens, people often living in luxurious Western-style "gated communities," and the millions of still deeply poor Chinese has grown enormously. Today, the richest 10% hold 45% of the country's wealth. The gap in average income between urban dwellers and those who live in the countryside is enormous. In some ways it has proven to be the most transformative of the social differences that separate today's China with the Maoist China of only a few decades ago.

Overall, the transformation has been astounding. If 88% of the country was considered to live in poverty in 1981, by 2012 the number was down to 6.5%, an incredible change given the numbers involved, literally unprecedented in human history.

In yet another sign of China's transformation the leading cause of death was recently reported to be cancer, an affliction more often associated with developed countries than the less developed nations. Sadly, in China's case it is the high level of air pollution from the nation's generation-long coal-driven industrialization, together with the vast increase in motor traffic, that has increased the cancer rates.

Overall, the Chinese people certainly have plenty of reason to be pleased. For the older generation today's commonly improved lifestyles are truly remarkable. For the generation that remembers decades of war and economic turmoil it must be truly astonishing to see how much Chinese living standards have improved in recent decades. Five hundred million people, a figure much larger than the entire United States, has been pulled from poverty while the average income has quadrupled over the last generation. This is something to be very proud of.

There is though one irony of recent life that would surprise many. Given the enormous funds required to purchase a home, young Chinese, forced to borrow money from their parents, are finding the latter more influential in their lives than parents have been for decades.

Nevertheless, despite that reality enormous numbers of young Chinese have purchased their own homes. Indeed, given the dramatic gender gap caused by decades of the one-child policy it is often difficult for a Chinese male to attract a wife without already owning a home. But as is common elsewhere in the developed world marriages themselves are going down while divorce is becoming more common.

## Chinese Women

Chinese women were among the biggest winners of the 20th century. Beginning the century with almost no rights or education, they were more often than not controlled partly through the painful process of foot binding. Yet by the early years of the century, women's education, even at the college level was much more common and foot binding, long outlawed, was less and less practiced, although it was still possible in the 1980s to meet women with bound feet. The Communist Revolution of 1949 moved as well to improve their status and the next year laws were passed giving them more rights. At the height of Mao Zedong's influence, the circumstance of women and men did not widely vary. Neither gender had much personal freedom.

On the other hand, it was difficult for those who controlled the factories

**Shanghai's stock exchange building**

Courtesy of Steven A. Leibo

to dismiss anyone, so at least more economic security was possible. The more recent economic changes though have again altered the circumstances of many women and given the progress made in earlier years of the century have at times seemed to have slowed the momentum toward improving women's rights. For example, given the decision-making powers to hire and fire, many employers have made it clear they prefer males as workers to avoid the expenses associated with maternity leave. Industries that have been associated with female labor have been especially hit by cutbacks. This was despite the fact that women, in the rural areas, generally get only around 77% of men's wages for the same work. Moreover, in the rural areas, given the incentives for families to take responsibility for growing more on the land and the common migration of men toward city work, agriculture itself is increasingly becoming a female activity.

Since enormous numbers of Chinese women still live in rural areas, traditional attitudes toward women still strongly affect their lives. Most importantly, it is still the common practice of women to leave their native villages and move to the village of their new husbands, thus making their own social position less secure than that of their spouses. Sadly, rising school fees are making it more and more difficult for families to afford to send their daughters (and sons) to school. Another issue, of course, is the simple reality that the schools are often too far away to make it convenient to send one's daughters. These pressures often mean keeping the girls out of school.

Among the urban and more educated classes, women have made important strides, but they are limited. They constitute around 23.8% of the Communist Party's membership, but their representation goes drastically down as one looks at the higher ranks of party administration. Although traditional values often prevail with regard to women's roles, the new openness has allowed Chinese women far more outlets to reflect on their circumstances. The new social and political openings have allowed for an enormous expansion of media outlets from radio talk shows to magazines that often frankly discuss women's concerns. If issues like sex, domestic violence, and

individual self-fulfillment were hardly discussed at all a generation ago, today they are often a common part of the public culture.

Moreover, as has happened in other parts of Asia, fetuses, once determined to be female by modern technologies like ultrasound, are more likely to be aborted. And when such drastic choices are not taken it is also common for rural families to simply not register their newly born daughters, a decision that can have drastic effects on the young women later when their lack of legal existence will hurt their chances for education and health benefits. Here again, China is following the path common elsewhere in Asia, where the number of boys sharply exceeds the number of girls. For China, official reports suggest there are 100 women for every 118 males.

Clearly these "missing" Chinese females may merely be unreported, but it is clear as well that in China, as with many other Asian countries, the traditional preference for boys still determines the numbers of female fetuses that will be carried to term and eventually raised. Given the extraordinary imbalance between males and females that is developing in parts of the country the nation's leaders are finally coming to the realization that they have to act decisively to deal with the problem. The rules against using modern technology to make gender-based abortion decisions have been significantly strengthened.

Previous President Hu Jintao officially addressed the need to deal with the problem while a commission was appointed to investigate the growing crisis, that has seen the gender imbalance grow so dramatically that by 2018 it was reported that China had 34 million more men than women. A situation that is likely to add enormous strains on Chinese society over the upcoming decades and will not be immediately addressed by the easing of the one-child policy, or even the announcement in 2021 that, in future, urban families would be allowed three children. Indeed, many young people have been reported as saying that economic independence is more important than having any children, never mind three.

Ironically the gender imbalance has impacted the role of women in that it has given women relatively more power in so far as they able to make more demands of those who seek to marry them.

Still despite the advantages of being more in demand as wives given the gender gap, Chinese women have higher rates of suicide then their male counterparts a trend quite different from the West.

In short, Chinese women have experienced extraordinary changes since 1900

**Sunday crowds at the entrance to the Forbidden City**     Courtesy of Steven A. Leibo

# China

**Solar energy in use in Weihai, Shandong Province, China**

although those changes have been most obvious in more urban areas and especially in large coastal cities like Shanghai and, of course, on Taiwan and in Hong Kong.

### The Internet

Like so much of the rest of the world Chinese society ended the 20th century grappling with the meaning of the emergence of the personal computer and the networking of much of the globe through the Internet. Even in the People's Republic, which initially lagged behind in computer use, sales are booming as parents buy PCs hoping to give their children an edge in the future job market. The government itself has committed the country to a major Internet presence as it moves into the new millennium. The Internet, which included no more than 100,000 people in 1996, was said to have reached over 253 million users by 2008 and between 300 and perhaps 500 millions more recently. In short, the Internet may have begun largely in America and among English language speakers. But today there are more Chinese using it than there are Americans. Blogging has become very common with some bloggers having well over a hundred million follows, a figure only understandable within a population the size of China.

While it is more and more common for Chinese citizens to have Internet access from their homes today, the country also has almost two million Internet cafés. In fact, the Chinese are apparently now the most prolific users of the Internet globally. The leadership has joined in. In 2008 both Premier Wen Jiabao and President Hu Jintao signed up for their own Chinese- language Facebook pages. Nevertheless, direct access to Facebook itself for Chinese users can be very difficult.

The government, while well aware of the importance of the Internet to its goal of building a modern economically sophisticated nation, is also aware of how easily the Internet can bring in unwanted outside influences and undermine the communist party's power. For example, when mainland Chinese students used the Internet to create their own organizations dedicated to protesting Japanese occupation of controversial islands, the leadership became uncomfortable and closed down the student networks. The year 1998 saw the first arrest of a Chinese businessman specifically for the crime of distributing Chinese e-mail addresses to overseas organizations.

Citing the growing number of sites devoted to vices from gambling to pornography, the government recently ordered 18,000 Internet cafés to close down temporarily, accusing them of having allowed children to play adult-only games. This is an issue about which many Americans are themselves concerned. The effort to keep the Internet under control continues. The authorities have decreed that anyone who writes a web blog or keeps a personal webpage must register with the government. They also employ thousands of people to browse the web and block "questionable" material. Still their effectiveness has frequently been shown to be relatively limited, given the availability of various software resources that allow for accessing supposedly "forbidden sites." But little has been accomplished. Hundreds of millions of Chinese regularly receive information, however rumor or reality-based, that the central authorities simply cannot prevent.

Clearly, the Chinese government is concerned about both the positive and negative aspects of the Internet. It is worried about its potential to cause internal disruptions. But it is equally concerned about losing out on the new globalized world economy that is emerging partly through the Internet. It represents both a tool to integrate China further into the world economy and a threat of further Westernization of the sort the government found so threatening in 1989.

Not surprisingly, the authorities had no intention of allowing the various Internet-based social media sites to allow the popular uprisings of spring 2011 in the Middle East to spread to China. But its ability actually to stop the flow of such information has diminished. Try as it may, though, the Chinese government works to monitor the Internet and is quite willing to intervene on a regular basis in the web itself. China is simply too open to enable the regime effectively to control its use by the nation's scores of millions of tech-savvy citizens. In short, the Chinese government has largely lost

**Shanghai urban street mall**

Courtesy of Steven A. Leibo

the ability to control the flow of information to its population. In the 21st century even a regime as overwhelmingly controlling as North Korea is no longer able to control the information available to the public within its borders. That China, an enormously larger and more open society, could really do so effectively seems highly unlikely.

But that has not stopped the Chinese authorities from trying to do so. Indeed, utilizing the growth of the same computer networks that have allowed the Internet to flourish the Chinese have of late been experimenting with using the power of computers and their abilities to analyze massive amounts of data to track the behavior of the nation's citizens. Modeled somewhat on Western-style financial credit recording agencies, Chinese authorities are apparently hoping to track and "score" the citizens behavior as complement Beijing's hope to eliminate corruption and to more tightly monitor society. For individual citizens that would apparently mean financial and social advantages for those positively rated and significant controls over the lives of those deemed more questionable societal elements. While the system might make sense given the CCP's interest in maintaining its authority it certainly challenges the momentum of recent decades in creating a more open society for the Chinese people.

### Looking Closer:
### The Human Rights Question

Certainly one of the most difficult issues in Chinese relationships is caused by tensions over human rights. Here, as with questions over Tibet, emotions sometimes get in the way of thoughtful analysis of the situation. From the U.S. side, many Americans have been appalled by various reports about the far fewer personal, religious, and political freedoms the Chinese enjoy compared to citizens of most Western countries. Of course, images remain powerfully charged by memories of Chinese tanks sent to drive peacefully demonstrating students from Tiananmen Square in 1989, the violent suppression of the 2008 uprising in the Tibetan populated areas of southwestern China, or the somewhat similar developments in the Muslim areas of the Far West.

The many reports Americans hear of forced abortions in the People's Republic, imprisoned democratic activists, minority peoples, such as the Uighurs and Tibetans, and the persecution of some religious figures are true enough. But these reports alone often fail to project an accurate image of developments in the People's Republic where the general trend has until recently been toward a far more open society than the Chinese had experienced in their entire history. Today's China, despite the very real issues

Western human rights activists decry is a far freer place than is generally understood. Millions of people have much more control over their daily lives, worship openly with little interference from the state, have the power to sue the government, and even take part in political elections at the local level.

That momentum toward an even greater level of individual freedom largely continued into the opening years of the new century as today's Chinese citizens no longer need, as they once did, permission from their work units either to marry or to apply for a passport. For those citizens who find themselves on the wrong side of the law, more legal aid resources have been established by the government. Unlike in the past, criminal lawyers are now officially allowed to represent their clients, rather than the state. People have successfully sued the government for false arrest and detention. However, the evolution toward a more open society has not always continued smoothly. Certainly under Xi Jinping, the government has seemed less and less tolerant of dissent and in the opinion of some observers has backtracked significantly. Repression in Hong Kong since the mid 2010s, with a widespread crackdown on demonstrations and increasingly draconian measures against the former colony's once-vibrant media outllets, has struck a particular chord.

Still, if a generation ago the Chinese leadership insisted on controlling practically every aspect of people's lives, the formula today seems a narrower one. The government allows people far more social, religious, political and intellectual rights as long as they do not challenge the unity of China or the power of the Chinese Communist Party. Thus, for example, religion—Catholicism and even Tibetan Buddhism—have been allowed to flourish as long as its followers do not tie themselves to the leadership of outside figures, such as the Dalai Lama or the Pope. But even that toleration has faded a bit more recently as once again Christianity, as so often in the past is being seen as a negative outside influence.

It is of course, still dangerous to question the national leadership itself. That last point was graphically demonstrated in the fall of 1998 when several democratic activists were given long prison terms for attempting to form a new political party, the Chinese Democracy Party. Of course, the People's Republic remains a country of swift justice. Every year thousands of convicted criminals are immediately executed after their sentences are handed down although it should be noted that the government seems to be rethinking that practice as well.

# China

Clearly, despite the much greater freedoms available to the Chinese people, the government is determined to maintain the right to decide how far and when those freedoms might expand. It is clear as well that Beijing's leaders have been quite willing to withdraw some of those liberties when they felt compelled to do so.

An issue that rose to particular prominence was Beijing's harsh reaction toward religious movements that were perceived to be beyond state control. From the Falun Gong group to Tibetan Buddhists and Catholics who continue to associate with the Vatican, China's leaders have shown little hesitancy in suppressing any religious movement they considered capable of challenging their authority. More recently, spiritual communities that have operated outside of the structure of the official religious establishment have seen their church buildings demolished.

One of the most obvious signs of China's internalization of the phenomenon of globalization as it relates to human rights was the proclamation on December 10, 2008—the 60th anniversary of the Universal Declaration of Human Rights—of a new Chinese call for a fundamental transformation of Chinese political life. The document was signed by hundreds of people, many of them in positions of relatively significant importance, calling for an end to China's system of one-party rule and its replacement by a more democratic system built on the usual checks and balances common to true democracies. To no one's great surprise, the proclamation's signers soon found themselves harassed and often imprisoned by the regime.

A year later, in 2010, the well-known writer Liu Xiaobo, who had organized the Charter 08 Manifesto, was sentenced to an eleven-year prison term. But, that hardly negated Mr. Liu's indirect ability to highlight China's human rights challenges. In fact, his activities and subsequent incarceration eventually earned him the Nobel Peace Prize. This was yet another significant embarrassment to China's leaders. That embarrassment, against which Beijing responded with a particularly heavy-handed effort to undermine the prize, only made the situation worse, as did the leadership's later arrest of the internationally prominent activist artist, Ai Weiwei. Perhaps even more ominous has been the regime's growing intolerance of those lawyers willing to defend individuals who have crossed swords with the government.

Perhaps the most obvious manifestation of the Party's commitment to maintaining its political hold on the country is its reaction to the calls for a more formal constitutional system for the country. Given that the Party has always held itself up as the ultimate arbiter of power and policy, those who have spoken of establishing a more politically neutral constitution have not been appreciated. Indeed just recently some prominent professors from Shanghai and Beijing lost their academic positions for advocating such ideas.

The extent of Beijing's nervousness about its own position became especially obvious as the nation did everything it could to avoid letting what became known as the "Arab Spring" spread to China. Apparently, they had reason to be concerned. In those dramatic months of early 2011 that saw so many uprising across the Arab world, from Tunisia to Egypt, from Bahrain to Syria, several of them successful. Predictably there were those within China who hoped to see their own "Jasmine Revolution" emerge. The authorities, though, had other ideas and did everything in their power to stem the momentum that never amounted to much anyway.

In short, the Chinese still have far fewer freedoms than Westerners, but far more than many Westerners believe they do. In fact, the state is simply less involved in the lives of average Chinese.

Perhaps the easiest way to understand today's Chinese "social contract" is simply to say that the Chinese have an enormous number of new rights as long as they do not challenge the domination of the Chinese Communist Party or question the unity of the country, as Tibetans or far western Muslim Uighurs often do. Still, despite the above, the general trends of late seem headed toward more control over people's lives rather than less.

### From China's Restive Far West to Labor Unrest

Other important issues to monitor are developments in Western China especially in Xinjiang, where outbreaks against Chinese rule have resulted in

**Spring 2008's earthquake**

# China

riots followed by harsh retribution by officials. Ironically, the September 11, 2001, terrorist attack in the United States turned out to be somewhat advantageous for Beijing. It allowed it to align its ongoing effort against the Muslim separatists of Xinjiang with the larger American-led War on Terrorism. In fact, the PRC's leadership even claimed, probably with some justification, that the infamous al-Qaeda had trained large numbers of Uighur militants. That is not surprising given the complications of life for the region's non-Han largely Muslim community.

For the most part, Beijing remains very suspicious of the influence Islam could potentially have on the region's inhabitants, and it closely controls it. Neither students nor government workers are allowed to fast during Ramadan, and taking part in non-officially sanctioned religious activities can put a person's career prospects in jeopardy. The effort is quite invasive ranging from limiting how long sermons can be to outlawing private teaching of either Arabic or the Quran. Long-standing tensions erupted dramatically in July 2010 after an incident in a factory in Uumqi, Xinjiang's capital. Sadly, the incident resulted in vicious ethnic fighting and the deaths of almost 200 people while about 2,000 were injured. Eventually the government executed many of those thought

**Professor Leibo visiting Chinese Carbon Capture Company** Courtesy of Steven A. Leibo

primarily responsible for the violent disturbances but that has hardly eliminated the problem.

A low-level insurgency of sorts has continued. Most recently, during the winter of 2014 came reports of yet another confrontation between local separatists and Chinese security forces. It included not only the use of a suicide belt, but it resulted in the death of 12 individuals, according to press reports. The violence has not confined itself to the Far West. One recent assault that took the lives both of attackers and tourists occurred at the very center of Beijing in the heart of Tiananmen Square. Far more horrific was an assault in the late winter of 2014 as a gang identified as radicalized Xinjiang separatists rampaged through the local train station killing almost 30 people and wounding another 100. It was yet another clear sign that the ethnic tensions in China's far west were not only growing in intensity, but were moving far beyond the region itself. Perhaps equally important is that many within China are in part blaming not only international Islamic activists but the Western based human rights organizations that have helped finance and organize movements that highlight the region's human rights concerns. Thus rather like Tibet, tensions within Xinjiang have the potential to be both an internal and international issue.

Not surprisingly, the general tightening of government controls throughout China in the years since President Xi came to power have had an impact on Xinjiang as well. In fact, in the view of many observers the crackdown has been draconian with the local authorities demanding that the region's largely Uighur residents turn in their passports and gain official permission if they wish to travel abroad.

Even more dramatically in the years since 2014 China has established a large number of detentions camps deeply reminiscent of the "re-education camps" of the Maoist years to try to forcibly "wean" their prisoners, mostly Uighurs, away from Islam and toward a more secular embrace of the values of the Chinese Communist Party.

Not surprisingly the situation of China's far western Muslim community has increasingly become better known outside of China and within the larger Islamic community. Indeed, their plight is starting to rise as a major issue of concern among the world's Muslims in a fashion similar to that the Palestinians have long attracted. Harrowing details of what happened in those camps, and of the oftern trivial reasons for detaining people, came to light in May 2022, after hackers pierced a state security system.

## The Price:
### China's Environmental Crisis

But if ethnic issues have long had the potential to cause social unrest and potential instability, the nation's environmental situation has emerged in recent years as yet another especially significant cause. Certainly China, as one of the largest and oldest of human civilizations, has long had a profound impact on its physical environment; the condition of Hainan Island after years of exploition could be described as like a moonscape in 1990 by one local official. In the years since China began its efforts to dramatically industrialize, at first chaotically under Chairman Mao and even more profoundly under Deng Xiaoping and his successors, the level of environmental degradation has begun to dramatically impact on the lives of people across the nation while arousing a growing backlash that at times challenges the stability of the nation itself. In short, when rivers and streams which communities have relied on for generations begun to dry up or are too polluted for people to use, even the jobs available from the nation's growing economic strength cannot compete for people's attention.

Certainly China has plenty to feel proud about. Its decision over the last generation to turn itself literally into the workshop of the world has brought enormous gains in economic growth and a significant improvement in the lives of its people. But that growth has had a tremendous impact on the physical environment upon which the current and future health of the entire nation depends. Ironically, the economic policies of Mao Zedong, who was considered by some to have carried out a "War on Nature", were enormously different from those carried out by his page-turning successor Deng Xiaoping. But both leaders, despite their differences, wanted rapid economic growth. Those policies were infinitely more successful in Deng's case, but they have cost the environment of China enormously.

That more recent environmental impact has happened in one of the most unusual physical environments on the planet. Indeed China's environmental history is almost unique among the nations of the world not only for its physical elements, but for the sheer level of detailed information we have available about the Chinese people's long-term relationship with their physical environment.

China is one of the largest and most climatically diverse countries on the planet. It is a nation that includes an extraordinary range of physically different terrains from southern rain forests and central Asian steppes and deserts to the majesty of the Himalayas. But that is true

# China

elsewhere as well. What is especially interesting, though, is that China, unlike so much of Eurasia and North America, was not covered by ice during the last ice age. This allowed a more continuous and flourishing biological diversity than other areas that saw more species go extinct during the glacial eras.

Adding to the uniqueness of China's environmental circumstances is that simple and obvious reality that for most of the human story, people were rare and nature was large. On the other hand, China's population, which is historically and contemporaneously ever so much larger than most societies, has seen Chinese territory significantly more impacted by human activity than the usual situation elsewhere.

Lastly is the extraordinary longevity and literacy of Chinese civilization. To make a long story short, we have far more records on Chinese environmental history, better and older historical records than we have for most societies. Significant deforestation, for example, began some 10,000 years ago. The record of that deforestation as well as more recent and important efforts at reforestation is well documented. Indeed, to understand the Chinese environmental experience is in many ways a key to understanding humanity's future as larger and larger numbers of humans make demands on their environment and on what was earlier the finite resources of China and today on the even more finite resources of the planet (the Chinese could, after all, call on the natural resources of other regions; the people of earth cannot). For those interested in how humanity can deal with the challenges of a changing climate, China's historical record is especially helpful. It offers a close look at how the Chinese have experienced changing climates over the several thousands of years.

Of course, it was the enormous rise of its population, even by Chinese standards, and the single-minded commitment to economic development, whether of the poorly thought-out sort of the Maoist years or the more practical and systematic since 1978, that has especially challenged the Chinese environment. Given the importance of understanding China's environmental evolution for gaining insights useful for the larger global community in the 21st century, an especially close look at current realities of China's environmental circumstances is especially appropriate with a focus on several immediate topics from water and soil to air quality.

## Contemporary China's Water Realities

Probably the most immediate reality of China's water situation is that it has significantly less water than the international

**Inside Shanghai's Science Museum**          Courtesy of Steven A. Leibo

average for most nations. Indeed, it has about 7% of the world's water supplies available for 20% of the planet's people. Moreover the usability of the water the Chinese do have is often especially problematic. Like elsewhere a considerable portion of that water is used for industry, but at significantly less efficient rates,

Parts of China, such as the north central plain, often suffer from water shortages while Southern China, especially in the era of climate change which will be discussed below, often experiences precipitation that arrives so quickly and in such a deluge that it is frequently useless. But the reality of too much water in some regions and too little in others and the role people have had in impacting the environment are complicated and need to be broken down more precisely.

In some very real ways, people in China have more water available than their ancestors. The modern era, of course, has enabled a technology previously unavailable: very deep drilling using technology developed by the oil industry to find reservoirs of water deep below the surface. Like so many other nations, China has taken advantage of these new sources. Unfortunately many of those underwater water resources are not sustainable. In fact some are only replenished in geological time even as humanity readily drains them daily with modern pumping techniques. It looks like some 130 million people on the north central Chinese plain are growing and surviving on grain drawn from unsustainable water sources.

The challenge of this obvious unsustainable reality has been known for some time. Geological surveys have for years

found the water tables in North China dropping significantly. Around the capital in Beijing it was reported that the city was now drilling over a thousand feet down to find water, five times deeper than they were a couple of decades ago. Under the circumstances, it is not surprising that the World Bank has warned of dire consequences in the future if water use and supply cannot be brought back into balance.

Moreover even when water is available, that water, especially in recent years, has often become very polluted by industrial wastes. Urban dwellers are forced to dramatically filter what water is available while farmers often face the choice of not watering their crops or doing so with industrial waste water that can literally be toxic. Many in the world were horrified in late 2005 by images of the Songhua River in China's far north saturated with carcinogenic chemicals floating by Harbin, a city of 3.8 million people, that suddenly found itself without water for days. Even more recently, in early 2013 came word that the carcasses of well over 10,000 rotting pigs had been dumped into the upper part of the Huangpu River that supplies some of the water for Shanghai.

As we will see below, the demands on China's water are growing even as the amount and quality of water is decreasing. That, of course, is also occurring because many of the new energy production efforts, from the obvious need for water required for the many planned hydroelectric damn projects to newer procedures like hydro-fracking for natural gas, require significantly greater amounts of water.

**High-speed trains ready to leave Beijing's South Station**     Courtesy of Steven A. Leibo

Ironically although China's traditional leaders were often judged by their ability to maintain adequate levees against the all-too-frequent floods caused by the Yellow River, today's leaders are more likely to be judged by their ability deal with the problems associated with a very different Yellow River than dominates Chinese historical memories. Today a combination of factors, from poorly planned economic development to over pumping and the slowly rising temperatures, has created a situation that has seen extended periods when the Yellow River has not even made it to the open sea.

In fact, in 2003 the river reached such a low level that 12% of the entire country was short of water while one-third of the fish that once lived within its waters are said to have become extinct. Broadly the river now regularly dries up more than 500 miles from the sea. Clearly the role of the river that has played such a role in the development of Chinese history has changed dramatically for reasons that have not made its common name "China's Sorrow" any less meaningful. Perhaps even more thought-provoking is the reality that drought is also becoming more and more common in Southern China, which usually has more than enough water, often too much water.

There were serious droughts in the south in 2006, 2007, and 2010. And the problem continues. In February 2021, south and east China saw 330,000 people with inadequate drinking water, while in December 2021, Shenzen on the border with Hong Kong was hit by its worst drought since 1963.

Chinese leaders are not unaware of those challenges. As often in the past, they are trying to find hydro-engineering projects to address China's growing water problem. Most notable is the ambitious south-north project to pump water to the north from China's southern water-plentiful region. The project itself not surprisingly has attracted the attention of environmentalists who have focused on the negative environmental impact of the project.

### Contemporary China's Soil Realities

Soil erosion is another significant problem. Historically deforestation makes soil more likely to flow away with strong rains or winds. But the explosion of animal husbandry over the last few decades has added to the stress on the land. The number of animals, especially sheep and goats, has grown enormously, 285 million by one count compared to 9 million for the United States. And those vastly increased numbers of grazing animals are quickly removing the surface grasses and plants that keep soil in place across much of western and northern China. Not surprisingly significant amounts of formerly useful land are turned into desert each year. The general estimate is that about 150 square kilometers of previously cultivated land is lost to desertification annually.

In short, far from the headlines has been the growing desertification of much of the country literally from north-central China to Inner Mongolia and Gansu Province. Desert landscapes, which once competed with rivers and lush grasslands for space in these regions, are now growing enormously. Today the residents' lives are dominated by the drying out of the land and the ever-present threat of huge dust clouds that can easily kill those caught within their grasp. While this has an immediate impact on those who live in the area, the growing number of dust storms common in the north makes the problem obvious to hundreds of millions more within China and well beyond its borders.

### Contemporary China's Air Pollution Realities

The fact that 7 of the 10 most polluted cities in the world are in China would hardly be a big surprise to anyone who has spent more than a few minutes in the People's Republic during the last few decades. Indeed, the world heard about the problem almost nonstop in the run-up to the 2008 Olympic Games. As was well publicized at the time, the Chinese government did everything it could, albeit with mostly temporary measures, to make the air as clean as possible for the weeks during which the games took place. But that moment of extreme attention hardly changed the larger reality: decades of burning massive amounts of coal have reduced the Chinese skyline to a drab and pulmonary-threatening experience not only for the residents of the country, but for almost everyone else close enough to China to be impacted. The situation is so bad that one Chinese entrepreneur is selling cans of air to any willing to buy. According to reports, the cans of air marketed like the long-popular cans of water come in three different flavors. While the idea might sound curious from a marketing perspective, the problem is very real. The air pollution in Northern China is so bad that it is said to reduce the average life expectancy by more than five years and significantly raised the number of other afflictions, including strokes, heart disease, and cancer.

The core of the problem is China's abundant use of coal, the world's highest, to fuel most of her industrial growth. In fact, coal generates about 70% of China's energy, and its use about equals the rest of the world's coal use. That coal-burning process in China, probably more so than almost anywhere in the world in recent decades, has been a particularly polluting version given how old and often unregulated its coal-driven energy industry has

# China

been for most of that time. As we will see below in the energy section, China has been moving to address the problem. But the reality of China's frequently horrific air quality problem remains to this point unchanged.

Beijing's air quality even at the best of times is enormously challenging for the millions who live there. But the early winter of 2013 put even those unacceptable standards to the test as the city was overwhelmed by a blinding haze that was so bad that the graphic images of the situation attracted the attention of a worldwide audience. Perhaps more surprisingly, they also provoked an outpouring of local public outrage rare in the People's Republic. The fury that burst out not only in social media but in more traditional forms of media was probably not all that surprising because the level of environmental degradation was not playing out in some obscure city in the interior affecting only the nation's least advantaged, but in the nation's elite capital. In short, it did not matter if one were a politburo member or a taxi driver. Not surprisingly the leadership is finally showing signs that the "get" the problem. Officials issued a statement last year offering over 10 billion renminbi to cities and areas that made significant progress in confronting the problem of the nation's increasingly unbreathable air.

Almost no one could escape the truth of the situation. Economic growth is meaningless if one cannot breathe.

## A Growing Environmentalism in China

For decades the issue of environmental degradation was simply not on the agenda for most people in China, neither among the population nor the leadership. The goal, whether it was under Mao or Deng, was production. The necessity of producing a sustainable environment was not on anyone's radar. But that has changed dramatically in recent years both on the governmental level and among the population at large. Happily when dealing with environmental issues, from soil degradation to the atmospheric science associated with global climate change, China's government has one major advantage over Western, especially American, leaders.

Unlike the attorneys who usually dominate American government legislatures and executive officer buildings, their leaders usually have a scientific background. When dealing with the more technical and scientific challenges of the sort that have often become dominant in the 21st century, they are often at a unique advantage over American leaders who frequently do not have the same internalized knowledge base.

Moreover, like political leaders everywhere, China's leaders want to stay in power. Even if they don't have to worry about reelection, they still understand full well that political upheavals can topple the party if people become angry enough. While in China there is not a huge base of people pushing for a more democratic governing system, anger at political corruption and especially environmental degradation has been quite capable of provoking considerable public outrage.

Perhaps as important is the growing realization at the level of the nation's leadership that economic growth, itself so vital for the nation's future and the communist party's longevity, is being undermined by poorly planned economic activities that have not taken environmental concerns into consideration. In short, for all the above reasons the leadership of the People's Republic has recently shown an environmental consciousness that would have shocked many of their predecessors. Indeed, outgoing President Hu, in his last formal speech before leaving office, put a major focus in his remarks on addressing environmental issues.

For the population at large, of course, environmental degradation has become a very important part of the daily challenge people face, especially over issues of water. Some water resources are increasingly unavailable. River waters that have run for generations are often no longer available, or the water, by virtue of uncontrolled industrial waste, is either simply unusable or used anyway to irrigate crops. Not surprisingly these growing stresses have created a regular series of local protests and a growing environmental consciousness. It is now going well beyond the rural peasantry to the urban middle class, which is being aroused by the sort of air pollution issues discussed above.

Recent changes in attitudes among the population at large and the government give one reason for optimism. On the other hand, China remains a single-party-dominated state. That can complicate dealing with environmental issues because historically many environmental organizations around the world have morphed into successful political movements. This is something the Communist Party is determined to avoid. Thus it is reasonable to assume that China's ability to deal successfully with its many environmental challenges is perhaps hampered by the national leadership's concern about the emergence of movements that might effectively check its authority. For the moment the authorities have attempted a balancing act of sorts, encouraging local environmental activism to pressure regional authorities to consider more than immediate economic growth while discouraging larger national environmental movements. That said, it is clear the authorities understand that the problems are quite real. Indeed they have been offering a sort of carrot-and-stick approach of late not only offering local areas financial rewards for addressing air pollution problems, but threatening far more severe punishments up to and including death to the worst violators.

## China's Environment, and the Global Community

In some ways the Chinese find themselves in a very unique and especially difficult situation. Decades ago the Western industrial nations began to develop a new consciousness about maintaining a decent environment even in the face of the needs for immediate economic growth. In the United States that resulted in the flurry of legislation like the clean air regulations of the 1970s and in Western Europe the emergence of politically powerful "green" political parties which were especially committed to environmentalism. Western

**Shanghai's New Science Museum**

58

# China

Europe has moved more quickly and the United States more slowly. More recently the West began to move beyond more local and regional issues like clean water and air to take on more complex challenges like climate change caused by the emissions of carbon-based fossil fuels into the upper atmosphere. In a sense the West took on one challenge and made considerable progress, and only more recently has it taken on the larger global climatic challenge.

China's situation is completely different but deeply linked to developments in the West. While the 1950s saw an explosion of economic growth in the United States and Western Europe, which was recovering from the Second World War, China was also carrying out its own economic drive for Western-style industrial modernity in the disaster better known as the Great Leap Forward. By the 1970s that same desire to build a modern industrialized society began anew under a better thought-out plan that has transformed China and the world. But if by the 1970s the West was starting to address not only the needs for economic growth but an environmentally sustainable one, China was stuck in the first stage until the opening years of the 21st century.

Thus China's leadership has had to take on the local and regional environmental challenges and at the same time the often very different carbon pollution-based challenges of recent years. In short, if America worked to deal with the more immediate issues of polluted air that caused pulmonary problems in the late 1970s and only more recently moved to take on carbon pollution, China is stuck trying to address both problems at the same time and under considerable international pressure.

One of the least appreciated aspects of the Sino-Western and especially Sino-American relationship is that China's decision to enter the globalized world economy and position itself in so many ways as the world's manufacturing center nicely complemented the new Western concern about environmental pollution. Thus moving factories might offer, as one hears so often, access to lower wage bills and eventually an increasingly more prosperous Chinese consumer. But one of the less well discussed but more immediate advantages was that moving factories to China, which was not like the West seeing more and more environmental and specifically air pollution regulations, could resolve some of those new challenges for western businesses as well.

Thus, while new environmental technologies were being introduced in the West, a considerable part of the environmental price of western manufacturing was simply transferred to a China eager at that point for new investment. A generation later, of course, the deterioration of China's environment, especially in the case of the enormous dust clouds that have entered the global atmosphere, are putting China under considerable western scrutiny however ironic that might seem. It is also worth noting that given the common international condemnation of China's environmental problems, estimates are that between 20% and 25% of the pollution the Chinese emit is released while making goods for foreign countries. In a sense, those foreign consumers are enjoying the fruits of Chinese manufacturing while exporting their own pollution back to China.

## China and the Climate Crisis

China has not been burning massive amounts of carbon-based fuels for very long. Moreover, even today its per capita carbon emissions are a mere fraction of the average Americans. Still, in terms of annual emissions, China surpassed the United States in $CO_2$ in 2007. While it remains true that per capita the Chinese still do not emit as large a percentage of the world's greenhouse gases, the sheer size and extraordinary growth the nation has experienced over the last few decades have made it a major contributor to the problem.

It is not just the enormous amount of coal that is used to provide the energy to fuel China's explosive growth, but the construction industry, which is seeing not just new buildings but entire new cities emerge. Since 2007, China has engaged in over two billion square meters of building construction each year, comprising half of all new construction in the world. That is more than the total existing building floor space in Canada. This means China has, in a sense, been building a new Canada every year for the past six years and is projected to continue doing so until 2020. Such an effort requires massive amounts of cement, the manufacture of which is especially problematic in terms of greenhouse gases production. Since the country's carbon footprint skyrocketed in 2011, China's per capita carbon emissions are now on par with those of Europe. However, that does not mean the majority of Chinese people are enjoying quasi-European living conditions. Such fast growth in energy consumption primarily comes from two sources. One is the large amount of embedded energy in the "Made-in-China" products that China manufactures for the world. The other is the handful of highly developed cities like Beijing, Shanghai, and Guangzhou that lie along China's eastern and southern coast. On the other hand, given China's huge geographic disparity in economic development, the enormous urbanization process has really just started in the midwestern areas. People from these areas are hardly likely to forgo the right to improve their living standards. As a result, China's contributions to the greenhouse effect (see below) are projected to grow enormously over the next few decades despite efforts to produce energy more efficiently.

Thus, across the planet, and at a faster rate than previously expected, the industrially augmented build-up of greenhouse gases is beginning to transform planetary conditions in an enormous variety of ways. Within China proper the mean temperature has risen 1.38°C over the past 50 years, and it is expected to reach 3–4°C

**Shanghai fast food**

Courtesy of Steven A. Leibo

# China

by the end of the century. Not surprisingly such changes, however mild they might superficially seem when averaged out, are already having their effect. Examples abound from melting mountain glaciers to increasing desertification and the spread of invasive species that are having a significant impact on both animals and vegetation.

More dramatically and often more immediately dangerous is that rising heat and thus the atmosphere's ability to hold more water in recent decades are allowing storms like hurricanes and tornadoes to carry more destructive power. That enhanced destructive power comes in the form not only of more powerful winds but also more regular flooding of the sort that is more and more common and increasingly referred to as "extreme" weather although it probably represents less a series of weather anomalies than a new emerging climate reality.

In China's case, the challenges have been quite different depending on the region. Southern China, always vulnerable to damaging typhoons, experienced a growing threat of floods of unprecedented dimensions. But even that threat is not confined to the south. Indeed as this was being written Beijing was experiencing some of the worst flooding in Beijing for half a century in July 2012. The waters that arrived during a 20-hour deluge killed 77 people while destroying 8,000 homes, hundreds of miles of roads and causing billions in damages.

Meanwhile yet another problem has emerged dramatically. North Central China, long a relatively dry region, is seeing an explosion of desertification, which is already creating large numbers of climate refugees. Ironically, the north, normally a drier region, has experienced unfamiliar torrential rainfalls while the south, which usually suffers from too much water, has in recent years had to deal with a regular series of droughts as well. With such developments it is not surprising that the internationally famous *New York Times* writer Tom Friedman suggested that global warming might better be thought of as "global weirding!"

Within China itself, as elsewhere in Asia and indeed around the world, long-familiar climate patterns are dramatically changing in a fashion that it has hardly taken a scientific background to appreciate. Of course, in a country like China, where a very large number of people, despite recent urbanization, still live as farmers, the impact of a changing environment is especially obvious. City dwellers might be slow to appreciate a changing climate, but farmers never are. Still, trying to unravel environmental changes in China from the more immediate to larger

**Beijing mass transit**

Courtesy of Steven A. Leibo

climatically based ones can be quite a challenge.

Clearly, isolating the specific impact of climate change on China's environment from the decades-long industrial drive across the country is a challenging task indeed. Certainly global warming is having an impact on surface water availability in many parts of the country, but so is simple over pumping, another different and often more immediate challenge to water resources. Nevertheless, it is easy enough to isolate some of the most obvious impacts a changing global climate is having on China itself. Certainly the most disturbing element of the climate crisis's impact on China is the slowing rising temperatures on the Tibetan plateau, which holds the largest accumulation of glaciers outside of Antarctica and the northern Artic. These glaciers feed the great rivers of Asia and perhaps 50% of humanity. And those glaciers are slowly melting, some 7% in the last 40 years, according to one researcher. The expectation is that they will melt even faster over the next few decades leading to a point when by the end of the century half of them might be gone. Yes, this applies to half of the glaciers that provide water for the great rivers, from the Mekong to the Brahmaputra as well as China's own Yellow and Yangtze. Overall China including Tibet has over 46,000 glaciers, the vast majority of which, more than 80%, are in a state of retreat. The largest glacier in China, the Urumqi Glacier No. 1, is said to have been losing mass at more than 230 meters a year for the last half century.

Most dramatically, the spring of 2011 saw water levels on the Yangtze so much lower than they had been in generations

that the authorities were forced to intervene in a major way to avoid ship collisions and groundings. The drought that impacted on the river's water levels has, of course, also imperiled water and electrical supplies. Clearly, the era of dramatic climate change is impacting China today rather than in the future, as so many have speculated.

Even more visually dramatic, though, can be the threat of flooding waters. China is especially vulnerable to the temporary but often devastating storms that, carrying the additional water that rising temperatures allows, have become especially devastating in parts of southern China. This is not forgetting the threat of more permanent flooding along China's very valuable and productive Eastern Coast. Consider Shanghai, for example. The city's very name means above the sea. It sits precariously alongside slowly rising coastal waters. Shanghai is approximately 13 feet above the level of the sea and is being impacted not only by rising waters but the draining of groundwater. This is causing in Shanghai and other global cities, from Bangkok to Venice, to experience a gradual leveling of the coastal lands on which the city is located. Of course, this phenomenon is not caused directly by climate change. But it is another example of humanity undermining itself by poorly thought-out environmental decisions. Shanghai is not the only city in China so threatened. Nationally the area less than two meters above sea level along China's eastern coast is said to be about the size of the entire nation of Portugal although millions more live along that coast than within the relatively small nation on the Iberian peninsula.

Overall, the average temperatures in China have gone up somewhat more than a centigrade since 1960 while the patterns are much like those found elsewhere. The more northerly parts of China are warming faster than the southern regions while winters are warming significantly faster than summers. These changes are causing the same sort of changes found around the world. For example, Northern China currently received 12% less rainfall than it did in 1960 while severe droughts have become even more common. Meanwhile southern China is experiencing even more rainfall, often resulting in devastating flooding. Having said that, it is also true that drought has also become a feature of life in the south as well.

In short, China, like much of the world, is experiencing a water problem, sometimes too much, sometimes too little. Either way it is difficult for humanity to continue as previously. Aside from water itself, humanity survives only by virtue of available food. Although China set out some years ago to make itself more self-sufficient in wheat, the annual production has gone down by 4.5% due to rising temperatures, according to scientists. These developments are ominous. But for the moment they have been offset by the general improvements introduced in recent years for Chinese agriculture in general and even by the positive expansion of some food crops farther north than they were traditionally viable.

## China and the International Climate Negotiations

When the first efforts began to confront the climate crisis in the mid-1990s, China was still only just emerging from its long period of economic stagnation. It was categorized, as much of the non-Western world was, as a "developing" country. Considered as such, along with the other planetary giant India, it was therefore not obligated to carry out the carbon emissions cuts demanded of the long-developed powers.

At the time that made sense. After all, the Western countries, themselves long industrialized, had for generations emitted vast amounts of the long-lasting greenhouse gases like $CO_2$ that were causing the problem. Most of the peoples of Asia and Africa, with a few notable exceptions like Japan or South Africa, had simply not been industrialized that long or had hardly yet begun pumping dangerous amounts of $CO_2$ into the atmosphere at anything like the levels emitted over the generations by the Western Industrialized world.

It is important to add that despite the fact that China's current contributions to the global CO2 emissions are adding significantly to the problem, China indeed has caught up and passed the United States as the largest "annual" emitter of CO2 gases. Its cumulative contribution of these greenhouse gases—that last over a hundred years plus in the atmosphere—will continue to be far less than the United States. Nevertheless the issue of cumulative emissions is rarely discussed in public. What the world so often does hear, though, is that China remains deeply committed to using coal as a fundamental part of its energy generating mix. Indeed China's actual CO2 emissions went up 34% in recent years. Attitudes are changing but not nearly as quickly as some would like.

The world has often heard of the problems the United States has had in taking on the challenge of climate change. Most notably a fossil-fuel industry funded an anti-regulatory and ideologically driven campaign to convince the American public that no such phenomenon as anthropogenic climate change is occurring. Given its different historical evolution, the Chinese government has also had its own difficulties in taking up the challenge.

Unlike within the United States, where taking on national regulations to confront the climate crisis or almost anything else is a major issue, proposing such regulations has not been a significant ideological problem. China, after all, has moved only so far from its earlier roots in the command economies of communism. For the Chinese the challenge has been quite different. Quite simply China has had other priorities, most immediately improving the living standards of its enormous population while building the national infrastructure necessary to operate a modern 21st-century society.

When one adds the historic reality that the destabilization of the planet's heat balance has largely been the "accidental accomplishment" of the developed world, a world that until the last generation used enormously greater amounts of fossil fuels than China, it is not hard to see why China has been reluctant to distract itself from the great work of modernization, largely on the Western model, by activities that were until just a few years ago seen as activities likely to slow down that accomplishment.

Nevertheless, attitudes are changing. Within China's leadership, a greater sense than perhaps yet exists in the United States has emerged that converting to clean energy may not be a drag on the nation's economic development, but a new and successful way forward to the jobs of the 21st century. Nevertheless, while the national leadership has increasingly shown a deep commitment to sustainable development and to confronting the climate crisis, it is also true that much of the mid-level Chinese establishment, both private and government, has been significantly less committed. However, even as China is becoming more committed to making the decisions necessary to confront the climate crisis, it also remains committed to the idea that its responsibilities as a developing nation significantly less guilty of creating the problem than the western nations should be seen differently. The formal description is usually "common but differentiated responsibilities."

As we have seen previously, the early international agreements on confronting climate change, most notably the famous Kyoto Accords, divided international

**Harry Potter store**                                              Courtesy of Steven A. Leibo

# China

responsibilities quite differently between the largely western developed world, which had historically caused the problem, and the significantly less "guilty" developing world. From China's perspective, that was seen as entirely reasonable. Early on, at least before the real explosive growth of the Chinese economy in the last 20 years, it was not terribly problematic. But that international perspective hardly lasted beyond the initial talks. The fact that an increasingly industrialized and economically competitive China was not required to take on the same economic burdens regarding greenhouse gas reductions as the ever influential United States made ratifying the treaty by the American government even more difficult than it might have been.

Given American ambivalence about taking on the challenge of climate change, China's lesser responsibilities were only one more impediment. As is well known, the Kyoto Climate treaty was never ratified by the United States during the Clinton administration, which had helped negotiate it. It was then more formally rejected by the subsequent George W. Bush administration. In many ways quietly abandoned by the Obama administration that had initially appeared to ready to take on the challenges of a destabilized climate, most notably in the long-awaited Copenhagen climate talks that were scheduled for the fall of 2009.

In December 2009, then Chinese premier Wen Jiabao arrived in Copenhagen as part of the more than hundred world leaders to take part in humanity's effort to confront a warming climate. That challenge, of course, has been caused by the burning of fossil fuels that have dramatically increased the ability of greenhouse gases to maintain the earth's long-term temperature balance. Over the previous decade, despite the lack of cooperation from the United States, much of the world had ratified the Kyoto Treaties and begun the effort to confront climate change along the lines of the Kyoto Treaties, which as we have seen, had prescribed very different obligations for the developed and developing worlds.

However, this time China's circumstances were quite different from previous meetings. China itself was now much more industrialized than it had been only a generation before. Moreover, it had become the leading emitter of greenhouse gases. It had become obvious that developing countries, of which China was the most important member, had to be brought under the carbon reduction regime if the world were to have any chance of staving off the worst aspects of dramatic climate change. From the perspective of many developing countries, though, that

reality seemed quite unfair. After all, their populations per capita used infinitely less energy than citizens of the developed countries, and they were themselves in the process of bringing their citizens' lifestyles up to western standards.

Fair or not, the Chinese government had come to recognize that China itself was deeply vulnerable to the threat of climate change and had to act. It began to speak, if not of exact carbon reductions, of efforts to make their economy more energy efficient by dramatically lowering the amount of energy they used relative to GDP growth. In short, it was willing to make the economy much more energy efficient, but not to offer exact reductions. It was a compromise that complemented their status as a still developing country. But it was not well received in many quarters, especially Washington. Of course, Washington's approval of China's policy is an absolute prerequisite for meaningful American carbon reduction targets.

By 2009 China's own reputation took a significant hit when it was widely blamed for playing a significant role in the "failed" Copenhagen climate talks. Apparently, Chinese officials were particularly unhappy with demands for formal monitoring of their emissions being included in any potential international treaty to succeed the earlier Kyoto Accords. More importantly, they were more interested in offering improvements in energy efficiency as measured against GNP than more absolute reductions. The reasons are obvious. China still adhered to the belief that it should be held to a different standard because historically it had contributed significantly less to the problem and was still a developing nation. Thus it was quite willing and committed, as we will see below, to make its economy more energy efficient, but unwilling to commit to an absolute reduction. All is entirely logical except for the simple reality that it is that absolute reduction in greenhouse gases that humanity needs to address the problem not progress.

Thus at the Copenhagen Conference itself, China was widely criticized in some quarters for resisting calls for international monitoring of its emissions and for demanding that the developed world contribute more to the developing nations' efforts to reduce their carbon emissions. Eventually, the conference ended without the world reaching a consensus on legally binding international carbon emission caps. While many blamed China for contributing to that failure, it was true as well that the American president arrived at the conference unable to commit his own country to the level of international cooperation necessary to confront the challenge of climate change.

Eventually the United States and China, as well as an increasing number of other nations, signed the much weaker "Copenhagen Accord." Happily by the following year the "Accord" had become much more meaningful as more and more nations at the subsequent Cancún Climate Conference signed on.

Eventually, China indicated a willingness to accept not merely voluntary commitments but legally binding ones and even more impressively to discuss not just making its economy more energy efficient in terms of $CO_2$ emissions and GDP, but of absolute emissions reduction targets. More excitingly, as we have seen elsewhere by 2015 China and the United States worked cooperatively to help the world community accomplish the first really successful international climate agreement signed in Paris and by 2016 both had officially approved it.

A further U.S.-China agreement at the November 2021 Glasgow climate conference, to work together to achieve the 2015 Paris goal of a 1.5°C maximum temperature rise and other climate issues was also widely welcomed.

### China's Emerging Energy Priorities

If China had initially been less than cooperative in forging a new international consensus, its leaders were making extraordinarily significant unilateral decisions about the nation's future energy policies by using their influence to nurture the nation's green industries and to position the economy to be a major player in the production of new non-carbon-based technologies.

Like the rest of the world, the People's Republic faces critical energy choices over the next several years. It is growing very fast, and the growth of its energy needs is one of the most important features of our modern world. This is not only for China itself because it will be remembered that about a quarter of China's energy use is to produce goods as part of the nation's role as the world's manufacturing center. Moreover as currently structured China's economy tends to focus on especially high energy activities, from steel production to cement, which add to the nation's massive energy appetite.

Before we look at more recent trends, a little energy background is called for. Overall, the story of China's energy use is a mixed one. In fact, the best way to understand the patterns of recent Chinese energy usage is to recognize a series of distinct periods. From 1949 to 1980, it followed the Soviet model that basically

# "Energy Consumption in China"

By Toby Michelena

Over the last several decades, energy consumption patterns and quantities have changed dramatically in China. A sustained high economic growth rate has driven industrial expansion, increased personal income and economic opportunities. These societal changes have resulted in a significant increase in energy consumption. China is currently the largest consumer of energy worldwide, consuming approximately 25% more energy than the US in 2016. However, based on World Bank data, the United States consumed more than three times the amount of energy than China on a per capita basis. This statistic, particularly in light of China's ever-growing population and it's continued economic development, indicates the potential for continued significant growth in energy consumption. It also demonstrates the ongoing need to develop new and more efficient energy production. In addition to continued growth in consumption of energy, there have been significant changes in the mix of fuels and energy production methods have continued to evolve. While coal and to a lesser extent oil, continue to be the dominant fuels for energy production, natural gas, hydro-power and a variety of renewable sources continues to make in-roads into the energy sector.

Traditionally, much of the country had energy systems that were not connected to a central grid. This type of energy consumption relied upon traditional fuels such as wood and coal. Economic growth, specific efforts to develop and modernize distribution efforts, governmental policies that encourage urbanization, and the associated move from individual housing to large apartment complexes have resulted in more and more of the population utilizing centralized power. According to World Bank Data, over the last 20 years, China has improved production capacity and distribution networks to the point that 100% of the population now has access to electricity. People living in individual homes, still found in rural areas or older sections of large municipalities, have also begun to shift from using traditional fuels as the primary or supplementary energy source to exclusively using energy from centralized sources.

More disposable income has also resulted in a change in personal energy consumption. Historically, cultural mores and limited access to abundant energy supplies have resulted in behaviors that have to some degree, limited energy consumption. Much of the south and southeastern portions of the country have typically only minimally used heat during the colder winter months and rarely used cooling systems in the summer months. Even with adequate energy supplies and buildings fully equipped with heating and cooling systems, it is still quite common for these systems to be turned off or only minimally used. Traditional practices continue to influence personal consumption. However, this is changing. There is an growing desire to maintain personal heating/cooling systems with both individuals and businesses increasing the use of energy systems to moderate building environments. As the use of heating and cooling systems continues to grow, energy demand will also increase. This is further magnified by the increase in electrical lighting and appliance use. Again, this continues to point to a significant growth in energy consumption within China. Changes in the economic condition of individuals as well as urbanization has resulted in a large surge in automobiles. A rapid succession in personal transportation from a population that primarily used non-motorized transportation to one that is developing a seemingly insatiable desire for automobiles has resulted in significant increases in the consumption of gasoline related products. As of 2014, it was estimated that China consumed about 25% of the amount of gasoline as did the United States. However, as the personal automobile purchases continue to expand by as much as 13% per year, gasoline consumption continues to grow. Efforts are underway to slow the growth in gasoline consumption by implementing policies that advocate for use of alternative fuel vehicles. But in the near term at least, gasoline consumption will continue to increase as the population becomes more mobile.

The production of energy to fuel economic growth and modernization has led to a number of challenges. Specifically, increased air pollution, which translates into significant health issues and high carbon emissions with the associated significant contribution to climate change plague the population. China has well documented bouts of severe air pollution and the associated environmental and health related issues. Most frequently found in the north and northeastern sections of the country, but also common all along the densely populated eastern portion of the country, the health issues have become a social and economic point of concern. World Health analysis of data from 2012 attributed more than 1 million deaths in China to air pollution with 76 deaths per 100,000 people attributed to PM 2.5 pollution. Further, China ranks atop the global lists in the Diability-Adjusted Life Year (DALY) resulting from air pollution. In addition to the health costs within China, energy, China is the largest emitter of $CO_2$ accounting for as much as 30% of global emissions. These emissions, primarily from the burning of fossil fuels for energy, are a leading contributor of global greenhouse gas emissions. Controlling emissions carbon emissions in China will be necessary to slow the change in the global environment.

In order to continue to expand options for internal energy production and to combat the deleterious effects of fossil fuel consumption, China has made a major move away from coal to less polluting forms of fossil fuels such as natural gas. In addition, the Central Government has initiated significant investment in alternative technologies. Voltaic energy production is growing rapidly, and wind and solar farms are appearing throughout the country side. With government investments in green energy technology estimated to approach $400 billion USD between 2017 and 2020, China is becoming the global leader in the green energy sector. This is aimed specifically at addressing both the continued growth in energy consumption and reducing the health and environmental impacts from fossil fuels.

Overall, China has become the dominant energy consuming country, and this will not change in the near future as society changes due to both the continuing economic and population growth However, increased consumption and the economic benefits it accrues continues to come at a significant cost to the health of the population and the global environment. China will need to pursue a very aggressive energy technology development program to provide for the continued energy demand and to reduce the social and environmental costs of energy production and consumption. Failure to move forward with aggressive alternative energy policies will put at risk both the economy and the health of the nation.

# China

meant state-subsidized energy prices and no concern about the environment. Moreover, following the practice of the early industrializing countries, such Great Britain, the United States, and Japan, it did so using fossil fuels, most notably coal, oil, and natural gas. Not surprisingly coal has remained the preeminent fossil fuel, although its usage has declined from about 70% of China's energy needs in 2006 to about 55% in 2021..

In the early 1980s China began an aggressive effort to manage energy much more efficiently and did so even as it had also begun going down its now famous path of explosive economic growth. Initially this effort was successful. Even as the nation's GDP doubled over the decade of the 1990s, its energy use only went up by a fourth. Unfortunately, in the years after the new century began, the commitment to energy efficiency seemed for a time to collapse even as its energy needs continued to grow.

More recently, China has begun again a major commitment to improve its energy efficiency. Impressively, the nation's energy-to-GDP ratio improved by somewhat over 19% in the last formal planning era, but that was in the context of a growing Chinese GDP. This still creates a greater and greater demand for energy. Recent reports are that China's coal use about equals that of the rest of the world, and its percentage of the world's energy consumption went up from around 15% to 19%. To fill that growing demand for energy, the Chinese have already begun to import additional coal to meet their demands and are investing billions in an Iranian oil field while becoming an even bigger importer of Saudi Arabian oil than the United States. In late 2009, a new pipeline to transport natural gas from Turkmenistan to China was also opened with great fanfare. As in the United States the controversial procedure called hydro-fracking, a newly emerging technology to extract natural gas, is being widely adopted as well.

Thus for the immediate future China remains as deeply committed to ever more problematic climate change and dirtier fossil fuels as any of the earlier industrializing western powers. Furthermore the development of those industries is especially ambitious, for example in China's northwestern region, which is said to have plans to increase coal production by over 600 million tons. That effort, when coupled with various projects going on in Australia, make humanity's effort to stave off the worst of fossil-fuel-driven climate change even more problematic.

On the more positive side, there is significant evidence that China is beginning to confront the challenge of

transforming its energy production base more seriously. Indeed, the government has made the goal of improving energy efficiency by 40% over the next 10 years a priority with the ultimate goal of seeing fossil fuel energy use decline as green energy advances. The announced long-term goal is to have the nation's carbon emissions peak by 2030 and then begin to decline.

But for the immediate future finding a way to cleaner fossil fuels also remains a priority. Most immediately China has begun aggressively to shut down sites that process energy in an inefficient fashion. This includes closing down everything from older iron smelting plants and cement production facilities to smaller thermal power plants.

Of course, coal remains fundamental to Chinese energy needs and is likely to remain so for a very long time. Given that reality, the country has already closed a significant number of less-efficient coal energy plants. It is also emerging as a major player in the effort to process and clean coal enough to gain its energy advantages without further damaging the environment or transforming the global climate. The effort to make coal usable, a process known as carbon capture and sequestration, is especially important given the estimates that if China's emissions continue to grow at the rate of 10% a year as it was about 2010, the country itself will by 2040 be emitting as much as the entire world does today.

Coal does not power the world's transportation industry; petroleum does. China has become very involved in the transformation of this energy arena as well. Most immediately, as a nation with an emerging car culture and industry, it is moving aggressively to push up mileage standards on vehicles. This is particularly important since China surpassed the United States in 2009 as the largest global market for automobiles. In December 2012 China surpassed the United States as the largest importer of oil. Happily, it is also embracing vehicle energy standards that American car manufacturers have long resisted, and which remain caught in the complications of partisan American politics.

Many Chinese businesses have also made significant progress in developing sophisticated technologies to convert coal to a liquid form usable for transport. The question remains in what final form such efforts will emerge. Limited technology does exist to carry out coal liquefaction in a fashion that removes atmospheric pollutants, such as from sulfur and $CO_2$. Nevertheless, it is significantly more expensive than making the conversion from coal to liquid without such environmental concerns.

While hardly a move that would encourage those who see any expansion of fossil fuel production as contradictory to the goal of moving decisively away from fossil fuels, China, much like the United States, has begun developing the new hydro-fracking technologies necessary to expand natural gas production. Certainly, doing so when it replaces coal, a much dirtier fossil fuel, has its advantages. But natural gas still adds to the planet's growing heat retention problems.

## China's Move into Green Energy Technology

China may for the moment be the earth's most prolific burner of coal, but it is also clearly making a significant effort to transition to a cleaner energy mix as well. Efforts are underway to introduce alternative energy methods and to design "greener" communities. The commitment to such a transition began only a few years ago. As in much of the world, it was partly prompted by more immediate economic demands. Under the pressure of the world economic downturn of 2008, Beijing, like so many other nations, began to "prime" its economy with billions of dollars in stimulus money. Coincidently the economic downturn occurred at a time when attitudes about the significance of the challenge of climate change were growing and when the new appreciation that a green energy transformation could promote new jobs became especially attractive.

Thus it is not surprising that a particularly large percentage of Chinese stimulus money was directed toward building the nation's green energy infrastructure and reevaluating the nation's physical resources with those needs in mind. For example, while its growing deserts are a major threat to society, they are also important areas for solar production. Although its production has still largely been for the foreign market, China has already become by far the largest producer of photo-voltaic cells. By 2009, it was investing more in clean energy than even the Obama administration. The same year it became the world's largest national investor in green energy overall. The government has also done a good job in creating a pricing system that makes long-term investment in green energy attractive for many businesses. Of course, the sheer size of China and its ability to engage in large-scale manufacturing make it more possible to see lower prices based on larger production.

By early 2017 the combination of China's horrific coal-fired atmospheric pollution, a growing commitment to confronting the climate crisis and the advance of green energy technologies saw Beijing announce that by 2020 they planned to spend over $360 billion on expanding wing and solar energy.

## Capturing Wind Energy

What is really amazing is that over the last decade China has gone from a country with only a few wind turbines to the largest wind turbine market in the world. The first foreign-produced turbine was installed domestically in 1986, and the first Chinese-produced system was exported to the United States as recently as 2008. Amazingly that transformation was done in the context of a world where the United States had invested significantly in wind technology generations earlier, and nations like Denmark had developed the most impressive wind energy company in the world. Nevertheless, in a relatively short number of years China has dramatically jumped into the market and become the world's leader in wind-energy technology.

In fact, China is the world's leader not only in wind turbine technology but number one in terms of actual installed capacity. Even more impressively it was reported over the last year that wind energy production had surpassed nuclear energy production to become the nation's third most important source, after coal and hydroelectric, of energy production. And ambitious goals have been announced. The goal is to double wind energy production by 2020.

## China's Solar Energy Growth

As with wind energy, China has embraced solar energy with considerable enthusiasm. Indeed, government industrial policy sees its development as important to the nation's future.

Of course, given that national government support and the relatively low wages within China, an impressive industry soon emerged. For a time though that emerging industry was hampered by problems associated with over supply. The more recent announcement of massive new investments by the government are likely to eliminate those initial problems.

## Hydroelectric Energy

Certainly the most famous or, in the view of some people, the most infamous of China's efforts to develop green energy are its deep commitment to developing new hydroelectric dams, the most famous of which is the Three Gorges project. While China has long been among the international community's most interested nations in harnessing the power of water, dams in recent years have also been promoted as a sort of technological fix to deal with the challenges of climate change. The argument as it is presented is that climate change is caused by prolific burning of fossil fuels and creates among other things significant water resource problems. In some areas drought and other explosions of rain water are as uncontrollable and dangerous as they are useless for careful irrigation. Thus some have justified the recent enthusiasm for dam building as technology that not only reduces the burning of carbon fuels, but as a way to provide more water in times of drought and to tame the torrential waters that are associated with a global atmosphere that through warming simply carries more water. Whether dams can really be claimed as a logical response to a changing climate, it has certainly become obvious that the recent Chinese enthusiasm for dam building especially on the enormous Tibetan plateau is making many of their downstream neighbors who rely on those waters, such as India and Vietnam, increasingly concerned. There is good reason since the Chinese government has plans to build sixty more large dams. It has announced plans that include doubling hydro-generating power by 2020, which will require an enormously ambitious construction schedule to accomplish.

But what is not often mentioned in the controversies associated with hydroelectric energy production is the simply reality that hydroelectric dams cannot produce green or any other sort of electrical energy if the rivers that turn their turbines are less and less full of water. That reality has already begun to impact on dams along the Yangtze River, for example.

## China's Auto Industry

As has long been the case in the United States, China in recent years is developing a very large private car culture that has seen millions of Chinese take to the roads in their own vehicles. Initially those cars were built to a particularly poor environmental standard. But recent years have seen pollution and mileage standards emerge that are more stringent than currently in place in the United States. Moreover the nation is also making a major commitment not only to follow the United States and Japan as leading car makers, but as leading car makers of all-electric vehicles of the sort that are only just emerging elsewhere. All electric cars are still partly defined by what kind of energy supplies the grid that powers them. In China, the first major "green energy" source, as elsewhere, was hydroelectric dam production. Realistically, for the near term coal will still generate much of the energy needed for China's proposed electric car industry.

## U.S.-China Energy Cooperation and Competition

Energy production is yet another area of important future cooperation between the United States and China. Some worry about a future geopolitical energy competition between the United States and China over fossil fuels found in nations like Venezuela, Sudan, and Iran. A much more positive outcome may well emerge as the world's two greatest energy importers begin to cooperate on green energy production. Signs of that more positive future are emerging. Already there exists the new private-industry-based Joint U.S.-China Cooperation on Clean Energy initiative created with exactly that purpose in mind. The Obama administration has also signaled an interest in establishing an even more formal energy cooperation model.

Unfortunately as the world moved more deeply into 2018, momentum began to change as China appeared to accelerate its movement into green energy as both a consumer of green energy and producer of the associated technologies while the United States, under the new Trump administration seemed ready for a renewed embrace of climate busting fossil fuels. Equally discouraging was news that despite Beijing's more public embrace of cleaner energy sources new coal plants were continuing to be approved at the provincial levels of government. The climatic and economic implications of such developments are likely to be enormous over the next few decades.

## COVID-19

The first COVID-19 cases in China were reported in Wuhan in Hubei Province in late 2019; many believe that there had been cases before then but that the information had been suppressed. It was claimed that the cases were related to a wet market (where seafood and live wild animals may be sold side by side). By the time the city was placed in lockdown on 23 January, there had been over 400 reported cases and seventeen deaths. The lockdown was total. All transport links to and from the city were closed and the population were confined to their homes. These measures proved effective and in April 2020, the lockdown was eased and then lifted. When in May that year, six new cases occurred, the city reported that it had tested all 11 million people there. Of course, by the time Wuhan entered

# China

lockdown, people from the city had travelled to many other parts of the country and even abroad, thus spreading the virus. When cases occurred elsewhere in China, similar draconian local measures were adopted, with equally successful effects. But it was rare for anything like the Wuhan approach to be adopted outside China.

In total, between January 2020 and June 2021, China had 114, 707 confirmed cases, with 5,133 deaths, very low figures considering the size of the Chinese population. From the early days, there were those who claimed that the outbreak was not the result of contacts in a market, but arose from a Virology Laboratory in Wuhan that specialized in such diseases. Such claims were rejected by China and by a WHO team that visited Wuhan in January 2021. But they were endorsed with some enthusiasm by US President Donald Trump, who had already begun to refer to the "China virus" or the "Kung flu virus." Trump also accused the WHO of being a China pawn and withdrew US funding from the organization. In May 2021, President Joe Biden, who had restored links with WHO as soon as he took office, asked US agencies to reexamine the evidence linking the Wuhan Virology Laboratory to the outbreak of the virus, to the fury of China.

Cases remained low for the rest of 2021, partly in response to the strict lockdowns imposed on areas where there were outbreaks. a strictly enforces vaccination program meant that by May 2022, 88.7% of the population were fully vaccinated. But from January to May 2022, there was a rapid rise in cases in cities such as Beijing and Shanghai. Once again, the chosen means of control was tight lockdowns, firmly imposed. Draconian measures were used, which sometimes involved isolating children from their families. There were protests at the difficulties of getting food and at the poor quality of the rations supplied.

In one sense it worked. Despite the country's huge population, there were only 1.19 million cases and 5,224 deaths. But the methods used caused much resentment and criticism.

## The Future: The People's Republic

For much of human history China was at the forefront of the human experience in both the arts and sciences. Indeed, in the early 19th century China's economy has been estimated to have equaled a third of the world manufacturing output. But, that extraordinary series of accomplishments ground to a halt in the mid-19th century as the West, newly invigorated by the Enlightenment and the Industrial Revolution, surged ahead. For almost 200 years, dramatic internal problems and external pressures ranging from Western imperialists and Japanese invaders to unsound Maoist economic policies, kept China from regaining its traditional place at the forefront of the human drama. However, things have now changed. The generation-long surge of economic building set off by Deng Xiaoping has helped China pull itself out of the two centurylong doldrums into which it had fallen. In fact, even as the world entered into what seemed likely to be an extended economic downturn during the late fall of 2008, China appeared better prepared than many to weather the challenge by virtue of its long built-up economic reserves and the decision to carry out a massive government stimulus package that not only put people back to work, but saw enormous investment in the nation's infrastructure. More importantly that infrastructure spending was done in a fashion more likely to make the 21st century more successful. Overall the nation had moved aggressively from a huge and ambitious expansion of the nation's high-speed rail systems to a green energy package significantly larger than what Americans were spending under their own stimulus efforts. Those were precisely the sort of investments the still developing nation would have needed in the coming decades, whether the recession had occurred or not. Even more importantly, they began efforts to make sure their own people's purchasing behavior would in the future be strong enough to lessen the dependence on international exports. But such government stimulus programs and efforts to redirect public purchasing habits were limited in their impact. China still needed a healthy world economy to thrive, and by 2015 that global recovery had not been reached. In fact, China, like much of the rest of the developed world, was experiencing some of the same pressures, from a slowing economy to inflation, that at times has been so common in the United States, Japan, and Western Europe. If anything, China was becoming a more "normal" nation subject to the same pressures other developed, rather than developing, countries experience. Still by 2018, despite various obvious challenges and perhaps significant systemic weaknesses, China's economic position was still significantly better than much of the world with growth just under 7%. However in China's case, unlike its giant neighbor to the South, India, the nation still lacks the sort of democratic mechanisms that can siphon off social pressures before they explode, as they did in 1989, for example.

If anything, the nation's leaders have been less open to reform over the last few years and more uncomfortable with dissent than they have been in recent memory. Indeed recent word that efforts are underway to eventually allow Xi Jinping to serve a third term in office only underscores the reality that much of the momentum of a more politically open society is currently being undermined.

That is a bad sign considering the number of local demonstrations stirred on both by official corruption and environmental degradation. Neither trend is particularly confidence inspiring.

The irony is that the leaders of the People's Republic have an enormous amount to be proud of. They have pulled a nation devastated by war, by ideologically destructive political campaigns, and simply by unproductive economic policies into the first ranks of the world's major powers. It is an astounding accomplishment that has transformed both China and the world. Ironically though there is a growing and significant sense among both the leadership and the population that some-thing is amiss, that everything from the growing inequality to corruption, from environmental degradation to dealing with the challenges of an increasingly aging population are tarnishing the glow of what has thus far been accomplished. That reality has no doubt played into the government's obvious focus on addressing environmental and corruption issues while largely backtracking in the arena of intellectual and political liberalization which has been so obvious in the years since Xi came to power. And of course the weakening of the economy that began to be especially obvious during the latter part of 2015 has no doubt also influenced the party's concern about maintaining its legitimacy and authority as it moves forward.

One of the most obvious examples of that growing level of discomfort with intellectual and political liberalization was the trial of Pu Zhiqiang, a well-known civil rights lawyer, who had aroused official displeasure with a series of social media comments that criticized Chinese officials and questioned official policies in places from Xinjiang to Tibet.

Looking forward clearly the greatest concern is China's recent turn away from the generally more open society it had slowly evolved toward since the dark days of Mao's Great Leap Forward and the Cultural Revolution. Unfortunately the recent about face on that momentum is likely not only to be something of a damper on China's long-term stability but more immediately play a role in a loss of confidence in the future by both individuals and corporations domestic and international.

Indeed, the recent efforts to allow Xi Jinping to run for a third term as president, in fact to completely eliminate the idea of term limits for those who hold the office of Chinese president, only adds to such concerns. Xi may have come under some criticism for the heavy handed approach to the pandemic, but he seems to have ridden that out. In any case, it is hard to see who might succeed him—he has carefully avoided bringing anybody forward to take on the role.

Perhaps of even greater concern is the increased likelihood of growing tensions with the United States. The days when both Washington, DC, and Beijing saw improved relations between them as helpful relative to their own often difficult relations with Moscow are long gone.

And of course China's more recent campaign against foreign cultural influences, including major efforts to discourage celebrations of ever so obviously Western holidays like Christmas is likely to add to suspicion of and criticism of Beijing in the United States.

These days the simple reality is that in an increasingly more nationalistic global environment we are seeing what some have called the "Thucydides Trap" that is the almost predictable clash that can occur when a long dominant major power finds itself challenged by a rising power. Avoiding such a clash will require a level of statesmanship that the world can only hope for.

More immediately though is the challenge of the growing trade war that has developed between the United States and China over the former's effort to rebalance trading relations through the implementation of a series of tariffs that not surprisingly invited Chinese retaliation.

# Hong Kong
## Special Administrative Region of the PRC (since July 1997)

**Hong Kong Harbor**                    Courtesy of Steven A. Leibo

**Area:** 398 sq. mi. (1,032 sq. km.)
**Population:** 7,549,390 (2021 est.)
**Chief Executive:** John Lee Ka-chiu (since July 2022)
**Per Capita GDP Income:** $59,770 (2022 est.) (purchasing power parity)

The former British Crown Colony of Hong Kong consists of four distinct areas. The first is the island of Victoria (better known as Hong Kong Island) immediately off the coast. The second part is the small area known as Kowloon, at the tip of the peninsula jutting from the Chinese mainland toward Victoria. Between Victoria and Kowloon lies one of the world's busiest and most beautiful harbors in the world though the air pollution in recent years has diminished the number of days when its beauty can be easily appreciated.

The third part is composed of the "New Territories," which extend northward from Kowloon to the Chinese border. Kowloon is connected by rail to the Chinese cities of Shenzhen and Guangzhou and during 2009 one of the big issues of the day was whether Hong Kong would take part in creating an ultra-high-speed railroad from the former colony northward. The first section of such a link was opened in December 2012 and the whole line opened in 2018, reducing the journey time between Kowloon and Beijing to 9 hours. There were also connections to Shanghai and Kunming. Because of COVID, the service

was suspended from January to March 2020. When it reopened, it did not run between Shenzen on the Chinese border and Kowloon. Later, a limited service on that section was restored, but was again suspended in January 2022 following further outbreaks of COVID in Hong Kong.

In recent years the largest of the islands, Lantau, has become much more developed. The relatively new and ultramodern international airport is located on the island as well as a Hong Kong's own Disneyland that has been successful enough to be planning an expansion of the property.

Most of the area of Hong Kong consists of hills and low mountains, but there are enough level lands in the New Territories for large quantities of food to be harvested. It is actually dependent for much of its food and water on the mainland of China. The population is almost totally Chinese, many of them having arrived since 1949 in order to find greater safety, freedom, and economic opportunity than was allowed on the mainland of China. The climate is subtropical and experiences monsoon rains in the summer, but is relatively cool in the winter.

Realizing the potential value as a naval base, although not seeing at first the commercial possibilities of Hong Kong, the British annexed it from the Qing Empire in 1842, after the first Opium War. Under an effective British administration, and sharing in the increase of British trade

with and investments in China during the 19th and early 20th centuries, Hong Kong experienced rapid growth as a port. Kowloon was annexed in 1860, after Anglo-French forces again attacked China. The New Territories were added in 1898 in order to provide agricultural land and living space for the growing population but were held on a 99-year lease.

It was the impending end of that lease that brought about the eventual return of Hong Kong to Chinese sovereignty in 1997.

### Toward Unification with the Mainland

Much of Hong Kong's recent economic success is directly tied to the changing policies of the People's Republic of China. The ideologically driven PRC of Mao Zedong hardly needed Hong Kong's economic strengths, but Deng Xiaoping's arrival to power in the late 1970s brought change. Deng was determined to open China up to the world and to begin that effort in the southernmost parts of China. Under the circumstances, the British colony, with its abundant knowledge of both China and the Western world was in a perfect position to contribute to and take advantage of Beijing's changing economic policies.

Just north of the Hong Kong border, Beijing established special economic zones that, coupled with Hong Kong's strengths, eventually became the earliest engines of China's resurgence. During those years Hong Kong's economy, which had earlier been less tied to the People's Republic, actually began its first steps, at that point economic, in its reintegration with the mainland. Thus, China's economic accomplishments became Hong Kong's as well, and the momentum toward 1997's reunification with China had already begun.

Ironically, given some of the tensions that arose in the years before the 1997 handover of Hong Kong to the PRC, it was the British who had pushed for treaties to resolve the impending end of the 99-year leases of 1898. In Beijing's perspective, none of the 19th-century treaties imposed on China by the imperialistic West had any validity, so there was no reason to consider 1997 any different.

However, the British wanted the fate of their colony, the last Asian remnant of their once enormous Asian colonial system, resolved, and insisted on negotiations. During those years the two powers worked well together and the Sino-British Joint Declaration on Hong Kong was signed in 1984. The United Kingdom even

**Harbor traffic**

Courtesy of Jocelyn Yau

an executive-dominated government for Hong Kong, where the legislature plays the role of an adviser. The British in contrast were moving to establish a strong, elected legislative assembly and more freedoms than they themselves had ever tolerated.

In December of 1996 Tung Chee-hwa, a shipping company magnate, was elected by the 400-member selection committee to be the first chief executive for Hong Kong after the transition. Almost 6,000 people had applied for membership in the committee and a final 400 eventually selected Tung. To many persons, Tung Chee-hwa seemed an especially appropriate choice. His personal background had well prepared him to deal with challenges ahead. A Shanghai-born Chinese who spoke the same dialect as many of China's leaders, Tung lived for a decade in the United States and has many ties there. He has been involved with the United States Chamber of Commerce, the Hoover Institution and the Council of Foreign Relations.

He was even said to count former President George H. W. Bush among his personal friends. Moreover he had already served as an adviser in the British administration of Hong Kong. That China's leader Jiang Zemin favored him was also known previous to the election and no doubt helped his candidacy considerably.

## A Not So Smooth Transition

Throughout early 1997 tensions ran high regarding the upcoming transition. Following through on its long-standing rejection of those political changes Britain had made since the handover agreement, Beijing repealed many of the new laws—some made within hours of the changeover.

agreed to coordinate its changes in Hong Kong with the People's Republic.

Within the agreements, Britain unilaterally gave up the right to change the Hong Kong political system. For more than 100 years that had meant being ruled undemocratically by British governors sent from London. For its part, Beijing promised to leave the existing economic and social systems essentially unchanged for at least 50 years after 1997 and to permit a degree of self-government.

In the years immediately preceding the handover, and especially after the suppression of demomstrations in Beijing and elsewhere in China in 1989,there was considerable concern among Hong Kong's residents about whether Beijing could be trusted to honor the promises it had made. For that reason, many people, especially white collar and professional workers, emigrated in considerable numbers. They numbered over 500,000 alone in the decade before the handover.

Unfortunately, during the last years before 1997 both Beijing and London showed an increasing willingness to violate the spirit of the 1984 treaty. Britain on its part, long happy with governing Hong Kong under its own benign colonial dictatorship, moved, especially under its last colonial governor, to transform Hong Kong into an increasingly democratic political entity, something Beijing had hardly agreed to. Even a bill of rights was introduced by 1991.

With the appointment of former Conservative Party MP, Chris Patten, to the post of Governor of Hong Kong in 1992, the British had apparently decided to take a stronger hand in determining the future of the colony's government prior to their

withdrawal. Even before Governor Patten's appointment, the British had taken steps to strengthen the democratic process in Hong Kong. In September 1991, elections were held for 18 of the 61 seats on the Legislative Council (Legco). Sixteen of those seats were won by pro-democratic candidates. That election gave a considerable boost to the pro-democracy movement although it did not make the Chinese on the mainland happy. Two years later, in 1995, the first truly free election took place.

Predictably, those last minute British changes aroused the anger of the Chinese government. The basic disagreement between the British and the Chinese had to do with the type of government Hong Kong would have. Beijing had in mind

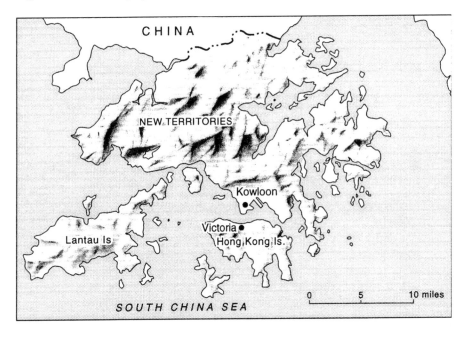

69

# China–Hong Kong

**Former Chief Executive Tung Chee-hwa**

During the transition there had also been considerable talk about the undemocratic aspects of Tung's election though with little appreciation that he was actually the most democratically elected leader in Hong Kong's history and the first Chinese. If anything, the tensions during the handover underscored how little the two groups had come to understand each other despite more than a century of interaction.

The last minute British efforts toward democratization clearly complemented Western political and social values though one might ask why Britain had waited so long to introduce them. What they did not complement was efforts to make a smooth transition from Hong Kong's earlier status as a colony to its future as part of the People's Republic, which despite Western preferences, continues to be controlled by an authoritarian single-party government.

## Hong Kong and China: The First Years

In the months leading up to the handover, commentators varied widely on what would occur next. Some predicted that China would dramatically transform the colony for the worst, stifling its freedoms and dynamic economy. Others insisted with equally great conviction that little would actually change within the former colony and that the doomsayers were raising unnecessary panic. They were both wrong. The first year after the transition turned out to be quite traumatic though for reasons few had predicted.

The principal menace arrived not from Beijing, but from the failing economies of her East and Southeast Asian neighbors. As well-known financial institutions faltered and the Hong Kong markets plummeted, Hong Kong residents found their lifestyles and hopes under siege. Throughout 1998 and early 1999 economic news continued to be very discouraging. Hong Kong, following the lead of its Southeast Asian neighbors moved into the worst recession since the early 1970s. Unemployment was up to a 15-year high and tourism, an important source of revenue, down.

Responding to the crisis the government not only expended considerable resources to defend the Hong Kong dollar but announced several economic stimulus packages. Ironically, considering all the Western rhetoric about how Hong Kong might be threatened by its reintegration into the People's Republic, Beijing now turned out to be a source of strength. Not only did the PRC's leaders work to defend Hong Kong's economy, they went as far as to threaten international currency speculators against efforts to weaken her currency and even began encouraging more mainland tourism there.

But what of all those fears of Beijing's new power over Hong Kong? The PLA soldiers who had marched into the territories with such fanfare in July 1997 withdrew from public eye. Perhaps most controversial were the new pressures upon the educational system regarding the expansion of education in Chinese. From the fall of 1998 the expectation was that Chinese, both the local Cantonese dialect and Mandarin, would become the principal language of instruction. Given the importance of English for international business, this demand was heavily criticized in some quarters.

Also of particularly significance was the furor raised in early 1999 over a ruling by the Hong Kong Court of Final Appeal that children born of Hong Kong residents had the right to reside in the former colony. Clearly a blessing for many Hong Kong parents of mainland children but one that raised considerable controversy over the local court's right to decide such important immigration issues and fears about a too large influx of new residents to Hong Kong especially as it was struggling with a financial turndown.

When, somewhat later, the Chinese National People's Congress, following a request by Tung Chee-hwa, chose to modify the Hong Kong court's decision, concerns were also raised about Beijing's growing power over Hong Kong. Eventually, by the spring of 2002 the news was filled with stories of the adult children of Hong Kong residents being forced to return to the PRC because they lacked the necessary papers to remain in Hong Kong.

Politically the long anticipated May 1998 elections brought the return to power of many of the former colony's most outspoken democrats. Martin Lee's Democratic Party did especially well in the elections, both in competition for those openly allocated seats and for those reserved for the professional classes.

**Former Hong Kong Chief Executive Donald Tsang Yam-kuen**

Overall, it is clear that a majority of the Hong Kong population would like to see a more democratic environment. In both the elections of 2000 and 2004, local democrats won clear majorities. Still, in the election that took place during the fall of 2004, supporters of Beijing won 34 of the 60 possible seats. However, this was not an unexpected outcome given that the majority of members are not chosen in open elections. The election results hardly changed public attitudes. In the late fall of 2005 Hong Kong's streets were again full of demonstrators demanding direct elections for the former colony's leaders. But that enthusiasm failed to achieve much beyond its early starts. As we will see below, more recent elections have not seen a significant growth in voting support for the more democratic parties either.

## Hong Kong between Two Worlds

In fact, Hong Kong's government has revealed no great commitment to expanding its residents democratic rights. For example, in late 1999, when new councils were formed at the local levels, they were even less democratic than their predecessors. Clearly, Hong Kong's new government, despite the gains made by some democratic activists, remained similar to the relatively open but also authoritarian regimes of countries like Singapore. In fact, when Anson Chan, who had long led Hong Kong's civil service, recently resigned she publicly decried the weakening of Hong Kong's publicly minded professional civil service.

The first Chief Executive, Tung Chee-hwa saw his popularity drop dramatically not only among the local population but among many of the former colony's most influential figures. For a time Tung managed to retain the all-important support of Beijing and was able to win his position anew when his first term expired in March 2002. Despite his lessening public popularity the situation was different administratively. Early on Tung saw his powers enhanced by the introduction of a new ministerial system consisting of a 14-person cabinet of policy officials whom Tung personally selected.

Beijing's unwillingness to consider expanding Hong Kong's very limited experiments with democracy was reinforced in the spring of 2004 when the National People's Congress ruled that only China's central government had the right to modify the former British Colony's political structure. But while some decried the decision it was also clear that Hong Kong's people still retained enough power to limit the authority of their own government if they exerted themselves enough.

That "people power" was especially evident during the summer of 2003 when tremendous numbers of Hong Kong residents took to the streets to protest a proposed anti-subversion bill law that would have given the Hong Kong's leaders the right to ban certain groups and allow the police to carry out searches without warrants. Eventually, under pressure from the population, Tung Chee-hwa agreed to modify the measure and remove its most onerous provisions. Nevertheless, the crisis had contributed to the weakening of Tung's support.

By the winter of 2005 Tung had become increasingly unpopular and eventually resigned his office a full two years before this term was set to expire. Meanwhile Beijing, once again asserting its authority, announced to considerable controversy that Tung Chee-hwa's successor as Chief Executive, Donald Tsang Yam-kuen, would only be allowed to serve out the final two years of Tung's term in office rather than the full five-year term of a new chief executive.

For many in Hong Kong, Beijing's decision was another example of China's willingness to interpret at its convenience Hong Kong's constitution. Public polls have also reinforced the impression that China is losing much of its popularity among Hong Kong's population.

As for Donald Tsang himself, he eventually won election in his own right in a contest against pro-democracy leader Alan Leong. Chinese Prime Minister Wen Jiabao then officially recognized the result by awarding Mr. Tsang the "instrument of appointment" at a ceremony that took place in Beijing at the Chinese leadership compound of Zhongnanhai. Mr. Tsang's new term began on July 1, 2007, exactly a decade after Hong Kong officially returned to China.

Within a few months Mr. Tsang found himself facing a particularly impressive critic. Anson Chan, Hong Kong's long serving head of its civil service under both British and Chinese rule, won election to the legislative council of Hong Kong in December 2007. Ms. Chan, a formidable politician and bureaucrat, had emerged in the period after Hong Kong's formal return to China as both a member of Tung Chee-hwa's government and one of its best-known critics. Later, after she left her position as the head of the civil service, Chan became for a time a leading advocate of constitutional and more specifically democratic reform in the former colony. This stance allowed her to consolidate opposition forces behind her electoral victory.

But Chan did not prove to be a long-term political foe. During the summer of 2008 she announced that she would not stand for reelection in the upcoming elections. When those elections did occur, many expected the democratic movement to weaken significantly, given Beijing's heightened status after its successful Olympics and growing public concerns that centered more on economic issues than democratic aspirations. In the end, though, the democratic movement, while weakened somewhat by the loss of two seats in Hong Kong's legislature, still retained enough to remain major players in Hong Kong's political life.

By March of 2012 in yet another very limited election, something over a thousand elite voters were allowed to take part, Leung Chun-ying (also known as C. Y. Leung), another former businessman who had apparently gained the ambivalent support of Beijing, was elected Hong Kong's new leader. In winning the "election," Leung Chun-ying defeated two rivals, including the democratic activist Albert Ho. Not surprisingly the pro-democratic forces loudly denounced the "election" as being exceedingly anti-democratic, given that the vast majority of Hong Kong's seven million residents had no say whatsoever in who would govern them next.

**Former Chief Executive of Hong Kong C. Y. Leung**

**Carrie Lam, Hong Kong's first female leader**

Leung's tenure though proved especially problematic as his efforts to strengthen Beijing's role in Hong Kong not only provoked some of the most significant popular challenges ever seen but apparently failed to win the approval of China's leadership either. Indeed, by the winter of 2016–2017 he announced, to considerable public satisfaction, that he did not plan to run again. Eventually in early 2017, Hong Kong residents watched, despite long standing calls for a formal democratic vote, Carrie Lam, the outgoing chief executive's deputy became their new leader. On one hand the choice was historic, Hong Kong's first female leader but in all other ways her selection was as undemocratic as all Hong Kong's recent elections, a situation Beijing certainly plans to continue.

### Hong Kong's Occupy Movement

Although Hong Kong's residents had frequently shown support for a more direct voting system to choose those selected to serve as the community's chief executive, Beijing had other ideas. In late 2014 it was announced that while local residents would be allowed to vote directly their choices would be limited to a small number of candidates carefully vetted by Beijing's supporters.

The announcement certainly made sense from Beijing's perspective. How could Hong Kongers be allowed genuine democracy by a system still controlled by the Chinese Communist Party? Many of those in Hong Kong though were outraged and a very emotional and confrontative movement in some ways reminscent of both the Tiananmen Square Movement of a generation previous and the more recent Occupy movement in the Unites States sprung to life stirred on by many young residents but with strong support from a much wider range of locals. Indeed, few in the ever so business-oriented former colony had ever seen such a level of political agitation. Relatively soon thereafter the Occupy movement morphed into a protest of a very different scale than almost anyone could have predicted, see the "Umbrella Revolution."

# China–Hong Kong

## Hong Kong's Umbrella Revolution

For outsiders long familiar with Hong Kong's reputation as a largely apolitical city dedicated to commerce, images of the extraordinarily large crowds, hundreds of thousands of people strong that filled the former colony's streets in mid-October of 2014 probably came as quite a surprise. But the roots of the challenge, to both the city's leaders and those in faraway Beijing actually ran quite deep.

On the surface of course the precipitating event was Beijing's announcement in late August of 2014 that rather than adhere to earlier promises for a genuinely democratic process for the upcoming 2017 election of a new chief executive, the new executive would be chosen in a fashion considerably less democratic than many had expected. The specific plan offered by Beijing, was that while it was willing to dramatically expand the voter base, Chinese officials still insisted on vetting the actual candidates of which only three would be allowed on the ballot. That decision, which was widely perceived as backsliding from the long-standing local promise of a genuinely democratic vote, initially helped spark an "Occupy Central" movement of activists who blockaded access to government offices and then quickly morphed into a much larger and

more widespread popular and largely student led movement that filled the streets across wide parts of Hong Kong with young people many of whom had the very formal support of academic administrators across the former colony.

But the technicalities of how democratic the next election would be were only part of the issue, after all even the oldest constitutional democracy in the world, the United States, has not yet accomplished true popular sovereignty in the election of its highest political leader, the American president. While the broken political promises associated with Beijing's insistence on vetting candidates was a precipitating event the larger challenge of history and identity played out dramatically in the background feeding the fires of discontent that were so dramatically on display as the world watched so many young Hong Kongers very publicly showing their contempt for China's rulers, flag, and the ruling Chinese Communist Party.

One of the core elements is the issue of memory itself and in Hong Kong's case, ironically both too much memory and too little. For a significant percentage of Hong Kong people their very arrival in the former British colony was often a result of the turmoil that the early years

of the People's Republic had let loose in neighboring Guangdong Province. For such individuals and more immediately their children any expansion of central Chinese control over Hong Kong, something they had fled precisely to avoid having to live under the control of the CCP was an anathema that had earlier seen many hoping to flee the colony before the 1997 deadline for its handover.

The handover of course, despite a worldwide media assumption that Beijing would interfere deeply in Hong Kong's affairs, actually went off relatively well precisely because Beijing had been reluctant to intervene during those first decades after the handover. Indeed many in Hong Kong often give the impression that they assumed that the handover had been merely symbolic—perhaps in denial sometimes acting as if they do not truly appreciate that the "handover" would sooner or later result in very real changes within the territory.

But Beijing's reluctance has significantly diminished in recent years with the decision about the upcoming elections only being the most recent and dramatic example. Indeed some of have feared that Beijing quite consciously hoped to more fully integrate Hong Kong long before the termination of the decades of autonomy

promised in the handover treaties that were negotiated between London and Beijing in the 1980s. Indeed occasional comments by senior Chinese leaders seem at times to confirm that impression.

And then there is the question of too little memory. Like so many in neighboring Taiwan, itself full of people who are ethnically Han but less self-consciously "Chinese" in a political sense, many Hong Kongers have little real sense of identification with China. After all, starting in the early 1840s, expanding in the 1860s, and even more at the turn of the century, the larger area known simply as Hong Kong to outsiders was drawn by the then powerful British Empire far outside of the Chinese political orbit. Indeed the memories that have so influenced people within the mainland, from the 1911 Revolution through the Communist Revolution of 1949, various traumas from the Hundred Flowers Campaign to the Cultural Revolution have simply not been part of most Hong Kongers' personal experiences. In short, they may be ethnically Han but many have no more of a sense of being "Chinese" in a political way than people from Taiwan to Singapore do. For such people, especially as the complications of the earlier association with Britain fade from memory they far more easily identify themselves simply as Hong Kongers.

It is of course in that context that many have experienced the growing pressures associated with the larger numbers of mainland visitors who have become a ubiquitous presence in the city. On one hand, the large numbers of visitors, newly moneyed individuals with wallets made flush by China's recent decades of economic growth have been deeply appreciated by the city's many merchants. On the other hand, as we have seen elsewhere, their very presence has frequently put severe strains on the territories' cost of living and resources, pressures that have often been deeply resented by local residents.

It is within that larger context that the so called "Umbrella Revolution" emerged which for weeks during the fall of 2014 saw at times thousands of Hong Kongers demonstrating while frequently living in an impromptu series of "tent cities" that sprung up in the heart of Hong Kong.

It was a standoff, by Hong Kong's standards of epic proportions with the demonstrators, especially inspired by one especially politicized teenager, Joshua Wong, demanding change and the Territory's then Chief Executive C. Y. Leung unwilling or perhaps unable to offer significant concessions. For a time many thought another confrontation of

that sort that had so dramatically caught the world's attention in 1989 in China's capital was about to occur with perhaps a similar level of violence.

In the end, though, cooler heads eventually prevailed. While there were occasional efforts to use violence against the demonstrators, tear gas attacks for example, such tactics were rare and the local leadership or perhaps Beijing itself chose to simply let the demonstrations largely run their course without making significant concessions. For those expecting Beijing to compromise and offer a more democratic election, it was a great disappointment. Still, for those hoping to avoid a bloody crackdown and most likely only a more immediate expansion of Beijing's control over Hong Kong, it was perhaps a significant relief.

As a practical matter, Beijing was never likely to make real concessions. Not only is the current leadership under Xi Jinping clearly less interested in allowing any significant expansion of political rights but doing so would have no doubt only complicated their relations not only with regions like Tibet but the increasingly restive Chinese far West. Not forgetting that the well-publicized tensions between Hong Kong residents and visitors from the mainland have reduced significantly the amount of sympathy many in China might have otherwise felt toward developments in the territory.

## The Struggle Continues and China Adopts a Tougher Line

That the government in Beijing was becoming increasingly exasperated with developments in Hong Kong was to become clearer in 2015-2016. An early sign was the apparent kidnapping of a number of booksellers from the territory, who had made a point of selling publications that could not be sold in China, usually because they were critical of the leadership. There were international protests, with Britain claiming that the action, which appeared to involve mainland officials operating in Hong Kong, was a breach of the Joint Declaration. All would resurface eventually.

The Legislative Council elections in 2016 also caused Chinese concern, with the election of six known pro-independence activists, who together with those favoring more democracy for the territory, formed a group of 29 in the 70-seat Council. Under the auspices of the Standing Committee of the National People's Congress, moves were made to disqualify the six pro-independence

activists. There were other signs of a tougher approach, reflecting Prime Minister Xi Jinping's developing nationalist agenda. In September 2017, a law passed by China's parliament, the National People's Congress, forbidding showing disrespect to the National Anthem, was extended to Hong Kong. At the 19th Communist Party Congress the following month, Xi, also Party general secretary, made a speech in which he said that Hong Kong and Macau could continue to govern themselves but "only with patriots playing the leading role." These developments, together with the elevation of the pro-China Carrie Lam to the position of chief executive and a decision by Hong Kong Radio and Television to drop the long-standing 24-hour feed of BBC World Service Radio, were seen as clear signs that Beijing intended to erode Hong Kong's separate identity.

The disqualification of the independence activists led to by-elections for four of the seats in March 2018, with two seats going to pro-China candidates and two to pro-democracy supporters. When the other two seats were contested in November, both were taken by pro-Chinese candidates. 2018 was also marked by regular protests at the increase of Chinese influence. The protests began on 1 January with demonstrations against a decision to put part of the new rail terminus for hi-speed trains from China under Chinese instead of Hong Kong law, which was seen as a means of facilitating Chinese police units into the territory. (The hi-speed link was intended as a major improvement in communications between Hong Kong and the Mainland, as was the world's longest sea bridge linking Hong Kong with the Chinese city of Zhuhai on the Pearl River Delta, and Macau.)

There was no letup in political tensions in 2019. In February, a bill—the "Fugitive Offenders and Mutual Legal Assistance in Criminal Matters Legislation (Amendment) Bill"—was proposed, allowing extradition to countries or territories with which Hong Kong had no such arrangements. This would have allowed extradition to China and led to demonstrations in June, demanding its abandonment. The government refused and the demonstrations rapidly turned to violence, including the occupation of the Legislative Council Chamber on 12 June. As the demonstrations continued, the police response was increasingly violent, and they continued even after the Chief Executive suspended the controversial bill, which was finally withdrawn in October. Demonstrators now called for the end of

# China–Hong Kong

police violence, withdrawal of the claim that there had been riots, the resignation of Carrie Lam, and the franchise for all. University campuses were occupied. For a time, the People's Liberation Army was stationed on alert outside the territory, but it did not intervene.

The extent of anti-Chinese feeling was clearly shown in the results from the District council elections in November. The turnout was high; 71 percent compared with 47 percent in the 2015 elections. Pro-democracy supporters won 390 seats out of 452, gaining control of 17 out of 18 councils. Foreign condemnation of China grew stronger. The United States passed a "Hong Kong Human Rights and Democracy Act" and began applying sanctions to some of those involved in the suppression of the activists.

Among those sanctioned was John Lee Ka-chiu, a former Hong Kong police officer, who had become underdecretary for security on retirement from the police force in 2012, and then secretary for security in 2019. (At that point, he had given up his British passport.) Lee had authorized the heavy-handed tactics used by the police against demonstrators, including water cannons, rubber bullets, tear gas, and live ammunition.

Demonstrations continued into early 2020 but faltered somewhat as concern rose over COVID-19 (see below). However, as early as January, the appointment of Luo Huining to head the Chinese Central Government Liaison Office in Hong Kong signaled a more aggressive approach from the authorities. Luo had the reputation of a firm supporter of central government policies in difficult situations. A series of arrests of those accused of "unlawful assembly" began. Those involved included Jimmy Lai, and entrepreneur and media owner, former legislators and democracy activists such as the lawyer Martin Lee. In June, the National People's Congress bypassed LegCo and passed the National Security Law. This criminalized any activities seen as promoting secession, subversion, terrorism or collusion with foreign countries. It allowed the central government to appoint judges and to establish security forces in Hong Kong. At the beginning of July, a 10-member Committee for Safeguarding National Security of the Hong Kong Special Administrative Region was formally established with Luo Huining as National Security Advisor to the committee. That same month, the chief executive, Carrie Lam, announced the postponement of the September 2020 LegCo elections, citing a COVID-19 surge, to September 2021. Meanwhile,

organizations were being dismantled and people dismissed. In December, Jimmy Lai became the first person to be charged with conspiracy and collusion with foreign forces.

International protests grew and the US imposed further sanctions on named individuals. Such moves were dismissed as interference in China's internal affairs. In January 2021, Britain, which had been issuing many more British National (Overseas) Passports (BNOP) in 2020, announced that it would expand its visa quotas for Hong Kong. The Chinese reaction was swift. China would no longer recognize such passports. If Hong Kong people wished to travel, they should use Hong Kong passports and they would not be allowed to leave or enter the territory with them. Action was taken against the BBC, with all World Service transmissions in Hong Kong stopped in February. New rules governing LegCo were introduced, reducing the number of directly elected members and increasing the number chosen by an electoral committee.

In April, a series of custodial and suspended sentences were given in the trials of senior pro-democracy figures who were accused of organizing illegal assemblies in the form of election primaries in 2019. Organizers of Hong Kong's annual vigil to mark the events of 1989 in Beijing were arrested. The Hong Kong Alliance, which had organized the events, was increasingly subject to police harrassment and decided to disband in September 2021. By then many of its leading figures were in prison. To many in Hong Kong and elsewhere, the 1984 Sino-British Joint Declaration was effectively dead.

And the repression continued. By spring 2022, there had been over 150 arrests under the National Security Law. An organization originally established in 1989, the 612 Humanitarian Aid Relief Fund, had been forced to close in 2021. Yet in May 2022, some of its former members, who had been helping detained protestors, including the 90-year-old Roman Catholic Emeritus Joseph Zen and the senior barrister Margaret Ng, were arrested and charged with "foreign collusion." There were international protests, with the Vatican expressing concern. The authorities remained indifferent to such actions.

By that time, Hong Kong was about to change leaders. Carrie Lam, who became chief executive in 2017, but who had spectacularly failed to live up to her promise to heal the divisions in Hong Kong, announced on 4 April 2022 that

she would not stand again for the post. She cited family reasons for her decisions but there was widespread belief that Beijing was disappointed with her performance. An election process got under way, at considerable expense, with one candidate approved by Beijing, the secretary for security, John Lee. Unsurprisingly, he was duly elected on May 8, to take office on July 1. For the first time since 1997, Hong Kong's chief executive would be from a security background.

## COVID-19

As news came out of China of this new virus, Hong Kong, with its close links to the mainland and its role as a major travel center, was seen as highly vulnerable. Small numbers of cases were detected but the expected massive increase did not happen. After a brief medical workers' strike, all but three crossings into China were closed in February. The Beijing–Hong Kong high-speed train service was suspended. The wearing of masks in public places, which had become a regular practice after the 2003 SARS outbreak also kept transmission low. Other measures included 21 days' quarantine, a limit on public gatherings to four people—a rule often broken because of political demonstrations—and limits on opening hours of bars and restaurants. By early April 2020, there had been 854 cases and four deaths. Cases then subsided until July-August. Both these developments were attributed to local people returning from overseas. Numbers from August to November were never more than 20 a day, but in November, they began to rise to over a 100 a day, until falling away in January 2021. By mid-May 2021, there had been a total of nearly 12,000 cases and 210 deaths. Only in May 2021 was there an easing of quarantine rules. Vaccinations began in late February 2021, with some 1,700,000 doses delivered by mid-May.

Cases remained low until February 2022. But then, despite continued tight controls on movement and meetings they suddenly took off, in a surge that lasted until the end of April. The hospitals came under severe strain, with oxygen running out and patients lined up in corridors. Many of these were elderly and unvaccinated. In mid-March, government statistics showed that only 53% of those over 80 had been vaccinated.

By mid May 2022, there had been 1.21 milllion cases and 9,370 deaths. Vaccination rates had improved, however, with 89.1% having had one dose, 83.6% two, and 47.25% a booster.

### The Environment

The environment is becoming more and more of a problem. The air pollution that has been growing over China's cities is severely affecting the living conditions in Hong Kong. Most recently, it was announced that during 2009 the air quality at street level in parts of Hong Kong was at life-threatening levels one in eight days of the year. While air quality at the higher levels was somewhat better, the murky haze that floats above Hong Kong has gotten so bad in recent years that it is not only threatening human health, but depressingly the views within Hong Kong's harbors, which were once among the most beautiful in the world.

But all of this is hardly China's fault. Indeed authorities claimed that the worst increases were the result not of regional pollution coming in from the People's Republic, but locally produced pollutants stemming from Hong Kong's own fossil fuel energy use. Local medical experts report that the increasingly foul air contributes to as many as 2,000 deaths a year. The employees of the many international companies that have bases in Hong Kong are becoming more and more vocal about the problem. Indeed, as within China itself, the last few years have seen a growing environmental consciousness starting to emerge within the colony's residents, which is being taken more and more seriously by the special administrative zone's leadership.

Today, the leading environmental concerns seem to revolve around the question of air pollution and waste management. In both cases there is some reason for optimism. Hong Kong and neighboring

**Inside Hong Kong's famed Star Ferry**

Courtesy of Steven A. Leibo

Guangdong Province have begun to work together on air pollution issues, and a series of monitoring stations is now in place. Moreover, a series of as yet volunteer air quality targets has been created as a result of the cooperation.

The results have been positive. In 2013, there were 150,000 medical cases attributable to air pollution, and 3,000 premature deaths. Although air quality is not always good, there was a steady fall in both numbers over theyears, with the deahs more than halved. An even sharper fall took place in 2020 as a result of COVID restrictions, although figures went up again in 2021.

On the question of waste management, Hong Kong's seven million inhabitants have a record of producing far more waste than many of their neighboring regional cities. Significant sums are being spent to take on that challenge as well. In short, a growing sense of the need not only for economic growth, but sustainable economic growth is starting to become more widespread.

### The Future

Hong Kong's future is looking much bleaker than would have seemed possible at the time of its reversion to China in 1997. Developments since Xi Jinping became leader of China in 2012, and the local reaction to them, have led to a steady deterioration in the concepts of "one country, two systems" and the preservation of the territory's separate status until 50 years after 1997. Freedom of the media has been eroded, as, to a lesser extent, has been academic freedom. Dissident views are no longer tolerated, even if peacefully expressed. There is much disillusion in Hong Kong, and many will try to leave, despite possible draconian methods to prevent this.

There is likely to be a reduction in its international position. This was already beginning to happen before the events of recent years, as new Asian centers such as Singapore and Shanghai have come into their own. The United States has stripped Hong Kong of favored trading rights, and it is now to be treated the same as China. The disruption of international trade and travel brought about by COVID-19 has clearly had a short-term negative impact on its economy.

Of course, Hong Kong has bounced back before. But the damage now is deep and may not be easily overcome.

**Hong Kong apartment blocks**

Courtesy of Jocelyn Yau

# Macao
## Macao Special Administrative Region of the People's Republic of China (Portuguese Dependency until 1999)

**Senato Square, Macao**

**Area:** 12.7 sq. mi. (32.9 sq. km.)
**Population:** 683,100 (2021 est.)
**Chief of State:** Xi Jinping, president (since March 2013)
**Head of Government:** Chief Executive Ho Iat Seng (since December 20, 2019)
**Per Capita GDP Income:** $54,798.9 (2021) (ppp)
**Languages:** Chinese (Cantonese), Portuguese, English
**Religions:** Buddhist, Daoist, Christianity.

Until its late 1999 return to the mainland, Macao (or Macau) was Portugal's only remaining overseas territory. Macao is divided about equally into Macao proper, which has a common land frontier with the Chinese mainland, and two nearby islands. The terrain is mostly flat. The offshore waters are muddy with silt carried by the Pearl River. The climate is subtropical with a summer monsoon and a relatively cool winter. Except for a small community of Portuguese (officials, soldiers, police, missionaries, businessmen,

etc.) and other Europeans, the population is overwhelmingly Chinese.

Portugal acquired Macao in the mid-16th century for use as a base from which to trade with nearby Canton by an agreement with the Ming dynasty of China. It prospered in the 18th century, but during the 19th it was rapidly overshadowed by Hong Kong. From its earlier days of prominence, Macao has retained some beautiful old buildings and something of a Mediterranean flavor. It has a reputation, partly justified, as a center of opium and gold smuggling and assorted vice. Gambling is unquestionably the major feature of the economy, and auto racing and bullfighting have been introduced as well.

The new government of Portugal after 1974 wanted to return Macao to China, but Beijing would not accept it because of the disturbing effect such a transfer might have had on Hong Kong. Portugal did agree to allow more internal autonomy to its former colony in 1976 and granted it increased powers in 1990. After

the Sino-British agreement was reached on Hong Kong in 1984, negotiations began between Lisbon and Beijing for the reversion of Macao to Chinese control. It was agreed in April 1987 that reversion would take place in December 1999, along lines similar to those already worked out for Hong Kong. Certain concessions were granted to Macao's leaders. For example, it was later agreed that capital punishment, common in the People's Republic, would not be employed in Macao.

In the months leading up to the handover two issues dominated the life of the colony. First the ongoing gang violence and the question of who would lead the colony after its return to mainland control. As in Hong Kong, a special committee of 100 notables was formed to plan for Macao's future leadership. Edmund Ho, the 44-year-old son of a well known diplomat and banker, was selected. More recently Fernando Chui Sai-on, who had served as the secretary for social and cultural affairs in Ho's administration, declared his own

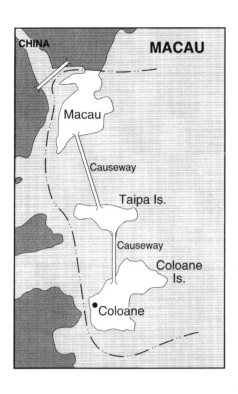

**Macao Chief Executive
Fernando Chui Sai-on**

a crackdown that drastically reduced the violence.

Politically the former colony has evolved in a fashion somewhat similar to its neighbor Hong Kong. The fall 2001 direct elections, which provided some of the representatives to the 27-seat assembly, resulted in a body filled largely by candidates primarily concerned with either business issues or ties to Beijing. The pro-democracy candidates did manage however to capture 21% of the vote and doubled their representation from one to two members. The four subsequent elections, in 2005, 2009, 2013 and 2017, have seen a modest shift away from the business interests towards a slightly more democratic base. But this was far removed from the shift within Hong Kong.

But the fact remains that within Macao there has been no more of a renaissance of democracy than there has in Hong Kong. The largely anti-democratic tone was particularly obvious in the transition from the leadership of Edmund Ho to Fernando Chui Sai-on. It saw no real competitive contest for leadership and only a few blank ballots and absenteeism offered in opposition to Chui's election.

It is also true that the less populated Macao has had fewer problems than Hong Kong in reintegrating into the People's Republic. That does not mean that issues have not emerged from time to time to complicate matters. Most recently there have been tensions over the former colony's system for legal education. Ironically students whose training has focused on the legal system of the mainland have fared far less well than those who have specialized in the more Portuguese-based system long in effect. Clearly those with a better knowledge of mainland law will most probably have an advantage in the future. But for the moment their options apparently remain limited compared to those who were trained in the more traditional legal system. This problem has emerged even as the lack of lawyers has become a significant problem given the growth of the casino industry.

Overall, Macao entered the millennium with a positive outlook. The economy has done relatively well in recent years although it too was hit hard by the world economic recession that began in the fall of 2008.

There has also been considerable progress in improving transport links between Macao and the outside world with particular progress made in linking Macao to Taiwan. Tourism is also looking up, and efforts to have Macao listed as one of UNESCO's World Heritage Sites are in progress. Tourism has benefited since "The Historic Centre of Macau" was formally inscribed at the 29th Session of the

UNESCO World Heritage Committee in July 2005 . It is known locally as Macau World Heritage.

In another sign of Macao's evolution, the government's decision in 2001 to open up the former colony's gambling industry to international investment has attracted investors hoping to transform Macao into a Las Vegas-like gambling and resort destination capable of attracting a much larger number of visitors than ever before. Because Macao is the only place in the People's Republic where casinos are legal, people flock there from mainland China and Hong Kong, and by 2007, it had overtaken Las Vegas as the "gambling capital of the world." Beijing is also aware of the potential problems and has forbidden officials from gambling in Macao. Beijing's concern about its own officials' potential corruption was not the only impact of Macao's greater involvement in the globalized world economy as became clear during the 2008 world financial crisis. Just as some American casinos invested in Macao when they had been financially stronger, by 2009 there was talk of those same businesses selling off Macao-based properties to make up for their own recent losses.

The momentum, however, quickly built up again. Most notable was a new casino, the Galaxy, which opened in May 2011. Built by a Hong Kong cement magnate, it cost around $1.9 billion and is said to be covered with enough gold leaf to impress even the most jaded gambler. Additionally, the international hospitality giants, Marriott International, Inc. and Galaxy Entertainment Group, have expanded their presence. While Macao remains the biggest gambling destination in the world, its gambling revenues suffered a major dip

candidacy for chief executive in June of 2009. The following July he was "elected" by 282 of the potential 300 votes possible in the election committee. There were no "NO" votes. Chui may have had few democratic credentials but, with a PhD in public health, he was a good technocrat. His 2019 successor, Ho lat Seng, who was elected unopposed, was both a member of the Chinese parliament, the National People's Congress, and the president of the Macau Legislative Assembly, but gave up both positions on becoming Chief Executive.

In sharp contrast to Hong Kong's reversion to China, Macao's was a much smoother transition with a considerably more cooperative attitude on both sides. Nevertheless, there were some features of the transition that were harder on Macao than Hong Kong. For example, unlike Hong Kong that had already put into place a largely home-grown bureaucracy, the departure of the Portuguese left Macao without as many trained administrators in place. To deal with the problem, the government arranged to have some of its civil servants trained in Singapore.

One important controversy was the mainland's decision during the fall of 1998 to station troops in Macao after the handover. It was a decision that clearly contradicted previous understandings, but one that was probably a logical outcome of Beijing's concern about criminal violence. For a time just before the turnover, gang warfare became a particularly violent part of the life of the colony. Once the turnover occurred, Beijing carried out

# China–Macao

**Former Macao Chief Executive Edmund Ho Hau-Wah**

in 2015-2016, possibly because many Chinese, perhaps concerned about the mainland's crackdown on corruption, seem to have been spending their money elsewhere. The downturn proved short lived and by 2019, when there were 41 casinos, revenue had built up again, only to be hit by the outbreak of COVID-19 (see below). Although casinos were only closed for two weeks and enjoyed something of a revival once they had reopened, regular travel restrictions to prevent the spread of the disease, tighter visa processes—Chinese need visas to enter Macao—and stringent test requirements kept many away. Gambling revenue fell by 80%. In early 2021, it began to pick up but the recovery was slow. Visitor numbers, an indication of the likely health of the gambling industry since most come for that purpose, have fluctuated as COVID has waxed and waned in the neighboring regions. By March 2022, numbers from China had dropped by some 30% year on year.

Gambling has not been the only issue bringing Macau into the international limelight. In 2005, as the Six Party Talks seemed to have reached agreement with

North Korea to end its nuclear weapons program, in a possible spoiler move from within the Us administration, the U.S. Treasury designated a Macau bank, the Banco Delta Asia (BDA), which handled many of North Korea's overseas accounts, as a money laundering organization. In 2007, it was official placed under U.S. sanctions. Its accounts were frozen and its access to the US-controlled international money system. Although the North Korean funds were eventually returned, the bank, which always denied the claims, was unable to get the sanctions lifted until 2020.

There is also some sign that Macao's growth as the new "Las Vegas" of Asia is putting some strains on its relationship with Hong Kong. Some within the former English colony are clearly concerned that Macao might soon become a serious rival for foreign tourist dollars. For its part, Macao has taken to refusing entry to Hong Kong residents it finds unacceptable. Those recently rejected include a number of relatively influential Hong Kong political activists.

In 2014, though, differences between the Chinese territories focused on quite a different matter. Two very prominent, well connected and wealthy Hong Kong businessman, billionaire Joseph Lau and Steven Lo were found guilty of bribery and money laundering and sentenced to five years in jail. Happily for the two, there is no extradiction treaty between Hong Kong and Macao and no doubt was areas on why the two fled to Macao to avoid punishment.

But while there may at times be tensions with their Hong Kong neighbor, the two former colonies have a lot in common. The most immediate is the impact of the regular presence of large numbers of visitors from the mainland. In Macao's case, as a community especially committed to tourism because of its gambling industry, that is not necessarily a bad thing. On the other

hand, the sheer numbers of visitors to Macao's relatively limited physical space have prompted serious consideration within the local community of setting limitations on the number of visitors who can be accommodated at any one time.

Economically, as 2017 opened, Macao's finances seem to be improving with the arrival of more Western tourists even as the number of mainland Chinese visitors appeared in decline. That Macao had decided to complement its effort to transform itself into the Las Vegas of Asia with a bit more of a family friendly tone was most obvious in the erection of a half sized Eiffel Tower by one of the local hotels.

But easily the most important development was the inauguration in late 2018 of the world's longest 34.2 mile sea bridge that will now link Macao, Hong Kong, and the mainland city of Zhuhai. Although passport controls will continue the new bridge will dramatically cut travel times and link both Macao and Hong Kong even more closely to the People's Republic than they are now.

As noted above, COVID-19 had little effect on Macau. Macau is a long way from the main centers of outbreak in China and adopted tight border controls. These included testing before entry. By April 2021, according to the WHO, cases totalled 49, with 48 making a full recovery. There were no deaths. Casinos closed for a brief period but reopened in August 2020, though with reduced customers. By April 2022, there had been 82 confirmed cases, all of which had recovered, and no deaths. Vaccination levels were high. 92.2% had at least one dose, 85.1% two doses, and 33.5% a booster. Tight restrictions on entry continued.The economic consequences were the most notable, with unemployment hitting the leisure and tourist industries. Construction projects also slowed. GDP per capita at ppp rates fell back.

**Constructing Macao's new MGM Grand . . .**   Courtesy of Steven A. Leibo

**. . . and as it looks today**   Courtesy of Wikimedia Commons

**Globalization meets Lhasa's Potala Palace**

**Area:** 1,200,000 sq. mi., most above 14,000 feet (3,107,985 sq. km.)

**Population:** 3.9 million (2019); officially Tibetan (95%, probably misleading because official Chinese sources only list Han Chinese with official permission to live in Tibet). Other ethnic groups are Han, Hue, Melba, Luoba, Naxi, and Nu.

**Status:** September 1, 1965, declared Tibet Autonomous Region (TAR)

Note: The term Tibet and Tibetans can have many meanings. On one hand, it usually refers to what the Chinese now call the Tibetan Autonomous Region (TAR), roughly the area the modern Dalai Lamas governed. It is that region on which this "looking closer" section of our text focuses. But the term can have broader meanings. Of the 4.6 million ethnic Tibetans reported in a 1990 census, only 46% lived in the TAR while 54% lived in Western Chinese provinces from Qinghai and Gansu to Sichuan and Yunnan. This latter area might best be thought of an ethnographic extension of the Tibetan community. Of course, one cannot forget the influential Tibetan community that followed the 14th Dalai Lama into exile in the years after 1959 and established itself in nations from Nepal to India.

### Introduction

Whether one arrives by bus, airplane, or perhaps the world's first pressurized railroad train that began operating in July 2006, it soon becomes obvious that Tibet is something truly astonishing. Situated at an average height of 4,000 meters, most of the country is over 14,000 feet high. Tibet is found on what is known as the Qinghai-Tibet plateau, to which many have long referred as the "roof the world." It is surrounded by four different mountain ranges: the Qilian Mountains, the Mt Kunlun-Bayan Har Mountains, the Mt Karokoram-Tanggula Mountains and, of course, the internationally famous Himalayas. The Tibet Autonomous Region itself is located on approximately half of this enormous region.

Sadly, for those interested in understanding the Tibetan situation, discussion of the issue is often marred by the emotionalism that both Tibet's supporters and the representatives of the People's Republic tend to carry into each discussion. The result is that all too often it is difficult to find an objective account of Tibetan-Chinese relations.

On the Tibetan side, charges from violations of human rights to genocide are often bandied about. The Chinese usually vehemently defend their control of Tibet and speak with pride of their liberation of the Tibetan people from the previously existing system of serfdom and peasant exploitation under which many had previously suffered. Putting the relationship in the context of larger global trends, it is often apparent that China's relationship with Tibet is similar to that found during the colonial era. That is, China frequently exhibits a recognizable "colonial" attitude of superiority toward the Tibetans. Tibetans for their part deeply resent that obviously unequal relationship.

More fundamentally, Beijing has usually viewed supporters of the exiled Dalai Lama as enemies seeking to dismember the Chinese homeland. When that support has come from official U.S. sources, such as the American Congress or even more dramatically from U.S. presidents, Beijing has felt particularly threatened. As a practical matter, premodern Tibet's cultural and ethnic identity long existed outside the direct control of China's many imperial governments. In fact, until recently Tibet's population did not include Han Chinese. Nevertheless, Tibet has long been under either direct or indirect Chinese influence. As so often is the case, zealots from both sides of the argument cite the historical record to justify their claims. It is to that early Tibetan history that we turn first.

### Tibet's 7th-Century Unification

Tibet has had a long and impressive national existence separate from that of China. This distinguishes it from other communities designated by Chinese authorities as separate "autonomous" or "administrative" areas, locations from

# China–Tibet

**His Holiness the Dalai Lama of Tibet**

Macao to Hong Kong and or even the physically independent Republic of China on Taiwan, all which are products of recent historical developments.

The emergence of a unified Tibet occurred during the late 7th century as regional tribes were brought together under the leadership of Songsten Gampo who is today considered the first ruler of Tibet. Ironically, given later developments, Tibet's leader chose to solidify his relationship with his powerful Chinese neighbors by a marriage with a princess from the Tang dynasty. What is particularly interesting about the marriage is that while Buddhism was to that point relatively unknown in Tibet, it is thought that under the influence of the newly arrived bride, Wen Cheng, Buddhism began to grow in influence. During those years Buddhist missionaries from India, China, and Nepal were apparently welcomed in Tibet, and it was scholarly Indian Buddhists who over time would have the most influence on the evolution of Tibetan Buddhism. Eventually Tibetan Buddhism would become far more important than the indigenous Bon tradition, and by the 8th century it was declared the official state religion. The transition did not come without considerable internal strife between the adherents of the two religious traditions.

During those early years of a unified Tibet, the nation was a major player in central Asian politics and drew cultural inspiration from both of its huge neighbors, China and India. Such basics as the use of butter, tea, cheese, and knowledge of astrology came from China. Policies on monasteries and their financial arrangements were adopted from India. Also because of Indian influence, the Tibetans began using a written alphabetic writing system quite different from the ideographs that might have been borrowed from China, as so many other Eastern Asians eventually did. Today's Tibetan alphabet

was adapted from an Indian script studied by one of Songtsen Gampo's ministers. Meanwhile ties with China remained very strong. More than 150 missions were undertaken between the two capitals, and many treaties were signed. But that relationship eventually ground to a halt by the early 10th century as both kingdoms, Tibetan and Chinese, collapsed.

## Relationship with the Mongols

In contrast to the complicated relationship between China and Tibet in the late 7th through 9th centuries, by the time the Mongols rose as a power the two often competing nations had not been in contact for generations. But the emergence of the Mongol empire was to change all that dramatically.

By the 13th century Mongol tribes under Genghis Khan had burst out of central Asia, intending to conquer all whom they encountered. Arriving in Tibet by 1207, they forced the Tibetans to submit without a fight. The latter agreed to accept Mongolian suzerainty over Tibet and to pay tribute to the great khan in order to avoid a bloody invasion. But the decision only put off the violence to a later era when, after Tibet had stopped sending the required tribute, the forces of the new Khan Ogedai advanced toward Lhasa looting monasteries and killing all who opposed his forces.

In the aftermath, not only did Tibet make a full submission to the Mongols, but the Mongolian leaders decided to adopt the Tibetan religious traditions. Eventually a fortuitous tradeoff emerged: Mongolia would help Tibet in secular matters while the Tibetans served as Mongolia's spiritual guide. Thus began that complicated relationship that eventually saw Tibet's leaders serve as Mongolia's religious teachers, carrying out religious obligations, doing divination and other rituals deemed necessary for the good health of the Mongolian leadership. Within Tibet itself the Mongols chose to grant the Buddhist religious leaders from the Sakya monastery secular authority, thus creating the tradition of theocratic rule that would become the norm for most of Tibet's history until modern times.

By the time Kublai Khan arrived on the scene, Tibet was administered by a Tibetan leader who had once served as tutor to the great khan and was able to gain recognition from the Mongol ruler of his superior status as a religious leader. The best example of the relationship is the term Dalai Lama itself. The title is an obvious reflection of the relationship combining as it does the Mongolian word for "ocean," *dalai*, with the Tibetan word *"lama"* for spiritual teacher.

By the 14th century Sakya rule over Tibet ended, while the Mongols, during the same period, lost their control over China. During the following years, an era that paralleled the famous Ming dynasty, the Chinese had no administrative influence over Tibet. Ignoring that reality, Ming emperors continued to confer titles upon the Tibetans as if they still did.

## The Emergence of Modern Tibet

It was not until the rise of the Geluk Sect (system of Virtue) that Tibet's modern history really began. That reforming tradition began with the career of the scholar, Tsongkapa, whose travels in the late 14th century convinced him of a profound moral decline. Eventually, he began to preach a revived Buddhism that emphasized strict monastic celibacy and academic study as the truth path to enlightenment. By 1409 Tsongkapa founded his own monastery: the famous Ganden Monastery just outside of Lhasa. It was the sect's choice of the Yellow Hat to distinguish themselves from the older "red hats" that was to give Tsongkapa's followers their best known name, the Yellow Hat Sect. Within only a few years two more monasteries, the Drepung and Sera, were constructed. These were religious settlements that housed over 15,000 monks on the eve of the 20th-century Chinese occupation. Even today, though they operate with significantly reduced numbers living in buildings that were only recently rebuilt, the monasteries continue to house hundreds of members.

Predictably, the rise of the Yellow Hat Sect aroused considerable tension with the older monastic Tibetan sects. During the following centuries, significant strife developed between the differing religious communities. By the early 17th century tensions had become so great that Karma Kagyu sect Tibetan king ordered the Geluk monasteries occupied. Moreover, the search for the newest reincarnation of the fourth Dalai Lama was forbidden. Eventually, with the help of the Mongols, who were still influential despite their withdrawal from China, the Yellow Hat Sect reasserted itself.

## Early Modern Tibet and the Outside World

In 1644 China's new leaders, the Manchus, established themselves in power. Unlike their Ming predecessors, the Manchu Qing dynasty was to be quite involved in Tibetan developments. It was in this period that the first Chinese imperial magistrate was stationed in Tibet while Qing forces regularly intervened within Tibet during periods of internal strife. They also dispatched an army to

**Lhasa pilgrim**

Courtesy of Steven A. Leibo

defend Tibet when Hindu Gurkhas threatened the nation from their base in Nepal. The Manchus were not the only regional power interested in Tibet.

From the perspective of the India-based British, Tibet was for centuries seen as a potentially significant route to Western China and an important buffer between themselves and growing Russian strength in Central Asia. During the late 18th century British diplomats and missionaries were able to enter Tibet relatively easily, a situation that the Manchus stopped by the end of the century. The Qing did so in part because, as so often before and after, China's leaders saw Tibet as deeply within their sphere of influence. They were understandably concerned about the presence of the British, who were by then becoming more and more powerful in India.

But Qing efforts to exclude them hardly diminished British interest. From the British perspective, a foothold in Tibet would make the growth of Russian influence in Central Asia easier to contain. Thus, by the early 20th century, British forces under Colonel Francis Younghusband invaded Tibet and easily destroyed the weak Tibetan forces sent against the invaders. By the summer of 1904, Lhasa was occupied by the foreign troops while the 13th Dalai Lama fled to Mongolia. While insisting that Tibet was part of China, the Qing government was powerless to oppose the British advance toward Lhasa. Once there Younghusband forced a treaty upon the Tibetans that in effect made Tibet a protectorate of the British Empire. This was something the colonel's superiors in London had hardly authorized. Once word of the settlement

arrived in England, the decision was made to repudiate significant parts of the agreement. Britain even officially agreed that Tibet was part of China, regardless of what the Tibetans themselves might think.

In the aftermath of the reasonably successful resolution of the crisis created by the Younghusband expedition, Beijing, in a burst of renewed confidence, sent troops to forcibly reenter Tibet. Following their arrival, the Qing forces worked to administer Tibet directly in a fashion that Chinese governments had not done for centuries. This time it was China, not Britain that was imposing its will on Tibet. Ironically, given earlier events, the Dalai Lama then fled to British India for support.

That renewed Chinese claim to Tibet in the early 20th century could not be maintained. In the aftermath of the Chinese Revolution of 1912, the Tibetans expelled the Chinese forces. The new Chinese Republic, the successor to the Manchus, was not in a position to challenge Tibet's assertion of independence, although it continued to maintain that Tibet was part of China. For the next several decades, two different Dalai Lamas successively governed Tibet as an independent, if not internationally recognized, sovereign country.

## Tibet's Era of Independence 1912 to 1951

Unfortunately for Tibet's long-term future, during the several decades of Tibet's de facto independence the government failed to establish for itself either an internationally recognized legitimacy or the military power necessary to resist China if Beijing ever again chose to reassert its authority. Most importantly, the government was unable to move forward with a military modernization program that was opposed by Tibetan conservatives. Even more enervating was an explosion of internal violence that broke out between forces based at the famous Sera monastery and those in Lhasa. Nevertheless, Tibet did manage to defend itself successfully from occasional Chinese encroachments through the early 1930s.

Overall, those years represented an era when Tibet remained especially isolated from the outside world. But it has ironically become particularly well known today because of the writings of visitors like Heinrich Harrer and famous films from *Seven Years in Tibet*—made from Harrer's memoirs—to the movie *Kundun*. Both are set during this period of Tibetan independence.

After World War II ended, the situation in central Asia became considerably more complicated. The Chinese Communists were moving closer and closer to a defeat of their longtime enemies, the nationalists, while below Tibet's southern border

the long-influential British were preparing to leave India. With that decision, a significant part of their long-term interest in Tibet's fate began to fade.

Accordingly, Tibet's leadership began making efforts to develop relations with the outside world including a successful invitation to the internationally famous broadcaster and explorer, Lowell Thomas, to visit and report on Tibet. As a practical matter, given the sorry state of Tibetan military preparations, hoping the support of the larger international community might protect them from China was probably their only option. Moreover, Lhasa's leaders, in what would eventually seem a vain effort to maintain their authority in the waning days of the Chinese Civil War, expelled all those Chinese associated with the Nationalist government of Chiang Kai-shek. Ironically, the gesture provoked one of the few moments of agreement between the increasingly ascendant Chinese Communists and the nationalists. Both Chinese political parties, true to their mutual assumption that Tibet was part of China, denounced the decision.

### The Chinese Return to Tibet: The Early Years

One of the primary goals of contemporary Chinese civilization has been to piece back together various regions perceived to be "Chinese" that were lost during the years of China's greatest weakness in the era from the Opium Wars through the Second World War. During the late 20th century, that goal meant the successful efforts to reabsorb Hong Kong and Macao not forgetting, of course, the long-term desire to bring Taiwan back into the fold.

The Chinese have seen Tibet no differently. For most Chinese it remains a fundamental part of China. That perception helps explain why China, in October 1950, only a year after the People's Republic had come into power and while the Korean War was getting more and more bloody, the forces of the PRC entered Tibet. The Chinese military was easily able to overcome the poorly equipped Tibetan forces and once again, as so often in the past, to reoccupy Tibet, destroying the de facto independence it had enjoyed for the decades since the Chinese Revolution of 1912.

As for the Dalai Lama, he temporarily left Lhasa with an apparent intention of going into exile. Eventually, though, the young leader chose to return to his capital while his representatives soon found themselves in Beijing forced to agree to Chinese military and administrative authority over Tibet. Known as the Seventeen Point Agreement, the document called for the establishment of Chinese civil and military facilities at Lhasa while promising Tibetan domestic political autonomy and recognition of its religious heritage. Most important to later developments was the first point, which stated that the Tibetans were officially recognizing Chinese sovereignty over their land. This was something they had never done before. For its part, China promised to recognize Tibet's traditional political and economic system as headed by the Dalai Lama.

As for the outside world, while nations from Britain to the United States understood that Tibet had quite obviously been independent during the decades before China's return, neither Western power had ever recognized Tibet's official independence nor would they now come to its aid. Behind the scenes, though, the United States would eventually become increasingly involved because of the growing tensions of the Cold War.

Still, in the early years of China's reoccupation, Beijing's control over Tibet was relatively light. Reportedly this was the case because Mao Zedong understood that Tibet's situation was different from other regions in China and that caution would have to be exercised. For example, during those early years, no Tibetan aristocratic or monastic property was confiscated, and the local landlords, long dominant over Tibet's deeply feudal and theocratic system, maintained their judicial authority. The long-term goal of transforming Tibet and integrating it into the People's Republic did not, of course, change. However, Mao was willing to approach the challenge with a relatively moderate initial hand.

That early caution did not last long. Nevertheless, during the early years there was general agreement among both Tibet's secular and religious leaders that they could successfully co-exist with the new leaders of the People's Republic. As for the Dalai Lama, he was apparently confident enough with developments that he had a new and quite impressive mansion built for himself within the famed summer palace retreat of Lhasa's leaders. This was an impressive building that included the first Western style toilet in the entire country.

## Tibet and the International Cold War

The roots of the later estrangement between Tibet and the Chinese were embedded in both the Cold War then engulfing the world and the more immediate circumstances of the ethnically Tibetan people who lived in those regions that lay beyond the area the Dalai Lama's government had previously controlled. Unlike within "political Tibet," Beijing had no reluctance whatsoever to intervene in those places. Thus, the revolutionary social transformation of the mid-1950s that was then raging in much of China affected as well on Tibetans in Sichuan Province. It eventually provoked a rebellion that quickly spilled over into Tibet proper.

By 1957 the United States was no longer dealing with the challenge of the Korean War, which had until 1953 seen America and China fighting a vicious conventional war on the Korean peninsula. It began to intervene more enthusiastically on behalf of those Tibetans willing to confront Beijing's power. Working with the Dalai Lama's brother, half a dozen Tibetans were trained on the American island of Saipan by members of the American Central Intelligence Agency. Other training facilities were established in the mountainous areas of Colorado. Meanwhile several dozen supply drops were made, and much more elaborate training facilities were set up in Nepal.

From the Chinese perspective, the fact that the United States, its longtime Cold War foe, had become involved was particularly alarming. It most certainly contributed to the much more violent crackdown Beijing imposed on Tibet in 1959, a crackdown that saw the 14th Dalai Lama flee to India. Eventually, within India, a relatively large Tibetan exile community developed. For a time their host, the new Indian democracy, itself having border tensions with China, would lend its support to the Tibetans. After the Sino-Indian clash of 1962, the Indian government began working closely with the Americans and Tibetans in these training efforts.

But American covert support for the Tibetan independence effort only lasted through the late 1960s. As for the Dalai Lama, he himself received generous American government funding at least through the early 1970s. Not surprisingly, U.S. support for the Tibetan independence movement dwindled as U.S.-China relations improved. Meanwhile, as it slowly improved its own relationship with Beijing, New Delhi also withdrew formal military support even as it continued to host the large

---

## "Tibetan Buddhism"

### By Jeannine Chandler

Tibetan Buddhism (also called Vajrayana or Tantric Buddhism) claims roughly 20 million practitioners around the world. Although most are found in the Himalayan region (Tibet, Nepal, Bhutan, Sikkim, Ladakh), Mongolia, Manchuria, China, and Russia, in the last half century converts have appeared in the West as well. In contrast to Mahayana or Theravada Buddhism, Tibetan Buddhism combines esoteric practices with the rigorous study of texts in order to hasten one's journey toward enlightenment. Tibetan Buddhists use meditation, deity visualizations, ritual prostrations, and the chanting of mantras to achieve this end. However, the defining characteristic of Tibetan Buddhism is its emphasis on guru (lama) devotion, as knowledge of and initiation into these practices is reliant upon one's relationship with a guru and his lineage.

In the 8th century, Indian master Padmasambhava brought the Tantric Buddhist teaching to Tibet and initiated Buddhism's integration with Tibet's indigenous religious tradition of Bön. Following a period of Buddhism's persecution and subsequent revival in Tibet, in the 11th century the adept Atisha introduced reforms to Buddhism in Tibet, intent on correcting what was perceived by many to be an overemphasis on tantric practices to the detriment of moral discipline. He also is known for reviving the monastic tradition in Tibet (for which it is now famous) as well as stimulating the creation of the New Translation schools in Tibet: Sakya, Kagyu, and Geluk. With the Old Translation School (Nyingma), these traditions remain today the four schools of Tibetan Buddhism.

The development of Tibetan Buddhism was influenced for centuries by secular political struggles as well as competition between (and within) religious schools, often with Mongol involvement. After centuries of sectarian conflict, the Geluk tradition eventually became the dominant school, headed by the Dalai Lama, a reincarnation of the bodhisattva of compassion, who came to be revered as the spiritual and temporal leader of the Tibetans.

Within the past 20 years, the 14th Dalai Lama has become the international embodiment of Tibet and the face of Tibetan Buddhism (and often of Buddhism in general). A winner of the Nobel Peace Prize (1989) and the United States' Congressional Gold Medal (October 2007), the Dalai Lama has campaigned for Tibetan independence, human rights, religious tolerance, and world peace. With his image behind the religion, Tibetan Buddhism has become globalized, with online sanghas and booming sales of Buddhist merchandise.

**Monks debating at the Sera Monastery in Tibet**

Courtesy of Steven A. Leibo

In the years after Deng Xiaoping came to power, much was done to rebuild Tibet's monasteries and reestablish its religious and cultural traditions. Families could again dedicate their children's lives to serve in the monasteries, and the Tibetan language was taught in primary schools though education in Mandarin became increasingly common and necessary for most careers.

For a time, under the relatively liberal communist leaders who dominated in the 1980s, efforts were made to find a compromise between Beijing's identification of Tibet as a part of China and the supporters of the Dalai Lama. Nevertheless, little was accomplished.

The horrors of the Cultural Revolution have passed, but the fate of Tibet still remains deeply in question. Though various Chinese governments have tried from time to time to find common ground with the Dalai Lama and his supporters, Beijing is absolutely unwilling even to consider Tibet's demands that have ranged from independence to complete autonomy. Thus while Tibetan cultural and religious life has been allowed to reemerge, any activities that have appeared to support the Dalai Lama and the independence movement have been ruthlessly suppressed.

The commitment to maintaining Tibet within the Chinese orbit was particularly evident in 1989 when Beijing violently suppressed an uprising. More recently, in March 2008, another series of demonstrations led to violence not only in Lhasa, but in the neighboring province of Gansu. This is an area of Tibetan presence, as explained above, that is beyond the frontiers of Tibet proper. The more recent tensions, which may have claimed more than 100 lives, were relatively predictable given Beijing's ongoing tight control over Tibet. Of course, many of Tibet's worldwide supporters used Beijing's expanding international profile during the run-up to the Olympics to highlight the plight of Tibet. This most certainly added fuel to the fire of discontent. That discontent continues today. Over the last years, Beijing has sent significant numbers of soldiers not only to Tibet, but into the larger ethnographically Tibetan regions. This has created a sort of unofficial martial law environment while smaller incidents from public demonstrations to bombings have continued.

As for the Chinese reaction, Beijing has behaved defensively over the last few years. It issued a series of reports outlining how much their control has improved the lives of the Tibetans. According to the documents, the 60 years since China assumed control have distinctively improved Tibetan infant mortality rates,

Tibetan community within its borders. If Britain's colonization of India earlier in the century had helped Tibet in its efforts to stave off China's demands, the fact that New Delhi chose not to assume Britain's role in Central Asia in the years after independence probably sealed Tibet's fate. Eventually, India's leaders would officially announce that also New Delhi considered Tibet officially part of China.

### Tibet under Chinese Rule: The Situation Becomes Complicated

If the early years of China's occupation of Tibet had been relatively successful, the situation changed dramatically in the late 1950s. Responding to what it saw as more foreign encroachment, the Chinese government dropped is previous reticence as it put down the rebellion. Even more tragically for Tibet's fate, China would soon enter the era of the Cultural Revolution, which by the mid-1960s saw enormous numbers of young Chinese attacking and destroying the symbols of China's cultural heritage. While it took place all over China, that assault was particularly destructive within Tibet. In those years, huge numbers of its cultural monuments were destroyed. Its monks were driven from the monasteries, and most of these facilities were devastated. Of course, feeding the assault was the fact that many of the monasteries had taken part in the earlier 1959 revolt. Moreover, their very existence as largely feudal theocratic organizations fundamentally clashed with the emerging Chinese communist sensibilities.

By late 1966, as the Cultural Revolution grew to a crescendo of chaotic political activism and violence across the rest of China, large numbers of Red Guards, despite the orders of leaders like Zhou Enlai, began to arrive in Tibet. They were ready to take on what was for them the quintessential feudal society they had long hated. Significantly, it was not just Han Chinese youth who became involved. Large numbers of Tibetans themselves, caught up in the enthusiasm of the moment, took part in the assault. People were even attacked in the streets for wearing traditional Tibetan clothing.

All across the country monasteries were attacked and destroyed while pitched battles took place between Tibetan monks and the assaulting Chinese and their Tibetan allies. All was done in the name of reforming the Tibetan consciousness from the traditional mindset to one more closely adhering to the new socialist "man" the leaders of the Chinese revolution had long striven to create. They believed this would require the complete suppression of Tibet's religious heritage in the name of building the new socialist society. In the aftermath of the wholesale assault on Tibetan identity, the once proud Tibetan society and religious establishment suffered an assault from which they would barely be able to survive.

# China–Tibet

lengthened life spans, and raised their incomes significantly. Unfortunately, from the Chinese perspective, while their impact on Tibet over the years probably has brought improvements, such developments have historically not lessened the sorts of tensions aroused by "foreign" occupations, as the Tibetans most certainly see the Chinese. Still the Chinese keep the focus on the positive improvements they believe they have brought to the Tibetans. They have even gone so far as to set March 28, the anniversary of the 1959 uprising, as a day officially to commemorate the liberation of Tibet's serfs.

Meanwhile, to facilitate the region's fuller incorporation into the People's Republic, Beijing has moved vigorously to extend and enhance its land-based communication routes to Tibet. In 2006 the world's only atmospherically sealed train began its first run from Beijing to Lhasa traveling the enormous distance and scaling the extraordinary peaks, at one point at a height of 16,640 feet. The train was expected to play a significant role in dramatically transforming Tibet, which was once one of the most isolated countries in the world. Meanwhile, the Chinese authorities have announced plans for an expansion of Tibet's airport facilities to link it more effectively with the rest of China.

But things have obviously not always gone smoothly for Beijing. China's efforts to weaken the influence of the Dalai Lama suffered an enormous setback in 1999 when the 17th Karmapa, the third-most important leader in Tibetan Buddhism, fled Tibet complaining that the Chinese authorities had denied him the ability continue his studies. The Karmapa Lama was hardly the only Tibetan to flee. Since 1990, thousands of Tibetans have arrived in Nepal as refugees. Moreover, in recent years the largely passive resistance of the Tibetans has moved to a new level with the emergence of terrorism being carried out in the name of Tibetan independence. Predictably, Beijing has struck back harshly, and in early 2003, it executed a former monk, the first Tibetan executed for such activities in a very long time. How many others might have died as a result of the more recent disturbances of 2008 may never be known. What we do know is that 19 people, mostly Han Chinese, died in Lhasa, but the rioting went far beyond the capital.

Indeed, the reasons for such concerns became even more obvious by the fall of 2010 when a series of very public protests broke out in Qinghai Province, where significant numbers of Tibetans reside. The issue was the government's efforts to deemphasize the teaching of Tibetan while carrying out a renewed effort to promote Mandarin Chinese. The protests were

**Chinese reestablish order in Lhasa, 2008**

apparently significantly more peaceful than those of 2008 and occurred mostly among the region's Tibetan student population. Sadly those tensions have not abated. They have continued not only in Tibet proper, but in the Tibetan areas outside of Tibet as well.

In March 2011 a young Buddhist monk burned himself to death to protest Chinese rule. This set off yet another round of protests, repression and several deaths in Sichuan Province. Elsewhere in 2012 tensions again rose steeply over the decision by local authorities in Gansu Province to switch from Tibetan to Chinese as the primary language of instruction in the region's schools. Especially dramatic have been the number of people setting themselves on fire, indeed over two dozen, to protest Chinese policies. More recently Chinese authorities, concerned about the spread of self-immolations, put two men on trial for encouraging such dramatic protests. Still the self-immolations continue, as recently as late 2014, when Facebook entered the controversy because of its unwillingness to retain posted photos of the deaths.

Even more recently thousands of Tibetan's defied the Chinese authorities by traveling to Bodh Gaya, the site in Northern India where the Buddha is said to

have first reached enlightenment. Mainland authorities would have been particularly unhappy with those who crossed into India for the event because the Dalai Lama himself presided over the ceremonies, and Tibet's new secular leader took part as well.

Not surprisingly China's efforts to address the tensions have often dramatically backfired. Demands that Tibetans formally express "patriotism" and "gratitude" " toward China have resulted in greater unrest in rural areas, a stronger presence of the security forces in monasteries, confiscation of materials form laptops to cell phones, and in general, a growing atmosphere outside Tibetan observers have linked to the excesses of the Cultural Revolution. Tibetans also claim that their language is slowly dying due to the overwhelming pressure to use Mandarin.

Indeed, according to locals, the Chinese government has been making it increasingly difficult for Tibetan language schools to operate.

Beijing for its part argues that it has merely imposed a new focus on Chinese in an effort to make it easier for locals to take part in the larger Chinese society within which they live. Chinese officials vehemently insist that they are trying to preserve the local language through the encouragement of bilingual education. The result of course is the same. It is becoming increasingly difficult to preserve the traditional cultures of China's ethnic minorities.

As a practical matter, Tibet's internationally respected but exiled leader would probably be better off cultivating more friends in Beijing than in Washington, DC. Only in Beijing could a path be found that would offer a compromise that would see Tibetan culture thrive in the 21st century. But that path of reconciliation appears long closed. Indeed at times the situation seems to just deteriorate. The Dalai Lama himself has spoken of teams of assassins he believes have been trained by Beijing to poison him. His recent reference to the internationally famous and controversial Diaoyu Islands by their Japanese name, the Senkaku Islands, saw him denounced with a particular level of vehemence by Chinese authorities.

Sadly, while the Dalai Lama has been extraordinarily successful in building support in the Western world, Beijing appears to have lost interest in seeking a compromise. It is perhaps merely waiting for his death in exile to help resolve the problem. That approach was particularly obvious in 2012 when the Chinese-appointed Panchen Lama, the second most revered figure in Tibet, made his first appearance outside of China proper at a conference in Hong Kong. In short, Chinese authorities appear quite ready to promote the Panchen Lama as an alternative leader of the Tibetan people. From Beijing's perspective it would probably solve a lot of problems.

Chinese economic policy in recent years has encouraged large numbers of Chinese to move to Tibet. While it is true that only a small percentage have official permission to live there, the number of "illegal" migrants has grown enormously. This has swamped the region's original inhabitants while developing those Tibetan community leaders, both secular and religious, who have shown themselves more cooperative and supportive of Beijing.

Most significantly, the politics of Sino-Tibetan relations has of late begun to focus not only on the 14th Dalai Lama, but on the question of who will succeed him after he leaves the scene. During the summer of 2007 Chinese authorities issued a new regulation outlawing anyone from recognizing a child as the official reincarnation of the Dalai Lama. This is obviously an effort designed to allow the PRC—at least within its borders—the power to control the naming of the next Tibetan leader.

Meanwhile, taking a page from his more western allies and despite the obvious contradictions with Tibetan tradition, the Dalai Lama has began to talk of having the next Tibetan leader chosen by more democratic means. Following through on that suggestion, he announced in the spring of 2011 that he planned to step down as the political leader of Tibet while continuing to serve as the community's spiritual leader. According to Tibet's spiritual leader, the decision was based on his desire to nurture the growth of the democratic tradition among Tibetans.

Within months, the next steps were implemented. By late April 2011 Lobsang Sangay, an American-educated doctorate in law from Harvard University, was elected to head the Indian-based Tibetan government in exile. Elected by those Tibetans living outside of China, the new political leader announced his willingness to open discussions with the Chinese at their convenience. Predictably, the Beijing government, which has never recognized the Tibetan government in exile, showed absolutely no interest in taking up the offer for talks. But, of course, his election has more to do with Tibetan politics in exile than anything directly linked to Tibet itself. Lobsang Sangay has himself never even been to Tibet. Nor has any foreign government ever officially recognized his government which operates largely from donations.

Nevertheless the Tibetan exile community has been satisfied enough with Lobsang Sangay's efforts on their behalf to reelect him in 2016.

Meanwhile the Dalai Lama, who will be 87 in 2022, is himself openly talking of the challenges of finding his successor. That individual, who in theory would eventually become the 15th Dalai Lama, will no doubt remain the official spokesperson for the Tibetans, at least in regards to Beijing.

Of course, as we have seen, Beijing is already promoting the role of the current and younger Panchen Lama. How all this might turn out is anyone's guess, but the odds are that Beijing, with its territorial control, is likely to win this battle.

Indeed, there is good reason to think that the man born as Tenzin Gyatso, today of course internationally famous as the Dalai Lama, may be the last official recognized Dalai Lama ever.

Moreover it seems likely that if a compromise cannot be found regarding the selection of the next Dalai Lama, the Panchen Lama, himself named after a very controversial selection in 1995, might well become the next spiritual leader of Tibet.

Meanwhile the fires of nationalism can burn both ways. It is true that Tibetan nationalists can cause Beijing significant problems. However, ethnic Han nationalist sentiment that Tibet is indeed part of China and a sense that the Tibetans have not been sufficiently grateful for the People's Republic's development efforts often pushes the PRC leadership's popularity higher when they energetically reject Tibetan calls for greater autonomy or, in some cases, independence which the Chinese leadership considers to be the real goal anyway despite the Dalai Lama's claims to the contrary.

As a practical matter, the real threat to Tibet's cultural traditions appear to be that the new generation of Tibetans is simply becoming more socialized as members of the larger Chinese cultural orbit than

**Tibetan woman and child**                    **Courtesy of Steven A. Leibo**

# China–Tibet

their parents. Retaining Tibet's cultural distinctiveness under the circumstances in understandably especially difficult as the people of Tibet move more deeply into the 21st century.

### Tibet's Central Role in the Climate Crisis

It is well known that China's decision to transform itself into the manufacturing base for much of the world has tremendously threatened its own environment and made China the largest annual producer of greenhouse gases. But what is less well known is how central Tibet is to the world's environmental challenges. In short what happens in Tibet is now critical to what happens in the rest of China, most of Asia, and indeed the world. That is a truly ironic development given that for much of Tibet's historical existence it was one of the most isolated places on the planet.

The root of that irony, though, is not surprisingly also linked to Tibet's mountainous geography. Indeed, Tibet is found at the highest elevation level of any major civilization on the planet. So high and expansive is the Tibetan plateau that, not counting the polar ice caps, it holds the largest amount of ice of any region in the world. The annual glacial run off from the Tibetan plateau feeds most of the major regional rivers, the Indus, the Ganges, the Mekong, and the Yellow River, not only in China but South and South East Asia as well. Thus rising temperatures on the plateau can easily create torrential flooding downstream before one would eventually see the runoff end completely leaving the lower lying areas in drought. Neither proposition is very attractive to the billions of Asians who live downstream from the Plateau.

Perhaps even more ominously is that alongside the famed glaciers of Tibet are enormous regions of frozen permafrost whose increasing melting not only negatively impacts the fertility of the land, but

are releasing even more greenhouse gases in the form of methane. This gas is not as long lasting in the atmosphere as $CO_2$, but it is significantly more potent in retaining global heat.

Interestingly in that context is the Chinese government's current experiment with trying to create a huge artificial forest on the plateau by burying piping heated by solar panels to make it more possible for trees to grow. How that will impact the fragile ecology of Tibet has been a matter of considerable controversy.

But far above the lower altitude civilizations of South, Southeast, and East Asia, which rely so heavily on the predictable and seasonable melting of the plateau's glaciers is the enormous lands of Tibet itself. It has been experiencing the growing desertification of an already fragile landscape apparently caused by the slowly rising temperatures and a changing pattern of rainfall locally.

### The Future

Even as Tibet is changing dramatically with each coming year, the underlying tensions between the Chinese authorities and many of the region's Tibetan residents will not subside anytime soon. Beijing continues to believe that its ongoing effort to improve the Tibetan region's economic prospects will eventually gain them more support among the indigenous Tibetans.

Since 2016, as part of Chinese President Xi Jinping's policy of the "Sinicization" of religion in China, thousands of Chinese officials were sent into temples and monasteries to enforce such a development. They even hoped to entice some to be more cooperative with promises of improved social benefits while moving against those the Chinese authorities see as "trouble makers." The effort, which purportedly included 21,000 officials, was interestingly referred to as the "monastic management system."

The bottom line of course is that Tibet's status as an official part of the PRC and

Beijing's long-term antipathy to the Dalai Lama remains ever so often on display most notably in the recent cancellation of a series of concerts by the well-known rock singer Bon Jovi who was discovered to have used the former Tibetan leader's image in the background of an earlier concert in Taiwan.

As a practical matter, China's growing influence in the world makes it almost certain that Tibet will remain deeply integrated within the People's Republic of China. Indeed, the real issue is whether the Tibetans themselves will continue to be the primary ethnic community within Tibet and thus avoid being totally swamped by Chinese immigrants.

Tibet's situation also needs to be understood within the context of a general effort, especially since the rise of Xi Jinping, to put a lid on all sorts of liberalization efforts that so many of his predecessors had at least tolerated. In Tibet, as well as the moves to control the monasteries, this has also led to an insistence on the use of standard Chinese (Mandarin) rather than the Tibetan language and to increased surveillance of cellphone and internet usage. After the outbreak of COVID in 2019, the increased COVID-related controls were also applied as a means of control in Tibet, although the Tibetan Autonomous Region had only one, non-fatal, case up to April 2021. Indeed, Beijing seems increasingly intolerant of any challenges to its authority regardless of whether such challenges come from Hong Kong, Tibet, the Muslim Far East, or simply Beijing's civil society reformers.

More immediately, Tibet itself has become less of an international concern as China's treatment of its far western Muslim minorities has become better known. Not forgetting that increasingly complicated domestic political concerns from the United States to the United Kingdom have made pushing the international human rights agenda more complicated in recent years as well.

# Taiwan

**Taipei 101, among the world's highest buildings**

Courtesy of Steven A. Leibo

communities practice various forms of Christianity.

**Main Exports:** (to the U.S., Japan, Hong Kong, and China) Textiles, clothing, plastics, metals, electronic equipment, and processed foods

**Main Imports:** (from U.S., Japan, Kuwait) Industrial equipment, automobiles, oil, minerals, and precision instruments

**Currency:** New Taiwan dollar

**Former Colonial Status:** Taiwan was a Japanese colony from 1895 to 1945

**National Day:** October 10, anniversary of the Chinese Revolution of 1911

**Chief of State:** Tsai Ing-wen, since May 2016

**Premier:** Su Seng-chang (since January 14, 2019))

**National Flag:** A red field with a blue rectangle in the upper left containing a 12-pointed white star

**Per Capita GDP Income:** $59,398 (2021 IMF est.) (purchasing power parity)

Note: Unlike the Hanyu Pinyin Romanized transliteration of the mainland, Taiwan has long used the older Wade–Giles and postal system spellings. For consistency this chapter will follow the style used on the island except for well-known mainland terms. Former President Ma indicated that he wanted to have the island adopt the Hanyu pinyin system used on the mainland but nothing has been done to make the change.

## History

Although the bulk of the population of Taiwan is and has been for centuries ethnic Han Chinese initially from the continent, the island's evolution through time has been significantly different from that experienced on the mainland. Archeological evidence suggests that people have lived in Taiwan for at least 15,000 years, and, in fact, it was not until the 17th century that the arrival of large numbers of ethnically Han people from the mainland began significantly to impact the island's demographic balance.

Before that the island's predominant population, like other relatively nearby Pacific communities, consisted of a wide variety of Austronesian peoples whose descendants today constitute about 2% of the population. But even after the island became predominantly Chinese in ethnicity, it long remained outside the direct control of China's many imperial and more recently republican governments. This is a historical evolution quite different from the mainland. That very different historical experience constitutes one more element in the perspectives that have separated Taiwanese from their mainland cousins.

**Area:** 1,389 sq. mi. (35,980 sq. km.)

**Population:** 23,854,196 (2021 est.)

**Capital City:** Taipei City, pop. 2,646,204 (2019 est.)

**Climate:** Subtropical and humid in the lowlands, with an 11-month growing season; in the higher elevations of the central mountains the temperatures are cooler.

**Neighboring Countries:** The Republic of China has been on the island of Taiwan, located 100 miles from the southeast China mainland, since 1949. It is about 300 miles north of the Philippine island of Luzon.

**Official Language:** Chinese ("Mandarin" also known as Guoyu or Putonghua)

**Other languages:** Taiwanese (Min), Chinese Hakka dialects. Indigenous tribal communities speak a number of Austronesian languages.

**Ethnic Background:** Chinese, also known as Han. The highlands are occupied by relatively small groups of Austronesian ancestry who resemble other indigenous people found in parts of Southeast Asia. They make up around 2% of the population.

**Principal Religions:** Confucianism, Taoism, and Buddhism. These three, which migrated with the earliest Chinese from the mainland, are generally intermixed. The indigenous

# Taiwan

### Taiwan's Premodern Historical Experience

Taiwan's formal encounter with Western colonialism began at the end of the 16th century when a group of Portuguese was shipwrecked on the shores of what they would come to call "Ilha Formasa," Portuguese for "Beautiful Island." But it was the Dutch who would be the first Westerners to establish a lasting presence on the island, an effort that began in 1624 and that eventually saw them drive their primary European competitors, the Spanish, from Taiwan by the early 1640s.

During the years of Dutch domination a significant transformation of the island's demography began as they encouraged mainland Chinese to resettle on the island as sugarcane and rice production workers. The newly arriving Han Chinese added to the number of ethnic Chinese already on Taiwan. Those newcomers were soon joined by other mainlanders who arrived after fleeing from the chaos associated with the collapse of the Ming dynasty and

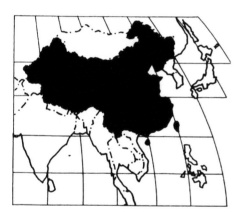

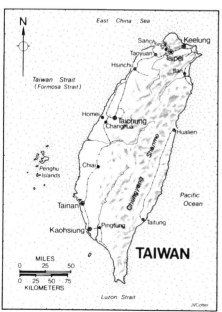

the subsequent arrival to power in 1644 of the Manchu Qing dynasty.

If the Dutch encouragement of Han migration to the island had a significant impact on the ethnic balance of Taiwan, it was the arrival of the anti-Manchu, Cheng Cheng-gong, better known as Koxinga, who even more profoundly moved the island into a Chinese political and cultural environment. A Ming family loyalist, Koxinga's forces were among those who resisted the Manchu conquest of the mainland by establishing themselves on Taiwan and creating the first formal Chinese administration the island had ever experienced. Koxinga's forces drove the Dutch from the island and were themselves able to resist the Qing forces for a generation. Eventually, though, by 1683 the effort failed and Taiwan was absorbed into the expanding Qing dynasty.

Over the subsequent decades Taiwan was considered part of Fujian Province. Meanwhile the population continued to grow significantly. By the mid-19th century it was estimated to have reached 2.5 million people while once again Western interest in the island was aroused. As a result of the 1858 British Treaty of Tianjin, two of the island's ports were designated treaty ports, adding to those that had already been established on the mainland from Hong Kong to Shanghai. But it would not be the imperialist Western powers that would ultimately make the biggest impact on Taiwan during the era. Rather it would be imperial Japan, which by mid-century was already beginning the steps that would see it emerge as a major colonial power by late century.

### Taiwan and the Emerging Japanese Empire

Almost as soon as Japan's own modernization effort began in the aftermath of the Meiji Restoration, Tokyo started showing interest in the island. That was most dramatically demonstrated in 1874 when Japanese soldiers arrived in Taiwan claiming that the island's indigenous inhabitants had attacked fisherman from the nearby Ryukyu island chain, which Japan also claimed. From Beijing's perspective, the temporary Japanese expedition was of real concern. A Chinese force was then dispatched to the island to help settle the conflict. Subsequently Beijing upgraded the island's status to that of an independent province. But its growing concern about the island's status did not stop the Qing Empire from eventually losing control of the island completely.

In 1895 as a consequence of the Sino-Japanese War of the previous year, Taiwan was absorbed by the emerging Japanese empire. The initial occupation was quite

**Former President Ma Ying-jeou**

traumatic. Some locals vigorously resisted the Japanese even as they vented their anger against local Qing officials, who, it was felt, had abandoned them. To some extent that was true. Officially Beijing chose to accept the loss of Taiwan though some of its local forces attempted to carry out their own resistance under the banner of a newly proclaimed "Taiwan Republic." That effort failed after only a few months. But if both the official and unofficial Qing defense of island was short lived, locals, both Chinese and the indigenous Austronesian community, continued their resistance for years. The violence was at times so intense that at one point over 6,000 Taiwanese were massacred by the Japanese. Despite that opposition, the Japanese managed to repress the resistance and establish themselves on the island. The occupation would last until the middle of the next century.

Like Korea, whose absorption into the growing Japanese empire took place during the same era, the people of Taiwan were pressured over time to become assimilated into Japanese culture. Initially there had been some ambivalence among the Japanese about making such an effort, literally to turn the native Taiwanese into second-class "Japanized" citizens of the new Japanese empire. But by the middle of the 20th century the effort was well underway.

Japanese was designated the language of instruction, and the new generation became increasingly literate in the language of their conquerors. Many locals even studied in Japan. Economically, the Japanese worked to enhance the island's infrastructure and to use it as an area for agricultural production, particularly rice and sugar for the Japanese home market.

Nevertheless, given how traumatic the next decades were to be on the changed dramatically during their years of separation.

Initially, though, while there was some ambivalence, certainly most Taiwanese had accepted Japanese control, and many served in their war effort. The arriving nationalists were greeted enthusiastically. Beneath the surface, though, the seeds of future tension already existed. During the war itself, many Taiwanese on the mainland had experienced discrimination by the nationalists, who frequently saw them as potential agents of Japan. While the island's citizens had already come a long way in developing a new identity that was neither Chinese nor Japanese, it was one that would eventually give the name "Taiwanese" new meaning.

If the nationalists' initial welcome had been enthusiastic, some of their earlier decisions were less appreciated. The island was placed almost exclusively under the direction of mainlanders cutting off the upper administrators from a more sophisticated knowledge of the sentiments of the locals. Particularly important among those perspectives lost would be the experience the Taiwanese had previously gained in working with and pushing for greater rights under Japanese colonial control.

But it was not merely prejudice that kept the mainlanders from understanding the locals. After half a century of Japanese control, significant numbers could not even communicate with the new arrivals. Japanese had become commonly spoken, and Mandarin, the newly designated "national language" of the government, was very different from the southern Chinese dialects better known in Taiwan. Given official insistence that those who worked for the new government understand the national language, many Taiwanese lost their jobs and were not even deemed eligible for official employment.

Unfortunately for the newly arriving nationalists, they were soon seen by many locals as simply another colonial force and one that governed less well and with more corruption than the departed Japanese. The charges were, of course, quite understandable. The nationalists, long infamous for the level of corruption among their ranks, were also increasingly distracted by the struggle on the mainland. Under the circumstances, there emerged among local Taiwanese the goal of winning greater local governing autonomy. This was a movement that was for the most part continuing the momentum already begun under the Japanese.

Ironically, given how passionately the nationalists had resisted communism, their own ideas about the role of government in the economy clashed deeply with the Taiwanese, who often resented the

**A Taiwanese man from the Austronesian community**

Courtesy of Steven A. Leibo

mainland—the several civil wars and brutal Japanese invasion—Taiwan's people were to be spared much of that horror. Ironically Taiwan ended the period in significantly better economic and social circumstances that their ethnic cousins on the mainland. Especially helpful were the implementation of new health regulations that allowed for dramatic improvements in the rates of disease, from cholera to small pox. At least that was true until the era of the Pacific War when Tokyo used the island as a staging area for its thrust toward Southeast Asia. During those years many Taiwanese served in the Japanese military, and the islands themselves were bombed by allied forces.

### Taiwan's Reunification with China, 1945 to 1949

After Japan's Second World War defeat at the hands of the Allies, the nationalist government, which had emerged while Taiwan's people were still living under Japanese rule, arrived to take control of China's long-lost possession, even if, in strictly legal terms, a formal transfer of sovereignty could not take place without a Japanese peace treaty. It was just as abrupt a change in administration as the previous one had been in the 1890s. Suddenly Taiwan was Chinese again. As time would reveal, both China and Taiwan had

# Taiwan

nationalists' intrusions into the local private economy. Squabbles over the fate of abandoned Japanese holdings only added to the tensions.

### An Open Conflict Erupts

The developing tensions exploded in February 1947 when the nationalist administration was temporarily swept aside by a local revolt initially sparked by economic tensions complemented by reformist demands for greater autonomy. General Chiang Kai-shek's forces, already hard-pressed on the mainland would have none of it. Nationalist soldiers arriving from the mainland massacred thousands of local Taiwanese—estimates suggest some 8,000 people died—and quickly crushed the revolt. Of course, this created a legacy of bitterness that would continue for decades. It is not surprising that the nationalist forces were hardly in a mood for careful negotiation and fence building. Their soldiers on the mainland were trapped in a life or death struggle with the communists. Taiwan was seen as the location of what might become their last stand. They were right. By 1949 Chiang Kai-shek's nationalists had been decisively defeated on the mainland, and the last remnants of their forces retreated to the island.

From Chiang Kai-shek's perspective, the situation could have been worse. His forces had, after all, reestablished themselves on a productive and relatively well developed island—at least compared to the mainland. It was an island whose infrastructure had been carefully nurtured by the now departed Japanese. Certainly, there was much wartime damage to be repaired, but compared to the problems on the mainland they were manageable.

For the locals themselves, though, many would soon evolve from seeing themselves as liberated by the land of their ancestors to simply living under a new foreign occupation. Most significantly, the mainlanders had shown with what brutal force they were willing to suppress Taiwanese demands for autonomy.

A change came with the outbreak of the Korean War in June 1950. While Secretary of State Acheson had not mentioned either Korea or Taiwan in his speech of January 6, 1950, on the parameters of US interests in Asia, President Truman decided to act to prevent the wider spread of communism in Asia. To avoid extended conflict in the region, he decided that the neutralization of the Straits of Taiwan—between Taiwan and the mainland—would serve the best interests of the United States. So the U.S. Navy's Seventh Fleet moved into the straits to prevent conflict between the two sides.

Japan formally renounced sovereignty over Taiwan in the 1952 San Francisco Peace Treaty, but the treaty left open the status of the island. The Chinese Nationalists, who had occupied Taiwan in 1954, who still claimed to be the legitimate government of China, were still in control of the island. Both claims were challenged by the People's Republic of China (PRC) since its takeover of the Chinese mainland in 1949 after winning the Chinese civil war, and in early 1950, there were clear signs that the PRC planned to invade Taiwan to defeat the Nationalists once and for all. It seemed unlikely that there would be any intervention to stop such a move. As noted, athough the United States had backed the Nationalists in the civil war and continued to recognize their government as the legitimate government of China, in January 1950, Dean Acheson, then U.S. Secretary of State, had made no mention of defending Taiwan in a speech on U.S. interests in Asia.

### Taiwan and the Cold War

The outbreak of the Korean War in June of 1950 proved a disaster for the people of Korea and for the many Americans who were soon caught up in the struggle. But for Taiwan's nationalists, the war brought real advantages. If the United States had earlier been reluctant to become involved in the ongoing competition between the nationalists and the communists, its support for Taiwan now became much more open. By 1954 a defense treaty was signed with the United States, and the island's fate clearly became linked to America's Cold War struggle with the communists. No longer would the Americans see Beijing's desire to retake Taiwan as merely a potential last act in the Chinese Civil War.

Taiwan's eventual fate had now become an issue of international Cold War tensions. This was particularly so during the American presidential election of 1960 when the defense of Taiwan's few remaining near mainland islands curiously emerged as a fundamental part of the debates between the then presidential contenders Richard Nixon and John F. Kennedy. But America's solidarity with Taiwan would experience a diplomatic revolution by the early 1970s.

### Taiwan's Fate and Sino-American Relations

By the late 1960s Taiwan's fate was again buffeted by forces beyond the island, as so often before. The United States, its longtime ally, was trapped in the Vietnam War, and the new Nixon administration was committed to using the growing rift between Moscow and Beijing to pressure

**Former President Chen Shui-bian**

North Vietnam to make the concessions the US required to withdraw from Vietnam. But gaining Beijing's cooperation required a significantly improved relationship with mainland China, which Richard Nixon's administration set out to accomplish. The price, of course, was Taiwan.

In July 1971, Henry Kissinger, special adviser to President Richard Nixon, made a secret visit to China. This was a contributory factor to a decision by the United Nations General Assembly in October 1971 to pass a resolution removing the China seat from the Chinese Nationalists in favor of the PRC. Then came Nixon's own visit in 972, a move that would eventually lead, in 1979, to a United States switch of diplomatic recognition from the Chinese Nationalists to the PRC. By then, the Chinese Nationalists had already lost control of the China seat at the United Nations. By the late 1970s it would see the official withdrawal of formal ties with the United States. None of that meant that America had completely abandoned Taiwan. Unofficial ties continued, including arms' sales, but on a strictly limited basis until the Trump administration. Immediately after his election, the incoming president took an unprecedented call from President Tsai, which he then publicized on Twitter and Facebook. China dismissed the event as a "small trick" played by Taiwan. Just before the Trump administration left office in 2021, it allowed US officials to have contact with their counterparts from Taiwan and even to visit Taiwan, although COVID-19 meant few visits took place. (See below, under Foreign Affairs for more detail on recent US-Taiwan relations.)

### Political Developments on Taiwan

Politics in the Republic of China constitutes one of the most encouraging cases

**Wind power facility at Taiwan's Changhua Coast Industrial Park**

of how democratization can take place over time alongside a modern, rapidly developing economy. Even critics of the Guomindang, the Nationalist Party that completely dominated the political system from the break with the mainland in 1949 until recently, would acknowledge that substantial progress has been made.

But those more democratic changes did not occur for decades after the Guomindang's abrupt withdrawal from the mainland. In fact, for the first several decades, the island's inhabitants, both the newly arrived mainlanders and the locals lived under a dictatorship dominated by Chiang Kai-shek himself and then his son Chiang Ching-kuo. That dictatorship could at times be quite harsh. During the era of martial law, formally begun in 1949, the government imposed censorship over the media, refused to allow competing political parties and suppressed any political activities it found suspicious.

But Chiang Ching-kuo's policies were not limited to suppressing all potential opposition. He also took care to encourage as many Taiwanese as possible, at least those who were thought loyal to the Nationalist Party, to become part of the GMD's ruling elite. Thus it was through a combination of repression and co-option

that the nationalists worked to retain their authority over the island.

Over the years, though, their harsh control would diminish significantly. Especially important in that evolution was the lifting of martial law in 1987 in the last years of Chiang Ching-kuo's administration. But even in the years before the ending of martial law, more informal political opposition groups were beginning to emerge. Most significant was the more tolerant legal environment that allowed the formation in 1986 of the Democratic Progressive Party. It would eventually become the Nationalist Party's biggest rival. As so often has been the case, developments on Taiwan have been deeply linked to both international events and, more specifically, to its critical relationship to the Chinese mainland.

## Taiwan's Democratic Emergence

In late 1989, the world was riveted by the image of peoples throughout the world of Eastern European communism casting off their anti-democratic leaders while some even within the Soviet Union were starting down the road of more open elections. Given that international environment, it is not surprising that Taiwanese political activists began to agitate aggressively for

more democratic reforms. By the spring of 1990, the pressure became such that critical decisions were made to move toward a more open system. Particularly important was the support of Lee Teng-hui, a native Taiwanese, who succeeded Chiang Ching-kuo as president and who would eventually become the first democratically elected president.

All this was going on in the aftermath of Beijing's violent suppression of the Tiananmen Square demonstrators of June 1989. Surely, it was argued that having Taiwan move toward a more open democracy, just as Beijing's international prestige was at its nadir, would be advantageous to the island nation. Of particular interest was that Taiwan saw its own version of the confrontation between students and the government, which had riveted the world the previous year.

In March 1990, just as the first anniversary of the Beijing confrontation was approaching, Taiwan students began their own demonstrations and hunger strikes demanding more political opening. But this time both the Taiwan government and the students themselves had the benefit of hindsight. They carefully avoided the mistakes made the year before. The students' demands were more reasonable that those made in Beijing, and the GMD government approached the challenge from a more flexible position. Indeed many of the demands for a more open political system complemented the goals of then President Lee. Finally the confrontation ended in a reasonably amicable fashion, and Taiwan moved further along a path toward democratization.

The upshot of the changes was the end of the Guomindang's decades-long domination of Taiwan's political scene. By the mid-1990s, most of the holdovers from the National Assembly—originally elected on the mainland in 1948—had retired. Discussion of politically sensitive issues, such as whether Taiwan should be independent of the People's Republic, was at last permitted.

More significantly, the Democratic Progressive Party had grown more influential, and relatively clean elections became more and more a common part of the political landscape. Eventually the Guomindang even lost its hold over the presidential office. But those changes occurred slowly and revolved around issues ranging from which party should lead the country to its relationship with the mainland.

Not surprisingly much of the contention among the competing parties has centered on the independence versus unification issue. The New Party that emerged for a time was more representative of the old line GMD, in its claim that it had the right to rule over all of China. However,

# Taiwan

**Commuting in Taipei**

Courtesy of Steven A. Leibo

the GMD, under the direction of former President Lee, took a more centrist approach. Meanwhile, the DPP was openly supportive of an independent Taiwan.

Further evolution of the political system also came about when steps were taken to strengthen the position of the president. New constitutional amendments provided for the direct election of the president. They also granted the president the authority to appoint and dismiss high-ranking government officials without the consent of the prime minister.

Taiwan held its first ever direct presidential election in March 1996. Lee Teng-hui, the longtime incumbent, was elected with 54% of the vote. The voters rallied around their president, who had skillfully raised Taiwan's diplomatic profile by meeting with several ASEAN heads of state, and who had visited the United States. Peng Ming-min, the Democratic Progressive Party candidate that year, came in second. Peng himself was known as an open supporter of Taiwan's independence, a stance of which leaders on the mainland have long been very wary.

During the election Beijing, no doubt concerned about the rising popularity of efforts to disassociate Taiwan further from the mainland, made a crude effort to intimidate voters by staging provocative military maneuvers in the weeks leading up to the election. While Beijing's exact motives are not completely clear, the result of its threats was to complement President Lee's efforts to fix his candidacy in the middle of the Taiwan political spectrum. Thus he became the election's big winner while the votes of both those openly advocating formal independence

and those encouraging closer ties to the mainland went down.

Even as Taiwan's evolution toward a more democratic system has progressed smoothly in recent years, the ever-present issue of relations with the mainland has continued to complicate matters considerably. In fact, there has at times been a growing popular support for the Democratic Progressive Party's calls for more formal and official independence from the mainland. For a time that momentum seemed to be waning when in late 1998, Chen Shui-bian, the DPP mayor, was defeated by Ma Ying-jeou, a member of the GMD.

All that occurred before the presidential election of March 2000. To the frustration of outgoing President Lee Teng-hui and

his GMD, hopes of a smooth transition from President Lee to another GMD president were dashed when former Provincial Governor James Soong declared for the presidency. His challenge was particularly galling to some party members because he had once served as their own party's secretary-general before falling out with his former colleagues. By early spring 2000 the race had become a three-man struggle between Soong, the pro-independence candidate, Chen Shui-bian of the DPP and President Lee's hand-picked successor, Vice President Lien Chan.

When the results of the 2000 presidential election were finally announced, they proved to be far more of a watershed than almost any analyst had predicted. Chen Shui-bian, the former mayor of Taipei and leader of the pro-independence forces, had won election to the presidency. The split within the ranks of the ruling nationalists had made Chen's victory possible. More important than the details of the win was the reality that after half a century of rule by the Nationalists, who had moved their government to the island after their defeat on the mainland, the Guomindang no longer held the presidency of the Republic of China. This was an astounding step forward in Taiwan's path toward building a more modern democratic society. While some were celebrating this demonstration of the growing vitality of Taiwanese democracy, many were concerned about how Beijing would respond to the arrival to power of the Democratic Progressive Party, which had been so much blunter in its calls for a formal declaration of official independence from China than had the Nationalists.

As a practical matter, Chen appeared to have won far more of the votes of those who were angry about corruption in Taiwan than any specific support for a

**The new high-speed train**

Courtesy of Steven A. Leibo

confrontation with China. Needless to say, Beijing was very unhappy with the results. Nevertheless, initially cautious statements by Chen and soothing diplomacy by the United States kept the "fallout" to a minimum. To the surprise of many, the arrival to the presidency of a representative of the independence-minded Democratic Progressive Party was at first received with far more toleration by Beijing than many would have predicted.

However, surviving Beijing's initial reaction was hardly the new President Chen Shui-bian's only problem. He himself had won a three-way race to become president, but the GMD still controlled the country's legislature. By the end of the following year, Taiwan's political system continued its dramatic evolution. His party, the DPP, won the parliamentary elections thereby becoming the largest party in the country. Meanwhile the old GMD Nationalist party saw its influence, which had been paramount in Taiwan so long, shrink further.

By spring 2004, Taiwanese political life was dominated by yet another presidential campaign that saw the incumbent, Chen Shui-bian, running once again against the GMD's chairman, Lien Chan. The campaign was a heated one. As so often before, it was dominated by questions surrounding Taiwan's relations with the People's Republic and the concern among some of the president's opponents that his ongoing effort to move Taiwan farther from Beijing might one day provoke the mainland to attack.

As the election neared, popular interest was so high that thousands of voters headed back from the mainland to cast their votes. More than the choice of parties and presidents faced Taiwan's voters as they anticipated the spring 2004 electoral choice.

On the ballot were two very significant measures: first, Taiwanese voters were asked to offer an opinion on whether Taiwan should strengthen its anti-ballistic missile defenses if the People's Republic did not withdraw the hundreds of missiles it had aimed toward the island. The second ballot initiative dealt with the question of whether Taipei should reopen peace talks with the PRC. Beijing itself made it very clear that it considered both ballot initiatives provocative. In the end neither initiative gained enough votes to validate them, but by then the election had become even more complicated and impassioned.

On the final day of campaigning both President Chen and Vice President Annette Lu were shot by a gunman who fired at their motorcade in the southern city of Tainan. Although both leaders experienced only minor injuries, the next day's election results, which saw Chen and his Democratic Progressives very narrowly

defeat the GMD leader by a mere 30,000 voters, set off a dramatic campaign of demonstrations and protests by Lien Chan's supporters.

Over the following weeks Taiwan's politics were convulsed by tensions as Lian Chan's supporters denounced the election results and demanded that army personnel who had been unable to vote at the last minute due to the assassination attempt be allowed another opportunity to do so. Eventually, though, the GMD withdrew their demand, and it became obvious that President Chen would indeed have another term. But even as Chen claimed he was theoretically open to the idea of a recount, he also proclaimed that his reelection victory had vindicated his efforts to move Taiwan even farther toward full legal independence, a move Beijing vehemently opposed.

Moreover, newly elected President Chen proposed creating a new constitution that would replace the one that has governed the island since the 1940s. More specifically, Chen wanted to create a constitution that more closely reflects the reality of Taiwan's separate existence from the mainland. When the vote was finally held to elect representatives to the ad hoc assembly needed to ratify the proposed constitutional changes, Chen's supporters once again out polled those of the GMD. But that hardly solved the ongoing internal debate over Taiwan's relationship with the mainland.

During the same period the leader of the GMD made a dramatic and historic visit to Beijing. This officially ended six decades of animosity between the Chinese Communist Party and Taiwan's former ruling party. In the course of the trip the

two leaders agreed to cooperate in opposing efforts to declare Taiwan independent. In the same period members of Taiwan's other opposition parties made their own trips to Beijing and announced that they too agreed that Taiwan was part of China.

For its part, Beijing, which was encouraged by the activities of Taiwan's main opposition party, went so far as to offer the GMD previously unreported credit for their role in resisting Japanese aggression during the Second World War and offered Taiwanese students the same tuition rates as mainlanders in the People's Republic's universities. Unfortunately for Taiwan's then current government, tensions between it and the GMD continued unabated. President Chen himself seemed caught between the proverbial rock and a hard place. His hard-core supporters wanted him to keep pressing his campaign to disengage Taiwan from the mainland while the population at large apparently preferred a more conciliatory approach.

Moreover, charges of corruption continued to hound President Chen's administration. His son-in-law was indicted during 2006 for insider financial trading while his wife faced charges of having mishandled diplomatic funds. The charges did not remain exclusively focused on the president's close associates. He himself was charged with misusing state funds and ended up handing over some of his presidential powers to the premier while he just barely survived a parliamentary recall vote during the summer of 2006.

During his last years in office President Chen's problems became even more dramatic. The parliamentary elections of early 2008 saw his GMD opponents win a

**Presidential Palace**

# Taiwan

strong majority of seats in the parliament. The vote was a clear repudiation not only of the corruption that has plagued his government, but of his frequently provocative policy toward the mainland, which Taiwan's former leaders so obviously rejected during their well publicized visits to the mainland.

As for the spring presidential elections, the only thing that appeared clear even before the election took place on March 22 was that the era of President Chen's more confrontational approach with Beijing was likely to be coming to an end. His own DPP nominated Frank Hsieh, the former prime minister, who had already made known his desire to lower the level of tension with Beijing. At the same time, Ma Ying-jeou, the Guomindang's presidential candidate, had long made it clear that his party rejected the politics of confrontation. In fact, the GMD promised that if their candidate was elected, they would terminate Taiwan's provocative official independence drive and move vigorously to improve relations with Beijing.

Once again Taiwan's population made its choice. The earlier January 2008 defeat of the DPP parliamentary candidates by the newly revived GMD was reconfirmed by the election of the latter's presidential candidate, Ma Ying-jeou, who won by an overwhelming 60% margin. The decision, which some had thought in jeopardy due to Beijing's then ongoing harsh crackdown on dissidents in Tibet, apparently did not turn Taiwan's voters away from Ma's calls for improved relations with the mainland.

In early 2012 Ma Ying-jeou's mandate to normalize relations with the People's Republic was endorsed again as the president won reelection, defeating the first female candidate, Tsai Ying-wen, whom the Democratic Progressives had promoted as their candidate. Once again, as so often in the past, relations between Taiwan and the People's Republic and the different ethnic and cultural experiences of the candidates played out during the campaign. Ma is, as is common among GMD figures, the child of those who had fled the mainland in 1949 while his female opponent, Tsai, focused on her Hakka and aboriginal background. Not surprisingly Ma strongly supported improving relations with the mainland and even spoke of signing a treaty with Beijing if he were reelected. Meanwhile Tsai questioned the relationship and challenged President Ma on the increasing levels of inequality found within the country.

When the January 2012 election occurred, and despite the distraction of the entrance once again of the former GMD leader James Soong into the race, Ma won handily over his Democratic Progressive

**At the National Health Service**

Courtesy of Steven A. Leibo

Party opponent. He won a clear majority of voters, a bit over 51% of the votes cast and was more than six points ahead of Tsai despite Soong having won slightly under 3%. Ma's victory might have been even greater if the economy had been doing better, but Taiwan, like much of the world, had been dragged down by Europe's continuing economic problems. Still, given the circumstances it was clear that Taiwan's voters were relatively satisfied with President Ma's policy of retaining strong relations with the mainland despite Taiwan's commitment to its own independence and budding democratic tradition.

Despite the DPP's inability to retake the Taiwan presidency in 2012's election, one thing remained very clear. Taiwan has continued down the path of creating a more stable two-party system than had existed in the early years. Former President Chen's tenure in office apparently had a significant impact on the island's citizens. By the time President Chen left office, the island's citizens had come to think of themselves more commonly as Taiwanese rather than Chinese. This is a transition likely to have profound implications in the future if it continues. It is worth mentioning, however, that Taiwan's then President Ma seemed to have significantly less interest in promoting an especially unique "Taiwan" identity among the island's people.

It would be a mistake, though, to assume that only the question of relations between Taiwan and the mainland separate the two competing parties. Ethnic differences often split them as well. While the Guomindang has evolved into a more Taiwan-based, rather than mainland-oriented political party its roots tend to be stronger among those of the distinctive Hakka background. The DPP usually gains wider support among those groups that distantly hail from China's Fujian Province. But it is also true, as is often the case, that one's political preferences can be tied to location. Regardless

of ethnic background, people who live in southern Taiwan have tended to be more supportive of the DPP than the GMD, which counts on strong support from the economically better off northern part of the island.

The GMD Nationalists had of course focused on improving relations with the mainland and thus gaining the associated economic gains from that relationship. But that policy also undermined the GMD's support at times.

In fact, frustration with Ma's policies toward the mainland helped Tsai Ing-wen, the first female leader of the DPP, to win the presidency with an impressive 56% in the presidential election of 2016. Unfortunately for the DDP, the party's focus on independence provoked a predictable backlash from the mainland and a considerable portion of the Taiwan electorate that seems quite satisfied with an ambiguous status quo. So much so that in the local elections of 2018 the GMD came roaring back with major electoral victories so impressive that President Tsai had to quit the leadership of her own party.

But as Chinese pressure intensified in response to Tsai's rejection of reunification demands, so her popularity bounced back. By December 2019, shortly before the scheduled presidential elections, polls showed her at 40 percent compared with 25 percent the year before. At the January 2020 elections, she won by 57.1 percent, trouncing the GMD's Han Kyo-yu, who had favored a more conciliatory approach to China. The DPP also did well in the Legislative Assembly elections, winning 61 of the 113 seats.

With no elections scheduled since then, the DPP has successfully seen off a series of challenges from the GMT to its proposals. Meanwhile, the GMT held its leadership election, delayed because of COVID, in September 2021. It was won by Eric Chu, who previously held the post in 2015-2016. The Chinese leader, Xi Jinping, sent a congratulatory message expressing

**Direct flights to China began in 2008**

the hope that China and Taiwan could work together for unification. Chu responded by saying he was against Taiwan independence and hoped the two sides could find common ground. It did not go down well in Taiwan.

### Taiwan's Foreign Relations

For decades the longtime goal of Taiwan's foreign policy was to gain international recognition. This has been seen as essential to the island's survival as an independent state, and this goal became even more important under the DPP party. Because of its huge investments on the mainland, the majority of Taiwan's overseas investments are located there. Indeed, during 2012 that growing economic relationship was reinforced by the signing of a new investment pact that was designed to facilitate conflict resolution when problems did arise associated with Taiwanese businesses on the mainland. That was not the only new agreement. In general, economic relations between Taiwan and the People's Republic grew significantly with the return to power of the GMD with its more conciliatory policies toward the mainland.

Still Taiwan's leaders also know that they need a counter-balancing political legitimacy capable of preventing the country from being swallowed up. There is also a growing sense that the question of Taiwan's separate status needs to be resolved as soon as possible, given the PRC's extraordinary growth in economic power and influence. Otherwise it would become impossible as time goes on. But while both sides have generally agreed with the above, there have, of course, been many tactical differences that separated the different political parties—GMD and

DPP—that have dominated Taiwan's political life in recent years.

There is no question that Taiwan is an independent entity in economic terms. But the issue of its official political standing has not yet been settled. Nevertheless, with its impressive economic power Taiwan has long been viewed as an independent actor by much of the global community. However, things are much more complicated politically. Over the years Taiwan's efforts to gain further international recognition have regularly met with Beijing's active opposition.

Beijing's influence has long worked to ensure that Taiwan's president is not able to take part in the annual meetings of the Asia-Pacific Economic Cooperation (APEC) forum. Nor has Taiwan been able to make any progress in regaining admission to the United Nations. Among the significant disappointments was South Africa's decision to withdraw its recognition and open relations with Beijing. Taiwan also lost official recognition from nations from Tonga and the Central African Republic to Guinea-Bissau and Macedonia. By 2013 only 22 nations officially recognized Taiwan's separate status with Gambia the most recent defector. By 2021, when Nicaragua switched recognition to the PRC, the number was down to 14.

The GMD presidencies of 1988-2000, and 2008-2010 put less emphasis on the political struggle over diplomatic recognition. This was a step in its efforts to lower the level of tension with Beijing. Taiwan—as the Republic of China is now increasingly calling itself—finally managed to enter the World Trade Organization (WTO) in 2002 as a "separate customs territory."

This was part of the generally improving relationship with Beijing. But Beijing

still opposed any general acceptance of Taiwan as an independent actor in the world, which could be a an inconvenience or a danger. Not being part of the WHO, for example, has at times put Taiwan at a significant disadvantage in dealing with quickly developing health threats. Taiwan's unusual political status can also be a very significant problem for its international business community. It can be very frustrating for Taiwan's businessmen to have to obtain individual visas for countries they would like to visit when their competitors from nations like Japan and Singapore enjoy much greater ease of international travel. On the more positive side, the complications associated with visas became somewhat less of a challenge during 2012 when the United States granted the citizens of Taiwan the right to visit without having to gain a visa in advance.

On the diplomatic level former President Lee was especially active working to distance the island further from China. In fact, he spent a lot of effort publicly emphasizing Taiwan's independence in tones that often antagonized Beijing. Lee's campaign even included a warm reception for the visiting Dalai Lama in 1997, Tibet's exiled leader. Interestingly, that visit had a significant impact that had perhaps not been anticipated. After the visit Beijing added a new demand to those it expected of the Tibetan leader. If he wished to work with Beijing, he was to officially announce that Taiwan was part of China.

Former President Lee also infuriated Beijing before he left office in 2000 by announcing that henceforth relations between the island and the mainland should be carried out in the manner of "state-to-state" relations. Although it was not quite a declaration of independence, the pronouncement set off another firestorm of denunciations from Beijing, which was as determined as ever eventually to integrate the island into the People's Republic.

Of course, once the DPP party won the presidency in 2000, under Chen Shui-bian, its new government continued, however cautiously, to carry out an agenda designed further to distance Taiwan from the mainland. That commitment and the dangers of such a stance were particularly obvious during the summer of 2002 when President Chen both suggested and backtracked on the idea of a referendum on independence in the same week. Despite the setback, he continued to make publicly clear his opinion that Taiwan was already an "independent state." He even went so far as officially to dismantle a government committee responsible for overseeing an eventual reunification with China.

From then, the Chinese naval and air forces began to operate regularly near

# Taiwan

Taiwan. Chinese missile units were established opposite the island. New flight paths cut across existing Taiwan routes. Any change to Taiwan's already limited access to international bodies was blocked. Even with the outbreak of COVID-19 (see below), which Taiwan seemed to handle with great success in 2020, China prevented it from any form of participation in the WHO. China also worked steadily, using its economic power, to cut Taiwan's diplomatic contacts. The Dominican Republic, El Salvador and Burkino Faso switched recognition in 2018, to be followed by the Solomon Islands and Kiribati in 2019. China also began to press some countries to compel Taiwan's formally "unofficia" offices to change their titles. Yet there was no evidence that this pressure changed public opinion in Taiwan. By the end of 2019, President Tsai's position in the polls had moved from a low of 25 percent to 49 percent, and she won the 2020 presidential election with an unprecedented 57.1 percent of the vote.

As noted, when the GMD were to power after 2008, they pursued a less confrontational approach to the mainland. They no longer pursued collecting diplomatic recognition—they were aware that Taiwan was beginning to lose that race already, as China became wealthier and spent more on persuading countries to change sides. China for a time took a more relaxed attitude to Taiwan's wish for membership of some major international organizations, as "Chinese Taipei." But, with China a Permanent member of the United Nations and thus able to exercise a veto, Taiwan took part essentially on China's sufferance. Thus, while Taiwan was invited to the World Health Organization's annual assembly, this was only on a year by year basis. Following the election of the DPP's Tsai Ing-wen, the Chinese stopped this arrangement.

No doubt this relatively softer approach was part of a general policy of achieving unification by peaceful means and the belief that the GMD, which was, after all, originally a mainland party, was likely to favor this. A meeting between Taiwan President Ma Ying-jeon and China's Xi Jinping in Singapore in November 2015 seemed to put the seal on this less fraught relationship. However, with the DPP victory in 2016, with the party's stress on independence, Chinese policy reverted to a more belligerent approach. This also increasingly chimed with Xi's more nationalist domestic policy. Cross straits links were cut. In October 2017, Xi adopted a tough line on Taiwan independence at the 19th Chinese Communist Party conference: "We have the resolve, the confidence, and the ability to defeat separatist attempts for 'Taiwan independence' in

**National Palace Museum**

any form. We will never allow anyone, any organization, or any political party, at any time or in any form, to separate any part of Chinese territory from China!"

This led to increasing pressure on Taiwan. China began regular incursions into Taiwan's air defense identification zone. These steadily increased in intensity, reaching almost daily incidents in 2021. However, most of these were around islands held by Taiwan forces in the South China Sea, with relatively few in the Taiwan Straits.

It was the Straits, where maritime incidents took place, that was the focus of international attention. The Britain, Canada, France, and the US conducted freedom of navigation operations in the Straits in 2021. Following the passing of China's coast guard law on February 1, 2021, Taiwan and the United States established a coast guard working group. The US has also sent its coast guard to the Taiwan Straits' area.

Chinese pressure has led some to speculate that the Chinese leader, Xi Jinping, who has been pursuing a more repressive policy in Hong Kong and Xinjiang, while modernizing China's armed forces, may be planning some form of attack on Taiwan. Anxieties increased following the Russian attack on Ukraine that began in February 2022. But the general conclusion is that whatever Xi's long-term plans, the country's military is not yet in a position to take the island. The international reaction to the Russian action, the willingness of Western countries to supply the Ukrainian armed forces with weapons and intelligence, and the support Taiwan gets

from the United States (see below) will also give the Chinese reason to hold back.

## Taiwan and America

Relations with the United States have remained strong since 1978 despite occasional irritation in Taiwan, for example, over President Clinton's comments during his official 1998 visit to the People's Republic of China. He unambiguously stated that the United States did not support moves toward official independence for Taiwan. Obviously aware of how easily the United States could be dragged into a crisis between Taiwan and the People's Republic, the American president wanted to eliminate any uncertainty that might make confrontations more probable in the future. But that hardly calmed Beijing, which was also hearing a contrasting and decidedly more pro-Taiwan tone from members of the United States Congress. Many had been working to strengthen American-Taiwanese military ties.

With the arrival to the White House of George W. Bush in 2001, many on Taiwan had reason to feel pleased. This was especially true because the new American president, far more than many of his predecessors, had made his support of Taiwan more public. The US even suggested a willingness to take part in Taiwanese war "games," something that had not occurred in a generation. Moreover, for the first time in years Taiwan's defense minister had an unofficial meeting with the American Deputy Secretary of Defense. The fact that Washington was willing to make such gesture was yet another sign

**Historicnewspaper edition, 2008**

of its increased commitment to Taiwan regardless of what Beijing thought.

Nevertheless, the new and apparently more pro-Taiwan government of George W. Bush, like its predecessor in the White House, was just as concerned that Taiwan might drag the United States into an unnecessary confrontation with the People's Republic. That was especially obvious during the spring of 2004. When Taiwan's voters cast their presidential ballots, they found themselves also voting on a referendum sponsored by President Chen that queried them on whether they felt threatened by the mainland's military posture toward the island. Predictably, Beijing was less than pleased with the ballot initiative.

More surprisingly, President George W. Bush also cautioned Taipei on the inadvisability of holding such a vote. This was a bit of advice Taiwan's president chose to ignore. Certainly the negative attitude of both Washington and Beijing regarding Taiwan's apparent gestures toward an official declaration of independence is important.

It was also true that the majority of Taiwan's citizens have made it clear that they too wanted a relaxation of tensions between the island and the mainland. Former Premier Frank Hsieh clearly had that in mind when he spoke of finding a less confrontational "middle way" between the various extremes found within Taiwan on the question of the Republic of China's relationship with the mainland. Interestingly when Hsieh resigned in early 2006, one of his last public statements reiterated his belief that as long as Taiwan benefited, the island itself should continue to find ways to work cooperatively with Beijing.

The departing premier made clear was not universally supported by his former government colleagues.

It was hardly surprising that Mr. Hsieh was willing to suggest that there was dissension within the government's ranks. Emotions regarding Taiwan's relationship with the mainland run deep and lie just beneath the surface. In fact, they can appear quite suddenly depending on events, such as the temporarily explosive environment that emerged after Beijing's national assembly proclaimed that the mainland retained the right to use force to reunite Taiwan with the mainland. On that occasion over 500,000 people in Taiwan went into the streets to protest. But developments on the island are only one element of the complicated relationship. The evolution of the mainland has also affected matters as well.

The rejection of the Maoist economic ideology under Deng Xiaoping has ironically had a deep impact on relations with Taiwan. Mao had been somewhat casual about Taiwan's fate in the years before he came to power. But with the establishment of the remnants of the GMD under Chiang Kai-shek claiming that they were the legitimate government of China, Mao became determined to regain control over the territory. Hopes were frustrated by the Korean War and US intervention, although hopes of regaining Taiwan never faded, even if Mao's primary emphasis was on the series of famous ideologically driven public campaigns, such as the Great Leap Forward and the Cultural Revolution.

Once Deng Xiaoping came to power and ended China's obsession with communist purity, the core legitimacy of the

CCP became an issue. To fill that void, mainland governments have over the years focused on nationalism and the party's credentials as the defender of the nation. In that context the question of Taiwan's fate has grown to the point where today's leadership no longer controls the issue, which the population has taken up as its own. Thus the CCP leadership has little choice but to take the hardest line possible on issues related to Taiwan's continuing ties to the mainland. Most important is Beijing's need to have Taiwan accept the idea that there can be only one China. The fundamental reality, though, is that regardless of who is in power in Beijing, the communist party would find a declaration of independence on Taipei's part to be a threat to the CCP's legitimacy. It would almost certainly feel compelled to act militarily against the island.

On the other hand, not coming to Taiwan's defense would be a geopolitical disaster for the United States. In short, Beijing and Washington have often found themselves trapped in a potentially explosive situation largely out of their control. Over the years, though, the situation has again evolved. On the one hand, the United States has continued to sell Taiwan billions of dollars' worth of new weapons that Beijing deeply resents. On the other hand, with the arrival of the less confrontational Nationalists to the Taiwan's leadership, Washington's own concerns about being dragged into an unnecessary conflict lessened. It is also true, though, that China's growing naval strength also makes the likelihood of a successful American intervention on Taiwan's behalf more problematic militarily. Perhaps in part because of that the U.S. has continued to remain an enthusiastic supplier of military equipment including only just recently an almost $2 billion additional sale in late 2015. At the same time Taiwan's government signaled its willingness to join the U.S.-sponsored Trans-Pacific Partnership pact.

But TPP, as the Trans-Pacific Partnership pact has been known and indeed, significant portions of the diplomatic agreements over China appeared to be in flux after the American elections of 2016 when America's incoming president, Donald Trump, initially signaled that his administration was likely to take a more unambiguously pro-Taiwan stance than Washington had taken for generations.

True many analysts observed the bi-partisan consensus that had been fashioned in earlier years by both the Nixon and Carter administration had often, during elections, been challenged followed by backtracking after various new administrations had established themselves in office. This was true of the Trump administration, for by

# Taiwan

early 2017 America's new president had, at China's request, reaffirmed its commitment to the one China policy.

But Trump, nothing if not volatile, had sent a different signal when he accepted a call soon after his election from Taiwan's President Tsai, to China's concern. For the rest of his presidency, as he became more hostile toward the PRC over trade and other matters, and more pro-Taiwan. There were more arms sales, including F-16 fighter jets, a new "unofficial" US office in Taipei, and more regular US Navy patrols of the Taiwan Straits. In August 2020, for the first time since the establishment of diplomatic relations with Beijing, two senior members of the administration visited Taiwan. And as he left office in January, he signed the Taiwan Assurance Act, providing further support for the island's defense.

If there had been concerns in Taiwan over the election of Joe Biden as Trump's succesor, they quickly disappeared, as he made it clear that he would be as supportive as his predecessor.The Chinese were warned that the US wished to see no change in the status quo. 2021 saw a relaxation of the rules govering contact between Taiwan's officials and overseas' representatives. Both Houses of Congress sent delegations to Taiwan. Biden's robust response over Russian aggression in Ukraine was also reassuring, as was increased co-operation on defense matters.

## Taiwan's Economy

As was common among several of its Southeast Asian neighbors, Taiwan's decision to turn itself into a relatively inexpensive exporter of products for the richer countries of the developed world was a key to its economic takeoff in the 1960s. Of course, doing so required not only taking advantage of its relatively low wage level, but also encouraging the improvement of the educational system. However, that decision to tie the nation's future to the international economy and especially in those years to the American economy did not come without significant challenges.

As for much of the world, the oil shocks of the mid 1970s forced Taiwan officials to begin to move the island's economy away from a more resource- and material- intensive economy to one more focused on high technology. In short, the decision was made to focus on the talents of Taiwan's human capital by nurturing a less resource-intensive, more scientific, and technological base for the economy. In that spirit, and somewhat based on California's Silicon Valley, the nation established its own technology incubation system, based at what would become Hsinchu Science Park. Today Taiwan's premier "science park" has

**Delta Electronics builds first green rated building in Taiwan**

become a centerpiece of government and private sector cooperation. It has played a major role in facilitating Taiwan's more recent economic development and its transition away from the older resource hungry and environmentally damaging industries.

Although Taiwan's economic record had been somewhat spotty in recent years, the economic turmoil of 1997–1998 saw the island relatively unaffected by the economic crisis that hit its neighbors so hard. In general, trends continued as before. In 1997, the economy repeated the performance of previous years with growth at about 6.7%. The year 1998 ended with a healthy growth rate of around 8%. This was a figure many of its neighbors facing negative growth rates surely envied.

Nevertheless, Taiwan has not been immune to the region's problems. It too has experienced weaknesses in its banking sector and a growing unemployment rate. Though Taiwan weathered the initial years of the Asian economic crisis, it entered the new millennium with a more negative economic environment.

Its economy declined dramatically in 2001 and only recovered slightly the following year. Not surprisingly, the slowing economy on Taiwan proper has proven to be an incentive for the island's business community to search for more opportunities within the People's Republic.

It also played a role in seeing Taiwan's Standard and Poor economic rating go down somewhat the end of 2002. By mid-2004, though, the economy appeared to be recovering. While lower than some had expected, Taiwan's growth rate for 2004 came in at a healthy 4.9%, a figure certainly helped by Taiwan's expanding ties to the still fast-growing People's Republic.

Although the figure for 2005 was a somewhat more disappointing 4%, 2007 came in at a healthier 5.7%. However, that was before the explosion of oil prices began to unhinge the international economy in the first months of 2008.

By late 2008, Taiwan, along with much of the world, was deeply impacted by the economic downturn that saw the island's export economy contract by just under 5%. Given that its economy is increasingly linked to the mainland's, which was one of the first countries to start emerging from the dramatic downturn, it is altogether logical that the current Nationalist government would use the last years to further strengthen the economic links across the Taiwan Straits. Of course, that was in large measure only continuing policies that had been growing for years.

In recent years, plans were formalized to allow direct shipping between Taiwan's largest port at Kaohsiung to Xiamen and Fuzhou. The initial arrangement was only for the ships of foreign nationals, and no direct cargo shipments were allowed from the mainland to Taiwan. But even those rules have loosened.

Most recently direct links have been allowed between China's Fujian Province and some of Taiwan's offshore island holdings. Influential businesses have been encouraging such direct trade. Acer, the well-known Taiwan-based computer maker, even opened a production facility in Guangdong Province.

By 2003 regular chartered flights became available to link Taiwan to Shanghai. Although the planes were still expected to touch down in Hong Kong or Macao before flying on to the People's Republic, passengers no longer had to go through the inconvenience of switching planes before going on to their final destination. Making connections even easier, direct flights between Taiwan and the mainland were temporarily allowed during the Chinese New Year holidays. Passengers, business travelers, and tourists alike did not even have to land in Hong Kong during the holiday period. Although only temporarily allowed, such flights clearly reflected the government's awareness that the majority of Taiwan's population wanted to be able to travel easily to the mainland.

Overall, significant progress was made under President Chen to make it easier for the residents of both communities, Taiwanese and Chinese, to visit and work with each other. Thousands of Taiwanese have worked in the People's Republic, and mainland tourists have regularly visited the island. One long-lasting impediment, though, was the absence of regular direct flights and ocean-going ferries between Taiwan and the coast.

By mid-2008, after the GMD reestablished themselves in power, even those last impediments rapidly fell away. In July, it became much easier to take a ferry from the mainland to China's Fujian Province. Regular direct flights that were not required to touch down initially in Hong Kong began.

The following year saw even more economic links forged under Taiwan's nationalist government. Almost 200 sectors of the island's economy were opened up to direct mainland investments, and PRC groups gained the right to purchase real estate. In Addition, the government moved vigorously to reduce tariff barriers between the communities. To no one's surprise, the DPP legislators were very unhappy with these efforts and vowed to oppose them.

Over time, the increasing ease of transportation and investment between these two long-estranged communities is likely to transform both peoples fundamentally. If in the recent past the lives of those who lived on Taiwan and the mainland often differed dramatically from each other, the current century is likely to see a major reduction of those differences.

On a more immediate level, Taiwan's effort to seek stronger ties with the mainland under President Ma and his nationalist GMD government clearly succeeded in linking the nation even more closely to the mainland's economic engine. Economic figures for 2010 showed that Taiwan grew at a very impressive rate of 10% over the year. Unfortunately, as both the economies of mainland China and the larger global community weakened again over the last year, economic stresses in Taiwan also intensified. This resulted in a growth rate for 2011 that was down by more than half. This trend continued until 2017, made worse by deteriorating relations with China after the DPP. regained power in 2016. Despite this, 2017 saw a surge in exports, which reached a record high of $29 billion in November, up 14 percent on the previous year. 2018 was less successful but annual growth picked up again in 2019, which saw an overall annual growth of 2.71 percent, partly due to Apple's new I-phone, with components sourced from Taiwan. And while COVID-19 clearly had some economic effects in 2020, with travel and tourism hit, the overall economic picture, with a 2.98 percent growth rate. is good. In 2021, growth bounced back to 6%, with strong growth in computer-related fields. At the same time, the pandemic and the economic downturn saw many businesses go bankrupt.

## Society and Culture

Taiwan's primary ethnic roots have long resided both in the Chinese mainland cultures that came to dominate the population over the centuries and in the indigenous Austronesian communities. The Taiwanese sense of identity remains an evolving concept. While a generation ago most Taiwanese, obviously of Han ethnic background, considered themselves "Chinese," today they are much more likely to identify themselves as "Taiwanese." In doing so they are reflecting a growing sense that the people of Taiwan represent a more diverse community with differing ethnic and historical experiences than those on the mainland.

Certainly the emergence of a Taiwan-based consciousness was one of the most significant developments of the DPP's years in office. Just how real that shift in self identity is, though, has been questioned. Some have suggested that it is less a substantive change in long-term self identification than a short-term reaction to the tensions with Beijing, a sentiment likely to diminish as relations improve.

The differences that separate those of Han ethnicity themselves are less rooted in recent political developments. Although intermarriage is more and more common, the non-indigenous population is made up of people from different communities within China. The most significant distinctions are between those whose families migrated generations ago from China's Guangdong Province, often known as the Hakka, and those whose lineage initially began in China's Fujian Province. The somewhat more diverse groups that arrived along with the fleeing Guomindang after the Chinese Civil War should not be forgotten. It is also true that many of the island's Han inhabitants trace part of their roots to the intermarriage of their ancestors with the indigenous communities that once dominated the islands.

One of the most interesting social developments in recent years has been Taiwan's entrance into the more globalized world of social media and its frequently progressive political stances. Those progressive movements, from advocating gay marriage to a stronger environmental stance, has seen the nation focus at least occasionally on issues beyond the usual argument over relations with the mainland that normally dominate Taiwanese politics.

### Taiwan's Indigenous Austronesian Communities

The vast majority of the Taiwanese are ethnically Han Chinese. However, approximately 2% of them make up a community of indigenous Austronesian peoples more

**Falun Gong protesters in Taiwan "greet" visitors from mainland China**

Courtesy of Steven A. Leibo

# Taiwan

**Tsai Ing-wen, Taiwan's first female president**

**Taiwan's student-led Sunflower Movement**    Courtesy of Wikimedia Commons

similar to those found in Southeast Asia. Their origins seem to lie not only to the far south, but among the non-Han peoples who previously inhabited the southern coast of China. Not a homogeneous group, the community is made up of some 14 officially recognized and quite distinctively different groups that have over the years often found themselves pushed into the mountains, particularly along the east coast of the island.

Often in conflict with the Han peoples arriving from the mainland, the diverse Austronesian communities were not completely subdued until the Japanese did so after they acquired the island at the end of the 19th century. Once that was accomplished, the Japanese initially set up a reservation system that isolated the various indigenous peoples from the majority Han community. Over time, though, the Japanese began to exploit indigenous land and encouraged them to assimilate into Japanese culture. Long isolated and often discriminated against by the dominant majority population, these communities have in recent years begun to assert themselves and even became active in the various groupings of indigenous Pacific peoples. Delegations have even traveled to Canada to confer with native peoples there about asserting their economic rights.

## Taiwan's New National Health Service

One of the most obvious signs of Taiwan's maturity as a society has been the successful implementation of a national health care system that covers all residents. Begun in 1995, Taiwan's Nationalist government, with some nudging from the emerging DPP movement, concluded that Taiwan's recent economic success had reached the point when a medical system that would cover the entire population

had become feasible. There was reason to do so. As was the case in the United States, a significant part of the population, something over 40%, had no medical insurance and were therefore eligible only for as much health care as they could afford.

More surprising was the fact that compared to the effort undertaken at approximately the same time in the United States, there was very little opposition. Unlike within the U.S. there has been a general consensus in Taiwan that health care is a human right with which the government should concern itself. Those that disagreed did not have the political clout to stop the effort. There are, of course, some who are dissatisfied. But the vast majority of the population is quite pleased with the system, which is both quite affordable and universal. Of particular interest was the fact that the government of Taiwan, as a sign of its continuing friendship, sent an expert on the Taiwan medical system to the United States as a resource just as the American government was itself—during the spring of 2009—taking up the challenge to provide its own population with such universal care.

## COVID-19

As it became clear spring 2020 that a new virus pandemic had begun in China, the Taiwan government acted promptly and effectively, drawing on experience and methods used during the 2003 SARS crisis. Following that, a Central Epidemic Control Center had been established. This promptly swung into action, introducing border controls, isolation arrangements

for anybody infected, screening of arrivals from mainland China—later extended—and the production of personal protection equipment. The school spring holidays were extended for two weeks but otherwise schools functioned as normal. The first case was detected in January, in a woman who had returned from teaching in Wuhan. She reported herself on arrival and was hospitalized. Numbers remained small, mostly people coming into the country. The first death came in February, a man with underlying medical conditions. Foreign travel or work continued to be the main cause of infections.

Numbers remained low, however, and some restrictions were lifted in June, with no resulting surge. On 29 October, it was reported that the island had been free of infections for 200 days. A year after the pandemic began, Taiwan's total documented cases was just over 1000, with 12 deaths. However, in February 2021, there was an outbreak among staff and their relatives at the Taoyuan General Hospital, north of Taipei, which created a cluster of about 30 people. A bigger outbreak developed in April at a hotel near Taoyuan International Airport, involving staff of China Airlines. There were also outbreaks in Taipei, leading to local lockdown measures, including the closure of schools. By mid-May, total numbers since the start of the pandemic had risen to 2260, with 14 deaths. While the majority of cases were in Taipei and the north, the whole island was affected, leading to tighter controls everywhere. Vaccination had begun but at a low level because after the success of 2020, it had been assumed that it would not be necessary to act quickly. New supplies have been promised, but the government was inititally unwilling to seek supplies from overseas, even if domestic supplies proved inadequate.

The earlier successes attracted much international interest, with a number of countries saying that they would draw on Taiwan experience for lessons. There was also some international criticism that Taiwan was not invited to the November WHO Assembly in November 2020, apparently because of Chinese objections. The low rate of infection continued to prevail, but suddenly took off in April and May 2022. By early May, the total number of cases reached 296,000 with 896 deaths. Low levels of vaccination had not helped.

**Taiwan and the Climate Crisis**

Although Taiwan's contribution to global warming is relatively small, it is still a highly industrialized nation. It was recently ranked as the 23rd largest producer of $CO_2$, the best known of the greenhouse gases that humanity keeps pumping into the atmosphere. Taiwan is particularly vulnerable to the effects of global warming because scientists believe it leads to the intensification of tropical storms, the kind that already cause considerable damage in Taiwan from time to time.

Many of its important urban centers are also located along the ocean's edge where water levels are steadily rising. A mere one meter rise in sea levels could, for example, see the ocean claim 272 square kilometers of land. Additionally, because Taiwan is located close to the equator, it is vulnerable to the arrival of new diseases as global warming permits these medical challenges to move further north into regions they had not previously inhabited. That problem has, in fact, already developed. Dengue fever, which plagues people in much of Southeast Asia, has begun to arrive in southern Taiwan much earlier each season. It remains longer and is expanding further to the north in its area of contagion.

On a more positive note, Taiwan's leaders have recently begun to address efforts not only to research the island's greenhouse gas emissions, but to work to reduce them. Legislation has been created to establish a national goal to keep emission levels from climbing above those of 2005. This is an important but not very ambitious goal. Thus far this has been a voluntary effort among the nation's top 200 energy producers. The year 2007 was designated Taiwan's inaugural year of carbon reductions, and authorities began a publicity campaign to teach the public how to reduce their own carbon energy impact. For professional men

this has involved the encouragement to dress down, ending the use of heavier suit coats that require more summertime air conditioning.

The nation has also moved to use more green energy. Major efforts are underway to encourage people to use mass transit, and Taiwan has become the third-ranking nation in the use of solar water heater installation density. Wind energy is also being installed, though largely as a way to augment, not replace, energy produced by fossil fuel.

One especially impressive example is the southern city of Tainan under the direction of its long serving mayor, Hsu Tain-tsair. He has been particularly aware of the threat of climate change and has worked not only to expand the city's green spaces, but to develop its mass transit facilities. Given that parts of Tainan are very close to sea level, that attitude is especially important.

The challenges of a changing global climate were especially apparent to islanders in August 2009 when the devastating Typhoon Morakot struck the southern part of the island killing over 600 people. The vast majority were from the island's indigenous community. While no single weather event can be directly attributed to man-made climate change, the devastation caused by Morakot was exactly of the sort one would expect from the more powerful storms scientists have attributed to a warming international climate.

**The Future: Taiwan**

As so often in the past, Taiwan's people have reason to be both concerned and satisfied. On the one hand, its budding democratic tradition survived the crisis of the 2004 election. Leadership of Taiwan was smoothly handed back to the Nationalists when they won the 2008 presidential election. Of course the next election, which saw the GMD reelected, proved equally smooth. Although President Ma won reelection with a six-point margin, his DP Party opponent captured a healthy percentage of the votes. This demonstrated that the era of two-party democracy has arrived in Taiwan. His policies toward the mainland remain deeply controversial.

For those who measure a democracy's viability by the real possibility of those in power giving it up to those who win at the ballot box, it was yet another marker in Taiwan's democratic evolution. On the other hand, former President Chen's efforts to further legitimize Taiwan's independence from the mainland had the potential of provoking Beijing into an aggressive policy that could, at the very least, have undermined Taiwan's economy and conceivably prompted a military response.

Complicating matters enormously is, of course, the fact that Taiwan's relationship with the mainland is so deeply linked to the more immediate political competition between the island's two main contending parties.

The growing number of mainland tourists with cash in their pockets and the ever stronger economic ties both argue for a stronger relationship with the mainland. But Beijing's increasingly more repressive internal administration undermined the nationalists' political strength while reaffirming the democratic progressive parties' long-term skepticism of the mainland.

Of course, it is worth mentioning that the greater interaction with the mainland also reinforces the sense of how different the Taiwanese national identity has become in the more than a century since the island's people have been a truly integral part of the mainland.

One of the most obvious ways that different identity has manifested itself is the momentum of Taiwan's growing social media–driven civil society. Especially dramatic in that context was the Internet-empowered student activism known as the Sunflower Movement that was critical in forcing the cancellation of the planned free trade agreement with China that was championed and abandoned by the government in the spring of 2014.

But while many in Taiwan value the economic advantages of closer relations with Beijing it was a lot easier to promote such policies when the PRC appeared to be embracing a more tolerant and liberal aproach toward civil society. That has been much less the case in recent years as conservatives in Beijing become more assertive. Under circumstances can it be a surprise people in Taiwan have become more suspicious of Beijing and that when the January 2016 elections were held the voters brought the DPP party, with its significantly greater cynicism about the advantages of stronger ties with Beijing, back to power at least temporarily so at least.

Perhaps the most obvious example of how much the tensions of earlier years have returned was Beijing's late fall 2017 unprecedented arrest of a Taiwanese activist Lee Ming-cheh, on the mainland who was accused of trying to encourage revolution through his use of social media.

The bottom line is fairly straightforward. Even as China becomes more and more powerful it has not lost its enthusiasm for seeing Taiwan once again integrated within the larger People's Republic and Taiwan is not in a position to do much about it.

In short, the best one can hope for is a continuation of the status quo and the

# Taiwan

avoidance of any crisis that might push the issue. That status quo became more doubtful under the Trump presidency (2017-2021), since the president showed little interest in commitments to long-time allies. Indeed, in the case of Taiwan, he is reported to have said that China could take it over if it wished, since it was on the doorstep, while the United States was thousands of miles away and could do nothing to stop such an action. But he acted differently, as has the new Biden administration. But it perhaps indicates the precariousness of Taiwan's international position.

# Japan

**Area:** 142,726 sq. mi (370,370 sq. km.)

**Population:** 125,747,062 (2022 est.)

**Capital City:** Tokyo, pop. 13,960,236 (2021 est.)

**Climate:** Sub-tropically warm in the extreme south, becoming temperate in the north. The high elevations have much lower temperatures than the coastal areas. There is a rainy monsoon from June to October.

**Neighboring Countries:** The islands of Japan are closest to Russia (North); Korea (West); and mainland China (Southwest)

**Official Language:** Japanese

**Ethnic Background:** Overwhelmingly Japanese (99.4%) and some Koreans. There is a very small community of Ainu on Hokkaido Island who are physically significantly different from the Japanese, possibly descended from the earliest inhabitants of the islands.

**Principal Religions:** Shinto, the earliest religious tradition, and Buddhism. The latter is especially widespread and split into many old and new sects; Christianity (less than 1%).

**Main Export:** (to U.S., nations of Southeast Asia, and Western Europe) Products of heavy industry, including ships and autos; products of lighter industry, including consumer electronics, and cameras; and a wide range of other items (i.e., textiles, iron, steel, and fish)

**Main Imports:** (from nations of the Middle East and Southeast Asia) Oil, raw industrial materials, foodstuffs, and textiles

**Currency:** Yen

**National Day:** February 23 (birthday of the Emperor)

**Special Holiday:** February 11, "National Foundation Day"

**Chief of State:** Emperor Naruhito (since May 2019)

**Head of Government:** Prime Minister Fumio Kishida (since October 2021)

**National Flag:** White, with a red disk representing the rising sun in the center

**Per Capita GDP Income:** $43,593 (2019 World Bank est.) (purchasing power parity)

The island nation of Japan consists of four larger bodies of land, Hokkaido, Honshu, Shikoku, and Kyushu and the smaller Ryukyu Islands south of Kyushu. The southern half of Sakhalin and the Kurile Islands to the north, which Japan possessed at the height of its World War II power, were lost to the Soviet Union at the close of the conflict.

Geographically, Japan is part of an immense hump on the earth's surface which extends from Siberia on the Asian continent through Korea and Japan southward, rising above water again in the areas of Taiwan and the Philippines and extending further south toward the eastern portions of Indonesia and Australia. As is true in other portions of the ridge, Japan is geologically unstable and subject to frequent and sometimes violent earthquakes. Thermal pressures from deep in the earth escape periodically through the many volcanoes that are interspersed among the mountains. Mt. Fuji, its lofty crater surrounded by a mantle of snow, is visible from the streets of Tokyo on a clear day—one of the most beautiful sights in Asia. It has not been active since 1719. All of the mountainous areas, volcanic and non-volcanic, are scenic—the taller peaks on Honshu have justly earned the name "Japanese Alps."

The mountains leave little level space; only about 15% of the total land area is level, and much of the only large plain is occupied by the huge and busy capital of Tokyo. As a result, farms are located in the hilly areas of the islands and are made level by the labors of the farmers, who have constructed elaborate terraces in order to win more land for their intense cultivation. Japanese farming is actually better called gardening, since the small units of land, an average of 2.5 to 5 acres per farm, are tilled with such energy that none of the soil or available growing season is wasted. This tremendous agricultural effort produces almost enough to feed the people, most of which live in densely packed urban areas.

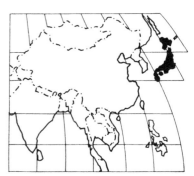

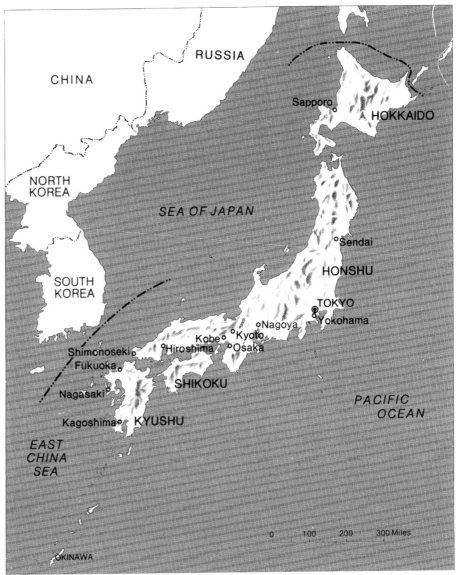

# Japan

**Tokyo Okajun**

Courtesy of Wikimedia Commons

The climate of the islands is totally dominated by the seasonal winds, or monsoons. Cold winds blowing from the Asian continent invade the land beginning in September each year. All of Hokkaido and some of Honshu lie buried in snow from December to March. In the spring, the winds shift, blowing from the warm equatorial South Pacific; the growing season of Honshu and Hokkaido then commences.

The subtropical island of Kyushu remains warm all year around, permitting two or three harvests of paddy rice each year. Only one crop of dry, or field rice, grows in the much shorter summer of Hokkaido. In the last half of August and in September, the southern monsoon brings typhoons (hurricanes), laden with rainfall and often destruction from the Pacific to the shores of Japan.

Rainfall and weather are also affected by the oceanic water currents that envelop the islands. The warm southern Kuroshio dominates the summer months; the arctic Oya Shio descends as far south as Tokyo in the winter. Both currents bring a huge number of fish to the offshore areas on the Pacific side, and an even larger number to the Sea of Japan. Depending almost wholly for animal protein upon this bounty from the sea, the Japanese raise only an insignificant number of livestock on the islands.

## History

The earliest known inhabitants of the Japanese islands were probably the Ainu,

a people who are physically very different from the Japanese. For much of Japan's history the Ainu people were driven steadily northward by settlers arriving from mainland Asia. The Ainu exist today in small reservations on the island of Hokkaido where in recent years they have tried to revive their ancient culture.

The men have much more body and facial hair than the Japanese. Archeological evidence reveals the existence of a Neolithic culture in Japan from about 10000 B.C. known as Joman, from the

rope-patterned ceramics they produced. This community was apparently displaced around 300 B.C. with the arrival of other people from mainland Asia who introduced a rice-growing culture known as Yayoi.

The people who eventually formed the community we know as "Japanese" had come primarily from the mainland of northeast Asia, by way of Korea, and are of the same linguistic ancestry as the Koreans. They were mainly of Mongolian stock whose ancestors had lived

**An Ainu elder**

Courtesy of Jon Markham Morrow

a nomadic existence on the continent of Central and Northeast Asia. This ethnic group became the predominant one, but there were also other elements from the South China coast and the Southwest Pacific.

All of these elements gradually blended into a people possessing very similar physical characteristics, considering the large size of the present population. In the first centuries A.D., the Japanese lived mainly around the Inland Sea, a body of water almost completely enclosed by three of the four large islands. They were organized into many warring clans and had no writing system with which to express their language, which is derived from dialects originally spoken in what is now Manchuria, Mongolia, and Siberian Russia.

Japanese tradition tells of the creation of the islands by the sun goddess whose descendants founded the Yamato clan that eventually emerged as the Japanese imperial family. Actually, there is considerable evidence to suggest that the real origins of the imperial elite are to be found, not in Japan itself, but in Korea. Some authors, going beyond the more vague references to "continental influences" have argued succinctly that the original Japanese ruling family was founded by the early southern Korean kingdom of Paekche. Whatever the specific ties to Korea, it is certain that the evolution of Japan was fundamentally altered by its leadership's decision to immerse itself in the culture of the continent in the 6th century.

### Encounter with China

The Japanese were greatly impressed by the tales told of Tang (618–907 A.D.) and China's power, wealth, prestige and culture. They quickly set about importing many aspects of Chinese civilization. Buddhism was at its height and it was through that medium that a range of cultural, linguistic, and political elements of Chinese civilization entered Japan. On a political level, the Yamato clan was interested in borrowing the Chinese imperial system since it offered the possibility of greatly enhancing their power far above the influence the clan had long held.

In an attempt to imitate the Tang dynasty, the Japanese imperial court built a capital at Nara, near the Inland Sea on the island of Honshu. They also worked to establish a centralized governing system along Chinese imperial models. For a time the influence of China was enormous. The Chinese language was adopted as the official writing system and played a role similar to that of Latin in the medieval west. Kyoto emerged as the new imperial capital in the late 8th century and became the home of a brilliant culture. Histories

were produced to "prove" the divinity and supremacy of the Yamato imperial clan. The 7th century B.C. was selected as the time that the sun goddess was said to have given the blessing of creation to Japan, and established the reign of her descendants on the islands.

Within court life at Kyoto, the arts flourished, especially a particularly distinctive literature that many believe to have been the world's first formal novels. The physical form of the novels, produced by women of the imperial court, was influential as well. Interestingly, although literary production was considered a fundamental talent for both men and women of the court, the men largely wrote in the adopted language of Chinese. Women, who in contrast, wrote using a system of modified characters known as kana to represent the sounds of Japanese, went on to write these profoundly influential works.

The best known of them, *The Tale of Genji*, a 1,000-page story about the romances of Prince Genji of the imperial court, is a sophisticated novel which deals with an extraordinary range of human emotions and sentiment. It is a far more personal and introspective work than the romances that had preceded it either in Japan or elsewhere. Written by Murasaki Shikibu during the early 11th century, it became the model of refined behavior for educated Japanese, a literary influence that could only be compared to that of Shakespeare in the West.

As time passed and Imperial Tang China itself faded, the more direct links

to China were severed. After the 10th century no more formal missions were sent to the Chinese court. By then the Japanese aristocracy was ready to build their own syntheses from both earlier Japanese traditions and the more recent borrowing from the court. If, however, many aspects of the period of tutelage continued to influence Japan over the centuries, the Yamato imperial family's attempts to establish themselves as Chinese-style emperors failed.

The creation of a true central government was not possible because many clans, particularly those in central and northern Japan, were strong and independent and were preoccupied with battling the Ainu people and each other. These clans did not attempt to overthrow the imperial court, however. They contented themselves with largely ignoring it. Moreover many had ties to powerful court factions that gave them additional autonomy.

Although the more martial, semi-independent clans outside the capital admired and imitated the cultural achievements of imperial Kyoto, they were primarily interested in the military power. The Taira, one of the two most powerful military clans, defeated the other, the Minamoto, in 1160 and then temporarily seized control of Kyoto. Shortly afterward, the Taira were in turn defeated by the Minamoto, whose leader Yoritomo was appointed as the first shogun, or generalissimo, of Japan by the emperor. Thus was founded the Kamakura shogunate, which remained in power for 150 years and an entirely new system of ruling.

# Japan

### The Shoguns

With the emergence of the Minamoto family and the Kamakura shogunate they founded, Japan moved into a new phase of its development, one that would last in various forms until the 19th century. Although it varied over the centuries, it usually operated as a generally feudal society dominated by successive shogunal families best thought of as military dictators. For the next 700 years real power usually existed in a somewhat precarious balance between regional lords and various shogunal families that emerged from time to time.

The imperial court remained largely irrelevant to the real issues of power. In fact, not until the 19th century, and then more in symbol than reality would power appear to gravitate once again around the emperor. For the feudal era even that appearance of power was gone.

Japan's "medieval" era has often been compared to feudal system in Western Europe, and indeed there were many similarities. Although Japan's feudal experience developed later than that in Europe it too was characterized by the dominating presence of an aristocratic military elite loyal to various regional lords or daimyo as they were known in Japan. In both regions, feudalism reflected the decentralized nature of power and a system that was built upon the labors of peasant farmers. Nevertheless, there were clear differences as well.

The ties between the military elite, samurai, and the daimyo tended to be more personal and based on kinship than that of the more contractual-minded Europeans who developed elaborate contracts to cement feudal relationships. Western Europe never developed the institution of the shogunate that eventually became a sort of "halfway stage" between feudal society and the centralized governments of a modern country.

The Kamakura shogunate was soon faced with the external threat of the powerful empire established by the Mongol emperor Kublai Khan in China in the 13th century. Two attempted Mongol invasions were defeated by a combination of Japanese military resistance and timely, violent typhoons. Interestingly, the Japanese perception that they had been saved by the intervention of divine winds, that is, Kamikaze, was an inspiration under far different circumstances many centuries later as young Japanese suicide bombers attempted once again to save their country from invasion during the last days of the World War II.

The 14th century fall of the Kamakura shogunate led to other weaker powers moving into the breach to establish their own dominance for a time. More importantly, the powerful regional lords known as daimyo came to dominate the life of the islands. These feudal lords were supported by highly trained and loyal samurai, that is by the soldiers, men who followed a warrior's creed of honor and loyalty known as Bushido. It was the bloody struggles among these regional leaders that made the late 16th century an exceptionally violent time in Japanese history.

### The Tokugawa System: 1603–1868

Japan disintegrated into a state of feudal warfare in the 16th century resembling that of the Wars of the Roses in England. Commercial interests continued, however, to promote trade and build roads. Warfare was gradually brought under control in the later part of the century by two persons—Oda Nobunaga and his brilliant general, Toyotomi Hideyoshi, who succeeded Nobunaga as dictator when his overlord was killed by a dissident general. After two unsuccessful attempts to invade China (see Korea section), Hideyoshi was assassinated. Though things were a bit unsettled for a time, Japan was about to enter into one of its most stable eras, the shogunate of the Tokugawa.

In 1603 Tokugawa Ieyasu, a feudal lord from the region where modern Tokyo is located, emerged triumphant. He established a new shogunate which lasted until the 19th century. The Tokugawa developed a complicated system that can be described as a sort of "centralized feudalism." On one hand the Tokugawa retained very considerable power, yet the regional lords, the daimyo, controlled their own domains. To retain power, the Tokugawa insisted that the lords maintain a residence and the permanent presence of themselves or family members at Edo. In short, the Tokugawa maintained control through a formal hostage system.

For generations thereafter, anyone on Japan's main thoroughfare was treated to the spectacle of aristocratic lords and their samurai entourages regularly traveling through the countryside to and from Edo. There is a curious irony to this system, sometimes known as the "alternative attendance" system. The Tokugawa Shogunate was powerful enough to impose it on the many feudal lords of Japan, yet weak enough to need such a system to maintain control. The system, designed to freeze the political and social structure of Japan under the Tokugawa, had the unexpected effect of vastly improving the resources of the despised merchant class that served this enormous and peripatetic nobility.

### The Arrival of the West

It was in the 16th century that the western ships, Spanish and Portuguese, began to arrive in Japanese waters and the various Catholic missionaries, from the aristocratic Jesuits to the more populist Franciscans, began to build commercial and religious ties to the islands. The Jesuits converted a large number of people, particularly on the island of Kyushu and its largest city, Nagasaki. Their position was enhanced by the conversion of a leading feudal lord of the island, which led many vassals and followers into the arms of the Church. Firearms and other Western methods of violence were introduced and eagerly adopted by the Japanese.

Spanish Franciscans, who arrived in 1593, began a period of even greater efforts toward conversion of the Japanese and also complicated the situation by periodic bickering with the Jesuits. Though the missionaries were often initially well received, such a positive reception did not last long. It was especially undermined by a growing Japanese awareness of the role they had played in supporting Western conquests in other regions of East Asia.

Hideyoshi, who was in domination by the 1580s, became convinced that Christianity was nothing but a veil concealing a future European invasion and embarked on a course of persecution directed toward the Western priests and their converts. Somewhat later, concerned that the Westerners could threaten their own power, the Tokugawa authorities moved

not only to persecute Christians but to close the entire country to the outside. The English East India Company withdrew in 1624, unable to compete with the Dutch. By the 1630s, only the Dutch with a factory at Hirado, and the Portuguese who were confined to an artificial island called Deshima in Nagasaki harbor, were left. In 1639, the Portuguese, closely associated with Catholicism, were expelled. The following year, the Dutch factory at Hirado was burned down and the Dutch moved to the now vacant Deshima. For the next 200 years the only Westerners allowed into the country were the 10 to 15 who lived at Deshima and those those on a yearly Dutch ship permitted to trade at Nagasaki.

A Chinese trading community also established itself at Nagaski for trade purposes.

Apart from those two groups, Japan had periodic contact with Korea and the Ryukyu kingdom, but under the Tokugawa chose to isolate itself just as the West was beginning to dramatically emerge. During this period of isolation, the clans, each ruled by a powerful daimyo, built ornate castles around which towns arose. Agriculture prospered, though sporadically interrupted by revolts of the peasants, who lived in abject poverty. Trade flourished and the population increased. A merchant class emerged which quickly acquired a great deal of influence over the daimyo and the martial samurai by making loans to them. There was much intellectual activity, which was conservative, to the extent that it advocated that the imperial clan, which had survived over the centuries, be restored to full power and to replace the "usurping" shogunate.

Over the next centuries sporadic attempts by the Western powers to "open" Japan to foreign trade were unsuccessful. This lasted until the mid 19th century when the Russians, British and Americans developed more serious plans to penetrate the islands.

For the United States, which was to take the lead in Japan's departure from isolation, the effort was a logical extension of its generation-long thrust toward the Pacific and beyond. In 1846 San Francisco had been taken and an eye clearly directed to the possibilities of commerce beyond. Though Japan was of less interest than the riches of China, it was seen as a stepping-stone to the Asian continent. Ironically, if the Americans who wanted to open the islands knew very little about Japan, many in Japan were quite knowledgeable about the outside world—they had had access to Western materials brought into Japan during the periodic visits of the Dutch ships at Nagasaki.

**Commodore Perry's fleet in Tokyo Bay**

### The Opening of Japan

The uncertainty among the Japanese when Commodore Perry of the United States sailed his fleet into Tokyo Bay in 1853–1854 is understandable. They had a good understanding of the military power the Westerners had demonstrated against China in the Opium War a decade earlier and knew they did not have the weapons to match the West. On the other hand, the policy of exclusion, now more than two centuries old, had become the accepted custom. No mere request by the arriving American flotilla could easily change that. The situation was even more complicated by the continuing antagonism of the southwestern domains of Satsuma and Choshu and the growing imperial sentiment which itself undermined the authority of the Tokugawa Shogunate.

The shogun's government, uncertain how to respond to Commodore Perry's demands, took the unprecedented step of asking the several hundred daimyo for their advice. Even though the answers received were not unanimous, they did demonstrate a generally anti-foreign tone. Nevertheless, the shogun's government, facing the potential military power of the Americans, signed the foreign treaties anyway thus even further alienating them from many of the feudal lords over whom they had so long dominated. Commodore Perry was therefore able to get the treaty desired by the U.S. The other Western powers soon had their own agreements. All of these were patterned after the "unequal treaties" that were then being imposed on the waning Manchu dynasty of China, although at first they were far more limited in scope, mainly taken account of the limited needs of naval ships and shipwrecked sailors. As a result, there was a further round of treaties that brought the full force of the "unequal treaty" system to Japan from 1858 onward.

The opponents of the Tokugawa, especially the powerful clans of the southwest, accused the government of weakness and continued an anti-foreign campaign under the slogan "Honor the Emperor—Expel the Barbarians." But their enthusiasm for driving the Westerners out proved militarily impossible. Western naval bombardments at Kagoshima in 1863 and Shimonoseki in 1864 convinced them of the folly of their demands. Eventually they did an about-face, becoming eager advocates of learning as much as possible from the West in order to be better equipped to resist its influence and power.

The immediate problem though was frustration with the Western pressures. The shogunal court found itself caught between the Western demands and the aroused samurai class. After a series of confrontations, 250-year-old Tokugawa shogunate collapsed in the face of a coalition of forces which included the southern

# Japan

domains of Satsuma and Choshu in alliance with the Kyoto-based imperial court. Known perhaps inappropriately as the "Meiji Restoration" (Meiji being the reign title of the young emperor who had come to the throne in 1867), due to the reemergence of the imperial court as a player, this truly revolutionary development was to be the central turning point in modern Japanese history.

### The Meiji Restoration

The Meiji Restoration was ostensibly the restoration of the Japanese emperor to power by the southern regions of the islands. What really occurred though was the arrival to power of an oligarchy of extraordinary young mid-level samurai mostly from the Southwest that was fundamentally committed to modernizing Japan in the face of the Western challenge. The leadership set up a strong central administration and governed in a style that nevertheless made some concessions to the concerns of those samurai elite left outside of the new constellation of power. Their fundamental goal was to build a "rich country and strong military" and to have Japan enter the Western family of nations as a full partner rather than, as was the case so often elsewhere, yet another victim of Western colonization.

Determined to make a dramatic break with the past, the new leaders issued a series of goals known as the "Charter Oath" which outlined their hope of reforming the social structure of Japan and to learn as much as possible from the outside world. The period of feudal isolation was clearly at an end. These new Meiji leaders wiped out the old clan system of authority and at the same time modernized land tenure. The landowning peasants were heavily taxed, however, yielding greater funds for modernization. Modern communications were established and new machinery was imported to manufacture textiles and other goods. An entirely new system of banking and other modern industrial techniques were imported, and many "foreign experts" were temporarily engaged to help in the transformation.

A modern education system, eventually geared to the production of literate and obedient subjects of the Emperor, was created. An effective army and navy and a modern legal system also emerged within a short time, eventually permitting the Japanese to renegotiate the "unequal treaties," but the leadership avoided foreign military adventures at first. On a political level, the Meiji oligarchies continued to dominate, though by the 1880s they found themselves pressed by a "popular rights"

movement led by wealthier members of the peasant class and former members of the samurai elite. Eventually, after studying Western governmental systems, the leadership adopted a modified version of the imperial German parliamentary system.

A Diet, or parliament, was created under a constitution of 1889 that proclaimed the emperor as the supreme ruler. Nevertheless, behind the scenes the governing oligarchy continued to rule. The period of indiscriminately adopting foreign institutions and techniques diminished and practically ended by 1890. After that, although the interest in Western science and technology continued unabated, more emphasis was now placed on traditional

**The late Emperor Hirohito at his coronation, 1926**

Japanese institutions and customs. The emperor became the object of still greater glorification, even though he possessed little more than nominal power. This veneration interestingly was less a product of traditional Shinto imperial myths than Japan's search for modernity. The oligarchy that created the new governing system felt that the nation needed some sort of unifying principle to support its modernization and the ancient system of the imperial dynasty seemed to suit their purposes.

Economically, a small group of zaibatsu (large family-owned holding companies) arose that dominated the beginnings of industry in Japan in a manner reminiscent of Carnegie, Harriman, and Morgan in the United States. But there was also abundant room for small business as well. This balance between central control and local initiative, coupled with the rapid

urbanization of Japan, its fairly low rate of population growth and the fact that the people demanded little in personal comforts, permitted a rate of modernization unparalleled in history.

By the end of the Meiji period (1868–1912), Japan had largely achieved its goal of modernization, a feat not duplicated by any other traditional nation in the world in such a brief period, or indeed anywhere on such a tremendous scale. Nevertheless, despite the changes in the material circumstances of Japan, many martial feudal values from the Tokugawa era would continue to be influential for generations.

It had also ended the era of "unequal treaties." It had sought to do this from 1872 onward, at first through a series of conferences between it and the foreign treaty powers. This had not been successful so Japan decided to negotiate separately, beginning with Britain. After hard negotiations, a new treaty was signed in 1894. The other treaty ports also fell into line. When the new treaties came into force in 1899, Japan had regained most of its sovereignty, although it would be another decade before it regained full control over its tariff.

### The Rise of the Japanese Empire

The international arena that Japan had chosen to enter during the late 19th century was an aggressive one of imperialism. After centuries of colonization, the imperial urge had continued to grow at an even faster pace. Africa and Southeast Asia were then being carved up by the Europeans and the Americans were beginning to turn an eye toward the Hawaiian Islands and eventually the Philippines. In central Asia, the Russians and English were competing for influence and China, the giant of traditional East Asia, was struggling to maintain even a modicum of influence. Within Japan, many argued that they too had to take their place among the imperial powers and begin to assert themselves abroad.

For many, the first goal was obvious, the Korean peninsula. In fact, as early as the 1870s some in government had forcibly argued for a move against the then closed "hermit kingdom" of Korea. That early effort had not been carried out but by the 1890s the Japanese were aggressively competing with China for influence on the peninsula.

By 1894 a full-scale war had broken out. The Japanese army and navy seized control of Taiwan and conquered Korea, which was annexed in 1910. In its war with China, Japan fought alone, without the support of any of the major Western powers and somewhat predictably

aroused the antagonism of the Russians who had their own interests in the area. Working with other European powers, Russia then forced the Japanese to give up at the bargaining table much of what they had won on the continent itself.

This lesson left a lasting impression on Japanese leaders. In their minds, the "Western imperialists" had their own set of rules; outsiders, like the Japanese, were not part of their "club" and were not permitted the same freedom of action as other world powers. Nevertheless, in 1902 , the Japanese concluded an alliance with Britain that lasted until the 1920s. The ensuing period saw a tremendous growth in Japanese military and political power at the expense of its neighbors, in part a result of its strengthened position as a member of a Western alliance.

The Japanese, of course, were not alone in conquering territory from the Chinese. By the turn of the century the dramatic episode known as the "Cutting of the Melon," had begun which saw the Western powers grabbing even more power for themselves throughout China. The Russians' actions particularly aroused Japanese anger. The two were competing for influence in northeast Asia. The Russians had, for example, established a "sphere of influence" in Manchuria dating from 1898. By 1904 the Japanese felt ready to challenge them and launched a victorious land and sea campaign (the Russo-Japanese War) thereby establishing themselves as the leading power in East Asia—in fact, one of the world's major powers.

A decade later, Japan did not waste the opportunity offered by the vulnerability of Germany during World War I. It quickly declared war and seized the German holdings in China's Shandong Province, as well as several small island groups in the Pacific. At the same time, it shipped considerable quantities of munitions to the Allied Powers, including Russia, its former enemy. A few years later after the Bolshevik Revolution of 1917, Japan sent a large military force to occupy eastern Siberia to see if the region could be added to the growing Japanese empire. By 1922, internal and external pressures eventually forced them though to withdraw from Siberia and Shandong.

## Taisho Democracy

The post–World War I period in Japan was one of transition. The original Meiji Constitution of 1889 had not worked quite as anticipated. The cooperation of the parliamentary parties had become more necessary than expected for the smooth operation of government and they had thus gained in power. Party leaders such

**Entrance of a Shinto temple at Nagasaki, c. 1880**

as Hara Kei emerged as prime ministers, and Japan entered an era where more experimentation was carried out in democratic decision-making. The voting lists were also enlarged to include almost the entire adult male population. The political parties became more influential than ever before. By the 1920s two political parties had rotated in power and a system of formal parliamentary government seemed to be at hand.

The parliamentary leaders found much of the real power needed to run the country still denied them. The military and bureaucracy remained extraordinarily influential and the aging oligarchic leadership still powerful. On the more positive side, the parliamentary governments were more open to negotiation regarding issues of international concern such as the growing naval arms race of the period. In fact, much to the irritation of the Japanese right wing, Japan signed a treaty that theoretically limited the growth of its navy.

But the speed of modernization in Japan left unsolved some problems and created many others. The rural population remained isolated from urban progress,

# Japan

while continuing to pay for it by increased taxes, rents, and difficult conditions in the countryside. All of this created considerable discontent.

Moreover, Japan had changed greatly since its days of isolation. The country's economy was far more integrated into the international order than ever before. Thus, the onset of the great depression hit the country very hard and the rural peasants especially so. The cause of the peasants was championed by ambitious army officers, who did so partly in sincerity but also for political reasons. Those officers, who were often of rural origin themselves, found allies among civilian nationalists. They adopted the position that rural poverty had two basic causes: poor government by the political parties and economic practices by the large combines. They criticized the political parties, which were more influential during the 1920s than at any previous time. The zaibatsu also came under fire for their "materialist devotion."

The military and civilian nationalists also blamed injurious and "insulting" tariffs and discriminatory trade policies of some foreign nations for the adverse conditions of the peasants. The answer to Japan's dilemma was, in their eyes, further expansion into the mainland which was seen as a "new frontier" one that be developed for Japan's benefit and receive its excess population.

This line of argument had a broad base of appeal, and the rightists strengthened their position by taking forceful action in the form of assassinations and coups. The more extreme of the right-wing groups never rose to power, but they were able to force the parliamentary parties from power.

## Toward War with China

From the early 1930s, although the extremists failed to gain power, Japan was again controlled by conservative leaders often drawn from the military. Within China, Japan took advantage of the conflict between the nationalist forces of Chiang Kai-shek and the Chinese communists. Increasing pressures, both diplomatic and military, were brought to bear in order to give Japan great influence over China. The Japanese army seized Manchuria in 1931–1932, soon after the local authorities had threatened Japan's interests by accepting the authority of Chiang Kai-shek's government. Renaming the area as the nominally independent state of "Manchukuo," the Japanese military established the youthful Henry Pu-Yi, the "last emperor" of the Manchu dynasty, as its puppet emperor. Frequent military clashes with China

**The newly installed *Orchid Emperor of Manchukuo* reviews Japanese troops at Dairen in 1934**

eventually led to an invasion of eastern China in 1937. During the invasion a multitude of atrocities were committed by the invading soldiers. The most infamous of these, in December 1937–January 1938, came to be called the "Rape of Nanjing" for the reign of mass murder and rape the Japanese soldiers inflicted on that city's helpless residents. With the start of the invasion, World War II had begun in Asia. Within two years it would be expanded by Hitler's invasion of Poland.

The merciless bombing of the mainland cities alienated the Chinese completely and enabled both Chiang and Mao to rally support for their separate struggles against the Japanese. Eventually an uneasy truce emerged between the two Chinese leaders because of the Japanese threat. The Japanese forces remained in occupation of the major cities of eastern China. The vicious Japanese assault led to increasing criticism and pressure from the outside world, including the United States. Unfortunately for the Chinese, only the Russians initially offered any significant official help.

Eventually, in an effort to limit the capability of the Japanese war machine, the U.S. and other Western countries gradually cut down shipments of oil and scrap steel. This reduced shipment of strategic materials caused the Japanese to look for sources elsewhere, particularly iron in the Philippines and oil in Indonesia. By the 1940s, the successful German victories provided an example of the rewards of aggression, and weakened those Western colonial powers the Japanese were soon also to challenge. Fortunately for the rest of the world, cooperation between Nazi Germany and Japan was always very unsteady even though they and Italy formed an alliance in 1940.

## World War II in the Pacific

In late 1941, Japan decided to force the issue with the Americans. It demanded an unfreezing of its assets in the United States, a measure that had been undertaken in response to the July 1941 Japanese invasion of Indochina. However, Washington refused and continued to withhold oil and scrap steel shipments. Washington encouraged the Dutch in Indonesia also to withhold sales of oil unless the Japanese agreed to a political settlement. That would have involved an end to aggression and withdrawal from China. Since the Japanese had no interest in such a dramatic retreat and the Americans were unwilling to compromise with a nation many felt would not dare attack, the die was cast for an even greater extension of the developing world war.

Believing that the U.S. would oppose any Japanese seizure of the resources of Southeast Asia, the Japanese decided to destroy the U.S. Pacific Fleet stationed at Pearl Harbor in Hawaii. On December 7, 1941, Japanese airplanes without warning almost completely wiped out the U.S. battleship fleet stationed at Pearl Harbor. The imperial forces of Japan then quickly attacked the many Western colonies in Southeast Asia. Initially, their superior might in the Pacific was impressive enough to cause fear of an imminent naval attack on California. That threat never materialized. But it did arouse enough popular sentiment on the American west coast to inspire a round up of the region's Japanese-American population, regardless of their U.S. citizenship, and their relocation to prison camps over the next several months.

The Japanese army met its greatest resistance in the Philippines, where the people cooperated with the U.S. defense force led by General Douglas MacArthur. But ultimately the islands fell. Apart from unwise attempts to gain still further

Japan

territories from Australia and India, the Japanese military settled down to occupy and exploit their newly won empire. The only land resistance during this period was sporadic and weak, from Chiang Kai-shek's forces, which were contained in southwest China, and from Mao Zedong's troops in the northwest.

Although many Japanese were convinced that they were on a great mission to free Asia from Western colonialism, their brutality against the local peoples very quickly alienated these communities and created an anti-Japanese sentiment in parts of the region that continues to this day. In the later years of the war, active resistance to the Japanese occupation formed in most of the Southeast Asian nations they had conquered.

As the war economy of the United States came into full production, the Japanese suffered increasing defeats in naval and air battles with the U.S. Australia initially served as the main base for the Allied campaign; it and New Zealand also contributed fighting units to the war. Island after island fell to American Marines and Allied Army units. U.S. aircraft and warships, principally submarines, cut the Japanese islands off from Japanese Southeast Asian and the Southwestern Pacific conquests by sinking tremendous amounts of shipping and by defeating the Japanese navy.

By 1944 General Tojo, who had led Japan to war with the U.S., was deposed as premier and disappeared from the circle of military officers who were in control. Important persons in the imperial court and the government saw that the war was lost and believed that peace should be negotiated as soon as possible in order to save the Emperor and avoid a communist revolution. The military however insisted on continuing the losing battle; the Emperor might have overruled them but chose to remain silent fearing that a move on his part might create an even more destructive civil war. The stage was set for the Americans to force a surrender without invading the Japanese home islands.

**The Atomic Bombs**

On August 6, 1945, the sky above Hiroshima was lit by the fiery destructiveness of the first atomic bomb used in the history of the world. The Japanese were already hard pressed by the Allied troops, who were being reinforced by soldiers arriving from the now ended European theater of war. Two days later, on August 8, the Soviet Union declared war on Japan. Moscow had agreed to do so the preceding February in exchange for postwar control of Outer Mongolia and territories like southern Sakhalin Island and the

**Children visiting "ground zero," Hiroshima**

Kurile Islands. A second atomic bomb was dropped on Nagasaki on August 9. The next day the war and peace factions went to the emperor and submitted the choice of war or surrender.

The emperor, in an act of great moral courage, chose surrender. The final terms of capitulation were agreed to by August 14, 1945, and the formal agreement was signed aboard the USS *Missouri* in Tokyo Bay on September 2, 1945. The islands had been terribly battered and exhausted by the war. National morale was almost completely crushed; some army leaders and high government officials chose seppuku, a formal suicide that eliminated the necessity of facing their conquerors or the people they had led.

The American decision to use the atomic bombs has continued to arouse heated controversy more than a half century after their use. Some have argued that Japan was already defeated—that the bomb was used more to intimidate the Soviets than to end the Pacific War. Considerable documentation exists to suggest the usual combination of mixed motives on the part of the American leadership. Nevertheless, regardless of the decision-making process then going on in Japan, which American leaders were not privy to, many believed then and now, however correctly or not, that the use of the bombs would eliminate facing a bloody invasion of the Japanese home islands with an accompanying loss of lives which was incalculable. Whether the war could have been ended without resort to either atomic weapons or an invasion we will never know.

**The Postwar Occupation**

The American Occupation of Japan after World War II was initially an ambitious attempt to remake Japan's political,

economic, and educational institutions in a way that would prevent the future re-emergence of militarism. In reality, the occupation can be divided into two distinct periods, the period of the transformation of a defeated enemy and the period, after the commencement of the Cold War, of working to revive their former foe and transform it into a loyal ally in the struggle against communism. During that early phase, the Supreme Commander of Allied Powers (SCAP), MacArthur's headquarters, rewrote the Japanese constitution, began to break up the powerful zaibatsu business conglomerates, and completely revamped the Japanese educational system.

In many respects, some of the reforms forced on Japan in the war's aftermath were more liberal than many comparable U.S. policies. Most importantly, the circumstances of the rural Japanese were vastly improved as the occupation forces moved to lessen tenancy and help establish the peasantry as a land-owning class.

The right wing of both the military and civilian sectors, were purged with the goal of rebuilding Japanese governance on a new more peaceful basis. The prewar parliamentary system, which had been largely suppressed during the 1930s, was revived and this time its authority was more clearly established and codified.

**Japan's Foreign Minister Shigimitsu signs the documents of surrender aboard the USS *Missouri*, while General MacArthur broadcasts the ceremonies**

# Japan

**Former Imperial Majesties Emperor Akihito and Empress Michiko**

Unions were encouraged as never before as the America sought to rebuild Japan largely in its own image. Women were granted the vote during this restructuring as well.

As the Cold War developed by the late 1940s many American reforms were abruptly curtailed as the U.S. hastily sought to firmly anchor Japan as an anti-communist bastion in the Far East. Union activities, earlier encouraged, were now often suppressed in the name of the supreme struggle against communism.

The war in nearby Korea that began in June 1950 also had a profound impact on the course of the occupation. The socialists, who naturally supported some of the liberal reforms proposed by the Americans, were now eyed with suspicion. Many were purged from government positions by SCAP authorities. Japanese moderates were genuinely frightened by prospects of political unrest and they feared a communist takeover right on their Korean doorstep. Discredited conservative politicians, removed from office due to their support of Japan's war effort, were rehabilitated as anti-communist allies.

The war had a number of other effects as well. While the Japanese adhered to the constitutional prohibition against maintaining armed forces, under U.S. pressure a national armed constabulary was formed. Heavily armed, these "police" effectively replaced U.S. occupation troops, freeing them for combat duty on the Korean peninsula. Japan's devastated industries were slowly revived by the Korean War boom, which allowed it to provide supplies and equipment for the U.S. war effort. Japan was not a combatant but but it was Japanese marine pilots who guided U.S. warships into Incheon harbor in September 1950. Almost overnight, the nature

of the U.S. occupation and U.S.–Japanese relations had changed dramatically.

In 1951 a peace treaty was signed with the United States and some other Western and Asian nations, which came into force in 1952, but the communist bloc refrained from concluding formal peace accords. Under the U.S. treaty, Japan regained its independence, but lost all of its empire outside the home islands. Further reparations were left to be determined between Japan and each individual country concerned. A security treaty was signed with the U.S. under which America was to maintain military bases in Japan and to administer Okinawa in the Ryukyu Islands, where the U.S. had established its largest military base in the western Pacific. Okinawa was eventually returned to Japanese jurisdiction in 1972.

## The Structure of Postwar Politics

The constitution introduced under the occupation in 1947 established a constitutional monarchy and a parliamentary system based largely on Japan's government as it had operated in the 1920s with modifications borrowed from Britain. It also provided (in the famous Article Nine) that Japan forever relinquished the right to make war and or to even maintain armed forces. This article though, which on the surface would appear to ban even self-defense, has significantly loosened over the years. In the early 1950s, Japan created an armed constabulary that, after being armed with heavy weapons, aircraft, and tanks, eventually expanded into today's sophisticated Japanese Self-Defense Force.

Over the years Japan's commitment to the U.S. alliance and its growing global importance has seen the responsibilities of the self-defense forces expand to

include responsibility for protecting vital shipping lanes to a 1,000-mile radius from the Japanese islands. Today Japan's navy (Maritime Self-Defense Forces) is one of the largest in Asia.

The new constitution also failed to mention, and in that way repudiated, any divine attributes or political power on the part of the emperor. In spite of this, or perhaps because of it, Emperor Hirohito remained a respected symbol of the nation for the rest of his life. In 1986 he celebrated his 85th birthday and also the 60th anniversary of his accession to the throne.

After one of the longest reigns in history, Emperor Hirohito died on January 7, 1989. He was succeeded by his son Crown Prince Akihito, who upon assuming the throne took the title Heisei or Achieving Peace.

In Spring 2019, Akihito decided in to take advantage of a law passed in 2017 that allowed him to step down at a time of his choosing. At 85, Akihito argued that he was too old to continue and abdicated in favor of his 59 year old son, Naruhito, who took the reign title Reiwa (Beautiful Harmony). The new emperor had been educated at the University of Oxford in Britain, and was married to Masako Owada, a Harvard-educated former diplomat. The couple have one daughter, which was seen as possibly leading to a constitutional crisis, since women are currently barred from the imperial succession. The new empress has not had another child, but the birth of a son to Prince Akishino (Naruhito's younger brother) and his wife in 2006 resolved the succession issue.

The transition evoked a great deal of soul searching in Japan about their responsibility for World War II in the Pacific and more specifically about Hirohito's own role in the origins of that bloody struggle. Some historians, such as the scholar Herbert Bix have suggested that Hirohito was considerably more involved in Japan's prewar imperialistic decision making that many had previously thought. Information that became available after his death does suggest that the Emperor had feared that an intervention on his part against the most extreme militarists within Japan might have provoked a civil war.

Ironically the parliamentary parties that had represented the moderate left wing of Japanese politics in the prewar era became in the postwar years, after the militant ultra-nationalists were purged, to represent a conservative front of big-business, pro-American politicians. Merging in 1955 into the Liberal Democratic Party, the domination of the LDP was so great that the opposition parties had no opportunity to come to power for years.

In fact over the next several decades, real politics within Japan played out within the LDP where the party's many factional leaders competed for power within the party and thus over the Japanese government itself. They continued to dominate the political scene until the late 1980s when their power began to weaken. Still, though the LDP's influence was enormous in the decades after the war, even as its power was dramatically limited by the extraordinary control of the entrenched Japanese bureaucracy.

Moreover, Japan, like so many other countries, has been dominated by "money politics." Politicians have very heavy expenses, since they are expected to offer presents to many of their constituents and to make outright gifts of money to their supporters. The funds for these transactions come mostly from business interests. For this reason, the political clout of the enormously wealthy business community has increased greatly over the years.

During the postwar era much of the wind was taken out of the opposition's sails by the remarkable growth of the Japanese economy which began in the 1960s and lasted until late in the century. Among the most significant foreign policy developments of those early years occurred under Prime Minister Eisaku Sato (1964–1972). In 1965 Sato announced his determination to regain jurisdiction over Okinawa. After prolonged negotiations with the U.S., the island as well as the rest of the Ryukyus, were returned to Japan in 1972. Sato also cooperated with the U.S. during the first years of the Vietnam War, a stance that helped Japanese firms make large profits by selling supplies and equipment to the U.S. for use in Vietnam as they had once supplied materials during the American struggle in Korean War.

But Japan's special relationship with the United States did not save it from the geopolitical dramas of the early 1970s. Long supporters of the pro-Taiwan stance of the United States, the Japanese were shocked when the White House, without any advance warning, set out to improve relations with the People's Republic of China. Although Prime Minister Sato hesitated, his successor moved quickly to establish relations with Beijing.

Kakuei Tanaka, a farmer's son and popular politician was elected president of the ruling Liberal Democratic Party in 1972, thus assuring him the prime ministership. He then paid a successful visit to Beijing and established diplomatic relations with the People's Republic of China.

Meanwhile Japan's vulnerability due to its limited national resources was especially demonstrated in 1973 when a temporary Arab oil embargo against Japan was imposed during the Middle East War. The LDP government had of course long supported American policies in the Middle East and that policy had usually meant a generally pro-Israeli position. However, Japan was then importing 80% of its oil from the Middle East. The price of oil quadrupled. Recognizing the situation, the government made statements critical of Israel and began to woo the Arab states. Moreover, it set out, as the United States was doing as well, to create a strategic oil reserve that, it was hoped, would make Japan less vulnerable in the future.

This crisis reduced Japan's economic growth and further weakened the Tanaka government. To recover, the ruling LDP spent large sums of money received from business contributions in an effort to influence elections for the upper house of the Diet, the House of Councilors. Despite that effort the party emerged with only half the seats they had previously held.

Over time the feeling grew that if the controversial Tanaka stayed in office until his term expired in 1975, he would bring disaster to his party. Meanwhile, the "Watergate Affair" in the United States and President Nixon's resignation in 1974 had heightened the Japanese public's interest in the behavior of its own leaders. The final blow fell that fall when a series of press articles exposed Tanaka's personal wealth and the questionable means by which it had been obtained.

Feeling that it might be facing its last chance to save itself from losing power, the Liberal Democratic Party dispensed with the usual jockeying for the premiership and chose the moderate Takeo Miki as its standard bearer. Nevertheless, in the years after the Tanaka scandal was exposed concern over corruption in Japanese politics and specifically within the LDP would continue to grow.

Worse news was to come. In early 1976 it was revealed that over the previous 20 years the Lockheed Aircraft Corporation had paid over $20 million in bribes to

**Houses and rice field**

# Japan

**Former Emperor Hirohito addresses the opening of the Diet**

Courtesy of the Japanese Embassy

various Japanese officials and politicians to promote the sales of military aircraft.

Over the next years the political domination of the LDP continued to flounder and a series of relatively nondescript leaders led the country until late 1982 when the energetic Yasuhiro Nakasone, emerged as Japan's new prime minister. Without opposition, Nakasone was later reelected to a second term as president of the party and prime minister.

While in power, Prime Minister Nakasone maintained a high profile abroad. He visited the United States and threw his considerable prestige and popularity behind an appeal to Japanese business and public to import and buy more foreign (especially American) goods, so as to reduce Japan's huge payments surplus. This appeal had little effect though and problems associated with Japan's balance of trade with the United States continued.

In the 1986 elections, helped by the premier's good image, the LDP made a significant comeback. Its main gains were in the cities and at the expense of the Japan Socialist Party. In an effort to make a fresh start, the JSP then elected a woman, Takako Doi, as its chairwoman, an unprecedented step for a major Japanese political party.

Despite Nakasone's accomplishments his premiership did not always go smoothly. His efforts to reform the tax laws and to privatize institutions like the Japanese railroads aroused opposition. He also damaged his prestige with remarks he made in 1986 to the effect that Japan's relatively homogeneous population and at that point, stronger economy, gave it a marked advantage over the America's more multi-ethnic society.

Thus, in spite of the July 1986 electoral victory, Nakasone's political career was weakening and by 1987 he resigned in favor of Noboru Takeshita, a low profile politician who had just taken over the leadership of former Premier Tanaka's sizable faction in the Diet. In the years that followed Japanese politics would be dominated by the efforts of the opponents of the LDP to end the party's long domination of Japan's political life.

## Contemporary Government

Japan is a constitutional monarchy, with the constitution dating to May 3, 1947. Administratively, the country is divided into 47 prefectures. Twenty is the legal age for voters. The legal system is modeled after European civil law with some English and American influence. The Supreme Court has the power of judicial review over legislative acts.

The Emperor is the ceremonial head of state. The Prime Minister heads the government and has the power to appoint the cabinet. The legislature, or Diet, is bicameral, consisting of the upper House of Councilors and a lower House of Representatives. New electoral laws took effect on January 1, 1995. Under the new system, the lower house consists of 500 members. Of these, 300 are elected from single member districts. The remaining 200 are chosen through a system of proportional representation.

## The LDP Falters

With the advent of the Takeshita government in 1987, Japanese politics became increasingly fragile. The years of domination and corruption charges had clearly

taken their toll on the LDP. No longer was the party the master of Japanese politics, and an era of instability, of revolving door prime ministers and governments, began. In fact, there were eight prime ministers in the period from October 1987 to July 1998, with the longest term in office being just over two years! By the late 1990s though Japan's political situation seemed to again be stabilizing.

Leading the LDP's comeback was Ryutaro Hashimoto, the reelected Prime Minister, who seemed posed to be a far more long-lasting leader than his weak predecessors. He first became prime minister in mid-January 1996. This was the fourth change in government since the July 1993 elections, and it had temporarily returned the LDP to control of the premiership. It then fell to Hashimoto to build on that temporary return to power.

Hashimoto was admired for his strong stand against former American Trade Representative Mickey Kantor in discussions over automobile imports and other issues. The prime minister also handled well the difficult negotiations over the American bases in Okinawa. In the end he built an agreement that seemed to satisfy at least some of the demands of each side.

Through mid-1997 Hashimoto, who was popular with the public, was well positioned to attempt major reforms of the economy. There were plenty of reasons to push for reform given Japan's poor economic performance during the 1990s.

For much of Japan's modern history, despite the domination of the LDP, the real governors of Japan were the prestigious bureaucrats that controlled the major government ministries. For a time it looked like the reign of the bureaucrats was at long last about to be challenged

**Former Prime Minister Naoto Kan**

114

and significant reforms about to be implemented. In fact, a strong conviction has been growing that over-regulation has not only hurt the economy but made day to day life for Japanese citizens harder as they struggled with extraordinarily high prices on consumer goods.

Missteps weakened Hashimoto's efforts and slowed the progress of reform considerably. Especially embarrassing was his early decision to appoint a known bribe taker to a cabinet position responsible for rooting out corruption. Though the decision was reversed, the slide in Hashimoto's popular support had begun.

But the core of Hashimoto's problems was the reality that Japan's economy continued its slide from stagnation to genuine recession and by the elections of 1998 the voters were ready to make their dissatisfaction known. In an especially high voter turnout, the LDP's vote totals went down as those of their opponents in the newly reorganized Democratic Party, the LDP's largest rival, went up. Anti-LDP sentiment was so strong that even the votes of the Communist Party went up.

Hashimoto resigned the next day and after an internal struggle within the LDP, Keizo Obuchi, leader of the largest LDP faction, emerged as the party's new leader and Japan's prime minister. Seen as a relatively bland individual, Obuchi presented himself as a leader committed to regaining Japan's economic momentum. He attempted to strengthen his position by enlarging his government with new members that included important segments of the political opposition. But, Prime Minister Obuchi's personal luck ran out during the winter of 2000 when the newly installed prime minister suffered a massive stroke that eventually killed him.

His successor, Yoshiro Mori, though apparently physically healthier than Obuchi, was no luckier. Coming from one of the most unsophisticated wings of the LDP, Mori alienated many within Japan and abroad by espousing ideas more reminiscent of Japan's prewar imperial past than that of a modern democratic society. And his nostalgic candor for Japan's imperial heritage hurt the LDP at the polls as well when, in the elections of June 2000, the opposition Democratic Party did particularly well capturing seats in Japan's lower legislative house.

Finally, amidst great public enthusiasm, Mori was replaced by the flamboyant Junichiro Koizumi, who became head of the LDP and thus Japan's new prime minister in the spring of 2001. Koizumi, who campaigned on a pledge to carry out needed reforms, was quite popular. He formed a coalition government that included not only his own LDP, but the New Komeito Party as well.

The new government's popularity did not last long. In the first year after he became prime minister, Koizumi and the coalition he directed saw its popularity drop by almost half in national public opinion polls. Koizumi's party, the LDP, lost some significant by-elections as well. Even more important, Koizumi then lost a major legislative battle to privatize Japan's massive postal-savings system. His loss was even more meaningful because the plan, part of his larger project for reforming Japan's economic system, was stymied not only by his political opponents, but by his supposed allies within the LDP. But those frustrations turned out to be temporary.

Responding to the setback, Prime Minister Koizumi called an unexpected election for September 2005. Using the rejection of his postal privatization plan as the center piece of his campaign to push reform even further, he impressively engineered a landslide victory that significantly renewed his reform agenda. It was a stunning reversal of fortunes not only for the prime minister, but for the LDP as well. The party won the highest percentage of votes since 1969. It was quite literally the biggest single election win ever. Clearly the nation at large was willing to support Koizumi's economic reforms, and the reformed postal legislation sailed through easily once the new government was formed. By September 2006, Koizumi was smoothly replaced by Shinzo Abe, who promised to continue Koizumi's

economic reforms. But there were significant differences.

The new prime minister, who was well known due to his strong stand on North Korean developments, was particularly unwilling to support progress on resolving the nuclear issues until the remaining questions about earlier North Korean kidnappings of Japanese citizens had been resolved. Nor did Koizumi's legislative momentum, drawn from the September 2005 elections, flow smoothly into Abe's tenure in office. During the late summer of 2007 the LDP decisively lost control of the senate, the upper house of the legislature, to the emerging Democratic Party. Impressively for the Democratic Party, its accomplishment marked the first time the LDP had lost its majority in the upper house since the party was founded in 1955.

But losing the Upper House was not the only problem facing new Prime Minister Abe and the LDP. A series of financial scandals, the suicide of one of his cabinet ministers and a controversy surrounding Japan's commitment to maintaining its support of NATO activities in Afghanistan eventually drove Abe to announce his resignation in early 2007.

He was succeeded by Yasuo Fukuda, a professionally trained economist who had worked in the energy industry before becoming one of the longest-serving Japanese chief cabinet secretaries in the nation's history. But as it turned out, his reputation for retaining his previous

**Urban life in contemporary Tokyo**   Courtesy of Joel Z. Leibo

115

# Japan

**The Democratic Party of Japan's short-term leader, Yukio Hatoyama**

political position did not carry through to his new position. Only a year after coming to power, Fukuda resigned citing his inability to make legislative progress, given the continuing divide within the national Diet. It will be recalled that the LDP only controlled the lower house while their political opponents, the Democratic Party, control led the less influential upper house. Such divided government may be commonplace in the United States, but for Japan's long influential ruling party, the LDP and its then leader Fukuda, it was a new and quite unfamiliar situation. Fukuda was followed in office by his LDP colleague, Tara Aso. Aso had previously served as Japan's foreign minister and is the first Catholic ever to serve as the nation's leader.

## Japan: Moving toward a Two Party System?

The uniqueness of Aso's background was not what finally determined his election to the LDP leadership and the prime ministership. His colleagues were clearly hoping that he would be able successfully to bring them through the impending elections for the lower house of parliament from which Japanese governments are formed. The LDP needed to do more than command a majority within the lower legislative body. Without two-thirds control, passing legislative proposals is especially problematic. Thus, the importance of new leadership was obvious. However, that all depended on the decision by Japan's population, which by the early summer of 2009 seemed only slightly to favor the LDP over their rivals. However, what mattered, of course, was the mood on election-day itself, which officially had to be set sometime before early September 2009.

Though the LDP's leadership had occasionally faltered in the years of its most formal domination, from the mid-1950s through beginning of the 21st century its leadership has never been so fundamentally challenged as it was in 2009. The fact that the LDP was in real danger of losing the election hardly came as a big surprise to its leadership. Prime Minister's Aso stalled until the very last moment before calling for elections in August of 2009. The delay hardly helped the LDP's prospects.

The campaign itself centered on fundamental issues like the relationship between the United States and Japan, with the Japanese Democratic Party challengers calling for a more equal relationship with the United States. Domestically the Democrats called for cutting what it called wasteful spending on LDP pet projects and a redirection of the funds toward increasing financial support for the nation's pension and child welfare programs.

When the results were reported, the LDP took a drubbing unlike anything they had previously experienced. They lost 177 seats in the Japanese House of Representatives while Yukio Hatoyama and the Democratic Party of Japan picked up an additional 195 seats and the right to form a new government. Certainly, the LDP had faltered in previous years. For example, it had temporarily lost power in 1993. However, that limited and temporary setback was nothing like the scale of its loss that year. Opponents of the conservative Liberal Democratic Party of Japan had waited for such a significant victory for a very long time.

The Democratic Party of Japan was formed in the late 1990s from a group of opposition parties that had never managed fundamentally to wrest power from the dominant LDP. But the elections of late August 2009 changed the situation dramatically. The new government that was formed by mid-September saw the DPJ holding the largest number of seats in both houses of the Diet, the Japanese parliament. Meanwhile the new government pledged to look with a fresh perspective at an entire range of issues from relations with China and the United States to climate change.

As is so often the case, in the years after they arrived in power the Democratic Party saw the initial enthusiasm that greeted their victory wane as controversies from their unsuccessful effort to renegotiate the Okinawa treaties with the United States to a noisy corruption scandal weakened them. By early summer 2010, the situation had become so critical that the newly empowered LDP Prime Minister Hatoyama was forced to resign his office in favor of Naoto Kan, his

finance minister and longtime rival within the movement.

The new prime minister came into office in a not terribly fortuitous fashion. He was after all the fifth prime minister in a row to succeed to his post in as many years. His own background as something of a maverick had been enhanced by his earlier role in revealing a cover-up related to HIV-tainted blood products. Within a year, though, his government also found itself linked to a series of scandals that forced the foreign minister to resign. By early 2011 it looked like Naoto Kan himself was becoming entangled in such a problem.

But then came the horrific earthquake and tsunami in March 2011 that changed the situation completely. Now in so many ways the future of Japan's experiment with two-party democracy depended on how well the Democratic Party of Japan handled the extraordinary series of crises that unfolded in the aftermath of the earthquake, the subsequent tsunami and nuclear meltdown.

Early indications were that Japan's newly emerging Democratic Party had been dealt an extraordinarily challenging hand as it tried to establish itself as a long-term alternative to the Liberal Democratic Party. Indeed Naoto Kan himself, the newest of Japan's increasingly common revolving door prime ministers, found himself out of office by September 2011. He was undone both by opponents within his own party and the volatility of the evolving Japanese political environment in the aftermath of the Fukushima disaster.

Of particular significance was the strong stand he took against nuclear power in the wake of the nuclear meltdown at Fukushima and his focus on green energy renewables that had undermined support within his own party. But more immediately the nation's second DJP prime minister was undone by the general perception that the government had not been forthcoming enough about the immediate dangers the public faced in the aftermath of the triple disasters that hit the country. The government, for example, had been incredibly slow and reticent to admit publically that the nuclear plants had experienced a real nuclear meltdown. Naoto Kan was followed in power by Yoshihiko Noda, who has been somewhat less supportive of his predecessor's rejection of nuclear energy and focus on renewables. But that was not enough to maintain the Japanese Democratic Party's hold on power. By the late fall of 2012 anger over higher sales taxes and the party's leadership in the aftermath of the Fukushima Crisis forced the government to call new elections.

When those elections did occur the Democratic Party was severely trounced by Japan's longtime national leader the more conservative Liberal Democratic Party led by former Prime Minister Abe. But it should be made clear that the election was much more of a referendum on recent Democratic Party leadership than the legacy of the Liberal Democratic Party's almost half century of leadership during earlier decades. Indeed less than 60% of eligible voters showed up to vote. For Japan, that was a record for the number of people who did not vote.

Once in power again the LDP moved aggressively in the direction of more formal economic reforms with a goal of reinvigorating an economy that had largely stagnated for a decade or more. That goal saw Abe, now back in power for the second time not only push for new leadership at the Bank of Japan but embrace the American idea of a Pacific-based free trade zone, from which the Trump administration backed off It is not yet clear (May 2022) whether the Biden administration will rejoin the pact, although it has created a new Indo-Pacific Economic Framework for Prosperity.

 The LDP's popularity waned, a victim of both the public's displeasure with Abe's efforts to expand the role of the nation's military and a new tax that unduly weakened the economy.

He was though saved by his decision to call parliamentary elections before the opposition could capitalize on the situation and won a new leadership mandate which brought the government into a much better position to lead.

Meanwhile the liberal opposition that the Japan Democratic Party had once represented, as the symbol of a truly two-party system in Japan, collapsed n 2016.

Although he had lost his two-thirds majority in the Upper House of the Diet in July 2019, Prime Minister Abe was expected to try to amend the rules so that he might seek a fourth term as prime minister in September 2021, after what he hoped would be a successful Summer Olympic Games in Tokyo in 2020. He talked confidentially of carrying on with his program of making Japan "a normal country" and in particular of amending Article 9 of the Constitution so that the Japanese Self-Defense Forces might become an ordinary military force. These plans would come to nothing. A scandal over the use of public funds to reward supporters and an attempted coverup, together with other scandals, damaged Abe's position. There was also criticism of his government's handling of the onset of COVID-19. But Abe carried on. Then, just after he became the longest serving prime minister in August 2020, he suffered a severe recurrence of ulcerative colitis, which had led to his resignation in 2007, and announced his resignation.

The Chief Secretary to the Cabinet, Yoshihide Suga, an Abe appointee in 2012, took over as prime minister, vowing to deal with COVID and to carry on with Abe's program. But COVID cases continued to rise, which led to the postponement of the Olympic Games to summer 2021, and took up most of the new administration's energy. Faced with an increasingly difficult situation, with major corruption scandals in the LDP, Suga came under criticism also for his handling of COVID. Measures to constrain the pandemic were seen as half-hearted or, in the case of "Go to Travel"—a scemem to revive tourism—postively dangerous.

Then there was the postponed Olympics. Suga insisted that these should go ahead and they did. But there were virtually no spectators and, while the games themselves passed off without incident, and the Japanese teams did well, he whole event was very subdued. It certainly did not produce the "feel-good" atmosphere that perhaps Suga had hoped might give him popular support.

Suga resigned in September 2021, just after a year in office. He was replace by Fumio Kishida, who had been foreign minister from 2012 to 2017, and was widely seen as a safe pair of hands. Kishida decided to test the electorate soon after taking over. Although the LDP lost 15 seats, the remainder plus the Komeito, which had long worked together with the LDP, gave him a comfortable majority. Perhaps as a sign of boredome with the frequent changes, the electoral turnout was low.

**Former Prime Minister Junichiro Koizumi**

## New Stresses

The last few decades have not gone smoothly for Japan. Frequent political and economic uncertainty has been complemented by other even more disturbing events and trends. For example, the country experienced an early "reality check" of sorts when its long assumption about being well prepared for earthquakes was severely challenged by the government's poor performance in responding to the Kobe earthquake of January 1995.

And of course, the 2011 earthquake, the subsequent tsunami and the nuclear disaster at Fukushima, far exceeded even that. It largely proved the absurdity of the proposition that any nation, even Japan, could truly prepare for the sort of challenges a huge quake could offer. Japan was very well prepared both in terms of its infrastructure and the population's emergency training. However, what Japan and the world were reminded of in the aftermath of that horror were the simple limitations to any nation's ability to prepare for the challenges nature so often presents us. But it was not merely earthquakes that in recent years have created problems for Japanese society.

More immediately, though, the extraordinary challenge the Japanese have faced since the triple disasters has been a mixed experience. In the immediate aftermath a great deal was accomplished. Debris was removed, new roads and railroads lines reestablished, and a general sense of the nation coming together to deal with the challenge emerged. But that newly found sense of purpose did not last long.

Since then a more profound sense of betrayal has become common as hundreds of thousands have not been relocated. The various lies and distortions fed the population about the extent of the ongoing dangers of, for example, radiation have added a considerable distrust of authority, from that of the private firm operating the nuclear plants to the government itself.

In fact, the previous sense that Japan was somehow free from the social ills that beset much of the rest of the world during the last third of the 20th century was crumbling. By early 2004 the sense of the change had become more common as Japanese TV audiences found themselves viewing images of their citizens held hostage in Iraq, one of which, a young tourist, was beheaded while several Japanese reporters were also killed. As had become more and more obvious, all of this seemed to suggest that Japan's role in the world was changing significantly.

For so many years such international incidents had been the problem of other nations, not Japan. Commenting on the

# Japan

full range of Japan's recent experiences, one writer even went so far as to write an article about Japan finally becoming an "ordinary" country. This was especially reinforced in the spring of 2008 when Japan experienced yet another mass horror as a deranged young man deliberately drove a truck into a crowd of people and then proceeded to kill even more with a knife. This massacre was worse than anything the normally so "safe" country had experienced in years.

Perhaps the most obvious example of Japan becoming an "ordinary" country has been the significant increase in the number of Japanese firms that have found themselves taken over by huge foreign multinationals. That more and more Japanese now find their employers to be foreigners is certainly something new for Japan but quite familiar elsewhere. A particularly graphic example of this evolution is the fact that a Welsh-American was named to be the head of Sony Electronics. Internationally Japan's image took a particularly strong hit during the last few years as its long-heralded and extraordinarily successful Toyota car company found itself temporarily pilloried for delaying recalls of some of its most popular models that were said to require important safety repairs. Eventually many of the most dramatic charges, that the cars refused to slow down, were proven incorrect, but not before the damage was done to the company's reputation.

### Foreign and Defense Issues

For much of the postwar-era Japan was uninvolved in most international issues and largely followed America's lead. That stance has modified in recent years as its foreign policy and defense planning have become more robust largely as a response to a range of developments from the American War on Terrorism, to the U.S. invasion of Iraq, and more regionally the ongoing threat of North Korean efforts to develop nuclear weapons.

Recognizing the changing realities, then Prime Minister Koizumi made it clear that he wanted Japan not only to consider changes to its post–World War II pacifistic constitution, but to aggressively lobby for Japan to gain a permanent seat on the United Nation's Security Council. Unfortunately, that is likely to be more difficult than some might have imagined only a few years ago. China's government has made it clear that it opposes Japan winning such a seat. Beijing's growing international influence ensures that opinion will be heard. The two Koreas also oppose such a move. Even the United States, which has been more supportive, has been unwilling to support Japan receiving

official veto power along with the potential permanent seat.

Looking more closely at Japan's all-important relationship with the United States, more often than not economic issues have been at the forefront of issues that separated the two powers. The trade imbalance between the two countries has long been an irritant in Japanese-American relations. Over the years, Japan has consistently had a sizable trade and services surplus. In 2011, it was around $40 billion with the United States. That rose to $69 billion in 2019, but fell back to $55.41 billion in 2020, as COVID hit. And while that imbalance is dwarfed by the imbalances associated with American and China trade in recent decades ,they have been at times an issue that stirred tensions.

In an earlier attempt to address this problem the U.S. Congress passed the Omnibus Trade and Competitiveness bill in 1988. The Special 301 section of that bill provided a powerful weapon in the form of heavy tariffs on U.S. imports from countries deemed to be engaging in unfair trading practices. The first Bush administration also introduced the Structural Impediments Initiative (SII). SII talks were aimed at eliminating the fundamental economic differences between the two countries that some claimed resulted in large trade deficits.

In a somewhat curious irony from the usual American association with free trade the Clinton administration, which followed the first President Bush in office, opted for an aggressive "managed trade" approach that insisted on establishing set targets. In 1994 and early 1995, the major issue was access to the Japanese market for American autos and auto parts.

There were also some newer developments that improved trade relations. The long-term weakening of the Japanese economy during the late 1990s added to the Japanese consumer's interest in less expensive goods and the drop in land prices combined to allow the introduction of more American-style superstores and even for the planning of U.S.-style malls. Changes in regulations regarding such investments also facilitated this development.

As the new century began Japanese-American economic tensions were simply less likely to make the headlines. China had become the country with which America has its largest trade imbalance. Thus, "Japan bashing" seemed to give way to "China bashing" as the U.S. deficit with that country grew.

The American media switched somewhat from concerns about trade imbalances between the United States and its trading partners in East Asia to more immediate complaints about U.S.

corporations that were increasingly "outsourcing" American jobs to factories in countries from India to the People's Republic. But if the once widely discussed Japanese-American trade imbalance receded from public attention, other issues of concern continued to affect the Japanese American relationship. Or at least it had so receded into the background until the new administration in Washington with its stronger focus on economic nationalism arrived in power.

Among the most important long-term issues was the controversy over the renewal of the American bases in Okinawa, which dated back to the era of the American occupation of the islands at the end of World War II. For years, resentments grew in Japan over the presence of the bases. Those sentiments are especially strong in Okinawa where the bulk of the American bases are located. Several factors have added to the tensions, some tied to a more general evolution of the international arena and others linked directly to events in Okinawa. The Cold War has been over for more than a decade and the Japanese public is no longer as supportive of the American presence as it once was. That said, worries about North Korea and most recently, the Russian invasion of Ukraine in 2022, have perhaps made the American presence more palatable.

Within Okinawa, American insensitivity and domination of some of the island's best lands added to the problem. The American establishment of an artillery range that once fired over a public road was only one of the most egregious examples. Accusations of rape against soldiers from the American bases by Japanese women have occurred far too often

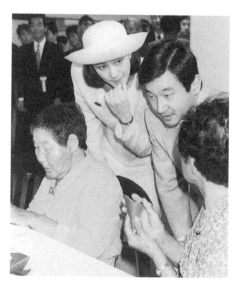

**Emperor Naruhito and Empress Masako (then Crown Prince and Princess) visit a nursing home**

# Japan

and dramatically increase tensions on a regular base.

Former Governor Masahide Ota had been particularly anxious to expel the Americans from Okinawa, but the elections of November 1998 brought to power a more pragmatic conservative, Keiichi Inamine, a businessman who argued for a more gradual approach to the problem and one that recognized that the Americans did pump a considerable amount of money into the local economy.

While Americans were probably relieved that Governor Ota was removed from the scene, the issues that had concerned the former governor did not go away. In fact, by the fall of 2002, when Inamine was reelected, he too was calling for a major withdrawal of American troops from Okinawa.

Finally, during late 2005 a treaty was negotiated that anticipated moving some Americans to Guam while relocating others to less populated parts of the islands. The cost of relocating the troops was expected to be borne by both the United States and Tokyo with the latter expecting to spend over $15 billion in the effort.

Eventually a formal treaty was negotiated in 2006. However, once the LDP left office, the new JDP leadership sought to revise the new treaty again. For the JDP the issue has been  an especially sensitive one since it had campaigned on a platform of realigning the relationship between Japan and the United States to a more equal footing. Meeting the expectations of Okinawans, who are dissatisfied with the presence of American bases on their islands, has been a daunting one. As we have seen, the issue eventually undermined the prime ministership of the JDP leader Hatoyama and helped facilitate the rise of Naoto Kan, who has also failed to solve the long-running controversy.

While at times, significant progress seemed to be made  made in resolving the long-running issue, with a new base being constructed away from urban areas, this has not proved to be the case.. While the fate of the American Futenma airbase had not been resolved,  a decision was taken to remove some 9,000 American marines from Okinawa and relocate them outside of Japan.

Another important issue of over the years has been the revision of the guidelines for the Japanese-American Security Pact, which dates from 1960. The 1999 revisions aroused considerable controversy within Japan and abroad. Though somewhat ambiguous, the guidelines suggested that Japan was willing to send military personnel abroad during times of crises. For example, elements of the Japanese military have played significant roles in South Asia alongside the United States.

After the September 11, 2001, terrorist attack in the United States, Japan agreed to allow its military to serve in a non-combat role in the American led war in Afghanistan. Tokyo also sent a naval destroyer to the Indian Ocean to support the American activities in South Asia as well. More recently, the two countries concluded yet another agreement that called for a major reorganization of military cooperation between them. Officially, it was said that the new relationship would be a global rather than regional relationship. The new plan calls for the armies, air forces, and navies of the two countries to work and train closely together.

Not surprisingly, the American decision in 2003 to overthrow the government of Saddam Hussein also complicated relations. A great many Japanese opposed their country becoming involved in Iraq even as they had already contributed to the struggle in Afghanistan. Nevertheless, Prime Minister Koizumi's government decided to send Japanese troops to Iraq to serve in non-combat roles. This was a decision that many of his parliamentary opponents did not support. Koizumi stood his ground, offering the United States all the support it could in Iraq. Eventually, only a few months before he left office, Koizumi brought the 600 Japanese troops home from Iraq even as they continued to offer logistical support. As for the Japanese activities in South Asia, their role in refueling ships in the Indian Ocean has continued to arouse tensions between the U.S. and Tokyo. It also emerged as yet another domestic political issue which the LDP and their critics argued over until Prime Minister Fukuda, in one of his few accomplishments in office, managed to get authorization for the renewal of the effort in mid-2008.

**Former Prime Minister Tara Aso**

Relations soured in in the Trump presidency over trade disputes and President Trump's belief that Japan, like South Korea, was taking the United States for a ride over its contributions to support of U.S.forces in the country. While there were plenty of voices pointing out that the U.S. also gained from these arrangements, Trump would have none of it.

Relations returned to a more positive level after Joe Biden became president in 2021, with Japan playing an active role in the QUAD, and informal linkage between the U.S., Japan, Australia, and India, designed to counter what is seen as growing Chinese influence in the region.

The conflict in Ukraine in 2022 has led to Japan further considering the issue of what the self-defense forces can and cannot do, especially as there are regional implications that directly affect Japan such as the China–Taiwan issue.

Relations between the United States and Japan have at times also been complicated by the question of North Korea's nuclear ambitions. In recent years, the most significant issue has been whether North Korea would continue on a path toward reconciliation with Japan and the larger world community, or, as often seemed to be the case, would decide to return to the policy of nuclear brinkmanship it usually embraced during the 1990s.

On August 31, 1998, North Korea fired what appeared to be a three-stage missile over Japanese territory. There was some uncertainty about whether they were testing an offensive missile or merely trying to put a satellite in space. What was obvious was that North Korea had demonstrated an ability to hit urban Japan with missiles. Especially upsetting for the Japanese was that they needed to depend on the Americans for technical information on the launch. Most significant recently was North Korea's successful October 2006 detonation of a nuclear device. This followed the equally alarming demonstration of its growing missile prowess with a series of short- and long-range tests.

Under the circumstances, Tokyo's reaction was hardly surprising. Not only was there a step-up of efforts to work with the U.S. on building a joint missile-defense structure, but for the first time the possibility of Japan joining the ranks of those countries that possess such weapons became more and more openly discussed. This is a development that in so many ways reveals a real "sea change" in attitude by the only country that has ever experienced a nuclear attack on its shores.

All of this was quite ironic given that relations during much of decade seemed to be improving. North Korea, in an apparent effort at "clearing the air" regarding their past policies, had finally admitted

# Japan

Prime Minister Shinzo Abe

travel with him back to Japan. But while relations have improved, questions about the abductions have at times continued significantly to strain Japanese-North Korean relations to the present. Those disagreements have at times also spilled over to Japanese-American relations as the two nations have sometimes promoted different policies vis-à-vis North Korea.

Not surprisingly one issue that the Japanese, South Koreans, and Americans have continued to agree on is the threat of North Korea's continuing nuclear and missile program. That concern was particularly on display during the spring of 2012 as North Korea announced plans for yet another missile test, this time said to be part of its developing "space program." Operating on the well-grounded assumption that North Korea's talk of a growing space program was simply not a very good "cover story" for furthering its missile program, the Japanese government not only condemned the effort, but it announced sophisticated plans to shoot down the missile. Japan considered this a forbidden test for North Korea, which is under the United Nation's sanctions regime. When the actual launch took place, though, none of those advance preparations turned out to be needed. The missile blew up shortly after its launch.

Since then, Japan's relationship with North Korea, like that of most of the Western world, has been minimal. As part of UN sanctions on the North, Japan stopped the movement of the pro–North Korean community in Japan from travel to the country. It has continued to condemn

Former Prime Minister Yasuo Fukuda

North Korean missile and nuclear tests, and has continued to raise the issue of the missing Japanese.

Japan's relationship with China has often been in the spotlight. Japanese ultra-nationalists have made efforts from time to time to stake claims to the Daiyou Islands, known to the Japanese as the Senkaku Islands. Predictably, Chinese from all walks of life, from Hong Kong to Taiwan and the People's Republic, have reacted angrily to such efforts. Of course, nationalism plays an important role in such tensions. But the issue is also a deeply economic one as well because the area around the islands, the East China Sea, includes energy resources both nations need.

The November 1998 visit of President Jiang of the People's Republic did not make much progress in improving relations either. Aware of the apology Japan had offered Korea a few months earlier China's leader made it clear he expected something similar regarding the brutal Japanese invasion of China earlier in the century. The Japanese government, apparently under pressure from its own conservatives, refused to offer a formal written apology. The educational establishment has also often played down the brutality of Japanese wartime behavior in China. The results have been quite predictable. Japan's efforts to become a permanent member of the United Nations Security Council have become considerably more difficult due to China's opposition.

But there have been occasional signs of an improving relationship. In November 2007, the first Chinese warship since 1934 sailed into Tokyo harbor to begin a long delayed visit dedicated to improving relations between the two East Asian giants. Given how complicated relations can be between Tokyo and Beijing, it will not be a surprise to learn that the visit had taken

that, as long had been rumored, they had actually kidnapped Japanese nationals during the 1970s and 1980s to serve as language teachers and intelligence resources.

Even more surprising was Pyongyang's decision to allow the 5 survivors of the original 13 kidnap victims to visit Japan. Predictably, the gesture backfired somewhat as tensions arose when the returning Japanese chose to remain in Japan and to demand that their North Korean children be given the right to join them. For a time the situation improved somewhat. During his visit to North Korea, then Prime Minister Koizumi even managed to convince its leader to allow five people, all children of the earlier kidnapped Japanese, to

Courtesy of Joel Z. Leibo

seven years to schedule. Still it was an important development in an environment that has seen the Japanese become more and more concerned about the growth of Chinese military power.

After Japanese Democratic Party took office, there was a flurry of contacts between Tokyo and Beijing that were so energetic that some speculated that America, which for so long enjoyed an especially close relationship with Japan, now had a real competitor in the People's Republic. Nevertheless, the initial JDP Prime Minister, Hashimoro, went out of his way to emphasize the importance of Japan's ongoing alliance with the United States. Since the return of Japan's Liberal Democratic Party's return to power that momentum coupled with a more general concern about a more assertive China has probably lessened the likelihood of weakened Japanese-American relations. On the more positive side, relations warmed somewhat after each nation found itself stricken by horrific earthquakes. That allowed them each respectively to help the other as they experienced these extraordinary human tragedies.

But those improved relations quickly dissipated as a more assertive China found itself facing a newly reinvigorated and conservative Japanese government under Prime Minister Abe. He called for a wholesale reevaluation of the nation's more passive attitude toward national defense. In this renewed and tenser atmosphere there have not only been a regular series of minor confrontations in the East China Sea, but a renewal of historical claims stemming from the 1930s.

Moreover, relations with the United States have been strained as well as Japan's newly reinvigorated LDP asserts a nationalist tone outsiders have not heard from Tokyo in half a century. One example in 2022 was Japan's decision to try to bring pressure on the Solomon Islands, as Australia has done, not to go ahead with an agreement to allow Chinese naval ships to dock and be serviced in the islands.

At base is a series of efforts to reevaluate the nation's wartime legacy, which not surprisingly has also seen many in Japan rethinking the Japanese-American relationship. In the same vein, in the United States, the Trump administration seemed interested in reevaluating America's historic relations with both Beijing and Tokyo in a fashion that many speculated could change the dynamics of the region for decades to come.

Prime Minister Abe also made it clear that his efforts to move past Japan's postwar legacy include a renewed effort to regain the Northern Islands the Soviet Union occupied at the end of the war. Following Japanese condemnation of the Russian invasion of Ukraine, relations with Russia have deteriorated, however. In March 2022, Russia suspended peace treaty talks and that it would suspend the visa-free concession for Japanese who wished to visit the Northern Isles. Then, in May 2022, Russia announced that it would not allow Prime Minister Kishida or members of his cabinet, as well as 63 other Japanese officials, to visit, which seems to rule out any movement on the Northern Islands for the foreseeable future. Japan protested at these moves but they can hardly have come as a surprise.

## Culture and Society

Before the arrival of Chinese influence, Japanese culture was, compared to its giant neighbor, rather unsophisticated; it was centered on the Shinto belief in spirits existing everywhere in nature. With the adoption of so many aspects of Chinese civilization Shinto was somewhat overwhelmed by the growth of Buddhism. In the modern era though, Shinto, experienced a revival of sorts with the Meiji Government's decision to use it as a feature of its enhancement of the role of the emperor. After the Second World War, "State Shinto" as it is sometimes called, was again de-emphasized.

Today both Shinto and Buddhism are somewhat eclectically interwoven in Japanese society which overall is quite secular. It is quite common for a Japanese to marry in a Shinto shrine and to venerate his ancestors at the Buddhist Temple. The Christmas season has also become an important time for socializing. It is an event hardly tied to the religious context the holiday carries in the West.

Overall, traditional Japanese society has experienced an extraordinary transformation over the years since the Meiji Restoration. Japan had begun the 19th century as a society that saw itself, largely divided hierarchically into classes of samurai, peasants, artisans, and merchants with the samurai the uniquely dominant elite. By the late 20th century Japan had become a much more homogeneous society more divided by intellectual and professional accomplishment than family background. Recent research has suggested that that too may be changing. Over the last few years a greater income disparity has emerged in Japan. In fact, according to researchers the gap between what the richest and poorest earn has grown by over 50% in recent years.

Since Japan was the first non-Western country to industrialize along Western models it faced earliest a dilemma that communities around the world continue to deal with—how to modernize one's society without simply becoming "Western." After considerable struggle they did manage to find a comfortable balance. Today, the older cultural patterns are not dead. In fact, they are often creatively blended with modernity.

The increasingly urban life of the Japanese is a distinctive one. The business sections of the city are usually constructed of reinforced concrete. Sadly, the simple, yet attractive wood and paper housing that so charmed earlier visitors to Japan, has given

**Morning traffic on Uchibori-dori Avenue**

# Japan

way in recent generations to long rows of concrete apartment blocks. The people who work in the city during the day commute to suburbs in the evening. Thus, the morning and evening commuting hours are as frantic as those in the cities of the United States. Very long commutes are the norm. The common pattern is one with which Americans who commute by rail into cities like New York could easily identify.

Happily for the Japanese their transport systems, particularly rail, are as modern as can be found in the world. The famous and efficient bullet trains run throughout the country. Television, radio, and computer games are widely enjoyed and while not yet quite as enamored of the Internet as many Americans, its use is growing very rapidly.

All of the fine arts are widely found in the cities, particularly Tokyo. Traditional European and Western musical works and ballet are heavily attended, as are cultural expressions that are distinctly Japanese such as the Kabuki and Noh theater performances.

On another level, bluegrass and country-western music sung in Japanese has a large following. Today, McDonald's and Kentucky Fried Chicken are quite popular restaurant chains in Japan. Underlying this shift to Western food is a far more significant outcome. Rice consumption has dropped considerably in the last quarter century. Consumption of meat and dairy products is skyrocketing and Japanese young adults are growing taller and bigger. It is not just American fast food that has attracted many Japanese. A version of

the popular American show *Sex and the City* was created for the Japanese entertainment market.

As Japan entered the 21st century, the single most important aspect of Japanese society is the reality that it is aging rapidly. Today, more than 14% of the population is over 65. This had risen to more than a quarter by 2020. Japan's population has officially also begun to decline. This is a reality that forces the question of how more and more pensioners are going to be supported by fewer and fewer workers.

On a social level, the news that the nation's population has continued to decline, officially down by almost one million over the last five years, is likely to arouse concern among some quarters who associate national strength with national vitality. More immediately some have linked the decline to the nation's recent economic challenges as demands for goods and services have declined.

The changing demographics that are affecting Japan are also significant in ways that are not as obvious. For example, Japan has always attributed part of its economic success to the high savings rates of its citizens. But the days of huge individual savings accounts that could be used to finance industry may soon be over as the rapidly aging Japanese begin to drain their accounts to support themselves in retirement.

Perhaps even more of a challenge for the relatively isolated and homogeneous Japanese society is the diminishing number of workers available to run its economy.

The most recent studies report that the percentage of Japanese under age 15 is now at a record low and that the nation has the highest ratio of elderly to young in the world.

The upshot is that the aging of the population and the lowering of the birth rate have combined to create a decline in the number of potential employees. The change is so significant that economists have projected that Japan, a country long uncomfortable with outsiders, will either have to allow thousands of immigrants a year to enter the country or fundamentally alter their society by encouraging more elderly workers to delay retirement and significantly more women to enter the workforce. The record thus far is not encouraging. Japan has long been one of the most homogeneous societies in the world. In the past, groups, such as the often despised Burakumin and Koreans, regularly faced discrimination from the larger majority society. In today's Japan, there are over 2 million foreigners among the 128 million population. The discrimination they often experience has been sufficiently obvious to attract the attention of United Nations observers who have studied the situation.

Despite Japan's obvious accomplishments in science and technology there are some unusual elements in its delivery of modern medicine. Until recently, Japan adhered to a more traditional definition of life that was defined by the presence of a beating heart regardless of the condition of the patient's brain. This definition has often made it difficult for Japanese medicine to offer its patients some procedures common in the rest of the industrialized world such as heart transplants. In contrast to the United States, procedures like abortion are not controversial in Japan while the use of the birth control pill has only just become legal for contraceptive purposes. It had previously been available for hormonal regulation.

### Japanese Women

On paper Japanese women have rights that American women are still struggling for. Indeed, a Japanese law similar to the American Equal Rights Amendment was passed long ago. As in the United States, the issue of sexual harassment has become an important topic in contemporary Japan.

Despite these gains, Japanese women still earn far less than men and hold far fewer seats in the lower house of representatives.

There have of course been gains. A woman directed the Japanese Socialist Party early in the last decade, and more recently Fusae Ota, a career civil servant was named the first female governor of the Osaka Prefecture. More impressively,

**earthquake damage**

Courtesy of Cecilia Fujishima

## Japan's Triple Horror

Few nations in the years since the Second World War have experienced a level of trauma of the sort Japan experienced in the first months of 2011. In the middle of the day of March 11, the fourth most powerful earthquake in modern world history, measured on the Richter scale at an unimaginable 9, struck just off the northeast eastern coast of Honshu. The earthquake was so powerful that it literally moved the entire island of Honshu almost eight feet further east! As is so often the case with such events, the largest of the earthquakes was preceded and followed by more quakes some as large as 7 on the same scale. What followed was a series of horrors that Japan's prime minister called the worst calamity since the end of the Second World War.

It is certainly true that Japan is far and away one of these countries best prepared for earthquakes. For decades it has done everything it could to modify its buildings and train its population for such challenges. Moreover, it was not just earthquake preparation for which Japan had planned. Indeed, along its coasts many of its cities were protected by what appeared to be impregnable tsunami walls that many other nations would have envied.

But all those well thought-out preparations were not enough. It turned out that even Japan's planners had not fully imagined the fury nature could throw at them. No, this time the situation was quite different, different because the extraordinary earthquake was followed by an enormous tsunami that was as high as 23 feet in places. This wave of water easily rolled over those tsunami walls destroying entire communities and carrying off more than 20,000 people.

As the world knows, the earthquake and tsunami were not the only horror Japan's population would face in the coming days. A significant part of the nation's energy grid was put in jeopardy as at least a half a dozen nuclear plants were caught up in the tragedy, and their operators lost control of the reactors within them. With the disabling of the several nuclear plants, yet another theater of tragedy unfolded as heroic Japanese nuclear workers struggled to limit the amount of radiation released into the atmosphere.

Eventually the slowly unfolding nuclear catastrophe was on the scale of such disasters ranked as a 7, the highest level on the nuclear event scale and the same number "earned" by the infamous Chernobyl disaster in the former Soviet Union almost a quarter of century before. All this, of course, played out as thousands of people beyond those impacted by the devastating tsunami found themselves evacuated from their homes and their agriculture crops declared inedible by the authorities who feared further radiation contamination.

Certainly, each disaster in itself—earthquake, tsunami, and nuclear—was enough to challenge even the especially wealthy and well organized Japanese. But, having so many cascading problems one after another was unbelievably difficult. What made the situation even more demanding was that while the fear of powerful aftershocks from the initial earthquake made some people nervous about remaining in their homes, the concern about the release of radiation into the atmosphere by the stricken nuclear power plants forced many to remain indoors. It was an impossible predicament under the best of circumstances. Even those far beyond the initial damage were drawn into the crisis as food supply lines broke down and the nation experienced rolling electricity blackouts.

By the time the nation had a chance to catch its breath, it became obvious that around 19,000 people had been killed outright by the earthquake and tsunami while hundreds of thousands of others will have their lives disrupted for years to come. Especially painful for the individuals involved will be the uncertainty about the fate of so many of their relatives, uncertainties that for enormous numbers of them will never be resolved.

If there was any silver lining to the horrors of the spring of 2011, it was the role of the Japanese military. Outlawed after World War II, the nation's military establishment, eventually renamed the Japanese Defense Forces, has long experienced suspicion from members of the public, who harbored memories of its violent role in the earlier part of the 20th century. But it was a very different Japanese military that made its mark in the early years of the 21st century. Its personnel played an important role in helping people deal with the most immediate aspects of Japan's spring of horror.

during the summer of 2016 Yuriko Koike, after a financial scandal involving the previous governor, was elected the first female governor of Tokyo.

Ms. Koike had previously served as defense minister of Japan and defied the leadership of the LDP party to run for and eventually win the post.

Studies of Japanese women's lives suggest that they face many challenges when trying to establish themselves as professionals. The general tendency on the part of employers is to assume they will quit their job once they have children and of course society often does pressure them to do so. Thus, it is difficult for women to advance as easily as men. And sometimes the discrimination can be quite blatant. In the summer of 2018 it was revealed that one of Japan's most prestigious medical schools was systematically lowering the academic records of female graduates to keep their numbers in the medical school lower.

Later in life they are expected to spend more time with aged parents than their male counterparts. For those Japanese women who do stay at home the demands of parenting are greater than for most Western women. Japanese men are not expected to take much responsibility in the home and even if they are so inclined, their work schedules rarely allow them enough time to actually do so.

As women age and find their children leaving the home, many are now spending more time and money on themselves. In fact, older Japanese women, often traveling in groups of other women are becoming an important market for the international travel industry while an increasing number of Japanese women are choosing not to marry at all. Given Japan's declining workforce, it also seems likely that more and more of them will remain in the workforce longer in upcoming years.

It is also true that working more does not necessarily offer the same advantages to Japanese women as it does for other women in the Asia Pacific region. According to a study published in early 2013, Japanese women rated second to last among their gender cousins. What the study especially highlighted was not their access to employment or relatively high levels of education, but the fact that they scored particularly low in leadership positions both in the public and private sectors. Only India had a lower score overall for women in the same study.

Japan has also finally begun to make some progress in dealing with its responsibilities toward the World War II–era

# Japan

"comfort women" it enslaved for sexual purposes during the war. Government-sponsored private charities are now funneling funds to its wartime victims, though the government's unwillingness officially to confront its treatment of women during the war is still a subject of considerable anger in some parts of Asia.

### Economy

The experience of Japan in the half-century since World War II has been one of extraordinary sacrifice, impressive accomplishment, and more recently frequent disappointment. World War II brought the virtual destruction of Japan's physical plant, but not of the human qualities that had built it. Among the most important of these were (and are) energy, persistence, a high level of education, impressive technical skills, a high rate of saving, and a willingness (somewhat declining at present) to accept relatively modest living standards.

The American occupation helped the Japanese economy by not imposing war reparations or other excessive burdens on it. The Korean War gave it a major shot in the arm (as did the Vietnam War in the next decade), in the form of official U.S. "offshore procurement" of supplies. By that time, various American specialists were beginning to advise Japanese industry on how it could increase its productivity.

The Japanese government, after the end of the Occupation in 1952, systematically pursued an Asian capitalist style of "industrial policy" aimed at stimulating Japanese recovery on the basis of "export-led growth." Anti-trust policy in Japan is much less severe than in the U.S., and this made it possible for Japanese industry to "rationalize" itself to a high degree in the mid-1950s.

The government, through the Ministry of International Trade and Industry (MITI), was much more involved in economic planning than is common in the United States (at least at the federal level). More concern was put on retaining workers and markets than shareholder's profits. "Sunset industries," such as textiles, were de-emphasized while industries using "leading edge" technologies were promoted: steel, automobiles, electronics, etcetera. This "rationalization" process had a spectacularly beneficial effect on Japan's industrial production and its export position, beginning in the early 1960s. So too did such domestic factors as political stability, social cohesion and a low defense budget, held by treaty to a bit under 1% of the GNP until 1987. External factors, such as the relative openness of the vast U.S. market, also helped greatly. These elements were accompanied by relatively high tariffs the Japanese government imposed on imports, by a maze of import regulations that were actually barriers, by a generally stable international scene and

by the conscious undervaluing (at least until 1971) of the yen, with its stimulating effect on Japanese exports.

But even from the Japanese point of view, there have been some real drawbacks to this process. The cost of living was kept unnecessarily high due to factors ranging from the undervaluing of the yen, the extensive system of middlemen in the distribution system, and barriers to imports, including agricultural products. The Japanese agricultural population is guaranteed high prices and protected from foreign competition for political reasons. Thus food is very expensive. The retail distribution system is very inefficient and costly. It is divided between chains of large, expensive department stores and a huge number of mom and pop corner stores. Housing, public utilities, and the like have been the victims of cumulative under-investment. Thus the average Japanese lives under conditions considerably less pleasant than the overall wealth of the country would suggest.

In spite of these problems, Japan is an industrial giant, third only to the United States. It has proved better able than other industrial economies to cope with the rise in the cost of imported oil. Its large trading companies have proved very effective in penetrating foreign markets, especially that of the U.S. They cope with import quotas, when imposed by foreign governments, through "up scaling" (keeping the number of exported units within the quotas, but improving their quality and increasing their price, while staying somewhat below the prices of competitive goods produced in the countries of destination).

Japan's regional economic role within Asia had also grown significantly over the past decades. In fact, Asia, rather than the United States, had become the principal area of Japanese trade before the drama of 1997's economic meltdown in much of the area. There were many reasons Japan had become so involved in the region.

Japanese corporations had turned to Southeast Asia to solve some of their own economic problems. Facing a tendency by Japanese workers to demand higher pay and shorter hours, Japanese industry moved much of its production overseas, especially to China and Southeast Asia. This Japanese investment, coupled with the opening of China under Deng Xiaoping, spurred impressive economic growth in much of Southeast Asia. Japan had also become a leading investor in Vietnam, a country that because of the long-lasting U.S. economic embargo had been unable to obtain U.S. investment for years. In short, for much of Japan's postwar history, while the individual consumer was

**Statue of Saigo Takamori, hero and nemesis of the Meiji Restoration**

often hard pressed to make ends meet, the economy as a whole had done well.

But that situation changed significantly in the last decade of the 20th century. Bank failures became more common, and the entire Japanese banking industry was being dragged down by a bad loans. The stock market also has weakened, and the economy lost the momentum that had once made it seem invincible. Moreover, the bubble burst on land prices and they too declined dramatically. Of course, the government tried to deal with the problem by employing a series of policies from direct "pump priming"—that is enhanced government spending—through more significant calls for major restructuring. In late 2002, for example, Tokyo approved a governmental spending package of more than $12 billion to be spent on public works and various "safety net" programs to ease the hardship of these difficult economic times. Particularly important has been the effort on the part of the Japanese government to pressure the banks into dealing with the rising level of bad debts. This pressure was backed up by threats to nationalize the banking industry.

Another significant economic development within the Japanese economy in recent years has been the growth in foreign control of some of her most important industries. The American Ford Motor Company recently took over a controlling interest in Mazda, and Britain's Cable and Wireless bought Japan's International Digital Communications. The idea of foreign firms purchasing domestic companies was something quite familiar to citizens of many other countries. But for Japan it was something quite new. Clearly, the weak Japanese economy of the previous decade made these dramatic changes possible.

These changes have had positive aspects, if not for Japanese corporations than for the Japanese public. Consumers have long shouldered the burden of artificially high prices for most of the goods they consumed from rice to electronics. The Japanese model seemed to be one of excellent service coupled with high prices regardless of what people actually wanted. But those days may be passing. The declining price of land coupled with changing consumer attitudes and regulatory changes made it possible for the larger American-style super store and malls to make significant inroads into Japan. These developments may not please the Japanese corporations or small businesses, but they will certainly have a positive impact on consumer satisfaction.

As the new century unfolded, the Japanese economy, after so many years of recession, finally started showing signs of a limited recovery. While part of the improvement was tied to the American economy, a more significant percentage is directly tied to Japan's growing exports to the increasingly large China market. In fact, "Greater China," that ethnic block that includes not only Hong Kong and Taiwan but the People's Republic, not long ago became the largest single market for Japanese goods. Even more recently China alone passed the United States as Japan's most important trading partner.

Perhaps the most dramatic example of Japan's economic recovery in the years before 2008 was the news that Toyota was on the brink of passing General Motors as the world's largest automaker. This is a reality made possible in no small part by the Toyota's willingness to embrace so much more enthusiastically the growing consumer demand for more environmentally green and economic hybrid cars.

But while embracing green energy hybrid cars was clearly an important strategic decision by the nation's automakers, it was in itself not enough to shield the nation's carmakers from the worldwide recession that began in late-2008 and drained consumer demand for Japan's products from nations as diverse as China and the United States. For a nation that lacks the energy resources some other nations enjoy, the recession came as part of a double-edged economic body blow. Before the economic crash, Japan's energy bills for imported fossil fuels had gone up extraordinarily fast. This was a burden that was only relieved as energy prices dropped in the wake of the even more dramatic crash in the demand for its products.

As in the United States and China, Tokyo immediately turned to the development of various government-sponsored stimulus programs that it hoped would keep the economy from doing a total tailspin and start moving the nation toward recovery. Eventually they implemented three different stimulus programs that totaled about $275 billion. The new Japanese Democratic government trimmed some of the spending after it came into power. Unfortunately, by late spring 2010 the Japanese economy had still not regained significant economic health. Rather, it was still plagued by a deflationary process that also saw significant unemployment.

More recently, though, Japan's economy received two very different shocks, one symbolic and the other far more fundamentally damaging. Only a few months after China passed Japan to become the world's second largest economy, the islands experienced a challenge significantly less symbolic and much more immediate. In March of 2011, one of the worst earthquakes in generations, a 9 on the famous Richter scale, hit northern Japan. The quake was bad enough. But it then created a devastating tsunami, literally a massive wall of water, slamming into the city of Sendia and a whole host of other smaller coastal communities. It caused a huge amount of damage, killing tens of thousands, while disabling some of the nation's nuclear plants.

The short-term blow to the economy was very significant especially as many of the nation's leading industries were unable to procure the supplies they needed to keep their factories operating. In the long term, of course, repairing the extraordinary damage caused by these horrific blows will take years. For a country that already has staggering debt levels to take on these new economic challenges will further weaken the nation's economic health for a long time.

With the return of the Liberal Democratic Party to power in late 2012 a new effort was instituted to try to reinvigorate the economy that included plans not only for further government stimulus spending to exploring the feasibility of a new regional pacts, and especially so after the American Trump administration withdrew its support for the trading pact it had long promoted.

The Kishida government that took over in 2021 has been long on economic soundbites but rather short on practical measures. It still has to cope with the ongoing effect of COVID but figures for 2021 were good and the recovery continued in the early months of 2022.

## The Environment and the Challenge of Climate Change

Among the major civilizations on the planet, the Japanese are perhaps the best known for their reverence to the environment. Indeed, who can even reflect on Japan without thinking about its Shinto-inspired reverence for the physical surroundings of the islands, from the nation's waterfalls to its beautifully mountainous terrain? Each spring, Americans head for their own nation's capital to enjoy the cherry blossoms that adorn the American capital, a gift of the Japanese people to the people of America that dates from 1912. The Japanese focus on the development of extraordinary gardening techniques is appreciated throughout world.

Japan also has the distinction of being one of the earliest peoples seriously to undertake an effort to preserve their nation's forests through a complicated series of local and regional efforts developed in the 1600s. They emerged out of a clear recognition of the demands a growing and increasingly urbanized society was making on the nation's forests. They eventually

# Japan

saw a sophisticated system of forest management emerge by the late 17th century.

But Japan's taking on the challenge of deforestation, even within the context of Shinto's gift of nature appreciation, which is so common to Japanese culture, did not prepare the nation for the challenges of modern industrial society and the dangers inherent in modern chemical processes. Indeed, by the 1950s many Japanese found themselves victims of one of the earliest and most famous of the postwar environmental disasters: the mercury-poisoned community of Minamata. In that now infamous case, extraordinarily dangerous amounts of mercury were careless dumped into the Minamata Bay. The mercury, which is extremely toxic, slowly worked its way through the local community causing profound birth defects and physical illnesses whose full effects and reach are only now being more completely understood. More recently Japan's most dramatic challenge has been less regional than global, the challenge of a radically changing planetary climate system impacted by the prolific burning of fossil fuels.

Japan was the first nation in Asia to fully industrialize. Not surprisingly it did so in the same fashion as the West, by burning prodigious amounts of coal to fuel the steam engines of 19th-century industrialization. Soon after, they began utilizing petroleum products in internal combustion engines. Given how long carbon pollution stays in the atmosphere, the longevity of industrialization can matter as much as annual emissions. Even today Japan might have an enviable reputation for energy efficiency (see below). The nation ranks fourth in carbon emissions.

Indeed, those emissions have been going up in recent years as problems within the nuclear industry have often forced more fossil fuel imports at times. Still its overall contribution is less than a quarter of either China or America's emissions. But not being as responsible for the problem hardly shields the country from the current and expected challenges to come.

As we have seen elsewhere, average temperatures are rising in Japan while heat waves are becoming more common. More immediately flooding and other water-related disasters have become more frequent as warmer air carries and discharges larger

amounts of water producing challenges from flooding to mud slides. Most dramatically the Itsukushima Shinto Shrine, a World Heritage Site particular vulnerable given its location, has increasingly become more often submerged.

Japanese agriculture has already been affected by changing temperature patterns that have negatively impacted farming caused by a range of problems, such as unusual heat spells and the arrival of more invasive species. The nation's fisheries have been impacted by the arrival of new fish species from more southern waters and the reduction of more traditional species whose numbers are diminishing, apparently in part due to climate change.

Most recently, heat waves have become more common. Indeed from the summer of 2012 to 2018 heat waves have become more and more deadly. And as we have seen, when rain does fall, it is more likely to do so more quickly with more devastating results.

Public polling reveals that well over 90% of the population understands that the global climate is clearly changing and that the assumption of negative consequences

Courtesy of Joel Z. Leibo

126

# Japan

is widespread. Nevertheless, transforming the nature of the nation's energy infrastructure is as complicated in Japan as it is anywhere else.

In other environmental issues, Japan's late 2018 decision to renew commercial whaling deeply hurt its international reputation among environmental activists.

### Energy

As a nation Japan has few sources of energy on its soil and has had to import almost all of its needs from abroad, especially the Middle East. Historically Japan met the vast majority of its oil needs from the volatile Middle East region. Indeed, the only nations that have recently imported more were China and the United States. In fact, China recently passed Japan and the United States to become the world's largest oil importer.

During the oil embargo in the early 1970s, the threatened cutoff of energy supplies proved particularly shocking to Japan's elites. In the years since, Japan has become not only one of the most energy-efficient nations on earth, but it has built up an impressive strategic reserve to help cushion such oil shocks. It is true as well that the Japanese government understands that meeting the current energy needs of the world's third-largest economy has become considerably more complicated in recent years.

With that in mind, the Ministry of Economy and Trade has regularly issued new National Energy Strategy documents to reduce fundamentally the nation's dependence on world oil resources while expanding its commitment to nuclear energy. A very ambitious goal at first to expand the percentage of power Japan gained from nuclear power from an impressive 29% to approximately 50% over the upcoming decades.

Of course, that was before the tsunami-based nuclear catastrophe hit Japan in the spring of 2011. In the aftermath of the crisis, Japan's then prime minister announced plans to move even more aggressively into the renewable energy field. The decision was not surprising given the Japanese people's experience with radiation during the Second World War, the more recent nuclear scares and its well documented history of the kind of earthquakes that can threaten such facilities. Still, Japan and the former Soviet Union are the only nations to have suffered the full-scale implications of a massive release of radiation into the atmosphere: for Japan after Hiroshima, Nagasaki, and more recently Fukushima, while the former USSR lived through the disaster at Chernobyl in 1986.

The expanded commitment to carving out a new green energy future had, of course, begun well before the horrific tsunami of 2011. In the transportation area, for example, the government mandated in 2010 that all new cars would be required to operate with fuel that includes 10% ethanol. In another sign of the future, Japan airlines carried out in January 2009 its first test of a new green energy fuel.

The most immediate issue, though, is how the Japanese perceive the experience of the summer of 2012 when the nation's entire nuclear-energy-generating facility went off line. The reader might ask how such a thing could happen. Japan's nuclear industry normally undergoes regular testing and recertification. By the summer of 2012 the entire nuclear industry, those plants that were on line and those destroyed by the earthquake and tsunami, were scheduled to go off line because the process of recertification had understandably become so much more complicated. By May of 2012 the last of them actually did so. For the first time since the 1970s Japan was without nuclear energy, a source which before the Fukushima disaster had been supplying almost 30% of the nation's energy needs.

For some it was expected to be an opportunity to demonstrate that Japan could meet its energy needs without nuclear power while others expected the demands of the summer to force people to recognize that nuclear energy had to be part of the nation's energy mix. In the long term, of course, a much more critical issue looms: whether Japan can supply its energy needs without nuclear power while not relying even more heavily on those fossil fuels that exacerbate anthropogenic climate change.

As so often happens in many societies and especially in democracies, the question of energy priorities has become a political issue between competing electoral groups. In Japan's case, the Japanese Democratic Party arrived in power committed to an especially ambitious plan to address climate change and the complementary green energy conversion. It was the Japanese Democratic Party that was in power during the many faceted Fukushima crises. In the two years after that horrendous series of disasters, the party saw its popularity plunge. Its subsequent loss at the polls facilitated the return of Japan's Liberal Democratic Party to power.

The former prime minister, Shinzo Abe, h ordered a reevaluation of his predecessor's, Yukio Hatoyama's, 2010 pledge to lower Japan's carbon emissions to 1990-level emissions by 25% and to do so by the year 2020. Abe also made it clear that he did not share his predecessor's distrust of nuclear energy. He initially reopened two of the nuclear plants that had been temporarily closed. That new start for the nation's nuclear industry has turned out to be less significant than some might have expected. Indeed most the plants that were operating before Fukushima are still off line.

### COVID-19

Japan's first case of the COVID-19 virus was found on15 January 2020, in a person in Kanagawa Prefecture, near Tokyo who had returned from Wuhan Cases rose slowly until the end of March, when people returning from Europe were the cause. The total number of cases remained low. By the end of October, there were some 100,000 cases. This rose to 200,000 in December, 300,00 by mid-January 2021, and reached 500,00 by mid-April 2021. Deaths remained relatively low until the end of 2020, reaching some 4,000 by the end of the year. This was followed by a sharp increase, taking the total to 10,000 by the end of April 2021. The relatively low number of both cases and deaths, despite some very large cities and an elderly population, was attributed to the early closure of schools, tight border controls, and the introduction of a partial state of emergency on 7 April 2020, extended nationwide two weeks later. Under this, people were requested not to go to bars or restaurants, which largely seemed to work, although there were some who ignored the rules. The Japanese tradition of mask wearing and avoiding physical contact were also credited with containing numbers. The 2020 Summer Olympics, due to be held in Tokyo, were postponed until 2021.

However, when the various measures were relaxed from May 2020, numbers rose again, leading to criticism of the government's actions. One particular issue was a scheme introduced in July 2020, the "GoTo Scheme" in which the government subsidized domestic travel for residents only, in an attempt to revive the flagging tourist industry. While it may have helped tourism, it also allowed the virus to spread. It was suspended in December 2020 and is unlikely to resume until June 2021 at the earliest. The handling of the disease had economic and political consequences. Exports were hit hard, and the prime minister's popularity went into a major decline. As the numbers infected rose steadily in Spring 2021, and the government continued to flounder, Suga's popularity continued low, Although plans for the Olympics went ahead, it was clear that these would be Olympics like no others. No foreign spectators would be allowed. While the Olympic Torch began its journey through all the 47 prefectures, starting in Fukushima in March, many places saw protests at its passage. By mid-May,

# Japan

with major cities, including Tokyo, in lockdown, opinion polls indicated that 66 percent of the people wanted the games cancelled.

In the event, as noted earlier, a rather subdued set of games went ahead, with few spectators and the athletes carefully confined to bubbles when not competing. Perhaps Suga's face had been saved but again as noted, it did not do him much good politically.

COVID did not go away. By late May 2022, there had been 8.63 million cases, with 30,336 deaths. There were spikes in August–September 2021, and a much bigger one that began in January 2022. By late May, it was tailing off, but figures remained high and controls remained in place. In May, however, it was announced that there would be a strictly limited resumption of tourism

After the slow start in 2021, vacciations began to pick up. By May 2002, they had reached 82.2% with one dose, 81% with one, and 57.9% had received a booster dose.

## The Future

Under Abe, Japan saw a major shift away from overt 70 years of pacifism. has coincided with a more assertive Chinese foreign policy. The result has been greater momentum than has long been the case toward not only reevaluating the nation's conduct during the Second World War, a struggle largely playing out in the nation's classrooms, to a more muscular role for the nation's military in light of China's growing assertiveness.

Significant over the last year was the successful passage of legislation promoted by Japan's conservatives to allow the Japanese Defense forces to serve overseas and take on a formal military role both in defense of Japan and its allies. The bill, which passed over strenuous objects of the opposition, aroused considerable public passion before it passed in 2015.

Clearly its passage was yet another example of how much the world order that prevailed in the half century after the end of the Second World War is fading into historical memory.

Indeed, as the world moved more deeply into 2017, it was becoming obvious that Japan's leaders were increasingly committed to expanding the nation's ability to defend the country and project military power. In the summer of 2016 Prime Minister Abe submitted a record military spending bill to the national parliament which represented the fifth year of requested growth for the nation's defense establishment.

Given the more assertive tone of recent Chinese foreign policy and the current enthusiasm in the United States for reevaluating its longtime alliances and global role that was probably a prudent move but one that is likely to add to tensions in the region over the upcoming years.

But as noted, Japan faces other major challenges, especially with a declining birthrate and an aging and declining population.

# The Republic of Korea (South Korea)

**Bulguksa, Buddhist temple dating from Silla Period**

**Area:** 38,452 sq. mi. (99,720 sq. km., somewhat larger than Indiana)

**Population:** 51,829,023 (December 2020 census)

**Capital City:** Seoul, pop. 9,985,562 (2020)

**Climate:** Temperate, with a short winter, hot and humid in the summer with a rainy monsoon from July to September.

**Neighboring Countries:** North Korea (North); Japan (East)

**Official Language:** Korean

**Other Principal Tongues:** English and Chinese. Very old Koreans may also speak Japanese.

**Ethnic Background:** Korean, related to Manchurian and Mongolian

**Principal Religions:** Buddhism, Confucianism, Christianity

**Main Exports:** (to U.S. and Japan) Textiles and clothing, electrical machinery, footwear, steel, ships, fish, automobiles, and electronics

**Main Imports:** (from Saudi Arabia, China, Japan, and the U.S.) Machinery, oil, transport equipment, chemicals, grains, petrochemicals, and electronics

**Currency:** Won

**Former Colonial Status:** Korea was a tributary state of the Chinese empires for certain periods until 1895; Japanese protectorate (1905–1910); Japanese De-pendency (1910–1945); South Korea was occupied by the U.S. from 1945 to 1948

**National Day:** August 15, 1945 (Republic Day)

**Chief of State:** Moon Jie-in, became president May 10, 2017

**Prime Minister:** Kim Boo-kyum (since April 16, 2021)

**National Flag:** White, with a center circle divided equally by an S-curve into blue and red portions; there is a varying combination of 3 solid and 3 broken lines in each corner.

**Per Capita GDP Income:** $42,251 (World Bank 2020) (purchasing power parity)

The predominantly mountainous peninsula of Korea is actually an extension of the mountains of southern Manchuria, from which it is separated by the Yalu and Tumen Rivers. The spine of the mountains runs from northeast to southwest, but remains close to the eastern coastline area of Korea. Eastern Korea is thus rugged, containing many scenic mountain peaks. The famous Diamond Mountains (Kimgansan) in North Korea are particularly spectacular, reaching their greatest height in the Changpai San at the northern border, where the peaks are snow-covered all year.

From these immense mountains, streams gather to form the Yalu River which empties into the Yellow Sea, and the Tumen River which flows into the Sea of Japan. The steep descent of these rivers provides one of the world's best sources of hydroelectric power, with a great potential that has only begun to be developed. The western coastal regions contain most of the peninsula's level plains, interspersed with frequent rivers. This is the agricultural belt where rice predominates, raised in wet paddies in the South, where

two crops are harvested each year, and grown in the North on dry plantations, where only one crop matures at the end of the summer.

Tidal variations along the west coast are extreme; there is sometimes a difference of 30 feet between low and high tide. The offshore islands, numbering about 3,500,

# South Korea

**Downtown Seoul around 1923**

Courtesy of Mark Jihun Suk

are the remnants of the mountain chain, standing with their shoulders above water. The long coastline and the nearness to some of the richest fishing grounds in the world have made the people, especially in the South, skilled fishermen. This has led to frequent tensions with individual Japanese fishing boats and with Japanese governments because the people of the overcrowded neighboring islands desperately need the same protein which the Koreans harvest from the sea.

The cooler climate of North Korea resembles that of Manchuria. It is better endowed with minerals, hydroelectric facilities, and capacity. The lower regions of the mountains support thick stands of timber. South Korea has a warmer climate, which supports a greater agricultural production. In December, the temperatures in Pusan may be mild at the same time that frigid blasts of below-zero arctic weather envelope the remote mountains of the North. Historically, the Siberian black bear and leopard mingled with fierce wild boars, Manchurian tigers, and smaller Korean tigers in the thinly populated northern region. In the more southern part of the peninsula the warmth increases as the animal life becomes more nearly tropical, dominated by herons, gulls, and other birds with colorful plumage.

## History

Given their appearance and language, the Koreans seem to have similar origins to the Turkic-Manchurian-Mongol people who have inhabited northeastern Asia for thousands of years and migrated to the island of Japan as well as to the Korean peninsula. People have lived in Korea from long before 10000 B.C. But the more specific origins of the Korean people lie with the arrival of two distinct groups to the peninsula: first a Neolithic culture of fishermen and shellfish gatherers who arrived around 8000 B.C. and later, from around the 1500 B.C., a community that lived as well by hunting. These early inhabitants of the peninsula were similar to other Altaic, Tungusic tribes that inhabited the regions now known as Manchuria and Siberia as is evidenced by comparing their various tools, from ceramics to daggers and mirrors. One particular type of knife associated with women was, in fact, common among peoples from East Asia to North American Indians and Eskimos.

Although the exact chronology is less than clear, it appears that the use of bronze metal technology came into existence somewhere between 1000 B.C. to 800 B.C. Archeological evidence suggests the presence of many tribal communities of limited size, the most important of which was eventually the state of Old Choson, which emerged around the 2nd century based in the northwestern part of the peninsula in the area around the present day North Korean capital of Pyongyang. Korean society then, as now, was intimately tied to developments within their enormous northern neighbor China and in the first centuries B.C. much of Korea came under Chinese control.

### The Chinese Commanderies

By 108 B.C., the Choson capital had fallen to the Chinese armies and their leaders the emperors of the famous Han dynasty which established several administrative divisions in the northern part of the peninsula. Especially important was the Chinese establishment of a base at Nakrang where an enormously sophisticated society, largely based on Chinese models, would emerge. New artistic and philosophical systems were introduced as well as the Chinese administrative styles. Significant numbers of Chinese colonists arrived as well, and Nakrang would remain important for the next several hundred years. Though the Koreans would strongly resist direct Chinese control and eventually regain their independence, the influence of Chinese cultural norms and the interest they would hold for Koreans would in many ways continue through the modern day. Like the Japanese, the Koreans would reject important aspects of Chinese civilization from the more merit-based Confucian examination system to its historical disdain for the military. Both Korea and Japan, despite their twin enthusiasms for Chinese civilization, would retain their emphasis on a hereditary aristocracy and honored military elite.

**Modern Seoul**

### The Three Kingdoms

By the 1st century B.C. three Korean kingdoms would establish themselves; Koguryo in the north, Silla on the southeast part of the peninsula and Paekche in the southwest. In each kingdom a powerful hereditary monarchy evolved that ruled with a centralized system of control. Each of these kingdoms was under strong Chinese cultural influence, including Mahayana (northern) Buddhism, Confucianism and the Chinese written language. Especially interesting is the fact that there is now considerable evidence to suggest that the original Yamato Japanese state that later developed on the nearby islands may have been an offshoot of the early Korean kingdom of Paekche.

During the 7th century, the Silla kingdom, initially working with the powerful Tang dynasty of China, defeated each of its rivals and emerged in domination. Later in the century, Silla's leaders even managed to drive out the Chinese and establish themselves dominant over most of the peninsula.

Over the next years, as Silla's leaders established themselves, a more centralized Chinese-style administrative trend was adopted that even included an exam system similar to what the Chinese were employing. The Chinese language was used as the principal means of written communication and even Tang clothing styles were adopted. It was during Silla's domination that the effort began to create a phonetic system for writing Korean which, by the centuries later become today's modern alphabet-like system known as han'gul (Chosungul in North Korea).

It was also during these years, inspired by the interest of Silla's leadership, that Buddhism became particularly important on the peninsula. A large number of Koreans studied in China itself and the Buddhist establishment grew enormously with the emergence of large numbers of monasteries.

Externally, Silla, although dominant on the peninsula, considered itself part of the Chinese world order. Practically, this meant sending tribute missions to the Tang capital and having their representatives perform the kowtow to the emperors, which meant to kneel and touch the forehead to the ground in deep respect. But if Silla managed to maintain Korea's independence from China it was less lucky with its own internal enemies, and by the early 10th century they had lost control of the peninsula to a new state that called itself Koryo, from which we derive the modern Western name for the country.

Korea's years of independence were brutally interrupted by the arrival of the Mongol armies who occupied the peninsula and used it as a launching pad for their two attacks against Japan in the 13th century. At the beginning of the 13th century the Mongol attack forced the Koryo government to withdraw to an island (Gangwha in Korean), north of modern day Inchon. Within a generation after more devastating attacks the Koryo leadership was forced to submit to Mongol demands that included taking part in what were fated to be the unsuccessful Mongol invasions of Japan. In two attacks late in the century, Mongol warriors, sailing in ships made by the accomplished Korean ship building industry, tried to expand their power to Japan. But as discussed in the Japan chapter, the attacks failed in the face of adverse weather conditions and Japanese resistance. For the Koreans, involvement in the campaigns was a disaster.

Even during the era of Mongol control Korean culture survived. Socially the aristocracy continued its influence and, now disdaining Buddhism, embraced a Chinese style neo-Confucianism, a particularly metaphysical form of the historical Chinese system of social relations.

Not surprisingly, the overthrow of the Mongol dynasty in China by the new Chinese Ming dynasty had ramifications within Korea that contained supporters of both ruling groups. For Korea itself, the ultimate outcome was the capture of the Koryo capital by General Yi Song-gye and the establishment of the longest lasting of Korean dynasties, which extended from 1392 to 1910 when it was abolished by the Japanese. Formally known as the Choson dynasty it is also known as the Yi dynasty after its founder. Its capital city, Hanyang, is today better known as Seoul.

### Yi Korea (1392–1910)

Violent power struggles within the ruling family marked the first years of the dynasty. Still, overall the Yi showed great creativity, wisdom, and artistry, advancing in the field of astronomy and perfecting han'gul (known as chosungul in North Korea), the alphabet-like system that by the 20th century would become the common instrument of writing Korean. Although governed by a local line of rulers, Korea remained a faithful tributary of the Chinese empire and one so devoted to Confucian civilization that it vehemently rejected the Buddhist orientation of previous generations. Eventually they were to embrace a neo-Confucian ideology so completely that most scholars believe them to have been far more Confucian than even the Chinese themselves. The government strengthened the Chinese-style administrative structure and examination system even more thoroughly than previous Korean regimes though the Chinese emphasis on true social mobility

# South Korea

never really took hold. For Koreans, the system of hereditary elites remained more attractive.

Despite their nobler births the Korean aristocracy in these years, like others in East and Southeast Asia, very consciously modeled themselves on China's scholar-gentry ruling class. Of course, as Japan would also do, they created their own distinctively Korean variation of the Chinese model. In Korea the elites were known as Yangban, a hereditary class whose members were most respected when they combined impressive ancestors, land and office holdings and, above all, devotion to scholarly accomplishments. This Korean version of elite society was to prove remarkably resilient and to survive well into the modern era. Given the introduction of han'gul, the phonetic writing and the educational priorities of the Korean Confucian elite, it is not surprising that these years saw an enormous growth in the production of printing, for the most part in Chinese, the first large-scale efforts anywhere in the world.

Socially, traditional Korea had differed dramatically from China in its earlier treatment of women. Korean women enjoyed a level of freedom that is said to have amazed visiting Chinese. They were able to inherit, and a new husband could marry into a woman's family and reside there among his in-laws in contrast to the usual Asian pattern of brides always being the ones to relocate.

As we have seen, during the 15th century Korea's new leaders embraced a neo-Confucianism that was more orthodox than even found in China itself. This closer embrace of Confucianism did not bode well for Korean women, whose status diminished over the centuries.

Technically, Korea was, throughout this era, more advanced than the West. From its accomplishments in printing to mathematics and instrumentation engineering, Korean society was very impressive on the eve of the Western arrival. But these accomplishments were dramatically interrupted when, once again, Korea's location between two powerful neighbors put its people at risk. Just as in the 13th-century Mongol armies had used Korea to attack Japan, by the late 1500s Koreans once again found themselves condemned by their location. In 1592 the Japanese, led by Toyotomi Hideyoshi, invaded the peninsula with almost 160,000 soldiers in an ill-fated effort to conquer China.

The Koreans defended themselves with a remarkable flotilla of the world's first armor-plated warships, the famous "Turtle Ships" which effectively destroyed the Japanese fleets. Moreover, with the help of the Ming they were successful in defending the peninsula, but the damage was

**Former President Lee Myung-Bak**

overwhelming. After a second assault in 1597 when, after Hideyoshi's death, the Japanese finally withdrew, both nations entered an era of increased isolation from their neighbors.

While life would soon calm in Japan, Koreans experienced more trauma. The recovery had hardly begun before Koreans faced yet another trial, the conquest of China by the Manchu and their own inclusion in this new emerging Sino-Manch Empire. From the Korean perspective, the fall of the much-admired Chinese Ming Empire to the Manchuwas an astounding cultural disaster that left many of them believing that Korea alone remained the last bastion of Confucian civilization. It was a sentiment many Russians had felt a century before when the exalted Christian Byzantine Empire had fallen to the arriving Ottomans. In Eastern Europe many Russians had begun to think of themselves as the new or Third Rome after Constantinople fell. At the other end of the enormous Eurasian land mass, Koreans, observing the collapse of Ming China, often felt themselves to be playing a similar role as the last defenders of true Confucian civilization.

Over the next centuries, although Korean pride in its Confucian accomplishments

**Former President Park Geun-hye**

soared, so too did intellectual and court factionalism that would eventually make the nation less prepared to deal with the challenges to come. On the international level Korea became intensely isolationist, as committed to its own inward looking perspective as its much disliked Japanese neighbors. Nevertheless, Korea did have its own scholars somewhat akin to the famous Japanese "Dutch Scholars," who also made efforts to understand Western technology and ideas.

Over the next centuries, Europeans who were occasionally shipwrecked on the rough coastline were held captive while Japanese and Chinese who happened upon Korean shores were expeditiously sent packing. It was a far cry from the Korea of earlier centuries which is said to have been much more open to the world. During these centuries that immediately preceded the arrival of the Westerners the Koreans were content with their many official expeditions to Beijing. Nevertheless even during those activities Korean concerns about the outside world remained profound. While they were able to roam freely within Beijing during their visits, the Chinese envoy's movements were severely restricted in Seoul.

### The Dawn of Imperialist Pressures

By the middle of the 19th century, Western pressures in East Asia had become intense. The Europeans during the two Opium wars forced open China and the Americans had done the same thing in Japan. It was now Korea's turn to feel the pressures of imperialism, but in her case it would ultimately be Japan that would determine its fate. But that thrust would be later. Early on it was the Westerners, specifically the French and Americans, who applied the first pressures. Within Korea, as we have seen, the Yi dynasty like Japan a generation earlier was vehemently committed to maintaining its isolation and the first contacts suggested that goal might be possible.

In 1866 a confrontation broke out with an American commercial vessel, the *General Sherman*, that ended with the death of all those on the American ship. Unfortunately, these early and successful efforts to resist outside pressures did not last. When a few years later the Americans retaliated against Korea for firing on American ships, the assault resulted in the deaths of more than 600 Korean soldiers. Some months later in 1866, the Koreans successfully drove a French force away from Gangwha island near Inchon. A generation later in 1882, the United States became the first Western nation to open treaty relations with the Koreans, followed by Britain and other Western countries. However, it was with Japan that Korea's external relations were to become particularly complicated and painful.

### The Beginning of the Japanese Assault

Koreans had long looked with disdain at their island neighbor, Japan's, efforts to remake itself on a Western model in the decades after Perry's arrival. In fact, their attitude almost provoked an indignant Japanese attack early in the 1870s. For the moment the Japanese decided against an expedition but a generation later Japan's attitude would be quite different. Over the next years, at China's urging, the court signed a series of treaties with the various Western powers. From China's perspective, which saw Korea as part of its own world order, Korean treaties with the Western powers provided some protection from Japanese demands.

Inside Korea, nationalists and the more educated youth often looked to Japan as a source of inspiration and direction. On the other hand, the elderly conservatives remained attached to the traditional Confucian empire of the Manchus. When an internal power struggle broke out during the 1870s the Japanese decided to intervene and dispatched a flotilla to the peninsula. It was an act not so very different from the American effort in the 1850s. This time, though, it was the Japanese who were making the demands rather than being the victims. The resulting treaty opened several Korean ports to the Japanese and not surprisingly aroused the ire of Korean conservatives and their supporters in China.

In the following decade an intense rivalry between the Chinese and Japanese over their relative influence in Korea was carried out and was paralleled within Korea by different factions who preferred one or the other of their neighbors. Ironically, given later events, the more progressive among the Koreans favored the Japanese having been impressed with that nation's willingness to embrace Western technical skills. More than once tensions and violence between the two groups encouraged further meddling in Korean affairs by China and Japan.

Given the intense imperialistic tone of the age a clash was inevitable. The explosion came in 1894. Initially it was internal developments, not international events, which set the stage. Within Korea a new popular movement, the Tonghaks, somewhat like the Chinese Taipings, had arisen. It was a movement that emphasized both traditional values, including Korean spiritualism, elements similar to Catholicism and was inspired by a general egalitarianism.

The Tonghaks were also anti-Japanese as well as antagonistic to the Westerners. More immediately it was driven by the distress of many in the peasant class who were hard-pressed by the exploitative demands of the Korean ruling classes. The new Japanese economic demands also added to the peasantry's plight and by the early 1890s a full-scale revolt had broken out. By the time the movement turned into an uprising it had become a major agrarian revolution.

In the ensuing turmoil, the Korean King Kojong called for Chinese help. Meanwhile, the Japanese used the occasion to rush troops to the peninsula. With little resistance, the Japanese drove the Chinese forces out of Korea. It was the first stage of what would become Korea's nightmare experience as a Japanese colony.

But the Japanese were not yet able to establish their undisputed control over Korea. The nearby Russians, whose empire bordered on Korea, had also developed considerable interest in the peninsula. But within 10 years the Japanese and Russians would also fight over the increasingly prostrate Korean peninsula. After more than a millennium of independence, Korea was once again caught by its own geography between more powerful forces.

### Becoming a Japanese Colony

When the short Russo-Japanese War of 1904–1905 resulted in a Japanese victory and the establishment of a Japanese protectorate over Korea, Tokyo was ready to make its move. With little opposition, Japan annexed the peninsula in 1910,

forcing a treaty on Koreans; arguments about the legality of that treaty are stil common. Korea became the largest dependency of the growing Japanese empire. It was, after all, the age of imperialism and such exploitative moves were common during these years. In fact, the Japanese had only just finished watching the Americans subdue those Philippine forces who had attempted to resist the American occupation of their land. Sadly, the Japanese occupation was to prove considerably more brutal than what the Americans imposed in their colony.

Japanese rule was very harsh and devoted to creating investment opportunities for Japanese capital, raising rice to feed Japan and establishing military bases and a railway system designed for further expansion on the Asian continent. Whether most Koreans agreed or not, the long-isolated peninsula was being transformed by the changes introduced by the Japanese.

On a purely technical level the Korea that eventually regained its freedom half a century later was the most developed of East and Southeast Asia's former colonies. But those industrial advantages hardly outweighed the humiliations of Japanese control.

Almost from the establishment of the Japanese protectorate in 1905, a committed Korean resistance movement began which did everything in its power to resist Japanese control. In 1909, they even managed to assassinate Ito Hirobumi, Japan's revered hero of the Meiji Restoration during his tenure as Japan's highest official in Korea. The Japanese were outraged

**The Gateway in the Ancient Walls of Seoul**

# South Korea

A game of Go-ban, or oriental chess. Korean Minister of War, Yun-Woong-Niel, is on the left (1900)

A young Korean and his wife in street dress, Seoul (1902)

and the peninsula's formal annexation occurred soon after.

The best-known resistance occurred in the spring of 1919 when, angered by open Japanese exploitation and inspired by newly learned democratic slogans used in World War I, hundreds of thousands of Koreans, many of whom had converted to Christianity, staged a massive, peaceful demonstration in favor of independence.

Outraged by the thousands of demonstrators who took part in declaring a Korean Declaration of Independence, Japanese officials brutally suppressed the peaceful demonstrations arresting and killing thousands. For Korea, those years were traumatic and resistance was common. Throughout the era, Koreans both within Korea and beyond its borders fought against Japan's control and hoped through efforts ranging from guerrilla warfare through international protests to force the Japanese out. But as with most other occupations it is true as well that many Koreans threw in their lot with the Japanese and attempted to advance by serving within the colonial administration. After all, by 1920, it looked as though

the Japanese were well-established in Korea and the end of their rule seemed far off.

Relaxing their rule briefly during the 1920s because of adverse Korean and world popular opinion, the Japanese intensified their exploitation when they undertook the conquest of Manchuria and China in the 1930s. In an effort to avoid further unrest, they attempted to absorb the Koreans by forcing them to adopt Japanese names and to speak the language of their conquerors. This had little lasting effect and actually served to further embitter the Koreans against the Japanese.

As the Pacific War developed in the 1930s the Koreans naturally found themselves caught up again in Japanese ambitions first to conquer China and later the assault on Southeast Asia. What the Japanese colonial authorities wanted of their Korean subjects was their labor. Millions were sent to Japan to serve as forced laborers during the war.

But working in Japan's factories and mines was not the only thing the Japanese demanded of their Korean victims. Along with young women from other parts of Asia, thousands of Korean women were

forced to serve as prostitutes for the Japanese army. Euphemistically referred to as "comfort women," somewhere between 100,000 and 200,000 Korean women were forced into sexual slavery during the Second World War. At the same time, a number of Koreans joined the Japanese armed forces, among them future president Park Chung-hye.

It was also during these years that Korea's postwar leaders, men like the American-oriented Syngman Rhee and his later communist opponent Kim Il-sung, made their reputations as leading Korean nationalists. The groundwork was prepared for their later arrival to power in the months after World War II.

### The Division of Korea

At the close of World War II, when Japan had all but surrendered to U.S. and British forces, the subject of the future of Korea was considered by the leaders of the "Big Three" at the Potsdam Conference in mid-1945. Russia's Stalin reaffirmed his promise that the U.S.S.R. would declare war on Japan, which it had refrained from doing prior to that time, and proposed that it would secure the Korean peninsula from the Japanese armies. It was ultimately decided that Soviet forces would occupy the northern part of Korea and accept the surrender of the Japanese troops in that region, and the U.S. forces would do the same in the southern portion. Since, at the time of the Japanese surrender in August 1945, the Soviet forces could have occupied the whole pennsula as it would be several weeks before American forces could get there, Stalin could have taken the whole peninsula but instead, he stuck to the agreement on division.

The American expectation was that the whole peninsula would come under the supervision of the then-infant UN. This decision, made halfway around the world from the helpless Koreans, was to be the basis of continued conflict and friction for years, and also was to cost the loss of thousands of lives. It also ultimately was to result in an economically harmful division of the peninsula.

Two days after the first atomic bomb had burst with a terrifying holocaust on the Japanese city of Hiroshima, the U.S.S.R. declared war on Japan. The Japanese accepted the Allied surrender terms on August 14, but during the few intervening days the Soviets had easily occupied North Korea. The boundary between U.S. and Soviet troops was fixed shortly afterward at the 38th parallel by two young colonels in the American army who were given about half an hour to pick a place on the peninsula to divide the two forces. It was a decision that Koreans themselves would think back on with bitterness from then until today. The division made little economic or political sense.

In the North, the Russians promptly installed a regime run by Korean communists under the control of the Soviet occupation forces. In the South, U.S. occupation forces, which operated a full military government from 1945 through 1948, followed a shifting policy primarily devoted to economic recovery and to the creation of a democratic government.

There were seemingly unending negotiations between the two powers in 1946–1947 on the formation of a provisional government for the entire peninsula. But events on the ground made most of these discussions irrelevant. The Soviets for their part had chosen to support Kim Il-sung, the well known anti-Japanese fighter, and the United States increasingly settled on supporting the aging Syngman Rhee who by then had lived in the United States for decades. In essence, the tensions associated with the Cold War of the late 1940s had already begun within Korea immediately after World War II.

The southern, American-oriented Republic of Korea was declared independent in 1948. Elections, carried out under the occupation's mandate, confirmed Rhee as the new president and the American occupation officially ended. The Russians reacted by establishing the "Democratic People's Republic of Korea" in the North and withdrew their own occupation forces. Soviet support of local communists were sufficient to maintain North Korea within the Soviet bloc with little or no Russian military presence.

During the Cold War, the two regimes were poles apart on what other nations they chose to associate with and on economic matters. But they did have an important concern in common. Each was led by committed nationalists who were determined to reunite their nations. Over the next two years activists in both parts of the peninsula hoped for some sort of clash that would ultimately reunite the peninsula under one or the other government's leadership.

### The Korean War

America on the eve of the Korean War was very involved in developments in the Republic of Korea (South Korea). Not only was it contributing more than $100 million a year to the country but it was also influential in practically every aspect of the new state's existence from government through cultural and educational affairs. Clearly the United States wanted the South to be well able to withstand a potential attack from communist North Korea. On the other hand, many Americans were more immediately concerned about those South Koreans who were anxious to

begin their own effort to unify the peninsula from the south.

President Rhee, the American sponsored president, was among those calling for an attack on the north. But despite Rhee's efforts to gain American support to unify the peninsula under his control, it was his northern rival Kim-Il-sung and the latter's Soviet allies that made the fateful decision to begin what would become a vicious civil war. In June of 1950, bolstered by a heavy dose of Soviet military aid, North Korean forces invaded South Korea. Their attack, well planned in advance, was very effective and they were barely prevented from overrunning all of South Korea.

Angered by the North's invasion, President Truman, despite earlier U.S. statements to the contrary, viewed the attack as an assault on America's national interests and ordered a military intervention on the side of the South Koreans. Choosing to work within the structures of the newly formed United Nations, President Truman arranged for the UN to condemn the aggressive acts of North Korea and to order military sanctions against the Soviet satellite. Ironically, the representative of the U.S.S.R., who could have employed its veto power, was not there to do so. The U.S.S.R. had been boycotting the council due to controversies surrounding the question of who should hold the China seat, the People's Republic of China or the recently defeated Nationalists on Taiwan.

The southern counter-attack, while nominally carried out by a UN force, was primarily an American military effort. General Douglas MacArthur

**U.S. Marines in Korea, November 1951**

# South Korea

commanded the UN forces. Demonstrating the same energy and self-will he had shown during most of World War II, MacArthur planned an aggressive campaign to drive the northern forces out of South Korea.

A combination of mass bombing of the North and a flank attack by an amphibious landing at Inchon, a coastal town near Seoul, succeeded in driving the North Koreans from the territory they had conquered. Then having successfully driven the northern troops from South Korea, MacArthur insisted, and found support among his superiors, for an attack on North Korea and yet another unification drive, this time from the south.

Even as the American forces were moving closer and closer to the Chinese borders, MacArthur, ignoring Beijing's warnings, and the views of American intelligence organizations. was certain that the forces of the People's Republic would not intervene. Sure of his judgment, MacArthur ordered his forces toward the Yalu River, the border that divided Korea from China. MacArthur was wrong. Perhaps if it had only been South Korean forces that carried the attack to the Yalu, China might not have intervened. But China was not prepared to accept foreign hostile troops directly on its borders. Moreover, both Moscow and Beijing wanted to save the communist regime in Korea.

Beijing's forces struck with great force, using the same successful tactics they had learned in their battles with the Japanese and Chinese Nationalists during the previous decade. The Chinese effort to drive the U.S. and UN forces out of North Korea succeeded, but they were ultimately unable to capitalize on their initial military successes and fully unite the peninsula. Nevertheless, they did temporarily manage to capture Seoul, the capital.

General MacArthur, realizing he had been put on the defensive, very publicly advocated a wider war effort, including the bombing of Chinese Manchurian bases and even the use of the atomic bomb. Eventually the famous general's utterances caused a public break between himself and President Truman who had lost faith in his judgment. MacArthur was replaced, but the war itself waged on.

Chinese forces tried to retake Seoul in April and May 1951, but their supply lines had become too long to support the effort. Armistice negotiations began in July 1951, but since neither side had won a clear victory, the talks dragged on for two years, while fighting continued. Each side sought to obtain a defensible position, and gradually the lines of battle hardened with heavy fortifications that would have made a major breakthrough by either side almost impossible.

**Myeongdong Shopping District**

A crisis over the repatriation of prisoners also prolonged the conflict. The Chinese and North Koreans disliked and refused to recognize the proposition that their soldiers, many of whom were former Nationalist soldiers, might not want to return to their homelands. Nevertheless, an armistice was reached on July 27, 1953, a few months after the death of Stalin which had led to a reduction of Soviet support for the war.

American politics also contributed heavily to this armistice. The popular military hero of World War II, General Dwight Eisenhower, was chosen by the Republican Party to oppose President Truman's Democratic successor. Eisenhower's promise during the campaign to use his influence to end the Korean War greatly influenced the American public. Privately, President Eisenhower threatened to use nuclear weapons to settle the dispute. The threat worked.

The eventual armistice was a stalemate of military might, and the demarcation is along about the same line as it was prior to the conflict. The real result of the struggle was the loss of several hundred thousand lives and an almost utter devastation of both Koreas. The fighting may have ended, but the two parts of Korea then settled in for a generation-long struggle for domination of the peninsula. Over the years that new struggle would take many forms.

### The Two Koreas in the Postwar Era

Shortly after the armistice, the Soviet Union and China began providing substantial economic aid programs to North Korea. As a result, it acquired a broad industrial base and a per capita industrial production that rose to a level higher than that of China. Kim Il-sung, the political leader selected by the Soviets in 1945 to lead North Korea, soon acquired exclusive control over the local communist party at the expense of his rivals.

Eventually the Korean War and subsequent Russian-Chinese ideological disputes over what is "true communism" gave Kim a much wider degree of freedom of action within the communist sphere. For a few years after 1960 Kim tended to favor the Chinese. After 1964 he swung back toward the Russians, then again toward the Chinese for a time, and after 1983, toward Moscow until the Soviet Union collapsed.

In South Korea, despite massive American aid, the postwar economy floundered and the elderly President Rhee grew increasingly senile, autocratic, and unpopular. In 1960 he resigned and left the country after his government faced demonstrations that began with student protests but which quickly spread to other groups. The army made it clear to Rhee that it would not suppress the demonstrations. There followed a year of political ferment and regrouping under a weak government that ended in 1961 when the army seized control of South Korea.

### South Korea Emerges Economically

After an initial period of direct military rule, the Japanese-trained General Park Chung-hee, the leader of the military junta

# South Korea

**South Korean children and video games**

that had seized power, nominally became a civilian and was elected president. He was reelected in 1967. In 1972, not satisfied with his authority as the elected president of South Korea, Park pushed through legislation that allowed him to become a dictator. With that development, the entire peninsula had fallen under the control of autocratic governments, the communists in the North and Park's supporters. Park justified his actions by citing the need to retain national unity in the south in the face of the northern threat. But if the political situation of the two Koreas was growing more similar, the beginning of their modern economic divergence was also gaining momentum.

The roots of South Korea's modern economic "miracle" are diverse, ranging from external to internal factors. What is clear is that the average per capita income in 1963 was around $100; by 2012 it was over $32,000; and by 2019, it had reached $37,000. It then fell back slightly in 2020 because of COVID to around $34,000. By 2000, some Korean laborers were earning salaries comparable to Americans in the Midwest. It should be noted, however, that these average figures hide huge discrepencies, with earnings in some major companies reaching $90,000. Obviously, such an economic transformation was caused by myriad developments, but for Korea, certain key factors can be noted. Especially important were ties with both the Americans and the Japanese.

Since the decision to intervene during the Korean War, the United States had

been committed to a stable South Korea and had helped create the conditions there necessary to such stability. By the 1960s, the Korean willingness to align themselves with the internationally unpopular American effort in Vietnam was also very lucrative. In fact, some of the most important South Korean construction firms profited greatly from the projects they carried out in South Vietnam during the war. Their role, in some ways, resembled that of the Japanese during the American involvement in Korea during the earlier Korean War.

Though the memories of the Japanese occupation remained bitter, the reality was that the Koreans, and especially many in the elite, were well positioned to take advantage of the economic growth then going on in Japan. These Korean leaders, including General Park himself, were fluent in Japanese and quite willing to gain the advantages of close economic ties to Japan. That strategy worked quite well as Japan invested enormously in South Korea. For example, Mitsubishi owned about 10% of the South Korean company Hyundai and supplied many of the most important parts.

These advantages would not have been realized if the Park government had not chosen to move his committed and inexpensive labor force into the world export market, an economic decision already well trodden by Japan itself. President Park's economic policy and the advantages of the international environment, especially after the early 1960s, were major benefits.

One has only to look at the Seoul's modern skyline to recognize the very real improvement in living standards and to appreciate how much was accomplished in those years. On the political level Park's leadership was much less successful.

President Park's increasing personal power aroused considerable opposition, especially from the intellectuals, students, and the powerful Christian churches. This opposition was cruelly suppressed on the grounds that it gave aid and comfort to North Korea at a time when American protection of South Korea was becoming increasingly unreliable. Kim Dae-jung, later president, though then an influential opposition leader who had received a large minority of the popular vote for the presidency in 1971, was kidnapped in Japan by the South Korean Central Intelligence Agency in 1973 and brought home. The next year President Park's wife was fatally shot in mid-1974 in what was officially described as an attempt on the life of the president himself. Since the assassin had some Japanese connections, the government launched a dispute with Japan. But there were reasons to believe that this quarrel, as well as tensions in North Korea-South Korea relations which existed in 1974, were at least partly inspired by the Park government's efforts to distract attention from its domestic difficulties.

Despite his easy victory in a rigged referendum held in February 1975, Park's heavy-handedness might have cost him crucial American support. For a time after Jimmy Carter became president, it even looked like the U.S. might withdraw its forces.

The fall of Indochina to communism in 1975 left South Korea the only non-communist nation on the East Asian mainland and intensified the sense of danger felt in the country. This was exploited by President Park to increase his rigid control through repressive measures.

Nevertheless, The ruling Democratic Republican Party came closer to defeat in a 1978 election when it won only 68 seats in the National Assembly to 61 for the opposition New Democratic Party. In reaction, President Park reorganized his cabinet and released a number of political prisoners, including Kim Dae-jung.

### President Park's Death

President Park was assassinated by the head of the South Korean Central Intelligence Agency in October 1979. After an interlude of confusion, the army under General Chun Doo-hwan seized power in December 1979. In mid-1980 it proclaimed martial law. Most existing political parties were dissolved, politicians banned from taking any further role in the ploitical

# South Korea

**Park Chung-hee**

process, and the media also came under attack. There were forced amalgamations and the closure of all news agencies except Yonhap, the official mouthpiece of the regime. Chun viciously crushed a revolt in the southwestern city of Kwangju. The Kwangju Massacre, as it was to become known, was one of the most violent incidents in recent South Korean history and has continued to affect the course of South Korean politics ever since. Chun then became acting president and began to install a new government. Martial law was finally lifted at the beginning of 1981.

Chun then launched a policy of "national reconciliation" under which thousands of people imprisoned or barred from public life were pardoned. New political parties emerged, including a Socialist Party; all were, in reality, under tight government control. Despite the repressive measures used by the government to control South Korea, the surging economic figures during the 1980s helped maintain a reasonable level of satisfaction among the population. Seoul's international prestige was helped as well when it was chosen to serve as the site of the 1988 Summer Olympic Games.

In many ways the assassinated president's emphasis on economic growth allowed the Republic of Korea to surpass its northern rival without a military confrontation. South Korea was increasingly able to demonstrate by virtue of its accomplishments that its own economic system was stronger.

### A Weakened Dictatorship

By the mid 1980s President Chun faced serious political problems. There were mounting student demonstrations against the government, and a leading opposition politician, Kim Dae-jung, had returned from exile in the U.S. Although Kim was placed under house arrest, a new political party with which he was affiliated, the New Korea Democratic Party, did unexpectedly well in National Assembly elections held shortly after his return, winning 50 out of 276 seats.

The events of February 1986 in the Philippines also had a considerable impact on South Korea, not only because Marcos, the dictator, lost power, but because the U.S. had withdrawn support from him in spite of its large strategic interest in the country. If the United States, reacting to popular Philippine democratic pressures, could turn its back on a longtime ally like Marcos, then it might just as easily do so in South Korea as well. Although there was speculation that Chun might try to stay on until after the Olympic Games, the military generals who dominated South Korea decided it was time to move toward opening the system before they were forced to do so.

An intensified dialogue ensued between the government and the legal opposition centering on the New Korea Democratic Party (NKDP). A deadlock soon developed, however. It related to the nature of a new constitution. The government and the ruling party, the Democratic Justice Party (DJP), wanted a cabinet (parliamentary) system, with the real power vested in the premier who would presumably be a DJP member; the opposition insisted on a directly (rather than indirectly, as at that time) elected president as the effective head of the government. The opposition however was hampered by disunity within the leadership of the NKDP.

Other elements of the opposition, including Christian clergy, lay believers, and activist students, demonstrated from time to time against the government. The demonstrators, although fairly numerous, were generally outnumbered by the huge numbers of police that the government deployed to cope with them.

South Korea's huge ally, the U.S., clearly favored compromise between the government and the opposition, and a further democratization of the political system. The activist elements of the opposition tended to view the U.S. as the main supporter of the hated South Korean "establishment," which they regarded as a military and police dictatorship. Many also blamed the United States for the continuing division of their country caused by the tensions of the Cold War.

### Toward a More Democratic Korea

In the summer of 1987, as Chun's DJP was preparing to hand over the reins of power to his designated successor, fellow former general and DJP politician Roh Tae-woo, a public outcry began. Recognizing he faced a potential disaster, Roh called for an end to press censorship and free elections. Roh was counting on a loyal (but minority) DJP rural political base and hoped he could count on a divided opposition to salvage victory. His assumption that he could still win the election given the splits in the opposition proved correct.

The first direct presidential elections in more than 16 years were held in South Korea in December 1987. The candidate of the ruling DJP was Roh Tae-woo. The two top opposition leaders, Kim Young-sam and Kim Dae-jung, were unwilling to cooperate, and the result was predictable: the winner was Roh Tae-woo with 39.9% of the vote, while the two Kims split the majority opposition vote 27.5% and 26.5%.

Amid anti-government protests, Roh Tae-woo was sworn in as president in February 1988. For the moment Roh, the former general, had prevailed, but the momentum toward a much more open system had begun. South Korea would never be the same.

In an election for the National Assembly held in April of 1988, the ruling Democratic Justice Party won only 125 of the 299 seats. Flexing its new power the opposition then held hearings on various abuses of power during the tenure of former President Chun Doo-hwan, and especially on the Kwangju Massacre of May 1980. Chun refused to testify, and President Roh refused to compel him to do so. Chun did make a public apology, turned over his assets to the state, and retired to the countryside. Dissatisfied, a number of opposition politicians and radicals continued to demand that he be put on trial. That demand, though, was to wait until

**Chun Doo-hwan**

more progress was made in the democratization of the country. Nevertheless, early in 1989, approximately 50 people, including two brothers of Chun, were arrested on charges of corrupt practices under his administration. President Roh had a better image than his predecessor, and made moves away from the tight controls that Chun had inherited from Park Chung-hee. Previously banned foreign books were allowed in, and for the first time ever, it became permissible to publish about North Korea that did not follow the government line. But the opposition in the National Assembly hoped to pass a vote of no confidence in his administration and compel his resignation.

The several years leading up to the 1993 presidential election was an important transitional period. Many did not trust the ruling party or President Roh Tae-woo. It was believed that he might seek extra-legal means of holding onto power. The new constitution was untested and the opposition was, for the most part, weak. There was also concern that the United States might significantly downsize its commitment to the republic. In spite of these concerns, 1993 did mark the beginning of a new, more democratic era for the country.

### An Emerging Democracy

The election of 1993 finally brought to power Kim Young-sam, a longtime democratic reformer who along with Kim Dae-jung had been especially involved in trying to bring about democratic reform. His election represented the arrival to the presidency of the first civilian elected leader in a generation, though members of the former ruling elite were still very influential. Upon coming to power, the new president, who was initially quite popular,

put forward very specific goals including the achievement of civilian control over the military, a more caring government, and an anti-corruption program.

By 1994 President Kim had initiated reforms to improve the political process. In a bi-partisan move, the National Assembly passed bills dealing with campaign spending, election procedures and local government. Government subsidies for political parties and candidates were increased. The overall limit on campaign spending was lowered (how much a candidate could spend on his/her own campaign). The legislation did not place a limit on how much a party could spend on a candidate. Overall, these changes made it easier for the opposition to compete on even footing with the ruling party. The legislature was also given increased authority over the budget and actions of the National Security Planning Agency (NSPA), as the Korean CIA had become after Chun seized power. (It would later become the National Intelliigence Service.)

President Kim Young-sam also succeeded in obtaining the agreement of all top military officials not to interfere in the political process. Charges of corruption were brought against top military figures and several were relieved of their positions, including the army chief of staff. The new government also moved to dismantle the National Security Planning Agency. A further significant move involved the release of almost 40,000 criminals and political prisoners. Helmeted riot police withdrew from the streets and the number of student demonstrations decreased. Anti-corruption measures were initiated against a number of high-ranking government officials. After 30 years of military participation in the political process, it is remarkable that the new president had as much success as he did.

South Korea had changed a great deal since President Park had ruled with an iron hand. President Kim was even named the winner of the Martin Luther King Prize for his contribution to building democracy and human rights in South Korea.

To the astonishment of many who had watched the longtime domination of South Korea by the military, President Kim even put on trial his two predecessors, Chun and Roh, for their roles in both the coup that brought them to power and the subsequent 1980 Kwangju Massacre. The trials ultimately concluded with former President Chun sentenced to death and President Roh to life imprisonment (lessened on appeal to a life sentence and 17 years, respectively). If President Kim had thought the trials would work to his advantage, he guessed wrong. The investigations also uncovered the depth of corruption inherent in the South Korean political system that eventually spilled over on to Kim's own administration and even his son.

### Economic Corruption Scandals

A flow of corruption revelations then swept over the political landscape in a tidal wave that has not ended. Former President Roh Tae-woo admitted receiving over $600 million in contributions from businesses during his term in office. Roh's admissions came after two of his associates, one of whom managed a secret fund, revealed its existence.

It then became apparent that in return for the huge payments, large corporations such as Hyundai, Samsung, Daewoo, and Lucky Goldstar received large government contracts. Another revelation was that Kim Dae-jung, an unsuccessful candidate for the presidency in 1992, had received over $2.5 million from Roh for his campaign.

The corruption charges though were not exclusively the problems of the former presidents Chun and Roh or even of President Kim Young-sam's longtime democratic rival Kim Dae-jung. Early 1997 saw charges of collusion between President Kim's closest advisers and even his son with the Hanbo Group industrial group. The president was struggling, as his last year in office began, to find a way out of the growing scandal with his own reputation intact.

But the corruption scandals that were rocking South Korea by mid 1997 were not the only thing that weakened President Kim's prestige. Well aware that South Korea's soaring economy of the 1980s had stalled, the president became convinced that new economic laws needed to be implemented to give South Korean

**The Olympic Highway in Seoul along the Han River**

# South Korea

businesses more flexibility over their workforces. That in itself might have been an understandable conclusion, but when President Kim's supporters called an early morning meeting of the Korean Parliament on December 26, 1996, and passed legislation allowing businesses to lay off workers or adjust their hours more easily, he aroused a huge civil disobedience movement.

For weeks, in late December and January of 1997–1998, the world watched as South Korea's democratically elected president was challenged by thousands of workers for reducing their economic security and acting undemocratically. Eventually, President Kim, his earlier insistence on standing firm notwithstanding, agreed to allow the parliament, including the opposition parties, the opportunity to review the legislation.

But the events of the fall of 1997 soon changed the international environment. As the economic collapse of Southeast Asia began to impact in South Korea, the economy, already faltering, went into a tailspin (see The Economy below). With the nation's confidence crashing, a long awaited presidential campaign began which would be among the most dramatic of Korea's long history.

### Kim Dae-jung: Korean President

The election campaign opened up with President Kim Young-sam's popularity in tatters and his government unable to take decisive action to deal with the

**General Roh Tae-woo**

nation's growing economic crises. Given the new situation it now looked like Kim Dae-jung, the three-time presidential candidate, frequent political prisoner and life-long opponent of the military regime, might finally have a real chance of winning. Recognizing that this was his last chance at the presidency, the former political prisoner, so long labeled a leftist radical by his opponents, moved decisively toward the political center and sought out allies on the middle and right of the South Korean political spectrum. Not giving up, South Korea's longtime ruling party, the Grand National Party nominated Lee Hoi-chang as its standard bearer who not surprisingly worked to distance himself from the extremely unpopular Kim Young-sam.

A third candidate, Rhee In-je, angry that the ruling party had not nominated him, emerged to turn the struggle into another three-way race. But this time, unlike in his previous efforts, the momentum was behind Kim Dae-jung. When he won the December 1997 vote, it was as astounding a political transformation as when Lech Walesa had become president of Poland or Nelson Mandela of South Africa.

Having waited a lifetime to lead South Korea and then at 73 winning power as his country experienced its worst economic collapse in a generation, the new president had his work cut out for him. Much to the relief of many, he seemed ready to begin. Recognizing that he had been elected by less than a majority and knowing the importance of unifying the country, he named as his prime minister Kim Jong-pil. Kim was a former army officer, who had married a niece of Park Chung-hee. In 1960, he and other army officers, including Park, planned a coup, but it was discovered and Kim was forced to resign. Behind the scenes, however, he continued to work on the project, playing a major role in the April 1961 coup that brought Park to power. He did not rejoin the army but instead established the Korean Cental Intelligence Agency whose main purpose was domestic surveillence. When Park established his Democratic Republican Party in 1963, Kim Jong-pil was one of its organizers and, after his election to the National Assembly, party leader. He also served as prime minister from 1971 to 1975. Purged in 1980, his political rights were restored in 1987, when he promptly returned to conservative politics. Yet in 1997, he threw in his lot with Kim Dae-jung, and supported the latter's presidential campaign. For some of his longtime supporters, Kim Dae-jung's decision was hard to understand, but the new president's decision to grant general amnesties not only to imprisoned political prisoners but to those who had been convicted of traffic violations certainly was popular.

**Former President Kim Young-sam**

Unfortunately, for the new president, the economic crisis of 1997 turned out to be far more difficult to manage. While Kim was able to replenish the country's foreign exchange reserves, which had been dangerously low in the months before he took office, real reform seemed far off. Initially successful in obtaining promises of cooperation from the labor unions, he soon found their leadership was quite unwilling to accept layoffs to strengthen the nation's businesses.

Thus, by summer of 1998 Korea was once again experiencing major labor unrest. Nor were the nation's economic leaders any more willing to cooperate with the government's plans for restructuring and thus despite considerable rhetoric on the new president's part little real economic reform has been accomplished.

One problem that also appeared to weaken the president's efforts was accusations that he was not only favoring his own political supporters but carrying out an anti-corruption drive against supporters of the previous regime. Not that his efforts were not warranted. One former director of the previous regime was even convicted of seeking to have the North Koreans take provocative acts that might have affected the results of the previous presidential election. Nevertheless, there were those who felt that the corruption drive was hurting the economic recovery effort. And those accusations of corruption were not merely the problem of members of previous regimes. Over the last few years some of President Kim Dae-jung's closest colleagues, friends, and even his sons were accused of similar crimes and he found his party, the National Congress for New Politics, losing ground politically.

# South Korea

South Korea's Blue House

Courtesy of Mark Jihun Suk

The situation became so bad that by Kim Dae-jung eventually felt it necessary to personally apologize for the scandals in his administration.

Reacting to the weakening of his power base, President Kim organized a new political grouping known as the Millennium Democratic Party that it was hoped, would do well in the spring 2000 elections. Unfortunately for Kim, when the elections actually occurred his new party came in a relatively distant second, 115 seats, to the 133 seats won by the former ruling party, the Grand National Party.

### The Sunshine Policy Renewed?

Meanwhile, as the new American administration of George W. Bush established itself in power, President Kim Dae-jung found his "Sunshine Policy"—the term used for his efforts to improve relations with North Korea (which eventually earned him the Nobel Peace Prize)—deeply undermined by Washington's renewed skepticism toward North Korea. In fact, the new American administration's stance not only undermined President Kim it eventually turned the next South Korean Presidential election into something of a referendum on Seoul's relationship with both North Korea and the United States.

That election occurred in November of 2002 when Roh Moo Hyun of President

Kim's Millennium Democratic Party and Lee Hoi Chang of the Grand National Party battled to succeed President Kim who was not legally allowed to run for a second term. And, quite an election it was as twin dramas played out during the struggle. On one hand, relations with North Korea, that had seemed so full of promise only a few short years before, continued to spiral downward as Washington's relationship with Pyongyang deteriorated.

Moreover, the deaths of two South Korean teenagers in a traffic accident with American soldiers (which subsequently saw the Americans acquitted of the charges by a U.S. military court) aroused considerable anti-American sentiment and a regular series of demonstrations against Washington's policies on the peninsula.

The Millennium Democratic Party's candidate, a labor lawyer, former political activist and supporter of President Kim, Roh Moo-hyun advocated a renewed effort to invigorate the Sunshine Policy and a less subservient and more equal relationship with the United States. His opponent Lee Hoi-chang stood for a policy much more in line with the Washington's and as an opponent of the outgoing president's efforts to improve relations with North Korea.

When the election of December 2002 finally took place, outgoing President Kim Dae-jung had considerable reason

to be satisfied. The final vote had been very close, but Roh had won. His victory reinforced the impression that South Korea's population remained committed to the policy of reconciliation on the Korean peninsula regardless of what the United States might think.

The election that brought longtime human rights activist Roh Moo-hyun to power by early 2003 may have resolved for the moment who would lead occupy South Korea's famous Blue House, but it hardly resolved the tensions that

**Former President Kim Dae-jung**

141

# South Korea

**Former President Roh Moo-hyun**

continued to exist within South Korean society and especially with the nation's conservatives that dominated the Grand National Party. While it is probably true that his decision to support the American effort in Iraq may have appeased some conservatives who felt Roh was likely to weaken South Korea's traditionally strong ties to the United States, which hardly satisfied his critics. And as so often before, the criticism of the new president was related less to relations with the United States or even with North Korea, but to financial and campaign scandals within South Korea itself. As a result, the Parliament dominated as it was by the Grand National Party voted to impeach the president who was temporarily removed from office amidst general public outrage that the parliament had misused its powers.

However, things did not quite work out as the leaders of the Grand National Party might have hoped. By April 2004, South Korea's political environment, already in turmoil, was again transformed by that month's parliamentary elections. The Grand National Party lost control of parliament, and the Liberal Uri party, which had been formed to support Roh Moo-hyun, enormously increased its representation and emerged as the dominant party. By the next month President Roh was back in office after the nation's constitutional court invalidated the impeachment efforts of the GNP and vindicated his leadership.

But political gains rarely last long in democratic politics. By early 2006 President Roh's influence seemed to be on the wane as his colleagues in the Uri Party began focusing on the upcoming parliamentary and presidential elections that, when they arrived in December 2007, saw the Grand National Party finally returned to executive power in the election of Lee Myung-bak, a former executive of the Hyundai corporation and a former mayor of Seoul. Lee was elected on a platform

that focused on the economy and the candidate's extensive business experience. However, once his election was secured, the next challenge was winning the upcoming parliamentary elections.

When those elections occurred, President Lee won the mandate he had hoped for. His revised conservative party, the Grand National Party, took 153 seats to the much lower 81-seat result for the United Democratic Party. It was a remarkable reversal of circumstances for South Korea's conservatives, who had not held such power in a decade.

Given that the transition from South Korea's left leaning politicians to the more conservative Grand National Party was accomplished smoothly, there is plenty to rejoice in how well the nation has made the transition to a more consistently democratic society. Nevertheless, the frequently "take no prisoners" nature of the system was unfortunately also demonstrated in the aftermath of the transition as well. In the early summer of 2009 South Korea's former president, Roh Moo-hyun, apparently depressed by the barrage of corruption charges leveled against him after he left office, committed suicide.

Things did not go wonderfully for President Lee either. In the aftermath of North Korea's more aggressive behavior, such as the sinking of the South Korean navy corvette, *Cheonan,* and subsequent shelling of a South Korean village near their disputed border, South Korea's aroused public began sharply criticizing President Lee's Grand National Party government for what was initially perceived as too timid a response to the North's provocations.

South Korea went into the parliamentary elections of 2012 with a general assumption that President Lee's Grand National Party or Saenuri Party faced a significant challenge while their more leftist challenger, the Democratic United Party, had a good chance of doing well. But the results surprised a great many observers. The Seoul metropolitan area voted with the DUP, but overall the Saenuri Party managed a slim victory. This was even more impressive given the low expectations observers had had of its chances. Especially interesting was the continuing strength of former military strongman Park Chung-hee's daughter Park Geun-hye. Ms. Park proved not only to be a successful politician in her own right, but the heir to her father's strong anti-North Korean stance, which seemed especially to help her with older voters.

By the time the presidential election was held in December, South Korea's conservative politicians, political heirs to the nation's earlier series of generals, once again secured the presidency in a fashion that highlighted their continuing ties to the previous era. Park Geun-hye, building upon her father's still appreciated legacy in many quarters and her own impressive political skills, was elected the nation's first female president. It was an election that evoked memories not only of her father's long years of political domination, but of the South Korean women's rights movement that only a few decades before had been in its infancy.

Whatever her skills at winning elections, Park proved less effective as a president. She was in many ways better abroad than at home. Although relations with China

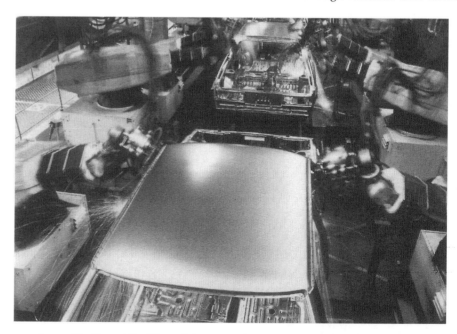

**Assembly line at the Hyundai automotive company in Seoul—the Excel**

142

### South Korea's "Rasputin"-Style Presidential Scandal by Mark Jihun Suk

The recent corruption scandal and subsequent impeachment of President Park Geun-hye, referred to among the South Korean public as "the Rasputin incident of Korea," sent seismic shockwaves throughout South Korea and the world since the news first hit the media in late October 2016. The fact that President Park had given Ms. Choi Soon-sil, her personal confidante, not only unlimited access to private government information, used to enhance Choi's financial interests, but significant control over national affairs raised enough of a public outcry to demand President Park's immediate resignation from office. Indeed, by the first week in January of 2017, the number of people joining the public rallies and protests in the streets of Seoul, demanding Park's resignation, reached over 10 million.

Choi had been Park's closest friend and confidante for more than 40 years, since they first met in the mid-1970s through Choi's father, the late "Reverend" Choi Tae-min. The elder Choi claimed to possess psychic powers, including the power to heal the sick and speak to the dead, which he exploited to become close to Park Geun-hye in the years after, first her mother and then her father, former South Korean President Park Chung-hee, were assassinated.

Park Geun-hye's own political career began after the death of Choi Tae-min, at which point her spiritual and personal confidence moved to Choi's daughter, Soon-sil, who also claimed to possess the same psychic powers as her father. By the early 1990s, Park Geun-hye's dependency on the Choi family became so serious that it resulted in the personal and legal estrangement from her remaining family, including her own siblings. Park herself won her first election as a National Assemblywoman in 1998.

After Park Geun-hye won the presidential election in 2012, Choi Soon-sil, like her father, began to establish a series of "nonprofit" foundations and used presidential influence to extort tens of millions of dollars. Ms. Choi, who held no government position nor had any credentials to serve in public office, would receive the president's plan for governance in advance, and then ran her own "shadow cabinet" that would make decisive comments on government policy. In doing so, Choi placed her cronies and others in significant policy-planning positions and dismissed or even retaliated against those who would not go along

with her plans with the authority "borrowed" from the president. During this process, "donations" coming from the Chaebols—Korea's supersized conglomerates, including Samsung, LG, Hyundai, SK, and so on—were sent to Choi and her "shadow cabinet" to earn favor with Choi.

Choi's two main foundations, the Mir Foundation and the K-Sports Foundation, received a total amount of 77.4 billion KRW (roughly $65 million USD) as "donations" from these companies. Lee Jae-yong, the CEO of Samsung and the biggest "donor" to this foundation, later admitted during the investigation that President Park herself arranged the meeting with the "Top 7" businessmen and personally compelled these CEOs to donate money. In exchange, the president encouraged the government to overlook legal problems such as tax evasions. In order to escape from possible disclosure by the law, Choi also established several "paper companies" in foreign countries, mostly in Germany, for money laundering her assets of roughly 11 trillion KRW ($9.3 billion USD).

However, the most serious aspect of this whole affair is the revelation that Choi practically controlled the presidential power all by herself. Through the investigations by the Special Prosecutors' Taskforce, it was revealed that Choi had received almost all her government policy briefings directly from the presidential residence. Then discussed the issues with her inner circle of a "shadow cabinet" including a K-pop music video director, a retired professional fencer who allegedly "moonlighted" as a male prostitute, Choi's personal trainer, and the figurehead president of her foundations. Choi and her cronies also received ultra-confidential information about South and North Korean military meetings, plus budget proposals for the government ministries. Indeed, President Park often asked her staff to get Choi's approval prior to making decisions with her "real" cabinet.

Although the scandal began to unwind over the revelations that Ms. Choi had used her influence to win a college scholarship for her daughter, it spun out of control after reporters discovered a Samsung Galaxy Tablet belonging to Choi Soon-sil in an abandoned office in Seoul which belonged to Choi's "paper companies." This turned out to be a "smoking gun." The tablet PC contained confidential data—presidential speeches

with Choi's editing remarks, presidential briefs for cabinet meetings, appointment information, correspondences between Choi and the presidential aides, and a lot of other evidence proving that Choi had been personally involved in numerous state affairs.

The subsequent public outcry turned into a fury—starting in late October with massive demonstrations mainly in the form of candle-lit rallies in the center area of Seoul every Saturday. Starting off with 20,000 protesters during the last week of October, the number of protesters in the streets of Seoul skyrocketed, reaching over 2.3 million by November 19—the biggest public demonstration ever recorded in Korean history. By February 2017, the total number of protesters exceeded over 16 million. Meanwhile, Park's approval rate dropped to a historic 4%.

The Supreme Prosecutors' Office began to investigate the Choi Soon-sil affair with a special taskforce, arresting Choi on November 3, and identified Park Geun-hye as her criminal accomplice. Park, in her two subsequent public apologetic statements, admitted that she had accepted "friendly suggestions" by Choi, but denied all the allegations against her and refused to resign. The National Assembly, including many from Park's own Saenuri party, decided on December 9th, 2016, that Park should be impeached. The vote was 234-56, with six abstentions.

Upon impeachment, President Park was temporarily stripped of her duties. A long series of public hearings then began in December before the Constitutional Court. Weeks later, after several fierce debates between the prosecutors and Park's lawyers, including a chilling remark from one of Park's lawyers claiming that there will be a "rebellion and blood will drench the asphalt" if Park is unseated—the Constitutional Court ruled to uphold the impeachment in a unanimous 8–0 decision, terminating Park's presidency, on March 10, 2017.

This decision marked the first time that a sitting president was removed from the office since South Korea set up the new democratic sixth constitution in 1987. Upon Park's removal from office, a new presidential election was scheduled for May 9, 2017, an election that eventually resulted in the election of Moon Jae-in, an attorney with a long established career in the field of human rights.

# South Korea

would sour later in her presidency, she made a good first impression when she visited that country and made a speech in Chinese. She got on well with the then U.S. president, Barack Obama, and on visits to Europe. Relations with Japan, however, already poor under her predecessor, grew even more frosty. And although she had visited North Korea in 2002, where Kim Jong Il had apparently expressed admiration for her father, her efforts at improving relations were desultory and rejected by the North in increasingly unpleasant and even sexist language.

At home, she was slow to act, taking a long time even to select her government. She hoped to improve education and encouraged creative industries. She also hoped to improve the lot of women. But she took limited advice, falling back on contacts from her father's day and coming increasingly under the influence of a businesswoman, Choi Tae-min. Her failure to issue an early apology or even to appear for several hours after the sinking of a ferry, the *Sewol*, in which some 300 people, mostly schoolchildren, were drowned in April 2014 led to a huge fall in her personal popularity. Eventually this led to huge protests, known as the "Candlelight Revolution," which embraced the growing scandals over the role of Choi Tae-min, as well as over a government black list of cultural figures deemed hostile to Park, her late father, and the government. She lost the support of her own party, many of whom proved willing to back her impeachment at the end of 2016.

The Constitutional Court ruled that the impeachment was valid, and Park was arrested in March 2017. She would eventually receive long sentences. The presidential election, scheduled for December, was brought forward to May. The result was a clear win for Moon Jie-in, leader of the main opposition party, whom Park had defeated in 2012, and he became president on 9 May. The new administration was marked by a number of imaginative appointments, including the country's first female foreign minister, Kang Kyung-wha. Moon took action on various election pledges, including improving the economy, reducing working hours and unemployment. State control over history textbooks ended. Moves were made to break the family control of the country's big conglomerates. The economy saw dramatic improvement, reaching three percent growth for the first time since 2014.

There were also successes in external affairs. Moon began working for better relations with the North, concerned at the increasingly belligerent exchanges between the North Korean leader, Kim Jong Un, and U.S. President Trump. He also

worked to reduce tensions in ROK-US bilateral relations, especially over the issues of trade and the ROK contribution to the costs of US forces in the country.

These various strands seemed to have been successful, as 2018 became the year of summits and apparent detente. North Korea made a late application to attend the Winter Olympics, to be held in Pyongchang, South Korea, in February. This was accepted, and a high-level delegation, which included Kim Jong Un's sister, accompanied the athletes. From this, there flowed suggestions of a North–South summit and, more surprisingly, a summit meeting between Kim Jong Un and President Trump. (For further details, see "Relations with North Korea," below.) There was some criticism of "pandering" to the North, but Moon's ratings in the opinion polls soared, reaching 80 percent a year a year after he became president. The euphoria did not last. By the end of 2018, it was clear that the high hopes raised by the summits were unlikely to be met. Old problems continued. The economy was sluggish, hit by the growing China-U.S. trade dispute. Youth unemployment remained high, people still worked long hours, especially outside Seoul, and there were public sector strikes. Relations with Japan plummeted, there was an improvement with China. Popular support for Moon and for the government fell and there were allegations of corruption.

Then came COVID-19 (for more detail, see below). The first case was reported in January 2020. The government response was swift and effective. Soon the disease seemed to be under control and the administration's popularity bounced back, winning the April 2020 general election. When restrictions were eased in May, however, there was a surge of cases. There followed periodic ups and downs, in particular linked to places of entertainment and religious centers. Localized controls began again and persisted into 2021. By mid-May 2021, there had been 135,000 cases, of which 8,500 were still isolating, and 1926 deaths. The government was criticized for its handling of the surges and for the slow beginning of vaccination, and its popularity dropped again. During the rest of 2021, cases dropped until early December, when a new rise led the government to introduce further controls. These were gradually eased in the New Year, as the principle of "living with Covid" was promulgated. Yet the numbers continued to rise during the early part of 2022, reaching 600,000 new cases daily in March 2022, but there was no change in government policy. Deaths remained relatively low and there was a good take-up of vaccines.

**Han Myung-sook, South Korea's first female prime minister**

### Economy

Despite the extraordinary economic growth of the 1960s and 1970s, South Korea's GDP rates over the last several years have been relatively anemic with each year bringing significantly lower growth figures. Indeed, for South Korea, like much of the world and especially its near neighbor Japan, the last few decades have frequently brought considerable challenges that began largely in the 1990s.

Certainly there were warning signs by the mid-1990s. But the drama that unfolded after the summer of 1997, when the Asian economic crisis began, was unprecedented. Still, it was hardly a surprise to close observers of the Korean economy. After spending a heady period as one of the exciting Asian "Tigers," South Korea, like Japan before it, saw its economic vitality lessen as the 1990s unfolded. South Korean wage bills had been going up faster than their Asian competitors, and productivity growth had not kept up either. They were losing markets to the newer emerging economies like the People's Republic of China and the smaller but until recently vibrant economies of Southeast Asia.

As we have seen, late in 1996, hoping to inject new life and flexibility into the system, then President Kim Young-sam, the first elected civilian president in a generation, reverted to a very undemocratic method of decision-making. In the early dawn hours after Christmas his party arranged for a secret parliamentary meeting where it used the absence of opposition delegates (who had not been informed of the meeting) to pass legislation that would have given Korean employers more leeway in firing workers.

The act, which on purely international economic grounds might have been defensible, only further undermined the

144

**A railroad station plaza in downtown Pusan**      Courtesy of CALTEX Petroleum Corp.

reputation of the government while doing little to add strength to the economy. Unfortunately, these moves may have strengthened democracy in the long run but they did nothing to make South Korea more economically able to compete with the other Asian economies with lower wage demands.

By the fall of 1997, the economic crisis that had begun in Thailand, a relatively minor player in the international economic arena, had hit Korea, one of the largest economies in the world. With confidence much weakened in the currencies of the entire region the Korean currency, the won, went into a slide making it all the more difficult for Korean businesses to meet their international debt. All this came at the worst possible time as the country moved into a presidential election campaign.

Unable to meet its international loan obligations, South Korea was forced after so many years of economic growth to request an enormous aid package of around $60 billion in loans from the International Monetary Fund. Korea had as well to accept stringent IMF demands that it institute major changes in its economy. Many of those demands, which would see unemployment rise considerably within the country, were very difficult to accept but given the circumstances Seoul had little choice. For the first time in a generation the South Korean economy had begun to shrink, and unemployment for 1998 doubled to 7.4%. The year 1997 had seen the economy grow by more than 5%, but 1998 registered a 5% contraction.

Fortunately, the President, Kim Dae-jung, after some initial hesitancy, heroically decided to accept the necessity of dramatic reform and took them on as his own. In sharp contrast to President Kim Young-sam's strong arm tactics of the previous winter, the new president used his long-term ties to the labor movement to help gain their initial cooperation. Those efforts were not though as successful as the president might have hoped.

By century's end there were clear signs of recovery. As the decade moved the South Korean economy successfully overcome the crisis of 1997. Indeed, its economy was humming along at a respectable 4.6% growth rate for 2004.

Unfortunately that momentum hardly lasted. The next economic downturn of 2008–2009 struck with a vengeance pushing the economy downward for a time. By the spring of 2010, however, the economic numbers were again looking quite positive. In fact, not only were unemployment and inflation figures down. The nation's growth rate for the year was around 6%, a very impressive figure and far better than many nations, such as the United States,

# South Korea

which were still struggling to find their way out of the economic crisis of 2008.

But as has happened throughout much of the region, from the People's Republic to Japan the European economic crisis and the United States anemic economic growth had begun to pull South Korea down by mid-2012 which eventually came in as a mere 2.7% and that down from the previous year's 3.5%. Since then the economy has continued at about the same pace of modest but hardly impressive growth.

Amidst the discouraging news there were at least some positive signs for the nations' economic future. The longtime effort to establish a free trade pact between the United States and South Korea was accomplished. In late 2011 South Korea's National assembly finally ratified the free trade agreement.

Another sign of South Korea's commitment to remain on the cutting edge of 21st-century economic trends was the nation's announced commitment of an $860 million fund to encourage local scientists to focus on the growing field of artificial intelligence. And the announcement was hardly something the public ignored given how many ordinary Koreans closely followed the contest between Google Deep Mind's self learning AlphaGo program and the reigning international Go champion Lee Sedol who was beaten by AlphaGo in four out of five games.

By 2016 though another mainstay of the Korean economy, the ship building industry seemed to be experiencing significant problems, indeed, by the late fall the industry was reporting very significant job lay offs of workers as demand for the ships and equipment associated with the weakening global oil exploration and transportation industry.

New pressures put further strains on the economy in succeeding years. South Korea's heavy economic dependence on China came under strain from 2017, following the decision to introduce the anti-ballistic missile system, Terminal High Alitiude Area Defense (THAAD) system. The ROK government maintained this was for defense against North Korea, but the Chinese claimed it was actually aimed at them. China applied strong economic pressure, including limiting tourism and banning South Korean goods, which had a severed effect on South Korea. The growth rate dropped to 3%, and there was widespread unemployment, especially among younger workers. By late 2019, the tensions and the Chinese measures had eased somewhat, only for the onset of COVID to set economic development back once more. At first, there was a major decline in the first two quarters of 2020. Tourism ceased and airline passengers fell by 58.8%, to their lowest level since 2008.1.3

million people were out of work, with the young once more particularly badly hit. Yet by the end of the year, there were signs of a recovery that persisted into 2021, when the growth rate reached 4% by the end of the year. A further sign of economic success was the announcement by the United Nations Conference on Trade and Development (UNCTAD) in July 2021 that the ROK would in future be classed as a developed country, the first time UNC-TAD had changed the status of a country since its founding in 1964. And although COVID came back with a vengence at the end of 2021, with a huge rise in cases in the first quarter of 2022, the economy continued to recover.

## Relations with North Korea

In the years since the collapse of the Soviet Union and the death of Kim Il-sung, the longtime leader of North Korea, people in the South have been divided about how to deal with their northern neighbor. It is clear that the North Korean economy has been failing and the regime has somewhat less control over what people think compared with the past. How the South should react remains less clear.

Basically three different approaches seem to be in the forefront of public thought. First, the northern regime might collapse suddenly. Such an eventuality would please some of those in the South who have spent their lives struggling against the North. But such a collapse would leave to the Republic of Korea the burden of integrating the much less

sophisticated infrastructure of the North into that of the South. The financial burdens would be enormous, as demonstrated in 1990 when West Germany had to do the same thing with East Germany. But South Korea does not have the same resources as Bonn did.

Others have hoped for a smoother transition, a so-called easy landing to North Korea's assumed collapse, emphasizing those programs that allow a smoother and less dramatic transition. Lastly, some people, aware of the enormous complexities of following either strategy, have understandably hoped for a simple stabilization of developments on the peninsula. But that is often difficult as incidents keep occurring that highlight both the tensions and the North's weakness.

Especially prominent among those incidents over the years was the landing and discovery of two different North Korean mini-submarines in South Korean waters. In the first incident in September 1996, a mini-submarine accidentally beached in South Korea. Recognizing the dangers of their circumstances, the sailors on board appear to have killed themselves or to have been murdered while the soldiers among them set off into the interior of South Korea. Before the incident was over, 26 North Koreans and several people from the South were dead. The North eventually apologized for the incursion.

The North Korean regime makes decisions on a regular basis that suggest it is more interested in confrontation than dialogue. For example, during the summer of 1998 they test fired a missile that passed

**South Koreans protest policies toward North Korea**

over Japan. That gesture came close to jeopardizing what limited trans-peninsula calm had been achieved, and it inspired South Korean efforts to expand their own missile program. A similar series of reconciliatory and aggressive gestures have continued to today.

As discussed earlier, after Kim Dae-jung, the former democratic activist came to power he established a more open policy dubbed the "Sunshine Policy" to improve relations with the North. Over the years considerable progress was made. For example, North Korea, in need of cash, has allowed South Korean tourists to make very controlled visits to its territory. For a time, this even included opportunities for South Koreans to enter the North in their own vehicles, including automobiles.

However, the most dramatic developments began when it was announced that Kim Jong-il of North Korea had agreed to meet with Kim Dae-jung in June of 2000. There had been summit proposals before. Indeed just before Kim Il-sung died in 1994, officials between the two sides had been discussing such a meeting between him and South Korean President Kim Young-sam. But although Kim Young-sam had been willing to meet his Northern counterpart, he refused to express any form of condolence on his death. The talks broke off and the North refused tio deal with Kim Young-sam during his remaining time in office. This time it was different, and meet they did. Later, it would be revealed that the summit had only been arranged through large transfers of cash to the North but at the time, what seemed to matter was the meeing. As people throughout the world watched, the two took part in the first summit ever between the leaders of the divided peninsula. Moreover, that dramatic meeting was followed by more reunions of individual family members many of whom had not seen each other since the Korean War began in 1950. For the first time in years not only did it appear that real progress was being made in North—South Korean relations but that for once events were being driven more by Koreans themselves than by outsiders like the Chinese and the Americans. Not only that but the U.S. government under President Bill Clinton not only supported Kim Dae-jung's approach to the North but also pursued its own policy of rapprochement toward the North. Secretary of State Madeleine Albright led a delegation to Pyongyang in October, and there was even talk of the president himself going.

For President Kim Dae-jung himself, 2000 must have been especially gratifying when his "Sunshine Policy" received

international accolades with his award of the Nobel Peace Prize for his efforts. (Again, there would be later claims that this had not come about without heavy expenditure and much effort.) Kim Dae-jung's engagement of the North continued under his successor, the progressive lawyer Roh Moo-hyun, despite North Korea's steady advance towards developing a nuclear weapon capability, including conducting what it claimed was its first nuclear test in October 2006. Although Roh condemned this move and backed UN sanctions, nevertheless, he accepted an invitation from Kim Jong Il to visit Pyongyang in October 2007, just before the December presidential election. Since he could not stand again, there was much criticism from his opponents of the decision to meet Kim Jong Il and fears that Roh would give too much away. This proved not to be the case. The two leaders signed an agreement which covered many issues and, which, if implemented, would have had significant benefits for both Koreas.

The victory of the conservative presidential candidate Lee Myung-baek in December 2007 saw a more edgy tone to North–South relations from the moment he took office in January 2008. There would be no more aid without a concrete response from the North. All aid projects would be examination and South Korea would take action over North Korea's human rights record. He did make some conciliatory noises, however, promising to raise the North's income to $3000 per capita in return for change. The North responded with a personal attack on Lee and a rejection of the income offer. Lee also found himself somewhat out of step with the U.S. as President George W. Bush's administration engaged with the North on the nuclear issue. So despite the North's contemptuous rejection of his first proposal, he promised on 11 July 2008 to work for mutual benefit and prosperity with the North.

The timing proved unfortunate. On the same day as Lee put forward his proposal, a South Korean female tourist was shot dead at the Diamond Mountains resort in the North after she allegedly entered a security zone. The North expressed regret but refused to allow a Southern team to investigate. The South suspended the tours, which never resumed. Eventually, the North took over all the assets at the resort. Tensions rose again in 2009 when the North conducted missile and nuclear tests, although subsiding somewhat after a high-ranking Northern delegation attended former president Kim Dae-jung funeral in Seoul in August.

An even more dramatic incident occurred in the spring of 2010. On 26 March,

the South Korean naval corvette *Cheonan* sank with the loss of all 46 crew members just south of the disputed North–South sea boundary. Although the North was widely suspected as being behind the incident, at first the South Korean authorities said there was no evidence for this and appointed a team of international civilian and military investigators to examine the evidence. This concluded that a torpedo from a North Korean vessel was responsible for the sinking. Russia, which had conducted its own inquiry but did not release the results, and China rejected the report. There is still debate, even in South Korea, about the matter.

President Lee imposed sanctions on the North but failed to get a UN Security Council resolution. The North, which denied involvement, reacted by ending all North–South arrangements designed to prevent clashes between them. Another incident in November that year added to the tension. The South announced a live fire exercise, south of the sea border, which the North demanded it call off. When this did not happen, North Korean onshore batteries shelled the Southern-held Yonpyong Islands, killing two marines and two civilians. Southern batteries returned fire, but it is not known if there were casualties. China blocked a UN Security Council resolution, and although the North said it would react even more firmly if there were further such exercises it ignored one in December.

Despite these events, the Kaesong Industrial Zone continued to function, although the North periodically applied pressure. Otherwise, as long as Lee remained president, relations made no progress. Indeed the North began a savage attack on Lee, depicted as a rat (a play on his surname) being killed in a variety of unpleasant ways. Tense relations continued under Lee's successor, Park Geun-hye, who was also subject to some unpleasant—and sexist—abuse. Following a North Korean missile test and claimed hydrogen bomb test in February 2016, Park announced the "temporary closure" of the Kaesong Industrial Zone and the withdrawal of all South Korean personnel. It has not reopened.

Relations seemed to improve under Park's successor, Moon Jie-in, after a shaky start in 2017. The year 2018 saw not one but three North–South summits, raising the possibility of the North Korean leader, Kim Jong Un, visiting Seoul.Work began on measures such as the removal of landmines from the Demilitarized Zone But hopes faded after the U.S.–North Korean summit in Singapore in February 2019 ended without agreement. Moon continued efforts at improving relations, with hopes being

# South Korea

raised occasionally, but without success. The South Korean presidential election in March 2022 saw the return of a conservative administration, which makes it hard to see any chance of a basic change in the relationship.

### Foreign Relations

A large number of South Koreans have become strongly dissatisfied with the status of the relationship with the United States. The major issues are the American responsibility for the partition of Korea in 1945 (even if the alternative might have been communist control over the entire peninsula), American support for a series of authoritarian governments in South Korea, and the alleged lack of American enthusiasm for reunification of the country. Moreover revelations about the murder of hundreds of South Korean civilian refugees by American soldiers during the chaotic early months of the Korean War as well as ongoing tensions regarding the presence of thousands of American troops within Korea today have added to the tensions.

Since the presidency of George W. Bush (2001-2009), the perception that the American government undermined the effort by South Koreans to improve relations with the North also emerged as a significant issue between the two nations. Certainly the most important element of the continuing tension between the United States and South Korea is the fact that, in large measure, the younger generation has become very skeptical of the Americans. In fact, until recently polls indicated that more South Koreans feared that the United State might start a war than North Korea, a perception that hardly helped American efforts to deal with the threat of North Korea's nuclear program. But such perceptions can be fleeting. As early as the summer of 2009,South Koreans were reportedly losing faith in the North's willingness to make the compromises necessary for a lasting peace.

How to deal with the reality of a weakening North Korea has added to the differences that divide these two longtime allies. Chief among them is the ambivalence among the South Koreans regarding the appropriate policy to take toward the North. For some Koreans this is believed to be the best time to push toward a complete collapse of the Northern regime regardless of the short-term difficulties involved in absorbing the communist government. Until recently though Washington with thousands of troops on the peninsula has at times seemed more interested in lowering the level of rhetoric and moving toward a smoother transition toward the future.

While the Clinton administration had been quite supportive of Kim's opening

**South Korean War Memorial**

# South Korea

toward North Korea, things changed dramatically after the 2000 American elections. Almost as soon as the new American Republican administration organized in Washington, DC, it pronounced itself far more skeptical about working with North Korea. Given the enormously close political ties that exist between South Korea and the United States, this posture made Kim's policy of reconciliation far more difficult.

In the months that followed George W. Bush's arrival in power the momentum toward reconciliation all but vanished and a new climate of tension began to emerge on the peninsula. Nevertheless, as we have seen, when the South Korean presidential elections of 2002 turned into a virtual referendum on Seoul's relations with both the U.S. and North Korea, South Korean voters turned to Roh Moo-myun, the candidate who advocated continuing not only the "Sunshine Policy" and a somewhat more distant relationship with the United States.

There was thus reason to think that despite the long-term ties with the U.S., relations in the future might not be as close as they were during previous decades. As was the case elsewhere in world, South Korea also had a great many skeptics about the US role in Iraq. Still it did commit itself to providing troops for the American effort there. It should also not be a surprise that relations have improved in the period since South Korea's conservatives returned to power.

On the American side, the war in Iraq has also affected very immediately relations with South Korea. In fact, by the summer of 2004 Washington had made known its decision to transfer some of those military units stationed in South Korea to the Iraqi theater of operations. Plans were also announced to relocate many of the American troops to locations further to the south, away from the border and away from the more populated areas of South Korea. This policy has continued, and American forces, once seen as a tripwire for greater American involvement if the North should attack, are now (2022), established well away from the Demilitarized Zone. But while President Donald Trump seemed to have toyed with the idea of withdrawing most of the American military presence in South Korea, his successor President Biden, has moved away from such a position. American troops seem destined to stay.

Not surprisingly, though, American concerns about the growing nuclear capabilities of North Korea have continued to be a major complicating element in Seoul's relationship with the United States. The Bush administration was adamant about the importance of creating a coordinated regional approach to confront North Korea's nuclear weapons capabilities. It insisted that North Korea dismantle its programs before considering any offers of economic assistance to the beleaguered northern government. In contrast, South Korea's governments have tended—at

**Moon Jae-in, president of South Korea**

least when the more leftist governments have been in power—to be much less demanding than the United States and much more interested in expanding regional and international cooperation. They have continued to carry out local initiatives from opening rail and bus lines between the divided nations to establishing more confidence-building measures than its huge American ally has usually been willing to contemplate.

From time to time, there has been some reason for optimism. After years of threats and very few accomplishments, the American administration of George W. Bush began to approach North Korea with more flexibility than it had previously shown. By the early winter of 2007 an agreement was concluded that officially saw North Korea promising to dismantle its primary nuclear facility at Yongbyon in exchange for a package of financial, security, and energy incentives. By the next year that had been accomplished.

There seemed reason for real optimism. Not only had North Koreans allowed international inspectors to begin dismantling their nuclear facilities at Yongbyon, but a series of summit meetings, first between the two nation's presidents and then between their prime ministers, started opening the door for real progress. Plans were finalized to open cargo rail service between the two long estranged nations. There was even talk of creating a formal peace treaty to replace the armistice that had ended the Korean War a half a century earlier. But of course, we have seen such developments on the Korean peninsula often turn out to

**Protest marchers**　　　　　Courtesy of Mark Jihun Suk

149

# South Korea

be quite fleeting. By 2008, North–South relations had sharply deteriorated under South Korean President Lee Myung-bak, and remained so under his successor Park Geun-hye. Once the American 2008 elections brought President Obama to power, the United States, South Korea's principal ally, at first indicated its willingness to open up a more meaningful dialogue with the North, but this came to nothing and Obama turned to "strategic patience," which in effect meant doing very little. Then came President Trump, who at first threatened the North with "Fire and Fury." This gave way to dialogue and summit meetings, the first ever between a U.S. president and a North Korean leader. Yet once again, the high hopes drifted away after the February 2019 summit in Hanoi, which collapsed over irreconcilable demands. Until he left office in 2021, Trump continued to hope that he could revive the earlier high hopes. His successor, President Biden, however, who had been vice president under Obama, had many other matters to consider, and faced with COVID, North Korea effectively shut itself down. The result was effectively, a return to Obama's strategic patience.

Overall, relations between Japan and South Korea seemed to be on the mend in the early years of the 21st century, as both countries worked to lessen the continuing tensions associated with the years of Japan's colonial control over Korea. Japan's government finally issued an official apology for its earlier imperialistic policies toward Korea. Former South Korean President Kim Dae-jung officially forgave Tokyo. Going further than previous presidents, Kim even promised to ease the barriers against Japanese cultural imports into the republic. Much of that was scuttled when yet another crisis developed over revisions in Japan's school books that failed to meet Korean demands for a fuller accounting of Japan's behavior during the colonization of Korea. Eventually it was agreed that the three countries—China, South Korea, and Japan—would work together to create a mutually agreed upon history of their often troubled relationship. As the most recent global economic meltdown unfolded, Japan and China both worked to help keep South Korea's financial house in order. This was a quite impressive example of regional cooperation. However, that momentum toward reconciliation lessened as more conservative and nationalistic politicians arrived in power in both Tokyo and Seoul.

One issue that has long aroused significant tensions between South Korea and Japan has been competing claims to the islands known as Tokto in Korean and Takeshima in Japanese. Although there are economic dimensions over fishing rights associated with the controversy, nationalist emotions have sometimes made the situation all the more complicated.

Unfortunately, relations have not improved in recent years, as South Korea has made demands for a more explicit apology regarding Japanese use of Korean women as sex slaves during the war and apparently President Park Geun-hye's political need to take an especially hard line stand on relations with Tokyo. Her successor, President Moon Jie-in proved equally hostile toward Japan, despite United States strong wish to see the two countries work together on security concerns over China and North Korea. Although this might seem sensible to Washington think tanks, it ignores history and so far has not made much headway.

Until 2016, relations between the Republic of Korea has steadily developed since the 1990s. Two-way tourism flourished and trade, once carried out clandestinely, now flourished. A free-trade agreement in 2014 helped, reaching over $100 billion annually. There were minor tensions, with a small dispute over some rocks claimed by both sides, jostling over fishing rights in the Yellow Sea, and issues such as the wish by some to invite the Dalai Lama.

Then, tension between China and South Korea rose in 2016 after South Korea and the United States began discussions about the introduction of the anti-missile Terminal High Altitude Area Defense System (THAAD) as part of the defense of United States' territory against a possible North Korean missile attack. There were worries in South Korea that such a move would provoke a Chinese reaction. These were overridden by the Park Geun-hye government, which in any case was not happy that China was not putting more pressure on the North to halt its nuclear program. The Chinese reaction was swift, hitting South Korean trade, tourism and popular culture. Sales of Korean goods in China were severely limited and Chinese tourists no longer visited. Matters improved somewhat after President Moon Jie-in took office in 2017 and promised South Korea would not participate in the U.S. missile defense system, there would be no additional deployment of THAAD, and Japan-U.S.-Korea security cooperation would not become a military alliance. The issue has not gone away, however. Koreans have become touchy over alleged Chinese denial that some of the peninsula's ancient states were Korean, and over claims that China has misappropriated the Korean traditional dish of kimchi. When a Chinese woman appeared as part of the opening ceremony of the Beijing Winter Olympics in February 2022 wearing the Korean dress known as hanbok in South Korea, there were protests at yet another appropriation of Korean culture. The explanation that she represented the sizeable number of Chinese of Korean origin, according to the Chinese embassy in Seoul, did not quell the protests, which were taken up by some politicians.

One of the most interesting developments in South Korea's regional relations is its increasing emergence as a model for other developing Asian nations. China's growth has been seen as impressive, but its circumstances are so different given its size. South Korea is being seen more and more often by its Asian neighbors as a particularly appropriate model to emulate. This has been especially obvious in the growing ties between South Korea and Cambodia, for example.

## Culture and Society

Korean culture, although distinct from that of Japan, resembles it in many respects. They have both also been exposed to Chinese influences over many centuries. Not surprisingly there are many cultural features that all three Confucian-influenced communities share in common. Nevertheless, Korea like Japan has also developed along its own unique cultural lines. As well as Chinese influence, the Japanese colonial period (1910–1945) has also left many traces, even if many of the most prominent ones, including major buildings, have been removed. Styles of work, and even some aspects of food culture, display clear links to the Japanese period and practices.

The ancient pre-Chinese aspects of Korean culture, such as shamanism—the belief in occult sorcerers and worship of demons—have a Northeast and Central Asian derivation. On this base the ingredients of Chinese culture, including Buddhism and Confucianism, were superimposed as a second layer. Since the 19th century there have been many conversions to Christianity. In fact, due to the support many foreign Christian missionaries gave to the Koreans during their years as a Japanese colony, the religion has an association with Korean nationalism not generally found elsewhere in East Asia. Today, the Christian community is a large and influential group that exerts a profound influence in the peninsula. Several prominent political figures, including former President Kim Dae-jung, a Roman Catholic, have been Christians.

## Health Care in Korea

The South Korean medical establishment has been deeply influenced by American medical practices. However, when it came to creating a health care delivery system that covered their entire population, the

Japanese model was chosen as a more appropriate system. The struggle was hardly an easy one. Before the late 1970s, medical insurance in South Korea was a voluntary decision by individuals who could afford it. But in his last years in office before his murder, President Park's government began the process of putting into place a mandatory health care system that would cover everyone. It was quite a battle. In fact, it was to last a dozen years as previously uninsured groups were added to the program until, by the late 1980s, the entire population was eventually covered. The funding has come from a combination of sources ranging from the individuals themselves to their employers and government subsidies to help pay the costs of the official medical societies that the government chose to administer the programs. The societies themselves were a conscious choice between the former voluntary private insurance programs and a full-blown government program that the administration wished to avoid.

## COVID-19

Then came COVID-19. This was probably inevitable, given the high volume of movement between South Korea and China. The first case was reported in January 2020, and the government response was swift and effective. A rapid program of test and trace, with quarantine for those affected was soon in place, with frequently daily checks to make sure people complied, and strict travel restrictions. By July, there were 12,904 positive test results and 282 deaths. The disease seemed to be under control but when restrictions were eased in May, there was a surge of cases linked in particular to places of entertainment and religious centers. Localized controls began again and persisted into 2021. By mid-May 2021, there had been 135,000 cases, of which 8,500 were still isolating, and 1926 deaths. The government was criticized for the slow beginning of vaccination, with only 3.8 million having received a first dose and 1.7 million both. Internationally, however, the South Korean management of the pandemic was seen as an overall success, with clear lessons for other countries.

Unfortunately, from June 2021, numbers began to rise again. By October, they had reached 2,300 new cases daily, and the trend continued, reaching 7,000 per day in mid-December. The government then acted, introducing new controls, and the numbers fell back. But the respite was only brief. By the end of January 2022, they had reached over 18,000 per day and were still rising, reaching 600,000 on 16 March. Numbers than began to show a stark decline. As with other countries, the

main cause of the increase was the spread of the omicron variant. And like most other countries that experienced a surge, this did not produce the same level of hospitalization or deaths as had happened in the early days. Also, after a slow start, vaccination levels had risen, with over 85% of the population vaccinated by March 2022. Like many other countries faced with increased infections in 2022, the government did not impose new restrictions and indeed, began to relax those in place, arguing that "we have to live with the virus."

## Korean Women

Like most of Asia, Korea remains a strongly patriarchal society. Traditionally some women's roles as shaman-like priestesses in the traditional religion of the peninsula did give them levels of influence not always possible elsewhere. More recently, partly as a result of women's activism, laws have been passed improving their status within society. In 1991, the South Korean Family Law was amended to give women more property and divorce rights. Of college-educated Korean women less than 20% are employed and usually in nonprofessional positions. Viewing the situation from a more global perspective offers important insights. On issues of gender equality, South Korean women recently scored only 92nd on a scale of 110 countries while they hit the 95th spot in wage equality.

Still, South Korean women today have access to the same higher education that young men do although few hold positions of executive level responsibility in the country's businesses. The situation is improving, though. The number of women in more senior management positions has doubled over the last decade although in real terms the figures remain small. Overall, women in employment rose from 47% in 1990 to 54% in 2019. There was then a slight fall back, to 53%, in 2020—about the same level as Japan—probably due to with the pandemic.

Women have served in positions of influence in the government bureaucracy, and the legislative elections of 2004 turned out to be truly revolutionary in terms of women's political roles. More than 150 women sought seats in South Korea's 17th national assembly, and 39 of them took their places among their male counterparts. This was a significant increase over the 16 women who had been part of the previous legislature. South Korea's women were also helped by a then new law that required political parties to nominate women for at least half of their proportional candidates. However, the victory went beyond that as 10 of the female legislators were elected directly by the

voters. More significant was former President Roh's naming of Han Myung-sook as the nation's first female prime minister. And of course the arrival to the presidency of Park Geun-hye in 2013, which of course probably did not help the cause of women in the long run given how disastrous her presidency turned out to be.

And of course South Korea is as much a part of the growing globalized cultural community as any other nation. In that context the #MeToo movement, originally begun in the United States, which focused on sexual abuse, especially by powerful males became an important social movement as well in the nation over the last couple of years.

The immediate future may not be so bright for women, however. South Korean yonger men, apparently, feel that too much has been done to advance women's rights, while the election of the antifeminist Yoon Suk-yeol as president by a narrow margin in March 2022, does not promise well. During his campaign, he said that he would abolish the ministry of gender equality and family affairs, established in 1988, as its work was no longer required.

## The Korean Peninsula and Climate Change

As one of the more industrialized nations on the planet, South Korea has contributed substantially to the growth of heat trapping $CO_2$ molecules in the upper atmosphere. In 2007, for example, South Korea's $CO_2$ emissions were the ninth highest in the world. As elsewhere, the climate of South Korea is changing in profound ways. Over the last 20 years, annual rainfall has risen 7% and heavy rainfall by more than 20%. But as is usually the case, the number of days that get no rainfall has also dropped. Meanwhile the nation has also experienced the worst drought in its recorded history.

More significantly, South Korean studies suggest that the patterns of agriculture are likely to change with some areas becoming more appropriate for cultivation while others should become capable of sustaining new crops. That is while other crops will likely become less sustainable. Similar changes are anticipated off the nation's coastlines as changing water temperatures impact the sorts of fish in them. Extreme temperatures have already impacted livestock and people as well. For instance, during the heat wave of 2012, around 800,000 chickens died as well as tens of thousands of ducks while the human population's efforts to cool themselves with air conditioning often failed due to the rolling electrical blackouts caused by the excessive demand.

# South Korea

Overall national studies suggest that for South Korea a one-meter rise in sea level will expose 1.2% of the nation's land and 2.6% of the population to flooding. But that more permanent water rise is more likely an event of the future. For now, the nation has had to contend with dramatic flooding incidents such as the devastating floods that hit Seoul, and can also cause severe damage in the countryside.

### New Energy Directions

As with many other nations, the importance of developing a sustainable energy based on renewable green energy sources has become an important goal for South Korea. In fact, in 2008 on the occasion of the 60th anniversary of the founding of the republic, former President Lee Myung-bak officially announced a policy of "Low Carbon, Green Growth" for the nation. The following year saw the establishment of an official presidential committee on the topic. Moreover the country has implemented a five-year plan to promote the reduction of fossil fuels and the enhancement of green energy technologies. It also broke ground in early spring 2007 for what was expected to be the world's largest solar energy plant. Once operational, it will complement a large tidal power facility that is already under construction.

The announced national goal is to raise South Korea's use of renewable energy from its current 2.28% to 10% by 2020. A particularly important element of the nation's commitment to the challenge of climate change was its hosting during the summer of 2009 of an international conference that dealt with the impact of global warming on some of the world's major cities.

Ambitious in itself, these plans were complimented by significant government investment in these new technologies and a stated goal of becoming a world leader in green growth. In that context South Korea has also become involved in helping African nations deal with the challenge of climate change.

Economically, what has been especially interesting was the decision in the same way the nation had initially taken on its post–Korean War industrialization effort. More specifically the approach now is to initiate a series of national five-year plans initially scheduled to run from 2008 through 2013. These include the goal of dedicating 2% of the national GDP to a comprehensive effort to deal with greening the economy. More realistically the plan also called for strengthening the ability of the nation to adapt to climate change. This is a decision that was probably reinforced later when, as we have seen, large parts of the Korean peninsula found itself devastated by horrendous flooding, in 2011 in South Korea and 2012 in North Korea. All were indicative of the sort of stresses a changing climate is bringing to much of the world.

### The Future: South Korea

South Korea faces many challenges in the decade ahead. The political transition from South Korea's liberals to the conservatives went very smoothly, and even more impressively the nation survived well the Park impeachment.

Most significant of course is the roller-coaster nature of relations between the two Koreas. There is, not surprisingly a growing skepticism among many in South Korea about their decade-long effort to engage the North. Today more and more South Koreans feel they have very little to show for the effort. Despite years of improved relations, family visits, joint ventures and even the award of a Nobel Peace Prize for their gestures toward Pyongyang, the North often acts in a very aggressive fashion. It is thus not surprising that the record of failure coupled with the North's growing nuclear capacity have raised voices in the South calling for a nuclear program of their own.

As we have seen as of early 2019 relations once again appeared to be improving and there was even a concerted effort to remove the extraordinarily dangerous mines that had long ago been deployed in the Joint Security Area that separates the two countries, but such hopes came to nothing.

Internationally, of course, the situation has become considerably more complicated. Indeed while relations with North Korea seem about as usual, swinging back and forth between occasional efforts at reconciliation and more tensions the evolving role of the United States has become a much greater issue than it was in recent decades. Indeed the combination of an American administration under President Trump that has become especially concerned about North Korea's growing nuclear arsenal and a more general American withdrawal from its three quarters of a century of global leadership has forced South Korea's leadership to reevaluate their own circumstances.

Ironically, or perhaps because of the tensions between the United States and North Korea both Korean governments decided to take the initiative to reduce tensions between themselves. Indeed as the world entered 2018 plans were dramatically underway to arrange a significant North Korean presence in the South Korean sponsored Winter Olympic games. Indeed during the games themselves the sister of North Korean leader Kim Jong-un arrived as a special guest of the southern government and officially invited South Korea's president Moon Jae-in to visit the north in a gesture that invoked memories of the short lived reconciliation of the mid 1990s. That visit took place in September of 2018 and a visit by North Korea's leader to South Korea was expected to take place sometime in 2019.

Still as tensions rise and fall on the peninsula some are probably relieved that the American-designed Terminal High Altitude Area Defense or THAAD system that has, after considerable controversy, been deployed in the South. All in all, there were three contacts between the two leaders in 2018, including Moon's visit to Pyongyang in September. Wide-ranging agreement was reached on measures to reduce tension and to turn the Demilitarized Zone into a really demilitarized area. Kim Jong Un also undertook to visit Seoul. But the North Korean interest was really better relations with the United States. That seemed hopeful in September 2018, when Kim Jon Un and President Trump met in Singapore, but a second meeting, in Hanoi in February 2019, broke up without agreement. That had a negative effect on North–South relations. Kim Jong-un has concentrated on developing his nuclear capability, with new means of delivery and regular missile testing. A liaison office, established in Kaesong (the North's southernmost city) in 2018, was blown up in June 2020, allegedly in protest over the South's failure to stop balloons with memory sticks and other material being sent into the North.

South Korean President Moon tried to keep up contacts, but despite the occasional positive response from his Northern counterpart, got nowhere, especially after North Korea sealed itself off from the world because of COVID. The failure of his policy toward North Korea saw Moon's popularity steadily decline, with some alleging that he had neglected urgent doemstic issues such as youth unemployment because of his concentration on the North. The result was that in the March 2022 presidential election, fought between two candidates with no experience of elected office, the former prosecutor Yoon Seok-yeol, a man of extremely conservative views, beat his more liberal rival, Lee Jae-myung, by a narrow margin (0.7% of the vote). Yoon has indicated that he will take a harder line toward the North. South Koreans will take some consolation from the fact that relations with the United States are better under President Biden than they were under President Trump. And, despite all the tensions and the North's regular announcments that it will no longer abide by the 1953 Armistice Agreement, it has continued to do so.

# Democratic People's Republic of Korea (North Korea)

North Korean leaders Kim Il-sung and Kim Jong-il

**Area:** 46,814 sq. mi. (121,730 sq. km.)
**Population:** 25,879,842 (May 2021 est.)
**Capital City:** Pyongyang, pop. 3,108,000 (May 2021 est.)
**Climate:** Temperate, with a longer and much colder winter than in the South; summer wet season from July to September
**Neighboring Countries:** China (North); Russia (Northeast); South Korea (South)
**Official Language:** Korean
**Other Principal Tongues:** Russian, Chinese, English. Japanese is spoken by a few very old people.
**Ethnic Background:** Korean, similar to both Manchurian and Mongolian
**Religion:** Buddhism, Christianity, Chondogyo (native syncretic religion), but all religions are under state control.
**Main Exports:** (to South Korea, Russia, China, Japan) Minerals, meat products, fish, and textiles
**Main Imports:** (from China, Thailand, Russia, Japan) Petroleum, machinery, grains, and coal
**Currency:** Won
**Former Colonial Status:** Korea was a tributary state of the Chinese empires for most of its history up to 1895; Japanese protectorate (1905–1910); Japanese Dependency (1910–1945); from 1945 to 1948 it was under Soviet occupation; after 1948 it developed an independent communist regime allied with both the Soviet Union and with China.
**National Day:** September 8, 1948
**Chief of State:** Kim Jong-un, chief of state (since December 17, 2011)
**National Flag:** Two blue stripes on the top and bottom separated by two thin white stripes from a broad central field of red which contains at left center a white circle with a 5-pointed red star
**Per Capita GDP Income:** $1,800 (2022 est.) (purchasing power parity)

### Political System

The Democratic People's Republic of Korea (DPRK) is one of the world's few remaining hardline communist states. The constitution was adopted in 1948 but has been amended several times since. In the most recent changes, in 2016, it became the Socialist Constitution of the Democratic People's Republic of Korea. This ended the role of the National Defense Commission, defined in the 1998 Kim Il Sung Constitution as the "highest organ of state," replacing it with the State Affairs Commission, headed by Kim Jong Un. It also signified a shift from military matters to the economy. The legal system is built on communist legal theory, German civil law, Japanese law from the colonial period and a significant amount of more traditional Korean Confucian and monarchial elements. The judiciary has no authority to review acts of the legislature. Suffrage is universal for everyone 17 years of age and older. The government has both a head of state and a Premier. The Supreme People's Assembly is the national legislature and has one house.

# North Korea

Candidates for office are chosen by the Korean Workers' Party (DWP) and run unopposed. The assembly itself rarely meets; in between meetings, a standing committee transacts business. For its entire history the state has been dominated by one family, initially Kim Il-sung, who died in 1994 and was followed by his son Kim Jong-il. Upon the latter's death in late December 2011, Kim Jong-un, Kim Jong-il's youngest son took over. The tools of that domination included not only the military and security services, but a cult of leadership that has regularly deified North Korean rulers in a way that might have even made Stalin or Mao Zedong blush.

### Politics and Government

The last few decades have generally been a disaster for North Korea, one of the last Soviet-style communist societies. The 1990s began with the collapse of its longtime supporter, the Soviet Union. And Beijing, its only other significant international friend, which had long been encouraging North Korea to transform its economy to survive, began to demand that it pay normal prices. While North Korea has a longtime reputation as the most isolated of national states, evidence of its dramatically faltering economy is everywhere. Those last decades have seen disastrous floods that have devastated important farmlands, while the regime has had to request enormous amounts of food aid from outside agencies. Undernourishment is rampant, and very real famine carried away enormous numbers of North Koreans during the mid-1990s. The actual state of affairs is becoming more and more known outside of the region, and it has added to the level of condemnation it receives.

Driven primarily by food shortages and the collapse of the old industrial base in the Northeast, thousands of people risked their lives to go to China, where many remained. The exact numbers of those who have left are not clear. Some return, and some may make multiple trips. Since Kim Jong Un came to power in 2011, there have been frequent efforts to stop the flow, which has declined somewhat. Some North Koreans make it to the South, but large numbers of North Koreans live in China, without official status, and others are scattered around East Asia and further afield.

### A Communist Monarchy?

In 1994, Kim Il-sung, the longtime exalted leader, died just before he was to meet with South Korean President Kim Young-sam. After that, in a fashion more reminiscent of an imperial dynasty than a

**North Korea's leader since 2011, Kim Jong-un**

modern socialist state, his son Kim Jong-il, who had been increasingly in charge for years, assumed power. For outsiders, the younger Kim's arrival to power had been of particular concern. He was not well known among North Korea watchers and rarely appeared in public. Moreover, he was thought to have been involved in some of the most egregious acts of North Korean terrorism. For most observers, though, the immediate issue was whether Kim Jong-il would be able fully to take control of the reins of power.

In the decade that followed, the answer to that question became clearer. The younger Kim successfully solidified his authority and slowly assumed many of his father's official titles. Eventually he was even named the official head of state. Nevertheless, the question of just how powerful any official leader of North Korea is remains somewhat of a mystery. One thing is clear: Kim Jong-il gave the nation's military significantly more power than it had held under his father.

Once in power North Korea's new leader showed a side few had suspected. For a time he devoted considerable energy to improving relations with South Korea and China. He even toured Shanghai, the People's Republic of China's showcase of economic and industrial accomplishments. In addition, the new leader, along with a large group of companions, traveled by

train to confer with Russia's leadership. Most interestingly, under Kim Jong-il, North Korea made a significant effort to establish ties with the outside world. That was something North Korea had been far less interested in during the long reign of his father, Kim Il-sung.

Clearly, such efforts were very different from those that North Korean watchers had been used to observing. Some even suggested for a time that that the younger Kim was interested in emerging as North Korea's Gorbachev. But given what happened to the Soviet Union under Gorbachev's care, it seemed safe to say that Kim Jong-il would probably have preferred to be North Korea's Deng Xiaoping. In the end, nothing of the sort happened.

Nevertheless, any real improvement was dependent on North Korea being able to move out from under the obsolete economic and geopolitical environment in which it has operated for more than a half-century. And for a time it looked like there might even be a real reconciliation between North and South Korea and perhaps with the United States as well. Sadly, though, most of that momentum dissipated during the first decade of the 21st century even as Kim Jong-il himself seemed to weaken physically.

The most immediate political challenge was of quite a different order. While Kim Il-sung had obviously groomed his own son to assume leadership, Kim Jong-il, who also had sons, did not initially appear to be grooming a successor. That oversight, if that was indeed the case, became especially important in 2008 when Kim Jong-il disappeared from public life for a considerable period. Speculation was rampant that he had had some sort of health crisis, most likely a stroke.

### A Third Generation of Leadership Emerges: Kim Jong-un

When Kim Jong-il did reemerge, the rumors appeared true given how much his physical appearance had deteriorated over the preceding months. Perhaps with a sense that the end was nearing, Kim Jong-il began to move more definitively to establish his chosen successor in power. Kim Jong-il quickly installed his youngest son, Kim Jong-unin this role. . Indeed the young man was named to the post of vice chairman of the national defense commission, an appointment that officially made him second only to his father in influence. Moreover, he was also named a four-star general in the nation's military.

But even the elder Kim's dictatorial powers were limited by human frailty. In December 2011, he died suddenly of a heart attack while traveling on a train. The news was withheld for about two days when it was finally announced by a tearful television news reader. Once the shock was over, plans were announced for a smooth transition to the leadership of his 20-something son, Kim Jong-un. But closer observers believed that both the military and Kim's uncle, Jang Song-thaek, would themselves take part in a much less personal joint leadership for at least the immediate future. It was not merely Kim Jong-un's inexperience that might have called for such a joint leadership, but simply the obvious young age of North Korea's new leader. Despite everything, North Korea is still a society where age itself carries authority, and the new leader carried very little of that. On the other hand, the fact that the young man did appear to resemble his revered grandfather more than his father offered a few advantages the young man was apparently willing to exploit.

Especially interesting initially was the new and quite young leader's relationship with his powerful uncle. The uncle, who was married to the younger Kim's aunt, had in the past had a reputation not only for factionalism, but for having his own opinions on leadership in the DRK. In fact, in the early years of the new century, Jang Song-thaek saw many members of his own family purged and himself dramatically demoted only to be reinstated as Kim Jong-il's health deteriorated. During

**Statue of Kim Il-sung and adoring children**          Courtesy of Bradley Martin

the months after Kim Jong-il's death, the uncle, Jang Song-thaek, initially seemed quite supportive. That was apparently appreciated. For a time after Kim Jong-un came to power, his uncle's influence appeared to grow significantly. Many outsiders speculated on who the real senior leader was. They continued to do so until late 2013 when the situation changed dramatically.

Suddenly, in late December 2013 North Korea's untested new leader had his previously powerful uncle publically arrested and summarily executed. The apparently bloody purge that followed included the deaths not only of Jang Song-thaek's followers, but members of his family while others apparently ended up in North Korea's infamous concentration camps. Over the next few weeks, often conflicting reports emerged as well about the fate of his aunt, Kim Jong-il's sister, who had herself once been quite powerful. (Nothing was seen nor heard from her until January 2021, when she was shown at a New Year Concert in Pyongyang seated with Kim Jong Un and his wife.) What had really caused the break was unclear although competition over the profits from seafoods, especially the oyster trade, was said to have played a role while Kim Jong-un himself spoke vaguely of stamping out factionalism. Jang Song Thaek failed to show the usual deference to Kim Jong Un in public, which may also have been a cause of grievance. More serious, probably, was Jang's apparent increasingly close links to China. He was a frequent visitor, and there were reports that the Chinese had built a special residence for him. Given persistent foreign claims that China might intervene in North Korea to avoid a collapse, Kim Jong Un might have been concerned that

Jang was plotting with the Chinese.

Similar suspicions may have been aroused over his elder half-brother, Kim Jong Nam. Although once said to be Kim Jong Il's favorite son, they had a falling-out. Since at least the late 1990s, Kim Jong Nam lived in Macau, although he made occasional visits to North Korea while his father was alive. In Macau, he was under Chinese protection, and there was international speculation that the Chinese might consider installing him in place of his younger brother, of whose succession he had been critical. In Macau or China, he was probably safe, but in February 2017 he visited Malaysia, apparently without any form of protection. While he waited for a return flight at Kuala Lumpur airport, a woman smeared his face with a cloth. He immediately became ill and died on the way to hospital. The next day, Malaysian police said that Kim Jong Nam had been killed with a nerve agent, VX. The Malaysian police arrested a North Korean, who was released but expelled for a visa violation, and two women, one Vietnamese and one Indonesian. North Korea denied any involvement, alleging a U.S.-South Korean plot. For a time, relations between the two countries were tense, but that began to pass after the body was returned to North Korea. The two women went on trial for murder. pleading not guilty and claiming they thought they had been taken part in a prank. One was released in early March 2019 and the other shortly afterwards, having pleaded guilty to a lesser charge.

If there was considerable speculation about the possibility of positive change when his father succeeded his grandfather, the early years of Kim Jong-un's reign did not offer the same optimism, even though

# North Korea

he had been partially educated in the West. He continued his father's "Army First" policy and for many years, made no attempt to change the formal state structure. Moreover, the numbers of those held in North Korea's concentration camps may have actually grown since he came to power.

### Life in North Korea

Until the middle of the last century, the lives of those who lived on the Korean peninsula were relatively similar whether they lived in the northern part of the country or the southern part. Both experienced the relative isolation of late Yi Korea and the traumas of both the Japanese occupation and the Korean War that ravaged the entire peninsula. From the mid 1950s though, their fate began to radically diverge. While South Korea moved unevenly toward becoming a major industrial power and by the mid-1990s a successful democracy, North Koreans lived their lives in a very different environment. However, in those first decades after the end of the Korean War, that divergence was by no means self-evident. Initially, North Korea was relatively better off both industrially and in terms of natural resources than South Korea. By the mid-1970s, after America's embarrassing retreat from South Vietnam, communism seemed to be on the rise.

Within North Korea, the government managed to meet the population's basic material needs while building up an enormous military infrastructure dedicated to the unification, of the peninsula. That military infrastructure was complemented by an extraordinarily sophisticated leadership

cult that was built around the accomplishments of Kim Il-sung, the nation's longtime dictator. That cult was rarely threatened, given the reality that for generations only a very few North Koreans had any opportunity whatsoever to learn what was going on outside the nation's borders. Within North Korea itself, while communism might in theory be a society that historically embraced an ideology of equality, in reality the North Korean society set up by Kim Il-sung was anything but equal. Rather it was a system as elaborately class and hierarchy-based as any found in the modern world. Having first demonstrated his ruthlessness in eliminating any potential rivals to his leadership, he had in 1958 turned to the effort to transform North Korean society itself. A scheme was put into place to categorize the entire population based on their assumed political reliability. Throughout society, people found themselves cataloged based on eight different criteria. The result was a *song-bun* or rating, perhaps a bit like a western credit rating, but with infinitely more important implications. Somewhat similar to both traditional Korean feudal models and class and caste systems found elsewhere in Asia, the system measured not only an individual but one's entire family. While enormously complicated and including more than 50 different categories, the system fundamentally broke down into three groupings: those who were at the core of the system; those seen as potentially wavering; and those seen, at least in theory, as hostile or in some fashion anti-social—even though under the circumstances no one could actually afford to be even slightly lacking in enthusiasm for Kim Il-sung and his government. Those who were placed in the

bottom rungs of society were not surprisingly former members of the South Korean army, people with formerly wealthy backgrounds, religious figures, and many others whose fate would be intimately linked to their ranking.

Where one fits into the system has an enormous impact on everything, from job prospects to housing. The latter applies not only within specific cities, but it affects the coveted right to live in Pyongyang, the capital. Not surprisingly, only the elite can travel or have any hope of living in the capital. Moreover, the entire system was buttressed by an ideology relatively unique to North Korea: the idea of *juche* or self-reliance. While North Korea was formally part of the communist bloc, it was something quite different as well. According to the theory of *juche*, an ideology vaguely similar in some aspects to some of the ideas associated with Turkey's *autarky*, North Korea was presented largely as an economically autonomous state that was not dependent on outsiders, whether within the communist world or the capitalist world beyond. The state ideology largely built from a powerful sense of Korean superiority, intense nationalism, the cult of Kim Il-sung and ideas borrowed from socialist theory enveloped the entire state and people in a mantle of an extraordinarily special status. For a long time, the isolation of the state, its control of the media and early relative economic success helped most of the nation's citizens accept state orthodoxy as truth. It should be noted that *juche* is seen by some scholars as a somewaht meaningless term, invented so that Kim Il-sung might present himself as an ideological figure, on a par with Stalin or Mao Zedong.

But North Korea's relative advantages over South Korea began to weaken in the 1970s. Its early industrialization faltered as machinery supplied in the 1950s as aid by the Soviet Union and Eastern Europe began to wear out. Workers, constantly encouraged to do more, actually became less productive. Conscious that Soviet production standards were lower than those in the West, the North Korean regime went on a buying spree for new, Western equipment. But it found that it could not pay for much of what it ordered. By the late 1970s, it had become the first communist country to default on its debts. Credit and the supply of goods dried up. Most of the debt is still outstanding. Around the same time, other international changes left North Korea behind.

On one hand, many of the nations of East and Southeast Asia began borrowing the export-orientated industrial policies Jadcpan and Germany had pioneered in the years after the Second World War and began to experience levels of extraordinary

**North Korean "Mass Games"**

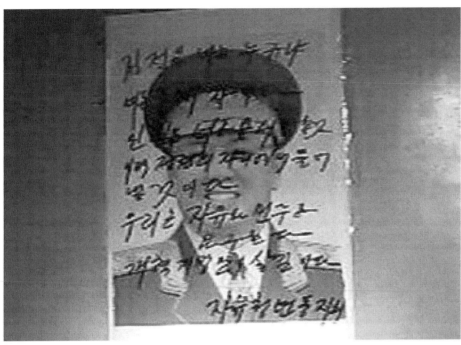

**Defaced photo of Kim Jong-il demanding his ouster**

growth. South Korea and Taiwan, and later nations from Thailand to Indonesia emerged economically and became known for a time as the new Asian Tigers. Meanwhile the socialist world, especially under the initially more tentative efforts of Deng Xiaoping in China and later more dramatically under Gorbachev in the Soviet Union, began to back away from the most obvious feature of communism's famous command economies. For tens of millions of North Koreans, the changes in the evolving socialist world would prove devastating, and for many, the changes would prove fatal.

### North Korea's Great Famine of the 1990s

As so often with such governments, the North Korean regime was built on an impossibly difficult lie. The state had taken responsibility for provide the masses with their basic food needs, including food, clothing, and housing. The policy also included making any sort of private economic activity absolutely illegal and doing so even as the government was announcing proudly that North Korea was economically self-sufficient. But that had never been the case. North Korea's leaders had relied very heavily on the generosity of their socialist brethren. However, it had taken advantage of the antagonism that steadily evolved from the 1950s on between the Soviet Union and the People's Republic of China. For Kim Il-sung, whose nation shared a border with both People's Republic and the Soviet Union, the situation offered an opportunity to play off one

communist giant against the other and gain the material advantages such efforts could offer. It was those circumstances, rather than the special unique circumstances within North Korea, that had allowed Pyongyang to appear relatively successful in its early decades. But everything changed for North Korea as both Moscow and Beijing started losing interest in North Korea. In the worst possible insult to the northern leadership's pride, each opened relations with the more successful South Koreans even as the subsidies from the socialist world stopped coming.

By the mid-1990s, the situation had become dramatically different for by then, given the collapse of Eastern European communism, the North found itself one of the last regimes still trying to maintain a Stalinist-style communist command economy. That effort, along with a series of natural disasters, severely damaged the economy of North Korea and created an environment of widespread hunger through much of the country by the last decade of the 20th century. For North Koreans, it was a horror to rival the worst of the famines in the 1950s associated with China's Great Leap Forward. The economy simply ground to a halt. The government was unable to meet even the most basic of the populations food needs, and there was simply no private economy to pick up the slack. Worse yet, until the government eventually relented and started tolerating individual entrepreneurial efforts, people found the mere act of trying to feed themselves by their own efforts to be largely illegal. As the famine developed, the

regime had little choice but to encourage the population to try to find ways to feed themselves. It was an immediate impact that eventually began a slow transformation of North Korean society itself.

Taking a page from the reforms in both the People's Republic and Vietnam, even North Koreans have been allowed to set up semi-private markets where people can buy a wide variety of goods from shoes to hardware. Meanwhile a significant percentage of the nation's foreign policy in recent years has been directed toward finding ways to repair the nation's deeply weakened economic infrastructure. And it is not just the buying and selling of goods considered legal in the West that contributes to the survival in North Korea. The production and sale of methamphetamines of the sort made famous by American TV show *Breaking Bad* are commonly available among the population that finds them not only a source of revenue, but a way to stave off the effects of hunger. But, of course, the drug is addictive and capable of adding to the misery so common in the country.

For North Korean citizens the relative isolation of the population has diminished as more and more of them have heard stories of the growing wealth enjoyed by their neighbors from China and Russia and the prosperity of their archrivals in the South. Not surprisingly more and more North Koreans have begun to cross into China in search of food. There they live furtive lives trying to survive and to avoid Chinese authorities who often send them back to North Korea. However, the movement back and forth across the Chinese–North Korea border has in recent years played its own role in opening up life in North Korea to outsiders. It has now become more and more common for cell phones to be smuggled into North Korea. Today reports about life in the North relayed to the South by those very cell phones have, to Pyongyang's great dissatisfaction, been regularly posted on websites. Another important source of information about the country has been until 2020, the presence of UN organizations and international Private Voluntary Organizations (known as Non-Governmental Organizations or NGOS outside the United States). UN reports, in particular, have provided detailed information about issues such as food supplies and health matters.

There is even a journal, published by Asia Press in Japan. *Rimjingang*, that claims that it has its own set of reporters operating secretly in North Korea writing on developments there, efforts that naturally put the individuals involved at great personal risk. But perhaps even more problematic for the regime itself are South Korean movies—and television soap operas

# North Korea

that are regularly smuggled in. Regardless of their story qualities, they reveal to a fascinated North Korean audience how radically different their own lives are from those of their southern neighbors. Perhaps even more predictably, as the numbers of North Korean defectors living in South Korea has grown and prospered, some, such as Thae Yong-ho, a former North Korean diplomat, who was elected to the South Korean National Assembly in 2020, have become more and more determined to undermine the regime.

While this new 21st-century penetration into North Korea has become a useful tool for outsiders, those North Koreans who take part in the effort are putting themselves at great risk of being imprisoned in one of the North's infamous prison camps.

### North Korea's Gulag of Prison Camps

While life for the average North Korean has become more and more difficult in recent decades, it is far worse for those who have somehow roused the regime's anger. That does not simply mean people who have individually aroused the regime's wrath. Taking a page from Korean tradition, Kim Il-sung, in founding North Korea, created a collective punishment system that included three generations of a family. Thus it was not a question of personally angering the regime, but of simply being related to someone who had at some point, perhaps decades earlier, done so. What is truly astonishing about the chain of prison camps in North Korea is that until recently, while the world knows a great deal about similar camps once operated by Hitler's Germany or Stalin's Soviet Union, those in North Korea have largely been ignored by outsiders. This is both because of the very limited information that was available and the general obsession with other matters from the North's missile and nuclear weapon's programs to its seesaw relations with South Korea. But those days are coming to an end as more and more information is emerging about one of the world's longest-lasting systems for incarcerating political prisoners.

From the information increasingly available, it appears that North Korea today operates six different prisons. They house about 200,000 people imprisoned over the decades for an enormous number of crimes from having been tainted by their presence or knowledge of the collapse of communism in Eastern Europe to being related to those who themselves possessed what the regime considers "wrong knowledge." Apparently, those in the camps are at times not only unaware of how their "relatives" have angered the regime, but that they were themselves even related to the offending individuals. One such camp is said to be three times the size of the American District of Columbia.Sometimes fellow inmates can end up having very curious "colleagues." For example, it has been entirely possible for orthodox communists whose more traditional Marxist views clashed with what goes for "Orthodoxy" in North Korea finding themselves housed with devout Christians whose religious convictions attracted the regime's anger.

What is new is the amount of information that is increasingly available about conditions within North Korea's concentration camps. This has come from the testimony of defectors, including some who have been prisoners and others who have been guards at such institutions. It has led to a number of academic studies, as well as collections of documents, documentaries and other material. There has also been a UN report from a former Australian judge Michael Kirby in 2014. These have painted a harrowing picture of life and death in the camps. However, there have also been disputes over some testimonies, as stories have been changed and challenged. This was the case with the account of Shin Dong-hyuk, who featured in the 2012 documentary by Marc Wiese, *Camp 14: Total Control Zone,* and the book by Blair Harden, *Escape from Camp 14,* published in 2013.

### Economy

Obtaining authoritative data for the government of North Korea is a very difficult matter indeed. Massive floods and mismanagement of the economy have been responsible for disastrous economic results. In the 1990s, the health care system collapsed and the hospitals had none of the modern medicines necessary to keep the population healthy. Surgeons were forced to operate without anesthetics. Since then, there has been some improvement, and government factories are again producing some basic medicines. But the severely underfunded health service, once on a par with those of the Soviet Union and Eastern Europe, has not fully recovered.

**"We will avenge anyone who hurts our self-respect wherever he may be!"**
Courtesy of Dave Pomeroy

158

# North Korea

South Korean watchers claim that the North's economy shrunk by 3%–4% for each year of the 1990s. The International Monetary Fund (IMF) estimated in the late 1990s that the country's gross national product (GNP) had fallen from about $21 billion in 1992 to $10.6 billion in 1996. The government itself said that the economy had shrunk by 50% during the late 1990s. Certainly, the collapse of the socialist economies of the USSR and Eastern Europe and the series of natural disasters in the 1990s.hurt North Korea greatly.

The situation improved in the new century. IMF estimates of GNP were $22 biillion in 2002 and $28 biillion in 2010. It then dropped back to $23.5 billion in 2016, and it continued to decline. Estimates for 2022, after two years of isolation because of COVID, are about $19 billion, although as a cautious opening up begins, it is expected to start to rise again after that. H The situation for the nation's residents remains precarious. In fact, what refugees from North Korea most commonly report are rising food prices and growing economic insecurity, Most such people come from the country's northeast, an especially poor area. The government's 2009 decision to devalue North Korea's currency had a tremendously negative impact on the population, which saw the value of their savings collapse. Kim Jong-un has repeatedly said since he assumed power in 2011 that economic development is a priority, but even he admitted at the Eight Party Congress in January 2021 that there were serious economic problems and he sacked several senior officials in charge of economic matters One solution offered was to involve the army more in the wider economy. Another was a new five-year plan because the current one had failed.

Recognizing their precarious economic situation, the government's struggle to find new funds has ranged widely from agreeing to allow international flights over North Korea in order to earn over flight fees from the airlines to the more controversial offer to accept some of Taiwan's nuclear waste. That deal which might have brought millions of dollars into North Korea called for Pyongyang to accept and bury on its territory thousands of barrels of radioactive material from Taiwan. While not of potential use for military purposes, the agreement aroused considerable tension within South Korea that was especially unhappy with the decision to place the material in mine shafts near their common border. Some reports suggest that the search for funds includes involvement in the international heroin trade and the counterfeiting of American currency, though official South Korean sources now claim the latter activity has been terminated.

To a very limited extent, North Korea began following the path long ago trodden by the People's Republic that of opening the country to global trade while liberalizing the economy. Following China's lead, North Korea has established free trade zones at Rason and at Sinuiju near the Chinese border, and for a time seemed to be planning others. Like those established a generation ago by China near Hong Kong, the goal has been to attract foreign investment with promises of cheap labor and tax incentives. However, the new special economic zones have attracted little international interest. The Rason zone became a center for a casino based at the Emperor Hotel (later Imperial Hotel) that attracted a large Chinese clientele. North Korea appears to have become ambivalent about their usefulness and is scaling back these tentative initiatives rather than expanding them.

A more successful special economic zone was the Kaesong Industrial Zone near the Demilitarized Zone (DMZ), established at the initiative of South Korea's Hyundai Group in 2003. Here South Korean companies managed North Korean workers producing goods for export. Over the years, this led to much cross border movement. But it always faced difficulties because of its position, which gave the North Korean military a powerful say in its operation. These included regular demands for increases in workers' pay and tight control over movement. Yet it survived until 2016, when it was closed by the South Korean government in protest at North Korean missile and nuclear tests. Although agreements in 2018 envisaged its reopening, nothing had happened by 2020, when North Korea effectively sealed itself off from the outside world because of COVID-19.

For the average North Korean, the most obvious example of the government's belated efforts to move away—if only slightly—from a communist style command economy has been the right now granted to allow the sale of goods at free markets. However, opening up the system is hampered by the internal perception that the introduction of capitalist reforms helped bring about the collapse of the Soviet Union. This is a road Pyongyang has no interest in following although for a time some thought that might be the case.

On the other hand, it seems clear that North Korea's third generation of rulers, despite the commitment to building up their missile and nuclear capabilities, do recognize the importance of moving more deeply into the 21st century. One sign of this was the 2013 visit by the chief of Google, one of the best-known Internet companies. While there, Google's leaders strongly encouraged the opening of the

Internet to the North Korean population. While some among the elite do have access, no real expansion is likely to happen anytime soon. It should be noted that the reception the Google executive received was nothing like the one accorded to the famous American basketball player, Dennis Rodman, when he arrived a few months later! But until 2020, there had been other signs of change. Tourism received, for example, much encouragement, and Chinese tourists could be seen all over the country. The pandemic ended that and other hopes of opening up as well.

### Foreign Relations: Survival North Korea Style

Although North Korea emerged after World War II as an independent state within the socialist world, it was long committed to maintaining something of a "distance" between itself and its largest allies the Soviet Union and the People's Republic. And that distance, nurtured by the regime's emphasis on *Juche* or self-reliance became particularly important after the outbreak in the late 1950s of the Sino-Soviet dispute that split the communist world.

Recognizing how much more complicated that rift made North Korea's international position Pyongyang's first generation dictatorial leader Kim Il Sung worked to create something of a balancing act between relations with Moscow and the Soviet Union. Nevertheless, those ties were very important to the regime as it received from both communist superpowers regular shipments of subsidized foodstuffs that helped sustain its economy. But that support began to change in the late 1980s and early 1990s as both Moscow and Beijing worked to develop ties with North Korea's archrival, South Korea. And more importantly by 1991 communism in the Soviet Union was failing even as Beijing continued to move dramatically away from the older Soviet-style command economy that Pyongyang still embraced. Suddenly North Korea's isolated leaders found themselves adrift in an increasingly capitalist and globalized world system that appeared to threaten its very survival.

By the early 1990s North Korea's leadership recognized that their long-term goal of growing powerful enough to unify the entire Korean peninsula under their control had now fallen to the wayside, and the North Korean elite found themselves increasingly concerned about the shear survival of their regime. With that in mind the Northern government began to tentatively reach out to the outside world. Kim Il Sung, for example, was engaged in organizing a meeting with his South Korean counterpart Kim Yong Sam the very

159

# North Korea

day he died in 1994. His son and successor Kim Jong-il spent much of the 1990s attempting to move the country more into the international community they had previously largely shunned. As we have seen, that effort culminated for a time in the award of the Nobel Peace Prize to Kim Dae-jung, South Korea's longtime democratic activist, for his efforts to improve relations with the North. (Later, it would emerge that both the North–South summit and the Nobel Prize had only been possible through heavy and secret expenditure.) As a rule, the South Korean left, long associated with the famous Sunshine Policy, has been more linked to efforts to improve relations with the North than their more conservative political counterparts. The engagement policy continued under Kim Dae-jung's immediate successor, Roh Moo-hyun, but when the conservative Lee Myung-bak became president in 2008, there was a steady moving away from engagement. The developing South Korean tourism to the North and other engagement policies ended. By the end of his time in office in 2013, Lee was being treated to a regular barrage of insults from the north, which refused to deal with him.

With the election in 2013 of Park Chung-hee's daughter, Park Geun-hye, there appeared to be ssome movement. She had visited North Korea and had met Kim Jong-il, who had, apparently, expressed admiration for the economic development of South Korea under her father. After assuming the nation's leadership, South Korea's new president spoke of making progress on improving relations with the North. Similar statements came from the North's leadership. But the relationship soon soured and Park reverted to a more hardline approach to the North. Only when she fell from power in 2017 and Moon Jae-in assumed office in South Korea, was there a change. After the bluster of US President Trump's "fire and fury" approach to the North, Moon worked hard to engage with the North. When North Korea attended the February 2018 Winter Olympics held in South Korea, there was a breakthrough, leading to three North–South summits and a series of new agreements, including the real demilitarization of the Demilitarized Zone that divides North and South. It also led to the first ever North Korea–United States summits.

The euphoria did not last. For Kim Jong-un, Moon was seen as a useful channel for improving relations with the United States, and he expected that this would bring positive results. When the Trump initiative foundered at the February 2019 Hanoi summit meeting, the North's overtures to Moon were replaced by a growing hostility. While Moon pressed on with trying to improve relations with the North,

his approach came under increasing domestic criticism. With the election of the conservative Yoon Suk-yeol as South Korea's president in March 2022, the pendulum is likely to swing away from engagement toward a more hostile policy toward the North.

Turning to China, relations with the People's Republic have also been quite strained at times. Beijing's decision to establish diplomatic relations with South Korea in 1992 was very disturbing to North Korea and probably of even more immediate concern was the PRC's decision to start demanding hard cash for goods, including foodstuffs, they supplied the beleaguered state. Perhaps most significantly Beijing has used its influence to encourage North Korea to implement economic reforms along the lines of those carried out by both China and Vietnam. It also made significant efforts to show North Korea's leaders through a series of visits the results of China's generation-long economic drive. Moreover, China has become very involved in facilitating international discussions over North Korea's nuclear program, even if by supporting UN sanctions, it has indicated its concern at the North's acquisition of nuclear weapons. More recently, in the aftermath of the seeming improvement in relations between North Korea, South Korea and United States relations with Beijing have warmed as well. The Chinese, however, became very concerned at South Korea's agreement in the wake of the January 2016 nuclear test, to allow the stationing in South Korea of the Terminal High Altitude Area Defense (THAAD) anti-missile system. While both South Korea and the US said that this was a preventative measure against a North Korean missile attack on the US, the Chinese argued that it could be used against their country. To bring pressure on South Korea, China hit at bilateral trade and the lucrative tourist industry. Tensions gradually eased but it took several years.

Some progress has even been made with Japan. In an effort to improve relations with Tokyo, North Korea finally confirmed during a visit by then Japanese Prime Minister Koizumi in September 2002 long-term Japanese suspicions that it had over the years kidnapped many Japanese citizens to serve as language teachers. Eventually a small group of surviving Japanese citizens, who had been kidnapped generations earlier, was allowed to return home to visit. Unfortunately, Pyongyang's decision hardly improved the "air" much as almost immediately more tensions emerged over the question of whether the "visiting" Japanese would return to their "adopted" homeland. It hardly helped when it was later discovered that some of the supposed "remains" of kidnapped Japanese

turned out to be phony, although there have been questions raised over the competence of the laboratory that carried out the tests. Many questions surrounding the kidnappings have still not been answered to Tokyo's satisfaction, and they continue to complicate relations.

North Korea's gestures regarding the kidnapped Japanese were clearly tied with Pyongyang's desire to clear the air with Tokyo, and to receive compensation for the Japanese colonial period as South Korea did in 1965. But their efforts to develop long-range missiles, the first of which was launched over Japan in 1998, have hardly helped matters. In addition, it's not just the developing missile technology that has caused international concerns. North Korea's hopes to move more deeply into the international community have also been enormously complicated by the regime's efforts to develop nuclear weapons that could be delivered with those increasingly sophisticated missiles North Korea has been developing.

## North Korea's Nuclear Program

Pyongyang's nuclear activities began with a civilian nuclear program with assistance from the Soviet Union in the 1950s. The country has deposits of graphite and uranium, and some Koreans had received rudimentary nuclear training in Japan toward the end of the colonial period. The Soviet Union provided training and an experimental reactor, which was built at the Yongbyon site 60 miles from Pyongyang in 1965. The Soviet Union did not provide nuclear weapons' training, and China, which detonated its first nuclear bomb in 1964, also refused a North Korean request for weapons' technology. The Soviet Union insisted that North Korea register with the International Atomic Energy Authority and was subject to inspection, but did not supply a list of facilities at Yongbyon until 1992. Also at Soviet insistence, North Korea signed the Nuclear Non-proliferation Treaty in 1987 but did not sign a safeguards' agreement until 1992.

It is not surprising that the North Koreans were interested in nuclear weapons. After all, the United States, its arch-enemy, had threatened to use nuclear weapons during the Korean War, and maintained hundreds of tactical nuclear weapons in South Korea, afterward. The United States, for its part, has long wanted to stop the North's nuclear programs. But little could be accomplished until America's own nuclear arsenal was removed from South Korea. The first Bush administration accomplished that goal in 1992.

In those years, it is not surprising that the North Koreans were interested in nuclear weapons. After all, the United

States, its arch-enemy, had hundreds of nukes in South Korea, and there was always the possibility that war could break out at any time. The United States, for its part, has long wanted to stop the North's nuclear programs. But little could be accomplished until America's own nuclear arsenal was removed from South Korea. The first Bush administration accomplished that goal.

Even as the American government was withdrawing its own enormous nuclear arsenal North Korea's leaders were coming to the realization that their nuclear program offered not only the possibility of deterring an attack, but could serve as well as a tool to gain economic and political concessions from the United States. Thus began the crisis of 1994 when Pyongyang publicly announced it was withdrawing from the Non-Proliferation Treaty, and apparently developing nuclear weapons at its nuclear energy plants at Yongbyon. It should be added that the situation with North Korea, as it is with countries like Iran, is complicated by the fact that international agreements do allow countries to develop nuclear capabilities if the facilities are dedicated to peaceful purposes such as electricity generation.

The crisis which brought Washington and North Korea to the very brink of war was eventually defused by the intervention of former President Jimmy Carter and the signing of what became known as the Agreed Framework. Under that agreement, North Korea promised to freeze its nuclear program in exchange for American promises of fuel deliveries to compensate for the loss of the electricity then supposedly being produced by the nuclear reactors. The agreement also provided for the construction of two light-water reactors that unlike the older Soviet-style reactors would not produce by-products that could be used in the manufacture of nuclear weapons-grade material.

The plan, loudly criticized in some conservative quarters in both South Korea and the United States, opened an era of relative calm that lasted for most of the following decade. Not surprisingly, there were many difficult issues involved in actually implementing the agreement. Still, ground was first finally broken in the summer of 1997 for the two new nuclear power plants that the international community had agreed to build in the north.

For a time things appeared to be going well. In fact, the last months of 2000 offered plenty of reason for optimism. Not only had the leaders of North and South Korea held a summit. American Secretary of State Madeleine Albright made a well-publicized trip to the Pyongyang. It even looked for a time as if President Clinton,

building on all the earlier progress, might visit North Korea. Unfortunately that trip did not occur. There were also problems at the Kumho site on the east coast, where the light-water reactors were being constructed. By the time the first concrete for the reactors was poured in August 2002, the project was years behind schedule. While some of this was their own fault, the North Koreans were not pleased. There were also problems in supplying the heavy fuel oil promised, mainly because of Congress' unwillingness to fund it.

Once the administration under George W. Bush established itself, Washington became quite reluctant to continue the diplomatic momentum of the Clinton administration. As the American War on Terrorism unfolded, it became clear that Washington's new decision makers considered the North Korean regime, as the new president put it in his January 2002 State of the Union speech, part of an "Axis of Evil."

Relations were hardly improved when during the fall of 2002 the North Koreans were said to have admitted that they had, in a somewhat ambiguous violation of the previous agreements, carried out a clandestine uranium enrichment program. Whether such a program had ever been actually realized or more importantly whether it had been aimed toward civilian electrical production or the production of nuclear weapons (a much more technically demanding accomplishment) has never been made clear. Nevertheless, once the issue was raised the relative progress made since 1994 seemed to collapse. By that stage, progress on the provision of light water reactors was several years behind schedule.

During the winter of 2002–2003 tensions only rose higher as Washington and Pyongyang took part in a series of escalating steps that saw not only the end of fuel energy deliveries to North Korea by the Americans but North Korea's announcement that the agreements of 1994 were "dead." They also said they planned to restart their nuclear programs.

From the American perspective, the most important issue has been the growing North Korean nuclear program that has probably produced enough plutonium for between 4 and 13 bombs. Adding to that concern has been Pyongyang's long-range missile program that may one day allow North Korea to threaten the American West Coast. Of more immediate concern has been America's fear that, given North Korea's economic situation, it could soon become a major exporter of weapons of mass destruction.

The most immediate impact of the increased role that China has been playing in the discussions was the agreement

reached in September 2005 that saw North Korea promise to end its nuclear weapons programs in exchange for guarantees that the principal countries involved would promote international cooperation with the North on matters from energy to trade and investment. As part of that agreement, South Korea even offered to supply North Korea with electrical energy. The agreement initially seemed to be a major breakthrough. But by coincidence—some thought design—the U.S. Treasury at that point imposed sanctions on North Korea for alleged money laundering and other financial infringements. North Korea's main link to international banking, the Macau-based Banca Delta Asia, was accused of assisting North Korea and all North Korean accounts with the bank were frozen. The nuclear deal fell apart.

### North Korea Crosses the Line

In the summer of 2006 North Korea began publicly testing its long-range missiles. While those tests were apparently less successful than Pyongyang might have hoped, they were more ominously followed up later that fall by its first apparently successful underground detonation. If this was not of a nuclear bomb, at least it was a nuclear device. A line had been crossed. On that day North Korea, one of the most brutal and closed society on the planet, entered the international nuclear club. This was a development that would immediately impact not only the Korean peninsula, but the international efforts to forestall the spread of nuclear weapons.

Still, for a time, during the winter of 2007 the momentum of negotiations appeared back on track. The American administration of George W. Bush, reeling from its defeat in the previous fall's congressional elections as well as setbacks in Iraq and Afghanistan, appeared anxious to make progress on the denuclearization of the Korean peninsula. Ironically, the soon to be ex-President Bush's new willingness not only to talk directly to the North Koreans, but to make concessions to the North's financial and security needs, was deeply reminiscent of the 1994 Agreed Framework developed by the Clinton administration more than a decade before.

Nevertheless, there were some differences. As in 1994, Washington promised to facilitate North Korea's access to fuel oil. Moreover, the Americans agreed to use their influence to release the monies the North had deposited in a Macao bank. Pyongyang, for its part, promised to dismantle its Yongbyon nuclear facility and to allow international inspectors to renew their monitoring of the North's nuclear activities.

# North Korea

Unlike 1994, the new agreement was much more incremental in its approach, promising the North specific gains for specific concessions over an extended time table. This time, the possibility of a continuation of the North's civilian nuclear energy programs was not on the table. Nevertheless, long interested in improving its relationship with Washington and anxious to regain access to its frozen financial resources, Pyongyang seemed initially enthusiastic to take part.

Amazingly, for longtime observers of the talks, for a time real progress was accomplished and by the fall of 2007 international nuclear experts were allowed to begin the work of dismantling the Yongbyon facilities. While the agreements dealt only with North Korea's production efforts, rather than with the nuclear weapons they had already developed, the agreements were a major accomplishment.

More ominously, by the time George W. Bush left office in 2009, North Korea seemed to have accomplished its long-term goal of developing a limited nuclear weapons capability. It was working to improve significantly its ability to deliver such weapons on long-range missiles. Meanwhile the North seems to have assumed a more proactive stance. In 2010 its naval forces destroyed a South Korean naval ship, the *Cheonan*, with considerable loss of life. The following autumn it bombed a South Korean island causing significant damage and death.

Although North Korea is under new leadership, the situation by the spring of 2014 had not changed much. Initially the country tested a new long-range missile that promptly blew up soon after launch. It then made preparations to test yet another nuclear device. Since then the situation, from North Korea's perspective, has improved.

By the fall of 2017 the North was claiming they finally had the ability to not only build atomic weapons, but also hydrogen bombs, and to target the United States with nuclear armed ICBMs. Indeed, that year was marked by increasingly hostile rhetoric between the U.S. under President Trump and North Korea. Some believed that the two countries were on the brink of war, although neither really moved to a war footing. Then came 2018, which turned into a year of summits (see above). Although there was no major breakthrough, the tension dissipated. While President Joe Biden has shown no sign of a softer approach to North Korea, some of the tensions have gone out of the relationship as the Biden adminstration has had other preoccupations.

## A Changing North Korea?

Until recently the population of North Korea remained quite isolated from the outside world and all the more vulnerable to the regime's enormous and sophisticated effort to control access to information beyond what the government's propaganda specialists dished out. But those days are long gone. Today's North Korean population is significantly more aware of the larger world around them and more specifically of life in South Korea. While quite dangerous they increasingly have access to DVDs and flash drives that carry a range of materials from commercial movies to variety shows specifically produced for the North Korean audiences by defectors in South Korea determined to undermine the northern regime. The result not surprisingly is a population that is much more aware of the outside world and more skeptical of the regime's propaganda about just how wonderful their own lives are compared to outsiders. Meanwhile websites in the southern neighbor South Korea regularly report on life in North Korea. These are based on reports phoned in from cell phones smuggled into the North. Even more courageously some North Koreans have at great personal risk taken to filming daily life and then passing those videos to the outside world though smugglers.

At the same time, North Koreans themselves live quite differently than they once did. More and more have been forced to fend for themselves as the state's financial support has been withdrawn, or is at best spasmodic, and there is more and more willingness to confront the authorities, at least over issues that are not politically sensitive. That cynicism apparently goes to the highest levels given that Korea is still a traditional society that revers age and seniority, something Korea's new leader Kim Jong-un quite obviously lacks.

## COVID-19

North Korea is ill-prepared to cope with a major health crisis. Although the health service was once of a standard with that of the Soviet Union or Eastern Europe, years of economic difficulties and lack of access to international medical practices have had a serious effect. To cope with earlier pandemics, the first reaction was to completely shut off contact with the outside world. When COVID-19 emerged in early 2020, that is what happened. Despite its close links with and heavy dependence on China, even that border was closed. Virtually no movement was allowed in or out of the country. Foreigners, including diplomats and aid workers, were confined to their enclaves. By summer 2020, this led to the withdrawal of most diplomatic and aid staff. Movement within the country was also strictly controlled. The North Koreans constantly maintained that the illness was not present, although defectors or those with contacts in the country told a different story. The reality was probably that any impact was limited. In 2021, a program of vaccination began using products from China and Russia. Tight restrictions continued into 2022, but there were periodic signs of a possible easing to allow more trade. But the moves have been tentative at best, with goods piling up at ports and airports as they undergo quarantine. Apart from Russia and China, the continued difficult conditions that made it difficult to operate led to the closure of many embassies in Pyongyang during 2020 and the total withdrawal of staff. The last European embassy remaining, the Romanian closed in October 2021. All UN agencies and foreign aid groups had also left by then.

## The Future: North Korea

The situation in North Korea remains quite ambiguous. On one hand the economy is in great difficulties, as the regime itslef admits. There have been reports from refugees in China that discipline has been breaking down among the ranks of the army. Moreover, protest leaflets have begun to appear occasionally within the cities. Even more significant has been the weakening of the wall of silence that has long surrounded North Korea.

The reality of life in North Korea's concentration camps has become far better known. Especially significant has been the highlighting of conditions in North Korea as a human rights issue as demonstrated by the UN Report of February 2014 that said the human rights situation in the north was "unparalleled in the contemporary world."

In the early years after the youthful and significantly less experienced Kim Jong-un came to power the momentum of improving relations was for a time lost and nuclear tensions rose ever higher. On the other hand, by 2017, of course, North Korea had mastered, after years of long and often frustrating efforts, the ability to manufacture not only nuclear weapons but also the ability to launch satellites into space. Its nuclear and missile programs have continued to develop, and it has resumed testing the latte, including an an apparent ICBM, with much publicity. While it claims to be able to hit the mainland United States, there is at present some doubts about how accurate such a strike would be at present.

By 2018, the chorus against North Korea's provocative weapons development program had grown stronger as demonstrated by the most recent UN sanctions voted against the regime. Especially interesting in that regard was China's evolving attitude toward North Korea's nuclear program. Beijing has apparently become much more interested in a nuclear-free Korean peninsula and increasingly critical of North Korea's ongoing program. But as we have seen none of that has mattered as North Korea has apparently accomplished its goals of creating a nuclear deterrent against what they see as the very real threat of an American assault.

Meanwhile the United States of course spent the last few years trying to use the threat of enhanced sanctions and military force to get North Korea to eliminate their nuclear weapons program.

Ironically, or perhaps because of the recent rise of tensions between the United States and North Korea both Korean governments decided to take the initiative to reduce tensions between themselves.

Indeed as the world entered 2018 plans were dramatically underway to arrange a significant North Korean presence in the South Korean sponsored Winter Olympic Games. And once the games began North Korea formally invited South Korea's new president to visit.

Eventually, in the early spring of 2018 many were astonished to see another round of reconciliation talks between North and South Korea's respective presidents, a development that was not terribly surprising given that both leaders had recently spoken of the importance of improving relations between them. More dramatic was the meeting in Singapore between the American president, Donald Trump, and the North's Kim Jong-un, which, culminating in yet another North Korean leader, as with so many earlier leaders, promising to move toward denuclearization. While heralded by many as a significant breakthrough, long-term observers of the region had plenty of reasons to be cynical and by early 2019 it was starting to become obvious that North Korea was not a committed to any sort of genuine denuclearization. It was equally obvious that the United States was unwilling to make any concessions in other areas, such as sanctions, unless the North met its demands on denuclearization. The result, as shown by the failure of the Hanoi summit to reach any agreement, was stalemate.

North Korea's continued goal is regime survival. It is not like Eastern Europe, where the abandonment of communism, led to a new political establishment. To the south, is South Korea, more economically powerful and with double the population, and backed by the United States. For the North Korean regime's elite, there appears to be no choice but to hang together and keep going. As the old saying goes, if they do not hang together, they risk hanging separately.

# Mongolia

Courtesy of Batbold Bayaraa

**Area:** 604,247 sq. mi. (1,564,619 sq. km., slightly smaller than Alaska, twice the size of Texas)

**Population:** 3,227,630 (2022 est.)

**Capital City:** Ulaanbaatar, pop. 1,645,000 (2022 est.)

**Climate:** Dry, with bitterly cold winters

**Neighboring Countries:** Russia (North); China (South, East, West)

**Official Language:** Mongolian

**Other Principal Tongues:** Turkic (mostly Kazakh, 5%), Russian

**Ethnic Background:** Mongol (about 97%); Kazakh (about 3%)

**Principal Religion:** The Lamaistic sect of Buddhism and a growing Christian presence

**Main Exports:** (to China, Canada, U.S., U.K.) Mining products, copper, coal, textiles, beef, meat products, hides, wool, minerals, and cashmere

**Main Imports:** (from Russia, China, Japan, South Korea, U.S.) Cars, food products, chemical, sugar, tea, machinery, equipment, petroleum, electronics, building materials, and clothing

**Currency:** Tugrik

**Former Colonial Status:** Tributary of the Manchu dynasty of China from end of the 17th century until the Chinese Revolution of 1911. The Republic of China (ROC) claimed Mongolia was Chinese territory but was unable to exercise control. Mongolia declared its independence in 1921, but the ROC continued to claim it as Chinese until 1946, a position it maintained even after it withdrew from the Chinese mainland in 1949. In 1949, the newly established People's Republic of China and Mongolia mutually recognized each other and established diplomatic relations. The ROC, which held the China seat at the United Nations until 1971, vetoed Mongolia's admission in 1955. It was finally admitted in 1961.

**National Day:** July 11th, in recognition of a communist/independence revolution in 1921

**Chief of State:** Ukhnaagiin Khurelsukh (since June 2021)

**Head of Government:** Prime Minister Luvsannamsrain Oyun-Erdene (since January 27, 2021)

**National Flag:** Three vertical bands of red, blue, and red. The band closest to the pole has a set of traditional symbols at the top in yellow.

**Per Capita GDP Income:** $14,309 (2019 est.) (purchasing power parity)

Note: Parts of this article have been adapted from Steven A. Leibo's winter 2014 article "The New Mongolia: From Gold Rush to Climate Change" published in *Education about Asia*

Mongolia is located in an area of extreme contrast in terms of geography. The arid rocks of the Gobi Desert in the southeast region of the country support almost no vegetation, and have a variation of temperature that splits the craggy rocks that interrupt the frequently monotonous landscape. Proceeding northward there is a gradual change, punctuated by the presence of mountains rising to heights of more than 13,000 feet. The desert gives way to mountainous forest areas whose own thick growth tapers off at the heights where perpetual snow dominates the landscape.

Water also becomes more abundant in the north, but the rivers are uncontrolled and rough, descending in cascades over rocky beds and resembling the swirling waters of the Pacific Northwest and Alaska. It is in this inhospitable part of the country that most of the people live. The traditional dwellings are constructed of felt that is made from wool and is stretched out over frames.

# Mongolia

### History

Prior to the 16th century, the people who inhabited Mongolia were famous as a world-renowned warrior community that had periodically conquered vast areas as far away as Eastern Europe. This was principally due to the superior horsemanship and cavalry techniques of the Mongols, acquired as a necessity due to their traditionally nomadic lifestyle. This pastoral existence also contributed to the superior stamina of their horsemen. Several Mongolian leaders became well-known. The most famous was Chinggis (Genghis) Khan. He and his successors were able to lead his men in the conquest of vast areas of eastern and southern Asia as far as Baghdad, now the capital of Iraq. From 1271–1368, a Mongol dynasty (the Yuan dynasty) ruled the Chinese Empire.

Although dynamic in the late middle ages, Mongolia entered the 20th century having long been part of the last Chinese empire, the Qing dynasty. But, of course, the first decades of the 20th century saw the collapse of both the Qing and Romanov dynasties and what might be called ethnographic Mongolia's subsequent emergence as both partially independent and partitioned.

But that ultimate fate was not immediately obvious as the century began. Indeed, in the early 20th century, while Outer Mongolia was relatively free of Chinese control, Russian imperial influence grew in the northern part of the traditional Mongolian lands. When the Manchu Empire collapsed in 1912, the princes and lamas of Outer Mongolia refused to recognize the claim of the Republic of China to the lands within the region. Concerned about China's continuing "interest," the leaders of Outer Mongolia then appealed to Tsar Nicholas II, who, in one of his government's last major agreements, negotiated a treaty with China's new republican government. Henceforth it was understood that while Moscow recognized Beijing's official claims to all of Mongolia, only Inner Mongolia would be administered by the Chinese while Outer Mongolia was to remain autonomous under local leaders. Meanwhile, to the south Inner Mongolia was being integrated within first the Qing dynasty and then later the Republic of China.

With the collapse of the Russian dynasty in 1917, China unsuccessfully attempted to exert full control over all of Mongolia. Meanwhile in 1921 Outer Mongolia was invaded by a force of White Russian anti-Bolshevik troops from Russia. Eventually the Bolshevik forces wrested control from the White Russians. By the early 1920s

**Prime Minister Chimed Saikhanbileg**

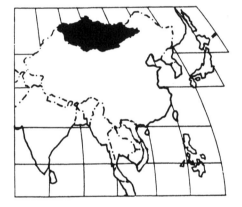

Outer Mongolia was being integrated into the emerging USSR. Mongolia had thus become the first Asian state formally to adopt communism's command economy. Meanwhile to the south its southern cousin, Inner Mongolia, remained in China's orbit.

### Soviet Mongolia

Within Outer Mongolia, Soviet domination was something of a mixed blessing. On the one hand, understandable Russian antipathy toward the Mongolian national hero, Genghis Khan, whose forces had so undermined Kiyvan Rus', made local displays of Mongolian identity and

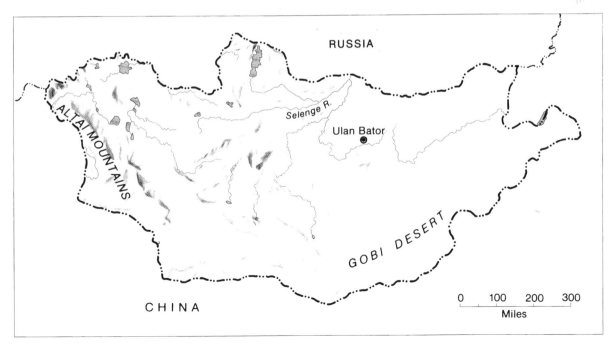

165

# Mongolia

**Former President Ochirbat's oath-taking ceremony**   Courtesy of the Government of Mongolia

nationalism at best awkward and at worst dangerous. Moreover, as was common under communism, the nation's Buddhist religious heritage was assaulted with a vengeance that saw thousands killed and large numbers of monasteries destroyed. Meanwhile, despite Mongolia's traditionally communal attitude toward the land, the attempt to impose a Soviet-style collectivist economy was strongly but ineffectually resisted by local herdsmen. Still, the initial and harshly imposed Soviet collectivist system also offered some unanticipated but distinct advantages that actually complemented the Mongolian lifestyle more than some had anticipated.

In short, for Mongolian herdsmen operating in the unforgiving climate of central Asia, there were real advantages to having access to a collectivist economy rather than surviving simply on their individual or family resources. Thus, during the era of communism a relatively strong social net was in place that supplied many social services, from health care to education, that made the life of Mongolia's traditional herdsmen economically more viable than it might have been. The Soviet Union, of course, helped the Mongolian state offer such resources. In effect, while the daily lives of most Mongolian herdsmen did not change much, their lives were cushioned somewhat within a larger collectivist economy.

From the Soviet point of view, Mongolia served as a buffer against an increasingly powerful Japan, as well as separating it from any threat posed by China to the south. Of course, the Soviet presence shielded Mongolians themselves somewhat from any potential Chinese interest in reacquiring their territory. A defensive alliance signed in 1936 between the USSR and Mongolia also allowed the former to drive a force of Japanese from eastern Mongolia in 1939. Somewhat later, in 1945, military units from both nations worked together to fight those Japanese troops still remaining in Inner Mongolia. At the same time, Stalin was able to obtain a Chinese promise to recognize Outer Mongolia's independence if a national vote showed that this was their desire. The proposed plebiscite was then held under

**Ulaanbaatar's new shopping mall**

Courtesy of Steven A. Leibo

carefully regulated conditions. The result, hardly a surprise, registered a "unanimous" vote for independence from China. Eventually, both the Nationalist and Communist leaders of China recognized Outer Mongolia's independence, and Beijing signed a boundary treaty in 1962. Still, China has over the years occasionally shown signs of wishing to increase its influence. These pressures caused Mongolia to cling to Russia for protection. Thus, the nation sided with the Soviet Union during the explosive Sino–Soviet dispute of the 1960s and 1970s. In return, Mongolia received substantial economic aid, which allowed the beginning of industrialization in the country.

## Mongolia's Transition Away from Communism

Under the influence of developments in the Soviet Union, especially after the ascendancy of Mikhail Gorbachev in 1985, the Mongolian leadership started down the path of political liberalization. By the end of 1989, the dramatic events in Eastern Europe led to the emergence of several opposition movements in Mongolia, who called themselves respectively the Mongolian Democratic Union (MDU), the Social Democratic Union (SDM), and the New Progressive Movement (NPM). They demanded an end to the Communist monopoly of power. Branches of these movements were established in every province of Mongolia, and street demonstrations began while the Communist government ordered troops to relocate near the capital. By March after more than a dozen demonstrators had begun hunger strikes, the nation's Communist leadership signaled its willingness to open negotiations.

The then Mongolian communist leader, Jambyn Batmunkh, formerly a professor at the State University, refused to authorize the use of troops. After negotiations the Communist Party Political Council resigned. The MDU tried to maximize its appeal to the voters by emphasizing nationalism, including praise for the medieval conqueror, Ghengis Khan, rather than communism. But to no avail. A few weeks later the entire Politburo of the ruling Mongolian People's Revolutionary Party resigned and was replaced by reformers; Batmunkh remained as chief of state for the time being. The ruling party then formally gave up its monopoly of power. The new General Secretary, Gombojavyn Ochirbat, was a relatively unknown figure. The beginnings of a new era of reform seemed imminent. By 1992 a new constitution was in place that allowed for multiparty voting. Even the term "People's Republic" was dropped, and the country was simply named "Mongolia." Political ferment and economic liberalization, of course, continued after these dramatic events. Freedom of the press brought a mushrooming of newspapers and magazines. Freedom of religion led to a resurgence of Buddhism and even of Christianity to some extent.

The new constitution provided for a popularly elected president and a Western-style parliamentary system of government, with a 76-seat unicameral legislative chamber, the State Great Hural. The president could introduce legislation before the Hural, and has a veto. The prime minister would be the leader of the dominant party or parties in coalition, which control the Hural while a Constitutional Court had the authority to review the legality of laws. The new constitution also allowed for private property, but pastureland continued to be under public ownership. After the mid-1992 elections, the former Communist Party (MPRP) still controlled 71 of 76 seats in the Hural. But their domination was beginning to weaken.

In 1993, Mongolia held its first presidential election. Candidates for the post had to be over 45 years of age and only political parties that held a seat in the parliament could select a standard bearer. The old-line Mongolian People's Revolutionary Party (MPRP) nominated the writer and academic Lodonguin Tudev, over the incumbent President Ochirbat. The opposition Mongolian Democratic Party (MDP) formed a coalition with the Mongolian Social Democratic Party (MSDP) and selected President Punsalmaagiin Ochirbat, who had been turned down by his own MPRP, to be their candidate. In the election, Ochirbat was elected president with 58.7% of the vote. The newly reelected president promised to speed privatization but also to protect those who were hurt most by the process.

During 1994, the MPRP continued to rule under Prime Minister Puntsagiyn Jasray, but not without challenges. Street demonstrations broke out in April. The primary issue was apparently corruption in the MPRP that reached as high as the prime minister. Demands that the government resign were ignored. Perhaps as a way of making peace, the MPRP sat down with the opposition parties in the Great Hural, the Mongolian Democratic Party (MDP), and the Mongolian Social Democratic Party to create important reform-oriented legislation. One part of the agreement between the three parties was to require electoral reform to allow for a fairer representation among the parties in the Great Hural. The MPRP also agreed to the creation of an independent media, not under government control.

The weakening of communist control which had been going on since the early 1990s was fully realized during the 1996 elections when a coalition of democratic parties swept the communist Mongolian People's Revolutionary Party from power. The MPRP, which had been in power since 1921, saw its legislative control destroyed as its opponents won 48 of the 76 seats in the parliament. With that vote Mongolia took its place along-side other former socialist states that have attempted to find a new future beyond their communist past. The new prime minister was the 41-year-old Mendsaikhany Enkhsaikhan, leader of the Democratic Union Coalition. Moving beyond the economic liberalization that had already begun, the new prime minister promised to reform the economy to attract more foreign investment.

### Building a Western-Style Democratic Capitalist Society

Simply glancing at Mongolia or its people might make the outsider assume Mongolia's fate once it left the Soviet orbit would begin to parallel its East Asian neighbors. While that might eventually turn out be the case it has certainly not been so during the first generation since Mongolia won its freedom. In fact, as during the Soviet era, Mongolia's development has more closely paralleled events in Eastern Europe than Eastern Asia. Thus the collapse of communism soon saw the arrival of numerous Western advisers eager to offer financial support. Over time Mongolia's transition away from communism closely paralleled the Eastern European economic shock-therapy approach, albeit within the context of an enormously larger and lightly populated rural society than was the norm in either Eastern Europe or Eastern Asia.

In short, Mongolia's new leaders were deeply committed to the idea of a free market economy and supported by an impressive array of influential outsiders, all quite willing to back Mongolia as long as its leaders adhered to the small government privatization model they saw as ultimately the most successful economic model. And adhere they did with an enormous array of privatization efforts and a reduction of basic social spending. Indeed the assumption was that democracy, another long-term goal of domestic and international reforms required such an approach.

Thus while the nation's democratic traditions began to grow the financial security of the population began to drop dramatically. Ironically, Mongolia's first decade of post-communist freedom offered not only more democratic freedoms, but considerably less economic security as the socialist safety net simply collapsed around the population. Given the enormous influence and financial resources outside groups carried with them, there was often little Mongolian dissenters could do. Not surprisingly, for many Mongolian critics it seemed perhaps that Mongolia had traded domination by the Chinese or Russian empires for that of the international aid agencies from the IMF to the World Bank and the Asian Development Bank.

**Sukhbaatar Square in Ulaanbaatar**                    Courtesy of Batbold Bayaraa

# Mongolia

**Former President Nambaryn Enkhbayar**

Meanwhile, even as Mongolian levels of employment, health care, and education began steep declines, the opening up of the nation's natural resources, especially minerals conveniently located not that far from the dynamic Chinese economy saw the country's overall growth eventually begin to climb dramatically, and a new Ulaanbaatar based middle class begin to emerge.

## Political Developments since 2000

The late 1990s saw political turmoil in Mongolia. The election of Natsagiyn Bagabandi, former speaker of the Great Hural, as president in 1997 marked the return of the Mongolian People's Revolutionary Party (MPRP) to office. But while Bagabandi lasted eight years in office, being reelected in 2001, prime ministers came and went in rapid succession. Building a political consensus was clearly difficult, while the assassination in 1998 of Sanjaasurengiin Zorig, who had been prominent in the overthrow of the one-party state, added to the sense of turmoil. (It would not be until 2015 that three people were convicted of the killing. In 2019, the former head of the intelligence agency, Khurts Bat, was secretly tried on charges of their torture.)

The issue of the prime minister was part of the ongoing competition between the market reformers and the former Communist Party members who make up the MPRP. Pushed from leadership by the results of the 1996 election, the former ruling party gained greatly from the reformist government's inability to cope with unemployment and inflation. Despite Mongolia's growing ties with the outside

world and increased investment, the MRRP has made great strides in its effort to return to its former position of prominence. And in the elections of 2000, both at the national and local levels, candidates from the former ruling party did well. In fact, winning 72 of 76 seats in the July 2000 elections for the national assembly.

As a result of their defeat the Mongolia's democratic alliance reorganized itself creating a new party, the Democratic Party (DP or the AN from its Mongolian initials) out of five former democratic groups. Nevertheless, the MPRP continued its electoral success. President Bagabandi was succeeded in May 2005 by another MPRP candidate, Nambaryn Enkhbayar. Overall, the MPRP seemed to be making a significant comeback, even if it was forced to operate within a much larger grand coalition for a time. But the coalition did not produce a stabilized political environment. In late 2005, the MPRP left the government and the coalition collapsed when. In early 2006 a new government, dominated again by the former communist era ruling party, organized itself under a new prime minister, Meyagombo Enkhbold.

For many observers this seemed a clear rejection of Mongolia's efforts to turn away from its communist past. All this, of course, was done legally as a result of political deal-making. But that did not stop thousands of demonstrators, upset about the reemergence of the MPRP, from taking to the streets of Ulaanbaatar to protest. Some observers noted that the ideological lines between the two major parties were not clearly drawn between communists and democratic capitalists, as some have

claimed. The latter, for example, had done particularly well in previous elections simply by promising to give each family government payments based on the number of children it had.

However, Mongolia's political environment remained in flux. Another crisis developed In the summer of 2007 when charges of corruption were alleged against the chair of the legislative assembly, leading to the dismissal of the Grand Hural. But the prime minister's hold on power was clearly on the wane, and by the late fall 2007 his party replaced him with Sanjaa Bayar as party secretary. But the 2008 elections failed to solve the problems. The early results were contested, and a riot broke out in the capital that resulted in the death of five people. Eventually, by the early fall, a new government was formed. Sanjaa of the MPRP retained his position as prime minister, and the new DP leader, Norovyn Altankhuyag, became the chief deputy prime minister. By the early summer of 2009, power relationships had begun to shift again as Mongolian Democratic Party's candidate, Tsakhiagiin Elbegdorj, won the presidency, replacing MPRP's Nambaryn Enkhbayar. In 2011, the Mongolian People's Revolutionary Party changed its name to the Mongolian People's Party (MRP, usually rendered MAN, from the initiials of its Mongolian title), although there was no change in its politics.

The political situation remains complicated and, at times, toxic. In April 2012 former president Nambaryn Enkhbayar was arrested and imprisoned. He was accused of corruption and human rights abuses.

# Mongolia

Interestingly, his treatment by the authorities seemed to suggest that the real motivations were a well-organized effort by his political enemies to weaken his influence. Enkhbayar, along with many in the public, was a critic of the lucrative contracts set up with international mining corporations even as so many Mongolians themselves remained in poverty. The charges attracted international condemnation but it did not keep him from jail. Despite health problems, the former president was sentenced to four years in jail. He did not remain there very long. He was soon transferred to a hospital and released altogether from custody by summer 2013. By then, a new Mongolian coalition government headed by Norovyn Altankhuayag of the Democratic Party was formed after the 2012 elections, but the struggle and the fact that political competition in Mongolia had been reduced to such a level was not a good sign for the long-term health of the nation's budding democracy.

The question of the control of assets such as copper and gold, and growing concern over increasing Chinese investment in the country, formed the backdrop to policy debates for the rest of the decade. It also had severe economic repercussions. Foreign investment fell by 85% in 2012-2015. A major cause was a dispute between the government and the powerful British-Australian conglomerate, Rio Tinto Mining Company. Faced with heavy demands for alleged unpaid taxes and rising costs, the company refused to invest further in the proposed underground expansion of the Oyu Tolgoi copper mine,

the country's largest, which was 34% government-owned, unless the dispute was resolved. At the same time, there was a fall in Mongolia's main export, coal, which had a knock-on effect foreign exchange reserves.

Russia and China seemed willing to provide alternative sources of investment, but there was concern at any increase in their possible influence, not least in the United States. The U.S. was also concerned that political and economic problems might cause Mongolia to end its assistance for the fighting in Afghanistan, where it had a small number of troops supporting the U.S.-led coalition. (It also had troops in Iraq from 2003–2008.) As a result, the U.S. Defense Secretary, Chuck Hagel, visited in April 2014, the first such visit for nine years, although there was no increase in U.S. assistance.

Things improved somewhat in 2015, at least on the economic front. There was fresh investment from India and China, and the Rio Tinto dispute seemed on the verge of settlement by the end of the year. But there was growing dissatisfaction at the wealth discrepancies, made worse for the agricultural sector, with an exceptionally dry summer and a hard winter. This probably explains the defeat of the ruling Democratic Party by the MPRP in the June 2016 elections, although there was no fundamental change as a result. Growth fell from 2.3% in 2015 to 0.4% in 2016. Unfortunately, China, which had helped in the past, was annoyed that the Mongolian government allowed a visit by the Dalai Lama in November 2016 and, as had

**Bush in Mongolia**

Courtesy of the White House

happened after earlier visits, instead of helping, made matters worse by raising duties on cross-border trade. That and an increase in international debt, led the new government to seek an emergency US$5.5 billion loan from the IMF. Negotiations became bogged down, however, partly because of objections from Rio Tinto, which was concerned at growing criticism of foreign involvement in mineral exploitation. This criticism had grown stronger after Kaltmaagiin Battulga of the Democratic Party succeeded Tsakhiagiin Elbegdorj of the same party as president, defeating the Mongolian People's Party (MPP) candidate by a small majority.

Whatever Battulga had said about curbing foreign influence rather went by the board as Spring 2017 saw new legislation that both extended licenses for mineral exploitation and eased rules for foreign investment. Rio Tinto began new prospecting in the Gobi Desert and the IMF loan was approved. Demand for copper and coal internationally helped with the balance of payments problems, as did a pickup in the Chinese economy. Domestic politics, however, were anything but settled. An internal split in the MPP led to the replacement of the prime minister amid allegations of corruption. Ukhanaagiin Khuralsukh took over in October 2017 but did not enjoy much of a honeymoon. Winter brought very harsh conditions, with a heavy loss of livestock, while before long, corruption charges were also being levied at the new prime minister. He survived a no confidence vote in November 2018, claiming that it was organized by elite groups that he was trying to curb.

Discontent over corruption did not subside. Large anti-government demonstrations took place in Ulaan Bataar in very cold conditions at the end of December 2018 and continued into 2019, while about half the members of the Grand Hural began a boycott of proceedings. Together, these developments led to the fall of the Hural speaker under legislation proposed by the president and his replacement by

**Reaching for Success!**

Courtesy of Steven A. Leibo

# Mongolia

an ally of the prime minister. Presidential power was increased by legislation passed in March allowing the president wide-ranging powers over judicial appointments, which he claimed to need to fight corruption. Some were skeptical of what was seen as a grab for presidential power, especially as he promptly dismissed the chief prosecutor and the head of the anti-corruption body, moves supported by the prime minister.

But increased presidential power did not last long. The Grand Hural passed new legislation, long debated, in November that strengthened the role of the prime minister and restricted presidential power over the judiciary. The new legislation also laid down that the benefits from mineral exploitation should be more fairly distributed. With the economy steadily recovering from the low of 2016, the prospects for 2020 seemed good. The ruling MPP reacted well to the start of the COVID-19 pandemic (see below), and was duly rewarded in the June 2020 elections, winning 62 of the 76 seats, while the Democratic Party could only manage 11. Unfortunately, Mongolia would soon find that early success in handling COVID would not necessarily last.

## COVID-19

As news came from China of a new possible pandemic, the Mongolian government took swift action, mindful of the long border between the two countries and the economic and social contacts. People were advised to wear masks as early as 10 January. Schools closed in early February, while public gatherings were banned. The Lunar New Year celebrations at the end of February were canceled, and the border with China was closed except for freight. The first detected cases came in May, imported from Russia and China, but numbers remained very low until November. That month saw the first death, and a full lockdown was imposed on the capital. Cases began rising in the middle of November, with 1584 cases over the period 20 November to 22 January 2021. By the end of March 2021, total cases had reached 8,070, with six deaths. Up until January, the government's efforts had been highly praised. Then a case came to light of the rough handling of a woman and her newborn baby, who were forcibly moved to hospital on a freezing winter's night after being diagnosed with the virus.

Protests began over that and the continuing restrictions, which included school closures for most of 2020 and limitations on movement that badly affected herdsmen. Senior health officials were dismissed and the health minister and the deputy prime minister offered to resign, but it was Prime Minister Ukhanaagiin Khuralsukh who went. He was replaced by the 40-year-old Luvsannamsrain Oyun-Erdene, the cabinet secretary and a graduate of the Kennedy School of Business at Harvard University. It soon became clear, however, that while the ostensible reason for the government's resignation was the heavy-handed approach to COVID, the real reason was to enable former Prime Minister Khuralsukh to stand in the presidential elections, scheduled for June 2021.

Meanwhile, despite the tight controls and Mongolia's early success in limiting the virus, numbers of cases began to rise in October 2021. They fell back, but reached another peak in January 2022, but then began to fall rapidly. Some restrictions were eased in 2021, and all restrictions came to an end in February 2022. By then a highly successful vaccination program meant that at the end of 2021, 91% of the adult population had received two shots, while 39 percent had also received a booster. Vaccines came from Russia and China, while the booster shots came from the international Covax vaccine distribution scheme. The costs of the booster program were met by a Japanese grant. All COVID restrictions were lifted on 14 February 2022. There continue to be cases, but the numbers are low. By April 22, 2022, according to the WHO, there had been a total of 920,361 cases, and 2,108 deaths since January 3, 2020.

### The 2021 Presidential Election

Meanwhile, from January to June 2021 were months of political manoeuvring. A 2019 constitutional amendment had limited incumbent presidents to one term, which meant that President Battulga of the Democratic Party could not stand again. He challenged this, but the Constitutional Court on 16 April 2021 ruled that the amendment was valid. Battulga responded by accusing the MPP of influencing the Constitutional Court and outlawed it by decree. The MPP ignored this and the election duly went ahead in June as planned. Battilga did not stand. In a low turnout, the Democratic Party candidate, Sodnomzudui Erdene, whose selected was disputed by some of his own party, did badly, receiving only 6% of the vote. A former Assembly member, now an internet entrepreneur, Dangasuren Enkhbat, of the Right Person Electoral Coalition, which held one seat in the National Assembly, came second with 22%. But it was Khurelsukh who won for the MPP.

### Society and Culture: Mongolia's Evolving Nomadic Lifestyle

Four times the size of California, Mongolia until recently only had a few hundred miles of roads (estimates ranged from 600 to 800 miles). Today, modernity is changing lifestyles quickly in Mongolia. On land once traversed by camels and horseback, Toyota Land Cruisers and Russian motorcycles are a common sight.

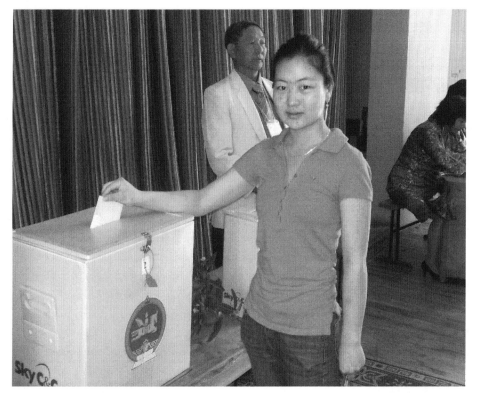

**Enthusiastic Mongolian voter**

The traditional lifestyle of the Mongolians was that of a pastoral people largely living outside of cities. Even today, significant percentages of the population of Ulaanbaatar still live in traditional *gers*, the world famous Mongolian tent-like structure. Indeed if there is any image of Mongolia aside from that of the 13th century's famous conqueror Genghis Khan that has captured the imagination of outsiders it is that of Mongolia's nomadic herdsman. Increasingly though, that lifestyle is becoming especially difficult to maintain. The record of an expanding urbanization gives part of the story. For example in 1958 Mongolia was 78% rural while by 1989 it had become 58% urban. Today's Mongolian rural population is only about 38% with an almost 2% annual increase of urban residents. And as to those famous *gers*, in recent years it is true those *gers* are more often then previously found not in the rural countryside but just outside of the capital. Many of them are now occupied by former herdsmen who currently live in poverty amidst the growing consumer society enjoyed by their better-off countrymen.

Clearly urbanization has been a global phenomenon but one that has had a particularly profound impact on the traditional and nomadic lifestyle of Mongolia's famous herdsmen. That urbanization has not taken place in a context of simply a modernizing society, but of much more immediate and transformative pressures on the Mongolian lifestyle.

The roots of the deterioration of that lifestyle can be found in two primary areas; the end of the collectivist economic safety net that had smoothed out, so to speak the demands of Mongolia's extraordinarily harsh environment. Moreover, as we will see below, the reality is that the environment particularly the climate is changing in ways that evolving economic policies aside, are, deeply undermining the lifestyle that has for so long sustained the herds. But those changes have impacted individuals in a variety of different ways.

Women, for example, have long been respected in traditional Mongolian society. The socialist state carried out proactive efforts to raise their status further. Today, the vast majority of women are literate and they constitute significantly more than half of the graduates of higher education. Women play important roles in the professions and represent the majority of the physicians and academics and over 40% of the agronomists, public servants, economists, and engineers. Mongolian woman also play important roles in the nation's governance holding ministerial positions responsible for issues from tourism to the environment. Still, although

recent years have seen a greater openness in the country's political system the end of the formally free health care system has especially hurt women, particularly pregnant and nursing women. Not surprisingly the maternal mortality rate has risen. Moreover, as with other collapsing socialist regimes, the withdrawal of government support for childcare facilities has inflicted additional burdens on women.

In terms of religion, quite predictably, decades of Soviet control played a role in turning Mongolia into a very secular society. Despite that experience a significant percentage of county's population still considers itself Buddhist. For example, the former president and occasional political prisoner, Enkhbatyar, is reported to be a devout Buddhist. Mongolia's emotional links to Tibetan-style Buddhism are strong. The present Dalai Lama first visited in 1979, and went again in 1982, when the country was still communist. In 1995, after the end of the communist regime, he again visited and attracted an enormous outpouring of interest. People from all over the country came to hear him speak. Clearly his presence signaled something of a rebirth of the country's religious heritage. During his 10-day visit, he conducted a mass initiation to replenish the dwindling number of Buddhist monks. That very successful visit was followed up during 2002 by a another visit to Mongolia. Unfortunately, though Chinese

authorities, who have long accused the Dalai Lama of working to weaken China, showed their irritation with the visit by apparently stopping train traffic into Mongolia for two days. The Chinese also reacted with heavy economic sanctions in 2016, when the Dalai Lama again visited Mongolia. After that, the Mongolian government said that there would be no more visits.

### Foreign Relations

The new Mongolia has also been moving to improve its relationship with the outside world. Diplomatic relations with the U.S. were established in the late 1980s and Mongolia opened its own embassy in Washington in the summer of 1990. At about that time, it also received a visit from the then American Secretary of State James Baker, who was anxious to show support for the long-isolated central Asian communist state's effort to start moving away from the centralized economic and political control typical of communist societies. More recently meetings have been held with world leaders from Bill Clinton and François Mitterrand, to Boris Yeltsin, Vladimir Putin, George W. Bush, and Joe Biden.

Relations with Russia are especially important though not always smooth or as close as they were in Soviet times. Russian is no longer the favored foreign language,

**Taking a break**                                                                 Courtesy of Steven A. Leibo

# Mongolia

although it is still widely spoken. Officials spent many years discussing the terms under which Mongolia would repay its Soviet-era debt to Russia. The two parties disagreed on the amount and the terms. Eventually, the two sides reached an agreement in 2010 by which Russia agreed to write off the bulk of the debt. It was not until 2016, however, that the elaborate processes involved allowed President Vladimir Putin to sign off on rescinding US$174.2 million, or 97% of the debt. Cross-border smuggling and rustling remains a concern. Trade is important, with something like 90% of Mongolia's energy needs coming from Russia.

In 1993, the two countries signed a Treaty on Friendly Relations and Cooperation. In September 2019, this was replaced during Putin's third visit to Ulaanbaatar by the Treaty on Friendship and Comprehensive Strategic Partnership. Military ties were resumed in the spring of 2008, and plans were put into place to develop a broad-gauge railroad that should, once built, facilitate economic relations between Russia and Mongolia. Mongolians still seem to harbor relatively warm feelings about Russia, possibly because of the sense that the Russian presence helps to shield Mongolia from the growing Chinese interest in their lands.

However, relations with Russia have been strained following the Russian attack on Ukraine that began in March 2022. Mongolian relations with Ukraine had generally been good. Ukrainian President Volodymy Zelensky even spent some time in Mogolia as a child, when his father was working there. Like Ukraine, Mongolians have long been concerned about the large powers on their doorstep but tended to see the threat as coming from China and the USSR and now Russia as a balancing factor. Since the beginning of the conflict, however, and following the ending of the COVID restrictions, Mongolians have begun to stage protest demonstrations, which have included pro-Ukrainian ones. At first, the police tried to stop these but eventually gave up. There have been calls for the Russian ambassador to be expelled. The government abstained on the UN General Assembly vote on March 2, 2022, condemning the Russian invasion.

As for China itself, relations with the PRC have grown significantly in recent years. A treaty of friendship and defense cooperation pact have been signed, and Chinese officials have reiterated their respect for Mongolia's sovereignty and territorial integrity. Still, the deep cultural links that exist between the Mongolian and Tibetan peoples, who have had their own problems with the PRC, reinforces the concerns some Mongolians have about China's long-term interest in their country.

Such concerns have been reinforced in the 2020s by a Chinese campaign to encourage the use of standard Chinese rather than Mongolian in the Inner Mongolian region.

Relations between Mongolia and the People's Republic are marked by regular high-level visits. When China's President Xi Jinping visited in 2014, he signed a new comprehensive partnership agreement that saw Mongolia promising to support Beijing's position on both Taiwan and Tibet, while China agreed to allow Mongolian freight to transit through China. The two countries regularly agree plans for trade expansion and Chinese investment is important. Mongolia has signed up to China's "Belt and Road" initiative.

Among neighboring countries, Japan-Mongolian relations are relatively limited. A soft loan from the Japanese Bank for International Cooperation has funded the development of a new international airport for Ulaanbataar. Work on this began in 2012 and was more or less completed by 2017. It has still not become fully operational. As mentioned, Japan provided funds for Mongolia's anti-COVID booster vaccinations. The then Mongolian People's Republic was the second country after the Soviet Union to establish diplomatic relations with the Democratic People's Republic of Korea (DPRK) in October 1948. During the 1950-1953 Korean War and in the immediate post-war period, it provided economic assistance as well as care for orphans. During the Sino-Soviet split from the late 1950s, Mongolia sided with the Soviet Union, while the DPRK tended to favor China. Relations thus became estranged until the 1980s. A "Treaty of Friendship and Cooperation" was signed in 1986, and the DPRK leader, Kim Il-sung , visited in 1988. However, following the fall of the Soviet Union, Mongolia established diplomatic relations with the Republic of Korea (ROK), which again led to estrangement and the cancellation of the 1986 treaty. But relations warmed somewhat after Mongolia sent relief aid during the 1990s DPRK famine and high level visits resumed. Mongolia's tobacco became a major export to the DPRK, while many North Koreans went to work in Mongolia until stopped by UN sanctions in 2017. Relations with the ROK have not developed much, although then President Kim Dae-jung visited in 1999. For a time, both Koreas were involved in the Tumen River Development Project alongside Mongolia, which, as a land-locked country, hoped that it would give it access to ports. Both Mongolia and the ROK remain members of the successor project, but the DPRK has dropped out. Mongolia has indicated a willingness to assist in improving relations between the two Koreas and

in solving the issue of the DPRK nuclear weapons and missile programs, but nothing has come of this.

Looking beyond Northeast Asia, Mongolia has been attempting to reach out internationally. A major foreign policy initiative of 1995 was launched when Natsagiyn Bagabandi, then chairman of the People's Great Hural (national assembly), publicly expressed Mongolia's desire to join the Asia-Pacific Economic forum. The country's leadership has felt that APEC membership was essential to open the door wider for foreign investment and economic cooperation. As of 2014 that goal had not yet been accomplished but success has come in other areas.

In the spring of 1998 Mongolia was finally admitted to the ASEAN Regional Forum. By the next year, having paid its debts, Mongolia took up its seat in the United Nations' General Assembly. During 2002 United Nations Secretary General Kofi Annan visited Ulaanbaatar and officially thanked Mongolia for contributing two military observers to the United Nation's mission in the Congo.

Relations with Washington also continue to be strong. Mongolia was one of those few nations that agreed to contribute personnel to the United States' effort to transform Iraq. Somewhat later, a grateful Washington announced that Mongolia was among those "select" nations eligible to compete for Washington's new grant program, the "Millennium Challenge dollars." The program was created to foster development among some of the planet's less developed countries. Even more dramatic for this land-locked nation, whose existence is so often overshadowed by that of its giant neighbors, a grateful George W. Bush arrived in 2005 to mark the first official visit by an American president.

Many Mongolians study in the United States. The Mongolian government co-funds the Fulbright masters' program, while a large number of Mongolian students study at American universities, including the current Prime Minister Luvsannamsrain Oyun-Erdene.

### Economy

The economy of Mongolia was for generations driven by animal husbandry of the sort carried out by the nomadic tribesmen and their cattle herds as well as by agricultural production. But that world has been changing dramatically in recent years. Nevertheless it is important to begin with a discussion of that earlier economy. Agriculture and livestock production were for generations the backbone of the Mongolian economy. Much of the country's industry, including wool production, clothing, and leather goods was tied to this sector.

As with all people who live more directly off the land, changes in weather patterns or periods of particularly harsh weather could devastate the national economy. For example, during the winter of 2009–2010, the weather was so harsh that 20% of the nation's livestock died. The exact numbers lost was estimated to be around nine million head. This devastated an enormous number of families.

Much of the economy still remains dependent on remittances sent home by Mongolians working abroad, as well as on assistance from international organizations and foreign countries. International donors, including the United States, the PRC, Japan, and Russia, are deeply involved in Mongolia's economy. The same is true of organizations such as the World Bank, the International Monetary Fund and the European Union.

Evolving government economic policies, most notably the end of the communist style command economies, also impacted the national economy dramatically. With the 1990–1991 collapse of the Soviet Union, as much as one-third of the nation's income dropped as the support from the then defunct USSR simply stopped flowing. Meanwhile within the country the break-up of large collective farms had a negative effect on livestock production. In 1995 livestock production (28.6 million animals) was only slightly larger than the previous record set in 1941. In 1998 it had gone up somewhat to 31.3 million. As with so many other countries of the former Soviet Union, the mid-1990s were a time of considerable economic and social stress.

Despite the economic problems and political changes, efforts at privatization continued. The decision, for example, was made to privatize housing without cost to the owners. The sale of small shops to private owners continued as well. In fact, by the end of 1996 there were over 30,000 private firms that employed hundreds of thousands of people. Even a stock exchange was introduced, and Mongolia joined the World Trade Organization (WTO).

There are also other dramatic signs of the transformation of Mongolia's economy. The Mongolian Airlines purchased its first Boeing 737 aircraft recently and established its own Coca-Cola bottling plant. Mongolia's interest in becoming more involved in today's dynamic and globalized economy has been particularly evident in the recent discussions concerning making English a second language for the nation's school children. The lack of trained English language teachers is likely to make that a major challenge for years

to come. But that has not stopped Mongolia's increasing links with the outside world from growing significantly. By the spring of 2011 it had become possible to fly directly from Hong Kong, one of East Asia's more dynamic commercial centers, to Mongolia. This scheduling decision clearly reflected the continuing integration of Mongolia into the larger world beyond central Asia.

## Mongolia Enters the Gold Rush Era

But while the transition from communism saw more Mongolians open private businesses and buy stock in companies, the real change was brought about by the arrival of international mineral extraction corporations. What has thus emerged is a large industry built around the mining of minerals.

The mining of gold, coal, copper, molybdenum, tin, and tungsten figure very significantly in today's economy. In recent years the production of copper has also been especially important as world prices have grown higher.

Also of particular interest over the last few years was the arrival of large numbers of foreigners who wanted to mine for gold. They were hardly the only people mining for gold. An estimated 100,000 Mongolians have apparently abandoned their regular occupations to scour the country-side looking for gold.

Driven by the new mining industry, the Mongolian economy has finally begun showing signs of dynamic growth. Having registered growth rates of only around 1% in 2000–2001, its GDP jumped to 4% in 2002 and is officially said to have obtained a growth of 5.5% for 2005. Even more impressive were figures of around 9% that were recorded for 2007 and 2008. But of course, then came 2008 global downturn that lowered prices for the nation's mineral exports and pushed its growth figures into the negative numbers.

Eventually Mongolia began to recover with help from the International Monetary Fund. For a time growth rates were especially impressive: 2010 came in at over 6%, 2011 at an astounding 17% plus, and even 2012 at a very healthy 12.7%.

In more recent years the situation reversed with the nation's growth rate in a rapid decline. By 2014 the rate had dropped to under 7% and 2015 came in at an anemic 2.3%. Growth then picked up again.

Ironically, traditional mining is not the only sort of "mining" that has arrived in Mongolia of late. Because of the country's traditionally cool temperatures and very low electricity costs large high-speed computer based "cryptocurrency" facilities are increasingly being set up to within the country.

Those changes have come at an extraordinary price. Most immediately, while China professes to respect the long-established borders between the nations and is said to have left any claims on Outer Mongolia behind there were certain advantages to Mongolia's long association with the Soviet Union. It reinforced something of a distance from Beijing. Today in contrast, Mongolia's economy is deeply dependent on China, linked in a way they it has not been for generations.

Like most countries, COVID hit the Mongolian economy badly. 2020 recorded negative growth of GDP, as the country imposed travel and other restrictions. Agriculture and construction were especially badly hit. Inflation soared. 2021 saw something of a rebound. While these two areas did not recover in 2021, mining and services did, giving a 7.3% increase in GDP in the early part of the year, though it later slowed, giving an overall figure for the year of 4.9%.

## Environmental Concerns: Global and Domestic

Because they live in such a challenging environment and alongside nature even more than most farming communities Mongolians have a particularly strong link and awe about the natural world around them and that world that has been changing dramatically in recent decades. And as we have seen, despite the well-known faults of that long-discredited economic system, communism did often make it easier for traditional Mongolian herdsmen to make ends meet given the horrendously demanding climate Mongolia is situated within. That was due to its collectivist economic structure and basic safety net. Once the evolution away from communism's command economy began, the withdrawal of government services often made the economics of herding impossibly difficult, thus, forcing many from the grasslands.

While there may be a great many differences between capitalism and communism, both systems assumed during the 20th century that economic growth was infinitely more important than environmental protections and the record of Soviet Era damages to the environment remain a continuing source of tensions. Despite that record, the level of environmental degradation over the last two decades of Mongolia's reintegration into the world community has been of a different order and caused by a wider variety of circumstances.

Firstly, it has been the introduction of large scale mining, both done by amateurs and professional mining concerns, that had an especially profound impact

# Mongolia

on the landscape. That mining of minerals from gold to copper, done not only underground but with even more damaging open pit mining, has radically transformed the physical environment in ways. More dramatic has been the drying up of some 400 streams and rivers blamed largely on industrial mining enterprises. Still Mongolia's environmental challenges certainly began long before the 21st century. Indeed there had been considerable tension at times between Russians and Mongolians about the level of environmental degradation caused by the formerly large Soviet military facilities as well as the impact of Soviet era mining efforts.

Moreover, a changing regional climate caused by global climate change has added to the difficulties facing what was once the lifestyle of the majority of Mongolians. To clarify that challenge it is important to recognize the core realities of Mongolian herding, that only through fattening animals during the summer can the herds survive the incredibly harsh winters. For various reasons, that has become progressively more difficult. Of particular importance has been the decreasing availability of the grasses the herds thrive on. The reduction of available grasses has many causes not the least of which has been the introduction of significantly larger goat herds. All that is understandable given how important cashmere is to Mongolia's increasingly globalized economy but also deeply unfortunate because the very low grazing habits of goats especially undermines the fragile Mongolian vegetation.

Moreover, due to greater evaporation because of global warming, the soil that vegetation grows in is ever more devoid of moisture. The result is that it has become increasingly difficult for Mongolia's

traditional herdsmen to fatten their livestock enough for the animals to survive Mongolia's especially harsh winters. And those winters have become ever more problematic as more erratic freezing and melting has a tendency to form an icy glaze over the ground making it even more difficult for the animals to obtain the food they need.

## The Future

In the last years Mongolia has made remarkable progress toward the goal of creating a politically and economically more open society. Its rulers have been especially successful in integrating the once isolated nation into the world community. Of importance for the future of Mongolia may well be the efforts to recreate the ancient "Silk Road" that made travel across Eurasia relatively easy during the Middle Ages. The plan, called the "Asian Highway Agreement," is intended to integrate an existing series of roads and canals into a modern transport system to link nations from Japan to Bulgaria. Interestingly traffic along that ancient route for commerce has already begun with Dell Computers shipping their products from China through Mongolia to Eastern Europe.

Still, the possibility of tension between Mongolia's new "friend," the United States, and Mongolia's neighbor, China, has the potential to make things very complicated. For a time the improved relationship between the United States and the People's Republic made that challenge less of an issue for Mongolia. This is partly because of the "fall out" from the terrorist attacks of 2001. Nevertheless, by 2014 the growing tensions between the United

States and China revived that particular Mongolian challenge.

What has really changed the situation is how much more linked Mongolia has become to China's economic growth. The society that once survived largely on its domestic herding industry is now much more dependent on the production of minerals for the export market and as we have seen as a processing location for the new cryptocurrencies.

Environmentally the nation has been especially able to access the international Green Energy Fund and promoting renewable energy even as its capital remains one of the most polluted globally and the country especially impacted by the changing global climate.

Still, if only a few years ago, Mongolia's future seemed quite bright, today's situation seems a great deal more ambiguous. Growth rates have fluctuated dramatically, even as more and more of the population has left the countryside for jobs in Ulaanbaatar. Not surprisingly the drop in commodity prices has added enormous strains to the country as recent budget and spending had assumed growing rather than diminishing revenues.

Indeed, the situation had become so challenging recently that the government was forced to ask for aid not only from the IMF but its enormous neighbor China even as relations with Mongolia's former geopolitical overlord Russia were clearly improving. Moreover the fact that Beijing and Moscow were improving relations just as Washington seems to be abdicating its previously ambitious global role suggests a complicated future for Mongolia's leaders.

# Brunei Darussalam

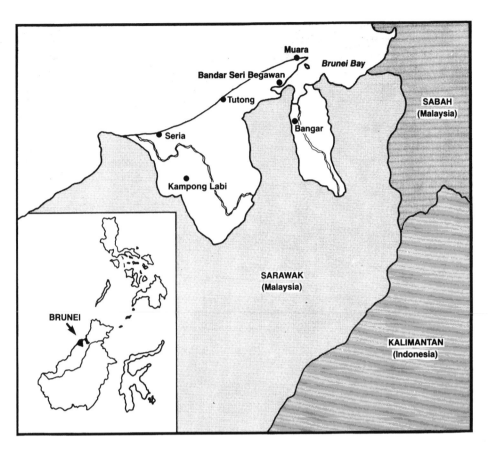

Education is free up to a doctorate. There are three streams in the educational program—Malay, English, and Arabic. Students may pursue advanced studies at schools at government expense. As of 2012 the latest trends are to enhance the national educational infrastructure's ability to offer more vocational education by founding a new polytechnic college.

Brunei has many splendid beaches, and hotels that provide excellent service and delectable foods, often combinations of rice, meat, and vegetables. The country's cattle are raised on a ranch in northern Australia, which is larger than Brunei itself. The cattle are flown into the country and slaughtered according to Muslim customs.

### History

From the 14th to the 16th century, Brunei was the cornerstone of a powerful Muslim empire that encompassed most of northern Borneo and the Philippines. However, the advance of the Dutch and the British, internal corruption, and warfare took their toll as the 17th century dawned. Brunei's rule was confined to an area today formed by Sarawak and part of Sabah. Toward the middle of the century, in 1841, in a rather desperate move to secure military help against marauding South China Sea pirates, the sultan ceded to the English adventurer Sir James Brooke the entire region of Sarawak. Brooke styled himself *rajah* ("prince" or "king") of the area and was succeeded by his nephew and the latter's son until 1946.

By 1847 the British secured from the sultan the island of Labuan off the northwest coast of Borneo. They speculated that it could become an important naval base, but the plan was never realized. There were further concessions and treaties. In 1865 the United States government under President Abraham Lincoln's administration concluded a treaty with the sultan. The American Trading Company of Borneo was created and granted vast land holdings, but this venture was soon thought worthless and was abandoned. Sixteen years later the British set up the North Borneo Company, which acquired the assets of the U.S. firm and pushed further land concessions from the sultan who had little power to refuse the mighty British Empire. Brunei was thus reduced to its present size.

With a fragile economy and no way to defend itself against the many European powers that were continuing to colonize the entire area, Brunei chose British protection in 1888. In 1906 it permitted a British commissioner to take up residence in the country. The sultan was required to take his advice in all matters involving defense and foreign affairs, but not on matters of faith and Malay customs.

**Area:** 2,226 sq. mi. (5,765 sq. km., about the size of Delaware)

**Population:** 437,479 (July 2020, UN est.)

**Capital City:** Bandar Seri Begawan (named in honor of the present sultan's father), Pop. 241,000

**Climate:** Tropical

**Neighboring Countries:** The East Malaysian states of Sarawak and Sabah enclose Brunei on the large island of Borneo, also known as Kalimantan, two thirds of which is Indonesian.

**National Language:** Malay; English is the second language

**Other Principal Tongue:** Chinese

**Ethnic Background:** Malay (67%), Chinese (15%), indigenous (6%)

**Principal Religion:** Muslim (60%, official state religion), Buddhist, Christian, traditional native beliefs

**Main Exports:** Crude petroleum, liquefied natural gas, methanol, and apparel

**Main Imports:** Aircraft, electronics, other manufactured goods, and foodstuffs

**Currency:** Brunei dollar

**Former Colonial Status:** Previously independent, it was a British protectorate (1888–1983)

**Independence Day:** January 1, 1984

**Chief of State:** His Majesty the Sultan and Yang di-Pertuan Agong of Brunei Darussalam, Sultan Haji Hassanal Bolkiah Mu'izzaddin Waddaulah (b. 1946)

**National Flag:** A yellow field crossed diagonally by single white and black stripes upon which is centered a red crest

**Per Capita GDP Income:** $66,590 (2020 est.) (purchasing power parity)

Brunei *Darussalam* (meaning "abode of peace") is one of the most unusual nations in the world. Having two distinct parts, with Malaysia's state of Sarawak plugging a 15-mile gap between the two, it is also one the wealthiest sovereign nations per capita on earth.

Much of inland Brunei is dense jungle scattered with remote villages and alive with brilliantly plumaged birds, but its gleaming capital city, Bandar Seri Begawan, on the Brunei River about nine miles from its mouth, is sleekly modern, and has several international-class hotels. The country's main port is bustling Muara.

Malays form the majority of the population, but there are also thousands of non-ethnic Malays, most of them Chinese involved in trade and commerce. In 1961 Brunei passed a law allowing local Chinese to become citizens if they had resided in the country for 20 of the previous 25 years and could pass a Malay language test. There are also small groups of British, Dutch, Americans, and Australians associated with the oil and gas industry.

# Brunei

**His Majesty The Sultan of Brunei, Hassanal Bolkiah Mu'izzaddin Waddaulah**

During the next few years the country's economy began to grow, first with the cultivation of rubber. Then the economic picture drastically changed as vast oil reserves and natural gas were discovered in the 1920s in the western part of the nation, followed by offshore deposits in the 1960s. Brunei was on the road to enormous wealth.

When the Federation of Malaysia was established in 1963 to be composed of Malaya, Sabah, Sarawak, and Singapore, the sultan of Brunei was urged to join. The then sultan rejected the plan, fearing for the erosion of his political position and determined that Brunei's oil and gas revenues would be reserved for the benefit of native Bruneians rather than becoming available to the proposed federation at large.

Brunei regained its independence after almost a century of colonialism on January 1, 1984. A member of the British Commonwealth, Brunei has since joined the UN and the Association of Southeast Asian Nations (ASEAN) among others. At the sultan's request, the Gurkha army units from Nepal stationed in Brunei while it was under British protection stayed on to aid the Royal Brunei Armed Forces. Decades later, they remain there with their own radio station, Gurkha Radio, available to fill their information needs.

The present sultan, Hassanal Bolkiah, heads the government, serving as prime minister, defense minister, and more recently as finance minister. The other key government posts are held by members of his immediate family. Born in 1946, the sultan has more than one wife, as Muslim custom allows. A few years ago he divorced his second wife and more recently remarried a much younger Malaysian woman. The decision apparently irritated many of his female constituents. That third marriage to a former television reporter from Malaysia also ended in divorce.

The sultan has three sons and six daughters. Educated in Brunei and Malaysia, he then enrolled as an officer cadet at the Royal Military Academy at Sandhurst, England.

He was crowned the 29th ruler of Brunei by his father in 1968 upon the latter's abdication. Easily one of the richest men in the world, the sultan controls the finances not only of his own family but that of the state itself. With such resources he can be quite lavish. For example, in 1996 to celebrate his 50th birthday, the sultan threw a party that cost over $25 million and included Prince Charles, an old friend, as a guest. The late American entertainer, Michael Jackson performed for the guests.

In 2004, in a wedding some called the Asian "wedding event of the year" his son Crown Prince Haji Al-Muhtadee Billah was married in a very elaborate ceremony to Sarah Salleh, a young commoner whose mother is Swiss. At that time, there was some speculation that the Sultan might be preparing to devolve some power to his son. This proved unfounded, and although the Sultan celebrated his 50th anniversary on the throne in 2017, making him the second-longest reigning monarch in the world after Queen Elizabeth II of Britain, he has shown no desire to step back from power. But if the wedding was part of the process of succession it is clear as well that the sultan has even more wide ranging political changes in mind for his kingdom.

## Politics and Government

According to its constitution Brunei is a "democratic Islamic Malay monarchy." However, it does not constitute a true

**Wedding of Crown Prince Haji Al-Muhtadee Billah**

**The Sultan Omar Ali Saifuddin Mosque**

democracy. The sultan and his family dominate the political life of the country. Although the constitution of 1959 did allow some sharing of political decision-making, the nation's legislative council was disbanded in 1962 after left-wing parties won a major victory at the polls, a victory which was complicated as well by an unsuccessful military coup. In the aftermath, the then sultan dissolved the legislature and suspended the constitution. By the mid-1990s though after a generation of absolute rule things appeared to be changing.

In February 1995, Haji Abdul Latif Chuchu, a political activist, was elected president of the Brunei Solidarity National Party, the country's only legal political party. Haji Latif and other party officials then called for democratic elections in a meeting with the sultan. That effort did not initially accomplish much. Haji Latif was subsequently banned from all political activity.

Things began to change again during the fall of 2004 when the sultan announced that he was creating a 21-member State Legislative Council with the stated goal of strengthening the monarchy and making the government more efficient. The move can hardly be considered a terribly dramatic step given the fact that the appointed members include the sultan and his brother as well as other family members and business elites. Still it was a gesture not to be discounted.

By the following year he introduced even more changes. New cabinet positions were added, and the State Legislative Council expanded in size while specific five-year terms were set for the individual members of the cabinet.

These changes were not insignificant. Brunei had not had an elected legislature since the early 1960s or even an appointed one since the mid 1980s. While the renewed State Legislative Council is hardly likely to call for dramatic changes in official policy, all this is said to be part of a process that will eventually lead to more open elections.

Despite the proposed changes, one thing remains absolutely clear. Sultan Hassanal Bolkiah, chief of government and head of state, still largely rules the country himself with the help of the Council of Cabinet Ministers, most of whom are family members. In fact, the government has said that although the State Legislative Council has now been revised to play a renewed role in the nation's governance, the sultan's goal is for it to improve the ties between the government and the people and to strengthen the monarchy rather than to make the state more democratic. A more obvious example was revealed over the last year when legal papers were released that showed that the new constitution has specifically claimed the sultan could do no wrong "in either his personal or any official capacity."

The sultan's desire to strengthen the monarchy was also evident in his efforts to start the formal introduction of the crown prince into the decision-making process. His son, Al Mutadee Billah, was appointed to the newly created position of senior minister.

He has also been emphasizing a more religious tone in some of his public talks, reminding his subjects of the importance of adhering to their Muslim duties. This approach has been a long-standing one. After his father's death in 1986, the present

sultan devised an ideology designed to reinforce the monarchy. Known as *Malaya Islam Beraja* or MIB it is mainly an affirmation of Islam and the monarchy. The sultan's ideology, MIB, was brought into the secondary schools in 1992. More recently constitutional amendments were introduced to make more explicit the sultan's right to make laws related to Islam itself.

But though there may still be little "public" politics within Brunei, there is certainly controversy within the ruling family that occasionally becomes more publicly known. In the late 1990s, an open conflict broke out between the sultan and his brother, Prince Jefri Bolkiah, who had been finance minister between 1986 and 1997, was accused of financial mismanagement and removed as finance minister and director of the Brunei Investment Agency (BIA). Surprisingly the break became very public, and Prince Jefri went into self-imposed exile for a time.

Tensions became so profound that for a while the public was witness to the spectacle of members of the royal family actually suing each other in court. This was a development that clearly added to growing public discontent. Finally the sultan stepped in to quell the lawsuits by settling the claims left by the collapse of Prince Bolkiah's business activities. Apparently family harmony has returned as Prince Jefri seems to be once again in the family's good graces. But the prince is not financially off the hook. The government is still trying to get him to surrender assets he owns around the world in compensation for his previous financial mismanagement. The saga continues. In 2008 Britain's High Court of London issued an arrest warrant for the prince. Again, he has been

# Brunei

accused of financial misconduct. It would seem the Sultan's expectations for the next generation are more positive.

While Brunei may be an island of relative tranquility compared to many of its neighbors, it too has experienced a renewal of Islamic political activism. In the fall of 2003 it was reported that the government had detained a number of individuals because of efforts to revive the banned Al-Arqam movement, which had previously had many followers in Brunei and Malaysia. The regime was understandably quite concerned about whether the wave of revolutions and uprisings that spread across North Africa and the Persian Gulf starting in l2010 would eventually impact Brunei itself. Attempting to act proactively, the government convened a major national conference in May 2010, hoping to reinforce the regime's home-grown ideology and limit the impact of what were seen as divisive ideas emitting from further west in the Islamic world. As we have seen, it has also moved to enhance the regime's Islamic credentials by expanding the scope of Islamic law within Brunei.

With that in mind, the government announced that Islamic or Sharia law would be expanded. Previously, Sharia was only applied in cases dealing with civil law. That is no longer the situation. In 2012 the Sultan announced that Sharia would be extended to criminal law including charges ranging from theft and illicit sex to apostasy. Politically it would seem that the Sultan believes that his reign would be strengthened by the embrace of a more Islamic tone to life in the country.

The introduction of wider Sharia law to cover criminal offences appears to have not been without difficulties. The move was widely condemned internationally, especially after it was announced on 30 April 2014 that the first phase, covering pregnancy outside marriage and failure to perform Friday prayers, would begin the next day. The Sultan ordered that criticism of the move on social media should stop. As a minor move toward Sharia was the banning of public displays of Christmas. Yet in February 2016, the Sultan demanded to know why nothing had happened and was told that the need to amend criminal procedures was the cause. In the event, it was not until April 2019 that Sharia law was finally in place.

There was a huge international outcry against the move. Human Rights Watch said new codes posed threats to fundamental human rights, violated the country's international obligations, and discriminated against vulnerable groups, including children, women, and religious and sexual minorities. The United Nations called the punishments cruel and inhuman. The Brunei foreign minister replied that the change was intended to prevent rather than punish. The United States urged Brunei to ratify the International Convention of Human Rights, which it had signed, and was assured that this would happen. The country also indicated that the de facto moratorium on the use of the death penalty, in place since 1957, would continue, despite the new laws containing specified death for adultery and insulting the Koran.

The criticism did not stop, however. The Brunei-owned Dorchester Collection of international hotels found that bookings for rooms and functions were cancelled, with some governments forbidding all use of such premises by their staff. Royal Brunei Airlines was similarly boycotted. The Sultan, who had been partially educated in Britain, was stripped of his honorary degrees by some British universities.

## Defense

While tiny in size, Brunei has a modern and capable defense force. Internal and external security is under the control of the Royal Brunei Armed Forces (RBAF), the Royal Brunei Police, the Gurkha Reserve Units, and the British Army Gurkha Battalion. Recent defense expenditures have been around 10% of the national budget.

The air force and navy are small but well equipped. Joint military exercises are held with Malaysia, Thailand, Singapore, The Philippines, Australia and New Zealand. The Singapore and British armies conduct jungle warfare training. A Gurkha Reserve Unit is directly under the control of the sultan. The Royal Brunei Police Force is the fourth component of national defense.

But as the world has learned in recent years, "defense" issues are not necessarily merely about the possible assault on one's nation by the forces of other countries. In July of 2003 ASEAN met in Brunei and agreed to work together to fight terrorists who have been active to various degrees in nations from Thailand and Malaysia to Indonesia and Singapore. Going beyond even that level of joint anti-terrorist activity, there is even talk of creating an ASEAN peace keeping force to deal with regional problems. More locally, the authorities in Brunei, following a similar effort in Malaysia, have begun efforts to eliminate illegal immigrants from Brunei and to make sure that their kingdom does not become a haven for terrorists.

**Modern homes on stilts**

### Foreign Relations

Brunei foreign policy stresses the security of the nation. A true mini-state, the country must rely to a considerable extent on the goodwill of its neighbors. The fact that it is surrounded by its two Muslim brother states, Malaysia and Indonesia, is advantageous. Brunei joined the Association of Southeast Asian Nations (ASEAN) just after independence in 1984. Membership has helped the country establish close diplomatic and military ties with the other ASEAN states. Brunei took the ASEAN chair in 2001 and 2013 and again in 2021. It is also a member of the ASEAN Regional Forum (ARF), a regional body focusing on Asia-Pacific security matters, and has chaired its annual meeting in 1995, 2002 and 2013. As ASEAN chair, Brunei had to handle the association's response to the 2021 military coup in Myanmar. Pleas for more moderate policies and for the release of all political prisoners were ignored by the Myanmar military. In August 2021, ASEAN foreign ministers agreed to appoint Brunei's second minister of foreign affairs, Erywan Yusof, as the organization's special envoy for Myanmar. His role was to seek a dialogue between the military and the opposition, ending violence and overseeing a humanitarian aid program. This proved to be a complete failure, with the Myanmar junta carrying on as before.

Brunei was the first Muslim state in the region to recognize Israel. Earlier on it had established ties with the Palestine Liberation Organization and opened an embassy in Iran. More recently Brunei has been strengthening its ties to other Muslim Middle Eastern states from Saudi Arabia to Morocco especially so with the hope of establishing Brunei as a safe haven for Muslims seeking to invest funds outside of the Western countries.

During the economic crisis of 1997 the sultan attempted to use his vast financial resources to shore up the collapse of his neighbors' currencies. Even his efforts failed to stem the tide of the currency debacle that hit the region. In years since the Asian economic crisis settled in, the sultan, despite weaknesses in his own economy caused by then falling oil prices, has vowed to take a more active role in helping the region progress. Not only has he been significantly involved in helping Malaysia and Indonesia recover financially, but he made his first official visits to his northern neighbors Myanmar, Laos, and Vietnam. Going far beyond his region during 2002, he made an around-the-world trip that saw him meeting with leaders from George W. Bush in Washington to the leaders of Germany and Mexico.

The major recent complication in Brunei's foreign relations was a dispute over the rights to a huge oil field off the coast of Borneo that both Brunei and Malaysia claimed. Compounding the problem was the fact that both countries had contracted with different oil companies to survey the area in anticipation of drilling in the disputed area. Not surprisingly, both Brunei's sultan and Malaysia's outgoing Prime Minister Mahathir became directly involved in the talks. Those talks were complicated still further by Malaysia's attempt to link the question of the off-shore oil resources to another sensitive regional issue, the question of Limbang, which Malaysia controls and which divides Brunei in two. Despite the tension, both nations have managed to keep the controversy from getting out of hand. Eventually a deal was completed. Brunei agreed to drop its claim on Limbang. The two nations came to an agreement on sharing the profits from two oil-rich marine areas for the next 40 years.

Despite its claim to economic interests around Louisa Reef in the Spratly Islands, an area also claimed by China, Malaysia, the Philippines, Vietnam, and Taiwan, Brunei has good relations with China. Diplomatic relations were established on Brunei independence in 1984. As it has faced economic problems in recent years (see below), Brunei has turned to China for investment and assistance. Chinese President Xi Jinping visited in November 2018, when the two countries agreed to update their relationship to a "strategic cooperative partnership." Brunei has joined the Chinese "Belt and Road" initiative and China has constructed an oil refinery and Asia's longest bridge, the 18.6-mile (30 km) Temburong Bridge. This opened in March 2020 and links the Temburong district to the capital. This has reduced travel time and allows travelers to avoid Malaysian territory, an important advantage because of COVID restrictions.

As well as condemning the military coup in Myanmar, Brunei also condemned the Russian attack on Ukraine in that began in February 2022.

### Culture and Society

The country is ruled by the royal family. The family line goes back some 29 generations farther than any of the other 28 monarchies in existence today. Brunei Malays are similar to the Malays of Malaysia and Indonesia. All are followers of Islam and speak the Malay language. They differ significantly from other ethnic groups in Brunei. Traditionally, Brunei Malays were fisherman, traders and craftsmen.

Today's generation is seeking more "modern" means of employment. About 10% of the Brunei Malays claim royal blood, having been descended from one of the sultans. Many of the Malays live in Kampong Ayer, the Malay community consisting of about 35 villages. Although under Muslim law a man is permitted to have up to four wives, this is actually rare in Brunei.

Contemporary life in Brunei for its citizens is one that many would envy. Perhaps to keep dissatisfaction with the sultan's political control to a minimum the state has used its oil resources to create a cradle-to-grave social security system. Almost every urban family owns at least one car, often more, and there is no income tax. Both education and health care are free.

The Kedazans are the second most populous indigenous group. They are similar to Malays in their practice of religion, language, and appearance. The greatest

**The Sultan Omar Ali Saifuddin Mosque**

# Brunei

difference is that they have tended to be rice farmers. They do not have the same status in society as the Malays. Other smaller indigenous groups include the Bisayas, who follow indigenous religious traditions; the Penans, nomads of the jungle; the Muruts, who once populated the military for the sultan; and the Ibans, whose numbers are increasing compared to the other smaller groups and who are known for their past head hunting activities.

The Chinese are far more important than their numbers would suggest. They dominate the sultan's commercial sector. They also provide the managerial and technical talent for the country. The older generation follows Taoist-Buddhist traditions. Less than 10% of the local Chinese have been granted citizenship. Still, their importance was recognized recently when the government's agreed to the founding of a Chinese-language newspaper in the kingdom. Like Malaysia and Singapore, Brunei is a multiethnic society that can only survive with a good bit of tolerance and acceptance of diversity. But maintaining tolerance is not the only thing that can offer challenges for Brunei. As the sultan has emphasized in his public talks, Brunei, like much of the world, is faced with the challenge of maintaining its cultural identity in the face of globalization.

### Women

As is the case elsewhere, the experience of women in Brunei is a mixed one. Until recently, no women held leading positions in the bureaucracy although large numbers do have jobs at the lower levels. That situation changed somewhat last year when a woman ascended to the nation's cabinet as a deputy minister for culture, youth, and sports.

Today nearly two-thirds of the student body at the national university is female. They also serve in the military, though not in combat positions. However, since Brunei is officially a Muslim society, Islamic domestic law governs the life of women. Women have fewer rights in such important areas as divorce and inheritance, and, as is common in the region, they cannot pass on their citizenship to their children. Men also have considerable advantages over women in the government's civil service jobs.

### Economy

Oil and gas provide Brunei with more than 90% of its export earnings. The nation is the third-largest oil producer in Southeast Asia after Indonesia and Malaysia. The Seria oil field was discovered in 1929, and by the 1950s it was producing 115,000 barrels a day. Offshore production began in 1964, and today there are hundreds of oil-rigs operated by Brunei Shell Petroleum Company, jointly owned by the government and Shell. Actual oil production is carefully watched since Brunei wants to conserve this source of income for the future. Almost half of its oil is exported to Japan, and the rest goes to other nations, including the United States. Brunei uses only about 3% of its production for domestic use.

Brunei is a major supplier of liquid natural gas, a venture owned by the government, the Royal Dutch Shell Group, and Japan's Mitsubishi Corporation. Millions of tons are exported annually to Japan and Korea alone. During 2002, for example, Brunei sent over 200 cargos of natural gas to their East Asian neighbors earning an estimated $2 billion. Overall, the petroleum sector—crude oil and natural gas—account for an enormous percentage, almost half of Brunei's gross domestic product (GDP).

The uncertainties surrounding the ongoing Middle East crisis and American Iraqi relations have made long-term economic planning for Brunei quite difficult. Certainly short-term hikes in the price of oil have been quite helpful for the kingdom. Still Brunei also needs its principal customers, such as Japan, to be economically healthy enough to pay those prices. On the other hand, a satisfactory resolution of the long-running Iraqi crisis could also see Iraq once again becoming a major oil exporter. This would lower the price of oil and hurt Brunei's government revenue. At least it would be the case until the longtime price pressures of China's and India's growing movement into the petroleum market has an even larger impact.

As of the late spring 2007, though, the concern that oil prices might drop once Iraq stabilized seemed a long way off. China's growing demand for oil, natural disasters in the oil-producing regions of the United States, and instability in the Persian Gulf combined to keep oil prices high and Brunei's energy revenues flowing nicely. At least that was the case until the global slowdown of late 2008 dragged down the demand for world's oil with it and, of course, the revenues those who sold it earned. Eventually the impact of the declining demand for the nation's energy products saw Brunei's GDP drop by almost 2% in 2008 and only slightly improve during 2009, a year that came in at a somewhat less negative growth rate while 2011 showed a stronger growth rate of around 2.2%. By 2012 the global economy seemed to be slowing down again. In the years since then, growth rates have hovered between 1% and more recently negative numbers.

The nation is also moving to play a bigger part in world petroleum production. The current plan is to go from a focus on selling crude oil to more emphasis on refinery activities and developing petrochemical industries within the kingdom. But of course raw production of fossil fuels remains at the heart of the national economy. In fact, Malaysia and Brunei managed during 2010 to resolve a long-standing territorial dispute that opened the way for more oil exploration in the waters shared by both Malaysia and Brunei. By 2012 Shell was working with its various affiliates to begin testing deep water drilling about 50 miles off the coast.

Another source of revenue is foreign investment, which is now producing almost as much money as the petroleum sector. In 2002, for example, over a billion dollars U.S. was invested by outsiders in Brunei as opposed to only about half that amount the previous year. More recently the government has been in talks associated with expanding into cement production.

Overall, the government has spent much time working on various plans to diversify the economy and more recently even moving toward privatizing some government agencies. One goal has been the plan to steer the economy away from dependence on oil and natural gas. They have reason to do so because current estimates are that the country's reserves will run out by 2025. For the moment, though, the efforts to diversify the economy have still often been tied to the energy industry. But even that is changing. In 2010, the nation moved into a new greener area of energy production by beginning to export methanol as well. Not surprisingly, the initial shipments went to the People's Republic of China while other customers included the United States, South Korea, Taiwan, and the Philippines.

There is an interesting aspect of the kingdom's reaction to developments since September 11, 2001, and the subsequent tensions between the United States and large parts of the Islamic world: Brunei decided to offer itself as an attractive banking alternative for those Muslims who are no longer comfortable having their investments in Western banks. That effort has led to a reorganization and merger of parts of the nation's banking industry and the emergence of the new Islamic Bank of Brunei Berhad.

Brunei is also developing plans to create a giant Mega port hub for handling the enormous container shipping that so dominates the region. Moreover, in yet another challenge to Singapore's accomplishments the government is also planning to push Brunei deeper into the Internet revolution with the creation of a cyber park to encourage the nation's involvement in the emerging e-market developments.

Another factor that complicates Brunei's economy is that the government employs more than half of the labor force. A new joint-venture garment manufacturer was forced to import Philippine and Thai workers because locals were either too few in number or not willing to do such work. In reaction to such problems the government froze civil service pay in an attempt to make state employment less attractive. However, in a country where health care and education are free, and where subsidized loans are readily available, there is little pressure to change. There may be some ambivalence on the part of national leaders concerning economic change. An influx of foreigners and new ventures would disturb the comfortable and traditional environment of this Islamic mini-state.

The economy is already suffering a decline, as gas and other natural resources run down. This has led to youth unemployment and the situation has been made worse by COVID-19. While Brunei escaped lightly at first, the closing of international borders and the decline in international tourism affected it. Per capita GNP (ppp), which had been generally growing, has plunged dramatically. It was $85,790 in 2019 and $66,590 in 2020.

## COVID-19

As COVID spread internationally, Brunei banned all foreign travel from 16 March 2020. Like its neighbors, the ban included pilgrims who planned to go on the annual Hajj pilgrimage to Mecca in June. The general effect on the country was small in 2020. There were only 203 cases, of which 186 fully recovered; the last local infection case was in May 2020. After that, there were 42 imported cases but no locally transmitted cases and no few deaths recorded. In February 2021, it was announced that China had made a donation of the Sinopharm COVID-19 vaccine. Vaccination would be free to Brunei citizens and long-term residents. The vaccination program got under way in April, mainly for key workers and the elderly. In July, it was extended to all over 18. Travel to Mecca for the Hajj was again banned.

By May 2021, Brunei had gone a year without without a single transmission of the virus, although some travellers did have it. But the long run of no COVID came to an end in August. Despite all precautions, which included the closure of schools, mosques, and many businesses, together with an instruction to stay at home as much as possible, and which continued until October, people began to get sick. By the end of 2021, there were 15,000 cases and 98 deaths.

February 2022 saw the beginning of another spike. By the end of April, the WHO reported that there had been a total of 141,629 reported caes, and 158 deaths between January 3, 2020, and April 29, 2022. By then, most restriction had been lifted and a total of 1,084,543 vaccination doses had been administered.

## The Future

With a per capita income of around $66,590, the country is doing far better than many of its neighbors. Although for a time, there was some economic distress as unemployment grew significantly, things improved until COVID struck, but the likely effect of that may be short-lived. However, income from oil fields has gyrated dramatically and the nation's GDP has been dropping into negative numbers at times. The war in Ukraine and sanctions on Russian energy supplies may help increase Brunei's share of the world energy market.

As always, the fluctuation of oil prices has added to those calling for the nation to diversify its income streams. And given the fact that oil and gas represent 90% of government revenue that is an important issue.

Overall though the primary economic challenge still remains to diversify the economy enough to prepare it for the day when the oil lines run dry, or realistically, when the world starts fundamentally to shift away from the fossil fuels on which Brunei depends for its livelihood. Given the generally growing global urgency about the importance of lessening our dependence on fossil fuels, that reality seems more likely today than it was only a few years ago. It is an example of the evolving global energy regime for which a nation like Brunei will have to plan carefully.

However, the long-term impact of the planet's weaning itself from fossil fuels is not the only concern. Beside humanity's long-term use of fossil fuels that enhance greenhouse gases, the kind of massive flooding that is so often associated with climate change has periodically hit Brunei. .

Such floods can lead to significant landslides and power outages. For Brunei there is a clear irony: the very fossil fuels that nurture its economy are making the entire region it inhabits and the nation itself increasingly vulnerable to the sorts of climatic changes, more powerful storms, and more frequent flooding that are becoming ever more common around the world.

# The Kingdom of Cambodia

**The temple of Angkor Wat built by Khmer warrior kings a thousand years ago**

Courtesy of AP Images

**Area:** 68,898 sq. mi. (181,300 sq. km., slightly larger than Missouri)

**Population:** 16,486,540 (2019)

**Capital City:** Phnom Penh, pop. 2,129,371 million (2019)

**Climate:** Tropically hot with a rainy monsoon season during the summer from May to October

**Neighboring Countries:** Thailand (North and West); Laos (Northeast); Vietnam (East)

**Official Language:** Khmer (Cambodian)

**Other Principal Tongues:** French, Chinese, and Vietnamese

**Ethnic Background:** Cambodian (Khmer, about 90%), Vietnamese (semi-permanent or permanent, about 5%), Chinese (1%), other, (about 4%)

**Principal Religion:** Buddhism

**Main Exports:** (to China, U.S., Germany, U.K., Vietnam, and Canada) Natural rubber, rice, pepper, timber, rice, fish, footwear, and tobacco

**Main Imports:** (Thailand, Singapore, Vietnam, Japan, Taiwan, and Australia) Cars, pharmaceuticals, cigarettes, gold, construction materials, oil, and machinery

**Currency:** Riel

**Former Colonial Status:** French protectorate (1863–1949); Associated State within the French Union (1949–1955)

**Independence Date:** November 9, 1953

**Head of State:** King Norodom Sihamoni (since October 29, 2004)

**Head of Government:** Hun Sen, premier (since 1985)

**National Flag:** A plain red field upon which is centered in gold the ancient temple Angkor Wat

**Per Capita GDP Income:** $4,000 (2017 est.) (purchasing power parity)

Cambodia has a rather short coastline that runs about 150 miles along the warm waters of the Gulf of Thailand. The land stretches from this coast in a wide plain, which is traversed in the eastern part by the broad waters of the lower Mekong River. The western part of the plain is dominated by a large lake known as Tonle Sap, 20 miles wide and 100 miles long. It is a body of fresh water that produces a heavy annual harvest of fish needed by those Cambodians, who do not eat meat because of Buddhist beliefs.

The borders with Laos and southern Vietnam run through thickly forested foothills that rise to highlands at the demarcation lines. The greater part of the northern border with Thailand consists of a steep series of cliffs; the part of Thailand closest to Cambodia is a plateau that is situated about 1,500 feet above the plain. The western border with Thailand and most of Cambodia's coastline is occupied by the Cardamom, Kirimom, and Elephant Mountains, which rise to heights of 5,500 feet.

Much of the large central plain is regularly flooded by the mighty Mekong River in an uncontrolled fashion. There are no elaborate dikes to contain the waters such as are found along the Red River in northern Vietnam. The rains that begin in May are the first cause of flooding; melting

# Cambodia

snows in Tibet and China in July add to the volume of water, which is also joined by monsoon waters from Thailand and Laos. By mid-September the floodwaters may cover as much as 8,000 square miles of land. These are not violent waters. Rather they deposit silt which enriches the land and they also bring huge quantities of fish to the Tonle Sap Lake, permitting annual harvests of up to 15 tons per square mile of water surface. The waters recede in October. The winter season begins in November, bringing slightly cooler and much drier weather except in the western and southern mountains, where there is sporadic rainfall.

### History

The civilization of Cambodia first emerged as a product of indigenous communities of peoples and their interaction with peoples from South Asia. The Khmer people, from whom the modern Cambodians (Kampucheans) are descended, first organized themselves under a state usually known by its Chinese name of Funan, which emerged about 500 A.D. in southern Cambodia. This was apparently a result of trade with, and immigration from, India to Cambodia via the Kra Isthmus, which is now the southern part of Thailand. These early contacts were brought about by Southeast Asia's geographic location on the trade routes between South Asia and China. More significant for the development of society in Southeast Asia was that the region's powerful monsoon rain storms often forced the ships to spend long periods on the peninsula waiting for weather conditions to change. It was under these circumstances that the spread of Indian culture, including traditions like Hinduism and Buddhism, could spread widely.

Although Funan was not a centralized state as would later develop, it did have tributary relations with the Chinese to its north. But it would be Indian, not Chinese, society that would have the most profound influence on the region during these years. Just as Koreans would in these years model themselves after Chinese society, the Cambodian elites in the first centuries of the modern era strove to become more like their Western neighbors. They took Indian names and developed literary works in Indian languages. Hindu Gods, from Shiva to Vishnu, were worshiped, and local leaders strove to associate themselves with these powerful Indian images.

### The Khmer Civilization of Angkor Wat

From the era around the early 9th century through much of the 15th century,

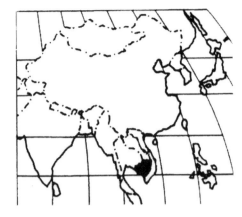

Cambodia was home to one of the world's most impressive civilizations. Located in Cambodia and parts of today's Thailand, this civilization, associated most with the extraordinary building structure at Angkor, has left us an enormous amount of information to try to understand it. Early leaders of this civilization were strongly influenced by Hinduism and identified themselves with the Hindu god Shiva. Because the temples were made of stone, many of which can be studied today, we tend to know more about elite religious society and less about the average "Cambodians" of the era. What we do know is that they were used by the monarchy to supply labor to the building projects of the empire. And their labor was impressive indeed. Angkor Wat, built in the 12th century, remains the largest religious building in the world today.

The people were converted after 1000 A.D. to the older school of Buddhism now generally referred to as Theravada Buddhism. Mahayana, or Greater Vehicle Buddhism, was also influential but less so than the more austere Theravada (the way of the elders) Buddhism which prevailed over time. At its height in about 1200, the Khmer Empire controlled much of what is now Vietnam, Thailand, Laos, and Burma. One of the main features of Angkor Civilization as we now understand it was a very attractive commitment to religious toleration.

In the later years of Angkor Civilization, the Cambodians were much influenced by

the arrival of Muslim traders from India. They not only converted many Southeast Asians to Islam, but played a significant role in reorienting the inward-looking rice-based economy of Angkor to one that was also interested in international trade.

In foreign affairs, the Angkor civilization found itself by the 1200s under pressure from Thai forces as well as the Vietnamese, a community whose tensions with Cambodia lasted well into the modern era. Sadly, having flourished earlier, the Khmer civilization of Angkor had collapsed by the 15th century and its people dispersed. The city itself lay forgotten until the 19th century when it was rediscovered.

For the next 350 years, Cambodia was sandwiched between the Annamese of Central Vietnam and the Thais to the north and west. The once mighty Cambodian

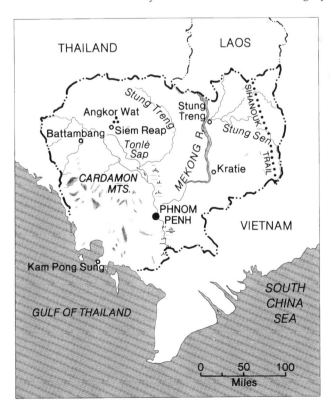

183

# Cambodia

**Young King Sihanouk, 1946**

people were, over the centuries, to be almost continuously dominated by one or the other, or both.

### The Arrival of the West

By the 1500s, Western missionaries had begun to arrive in Cambodia seeking converts to Christianity and influence for the Spanish Empire. They were not terribly successful and unlike their brethren in the Philippines, had little success in attracting converts. But while Western missionaries from the Iberian Peninsula were the first to appear in Cambodia, the Indochina's more fundamental encounter with colonialism would come from the forces of imperial France.

The beginning of formal French influence in Indochina was initially an offshoot of their activities in China during the Second Opium War. Once the Anglo-French forces had captured the city of Canton in southern China, French officials made the decision in 1859 to send a fleet to Vietnam to establish a presence there. From the French perspective, it was a way to successfully compete with their archrivals, the English, in the rush to establish themselves in East and Southeast Asia. French-specific interest in Cambodia was stimulated in the late 1850s by British advances in Burma. Both powers thought of Southeast Asia principally as a stepping stone to the supposedly vast treasures and markets of southwest China.

Although it established a protectorate over Cambodia in 1863, France did not dethrone the reigning family; the area was increasingly drawn into the Indochinese colony created at the end of the century in

an attempt to rival the much larger British Indian Empire. The French prevented the Thais from moving against Cambodia and protected it also from its other overlord, the Vietnamese, who had themselves become part of the French Indochinese Empire. Because this protection was welcomed by the Cambodians there did not develop the violently anti-French attitude that existed in neighboring Vietnam during the same era. Nevertheless, when the French in the early 1880s attempted to modify tax rates and introduce other administrative changes they provoked a revolt in 1885 that lasted for more than two years and required large numbers of French troops to suppress it.

During those early years of the French presence they ran Cambodia as a trusteeship and allowed the indigenous monarchy and its officials to largely administer the country. Nevertheless, the French held the ultimate strings of power and were usually instrumental in choosing who actually held the Cambodian throne during their years of colonial control. The hands-off policy was abandoned by the late 19th century as French officials began to interest themselves in internal developments and to more directly control it as a colony.

As in other parts of Southeast Asia, the existence of a stable colonial administration attracted a sizable number of Chinese immigrants, who quickly emerged in a virtually dominant position in profitable ventures as commercial middlemen. Many Vietnamese also immigrated to Cambodia during these years. Because they were more likely to speak French they were more able than the native Cambodians to advance themselves through links with the French.

Initial French enthusiasm for Cambodia lessened after it became clear that the colony itself lacked the rich mineral resources many had hoped for nor provided a convenient "back door" to the southern provinces of China. By the interwar period, the Cambodian economy, like many of its neighbors in Southeast Asia, was increasingly integrated into the world economy. For Cambodia this meant producing rice for the world markets and becoming, under the control of French companies, a major exporter of rubber.

### The Second World War

Japan quickly overran Cambodia in 1941, and as a token of appreciation, two of the Cambodian border provinces were awarded to Thailand, by then an official ally of the Japanese. They were returned to Cambodia after the defeat of Japan, but the Cambodians have maintained a lingering suspicion that Thailand still covets

**King Sihamoni**

them. In theory, Cambodia remained under French control after the establishment of the Vichy regime in 1940, but in practice, from 1941 to early 1945, it was ran by the Japanese military.

After the return of the French in 1946 politics in Cambodia were dominated by a popular yet unpredictable individual who initially ruled until 1970: Prince Norodom Sihanouk. He had been made king by the French in 1941, despite his age (18) and the existence of better candidates, including his father. Sihanouk was something of a playboy, seemingly more interested in his wives and consorts—he had at least six known ones—jazz, especially the saxophone, and film making. But he also became impatient with the conservative traditions of the monarchy and increasingly interested in the liberal political movements within the country. This led to the French, who had come back after the defeat of Japan, to grant a more democratic constitution in 1947, althought they still maintained overall control. During the early 1950s he successfully convinced the French to grant full independence for Cambodia, an effort that gained him even more public appreciation. He abdicated the throne in 1955 in favor of his father so that he could organize his own political movement, the People's Socialist Community which he expected to replace the existing political parties. Building on his widespread support among the population, Sihanouk dominated Cambodian political life for the next generation.

He skillfully used this popularity to cope with what he regarded as major domestic problems: the traditional aristocracy, the partly westernized intellectuals, the businessmen, the small communist movement, and a segment of right-wing opponents who he believed were supported by Thailand. Initially, his efforts were almost uniformly successful. He continued to lead the Sangkum, or the People's Socialist Community that was the only significant political party. Sihanouk's sense of his own talents is difficult to exaggerate. During the same years he wrote and produced a number of feature films with himself as the leading man.

But for the popularity of Sihanouk at home, Cambodia would never have been able to deal with the external pressures with which it was faced. In order to keep open the largest number of possible alternatives, Sihanouk remained "neutral" in the international "Cold War" and aloof in the hot war in Asia. He engaged in active and skillful diplomacy that often puzzled the most astute foreign ministries.

### The Vietnam War Era

To counterbalance the threat of North Vietnam, Sihanouk established close relations with the People's Republic of China, a nation that was not anxious to see Ho Chi Minh's Vietnam dominate Cambodia. Overall, Sihanouk hoped he could play off the powerful forces around his country to keep Cambodia safe and independent. But given the tensions of the Cold War era, Sihanouk's efforts to find a middle ground between the contending forces was complicated indeed and aroused the suspicions of the United States which saw him as an impediment to their own plans for the peninsula, especially after he terminated US military and economic assistance in 1963.

He was supportive of both sides in the Vietnamese struggle during the early 1960s. For example, he allowed the North Vietnamese to use Cambodian territory in their efforts to supply their troops in South Vietnam while keeping open his relations with the Americans.

For this reason, relations between Sihanouk and the U.S. were strained after the early 1960s. Complaints by the U.S. increased sharply in late 1967 as the fighting in South Vietnam became more intense. Clearly the United States wanted to pursue the Viet Cong into the eastern provinces of Cambodia. The whole situation was made even more complicated by Cambodia's claims to areas in South Vietnam, claims Sihanouk put forth at the bargaining table repeatedly when dealing with the U.S. Eventually Sihanouk did secretly agree to allow the Americans to bomb North Vietnamese supply lines in Cambodia.

The ever-changing diplomacy of Sihanouk worked to the extent that its

**Along the Tonle Sap, Cambodia's Great Lake**

Asian neighbors did not constitute a direct threat to the survival of Cambodia. Nevertheless, the unity of Cambodia and Sihanouk's direct control were weakening. There was a significant increase in communist-led revolts in the provinces bordering Thailand and Laos in the latter part of 1968, as well as the number of Viet Cong illegally present within Cambodia. The displeasure of anti-communist Cambodians grew so great that in 1970, while Sihanouk was out of the country, major anti-Hanoi demonstrations broke out in Phnom Penh. General Lon Nol and Prince Sirik Matak, an older cousin of Sihanouk, proclaimed the ouster of Sihanouk and a new government under their leadership. The communist problem, however, was not the only issue—there had been disputes over Sihanouk's socialist economic policies that were thought to be hurting the economy as well.

Recognizing the more pro-American tone of the new Cambodian administration, the North Vietnamese and Cambodian communist forces, now supported by the ousted Sihanouk, promptly began to expand their military activities in various parts of the country. That same year, in April of 1970, 20,000 American and South Vietnamese soldiers entered Cambodia to attack the communist bases along the border from which the communists had been conducting raids into South Vietnam. To their disappointment they found the bases had been abandoned weeks before. The Americans soon pulled out, but their bombers would return in coming years to

carry out a massive campaign against leftist forces within Cambodia.

The country suffered severely as a result of this military campaign. Although Lon Nol was in poor health and under heavy military pressure from the communist forces he managed to remain in power until 1975. However, long before that Lon Nol had already dissolved the National Assembly and begun to rule by decree. He also proclaimed himself President. But none of these efforts helped. Public confidence in the government eroded badly. Meanwhile the expansion of the Vietnam War into Cambodia had further outraged many Americans and by mid 1973 the bombing partly undertaken to support Lon Nol's pro-Western government was halted.

### The Cambodian Genocide

Meanwhile the communist forces of Cambodia, dubbed the Khmer Rouge by Prince Sihanouk, who was quite publicly working with them, were growing stronger. Although fiercely nationalistic, they initially also had the support of the North Vietnamese. The Khmer Rouge's most influential leader was Solath Sar, better known as Pol Pot, a Western-educated Cambodian whose family had earlier had significant ties to the Cambodian court.

Communist Khmer Rouge military efforts came close to isolating Phnom Penh by early 1975. Undermined by his own shortcomings, political bickering, and uncertainty about American support, Lon Nol's government evaporated. The rebels refused to negotiate, leaving

# Cambodia

**Cambodian Prime Minister Hun Sen**

it no alternative but to surrender amid ominous proclamations of a collection of "blood debts" from the leadership. The final collapse came in mid-April 1975, when Phnom Penh fell to the Khmer Rouge. It was to be the first step in the darkest chapter of Cambodian modern history.

The policies of the new Khmer Rouge regime, which was pro-Chinese and soon became anti-Vietnamese, reflected the ideological mentality of its leaders and personnel. Once in power the Khmer Rouge set out to brutally transform Cambodia, which they now renamed Kampuchea, into a classless agrarian society. It was to be an experiment in social engineering more radical than ever tried in modern human history. Going beyond the social reorganizations of Asian groups like the Chinese Taipings or what had gone on elsewhere in the communist world, the Khmer Rouge was determined to remold all Cambodians to fit their "idealistic" images. Those who were not perceived as "appropriate" for the new order were simply murdered. Over the next several years, civil society as Cambodia had known it simply disappeared. Money and wages were abolished, the cities largely emptied and all forms of religious life, freedom of the press, and much of the middle class were simply eliminated from the life of the nation.

To build their new classless agrarian society the Khmer Rouge closed down institutions from hospitals to educational facilities and even monasteries. Private property, even down to the most personal hygiene supplies, was communalized while a policy of systematic mass murder was put into place. Over time what emerged was a genocide that rivaled the horrors experienced by Armenians and Jews earlier in the century or that experienced by others in Central Africa later on. As one writer has put it,

Democratic Kampuchea was less a nation than a state prison camp.

The major cities, including Phnom Penh, were forcibly evacuated, allegedly on account of food shortages. There were executions of supporters of the former regime and widespread atrocities, mainly against persons of middle class background. Anything, even the wearing of glasses, could mark someone as too bourgeois and thus bring on a death sentence! Cambodians found themselves brutalized by one of the harshest governments of the 20th century. A veil of secrecy shrouded the nation. The formerly beautiful capital of Phnom Penh with 1.3 million people was left with 90,000. Boarded-over storefronts and virtually deserted streets told the story. The new regime wanted to stifle religion, wipe out any education system conflicting with the hopes of the "new order," and stamp out family ties.

Families were driven from the cities to labor from dawn to dusk in the fields. First priority was the destruction of the intelligentsia and middle class. Although estimates regarding the number of dead vary widely, the best scholarly estimates now put the number at between 1.5 and 1.7 million people dead from execution, starvation, and overwork. Of the seven to eight million Cambodians before the genocide began, some have estimated that the death toll ranged from 15% to 40% of the entire population.

The regime's atheistic and racist mentality was particularly devastating for the nation's Buddhist community whose monks and properties were regularly singled out for destruction. Although much of the killings were of Cambodians by Cambodians, the nation's ethnic minorities were not spared; hardly surprising given the vehement racist/nationalist mentality the Khmer Rouge usually displayed. Previous to the Khmer Rouge's arrival to power the largest ethnic communities in Cambodia were the Muslim Chams, the Chinese and the Vietnamese. Together these minorities had traditionally made up about 15% of the nation's population but once in Cambodia the new leadership was determined to change the situation. The Vietnamese, who were particularly hated, were completely eliminated with many dead and others fleeing to Vietnam. Recent researchers have failed to find a single Vietnamese who survived the assault on their community in Cambodia. The Chinese, whose traditions as city dwellers made them particularly unpopular with the new rulers, saw more than half, about 200,000, of their numbers die during these years. The Muslim Chams fared no better. After first experiencing the Khmer Rouge's efforts to destroy their Islamic traditions, their people were systematically massacred after they attempted to resist.

Pol Pot's preferred method of execution even saved the cost of a bullet: a skull-penetrating blow to the rear of the head by a pickax used on a kneeling person. Massive piles of bones throughout the

**Mekong River tour boat**

186

country attest to this grisly activity. Others simply starved to death.

Once Lon Nol's government was overthrown, the still popular Prince Sihanouk, who had spent the interveing years between lavish palaces provided for him in Beijing and Pyongyang, returned home. Khmer Rouge rule Cambodia was not run by Sihanouk, though, but by a shadowy leadership of the Cambodian Communist Party known as the Angka ("organization"), of which Pol Pot was Secretary General. An election held in 1976 filled 250 seats in the People's Representative Assembly. All of the 515 candidates were picked by the Angka. Sihanouk then resigned, together with the rest of the government. The former king was placed under house arrest, while at least three of his children died at the hands of the Khmer Rouge. A government entirely of communists was announced, with Pol Pot in actual control.

### Cambodia's Vietnamese Interlude

The new Cambodian regime had immediate friction with all of its neighbors, the most serious with Vietnam, which erupted into continuing border warfare from early on until late 1978 when Vietnam invaded. By early January 1979, Pol Pot had fled to western Cambodia, and a new pro-Vietnamese government known as the People's Republic of Kampuchea had been set up in Phnom Penh. Despite their defeat, Pol Pot's forces would then carry on a guerrilla war against the Phnom Penh government until the late 1990s.

Though Hanoi probably viewed its invasion as both a reaction to the Khmer Rouge's assaults and as an effort to free the Cambodians from Pol Pot's murderous regime, few in the international community viewed the invasion in that light. In general the world community viewed the invasion as an unprovoked Vietnamese aggression and responded negatively. Ironically, the world reaction produced some very strange informal alliances as both the United States and the People's Republic of China condemned the invasion, and to various degrees were supportive of the defeated Khmer Rouge.

The Chinese, long unhappy with Hanoi's ties to the USSR, staged a brief invasion across the Vietnamese border in early 1979 with the announced purpose of "teaching Vietnam a lesson." Unfortunately, for the PRC the only "lesson" learned was their own forces were ill prepared to deal with Hanoi's experienced troops. The attack had no impact on Vietnam's control of Cambodia.

For the next decade, regular fighting went on in western Cambodia between Vietnamese troops and Pol Pot's forces.

Tension also arose between Vietnam and Thailand over the Cambodian refugees grouped near the border. A coalition under Sihanouk, including what was left of Pol Pot's regime, emerged in opposition to the Vietnamese-dominated government in Phnom Penh. This group retained Cambodia's seat in the UN.

The Phnom Penh government, while hardly the genocidal regime of the Khmer Rouge, was itself repressive. Moreover because it was dominated by the Vietnamese it was understandably not very popular with the Cambodian population. For a time the government attempted to carry out socialist agricultural policies somewhat similar to those common during Pol Pot's years and within Vietnam itself, but these were eventually phased out. The anti-religious policies of Pol Pot were also ended. Once again Buddhist activities were allowed. Monks could retake their traditional place in Cambodian life despite

some restrictions. Though many Cambodians had been very relieved to have the Vietnamese drive out Pol Pot's murderous regime, the new Vietnamese-backed government was unpopular and thousands of Cambodians continued to flee the country.

It was during these years that Cambodia's later "strong man" Hun Sen emerged in importance. Originally, from a middle class family, Hun Sen had initially been part of the Cambodian Communist resistance to Sihanouk's government. He later joined the Khmer Rouge only to break with the regime in 1977. Hun Sen returned home as part of the Vietnamese invasion force. By 1985 he was prime minister.

Eventually, in May 1988, the Vietnamese Government announced that it would soon withdraw its troops from Cambodia. Hanoi had done so by 1989. The reasons for this major policy shift included the dismal state of the Vietnamese economy, the small chances of attracting aid from

**Monument filled with skulls at the infamous "Killing Fields"**
Courtesy of Steven A. Leibo

# Cambodia

**Their Majesties the former King and Queen of Cambodia**

abroad while the Cambodian occupation continued, and Soviet pressure, or at least persuasion. It is probably not a coincidence that only the month before Moscow had formally agreed to remove its troops from Afghanistan by February 15, 1989. Hanoi also wanted to improve its relations with the United States, something that its continuing hold over Cambodia made impossible.

The prospect of a Vietnamese withdrawal naturally accelerated the pace of political and diplomatic activity relating to Cambodia, both within and outside the country. Having lost its more immediate Vietnamese support, Hun Sen's government was faced with the necessity of building a strong popular base of its own within Cambodian society. It was thus during this era that he moved to reintroduce private property and expand further the role of Buddhism which had been allowed to revive in the years after Pol Pot's defeat.

The main problem that the Vietnamese evacuation created was the fear that it might lead to another seizure of power by the bloodthirsty Khmer Rouge. Of course, the other contenders for power were Hun Sen's government in Phnom Penh, the Royalists around the former king, Prince Sihanouk, and a non-communist resistance group directed by the former Prime Minister Son Sann. The latter two in fact had received international recognition as a Cambodian government in exile but represented little of practical importance within the country.

## The UN-Sponsored Elections

As the 1990s unfolded a complicated series of international negotiations took place with the goal of establishing Cambodia on a healthier and more stable road to recovery. On October 23, 1991, the Paris International Conference on Cambodia adopted an agreement on a Comprehensive Political Settlement of the Cambodia Conflict, which created the United Nations Transitional Authority in Cambodia (UNTAC) with a force of 16,000 military and 6,000 civilians that began arriving in Cambodia in early 1992. UNTAC's function was to disarm the Cambodian warring factions and create a political climate where free elections could take place.

The long awaited free elections took place in 1993. But the victory of the royalist forces under Prince Ranariddh, the son of King Sihanouk, was overturned by Hun Sen, whose military forces remained stronger. Refusing to accept his party's political defeat at the polls, Hun Sen forced the creation of a very convoluted political system with two prime ministers.

Thus, from 1993 through 1997, Cambodia operated under the coalition government formed in the aftermath of the 1993 United Nations sponsored election. After more than a generation of civil war and totalitarian governments this was a remarkable improvement. Officially its

government was a constitutional monarchy headed by Norodom Sihanouk, who was once again officially sworn in as monarch in September of 1993.

Sihanouk's sons directed FUNCINPEC, the "royalist" party and Prince Norodom Ranariddh held the position of first Prime Minister. Hun Sen, the longtime leader of Cambodia, held the title of second prime minister although he actually held more power than his rival. The cabinet also featured dual ministers representing both parties.

The country operated as a parliamentary system though the judiciary was not as independent of the government as the constitution required. The unusual system of two prime ministers certainly helped get the government operating, but the more common pattern of having rotating prime ministers, as has occurred in Israel and Turkey, might have worked more efficiently.

From the start the two prime ministers were frequently estranged and actual fighting often broke out between their supporters. Only the most optimistic believed the unstable coalition could survive. Norodom Sirivudh, half-brother of King Norodom Sihanouk, was "encouraged" to go into exile for allegedly planning to kill co-prime minister Hun Sen. Many believed the Prince was framed in an attempt to silence his criticism of the government. The murder in 1996 of Hun Sen's brother-in-law was another example of the tension. Nevertheless, the coalition might have survived if the third factor in Cambodian politics, the bloodthirsty Khmer Rouge, had not complicated the situation enormously.

The Khmer Rouge and what to do about it had, of course, long been the major issue that faced the government. Attempts to end the fighting took different forms over the years. The approach ranged from fighting to occasional efforts to reconcile with the Khmer Rouge, despite its bloody record of mass murder. Of those contending for power it was the royalists who were most willing to associate themselves with the Khmer Rouge. There was also a move to have Sihanouk form a provisional government of reconciliation that would have included the Khmer Rouge. Hun Sen's supporters opposed the plan, and Sihanouk withdrew his offer. Nevertheless, by the late 1990s the dynamics of Cambodian politics started changing dramatically.

## The End of the Khmer Rouge

The year 1996 saw major progress in the government's efforts to end the longtime insurrection of the Khmer Rouge. In August, Ieng Sary, a senior leader of the Khmer Rouge, said to be second only to

Cambodia

the infamous Pol Pot, broke ranks and offered to end his role in the insurrection. The offer, while greeted as an important step in the final reconciliation of the country, was complicated by the former Khmer Rouge officer's direct role (vehemently denied) in the genocide of the 1970s. After complicated negotiations, he was granted a royal pardon.

That Ieng Sary's defection indicated a weakening Khmer Rouge was highlighted by the remaining leadership's willingness to allow a formal radio talk show discussion on maintaining Khmer Rouge solidarity. This was a remarkable step to take for a party with one of the most totalitarian records of the 20th century. These developments highlighted a blow to the Khmer Rouge as profound as their earlier loss of power after the Vietnamese invasion of 1979 and which later events showed they would not recover from.

By early 1999 the last of the major Khmer Rouge leaders had fallen into the hands of the government though it was unclear how many of the actual killers would ever come to trial before either a Cambodian tribunal or one organized by the international community. Over the years, though, there has been an almost constant effort to create a tribunal, rather like those that have dealt with crimes in the former Yugoslavia and the genocide in Rwanda, to confront the horrors of the Khmer Rouge years.

The world community had by 2006 finally agreed upon an institutional framework to accomplish such a goal. In January an international tribunal, which included both Cambodian and foreign nationals, was established just outside of Phnom Penh. The following summer prosecutors and judges were sworn in. In mid-summer of 2007 the new tribunal officially recommended that the Khmer Rouge leaders be tried for genocide and crimes against humanity. By the fall some of the most notorious of the surviving Khmer Rouge leaders had been arrested and began appearing before the newly established tribunal. By 2008 more formal trial procedures had begun against some of the most infamous of the members of the Khmer Rouge who still survive. They include Kang Kek Leu, known as Duch, who had once directed the horrific Tuol Sleng detention camp and was eventually sentenced to life imprisonment.

Of course, the simple passing of time has allowed many to evade justice. In early 2013 Ieng Sary, one of the founders and a principal leader of the Khmer Rouge, died during his trial. He was eighty-seven at the time of his death, and his co-defendants are also in their eighties. Indeed, by early 2014 there were only two potential defendants remaining. The likelihood that any of those who played major roles in one of the late 20th century's worst cases of genocide and mass murder will ever be formally punished seems more doubtful with each passing day.

**The Search for Political Stability**

The unstable coalition government that had operated since the United Nations' sponsored elections collapsed during the summer of 1997. The actual break was caused not by tensions with Sam Rainsy's group but, as so often in the past, over relations with the then weakening Khmer Rouge. In early July, Hun Sen's forces carried out a coup against the supporters of his rival Prince Ranariddh. The second prime minister claimed that the Prince had finalized an alliance with elements of the Khmer Rouge and was planning to integrate them into his own forces. All this took place in the middle of a "circus" of international media attention as the Khmer Rouge itself seemed close to collapse and rumors abounded that the notorious Pol Pot might become available for trial at an international tribunal against genocide. What was actually going on behind the scenes was quite uncertain. What was clear was that after the dust settled Hun Sen's forces had driven the Royalists from the capital and Prince Ranariddh was in exile.

By mid-July 1998 most of the major aid donor countries had temporally halted aid to Cambodia in protest against the coup and the country's hopes to join ASEAN were dashed as the leaders of the Association of Southeast Asian Nations decided to postpone the planned admission of Cambodia. Apparently the proposed alliance between the Cambodian Royalists, assuming we accept Hun Sen's claims, caused major political waves within the Khmer Rouge as well. By the end of the month the movement's longtime leader, Pol Pot, had fallen from power, denounced by his former followers. Later that summer the world got its first glimpse in a generation of the fallen leader when Pol Pot was given a "show trial" by his former colleagues and sentenced to life imprisonment. Within months word came that the former ruthless dictator had died, apparently by his own hand.

In the months after the coup Hun Sen worked to establish his authority

**A young Buddhist monk**

189

# Cambodia

**Victims of the Khmer Rouge**

Courtesy of Steven A. Leibo

throughout the country while claiming he was ready to allow the continuation of parliamentary elections. He even retained the title of second prime minister while allowing a one-time Royalist, Ung Huot, to replace Ranariddh as the first prime minister. As for King Sihanouk, the man who had spent his entire life trying to retain his influence within the Kingdom he had inherited, there was little room for hope. His comments seemed to suggest an exhausted leader who had lost faith in the future.

Given the international community's negative reaction to Hun Sen's actions, Cambodia's strong man found himself still required to present to the world a Cambodia willing to continue the process of democratization. Well aware that the long-planned parliamentary elections of mid 1998 would not be accepted as valid unless Prince Ranariddh took part, the world was entertained in the months before the election with a show of the former first prime minister and his associates being tried for smuggling weapons and plotting a coup against Hun Sen. After being found guilty, the prince was sentenced to 35 years in jail and fined millions of dollars. Once that was done, the plan, arranged in advance, was carried out. The prince's father, King Sihanouk, granted him a full pardon that allowed the ousted first prime minister to compete in the elections of July 1998.

Cambodia's election of the summer of 1998 did not though improve conditions much. Once again, the players remained largely the same: the supporters of Hun Sen, the Royalists led by Prince Ranariddh and Sam Rainsy's followers. As expected Hun Sen's backers dominated the country's media outlets making it hard for the opposition to get their electoral message out to the voters. Discouraging to supporters of the opposition was the decision by both Ranariddh and Rainsy to attack Hun Sen by stirring up anti-Vietnamese sentiment. Certainly, it was a tactic that could be effective against Cambodia's longtime leaders who had initially been installed in power by Hanoi. Nevertheless, given Cambodia's recent history of ethnic-based genocide, few could find the decision an admirable one and it eventually caused several deaths among the local Vietnamese community.

Once the voting took place, a new controversy exploded over the counting of votes that eventually saw both opposition parties refusing to cooperate in the creation of a new government. Their cooperation was needed because Hun Sen's supporters had failed to gain enough seats in the national assembly to form a government on their own.

Officially the vote tally had given the government party, the CCP, 41.1% of the vote to 31.7% for the Royalists and 14.3% for Sam Rainsy's party. Whether the actual vote counting had been corrupt, the result was more months of political strife and public demonstrations before it was agreed that a new coalition government would be formed. Not surprisingly the compromise left Hun Sen as the main

political leader and prime minister with Prince Ranariddh as the new president of the National Assembly.

Nevertheless, over the years, the most obvious development in Cambodia's political life has been the increase in longtime Prime Minister Hun Sen's power and influence. In recent local elections, his followers won the vast majority of votes. Although many have questioned the honesty of those polls Hun Sen's power has continued to increase.

The elections that took place during the summer of 2003 did not fundamentally alter the situation at all. As before, Hun Sen's CCP won 58 of the parliamentary seats while his rivals, the royalist party FUNCINPEC and the SRP of Sam Rainsy, got 26 and 24 respectively. On the positive side, a huge number of local and international observers testified that the election had been carried out in a reasonable fair manner.

At the time the Cambodian constitution required that a government could only be formed if a political party controlled a two-thirds majority, something Hun Sen followers lacked. Thus began, as it has so often before, months of political struggles over how the new government would be formed. FUNCINPEC and the SRP jointly insisted that they would not offer the required support unless a tripartite governing coalition was formed under someone other than Hun Sen.

The longtime prime minister absolutely refused to step down or allow more than a two-party coalition to form the new government. Eventually, FUNCINPEC broke with its ally the SRP and joined yet another coalition government. Fundamentally little had changed except that valuable time had been lost. The nation's entrance into the World Trade Organization had been delayed as were completion of plans for a joint Cambodian-United Nations tribunal to address the horrors of the Khmer Rouge era.

FUNCINPEC, the royalist party, was clearly losing its ability to be an effective national opposition. It had been additionally weakened by internal divisions that most recently saw Prince Ranariddh driven from the party's leadership. By early 2006 it was obvious that its members were reconciling themselves to a clearly secondary role and becoming less confrontational toward the government. They had good reason to do so. A new constitutional change reduced the number of parliamentarians whose support is needed to establish a government. The significance is that, in the future, the CCP will no longer need FUNCINPEC's support to form governments. The situation was further complicated in the late summer of 2007 when an entirely new opposition party, the Human Rights Party, was founded by a former political prisoner. However, that hardly affected real power in Cambodia. Indeed, during the summer 2008 election the CPP managed to win 73% of the seats in the national election. By the spring of 2012 local elections were again held and as expected, Hun Sen's Cambodian People's Party (CPP) won easily.

Nevertheless, on the surface the situation continues to evolve. For example, in 2012 yet another new alignment emerged as the former Sam Rainsy Party and the more recently formed Human Rights Party merged to form the new Cambodian National Rescue Party. But while the newly formed Cambodian National Rescue Party did relatively well in the summer elections of 2013, Prime Minister's Hun Sen's party retained control of the national assembly despite enthusiastic opposition from younger people and new social media outlets. Not surprisingly, opposition figures like Sam Rainsy who once again protested what they saw as a flawed election process. More recently the government gave itself the power to dissolve political parties. By late fall of 2017 they had actually done so by officially outlawing the National Rescue Party and forcing some of

its leaders like Ms. Mu Sochua, the party's deputy leader into exile.

More recently Cambodian elections have become more of an international farce rather than anything resembling a real electoral choice. Indeed in the last elections, those held in the summer of 2018 the government party claimed to have won all of the seats in parliament and 77.5% of the national vote.

In the aftermath both the United States and the European Union openly spoke of imposing sanctions over what the US administration referred to as "flawed" voting.

In short, very little is new on the Cambodian political scene. More to the point, Cambodia's UN sponsored experiment in real democracy during the early 1990s has clearly failed. Today Cambodia is most accurately identified as a single-party dictatorship. Moreover, in a world where open dictatorship appears to be making a comeback, from Russia to China, from Turkey to Eastern Europe Hun Sen has little to be concerned about regarding a significant push back against his continuing domination of Cambodia's political life.

Not content with his claimed election victory in 2018, Hun Sen continued to pursue opposition leaders at home and

abroad. When Sam Rainsy tried to return to Cambodia in 2019, he was prevented from entering the country. Hun Sen alleged that this was part of a plot to overthrow the government and trials began of those accused of involvement, including the president of the now banned National Rescue Party, Kem Sokha, who went on trial in January 2020; it was eventually adjourned in March 2021. Meanwhile, a trial of over 100 opposition figures began in November 2020. Because of the numbers, this attempt ended in chaos, so in January 2021, the defendants in the country were divided into two groups for trial. A large number of heavy sentences were handed down, including a 25-year one on the exiled Sam Rainsy.

COVID-19 provided further opportunities for government restrictions, once it was decided to take it seriously. In April 2020, Hun Sen was given extra powers to deal with the pandemic. Peaceful demonstrations were violently broken up. The media and other forms of communication came under tighter controls. International protests were brushed off as unacceptable attempts to interfere in the country's internal affairs. Repression continued into 2021, with members of the "Mother Nature" environmental monitoring group

**Boat racing at the Water Festival in Phnom Penh**

Courtesy of Serge Corrieras

# Cambodia

receiving prison sentences for allegedly inciting protests over illegal logging and other environmentally degrading activities.

### Society and Culture

The art and culture of the Khmer Empire, based largely on its Indian, Hindu, and Sri Lankan Buddhist origins, were an elaborate and highly developed combination to which distinctly local elements were added during the centuries that have passed. The surviving specimens of the Empire are mainly of stone and bronze that display highly stylistic and ornate techniques. The modern Cambodians are justifiably proud of their historical heritage. The Khmer (Cambodian) language was spoken prior to the arrival of Indian influence and is now written in a script derived from India. Sadly for Cambodia's cultural heritage an enormous percentage of the country's cultural leaders were murdered by the Khmer Rouge, a blow few nations could easily survive.

While it will take years for the nation's cultural heritage to recover, the damage goes far deeper. Cambodia remains a country where the ratio between men and women was distorted by years of civil war and genocide. This is even more pronounced among the older generation where the loss of males to warfare and violence remains significant.

Perhaps worst of all, Cambodia may have survived the Khmer Rouge years and even seen its economy slowly improving, but infant mortality rates have actually climbed in recent years. According to the United Nations, the primary cause of this worsening of infant mortality has been the rising level of AIDS and a weakening public health service. No doubt recognizing the severe strains Cambodia's exceptionally high birth rate causes (the second highest in Southeast Asia), the government has introduced a program to encourage families to plan their childbearing decisions more carefully.

Life for minorities, especially the Vietnamese, remains especially difficult. Long-time antagonisms and current political tensions both play a role in keeping Cambodian hostilities toward Vietnam and their own Vietnamese residents strong. On the other hand, Cambodia's Chinese community has recovered from the blows it experienced during the Khmer Rouge era and has been growing rapidly in recent years.

There is also relatively good news for the Cham community, those Cambodian Muslims who found their ranks decimated during the Pol Pot years. Money has been flowing in from the Islamic world to help rebuild mosques and to found Islamic schools although there has been some concern that those schools may be fostering the sort of intolerance

that has at times brought so much grief to people from the Middle East to South Asia. No doubt in response to those concerns, the United States itself has started to provide funding and training for Cambodian Muslims in the values of human rights and democracy.

Perhaps one of the most telling signs of Cambodia's return to normalcy has been the emergence of a problem with teenage drag racing. Where Khmer Rouge thugs once murdered people in the nation's capital, today's population has become more concerned about dangers from wealthy teenagers racing through the streets disrupting traffic.

### Women

Women make up the majority of the population and the largest percentage of the workforce in most sectors, from agriculture to business, industry, and service sectors. Because of the years of violence, women today head a quarter of the households in Cambodia. They do not, however, hold many significant positions of influence. Men continue to dominate decision-making.

The country's new constitution explicitly contains language offering women equal rights, but in practice these are not normally carried out. According to a new report by the United Nations, the inequality between men and women has actually

**Downtown Phnom Penh**

Courtesy of Steven A. Leibo

192

# Cambodia

grown greater in recent years. Cultural traditions that emphasize male authority are still strong. Moreover, as is often the case, the return to a less authoritarian socialist economy, despite the many advantages, also frequently has the impact of reinforcing traditional attitudes that value females less than men. There are, however, many non-governmental organizations that are quite active and emphasize improving the lives of women. As in other Southeast Asian countries, stories of the trafficking in women are very frequently reported. The unfortunate young women and girls far too often end up as part of the region's well-known sex trade.

But new opportunities are also opening up as Cambodia enters more deeply into the globalized economy. Local workers, as part of a program to help Cambodia's least advantaged citizens have been trained to digitize Western literary classics by typing them into computers, activities that not only help them earn money but develop valuable computer skills.

Unfortunately it is also true that nations as poor as Cambodia can also become victims of unscrupulous individuals who are only appearing to help. During the early spring of 2013 an orphanage run by an Australian group was raided by government officials and accused of abuse and neglect. Since then a very public scandal has developed regarding various so-called "orphanages." Their founders organized them merely to earn money from sympathetic Westerners.

## COVID-19

As news of COVID-19 began to spread world-wide in early 2020, Hun Sen played down its significance. He refused to ban flights from China, arguing that it would severely damage the economy. During a visit to China in February, the first foreign leader to do so since the pandemic began, he said that the two countries were "stalwart friends" and criticized those countries that had banned travel to and from China. As it became increasingly difficult to ignore the devastating effects of the illness, however, there was soon a change of approach. At the end of March 2020, tourist visas were banned. In April, the National Assembly authorized sweeping new powers to contain the virus. Heavy sentences could be imposed for new offences such as obstructing the authorities, causing social unrest or threatening national security. This included critical comments on social media. Before long, this led to complaints about the heavy-handed police approach to protests, which, in turn, led to instructions to the police to use less-violent tactics.

Tourist visas remained banned; only diplomatic, official, and sponsored business visits were allowed. Flights from neighboring countries were stopped. Hand sanitizer, social distancing, and a ban on gatherings of more than 20 people were put in place. Exposure to the virus meant self-isolating, even for Hun Sen, who spent 14 days in quarantine in November. It was a successful policy, with less than 400 hundred cases in the first year, and no deaths reported. It came at a high cost, however, with families complaining about the difficulties of getting food during lockdowns. In February 2021, however, the policy fell apart as numbers began to rise, reaching 1578 by mid-March. One death was reported during this period. Around the same time, vaccines arrived, and vaccinations began on February 10. Health workers, the elderly and the medically vulnerable were the first recipients.

That outbreak lasted until September 2021, with periodic lockdowns in various parts of the country, including the capital. Another wave followed between January and April 2022, despite a good record on vaccinations. By the end of April 2022, there had been 136,200 cases reported, with 3,056 deaths. By then, however, the government seems to have decided, as alsewhere, that it would have to live with the virus, and most restrictions were lifted. This included international travel restrictions.

## Foreign Relations

Throughout its history, Cambodia has been in the unfortunate position of being caught between contending forces beyond its borders. In the precolonial era both the Thai and Vietnamese empires occupied parts of Cambodia. The country was also caught between the United States and the pro-communist Vietnamese during the Vietnam War. The North Vietnamese used overland routes through Cambodia to transport war materials. The U.S. bombed those same North Vietnamese supply lines through Cambodia thus disrupting life in many parts of the country.

Prince Sihanouk could neither prevent the North Vietnamese from using his territory, nor satisfy the United States that his policies were not pro-Hanoi. Later, during the Vietnamese occupation which was backed by the Soviet Union, Cambodia was again a pawn between the Vietnamese and their Soviet ally, on the one hand, and the Chinese, who backed the Khmer Rouge, on the other. Even today relations with Vietnam remain difficult as both nations continue to argue over where the border between the two states should be.

For many years, there were also clashes with Thailand over their mutual borders.

The Thais have been angry about the establishment of casinos near their mutual border. Tensions reached a violent crescendo in 2003 after a Thai actress was said, incorrectly, to have claimed that the revered local heritage site, Angkor Wat, should belong to Thailand. In subsequent outbursts of Cambodian anger, Thai properties were attacked in the capital, and Bangkok had to evacuate its citizens quickly.

Both Cambodia and Thailand have long-standing claims to the ancient temple structure of Preah Vihear and a dramatic confrontation developed over their competing claims in 2008. There were regular military clashes in the area until 2011. Making matters worse, the issue became even more complicated when the question of how supportive the Thai government was to Cambodia's plans to have the temple proclaimed a UNESCO World Heritage Site became yet another political "wedge" issue separating Thailand's "warring" political factions. Unfortunately the confrontation took on a very nationalist and populist tone within Cambodian society.

Eventually, the International Court of Justice at The Hague became involved, as it was aksed to uphold a judgement made in Cambodia's favor in 1962. In 2013, the court unanimously upheld the 1962 decision. Gradually, tensions between the two sides eased, although the there are still questions about which country owns some of the land in the area.

Relations have also continued to be tense at times with Vietnam. Hanoi has, for example, continued to be suspicious about whether Cambodia has allowed access to its territory by groups the government considers anti-Vietnamese. On the other hand, the two governments have been cooperating on road building in the area near their shared borders.

The most important development for Cambodia in recent years has been the slow improvement in its relations with many of its Southeast Asian neighbors. In 1995, Cambodia secured "observer status" within the Association of Southeast Asian Nations (ASEAN) and was then expected to become a full-fledged member. However, the 1997 coup delayed Cambodia's entrance until 1999, when it finally gained full membership. Chinese investment and assistance have continued as other countries have withdrawn because of Cambodia's political situation, and Cambodia is now firmly embedded in the "Belt and Road" initiative.

Cambodia's positive relationship with China was graphically on display during 2009 when the government very publically

# Cambodia

deported more than a dozen Uighur men and boys. On the run from China's crackdown in its central Asian territories, they had been smuggled into the country by Christian missionaries. In fact, the government did more than merely deport the refugees, whom the Cambodians deemed illegal immigrants rather than potential asylum seekers. They had them placed on a special flight back to China provided by the Chinese authorities. Despite the accompanying protests from both the United States and the United Nations, the government's decision is probably understandable given that China has become the single largest investor in Cambodia's economic development.

For years, Cambodia's relationship with the larger international community beyond Asia has been complicated by differing attitudes toward the creation of tribunals to try the former members of the Khmer Rouge for their genocidal acts during the late 1970s. The Cambodian government resisted calls for international trials by claiming that such trials might destabilize the admittedly new and fragile peace that Cambodia has been enjoying. Nevertheless, efforts to reach an agreement regarding future criminal proceedings against the surviving leadership of the Khmer Rouge remain a major issue. By 2005, this culminated in an agreement to establish a special tribunal within the Cambodian judicial system. It would include international judges alongside local jurists to address this most horrid chapter in human and Cambodian history. As we have seen, by 2008 those trials had begun. By 2009, the infamous Kaing Guek Eav, better known as Duch, once the head of the horrific concentration camp S-21, had publically confessed in court. In 2010 he was finally sentenced to an additional 19 years in jail. But due to technical complications, that appeared likely to reduce his eventual jail term.

On the other hand, as noted above, the simple passing of time is removing many of the more important former Khmer Rouge defendants from the arms of justice. For example, Ieng Sary, a founder of the Khmer Rouge and important leader, died in early 2013 while he was standing trial.

### Economy

A major challenge for the government is to establish a national economy. Two decades of conflict and revolution have destroyed much of the country's infrastructure. But finally significant progress is being made in replacing what was lost and damaged. The presence of UNTAC, the United Nations force, also caused distortions in the economy. The Asian economic crisis of 1998 also affected Cambodia though it had, one might say, less far to fall given the long-term weakness of the economy compared to its neighbors.

As might be expected, the military commands about 20% of the entire budget though plans are now being made to scale back the military. Plans to demobilize the military have not gone as well as hoped and large numbers of former soldiers have not gotten the bonuses they were promised to help them rebuild their lives.

About half of the country's operating budget comes from foreign aid. The country has continued to receive substantial amounts of aid and loans from individual donor countries, the International Monetary Fund (IMF), World Bank, and the Asian Development Bank (ADB). For a time in recent years one bright spot for the Cambodian economy was the jump in foreign investment that included several major hotel chains.

By the new century Cambodia's tourist industry was again clearly on the mend. The number of new visitors grew rapidly, and foreign investment was again rising. Creating that sense of stability is particularly important given that outside aid remains so important to Cambodian success despite recent economic gains.

**Statue at Angkor**

194

International aid agencies have been hard pressed to provide larger and larger amounts of aid for new problems, such as the Asian tsunami victims. Given those new demands on the donor community, it has been particularly important for Cambodia to achieve economic success.

For Cambodians the end of the Khmer Rouge has allowed for Cambodia to start healing economically. Inflation has lessened and economic momentum has once again begun.

The World Bank says that Cambodia's growth rate between 1998 and 2019 was 7.7% per annum, making it one of the fastest in the world. This was largely due to the growth in the garment industry and tourism. Indeed, the growth rate in 2007 came in at over 10%. But in 2020 the effect of COVID-19, as in other countries, caused a steep fall. A rate of -3.1 % was the result, caused by the collapse of the tourist trade, and widespread disruption in the garment and construction industries. The rate picked up in 2021, coming in at 3% but is not expected to recover before the end of 2022.

One success story is that the numbers of those in poverty has been reduced over the years, and is now (2022) about 18%. The lowest rates are in the capital city while in some rural areas, it is much higher.

As is the case for so much of the world, the emerging economic giant China affects Cambodia as well. Cambodia entered the World Trade Organization (WTO) in 2003. This was a change that offers many advantages. However, the nation has to compete even more for sales with the growing efficiency of Chinese factories. On the other hand, China's success has in part also been Cambodia's because the PRC has become the largest single investor. Among other projects, it is constructing the country's first expressway, expected to be completed in 2023, which will connect the capital to the southwestern province of Preah Sihanouk as well as extensive building works in the port city of Sihanoukville. Chinese tourism, which is also important, has been badly affected by COVID-19, but that may pick up in due course.

Perhaps somewhat macabre has been talk of capitalizing on international interest in the Khmer Rouge years by creating a fancy "theme" park to receive visitors to various sites associated with the atrocities. The plans including the restoration of the buildings associated with the Khmer Rouge as well as the creation of a high-tech museum complex and tour guides apparently chosen from among former members of the Khmer Rouge. By the spring of 2010, plans were even in place to turn Pol Pot's final stronghold and the site where he died into a tourist site to include a guidebook commissioned by the prime minister. As a practical matter the plans are probably not all that different than the museums dedicated to the memory of the European holocaust. Given a thoughtful approach, the sites can become not only important memorials to the victims, but a source of additional revenue for the nation.

More predictably, the growth of tourism around Angkor Wat, the nation's extraordinary medieval religious site, has grown enormously in recent years. It is likely to continue to do so as more and more tourists grow comfortable visiting Cambodia. It seems likely that a percentage of those tourists might also be interested in learning more about the trauma of the Khmer Rouge years.

Even more exciting in terms of revenue has been the growth of Cambodia's offshore oil industry. Current estimates suggest that in the next several years Cambodia could start seeing several hundreds of millions of dollars of income as a result of these resources. Obviously this is not great news for those hoping to wean the planet from its addiction to fossil fuels, but it is very good news for a nation sorely in need of new revenue streams.

But there are some real concerns. The growth of Cambodia's role in the world drug market is discouraging. Cambodia is rapidly earning a reputation as Asia's newest "narco-state." In 1996, Washington placed Cambodia on its "watch list" of trafficker states. As a demonstration of Cambodia's increasingly deep involvement in the globalized community its government found last year that it had to expel a large number of foreigners for using Cambodia as a base for Internet financial scams.

### Cambodia: From Environmental Degradation to Climate Change

Cambodia may be experiencing a level of stability the nation has not seen for decades, but that is not the case for much of its environment. It is currently thought that about half the nation is covered to some degree by natural forest cover. But that is changing rapidly as more and more forests are removed to make way for agriculture. Moreover, logging, both legal and illegal, is having an impact on marine and freshwater resources.

Of particular concern has been the fate of Cambodia's flooded tropical grasslands. A new report offers the startling conclusion that over the last decade almost 46% of the nation's flooded grasslands have been lost to commercial rice growing. This is a change that is dramatically impacting the livelihood of both the local residents and the bio-diversity of the region.

As is common elsewhere, tensions over how best to build the economy and preserve the environment are becoming intense. In 2012 Chut Wutty, Cambodia's best known environmental activist, died in some sort of confrontation with local security officers who had been operating on behalf of local logging companies. Chut Wutty was a well-known critic of the sale of the nation's parks to the logging industry.

Although its sincerity might be questioned, the government has responded

**Bayon temple at Angkor Wat**

# Cambodia

to the growing tensions by announcing a moratorium on the granting of such land concessions. It is in the process of initiating a survey of people who farm on what is considered government land.

As with many of its neighbors, Cambodia is particularly vulnerable to the threat of rising waters and more powerful storm systems associated with the phenomenon of global warming. One province, Koh Kong along the south west coast, is particularly valuable due to the presence of tourist attractions and new port facilities. It is especially vulnerable. Indeed, a mere one meter sea rise would flood about half of it, according to studies. Of course, while a more permanent sea-level rise is a real issue for the moment, the most immediate threat caused by rising temperatures is the shorter-term water surges that impact the region's coast lines caused by ever more powerful storms. In Cambodia's case, such storms have killed hundreds of people and deeply hurt the economy. Only a year or so ago, some $30 million worth of food was destroyed by flooding, and a million people faced food shortages.

More immediately the ongoing deforestation, while impacting the ability of the planet to absorb the increase of atmospheric greenhouse gases, also deprives thousands of Cambodian villagers of the resin they harvest from the trees to sell for a variety of purposes, including boat sealants and fragrant oils. As is so often the case, the sale or theft of trees might be making some people richer, but they are depriving others, usually poorer citizens, of long-term and more renewable economic resources.

## The Future

In a fashion so different from much of Cambodian history during the latter half of the 20th century, the early years of the new century have been relatively kinder to Cambodia. Not only did the Khmer Rouge collapse long ago, but a reasonable level of stability and cooperation has been reached. Unfortunately, that stability has emerged from the increasing strength of the ruling party, the CCP, which has largely eliminated the influence of the other smaller parties.

In fact, international organizations have publicly condemned the government's use of lawsuits to intimidate the opposition, which has had little influence. In one especially notable case, Hun Sen sued the former minister of women's affairs when she demanded an apology from the prime minister after he made sexual comments about her in public. Not surprisingly, the court sided with the powerful prime minister and fined the former lawmaker thousands of dollars. By early spring 2010 the former minister, Mu Sochua, had unsuccessfully appealed to the nation's Supreme Court and her party had been outlawed.

Curiously one of the most surprising aspects of Cambodia's current international relations is the continuing demand by the United States to be repaid funds lent a half century ago to the American government's Cambodian ally Lon Nol during the Vietnam War era. Needless to say, Cambodia's current leaders, pointing out the massive damage American bombers did to the country during the war, have rejected demands to repay the funds. The larger reality is that Cambodia's increasingly dictatorial government is likely to move closer and closer to China in upcoming years.

Still, Cambodians have much to be grateful for. Unlike others in the region the economy has been relatively stable in recent years and a sense of normalcy reinforced by the reestablishment of a train service from the capital to the southwest coast's tourist areas is of both real and symbolic significance. Further complementing Cambodia's move into the 21st century's globalized world is news that the country has now been successfully linked by undersea fiber optic cables to the rest of Southeast Asia.

Perhaps of even greater significance is that real estate investment has become not only an important local development but is attracting significant international interest. Indeed, for those familiar with the modern history of Cambodia, that idea that the country is now seen as being appropriate for the sort of long-term investment real estate requires is quite gratifying.

# East Timor

**Executive office building in Dili**

Courtesy of Marc Cassidy

**Area:** 5,743 sq. mi. (14,874 sq. km.)
**Population:** 1,364,668 (2022 est.)
**Capital City:** Dili, pop. 234,000 (2021 est.)
**Climate:** Tropical
**Neighboring Countries:** Australia and Indonesia
**Official Languages:** Portuguese, Tetum
**Other Principal Tongues:** Bahasa, English
**Ethnic Background:** Indonesian-Malay and Melanesian
**Principal Religion:** Catholicism
**Main Exports:** Coffee, sandalwood, marble, and natural gas and oil production is being developed
**Main Imports:** Food, gasoline, kerosene, and machinery
**Currency:** U.S. dollar
**Former Colonial Status:** Previously controlled by Portugal and Indonesia
**National Day:** Independence celebrated May 20, 2002
**President:** Jose Ramos-Horta (since May 2022)
**Prime Minister:** Taur Matan Ruak (since June 22, 2018)
**Per Capita GDP:** $3,123 (2019 est.) (purchasing power parity)

Among the newest members of the community of nations, East Timor occupies only part of one island in the vast Indonesian archipelago. The other half of the island, "West Timor" remains part of Indonesia. To understand the origins of the region's newest independent nation requires a close look at the centuries of Portuguese and then Indonesian colonial control of East Timor.

## History

East Timor, is approximately the size of the American state of Maryland. Historically it included about two-dozen different linguistic communities, most of which practiced an animistic religious tradition until quite recently.

The colonial history of East Timor began with the arrival of the Portuguese in the first years of the 16th century. Those early arrivals from Europe were initially interested in the sandalwood of the area and had little impact on the lives of the inhabitants who lived largely in small villages in the interior. By the late 16th century, Dominican friars from Portugal had begun to establish themselves as did people known as "Black Portuguese," a reference to the peoples of mixed Portuguese and local ancestry from the surrounding area. Long known for the sandalwood produced there the island found itself fought over by both the Portuguese and the Dutch during the era of colonial expansion. Eventually, but not until the early 20th century, the present boundaries were established between Dutch administered west Timor, part of the larger Dutch East Indies colony, and East Timor which was controlled by the Portuguese. As with the rest of the area, the British occupied the region during the Napoleonic wars. After the defeat of the French, the Portuguese reestablished their control.

Within East Timor, the Portuguese colonizers made little effort to develop their holdings. In fact, according to one 19th-century visitor no roads had been developed at all beyond the settlement of Dili itself. Lisbon put very little effort into East Timor until late in the 19th century when they feared losing it to the other, more aggressive, European powers.

As tensions built toward the Second World War, a group of Australians landed in East Timor and prepared to resist the advancing Japanese forces. Later, as with the rest of the enormous Indonesian archipelago, the advancing Japanese army occupied East Timor. Over the following years Western forces, frequently with the help of the East Timorese, worked to sabotage the Japanese holdings. After the war the Portuguese once again reestablished their control.

A generation later, in the mid 1970s, another even more dramatic trial began for the East Timorese when Portugal's authoritarian government fell from power, replaced by a more liberal government less committed to retaining the country's colonial holdings. The new government declared its intention to allow East Timorese to decide their own future in a referendum planned for the fall of 1976.

### Indonesia's Invasion and the Cold War

The promise of independence would sadly be forestalled for a quarter of a century as developments within East Timor and the larger international Cold War intervened to alter its fate. To understand the roots of the disaster that soon befell East Timor it is important to look at the colonial history of the larger Indonesian island chain that surrounds it.

But just as India's government had moved into Goa in the early 1960s, and as China took back Macao in December 1999, Indonesia decided to absorb East Timor in 1975. Ironically, Indonesian leaders had not been particularly interested in East Timor before the mid 1970s. It was often outsiders like the Australians who had at times encouraged them to integrate East Timor into Indonesia.

Other international forces and themes played out as well. The Cold War struggle between communism and democratic capitalism influenced events in East Timor also. During the mid 1970s communism was in ascendance in Southeast Asia. From Vietnam to Cambodia left-wing political forces had advanced and as we have seen elsewhere in *East and Southeast Asia*, communists came to power in both countries during the spring of 1975.

Within East Timor its own resistance group the Fretilin, the main independence group, was a nationalist party with a clearly leftist orientation. From the perspective of the very anti-communist Indonesian military and the Western democracies, the potential rise of the leftist East Timorese independence movement to power within a free East Timor was simply unacceptable. Thus, their support for Indonesia's occupation was quite predictable.

### An Era of Mass Murder

When the Indonesia invasion began in December 7, 1975, the East Timorese were

# East Timor

more prepared to resist Jakarta than one might have imagined. As a former colony of Portugal—a member of NATO—some East Timorese had had professional military training. The departing colonial power also left weapons behind that were later used effectively against the Indonesians.

But these advantages hardly made them a match for Indonesian forces. Unlike the East Timorese, Jakarta had the military support of the United States and thus the ability to impose its will upon the resisting East Timorese. In the years after 1975, despite considerable efforts at infrastructure building and impressive educational gains made by the East Timorese under control from Jakarta, many East Timorese continued to work for independence. Meanwhile, the Indonesian military maintained a very brutal control there. In fact, estimates of the numbers killed over the years either directly or indirectly as a result of the occupation are, according to a recent independent report, from 84,000 to 183,000 people.

Sadly for the people of East Timor, there was almost no international awareness of their plight from the mid 1970s through the early 1990s when word of the horror going on there began to be better publicized. Most important in that growing international awareness of the crisis in East Timor was the massacre that took place in Dili in 1991. On that occasion, hundreds of East Timorese, perhaps emboldened by the presence of members of the world press, openly defied Indonesian authorities while attempting to commemorate the recent death of an East Timorese activist.

At the cemetery, ignoring the presence of western reporters, the Indonesian military opened fire killing an estimated 70 to 200 people. Despite the horror, it also marked the beginning of a greater global awareness of events in East Timor because of the coverage it received. Thus, after a generation of suffering the East Timorese finally found a growing body of international supporters after what became known as the Santa Cruz Massacre.

Later the East Timorese nationalists got a much needed boost in 1996 when two of their most prominent members were awarded the Nobel Peace Prize for their efforts. Bishop Carlos Filipe Ximenes Belo, who continued to live in East Timor, and Jose Ramos-Horta, a militant leader of the movement in exile, shared the award which gave the struggle of East Timor much more global attention.

Saluting the flag of the new nation of East Timor

## Asian Economic Crisis and the Fall of Suharto

East Timor's fate began to change dramatically only in the years after the Asian economic crisis of 1998 that saw the authoritarian government of former General Suharto finally fall from power. His successor, B. J. Habibie, perhaps seeking a dramatic gesture to respond to the long running crisis of East Timor, announced in January 1999 that the unhappy province would be allowed to have a referendum on staying within Indonesia. The decision, while greeted enthusiastically by most East Timorese was seen as a disaster by many Indonesian immigrants to East Timor and the Indonesian army that had fought to retain the area. Indonesian attitudes were not surprising. Not only had many Indonesians in the military served in East Timor. Many were heavily invested in the region's economy. There was also a reasonable and understandable fear that East Timor's freedom might provoke the many other restless parts of Indonesia to secede.

## The Referendum

The months leading up to the August 1999 referendum were both a time of crisis and excitement for the East Timorese. On one hand international observers arrived to supervise their long awaited opportunity to vote on ending their relationship with Indonesia. On the other hand, local militia, supported and supplied by the Indonesia military, violently attacked those supportive of independence and threatened a bloodbath if the vote resulted in a choice to leave.

The actual referendum went fairly calmly. However, as soon as it became clear that the East Timorese had voted against autonomy within Indonesia and more specifically for independence, an explosion of violence racked East Timor. Pro-Jakarta militias clearly backed by

elements of the Indonesian military went on a rampage that saw perhaps 1,500 people slaughtered. Thousands more fled to West Timor, where they ended up in refugee camps often still harassed by the pro-Jakarta militias that opposed East Timor's independence.

Eventually, as the outrage grew and public awareness of the crisis expanded, the Australians agreed to lead an international force, which included troops from Thailand, Singapore, Malaysia, and the Philippines to East Timor to help restore order. Even China sent members of her security forces to work in East Timor. In the following months the United Nations established itself in East Timor and administered it with funds provided by nations ranging from Norway and Sweden to the Netherlands and Portugal.

After most of the violence ended, thousands of East Timorese returned home from refugee camps in West Timor even though reports of continued harassment and persecution of those still in West Timor are common. It is also clear that the militias have not only made it very difficult for the refugees to return to East Timor. They have also murdered foreign peacekeepers. Those refugees who have returned went home to a devastated land.

## From UN Control to a Free East Timor

Meanwhile the East Timorese under their most popular leaders from Xanana Gusmao to Bishop Bello built the rudiments of a future government that would administer East Timor when the United Nations forces known as UNAMET pulled out. In the period after the departure of the Indonesian troops East Timor did not experience its long anticipated calm. There was considerable tension between the UNAMET administration of East Timor and local leaders who have vehemently complained of being ignored by the United Nations professionals. East Timorese leaders have also accused the aid agencies of underpaying their own workers and being more interested in earning money than delivering aid. Some East Timorese have also been upset with the number of outsiders the United Nations authorities hired to administer programs there.

By the time the United Nations officially turned power over to the incoming East Timor administration, an enormous amount had been accomplished during its 32-month tenure. Large numbers of building had been rebuilt and many businesses reopened. Thousands of new civil servants were hired and trained to administer the new country. While a new central bank, a new public television station, and customs service was established. Moreover,

**President Jose Ramos-Horta**

hundreds of schools were repaired and teachers hired. There was still much to do, but considering the state East Timor had been after the initial and devastating Indonesian departure, it was all quite impressive.

### Forming a Government

In late August of 2001 East Timorese went to the polls again in the ongoing effort to build a new political future. At stake was the election of an 88-person assembly that was being chosen to write a constitution for the new government and to set a more specific timetable for the nation to emerge beyond the controls of the UN. Over 425,000 voters were involved and a wide range of parties offered themselves up for the voter's choice.

Not surprisingly, once the votes were counted Fretilin, now led by Mari Alkatiri, won 55 of the possible 88 seats. This win allowed Alkatiri to become the prime minister. Fretilin's count might have been even higher if tensions had not developed between the national liberation party and its former leader Xanana Gusmao. He decided to campaign for the more minor parties based on the argument that it was important that no one party dominate East Timor's immediate future.

Xanana Gusmao's behavior was unusual in other ways as well. Unlike so many independence leaders who have anxiously awaited the opportunity to finally lead their nations, Gusmao appeared to be a very reluctant leader. In fact, he initially seemed quite reluctant to stand for election at all. Nevertheless, once committed Gusmao went on to win the April of 2002 presidential contest easily.

Most dramatically, East Timor's real day of reckoning occurred on May 20, 2002, when it celebrated its official independence. While its resources were limited, there was no shortage of hope. Certainly,

that seemed apparent during the spring of 2002 when thousands of East Timorese refugees began returning home in anticipation of beginning life anew under their new government.

While East Timor had finally gained its independence, enormous problems still faced the society. Unemployment was very common, and there was considerable concern about the upsurge in criminal violence. More significant politically was the rising anger against the new government's inability to deal effectively with the nation's many problems. That frustration became abundantly obvious at the end of 2002 when angry crowds burned down not only Prime Minister Alkatiri's home, but those of his relatives and several Western businesses.

Perhaps most discouraging was that the local security situation forced the decision, during the late spring of 2004, to ask that the United Nations put off the departure of its security forces, originally scheduled for May 2004, for another year. That request was granted. By the spring of 2005 the last of the United Nations 450 peace keeping forces—of a contingent that had once numbered around 11,000 people—departed, leaving only a group of around 150 civilian administrators and security advisers. But that has hardly calmed matters completely. By the spring of 2006 East Timor's internal problems had once again made the international news as members of the security forces went on strike. Their eventual dismissal by the government then set off a series of riots that initially culminated in the prime minister's resignation.

Over the last few years a new alignment of political power had been forming in East Timor. The internationally famous Nobel Prize winner, Jose Ramos-Horta, replaced Alkatiri as prime minister and then subsequently won an election to replace outgoing President Xanana Gusmao. As for the former president and leader of East Timor's national struggle for freedom, by mid-summer 2007, he was campaigning to become prime minister, a position that in

East Timor holds more executive power than that of the president.

Unfortunately, when the election took place, the results only created more tension. Fretilin, the former national resistance party that led the national resistance struggle and dominated politics in the years since nationhood, won the elections. But the final numbers did not give them enough of a parliamentary majority to create a government.

Over the next several months Fretilin was unable to reestablish a working coalition. Eventually Xanana Gusmao, with the support of his political ally Jose Ramos-Horta, formed a governing coalition with his own newly formed party and two other allied parties. From the perspective of Xianana Gusmao's previous allies in Fretlin, that was completely unacceptable. The formation of the new government, with Gusmao as prime minister, set off yet another round of riots.

But riots were the least of the new leadership team's problems. In February 2008 a rebel army commander attempted to assassinate both Prime Minister Gusmao and President Ramos-Horta. Luckily, for the longtime resistance leader, Gusmao managed to avoid injury. But President Ramos-Horta was critically wounded and flown to Australia for treatment. After a very dramatic recovery effort, the nation's president was eventually able to return home having barely survived the ordeal. What is perhaps even more impressive is that Ramos-Horta eventually granted the conspirators, who had almost killed him, official clemency for their acts.

It should be noted that the position of president in East Timor is largely ceremonial. Despite that, East Timor's only Peace Prize winner and recent target of an assassination attempt was interested in serving another term. Unfortunately for him, the East Timor electorate had other ideas, and Ramos-Horta only came in third in the voting that took place in March 2012. By May he had been succeeded by Taur Matan Ruak, another resistance leader.

**East Timor coastline**                    Courtesy of Marc Cassidy

# East Timor

**Former Prime Minister Rui Maria de Araújo**

But East Timor's other longtime leader, Xanana Gusmao, retained the more important position of prime minister.

Political uncertainty continued, however, as the 2017 elections had not created a clear governing majority, and the prime minister called another election in May 2018. Turnout was high, at 81%, and victory went to a newly formed Alliance for Change and Progress (AMP), which brought three existing parties together. The AMP won 34 seats, giving it a clear majority in the 65-seat assembly. Former president Taur Matan Ruak became prime minister. Francisco Guterres, who had twice before stood unsuccessfully for the presidency, in 2007 and 2012, this time won it.

Despite its majority, it proved no easy task to keep the coalition working together. After failing to get approval for the budget, the prime minister offered his resignation in February 2020 but agreed to stay on until a new government could be formed. This proved difficult even though there were urgent financial needs as the country began to cope with COVID-19. After discussions with President Guterres in April 2020, the prime minister formally withdrew his resignation in order to deal with the problems caused by the pandemic. By March 2021, this new arrangement seemed to be working. As life returned to normal, however, the old tensions returned. When President Guterres sought a second term in March 2022, he was up against Jose Ramos-Horta. The first round proved indecisive and a run-off was held on 19 April, which Ramos-Horta won, meaning he would become the next president in May 2022.

There were other problems, including Cyclone Seroja, which struck in April 2021, causing heavy destruction in Dili and killing 50 people.

## Defense and Foreign Relations

Aside from the United Nations and the international donor community, the nation's most significant foreign relations are with Indonesia and Australia. With Indonesia, there was at first much tension, for understandable reasons. But Indonesia has shown no disposition to make life more for complicated for East Timor by supporting those who retain desires to undermine it. A Truth and Friendship Commission, established in 2005, reported in 2008 that there had been crimes against humanity by Indonesian forces. Not all the issues raised have been addressed, but it helped to improve relations. In normal times, all border crossing points are open. Both civilian legislators and military officers from the two countries have worked to improve cooperation. Indonesia is East Timor's largest trading partner, accounting for some 50% of all trade.

Relations with Australia are equally important but for quite different reasons. Tourist dollars and lucrative investments that will help East Timor make in building a new and stable community are expected from Australia. And Australia has been committed to that relationship. It is the country's largest development partner, accounting for 3% of Australia's ODA. This amounted to US $120.7 million in 2019–2020 and a commitment of $105.2 million budgeted for 2020–2021. Australia has also been East Timor's primary partner in coping with COVID-19. Other forms of cooperation include training for the East Timor military and police. That said, there have also been tensions in the relationship, mainly over maritime boundaries and access to maritime natural resources. Although the two countries reached an

**Both Former President and Prime Minister Jose Xanana Gusmao**

agreement formally delineating their boundaries in the Timor Sea in February 2018, there continue to be problems. The persistence of the tensions, exacerbated by claims about Australian bugging of Timor's cabinet during negotiations.

Beyond relations with their more immediate neighbors, East Timor has long wanted to join ASEAN. It achieved observer status in 2002 and applied to join in 2005. There are doubts among ASEAN leaders about the application, including concerns that the country's poverty would make it difficult to take meet the costs of membership, and so far (March 2021) the application has not been accepted. In another move, perhaps to move away from overdependence on Indonesia and Australia, East Timor has begun to make tentative moves towards China since the mid-2010s. Work began on an expressway and other projects. In 2019, the Timor Gap E.P., the country's natural oil company, sought a Chinese loan to construct onshore facilities. Although there is apparently little current Chinese activity, such developments have worried a number of countries, including Australia, which are concerned at the possible increase of Chinese influence in the region.

## Society

Like their neighbors in Indonesia most of the peoples of East Timor are of Indonesian-Malay stock while within the mountainous regions live peoples of Melanesian ethnicity. In contrast with their neighbors though, Catholicism rather than Islam is particularly widespread and in fact grew significantly during the years of Indonesian control. Animism, Protestantism, and Islam are present. Although Muslims constitute only about 5% of the population, East Timor's first prime minister was a Muslim.

The vast majority of East Timorese work in subsistence-level agriculture in the countryside. While agriculture has recovered from the devastation brought about during the Indonesian withdrawal, much of the rest of the society remains deeply impacted by those events. Most people speak either Indonesian or Tetum. The language of the former colonial power, Portuguese, is still spoken by the older generation. The effort to make it the official language has caused considerable tension among the many people who do not know it.

As we have seen, the struggle produced thousands of refugees and the separation of many families, including children separated from their parents into various camps in West Timor. Over the last several years many of those families have attempted to make their way back to East Timor again. Jose Xanana Gusmao has

**Political rally for East Timor**

been especially involved in encouraging them to return. The fact that the country has one of the lowest per capita crime rates in the world probably helps.

The strong sense of family in East Timor has also had an impact on how it has sometimes been perceived on the broader world stage. Responding to both its strong Catholic heritage and to unpopular family planning efforts carried out by its former Indonesian occupiers, the people of East Timor have often been displeased with international calls discouraging them from criminalizing abortion. But those calls have been largely ignored as East Timor prepared its new legal code. Moreover practices from contraception to efforts to enhance the rights of women have often been frowned upon by the citizens of this society, which in many ways is still quite traditional.

The people of East Timor remain among the least privileged in the world. Only half are literate and more than 40% live below the poverty line. Those are the core realities. Nevertheless, in the years since they gained their freedom and started to develop their own natural resources, the situation has improved considerably. Infant mortality has dropped significantly, and life expectancy is going up. The people of East Timor have much by which to be encouraged.

## Economy

The most obvious reality is that East Timor's economy was until quite recently in a disastrous condition. Not only was it largely undeveloped before the violence of recent years, but it also needed to set up a legal system to attract outside investors. The most basic issues are on the table from laws on buying and selling goods to the question of whether foreign firms will be able to buy land. Making progress is incredibly important as the urban areas are said to have an unemployment rate of around 80%. Of course, refugees, who need employment, have returned home in large numbers.

News of riots and the well known United Nation's concern about the new country's general level of security will not make it easier to attract outside money. But things are not all bad. Outside donors have promised some $360 million. Such foreign aid is not always as impressive as it might sound when one only considers the raw figures. An outside monitoring agency reported in 2010 that relatively little of the approximately $8 billion that had been donated to East Timor in the years since independence had ended up in the local economy. Most of it was spent for the salaries of foreign administrators, imports, and administration.

The new nation has also developed an important revenue stream through monies earned from natural gas and oil from the Timor Gap. Unfortunately, working out that oil and gas deal with Australia was quite difficult. The government refused to ratify a proposed treaty that would have given East Timor only 18% of the potential oil revenues while Australia was to have received 82%. The core problem was just where the proposed line between the two nations was to be officially demarcated. Dili insisted that the line lie at the midpoint between the two nations rather than where it had been designated in 1975. Given the extraordinary financial needs of the East Timor government, it was not surprising that Dili continued to insist that the final arrangements maximize their small nation's future oil income. Eventually a compromise was worked out for the two nations to share the potential financial gains while they put off further discussion of the territorial borders between the two nations for 50 years. That hardly solved all the problems. More specifically the government of East Timor wanted the gas drawn from the new offshore wells to be processed on shore within East Timor itself. The Australian energy company, Woodside Petroleum, refused to accept the idea and opted for building an offshore floating facility. Meanwhile East Timor officially charged Australian officials with spying on them during the negotiations. This was an act which Timor claimed should invalidate the agreement. The charges understandably added to the tensions between the two nations. Australian officials specifically warned Timor's representatives to withdraw their charges or "face the consequences."

Eventually East Timor and Australia settled their differences and progress was made in developing the local oil fields. But they have still not finalized the long-term agreements over whether the fuels will be processed within the country and other related expenses that continue to complicate the nation's budget making

ability and the stability of the government itself. Indeed, in early 2019 the government itself was once again in crisis over a battle over spending priorities.

## From the Environment to Climate Change

The best news for East Timor in recent years has been the new enormous revenues flowing into the country from earnings associated with offshore drilling of hydrocarbon fuels like natural gas. Ironically all this comes at a time when the cost of humanity's burning of fossil fuels has become more and more apparent around the world and especially for nations in locations such as East Timor. For it, as with many of its surrounding island communities, the rise of sea water is a significant issue. Locally the waters around the nation have been rising at the rate of .9 mm a year since 1993. Future projections regarding sea levels, depending on the growth of greenhouse gases, suggest much higher levels in the future. As elsewhere, given the nature of a warming global atmosphere, wet seasons are expected to become even wetter and dry seasons even drier as water patterns are transformed by a warming atmosphere's ability to hold more water. Given that reality the number of days of intense heat and/or extreme rainfall are also expected to grow. On the positive side, there is some reason to believe that the frequency of tropical storms hitting the island might decrease.

## COVID-19

East Timor began precautions against COVID-19 in February 2020, although at that time there were no known cases within the country. From 10 February, limited border controls began, at first aimed at those coming from China but soon extended more widely. On 19 February, all border crossings with Indonesia closed. The first case within the country was detected on 21 March. The next day, a state of emergency began. Schools were closed, gatherings limited to five people, and the Roman Catholic hierarchy closed all churches. International travelers were to be quarantined for 14 days. The second case was detected on 9 April. Infections remained very low, and some restrictions were lifted in August. By September, there were 27 cases, all but one of which had fully recovered. Numbers then slowly crept upwards, reaching 119 by early March. Of these, 94 had recovered and 24 were active. Then numbers began to rise again, for a total of 326 cases. There were no deaths. It was claimed that all cases were brought in; the sparse and

# East Timor

scattered population prevented community transmission.

But the early success in handling COVID proved deceptive. The border with Indonesia could not be closed completely and Indonesia was the worst affected country in the region. Infections began to rise steeply in April 2021, and by the end of the year, the total number of cases was 20,000 with 120 deaths. A steep decline was followed by another surge in February 2022. By the end of April 2022, there had been 22,885 cases and 130 deaths.

Australia provided technical and logistical assistance and funds. East Timor began to receive vaccines via the International Vaccine Alliance. By April 2022, 48.9% of the population had two doses and 3.9% booster jabs. Restrictions were eased, including for fully vaccinated international visitors.

The strict measures taken to control the virus were opposed by Jose Xanan Gusamao and his opposition Nacional de Reconstrucao de Timor, but the government, with 36 of the 65 parliamentary seats, prevailed.

## The Future

It will not be easy for East Timor to establish itself as an economically viable nation. Still, of course significant money, reportedly in the several billions, has already begun to flow in from East Timor's energy resources. Such revenues will be absolutely vital to a nation's future. But merely having the money is not enough. It is vitally important that the money be spent well, not only in building up the nation's current infrastructure, but in holding funds aside for the benefit of future generations. Unfortunately, as we have seen, despite the new monies flowing into the country, now, long after becoming an independent nation, a large percentage of the population still lives on only $1.25 USD a day.

Moreover, as we have seen the continuing inability to finalize long-term agreements with the various oil and gas companies complicated the effort to fully utilize those resources and the nation's finances.

Discouragingly the political crisis and attempted assassinations hardly attract the foreign investment that East Timor's growth requires. The United Nations forces that assumed security responsibilities in the first days after the crisis have withdrawn in favor of local forces. This is clearly a sign of renewed confidence.

Perhaps more important is that the new revenue sources available to the nation have allowed a significant amount of infrastructure, from electricity to roads, to be put in place. Mostly located around the capital, they will most certainly improve the nation's long-term economic viability.

All in all East Timor has a great deal to be proud of. The nation has stabilized and the nation has developed a sophisticated civil society committed to promoting human rights within and beyond the nation's borders. On the more negative side, the recent inability of the nation's political parties and their leaders to cooperate enough to form a government capable of truly governing the country is discouraging.

One can also assume that once the plans for further exploitation of the nation's potential fossil fuels are finalized, the economics of the nation, still one of the poorest will finally improve, at least as long as the world community continues to use such climate-busting energy resources.

# The Republic of Indonesia

**At the Mall in Bandung, Indonesia**

Courtesy of Steven A. Leibo

**Area:** 741,040 sq. mi. (1,906,240 sq. km.)
**Population:** 276,144,111 (mid-year 2021 est.)
**Capital City:** Jakarta, pop. 10,915,000 (2021 est.)
**Climate:** Tropical, with a monsoon season from November to March
**Neighboring Countries:** Malaysia and the Philippine Republic (North); Australia (South); Papua New Guinea (East)
**Official Language:** Bahasa Indonesia (a formal version of the Malay language)
**Other Principal Tongues:** Malay, Common Malay (a dialect), and about 250 other Malayo-Polynesian languages and dialects, such as Sundanese Madurese, Japanese, Dutch, and Chinese
**Ethnic Background:** Javanese (45%), Sundanese (14%), Madurese (7.5%), coastal Malays (7.5%), other (26%)
**Principal Religion:** Overwhelmingly Muslim, with small groups of Christians, Hindus, and Buddhists
**Main Exports:** (to Japan, Singapore, South Korea, China, Germany, Malaysia) Petroleum, liquefied natural gas, carpets, fruits, nuts and coffee, plywood, textiles, rubber, and electrical appliances
**Main Imports:** (from U.S., Singapore, Japan, China, Thailand, Saudi Arabia) Aircraft and equipment, cotton textile fibers, engines, civil engineering equipment, pulp, chemicals, foodstuffs, and fuel
**Currency:** Rupiah
**Former Colonial Status:** Dutch Colony from about 1625 to 1949
**Independence Day:** December 27, 1949 (August 17th, the anniversary of the 1945 date when revolutionaries proclaimed the Republic of Indonesia)
**Chief of State:** Joko Widodo, president (since October 2014)
**National Flag:** Two horizontal bands; the top is maroon and the bottom is white
**Per Capita GDP Annual Income:** $12.072.7 (2020 World Bank) (purchasing power parity)

Stretched along the Equator between Australia and the Asian mainland for a distance horizontally of about 3,000 miles, Indonesia consists of some 13,000 individual islands. The actual number seems to change frequently as improved visual technology reveals more islands even as rising waters submerges others. The largest are Sumatra and Java. Kalimantan occupies the southern portion of the Island of Borneo, and Irian Jaya is the western portion of the island of New Guinea. About one-fourth of the land is covered with inland waters.

If Indonesia did not have a great variation in elevation, its climate would be uniformly oppressive because of its equatorial location. The heat and humidity of the coastal areas give way to more moderate temperatures as the altitude rises to breathtaking heights. Although Irian Jaya is predominantly low and swampy, as is Kalimantan, there are mountains that are snow-covered throughout the year on New Guinea.

This is an area of volcanic peaks—some dormant and some active—that have enriched the soil greatly during their centuries of destructively explosive activity. Krakatoa, located on a tiny island between Java and Sumatra, exploded with such force in 1883 that it produced a tidal wave that was felt around the world and that inundated parts of nearby seacoasts. In other areas of the world, torrential rainfall such as occurs during the monsoon season is the enemy that washes valuable topsoil to the sea, exposing infertile land to the sun. In Java, the downpours are welcome. They wash away old soil and expose even richer volcanic ash and dirt which is fertile almost beyond belief.

The wildlife of Indonesia is more interesting and varied than in almost any other country of the world. The Komodo dragon, 10 feet long and a remnant of prehistoric times, inhabits the island of Komodo east of Java. The Javanese rhinoceros makes increasingly rare appearances in the Udjung Kulon ("western tip") preserve on the end of Java, where successive governments have tried to maintain the natural setting of plants and animals. The gibbon, most agile among the primates, swings overhead in the tall trees that provide thick shade for the banteng, a native ox with white legs that resembles an

# Indonesia

ordinary dairy cow. Although crowded by a multitude of species adapted to its character, this area, as well as most of the interior of the Indonesian islands, is extremely inhospitable to modern man.

### History

Fossils and other prehistoric remnants of human skeletons indicate that Indonesia was one of the earlier areas of the world to be inhabited by humans. The present population of the area acquired its somewhat uniform appearance about the second millennium B.C., a time when there was gradual intermarriage and mixture between native Polynesians and people from the Asian mainland. This combination, relatively stable since that time, is now referred to as Malayo-Polynesian.

Early Indonesian history is best seen as a regional history of diverse communities rather than as a unified early state directly tied through time to modern Indonesia. In fact many different communities existed though there were several commonalities among them, especially the presence of Hinduism and Buddhism, and their role in early international trade.

The arrival of Indian cultural, religious and commercial influences around the 1st century A.D. greatly influenced the people. Eventually Hinduism and Buddhism mingled with the ancient animist background of the Indonesians and produced an extremely complex, varied, and unique culture, especially on Java and nearby Bali. The advances brought by the Indians and the availability of good harbors in the

Malacca and Sunda Straits were the basis for the rise of two powerful commercial and naval empires at the beginning of the 7th century, A.D. Srivijaya was based on the island of Sumatra; Sailendra arose on neighboring Java. The empires thrived on a lively trade centered on the production of spices treasured throughout the rest of the world, though available only here. Especially important was the islands' control of the trade routes between India and China and, in Srivijaya's case, its ties to imperial China. Taxes were imposed on passing ships based on the number of passengers and the cargo carried.

If Hinduism and Buddhism were prevalent in the early traditions of these island kingdoms, their modern heritage lies elsewhere. Indian merchants also brought Islam to the islands at the beginning of the 11th century, but it did not have much influence at first. The development of the Indonesian empires was briefly disrupted in the 13th century by a naval expedition sent by the powerful Mongol emperor of China, Kublai Khan. Shortly afterward, a new empire, known as Majapahit, became dominant, and seized control of the valuable spice trade. Majapahit was the last major Indonesian kingdom headed by a Hindu.

After their departure from the scene, Islam became more and more common. It had long been spreading, and by the end of the 16th century the vast majority of the people had become Muslims. In a sense the early South Asian influence continued, but now in its Islamic, rather than Hindu form. Today only Bali, the famous tourist destination within Indonesia, remains

deeply committed to its traditional Hindu heritage.

### The Colonial Period

Though Europeans had longed for the spices of the East for centuries (European spices were limited to salt, garlic, and vinegar), the profits from those valuable commodities were largely in the hands of Muslim middlemen during the premodern era. What the Europeans wanted was to gain access to those profits. This explains the push in the 15th century to find new trade routes to the East. These images of fantastic wealth to be earned in the spice trade first brought Europeans to the East Indies, or Dutch East Indies as the islands were later called. The spices were, and even now are, grown principally in the Moluccas (Spice Islands) and on Java.

There was a keen interest in the area on the part of Portugal and Great Britain, but it was the Dutch who were ultimately successful in dominating Indonesia, controlling the area through a commercial organization, the Dutch East India Company. By then the Majapahit Empire was already in decline leaving the island of Java as a relatively easy conquest. It was quickly identified as the most strategic and fertile of the islands and one that could produce coffee, indigo, and some spices. The local leaders were either militarily defeated or intimidated by the Dutch, who compelled them to deliver produce to the Company.

The colonial experience of the East Indies, as Indonesia was then known, was much the same as in other parts of the

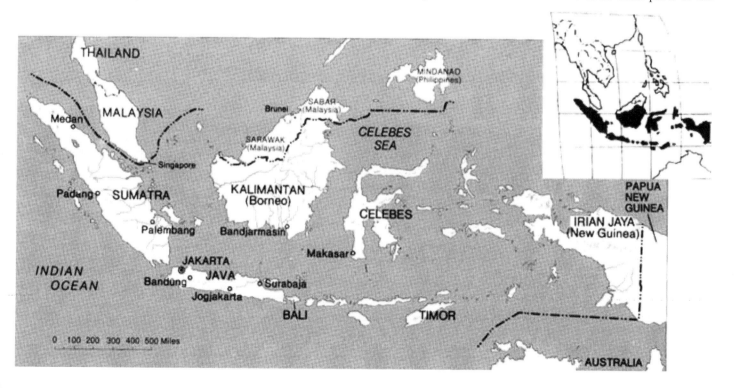

colonized world: centered on the process of extracting wealth from the colony. As was so common during colonialism, this was often carried out without any concern for the welfare of the indigenous peoples. Thus for example, in an effort to drive up prices, the Dutch destroyed some island communities' ability to produce spices, devastating their economies and people in the process.

With the wealth gained, the Netherlands emerged as one of the most powerful European countries of the early modern period and one that supported an impressive navy. But as would be the case in the 20th century their control over the East Indies was temporarily interrupted in the 19th century due to developments back in Europe.

The Napoleonic Wars resulted in a brief period of British occupation of Java from 1811 to 1816. But once the Napoleonic war was over the Dutch were able to reestablish their control partly because the British, wanting to maintain a balance of power on the European continent, knew that Holland would need Indonesian wealth to contribute to European stability. It would not be the last time the states of Southeast Asia were sacrificed to the needs of internal European politics.

By then the East Indies had passed from administration by the Dutch East Indies Company to that of the Dutch crown. However, direct crown control proved difficult as it undertook administrative and judicial changes that challenged the power of the Javanese aristocratic class and provoked a war in the 1820s. The Dutch won but only after great loss of life. An especially exploitative economic system known as the Cultivation System was introduced. It was designed to gain maximum economic advantage for the Dutch from their control over the islands. This system added further to the hardships of the native Indonesians.

Eventually, in the last part of the 19th century there was a return to free economic development based on private investment. During this era there was considerable Western investment and the introduction of railroads. Large amounts of new land were put under cultivation. Indonesia emerged as the world's largest producer of tin and rubber. The islands became so associated with the production of products such as coffee that the term "java" became synonymous with the drink itself.

By the late 19th century, feelings against Dutch control were growing in both Indonesia and the Netherlands itself. Responding to these new sentiments, the colonial government adopted the "Ethical Policy," under which strenuous efforts were made to promote the welfare of the Indonesians through public works and health

**Farming in Indonesia**

measures. The government even announced that it would no longer take any surplus revenues generated by Indonesia and canceled the colony's debts.

Direct control over the East Indies grew during the early 20th century even as new transportation methods allowed the Dutch themselves to become increasingly more remote from Indonesian society. They could, after all, send their children to schools in Europe and develop their own society more distant from that of the Indonesians they ruled. The phenomenon was a common one throughout much of the colonial world.

Local education was neglected and little serious effort toward preparation for self-government occurred despite the more general calls in the post–World War I era for national self-determination. There was thus a rapid growth of both nationalism and communism in the interwar period in spite of increasingly harsh Dutch police measures.

## World War II

When the Pacific War began in December 1941 Indonesia was, due to its great natural wealth, a prime target for the Japanese offensive in Southeast Asia. Weakly defended by a Dutch government-in-exile that had been driven from its own European homeland by the Germans, the islands rapidly came under Japanese control in early 1942.

As was the case elsewhere, many Indonesians warmly greeted the Japanese and sincerely believed their claims that they had come to free Asia from Western colonialism. Many Indonesians, either for convenience or commitment, made the decision to work with the Japanese. One was Achmed Sukarno, the long-term Indonesian nationalist, who decided to use the

occupation as a tool to help realize Indonesia's goal of national freedom. Eventually, he even managed to convince the Japanese authorities to help arm and train Indonesians in the struggle against the West.

The initial enthusiasm notwithstanding, the Japanese administration soon convinced many Indonesians, as was to occur elsewhere in Asia, that they were hardly liberators, but merely new conquerors come to exploit the resources of Indonesia as the Dutch had before them. If the Japanese hoped to build a new colonial base in Indonesia, their real impact was rather in fundamentally destroying the old colonial mentality rather than building a new one.

Moreover, although they were foreign conquerors, the Japanese not only destroyed the prestige of the Dutch in the eyes of the Indonesians, but also gave the latter valuable experience in political activity and public administration.

## A New Nation

As soon as the war was over, Sukarno and fellow nationalist leader Mohammad Hatta immediately proclaimed the independent Republic of Indonesia. This move had widespread support of other leaders and among the population of the outlying islands. It paralleled similar anti-colonialist developments elsewhere such as those of Ho Chi Minh in Vietnam. But declaring independence and actually winning it were not the same thing.

British forces soon arrived and used their power to help the Dutch reestablish themselves, though not before a massive public outbreak of anti-Dutch feelings and considerable violence. For the moment, the Dutch would be able to reestablish themselves, but over the next four years a major independence struggle took place, which eventually saw the Dutch

# Indonesia

**Richard M. Nixon (right) meets with Indonesia's leader Sukarno**

Courtesy of Special Collections, University of Virginia Library

withdraw. A settlement was reached at the end of 1949. It recognized the independence of Indonesia, which was supposed to be linked to the Netherlands through the Dutch Crown. West Irian, part of the island of New Guinea, was not included in the agreement. Dutch-owned industry and investment were to remain intact.

The new Republic of Indonesia, based on Java, promptly abolished the federal system created by the Dutch administration and established a unitary republic that later cut all ties with the Netherlands. Over the first several years, it would operate as a parliamentary democracy with the charismatic Sukarno at its head.

The Indonesians faced independence under almost insurmountable difficulties. There were geographic and cultural differences, poor communications between the islands, and the dominant power of the Javanese was resented in the other islands—referred to as "Outer Islands." The political turmoil left by the years of Japanese occupation followed by battle against the Dutch, and the primitive state of economic and political development, were adverse influences. In addition to these liabilities, there was the leadership role of Sukarno himself.

### The Sukarno Years

Flamboyant, popular, unpredictable, self-indulgent, articulate, dictatorial, and lovable are all adjectives that have been used to describe Sukarno. During the years of his control he moved Indonesia from a parliamentary system to a more authoritarian one called "Guided Democracy." Denouncing Western democratic traditions, he practiced a political leadership that stressed Indonesian nationalism above regionalism and non-alignment in the Cold War between Washington and

Moscow. Although not a communist, he frequently worked closely with the PKI, the Indonesian Communist Party. The U.S., alarmed by this, arranged a tryst for Sukarno with a beautiful woman at his hotel in New York while he was appearing at the UN. Cameras recorded the whole event in detail. When confronted with it, accompanied by threats of being disgraced, he was delighted. He asked for a copy to play publicly in Indonesia to visually demonstrate his sexual prowess.

Politics in those years became a complicated mixture of PKI communists led by the young and energetic PKI secretary-general, Dipa Nusantara (Achmad) Aidit, the army and Sukarno. The charismatic Sukarno was usually able to command the support of both the communists and the army. But his economic policies weakened the country. Promises had been given to leave foreign investment intact, but these were not kept. Dutch assets were seized in 1957. Some Chinese investment was nationalized in the following years. Most American assets were confiscated in 1963–1964.

Supported by Soviet diplomacy, Sukarno, in 1962, threatened West Irian, today known as Irian Jaya, with a substantial Soviet equipped military force. Under American pressure and mediation, the Dutch finally surrendered the western portion of New Guinea that they had until then continued to hold.

Sukarno then turned his attention toward Malaysia, which had been created by the British when they united Malaya, Singapore, and North Borneo (Sabah and Sarawak) into a single, independent nation in 1963. In contrast to the Dutch in West Irian, the British were willing to fight to protect Malaysia.

The confrontation with Malaysia, launched in 1963 by Sukarno, led the PKI,

which already had achieved considerable power, to demand the arming of communist-led "workers and peasants." That demand was resisted by the army, but endorsed by China and given an increasingly enthusiastic reception by Sukarno in 1965.

The events that followed remain unclear to this day although their impact transformed the country. What we do know is that a group of dissident military officers plotted to overthrow their more senior commanders. The exact relationship between the PKI, Sukarno, and the plotters remains uncertain. However, the results are not.

As dramatized in the film, *A Year of Living Dangerously*, events moved quickly during the fall of 1965. The coup attempt failed, and the army, now under the leadership of General Suharto, emerged in power. Suharto then crushed the rebellion. Resentment against the PKI, which had been smoldering in the islands for years, erupted into a massive slaughter of hundreds of thousands of people suspected of being communists or their sympathizers, including Audit. While the army itself was directly involved, a large percentage of the deaths seem to have actually been carried out by civilians with the military's encouragement. The total number killed remains unclear. The PKI was almost annihilated and was outlawed as a political party. The army soon stripped Sukarno of all power. He died in 1970.

**Former President Suharto**

### Suharto

If Sukarno had led an authoritarian government with leftist-leaning nationalist sentiments, Suharto would now offer his own version of authoritarianism but one that was more open to the West and based on the military. Ideologically it had been built around the idea of Pancasila. This state ideology incorporated the five principles of nationalism, democracy, internationalism, social justice, and belief in one God. All political parties were required to accept them, and the armed forces had been given a legitimate role in the political process through the official government party, Golkar.

After the 1965 coup, the appointed Provisional People's Consultative Congress (MPRS) was purged of pro-communist elements. Later in March 1967 it proclaimed Suharto president for five years.

Having achieved effective control of Indonesia, Suharto and the army ended the confrontation with Malaysia and began to tackle Indonesia's massive economic problems. Steps were taken to rejoin the UN, from which Sukarno's government had withdrawn in 1965. An interest was shown in resuming normal economic relations with the non-communist world, including the Netherlands and the United States.

Communist China, in contrast, denounced the new military regime as a gang of fascists, particularly after the extensive anti-Chinese violence following the military seizure of power. The Soviet Union had more mixed feelings; it did not wish for communists to be slaughtered, but since the PKI had adopted the Chinese side of the disputes in international communism, the Soviets undoubtedly were gratified by the example of its failure—an example to other communist movements of the world which had sided with Beijing.

Unlike his rejection of Sukarno's anti-Malaysian foreign policy, Suharto's regime continued the latter's interest in West Irian. When the Dutch withdrew from West Irian in 1962, the UN promised that a popular vote would be taken to determine the will of the people. The alternatives were independence or union with Indonesia. However, Indonesian military officers present in West Irian in 1969 rigged a unanimous vote for union with Indonesia. Thus the region, known today as Irian Jaya, came to be part of Indonesia though even through the 1990s problems of anti-Jakarta regionalism have continued.

After the failure of the 1965 coup in Indonesia and the end of the confrontation with Malaysia, Indonesia joined with Malaysia, Singapore, Thailand, and the Philippines to form the Association of Southeast Asian Nations (ASEAN). Brunei joined in 1984. The original purpose of this organization was to help stabilize regional power, develop the area economically, and support the American struggle in Vietnam.

Its main visible functions were to maintain easy access for its members' raw materials to the markets of the developed countries, and to cooperate to a limited extent against communist insurgency. After the Vietnamese invasion of Cambodia at the end of 1978, ASEAN, with Thailand as the "frontline" state, began to play an important role in trying to negotiate an end to the struggle on terms that would include a Vietnamese military withdrawal.

It was announced in late 1969 that general elections would be held in mid 1971 in Indonesia. The result was an overwhelming victory for the government party, the Sekber Golkar, a federation of about 260 trade, professional, and regional groups which enjoyed an overwhelming advantage over the other legal parties.

Widespread discontent over the lack of political freedom and social justice erupted in serious riots in early 1974. Most of the anger was nurtured by inflation, commodity shortages, and was mainly aimed against the government. Other elements included dissatisfaction with the growing economic influence of Japan, and the commercial influence of local Indonesian Chinese whose preeminent role in the economy has often led to outbursts of anti-Chinese sentiment.

In the wake of the riots, President Suharto made some changes, but government corruption, food shortages, a weak educational system, tensions between the Indonesian majority, and the important Chinese minority continued to plague the country.

Nevertheless, in Indonesia's third general election in 1977, Golkar won 230 out of 360 seats in the House of Representatives. A few years later, in 1982, Golkar was again predictably victorious. Overall the system allowed for the appearance of a more democratic system while maintaining military domination.

Despite the authoritarian and military nature of the regime, Suharto's generation-long control over the country was economically successful for most of his tenure in power. In fact, the government specifically defended the lack of political progress made over the years precisely on the grounds of economic development. And those boasts were not without merit. Very real social and economic progress was made in Indonesia during the last quarter of the 20th century. The Suharto government, despite its many faults dramatically improved the educational level of the Indonesian people. Real wages went up as social conditions improved markedly. Per capita GDP had, for example, risen more than 4% annually for the first 20 years after 1965. After 1988 the figure for the last decade of Suharto's control was closer to 7%—impressive figures indeed.

These changes occurred in part because Suharto's regime was committed to integrating Indonesia into the world economy. During these important years Indonesia was able to successfully offer its services as an assembly area for products produced in the dynamic Asian economies of its neighbors from South Korea and Taiwan to Singapore and Hong Kong. Indonesia had long had the advantage of having considerable oil, gas, and timber reserves. Now these additional efforts at diversifying the economy were quite

**Children at play in a poorer part of Jakarta**

# Indesia

effective and improved the lives of Indonesians a great deal.

Still, Suharto's rather heavy-handed rule had naturally aroused opposition. There were two small legal opposition parties: the Indonesian Democratic Party and the United Development Party (the latter is Muslim-based). Interestingly those parties were not even officially allowed to call themselves "opposition" parties nor were they in a position to seriously challenge Golkar and the military due to the latter's overwhelming political and financial advantages.

Administratively, the general trend from the 1960s was toward a greater centralization of authority at the national level in Jakarta. But, perhaps under the impact of democratic developments in the Philippines and South Korea, there was, during Suharto's last decade in power some liberalization of the authoritarian political system. One form this trend took was a lessening of some central control—at least in the politically less sensitive areas of fiscal and technological authority. Another form was the revival of unofficial, as well as official, interest in the personality and career of the late President Sukarno, a development that has played a role in the recent prominence of his daughter.

One feature of the tensions that became more evident in recent years was anger at the ability of well-connected individuals and groups to dominate the economy. This was hardly new. Both the Dutch colonial system as well as that employed during the years of Japanese occupation and under Sukarno had seen the economy tightly controlled by those with special advantages. But by the 1990s, expectations had changed, and these long-established economic controls were no longer acceptable.

The longtime domination of Suharto's family and friends in the Indonesian economy particularly aroused concerns that their activities were actually stifling the economy. These concerns were so significant that they, at times, even provoked challenges to Suharto from within the ranks of the usually supportive Indonesia military. Most of these tensions however remained fairly subtle till the crisis of 1998.

Suharto's government also kept the pressure on the media. In 1994 it arrested three members of the Alliance of Independent Journalists for slandering the government through their publication *Independent*. The government even set up an Association of Indonesian Journalists that all reporters were required to join. But things have not always gone as smoothly as the government wanted. In fact, Suharto's regime was already looking vulnerable even before the 1998 crash.

**Morning exercises in Jakarta**　　　　　　　Courtesy of Steven A. Leibo

### The Fall of Suharto

After the bloodbath of 1965, Indonesian politics remained reasonably calm until the economic turmoil that developed in late 1997. The military and its partner, Golkar, allowed the impression of political harmony while maintaining a tight grip on political power. Nevertheless, even before the economic meltdown of the region during late 1997 and early 1998 Suharto's grip was being challenged.

The military's long-term domination of the country, the growing disparity between rich and poor, the economic domination of Suharto's family and more general frustrations with pervasive levels of corruption all played a role in the developing tensions. But the more immediate cause was the entrance into Indonesian politics of the daughter of Indonesian nationalist hero Sukarno.

Until 1987, Megawati Sukarnoputri, the former president's daughter was not involved in politics. Only in the late 1980s was she elected to parliament. Somewhat later, in 1993, she emerged as the leader of the Indonesian Democratic Party, one of the two parties the government allowed to exist. But while many had dismissed the college-educated former housewife, President Suharto did not. He moved to weaken the political base of this cautious leader who carried with her the legacy of a powerful name in Indonesia's national memory.

Not content to harass her, Suharto's government engineered her ouster as leader of the PDI by pro-government supporters within the party. No doubt the hope had been to remove Megawati's official base but doing so appeared to backfire when, in the summer of 1996, government

backed hoodlums attempted to force her supporters from the PDI headquarters. Rather than go quietly, her supporters quickly gathered and a confrontation ensured which eventually saw several deaths and hundreds wounded.

The government's strong-arm tactics had done no more than solidify her leadership before her followers and raise the international prestige of her movement. By late fall she was being coupled in the public mind with other Southeast Asian women who have challenged dictatorial governments, such as Corazon Aquino of the Philippines to Aung San Suu Kyi of Burma. In late 1997, as the economic meltdown began to hit throughout the country, Megawati Sukarnoputri even announced she was ready to replace the president when his term ended in March 1998.

Her offer was not taken up. Rather, the government's political arm, Golkar, backed by the army, proceeded to reelect the 77-year-old president once again. Far more significant for the nation's future, Suharto chose Research and Technology Minister B. J. Habibie as his vice-president and presumably his successor.

Habibie, a 61-year-old engineer, had the confidence of the president and the technical background Suharto was said to have been looking for. Unfortunately, his reputation among the international financial community was not very positive. He was seen as a volatile leader and an economic nationalist too infatuated with unrealistic showcase style industrial goals. Nor did the ever-influential army have any affection for him. Suharto favored him and that was enough. By March 1998, newly elected President Suharto and his new vice-president were in place. But by then Indonesian politics were starting to move far beyond Suharto's control.

By mid-May 1998 the loss of confidence in Suharto's regime had become simply too great. Initially aroused by the rising prices of basic commodities, as mandated by the IMF's recovery program, Jakarta and other cities saw demonstrations by at first students and then others against the regime. After more than a quarter of a century in power, Suharto had lost the confidence of more than just the younger and poorer members of society. By late May, even his most trusted loyalists and many of the country's leading political, intellectual and religious leaders had withdrawn their support. After one bloody clash between the students and the army, many even within the army leadership itself, were apparently ready to abandon Suharto and more importantly to help the country make the transition toward new leadership. With encouragement of General Wiranto, the Chief of the Indonesia Armed Forces, President Suharto finally resigned on May 21 and allowed his newly chosen vice-president Habibie to assume office.

We still have much to learn about the details of Suharto's fall, but it appears that members of the Indonesian military, most notably those led by Suharto's son-in-law, were probably working to bring about a situation which would have allowed the military to suppress the demonstrations and retain its influence. General Wiranto, the Minister of Defense and Security apparently had other ideas and threw his weight behind those hoping for a more peaceful resolution of the crisis, including the newly installed president.

### Indonesia Enters a New Era

The 76-year-old Suharto had stepped down after 32 years in power. But the Indonesian establishment, military, political, and financial was still largely in place. The new president, Habibie, had no popular mandate or even strong support among the military to help him lead. Unfortunately for the new president, nor was he able in the months following the fall of Suharto to develop such a following. In fact, his attitude, relatively cautious and incremental did little to build popular support and merely reminded many of his fundamental ties to the Suharto years.

Habibie did manage to move the country toward new elections. First parliamentary elections took place in June 1999, and then the presidential contest was followed later that year. The earlier elections proved to be a vindication for Megawati Sukarnoputri, whose Indonesian Democratic Party won 34% of the votes and 153 seats in the legislature. Despite those who thought Golkar's strength had totally

**Former President Abdurrahman Wahid**

**Former President
Megawati Sukarnoputri**

failed it, the former "government" party came in second with 120 seats. Altogether 21 parties managed to win seats in the 500 seat Indonesian House of representatives—down from the 200 parties that were competing earlier in the year.

Though Golkar's continuing strength was a surprise to some observers the really big winner in the contest was Megawati who seemed on a clear path to the presidency. But the presidential election that occurred the following October turned out quite differently from what many expected. Sukarno's daughter may have been very popular with the Indonesian public, but winning the presidency required far more than that. Megawati was hurt by a reputation for indecision. Most importantly she was far less effective than others in building the necessary support within the legislature. When the vote took place, the aging and partially

blind Muslim leader, Abdurrahman Wahid, outmaneuvered not only Megawati but Suharto's chosen successor, Habibie, to emerge as Indonesia's new president.

That Indonesia had moved beyond Suharto and Habibie was certainly exciting for those who had hoped for a more open Indonesia. Wahid had long been known as an open-minded and tolerant leader. Nevertheless, Megawati's supporters were very disappointed. The newly elected president's decision to tap her as the nation's vice-president satisfied many, and the new team was duly sworn in.

Indonesia sorely needed a period of stability following the Asian economic collapse and the parallel fall of Suharto's long-lived dictatorship. Unfortunately Abdurrahman Wahid's presidency proved to be a disaster. Almost from the start, the new president failed to establish himself as an individual capable of guiding Indonesia. Many of his comments and acts were erratic, and corruption charges weakened his hold on power. Not only did he manage quickly to anger his own vice-president, Megawati, but his relations with the influential House of Representatives deteriorated rapidly over the months.

By the summer of 2001 Wahid, acting as if Indonesia remained the dictatorship it had once been, attempted to use his presidential authority to declare a state of martial law that would have allowed him to suspend the legislature. But support for the president had collapsed by then. In July the newly empowered national legislature voted to remove him and allow Megawati to take over as president.

Thus, in one stroke, the daughter of Indonesia's founding figure, the woman who had risen from the position of President Suharto's most vocal opponent to the biggest winner in Indonesia's first post-Suharto elections, had finally become president. In doing so she became the first female leader of the world's largest Muslim nation.

Once she assumed office, though, Megawati's presidency proved something of a mixed blessing. Some, for example, found her indifferent to the details of government. Moreover, a reputation for excessive caution surrounded her leadership. Still, Indonesia's political transformation has gone far beyond the question of what particular individual will lead the country next.

In the years following the election Indonesia worked vigorously to reorganize its political selection process. Most importantly, it adopted a more direct and democratic voting procedure to pick the country's leaders. Thus, unlike the preceding elections, Indonesia's next president was to be chosen after a two-part direct election.

As the time for the new parliamentary and presidential elections grew closer,

# Indonesia

hundreds of parties began to play a role in the campaign. Eventually two dozen parties qualified to contest the election of April 2004. Not surprisingly the PRI-P of President Megawati and Golkar, the former ruling party, were at the forefront of the struggle.

Initially President Megawati retained considerable popularity, and many assumed she had a good chance of being reelected. But that became less certain as her government found itself facing a wide variety of challenges. Among the most immediate problems she had was the challenge raised by the American campaigns in Afghanistan and Iraq. On the one hand, Megawati's government understood the importance of maintaining close ties with the influential Americans. Given the frequent terrorist attacks in the country, such as the bombings in Bali 2002 and 2005, it was understandable that she committed her country to supporting the American War on Terrorism.

On the other hand, many of Indonesia's hundreds of millions of Muslim voters were vehemently opposed to Washington's military campaigns in Afghanistan and Iraq, a sentiment that forced Indonesia's leaders into a complicated balancing act between Washington, DC, and their own people. The most obvious example of that tension was the original ambivalence that Jakarta showed to Washington's claims of an al-Qaeda's presence within Indonesia. Eventually, of course, the fall 2002 terrorist bombings in Bali did stir Indonesia's leadership toward a crackdown on some of the most extremist Islamic militants within the country.

Those difficulties and others played a role in the outcome of the parliamentary elections of April 2004. To the surprise of many pundits, Megawati's political party, the PDI-P, which had won 34% of the votes in the previous parliament, saw its share drop to a mere 19.67%. Golkar, the former ruling party, emerged triumphant with 20.99% of the vote. Given the outcome, it was now clear that the president's own reelection was likely to be a far more difficult challenge than many had previously assumed. Even worse was the news that according to polls more than 80% of the Indonesians claimed to want her to be replaced. Such a candidate was at hand to do that.

During the spring of 2004 Megawati's former security minister, retired General Susilo Bambang Yudhoyono, surged ahead in the polls as the candidate most likely to win the upcoming presidential elections. There were other candidates as well jockeying for position, including another military officer, General Wiranto, whom the newly triumphant Golkar chose to lead their effort to recapture the presidency.

By the time the presidential elections of 2004 finally arrived it was clear that the vast majority of Indonesian voters wanted a change in government. In the first round of voting that took place in July the 55-year-old Susilo Bambang Yudhoyono received 34% of the vote while Megawati trailed by seven points, enough to retain her status as a candidate for that fall's run off but certainly a deep disappointment for her followers. That disappointment would continue though the fall when, despite the decision by the former ruling party Golkar's to support her reelection, Megawati was trounced by Susilo Bambang Yudhoyono in the late September 2004 run off.

Politically, the two finalists had a great deal in common. Both were secular nationalists committed to economic growth and resisting the forces of secession that have so often complicated Indonesia's political life. Nevertheless, Megawati had become quite unpopular and the reality that 40% of the working population remained underemployed, despite the very real economic improvements experienced by the country in recent years, deeply hurt her.

For his part, the new president, Mr. Yudhoyono, brought an impressive background to his new challenge. He had a newly minted doctorate in agricultural policy, (earned during the campaign itself) coupled with many years as a professional military officer. Plus, he had served in Megawati's cabinet where he was her minister of security, a position that allowed him many opportunities to serve as the government's principal spokesperson before his resignation. Indonesia's new leader also has another major advantage. He also spoke fluent English, an absolutely essential skill in today's globalized international community.

Significantly, Susilo Bambang Yudhoyono had taken office as the first directly elected president since Suharto fell. He leda government that undertook profound reforms in order to make the system more democratic. In fact, those changes were as dramatic as the election itself. Known collectively as Reformasi, the reforms ranged from a formal separation between the police and army, to fundamental alterations of the structure of parliament to make it more democratic. In the same vein, Indonesia introduced a constitutional court and basic human rights protections. Of particular significance given their past role in national politics, Indonesia's parliaments no longer have special seats reserved for the military establishment.

But the new president hardly had time to get his administration formed before one of the worst natural disasters in modern history pummeled the islands. On December 26, 2004 an undersea volcanic eruption led to an enormous tsunami. Although the exact numbers will probably never be known, estimates were that around 132,000 people in Indonesia were killed, particularly in the long-troubled Aceh Province, while another 700,000 were left homeless. Moreover, almost 40,000 remained missing long after the disaster. Half of the capital city of Banda Aceh was leveled, and an enormous percentage of the community's infrastructure from homes and roads to universities was destroyed. It was a challenge with which any leader, let alone a newly inaugurated one, would be hard pressed to deal.

To make matters worse, the president had to deal with the challenge without

**Fast food lunch in Bandung, Indonesia**

Courtesy of Steven A. Leibo

full control of the government of the nation's parliament. President Susilo Bambang Yudhoyono's party had won 7.5% in the elections, leaving him with control over only 120 seats in a parliament of 550. Still the president had important allies. His vice president, Jusuf Kalla, an accomplished businessman and politician in his own right, emerged as one of the principal organizers of the massive relief effort that saw outside agencies and numerous Indonesian organizations rushing in to offer help.

Despite such challenges, Indonesia's President Yudhoya was a formidable leader. Particularly important in his initial popularity was the anti-corruption campaigns his government carried out and his accomplishments dealing with the troubled province of Aceh. Public frustration with the government's belt tightening apparently did not weaken the president significantly. Indeed, during the spring elections of 2009 his party did exceptionally well while those of the more religious parties went down dramatically.

Months later the president himself was reelected, and remained quite popular with a continuing approval level of over 50%. His popularity was such that some of his backers even talked of him possibly circumventing the nation's constitution by seeking a prohibited third term.

Still the general momentum toward building a stable democracy continued unabated. By the early summer of 2012, the race to follow Yudhoyono had already begun in earnest.

Indeed, a hint of a new era was initially signaled by the election of a less traditional politician, Joko Widodo (usually known as Jokowi), to be the governor of Jakarta. What made the emergent political leader especially unique was that he was the first contender for power not to come from the traditional Indonesia political elite.

Whether the unconventional Joko Widodo would actually become president was not at all clear in the months before

**Jakarta street scene**

Courtesy of Steven A. Leibo

the presidential poll. Indeed his enemies were trying to claim he was really an ethnic Chinese Christian. These are two different identities that would most certainly make him less attractive among many Indonesian voters.

By the time the voters went the polls, though, it was obvious that Indonesia, despite the drama of the final weeks of the campaign, had taken yet another step forward in its democratization process as Joko Widodo, the son of a simple wood seller, who had grown up largely in poverty, was elected president by a 53% margin over his rival a member of long influential Indonesia military elite.

In the 2019 elections, Jokowi received 55.5% of the vote. His opponent, the son-in-law of former President Suharto and ex-army general, Prabowo Subianto, got 45% and unsuccessfully challenged the result in the Constitutional Court. The resulting riots left eight dead and hundreds injured. But the result stood. The president's runningmate was an elderly Islamic cleric, Ma'ruf Amin, with a reputation for religious intolerance. In a surprise move, Prabowo Subianto became defense minister in September, much to the concern of human rights activists.

Among the early pronouncements of the new administration was the move of the capital from Jakarta to East Kalimantan in August 2019. This was not unexpected. Modern Jakarta was originally the Dutch colonial city of Batavia, itself built on the site of the indigenous city of Jayakerta, which the Dutch razed to the ground after its capture in 1619. Built on the coast, Jakarta was slowly being destroyed by the sea. The new capital would be built on East Kalimantan, and would be named Nusantara, the Javenese word for "Archipelago." The plan was that it would be ready by 2024.

COVID and its devastating effects may have slowed the process so that it was not until February 2022 that a law was passed to create the new capital. 2024 remains the target year for completion.

More controversial were new laws introduced in September 2019 against criticism of the government and imposing limits on personal conduct. These led to student-led protests, and the government postponed them in November. But they were not withdrawn.

Longstanding problems did not go away. The minister for security was stabbed in an Islamist attack in September 2019 and there was separatist activity in West Papua (Indonesian New Guinea); this continued in succeding years. As usual, smoke from forest burning in the second half of the year not only affected large parts of the country, but also brought complaints from neighboring countries, including Malaysia.

Unfortunately, whatever plans the administration had, 2020 saw Indonesia knocked sideways by COVID-19 (see below). The central government floundered, torn between health needs and the economy; local authorities performed better. But the cost was heavy. Tourism dried up and the economy was badly hit. There was widespread unemployment and underemployment. Work on the movement of the capital was put off to some unknown future date; by early 2022, it was argued that the success of the vaccine program would allow work to begin, with, as noted above, the target date of 2024 still in place. Another major project, informally known as "Komodo Jurassic Park," aimed at increasing tourism, was resumed, but there were growing domestic and international doubts about the project after photographs were published that seemed to indicate that the "Komodo dragons" were reacting with hostility toward the work. Economic growth plunged although at the end of the year the IMF was predicting a revival in 2021.

The relentless toll from the pandemic continued into 2021. On 26 January, there were over one million cases, the highest in Southeast Asia. By June, it was 1.83 million, with a widespread acceptance that this was probably an underreporting. After the Ulema Council declared that the Sinovac vaccine was halal in January, a program of vaccinations began, including the Oxford AstraZeneca vaccine from March. The government continued to send different signals. The Hajj pilgrimage was banned for the second year yet there were optimistic announcements about restarting tourism in the summer, for example. And the toll went on. By early May 2022, official figures said that there were around 6,050,000 cases since the start of the pandemic, with 156,000 deaths. As elsewhere, these figures were underreported.

Hospitals struggled and, as elsewhere, some saw an opportunity to make money The minister of social affairs was arrested

**Men on the way to work**

# Indonesia

in December 2020 for allegedly taking $2.75 million in kickbacks for COVID-related procurements, and he was sentenced to 12 years in prison in August 2021.

### Indonesian Regionalism and East Timor

When studying the modern history of communities like Indonesia it is important to remember that they were not single ethnic/linguistic/political communities before the colonial era. Rather, it was often the colonial experience itself that helped create the generation of nationalists like Sukarno or Hatta who led the struggle for independence. But like nations throughout the world, whose political borders were shaped by outside colonial powers, it has often been difficult to keep focused on their identities as Indonesians in the face of strong regional and ethnic ties. During the heady days of economic growth, pride in those accomplishments helped to strengthen Indonesia's national identity. Nevertheless, strong separatist sentiments and movements continued to be influential in regions from Aceh, near Malaysia, to Irian Jaya far to the east. And it was not just the power of separatism that challenged Indonesia's leadership in recent years. The larger geographic region also included militant Muslims who advocated the creation of an entirely new Islamic nation that would include countries from Indonesia and Malaysia to Singapore, Brunei and the Southern Philippines.

No Indonesian area experienced as much international attention for the level of its struggle and suffering as East Timor. Unlike much of the rest of Indonesia, which had been administered as the Dutch East Indies, East Timor had been a Portuguese colony for hundreds of years. Rather like Portuguese Goa in India or Macao near Hong Kong, it was a small reminder of the once energetic Portuguese role in colonization.

But just as India's government had moved into Goa in the early 1960s, and China took back Macao in December of 1999, Indonesia decided to absorb East Timor in 1975. The logic of Indonesian nationalism might have made the move seem appropriate, but culturally Indonesians and the East Timorese were quite different. Indonesia, although it includes many religions including millions of Christians, is largely Muslim, while East Timor, by grace of its centuries as a Portuguese colony, and more importantly the tensions which existed after Indonesia occupied it, is primarily Catholic and animist.

However significant the religious differences are, the real problems were probably the lack of a shared historical experience between the two peoples and especially

**Former President Susilo Bambang Yudhoyono**

the brutality of the Indonesian occupation. The Indonesian move into East Timor was resisted by a leftist-nationalist movement called Fretilin, the Revolutionary Front for an Independent East Timor, and widely condemned internationally. In fact, only Indonesia's ASEAN partners and Australia actually recognized the legality of the occupation. Throughout the 1990s, reports of significant human rights abuses continued to be a problem for the Suharto government and aroused the sympathy of an increasingly large group of international sympathizers.

But it was not until the fall of Suharto in 1998 that the situation began to change. Once in power the new government of President Habibie indicated interest in trying to resolve the long-standing struggle. Clearly hoping to move toward some sort of autonomy, the regime made a series of dramatic admissions regarding its previous role in East Timor and claimed to be withdrawing some of its troops from the region. Not surprisingly leaders in East Timor were more interested in real independence than Jakarta's offer of greater autonomy.

Habibie blundered deeply by not ensuring that the Indonesian military was on board before offering the East Timorese an opportunity to vote on their future. In the months leading up to the August 1999 vote, it became clear that elements of the Indonesian military were supporting a terrorist campaign within East Timor to disrupt the referendum.

Eventually the violence, after the results of the vote for independence were announced, became so blatant that the United Nations supported by a force from Australia and other regional powers assumed control over East Timor from an extremely embarrassed and humiliated Indonesian military leadership (for more information on East Timor, see the section dedicated to its recent development).

Indonesia's former president, Megawati, came to power after East Timor had departed from Indonesia. While we have

no way of knowing exactly what she might have done had she arrived in power earlier, once in office, she allied herself with those nationalists who wanted to ensure that East Timor would remain the exception to the continuing unity of the nation her father did so much to build.

That understandable commitment to maintaining the territorial integrity of Indonesia, despite the loss of East Timor, was particularly obvious in her government's relations with the other rebellious province of Aceh. Thus, while formally apologizing to the people of Aceh for human rights abuses of the past, Megawati

**Statue of the young Barack Obama who grew up, in part, in Jakarta**

Courtesy of Steven A. Leibo

# Indepedence

made it clear, she would oppose any independence efforts they might mount.

Nevertheless tensions continued. By the early spring of 2003 Jakarta began yet another military campaign to ensure that Aceh remained under its control. By the early summer hundreds of people from Aceh had been killed and thousands more made homeless as the central government made a dramatic effort to wipe out the region's nationalist movement.

Worse yet, the government moves against Aceh's separatists turned out to be the least of their problems when the horrific tsunami that hit the Indian Ocean in late December 2004 particularly devastated Aceh, destroying many of its population centers. But that horrific crisis did turn out to have a positive dimension as well.

In the aftermath of the tsunami, an agreement was worked out during the summer of 2005 to end the insurgency that had lasted over 30 years and killed more than 15,000 people. According to the agreement, the Achenese would disarm their forces while the government agreed to withdraw its troops, grant the province more autonomy, and allow the formation of Achenese political parties. By 2006 that agreement was apparently working, and plans were underway to integrate the former rebels into the provincial political system.

But if the tensions in Aceh have lessened in recent years, Indonesia still has plenty of other regional challenges. Most notable is the continued agitation in Papua province (called Irian Jaya from 1963 to 2000), which has remained disaffected since it was taken over from the Dutch in 1963. The total number of those killed is unknown, but has led to claims of genocide in the province. When the name was changed in 2000, a promise was made that Papua

would enjoy "special autonomy," but this failed to end demands for independence. The government also attempted to end such demands by moving people from elsewhere to Papua, which only added to the discontent. At least 20 people died during one demostration in 2019. In April 2021, the local head of the National Intelligence Agency was assassinated.

Protests continued in 2022. In March, a demonstration against a plan to create six new provinces in the region led to two deaths, and another demonstration in May was broken up with heavy-handed police tactics, though no deaths were reported.

Islamic terrorism has also been notable, especially since the release in January 2021 of one of those implicated in the 2002 Bali bombing, Abu Bakar Bashir. A Roman Catholic Cathedral in South Sulawesi Province was the target of two suicide bombers. While there were no deaths, many were injured. An attack on the central police HQ in Jakarta in the same month left one person dead.

## Society and Culture

Indonesia is a nation of islands that traditionally had mainly indirect contact with each other—a nation more recently ruled in effect by a cultural minority located on the island of Java. The vast majority of Indonesians are Muslims though other important groups of Christians and Chinese Buddhists are also present. Animism, a common tradition throughout Southeast Asia, is also found among some of the more isolated communities. Bali, the island fabled in story and song in the Western world, is the one significant part of Indonesia that still practices Hinduism, the tradition that once dominated the entire region.

Thus, Indonesia is a country of great cultural differences. More than 300 specific groups are recognized and over 350 different languages are spoken. The dominant Javanese themselves constitute about 50% of the population. The largest non-indigenous community is the ethnic Chinese who, while constituting only around 3% of the population, are especially dominant in private economy.

The economic accomplishments of the era from the 1970s through the mid 1990s brought into being a new middle class that enjoyed many of the material comforts such groups enjoy elsewhere. Unlike the middle classes in other parts of East and Southeast, though, they did not appear to be particularly politicized or willing to challenge Suharto's regime until the drama of the late 1990s. Now the situation is quite different.

Modern Indonesia has developed as a community that draws sources from many different groups from Javanese and Malay traditions to those from the West and derived from Islamic society. Normally, non-violence and courteous agreement are a tradition in Javanese culture. Open disagreement is avoided—differences are buried in an atmosphere of agreement, no matter how unreal. Still, once it becomes apparent that differences cannot be hidden, violence has at times become painfully real.

In recent years a revival of an Islamic emphasis by some Javanese has tended at times to make the Christian and Chinese communities feel more insecure than in previous years. Of course, within the Indonesia, the tendency has long existed to blame the nation's economic crises on its influential Chinese minority a phenomenon that has sometimes resulted in violent attacks upon that community.

More positively Indonesia's large Chinese community has seen its circumstances evolve dramatically in recent years. It has now become not only legal but common for the local Chinese community to embrace their ethnicity and culture publicly. This is a far cry from the years when under the Suharto military dictatorship any show of Chinese culture could bring severe retribution.

But that does not mean ethnic relations are uniformly improving. Over the last few years, and especially as Indonesia's economic has weakened, there have been more and more outbreaks of communal violence. Especially violent outbreaks of fighting between Dayak tribesmen against Muslim Madurese settlers in Kalimantan have regularly created thousands of casualties and refugees. Dramatic and bloody confrontations between Indonesia's Christian and Muslim communities have broken out as well.

**Bandung side street**                    Courtesy of Steven A. Leibo

# Indonesia

Most dramatic was the recent confrontation over a Christian Church located on the outskirts of which was ordered demolished in front of its very upset congregants. While the order was justified by officials because the Church had never received official permission for its initial construction the local Christian community clearly believed, and the very public attitudes of many of those who gathered the cheer the demolition clearly suggested an ongoing problem with the activities of the small Christian community within the overwhelming Muslim nation. Clearly Indonesia is a country deeply affected by various communal tensions.

Less well known have been attacks against members of the Ahmadiyah set, which sees itself as part of the Islamic community despite that fact that many locals consider the group heretical. It has experienced not only direct attacks, but calls for it to be legally banned.

As is often the case within Muslim societies, the question of how closely secular law should parallel Islamic Sharia law is a regular issue, with legislature introduced from time to time. But generally, such moves have not made much progress. Not only secular groups but even some non-Muslim traditional organizations have opposed them.

Still, the clash between traditional society and modern international trends can be just as complicated in Indonesia as they are elsewhere in the world. Most dramatically, the authorities in Aceh, disturbed by the rise of a local contemporary punk rocker generation, in 2011 rounded up a large number of them. Despite international condemnation, it shaved their heads while forcing them to go through a re-education campaign. According to reports, the effort was not very effective. In fact within months the punkers were back in the streets with new protest songs and their heads no longer shaved.

## Indonesian Women

As is the case in many countries throughout the world, Indonesian women have many disadvantages when compared to men. Officially, they have the same rights but reality is often quite different. Those who work in industry usually get lower pay than men and often without the benefits men receive. Traditional Islamic family law prevails, making it legal for men to have more than one wife. Nevertheless, during President Suharto's period in power, the practice was that senior level officials and officers were forbidden to do so. At the lower levels of the civil service it was tolerated, but men wishing to take another wife were required to get the permission of their supervisor as well as of their first wife.

Women's lower status is especially evident in the laws of citizenship. Women are not allowed to pass on their citizenship to their children. Thus a woman who becomes pregnant by a non-Indonesian citizen takes the risk of seeing her own children deported. In contrast to some other Asian societies there is much less social preference for boys over girls.

Some real improvements were being made in recent years. The number of young women graduating from high school went up enormously in the last generation, and the number graduating from college tripled in the years from 1980 to 1990. Additionally, a number of women's organizations have appeared to help improve the lives of Indonesian women.

Moreover, at the upper more educated levels, the gap between women's and men's salaries lessens. Many women now work at important mid-level positions in both government and the private sector. Unfortunately, the lives of both women and men were dramatically affected by the economic collapse of the late 1990s. Spousal abuse was reported to have risen as families experienced more tension, and women were less able to afford the contraceptives they previously had used to help control their own fertility. In the last year the role of one particular female Indonesian has been seen as especially critical, that of Sri Mulyani Indrawati, an Indonesian economist originally trained at the University of Illinois. As the nation's finance minister, she was a particularly strong voice against corruption and economic restructure.

Although President Megawati was not able to win reelection in her own right after inheriting power from President Wahid, her tenure in power represented an enormously significant development. Under her leadership Indonesian Muslims had had the opportunity once again to show to the world that despite the common believe that women have no place in the politics of Islamic societies, that was hardly the case in Indonesia. A woman there had risen to ultimate power within the largest Muslim country in the world, as they already had in other parts of the Islamic realm.

Not surprisingly modern pop culture has impacted Indonesian youth as much in this relatively conservative society as elsewhere. Indeed, one of the recent sensations, however controversial in some quarters, was the growing popularity of a group of young hijab-wearing female heavy metal musicians.

A further sign of a less-tradtional approach to the status of women was the passing in May 2022 of a new law outlawing sexual abuse and forced marriage, despite opposition from some conservatives who argued that such "liberal values" would allow "deviant " sexual behavior. This was introduced partly to try and stem the rising incidence of reported violence against women. Cases increased from 220,000 in 2020 to 338,496 in 2021.

## Foreign Relations

Recent years have been a very complicated for Indonesia's relations with the outside world. Not only have Indonesian based forest fires often filled the entire region with choking smoke that hardly endeared her to her neighbors, but her ongoing battles during the late 1990s with the International Monetary Fund often complicated the regions efforts to recover from the Asian economic collapse of the late 1990s. And of course the struggle over East Timor not only soured relations with Australia and much of the international community but forced Jakarta to accept a humiliating presence of foreign troops on

**President Joko Widodo**

land she had until recently vehemently insisted was her sovereign territory.

That was ironic given that Indonesia has usually played an important and respected role in the region. As the fourth most populous country in the world, Indonesia has always considered itself to be number one among equals within the Association of Southeast Asian Nations (ASEAN). It is fair to say that the other ASEAN states have usually accepted the "big brother" role of Indonesia. The ASEAN headquarters is located in Jakarta. For its part, Indonesia has worked within the context of ASEAN although Jakarta has often been less enthusiastic about the rapid elimination of trade barriers since it is the least developed of the member states.

In the past Indonesia prided itself on being an arbiter of disputes and a conciliator. Indonesia played a role in the settlement of disputes in Cambodia and was helpful in having the Burmese activist Aung San Suu Kyi released from house arrest during the mid-1990s. Efforts to play a similar role after the 2021 military coup in Myanmar have helped to shape the ASEAN response—even if this time, Indonesia was unable to change the new junta's policies. Indonesia has also sponsored several seminars on the conflicting territorial claims in the South China Sea, and especially the Spratly Islands.

During the Cold War Indonesia was a key player in the Non-Aligned Movement that traced its beginnings back to the Bandung (Indonesia) conference of 1955. Nevertheless under former President Sukarno, the policy definitely leaned left. Sukarno tried to organize the New Emerging Forces that linked Indonesia to such countries as China, North Korea and Vietnam. After Sukarno's fall, President Suharto placed the country on a much more centrist path and one more tied to Western economic ideas. This generally non-aligned policy was evidenced for example in that the country did not develop defense treaties with any major outside power or group of powers. This set Indonesia apart from most of her ASEAN neighbors.

The country's territorial waters expanded greatly when the UN Law of the Sea Convention went into effect. Under the convention, all of the waters between the country's numerous islands, officially set at 17,500, now became Indonesian territorial waters. But Indonesia's important and influential role regionally and economically began to unravel in late 1997 as her economy was struck by the same economic crises that had begun in Thailand and swept on toward South Korea. But unlike the situation both in Thailand and South Korea, there initially seemed no new or alternative leadership ready in the wings to take charge of getting the country back on track.

Unfortunately for Indonesia its long entrenched leadership, led by Suharto, seemed unwilling to find a way to work with the International Monetary Fund even as it requested funds from the agency. Thus by early 1998 the world was treated to an ongoing series of major world financial figures each making their way to Jakarta to meet its aging leadership hoping to encourage a more cooperative stance from the Indonesian government.

Certainly there were reasons for Jakarta to balk at some of the IMF's stringent financial demands for economic restructuring which would only add to the financial distress of the Indonesia people and hurt Suharto's own family's financial interests. Nevertheless, the open struggle with the IMF only added to those doubts about whether Indonesia's leadership would be able to make the hard choices necessary to recover and gain the confidence of the world financial markets.

Relations with the People's Republic of China, which were strained by the anti-Indonesian Chinese riots of 1998, were steadily improving in the years afterward. In fact, former President Wahid even indicated an interest in improving relations with neighbors from China to India in order to offer a counter-balance to the enormous Western influence in the region. That momentum seems to have stalled as China itself has emerged less as a friend than as a potential threat through its recently more assertive claims over the South China Sea. Those growing tensions have seen Indonesian leaders talking of putting more and more financial and military resources into place specifically to counter that growing concern.

Like much of the world Indonesia was deeply impacted by the September 2001 terrorist assault against the United States. But for Indonesia the challenges were particularly daunting. Especially so as its secular and nationalist minded leader Megawati publicly supported the United

**Former editor Steven Leibo meeting with Indonesian climate change activists**

# Indonesia

States, while many others, in this largest of Muslim countries on the planet, including her own newly chosen vice-president were publicly critical both of her association with the United States and the latter's military activities in Afghanistan.

Those tensions only became more complicated when in the spring of 2003 the United States used its enormous power to overthrow the government of Saddam Hussein in Iraq. While most Americans seemed to support the campaign, within Indonesia Washington's efforts were enormously unpopular.

Although tensions over American policy in Iraq had an impact on Indonesia's international position, it played out as well on a regional level given the fact that Australia not only supported Washington's efforts, but it sent its own contingent of troops to the struggle. Clearly all this is yet another complication in Indonesian-Australian relations that were already complicated enough by Australia's role in the loss of East Timor only a few years earlier. On the more positive side, Indonesia's recent evolution toward a more democratic society and its increasing commitment and success in the war against Muslim Jihadist terrorism, despite the obvious setbacks, have helped enormously in improving Indonesian Western relations.

But as we have seen elsewhere, in the emerging 21st century that is not enough. Like other nations in the region Indonesia has needed to rethink its foreign policy in the light of the growing strength of the People's Republic of China, especially her navy and the relative weakening of the United States. Of course, improving relations with China is complicated by the conflicting claims of the two countries in the South China Sea, as it is for other claimants.

Indonesia has been concerned at Chinese air and maritime incursions into its sea areas. China has contested the Indonesian claim to the waters around Natuna island, which Indonesia has named the Natuna Sea, since around 2015. Under the Law of the Sea Conventions, this area is part of the Indonesian Exclusive Economic Zone. But when Indonesia began to exploit the area, the Chinese protests began and the dispute has rumbled on ever since, coming to a head most recently in December 2021.

## Economy

Until very recently the local economy was in shambles. Long proud of the steady economic progress they had made over the last generation, Jakarta suddenly found itself caught in the currency collapse begun in Thailand in the summer of 1997.

Initially working closely with the IMF, an enormous aid package of $43 billion was arranged. Suharto's government started to act decisively by promising to close banks that were insolvent and to take "belt tightening" economic decisions. While the economic crisis grew, social and political cracks within the society, long present, added to the tensions. As the century drew to a close, riots broke out as people protested higher food and fuel prices. All this was in such contrast to the economic experience of Indonesia over earlier decades.

For much of the previous generation Indonesia had had a diversifying economy. Economic growth in Gross Domestic Product (GDP) had averaged about 7% annually since the 1970s. Foreign investment grew enormously. Indonesia's participation in the "growth triangle" with Singapore and Johore state in West Malaysia appeared to prove the merits of the private sector in the development process.

Despite the enormous economic growth and social improvements accomplished over those decades, 26 million of the country's 200 million people were said to be living in poverty, as defined by the World Bank even before the economic problems of 1997–1998. But with the onset of the Asian economic crisis, the situation grew dire. Millions were pushed back into poverty as unemployment soared and more than two thirds of the population fell below even the more modest Indonesia poverty line. Unfortunately, as Indonesia moved more deeply into the new century, its recovery clearly lagged behind many other East and Southeast Asian nations that have already managed the recovery from the debacle of 1997.

Happily Megawati's arrival in power ended the uncertainty that surrounded her predecessor's chaotic administration and things began to improve. While growth rates have hardly returned to the heady figures of the 1980s, recent years have seen the GDP rise modestly. Domestic consumption has risen and the banking sector has seen significant improvement. Though concerns about domestic terrorism did impact the economy as well.

More positively, Indonesian authorities were relatively successful in their efforts to deal with local terrorist networks. But these efforts have also been very controversial as significant elements within Indonesian society have seen the American War on Terrorism as a campaign designed to weaken Islam itself, a perception hardly helpful to Indonesia's leaders.

If the concerns about terrorism, and sectarian violence were not enough of a problem for both Indonesians and their economy, the horrendous earthquake and subsequent tsunami that hit the country, especially the Aceh Province of Northern Sumatra during late 2004, were particularly horrific. A hundred thousand were said to have been killed in Indonesia alone while perhaps up to 200,000 died throughout the region.

By the spring of 2008 the economy was still moving on the path of solid economic expansion. The growth figures around 6.3% were certainly positive, but

**The capital's business district plays the stock market**

unfortunately they were not high enough to create the new jobs its growing population required.

Despite 2008's global economic crash, Indonesia did relatively well in the following years. GDP growth stayed at about 6% and foreign investment grew significantly. Meanwhile domestic demand, usually a sign of local confidence, continued to be strong. Other growth areas were in both palm oil and coal though as we have seen elsewhere both can be very problematic for environmental reasons. One issue, though, that troubled some was a series of economically nationalist policies designed to reduce the role of outsiders in Indonesia's national economy. Some believed this might have the effect of weakening the economy and making the nation less attractive to foreign investors.

Until 2019, the economic outlook has been reasonably stable at around 5% per year. But the onset of COVID hit it badly in 2020, when it dropped to -2.1%. By 2021, it had bounced back to 3.5%, with Asian Development Bank predictions of returning to around 5% in both 2022 and 2023. The resumption of construction work and,

perhaps, a revival of international tourism could be key factors.

## Environmental Issues

The late December 2005 tsunami that so devastated the Ache region of Indonesia reminded Indonesians of how vulnerable we all are to natural phenomena like those deadly earthquakes that sent those huge waves toward the nation's shores. In two very different ways nature's demonstration of its power to disrupt our lives continued unabated over the last year. In October 2010 another tsunami hit Sumatra killing around 500 people. Within hours, the nation's most dangerous volcano, Mt. Merapi on the island of Java, erupted killing hundreds more and forcing over 100,000 people from their homes.

Such disasters continue. In 2021, a landslide in West Java killed 50, and an earthquake in West Sulaewesi left more than 100 dead. That same month saw thousands displaced by floods in South Kalimantan. In April, Cyclone Seroja caused floods and landslides that killed hundreds of people and displaced many more. Mount Semeru

in East Java erupted in Dember 2020 and again in December 2021, killing many on the latter occasion. In January–March 2022 alone, Indonesia reported 1,137 disasters, with 29 dead or missing.

But not all environmental threats emerge beyond humanity's influence. Within Indonesia decisions are regularly made that have immediate and long-term implications for the nation. Most important is the burning of Indonesia's forests, which regularly send huge plumes of smoke throughout the regional atmosphere hurting not only locals but their national neighbors. Of course, the smoke they create is only part of the problem. The cutting down of Indonesia's forest coverings, like similar activities in Brazil, is also contributing to the destabilization of global climate patterns by adding to the greenhouse gases that cause global warming.

This happens in two ways. First, the burning of Indonesia's forests, particularly serious in the aftermath of the Asian economic crisis of the late 1990s, releases massive amounts of $CO_2$ that had been retained by the trees. Second, the cleared land no longer absorbs $CO_2$, thus keeping more in the atmosphere. Moreover, Indonesia is home to huge peat swamps that also contain enormous amounts of $CO_2$ that are now slowly being released as the swamps are drained and the resulting drying-out process releases their long-stored gases.

In Indonesia's case, the expansion of palm oil production on land that was previously forested or covered by peat bogs has been particularly problematic environmentally. For example, on the island of Kalimantan alone deforestation during 2010 had the carbon equivalent of an additional 28 million vehicles on the roads. The situation is so dramatic that Indonesia is among the top three emitters of greenhouse gases in the world. This is true even though its output of the industrial-based greenhouse gas emissions, while rising, remains relatively small.

In a dramatic gesture in the build up to the late-2007 meeting in Bali to expand the international efforts to confront global warming, the nation's president along with huge numbers of his fellow citizens worked to plant millions of new trees. It was a dramatic effort that President Bambang Yudhoyono proclaimed as Indonesia's gift to the international community.

At the conference itself significant progress was made in creating an international formula that, it is hoped, will eventually offer financial incentives for nations like Indonesia to preserve their tropical forests. Developing such an international system is vitally important because forests play an important role in maintaining the

# Indonesia

world's current climate balance. Since the Bali Climate Conference, Indonesia's commitment to dealing with the related energy challenges has continued unabated. In the early spring of 2010 the World Bank announced efforts to help the nation develop its geothermal energy capacity. According to Bank officials, Indonesia has the largest potential geothermal sources in the world.

Meanwhile, officials have announced plans to reduce the growth of Indonesian-produced greenhouse gases by 25%. Complementing that goal was the recent announcement of a new set of green energy building design guidelines. Unfortunately, though, that progress has been diminished by the continuing deforestation that has paralleled Indonesia's growing role in the production of palm oil, a common ingredient in a great many commercial products.

Meanwhile the general population is also getting deeply involved. Recently dozens of climate activists who had been personally trained by Al Gore fanned out across Indonesia to offer a series of presentations on the impact of climate change globally and within the country itself. This important momentum was complemented by a presidential announcement in the spring of 2011 that he was instituting a moratorium on new cutting concessions in peat lands and primary forests. The goal is to give the nation the time necessary to enact reforms that will slow deforestation.

Compared to some other countries, the people of Indonesia have become increasingly active in the fight against climate change. There is an important youth movement that is quite active while the government has been quite supportive. There has even been the implementation of car-free days in Jakarta that over time have been expanded. This is an issue that has not only an immediate impact on Jakarta's impressive traffic congestion, but it raises national awareness of the various problems associated with automobile use.

Of course, it is not surprising that the Indonesians have been especially sensitive to the world's most dramatic environmental challenge. As a nation of relatively low-lying islands, Indonesia is thought to be particularly vulnerable to the rising waters brought about by climate instability. Most dramatically, its people experienced the power of the early 21st century's increasingly powerful rainstorms in February 2007 when around 400,000 residents of Jakarta were displaced by huge floods released by horrendous rainstorms. Even more recently during April 2012, Jakarta experienced flooding that was in some parts of the city as high as five feet. Unfortunately flooding has now become a regular feature of life for many of the

residents of the Jakarta. Indeed while the world tends to focus on the slow flooding of the more famous Venice, Jakarta's problem is considerably worse and like Venice caused not only by global issues like climate change but local drilling by residents who are draining regional underground aqueducts causing the entire city to sink even as waters rise.

## COVID-19

COVID-19 was first detected in Indonesia in late January, brought in by international travellrs. The first death, of a Briton, took place in late February, and the first domestic deaths came in March. Numbers infected and deaths rose swiftly. By the last week of January 2021, total reported cases had passed the million mark, the highest in Southeast Asia. On the 21 January, there were over 2000 deaths. At the end of May 2021, there had been 1,837,126 reported cases and over 51,000 deaths.

As noted, the government response was less effective than that of local authorities. There was at first a reluctance to close borders for fear of the economic damage but eventually it became necessary, as did rules on gathering, social distancing and so forth. Tourism ground to a halt, even as the government pushed a campaign to encourage people to visit. The economic toll was heavy, with millions out of work and millions of others on short time. One decisive decision was to release 30,000 prisoners to prevent massive outbreaks in jail.

Vaccinations began in January 2021, made easier after the Indonesian Ulema Council declared on 8 January that the Sinovac vaccine was halal and could therefore be used by Muslims. In March, the Oxford AstraZeneca vaccine was also approved and came into use. By the end of May 2021, around 10% of the population had received at least one dose. The government optimistically talked of tourism reopening in March, and there are also hopes that the economy would bounce back in 2021. .

But the virus did not go away. There was a spike between June and October 2021, with a huge rise in deaths, and a much smaller one in February–April 2022. By early May 2022, total reported cases reached 6,050,000, with 156,000 deaths. But there had been a gradual lifting of restrictions, as in most other countries. As we have seen, the economy was beginning to recover. International tourism restarted for those fully vaccinated or who had a negative test.

## Future

Indonesia has experienced a great deal since the Asian economic crash and the

fall of Suharto. For a time previous to those dramatic days, continued growth appeared almost to put Indonesia firmly into the mid-level developing nation's category. But the 1997–1998 economic crash and resulting political transformation ended those hopes. Once Suharto fell, the immediate challenge was to establish a stable transition toward a more open society. However, the first three presidents after Sukarno—Habibie, Wahid, and Megawati Sukarnoputri—were all unable to generate enough lasting popular support and stability to allow that to happen.

The next president, Susilo Bambang Yudhoyono, did manage to create a much more politically stable environment and of course was reelected.

The following election, as we have seen, pitted a member of the old guard from the Indonesian military with a man, Joko Widodo who repesented a new more populist chapter in the nation's democratic evolution.

The election itself eventually proved to be one of the most bitterly fought campaigns since Suharto fell from power but in the end, Joko Widodo's elevation to the presidency went relatively smoothly. Indonesia has much to be proud of.

Nevertheless, things have not gone as President Joko Widodo might have hoped. While running for office he promised to lift national growth rates to an average of 7% a year, while as we have seen they have actually been declining somewhat each year and usually average a bit under 5%.

Moreover, while the election of the more populist Joko Widodo, may have been a signal that the nation was moving past its militarist years it also opened the door to reinforcing some even more fundamental divides within the country as Joko's resignation put his deputy a Chinese Christian, Basuki Tjahaja Purnama into the sensitive office of major of Jakarta, the first non-Muslim mayor for more than a half century. Not surprisingly, the new mayor found himself embroiled in a blasphemy case and was decisively defeated in the spring elections of 2017 and for a time jailed.

There have also been questionable decisions regarding the importance of retaining a balance between promoting economic growth and environmental concerns most notably in the ambitious effort to develop the Trans-Papua Highway through some of the largest and still intact rain forests in the world.

Internationally, of course, Indonesia faces the same challenge its neighbors do, adjusting to a regional environment within which China and its growing naval presence slowly replaces the influence that the United States once held.

# The Laos People's Democratic Republic

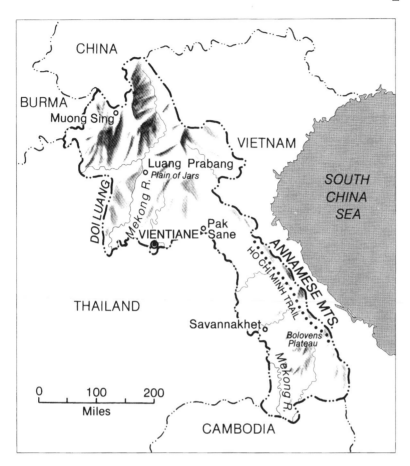

**Area:** 91,400 sq. mi. (234,804 sq. km., somewhat smaller than Oregon)

**Population:** 7,275,560 (2021 est.)

**Capital City:** Vientiane, Pop. 948,477 (2020 census)

**Climate:** Tropical, with a rainy monsoon from May–October and a dry season from November–April

**Neighboring Countries:** China (North); Vietnam (East); Burma (Northwest); Thailand (West); Cambodia (South)

**Official Language:** Lao

**Other Principal Tongue:** French and some English, ethnic languages

**Ethnic Background:** Lao Loum (lowland, 68%), Lao Theung (upland, 22%), Lao Soung (highland, including the Hmong [Meo] and the Yao [Mien], 9%), ethnic Vietnamese/Chinese (1%)

**Principal Religion:** Buddhism; animism is predominant among the tribes

**Main Exports:** (to Thailand, Vietnam, France, Germany, U.K.) Electric power; (to Thailand) timber, textiles, garments, wood, and coffee

**Main Imports:** (from Thailand, Russia, Japan, France, China, Singapore, Vietnam) Rice, petroleum products, machinery, and vehicles

**Currency:** Kip

**Former Colonial Status:** French protectorate (1893–1949); member of the French Union (1949–1954)

**National Day:** December 24, 1954

**Chief of State:** President Thongloun Sisoulith (since March 2021)

**Head of Government:** Phankham Viphavan (since March 2021)

**National Flag:** Two red stripes (top and bottom), a wide blue stripe between them upon which is centered a white circle

**Per Capita GDP Income:** $8,111 (2020 est.) (purchasing power parity)

Laos is a landlocked country, largely covered with mountains and tropical forests, interrupted by patches of low scrub vegetation in the areas where the soil is poor. It is an extremely undeveloped country with few roads where the natural beauty has not been greatly altered by the presence of man.

Most of the fertile land lies along the valley of the Mekong River, where it is eroded and flows as silt to the rice paddies in the Mekong Delta in southern Vietnam. The land receives ample rainfall, but the sandstone soils have little capacity to retain the moisture. In the last part of the dry season from November to May, the air becomes oppressively hot and very dry. This is when tribesmen living in the mountain forests burn the trees to clear the land. The practice, coupled with natural forest fires, sadly robs the land of much of its fertility.

**Loatian landscape**

219

# Laos

## History

The Lao people moved into northern Laos from the southwestern Chinese province of Yunnan beginning in the 11th century A.D. During the succeeding centuries they slowly expanded toward the south, founding two communities in central and southern Laos. In their efforts to settle, the additional lands they came into frequent conflict with the Burmese and Thai who were also active in this part of Southeast Asia.

The French established their colonial authority over neighboring Vietnam by 1893. When there was a dispute between Thailand and Laos over demarcation of the border, the French proclaimed a protectorate over Laos in 1893, making it a dependency within the French Indochinese Empire. Because of its remoteness and lack of natural resources, the French did almost nothing to develop Laos; they did succeed in ending the payment of tribute to the kings of Thailand, however.

When the Japanese soldiers conquered Southeast Asia in 1942, Tokyo supported their Thai ally in taking some border territory from Laos. A nationalist movement, known as the Lao Issara and directed mainly against the Japanese occupation forces, arose during World War II. When the French reentered after the defeat of the Japanese, Thailand was forced by Britain and the U.S. to return the territory it had acquired while allied with Japan. The Lao Issara promptly started anti-French activity from bases in Thailand. Preoccupied with resistance movements in Vietnam, the French granted Laos internal self-government within the French Union in 1949, thus splitting the resistance movement while the non-communist majority took a leading role in the new government.

Meanwhile the pro-communist forces formed themselves into a new party known as the Pathet Lao which became increasingly associated with Ho Chi Minh's movement in North Vietnam. By the mid-1950s, The North Vietnamese help allowed the Pathet Lao to gain control over provinces along the border with Vietnam, even as Laos finally gained full independence from France in late 1954.

Within Laos a small-scale civil war broke out with both sides the United States and North Vietnam contributing respectively to their different allies. By the early 1960s Laos had become a hot bed of coups and countercoups as each side sought to gain advantage.

Evidently realizing that such chaos did not serve the aims of either side, U.S. President Kennedy and Soviet Premier Khrushchev agreed in 1961 that Laos should be neutralized. Following intense jockeying for position, the Pathet Lao withdrew from the coalition government that had just been set up. The result was continuation of a highly complex and somewhat obscure, undeclared civil war.

During the following years most military activity was directly tied to the Ho Chi Minh Trail, which was vital to the North Vietnamese war effort in South Vietnam. Hanoi sought to keep it open, while the U.S. tried periodically to close it. Later, as part of the accord supposedly settling the Vietnamese conflict, an agreement was reached regarding Laos. It included many of the Pathet Lao demands and tended to lessen the influence of the right wing in the central government.

A coalition government was not installed until April 1974. It became a means whereby the Pathet Lao greatly strengthened its political influence. Prince Souvanna Phouma, a non-communist who had joined the anti-Japanese Lao Issara, and who served as prime minister four times between 1951 and 1975 had to reduce his activities because of age and ill health, and his half-brother, Prince Souphanouvong, the leading Pathet Lao in the coalition government, assumed the chairmanship of the Political Council. He in effect made it, rather than the National Assembly, the real legislative body. Although the Pathet Lao military located themselves in the government areas, non-communists were not allowed to function politically in or even to enter areas held by them. North Vietnamese troops remained in the highlands after the coalition government was formed.

A heart attack suffered by Premier Souvanna Phouma in mid-1974 made things easier for the Pathet Lao. The early months of 1975 saw demonstrations by pro-communist elements (students, etc.) in some towns, as well as fighting in remote areas. But the fall of South Vietnam and Cambodia, in the spring of 1975, made a Pathet Lao takeover inevitable; the right-wing

**Former Prime Minister Bouasone Bouphavanh**

**President Bounnhang Vorachith**

members of the government resigned in May. Soon there was a shift in favor of "hardline" communism. The monarchy was abolished and a new government was created with Souphanouvong as President. By 1977, the ex-king was under arrest.

By 1976, the political "re-education" of the Lao people had begun. Additionally a sizable Soviet aid program, including the building of an airfield on the Plain of Jars, was developed. Vietnamese influence was also very great, and their troops remained on Laotian soil. Using "yellow rain" (Soviet-made natural poisons) for a time, they fought Lao insurgents, some of whom were supported by China. The new socialist government also attempted to put in place a communist command economy though the efforts were not sustained and the commitment to a centrally planned economy did not last.

By the 1980s, the situation had begun to evolve again. At a congress of the ruling Lao People's Revolutionary Party held in November 1986, there were some leadership changes, with younger and better-trained men rising to the top. The change reflected new attitudes on economic development. The party, in line with developments elsewhere in the communist world, and concerned by the poor state of the Laotian economy, called for better relations with China, Thailand, and the U.S. They also began to move away from a rigid communist economic system in favor of a more open system along the model of the People's Republic of China and the economic renovation then going on in neighboring Vietnam and other former hard line communist systems. To that end, in 2003 the government added official protections for private property to the national constitution and become more interested in bringing Laos more deeply into the world

# Laos

**Pha That Luang, the major stupa of Vientiane**

economy. In 2019, for example, a new law allowed foreigners certain property rights in the country.

### Politics and Government

Under the 1991 Constitution, the Laos People's Democratic Republic (LPDR) continues to have a Marxist-Leninist style political system, though in reality its economy is more and more open to capitalist style practices as well. Political power rests with the Pasason, the central organ of the Lao People's Revolution Party (LPRP).

This control is somewhat tempered by a focus on eliminating corruption and ostentatious living among the nation's political elite, and a general move toward decentralization of the Laotian governing system. These efforts include the opportunity for the various local areas to retain a higher percentage of the tax revenues they collect. If successful, it could have a significant impact on how Laos is governed, especially as individual provinces are now allowed to compete with each other to attract foreign investment.

After Khamtay Siphandon, a military leader, became president in 1998 and brought a number of generals into the government, there was some speculation that Laos was moving towards the same sort of military dominance as Thailand and Myanmar. That fact that, during 2005, 8 of the 11-member politburo were either active duty military or retired officers certainly seemed to reinforce that impression.

Regardless of the military ties of many politburo members, the Lao People's Revolutionary Party has continued to be firmly in control. Senior leaders move up the system in an orderly fashion through elections every five years. In the March 2021 elections, the immediate past prime minister, Thongloun Sisoulith, became president and party secretary general, while Phankham Viphavan, previously vice-president, became prime minister.

The unicameral Assembly, also elected in 2021, operates under the principle of democratic centralism, which allows the leadership of the LPRP to control the legislative process. The party holds the vast majority of seats. Opposition is firmly discouraged. A civic activist, Sombath Somphone, was abducted on the streets of Vientiane in 2012, even though he had avoided becoming involved in political issues, and has never been seen or heard of again, despite the UN taking up the case with the Lao government. Cell phones are popular but a decree issued in 2014 banned users from spreading "false information" including criticism of the government or the party.

### Foreign Relations

LPDR foreign policy had a decided "Look East" orientation for years. The country has had a long-standing relationship with Vietnam. In 1977 the two countries signed the Treaty of Friendship and Cooperation. The agreement gave the Vietnamese, among other things, the authority to enter Laos whenever it is deemed necessary. Though the Vietnamese troops were withdrawn from Laos in 1989, there are credible reports that the Vietnamese remain involved in helping Lao's authorities deal with the challenge Hmong insurgents have put up against the regime.

Laos is also especially involved with its neighbor to the West, Thailand, which has been a major investor in the Laotian economy. The first Lao-Thai Friendship Bridge, opened in 1994, spans the Mekong River, linking Vientiane, the capital of Laos, to Nongkhai, Thailand. Since then, three more road bridges have been added, in 2004, 2009 and 2013. These was complemented in 2008 by the opening of Laos' first international train link. It is hoped that it will eventually become part of a long-planned international train line throughout much of eastern Asia. Given that Laos is landlocked, the railroad has the potential to play a very significant role in the nation's future. Because of Laos' interest in selling the energy from its hydroelectric industry to Thailand, these ties are likely to become even more important over the years. At the same time, the two countries are in dispute over the Lao wish to construct large dams on the Mekong River to increase hydroelectric power. The Thai government is concerned about the possible impact on people and the environment. There is also some international concern over the possible negative effect on historic sites, including the former royal capital, Luang Prabang, a World Heritage Site.

As elsewhere in the region, the influence of the People's Republic of China has grown in Laos although the relationship has not always worked out well. Laos

# Laos

faced a dilemma in 1979 when China went to war with Vietnam, eventually supporting the latter. Relations with China suffered and were not restored until 1989. Since then, relations have been good, with frequent high-level visits, including Chinese President Xi Jinping in November 2017. Although a 2000 joint venture between China's Yunnan airline and Lao National Airline did not work out, China is heavily involved other transport projects, including a high-speed link agreed to in 2016, which is due to be opened in 2021. Bilateral trade and investment have grown steadily since the Asian economic crisis of the late 1990s made it obvious that the country would be better off not exclusively dependent on Thailand for its economic health.

Relations with the United States have been on good terms in recent years, despite some concern over the country's human rights' record. In 2005 the U.S. granted Laos "most favored nation" status, which made it much easier for it to export its products to the United States. The two countries have worked together successfully in the areas of refugee repatriation, curbing the production of opium for export, and resolving the status of Americans missing in action since the Vietnam War. In September 2016, President Barack Obama made the first ever US presidential visit to Laos. He acknowledged the damage done to the country by U.S. bombing during the Vietnam War and made US$90 million available to clear unexploded bombs.

Relations with the Soviet Union were close but faded after the re-emergence of Russia in 1991. They have gradually improved again, with developing trade, technology, education, and cultural relations. In 2016, Laos and Russia signed an agreement on cooperation in the field of peaceful nuclear development, including the construction and operation of nuclear power stations. This commitment was reaffirmed in July 2019. Laos has also bought Russian military equipment. Laos and Ukraine established diplomatic relations in 1992. When the Russian attack on Ukraine began in February 2022, the Lao government issued a call for a peaceful resolution to the fighting. But it abstained on the March 2022 UN General Assembly resolution condemning Russian actions.

The most obvious sign of Laos' emergence from its self-imposed isolation is the fact that it finally became a member of the Association of Southeast Asian Nations (ASEAN) during the summer of 1997. It was the ASEAN chair in 2005 and 2016. A further sign of the move away from isolation has been the willingness in recent years to host a wide variety of international gatherings.

## Culture and Society

In physical appearance and culture, the Lao are regarded as "cousins" of the Thai. In fact the two people groups are so similar that Laos has even asked Bangkok for special consideration for Laotians in matters related to visas and work permits. Overall the Lao are an extremely easygoing people and their country was relatively peaceful in modern times until the turmoil brought about by the Vietnamese revolutionary struggle nearby.

Although the government abandoned formal communist economic controls for a more open economic system after 1986, real changes in people's living standards are only just now beginning to be felt. Some wealthy urban dwellers now have the money for cars and TVs. The capital, Vientiane, has itself seen important changes. Foreign newspapers are now available along with the relatively new *Vientiane Times*. Laos even saw the establishment of its own stock exchange in 2011. Laos is now available on the Internet and has its own e-mail service provider and more people live in the cities.

Still only around 33% of the population is urban. Most of them are in the area around Vientiane, the capital. The major-ity of the population still lives in the rural areas. Nevertheless, Laos is changing as well. Over the last 20 years poverty has declined from a number that included almost half of all Laotians in 1990 to around 21% in 2009. More and more are now literate with recent figures setting the number at something over 70%.

Since the majority of the population still lives as subsistence farmers, they have to deal on an almost daily basis with the perils of unexploded military ordnance. Explosions have killed over 12,000 people since the end of the Vietnam War era, and to this day they make tilling the soil in large parts of the country very dangerous.

Laos's recent growth had its impact on society, most significantly on the emerging economic gap between the nation's rural poor and growing urban rich. If development continues as it usually does—with the cities initially growing wealthier than the countryside—Laos is likely to face the same sort of increased tensions that both China and Vietnam did before them.

Over the last dozen years or so, domestic tensions have begun to surface. A bombing campaign began even as some students started taking to the streets to question the government's authority. In the rural area rebels from the minority Hmong people

**Lane Xang Avenue in Vientiane**

**Buddha**

moved to educate young women about the dangers of labor recruiters who lure young girls to the sweatshops and brothels of Thailand. As is frequently the case, the more educated urban women have more opportunities than the majority of the women who live in the countryside where many remain illiterate.

On the other hand, after Thailand and Cambodia recently banned the practice of allowing couples to hire local women to serve as birth surrogates for them many in Laos have moved into the business, a development that might offer economic advantages to poorer Laotian women but has proven problematic enough for the practice to be banned in neighboring countries.

### Economy

From the standpoint of economic geography, Laos falls into two clearly divided areas. In the Mekong Valley, agriculture centered on rice prevails. In the hills, the remote tribesmen sporadically cultivate the poor soils in a migratory fashion. Development is retarded by the poorly developed infrastructure of roads and other means of communication and transportation around the country. Like the adjacent highlands of Burma, Thailand, and China, the Laotian mountains are among the main opium producing regions of Asia. Most of this narcotic substance is smuggled out by air, though increasingly addiction is becoming a problem for the Laotian people as well.

In the years after the communists came to power, they enforced a socialist economic system but by the mid 1980s, that system began to change. The People's Democratic Republic (LPDR) launched the New Economic Mechanism (NEM) in an attempt to modernize the country's economy. By mid-1990s the political landscape began to change with the passing of 86-year-old Souphanouvong, known as the "Red Prince" and Phoumi Vongvichit, a leader of the Pathet Lao, who died in 1994. Virtually all of the founding members of the LPRP have now either died or retired and the general trend of Laotian politics has since them moved rather dramatically away from its recent history. Since 1990, reforms have included the introduction of a new accounting system for production and domestic trade, assigning a permanent staff to monitor budgetary revenue, creation of central banking laws, and the integration of official and parallel exchange rates. The number of state-run enterprises has dropped dramatically as well. More recently serious efforts have begun to train civil servants in English so they can more easily work with their counterparts in ASEAN. As is common elsewhere in the region the Laotian military

have attacked Laotian targets. As of spring 2012 those attacks did not appear to be significant enough genuinely to threaten the nation's leaders. But news of the occasional assaults that have killed civilians and foreigners alike has hardly helped the effort to attract outside investment or tourism. Reports more recently have suggested that agreements may have been made with some of the Hmong insurgents to lay down their arms, but the details appear far from certain.

As has become so common in recent years throughout Asia, recent tensions have been less political and more about the transformation of land use from environmental degradation to the confiscation of land for large commercial ventures. As we will see below, this phenomenon has also become common in Laos.

In sharp contrast to the socialist government's previously antagonistic stance

toward the nation's monarchial past, the country's leaders have more recently been showing considerable respect for that very past. That is quite ironic given that relations with the surviving members of the Laotian royal family remain quite tense. Nevertheless today's Laotian leaders have been making significant efforts to enhance the population's awareness of Laos' imperial past and to link the current government to that heritage.

### Women

The new constitution provides equal rights for women though the traditional culture still favors men. Today women occupy positions of responsibility in business and government. In addition, they have improved their representation in the latter recently. The government, working through women's organizations, has also

# Laos

has been a major player in Laos' economic development. Dividing the country into three regions, the military has been deeply involved economically in everything from tourism to timber products.

The military may well be the only organization with the skills necessary to administer the process of economic modernization. Nevertheless, their control is hardly likely to allow the sort of vigorous economic growth that a more open system might offer. Still Laos clearly appears on the road to a more open economic system and this has included creating, as China started a generation ago, the opening up of its own Special Economic Zone to facilitate foreign investment.

Foreign investment regulations were also liberalized in 1989 and again in 19941995. The growth of such investment continues at an increasingly breathless pace from around $51 million at the dawn of the new century to a staggering $13.6 billion in 2010. Laos's nearest neighbor—China—is especially involved. The US State Department said that Laos received $1.07 billion from China alone in 2019. FDI fell in 2020–2021 as a result of COVID, but is expected to pick up as the world economy recovers.

The country has attracted significant foreign investment for the development of hydroelectric power. The second-largest sector for investment is tourism, followed by mining and manufacturing, including clothing. One of the hydroelectric projects is expected to be the world's second-highest concrete-faced, rock-filled dam. The government has planned to sell a significant percentage of the newly generated power to Thailand although progress on the dams was not initially very rapid. Hopes for the project were finally enhanced in 2005 when the World Bank gave its official "go ahead" for the effort. By 2006 two major hydroelectric projects had begun construction. A year later the projects began to have a significant impact on Laos's economy.

Especially important was the beginning in March 2010 of official operations for the Nam Theun 2 hydroelectric power station. It is the largest in Laos and is already selling energy to Thailand. While dam building has brought increasing revenue into the country, these efforts are not without controversy. In fact, a significant amount of resistance has developed over such projects along the Mekong River.

For most of the last decade, the nation's GDP growth has hovered around 6% and more recently around 8% annually. Unfortunately, that growth has been quite uneven. Wealthier Laotians exist but more than 75% of the people earn less than $2 USD a day and while many of the people living in the lowlands of Laos are doing better, the poorest still live in the upland areas farther away from the Mekong River. Overall, Laos remains among the poorest countries in the world with a life expectancy of only about 60 years for males and 64 years for women. However, both numbers have risen in recent years.

Tourism, another important revenue source in Southeast Asia, has begun to pick up. Most recent estimates are that more than 3.7 million people visited the country in 2013, and the numbers and impact on the economy are expected to grow. As with other countries, COVID affected the tourist trade in Laos in 2020–2021 but it is expected to recover gradually.

One of the more positive, if controversial, economic developments in recent years was the introduction in 2009 of a plan to develop the northern-most provinces using significant amounts of Chinese investment. The plan is to develop a zone of industries from mining and agriculture to tourism although the level of Chinese investment has raised concerns in some quarters. But such plans do not always work out as expected.

In the early 2000s, many had great hopes for the project known as Golden City in Boten, Laos, just across the border from the People's Republic of China, where most of the population is Mandarin-speaking. The project began in 2003 with money and expertise from both Hong Kong and the mainland. The goal was to develop the infrastructure to nurture both tourism and trade. For a time a thriving gambling facility with the complementary hotel and resort facilities emerged. But strong-arm tactics, including murders and beatings of wayward customers forced the Chinese government itself to intervene by discouraging its citizens from crossing the border to gamble and pressuring Lao authorities to shut down the place. It now is abandoned.

During recent years ambitious plans for the construction of a high-speed train from the Chinese border to Vientiane were also put in place with the Chinese providing most of the funding as part of their goal of extending rail road lines from China to Singapore. In December 2021, the lines connecting Vientiane and Boten on the Lao side of the border, and Yuxi-Mohan on the Chinese both formally opened, thus connecting Kunming in China with Vietiane in Laos. Meanwhile, the Japanese funded the construction of a new airport to link the capital with some of the more remote parts of the country to the southeast and along the Vietnamese border. It opened in the summer of 2018.

Perhaps one of the most important economic issues facing the Laotian government was joining the World Trade Organization. By February 2013, the nation had become the WTO's 158th member.

**The Patouxai or "victory gate" Vientiane**

Like their Vietnamese and Chinese neighbors, the Laotian leadership apparently wants economic reform while maintaining their hold on political power. Still the move away from a communist system is relatively new and remains controversial in some quarters. Increases in crime have been noted with fears that the reforms may have gone too far. Those concerns were acted upon during 1999 as the government made a conscious effort to emphasize what it called "traditional Lao values" as a counterweight to the growing obsession with making money. That effort to draw upon Laotian tradition to shore up the nation's leaders has continued.

One of the most profound economic changes has been the government's efforts to commercialize the rural economy. Large parcels of land that were traditionally farmed by peasants have been leased out to larger local and international investors for the production of commercial crops, including rubber, sugar, and eucalyptus. These land transfers have provoked considerable anger among the rural population who have often claimed they were unfairly compensated. The tensions have been significant enough for the government to announce in June 2012 a four-year moratorium on new leases. Estimates are that approximately seven to eight million acres have already been turned into large-scale agricultural plantations.

One of the most troubling occurrences associated with this topic was the disappearance in late 2012 of one of the best known Laotian experts on rural development, the internationally respected Sombath Somphone who, after an education in the United States, had returned to his native Laos to become a very well-known expert on rural farming. His work had ranged from encouraging eco-friendly farming methods to new types of agricultural production. However, somewhere along the way he seems to have angered those in power. Since being arrested by local police, he has not been seen despite the many efforts of various international figures, from Hillary Clinton to Desmond Tutu, to determine his fate.

### From Environmental to Climate Change Challenges

Given the enormous economic changes that have impacted the entire region from East to Southeast Asia over the last generation, Laos remains something of an anomaly. It has not experienced the explosive economic and social transformation as have countries like China, Thailand, Indonesia, and Mongolia; nor has it had the dramatic political changes that some of its neighbors have experienced. Indeed, Laos

remains today, much like it has long been, a largely agricultural country where most people live by food they themselves have grown. Something over 70% of the people still work in agriculture.

The core of Laos's environmental basis is changing as well. As elsewhere deforestation has had a significant impact. Illegal logging and growing populations in need of more farm land have taken their toll. In 1940 forests covered around 70% of the country. By the beginning of the new millennium they were down to only a bit over 40%. On the more positive side, the government claims to understand the problem. It has designated various protected areas and committed itself to expanding the forested areas significantly over the next decade.

Laos and its people might be significantly more isolated than many of their surrounding communities. But that hardly insulates them from the most dramatic global changes occurring because of climate change. Indeed they are especially vulnerable because the local population is so much more immediately dependent on agriculture and on the climate and because they lack the financial resources to adapt to the challenge. In issues like the behavior of water, too much water at one time, as is frequently the case in the era of climate change, or even drier seasons impact agriculture workers even more immediately than city dwellers. But Laotian city dwellers are not off the hook either. The number of people who live in cities has grown in recent years, and most cities in Laos are located on extremely vulnerable river flood plains.

On the more positive side, the officials have recognized the threat of climate change. They have begun an effort not only to help mitigate the problems as they develop but have launched an educational

**Young Laotian monk**
Courtesy of Rusty and Marilyn Staff,
Asia Transpacific Journeys

campaign to help the general public understand the challenge.

### COVID-19

As the news came from China of a new form viral disease, the Lao authorities took drastic measures to prevent the spread in the country. All flights to and from China were canceled. All hotels, casinos, and other places of entertainment were closed. People were advised to avoid all unnecessary social events, including weddings. Lunar New Year celebrations were canceled. Starting on 15 March, some border crossings with Vietnam were closed, and after the first cases in March 2020 all border crossings were closed. There were no cases between April and the end of March 2021. The total number of cases reported was 49, and there were no deaths. Chinese-supplied vaccines began to arrive in March 2021, as did COVAX-supplied AstraZeneca.

The first two deaths in May 2021 led to a national lockdown. This failed to stop the spread of the virus however, and by December 2021, there had been a total of 110,000 cases and 360 deaths. Cases then began to fall back. By April 27, 2022, the total number of cases had reached 206,512 and there had been 737 deaths. The problem seems to have been poor personal hygiene and an underfunded health service. There may have also been a certain amount of complacency over the handling of earlier pandemics. The relatively underdeveloped nature of the transport infrastructure led to difficulties in providing healthcare and getting vaccines into remote areas.

### The Future

Laos faces many challenges. The combination of divisions within the ruling elite and external challenges to their rule suggests that the relative calm of Laos during recent years may not last. People are apparently more willing to criticize the government's inability to improve the economy fundamentally. The recent willingness to re-embrace traditional Laotian values and to allow greater decentralization may very well reflect the regime's general concern about maintaining its authority. The fact that there has also been a significant effort to bring younger and more educated leaders into the power structure is certainly another sign of that concern.

Moreover relations with Thailand continue along their complicated "love-hate" route, but they have been improving significantly. Still Laos is now a member of ASEAN and is likely to benefit from those improved ties. It is also attempting to broaden its relations by strengthening

# Laos

links with other countries, especially the People's Republic of China and Vietnam.

The long-term efforts to revitalize the entire Mekong river area and to make it a more effective tool for trade throughout the region are eventually likely to be very beneficial to Laos. The regional development of the Mekong region, coupled with efforts to build new highways and railroads that would run through Laos and more directly and conveniently link the nation with its neighbors from China and Vietnam to Thailand, are likely to have a major impact on Laos' future.

Overall, the government has increasingly committed itself to further integration in South East Asia. This was best exemplified by its sponsoring of the 2009 games in Vientiane. It also succeeded in joining the World Trade Organization. Meanwhile, growth rates have remained relatively stable and reasonably healthy with recent growth rates coming in at around 7%. Not forgetting that the new airport will make Laos much more able to accommodate the larger number of tourists they are hoping to attract in coming years.

Of course Laos's economic future continues to be linked to that of China especially with the construction of a railroad linking the two nations expected completed in 2021. And that linkage with China will no doubt become even more important over the coming years as China strengthens and the influence of Western countries like the United States diminishes.

# Malaysia

**The modern city of Kuala Lumpur**                    Courtesy of the Embassy of Malaysia

**Area:** 128,775 sq. mi. (333,525 sq. km.)
**Population:** 33,221,122 (2022 est.)
**Capital City:** Kuala Lumpur, pop. 1,809,699 (2022 est.)
**Climate:** Tropically hot and humid
**Neighboring Countries:** Thailand (North); Singapore (South); Indonesia (South and Southwest)
**Official Languages:** Malay and English
**Other Principal Tongues:** Chinese, Tamil
**Ethnic Background:** Malay and other indigenous (58%), Chinese (24%), Indian (8%), others (10%) (2000 est.)
**Principal Religions:** Islam, Buddhism, Hinduism, and Christianity
**Main Exports:** (to Japan, Singapore, U.S., China, Thailand) Natural rubber, palm oil, tin, timber, petroleum, and electronic goods
**Main Imports:** (from Japan, Singapore, China, Thailand, Taiwan South Korea, Indonesia, Germany, U.S.) Chemicals, machinery, electronics, transportation equipment, plastics, iron, and steel
**Currency:** Ringgit
**Former Colonial Status:** The British East India Company acquired the islands of Penang in 1786 and port city of Melaka in 1824. The various states of Malaya

entered into protectorate status from 1874 to 1914; they remained British colonies or protectorates until 1957 with the exception of the Japanese occupation from 1942 to 1945. Sabah was administered by the British North Borneo Company from 1881 to 1941, occupied by the Japanese from 1942 until 1945 and was a British Colony from 1946 to 1963. Sarawak was granted to Sir James Brooke by the Sultan of Brunei in 1841; it became a British protectorate in 1888; after the Japanese were expelled in 1945, Sir Charles Vyner Brooke, the ruling Raja, agreed to administration as a British Crown Colony, which lasted until 1963.
**National Day:** August 31, 1957
**Chief of State:** Sultan Abdullah of Pahang (since January 24, 2020. Note: the official title is *Yang di-Pertuan Agong*, unofficially known as King)
**Head of Government:** Prime Minister Muhyiddin Yassin (since March 1, 2020)
**National Flag:** 14 horizontal stripes of red and white with a dark blue rectangle in the upper left corner containing a yellow crescent and a 14-pointed star
**Per Capita GDP Annual Income:**

$27,923.70 (2020 World Bank est.) (purchasing power parity)

Located at the southern end of the Malay Peninsula, the mainland portion of Malaysia consists of a broad central belt of forested mountains. In the areas of Malaysia where the mountains give way to low plains the vegetation turns into a thick green jungle situated on swampy plains, particularly in the coastal area. The climate is uniform during the year because of the closeness to the equator—hot and humid.

The Borneo states, also known as East Malaysia, contain wide coastal lowlands that have relatively poor soil and are interrupted by frequent rivers. The altitude rises in the south as the border with Indonesia is approached. The division between the two occupants of the island straddles a scenic range of rugged mountains the highest of which is Mt. Kinabalu, towering majestically to a height of 13,000 feet. Few people of the western world have penetrated Borneo to view this remote area, which is inhabited by an indigenous people who have advanced little beyond Stone Age life. The people of Malaysia are quite similar to their Indonesian

# Malaysia

neighbors—a mixture of Polynesian, Mongol, Indian, and Caucasian origins. There is also a large minority of Chinese who are descendants of laborers brought in by the colonial British.

### History

The history of Malaysia, as a country, really begins during the colonial period, when the British started to establish their holdings in the area. Before that, the various regions that today are associated with Malaysia were part of several different political communities ranging from the mainland based Siamese kingdom to the north to the various commercial empires in what later became Indonesia.

The Malay language was prominent enough in the region's early life to serve as the principal language for commercial activities until the early modern era. Throughout the region, regardless of a person's ethnicity, knowing Malay was absolutely necessary to take part in the international trade of the region.

Malaya might have been colonized sooner. The Portuguese captured Melaka (Malacca) in 1511 but lost it to the Dutch in 1641. Dutch interest was focused on the fabled riches of Indonesia. The absence of Dutch control permitted the British East India Company to enter the area without opposition. They took Penang in 1786 and Melaka itself in 1795, those gaining control of the Straits of Malacca, an important route on the way to China. Singapore was added in 1819, and the three settlements became the Straits Settlements, still under the East India Company, in 1826. The East India Company's interest in the area declined after it lost its monopoly of the China trade in the 1830s and its command of the Indian trade after the Indian Mutiny of 1857.

In 1867, the Sraits Settlements became a Crown colony. Thereafter, in order to protect their trade routes, the British compelled the rulers of the small individual states of Malaya to accept "protection." This included the presence of a British adviser at each Malay court to ensure that British goals were achieved. Four outlying, impoverished states of Siam (Thailand) in the north were added to Malaya in 1909.

The sultanates were arranged in two groups. A group of four became the Federated Malay States, created in 1896, had a British administrator who had the final say on non-religious matters. After the last independent sultanate, Johor, came under British administration, it and four others became the Unfederated Malay States in 1914. These had a British advisor who had less power than the administrators. The local rulers were treated as royalty, with court ceremonial protected and the rulers treated with great honor. But the British were in control.

The rubber tree was brought from Brazil and planted in the rich soil to grow in an almost ideal climate. Drawn by the natural resources and the stability of the area,

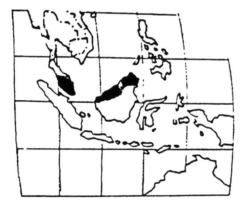

British capital poured in. There was also a mass influx of Chinese and Indian laborers to work the rubber plantations and the tin mines. In many cases the Chinese soon entered commerce and some became extremely wealthy and influential.

The arrival of immigrants from China and India created the ethnic mix which has been the most fundamental feature of modern Malaysian social and political life. By 1939, 45% of the population were Malay, 39% Chinese, and the rest Indian and Westerners. This tripartite division of the population between native Malays who constitute around half the population and the Chinese and Indian communities, remains to this day.

During the British rule the later "division of labor" also began to appear as Chinese moved into the economy with the Malays largely remaining less urbanized or in some cases becoming part of the British civil administration of the area. The British often favored the Malays, at the expense of the Chinese, a preference that more recent Malaysian governments have also followed. More importantly, British rule not only saw the evolution of the region from one that was relatively homogeneous to the more multi-ethnic society of modern Malaysia. As elsewhere British policy was to retain its authority by "divide and rule" processes that have certainly contributed to the problems that have affected Malaysia in later years.

### World War II

Malay, with is rubber and tin, was an obvious target for Japan once the Pacific War began. When the Japanese arrived in 1942, they treated the Chinese with much greater brutality than they did the Malays. In reaction, the local Chinese, whose own politics were more tied to developments

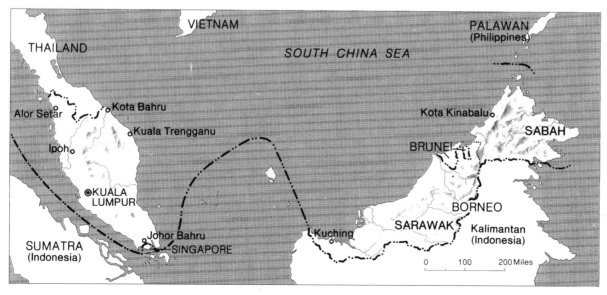

228

within China, formed an anti-Japanese guerrilla force of Chinese, most of them communists, who operated from bases deep within the thick jungles. Receiving weapons smuggled in by the British, the guerrillas fought their non-communist rivals as well as the Japanese. In contrast to the Chinese community, there was some sympathy among Malayans for the Japanese activities. Many people in Southeast Asia had been attracted to the Japanese calls to free the region from Western colonialism. The Chinese, well aware of the atrocities the Japanese had committed in China, did not view Japan's forces so positively.

After the war, the British moved to unify the various regions that would later come to form modern Malaysia. A major problem, though, was the indigenous Malay concerns about maintaining their own dominance in a future independent Malay state. The eventual compromise offered freedom within a constitutional structure which included support for the traditional Malay leaders, the recognition of Malay and Islam as the official language and religion respectively, and an overall structure that favored the Malay over non-Malay peoples.

The arrangement, as it was called, included an understanding that, while the Malays would control politics, the economy would be dominated by the non-Malay citizens. Not all members of the Chinese community were happy with the agreement, and for the next decade a major insurrection developed led by local Chinese communists who had earlier been active in the resistance against the Japanese. While the entire period, known as "The Emergency," was very traumatic for the region, the rebellion was never able to draw much popular support and especially not from the Malay community. The British mounted a huge military effort that reduced the rebellion to almost nothing within a few years.

### A New Nation Emerges: 1957

The British granted Malaya internal self-government in 1955 and full independence in 1957. Under the able leadership of Prime Minister Tunku Abdul Rahman, head of the dominant Alliance Party, (now known as the National Front), which included then and now, a dominant Malay party known as the United Malay National Organization (UMNO) as well as other parties representing the Chinese and Indian communities. UMNO, which has dominated Malaysian political life ever since, originally emerged as a reaction to British efforts to grant more rights to non-Malays. The party has not, in the years since, lessened its commitment to

strengthening the position of Malay peoples within modern Malaysia. As we will see below, UMNO has dramatically improved the social and economic standing of the average Malay citizen but tensions over such favoritism continue to plague the country.

By the early 1960s Malaysia's chief problem, though, was not about indigenous ethnic tensions but with their immediate neighbors, especially with Sukarno, the fiery nationalist leader of Indonesia. Faced with Sukarno's increased interest in dominating the region, and a marked swing to the left in Singapore politics, Rahman and the British devised a plan to unite Malaya, Singapore, Sabah, and Sarawak into the Federation of Malaysia. The tiny, oil-rich Sultanate of Brunei was also invited to join, but declined. After many complicated negotiations the federation came into existence in September 1963.

Sukarno, encouraged by his success in acquiring West Irian, (now Irian Jaya) from the Dutch without a fight, was furious about the federation's formation. A confrontation with Malaysia began. This involved sporadic fighting in the remote parts of Borneo, and unsuccessful attempts to land Indonesian guerrillas in Malaya. The confrontation was quietly discontinued in the mid-1960s after General Suharto seized power from Sukarno.

The new Malaysian Federation faced significant domestic problems as well. There was continuing tension between the Chinese and Malays, especially over the role of Singapore, whose population is overwhelmingly Chinese, and which resented Malay domination of the central government. When Prime Minister Lee Kuan Yew of Singapore tried to increase his party's influence and power beyond Singapore and within the Malaysian Federation at large, a crisis erupted. It led to the expulsion of Singapore from Malaysia in August 1965.

**Former Prime Minister Dato Seri Dr. Mahathir Mohamad**

### A Challenge to the System

If Singapore's expulsion from the federation only two years after its formation

had lessened tensions between Kuala Lumpur and Singapore, the core issues of Malay, non-Malay relations continued. As will be recalled, the compromise of the late 1940s has seen a political system which favored ethnic Malays while allowing the non-Malays to dominate the economy.

In the years leading up to 1969, the Malay leadership had been able to successfully dominate the country's political system. But the elections of 1969 challenged the political and economic compromise that had been at the root of the new nation's stability. Non-Malay parties won more votes than those of the Malay allies. While no dramatic change in government direction was immediately in the offing, it aroused the concerns of the Malay population, and hundreds died in the resulting communal violence.

This led the government to proclaim a state of emergency and to suspend the constitution; parliamentary government was, however, restored in early 1971. In the following years the government committed itself to improving the status of Malays, economically and socially. The hope was that if Malays were more integrated into the economic life of the community there

Mahathir originally gained public attention with a series of articles and then a book dealing with what he called *The Malay Dilemma*, which dealt with what he described as the second-class status of Malays. A fervent nationalist, who wrote in English and even addressed such controversial subjects as the emancipation of women, his work was banned by the authorities when it came out in 1970. For a time he even had to go into hiding from the authorities for his outspoken comments against the leadership.

But given his support among younger Malays he was eventually invited back into UMNO and by the mid 1970s began his assent toward the premiership. In the years since, Dr. Mahathir has become one of the most outspoken leaders of his generation and a frequent and regular critic of the West even as he has successfully worked to integrate Malaysia itself into the modern industrialized world economy. Since his retirement he has emerged as a frequent critic of the government and his successors. Indeed, most dramatic was his decision in 2018 at the age 92 to come out of retirement and successfully lead the opposition in challenging Prime Minister Najib's ruling coalition in the elections.

# Malaysia

**Petronas Towers, among the tallest buildings in the world**

would be less cause for the sort of social tensions that so commonly existed.

In the general elections of 1974 the National Front (the Alliance Party plus some smaller ones) won a sweeping victory. During the elections, strong precautions were taken to avoid the violence of 1969. In fact, to preserve social peace it became illegal to even discuss the issues that separated the different ethnic communities or the various programs designed to promote the economic life of the Malays.

### Dr. Mahathir Emerges

In the mid 1970s a new political activist emerged who would eventually dominate Malaysian politics over the next generation. First chosen as prime minister in 1981 Dr. Mahathir Mohamad, a physician by training, was the first non-aristocrat to become first minister and a man whose political views have led him, along with Singapore's Lee Kuan Yew, to be seen as one of the most articulate, if at times deeply controversial, spokesmen for an "Asian Voice" in world affairs.

In the years after his arrival to power, Mahathir managed to grow increasingly influential. He consistently prevailed over opponents within his own party, UMNO, and over other centers of power within Malaysia. Over the years the Mahathir government also tried to curb the constitutional powers of the various Malay Sultans. In January 1984 it was successful in abolishing the Yang di-Pertuan Agong's power to veto legislation.

Several political problems of fairly serious proportions appeared in the 1980s. One was leadership struggles within both the main components of the ruling coalition which governs the country: the dominant UMNO, and the less powerful Malayan Chinese Association (MCA). Another was a rise in the activity of militant Islam, especially among the 20,000 Malaysian students in the United States and in Sa-bah (North Borneo), where there were violent Muslim demonstrations early in 1986 against the state government.

There were serious tensions within UMNO in 1987, reflecting a leadership struggle, a generational gap, and a growing

feeling that the party was strong enough to govern without the inconvenience of a coalition with other parties representing different races. Prime Minister Mahathir won a close vote for the party leadership in April and then purged some of his rivals. The relatively passive Malayan Chinese Association was troubled not only by a leadership problem, but also by a challenge from outside the National Front by the Democratic Action Party (DAP), a younger and more vigorous party.

In a series of sudden arrests that were strongly criticized within and outside the country, the government cracked down on its opponents in 1987. Some of them were UMNO members, but more of them belonged to the DAP.

Prime Minister Mahathir long admired the economic dynamism of Japan and South Korea and often sought to use them as models for Malaysia. More broadly, he emphasized an "Asian" approach to economic issues. He spoke enthusiastically of an economic organization (the East Asian Economic Grouping) that would include the ASEAN states, China, South Korea, Taiwan, Hong Kong, and Japan, but would exclude other nations particularly the United States. During the economic crisis of mid-1997 it was Mahathir who was most ready to propose regional solutions to the area's problems from the use of local currencies for trading to a regional equivalent of the International Monetary Fund.

Dr. Mahathir's ideas were not always well received in either Australia or the United States or even among his Asian economic partners. Still, he was

**Peninsular Malaysia
The nine states with hereditary rulers,
and Penang and Malacca**

increasingly admired as an outspoken voice for the "non-Western" and specifically Asian communities. After the infamous terrorist attacks of September 11, 2001, many in the West predictably gained a new appreciation for Dr. Mahathir, who was increasingly seen as a more moderate and "modern" Islamic leader in a world increasingly influenced by radical Islamic militants like Osama Bin Laden or those who had only recently dominated Afghanistan's then Taliban-led government.

### Contemporary Politics

Malaysia, a member of the British Commonwealth, is nominally a constitutional monarchy with a bicameral legislature composed of the Senate, Dewan Negara, and House of Representatives, Dewan Ra'ayat. The parliament in Malaysia is not an effective institution for the discussion of public policy. The opposition has limited time to speak and often receives bills for consideration the same day on which they are to be voted. The Standing Order of Parliament prohibits treasonable or seditious words, the interpretation of which is left up to the Speaker of the Dewan Ra'ayat who is appointed by the government (prime minister). Questions about how representative the system really is were raised when a new law was passed that made it illegal to question voting roles. The opposition parties, which opposed the new legislation, had argued that checking the roles was important as many claimed they continued to list people who died.

Certain topics such as the special rights of Malays are not subject to discussion. Tough questioning by the opposition is rare and would not be widely reported in the media in any case, since it is either owned or licensed by the government. Overall, the prime ministership of Mahathir, who served from 1981 to 2003, evolved into a particularly powerful position.

The country has an unusual system for selecting the ceremonial leader the Yang di-Pertuan Agong (King). The Yang di-Pertuan Agong serves for five years and is selected on a rotational basis from among the hereditary rulers from 9 of Malaysia's 13 states.

Elections in Malaysia have generally been clean, unlike those in many other developing countries. The single-member district formula benefits the government as does the fact that districts are often gerrymandered to favor the Malay voter.

Although important opposition parties are quite active Malaysian politics have long been dominated by the UMNO that has ruled in coalition with other small parties. In practical terms, really significant political issues and the fate of individual

**Parliament House, Kuala Lumpur**

governmental leaders has largely been determined more within the UMNO itself rather than between UMNO and her coalition partners. Among the opposition parties PAS, the Parti Islam Se Malaysia, has been openly advocating the creation of an Islamic State in Malaysia.

The PAS's momentum, though, was somewhat weakened after the September 11, 2001 terrorist attacks in the United States and the commencement of the worldwide campaign against terrorism that Malaysia's own government, under the strongly secular-minded Dr. Mahathir took part in. PAS has become a significant player in Malaysian politics. It may become even more so under its new more radically conservative leader Abdul Hadi Awang if the PAS's new, more outspoken leadership does not backfire by alienating the more moderate Malaysian voters.

Certainly among the most significant issues of the 1990s was the question of who would assume the mantle of Prime Minister Mahathir's authority after the long dominant leader left the scene. One early element of that issue was addressed in November 1993 when the UMNO was involved in selecting a deputy president. This post, within Malaysia's dominant political party, was tantamount to a guarantee of gaining the post of deputy prime minister, and eventually the prime

ministership. The contest involved the Minister of Finance, Anwar Ibrahim, and the then Deputy Prime Minister, Ghafar Baba. The Prime Minister, Dr. Mahathir seemed to prefer Ghafar Baba, but Anwar won a decisive victory and was appointed deputy prime minister.

Thus began a complicated relationship that has seen Anwar over the years become the most obvious heir to Mahathir's leadership and then later the powerful prime minister's most implacable opponent, an imprisoned felon, and a contemporary political opposition leader. More than personalities initially separated the two leaders. For example, relations with the more activist Islamic community have often been problematic. One significant challenge for the government in recent years came from the radical Islamic group, Al-Arqam. The sect was eventually banned. Al-Arqam had been operating hundreds of schools and many businesses throughout the country. As mentioned above, PAS, the party most openly advocating an Islamic state, has become more important in recent years.

As with other issues, the style of Dr. Mahathir and his former ally Anwar differed. The prime minister, at times, seemed to go out of his way to challenge conservative Muslims by suggesting that a too rigid adherence to Islam might impede economic

# Malaysia

growth. Interestingly, the question of whether one wore a beard became an important issue in measuring the growth of Islamic influence in party politics. Anwar, a former Muslim activist, wore a very discrete goatee, while Mahathir went clean shaven, a subtle difference, but one that does carry considerable symbolism. The issue was reflected as well in the clothing choices of their wives. Mrs. Mahathir wore her hair uncovered while Anwar's wife covered her head in public.

For most of his period in power, Mahathir's leadership was largely unquestioned. Nevertheless, in October 1996, the party's convention saw very real competition between the prime minister's followers and those of Anwar Ibrahim. For a time it even looked like Anwar's supporters were pulling ahead. By the time the polling was completed a balance had been maintained between the two groups and Mahathir's power to sway his party's loyalists confirmed.

The following year, as the full brunt of the economic crises hit Malaysia, the long outspoken Mahathir lashed out at those he felt had brought on the crisis. His primary target was international currency traders. While many perhaps more objective economists have come to the same conclusion, his comments, coupled with suggestions about controlling the financial markets with new laws, seemed to make the situation worse. Fear that such laws might hamper international currency movement caused Malaysia's currency to drop even further.

Meanwhile, provoked by the worsening situation, Anwar stepped forward to calm the markets by denying any such plans. Anwar was wrong. Mahathir not only introduced controls on some currency and stock exchanges but imposed price controls on a limited number of commodities as well. As for his longtime deputy, while Anwar's monetary policies as the nation's longtime finance minister had put him largely within the range of international opinion on economic decision-making, they contrasted deeply with those of his boss, Prime Minister Mahathir.

Over the summer of 1998, it was clear that behind the scenes the prime minister was moving against Anwar's supporters. By early September, the strong-minded leader had driven his most important financial advisers from power including his longtime heir, Anwar Ibrahim. In fact, over the next week, Anwar found himself not only imprisoned, but beaten by his jailers and charged with an enormous range of sexual and corruption charges. The arrest and subsequent conviction of Anwar on charges of corruption sparked considerable international media attention and inspired large pro-Anwar demonstrations

**Former Prime Minister Datuk Seri Abdullah Badawi**

**Prime Minister Mohamed Najib bin Abdul Razak**

throughout Malaysia. The former deputy prime minister himself was to remain imprisoned until he was released by the courts in the months after Dr. Mahathir left office.

In the elections that followed the crisis Mahathir's ruling National Front Coalition still did quite well, winning 148 seats of a possible 193. Nevertheless, it was clear that significant problems were brewing below the surface. For the first time most Malays voted against Mahathir's own UMNO organization. In fact, Mahathir's coalition had won due to the support of Indian and Chinese voters. Some of them were apparently nervous about the influence of Islamic groups among the opposition.

Dr. Mahathir had clearly survived the many challenges he faced not only from the internal politics of Malaysia but the impact of the Asian economic crisis. By the summer of 2002 he was ready to make

his future plans publicly known. He did so in a particularly dramatic fashion, announcing tearfully in June that he was resigning from government a move that apparently shocked everyone in attendance. What happened next, though, was enough to make observers quite skeptical as within the hour he had taken back the resignation and announced that he would temporarily put off his departure. Moreover, he was supporting as his replacement his new deputy prime minister, Abdullah Badawi.

## Malaysia Enters the Post-Mahathir Era

Dr. Mahathir was Malaysia's fourth prime minister and in that capacity served the country for over 20 years. These were years that saw the nation transformed in countless ways. While he was at times extraordinarily controversial both within Malaysia and on the international scene his impact on Malaysia was largely a positive one. He promoted a multi-racial society while maintaining the centrality of the Malay community. Moreover he worked diligently to bring Malaysia into the world economy and encouraged an important role for a moderate and modern minded Islamic experience.

By October 2003 it was time for the sometimes larger than life Dr. Mahathir to leave office, replaced by his chosen successor Datuk Seri Abdullah Ahmad Badawi. Early impressions can be deceiving, but it initially appeared that Prime Minister Badawi's differences with Dr. Mahathir's would be more those of style than substance. He remained committed to most of his predecessor's policies, including the controversial decision to introduce the teaching of science and math in English. The purpose was to prepare Malaysian students better for the globalized competition they would soon face, while being more closely linked than Dr. Mahathir to his nation's Islamic heritage.

However, Abdullah's approach to Islam was hardly that envisioned by Islamic hardliners. Although he was an Islamic scholar, after coming into office, he worked to promote a vision of Islam that is as much cultural as religious. He strove to encourage better dialogue between the Islamic community and the West. At the same time, he was quick to shut down a Malaysian newspaper that printed copies of the infamous Danish cartoons that provoked such international outrage in 2006.

If the new prime minister's basic policies were a continuation of those of his predecessor's, his personal style was more conciliatory. This approach won him improved relations with countries from Australia to the United States. Coupled with Abdullah's early initiative, an anti-corruption campaign especially centered on the police—it was popular enough to give UMNO a major victory in the 2004 parliamentary elections.

His success though did not turn out to be long lived. During the late fall of 2007, the largest political rally in over a decade took place in Kuala Lumpur. Tens of thousands of people, led by the controversial former deputy prime minister, Anwar Ibrahim, called for electoral reforms. This is hardly a surprising demand given that Malaysia likes to think of itself as a democracy. Nevertheless, it has been governed by the same political party since 1957.

By the spring of 2008 the calls for reform had culminated in a humiliating showing by the government at the polls. The elections that took place in March resulted in a huge defeat for UMNO. It lost control of several state governments, from Penang and Selangor to Perak and Kedah, while the current coalition, which has led Malaysia since 1969, dropped a significant number of seats in the national parliament. The primary defectors were the government's ethnically Indian and Chinese supporters.

Opposition votes went to a coalition of different parties that had forged an alliance against the UMNO. Especially significant was the political reemergence of Malaysia's former deputy prime minister, Anwar Ibrahim, who had earlier endured six years in jail after his falling out with Dr. Mathathir. To make matters even more complicated, not only had Dr. Mathathir's disgraced former deputy begun a major comeback, but the nation's outspoken former leader had been feuding with his chosen successor, Prime Minister Badawi, whom he blamed for the weakening state of the UMNO.

By August 2008 Anwar Ibrahim's effort to stage a fuller political comeback was

**Seeking public awareness of AIDS**

well underway. He won a seat in parliament while Badawai lost control of his party and eventually the prime ministership when his former deputy, Mohamed Najib bin Abdul Razak, assumed leadership of the party and government. In some ways, the new prime minister offered a fresh perspective. He spoke openly of the need to discuss publicly some of the more controversial elements of Malaysian society, such as the deep ethnic tensions that can bubble dangerously to the surface. His predecessors had been silent about this. More dramatically, he proceeded to remove some of the more discriminatory government policies that reserved special hiring privileges for ethnic Malays.

On the other hand, his government continued the authorities' long long-term efforts to undermine Anwar Ibrahim. In what appeared to be yet another attempt to destroy Ibrahim's electoral popularity, the government again accused him of the sort of sexual misbehavior reminiscent of the dubious charges that had caused him to languish in jail earlier in the decade. Another trial, much like that of the late 1990s,

started again during 2010 with the obvious goal of weakening him and his supporters. Of course, the government had plenty of reason to be concerned. After all, its ruling coalition had found itself significantly less powerful after the last elections. Indeed, it lost its two-thirds majority domination.

More dramatic has been the rise of a very energetic reform movement—the Coalition for Free and Fair Elections or more simply Bersih ("Clean" in Malay). It was able to organize mass rallies. In July 2011, one attracted tens of thousands of demonstrators and resulted in a confrontation with security forces who used tear gas and water cannons and arrested thousands of people. A similar confrontation took place almost a year later when another large demonstration by Bersih was attacked by police who used everything from tear gas and water cannons while arresting hundreds. Predictably, the government also charged its tenacious nemesis, Anwar Ibrahim, for his involvement in the rallies. To no one's surprise, Anwar denounced the latest legal assaults on him as simply more political harassment.

By the spring of 2013 the substance of Malaysia's politics had not much changed from the fault lines of the previous decade. Prime Minister Najib's center-right coalition government, led by his National Front, promoted national unity and economic development. Unfortunately while the prime minister himself has continued to enjoy relatively widespread popularity, the government has lost support. This was not good news for the Malaysia's leadership given that elections were scheduled for May 2013.

Hoping to retain a semblance of popularity and with the upcoming elections in mind, the government moved to arouse conservative support by a wide variety of measures, from banning books on sex education to forcing the cancelation of a gay arts festival. Clearly, the old ways were not working as they once had. In truth, it

**Rural life, Penang**

# Malaysia

**Malaysia's "come back kid," Anwar Ibrahim**

was not just the popularity of politicians like Anwar Ibrahim that changed the situation. Especially significant was the emergence of the website, *Malaysia Now*, that attracted around 300,000 visitors a day. It is significantly less monitored than the traditional Malaysia print media. It is within the web and, of course, in the streets that Malaysia's dissident community has found its voice.

The ruling coalition does seem to be aware that Malaysian politics is evolving. Even as they have moved to enhance their Islamic credentials, they have also implemented reforms allowing for more peaceful political gatherings and for college students to join political parties.

The opposition, led by Anwar Ibrahim, proved unable to form a winning coalition, as was shown in the May 2013 elections, one of the hardest fought in the country's history. While the coalition gained an impressive 89 seats, thus denying the governing party a two-thirds majorityt. Nevertheless, Prime Minister Najib's supporters took 133 seats in the parliament, enough to allow him another term as leader.

But the victory was not the triumph that Prime Minister Najib Razak hoped for. By 2015, his popularity plummeted, not the least because he was involved in the fraudulent receipt of enormous amounts of money derived from state funds. There was also disquiet about a new goods and sales tax (GST). The government responded to the widespread criticism with threats to stop activists going abroad "to safeguard the country's image." Before long, former Prime Minister Mahathir emerged from retirement to challenge the government

with a newly organized coalition, Pakatan Harapan (Pact of Hope), which was successful in the May 2018 elections, thus ending the 61-year rule of the Barisan Nasional (National Union). The Pakatan Harapan also won a majority in seven of Malaysia's states, which meant that, for the first time since independence, the majority of states were not led by the UMNO (United Malay National Organization) party, the main component part of the Barisan Nasional.

The day following the election, the outgoing prime minister, Najib Razak, resigned as the UMNO chair and the Barisan Nasional president. Immediately, he and several other former officials were barred from leaving the country. Later, Najib and his wife, Rosmah Mansur, were arrested on a number of charges, including money laundering and corruption, while large amounts of cash and valuables, including 300 handbags—gifts, according to Rosmah Mansur—were taken from their house. In July 2020, he would receive a series of prison sentences. Anwar Ibrahim was released from jail and pardoned on the 2015 sodomy charge, and on May 21 his wife, Dr. Wan Azizah Wan Ismail, was elected deputy prime minister. Anwar in turn won a landslide victory in a by-election in October and returned to parliament, apparently reconciled to Mahathir.

The new government repealed the unpopular GST, electoral districts were withdrawn to be more equal, the "Anti-Fake News" Law was repealed, and the death penalty was abolished, with pending executions cancelled. But in other ways, things continued as before. Two women were sentenced to be caned for "unnatural acts" in August, while that same month the minister of religion, who sent out rather mixed messages on the subject, said that Malaysia had never recognized the existence of LGBT people.

On January 6, 2019, there was a bombshell. Sultan Muhammed V, elected king in December 2016, became the first king to resign before the end of his five-year term. No explanation was offered, but there were widespread rumors about a lavish lifestyle and not welcoming the 2018 change of government. In his place, Sultan Abdullah Sultan Ahad Shah of Pahang, became king. During the course of the year, there was a decline in the popularity of Mahathir's government, which lost a by-election. The LGBT question did not go away. Questioned at a trade conference in March, the minister of tourism said that he did not think there were any people like that in Malaysia. Nevertheless, the religious courts continued to take a different view, with five men accused of "unnatural offenses" sentenced to be caned, fined and imprisoned. There were also problems in international affairs (see below).

The coalition that made up Pakatan Harapan was in trouble. This was partly because the reconciliation between Mahathir and Anwar Ibrahim proved fragile. Despite promises, Mahathir would not name Anwar as is successor, the 2018 coalition collapsed in February 2020. During the week of turmoil that followed, UMNO staged a return. The new prime minister, elected on March 1, was Muhyiddin Yassin, the minister of home affairs and president of Bersatu, a Malay nationalist party formed in 2016 to oppose Najib. Dr. Mahathir was also a party member, but he turned on Muhyiddin, claiming that the election was a fake. In fact, it took until mid-July 2020 before the new prime minister could muster a parliamentary majority. Even then, there were difficulties. As the country faced COVID 19, the king in October refused a prime ministerial request for a state of emergency, while the government faced claims that it was using the pandemic as an excuse to crack down in dissent. COVID-19 continued to dominate the first half of 2021, although there were other problems, such as heavy flooding. Mahathir continued to snipe at his successor, repeating the charge of using the pandemic to stifle opposition.

Muhyiddin claimed he could survive but when he criticized UNMO over corruption, the party withdrew its support and he resigned on 16 August. His deputy, Ismail Sabri Yaakob, who was also UMNO deputy vice-president, took over and

**Tri-shaw in Malaysia**

UNMO returned. The new prime minister concluded an agrreement with the opposition under Anwar, which included a number of electoral reforms. The voting age was lowered from 21 to 18, and party defections would be prevented.

### Foreign Relations

Malaysia has been an effective actor in international politics for some time. In fact, Malaysia has increasingly taken the liberty of speaking for the developing countries in the world community and particularly in international forums like APEC and the WTO. Malaysia, along with Singapore, have emerged as the most effective representatives of an Asian vision for the future and one that was strongly backed by the economic accomplishments of both regimes over the last generation. The government has also moved to strengthen its ties to the People's Republic of China.

Relations with neighboring countries are often strained over the question of illegal immigrants, who play an important role in areas such as the construction industry. There are periodic crackdowns, with roundups of those without the proper documentation. Usually, domestic pressure for the release of workers frees up some of those detained, but others are held in camps, often in poor conditions. Tensions with Thailand are increased by alleged Malaysian support, including training, of Islamic groups from southern Thailand.

Other issues have as well affected regional relations. Disputes continue over the many islands that dot the area. The disagreement with Indonesia over Sipadan and Ligitan islands off the coast of Sabah, East Malaysia, remained causes of concern during the 1990s. The dispute over Pulau Batu Putih ("White Rock Island") with Singapore was referred to The Hague by mutual agreement. In 2008, the International Court split the claims between the two countries, to which both agreed. However, since 2017, Malaysia has sought to reopen the case. The claims and counter claims continue throughout the region. For example, China, Malaysia and four other countries claim all or part of the South China Sea and the Spratly Islands.

As we have seen elsewhere in the region, relations between the various nations located around the South China Sea have been particularly tense due to China's growing assertiveness regarding its sovereignty in the area. But for Malaysia, tensions with China were particularly strained in 2014 given that Malaysia's infamously lost commercial airliner was largely carrying Chinese civilians on its ill-fated flight to Beijing. The lost flight has not been located. A new problem arose in August 2018 when the Najib government put on hold two major Chinese-backed projects, an East Coast rail link to Thailand and a gas pipeline in Sarawak, because of costs. Then Prime Minister Mahathir agreed to restart these in 2019 and also to rejoin China's "Belt and Road" plan, with which they were associated.

But in 2021, there were further tensions with China over the South China Sea, when Malaysia protested over Chinese air incursions into its airspace.

Malaysia maintains strong ties with the Islamic countries of the Middle East, but it has also officially attempted to improve relations with Israel. On a more practical level, that has not always been easy. A visiting Israeli cricket team was greeted with protests during its spring 1997 visit to this heavily Muslim country. Nevertheless, as within practically all Islamic societies, sympathy with the Palestinians in their struggle with Israel as well as a criticism of recent American policies in Iraq and Afghanistan find many in agreement. Islamic-related tensions also increased after Mahathir returned to power in 2018. The following year, Malaysia lost the right to hold the 2019 World Para Swimming Championships, which had been awarded in 2017, when it announced that Israeli athletes would not be allowed to compete. The championship went to London instead. Also in 2019, both Myanmar and India accused Malaysia of interference in their internal affairs after adverse comments on the treatment of Muslims. In December 2019, there was much criticism from the Organization for Islamic Co-operation of Mahathir's proposal to hold an Islamic summit. The organization argued that only it had the power to convene such a meeting. In the event, only 20 of the 57 members of that body attended.

Relations with America have usually been quite complicated as well. Prime Minister Mahathir seemed at times to go out of his way to arouse the concerns of many in the United States, the last superpower and an important Malaysian market. Not only did he charge in 1997 that Western financial speculators had caused the economic meltdown, but went on to claim that Jews were behind the "attack" against Muslim countries like Indonesia and Malaysia. If that were not enough to arouse the ire of many in Washington, he subsequently led a large entourage to Cuba to encourage trade with the Castro regime.

The Americans retaliated when the former U.S. Vice President Al Gore chose the fall 1998 meeting of APEC, which took place in Kuala Lumpur, to denounce the Malaysian government's treatment of Anwar Ibrahim. Some might have wondered if the Americans were more upset about Mahathir's anti-democratic activities or his effort to impose currency controls. In either case, having Gore act as if Anwar were a hero not unexpectedly turned to the prime minister's advantage as many Malaysians resented the American interference.

Although many in Malaysia have sided with the more anti-American Islamic activists and denounced the American bombing in Afghanistan and the invasion of Iraq, the prime minister found himself in a complicated situation. On the one hand, he remained a vehement critic of the West. On the other hand, Mahathir also spoke out against the dangers of Islamic activism in politics and most recently against suicide bombers. Because of that stance the American administration, which has often shunned him, began working to improve relations with Malaysia's particularly

**National Planetarium**

# Malaysia

influential moderate and secular Muslim national leader.

He was even received as a guest in Washington, DC, during the spring of 2002. That is not surprising because while Malaysia under the leadership of Dr. Mahathir often irritated the United States with his vehement criticism of both America and Israel. He has as well been a genuine voice of moderation within the Islamic world and has not hesitated to criticize his fellow Muslims for not advocating policies that would better integrate people into the modern technologically advanced world.

Overall, foreign relations have been relatively successful for Malaysia especially with respect to ASEAN. Singapore and Malaysia came to an agreement on their territorial waters boundary. They also reached agreement over Malaysian restrictions of the importation of Singaporean petro-chemicals. Still, as often in the past, issues such as water can make relations between Singapore and Kuala Lumpur complicated. Fairly recently, Singapore finally agreed to significantly raise the fees it pays for Malaysian water.

Although perhaps more a decision associated with domestic rather than international issues, the government established relations with the Vatican in mid-2011. According to observers, it was done as a gesture toward Malaysia's Christian community, which has felt itself under pressure recently over issues such as the use of the term "Allah" in Christian Bibles. This is a historically logical but politically controversial term in some Islamic quarters in Malaysia.

One other international incident that could have cause difficulties but in the end blew over was the killing at Kuala Lumpur airport in February 2017 of Kim Jong Nam, eldest son of Kim Jong Il,

and half brother of the current leader, Kim Jong Un. He died after two women smeared his face with a toxic agent. North Korea claimed that the dead man was not Kim Jong Nam, but Kim Chul (a name under which Kim Jong Nam was known to travel) and demanded the release of the body. Malaysia ignored the claim. Two women were held, one Vietnamese and the other Indonesia, together with a North Korean man. The latter was eventually released but expelled for visa violations, and the two women went on trial. North Korea insisted it was a South Korean and U.S. plot, and for a time the two countries refused to allow diplomats to leave. But eventually the body was handed over to North Korea and the crisis passed. By summer 2018, full diplomatic relations had been restored. The women were eventually freed in 2019.

But relations with North Korea soured again in 2021, when the Malaysian courts allowed the extradition of a North Korean national to the United States on money-laundering charges, and North Korea severed diplomatic relations.

## Society and Culture

Malaysia's population is very young. About 30% are under the age of 15. A high percentage of the people are literate; primary and secondary school education is provided for all, and there are a number of colleges and five universities. Although Islam is the state religion and Muslims enjoy certain special privileges by law, there is complete freedom of worship for other faiths. Nevertheless, Islamic departments within the government do have the power to arrest people for inappropriate behavior although after a recent incident they were formally told they would need official

police permission to do so. The government has also made it clear that critics of Malaysian family law could be charged with sedition of they were seen as attacking Islam itself. But that hardly ended the tension.

Tensions that have long existed quietly within Malaysia have come to the surface more and more frequently. This was demonstrated in an especially dramatic fashion when Muslim activists destroyed a Hindu temple that was said to have been built illegally in the 19th century. During 2009 Muslims in Selangor State provocatively protested the construction of a Hindu temple by marching through the streets carrying the head of a cow, the animal held sacred by Hindus. Not surprisingly, boar heads have been found on the grounds Muslim mosques, and a regular series of bombings has been directed toward churches. One of the most explosive recent issues has been Muslim displeasure with Christian use of the word "Allah" to refer to Christian God. While correct, given that Jews, Christians, and Muslims, despite their different religious practices, technically worship the same God, such scholarly explanations have little impact when emotions are aroused.

In early 2010 a Malaysian court finally ruled that Christians could continue their long-standing policy of using the term "Allah" to refer to their own God. That ruling, though, hardly ended the controversy. Meanwhile tensions continue between Malaysian Christians and those within the Muslim community who find Christian usage of the term offensive. Eventually some progress was made when in early 2011 the government officially released thousands of Malay language Bibles that had been confiscated because they had used the term "Allah" to refer to the Christian idea of God. But the controversy over the use of "Allah" within Christian publications has in no way gone away.

Malaysians are also great sports enthusiasts. Although more traditional ball game forms have dominated in the past, soccer is now the nation's most popular pastime. There is also tremendous interest in horseracing as seen by the country's five first-rate turf clubs. But here, too, religion can cause complications. In November 2021, for example, the World Squash Federation canceled the December 2021 Men's Squash Championship, due to be held in Malaysia, because the latter refused to allow Israeli athletes to take part.

The majority of the Malay community used to live in a fairly traditional manner, principally engaged in farming and fishing, but modern Malays are increasingly entering the trading, professional, and other sectors of the modern economy. Today, Malaysia has a significant Malay

# Malaysia

middle and upper-middle class. There are also a significant number of very wealthy Malays, some of whom have made fortunes by having access to lucrative government contracts. With the exception of Singapore, Malaysia also has the highest percentage of Chinese in Southeast Asia. The community is divided into several linguistic groups that reflect the origins of their ancestors who migrated from China. Many educated Chinese, particularly among the younger generation, learn English and Malay. The more educated Malays usually speak English. That is likely to become an even more significant reality in upcoming years as the government, hoping to improve Malaysia's long-term economic prospects, has begun insisting that subjects such as science and math be taught in the English language.

Despite crises, the impact of sustained economic growth over the last generation remains very visible. Longer life, improved health care, a significant increase in the number of people owning telephones, and an expanding national highway system were all indicators of the country's economic success over the last

decade. Sadly, one effect of the economic problems is the reduction of the number of Malaysian families able to send their children abroad for higher education. While staying at home to save money might be a logical option, Malaysian universities have not been able to accommodate the larger numbers of potential students. Nevertheless, Prime Minister Mahathir did improve his standing among many non-Muslim Malaysian citizens by making it easier for outstanding non-Malay students to win places at the nation's universities.

Overall, in recent years there has been a growing sense that the official policy of Malay Rights, the preference for Malays over other Malaysian citizens, has been something of a drain on the economy. As we have seen, Malaysia's most recent prime minister moved to lessen some of those preferences, at least for a time. But that effort did not last long when it became obvious that the government's continuing support required more cultivation of the core Malay voters, who very much approved those same preferential policies.

Ironically, the really explosive potential of ethnic tensions that was revealed over

the last year came from quite another unexpected source. Early in 2013 hundreds of Philippine gunmen arrived in Eastern Malaysia and made a dramatic bid to conquer the region as an extension of their long-running separatist movement within the Philippines. Eventually the Malaysian military was able to destroy the group, killing and capturing them. But the incident was sober reminder of how easily ethnic tensions can spill over from one nation to another.

### Women

In Malaysia, Muslim women are subject to Islamic legal codes. In contrast, non-Muslim women are subject to the more secular civil code. For Muslim women that means that practices such as polygamy are allowed. On a practical basis of course the situation is more complicated. While at least one Malay state has made it somewhat easier for a man to meet the requirements to take more than one wife (not, for example, having to gain the first wife's permission), Former Prime Minister Mahathir made it clear that he

**One of many beautiful mosques for the large Muslim population**

# Malaysia

disapproved of the practice as have other national leaders elsewhere in the region. Mrs. Mahathir would not even welcome second wives into her home.

Dr. Mahathir's daughter has also made her opinions known. Marina Mahathir has emerged as a well-known AIDS, human rights, and democracy advocate. She has also spoken out against a too strong emphasis on Islam in Malaysian life and insisted that Malaysian Muslim women are still being treated as second-class citizens by Islamic family laws that do not even apply to non-Muslims. Most dramatically Ms. Mahatir set off a firestorm of controversy when she likened the situation of women in Malaysia to that of blacks under South Africa's former apartheid regime.

The fact is Islamic domestic law is widely used and it does favors males in matters of inheritance, but its application in Malaysia has varied from that practiced elsewhere. In 1989 the Islamic Family law was revised to give Muslim Malaysian women more rights in such personal matters as divorce. Nevertheless, in some regions, where Islamic parties have been influential, in Kelantan, for example, their rights have been lessening lately. Overall, one notes that the nation's Islamic heritage has been more reinforced in recent years. For example, in one state, Terengganu, the government established a phalanx of religious monitors to make sure that at least in public appropriate behavior between the sexes was enforced.

Malaysian women's rights and the nation's Islamic heritage have been particularly in the news lately because of the attempt by a young female Christian convert to have her former religious affiliation—Islam—removed from her identity card so that she can marry her Christian fiancé. Her longtime legal battle ended abruptly during the early summer of 2007 when Malaysia's high court dramatically ruled against her wishes. In doing so the high court specifically rejected the constitution's guarantee of religious freedom.

Looking at today's Malaysia, women are still under-represented in decision-making positions and their role in the professions is only recently growing. Happily, as has been the case so often elsewhere, the next generation of Malaysian women seems well situated to gain more control over their lives than women of earlier generations. Today's civil law grants them equal rights in work and education and today they are well represented among university student ranks. Women have served in cabinet level positions and they represent between 6% and 7% of those who serve in the various regional and national legislatures and a women, Malaysia's first astrophysicist even serves as the director-general of the nation's National Space Agency.

But more than Malaysian citizens find themselves within the country. For many foreign women the experience can be quite different. Malaysia has been accused of being part of an international network of human sex trafficking that often sees refugees from Myanmar being sent off to work in the brothels of Thailand.

## Economy

Until the economic crash of 1997, Malaysia had one of the strongest and fastest growing economies in the Asia-Pacific region. Many expected Malaysia to become the "fifth tiger," joining Hong Kong, Singapore, South Korea, and Taiwan in the developed country ranks. Under Dr. Mahathir, the country had even developed enormously ambitious plans from the erection of the world's tallest building to hopes of turning Malaysia into a center for world telecommunications. The Malaysian national development plan had called for the country to achieve fully developed status by 2020. Under an earlier economic policy, the government was also able to substantially raise the level of Malay (rather than Chinese) participation in the non-agricultural sectors of the economy.

When the 1997 economic crises hit, Malaysia suffered the same fate as many of her neighbors. Its currency value dropped dramatically as did the local stock market. Initially, the government seemed confident it could manage the crises and unlike so many of her neighbors, Malaysia chose to confront the crises without borrowing funds from the International Monetary Fund. Given how strongly Malaysia's leadership has long felt about continuing Western influence within the world's financial institutions such as the IMF and the World Bank, this was a fairly predictable decision.

In response to the deteriorating situation, the government finally decided to cut its budget by a fifth and delayed some large infrastructure projects like the $550 million monorail system that had been planned for Kuala Lumpur. By the fall of 1998 Mahathir, decided to go much further. Defying the international trend toward greater economic liberalization, he imposed controls against the trading of Malaysian currency or stocks outside the country. His goal, of course, was to shield the country from the sort of outside financial speculation he believed caused the crisis in the first place. The problem is that such a move can also end any hopes for outside investment. This is something most countries have felt necessary to help growth. The decision caused enormous and immediate political problems for the prime minister.

Despite the controversy, economic and political, Malaysia's economy in the

following months did respond favorably. Although it was not clear if Malaysia's economy started to recover because of or despite the financial controls Dr. Mahathir imposed, they did improve. The year 2000 saw significant growth rates that by 2002 had become just over 4% annually. For a time though last year the nations' growth rate was expected to slow due to the financial setbacks associated with SARS outbreak that hit much of East and Southeast Asia during the winter and spring of 2003.

Recognizing the problem Dr. Mahathir's government responded with a combination of tax cuts and interest rate reductions in order to offer some relief to those hurt by the a potential economic downturn. Happily neither the dislocations caused by the U.S. war in Iraq nor the SARS virus significantly impacted on Malaysia's growth, which has continued its steady recovery from the crisis of 1997. The growth rate for 2004 came in at just over 7%, which is very healthy indeed.

One predicable problem has been higher international oil prices although Malaysia's government has been working hard to promote the production of palm oil as a fuel as well. Moreover, hoping to expand the economy further, government leaders have been working out stronger trade relationships with nations from Japan to Australia. Exports to both the United States and the People's Republic of China have also gone up significantly.

Abdullah Badawi, the former prime minister, also promoted agricultural improvements as a way to enable that industry to complement the contributions of the service and manufacturing sectors. In mid-2005, his government introduced a new "Malaysia Plan" that focused somewhat more on human "capital" improvements, laid greater stress on education, and tried to improve economic conditions in the rural areas.

There has also been hope that Malaysia, given recent Western-Islamic tensions, would be able to attract more Muslim tourists over the next few years who might otherwise have done their leisure travel in the West.

The world economic downturn that began in the fall of 2008 posed a major challenge. Like so many nations, from Japan and America to Britain and China, Malaysia developed its own $18 billion stimulus program to help the local economy weather the developing global recession. Some of their policies went further than those found elsewhere. For instance, the government ordered businesses to lay off foreign workers before local citizens.

Nevertheless 2009's growth rate declined by a depressing 2.2%, a far cry from those healthier numbers that ranged somewhat over 6% in the years before the onset of the global recession. Like much of Asia, though, the impact on the local economy of America's financial crash did not last terribly long. The economic growth for 2010 is reported to have been a very healthy 7.2%, a figure higher than it had been before the 2008 crash. Since then, though, growth has slowed somewhat in each succeeding year, and 2012 came in at a bit under 4.5%, down again from the previous year's 5% plus. This is clearly a reasonable growth many countries might envy, but it is very different from earlier decades.

The challenge now is to move forward the stated national goal of bringing Malaysia more into the ranks of the economically middle-class countries. To that end the government has created the first minimum wage law and raised salaries and pensions, all hoping to improve living standards.

One of the more interesting aspects of Malaysia's recent economic activities is the creation of a western university zone in the city of Johor just opposite Singapore. The goal, thus far quite successful, has been to convince Western, largely English, colleges to set up branch campuses in Malaysia to provide the very popular Western-style educational experiences at lower prices and to ensure that Malaysia's brightest will more likely remain at home.

The economy continued to do well up to 2020. Growth in 2019 was 4%. Wages may have not moved very much, but Malaysia's labor force was generally better educated and more productive than those of most of its neighbors. By then, according to the IMF, Malaysia had the forth largest economy in Asia. The World Bank has described it as one of the most open countries in the world, with a good record in reducing poverty. Its growth after it recovered from the 1998 economic crisis averaged about 5.4% per annum.

However, the World Bank has also indicated that there will need to be strong government intervention to counteract the effects of COVID-19, which has resulted in the resurgence of poverty in some groups. The immediate economic effect of COVID was a dramatic fall in the growth rate in 2020, which plunged from 2019's 4% to -5.6%. As world trade began to pick up in 2021, things improved, with growth at 3.1%, according to the IMF. The IMF predicted that there would be an even better performance in 2022, at around 5.75%. Certainly, the first quarter of 2022 promised well, with trade up 17% year on year.

### Environmental Issues

Like the rest of the region, environmental problems are increasingly plaguing the country. The Science, Technology, and Environment Ministry reported in late 1995 that two out of three rivers in Malaysia were polluted and that those left unpolluted were deteriorating rapidly as a consequence of industrial waste. It was estimated that seven million fish died off the coast of Perak state from exposure to potassium cyanide.

Another problem, which one finds throughout the region, is deforestation. It has even been estimated that the rain forest in the East Malaysia state of Sabah will soon have no more marketable timber left. Sadly native peoples are losing their lands to greedy state politicians and Japanese plywood manufacturers. Within Malaysia a growing environmental moving is also emerging. More recently environmental activists have been involved in opposing not only unsustainable logging in the state of Sarawak as well as a proposed processing plant for rare earth minerals.

Public health challenges are, of course, well known elements of the challenge of climate change. That has certainly been the case in Malaysia as well. Indeed the country has experienced a major uptick of dengue fever infections, a phenomenon increasingly common as so-called tropic diseases spread further north.

On the more positive side, the governments of Malaysia, Indonesia, and Brunei recently pledged jointly to protect 200,000 square kilometers of rain forest. This is a significant decision given how important rain forests are to the health of our planet. In addition, had the round of international climate talks held in Copenhagen at the end of 2009 been successful, the nation would have been in a good position to reap the benefits of the proposed plans to offer financial incentives to preserve their tropical rain forests. Unfortunately, no binding agreements came out of Copenhagen. More recently of course the world made significant progress with the signing of the Paris Climate Agreement in late 2015 which did include a plan for forest preservation.

### COVID-19

The first COVID-19 cases in Malaysia were detected in early March 2020. Although numbers and the death rate would remain low in April and May, the government introduced a two-week national control order, with restrictions on movement, religious gatherings and arrests of undocumented migrants. This was later extended. In June, cases rose to nearly 300 a day but then fell until September. From then until the end of January, cases were running at over 3000 a day, then fell back to about 1500 a day. But hope that the pandemic was over soon passed. April 2021 saw the on the rise again, to reach over 9000 daily by the end of May. By then, there had been some 622,000 cases, and 3,460 deaths. By the end of the year, the figures were 2.7 million cases, with 31,000 deaths. Borders had been closed for much of the period, with strict limitations on internal travel and gatherings. But the continued rise was of great concern, and to try to break the cycle, a total nation-wide lockdown began on 1 June 2021. Around that time, cases dropped below 6000 daily. Vaccinations began in February 2021. By the end of May, some 3.64 million had received one dose, and 1.14 million two. This meant that 3.6 of the population was fully vaccinated. An intensive campaign began to improve these figures.

Despite all the efforts, however, by mid May 2022, cases totaled 4.49 million and 35,641 deaths. Vaccination rates were high, with 86.3 having had one dose, 83.4% fully vaccinated, and 49.7% had booster doses.

With international trade and tourism in disarray, the economy took a major hit, with many families slipping back below the poverty line. The government was reported to have spent $82.31 billion up to May 2021, to counter the worst effects, and in June 2021 announced a further $9.68 billion package. It is widely expected that the underlying strength of the economy (see above) will ensure that it will eventually bounce back. But there will be a lot of lost ground to make up.

### The Future

In the more than five years after he succeeded Dr. Mahathir, Abdullah Badawi clearly put his own stamp on the Malaysian administration. He worked to encourage a moderate cultural Islamic emphasis instead of the more controversial secularism often promoted by his successor. In practice, the effort had as its goal to limit the influence of the more radical Islamic activists. But as time went on, his leadership and that of the United Malay National Organization faltered while the formerly deposed and humiliated ex-deputy prime minister, Anwar Ibrahim, made at least for a time, something of a comeback. Badawi himself was replaced by Mohamed Najib bin Abdul Razak, who, while leading a diminishing coalition, still managed to retain the longtime National Front's domination of political power.

Unfortunately, Najib's term in office proved more and more divisive as long simmering tensions, ethnic, economic, and political came bubbling to the surface. Indeed Najib was regularly criticized for not only working to suppress the voices of his critics but tolerating a more public role for the Malaysia's own Ultra Nationalist Islamic groups even as he himself was seen as financially corrupt by larger segments of Malaysian society.

# Malaysia

And of course domestically, even as the government managed for a time to remain in power two previous leaders, Mahathir Mohamad, and Anwar Ibrahim, the latter from his prison cell emerged as major symbols of those who would challenge the government's authority.

By 2018, that symbolic opposition had become considerably more as Dr. Mahathir reentered the political arena as the leader of a coalition which included his former colleague and political competitor Anwar Ibrahim in an ultimately successful bid to pull down the government.

Indeed, those elections culminated not only in the 93-year-old Dr. Mahathir reclaiming his position as prime minister but Najib, the previous prime minister being charged with corruption.

Mahathir's departure in 2020 and the subsequent political struggles, plus the the onset of COVID-19 have made it more difficult to foresee Malaysia's short-term future. The political pattern now seems to be the likelihood of short-term coalitions, even if many of the principle players remain the same, unless there is agreement that the need for a return to economic prosperity means working together. Malaysia should eventually get back on the path to economic growth but much depends on getting the pandemic under control.

# The Union of Myanmar
## (*Burma*)

The ancient city of Bagan is located in Mandalay region

**Area:** 261,700 sq. mi. (676,600 sq. km.)
**Population:** 55,096,098 (2022 UN est.)
**Capital City:** Naypyidaw, pop. 683,265 (2022 est.)
**Climate:** Tropical, with torrential rains during the summer monsoon (June–November) in the coastal areas

**Neighboring Countries:** China (North and East); India, Bangladesh (West); Laos (East); Thailand (East and South)
**Official Language:** Burmese
**Other Principal Tongues:** English, Chinese, Karen, and Shan
**Ethnic Background:** Burman (68%), Shan (9%), Karen (7%), Rakhine (4%), Chinese (3%), Indian (2%), Mon (2%), other (5%)
**Principal Religion:** Buddhism (89%) and other traditions, including Christianity, Islam, and animism
**Main Exports:** (to Japan, Singapore, China, Thailand, India and Hong Kong) Beans, teak, rice, hardwood, natural gas, and fish
**Main Imports:** (from Japan, China, Thailand, Singapore, South Korea, Malaysia) Machinery, transportation equipment, chemicals, food products, plastics, and construction supplies
**Currency:** Kyat

**Former Colonial Status:** British dependency (1886–1947)
**Independence Day:** January 4, 1948
**Chief of State:** Myint Swe (since February 1, 2021)
**State Administration Council Chairman:** Senior General Min Aung Hlaing (since April 6, 2016) (Also Commander-in-Chief of Defense Services)
**State Counsellor:** Aung Sann Suu Kyi (since April 6, 2016; reelected November 2020; detained February 1, 2021)
**National Flag:** A five-pointed star in the middle with three stripes of green, yellow, and red signifying peace, tranquility, courage, and decisiveness
**Per Capita GDP Income:** $5,123 2020 World Bank est.) (purchasing power parity)

Note: The government of Burma has changed the name of the country to

241

# Myanmar

Myanmar. Where appropriate, that term will be used in this text.

The long western coastline of Myanmar faces the tropical waters of the Bay of Bengal in the north and the Andaman Sea in the peninsular southern regions. The northern part of the country is actually a moist and hot basin. It is separated from India and Bangladesh by high, forested ridges and lower valleys, and from China, Laos, and Thailand by the mountains and by the Shan Plateau, which combine to form a crescent nearly enclosing Myanmar.

The mountains of the plateau region are not particularly high when compared to those in other countries of southern Asia; they reach a maximum height of about 9,000 feet. The Irrawaddy River originates in the mountainous region of the north, turbulently descending to the lowlands where it is transformed into a sluggish, muddy stream of water. It is along this river and the Sittang River that the largest cities of Myanmar are located, including Yangon and Mandalay.

The northern mountains are thinly inhabited by people who are mostly non-Burman. They live principally in the thick forests where teak and other valuable trees grow. The great majority of the people live in the crowded central valley where great quantities of rice are raised each year, much of which is exported. The comparatively cool and dry season, which starts in November, ends in about mid-February when the wind changes from the north and begins to blow from the Bay of Bengal. The air becomes hotter during April and May, and periodic storms appear on the horizon.

In June, the full force of monsoon rains inundates the coastline. An average of 200 inches of rainfall each year, but the further inland regions receive less rain as their distance from the coast increases. The rains abate in late October; the wind again comes from the North, providing a cooler and drier relief from the oppressive moisture of the preceding months.

### Historical Background

In the early centuries A.D., the fertile coastal region of Myanmar was inhabited by the Mons, who had cultural characteristics quite similar to those of India. In about 1000 A.D., they converted to Theraveda Buddhism which had come from India by way of Ceylon (Sri Lanka). The Mons in turn transmitted this tradition to the other people living in the region, including the Burmans.

The term "Burmese" is often used by outsiders to describe all of the people living within the country of present day Myanmar. "Burman" is correctly used to designate the largest ethnic group.

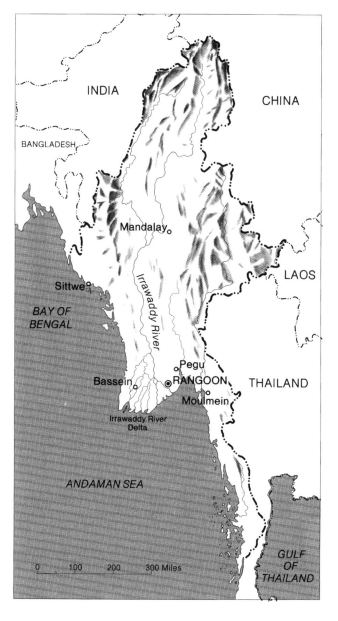

Burmans are closely related in terms of language and appearance to the Tibetans, and seem to have moved southwest into Myanmar from the remote regions of eastern Tibet beginning about 800 A.D. Although they have oriental features, they usually do not have the eyelid fold of their Chinese neighbors; the color of their skin varies from deep brown to extremely light in color.

The Burmans emerged as the most powerful force in the country by the mid-11th century under King Anawrata, who established a national capital in the central city of Pagan, from which most of the country was subdued. The Shan (Thai) people, who lived in the northeastern part of Burma, disliked Burman rule, and in the late 13th century requested the protection of the Mongol empire which ruled China. The emperor Kublai Khan sent a large

force of cavalrymen who invaded Burma, totally destroying the Burmese kingdom.

From about 1300 to the mid-18th century, Myanmar history is one of repeated destructive civil wars among the various ethnic groups that made up the population. No one emerged victorious; the wars served only to limit the development of what was to become Myanmar.

European merchants and explorers first appeared along the coast after 1500. Although the Dutch had trading bases there for a brief period, there was no early colonization of Myanmar. In 1753 a new Burmese kingdom emerged, rapidly reuniting the several small states into which Myanmar had been split by civil war. This warlike kingdom raided Thailand, fended off two invasions by the Manchu dynasty of China, and in the early 19th century, invaded Assam to the west.

**Lord Louis Mountbatten, supreme allied commander in Southeast Asia (1943–1946), later Earl Mountbatten of Burma, talks with British troops near Mandalay in April 1945**

The British East India Company, which controlled Assam, sent troops to push the Burmans out of the area in the First Burmese War (1824). The British then took over the Arakan and Tenasserim coasts and advanced up the Irrawaddy River. Faced with defeat, the Burmese surrendered those coasts and permitted the British to maintain a minister at the Burman capital of Ava. Relations with the British remained tense and eventually resulted in the Second Burmese War of 1852. A decade later, 1862, a commercial treaty gave the British the right to trade throughout Myanmar. Thibaw became king in 1878, and rapidly alienated the British by again interfering with their trade and establishing relations with the French. This resulted in the Third Burmese War (1885–1886), which ultimately ended Burman rule. The country was then governed as a province of British India until 1937 when it became a Crown Colony.

### Myanmar as a British Colony

The emphasis during the British colonial period was on profitable trade rather than the welfare of the various ethnic groups in Myanmar. In depriving the Burmans of control, the British aroused the hatred of this the largest group. The minority Karen, Shan, Chin, and Kachin peoples however looked to the British for protection from the Burmans, and thus were less antagonistic toward their colonial rulers. The British also undermined the influence of the Buddhist monasteries and imported large numbers of Indians to perform skilled and semi-skilled tasks rather than training the Burmans for these jobs. Thousands of Chinese also entered to engage in trade. The presence of these foreign minorities provoked anti-Indian and anti-Chinese riots in 1931. The anti-foreign Burmese resisted adoption of European skills and cultural patterns more successfully than the people in almost all of the other British colonies.

Nevertheless there was considerable economic growth during the colonial period. Myanmar became the chief rice exporter of Southeast Asia; the lower Irrawaddy Valley was cleared of its dense forests and brought under cultivation.

Burmese labor was used for the cultivation of the huge crops.

The British granted a degree of self-government to Myanmar in 1937 that included an elected legislature and a cabinet. Unfortunately the lack of experience in government on the part of the Burmans created a basic instability. Predictably there was little support among the people for the elected members and officials.

Thus, when the Japanese invaded Myanmar in 1942, they were welcomed by the people and Chief Minister Ba Maw of the colonial government accepted leadership in a puppet government later established by the Japanese in 1943. Even though the people had welcomed their conquerors, the Japanese quickly set up a very oppressive administration designed to exploit Myanmar's capacity to produce rice. Active resistance soon formed around the Anti-Fascist People's Freedom League (AFPFL), a political movement composed of left-wing nationalists and some communists, leading a guerrilla army under the Burman popular hero Aung San.

During the war the Allied forces, in an effort to establish a supply route to southwest China, slowly fought their way through Myanmar. The country was eventually liberated by mid-1945. The British then tried to establish a government along prewar colonial lines, but friction erupted immediately with the AFPFL by then led by Aung San. The British were then living under the anti-colonial Labor Party government of Prime Minister Attlee, which was in the process of giving up its control over India and Pakistan. It agreed in 1947 to give Myanmar its independence; the AFPFL chose then to leave the British Commonwealth entirely.

Tragically, Aung San was assassinated in 1947. The death of the country's popular independence leader complicated the situation considerably. Aung San had led independence struggle and was viewed by many as the founder of modern Myanmar. He had been an effective leader of the nationalist movement and was expected to lead the first postcolonial government, but his death ended that possibility. Later, of course, his memory would help galvanize Burmese behind the pro-democracy movement of his daughter Aung San Suu Kyi, the 1991 winner of the Nobel Peace Prize.

In the aftermath of the assassination, U Nu, a fervently Buddhist member of the AFPFL took control of the government. At the time, Burmese communists threatened the government of Myanmar, so much so that the government controlled little of the nation outside Rangoon. However, the lack of cooperation among the insurgents enabled the Burmese army under Ne Win to reduce the rebellion to a much lower level by 1951.

# Myanmar

The Burmese, although independent, were not experienced in operating an effective government. Meanwhile the AFPFL split and became a coalition of parties with a high degree of inefficiency, corruption, and factionalism. The leftist-socialist group was led by U Nu while the more conservative wing was led by Ba Swe. The split between the two factions resulted in the forced resignation of U Nu in the fall of 1958; Myanmar was then ruled by the military, led by Ne Win. Little progress was made toward solving the political problems of the country, or toward getting the sluggish economy moving during this period of military rule.

Elections were permitted in 1960 that resulted in U Nu's faction being returned to office, but by 1962 adverse political and economic conditions again caused the military to intervene. This time, Ne Win abolished the existing political parties, imprisoned a number of political leaders, including the highly popular U Nu, and established a military dictatorship under the Union Revolutionary Council. He then announced that he would make Myanmar a socialist—though not a communist state. Meanwhile the internal revolts had continued, particularly in rural areas during the post-independence years. Ne Win was unsuccessful in negotiating an end to these revolts despite new military operations.

Ne Win invited some of the former political leaders in early 1969 to advise him on Myanmar's political future. They urged a return to elected government instead of military rule. When Ne Win refused, U Nu went into exile and announced that he would lead a political movement for the overthrow of Ne Win; however, he eventually gave up the plan and returned to Myanmar. Meanwhile Ne Win launched an effort to make Myanmar a one-party state, controlled by the Burma Socialist Program Party, a leftist movement with some communist elements.

A new constitution was adopted by referendum at the beginning of 1974. Myanmar was renamed the Socialist Republic of the Union of Burma. Real power though was exercised by a 29-man Council of State, chaired by President Ne Win. The government remained repressive, unpopular, and inept.

Inflation, shortages of rice, and floods contributed to political unrest in the mid 1970s. In December 1974, the funeral of U Thant, former Secretary General of the United Nations, provided the occasion for Buddhist and student organized riots that were quickly suppressed by the military. In 1983, Myanmar found itself dragged into the violent politics of the Korean peninsula when North Korean agents planted three bombs, aimed at South Korean President Chun Doo-hwan, at the Martyr's

**Former President Thein Sein**

Mausoleum that killed 17 visiting South Korean officials and journalists on October 9. High Burmese officials were narrowly spared from this terrorist attempt. Infuriated, Ne Win shook up the security services and broke diplomatic relations with North Korea.

## Contemporary Government and Politics

For years the dominant political figure was General Ne Win who ruled from 1962 through 1987 through the country's only political party, the Burmese Socialist Program Party (BSPP). But the party was in large measure merely a front for the nation's real rulers its military establishment.

Under military rule in the years since impendence, Burma as the nation was known before the generals renamed it Myanmar went from an economic status as one of the richer countries of Southeast Asia to one of the worst off economically a victim of horrendously bad economic management and international isolation. Politically though the situation did not change much. The military dominated the country.

## An Epic Struggle for Democracy

In spring of 1988, a series of massive demonstrations took place against the ruling regime by students, monks, and urban residents that seemed to offer the promise of more democratic rule of the sort then emerging in the Philippines and South Korea. The army however was determined not to allow such an outcome. Unlike similar struggles elsewhere, Myanmar's military leaders did not have the world's press to worry about. Rangoon was neither Manila nor Seoul. It was far easier to use brute force with impunity.

At the end of July, Ne Win was succeeded by a close associate and tough former general, Sein Lwin, who became president of the Union of Myanmar. He proclaimed martial law in Rangoon and tried to control the pro-democracy demonstrations by military force but failed. The leadership then turned to a relatively moderate civilian, Maung Maung, who pledged multiparty elections in which none of the current leaders would run for office. There was great popular joy at this, but also a widespread demand for an immediate interim government. In September of 1988 former Prime Minister U Nu proclaimed such a government, composed largely of opposition leaders.

The nation's military leaders had other ideas. Defense Minister Saw Maung seized power on September 18, 1988, and assumed both the chairmanship of the ruling party (the State Law and Order Restoration Council (SLORC) and the presidency of the state. Protest demonstrations were then violently and brutally suppressed by the army. Thousands of people died as the army drove the pro-democracy crowds from the streets. The military assault that followed was even more brutal than the internationally televised repression that occurred in the People's Republic of China the following year. Thousands of refugees eventually headed for Thailand and various border areas beyond the control of the government.

For the moment, efforts to end the generation long military dictatorship had failed but Myanmar's democratic activists soon had another opportunity to expand the nation's democratic base. The opposition, calling itself the National League for Democracy, discarded U Nu as its head and selected the increasingly popular, Aung San Suu Kyi, the daughter of the national hero Aung San (assassinated in 1947). She benefited not only from his name and memory but also from the atmosphere surrounding the funeral of her mother in January of 1989, which amounted to a peaceful demonstration against military rule.

In preparation for the supposedly free election scheduled for 1990, the military leadership disqualified Aung San Suu Kyi, from running. It placed her under house arrest in July of that year, together with other leading members of the opposition. Still, the opposition parties won over 80% of the vote for the National Assembly in the May 1990 elections. But the army refused to surrender power and intensified its campaign of repression. Attempting to assert themselves, Aung San Suu Kyi's party and the Karen guerrillas then symbolically proclaimed a coalition government in opposition to the army-dominated one.

In spite of the brutal repression by the military, unrest continued to grow, both in the cities and in the rural areas. The government responded by closing the universities in 1991. The army, strengthened by purchases of more than $1 billion in arms from China, launched a series of offensives in ethnic minority areas. One result was a stream of refugees out of the country, including Muslims fleeing to Bangladesh.

In the following decades the military repeatedly and often violently sought to maintain its control. This is not a surprising attitude given that historically the political culture of the country has been both hierarchical and paternalistic. This is a tradition the military was apparently committed to maintaining despite the results of the 1990 elections.

In short, effective control of the government long rested with the military junta that was officially known as the State Law and Order Restoration Council (SLORC) until it renamed itself the more benign sounding "State Peace and Development Council" in late 1997.

However, a military junta by any other name is still a military junta, and no real political openings followed the change of names. In fact, over the years the various minor transformations appeared to have indicated more of a generational change among the country's military leaders than any movement toward a greater political opening.

There were at times evidence that there was tension among the military elites. For example, in early 2002 the junta claimed it had suppressed a coup attempt by relatives of the former leader, Ne Win. Those involved were subsequently condemned to death although the executions were not immediately carried out.

Certainly the most important political issue since the late 1980s has been the status of Aung San Suu Kyi, the most famous opposition figure in the country. In the aftermath of the government's refusal to recognize her party's 1990 political victory she ended up in a state of "on again off again" house arrest that lasted for decades.

In 1995, she was for a time released to great fanfare. But that turned out to be of little significance. Despite Aung San Suu Kyi's temporary release from house arrest, it soon became clear that the government had no interest in allowing her to carry out her political activities. In fact, for all practical purposes she still remained under house arrest until the spring of 2002 when once again, to more fanfare, she was temporarily released from confinement.

Overall, despite the occasional efforts at reconciliation, Myanmar's military leadership remained unwilling for years to allow her to play any role in the political life of the country.

**Aung San Suu Kyi (1991 Nobel Prize winner)**

Courtesy of Leslie Kean, The Burma Project USA

Throughout the late 1990s, her efforts to address her supporters were constantly interfered with and confrontations between students, monks, and the government forces were a regular feature of life in the capital. During the fall of 1996, for example, the NLD attempted to hold an official meeting within Myanmar that resulted in hundreds of arrests. Attempts in 1997 and 1998 fared no better and NLD supporters found themselves under major pressure from the government.

By the spring of 2003, most of the pressures against Aung San Suu Kyi and her party were put back into place. Most dramatically, the backers of the junta attacked her convoy, which had been traveling in the countryside and arrested the famous democratic activist in a bloody assault that saw an unknown number of her supporters killed.

Over the following months Aung San Suu Kyi remained in "protective custody" while governments and people from around the world, most importantly from within the region, called for her release. While all this was going on, the junta went through a transition that saw long-time strong man, General Khin Nyunt, emerge temporarily as the prime minister.

Once in power the new prime minister announced a "road map" toward a more open society in order to placate some of the junta's critics. Eventually, by the fall of 2003, Aung San Suu Kyi was allowed to return home. Given these government actions, there were some who speculated that the new prime minister might even be considered a relative "reformer" within the context of the extreme hard liners who dominated the junta. Whether or not that was true, what was clear was that no real change was going to be allowed.

By the fall of 2004 Khin Nyunt himself had been removed from power by his opponents who accused him of "violating discipline." Eventually the fallen leader was given a 44-year suspended sentence for corruption in a move that sent a clear signal even to those in the military that the top leadership would accept no deviation from their control. He was to remain under that detention until late 2011 when the situation began to evolve again.

Still, in the spring of 2004 before Khin Nyunt was removed from power, the government, perhaps at his urging, had convened what was presented as an historic meeting of the national convention, which was charged with creating a new constitution. Aung San Suu Kyi's NLD refused to take part unless its leaders were released from jail. The government, though, continued with the initiative claiming that

# Myanmar

the groups it had brought into the process were more representative than the NLD.

What actually seemed to be occurring was an effort by the junta to create a political system that would eventually allow the appearance of democratic governance even as it remained in absolute control. Those efforts at "window dressing" hardly fooled any of the regime's closer observers. After all, Khin Nyunt himself was initially replaced as prime minister by Lt. Gen. Soe Win, who was said to have been directly involved in the earlier and quite deadly 2003 attack on Aung San Suu Kyi's convoy. Meanwhile, his close ally, General Than Shwe, the chairman of the State Peace and Development Council, remained deeply entrenched in power.

## 2007's Dramatic Challenge to the Military Junta

The junta's efforts to present the impression of a more open society was clearly not convincing to those who actually lived under its dictatorial control. In August 2007 the largest demonstration in decades began. Initially stirred by a dramatic rise in the price of fuels and public transportation, thousands and eventually tens of thousands of Burmese, led by Buddhist monks, took to the streets to protest peacefully against the military junta that controlled their lives.

Quite dramatically, they even marched in front of the home of Aung San Suu Kyi who, of course, remained under house arrest. As expected the junta struck back. Beginning in late September, the troops were sent against the crowds, and late night arrests began against the demonstrators, Buddhist monks and civilians alike. Eventually thousands were detained and many killed. Just how many died in the crackdown is not known. Clearly, it was less than the larger numbers who died in the crackdown of 1988, but by the time it was over, the junta was just as much in control. However, it had been forced by both regional and international condemnation to open talks again with Aung San Suu Kyi.

Sadly, the suffering of the people of Myanmar had hardly just begun. By the spring of 2008, the nation was hit by a devastating cyclone that killed an estimated 140,000 people. It also left sections of the nation devastated, especially the Irrawaddy River area that historically has supplied much of the nation's food.

While weather had initiated the crisis, the junta's own incompetence almost immediately made it worse. Extraordinarily hesitant to allow outside foreigners to help bring in critically needed supplies, significantly more people ended up suffering far greater losses. In fact, it took weeks before the country's leaders made

the concessions necessary to allow relatively large relief efforts to begin. The entire experience was a graphic example of the human consequences of Myanmar's political isolation from the larger international community. This is a situation that may have been part of the junta's decision to make yet another effort to offer the international community an image of a more open Myanmar.

By mid-2010 Myanmar's military leaders were once again deeply involved in what appeared to be another effort to create the facade of a more open government. More specifically, they restructured the nation's constitution to create a system that would ensure continuing military domination while formally allowing elections. For example, the system guaranteed the military 25% of the nation's newly elected assembly. But from the junta's perspective, that was hardly enough to ensure the victory it apparently craved. Anticipating the elections the junta first moved to ensure that Aung San Suu Kyi would not be in a position to impede their efforts. It put the Nobel Peace Prize laureate on trial after an American fan successfully and illegally visited her compound.

Eventually the trouble-making American was released to the custody of a visiting American senator while Aung San Suu Kyi found herself back under house arrest with more formal jail time. Meanwhile the largely cowed nation moved toward yet another round of elections completely orchestrated by the junta. And orchestrated they were. As always, the local media was carefully controlled, and no outside

**Former Prime Minister Soe Win of Myanmar**

election monitors or western journalists were allowed to take part.

Surprisingly, on the surface at least the election appeared lively enough. Although no formal debates were allowed, over 37 political parties took part even as around 3,000 individual candidates competed for positions in the new government. Not without controversy, some of Aung San Suu Kyi's political supporters even agreed to take part. The elections themselves, which took place in November of 2010, turned out as expected with the military using every means at its disposal to ensure its own victory and the marginalization of any dissident voices.

When the election results were eventually made available, no one was surprised that the military's Union Solidarity and Development Party (USDA) took more than 60% of the seats. That was above the 25% directly reserved for the military. Clearly, Myanmar's ruling junta or oligarchy planned to remain in a position to dominate the nation even longer. Of course, the international reaction was equally predictable. Mild criticism came from UN leader Ban Ki-moon while the western nations uniformly denounced the balloting as largely a fraud. Equally predictable, Myanmar's less than democratic neighbors, from China to Vietnam, were supportive of what they described as a significant step toward a more open and democratic Myanmar.

Once the elections were safely behind them, the junta, with great international coverage, again released Aung San Suu Kyi from house arrest hoping perhaps to signal yet again another "new era" in Myanmar's political evolution. Unfortunately most of the international coverage failed to note how much of a revolving door policy had surrounded the famous Nobel laureate's frequent confinements. Nevertheless, to the surprise of many the situation really did for once seem to be evolving in a positive direction.

## Changes from 2010 to 2020

In the months following the November 2010 elections, a number of elements about the Myanmar's emerging new/old government were becoming clearer. First, the military and its political allies would remain absolutely in control.

On the other hand, a considerably more open atmosphere was allowed to emerge. Especially important was the regime's dramatic release from prison of large numbers of political activists. Many were part of Aung San Suu Kyi's movement, and others had been imprisoned since the confrontations of 1988.

In fact, so significant have been these changes that the American government

**A new electoral start for Myanmar?**

Courtesy of Htoo Tay Zar from Wikimedia

somewhat more open society was in both its and the nation's best interests.

Clearly the military had come to recognize that its long-term fate depended on not provoking the sort of unrest that had overwhelmed so many governments in the Middle East over the last few years.

Of course, many in the military still consider that the democratic electoral process is no more automatically capable of producing good leadership than the military. Recent events in Thailand and Egypt have perhaps reinforced that impression.

Nevertheless, Myanmar's military leadership still seemed to believe that their best option was an opening to the West, something that is only possible if aspects of the especially repressive military regime were shed.

### Historic Elections?
### November 2015 and 2020

In the months following that election, there seemed to be an extraordinary transition away from purely military rule. Aung San Suu Kyi's's colleague Htin Kyaw successfully ran for the office of president, while she herself assumed a new and apparently influential role as the nation's "State Counsellor," foreign minister and minister to the office of the President. But the apparent transformation was superficial. The military remained powerful in both the economic and political spheres. They still had a veto power on any constitutional change through their nominated representatives in both houses of parliament. Despite her immense popularity, Aung San Suu Kyi made no attempt to challenge their power. Indeed, she supported them in international charges of brutality and possibly genocide against the Muslim Rohingya in Rakhine state, even before the International Tribunal at The Hague in 2019

The military leaders remained suspicious, however, and when Aung San Suu Kyi's National League for Democracy again won in in the November 2020 elections, while the military's Union Solidarity and Development Party only won six percent of the vote, they began to make ominous noises about electoral fraud—perhaps influenced by President Trump's similar claims in the U.S. presidential election. While there were minor issues, the Electoral Commission dismissed the broader claims, as did international observers. But they still went on and in January 2021 began to be accompanied by hints that the military might act. Act they did. On February 1, 2021, the elected members of parliament gathered in the capital, Naypyitaw (created by the military between 2002 and 2006) to be sworn in, but they were all detained on the orders

has reopened relations with Myanmar and dramatically begun to rethink its relationship with the formerly isolated military regime. Especially significant was the late 2011 visit by then Secretary of State Hillary Clinton to Myanmar where she met not only with the nation's new leader Thein Sein, but with Aung San Suu Kyi herself. From the perspective of the United States, Myanmar's leadership had finally started to take decisive steps to move the nation away from its repressive past. The Obama administration quite enthusiastically moved to reinforce those trends. In fact, not only did Hillary Clinton visit, her efforts paved the way for the even more important visit that took place some months later in November 2012 when President Barack Obama visited. This was an obvious gesture to recognize the important political evolution going on in Myanmar.

In the spring of 2013, Thein Sein made an official visit to the United States. This was the first time in half a century a leader of Myanmar had done so. Of course, both visits highlight how much Myanmar is currently making a genuine effort to emerge from international isolation, as well as America's willingness to support that effort.

That dramatically more supportive American attitude was inspired by very

real changes within Myanmar. Perhaps of greatest significance was the fact that after literally decades, Myanmar's Nobel Prize–winning symbol of the nation's democratic aspirations had announced that she planned to compete for electoral office in the elections scheduled for April 2011. And compete she did. Aung San Suu Kyi not only won a place for herself in the nation's new parliament. Her party won 43 of 45 of the contested seats making Myanmar's long-imprisoned democratic leader the head of Myanmar's official opposition.

This was an extraordinary development given the country's history during the last few decades. Indeed, for a time she spoke openly of running for president in 2015 if certain legal restrictions complicating such a run were removed.

The problem was that Myanmar law forbids candidates to have either children or spouses who hold foreign citizenship. Aung San Suu Kyi had married a British academic, Michael Aris in 1972, and their twochildren are British citizens. (Aris died in 1999.)

There was at that point no reason to believe the Myanmar military was ready to move aside in favor of a system of purely democratic rule. However, it was obvious that the nation's leadership had determined that experimenting with a

# Myanmar

of Senior General Min Aung Hlaing, commander-in-chief of the Defense Forces since March 2011. Min claimed he was acting under articles 417-419 of the Constitution, which allowed him to take over if the country was in danger from "insurgency, violence and wrongful forcible means." In fact, such powers are reserved to the president, who was in military custody, along with Aung San Suu Kyi. Both were later charged. President Win Myint was accused of having broken COVID restrictions. Aung San Suu Kyi was first accused of having illegal walkie-talkies and later of bribery and corruption. Vice-president Myint Swe, a military protégé, became president.

Almost immediately, demonstrations against the coup began across the country. The police and military responded with force, using live ammunition. By mid-March 2021, some 80 people had died, with the number increasing daily. There were widespread strikes, and martial law was imposed in some parts of the country. The response from the military leadership to criticism of its tactics was that the unrest was the fault of the detained (and incommunicado) Aung San Suu Kyi. Demonstrators made extensive use of social media, despite attempts to shut down such channels. On 14 March, the deposed speaker of the National Assembly and supposed leader of a group of its ousted members, Mahn Win Khaing Than, appealed via a recorded message on Facebook for the demonstrations to continue. The demonstrators called for international support and action against the military leaders. A number of countries, including the United States and the United Kingdom responded by adding to the sanctions already in place on military leaders and their economic interests, which were imposed in response to the crack down on the Rohingya in 2017. There was little support for such action in Asia. ASEAN said the matter was an internal affair. Russia and China worked to prevent an attempt to impose United Nations sanctions. In late May 2021, the head of the military junta said that Aung San Su Kyi was well and would go on trial shortly.

Although the military clearly have never withdrawn from the political scene, developments in the last ten years did seem to offer hope that such a process might be under way. Events since the November 2020 elections have shown that such hopes were premature. Although General Min Aung Hlaing has said that the military would withdraw from politics after 12 months, old habits die hard.

In the early days after the coup, there were occasional signs of apparent moderation. In March 2021, 628 people detained for taking part in demonstrations were released. But they were all recent detainees; none of those held since Febraury 1 were included. And the repression continued, with troops firing on crowds. International reaction included sanctions on coup leaders and official protests, while ASEAN excluded Min Aung Hliang from its August summit meeting. All had little effect.

Aung San Suu Kyi was tried and sentenced on multiple counts, as were several others. And the repression went on. A Christmas Eve attack in the eastern part of the country, in which two Christian Aid workers may have been killed. Demonstrations and killings have continued and show no sign of stopping.

## Defense and Foreign Policy

Until recently much of Myanmar's defense policy was internally directed against the various ethnic groups that sought either total independence or some degree of autonomy. Progress, though, has been made at times. On January 14, 1996, SLORC improved its hold on the country when Khun Sa, the number one opium and heroin producer in the Golden Triangle, the area where the borders of Myanmar, Thailand, and Laos meet. surrendered his 10,000-man Mong Tai army to Burmese officials. In return for the surrender, Khun Sa was apparently assured that he would not be extradited to the United States. Amnesty from Rangoon and the right to maintain control over part of the Shan state with a downsized army may also have been part of the deal.

The Burmese government has also signed agreements with the New Mon State Party (NMSP). The military agreement gave Mon rebels control over 20 designated areas in their home state in return for a cease-fire. Karen groups have been fighting the Myanmar central government since 1949, sometimes encouraged by Thailand. While the Myanmar military have had some successes against the Karen National Union, the struggle continued. A temporary ceasefire 2012 quickly fell apart, and the struggle resumed. Another ceasefire in 2015 lasted until 2018. Fighting then resumed when the Myanmar military moved troops into Karen territory to protect a road-building project between two military bases. Over the years, large numbers of Karens have sought refuge in Thailand, as have people from the Shan state, another area of ethnic conflict.

The military situation along the Thai border can be tense. Yangon has in the past accused Thailand of providing not just sanctuary and help for both the Karen and Shan rebels. Burmese military forces also have conducted raids against refugee camps across the border. Issues ranging from the flow of drugs into Thailand to Bangkok's forced return of thousands

**Young monks eating**

248

# Myanmar

of illegal workers to Myanmar as well as incidents associated with anti-Myanmar activists in Thailand have strained relations. Sometimes the issues that separate the two peoples are less geopolitical and more tied to popular culture. During both 2001 and 2002 the border was closed for a time, a move that especially hurt those Thai merchants who depend on trade with Myanmar. A dramatic development in Thai-Myanmar relations was the visit by Aung San Suu Kyi to Thailand in June 2012. Unwilling to leave Myanmar for a generation because she was concerned that the authorities would not allow her to return, she finally felt that the situation had changed enough to allow her to visit Myanmar's neighbors. There she met not only with Thai figures, but with the Burmese refugee community.

Relations with the People's Republic of China are generally quite positive and improved as the country's international isolation faded after 2011. In January 2020, President Xi Jinping made the first Chinese presidential visit to Myanmar for 19 years. Since the early 1990s, Myanmar has reportedly received huge amounts of military equipment from China. Trade between the two countries has long been an important factor in Myanmar's economy. Along with India and Russia, China also used its international influence to help shield the military junta from some of its international critics. It also seems likely that China, concerned that its support of the junta might mar its international reputation, counseled Myanmar's generals against using the sort of force they had employed in 1988. Whether that is true or not, when the inevitable crackdown did happen, it was significantly less violent than the previous clash between the population and their military rulers.

The growing ties between Myanmar and China aroused concern among regional neighbors. India and Indonesia, as well as the other ASEAN states, appear concerned about Chinese access to three strategic islands off the Burmese coast. For their part, as Myanmar's leaders began to make efforts to improve relations with the West, there were signs of them wishing to be less dependent on China for international support. But following the February 2021 coup, where China has, like Russia, prevented the United Nations from adopting a tough approach, and advised against additional sanctions, the military may once again turn to China for continued support.

For years, the story of Myanmar's foreign policy was one of exclusion from the outside world but as Myanmar emerged from its self-imposed isolation, it faced a complicated international environment. Its efforts were especially complicated by

a split between many Western states and Myanmar's more immediate Southeast Asian nations on the question of relations with Myanmar and the military government that controlled it for so many years.

Until the second decade of the 21st century, Myanmar's international support had practically vanished. In the eyes of many Westerners, Myanmar had emerged as the "South Africa" of contemporary human rights concerns. Within the United States, states such as Massachusetts banned their governments from working with any corporation active in Myanmar and efforts to boycott the developing tourist trade were active. In April 1997, the United States government officially banned all new American investment

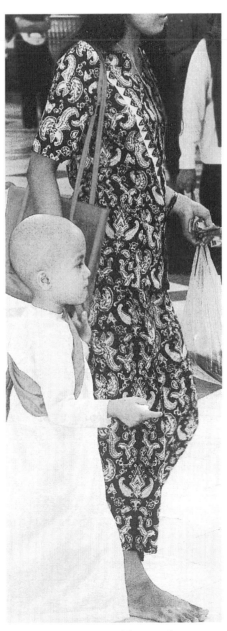

**Young nun and her mother**

in the country. The United States, along with other Western nations became even more critical of Myanmar's military government. Meanwhile, the fame of Aung San Suu Kyi as a campaigner for democracy had spread throughout the Western world. She was awarded the Nobel Peace Prize in 1991 and was no doubt helped by the success of the 1995 film Beyond Rangoon, which, along with the country's bid to join ASEAN, led to what proved a temporary release from house arrest. In early 1997, she appeared on the cover of the influential *Parade* magazine, a newspaper magazine that reaches millions of Americans every Sunday.

In 1995, Madeleine Albright, U.S. ambassador to the United Nations, visited Yangon and delivered the message that there would be no significant change in U.S. policy toward Myanmar until the government changed the way it treats its people. Somewhat later secretary of State Condoleezza Rice called the country an "outpost of tyranny." Then in the aftermath of yet another condemnation of Aung San Suu Kyi to house arrest, the Bush administration extended the economic sanctions against Myanmar for another three years. The combination of consumer boycotts of textiles and official sanctions have made it very hard for Myanmar to sell its products within the enormous American market. Significant progress in improving relations with the United States finally began in the fall of 2011 after changes by the Myanmar government were deemed sufficiently significant for Washington to renew relations. The most dramatic step initially, of course, was the visit by Hillary Clinton, then Secretary of State, in late 2011. She held meetings with both Myanmar's new and apparently more flexible leaders and with Aung San Suu Kyi herself. The latter appeared from news photographs to have been an especially gratifying visit.

Myanmar's relations with its neighbors are complicated. Overall, the closer nations, especially those in ASEAN, are interested in a policy of "constructive engagement," which finally allowed Myanmar to enter ASEAN as a full member in 1997. The decision to allow Myanmar to enter ASEAN aroused considerable concern in the Western world and created tension between the European Economic Community (now the European Union) and ASEAN. ASEAN itself is keen on bringing Myanmar into the organization as a means of providing Yangon with other alternatives to China. While Myanmar's rulers wanted to join, they probably did not appreciate the widespread criticism they have received from many regional colleagues who have been quite outspoken in their negative comments about Myanmar's human rights practices.

249

# Myanmar

That criticism became at times very specific as when Malaysia's then Prime Minister, Mahathir Mohamad, visited Myanmar in July 2003 and took the opportunity to tell his hosts quite openly that their membership in ASEAN was causing significant problems between ASEAN and other international group. Others were less critical, stressing the value of engagement but in 2005, Myanmar chose not to serve as the head of ASEAN's influential standing committee, as it was scheduled to do, to placate some of its critics. Some members of ASEAN continued to be critical of Myanmar, especially at the time of the "Saffron rebellion" led by Buddhist monks in 2007. But there were no sanctions and no move to expel Myanmar from the organization. The following year, ASEAN played a positive role when southern parts of the country, including Yanggon, were hit by Cyclone Nagis. The government declined international aid, since it would involve large number of foreigners in the country. This led to international criticism, with a number of countries calling for forcible intervention. ASEAN then offered to act as a channel for aid, however, and the crisis was defused. The opening to the West after 2011 brought major and early benefit as it lessened the complications of membership in ASEAN. By 2014, it was able to assume the annual chair of the association. Despite later setbacks such as the 2017 Rohingya crisis, ASEAN has continued to argue for engagement rather than confrontation, even at first in the face of the 2021 military coup. But faced with the intransigence of the coup leaders, it has adopted an increasingly tougher line.

Chinese influence in Myanmar is longstanding and significant. This is partly due to the military assistance described above and China's refusal to criticize internal politics, and partly because of significant immigration and trade. Insurgencies and their handling by the military in the border states has caused difficulties in the past. Chinese influence has created other problems. As well as United States' concerns about Chinese expansionism, India is worried by the extensive Chinese presence in Myanmar and the possibility of military cooperation. India has had a Treaty of Friendship since 1951. It has been concerned at Chinese influence in Myanmar since the deterioration in its own relations with China since the late 1950s and has worked to keep up a good relationship with Myanmar to counter such influence, as well as to gain help dealing with its own insurgency movement along its northeastern frontier. worked to warm relations with the junta perhaps to balance Chinese influence. There has also been some military cooperation, with the first ever joint military exercise in 2017. Myanmar is the only one of India's neighbors that shares a border with ASEAN, which it sees as a useful channel to that organization, despite the latter's own problems with the country.

On the principle of non-interference in internal affairs, India has avoided comments on Myanmar's political developments. It has provided humanitarian aid from time to time. There have been some high-level visits. Then Prime Minister Rajiv Gandhi visited Myanmar in 1987. In the fall of 2004, General Than Shwe, then chairman of Myanmar's ruling junta, made the first visit by a Myanmar leader to India in almost a quarter of a century. India's Prime Minister Narendra Modi went to Myanmar in September 2017, while then State Counsellor Aung San Suu Kyi was one of the foreign guests at the Republic of India Day parade in January 2018.

Relations with another neighbor, Bangladesh, began when the latter was still part of Pakistan. After Bangladesh gained independence in 1971, the two countries established diplomatic relations early in 1972. Since then, the relationship has seen periods of cooperation interspersed with periods of tension, mostly over incidents along the land and sea borders. The most difficult of these issues, that of the Rohingya refugees, which is deal with in more detail below, has put a huge economic and social strain on Bangladesh, a country with many problems of its own. It looks likely, however, that the situation will continue to cause problems for some time to come, given the military takeover in Myanmar in February 2021, since it was military action against that brought about the present crisis in 2017.

The Myanmar relationship with what is often seen as another isolated "rogue state," the Democratic People's Republic of Korea (North Korea), is also complex. They established diplomatic relations in 1975. But following a North Korean attempt to kill the visiting Republic of Korea president, Chun Doo-hwan, at the Martyrs' Cemetery in Yangon in October 1983, Myanmar not only broke off diplomatic relations but also formally withdrew recognition of North Korea. It is likely that some trade, especially in rice and other foodstuffs, either continued or soon restarted but this was not made public. Faced with increasing international isolation, the two countries agreed to resume diplomatic relations in 2007. Before long, there was growing signs of Western concern about North Korean supplies of weapons' systems to Myanmar. Rumors of underground defense-related structures and a possible nuclear program led to U.S. naval vessels turning back at least two North Korean ships bound for Myanmar. It is not clear if any of this was true and the stories have died away.

### Society and Culture

While Burmans constitute the largest ethnic group in the country, others such as the Karens, Shans, and Kachins are important. Much of modern Burmese history has been dominated by the efforts of these

groups to gain greater autonomy from the Burmese Government.

Theravada Buddhism pervades almost every aspect of Burmese culture. In fact, the military junta has made efforts to link itself to Buddhism as a way to reinforce its legitimacy. Monks are numerous and influential; most Burmese males spend at least part of their lives in monasteries. The countless temples and shrines have been constructed with great care and with precious materials that combine to create structures of exquisite beauty; the best known of these is the huge and ornate Shwe Dagon in Yangon. There is also a widespread belief in animism, especially with respect to the existence and activities of "nats" which are spirits within objects. Christian and Muslim groups also exist although they operate under heavy controls imposed by the government.

While these religious traditions reinforce Myanmar's links to its cultural tradition, the junta's political policies were hurting country's ties to the future.

Indeed, the regime was so concerned about the thousands of students who had so often protested against its rule that most of the nation's colleges were closed to keep the opposition under control. The result, of course, was that a generation of Burmese who have failed to gain the higher education they and their country needed to move into the 21st century, or of course many fled depriving the country of very people Myanmar needed for the challenges of the new century.

More recently among the youth of the larger Burman society, quite another direction has begun to emerge. Younger people who once felt it necessary to flee the country to fulfill their dreams are starting to establish themselves in the telecommunications industry, currently in its infancy. They are developing software applications for the day when a significantly greater percentage of the population will have access to mobile smartphones.

### Myanmar's Rohingya Crisis: 21st-Century Ethnic Cleansing

Unfortunately while the new more democratic government in Myanmar has been a great improvement for many people that has not been the case for others. Of immediate concern has been the explosion of tensions that have developed between the longtime Burman Buddhist residents and the people known as Rohingya, a mostly Muslim ethnic group who have for eons been a significant part of the population state of Rakhine State in the country's northwest.

The Rohingya people themselves speak a distinct Indo-European language that, while it shares similarities to Bengali is

**General Than Shwe**

in terms of actually communicating, quite different. The community appears to have deep historical roots in Rakhine even as many also arrived during the era of British colonial control from today's Bangladesh.

During the early postcolonial era the Rohingya were relatively well treated, indeed some served in the new nation's parliament but as the military took control in the early 1960s, the treatment of Rohingya grew dramatically worse. Indeed, today they are not even included among the official ethnic groups recognized by the Myanmar government that has for decades carried out a systematic and expanding suppression of the community all the while insisting they were simply unwanted foreign migrants from neighboring Bangladesh. This denial of citizenship has played a major role in depriving the community of rights from open travel to higher education while denying them any role in either the military or government. Not surprisingly, such treatment radicalized members of the Rohingya community leading to the formation of the Arakan Rohingya Salvation Army (ARSA) a resistance movement that has carried out attacks against Burmese officials and the non-Rohingya community in Rakhine itself.

The situation has grown dramatically worse after violent clashes instigated by the ARSA in August of 2017 that provoked a massive retaliatory strike by Burmese authorities that many are calling one of the most horrendous examples of ethnic cleansing of the 21st century. Indeed more than a half a million Rohingya were forced to flee to a not very welcoming Bangladesh having experienced horrendous violence at the hands of the Burmese authorities

Meanwhile in neighboring Bangladesh the largest refugee camp in the world has sprung up as those fleeing Myanmar find

themselves trapped in squalid conditions they are not likely to be able to escape anytime soon given the hardening attitudes against them at home and among government officials in Bangladesh itself.

Somewhat ironically but perhaps predictably, as is so often the case in such situations, the clashes have brought about a level of national unity among the majority Burman community, from Buddhist monks and the military to the more democratic supporters of Aung San Suu Kyi that would have seemed imaginable only a few years.

And, while that national solidarity might at first glance seem positive. In the face of an international community that has been deeply moved by the suffering of the Rohingya, even Pope Francis visited both Myanmar and refugees in Bangladesh, it seems increasingly likely that most of the good will Myanmar garnered in the Western World in its decades long struggle for democratic freedoms is rapidly being lost. As a practical matter the result will probably be that the nation in upcoming years will grow even closer to China given Beijing's frequently less than enthusiastic support for human rights globally.

### Women

In contrast to the customs of both traditional India and China, Burmese women have enjoyed a high degree of freedom and social equality; they can inherit property, keep their maiden names after marriage and have equal rights in contracting marriage and suing for divorce. Reports of spousal abuse are infrequent. Nevertheless, for many young Burmese women, especially among minorities that live near the borders, life can bring great trials. Many end up working as illegals in Thailand's agricultural or industrial sectors, becoming, especially for the latter, part of the increasingly globalized production chains that circle the globe.

There are also frequent reports of young women having been lured across the border to Thailand to accept jobs that turn out to be forced prostitution in Bangkok's brothels despite the original job offers. This is also true for members of the nation's various ethnic minorities, who have often ended up being sent by human traffickers to serve in those same Thai brothels after trying to flee the nation by sea.

Moreover, the government's longtime policy of demanding forced labor from its citizens often leads to abuses. There are no independent women's rights organizations nor are there government ministries responsible for women's issues. With the exception of Aung San Suu Kyi, women play almost no role in the political life of

# Myanmar

the nation. Until quite recently her role was, of course, largely symbolic.

As elsewhere in the world and within the region, the women of Myanmar are increasingly faced with the risk of contracting AIDS. Women are especially vulnerable to the disease since they tend to have less power than their male counterparts and frequently less access to the education necessary to prevent infection and later to the medications needed to deal with the disease.

## Economy

The news about the national economy has usually been quite grim. For a time, the situation improved somewhat, most notably with the suspension of most international sanctions. But those more positive changes have come to an end since the 2021 coup..

Indeed, a generation ago now, Myanmar's leaders made a rather feeble attempt to transform the economy from its earlier centrally planned socialist-style organization into a market-orientated one. But that quickly lost enormous momentum. By 1997, even before what is known as the Asian Economic Meltdown of 1998, the economy, having done somewhat better during the early 1990s, was again a disaster. Once that somewhat more open period passed, a new tone of corruption and patronage was reestablished. All this was made worse by shortsighted government

**Mother and daughter in front of Pagodas**

currency manipulation that only served further to weaken public faith in their country's money system. For example, the economy was significantly disrupted when the government limited how much money could be withdrawn from banks. This forced people who owed money to pay back half of their loans immediately. Meanwhile the World Bank ended its relationship with the regime and sent a clear message that investment should be considered especially risky.

Despite the fact that the nation is quite rich in natural resources, the combination of poor governmental economic leadership and the international sanctions its policies provoked for so many years combined to create very weak economic circumstances.

Nor did tourism, usually an important industry for the region, play its usual role either. Even the temporary and occasionally reconciliations between Myanmar's Nobel Prize–winning activist, Aung San Suu Kyi, and the government did not affect the number of tourist arrivals significantly. They still remained far short of Myanmar's tourist potential. Nevertheless, tourist numbers did climb in the early years of the new millennium as people who had originally planned Southeast Asian vacations to Indonesia redirected their sights toward Myanmar after the terrorist bombings in Bali.

While it is also true that a new Burmese middle class seems to be emerging, the average income is only a bit over $1,000 a year, and few get any advanced education. Very few have a high school-level education, and far fewer, only a bit over 4%, have a college education. As mentioned above, especially significant is the country's failure to produce enough college-educated professionals to meet the new economic challenges of the globalized world economy.

But there are areas where Myanmar has managed to meet global needs. Sadly, really significant economic gains have been made in the illegal but lucrative narcotics trade. Since SLORC came to power, Myanmar has become the world's main producer of opium and heroin. More recently it has added the production of methamphetamines to its infamous production schedules. The government itself claims it has been actively working to reduce the production of opium and even forcibly relocating peasants to areas where they can cultivate crops other than opium.

It is also true, though, that while the West may have spent years trying to use economic pressure to force the junta to improve its governing record, the country has weathered those pressures relatively well. Despite being largely isolated by the Western countries, Myanmar's neighbors,

from China to India and Thailand, have been more supportive. China, for example, is particularly interested in using Myanmar as an oil transport resource that might allow it to depend less on the potentially unreliable waters around the Straits of Malacca.

One legitimate area of Myanmar's economy that has seen impressive growth is that of pearl production. In contrast to other Myanmar businesses, the pearl industry has been able to attract foreign investment. The oil and gas industry has also attracted outside investment as well. A South Korean company was involved in exploring for oil off Myanmar's western coast. Despite the coup, which has led to widespread economic sanctions, there is still some foreign interest in the country.

Moreover, commitments have been made by Myanmar's neighbors, particularly China, Thailand, India, and the more distant Russians to invest directly in Myanmar's energy sector. China alone has seen a very significant growth in its trade with Myanmar while transportation links with India have been growing.

Perhaps one of the most important developments that may ultimately affect the economy is the growth of economic cooperation among Myanmar's neighbors. The recent trade fair held among the Greater Mekong Sub-region nations is only the most obvious example. Even more dramatically, the ongoing effort to dredge the Mekong to make it easier to navigate within the region occupied by China, Myanmar, Laos, and Thailand is eventually likely to offer considerable economic benefits.

Nevertheless, growth figures remain difficult to gauge. The figures occasionally issued by the Burmese government differ dramatically from those offered by outside agencies like the Asian Development Bank. Following the 2003–2004 financial year, Yanggon did not even publish growth figures, a decision that hardly suggests robust growth. More recently the situation has changed somewhat. The junta claimed very impressive double-digit growth rates while outsider agencies estimated the rates at somewhat over 2%. More recently the figure again set by outsiders has been a somewhat healthier 2.9% for 2006. But those plunged again in the aftermath of the recent series of disasters. The year 2008 came in at a weak 0.9%, and that was before the full impact of the world economic downtown was felt late that year. For years, growth figures seem to have hovered around a healthier 5% to 6% range of GDP.

But the effect of COVID and the 2021 coup have had a major economic impact. The World Bank has said that the economy has contracted by 30% as a result of these two developments, and predicts that growth in 2022 will at best be 1%.

The bottom line is that Myanmar remains a very poor country with an economy that seems to be getting worse by the day. And that was not just from poor economic policies or the nation's international isolation. Most notably, the nation was deeply challenged by the enormous damage caused by the devastating cyclone in 2008. Other problems include flood damage, significant foreign debt, unemployment, high inflation, an unrealistic exchange rate, a very poor infrastructure, (which is finally improving) a failed educational system, and until recently the prospect of little immediate assistance from the international community as a result of the junta's anti-democratic behavior. But by the spring of 2012, though, it was finally possible to imagine a different future.

## Environmental Issues

As is so common among its neighbors, protecting its natural environment and especially the nation's forest growth is an important challenge. In Myanmar's case timber smuggling remains a problem, and negotiations are currently under way to form a cooperative arrangement between the Myanmar and the Chinese government to deal with forestry issues along their shared border. Myanmar is also attracting unwanted attention from its Thai neighbors for the burning of rubbish and weeds that so often dramatically influences the air quality of its richer neighbor. These are, of course, practices that have gone on for ages. But in today's increasingly more environmental conscious world, it is more of an issue. Like many other countries whose tropical forests are being dramatically reduced by deforestation, Myanmar could potentially gain significantly if the world were finally to develop a system to make it financially advantageous to let forests remain healthy and capable of successfully absorbing the $CO_2$ greenhouse gases that are adding to the current challenge of climate change.

## COVID 19

Myanmar introduced preventative measures against COVID-19 starting 20 March 2020, banning international flights and large public meetings. It reported its first cases in April 2020, when the government also introduced measures to ease the economic burdens of the pandemic and better health care. By March 2021, the total of reported cases was 142,000, of whom 132,000 were said to have fully recovered. Total deaths reported were 3,203, with peaks in October and November 2020. By late February 2021, the daily reported death rate was said to be hovering around zero. Half the total deaths were in Yanggon, the most populous city. Vaccination began in late January, with supplies donated and purchased from India. There were, however, disruption to the program after the military coup. By December 2021, there were over 530,000 cases, with 19,000 deaths, according to official figures. By May 2022, the figures were 613,000 and 19,434. Vaccinations were estimated at around 52.7% of the population fully vaccinated.

## The Future

Until just recently it actually seemed, literally for the first time in decades possible to be generally optimistic about Myanmar's future. That is probably still true but as history has shown so often before releasing governmental pressures in a long repressed society can be an incredibly difficult and even explosive endeavor. Politically of course Myanmar's governing situation is opening up in a fashion that has not been seen in generations. Famous and influential leaders have come and gone and international donors and investors are again showing interest.

But of course, at the same time, a freer society also revealed rifts in the society that were previously hidden somewhat below the surface, most notably between Myanmar's Burman Buddhist majority and its minority communities. The assaults against the Rohingya Muslim minority have been so horrendous that the country has been accused of ethnic cleansing by the internationally respected group Human Rights Watch.

Meanwhile, the somewhat more open atmosphere has seen as well dramatic clashes between the nation's security forces and student activists demonstrating for educational reforms. Indeed scores of students recently clashed with police and were subsequently charged with offenses that could lead to years in jail for many of them. The core issue has been an attempt to centralize the nation's higher education system.

At least for outsiders, the nation's previous image of a closed society of oppressed and long suffering Buddhist community has been muddied by the more chauvinistic attitudes that many in that community have shown toward their nation's Muslim minority.

Complicating matters was the mixed message of Aung San Suu Kyi's arrival to power. On one hand, it represented the culmination of decades of suppressed democratic aspirations on the part of the people of Myanmar. On the other hand, many have been disappointed by her response to the the plight of the Myanmar's Muslims citizens in the face of nationalist Buddhist assaults against their community.

As a practical matter, regardless of what Aung San Suu Kyi's personal feelings might be about the situation of the Rohingya Muslims, her power to impact developments was quite limited. She does not control those security forces that have been most directly involved with dealing with the tensions. Moreover, her own situation is hardly that secure.

Indeed, the assassination in early January 2017 of Ko Ni a Muslim himself and an important adviser to Aung San Suu Kyi highlights how fragile even the progress that had been made in creating a more open tolerant Myanmar.

Now, faced with the military back in control, hopes for a more liberal country have faded. And, on past experience, the military are unlikely to give up power anytime soon. The propspects for the future look bleak.

# Papua New Guinea

**Shipping at Port Moresby**

Courtesy of Ray Witlin

**Area:** 178,260 sq. mi. (475,369 sq. km.)
**Population:** 9,256,576 (May 2022 est.)
**Capital City:** Port Moresby, pop. 400,051 2022 est.)
**Climate:** Tropical
**Neighboring Countries:** Australia (South); Indonesia (West)
**Official Language:** English
**Other Principal Tongues:** There are over 800 indigenous languages and a Pidgin English is spoken in much of the country
**Ethnic Background:** Melanesian, Papuan, Negrito, Micronesian, Polynesian
**Principal Religion:** Traditional tribal beliefs (34%), Roman Catholic (22%), Lutheran (16%), other (28%)
**Main Exports:** (to Japan, China, Germany, Australia) Oil, natural gas, copper, gold, timber, coffee, rubber, palm oil, cocoa, and crayfish
**Main Imports:** (from Australia, Japan, Singapore) Machinery, consumer goods, food, fuel, transportation equipment, fuels, and chemicals
**Currency:** Kina
**Former Colonial Status:** New Guinea was a German colony from 1884 to 1914. On the outbreak of World War I, it was seized by Australian troops. Post war, it was administered by Australia under a League of Nations' mandate from 1919 to 1942. Papua was a British protectorate from 1884 until 1888. It then became a British colony, administered by Australia until 1942. From 1942 to 1945, both areas were under Japanese occupation. Post war, the status quo was reinstated, with Australia's mandate over New Guinea continuing as , a United Nations trusteeship administered by Australia until 1975.
**National Day:** September 16, 1975
**Chief of State:** Her Majesty Queen Elizabeth II, represented by Sir Bob Dadae (since February 28, 2017)
**Head of Government:** Prime Minister James Marape (since May 2019)
**National Flag:** Divided diagonally from top left to bottom right, the top a red field upon which is centered a yellow bird of paradise, the bottom a black field showing five white stars in the Southern Cross
**GNP Per Capita GDP:** $3,861 (2020 est.) (purchasing power parity)

Occupying the eastern half of the large island of New Guinea, the western portion, Irian Jaya, being part of Indonesia, the nation was formed from Papua, the southeastern quarter of the island and the Territory of New Guinea, the northeastern quarter plus the nearby Admiralty, northern Solomon, and Bismarck island groups.

The terrain is covered largely with very high mountains, swamps, and jungles. The climate is uniformly tropical except in the more temperate altitudes of the mountains. There is an extremely small European minority; the indigenous inhabitants belong either to the Papuan group (on New Guinea) or to the Melanesian people (on the islands).

## History

Until two centuries ago the people of Papua New Guinea were still living a lifestyle thousands of years older than what the population experienced in 18th century Europe. Still their societies—and there are a great many different communities among them—were quite sophisticated and ancient. In fact, it has been estimated that people have lived in New Guinea for at least 50,000 years. The evidence indicates that intensive agriculture has been carried out—probably using sugarcane—as the primary crop for several millennia. It is also possible that the cultivation of taro root was an early part of the farmer's repertoire.

Archeological evidence suggests that such food production developed as early as 7000 B.C. and was accomplished indigenously rather than being imported from elsewhere. But that production accomplishment was not the work of a single group. In terms of human habitation, Papua New Guinea has long been one of the most diverse communities in the world. Even today, of the 6,000 known languages in the world, 1,000 of them are confined to New Guinea.

Despite that long historical presence in the region, the peoples of New Guinea lived in small villages without larger political organization or more sophisticated tools than those made out of stone. They did have the advantage of the taro root as something that humans could domesticate, but the island lacked any of the larger animals that other societies have been able to domesticate. The only relatively large animals were flightless birds and small kangaroos. Neither is suitable for human use as are horses or camels found elsewhere.

### The European Arrival

Prior to the late 19th century, apart from missionaries, New Guinea attracted two main types of Europeans: explorers and investors, lured by its supposedly substantial mineral resources. Dutch influence based on Indonesia became dominant in western New Guinea. The northeastern part of the big island and the smaller islands to the east were annexed by Germany in 1884, as the colony of German New Guinea. The southeastern part of the island known as Papua was annexed by the governor of Queensland, Australia in 1883, on behalf of Britain. The British government initially rejected this move, but in 1884, placed the territory under British protection. In 1888, the territory became a British colony. From 1902 onward, this was administered by the new Dominion of Australia.

The German holdings in northeastern New Guinea and the nearby islands were seized by Australia during World War I. They were then awarded to Australia under a League of Nations mandate that after World War II became a United Nations trusteeship. Despite the technical distinction between the two, it was not until the Australian parliament passed the Papua New Guinea Act in 1949, that they were merged into one legal entity.

In 1942, the Japanese conquered the islands east of New Guinea and invaded parts of the large island, including both of the eastern regions. Some of the bitterest fighting of the Pacific War occurred during the next two years as Australian and American forces drove the Japanese out of all but a few strongholds. Following the end of the war, Australian civil administration was restored. In response to UN criticism and a growing demand for self-government, an elected assembly was established in 1968.

In elections in 1972 to the House of Assembly (the parliament), the National Coalition, led by Michael Somare was

victorious. His program, which called for full self-government, was accepted by Australia soon afterward, even though it was opposed by many of the European inhabitants who were understandably concerned about the changing political environment. Following the passing of the Papua New Guinea Indepndence Act by Australia's Gough Whitlam government, Papua New Guinea became independent on 16 September 1975, joining the United Nations in October that year. It also joined the Commonwealth, and kept Britain's Queen Elizabeth II as head of state. Close ties continue with Australia, which is the country's major aid donor.

### The Bougainville Crisis

Even before Papua New Guinea formally gained its independence, it was faced with a major political challenge. The island of Bougainville is the largest of the Solomon Islands' group. In 1899, it became part of the German colony of New Guinea and was seized by Australian forces in 1914, becoming a League of Nations' mandated territory in 1919. Situated some distance from the rest of Papua New Guinea, it declared its independence on 11 September 1975, as the "Republic of the North Solomons." However, there was no international support for this move and in 1976, Bougainville agreed to join Papua New Guinea, with considerable self-government rights also granted to other regions.

The island's economy was heavily dominated by the foreign-owned Bougainville Copper Mine established in 1972. An attempt by landlords to get compensation

from the company, most of whose profits went abroad, for their loss of land failed in 1988. This, and concerns about the environmenatal damage, led to attacks by a group calling itself the Bougainville Revolutionary Army, led by Francis Ona, which also called for the island's independence, on the grounds that it belonged to the Soloman Islands, not Papua New Guinea.

The attacks escalated into an uprising in which over 15,000 were killed. Supported by Australia, the Papua New Guinea Defense Forces fought the uprising. But frustrated by the seemingly endless conflict, which the Defense Forces seemed to be unable to bring to a conclusion, Prime Minister Michael Chan in 1997 recruited a group of South African mercenaries. There was no extenal support for this move. When the chief of the Defense Forces refused to back the move, announcing that any mercenaries would be arrested on arrival, Chan was forced from office. In the 1997 election, he became the first prime minister to lose his seat.

Following these developments, New Zealand brokered peace talks, which led to an agreement between some of the rebel forces and the PNG government to end the fighting. To oversee this arrangement, a Peace Monitoring Group under Australian auspices was created. Although some elements of the Bourgainville Revolutionary Army would hold out until Ona, their leader died of malaria in 2005, the agreement held. Bourgainville was granted autonomous status in 2001 and a referendum on independence would be held in due course.

It was not until late 2019 that the promised—but non-binding—referendum was

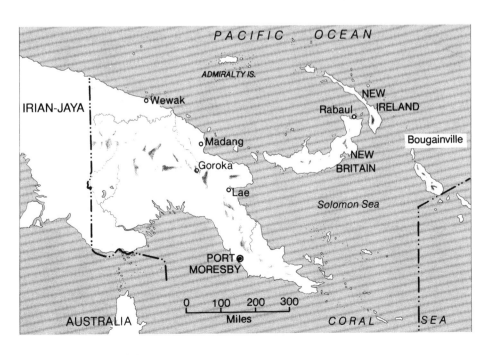

255

# Papua New Guinea

finally held. However, when it produced a 98.31% vote for independence, the central government agreed that Bourgainville would become independent in 2027.

The conflict took a heavy toll on the island. There were not only the large number killed in the fighting but a tight economic blocade mounted by the Defense Forces badly damaged the local economy.

### Politics and Government

The political system of Papua New Guinea is a federally based parliamentary system which offers universal suffrage for its citizens. The judiciary is independent from the executive branch of the government. Although democracy has been successfully maintained, little has been accomplished in terms of the daily living standards of PNG citizens in the decades since full independence. The government is currently made up of representatives from 13 different parties as well as 20 independents, a political diversity that makes it difficult to accomplish much politically. There have of course been efforts to reform the system. In 2002, for example it has been made illegal for politicians to change their party affiliation after elections, a move that it was hoped would offer more political stability. In practice, however, little changed.

Another governmental reform was undertaken, which resulted in the elimination of the country's 19 provincial parliaments. Unpaid local government officials, along with the national parliamentary representatives, formed local assemblies. They took the place of some 600 paid politicians who composed the provincial parliaments. The MPs in the new assemblies with the largest representation became governors. They are to be the primary link between the local assemblies and the capital. The move may also have some impact on the unstable political party system, where new parties appear frequently, and where members regularly shift from one party to another. Especially damaging over the years was the long running struggle with separatists from the island of Bougainville, which not only caused tremendous suffering but, as we have seen, dramatically impacted on the politics of the central government.

After Prime Minister Chan was forced from office, only to lose his own political seat in the July 1997 elections, he was followed in office by the flamboyant Bill Skate, who successfully held off a challenge by the nation's first prime minister, Sir Michael Somare, to return to office. Skate, the former Port Moresby governor, took office in July of 1997. His primary accomplishment, during what turned out to be a very short-lived administration, was ending the fighting in Bougainville by signing a peace treaty in early 1998. Unfortunately for Skate, within a year his tenure in office had become very rocky. The following July, Skate was ousted from his position by a whopping 99 to 5 parliamentary vote.

His successor was the well-known economist and businessman, Sir Mekere Morauta, who promised a more stable financial and international administration. Unfortunately, the prime minister's hopes to use his extensive experience to improve the economy did not work out. In August 2002, for the third time, Papua New Guinea's founding prime minister, Michael Somare, returned to office. By 2007, he had been reelected to yet another term as prime minister.

In December 2010, Sir Michael Somare, who had faced increasing hostility because of his autocratic ways, stepped down to face charges of financial irregularities and for heart surgery. In his absence, a former treasury minister and businessman, Peter O'Neill, was chosen to replace him. When Somare recovered and tried to resume office, O'Neill resisted. There followed a period of tension, with rival administrations claiming authority. Somare even attempted a coup d'état, but the security forces refused to back him, but the issue was not settled until O'Neill's party won a resounding election success in 2012. Somare never returned to office but continued in parliament until 2017. He died in February 2021.

PNG politics continued to be unstable and periodically violent; guns are widely available. But while O'Neill faced regularly parliamentary challenges, he remained prime minister until May 2019, when he was replaced by a former ministerial colleague, James Marape. O'Neill's time in office had been punctuated by regular charges of corruption. These caused trouble with aid donors as well as a crisis in 2016 when student protests were met with police violence, including suspected deaths, and the closure of universities for the rest of the year. A vote of no confidence was proposed, which O'Neill tried unsuccessfully to block, yet it was defeated by 85 votes to 21. As O'Neill left office, there were allegations that he had had dual PNG-Australian citizenship, which should have debarred him from office. Nothing came of this but in May 2020, O'Neill was arrested on charges of misappropriation, abuse of office, and official corruption in connection with the acquisition of Israeli generators in 2014. The case was referred for trial in December 2020. O'Neill maintained that the case was politically motivated, and in October 2021, the charges were dismissed.

Marape has not had an easy time in office but has survived, although with a steadily reduced majority. Suspension of parliament effectively from the end of 2020 for eight months because of COVID helped. He thus avoided a no-confidence vote that had been planned. Because a prime minister cannot be removed by a no-confidence vote in the 12 months before the next general election, he is safe until the July 2022 general election. It is widely expected that he will then lose to Peter O'Neill.

**Mountain children**

## Society and Culture

The vast majority of the population (around 85%) still lives at a subsistence level in isolated villages. Little headway has been made in developing the more industrial sectors of the economy or helping the villagers compete in the world agricultural market.

A small portion of the indigenous inhabitants still live at an Old Stone Age level-hunting and gathering for a living. The common impression that all of its citizens live under such traditional circumstances has—at times—made it difficult to attract foreign investment.

Most of people practice some sort of Protestant Christianity; the majority are Lutherans. The largest single Christian group, however, are Roman Catholics, who accounted for about a quarter of the population in the 2011 census. There are small numbers of followers of Islam, the Baha'i faith, and Hinduism. Traditional religious practices are also an important part of the religious environment, with some combining this with other religions. . Western missionaries, many of them American, are quite active in the area. Although there is in theory freedom of religion, there have been attacks on Muslims and other minority faiths.

In recent years, the combination of the growth in the urban population and significant levels of unemployment has produced a major growth in crime which has made it even more difficult for the country to attract tourists to its shores. In fact, the crime rate became so significant that the American Peace Corps decided in 2001 to pull its volunteers from PNG after 20 years' operation there.. So bad had the crime situation become that capital punishment, once abolished, was theoretically reinstated in 1991. However, nobody was executed and it was again abolished in January 2022 after the courts were prepared to allow a number of executions to go ahead.

### Women

Although government legislation gives women extensive rights, they are in practice still discriminated against, and some of the traditional cultural values that once offered women some protections have broken down in recent years. Polygamous marriages are allowed and often are at the root of domestic violence. It is, for example, not uncommon for a woman to be imprisoned for attacking another of their spouses' wives. The government has banned new polygamous marriages although the legislation does not affect previously established unions. Interestingly the new government has also introduced legislation designed to encourage the political parties to support female candidates. While this is a worthwhile goal, it will not be easy to realize. Since independence in 1975, only seven women have been elected to parliament. The most prominent of these, the Australian-born wife of the then Chief Justice, Lady Carol Kidu, was the only female MP 2002-2007 and 2007-2012. After she retired from politics in 2012, there were three female MPS 2012-2017. All lost their seats in the 2017 general election, and none have been elected since. This may change in the 2022 General Election, since Prime Minister Marape in August 2020 revived the idea of reserved seats for women. Rape appears to be quite common.

Only 50% of PNG women are literate (male literacy is around 63%), and a third do not attend primary school. Still, some women have established themselves in many upper level positions in business and government. Nevertheless, traditional practices still tend to treat women as property that adds to the perception of them as second-class citizens or even less.

Violence against women and children is widespread and tolerated. In 2019, for example, violence in the Highland region

**Mekeo tribesmen in ceremonial dress**　　　　　Courtesy of Colin Freeman

# Papua New Guinea

left some 30 dead, most of whom were women, some of whom were pregnant. The police have been known to target women and children when dealing with demonstrators, and they are often reluctant to investigate alleged violence. Accusations of sorcery are mainly directed against women, who are liable to be tortured and killed in brutal fashion. As well as the alleged sorcerer, their first-born child is also likely to be killed, in the belief that they will have inherited a parent's power to do evil. Before independence, a Sorcery Act was passed in 1971. This made sorcery illegal and a criminal offence but distinguished it from witchcraft, which was said to often be benevolent. But convictions were rare. The act was repealed in 2013. A replacement act required all sorcery-related killings to be treated as murder, but there have been no convictions. The outlook remains bleak. As New York-based Human Rights Watch noted in its 2020 report, PNG is "one of the most dangerous countries in the world to be a woman or girl. . . ."

## COVID-19

The first reported case of COVID-19 was on 20 March 2020. By then, the authorities had already taken preventive measures. Air arrivals from Asia ended in early February 2020 and the land border with Indonesia was closed. When infections rose in April, the capital district was locked down, with gatherings prohibited, schools closed, a night curfew and a ban on the sale of alcohol. Public transport, including domestic air travel, ceased to operate. As numbers reportedly fell, the lockdown was modified in early May, although gatherings were still prohibited. While these measures were undoubtedly effective, there was much scepticism both within PNG and more widely at the official figures. These claimed that at the end of 2020, there had been 800 cases, with nine deaths.

But any complacency disappeared in 2021. New cases began to appear in February and rose rapidly in March and April. The already fragile health service was overwhelmed, with intensive care units full, shortages of essential needs and only about 500 doctors in the country. By the end of April 2021, the number of cases was said to be 10,915, with 107 deaths but these figures were almost certainly too low. Australia sent 8,000 doses of vaccine in March 2021 and promised more. There were spikes in February–June and August–December 2021, and January–March 2022. By the end of April, official figures gave a total number of cases as 43,817, with 650 deaths, but the real figures were believed to be much higher. 441,214 vaccine doses had been administered.

## Foreign Policy

The most controversial aspect of PNG's foreign policy in recent years was former Prime Minister Chan's decision to resolve the Bougainville crisis by employing a mercenary contingent. The incident temporarily soured relations with Australia that had been especially angry about the employment of the South African mercenaries. Matters were not helped when a confidential Australian government document, which negatively evaluated PNG's leadership, was leaked to the press during the summer of 1997.

PNG's southwestern neighbor New Zealand played an important role in trying to reconcile the opposing sides in the ongoing Bougainville crisis. Later, PNG's neighbors contributed to the resolution of the problem by agreeing to supply troops from New Zealand, Australia, Tonga, Fiji, and Vanuatu. One of the most significant accomplishments of the former Prime Minister Sir Mekere Morauta was the completion of a final peace treaty on this issue which has so disrupted life in Papua New Guinea. The agreement that finally resolved the long-running crisis was to allow Bougainville to become a special autonomous region able to take more control over its own fate. And by the late spring of 2005 its people were doing precisely that. Over 130,000 of them registered to vote in the region's first ever autonomous election, a polling that was carried out smoothly under the watchful eye of a dozen international observers.

Among the most complicated of Papua New Guinea's international relationships is with its neighbor Australia. On the one hand, the Australian government contributes hundreds of millions of dollars in aid the frequently hard pressed nation needs. On the other hand, former Australian Prime Minister Howard made it clear that he wanted more accountability on how that aid was spent. He dispatched 200 Australians to help improve the nation's public administration, a move that was not well received by Papua New Guinea's Prime Minister Michael Somare.

Eventually a more formal "Enhanced Cooperation Program" was put into place. It allowed 300 Australian experts to serve in a variety of governmental posts from the local police and courts to immigration and customs offices. However, that agreement collapsed in May 2005 amidst more tensions between Prime Minister Somare and the Australians. Once Australia's next Prime Minister Kevin Rudd assumed office in 2007, there was significantly more effort on Australia's part to help PNG deal with the challenge of climate change and the all-important effort to reduce carbon emissions globally. In the most recent

Courtesy of Laura Tamakoshi

example, Rudd (whose party replaced him as prime minister in June 2010) offered help in reducing carbon emissions associated with deforestation in PNG.

Tensions also exist over the agreement Australia and PNG have regarding the resettlement of refugees Australia is unwilling to welcome. For a time, PNG agreed to set up a resettlement facility but by the spring of 2016 the nation's supreme court ruled that the facility was illegal. The process of closing down the center began the following year and was completed in 2019. Many of the refugees, who feared that a move to less secure sites would leave them vulnerable to attack, did not want to move. But Australia made no protest at the action.

In an attempt to move away from overdependence on Australia, PNG has since the mid-2010s began to make approaches to China. There have been frequent ministerial visits to Beijing, and in 2019, PNG proposed negotiating a possible deal whereby China would refinance the country's total national debt (then $7.95 billion, equal to 32.8% of GDP). These growing contacts with China have begun to worry Australia on both strategic and economic grounds.

## Economy

The economies of the two areas, Papua (in the south) and New Guinea (in the north), are similar except that most of the mineral deposits (copper, gold, and silver) so far discovered are located in New Guinea. The external trade of Papua New Guinea is largely with Australia, the United States, and Germany. More than 50% of PNG's economy is owned by large Australian firms.

Almost 70% of PNG's exports come from mining. There are also substantial oil and gas deposits. Regrettably, production has often been disrupted by bandits and local armed gangs.

In spite of the country's political difficulties, economic growth was impressive in the early 1990s, but it weakened in the following years. In 1995, the country narrowly avoided financial collapse. During the Asian economic crisis of the late 1990s, PNG was hurt as the economies of its neighbors went into decline. Its logging industry, which had thrived on the needs of the growing Asian economies, largely collapsed. The year 1997 saw the nation's growth rate drop by over 5% with 1998 dropping by another 3%. Those years, though, appear to have been the end of the economic slump, at least for the moment. By 2011 the nation was growing at an impressive 10.7% rate.

Indeed, as the new century has progressed, PNG's economic resources are increasingly becoming more available to the international market. In 2010, Exxon-Mobil was awarded a large contract to exploit the nation's natural gas resources for shipment to energy customers from Taiwan to China and Japan. A few years later, by the late spring of 2014, the facility shipped its first cargo of liquefied natural gas to Japan. This was an accomplishment heralded as a historic milestone for PNG. It is an important new resource for Japan, whose energy resources have remained so challenged since the tsunami and nuclear meltdown of a few years ago.

And for a time PNG's economy, as we have seen above really was doing quite well but the situation has again reversed itself over the last several years. Indeed, if in 2014 the growth was a healthy 7.4% by 2017 it dropped to 2.5%. It was badly hit by the onset of COVID, dropping to -3.9% in 2020. It picked up in 2021, and growth for 2022 is predicted at between 3% and 4%.

### The Environmental Challenge

Because Papua New Guinea remains one of the least explored areas in the contemporary world, it has drawn a lot of attention from those concerned about its fate if the world's climate changes as much as some have predicted. The glaciers on the island's highest mountain have retreated significantly in the last 30 years. It is also feared that further warming will eliminate many of the indigenous and poorly known species that live in the country's high elevations. As for the inhabitants themselves, responding to concerns about global warming and the more immediate rise in the price of expensive imported fuels, they are now producing automobile fuel from coconut oil. But such efforts have not held off some of the most dramatic changes brought about by climate change.

The people of the Carteret Islands, located in the easternmost part of Papua New Guinea, are already living through what may soon become a common plight for the hundreds of millions of people around the world who live close to sea level. Today the island's population of some 2,600 people is facing an environmental disaster. The ocean is progressively rising and slowly devastating their once beautiful island chain. Even when the waters recede, as they still frequently do, salt water is destroying the islands' vegetation making it increasingly difficult for this long isolated community to survive. Perhaps more ominously are reports that efforts by some of Carteret Island's threatened inhabitants to relocate to other nearby islands were rebuffed by locals. This is perhaps a hint of the challenges much of the world may face as rising waters limit livable land along the coasts.

Opinions differ about the exact cause of PNG's local challenge. It could be a more general ocean rise caused by the increase in greenhouse gases in the upper atmosphere. Or it could be a more immediate and local problem. Some believe the problem is the sinking of an ancient volcano. Regardless of the specific circumstances, the challenge of rising waters is one that more and more communities in the 21st century face.

Given that concern, it is not surprising that during the late spring of 2009 PNG's leadership participated alongside its regional neighbors in an effort to get the United Nations' General Assembly to encourage the UN Security Council to take more direct responsibility in confronting climate change. Although the vote was largely symbolic, it passed the assembly in early June. It was the first resolution specifically to link climate change to security issues. It was also recognition of how the "security" issues of the 20th century are evolving as we proceed in the 21st century.

### The Future

The best news for PNG is that its growing natural gas export industry is now fully operational. Given the growing need to decarbonize the world's energy resources, the fact that natural gas is believed by many to be less carbon intensive than fossil fuels like coal makes it likely to become an even more valuable financial resource for PNG over the coming decades. Estimates now are that the sales of PNG's natural gas could bring the nation over $30 billion over the next few decades.

Also on the more positive side, PNG's international reputation was certainly helped when it was chosen to host the November 2018 APEC summit which welcomed global luminaries from China's Xi Jinping to the American vice president.

Growth in 2014 was 7.4%, with gas exports the main driving force. It faltered in 2016 as energy prices fell world-wide but began to pick up again from late 2017 as the demand for energy resumed. GDP grew by 5.6% in 2019, but in 2020 it again faltered. While for much of the year, PNG remained relatively safe from COVID, the disruption caused by the disease to international trade hit the economy, with an expected fall in growth to 2.2% in 2021 and to 3% in 2022, according to the World Bank. The World Bank has repeatedly expressed concern over the overdependence on energy exports, arguing for more diversification, so far without success.

# The Republic of the Philippines

**Majestic Mayon volcano, the most symmetrical mountain on earth, looms mistily over Legaspi City at the southern tip of Luzon (still active, a curlicue of smoke issues from its summit)**

**Area:** 115,700 sq. mi. (300,440 sq. km.)
**Population:** 112,508,994 (2022 est.)
**Capital City:** Manila, pop. 14,406,059 (2022 est.)
**Climate:** Tropically warm with rainy monsoons in the summer
**Neighboring Countries:** The Philippines' closest neighbors are Republic of China on the island of Taiwan (North) and Malaysia (Southwest)
**Official Languages:** Filipino (a formal version of Tagalog) and English
**Other Principal Tongues:** Tagalog and tribal dialects of principally Malay origin, including Visayan, Ilocano, and Bicol
**Ethnic Background:** Christian Malay (91.5%), Muslim Malay (4%), Chinese (1.5%), other (3%)
**Principal Religion:** Christianity, predominantly Roman Catholic (about 83%), Protestant (9%), Islam (about 5%), Buddhist and others (3%)
**Main Exports:** (to U.S., Netherlands, China, Singapore, Malaysia, Taiwan, and Japan) Coconut products—copra, oil, and fibers, abaca—Manila hemp, timber, Philippine mahogany, sugar, iron ore, electronic equipment, optical equipment, and garments

**Main Imports:** (Saudi Arabia, U.S., Japan, Taiwan, South Korea, China, and Malaysia) Industrial equipment, wheat, petroleum, vehicles, plastics, and chemicals
**Currency:** Philippine Peso
**Former Colonial Status:** Spanish colony (about 1570–1898); U.S. colony (1898–1946); occupied by the Japanese (1941–1945)
**National Day:** July 4, 1946 (June 12, the anniversary of the proclamation of independence from Spain in 1898, is also a national holiday)
**Chief of State:** Rodrigo Duterte, president (since June 30, 2016)
**National Flag:** The left edge is the base of a white equilateral triangle containing a yellow sun and three yellow stars; the rest of the flag is divided into two horizontal stripes with blue on the top, red on the bottom.
**Per Capita GDP Income:** $8,389.80 (2020 World Bank est.) (purchasing power parity)

The land which makes up the territory occupied by the Republic of the Philippines consists of a portion of a mountain chain running from northern Siberia in Russia through the China Sea to Borneo

and New Guinea and the small islands of eastern Indonesia, and then southward through eastern Australia. Countless ages ago the sea invaded the lower part of these mountains—the Philippines are a small portion of the top of this mountain range that has sufficient height to rise above the surface of the tropical waters of the Southwest Pacific.

The nation includes 11 larger islands with more than 1,200 square miles of land on each island: Luzon, Mindanao, Samar, Negros, Palawan, Panay, Mindoro, Leyte, Cebu, Bohol, and Masbate. More than 95% of the nation's land and people are located on these islands.

The remaining islands, around 7,000 are desolate, jungle-covered, and mostly uninhabited. Few have an area of more than one square mile, and about 4,500 of them exist as land masses in the 21st century only because it is impossible to sail across them. They are dots on navigation charts not even possessing the dignity of a name.

The temperature is consistently warm. Much of the terrain lies above an altitude of 1,600 feet. Almost all of the islands are mountainous, containing a multitude of dead and active volcanoes. The eastern slopes receive ample rainfall during all

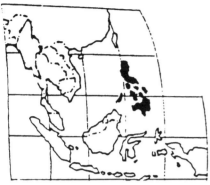

months of the year. The westward-facing parts are drenched by the southwest monsoon from May to October. All areas of the islands have periodic, often devastating typhoons which bring torrential rains.

The land is covered with vast expanses of thick jungle that grows with incredible rapidity and contains among its taller trees the timber from which Philippine mahogany is marketed to the world. The part that has been tamed by the population varies from a thick growth of poor grass that supports grazing to plantation producing coconut, rubber, pineapple, and other tropical crops.

## History

Unlike some of the communities discussed in *East and Southeast Asia*, the Philippines did not have a unified history before the arrival of the colonial powers. Rather, like Indonesia, it is made up of widely diverse groups of communities that had largely gone their separate ways before the conquerors, first the Spanish and later the Americans, forced them into a single administrative unity. What we know of the years before colonization is relatively limited.

Research has shown that about two centuries before the Common Era a fairly advanced people from what is now northern Vietnam and southern mainland China migrated to the large islands of the Philippines. They practiced a system of communal agriculture based on irrigation. Many of their descendants live in the islands today as small non-Christian communities. The larger number of Filipinos, who are of Malayo-Polynesian origin, arrived in the islands from the 8th to the 15th centuries from Java and the Malay Peninsula. Their migrations occurred principally during the period of the strong Srivijaya kingdom in the Indonesia-Malaya area and during the Majapahit kingdom on Java, which dominated a large area up to the beginning of the 13th century Muslim traders and pirates later arrived during the 14th

century. There has also long been a small Chinese community.

### The Arrival of the Spanish

Ferdinand Magellan, the famed Portuguese explorer who, sailing under the Spanish flag, directed the first successful voyage around the world, was killed in the islands in 1521. There was no serious attempt by the Spanish to establish a colony until 50 years later when the Spanish forces, based in their colony of Mexico,

dispatched an expedition to the Philippines. The initial settlement was small and had as its only contact with the European world the annual visit of the "Manila Galleon" sent to Mexico once a year. This is not very surprising because, unlike many of the other island communities to their south and east, the Philippines did not produce many of the spices that had attracted the Europeans to Asia in the first place.

As they had done in Central and South America, the Spanish gave large tracts of

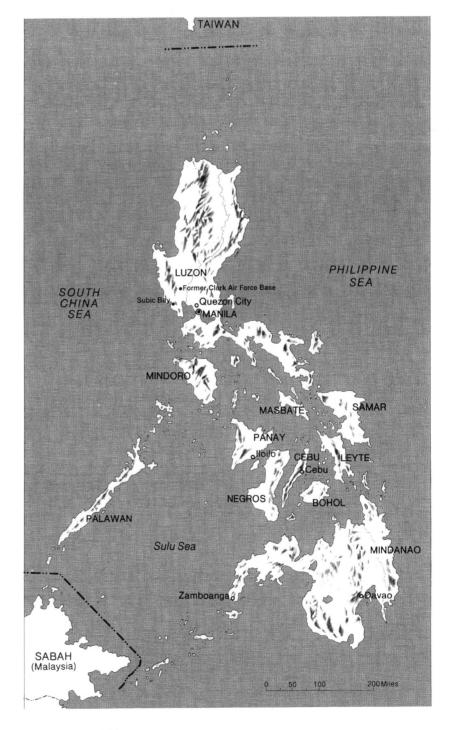

# Philippines

fertile land to prominent Spaniards who had almost complete authority over their domains, and exploited the native inhabitants without interference. Many of the native Filipinos, driven from their farms by the Spanish, went to the more hilly and mountainous areas of the islands to continue farming. Faced with the steep slopes of these regions they developed new agricultural plots based on intricate stone terracing of the steep sides to allow their crops to grow on artificially leveled land.

Given the especially harsh treatment the Filipinos received from their Spanish military occupiers, the best friends that the Filipinos initially had among the early Spanish were the Catholic monks who protested their treatment by the secular authorities. Eventually the harsh treatment of the natives reached the ears of King Philip who, by the mid 16th century, granted primary responsibility for the islands to the Catholic monastic orders. Over the next centuries, the various Catholic orders acquired huge estates and became increasingly resistant to efforts at reform.

Compared to the Spanish civilian officials the friars had far more power and influence, the most obvious example, their successful conversion of the islands over the centuries to their current status as the most Catholic country in Asia. In sharp contrast to the Americans who later made the teaching of English a major priority during their own colonial years or even their own brethren in Latin America, the Spanish religious authorities discouraged the teaching of Spanish which it was felt would make the Filipinos more difficult to control. Moreover, even as they converted many Filipinos to Catholicism, they resisted the ordination of native priests.

The Catholic religious establishment was involved in all aspects of the colony's civilian administration from collecting taxes and doing budgets through control over the recruiting for the army and the police. Predictably, the tight control of the ecclesiastic authorities eventually aroused tension with the indigenous Filipinos. Over time various leaders arose to challenge the Spanish Friar's authority, frequently over the latter's unwillingness to ordain Filipino priests. A trio of reformists, accused of questioning Spain's authority, were publicly executed by the authorities in 1872 in front of a huge crowd that watched the unhappy prisoners being slowly strangled to death.

Spain's attitude toward the islands had evolved during the century. After it lost its colonies in Central and South America during the first part of the 19th century, the Philippines assumed an even more important position. Nevertheless, efforts to develop the colony's economy were largely unsuccessful. So were the attempts to subdue the Muslims communities of the southern islands. Predictably, the slow but steady growth of education and the spread of European ideas like nationalism and unrest, which were caused by oppressive Spanish economic policies, gave rise to a small group of educated Filipinos who demanded independence from Spain.

Among the best known of these Filipino nationalists was Jose Rizal, a passionate intellectual whose fictional portrayal of life in the Philippines, in a novel published in 1887 and smuggled into the islands, aroused considerable public sentiment and the anger of the Church authorities. Eventually, associated by the government with another revolt that had broken out, Rizal was executed in 1896, yet another martyr to the Philippine nationalist cause. But his death did not end the cries against

**Jose Rizal y Mercado**

Spanish control. A late 19th-century insurrection would emerge even as international events beyond the Philippines were soon to transform the circumstances of the islands almost completely.

### The Arrival of the Americans

Taking advantage of Spain's preoccupation with Cuba during the Spanish-American War of 1898, local Philippine nationalists proclaimed an independent Republic of the Philippines and quickly adopted a European-type constitution. Given the well-known American feelings against colonialism, the Filipino leaders, assuming the United States supported them in their fight for independence, joined the Americans in a combined assault against the remaining Spanish forces in the islands. Their assumptions about America's intentions were wrong.

To the frustration of the Philippine nationalists, the U.S. government decided to keep the islands for itself. This was partly out of fear that some other power, such as Germany, would seize the Philippines, and this policy was influenced by the young American assistant secretary of the navy, Teddy Roosevelt. Understandably feeling betrayed by the Americans with whom they had fought against the Spanish for the previous six months, the rebel forces led by General Emilio Aguinaldo's immediately went into armed revolt against the United States.

During the Spanish-American War itself, the Philippine struggles had merely been a sideshow to the American war with Spain over Cuba. Few Americans, save the young Teddy Roosevelt and his colleagues, were even interested in following the European powers in the exercise of empire building. In fact, when the clash over the Philippines actually came, even the president of the United States had to use a map to find where the islands were.

Once the decision was made to conquer the islands, the United States committed itself to put down the forces of the Philippine nationalists. The resulting struggle was carried out in a fashion very similar to the Vietnam struggle of several generations later.

As the tensions began, Emilio Aguinaldo, the leader of the Philippine nationalists, declared his nation free and independent and moved to occupy as much territory as possible before the Americans established themselves. The goals of the movement were quite impressive for their age. They envisioned a democratic Philippines, which would even include votes for women. This was something that was not yet a reality in the United States. But Philippine aspirations were of little interest to the Americans, who by then had their own plans for the islands' future.

The inevitable clash finally occurred in February 1899 as fighting broke out between the American and Philippine forces. Over the next few years the United States was forced to commit three-quarters of its entire military, about 75,000 soldiers, to the struggle.

Before it was declared over by President Teddy Roosevelt in 1902, approximately 200,000 people had died. Most of them were Filipino civilians, but the figure also included more than 4,000 American soldiers as well. It was a bloody affair that included atrocities on both sides that would sound ominously familiar to later generations who came of age hearing horror stories about the Vietnam struggle. In the end, though, American power and divisions among the Filipinos weakened Aguinaldo's effectiveness. His capture, after a daring American raid, determined the fate of the islands. Among the most prominent of the Americans who commanded

**General Emilio Aguinaldo**

there during the struggle was Arthur MacArthur, father of Douglas MacArthur, whose boyhood experiences in the islands would affect the rest of his career.

Though the Americans had fought hard to establish their control over the islands, there was enough ambivalence about the blatantly imperialist effort for Washington also to commit itself to preparing the islands for eventual independence. Unlike some of the other colonial powers, the United States did make a clear effort to share administration with the Filipinos from the colony's earliest years. In fact, the American-sponsored assembly that was soon formed had the distinction of being the first elective legislative body in the entire region. But while the United States increasingly turned over internal decision making to the Filipinos, control over defense and foreign policy remained tightly in American hands.

Education was a major goal of the islands' new administration, and large numbers of young Americans were recruited to serve as teachers, especially English teachers. The program was in many ways rather like the Peace Corps efforts later in the century. The major emphasis on education and English soon had a considerable impact. Literacy rates improved markedly and English became in more common use among the island's inhabitants.

By 1916, the United States had committed itself to the goal of establishing eventual independence for the islands. It had also begun the creation of internally self-governing institutions. The colonial administration also made efforts in the fields of communication, public works and education.

Nevertheless, the emphasis was on creating areas for profitable American investment. There was little done to develop the economy as a whole for the benefit of the

**Grounds of the Pacific War Memorial, Corregidor**

# Philippines

Filipinos, especially the poorer classes. A foreign trade emerged that was almost totally linked to and dependent on the U.S. market. Sadly, while the Americans were quite influential in moving Filipinos into governing positions and improving literacy rates, their economic policies did little to address the economic domination the land-owning elite held over the population.

Feudal systems of sharecropping in the rural areas, which had arisen under the Spanish as a result of land grants, continued and became an even worse problem. The local elected governments permitted by the colonial administration drifted toward control by Filipino political machines and bosses who bore a remarkable resemblance to some of their contemporaries in Latin America.

In the 1930s, Manuel Quezon, who formed and led the Nationalist Party, emerged as the leading politician and eventually president. Political idealism was one factor that prompted the United States to adopt legislation providing for an almost fully self-governing Commonwealth to be established in 1935. The other was pressure from U.S. sugar interests for protective tariffs against Philippine sugar, which were impossible unless it was independent.

## Toward World War II

The growing threat of the Japanese in Asia, in the late 1930s, lessened the desire for total independence on the part of the more radical Filipinos, who saw the need for U.S. protection. Partly as an assurance of further American support, Quezon hired Douglas MacArthur, son of the island's late military governor and former American army's Chief of Staff to serve as the Philippine's "Field Marshal." But despite MacArthur's reputation as an outstanding military strategist, the Philippines were not at all prepared for the assault they were to experience as the forces of imperial Japan attacked in December of 1941.

The islands were quickly overrun by a force of well-trained Japanese soldiers who inaugurated, in 1942, the same harsh military rule that was their policy in the other areas of Southeast Asia they conquered. As was the case elsewhere, many Filipinos, including the father of the later martyred hero, Benigno Aquino, took the Japanese at their word about freeing Asia from the Western colonialists and collaborated with them. This was often true of the Philippine elite that had earlier worked with the Spanish, then the Americans, and now the Japanese occupiers. Many other Filipinos eventually took up arms against Japan's forces.

This resulted in a limited guerrilla movement operating clandestinely in the rural areas to sabotage the military installations of the Japanese. Quezon and his government went into exile in the United States, where he died in 1944. His successor, Sergio Osmena, was eventually able to return to the Philippines as a result of the progress of General Douglas MacArthur's forces in liberating the islands.

MacArthur, in sharp contrast to his later role as a social revolutionary in Japan, chose to reestablish the Philippine land-owning elite in power even overlooking their role as frequent wartime collaborators with the Japanese. Not surprisingly, that enraged many of the leftist guerrillas who had fought Japan and had long harbored hopes for a more equitable land distribution after the war. Given American concerns about socialism and fear of communism, the likelihood that the U.S. would have supported their wartime peasant allies in efforts at significant land reform was small indeed. Most groups, like the leftist Huks, were simply demobilized and sent home only to emerge in later years as a new threat to the government. On a political level though, the United States did officially grant the islands their independence on July 4, 1946.

The economy had been devastated by the war, and it was necessary for the United States to pour in huge sums for relief and rehabilitation and to grant duty-free status to Philippine exports in the American market until 1954. Much of the aid did not reach those who needed it. Osmena died in 1946. For the next 20 years the Philippines were ruled, with one exception, by a succession of colorless, corrupt, and inefficient leaders, and behind the scenes the United States remained especially influential.

Ramon Magsaysay, who served as president during the mid-1950s was, for example, especially close to the American intelligence community that had sponsored his rise in Philippine politics. Once in power he maintained a consistently pro-U.S. policy and took the Philippines into SEATO, the Southeast Asia Treaty Organization in 1954. In spite of his strenuous efforts the power of the small group of families who dominated agriculture, industry, and trade—the descendants of the Spanish aristocratic class, continued. Unfortunately for the Americans who valued their ties to him, Magsaysay was killed in an airplane crash in 1957.

The next few years saw little change in the Philippines. There was a limited growth of anti-Americanism as some of its leaders dabbled in an active, anti-U.S. foreign policy intended to make the Philippines more popular, powerful, and acceptable in the Asian community.

## The Marcos Years

Ferdinand Marcos of the Nationalist Party was elected president in 1965 amid a general sense of an urgent need for change among the people. His election was helped by his claim, later disproved, to have been an influential leader in the anti-Japanese guerrilla movement. Marcos embarked upon a reform platform similar to that of Magsaysay, but met the same intractable obstacles as his predecessor. Corruption remained a virtual custom among minor government officials and employees for the next 20 years. The Communist Party (PKP) abetted by discontent among the poverty-stricken rural people, also resumed its guerrilla activity against the state. Traditional rivalry between the Nationalist Party and the Liberal Party continued.

President Marcos was reelected in 1969 over a Liberal Party opponent by a large majority and became the first Philippine president to win a second term. Nationalist majorities in both houses of the Assembly were sizable. But student and labor demonstrations in Manila were symptoms of the country's malaise. Some of the dissent had an openly anti-U.S. tone.

Among Marcos' most outspoken opponents was the young Benigno Aquino, a former journalist and popular politician. Aquino and his later internationally famous wife, Corazon Aquino, came from elite Filipino families. Having been unable to run against Marcos in the 1969 election, it was expected that Benigno Aquino would run for president in the next elections but those elections never came about. Ferdinand Marcos, already the first Philippine president to serve two full terms, had other plans.

Marcos had no intention of running for office again. Rather, after staging a series of violent incidents that added to the sense of crisis in the country, he declared martial law and canceled the upcoming elections. Large numbers of his political enemies were imprisoned. Aquino was to spend the next seven years in jail where much to Marcos' displeasure he came to be seen as the principal martyr of the developing dictatorship. Marcos justified his actions by claiming the islands were threatened by communism and needed authoritarian government for the moment.

Despite these actions, the influential Americans and the local business community as well as much of the population initially approved of the move. In the ensuing years Marcos had some success in improving the state of law and order except in Mindanao, where an ongoing Muslim revolt had been in progress for years. Of greatest importance, however, he received additional support by rigging a referendum on a new constitution under which he awarded himself virtual dictatorial powers for an unlimited period.

Principal opposition to the Marcos regime came from the Catholic Church and insurgent Muslims in the southern islands. The latter received support from other Muslim countries. Little progress though was made dealing with those problems until years later. Under Marcos, martial law delegated great political power to the armed forces, which became repressive and corrupt, even while providing a semblance of order.

Imelda Marcos, the flamboyant wife of the president, became Governor of Manila and announced ambitious plans for its redevelopment. Even as she set up her own power base, she remained loyal to her husband. Still, her plans to succeed him were widely known. For a time the powerful couple seemed to be a Philippine equivalent of the glamorous Kennedys of American political life.

In the 1980s, the militant wings of the opposition groups began to resort to terrorist bombings. Insurgency, particularly Muslim and communist, became a continuing problem as well.

Despite the end of martial law in 1981, there was little improvement in the political situation. The country continued to be run by an alliance led by the aging Marcos, his wife Imelda, the armed forces, the ruling New Society Party and rich and powerful men close to the president who operated an economic system known informally as "crony capitalism." By the early 1980s more and more of the Philippine elite had lost faith in Marcos's government and its ability to deal with the economic crisis brought on by the rise in oil prices in the mid 1970s.

Marcos often talked of forcing the U.S. out of its huge air and naval bases in the Philippines, but that was almost certainly to divert popular attention from his domestic policies as well as to get greater concessions from the United States, including higher rents. In addition, he was determined to appear at home and abroad as entirely independent of the United States and as the leader of a truly Asian nation. Partly for this purpose, he visited and granted diplomatic recognition to the People's Republic of China in June 1975; another consideration was that he wanted, and apparently thought that he got, a pledge from Beijing not to support the small Philippine communist insurgent movement, the New People's Army. Marcos also established diplomatic relations with the Soviet Union in 1976.

Despite the occasionally nationalistic rhetoric, relations with the United States were reasonably good; President Ford visited in late 1975. During the late 1970s the United States' primary concern in the

**Ferdinand and Imelda Marcos
at their zenith in 1972**

Philippines, especially after its loss in Vietnam, was to maintain its access to the bases. Marcos knew that and often offered himself to the Americans as their only guarantee that the bases would be maintained—assuming the Americans were willing to pay enough. An agreement concerning the base leases was finally concluded with the United States in 1978, and a second in late 1983.

## The Aquino Challenge

The forces of opposition to Marcos' rule continued to grow. Had he been able to offer a record of continuously strong economic growth, as had other Southeast Asian rulers of the era, his authoritarianism might have been tolerated. But that was not the case. As in the early 1980s, other regional economies started to take off, and the Philippines lagged behind, mired in economic problems.

In 1983, longtime opposition leader Benigno Aquino, probably encouraged by false reports that Marcos was about to undergo surgery, decided to return to Manila from the United States, where he had been serving as a fellow at Harvard University. Sadly, he had misjudged just how dangerous his decision was. As he was getting off the plane Aquino was summarily gunned down.

The opposition blamed the government, and more specifically, the armed forces, for the assassination. Huge demonstrations occurred in the cities against Marcos and in protest at the sham official investigation of the murder.

After an unnecessarily lengthy inquiry, armed forces Chief of Staff General Fabian Ver and 25 others were indicted in January 1985 for complicity in the assassination of Benigno Aquino. The trial began in February and continued for months. But when all the evidence was in and after the jury had retired to deliberate, the Philippine Supreme Court took the unheard of step of dismissing the charges on the grounds that there was insufficient evidence.

Despite their success in dealing with the events surrounding the assassination, the Marcos regime seemed to be unraveling. Marcos still had some major advantages, the influential Americans were, as always, more interested in the security of the American bases than the welfare of the Philippines themselves. They still

**Inside the Pacific War Memorial Museum on Corregidor**

# Philippines

believed that his remaining in power was their best defense against losing the bases.

In fact, even as many officials among the Americans had lost faith, Marcos's long-term relationship with Ronald Reagan kept the United States from openly siding with his enemies until his regime was almost completely spent. Eventually, under American pressure, Marcos called a presidential election for early 1986.

By then, though, the opposition had managed to unite behind Corazon Aquino, the widow of Benigno Aquino. Her candidacy, which had the support of the Philippine Catholic hierarchy and its influential Archbishop of Manila, Cardinal Jaime Sin, soon attracted widespread support, especially in the cities. She also had, at least for the moment, the support of her vice-presidential candidate, Salvador Laurel's powerful political organization. Although Marcos was officially declared to have won the election, which had been monitored by large numbers of mainly American official and unofficial observers, it soon became obvious that his supporters were guilty of massive fraud and that Mrs. Aquino had actually won.

The United States government was by now finally convinced that Marcos' time had passed and switched its support to Mrs. Aquino. A group of army officers belonging to a military reform movement usually known by its acronym RAM then began to plan a coup against Marcos.

Hearing of the plans for a coup, Marcos concluded that it was the work of Defense Minister Enrile and Vice Chief of Staff Fidel Ramos and began to move against them. They and their supporters, now including many Americans, promptly came out in support of Mrs. Aquino. Privately, the Americans supplied important intelligence to the insurgents. Cardinal Sin, meanwhile, urged the Catholic faithful to block the streets of Manila to prevent the movement of troops loyal to Marcos. This tactic was effective and later came to be known to the world as an example of "people power." Marcos had lost. After gaining an offer of asylum from the United States, provided he did not use force against his own people, Marcos went into exile in Hawaii and Mrs. Aquino was inaugurated President.

Ferdinand Marcos died in Hawaii in 1989. Many people wanted to bring his body back to the Philippines, but it was four years before this was allowed. Moves to have him interred in the Heroes Cemetery were rejected, and he was buried in at a temporary site until 2016. Then, despite continued protests, supporters re-interred the body in the Heroes Cemetery. His wife returned to the Philippines in 1991 and for a time pursued a political career of her own, including running for president. She

failed but did sit in the House of Representatives for some years. She was forced to give up much of her wealth and received a jail sentence for corruption.

As president, Aquino repealed Marcos' repressive regulations and released his political prisoners. She also initiated steps to recover the enormous wealth—put at $10 billion by the CIA—that he had stashed abroad, mainly in the United States and Switzerland. President Aquino and her middle-class cabinet, faced with a pro-Marcos majority in the Assembly and the Supreme Court, then declared a "revolutionary" government in order to be better able to eliminate the legacy of Marcos' rule.

About six months after her election, President Aquino began to move on her major challenges. She visited the U.S. in September, and the American Congress

**Former President Corazon Aquino**

voted an extra $200 million in aid for the Philippines. She began then to work on an ambitious and difficult land reform program, which was badly needed. In late November she broke with her former supporter Defense Minister Juan Ponce Enrile, who had apparently been threatening a military coup against her. At that time, General Ramos ensured that the armed forces remained loyal to President Aquino. Aquino's most important military supporter, Fidel Ramos, later President Ramos, also pressed her to take a stronger line against the communists and their New People's Army (NPA).

After long negotiations, the communists agreed to a 60-day truce, beginning in December 1986. The PKP used its interlude

of legality to make energetic propaganda in the cities, but it ended by apparently alienating more people than it impressed. Accordingly, it refused to renew the ceasefire. President Aquino countered with an offer of amnesty to any insurgent who surrendered. In January 1987 another dissident movement, the (Muslim) Moro National Liberation Front (based in Mindanao), signed a peace agreement with the government. Unfortunately, it hardly solved the ongoing problems in the largely Muslim island.

There were also some serious disorders just before a referendum was to be held on a new constitution, but they were suppressed. Despite these problems Aquino's constitution got an unexpectedly high vote (about 75% of those casting ballots). It limited the president to one six-year term, created a bicameral legislature, granted the courts the power of judicial review of laws and provided that the U.S. bases be non-nuclear and could be continued after 1991 only on the basis of a treaty approved by at least two-thirds of the Philippine Senate.

President Aquino's supporters won a sweeping victory in elections for the Senate and House of Representatives held in May 1987. But in August of the same year, in the most serious of several attempts to overthrow President Aquino, a colorful paratrooper, Colonel Gregorio (Rambo) Honasan, led an attempted coup against her. It failed due to energetic action by loyal forces under Chief of Staff Ramos (made Defense Secretary in January 1988). For a time it appeared that President Aquino's position might be untenable. Increasingly, her former political allies were moving against her.

Despite the great hopes that had accompanied her arrival to power, the new president had difficulty living up to those expectations. The army disliked her efforts to reconcile with the long running communist insurgents. Those that hoped she would move against the entrenched landowners and institute true land reform were equally unhappy.

Given the unequal land distribution of the Philippines, it is hardly surprising that the communist insurgency continued to grow to the point where President Aquino apparently considered proclaiming a state of emergency. Frequently brutal anti-communist vigilantes also emerged in many areas.

Despite the victory of the democratic forces, Philippine political life remained riddled with corruption and factionalism on the part of elected and appointed officials. From Aquino's perspective, actually accomplishing something was quite difficult. The lower house of Congress was subservient to the popular Aquino,

# Philippines

Workmen cut the bananas from the stalk and place them in a washing vat

of Imelda Marcos was something of a distraction, much more important issues demanded the government's attention.

In 1991 the Philippines suffered a series of natural disasters, including a storm that struck the central islands in November and caused unusually heavy damage (runoff and mud slides) because of heavy illegal logging and more dramatic, a volcanic eruption. Mt. Pinatubo, a volcano about 55 miles north of Manila, and only 10 miles from U.S. controlled Clark Air Force Base, erupted in June of 1991 and fatefully determined the outcome of the long and complex negotiations between Manila and Washington on the future of the U.S. bases in the Philippines.

Before the eruption, Manila had been demanding $825 million per year for seven years in aid, in exchange for continuation of the base agreement. The American Congress was unwilling to appropriate that much, and Washington had been offering $520 million per year over 10–12 years. Certainly there were lots of reasons the Americans wanted to keep their bases in the Philippines. They were very valuable for repair and refueling of ships and aircraft and for training of personnel. Moreover, Filipino labor was plentiful, cheap, and skilled.

But as was said at the time, the volcano had its own agenda, and it was clearly not the same as that of the negotiators. The eruption, apparently the most powerful anywhere in the 20th century, heavily damaged the town of Angeles, near Clark, and covered the base with about a foot of ash, rendering it virtually useless. Subic Naval Base and its environs also suffered damage.

After the eruption, some haggling continued between the two sides, but the negotiations were basically over. The bases had also become much less important to U.S. strategic interests since the collapse of the Soviet Union, the main regional threat.

In September of 1991, the Philippine Senate, in a nationalistic mood, voted not to ratify an agreement incorporating the U.S.'s final offer (Clark to be turned over, Subic to be kept for 10 more years for $203 million per year). American forces then began to withdraw. The most graphic reminders of the American occupation of the Philippines were now to fade into history.

## Politics and Government

The Philippine political system resembles that of the United States. Prior to 1987, the Philippines were governed under the U.S.-modeled 1935 constitution. That constitution provided a bill of rights, a bicameral legislature, an independent judiciary and a president with a four-year term. A

whereas the Senate, whose members were elected by the national electorate, rather than from local constituencies, was highly independent.

According to analysts, the core problem is that politics in the Philippines may appear democratic, but they are still largely tied to families and personalities rather than parties. Thus, the vast majority of the nation's politicians are not linked to particular parties or, more importantly, to specific policies whose success or failure can be used to judge their performance in office. For that reason it has been very difficult for any national leader to build a stable and strong coalition around specific reform policies. For example, in June 1988, the Philippine Congress finally voted a moderate land reform program that managed to please neither the landlords nor the land hungry tenants. Social unrest and communist insurgency continued.

During these years, the presence of the U.S. bases, holdovers from the years when the Philippines were an American colony, became especially controversial in the eyes of the Philippine political elite and intellectuals. After difficult negotiations, an agreement was reached in October 1988, under which the U.S. was to give $481 million in economic aid (one-third of what the Philippine side had been demanding) in 1990 and again in 1991, when the base agreement was set to expire.

Under the new constitution, any new agreement would have to be ratified by the Philippine Senate, and perhaps by a popular referendum. In May 1988, the Senate voted a ban on storage of nuclear weapons on the bases, but it appeared that in practice they could still be taken through in transit.

A series of developments, in late 1989 and early 1990, heightened the general impression that, under Aquino's indecisive leadership, the country was drifting or even regressing. In early December the sixth and most serious attempted military coup against her was quelled, but mainly because U.S. combat aircraft flew over the rebel positions. The fact that the United States had effectively used its Philippine-based military resources to intervene in local politics added a new and complicated dimension to the base issue.

The American side wanted continued access even after the bases passed to Philippine control. Manila wanted to get as much money as possible out of the entire transaction. Philippine nationalists found the presence of the bases to be a source of national shame. Filipinos employed at the bases were, of course, concerned about their continued employment.

Political unrest and attempted military coups continued to be a serious problem. As the end of President Aquino's term approached, various political figures began to jockey for succession. One of them was Imelda Marcos, the widow of Ferdinand Marcos. She returned from exile in November 1991 and gained government permission to bury her husband in his native province, Ilocos Norte. Although facing criminal proceedings on charges of corruption, she soon began to campaign as the champion of the poor, notwithstanding her vast fortune. But while the return

267

# Philippines

new constitution was approved in 1987. It limits presidents to single six-year term. Close relatives of the president cannot be appointed to public office. Both the legislature and the judiciary may review the legal reasons for the imposition of martial law. The constitution also provides for civil liberties and is democratic in form. The legislative branch has a House of Representatives and a Senate. Under the constitution congress has the power to declare war, restrict presidential emergency powers, and control the appropriation of revenue. The Senate has 24 members with six-year terms that are limited to two consecutive terms. The house can have up to 250 members elected from legislative districts apportioned by population. Some of the seats (20%) are filled through a party-list system. Although the American-style system as modified in 1987, has continued to function, there are periodic suggestions that it should be replaced by a more European-style parliamentary system.

The Philippines have historically been a two-party system. The Nacional and Liberal parties traded control of the government between 1946 and 1972. Both parties tended to serve the interests of the political elites in the country. During much of the Marcos era there was no effective political party opposition. Strong opposition began to emerge around 1980 with the formation of UNIDO which had the backing of anti-Marcos elites. Benigno Aquino Jr. established LABAN ("Fight") as a vehicle for his political ideas. The political party landscape fragmented somewhat during the Aquino years. Today politics continues to be highly personalized. Support is given to individuals, not platforms, programs, or ideologies though that can be more complicated lately given the fact that presidents are not eligible to run again.

As in many other communities in Asia and elsewhere, Philippine politics are much influenced by the presence of "patron-client relationships." Essentially, this means that political life centers on relationships that are personal and hierarchical. Political relationships are also built on the concept of "utang na loob," obligations of indebtedness. Politics is therefore frequently dominated by personal loyalty to a hierarchical group. Patrons must provide resources to their clients to keep their loyalty. This has been a motivation for the corruption that has often weakened the Philippines. On a more practical level it also means that only the nation's president is particularly associated with specific policies against which they are eventually judged.

In this type of environment, institutions like interest groups, political parties, and other organizations that could unite large segments of society are less effective than

**Philippines street scene**

they might be. Thus, such institutions which have at times been so effective in countries from South Korea to the United States are of less value in the personalized political culture of the Philippines.

## A New Beginning for the Philippines

Fidel V. Ramos was elected president of the Philippines in May 1992. However, as one of seven candidates, Ramos, in winning, received only 23.4% of the vote. To make matters more complicated, his closest challenger, Miriam Defensor Santiago, claimed fraud and managed to have the Supreme Court consider the charge. Ramos, in short, did not start off with a lot of support, though Mrs. Aquino backed him strongly. Still, for most of his term, he was quite effective.

During the first years after his election, President Ramos and his government faced several significant challenges: the need to establish law and order, opposition to the current political process by groups including the National Democratic Front (representing the communists), the Muslim National Liberation Front, the Muslim Islamic Liberation Front, the military officers' group RAM-YOU and the continuing entrenched position of the old political elite. By his last year he also had to face the challenges of the Asian economic crisis of 1997, but that was much later. Initially, he was quite successful in dealing with the issues that faced him.

In fact, by early 1996, there were still plenty of problems but also signs of improvement. President Ramos and the MNLF leader, Nur Misuari, finally concluded an agreement that many hoped would contribute to ending the generation-long struggle that had taken more than 120,000 lives. Overcoming the opposition

of minority Christian communities in the south, Ramos and Misuari agreed to form a special presidential council headed by Misuari which would have responsibility over development issues in 14 of the southern provinces. The deal, part of a larger plan that included the formation of a more autonomous Muslim-dominated region after three years, marked a major breakthrough for efforts to reinforce Philippine stability. It was later to prove less successful in bringing in Misuari's more militant Muslim co-religionists.

Ramos even managed to gain an agreement with the Communist National Democratic Front in April 1998 which projected a series of negotiations intended to end the generation-long communist rebellion. Economically, the Ramos administration had moved to reform the Philippine economy and further integrate it into world.

But, despite a very impressive record for most of his administration, President Ramos's last year in office was hurt both by forces he controlled and those he did not. Although Ramos never publicly said he wanted a second term—a clear violation of the new constitution—he let his followers try to modify the constitution in order to allow him to do so. The decision was inadvisable and he soon found even his former allies, President Aquino, Cardinal Sin, and much of the population aroused against the idea. In the end he backed down and disavowed the idea, but not before he had damaged his reputation. Then President Ramos, understanding his time at the helm was really up, chose House Speaker Jose de Venecia as his successor.

But while having Ramos' support was important, de Venecia still had to win the election. And that turned out to be a very daunting task, especially when facing the vice president Joseph Estrada. Estrada was a former actor, who wanted the job himself, and campaigned hard to get it. In contrast to the organizational skills of de Venecia, Estrada, despite his personal origins among the Philippine elite, campaigned as a populist and was much more flamboyant as a public campaigner, a skill especially important in the May 1998 election which included not only Estrada and de Venecia but nine other candidates.

In the end, as the polls had long predicted, the people chose Joseph Estrada. Estrada may not have had the support of many Philippine elites. In fact much of the leadership, from the military to the church, was skeptical; nevertheless, he won the presidency with an impressive 40% of the vote and drew his support from a wide range of voters. It was. In fact, a far better performance than Ramos had done in his own earlier effort. The victory was coupled with both President

Ramos's willingness to accept the end of his term and with Estrada's decision to continue Ramos's economic policies. This seemed to put the Philippines on the verge of a much brighter future than many had expected.

President Estrada's popularity did not last as long as he probably hoped. As the months went on, his poll ratings dropped steadily. His administration was plagued by rumors of economic corruption, inattention to detail, favoritism, and unpopular policies. The president soon found himself almost abandoned save for some members of the poorest classes. He was impeached by the Senate. The influential Philippine Catholic Church got involved as well as it denounced the besieged president for setting a bad moral example for the nation.

Eventually the backlash against Estrada grew so great that the President's support collapsed and his vice president, the American trained economist and daughter of former President Macapagal (president 1961–1965), Gloria Macapagal Arroyo became president. Despite her assumption to power, the former president still had supporters. For years after his departure she faced a series of pro-Estrada demonstrations and various legal challenges to her authority which made it difficult for the new president to fully establish her authority.

While the Philippines' new president and Asia's newest contribution to the

**Former President Fidel Ramos**

ever growing number of female national leaders may not have been nearly as flamboyant as her disgraced predecessor, she presided over a reasonably successful period in the life of the Philippines. Arroyo, an economist, who had once been a Georgetown University classmate of U.S. president Bill Clinton, kept the nation's inflation under control while making important progress in the areas of agricultural

funding and an expansion of insurance coverage for the population. Her administration also worked toward lowering the cost of electrical power. Somewhat more controversial was her direction of Philippine–American relations.

In contrast to many Asian leaders President Arroyo was particularly supportive of the American War on Terrorism. In fact, her administration received considerable public criticism for inviting the American military to become active in the struggle against the Abu Sayyaf, the militant Muslim nationalists that have been so active in terrorism in the Southern Philippines.

Overall, it would be hard to argue that President Arroyo did not perform the functions of her job with an enormously greater commitment and professionalism than her "playboy" predecessor. But international and domestic challenges made her tenure in office very challenging. Within the Philippines, the levels of crime, drug use, and urban violence have become particularly significant with almost a score of gangs in Manila specializing in kidnapping the rich for ransom. The problem had become so great that the President declared that crime problems had gone beyond being simply law and order issues and become fundamental threats to the National Security. Other problems also made life difficult for the new president.

Like her predecessor Corazon Aquino, President Arroyo had to deal with the

**A panoramic view of the Sierra Madre slopes**

# Philippines

threat of military coups. In fact, during the summer of 2003, a group of some 300 soldiers took over a shopping mall in downtown Manila and demanded that the president resign. The group's mutiny, (they had apparently hoped to establish a military junta) was dealt with in only a few days, but it was only one example of the problems the president has faced since coming into power in the aftermath of President Estrada's departure in disgrace. The problem of violent challenges to her rule has not gone away. More recently, in 2008, the president reportedly was the target of another foiled assassination plot devised by the notorious Abu Sayyaf.

As the time grew closer for the presidential elections of 2004 the Philippines' "accidental" president initially announced that she did not intend to run for office again. Her public explanation was that she has wanted to save the country from a "prolonged period of political infighting." That explanation of course sounds good but it was hard to see how her not running would avoid that problem. And upon further reflection she apparently agreed because, by the fall of 2003, she reversed herself and declared her candidacy.

**Former President Joseph Estrada**

By the time those elections rolled around the President found herself facing a very wide range of opponents, from her own former education secretary Raul Roco to the controversial senator and former Chief of Police who ran for office even as the Supreme Court reopened a case against him which dealt with the alleged official murder of a number of criminals who had been in his custody. One candidate even had to drop out for a time when he learned he had developed a case of prostate cancer.

In the end her chief competitor declared his candidacy. Fernando Poe was a man whose background closely resembled that of her predecessor, President Estrada. He was a popular film star, who had dropped out of high school. As the time approached for election, the two of them were neck and neck in the polls.

Once the voters went to the polls, though, it soon became clear that Gloria Macapagal Arroyo had managed to win the presidency herself. At least that seemed to be the case. Unfortunately for the newly elected president, charges soon surfaced that she may have tampered with the counting process. For a time, as demonstrations grew in the streets and influential figures called for her resignation, it even looked like her situation was increasingly precarious. In the end, though, the president survived a call for her impeachment and remained in power.

But there was a clear price to pay. Both her son and husband ended up leaving the country to alleviate some of the charges of corruption that had surfaced although the antagonism against President Arroyo continued unabated. By early 2006 yet another military coup was apparently attempted against her. The effort was headed off by prompt government action. But it was obvious that the president's unpopularity went far beyond the military plotters. In the aftermath of the failed coup attempt, thousands of people, including former President Corazon Aquino, went into the streets to call for her resignation.

Despite the complications of her initial election, the president's support did not wholly fail her. In the elections of May 2007, her supporters won 200 of the possible 219 seats that were up for reelection. This put them in a commanding position to control the new House of Representatives. However, her success in the lower house did not stop her many opponents from winning the majority of seats in the upper house. Unfortunately while the results of the elections were relatively positive for the government, more than 100 people died in associated violence. The unrest reopened the anger associated with the controversies of the 2004 election battle.

By the early summer of 2008 the president's long-term goal of rewriting the 1987 constitution was gaining steam. The lower house of congress voted to transform itself into a constituent assembly in order to revise the constitution. But it was not just been members of the senate who opposed the idea. Large popular demonstrations against the effort regularly occurred. Part of the problem is that many of the president's critics claimed the plan is merely a gimmick designed to maintain Arroyo's

power. Others claimed there was a secret plan to delay the 2010 elections with the hope of using a revised parliamentary system to allow Arroyo to return to power as a prime minister chosen by the lower house of congress.

Despite the fears of some, the presidential elections were held on schedule in the spring of 2010 with a campaign that featured very familiar names. Joseph Estrada, the former president whose failed administration had led to Arroyo's initial rise to the presidency, ended up running unsuccessfully against Senator Benigno S. Aquino III, son of the couple who had battled so dramatically to terminate the presidency of former Philippine Ferdinand Marcos in the mid-1980s.

The new president, who won an impressive electoral victory, campaigned on a platform that highlighted his family and anti-corruption policies. While his election over Estrada may certainly have reflected such hopes, it was also true that his rise to power was yet another example of the influence of the small number of elite families who have dominated Philippine politics over the decades.

Indeed the charge not only of nepotism but corruption continues to dog the Philippine election process. In fact, when Benigno S. Aquino III's term ended in mid-2016 the contenders for the presidency included a range of candidates, many of whom were either implicated in corruption scandals or had major ties to the families of Philippine elites.

Once the dust was settled from the 2016 presidential election, the outspoken mayor

**Rodrigo Duterte, president of the Philippines**

of Davao, Rodrigo Duterte, who has at times been compared with the American Donald Trump, was elected. After his election there were two major trends. One was a move to improve relations with China (see below), the other was an expansion of his local war on drugs nationwide. The police and civilian vigilante groups were given carte blanche to kill suspected drug dealers and users. Nobody can be sure how many were killed; estimates range from 5 to 8,000. Even when claims were raised in the Senate in 2017 that one of his sons was involved with a Chinese trafficker, Duterte's response was that if any of his family was so involved, they should be killed. The incident blew over. In 2019, Duterte handed over the running of the anti-drugs' campaign to Vice-President Leni Robredo, a former human rights' lawyer who was known to oppose the campaign, which began to ease off. In 2020, Robredo was absolved by the department of justice of sedition charge arising from her opposition to Duterte's policies.

That Duterte still believed in violent responses to law breaking was shown in 2020. One of his reactions to COVID-19 (see below) was to suggest that curfew or quarantine breakers should be summarily shot. The suggestion was not, however, taken up.

The 2022 presidential election clearly indicated that the power of the old political elites had not waned. One candidate was the vice-president Leni Robredo. But it quickly became clear that the frontrunner was Ferdinand "Bongbong" Marcos Jr., son the the former dictator, whose running mate as vice-president was Sara Duterte, daughter of Rodrigo Duterte. Marcos Jr. avoided traditional electioneering platforms, using instead social media to praise his father's time in office and his mother's great contribution to the country. Despite doubts about his abilities and qualifications (partly educated

in Britain, his supposed University of Oxford degree turned out to be a diploma in social sciences after he had failed his degree exams and he was better known as a playboy than a politician) and a campaign short on policies but long on nostalgic references to his father's rule, the election went to the Marcos–Duterte team. While Marcos pledged to heal the divisions in the country, there were demonstrations against the election outcome from the beginning.

International commentators are generally agreed that there will be no great changes under the junior Marcos. Policies will continue to favor the interests of the elites rather than the mass of people.

### Culture and Society

Like so much of the developing world the contrasts in society are striking. Manila, a busy, modern city, has a sophisticated cultural atmosphere that can compare with most Western cities. In recent years, a building boom has made it look even more like some of its more economically vibrant East and Southeast Asian neighbors. Still, many peasants live at poverty levels that are as extreme as anywhere in the world. The Philippines remain one of the most stratified countries in the world. It is a society where a significant percentage of the population cannot meet their basic nutritional and other needs while the richest 10% possess 36% of all personal income. Despite the economic growth, the number who live in poverty has actually grown over the last few years. For example, in 2003 the official number living in poverty was reported to be around 30%. By 2008 it had risen to almost 33%. Ten years later, it was 21.1%, according to official government figures, but as COVID struck, the same source noted that it had fallen back to 23.7% in early 2021.

The Filipino language, a refinement of the Tagalog spoken by many Philippine people, serves as the official language. Spanish is spoken by a dwindling number of descendants of the Spanish aristocracy. English is well known, and many educated Filipinos, unable to find work in their homeland, have left the country. For example, many Filipino medical doctors and nurses have settled in the United States. Large numbers of them work in the various countries of the Middle East, a fact that makes the Philippines especially sensitive to what happens in that frequently volatile part of the world.

The influence of the Catholic Church is very important. The church controls enormous holdings, and, the late Archbishop Jaime Cardinal Sin, who was instrumental in helping to end the Marcos dictatorship

and making sure President Ramos honored the constitution by not running again, was very influential. President Estrada weakened his political base by antagonizing the church officials due to his support of population control programs and the death penalty and to his leading a personal lifestyle the church leaders found morally unacceptable.

The church has also played an important role in condemning corrupt political practices and campaigning for greater support for the poor. The church's strong stand against birth control has, in theory, also made it very difficult for the Philippines to limit the country's soaring population, although there has in fact been a steady decline over the last 70 years.

In recent years the administration has frequently come under fire for human rights violations. It has been reported that more than 1,000 people have disappeared, been killed, or gone missing as a result of actions taken by the Filipino security forces. The nation's Supreme Court has accused the government of tolerating their behavior. The assaults have had their targets not only relatively young children but activists perceived to be threats to government.

Since 2016, the situation has deteriorated even further under the Duterte administration, with widespread, officially authorized killings of alleged drug dealers and users leading to domestic and international condemnation. This has been brushed off by the president, who has said that his opponents, which include the Roman Catholic Church, can "go to hell."

### A Generational Struggle: The Muslim South

The biggest challenge to people's lives in the recent years has been the enormous number, reports suggested over 500,000, who were forced to flee their homes in the wake of yet another failed effort to resolve the tensions between Manila and the Islamic southern providences. Former President Arroyo's government reached an agreement with the Moro Islamic Liberation Front that would have allowed local Muslims greater autonomy in an expanded area on the southern island of Mindanao. But that agreement was opposed by the Roman Catholic community of Mindanao, which eventually managed to get the nation's Supreme Court to block the settlement.

Predictably the frustrated MILF began a new series of assaults on government troops and others. Eventually another cease-fire of the sort that had been implemented in 2003 was reinstated, but not before almost 100 people had died. And that didnot really stop the fighting.

# Philippines

**Former President Benigno Aquino III**

During the presidency of President Aquino III (2010-2016), he met with the leader of the Moro National Liberation front in meetings that took place in both Japan and Malaysia. Eventually an agreement was hammered out that once again appeared to reduce the likelihood of future violence. President Aquino announced an agreement that would allow for the creation of an autonomous Muslim region in the south to be called Bangsamoro. He apparently won the approval of the Moro Islamic Liberation Front. According to the new agreement, the southern region would gain greater autonomy even as the national government retained important control over issues such as monetary and foreign policy and security. Still, long-term observers were well aware that earlier attempts at reconciliation between the northern Catholic Philippines and the Muslims of the south had frequently failed

It is not just tensions between the largely Catholic North and the Islamic community of the South that made Mindanao so dangerous at times. Rivalries between different Muslim clans have also provoked vicious fighting and killings. a

Sadly, the overall situation has not improved. Indeed, the violence has become so dramatic that President Duterte was recently forced to return from a trip to Moscow and declare martial law in the region. To add to the problems, since 1969, a revived military wing of the Communist Party of the Philippines, the New People's Army, has actively opposed the government. A peace agreement was arranged in 2017, but in 2019 the Duterte administration abandoned it.

## Women

Philippine women have not been influential in their country's politics. The careers of women such as Imelda Marcos, Corazon Aquino, and President Arroyo, are more representative of the power of family connections than women's influence. In the same vein the previous president, Arroyo, is the daughter of yet another previous president. In the 2022 presidential elections, the winning vice-president was Sara Duterte, daughter of President Rodrigo Duterte. This circumstance would hardly surprise most Americans.

In the workplace their salaries are usually one-third that of men. Philippine women often travel abroad to find work. They go to places like Singapore and the Persian Gulf States to serve as domestic servants. In the United States, they often serve as nurses. In fact, the Philippines supply more female overseas workers than any other country.

In the late 1980s a new family code was introduced in the Philippines to replace the older more traditional code that had earlier reinforced inequality between the sexes. Women gained the right to practice professions without having their husbands' permission. Women also gained more rights over their children and remarriage. As is the common case in East and Southeast Asia Muslim women are covered by separate legal codes that allow polygamy. Catholic practice is also very influential in the Philippines. Thus divorce is not legally available (though annulment is), and abortion is available only to save the life of a mother.

Former President Ramos made a significant contribution to the rights of women when he signed a new anti-rape law that

**Former President
Gloria Macapagal Arroyo**

offered more sensitivity to the rights of the victims. Still domestic violence against women, as elsewhere, is common. In contrast to most Asian countries, Philippine women go to college more often than men do. Around 10% of all women are college graduates. The figure is only about 7% for men. By 1992 women began to be admitted to the Philippine military academies.

Women's lives, of course, are especially impacted by how much control they have over their own fertility. Given the Philippines' relatively low socio-economic level and high birth rate, that reality is especially true for the women of the islands. But as a largely Catholic country, issues associated with birth control are especially controversial. Nevertheless the government did manage to pass legislation to establish the Responsible Parenthood and Reproductive Act in 2012. This was designed to make available both sex education and contraception to poor women. Unfortunately, the legislation was delayed by the Philippine Supreme Court, although a modified version was allowed in 2014. It is estimated that 7 million women in the Philippines were using some form of contraceptive in 2019.

About one-third of the workforce is female although women predominate at the lower levels earning the lowest wages. Women have made considerable gains in the field of law. They make up 26% of the trial court judges. They are also very involved in teaching at both the primary and secondary levels and outnumber men in civil service jobs though not at the highest levels.

Women have served both in the country's parliament and as cabinet level ministers though in relatively small numbers as yet. Of course, during the recent presidential election, Gloria Macapagal Arroyo, daughter of a former leader, was elected vice-president and later succeeded to the presidency with the collapse of President Estrada's administration. Somewhat later she won the presidency in her own right. Thus the Philippines have in recent years been led by two different women, Corazon Aquino and President Macapagal Arroyo.

More recently though under President Duterte the situation has evolved again with the current president quite openly expressing misogynistic comments more in keeping with earlier generations. Nevertheless, as noted, he did not oppose his daughter running as vice-president in the 2022 elections.

## Foreign Policy and Defense Issues

Philippine foreign policy has often wavered between developing closer ties to its regional neighbors and focusing on its relationship with the United States. During his term in office former President Ramos made it a personal priority to strengthen ties with his regional neighbors and traveled extensively to do so. Ramos felt it was particularly important for the Philippines to improve relations with other members of ASEAN, the Association of Southeast Asian Nations. President Ramos, for example, visited Indonesia to discuss the possibility of links between Mindanao, in the southern Philippines, and Indonesia. Eventually, the Indonesian government offered important help in his efforts to bring the confrontation with the MNLF Muslim leadership to resolution.

Once in office President Arroyo continued the focus on Asia by visiting many neighboring states with a special emphasis on improving relations with Malaysia. Unfortunately, relations with Malaysia were nevertheless strained for a time over Kuala Lumpur's abrupt decision to expel large numbers of illegal aliens, a move that caused considerable hardship to thousands of people, many of them from the Philippines.

Under President Arroyo, relations with the United States remained especially important. The president was educated in the United States and was among the first Asian leaders to lend her support to the Americans in the immediate aftermath of the September 2001 terrorist attacks on the U.S.

Later, as the American campaign in Afghanistan wound down, Arroyo made the controversial decision to invite American advisers to assist Philippine soldiers in the struggle against the Muslim Abu Sayyaf group that has long been known for its terrorist activities and kidnappings of foreign tourists.

Her decision offered benefits and problems. On the one hand, the American administration offered her government millions of dollars in aid. On the other hand, her approval of the return of American troops aroused considerable controversy and provoked massive demonstrations in the southern parts of the country. That commitment turned out to be a longer one than many anticipated. Washington, after sending the first troops during the winter of 2002, pulled most of them out again by the following summer. But by the spring of 2003, after President Arroyo made an official state visit to the White House, Washington announced that more American troops were being sent. The president also paid a political price for her controversial decision to send Filipino soldiers to serve in Iraq in support of the American occupation there.

In 2004, the Philippine role in Iraq took a more dramatic turn as a Philippine truck driver was taken hostage and threatened with beheading. President Arroyo then made the controversial decision to expedite the departure of her troops in order to win the release of the hostage. In doing so, she pleased many people in the Philippines, but she came in for considerable criticism not only from the United States but from her Australian neighbors as well.

Her successor, Benigno S. Aquino III, continued the policy of friendship with the United States and even consulted with Barack Obama, the former American president, about strengthening that longstanding relationship.

Once President Duterte arrived in power though relations with America began to deteriorate as the United States began raising concerns about a dramatic upturn in human rights' violations associated with Duterte's anti-drug campaign.

Although when Donald Trump became U.S. president in 2017 there was some tension, he and Duterte eventually established a positive working relationship. Trump said that Duterte was doing a good job and praised his war on drugs, although this did not stop Duterte becoming the first Philippine president to visit Israel in September 2018 in search of an alternative source to the United States for weapons. The relationship is unlikely to continue under Trump's successor, Joe Biden, although the latter has said that he looks forward to a meeting.

During the 1990s, relations with the People's Republic of China also proved complicated at times. By far, China's occupation of Mischief Reef in the South China Sea constituted the most serious problem. In early 1995, Manila discovered that one of the small islands in the Spratly chain about 150 miles off the Philippine coast had been occupied by members of the Chinese navy.

In May 1995 Philippine military officials tried to take a boatload of journalists to see the reef but a Chinese patrol boat blocked their path. The Philippine navy then detained a number of Chinese fishermen who were illegally in the country's territorial waters. Later, at the ASEAN Regional Forum, ARF, the ASEAN states spoke with one voice in raising concern about the Chinese occupation. Beijing though in the years since has continued to make relatively assertive claims in both the East and South China seas.

Over the years tensions grew dramatically as more and more confrontations occurred between the Philippine forces and those of the People's Republic of China. The Philippines have aggressively asserted its rights in what the international community has historically called the South China Sea and that the Philippines now refer to as the "West Philippine Sea." Unfortunately for the Philippines, it is easier to rename the waters than to develop the naval resources to defend them. With the help of the United States, they have been attempting to do just that. In that context, the United States has been especially supportive of the Philippines. Ironically, the tensions resulted not only in strengthening ties between the United States and the Philippines, but in reversing some of the trends of recent decades. Amazingly, an announcement was made that the Americans would again be welcome to use the facilities at Subic Bay and Clark airfield. A generation before that had been seen as so controversial that the Washington had abandoned those bases.

Clearly the growing concerns about China's recent assertiveness in the South China Seas changed how locals viewed the United States. That evolution was particularly obvious in the "Enhanced Defense Cooperation Agreement," which was signed before President Obama visited the Philippines in 2014. Unlike earlier arrangements, the US was allowed to station troops on the islands, but not establish permanent bases, as was the case in earlier years.

After President Duterte came to power in 2016, he shifted the country's approach to China. While not abandoning the claims in the South China Sea, Duterte has moved towards better relations with the PRC. This may be partly because China has refrained from criticizing Duterte or his policies. Soon after becoming president in December 2016, Duterte visited China. There he said it was time for the Philippines to move away from Washington, and Chinese leader Xi Jinping described him as "good guy." In November 2018, President Xi made a state visit to the Philippines. But as China continued to press its claims in the South China Sea, the mood began to change, shifting in 2020 back to a more conciliatory approach to the United States. Duterte let others make the running but did not disassociate himself from the shift.

Duterte condemned the Russian invasion of Ukraine in February 2022.

In one of his few policy statements during the 2022 presidential election campaign, Ferdinand Marcos Jr, the eventual winner, said he would work for a better relationship with China.

## Economy

The Philippine Republic is fairly rich in natural resources and, with the exception of the Manila plain, not overpopulated.

Still, much of the wealth winds up in the hands of a small group of rich individuals and families. Corruption and inflation have been a continuing problem. Under former President Marcos's "New

# Philippines

Society," a limited land reform program was in progress. Landlords, as part of the establishment, were well compensated by the government for what land they had lost, and this further inflated the economy.

Under President Aquino, a less stifling, but still harmful version of the "crony capitalism" that had flourished under Marcos emerged. Her successor, President Fidel Ramos, was much more successful with economic reforms and carried out a significant amount of land reform and other economic efforts. Called "Philippines 2000," the government strove to change its traditional agrarian-based, paternalistic economy to an industrial and market-driven one. They have moved, for example, to liberalize rules for investment, trade, and banking among other economic activities.

During the mid-1990s the economy was finally showing signs of strength. The 5.1% growth figure of 1994 paled when compared to double-digit numbers of some of its neighbors. But economic indicators were finally showing substantive growth that would continue at about the same av-erage rates over the next decade or so. This was true despite the occasional dramatic dip as larger regional and global events washed over the islands.

By the time President Ramos hosted the Asia-Pacific Economic Cooperation (APEC) forum in November 1996, he had plenty of reasons to be pleased. The facilities at the Subic Bay were ready to convince the arriving dignitaries that the Philippines, so long the laggard in the regime's economic spurt, was ready to make its own effort to become a new "Asian Tiger!" When the Asian economic crisis hit in mid-1997, the Philippines were as vulnerable as many of her neighbors and saw her own currency take a plunge. But unlike them the Philippines initially weathered well the international economic stresses and began not only to recover but pull ahead.

More recently the economy has shown a modest growth rate and inflation somewhat lessened, two factors which contributed to the generally improving situation. Unfortunately, news of scandals, financial and otherwise, became very common during President Estrada's term in office and hurt the country economically. With the arrival of the professionally trained economist Gloria Macapagal Arroyo to the presidency, the Philippine economy did relatively well. Growth rates averaged around 5%. The GDP rate for 2005 was a very healthy 6%, up from the previous year, while 2007 was over 7%. The year 2008 came in at 5.4% although that was before impact of the most recent global economic downturn was felt.

**Aftermath of Typhoon Haiyan**

Extreme weather events, frightening phenomenon that are becoming more and more common as the earth's atmosphere continues to heat as a result of humanity's prolific burning of carbon fuels, is, of course, impacting various nations throughout the world. But the Philippines, along with Australia, often seem to be at the front lines of those climate assaults. In the case of the Philippines, it has been, as we have seen, the regularity of ever more devastating storms. But 2013 turned out to be of quite a different order.

By the time Super storm Typhoon Haiyan slammed into the central Philippines on November 8, 2013, it was recording winds of around 195 miles per hour, the most powerful typhoon winds ever recorded to have hit land. A bit later the super-charged winds hit the city of Tacloban on the island of Leyte with horrifying results. When the storm finally passed, perhaps 8,000 people had died or simply vanished, and the city itself was devastated. Indeed it looked as if it had been struck by nuclear weapons, the destruction seemed so complete. As so common with such events, reminiscent of super storm Sandy, which had had such catastrophic impact along the shores of the American Northeast the year before,

it was not just phenomenal winds but surges of ocean waters that caused much of the damage. According to news accounts, walls of water about 20 feet high had rushed inland. It swept buildings and people aside. Later, as the waters receded, it pulled much of the same combination of people and building materials out to sea.

Sadly once the storm had passed, the plight of many of the residents remained desperate. Unlike the situation some years earlier during 2004's devastating tsunami, potential rescuers found it much more difficult to travel to the devastated areas with needed supplies. Along with the number of deaths was the sheer magnitude of the destruction that had created refugees of some 800,000 people. Eventually it became clear that even larger numbers estimated to be around four million had lost their homes. Months later, needed supplies to help the region recover were still only very slowly arriving. For the Philippines, Haiyan had become, in the eyes of many, the nation's worst natural disaster. Because science has shown that storms such as Haiyan have become more likely and even more dangerous due to carbon pollution, it is questionable how appropriate the term "natural" really is.

Even as the full impact of the global slowdown hit economic growth rates for the Philippines, growth continued at least in the modest positive area of

just un-der 1% for 2009. Happily, as the world's economy, especially that part that is based in Asia, began to rebound, local economic growth rebounded as well and came in for 2010 at a healthy 7.3%. More recently growth rates have remained relatively steady at just under 7%, among the healthiest in the region.

Like that of many of its neighbors, the economy in the Philippines is particularly tied to the international economic situation. From Malaysia to Israel and throughout large parts of the Middle East, many Filipinos work abroad and the money they send home plays a significant part in the health of the local economy. When various crises affect the lives of those overseas workers the nation itself suffers as well. As the world economy has improved those remittances have gone up and played a significant role in pushing consumer spending higher. On the other hand, the weakening of the global economy lessens those remittances and prompts the return of those same laborers from abroad thereby adding to the number of people looking for work locally.

The Philippines do at times have trouble competing for outside investment with many of its neighbors because the local minimum daily pay rate, at around $5.23 USD, while much lower than in countries like the United States or Japan, is not an advantage when competing with countries like China, where the going rate can be as low as 31 cents a day or even Vietnam which comes in at around 92 cents. That higher figure is unfortunately not complemented by utility rates for power that also exceed their rivals as well.

Still that reality has not always been an impassible barrier. Mitsubishi recently decided to make the Philippines the hub of its Southeast Asian production facilities for sports utility vehicles headed for markets from Southeast Asia to Latin America, a decision that certainly helped improve the local economy and complemented other positive trends.

Former President Arroyo made significant progress dealing with some economic issues such as inflation, and the recent opening of a new natural gas field has promised to be a very helpful boon to the economy. Despite the new natural gas field, the Philippines remain an importer of oil and, like so many other nations around the world, have been deeply hurt by the rising cost of oil.

Like much of the region, the Philippines has benefited from China's economic growth. Indeed bilateral trade between the two nations has been growing very steadily in recent years, and their respective leaders pledged recently to double the level of trade in the future despite the island tensions.

While the Philippines generally have reason to be reasonably satisfied with recent economic developments, it is also true that its relative position has fallen over the last half century. In the years before World War II, the Philippines had the highest per capita income in Southeast Asia. In the early 1950s its per capita income was far ahead of Thailand while today the average Thai has twice the income of the average Filipino. The real problem for the Philippines is not growth per se, but the fact that the society is especially divided along economic lines. The vast majority is quite poor and burdened by a birth rate that makes economic progress very difficult. While the poverty level has been reduced in the 21st century, it still remains high. It was 16.6% in 2018, but the impact of COVID-19 led to an increase. In February 2021 however, the Philippine National Economy and Development Agency hoped, that with an expected economic recovery, it would be back in the range 15.5% to 17.5% in 2021.

## Environmental Issues:
## From Local to Global

As is usually the case elsewhere, the environment of the Philippines has been severely impacted by the economic demands of its growing population. Deforestation has become a significant problem, and the air quality has been deeply affected. On a national level, the government has shown an interest in confronting these problems, but progress has been very limited. Efforts at reforestation have not been very successful. Those will likely be improved if the various international efforts to retain tropical forests are eventually implemented successfully as part of the international climate change negotiations. Momentum in that regard has not been great over the last two years. But it certainly seems likely to become a reality as the challenges of man-made climate change become even more obvious over time.

Like the rest of its neighbors, the Philippines are experiencing the slowly rising temperatures associated with the thickening of greenhouse gases. While the temperature rise is not as dramatic as recently seen in the higher areas of the northern hemisphere, changes are beginning to occur. The islands are becoming dryer, and tropical diseases like dengue fever are becoming more and more common. At base, the primary impact of man-made climate change is about water. In some places there is too little, in others too much. Thus even as parts of the Islands are becoming dryer, Manila itself has been hit particularly hard by ever more powerful hurricanes. Although the entire region of East and Southeast Asia is vulnerable to the power of typhoons, the Philippines by virtue of the physical geography and location are particularly so.

This happened most dramatically in the fall of 2009 when Typhoon Ketsana (Ondoy) flooded large sections of Manila and subjected the city to levels of rainfall not seen in generations. Those enormous typhoons, common in the region long before the era of man-made climate change, have become an ever more powerful and familiar presence in the lives of the Philippine people in recent years.

While Ketsana was especially dramatic, the more important reality is that enormous storms that inundate the Philippines and more and more commonly flood its capital city are becoming an even

**Philippine street traffic**

Courtesy of Raeann Rebanal

# Philippines

greater burden. Indeed such storms, much like Hurricane Sandy that devastated the American Northeast, have become so common that it is literally hard to keep up. In August 2012, for example, Manila was again inundated. Half the city was under water with scores of dead and once again hundreds of thousands displaced.

It is not just the torrential rains that challenge society, but the horrendous landslides caused by the loosening of saturated lands. Then came Hurricane Haiyan, which caused even greater devastation than the islands had experienced in recent memory (see the textbox devoted to the storm's destructive impact).

Indeed, Philippine citizens are becoming increasingly aware of the challenge of climate change. In the spring of 2008, around 10,000 people took part in a huge conference in Zamboanga City. It was addressed by an impressive array of scientists, NGO representatives, and political leaders. Since then a number of Philippine climate activists have been trained by America's former vice president and Nobel Peace Prize winner, Al Gore, to give updated presentations of his famous slide show on the climate crisis to better familiarize local audiences with the seriousness of the challenge.

On the "solutions" side of the challenge, locals have been working with Icelandic companies to introduce geothermal energy production on Biliran Island in the Leyete region of the country. Meanwhile the new president has implemented a policy of planting 1.5 billion new trees over the next several years. The encouragement of tree planting continues. In 2018, President Duterte announced a ban on further open cast mining, ordering the mining companies to plant trees. In 2019, a new law decreed that students could only complete graduation from schools after they had planted 10 trees each. Considering how much the Philippines have been subject to deforestation, that is an important contribution.

## COVID-19

The first cases of COVID-19 in the Philippines were detected in mid-February 2020. As the numbers began to rise, President Duterte declared a "State of Calamity" for six months in March. Borders were closed and there were major restrictions on domestic travel, gatherings, and other activities. He also said early on in the pandemic that the police should shoot quarantine and curfew breakers; if they did, there are no exact details of those killed. Numbers rose rapidly but subsided in

May and restrictions were relaxed. Inevitably, this led to a renewed spike and new restrictions. Now the president ordered the arrest of those without masks. In all, there were 120,000 arrests during that second wave. Numbers infected remained high into 2021, reaching 500,000 in January and then surged again from April. By the end of May 2021, there were 1,204,716 reported cases, of whom 1,167,426 had recovered. Over 21,000 had died. By the end of 2021, there had been 3 million cases and 51,000 deaths. There was a spike in January 2022, and by mid-May, there had been 3.69 million cases, with 60,452 deaths. The biggest concentration was in the capital region around Manila, which accounted for more than 50% of the cases. Vaccinations began at the end of February, using a variety of types, including Russian and Chinese. Take up was slow: by the end of May 2021, just under four million (3.7%) had received a first dose and 1.2 million (1.1%) the second. A year later, 62.8% were fully vaccinated, while 12.5% had received a booster.

Even though Duterte seemed more interested in the economic rather than the social consequences of the disease, as noted, the economic impact was severe. By October 2020, the IMF calculated that the economy had contracted by 8.3%. Unemployment rose sharply. 21% had lost their jobs by August 2020. Poverty and hunger increased.  By the end of 2020, there was an emphasis on vaccination—not yet begun—would solve the economic problems. Certainly, despite the continuing concern about the pandemic, there was some optimism that there would be a return to growth in 2021, but this proved not to be the case. Better things are expected in 2022.

### The Future

Benigno S. Aquino III came to power with a famous name and a great deal of good will. But he had a relatively limited record of real accomplishments. Once in office, he has begun a significant series of initiatives, including educational and environmental projects.

Especially important, of course, is addressing the nation's long-standing inability to reconcile the needs of the local Christian communities with southern Muslim demands for their own separate autonomous state, as represented by the Moro Islamic Liberation Front. As we have seen, the president had reason to feel a sense of accomplishment. For a time it even looked like much had been accomplished. But as has been the case for

generations, each step forward has seen the problem continuing in new ways or areas. In short, the ongoing turmoil in the Southern Philippines is not going away anytime soon.

Although the former president himself was not directly involved, perhaps the most important development in Aquino's time in office was the decision by the Philippine Supreme Court officially to break up the enormous estate owned by the president's family. Like so many Philippine leaders, the president hails from one of those families that have long dominated the Philippine economy and controlled huge amounts of land. Many leaders have spoken of land reform. But in the spring of 2012, after years of controversy, the court finally ruled that the Aquino estate itself, land linked not only to the current president but to his mother, the former president and her martyred husband, would be divided up among 6,000 tenant farmers. It was both materialistically and symbolically an enormous blow to the plantation economy, which has long held sway in the Philippines to the detriment of the larger population.

Perhaps even more significant, though, is the fact that after a long period of stagnation the Philippine economy has finally begun to grow energetically. Indeed its growth rate was lately second only to that of China. Perhaps more than any other issue, it is that growth that offers reason to feel somewhat optimistic. If it were not happening at the same time that the more powerful storms associated with a changing global climate were hitting the island with greater ferocity, one might feel absolutely optimistic.

For the immediate future, the most obvious challenges remain the same, managing the evolving power relations in the region, especially the growing power of China and America's diminishing influence as well as the destabilized global climatic system.

As we have seen the Philippine's record on successful presidential leadership has been a very mixed record indeed and Duterte's indifference to the human rights violations associated with his anti-drug campaign have not been encouraging.

Nevertheless, he remained relatively popular, especially given the steady economic growth of recent years. The election of Ferdinand Marcos Jr. with Sara Duterte as vice-president seems unlikely to change the pattern of the country's political development. With the easing of COVID pressures, there may be some economic recovery. But in most ways, things seem likely to go on as before.

# The Republic of Singapore

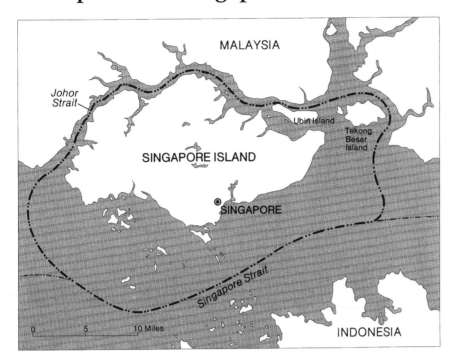

**Prime Minister Lee Hsien Loong**

**Area:** 239 sq. mi. (692.7 sq. km., somewhat smaller than New York City)

**Population:** 5,891,591 (2021 est.)

**Capital City: Singapore,** pop. 5,891,591 (2021). Singapore is a city republic, so the population of the Capital is the same as the population of the country.

**Climate:** Tropically hot and humid

**Neighboring Countries:** Malaysia (North); Indonesia (South)

**Official Languages:** Chinese (Mandarin dialect), Malay, Tamil, English

**Ethnic Background:** Chinese (about 77%), Malay (14%), Indian (about 7%)

**Principal Religions:** Buddhism, Hinduism, Islam, Christianity, and Daoism

**Main Exports:** (to Malaysia, U.S., Japan, China, Taiwan, Thailand, South Korea) Rubber, petroleum, tin, and manufactured goods

**Main Imports:** (from Japan, U.S., Malaysia, Taiwan, South Korea, Thailand) Manufactured goods, petroleum, fuels, chemicals, and foodstuffs

**Currency:** Singapore dollar

**Former Colonial Status:** Possession of the British East India Company (1819–1867), British Crown Colony (1867–1958), occupied by the Japanese (1941–1945), internally self-governing (1958–1963)

**National Day:** August 9, 1965 (Independence Day)

**Chief of State:** Halimah Yacob (since September 2017)

**Head of Government:** Lee Hsien Loong (since August 2004)

**National Flag:** Divided horizontally, with a white crescent moon and five white stars on a red field at the top and a white bottom

**Per Capita PPP GDP Income:** $93,397.05 (2020 World Bank)

The small island of Singapore is separated from Johor State at the southern tip of West Malaysia by a narrow strait of water; road and railway bridges provide access to the mainland. Although tropical, the island is highly urbanized. The city occupies the more agreeable part of the island on the southeast coast. Its harbor is naturally a good one, and it lies at the crossroads of Southeast Asia at one end of the Straits of Malacca. This is the best and shortest passage between the Indian Ocean and the South China Sea, and Singapore has been an important naval base and commercial port for almost two centuries.

## History

Prior to the arrival of Europeans, Singapore was a small insignificant part of the Malay world, inhabited by a few fishermen but not much more. Sir Thomas Stamford Raffles of the British East India Company occupied got permission from the Sultan of Johor and the local chief to establish a trading post at the mouth of the Singapore River the island in 1819 after realizing the commercial possibilities of the harbor given its very strategic location. In 1824, the island was ceded to the East India Company. The decision to make it a free port was quite important to the city's later growth. In 1826, the company united Singapore with its two other enclaves on the Malay Peninsula, Penang and Malacca, to form the Straits

Settlements. Then, after 1833, when the East India Company lost its monopoly of the China trade, it lost interest in Singapore although it continued to administer it. Unimpressed by the company's lack of interest in developing Singapore, British merchants petitioned the government in London to take it over. By 1867, it had been made a British Crown Colony. In spite of Dutch competition based on neighboring Java and Sumatra, the colony began to achieve the size of a major commercial port. The opening of the Suez Canal in 1869 attracted even heavier traffic from Europe to the Straits of Malacca.

This commercial development also resulted in the migration of many Chinese to the island. They quickly became the majority ethnic group as they labored to process rubber and tin. Unlike many other overseas Chinese communities, those in Singapore were not mainly young men. A British ordinance of 1939 restricted the numbers of Chinese men who could

**The late Lee Kuan Yew**

277

# Singapore

**Contrasts in urban Singapore**

come, but not women. As a result, Singapore was a city of Chinese families, which made it a very stable society.

Over time, Singapore became the principal British stronghold in the region. A large British naval base was constructed in the 1920s, equipped with coastal defenses designed to protect it from attack by sea. Unfortunately, the new defenses were not finished by the start of World War II and the Japanese assault. When World War II began, British plans came to naught. Three days after the attack on Pearl Harbor in 1941, Japanese torpedo planes sank the *Prince of Wales* and the *Repulse*, two mammoth British warships that had been dispatched to Singapore to help in the defense of the port. In addition, an invasion of Malaya was carried out by a large, highly trained Japanese army, which came not by sea, as expected, but by land, The mainland fell to the invaders within four weeks, and the siege of Singapore began. The British held out for two weeks before the Japanese finally captured Singapore and 60,000 prisoners on February 15, 1942. It was one of the worst military defeats ever suffered by Great Britain.

As elsewhere in Southeast Asia, the Japanese often mistreated the people they had conquered, particularly those of Chinese origin. Ultimately, as the war neared its conclusion, the Japanese were isolated in Singapore by American sea and air action. The British peacefully returned to the island soon after Japan collapsed in 1945, setting up a military administration that was replaced by a civilian one in April 1946.

After the war Britain used Singapore as its headquarters in the region. Although, over time, Britain began slowly to withdraw from the Malay Peninsula. It did retain its Singapore bases, but decreased their size as it embarked on a pullout.

Malaya moved toward independence as the Federation of Malaya, but Singapore, with its large Chinese population, was excluded and remained a Crown Colony. Although the U.K. maintained control over Singapore's external relations, it permitted increasing degrees of internal self-government.

The communist uprising known as "the Emergency," which began in Malaya in 1948, also affected Singapore. Following the launch of an armed insurrection led by the Malayan Communist Party (MCP), which called for the establishment of "People's Democratic Republic of Malaya," to include Singapore in February 1948. The Singapore government declared a state of emergency in June 1948. Singapore did not escape the MCP's campaign of attacks on property, murders, and attempted assinations of senior figures.

By 1953, the communist offensive was beginning to lose steam as the British fought back and the MCP lost support. In 1953, the governor appointed a commission to examine the future government of the colony. In 1954, this recommended limited internal self-government, which came into force with the 1955 General Election for a much expanded Legislative Council. The Labour Front, led by David Marshall, was the single largest party. Marshall became the first Chief Minister of Singapore. Among the first actions of the new government was a formal ending of the emergency regulations, which were replaced by a new set of security laws.

As the communists were beginning to lose the jungle war on the peninsula, the MCP leader, Chin Peng, who had come to prominence fighting the Japanese and who, ironically, had received the British Officer of the Order of the British Empire (OBE, later withdrawn) for his assistance to British clandestine forces,

tried unsuccessfully to negotiate with the Malay leader, Tunku Abdul Rahman and with David Marshall an agreement that would have allowed the MCP to operate legally. In return, Chin would help in the cause of indepndence. The talks failed, but may have been a useful bargaining point with the British, who conceeded full independence of Malaya in 1957.

Singapore continued as a Crown Colony, but a new constitution gave full internal self government. In the election that followed in 1959, the People's Action Party, led by Lee Kuan Yew PAP, came to power in an electoral landslide. It has remained in power ever since. Although he had ties to the communists, Lee Kuan Yew, quickly moved to lessen their potential influence. Sensing British and Malayan concerns over his election, he made strenuous efforts to improve relations.

A widespread and ambitious program of centralized economic development and social welfare programs began, which led the communists to redouble their efforts to seize control of the government. During those early years of the new state, the principal tensions were within the People's Action Party, between the moderate socialists who favored more ties with Malaysia, and their more extremist communist allies. Eventually the PAPs principal leftists quit to form the Barisan Socialist Party.

The apparent strength of the left in Singapore was a major source of concern to Britain and Malaya. Thus, Prime Minister Tunku Abdul Rahman of Malaya immediately proposed that Malaya, Singapore, and the Borneo territories of Sabah and Sarawak be joined into the Federation of Malaysia. His purpose was twofold: to protect the stability and progress of the entire region, and to control the leftist

**Former Prime Minister Goh Chok Tong**

278

# Singapore

trend in Singapore. Tunku Abdul Rahman had reason to be concerned. Had Singapore become a communist state, Malaya would have suffered a serious economic blow, since the island processed and shipped the bulk of the rubber and tin which produced most of Malaya's foreign exchange. It would have posed a political threat as well.

In spite of opposition by the Barisan Socialist Party, the Malayan Communist Party, and the vehement opposition of Indonesia's President Sukarno, the Federation of Malaysia came into existence in 1963. Sukarno immediately declared that Indonesia was in a state of "confrontation" (a sort of undeclared, irregular war) with Malaysia, severing all trade relations. Singapore suffered somewhat from this step, since Indonesia had been one of its most important trading partners, but Indonesia suffered as well. Actually, the economic needs of both gave rise to a widespread smuggling operation which helped to offset the effect of the official boycott.

The short-lived union of Singapore with the Federation of Malaysia came to an end in 1965. The Federation may have solved the immediate problems of a potential communist takeover. But it did not resolve the more basic antagonism between the Malays and Chinese that has long been the greatest internal problem within Malaysia. The Malay-dominated government of the Federation preferred to deal at arms-length with the Chinese-controlled regime on the island rather than to add more Chinese to the Federation's population. Lee Kuan Yew's vision of a more multicultural Malaysian Federation was clearly threatening to the Malay leaders of Kuala Lumpur. When he energetically tried to extend the activities of the PAP to mainland Malaya and to exert greater influence throughout the Federation, matters came to a head. Singapore was forced out of the Federation, left to survive on its own.

## Birth of a New City

Although the separation of Singapore from the Federation of Malaysia was described as a matter of mutual consent, in reality Singapore was confronted with a demand to withdraw. It had no choice but to do so. Within Singapore, leaders like Lee Kuan Yew had serious doubts that the newly independent country could survive on its own. There was, though, little choice but to try.

The immediate problem for Singapore was survival. But happily the new city-state had the advantages of excellent leadership under Lee Kuan Yew and a population committed to accomplishing that goal. In fact, under the paternalistic leadership of Prime Minister Lee and PAP, Singapore did more than survive. It prospered and became one of the most successful economies of Southeast Asia while maintaining a major commitment to improving the living standards of its people.

By the end of the century, its population enjoyed the highest standard of living in the region and was generally one of the safest societies. Some though have come to believe that Singapore's citizens have paid a high price in political freedoms for PAP's economic successes.

Political developments during the early 1960s complemented PAP's ability to dominate the new nation's political life. In elections held in 1963, the People's Action Party elected 39 representatives to 23 from the Barisan Socialist Party. But even then Prime Minister Lee Kuan Yew so dominated the political scene in Singapore that members of the opposition party angrily stalked out of the Parliament in 1966.

Since then the People's Action Party has been in almost complete charge although a new, leftist opposition party formed in April 1971, was successful in electing one member in 1981. In 1984 it doubled its holding to two, but that barely made a dent on the PAP's monopoly of political power.

In 1986, the debates in parliament began to be televised. This gave wide publicity to the speeches of one of the only two opposition members, an articulate ethnic Indian, J. B. Jeyaretnam, who in September of that year was expelled from the body for having allegedly defamed the impartiality of Singapore's judiciary.

From time to time, the government, which maintains a limited amount of censorship, has tried to penalize foreign publications that contain articles it does not like. Punishments have ranged from financial pressures to outright lawsuits.

As concerns about Singapore's immediate survival have given way to economic success, Prime Minister Lee, who ran the country directly till 1990, began to concern himself with slowing the spread of what he believed were negative Western values. Distressed by the materialistic outlook of Singapore's "yuppies," he has tried to revive a modern version of Confucianism. He and other government officials have enthusiastically embraced Confucianism's more communal values and hierarchal perspective as more suitable for Singapore's predominantly Chinese population than Western individualism.

While this emphasis on a Chinese approach to values has also encouraged the study of Mandarin Chinese in the schools of Singapore, the government has treated with considerable disdain and hostility those it perceives as pushing multi-cultural Singapore too far in the direction of being an exclusively Chinese nation. Important as well has been Lee Kuan Yew's concern that Singapore's people continue their commitment to learning English, an

**Singapore skyscrapers**

# Singapore

increasingly important language throughout the world.

Over the years Singapore's leaders have viewed their nation as particularly fragile because of its ethnic diversity and vulnerable because of its small size when compared to its neighbors. Accordingly, they have done whatever they considered necessary for domestic and external security. The armed forces are large for the size of the country and are impressively modern. The Internal Security Act—inherited from the British—is used by the Internal Security Department, to make dissent difficult.

### Government and Politics

Lee Kuan Yew, in office from 1959, retired as prime minister in November 1990 in favor of his handpicked successor, Deputy Prime Minister Goh Chok Tong. The change, though, made little difference in the political realities of Singapore. In fact, the nation's most obvious founding father would continue to serve as a senior adviser in various governments for the next 20 years.

Still, the January 1997 elections saw Prime Minister Goh move somewhat out from under Lee Kuan Yew's shadow. This time PAP even won a greater electoral victory than previously. The election though was more than a triumph of Prime Minister's Goh's new authority. PAP and the government used all their power to ensure a victory. They even announced that the government planned improvements in the city's housing infrastructure within which most of the city's citizens live and often own apartments. Interestingly, the government warned that those districts that voted against PAP would be last on the waiting list for improvements.

A new development was the emergence of Lee Kuan Yew's son, Lee Hsien Loong. He was deputy prime minister under Prime Minister Goh, becoming prime minister in August 2004.

The younger Lee was born was born in 1952. He joined the Singapore defense forces as an officer in 1971 and eventually reached the rank of brigadier general. He studied mathematics at Cambridge in England (1974) on a military scholarship and got a first-class degree, as well as a diploma in computer science. While still in the army, he took a master's degree in public administration at Harvard (1980). In 1984, he joined the People's Action Party, and his rapid rise to political power began immediately. That same year he became Minister of State in both the Trade and Industry and the Defense Ministries. Named Deputy Prime Minister in 1990, he was long expected to become prime minister, but how much of the nation's ultimate decision making would be in his hands was less than clear. While his father left the prime ministership more than a decade earlier, Lee Kuan Yew clearly remained influential in his son's government as "senior advisor" to the government.

It did appear though that the new prime minister was determined to make his own mark on the nation's leadership. He has spoken frequently of the need to build a more open and politically responsive system within Singapore, and laws that previously required police permission to hold indoor meetings have been rescinded. Such changes allow a somewhat more open environment for political activity.

During the August 2005 presidential election, the official election committee rejected all candidates for office save those of the incumbent S. R. Nathan. In the spring of 2006, the long-awaited general elections offered very few surprises. The ruling People's Action Party won 82 of the 84 seats in parliament although their winning percentage (66.6%) was significantly lower than their 2001 win, which had come in at 75.5%.

Responding to criticism, the government decided to follow the model made famous in London by authorizing the creation of a "Speaker's Corner" in Singapore, where people could voice their opinions in public. But it was hardly a genuine move toward a more open political debate. Aspiring speakers were told they had to register with the police in advance and could still be sued for libel for their comments. That change was one of several designed to reduce the pressures for more genuine reform.

Recognizing that the pressures were still building for a more open system the constitution was modified during 2010 to address those concerns. Voting and election procedures were modified to guarantee more clearly a voice for those beyond the People's Action Party. It was thought by some that the move had been engineered to open up more space for public dialogue without actually lessening the PAP's political strength. If that was the plan, it apparently did not work

In May 2011 yet another round of elections were held that proved quite historic. The PAP won the elections and still dominated the parliament in the aftermath. However, its vote tally dropped once again, as in the previous election, this time by something just over 6%. The Singapore Workers Party, led by Low Thia Khiang, made a relatively impressive showing.

Regardless of the results, what is most obvious is that PAP remained in control. Indeed, the government has long made it quite difficult for its opponents even to build support for their causes. One earlier opposition politician, Chee Soon Juan, was jailed for publishing and giving speeches the government did not support. Later, Chee spent 12 days in jail for giving a political speech without a permit. Longtime opposition leader, J. B Jeyaretnam, was no luckier in his opposition to government policies.

The parliamentary elections in 2011 revealed something of a crack in the PAP's armor. Some have even spoken of the Workers Party as perhaps one day

**Singapore**                                        Courtesy of Frank Conlon

**Singapore entrepreneur and family**

becoming part of a genuine two-party system. Especially significant was that in the aftermath of the election the government's longtime minister mentor, Lee Kuan Yew, finally and officially left his position as a senior adviser. He cited the need for the government to make a new start. In the aftermath his position was formally abolished. Lee remained a member of parliament, but he was already ill and died in March 2015.

In the September 2015 general election, the PAP bounced back. It got 70% of the popular vote, and took 83 of the 89 seats. The Workers' Party took held the remaining six. The following year saw a constitutional amendment to the method of electing the president. Under its terms, candidates were limited to members three ethnic groups, Chinese, Malay, and Indian, who had not had one of its members in the post for the last five terms. As a consequence, only a Malay could stand in the 2017 presidential election. In the event, Singapore got not only the first Malay to hold the post for 47 years, but its first female president. This was Halimah Yacob, a member of the PAP and a former speaker of parliament.

More typical was the pursuit of critical journalists. Lee Kuan Yew harried the Hong Kong-based *Far Eastern Economic Review* for many years. A naturalized American citizen of Singaporean origin was arrested in 2008 for insulting a local judge in his blog. In 2011, a British journalist was sentenced to six weeks and a heavy fine in jail for his book, *Once a Jolly Hangman*, which argued that the Singapore judiciary was not independent. He had returned to Singapore for the book launch. By that stage, the government was turning its attention to controlling social media and the internet. In 2016, a new law on contempt of court attracted international criticism

for restricting freedom of speech, while a 17-year old blogger received a jail sentence for critical comments on Christianity and Islam. In 2021, the prime minister received damages twice over alleged defamations on social media. He said that he would donate the money to charity.

There were occasional hints at more openness. The controversy over the 2010 decision to open two government casinos in order to attract more tourists sparked a lively debate. Open discussion was allowed, with even senior ministers joining in. But the project went ahead, whatever the views expressed.

Prime Minister Lee Hsien Loong indicated that he would retire around his 70th birthday in 2022, when the next general election was due. He began to bring new ministers into the government, no doubt with the aim of grooming one to take over from him. In any event, as COVID-19 struck in 2020, he announced that the 2022 elections would be brought forward to July 2021 under COVID-safe conditions. The People's Action Party won 83 of the 93 seats, while the Workers' Party won 10. The new Progressive Singapore Party received two no-constituency seats. But the PAP share of the vote dropped back to 61.2%, and Lee Hsien Loong's chosen successors performed poorly. In response to this result, Lee announced that he would stay in office to "see Singapore safely through COVID."

## Foreign Policy

Singapore, as an independent ministate, cannot hope to survive without friends. The strategy has been to make the country so valuable to the region that no one would wish its booming economy destroyed because of the repercussions that would be felt throughout the area. This approach has succeeded. Singapore is one of the world's busiest ports and is the center of economic activity in Southeast Asia. It intends to keep its value high by always being the best.

Relations with Malaysia, though, can at times be complicated. Singapore has though come to an agreement with Malaysia on its international sea boundary. A flap over a Malaysian tariff on Singapore petrochemicals in 1995 was reffered to the WTO, but the parties agreed to settle. Unfortunately, more problems surfaced early in the late 1990s when Senior Minister Lee Kuan Yew made disparaging remarks about crime problems in one of the Malaysian cities closest to Singapore. The comments were resented and Lee later apologized. Nor were relations improved when Lee later published the first volume of his memoirs about the early years of the city. Many in Malaysia were unhappy with his

comments about some of their previous leaders.

The reality is Malaysian-Singapore relations are often tense. Considering that Singapore gets most of its food and water from Malaysia, having a good relationship is especially important. In fact, the price of Malaysian-supplied water was taken to the International Court of Justice for arbitration. Given the leadership changes within both Malaysia and Singapore some analysts claim there is reason to expect the all too often tense relationship between the two neighboring countries is likely to lessen. Especially significant in that regard was the resolution of the long-simmering arguments between Malaysia and Singapore over railway rights. Just last year a land swap was worked out between the two neighbors that resolved the question of underutilized Malaysian railroad rights within Singapore. In the end, both nations agreed to the joint development of a block of commercial property. Periodic tensions arise over sea boundaries and air space, perhaps inevitable given the closeness of the two countries. A high-speed rail link connecting Singapore with Kuala Lumpur was proposed in 2010 and agreed in 2013. But following elections in Malaysia, it was postponed in 2018 and terminated in 2021. A Johor-Singapore link was originally proposed in 1991, but work did not begin on the Malaysian side until November 2020 and on the Singapore side until January 2021.

One of the most important challenges of recent years was to help Indonesia through the economic and political challenges it faced. Singapore had good relations with Suharto but with the dictator's departure a new and stable relationship needs to be developed. Here again, the outspoken Lee Kuan Yew at times complicated matters by making disparaging remarks about Suharto's designated vice-president and then successor, B. J. Habibie. Of course Singapore's citizens could hardly remain indifferent to the fate of so many Indonesian ethnic Chinese who found themselves threatened by the violence unleashed during Suharto's fall from power. While Singapore did not send troops to East Timor during the later crisis and intervention of 1999 it did send a medical team and provide aid.

In the months after Abdurrahman Wahid came to power in Indonesia Singapore attempted to improve relations with him. Wahid's government reciprocated, by asking Lee Kuan Yew to serve on a panel of outside advisers for Indonesia. In June 1996, Prime Minister Goh Chok Tong visited Indonesia to help coordinate a major new Singapore investment program there and to establish an agreement under

# Singapore

which Indonesia will supply natural gas to the Chinese city-state.

Relations with Indonesia had a hit in 2014, when the Indonesian Navy named a warship in honor of two commandos executed in 1968 after a bomb attack in Singapore in 1965. This led to the suspension of defense cooperation for time. After a semi-apology from Indonesia, relations were restored at the end of the year. Another regular source of tension is the annual forest burning in Indonesia that causes pollution in Singapore (and Malaysia).

Until recently perhaps the most profound aspect of Singapore's foreign relations was the influence it has had on the region as a model of economic and social growth under a non-communist but authoritarian regime. Despite Western preferences and claims that a free and vibrant economy cannot exist without a politically open system, Lee Kuan Yew and the PAP long seemed to have demonstrated that they apparently can. It is an example that countries as close as Malaysia and as far as the People's Republic of China have watched closely.

The Bush administration's "War on Terror" impacted Singapore as it did on other countries in the region. Singapore contributed forces to assist in Iraq and became a major U.S. ally. While there are obvious political and economic advantages to this, not least in giving access to U.S. military equipment, Singapore, surrounded by Muslim states, had to tread a careful line. The other area where Singapore has to be careful is with the People's Republic of China. It was not until October 1990 that Singapore switched diplomatic relations on Taiwan from the Republic of China to the PRC. The relationship with Taiwan had been quite close, with joint military exercises and Taiwan defense personnel training in Singapore. Even after the switch, there were still informal links. Thus just before he became Prime Minister in 2004, Lee Hsien Leung visited Taiwan and held meetings with senior Taiwan officials. In 2015 Lee invited the then Taiwan president, Ma Ying-jeon, "privately" to Lee Kuan Yew's funeral. China has protested at such behavior but was pleased that Singapore warned Taiwan's leaders of the dangers of pressing for independence. And in November 2015, Taiwan President Ma Ying-jeon and China's Xi Jinping met in Singapore, perhaps a sign that China could see some advantages in Singapore's links with Taiwan.

## Culture

Singapore is a more multi-cultural city than many people realize. The vast majority of the population is Chinese, but they emigrated from several parts of southern China and thus tended to speak mutually unintelligible dialects until the government began its emphasis on learning "Mandarin" Chinese. That is also one of the reasons English has long been used as the official language of instruction, business, and in government. Moreover, the community includes a significant minority of Malays and South Asians. The presence of large numbers of Muslims has resulted in the presence of terrorist cells in Singapore, and some have feared that this might result in an increased prejudice against local Muslims, a development that would hurt the social cohesiveness of Singapore and certainly add to the tensions which arise with Malaysia from time to time.

The main feature of society in Singapore today is that it is centered on the industry of a bustling port and its very urban citizens who enjoy the highest standard of living of the region. Rather than living in the countryside, they live in apartments that the government built and that they have been encouraged to purchase.

### A Very Well Organized Society?

Singapore's leadership has made extraordinary improvements in the life of its citizens. It has done so at a price that some might find excessive. The government has over the years intervened in many aspects of the lives of its citizens, thus creating an astoundingly regulated society. Still, as a result of the government's almost puritanical attitude, Singapore has been viewed as one of the safest and cleanest places in the world. Though, that reputation was tarnished somewhat when during the aftermath of the World Trade Center attack of September 2001 it became clear that a terrorist cell had been operating in Singapore. The crime rate (hardly significant when compared to many of its neighbors) has also tarnished that "squeaky clean" image somewhat.

However, the social success of Singapore has not always been sufficient to keep the country's best and brightest at home. Significant numbers of highly educated young citizens have left the country in search of greater political freedom. While some have returned, the fact that the usually prosperous environment alone has not been sufficient to keep younger people from leaving should give the government cause to ponder how much authoritarianism is appropriate for a modern, well-educated society.

Education is highly admired in Singapore, and the society is moving smoothly into the computer age. Increasing numbers of households have personal computers and more and more of them are connected to the Internet. Predictably, that has opened up yet another vehicle of potential disruption the government would rather avoid. There have been moves to liberalize the social policies that are so influential in Singapore as well. In recent years the government has become somewhat more tolerant of activities and behaviors from bungee jumping to same-sex couples.

**Singapore waterfront**                    Courtesy of Frank Conlon

Overall, the island has acquired a genuinely cosmopolitan atmosphere with people from all over the world present. The city-state serves as a major international port that lies at the crossroads of Asia. For a modern urban society Singapore is still a very safe city whose crime rates remain quite low—certainly lower than in many urban centers in America or many other places in Asia. In fact, until recently it could boast that the crime rate had gone down every year for almost a decade.

There are other concerns as well. The birth rate is declining, and the government has begun a concerted effort from making it easier for foreigners to become citizens to encouraging parenthood to address the problem. There has also been a growth in the gap between rich and poor. The nation's leadership has addressed this by introducing a compulsory annuity program that should help poorer citizens to retire with more of the funds they need to live.

While Singapore may be an unusually stable society, very public controversies of the sort common elsewhere certainly do break out from time to time. Most recently the question of homosexuality became a public topic when a dramatic struggle broke out among conservative women. They had became involved in a struggle over the question of whether an organization founded to support gender equality had become too involved in what some saw as promoting a gay agenda.

In other incidents, a Christian preacher had to apology publically for derogatory comments he made on YouTube about Taoist religious practices. Clearly, Singapore may pride itself on the sophistication of its multicultural society, but it is as vulnerable to outbursts of intolerance as many of its neighbors.

The presence of immigrants has over the last year become an especially often discussed topic as the government initiated a formal dialogue regarding immigration and its role in providing the nation with needed manpower. The issue, which was an important topic in the most recent elections, has revealed a wide divergence of opinions. Some focused on the advantages immigrants bring while others feared the negative impact they could have on wages and public services.

Another trend worth noting is the government's effort to mitigate some of the most extreme aspects of capitalism by instituting a stronger social net than had previously existed. These efforts have been wide-ranging. But in total they have sought to make challenges from education and housing to public health more accessible for those in the lower income levels. Clearly this is a philosophical approach more akin to social democracy than the recent focus on market forces. It is likely to also be attractive at the polls during the next election.

The most obvious feature of that somewhat more social democratic policy was the implementation of a new national health insurance program, as well as a series of social programs directly focused on Singapore's many senior citizens who have not benefited as much as the younger generation from the nation's recent growth. Indeed, given that Singapore is said to be the most expensive city in the world to live in such policies matter greatly.

## Women

Women in Singapore have the same civil rights as men. In contrast to some other parts of Asia, Muslim women are covered by most of the provisions of the Women's Charter although in matters of polygamy and divorce Islamic law prevails. The government has also mandated that women should get equal pay for equal work and no longer allows separate pay scales.

Interestingly Singapore was recently noted as the best place in Asia to be a mother, according to Save the Children, an international organization that studies issues from gender equality to maternal and child mortality rates. On the larger global scale, Singapore came in 15th among that world's nation's but first within Asia itself.

Problems do exist. For example, women do not have the same rights males have in automatically passing on their citizenship to their children. Moreover, medical benefits available to the families of male civil servants are denied to families of female employees. And quotas that limit the number of women in the nation's medical schools were only just being addressed. On the more positive side, two women currently serve as ministers in the nation's government.

## Economy

In a fashion similar to that pioneered in Japan, Singapore's economy has been developed along the lines some refer to as "Asian Capitalism," though without the corruption often associated with the term. In contrast to "Anglo-American capitalism's" ever present suspicions about government, Singapore's government has played an important role in guiding the nation's economy. Employing institutions like the Economic Development Board and the Trade Development Board, the leadership has helped guide and set priorities for the economic evolution of Singapore. Such institutions have been especially helpful as Singapore has moved through various economic stages from the processing of primary products to the new information technologies.

As one of the first nations to embrace what is now known as "globalization," Singapore is heavily dependent on foreign trade and investment, all of which it is doing its best to promote. Since the mid-1980s the economy had been growing at a rate of about 8% a year. Because of its high level of development and its "contribution" to the U.S.'s trade imbalance, Singapore lost its preferential tariff status under the United States' Generalized System of Preferences (GSP) in 1988. Nevertheless, in the mid 1990s the growth rates averaged around 9%.

Even before the onset of the economic crisis of 1997, the island suffered a glut of empty retail spaces and very high rents. Wages were high and rising because labor was chronically short. It was in the context of these problems that Singapore, along with its neighbors, experienced the many economic problems 1997 brought. Not only did its currency plunge, but tourist arrivals—no doubt frightened by the stories of the choking atmosphere of a few years before—dropped significantly.

Responding proactively, the government continued to develop new industries, such as those in information technologies, electronic commerce, and most recently biotechnology. In fact, the government has made it clear that it hopes to see Singapore become especially involved in new biomedical breakthroughs associated with stem cell research. As the island nation entered the new century, the economy initially appeared on track again with a growth rate of 9.9% for 2000. Unfortunately, 2001 turned out be a disaster, literally the worse GDP—it fell by 2%—in the nation's history. That downturn was clearly tied not only to the worldwide glut of electronic products, but to the more general international economic slowdown, especially within the United States and its important domestic market.

Responding to the problem, the government worked not only on long-term solutions like the diversification of the economy and moving away from the dependence on electronics, but also on immediate changes to the corporate tax system to make Singapore more attractive to business leaders. It was especially important to lower the local wage bills. To deal with the problem, new policies were put into place, including lowering taxes to encouraging new bilateral trade agreements with nations like Canada and Sri Lanka. Especially important in that regard was the signing of the long-negotiated Singapore-U.S. free-trade agreement.

The economy has also been helped by the growth of Southern India, with which

# Singapore

Singapore has deep cultural and economic ties. As a sign of how Singapore might evolve in the future, the controversial decision was taken to allow two casinos to be built. This was a clear recognition of the success nearby Macao has had with its own efforts to expand its gambling revenues and of the importance for Singapore to continue to diversify its revenues. One casino, run by the Las Vegas Sands Hotel group, was built in downtown Singapore.

Regardless of what combination of factors has been most influential Singapore's recovery, the economy in the early years of the new century was rebounding nicely. Economic growth for 2006 was around 7.4 %, and 2007 was about the same. Singapore of course had to deal with the late 2008 global meltdown like the rest of the world. Since then the economy has slowed with a declining pattern over the last several years. 2015, for example, came in at only 2.2% growth rate.

Singapore's status as one of the world's most globalized nations has a price. The global recession that set in so dramatically in the fall of 2008 deeply affected the local economy. By early 2009, the economy had dropped precipitously. Singapore moved quickly to put in place its own $13.7 billion economic package to revise the economy. Moreover, in the early spring the government moved to devalue its currency in hopes of making its exports relatively more attractive. Singapore impressively managed to pull out of the 2008 meltdown quickly. Since then, economic growth has been relatively slow ranging from 1.9% in 2015 to 3.6 %. Still that growth recently allowed each adult a one time bonus check from the government of around $200 US dollars.

## The Energy and Environmental Challenge

Given how often hot ash from the regular burning of Indonesian forests arrives to hang over the city, environmental issues are rarely far from people's minds in Singapore. As for the larger issues of energy use and the challenges of global warming, Singapore, unlike China, already generates the bulk of its electrical energy needs from natural gas, a cleaner technology than coal. Moreover a campaign to enhance energy efficiency is underway. Greater tax breaks for purchasers of hybrid cars have been implemented along with experiments with hydrogen cars. More significant is that the government plans to begin implementing a carbon tax in 2019 which over time will grow higher and encourage the use of alternative energy sources.

But while the small island nation's ability to influence global climate change in a fundamental way is relatively small, its vulnerability is great.

A good chunk of the nation's entire business district, airport, and important naval facilities is somewhat less than two meters above sea level. Of course, as a relatively small island surrounded by water, Singapore simply does not have the option that many other nations have when faced with rising oceans. Given that reality, the country's authorities have begun discussions with the Dutch government on what the Netherlands has learned in its long fight against the sea.

Moreover, Singapore is largely a city state that primarily features an urban lifestyle. Therefore it is particularly vulnerable to rising temperatures by virtue of what is known as the urban heat island effect. In short, rising heat is exacerbated by the nature of urban landscape often making cities especially uncomfortable during extended heat waves.

## COVID-19

Singapore took early action against COVID-19, with stringent rules on mask wearing, social distancing and gatherings. But as an international travel hub, it was perhaps inevitable that the disease would spread to the island. By mid-April 2020, a peak of over 1,000 a day new cases were being recorded. But numbers gradually subsided into the summer and the autumn saw daily figures of under ten. However, in May 2021, cases began to rise, with the biggest cluster at Changi International Airport, and control measures were re-enforced. Financial support for workers was also increased. Towards the end of May, the total number of cases since the start of the pandemic was just under 62,000. The vast majority made a full recovery Deaths were low. At the beginning of December, there had been 29.

But it did not go away. There were periodic surges in 2021 and by December that year, there were over 279,000 cases and 827 deaths. By May 2022, there were over 1,200,000 cases, and 1,340 deaths. But numbers were falling. Vaccination rates were relatively low at first, but steadily increased as more doses arrived. By the end of December 2021, 83% had received two doses. Each time there was a surge, control measures returned, despite opposition from some ministers, who argued that the virus would have to be lived with. And as the numbers vaccinated increased, the government began to ease back on controls, with most being lifted by April 26, 2022. Once again, travel across the causeway to and from Johor was allowed, and self-service buffets re-opened. For the first time in two years, the Muslim community was able to celebrate Eid.

Although the economy was badly hit in 2020, contracting by 5.8%, sending the country into recession, it made a good recovery in 2021, as imanufacturing, construction and nternational trade picked up, to grow by 7.5%. This continued in 2022, with the tentative reopening of tourism by early May 2022. For example, international passengers at Changi Airport reached over one million for the first time in two years. It was not all smooth sailing. Reopening links to Malaysia saw a drop in the workforce, but this might only be temporary.

The prime minister warned that Singapore cannot escape the economic consequences of the Russian attack on Ukraine, which began in February 2002.

## The Future

The citizens of Singapore can celebrate the more recent evolution of the nation's economic policies, which have been redirected somewhat toward a better balance between mere economic growth and the individual needs of its citizens, especially the more vulnerable among them. On the other hand, the city state has not forgotten its more wealthy citizens either.

Indeed, Singapore has always prided itself on being at the cutting edge of new economic trends and no better example can be cited than the creation in 2017 of a 15-story vending machine–like structure to sell, not candy bars or soda but high-end cars from Ferraris and Bentleys to Porsches for the especially wealthy and time conscious automobile consumer.

In political terms, the 2025 general election is now seen by many as the time when current Prime Minister Lee Hsien Loong finally retires. In 2022, his chosen succesor seems to be Finance Minister Laurance Wong, a loyal team player. But things can change.

# The Kingdom of Thailand
## (before 1935 known as Siam)

**River Traffic in Bangkok**

**Area:** 198,455 sq. mi. (514,080 sq. km.)

**Population:** 70,060,653(2022 est.)

**Capital City:** Bangkok, pop. 10,723,000 (2021 est.)

**Climate:** Tropically hot with a wet monsoon season (May–October) dry and increasingly hot (November–April)

**Neighboring Countries:** Malaysia (South); Burma (Northwest); Laos (Northeast); Cambodia (Southeast)

**Official Language:** Thai (about 75%)

**Other Principal Tongues:** Chinese (about 14%); other (about 11%)

**Ethnic Background:** Thai (about 75%); Chinese (about 14%); Malay (about 4%); inland tribal groups (about 2%); Cambodian refugees (about 2%); other (about 3%)

**Principal Religions:** Theravada Buddhism, Islam

**Main Exports:** (to Japan, U.S., China, Malaysia, Hong Kong, Singapore) Textiles, footwear, cars, computers, rice, sugar, corn, rubber, tin, timber, and fishery products

**Main Imports:** (from Malaysia, Singapore, Japan, U.S., Saudi Arabia) Machinery and transport equipment, petroleum, chemicals, fertilizer, and consumer goods

**Currency:** Baht

**Former Political Status:** Siam avoided becoming a European colony; it was a nominal ally of Japan during World War II

**National Day:** December 10 (Constitution Day)

**Chief of State:** King Rama X (Maha Vajiralongkom) (since 2016)

**Head of Government:** Prime Minister Prayut Chan-o-cha (since 2014)

**National Flag:** Five horizontal stripes from top to bottom; red, white, blue (wider than the others), white, and red

**Per Capita GDP Income:** $18,900 (2022 est.) (purchasing power parity)

The broad central plain of Thailand, through which flows the Chao Phraya River, is the most fertile and productive area of the country and contains the principal cities, including Bangkok. Viewed from the foothills, which are found on the western edge of the plain, the land resembles an almost endless window with countless "panes of glass" when the precisely divided rice paddies are flooded with water.

The northern areas are more mountainous, and are covered with jungles containing timber and mineral resources. Valuable teakwood is still brought from the jungle on the tusks of the Asian elephant. The northeast region is dominated by the arid Korat Plateau. Ample rainfall occurs in the plateau, but it is not absorbed by the sandstone soil—it quickly collects into streams and rivers and runs to the sea instead of enriching the land. More people live here than can be supported by the limited agriculture that is possible. The southern region consists of the narrow Kra Isthmus and the coastal belt.

### History

People of Thai origin today not only inhabit Thailand but also live in the adjacent regions of all of Thailand's neighbors with the exception of Malaysia. The original home of these people was in southwest China where they were ruled by a highly organized kingdom in the 7th century A.D. The pressure of the Chinese

285

# Thailand

and later the Mongols caused a migration of the Thais southward where they eventually founded a new state in what is now northern Thailand.

In sharp contrast to governmental traditions in China, the Thai kings ruled as autocratic divine beings. Although they had not ruled directly for much of the 20th century, elements of this earlier tradition continue in the deep reverence the Thai people still hold for their monarchy.

During centuries of slow expansion they were eventually able to crush the Khmer Empire in neighboring Cambodia. In the 16th century, Siam, as it was then called, was conquered by the Burmese. Apart from sporadic contact by French merchants, the Europeans did not enter the area during the early centuries of exploration and colonization.

There was another Burmese invasion in 1767, but shortly thereafter Burma was invaded by the Manchu empire of China. That development eventually allowed the Siamese to win their freedom again. The present reigning dynasty came to power in 1782, and moved the capital city to the more secure location of Bangkok. Siam again emerged as a strong state. But though Siam's relations were already complicated, they were about to get much more so.

### The Arrival of the West

Early in the 19th century, Siam began to have more extensive contacts, commercial and otherwise, with Westerners. Moreover, the British gradually established control over Burma, and the French asserted their power over Vietnam. Laos and Cambodia had formerly been tributary states of Siam, but the French were ultimately able to combine it with Vietnam in their colony of Indochina. Thus, Siam was surrounded with the British on

**Prime Minister Prayut Chan-o-cha**

the west, the French on the east, and the Manchu empire of China to the north.

Siam managed to avoid becoming a European colony by a lucky combination of factors. First were the advantages of having not one but two European colonial powers on their borders (who could then be played off against each other). Second was enlightened leadership, which moved to strengthen the country through an increasing degree of modernization. It was a combination too few other non-Western states enjoyed.

In Siam's case, two important monarchs, during the critical late 19th and early 20th centuries, helped shield them from the worst of imperialism. The first was Mongkut, who reigned in the critical mid-19th century, and his son Chulalongkorn who followed him in power. Mongkut who was the monarch described in the book *Anna and the King of Siam*, which eventually inspired a musical and two feature length films.

Phra Maha Chulalongkorn, his son, was king from 1868 to 1910. He gained fame not only by abolishing Siam's feudal system, but also by modernizing the government and the army and by introducing such conveniences as the telegraph and railroad. He also paid an extended visit to the European capitals.

Both monarchs, father and son, recognizing the seriousness of the Western threat, took significant steps to educate themselves in Western issues and to find ways to lessen the growth of Western power in Siam. Overall their policies were a combination of tactical acceptance of various legal and territorial demands made by the Europeans while working to maintain the ultimate sovereignty of the Siamese state.

As part of some early 20th century treaties the borders with Laos and Cambodia

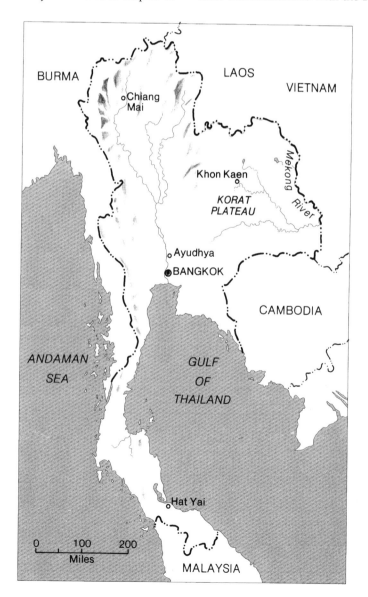

**Wat Po**

long history of protecting itself through power politics, began to change sides. An anti-Japanese guerrilla movement arose, and American military intelligence officers were able to operate almost openly in Bangkok during the last months of the war.

Pibul, himself, the pro-Japanese premier, resigned in 1944. At the end of the war, Britain took the position that Thailand was an enemy country and compelled payment of reparations in the form of rice, which was sent to Malaya. The U.S. however viewed Thailand as a more reluctant Japanese ally, and was able to persuade the British to adopt a similar policy.

Thailand's most immediate problem in the postwar years was to reintegrate itself into the world community after having been allied with imperialist Japan, and to establish a stable government. The former proved easier than the latter. The lands taken from France and Britain during the war were returned. Thailand was admitted to the UN in 1946.

Political stability, however, proved more difficult. The king, who had only recently been enthroned, was found dead of a gunshot wound in 1946. Premier Pridi, who was accused, apparently falsely, of having played some part in the slaying, was deposed. The army, still led by Pibul, again seized power. It was a pattern that was to continue into the 21st century. In total, there have been eighteen military coups between 1932 and 2022. .

### The Cold War

Initially, it appeared uncertain as to what position Thailand would take when the Korean War began in June 1950. Once it decided to support the American-backed UN troops, it began to receive U.S. military aid. This further strengthened the political position of the army in domestic affairs, making it more and more powerful within Thailand and, given the economic support of the wealthy Americans, helping to build the country's economic infrastructure.

The early 1950s saw many leaders like Nehru of India and Sukarno of Indonesia attempting to build a nonaligned movement during the height of the Cold War. Some governments accepted this position, but Thailand chose to align itself more directly with the Americans. Thailand became a founding member of SEATO, the Southeast Asian Treaty Organization (designed to be an Asian equivalent of NATO), and supported the American war in Vietnam.

Premier Pibul did permit freer discussion of political issues and began to encourage a growth of neutralism.

were adjusted. Under these treaties, regions were traded back and forth between France and Siam. In order to keep other colonial powers out of Siam, France and Britain established "spheres of influence"—the French east of the Chao Phraya River and the British west of the river. As a result of its somewhat limited, but significant, modernization program, and the fact that it escaped being a colony of a European power, Thailand today lacks the sense of resentment toward the industrialized nations that many people still feel in the countries of the former colonial world.

### A New Political System

After World War I there was a period of extravagant spending by the royal government, which was followed by a worldwide economic depression. This created discontent within Thailand and gave rise to intense political activity. The result was a bloodless overthrow of the autocratic monarchy in 1932 by a combination of civilian politicians and military leaders.

The two groups cooperated in the adoption of a constitution that limited the power of the king and established a parliamentary form of government. The first prime minister was a brilliant lawyer named Pridi Phanomyong. The king, dissatisfied with this system, abdicated in 1935, and was succeeded by his 10-year-old nephew and a regency council. This and other unsettling conditions, including the increased power of Japan in Asia, led to the overthrow of Pridi by Marshal Pibul Songgram. As World War II approached Marshal Pibul would

prove to be especially nationalistic and pro-Japanese.

In theory the country continued to be governed by a coalition consisting of the prime minister, the military, and Luang Pradit, the foreign minister. As the military acquired increasing political power, they displayed their nationalism by such means as legislation aimed at curbing the role of the Chinese commercial community, and changing the nation's name from Siam to Thailand, meaning "Land of the Free." In the years following the 1932 coup the Thai military, like the later Burmese and Indonesian military, would insist on an important place for itself in national decision-making.

### The Pacific War

Three weeks after the bombing of Pearl Harbor by the Japanese, Thailand signed a treaty of alliance with Japan. War was declared on the United States and Great Britain on January 25, 1942. With the support of Japanese troops, Thailand compelled the French to cede some border territories in Laos and Cambodia. The four southern states of Thailand, which had earlier been given to the British in Malaya were now returned to Thailand by the Japanese after they seized the British colony of Burma. Thailand probably had little choice in cooperating with the armies of imperial Japan. The Japanese certainly had the means to impose their will and had demonstrated their strength in early clashes with the Thai forces.

As the war began to turn against Japan, the Thai government, which has a

# Thailand

Concerned about potential Communist Chinese influence he also took steps against the local Chinese community that traditionally had been involved in the economy but refrained from taking part in politics. Nevertheless, Communist gains in Laos created more uneasiness in Thailand, which was dispelled when the U.S. pledged direct assistance in the event SEATO failed to fully support Thailand.

Pibul was overthrown in 1958 by Marshal Sarit, who kept Thailand firmly in an anti-communist posture. The country had an orderly, stable, and not overly intrusive government. As was true in so many nations, the military leaders were able to accumulate vast private fortunes through corruption.

Less effective military leadership continued after 1963 under subsequent leaders. Reliance was placed upon the ability of the popular royal family to maintain the unity of the Thai people, as well as on an increased degree of official respect shown for Buddhism and its various organizations. However, communist-inspired unrest in the poverty-stricken northeast region became more serious. The government treated this as a genuine threat, though perhaps partly to obtain additional American aid.

Once the United States fully committed to the struggle in Vietnam, Thailand permitted the Americans to use its air bases for attacks on North Vietnam and the Viet Cong. Thailand sent about 11,000 troops to fight in Vietnam and Laos. Having sided with the Americans, Thailand was able to gain enormous economic aid.

The reaction from the communist side was predictable: as Thailand increased its assistance to the U.S. and South Vietnam, the communists stepped up their guerrilla activities within the country. The increased U.S. military buildup in Thailand was thus paralleled by a greater flow of U.S. aid to the Thai armed forces. But if Thailand's association with the anti-communist side was clear in these years, its own domestic politics were less so.

The National Assembly was dissolved in 1968, leaving no representative body in Thailand. Eventually, a constitution was drafted by a Constituent Assembly and promulgated by the king in mid-1968. Elections in 1969 gave the United Thai People's Party, the government party, the victory. The Senate was appointed by the government.

But, the powerful military, unhappy with developments, suspended the parliament and reshuffled the cabinet. In 1972 a new constitution was proclaimed under which 299 members of a National Assembly were all appointed by the government, in other words by the army.

## Democratic Momentum?

The next year, the army-dominated government was toppled by student demonstrations that had the support of the king and at least part of the army. A civilian government was then ushered in, committed to greater freedom and reform. It was yet another step, such as in 1932, when the autocratic monarchy had ended, that gave Thailand the possibility of moving toward a more democratic form of government. In this case, it was partially as a result of the intervention of the monarchy itself that had not played a political role since 1932. As the new government was formed in 1973, Thailand seemed on the verge of taking yet another step toward more inclusive political decision-making.

But true parliamentary government was not to develop in Thailand. A combination of insecurity caused by the growing strength of communism in the region—Vietnam had been unified under Hanoi and Cambodia taken over the Khmer Rouge—as well as unhappiness about the open political battles within the new democratic government moved the military to once again reassert itself in 1976. In October of that year, with the backing of the King, the government was overthrown and the democratic constitution suspended.

Over the next years Thailand's politics were moved by several factors—the emerging democratic movement, which had its first real chance to govern in the mid-1970s, the ever influential Thai military and the King, who continued to be revered and demonstrated a willingness to intervene in the governing system when he deemed it appropriate.

An informal power-sharing arrangement between the army, civilian politicians, and officials has been common over the last few generations. Army leadership itself has been divided between those willing to work with civilians and those who are not. Rule has shifted between civilian and military-dominated governments, with and without ex-generals in the premiership, and outright military rule. Corruption has been commonplace. However, there were signs during the early 1990s that the military's domination of Thai politics was being increasingly challenged by the growth of a more politically conscious middle class.

In 1991 another civilian government was overthrown. Rule then shifted to the military dominated National Peacekeeping Council. In March 1992, a three-party coalition favored by the Council won control of the government with 53% of the seats in the lower house of parliament. The NPC then appointed all 270 members of the upper house with most having military backgrounds or connections.

When agreement could not be achieved on a new prime minister, the leader of the "junta," General Suchinda Kraprayoon, a key figure in the coup, and an individual especially unpopular with those who supported democracy, stepped into the post. Public demonstrations against Suchinda then led to severe repression by the Thai military. The level of violence against the civilian population was unparalleled in the recent Thai history.

The king stepped in to calm the crisis. On May 20, Suchinda appeared on national television kneeling before King Bhumibol. He was ordered to settle the crisis peacefully. After a short period of "caretaker" government, new elections were held on September 13, 1992. Chuan Leekpai was chosen as prime minister. The constitution now required that the prime minister be chosen from the lower house of parliament. The new government was ruled by a five-party coalition. This made it difficult to proceed with the legislative agenda that centered on constitutional reform. The army had been warned. It could no longer assume the civilian population would simply go along with anything it attempted.

In May 1995, Prime Minister Chuan Leekpai was forced to dissolve parliament when the Palang Dharma party pulled out of the ruling five-party coalition. Elections took place the following July which saw the prime minister's coalition lose.

**Traditional Thai dancer**

**Thailand is prone to regular flooding**

Thai voters then elected the Chart Thai party's Banharn Silpa-archa as prime minister. The Banharn government was built around a seven-party coalition led by his party, Chart Thai, and the Palang Dharma which defected from Chuan's coalition prior to the election. But the new government came under fire almost immediately for a kickback scheme involving the prime minister's party and a Swedish submarine manufacturer, and for protecting a minister involved in vote-buying.

The military's recent reticence to intervene seemed less sure when a military radio broadcast criticizing the government for its management of the economy raised concerns in Bangkok and abroad. A disagreement over military promotions between the Minister of Defense and the Army Commanding General, Wimol Wongwanich, also worsened civil-military relations. To make matters worse, the king criticized the government for the traffic chaos in Bangkok. By mid-1996 prospects were not looking bright for the Banharn government, and by November new elections brought Chavalit Yongchaiyudh, the Defense Minister, from the previous government, to power.

As a former Armed Forces Chief, Chavalit had close ties not only to the Thai military but to Burma's military junta as

well. The new leader was 65 and claimed he was committed to cleaning up corruption. That was probably a good idea since his own party, the New Aspiration Party, was said to have been the most involved in buying votes during the elections.

Chavalit had his work cut out. Even before the economic crisis of 1997 his government had to face calls for a new constitution in order to reduce corruption. As has been the case in so many other countries, Thai electoral politics has been driven by money. In fact, enormous sums are usually spent to influence elections including even the direct purchase of votes in rural areas.

To address the problem a group of former parliamentary members and legal experts were chosen to write a new constitution. The results were presented to the nation's legislature during the fall of 1997. At that point Chavalit, despite his earlier promises, seemed more in support of those who feared the new constitution would hurt their personal interests. Foremost among the changes were the direct election of senators, rather than appointment by the prime minister, more regulations to promote public accountability, and further guarantees of individual rights.

The rules for election to the senate were particularly creative. To make the election

as incorruptible as possible, those running were not allowed to make any public announcements about proposed goals once in office. Later after the early 2000 senate elections occurred, it became especially clear that the commitment to ensuring a more honest electoral process was still firmly in place. To the surprise and irritation of many senatorial candidates, the electoral commission, citing concerns about corruption, revoked the victories of more than a third of the winners and called for new supplemental elections. Happily, for those who supported the new constitution, the new charter had the support of both the population and the military.

It was a difficult fight and, in the end, one of the few significant accomplishments of Prime Minister Chavalit's term in office, even accepting his somewhat ambivalent support. As the battle over the constitution was going on during the fall, the more immediate crisis over the economy was raging. In that battle the prime minister, in office for less than a year, would not prevail.

The turmoil now known as the "Asian Economic Crisis" began in 1997 with a drop in the value of Thailand's national currency, the baht. Unfortunately, the Prime Minister seemed bewildered by the

# Thailand

crisis and many in the country quickly concluded he lacked the skills to take on the challenge. Thus Prime Minister Chavalit became the region's first political casualty of the economic crisis.

His replacement was former Prime Minister Chuan Leekpai, who returned to power in November. When Chuan Leekpai, 59, assumed office again, many in Thailand voiced a collective sense of relief that he would be better able to deal with the crisis than his predecessor. Certainly no one could single-handedly pull the country back from the brink, but Chuan did move quickly to build a strong support team around himself and then set off for an important meeting in Washington where he was successful in improving relations with the United States. Most importantly, he resolved a problem over new defense aircraft Bangkok had ordered and which it could no longer afford. The trip turned out so well that even his opponents seemed satisfied.

Despite the early confidence he had received from the public, Chuan Leekpai's popularity did not last as long. By mid-1999, much of his authority was weakened by revelations of corruption among some of his political coalition partners. The prime minister, working to retain his authority responded by inviting new partners into the ruling coalition.

Although Prime Minister Chuan offered sophisticated leadership during Thailand's struggle to recover from the impact of the Asian economic crisis, his efforts were not enough to keep in him office. In January 2001, Thais went to the polls for the first time since 1997 to elect a new government. This time they voted under the new electoral rules.

New electoral changes had been designed to reduce the influence of money in Thailand's electoral process. Nevertheless, money remained especially important to the final outcome of the election as the Thai telecommunications tycoon billionaire Thaksin Shinawatra used his abundant cash not only to form a new party, the Thai Loves Thai party, but to win a major victory at the polls. In fact, his electoral domination was the largest in Thailand's parliamentary history and ushered Thaksin into power with an extraordinary 70% popularity in the polls.

### Thai Politics at a Crossroads?

In the years after Thaksin Shinawatra came to office, he significantly increased his power. He initially did so by relying more on the nation's traditional elites and the military while, according to some critics, backing away from plans for more significant political reforms. The government

**Yingluck Shinawatra, Thailand's first female prime minister**

was also accused of using its power to pressure both the international and domestic media. Leading journalists reportedly had their bank accounts scrutinized, possibly a tool of intimidation while prominent writers and editors were forced from their positions.

Some observers even suggested that the prime minister's long-term political goal was to move his nation's political system closer to the one-party dominated systems of Singapore and Malaysia, rather than to a more genuinely open political system. The prime minister himself was quite open about his negative attitude toward democracy, which he clearly saw as "overrated."

There were certainly plenty of examples of the government's authoritarianism. The prime minister developed an almost dictatorial control over the parliament. Moreover he put his cousin in charge of the Thai army. His family's financial holdings also grew enormously after coming to power.

Nevertheless, much of the population remained quite supportive of the prime minister. Understandably, people were initially pleased by Thailand's recovery from the devastating economic downturn of the late 1990s. His very severe and violent crackdown against the Thai illegal drug industry was also largely appreciated by the masses. Many have also reacted positively to his promises of significantly reducing poverty and terrorism. Ironically, the tsunami of late 2004 further strengthened the prime minister as he was frequently shown in the media dynamically confronting the challenges brought by the raging waters. That publicity paid significant dividends only a few weeks later in early 2005 when the results of the general elections handed him and his party another big electoral boost.

With that second win, some feared that, given the prime minister's authoritarian

**Floating market in Ratchaburi Province south of Bangkok**     Courtesy of Karla Allan

predilections, Thailand would remain democratic in name only. However, that impression did not last long. Over the following months, as the economy lost its earlier momentum and the insurgency in the south failed to be resolved, much of Prime Minister Thaksin Shinawatra's momentum seemed to fade.

Making matters worse was the emergence of a huge political scandal concerning the questionable sale of the prime minister's family's media holdings to a Singapore company. Huge demonstrations became common in the streets of Bangkok while he found his political legitimacy collapsing. Hoping to renew his political mandate amidst the crisis, Thaksin called for a snap election in early April 2006.

However, the opposition candidates boycotted them. Not unexpectedly this created a situation where at least on paper Thaksin's political party, Thai Loves Thai, was in a position to dominate the parliament. Over the next few months, Thai politics continued to get more complicated, while in Southern Thailand the Muslim insurgency, another matter for which Thaksin's detractors blamed the prime minister, continued to worsen.

### Saving or Destroying Thai Democracy?

Suddenly in September 2006 the situation changed dramatically as the Thai military, so often a major player in the nation's political history, staged a coup as the now acting Prime Minister Thaksin was in New York attending the United Nations. While the role of the nation's deeply revered monarch, the late King Bhumibol Adulyadej, remains somewhat murky, it was immediately obvious once the military coup occurred that it clearly had the king's support.

Ironically, although much of the world initially condemned the actions of Thailand's military, the move was received relatively positively within the country and even among many of the nation's most ardent supporters of democracy. That was not surprising as many had come to believe that Prime Minister Thaksin himself had been fundamentally opposed to Thailand's democratic tradition.

Once the military fully established itself, Surayud Chulanont, a retired general with close ties to the king and a known supporter of Thai democracy was named prime minister. At the same time plans were announced for a temporary suspension of democracy. The world was told that the delay was necessity given the importance of modifying the constitution in light of recent developments.

Meanwhile, during the summer of 2007 the Thai courts officially banned Thaksin,

along with many senior members of his party, from taking part in the nation's politics for five years. The other political parties whose activities had also been banned were now allowed to resume them. As for the nation's political constitution, suspended since the coup, the new military-dominated government issued its own revised version, which won a 57% approval during the subsequent referendum.

Nevertheless, the divisions within Thai society clearly remained. The more than 40% of the population that voted against the new constitution usually lived in the rural areas that remained strongly supportive of Thaksin. Bangkok's population, on the other hand, was strongly critical of Thaksin's years in office.

By late 2007, the question became even

**Ousted Thai Prime Minister Thaksin Shinawatra**

more complicated whether Thailand would continue on the road toward the vibrant democracy it had become in the years before the pro-democratic military coup. New elections were allowed to proceed again. In a stunning reversal of fortune, the newly formed People's Power Party, the successor to the exiled former Premier Thaksin's Thai Loves Thai party, easily defeated its rivals and came very close to gaining a governing majority in the nation's parliament. While their actual win, only a few votes short of an absolute majority, was significantly lower than those they had won during the last few convoluted elections before the coup, it was nevertheless significant.

Clearly, the majority of Thailand's voting population, and especially those in the rural areas that had long supported Thaksin, had fundamentally rejected the military's intervention and had thrown their support to the former prime minister's hand-picked successor, Samak Sundaravej. By February 2008, the new prime

minister was able to form a cabinet, which the king then swore in.

A close look at the newly formed government revealed a few clues about Thailand's future. On the one hand, it was largely made up of the ousted Prime Minister Thaksin's supporters. On the other hand, many of his closest former colleagues were unable to take part because of laws that had officially banned them from politics for five years. Most interestingly, Samak Sundaravej himself took the post of defense minister, an unusual role for a civilian leader. However, it was an understandable decision given the tensions with the nation's military leaders.

Despite the fact that Samak himself, like his sponsor, had a checkered past, Thai voters clearly preferred the People's Power Party and its promises of a renewal of Thaksin's economic policies, which had included specific populist policies for the rural poor. Nevertheless, the election results, which could so obviously be interpreted as a vindication of ousted Prime Minister Thaksin, hardly ended the issue. In fact, the struggle merely entered another stage.

The simple fact was that while Thailand's rural poor may have continued to support Thaksin's political movement, it had developed over the years an impressive array of enemies. They came from diverse sectors of Thai society: from the military to the financial community and, more subtly but equally obviously, from the monarchy itself. Given that reality, it is not surprising that by August 2008 a new seemingly populist and certainly militant movement, known as the People's Alliance for Democracy (PAD), emerged to challenge the authority of the government and Thaksin's supporters.

Over the next month, the movement's middle-class supporters successfully occupied major government buildings and ultimately Thailand's ultra-modern international airport. The movement seemed at first glance to be quite rowdy. However, it was obvious upon closer inspection that it was linked to a very well organized and funded movement with relatively visible ties to those segments of the population that had risen to oppose everything Thaksin represented: the monarch, the police, and the financial elite.

Most significantly, Thailand's demonstration of what might be seen as pseudo-people power had real clout. After pushing one prime minister from power, the movement ultimately saw yet another pro-Thaksin prime minister, Somchai Wongsawat, his brother-in-law, forced from power by the Thai Supreme Court, which accused him of corruption. It dissolved his political party.

Eventually a new prime minister, Abhisit Vejjajiva, who hailed from the ranks of

# Thailand

**Lumphini Park, Bangkok**

those who have been so critical of Thaksin, took office in December of 2008. Almost three full years of political uncertainty—from Thaksin's bid to solidify his party's absolute control to the military coup that overthrew him to the new elections that brought his supporters back to power and more recently to the political activism of the PAD—all combined to ensure that Thailand's political future remained up in the air. A dramatic year it was.

The turmoil continued throughout 2009 and well into 2010 as the opposing forces, dubbed "red shirts" for Thaksin's rural supporters vehemently opposed the unelected new Prime Minister Abhisit Vejiajiva. They faced off with the "yellow shirts," the more urban-based royalist anti-Thaksin activists. By March a new populist movement, known as the United Front for Democracy Against Dictatorship, emerged from the ranks of the Red Shirt movement that carried out a series of mass demonstrations in the capital. Eventually the violence that included the assassination of a former Thai general who had become a leader in the Red Shirt movement was quelled. In May

the Thai military intervened to end the disturbances.

For many on the outside, the violent confrontation had been seen simplistically as a struggle between the masses supporting a democratic movement and an authoritarian military influenced by the monarchy. On the ground, the situation was much more complicated. It is perhaps best discussed in the context of populist rural forces supporting an anti-democratic former prime minister against more urban and democratically minded military, urban and royalist figures. This proves that in Thailand, as in so many other societies, it is difficult to simplify political battles into cartoon-like descriptions.

If the intervention of the Thai security forces finally ended the months of violent confrontation, their efforts did not bring the tensions within Thailand to any sort of a conclusion. Indeed the battle merely moved to yet another arena, the political and by the spring of 2011 the same forces were arrayed once again to go at it at the polls. Unfortunately the players had hardly changed. On the side of the so-called "red shirts" once again Thaksin

was deeply involved and from his perch in Abu Dhabi personalized the struggle even more than in the past.

Having seen most of his more experienced supporters banned from political life, the deposed former prime minister turned to his inexperienced younger sister, Yingluck Shinawatra, a businesswoman with no previous experience in politics, to serve as the figurehead leader of his party in the upcoming electoral battle.

The election was scheduled for early July. On the government's side, of course, Prime Minister Abhisit Vejiajiva remained at the head of his Democratic Party. He entered the election with a record of the kind of populist economic policies that in earlier years had made Thaksin so popular with the rural masses. If that was not enough, the government's control of the press had become so repressive that the human rights NGO Freedom Watch placed its media in its "not free" category. But those efforts on the part of Prime Minister Abhisit's Democratic Party were not enough to ensure him victory.

By the time the votes were tallied, Thaksin Shinawatra's supporters, now led by his younger sister Yingluck, had prevailed. Her PPT party, or For Thais Party, won a majority of seats in the parliament. She captured the same areas in which her older brother, still in exile, had been especially popular. In August, 44-year-old Yingluck Shinawatra, Thiland's first female prime minister, assumed office. Predictably her detractors accused her of merely serving as a stand-in for her controversial brother and criticized her for not having any political experience. The long-term fate of her six-party coalition government was not immediately obvious. What was clear was that the year-long see-saw of power between Thaksin Shinawatra's supporters and his enemies had entered yet another chapter in the ongoing battle over Thailand's future.

After assuming office Yingluck moved cautiously to reassert the influence of her and her brother's followers. By the spring of 2012 the ban imposed against members of the Thai Loves Thai party, which her brother had formerly led, was being lifted even as efforts were underway to modify the clauses built into the constitution that made it especially easy to ban political parties.

Predictably the effort set off another round of political uncertainty that soon saw the relatively inexperienced new prime minister dissolve parliament and call for new elections. Abhisit Vejiahiva, the former prime minister, was charged with murder for deaths associated with protests from several years before. Once again the nation's political environment was careering out of control.

In May 2014, Prime Minister Yingluck's government was driven from office. The Thai military once again reasserted control and announced yet another postponement of elections. They continued their decade-long drive to force the former prime minister and his supporters not only from power but from any influence in Thai life.

In the years since, the Junta's military leader Prayut Chan-o-cha has not only managed to stay in power but successfully promote yet another constitution, one that opened the door for a limited civilian role in governance while ensuring the predominate rule of the military. And the tally for the new constitution's approval in August 2016 was not even close. The military backed constitution was approved overwhelmingly, with 61% of a 59% turnout, thus opening the door to new elections which the military assumed would not threaten their influence.

The new constitution was due to come into force early in 2017 but hit a snag. King Bhumibol (Rama IX) died in October 2016 and his successor, King Rama X (Maha Vajiralongkom), objected to some clauses

in the constitution on the grounds that they interfered in the royal prerogative. Changes were made that gave the king increased powers, and the new constitution came into force on 6 April 2017, but it was not until October that the prime minister announced that new elections would be held, in November 2018. Meanwhile, legal proceedings moved forward against a number of former ministers, including Yingluck Shinawatra, who fled the country and joined her brother, former prime minister Thaksin Shinawatra, in Dubai. She was sentenced in her absence, while some of her former ministerial colleagues received heavy jail sentences.

In any event, the House of Representatives elections were postponed again and eventually held in March 2019, the first since 2014. While the opposition parties did not do badly, the pro-military groups dominated. Their approach to government was shown in February 2020 with the dissolution of the third largest opposition party, Future Forward, by the Constitutional Court because it had accepted a loan from its leader. This was deemed to be a donation and therefore illegal.

There were public protests at this action, which were stopped under COVID-19 restrictions (see below). Further protests began in July 2020, although they remained illegal. In August, the protests developed further, to include criticism of the monarchy, dangerous ground. Participants also got younger. Growing demands included resignation of the prime minister, constitutional revision and an end of harassment. Anti-monarchy voices grew stronger seeking a reduction of the monarch's powers, including the expression of political opinions—used to support military coups in the past. Questions were raised about the monarch's wealth and the fact that, since he assumed the throne in 2016, he has spent much of his

**Former Prime Minister
Surayud Chulanont**

time in Germany. Unlike his father, he did not appoint regents in his place when he was out of Thailand. The government's response became increasingly tougher. Meetings of more than four people were banned and topics touching on national security—the role of the monarch—were prohibited.

But the protests did not stop, even after the king returned to Thailand and continued into 2021, partly fuelled by the government's handling of the pandemic crisis. In parliament, the elected House of Representatives twice debated votes of no confidence in the prime minister but both were defeated. Public protests continued and were brutally put down but did not stop. Increasingly, the monarchy was coming under criticism, but proposals for reform were deemed by the Constitutional Court to be threatening a "pilllar of the nation" and thus unconstitutional. To cope with COVID, in April 2021, the cabinet handed all power to the prime minister.

The draconian control measures have reduced the protests but the issues have not gone away. And, with elections due in 2023 and the king likely to spend most of his time in Germany, it is unlikely that 2022–2033 will be peaceful.

### The Restive Muslim South

Going beyond the question of how Thailand will be governed, the last years have revealed an even greater challenge to the nation's fundamental stability. Outsiders tend to forget that although a large Buddhist majority lives in the north near the major cultural and industrialized parts of the country Thailand has a significant population of Muslims of Malay ethnicity who live in the southern part of the country. It is not just outsiders who have at times apparently forgotten about those who live in the south. For years many southern Muslims have complained about being ignored by the nation's leaders.

The long simmering tension erupted dramatically during the spring of 2004 when hundreds of young Muslim men assaulted several government facilities in an apparent attempt to find the military equipment necessary to support a separatist movement. It was the first significant outbreak of sectarian violence since 1993. Of even more concern was that the attacks demonstrated a growing military and organizational sophistication that suggested to some observers that local Muslim insurgents were benefiting from outside training.

The Buddhist dominated government based in Bangkok responded by declaring martial law in the three southern provinces. Unfortunately, the crisis that began anew in 2004 has turned into an ongoing

# Thailand

**Princess Maha Chakri Sirindhorn visited the Sage Colleges in May 2009**

Courtesy of Harvey Vlahos

crisis, the roots of which have been growing for years.

One of the more immediate causes was former Prime Minister Thaksin's decision, after some initial hesitation, to enroll Thailand as a major supporter of the American President George W. Bush's Iraq campaign. The decision to support the overthrow of Saddam Hussein was, of course, controversial around the world. But among Muslims it has been especially so, and it added to tensions within Southern Thailand. But recent political decisions have only been one element of the growing tensions.

For years the southern Muslim provinces have felt that Bangkok was not supportive enough of their cultural heritage that so obviously differed from the Buddhist dominated north. It was more than local issues that had changed the situation. As was the situation elsewhere within the Muslim world, local Thai Muslims had been drawn more and more deeply into the world Islamic community. Today, significant numbers of Thais have studied in the Islamic universities of the Persian Gulf and Pakistan.

Prime Minister Thaksin's approach was strongly to support the Thai military's efforts to suppress the insurgents while working to improve the southern economic infrastructure. Whether such economic growth can lessen the growing tensions in the south is something only time will tell. Certainly it has been obvious to the government that merely using strong-arm tactics has not worked.

In fact, General Sonthi Boonyaratglin, himself a Muslim and the general who initially led the September 2006 coup against the prime minister, was reported to have been partly motivated by his dissatisfaction with the prime minister's failures in dealing with the southern provinces. But once in power the military did not accomplish much more than the former prime minister had. The insurgency has continued and has managed significantly to weaken the economy of the region.

The insurgency continues, although religious motives are sometimes entangled with more criminal activities such as drug smuggling as well as political motives. However, the level of violence has dropped. Whereas up until the mid-2010s, those killed each year were measured in hundreds, more recently the numbers have been much lower.

## Governmental System

The Thai political system is nominally a constitutional monarchy usually governed with a democratic-style parliamentary system. The military remains very influential, but in recent years until the events of September 2006 it had chosen to remain largely out of domestic affairs. As we have seen, though, Thailand has struggled since 1932 to evolve a modern workable political system. But for most of that period, politics have been dominated largely by the military.

Civilian-led governments have been in place from time to time, but they have not always been very stable. In order for true democratic civilian government truly to establish itself, several things must take place. First, corruption must be curtailed. As Thailand's educated middle class grows, this segment of society, like elements of the military, will no longer accept the old ways of doing things. It has been revealed recently that the nation's extraordinarily revered king is especially concerned that the level of corruption is undermining the nation's future.

The aggressive effort of former Prime Minister Thaksin Shinawatra to expand the authority of his office and political party seemed for a time dangerously close to tipping the balance of power away from the more open system that had been evolving. However, the military coup of 2006 temporarily ended that threat with an equally undesirable and unfortunate return military rule.

But then the first elections after the coup brought Mr. Thaksin's authoritarian-minded supporters back to power leaving the prospect of Thailand's authentic democratic future still in doubt. That sudden reversal turned out to be only one more step in the emerging drama that would see over the past year a dramatic rise in street demonstrations in support of various governments that have rotated back and forth in power. While Thaksin's supporters at that point no longer controlled the prime minister's office, the change was more a product of court decisions than electoral politics. For a time Thaksin's influence was renewed in the form of his younger's sister's temporary rise to power. But of course Thaksin's "comeback" failed and the military for the moment seems to have successfully reestablished their control.

Indeed, the only thing that can be said for certain about the Thai governing system is that the momentum of stable democratic growth has fallen away as the society struggles to develop a new legitimacy that the majority of Thais can accept.

That effort is especially difficult these days as the nation's core symbol of legitimacy since the mid-1940s King Bhumibol Adulyadej, passed away in the fall of 2016 replaced by his considerably less experienced son the new King Vajiralongkorn. The fact that the latter prefers to live in Germany rather than Thailand has led to increasingly open criticism of the monarchy. Although this is often brutally suppressed, it regularly recurs.

## Foreign Policy

Thailand's foreign relations are driven by its geographic location and pragmatism. It has a fascinating history of keeping enemies at bay through diplomatic and other means that generally have not involved the direct use of force. Of particular importance has been the relationship with its enormous northern neighbor, the People's Republic of China.

Thai officials profess not to be worried about China's growing military might. However, there is concern over the potential for large scale Chinese migration into the country and the possible impact from a flood of inexpensive products from the north that could undercut sectors of the Thai economy. These concerns are long term and unpublicized but they are real. Nevertheless, rather than shut China out, Thailand wants to see relations between the two countries expanded. While still in office, former President Jiang Zemin of the People's Republic visited, and Thai Queen Sirikit made a state visit of her own to China. More recently overland transportation routes between the two nations were improved as well.

Because of its well integrated overseas Chinese community, which dominates the business sector, Thai officials and businessmen feel they have an advantage over other Southeast Asian states in opening up new economic links with China. Some even believe they can provide a link for the other ASEAN states to the People's Republic. In contrast to many other Southeast nations, the local Chinese community takes an active part in politics.

During the 1990s, the huge explosion in the study of Mandarin was welcomed in Bangkok. Beijing was also particularly helpful during the early stage of the Asian economic crisis when it agreed to buy large amounts of Thai rice to help the struggling economy. Beijing contributed $1 billion to the IMF bail-out funds that were arranged to help Thailand. It also avoided devaluing its own currency which would have made recovery much more difficult.

Thailand has moved to become more involved in broader international activities. During the crisis over East Timor, Bangkok decided to dispatch around 1,500 soldiers to reestablish stability in that troubled community. A Thai officer became second in command over the entire military operation.

Relations with Myanmar remain complex, despite the major role that the military play in both countries. The 1995 defeat of the Karen rebels in Myanmar sent thousands of refugees across the Thai border and which altered relations between the two countries. The Burmese believed the Thais were aiding the Karens. Bangkok was upset because of Burmese military raids on refugee camps inside Thai territory. Later that spring, Burmese officials closed a major border crossing at Mae Sod that resulted in a significant economic loss for businesses on the Thai side of the line. Following the 2021 Myanmar military coup, tensions rose again after a December 2021 Myanmar campaign against the Koreans. This led to about 10,000 Karens fleeing into Thailand. COVID, too has caused tensions, with some Thais blaming Myanmar for the spread of the virus.

Burmese authorities were also incensed over what they perceived to be the "gentle handling" of Burmese dissidents who, in the fall of 1999, took over Rangoon's Bangkok embassy. This resulted in yet another border closing which, unfortunately, has become a common occurrence. More recently, tensions associated with the production of drugs in Burma that eventually find their way across the border has added to the problems.

Other concerns, including competing offshore territorial claims, have also impacted in the region. There are periodic Thai–Myanmar clashes over three disputed islands. In May 1995, Thai and Vietnamese navy patrols exchanged gunfire off the Thai coast. Thai fishing boats and crews have also been seized by the Vietnamese. Since then, relations with Vietnam have improved considerably, and Bangkok and Hanoi have been working well together, especially in terms of a mutual understanding regarding their respective strategic and military circumstances.

To the south border tensions have risen between Thailand and Cambodia. Ironically, today's popular culture has also had an impact on Thailand's foreign affairs as locally produced historically based feature length films have managed to antagonize both their Lao and Burmese neighbors. Recently the supposed remarks by a Thai actress that the extraordinary Cambodian historic site, Angkor Wat, should rightfully belong to Thailand set off weeks of angry and expensive tensions and violence with Phnom Penh. Especially controversial has been the competing claims over the ancient temple of Preah Vihear that provoked a dramatic military confrontation in the summer of 2008 and caused several deaths. This was not just an international matter for Thailand. The controversy that swirled around the temple even added to the animosity of internal Thai politics. Prime Minister Samak's tenure in office was weakened as well when he appeared to support Cambodia's claims to the revered temple site. The fact that Cambodia's longtime ruler, Hun Sen, recently chose to hire Thailand's most controversial recent prime minister, Thaksin, as an advisor certainly did improved relations either.

The ties between Hun Sen and Thaksin were "problematic" while the latter's enemies were in power in Bangkok. The arrival of his younger sister to leadership in Thailand offered the very real possibility that some of the tensions could be resolved. Somewhat later, after her initial visit to Cambodia, there appeared reason to be optimistic.

**Class outing in Bangkok**

# Thailand

Relations with the United States are also important and at times difficult. During the early development of the Asian economic crisis many felt that the U.S. had been slow in reacting to the gravity of the economic problems that beset the region. Fortunately, as the crisis developed and the Americans became more actively involved in trying to resolve the situation, these concerns became less significant.

After the September 2001 assault and the "War on Terrorism" rose to the top of the international agenda, Thailand was initially unwilling to even admit the there was a terrorist presence within Thailand. As time passed, Bangkok's attitude changed. Thaksin's government eventually became a strong backer of the American military campaigns in Afghanistan and Iraq. Predictably, the decision to send military personnel to Iraq aroused considerable ire among many Thai Muslims and Buddhists alike. In fact, by the spring of 2004 the prime minister, aware of how controversial his decision to send military personnel to Iraq had been, was talking of removing them if the situation became any more unstable there.

Of course, the campaign against terrorism has hardly been something Thailand has watched as a disinterested observer. In the late spring of 2003 the prime minister officially admitted that there were members of the infamous, Indonesian-based Jemaah Islamiyah present in Thailand. Moreover, it has become increasingly obvious in recent years that the insurgency in the south has developed ties with other Muslim activists beyond the region.

## Society and Culture

Shortly after their arrival in Southeast Asia, the Thai were converted to the Theravada school of Buddhism, which came from the island of Sri Lanka. The numerous colorful festivals and the participating monks almost completely dominate the traditions of the people. Thai architecture is unique, colorful, and particularly elaborate.

The customs and traditions of Bangkok and the larger cities have been modified greatly by increased contacts with the West, particularly with Americans. In fact, Thailand is among those developed countries with the greatest divergence between the very urbanized middle classes of Bangkok and the peasant farmers in much of the rest of the country.

For years visitors to the city have had to put up with some of the worst traffic in the world. Today the situation is improving. The new Bangkok expressway system is open, and it is now possible to get from one part of the city to another far easier than it was only a few years ago.

Significant among social issues has been the government's aggressive campaign to ban smoking anywhere near the nation's schools. It is clear that Bangkok is quite serious in this effort to make smoking less common. By the fall of 2003 the plan was to extend the ban throughout many public areas, including Internet cafés and beauty parlors. Not surprisingly the effectiveness of the ban could be called into question by anyone who has been in Thailand lately.

On an even more serious matter—the use of illegal drugs—the government has been even more committed. During the spring of 2003 a major and quite aggressive campaign against drug dealers was carried out. It resulted in tens of thousands being arrested and hundreds dying in the crackdown. Then Prime Minister Thaksin Shinawatra said at the time that his goal was to eliminate the use of such drugs. This has not been achieved, despite severe laws, including the death penalty for trafficking, especially as newer drugs have emerged.

### Women

As elsewhere, Thai women have grown up in a region that generally values boys more than girls. Today, the situation of women in Thailand is especially complex and combines examples of considerable progress and proof of their continuing lack of control over their own lives.

The military has allowed a few women into their upper ranks, but women are still not allowed to attend the nation's military academies. Women have fewer rights than men in obtaining documents like passports, and domestic law favors husbands. Men, for example, also have more rights under the divorce laws. Women are less than 10% of those appointed to the Thai senate. On the other hand, young women have far more access to education today, and half of the college graduates are female. The problem is especially acute among the thousands of young women from Thailand's poorer neighbors, such as Vietnam and Myanmar, who are lured to Bangkok with offers of jobs and then find themselves in virtual debt slavery in the brothels of that huge city.

In the mid-1990s an ominous cloud appeared on the horizon. A report by an international organization revealed that Thailand had developed the fastest growing AIDS population in all of Asia. In spite of a very successful birth control program, there has been little public education about AIDS until recently. Figures for young women especially in northern Thailand are very high. In Bangkok, a significant portion of the prostitute community is infected. To make matters worse, a new more powerful strain of AIDS was discovered in Thailand in 1995. The Thai government has attempted to move against the traffickers, and various international organizations have attempted to improve the situation of these young women. Nevertheless, the situation remains a tragic one today. By 2016, Thailand was reported to have the highest incidence of HIV / AIDS in Asia.

In other areas of Thai life female monks recently began an increasingly popular campaign to win the same sort of religious and governmental recognition and support their male counterparts receive.

Politically as we have seen, Thailand's enormously controversial former political leader, Thaksin, appointed his sister titular leader of his party as part of his preparations for the spring 2011 election. When the dust settled after the election, whether genuinely in her own right or not, Yingluck Shinawatra had been elected Thailand's first female prime minister. The elevation of the first woman to the nation's highest political office, of course, did not last long.

**Demonstrations in Thailand, 2008**

## Economy

For years the Thai economy was one of the fastest growing in Asia. Many had expected it to become one of the "Asian Tigers," like Taiwan, Hong Kong, Singapore, and South Korea, which had so impressed the world during the last decades of the century. In fact, according to the World Bank Thailand's growth between 1985 and 1994 was a robust 8.2%, even better than South Korea in those years. Even in early 1997, things still looked good. The huge American company, General Motors, signed a deal for a new car plant said to be worth over $750 million and which promised 1,500 new jobs. Though the situation seemed to change suddenly during the summer of 1997, in truth the problems had been building for quite some time.

In the first half of the 1990s, it appeared for a time that the infrastructure of the country was simply unable to keep pace with the rapidly growing economy. Efforts were then made to construct a mass transit system in the congested Bangkok area. Progress in building up the country's infrastructure in a logical way was also made. New factories are being located outside the Bangkok area in industrial parks. Each is required to have its own wastewater treatment plant. The water coming out of these plants today is far cleaner than the water industries take in for their use.

Bangkok had been making progress in helping the country deal with its growing involvement in the world economy, and though the economy had slowed down, few anticipated the developments of July 1997. That summer, international currency speculators aroused by Thailand's huge private foreign debt began to speculate against the value of the baht. Though the government defended the price of the local currency through the summer, it was forced by July to devalue the baht. Thailand's economic bubble began to burst. Especially hurt were the many business people who seeking better loan rates abroad had gone heavily in debt over loans pegged in currencies like the American dollar. Whether the loans had been economically viable when they were originally made or not, they became impossible burdens when Thai locals had to buy much more expensive American dollars to repay them.

The economic crisis had begun. Thailand would not be the only nation caught in the collapse. Soon, Thailand had to turn to the International Monetary Fund to gain the financial resources needed to deal with the crisis though as always those funds came with demands for economic reforms and budget cutting that few countries take easily. By the spring of 1999, Thailand was gaining the reputation as one of the nations of the region that had most responsibly taken on the challenges of the economic crisis.

Thailand's leaders had reason to be pleased as the nation entered the new century. Once again, the economy was going strong. If the growth rates were not what they had been at points during the previous generation, growth rates of 3–4% were being projected. Clearly, it looked as if the worst of the 1997 crisis was finally over. But as the new century dawned, the economy remained very fragile, and the slowdown in the United States affected Thailand as well. Things became even more complicated during 2001 as Prime Minister Thaksin Shinawatra spoke openly of employing more economic nationalism. This tended to make outside investors nervous.

Even as Bangkok seems determined to crawl back from the brink, the country faced serious problems with its natural resources and a limited technological base. Because so much of the country's timber has been cut, erosion is rampant. The quality of the soil is being negatively affected, and flooding is common. While the environment remains a critical problem and will be for decades to come, there is now visible evidence of government efforts. One can now see miles of newly planted trees along major highways and the ban on cutting teakwood is apparently strongly enforced.

The most immediate challenge of course, is maintaining a stable economy. Considerable progress has been made, and the most recent gains have been in the area of growing domestic consumption that insulates the economy from too great a dependence on exports. Unlike the disastrous era of the Asian Economic Crisis, the Thai bhat has been considerably healthier. Large infrastructure projects that had been put on hold during the late 1990s seem again back on track as well.

Like all countries that have a heavy dependence on tourism, Thailand has been badly affected by the world-wide consequences of COVID-19. International travel quickly stopped and had not resumed by May 2021. One result was that the national carrier, Thai Airways, filed a bankruptcy plan. The wider economy was also affected by the general downturn in trade. Many were out of work. But the central bank was optimistic in early 2021 of an economic revival during 2021.

The economy had been recovering well from the economic setbacks of the late 1990s. Tourism, deeply hurt by the tsunami of late 2004, had begun to recover. Meanwhile the growth rate for 2005 came in at a healthy 4.4%, while the next year until 2008 averaged around 5%. Then came 2008, and by year's end the emergence of the international recession had hit Thailand especially hard. In fact, growth figures for 2009 came in at more than two percentage points in the negative. Of course, the economic shock in late 2008 only "complemented" the domestic political instability that had already undermined Thailand's earlier reputation as one of the most stable in Southeast Asia.

Like most of Asia, Thailand did manage to come through the latest international economic crash of 2008 relatively well. Having regained its momentum by the end of the year, 2010 came in at a very healthy growth rate of just under 8%. But as has been the case across the world, Later figures were more discouraging. In Thailand's case, the numbers for 2011 reflected hardly any growth at all.

Indeed over the last few years the nation's growth dropped by half to something just under 3%. Though more recently that is in 2017, it inched up to closer to 4%. But the pandemic hit hard. Growth was -6.2% in 2020. It climbed back to 1.6% in 2021 and is expected to reach 3% in 2022. A full recovery is not expected until 2023.

While there still remain many problems, one economic success story has been in tackling poverty levels. Although the progress made in this field has been slow since 2015, compared to earlier years, by 2020, only 6.8% were still below the poverty line. Of course, there are still large discrepencies between the affluence of urban areas and the countryside but this is a major achievement.

## The Environment:
## From Global to Local

As is the case elsewhere in the world, Thailand's economy has been buffeted by both regional and global economic trends. But it has been environmental challenges that have especially impacted the nation over the last year. Whether one considers them part of the growing climate crisis caused by humanity having accidentally upset the heat balance of the planet by excessive burning of carbon based fossil fuels or simply examples of "extreme" weather, Thailand proved especially vulnerable over the last year. In July 2011 the nation experienced flooding that was said to be the worst in half a century. The waters inundated 60 of the nation's 76 administrative provinces, killed over 650 people and dramatically hurt the national economy. While national production was deeply impacted, the most graphic images were those of Bangkok residents struggling to deal with the rising waters. The waters did not quickly recede. Indeed in some cases they stayed in place for months.

# Thailand

While the waters eventually receded from the nation's capital, Bangkok, like other regional cities form Manila to Ho Chi Minh City, are especially vulnerable not just to occasional flooding but to much more serious inundation. The primary problem is that waters are not only rising, but the land is settling as more and more water is drained from underground aquifers that are being tapped to supply water for the growing urban populations. That phenomenon is a dangerous combination that is also sealing the fate of even more famous cities beyond the region, like Italy's Venice.

Rising waters can, of course, be deadly, but they are generally challenges of a shorter time scale. More dramatic is the vulnerability to rising heat of the Thai rice crops. If, for example, the temperature rises above 25°C (around 95°F) during a plant's flowering cycle, it can be rendered sterile. That fact is an extraordinarily important reality given that Thailand is the world's sixth-largest producers of rice and one of the largest exporters in the world. In short, more regionally Thailand's rice exports are especially popular in Asia. Thus the weakening of the nation's ability to produce rice can have an impact on Asia's food security that cannot be overstated.

As a country that remains a popular tourist destination for international travelers, Thailand is interestingly also working to improve its green energy infrastructure. This is not only as a way to address the challenge of an increasingly destabilized global climate, but also to make itself more attractive to the "green-minded" tourist community. Complementary to the more immediate concerns, this focus has seen a growing government commitment to new solar projects as well as the emergence of campaign to have corporations adopt green "Corporate Social Responsibility" strategies. This strategy is not new. Back in 1997–2001 Thailand was the first Southeast Asian country to begin planning for solar power in the nation's development plan.

## COVID-19

COVID-19 first struck Thailand in February 2020, and a State of Emergency was declared in March. This allowed the prime minister to ban public assemblies, confine people to their homes, and suppress pandemic information or comment. This action was seen as being about as much about controlling dissent as about COVID in many quarters. From the beginning of April, all flights were banned. For much of 2020, cases and deaths remained low but from November there were signs of upward movement. This accelerated in February 2021, leading to new restrictions. Bars restaurants and schools were all closed. Cases continued to rise, however, in May. By then, total cases had reached some 154,000, of whom over 102,000 had made a full recovery. There had been about 1000 deaths. Vaccination was slow. Manufacture of the AstraZeneca vaccine was the monopoly of Siam Bioscience, virtually wholly owned by the king, which was criticized for a slow response. Chinese vaccines were also becoming available. By the end of May, 2,433,807 people had received one dose (3.5% of the population, while 1,094,523 (1.6%) were fully vaccinated. At the end of 2021, there were over two million cases and around 21,000 deaths. Vaccination rates had slowly increased, so that by the end of the year, 63% of people had received two doses.

Cases continued to rise in 2022. By mid-May, there were 4.39 million cases and 29,595 deaths. 74.2% of the population had received two doses of a vaccine and 38.5% had received a booster dose. While there were some relaxation in control measures, many still remained in place, including for international travelers.

## The Future

The years since 2000 have been very complicated for Thailand. Nevertheless, the national economy has performed relatively well considering the extent of both natural, political, and financial disasters the country has faced. The tsunami in late 2004 was an enormous challenge to overcome. The international financial crisis of 2008 was followed only a few years later by historic flooding in 2011. There were years of strife between the supporters of former Prime Minister Thaksin and his critics. Under such circumstances, Thailand can be complimented for its resilience.

On the political side, the situation since the fall of 2006 has become practically intolerable. It was obvious at that point that something dramatic was going to occur. In September it did so when the military, with the rather obvious support of the popular king, overthrew the popularly elected government of Thaksin Shinawatra. This set off a horrendously complicated set of revolving door governments and massive demonstrations for and against the various prime ministers who have come in and out of power over the last half dozen years. The elections of July 2011 saw Thaksin's supporters, led by his younger sister, Yingluck Shinawatra, swept back into power. But as we have seen, by 2014 she was out of office and for a short time merely a prisoner of the military, like so many others.

For now the military leadership has managed to solidify its leadership, indeed successfully promoting a new pro-military constitution in 2017 and its own formal political party. And in large measure the military has managed to maintain its domination despite some of the challenges raised by the most recent election in the spring of 2019. In that election, the most recent Thai national election, the military managed with the help of the military's guaranteed seats to emerge dominate once again and the current leader in a position to form yet another government. Nevertheless, the opposition won enough seats to complicate the military's efforts to dominate the nation for some time to come.

Other problems include a king who wants all the rights and privileges of his role but prefers to spend as much time as possible outside the country and the unknown long-term effects of COVID-19.

# The Socialist Republic of Vietnam

**Communist Party of Vietnam headquarters in Ho Chi Minh City**

**Area:** 329,560 sq. mi. (853,556 sq. km.)

**Population:** 96,208,984 (2019 census); 99,220,000 (2022 est.)

**Capital City:** Hanoi, pop. 5,067,352 (2022 est.)

**Climate:** Subtropical, with cooler weather in the higher elevations. The Mekong Delta area is hot and humid.

**Neighboring Countries:** China (North); Laos and Cambodia (West)

**Official Language:** Vietnamese

**Other Principal Tongues:** Some French and Chinese, mountain area languages (Mon-Khmer and Malayo-Polynesian)

**Ethnic Background:** Vietnamese (about 85%); Thai, Cambodian, Lao, Chinese, tribesmen (about 15%)

**Principal Religions:** Buddhism, Taoism, Confucianism subdivided into many sects, Christianity, animism, Islam, and syncretistic traditions like Caodaism, a blend of eastern and western traditions

**Main Exports:** (to U.S., Japan, China, Australia, Germany, Singapore, U.K.) Agricultural products, especially rice, coffee, coal, minerals, oil, clothing, shoes, and rubber

**Main Imports:** (from China, Taiwan, South Korea, Japan, Singapore, Thailand) Steel products, railroad equipment, chemicals, medicines, petroleum, fertilizer, cotton, grain, cement, and motorcycles

**Currency:** Dong

**Former Colonial Status:** French colony (1883–1954); occupied by the Japanese (1942–1945); anti-French struggle (1945–1954); civil war (1954–1975)

**National Day:** September 2, 1945, when independence from the French was declared and the Democratic Republic of Vietnam was proclaimed

**Chief of State:** President Nguyen Xuan Phuc (since April 5, 2021)

**Head of Government:** Prime Minister Pham Minh Chiuh (since April 5, 2021)

**General Secretary, Communist Party:** Nguyen Phu Trong (since January 2011)

**National Flag:** A red field with a five-pointed yellow star in the center

**Per Capita GDP Income:** $8,200 (2022 est.) (purchasing power parity)

Very narrow in the middle, the map of Vietnam is shaped somewhat like a dumbbell. The northern "bell" is an area formerly known as Tonkin. It is quite mountainous, with peaks as high as 10,315 feet, close to the southern Chinese border. The mountains gradually diminish in height as they approach the plains and river deltas closest to the Gulf of Tonkin.

The Red River originates in the lofty plateaus of the Chinese province of Yunnan, some 8,000 feet above sea level, and forms the border with China for a distance of about 30 miles. When it enters northern Vietnam, it is 260 feet above sea level, descending through a narrow gorge until it widens; after being joined with the River Claire it meanders 93 miles to the sea, flowing in a shifting, irregular course that is 140 miles of curving and twisting water.

The two principal cities of northern Vietnam, Hanoi and Haiphong, are situated on the river and flooded by its waters during the wet season each year. They are colored red by the silt washing to the sea from the highlands. It is in this river delta region that much of the food of northern Vietnam is produced by peasants laboring in the fields with the same basic tools used by their forebears.

The narrow middle part of the country is a thin, coastal plain, closely confined on the west by the Annam Cordillera, a north-south range of mountains forming a natural barrier between Vietnam and Laos to the west. This coastal belt is

# Vietnam

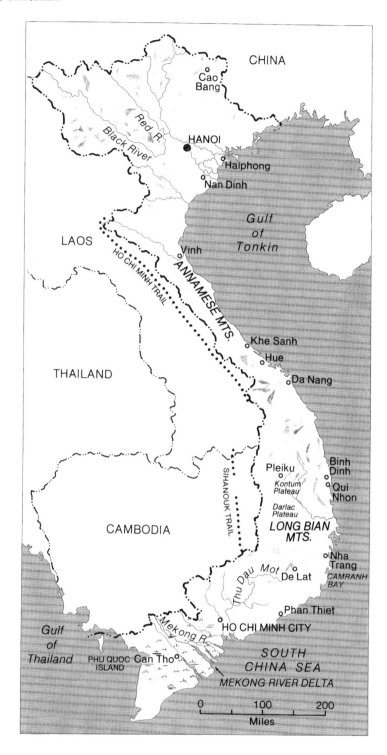

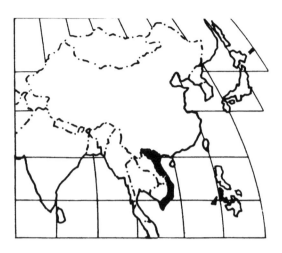

Cambodia during the dry season and even further upriver during the wet months each year.

Intensive agriculture, dominated by rice production, has enabled the people living in the Mekong River Delta to produce large surpluses of food in the past and present. Traditionally, two harvests of wet paddy rice are possible each year, a feat possible in very few places of the world. In contrast, only dry field rice can be grown in parts of northern Vietnam.

### History: Before the Chinese Arrival

Linguistically the Vietnamese speak a Mon-Khmer language that includes a lot of Chinese and French words. In appearance the Vietnamese most resemble other Asian peoples of mongoloid origin although their ethnicity seems more correctly tied to both the Mongolian peoples of their north and the Austroasiatic-Indonesian peoples to their south.

Among the non-Han peoples of Southeast Asia the Vietnamese were the people most influenced by Chinese culture. Nevertheless, Vietnamese culture had developed a sophisticated sea-oriented civilization long before the era of significant Chinese influence. Known as the Dongson Culture or Lac-Viet era, early Vietnamese civilization in those years was especially influenced by the more southern communities of the coasts and islands of Southeast Asia.

By the 3rd century B.C., pressured by both Chinese armies and arriving immigrants, Vietnam fell deeply under the influence of Chinese civilization. Eventually conquered by the powerful Han dynasty of China, Vietnam remained part of the Chinese empire for most of the next millennium. For the Chinese, in those years before the region around Guangzhou (Canton) was developed, controlling Vietnam was especially important as its occupation facilitated Chinese trade with the island communities of Southeast Asia.

narrow and somewhat inhospitable. Its lands are not enriched by the silt of any large river, and the typhoons of the South China Sea frequently do considerable damage.

The lower portion starts with an area of central highland plateaus that are heavily forested and inhabited by more traditional peoples who till the limited available land after clearing it by burning. These highlands gradually give way to the Mekong

Delta, near where Ho Chi Minh City (formerly Saigon) is located.

The Mekong River starts in remote Tibet where snows gradually melt in the thin, icy air, gathering into small streams. Before reaching Vietnam, the waters travel almost 3,000 miles through some of the most rugged country in the world. The river is yellow and sluggish by the time it enters the country. The tides of the sea are felt as far back as Phnom Penh in

300

**Town on the Mekong River**

Courtesy of William Garrett Stewart

It was natural that during those centuries the Vietnamese adopted many aspects of the Chinese political system and cultural patterns. The Chinese language and writing system became well known among the elite as did the Confucian social system. Eventually the Vietnamese developed their own version of the famous Confucian civil service exam system and used it as a tool to choose many of their elites. Despite China's enormous political and cultural influence, many core elements of Vietnamese civilization, from a greater role for women to the language itself, have survived to help define Vietnamese identity.

Not surprisingly, the Vietnamese often feel a combination of respect, dislike, and fear toward the Chinese. In fact, throughout history the Vietnamese have at times tried simultaneously to be "more Confucian than the Chinese" while vehemently working to avoid becoming too "Chinese like." Alternatively, as one well-known scholar has put it, "the Vietnamese could easily become Chinese but have no interest in doing so."

That attitude played a significant role over the centuries as various Vietnamese leaders, among them the famous Trung Sisters of the early 1st century A.D., led a series of unsuccessful revolts against Chinese control. The rebellion led by the two sisters is particularly notable not only because of its role in inspiring future generations to resist the Chinese. It also serves as an important reminder of how important women have been in Vietnam's long history of fighting for its independence from the era of the Trung Sisters (39–43 A.D.) to the struggles against the French and later the United States.

After the collapse of the Tang dynasty in China in the early 10th century, the Vietnamese finally broke away from direct Chinese control. Still, over the centuries China has attempted more than once to reassert its authority over its southern neighbor.

## Independent Vietnam

Somewhat after Vietnam's leaders established their independence in the late 10th century, the first more recognizably modern Vietnamese kingdom, known historically as the Da Viet, emerged under the leadership of the Ly dynasty, which located its capital at what would later be known as Hanoi. However, establishing a stable and unified Vietnam soon proved beyond the capacity of the Ly family. Over the next several centuries, Vietnam found itself regularly facing new threats from the north, such as when the Mongols sought to occupy the country in the 13th century and when the Chinese Ming dynasty effectively did so for a short time in the 15th century. Divisions existed as well among the Vietnamese themselves as many southerners resisted efforts to unify the country under northern control. In fact, it was not until the late 18th and early 19th centuries that Vietnam emerged under the unified control of the Emperor Gia Long. His dynasty would lead Vietnam from Hue, modern Vietnam's best-known imperial city.

Vietnam's relationship with its enormous neighbor to the north was not the only challenge faced by the Vietnamese. To their south lay the lands of Champa, a South Asian-influenced community of Malayo-Polynesian stock which had established a kingdom that lasted from the 2nd to the 17th century. Unfortunately, for the Cham peoples their kingdom slowly collapsed during a series of struggles with both the Khmer peoples of Cambodia and the Vietnamese. Finally, in the years from the 15th through 17th centuries the originally northern-based Vietnamese conquered the last of the lands once held by Champa. Today, the Cham people survive as a small Muslim minority community in both Vietnam and Cambodia.

## French Colonialism

French interest in Indochina, the name given to the eastern portion of mainland Southeast Asia, began in the 18th century. Initially taking the form of commercial and missionary contacts, the French effort did not become serious until the mid-19th century. Forces of Napoleon III conquered Vietnam in a series of military campaigns, beginning in the South and working slowly northward. Initially, the French navy was far more interested in the region than the French government, but over time the national commitment grew. The proclamation of a protectorate over the Annamese (Vietnamese) state in 1883 was followed by a short war with the Chinese to force the Manchu emperors to recognize the end of the tributary status of Annam.

The French divided their newly won possession into three segments: Tonkin in the North, Annam in the narrow middle belt and highland plateaus of the South, and the colony of Cochin China in the Mekong Delta. Those three areas were ruled by a governor-general who also presided over Cambodia and Laos after 1887.

301

# Vietnam

Actual administration of the colonies was by the French during the colonial period although an imperial court was permitted to exist in Annam. The French introduced a narrow-gauge railroad from Hanoi to Kunming in China that allowed them to extract mineral wealth from the North. In addition, intensive cultivation methods were introduced to produce large quantities of rubber.

During the early colonial period the French encouraged the migration of people from Tonkin in the north to the delta of Cochin China. Immigrant Chinese were also permitted in the southern colony although at times the European businessmen there resented their competition.

Considerable effort was put into the promotion of French culture among the Vietnamese. As a result, an upper class of Vietnamese eventually emerged that was fluent in French, at home in French culture, and often Roman Catholic. But over time they were often bitterly resentful of French political domination. It was a pattern that was followed frequently throughout the colonized world.

### The World Wars and Nationalist Struggles

Shortly after World War I, a nationalist group, composed of people supported by the French-speaking upper class emerged, competing with a communist movement led by a dedicated patriot known as Ho Chi Minh (real name Nguyen Tat Thanh). Both of these movements attempted unsuccessful armed uprisings against the French. In 1930, Ho, who had trained in Moscow just after the 1917 revolution, brought together the various communist groups into a single new movement known as the Indochinese Communist Party.

Once the Second World War had begun, the Japanese took Indochina by default after Germany installed the puppet French Vichy government. Japan demanded the right to land forces in the area, which was granted by the French. Within three months the Japanese controlled all of northern Vietnam. In July 1941 they occupied the south as well.

In contrast to other leaders of anti-colonial Asian movements, like Sukarno of Indonesia, Ho Chi Minh did not collaborate with the Japanese. Rather, being a fluent speaker of English (he had lived and worked in London), he aligned himself with the allied forces and spent the war years often working closely with the Americans.

In 1945, the Japanese ousted the local French authorities whom they correctly suspected of being in contact with General de Gaulle and the Allies. Direct Japanese authority, though, was short-lived. Surrender came within six months. At the Potsdam Conference in 1945, the Allied powers decided to divide Vietnam at the 17th parallel for the purpose of disarming and evacuating the Japanese. The southern region was to be occupied by the British and the north by the Nationalist Chinese. For Ho and other nationalists this was a serious development given the long Chinese interest in Vietnamese territory. For the immediate period one of Ho's most important goals would be to make sure the Chinese did not come to stay.

For him the moment he had long waited had finally come. He hastily proclaimed the Democratic Republic of Vietnam in Hanoi at a big public rally on September 2, 1945. Given later events, it is ironic that Ho, an admirer of the United States, began his speech with lines chosen from the American Declaration of Independence.

Shortly thereafter, the forces of the Chinese Nationalists moved into the northern region. Meanwhile, Ho expanded his power in the rural areas of the north, eliminating his Vietnamese Nationalist rivals and managing to co-exist uneasily with the Chinese occupation forces that gave every indication of wishing to remain in Vietnam. Ho's movement, known as the Viet Minh was certainly not the only nationalist movement in Vietnam. Indeed, there were others who were nationalist but not communist. But Ho Chi Minh was widely admired and helped by his reputation for having close ties to the increasingly powerful Americans.

Meanwhile in the south, the British suppressed activity by the Viet Minh and quickly returned the area to the French. Seeking a withdrawal of the Chinese in the north, Ho and the French put pressure on them. Fortuitously, the outbreak of civil war in China helped instigate a Chinese withdrawal in early 1946.

Ho permitted the French to reenter northern Vietnam, promising to keep the Democratic Republic of Vietnam within the French Union, as so long as its autonomy was respected and providing it was allowed to control all of Vietnam. He certainly wanted French economic aid, but the chief reason for this attitude was probably Stalin's attitude at the time. The Russians wanted a French communist victory at the polls in France, and did not wish to alienate French voters by supporting a communist revolt in Vietnam.

**Ho Chi Minh leaves the French Foreign Ministry, July 1946**

# Vietnam

**Ho Chi Minh**

### An Anti-Colonial Struggle

The French colonial regime, however, refused to allow Viet Minh control of Cochin China. France was committed to reestablishing its control over Vietnam, an effort Ho and his movement opposed. By the end of 1946, fighting erupted between the French and the Viet Minh, who retreated to the mountains above Hanoi to conduct a guerrilla war. In an effort to find a political cover for their desire to reestablish their former colony, the French selected Bao Dai, the hereditary Emperor of Annam and a descendant of the royal family that had once ruled from a massive palace at Hue, as the new official leader of the country. Bao Dai officially accepted the French offer in 1946. He then became provisional president and later permanent chief of state of a government obviously organized by the French to maintain their power in Indochina. The arrangement hardly pleased real nationalists like Ho, and the struggle continued.

The American attitude toward Vietnam in the immediate aftermath of World War II was ambivalent. America had a long-term commitment to anti-colonialism, and President Franklin D. Roosevelt had long made it clear that he did not favor the simple resumption of European colonies in Asia after the war. These American attitudes were well known. In fact, as early as 1919, the young Ho Chi Minh had attempted unsuccessfully to meet President Woodrow Wilson at the Paris Versailles Conference to discuss Vietnam with the influential American president who was so associated with the idea of "national self-determination." A generation later, Ho, having just finished working with the Americans during the war, still hoped to gain U.S. support for his fledgling nation.

However, in the years after World War II there was also an interest among the Americans in strengthening their erstwhile allies, the French. Paris wanted its former colony back. Thus, those U.S. officials who were concerned about ensuring that France remained strong as an ally in Europe prevailed over those who were more concerned about America opposing the anti-colonial Vietnamese communist movement.

As the tensions between East and West grew, American attitudes hardened. When the Cold War set in during the late 1940s, Ho's nationalist credentials loomed far less large in the minds of American decision-makers than his equally strong commitment to communism. Now many American decision makers would develop a strong antipathy for Ho and his movement. In their minds they were merely an extension of world communism directed from Moscow. However, it would be another generation before they would act directly on those attitudes.

In early 1950, the Viet Minh received diplomatic recognition from newly communist China. With Chinese military aid, they cleared French troops from the border areas of northern Vietnam later in that year. What had been an anti-colonial struggle was evolving into a major theater of the Cold War in Asia, a fact that led to increased involvement of the United States and of the People's Republic of China.

France initially had trouble convincing the Americans to support its efforts. Nevertheless, they had little trouble convincing America that France was now fighting on the front lines against communist expansion, as was the U.S. in Korea. Ho Chi Minh, a nationalist and communist, had not changed, but the "context" in which he was viewed by the powerful Americans had.

By the spring of 1953, the French prospects in Vietnam were bleak; the approaching end of the Korean War was expected to enable greater Chinese effort in Vietnam. In desperation, the French granted further political, economic, and military concessions to the non-communist Vietnamese state and substantially increased their own military activities. Their purpose was not to defeat the Viet Minh, since such a goal was unrealistic, but rather to obtain a "face saving" political settlement. The U.S., the Soviet Union, Britain and France decided that a conference should be held in the spring of 1954 in Geneva, Switzerland, to deal with the questions of Indochina and Korea. But developments in the battlefield were moving faster than diplomacy.

### Dienbienphu

The French had fortified a position at Dienbienphu in northwest Vietnam in response to a Viet Minh thrust into neighboring Laos. The Viet Minh then surrounded the French with artillery and mortars supplied by the Chinese and laid siege to the French camp. Although the decision to make Dienbienphu the central symbol of the struggle over Vietnam only came slowly, the battle eventually grew into one that symbolized the entire Franco-Vietnamese war. Overly confident, the French assumed their position within a valley surrounded by soldiers who held higher ground, would not be a problem. They were wrong. The Viet Minh quickly destroyed the airstrip to prevent reinforcements and supplies from being sent in, and the siege began in earnest.

Even as the battle raged, many within the American administration argued that as the symbolism of Dienbienphu grew, the United States should intervene. Though there was considerable opposition to doing so unilaterally, Washington did go so far as to approach London about a joint effort to save the French. But Winston Churchill, again the British Prime Minister, declined. The French were left to fight alone. The tiny base fell on May 7, 1954, the day before the matter of Indochina was to come before the Geneva conference.

There were few times in recent history when the fate of a small country so depended on world politics. The French wanted to get out of Indochina on any reasonable basis. The Soviet Union did not want to press France to the extent that it would join the European Defense Community, a multi-country army then being proposed. Russia desired even less a direct clash with the U.S., which had only recently completed a massive series of hydrogen bomb tests in the Pacific. The People's Republic of China also wished to avoid conflict with the U.S. and apparently did not want Ho Chi Minh to achieve too much power.

### The Geneva Settlement

Ho Chi Minh's delegation to the conference arrived with a demand that the three nations of Indochina be treated in such a manner that would have produced a communist victory not only in Vietnam, but also in Cambodia and Laos. But the Chinese delegation conceded that a final settlement would treat the three countries separately. Ultimately, the final settlement contained some minor concessions to the communist movement in Laos, but none in Cambodia.

# Vietnam

Vietnam was divided at the 17th parallel, considerably farther to the north than had been demanded by Ho Chi Minh. National Elections were scheduled for mid-1956. Military details of withdrawal, etc., were left to the French and Vietnamese. This was a defeat for Ho, who desired immediate elections before a non-communist government could solidify itself in the south. He was sure of victory in the north, since he was credited with expelling the French colonial government. In fact, it was generally agreed by most observers, including the Americans, that Ho Chi Minh, the longtime leader of the Vietnamese struggle for independence, would easily win the scheduled elections. Ho appeared poised to win at the ballot box what he had largely won on the battlefield already.

In order to exclude American military forces from Indochina, the settlement prohibited any foreign power from maintaining forces in Vietnam. A general political agreement was included in the final version in which many things were left subject to interpretation. The U.S., not surprisingly, was very unhappy with the settlement which appeared likely to bring into existence a unified Vietnam under communist control. It declined to sign the agreement. Although angered by this refusal, the Chinese agreed to accept an informal American promise not to "disturb" the agreement. The settlement was then "adopted" in July 1954 without actually being signed by the representative of any nation.

Ho Chi Minh's regime promptly took over North Vietnam from the French. It began to build a strong and effective regime with large amounts of economic and military aid from the Soviet Union and China. Exhibiting revolutionary zeal, the new government embarked on an extremely brutal program of collectivization that soon cost the party considerable popularity. In fact, the program provoked a peasant revolt in Nghe An, the southernmost province, which had to be suppressed by government troops in 1956. Ho was forced to moderate his programs in order to regain his popular support.

## Ngo Dinh Diem and the Americans

Nearly everyone at the Geneva conference had expected South Vietnam to collapse, or to go communist via the ballot box. Bao Dai had no real authority and was under the influence of corrupt military leaders. In mid-1954, however, he appointed Ngo Dinh Diem premier. Diem, an energetic Catholic and committed nationalist, had strong ties to the Americans. In fact he had only just recently returned from an extended stay in the United States. Having appointed the anticommunist

Diem, Bao Dai then resumed his luxurious life in France. Diem later deposed him.

In October 1956, Diem proclaimed South Vietnam a republic and assumed the office of president. From the time of his appointment, Diem had enjoyed the support of prominent U.S. officials. They hoped to strengthen his position enough to allow him to serve as a non-communist alternative to Ho Chi Minh.

Diem also received the support of the several hundred thousand of his Catholic co-religionists who, partially inspired by CIA propaganda, fled into the South in 1954. Diem gained as well the allegiance of the traditionally corrupt army and managed to impose his authority over South Vietnamese religious sects that were hostile to his government.

The United States backed Diem's 1956 decision against holding the national elections called for in the Geneva Convention and his efforts to establish South Vietnam as a separate country. For the Americans Diem's regime seemed a way to stop the unification of the country under Ho Chi Minh, which Vietnam-wide elections would probably have brought about. The U.S. now offered massive amounts of military and economic aid just as it had earlier supported the French effort against Ho.

North Vietnam was furious and called for international action against Diem, but it received no support from the Soviets or the Chinese. Initially hoping that Diem's regime would collapse from its own weight of dishonesty and corruption, Ho discouraged the communist guerrillas, who had remained within South Vietnam after the Geneva division of the country, from taking action. However, in 1957 the rebels, called Viet Cong, undertook a

terrorist campaign to force village support of their communist movement.

Diem and his supporters responded by setting up a virtual police state which smothered all opposition, non-communist and communist. He was able to withstand a military revolt in 1960 and tried to promote the regime's power in rural areas by use of anti-Viet Cong measures. Diem's crackdown against the Viet Cong was successful enough to push them to adopt new, more militant tactics. However, initial southern success turned into a virtual loss of control over much of the countryside as Viet Cong strength swelled and its military activities increased.

In contrast to the conservative American assumption of an unrelenting global conspiracy to spread communism throughout the world, there was no major direct support of the Viet Cong by North Vietnam until 1959 because of the reluctance of the Soviets and Chinese to provoke another crisis in the region. Moreover, because of serious economic difficulties in 1960, China sharply reduced its aid to North Vietnam. Despite the international situation, Hanoi did begin to give substantial and active support to the Viet Cong in the south.

In response, the United States, during the early months of the Kennedy administration, in 1961 increased its aid to the Diem government and raised the number of American military advisers to the South Vietnamese army. The Chinese, in return for Vietnamese support in their ideological disputes with the Soviet Union, also increased their support of Ho's effort to bolster the Viet Cong.

The dictatorial Diem government further alienated public opinion in South

**Eisenhower and Ngo Dinh Diem**

**Black smoke covers areas of Saigon during the Tet Offensive**

Vietnam, which resulted in growing support for the Viet Cong. Moreover, Diem, whose own background was among the minority Catholics, infuriated the Buddhist community by publicly allowing discrimination against their practices while supporting Catholic activities. By the spring of 1963, he had alienated the most influential segment of the public by his harsh measures.

Aroused by government attempts to ban Buddhist public religious displays, Buddhist demonstrators were fired upon by government troops. Soon the international news was filled with images of Buddhist monks burning themselves to death to protest the actions of the American-backed Diem regime.

Predictably, the U.S. government was becoming increasingly embarrassed and disgusted with Diem. An army group, with American support, deposed him in late 1963, resulting in his violent death. Over the next year or so, the government of South Vietnam was in uncertain hands. For a time, leadership was held by General Duong Van Minh, but he proved too independent for the Americans and was quickly deposed. Power was supposedly centered in Saigon, but local military leaders in the provinces were all but independent of the central government. Entering an election campaign in 1964, the U.S. did not want to disturb the shaky status quo.

That uncertain period after Diem's death was interrupted in August when news reports indicated that North Vietnamese torpedo boats had attacked a U.S. destroyer in the Tonkin Gulf. Public reports at the time suggested that on two different occasions North Vietnamese boats had threatened the American ships. More recent evidence suggests that, though no one was hurt, the American ships operating off the coast of North Vietnam may have provoked one attack and that the second reported assault probably never occurred.

Nevertheless, at the time, given the fact that the United States government had been actively looking for an excuse to step up its efforts, the reports were not questioned. President Johnson manufactured a crisis out of the event and secured a vague resolution from Congress authorizing him to take military action in response. Eventually, the Tonkin Gulf vote would be viewed as the single most important element in U.S. congressional support of the war. In fact, it became a de facto declaration of a war although such a formal declaration never formally occurred.

Because of their opposition to Diem's harsh rule, a great many non-communists also supported the Viet Cong and its political arm, the National Liberation Front. When he was deposed, this ended. Feeling the need of greater support and believing it more probable that military action would succeed after the downfall of Diem, the Viet Cong embarked on wider military efforts. In 1964, they were, for the first time, joined by regular units of the North Vietnamese army. There was

a rapid increase in the area under communist control, particularly in the central highlands of South Vietnam. The Russians, sensing an imminent victory, sent their premier to Hanoi in early 1965 to give assurances of support. The Americans feared South Vietnam would soon be lost. For the United States, which had been traumatized internally during the previous decade over the issue of "who had lost China?," such a development had to be stopped at all costs. More direct action was taken.

### The American War

By 1965, the United States was bombing North Vietnam and deploying U.S. Marine and Army combat units. The days of the "advisers" were over. Now American troops under U.S. officers would fight the North Vietnamese and their supporters directly. South Vietnam finally had the formal direct support of its major superpower ally, the United States. Given the changing circumstances, Hanoi would need similar help, but developments within the communist world were getting more complicated.

Ideological differences had led to a breakdown in Soviet-Chinese relations. The differences between the two communist giants now included disputes about what role each nation should play in aiding Ho Chi Minh's forces. After 1965, China's leadership resented the superior economic ability of the Russians to buy influence in Hanoi and limited its own assistance to the maintenance of the Chinese-North Vietnamese rail line and the shipment of infantry weapons. Although there was an agreement to ship Soviet equipment through China to North Vietnam, the trains were often delayed and harassed by "Red Guards" active in Mao's Great Cultural Revolution, then in progress in China.

Meanwhile, in Saigon a dashing young Air Force general, Nguyen Cao Ky, emerged as a leading figure in the military establishment of South Vietnam. In mid-1965, he became premier and retained that position for two years. This provided a welcome respite from the seemingly continuous change of rulers in the country. It became clear, though, that during his rule the armed forces exercised almost all-political power. This continued to arouse Buddhist opposition.

The cost to the U.S. rose to more than $30 billion a year, placing a serious strain on the American economy and on its political system. Within the U.S., opposition to the war began to grow more and more significant, especially among college-age students who did not share their leadership's obsession with anti-communism

# Vietnam

and who were more likely to view the struggle in South Vietnam as a civil war rather than as a part of a worldwide struggle between communism and capitalism. Moreover, the clearly undemocratic nature of the South Vietnamese regime made it hardly seem worthy of the sacrifices Americans were increasingly being asked to make. Recognizing that last issue, President Lyndon Johnson set out to improve Saigon's image.

Due to pressure from Washington to offer at least the appearance of a democratic regime, some political progress took place in South Vietnam. A constitution was enacted, and elections for a new National Assembly were held in 1967. Military intrigue reduced General Ky to the candidacy for vice president. General Nguyen Van Thieu, a Catholic, was elected president though in a relatively poor showing that saw a considerable number of votes going to an anti-military "peace" candidate.

The new government had a broader base, but the habit of jailing political opponents persisted. The military situation, bolstered by a half million U.S. troops, improved. The South Vietnamese army alone simply could not hold its own against North Vietnam and Viet Cong units. The government did gain control of half the land area by the end of 1967, but in many cases, its hold was shaky.

## Tet: A Battle Won and Lost

As 1968 began, both sides found themselves involved in a terribly costly and bloody conflict. Yet little was being accomplished to resolve the struggle. The U.S. was distracted by the 1968 elections, in which President Lyndon Johnson had declined to run, and the Soviets dared not appear to be less revolutionary than the Chinese. On Tet, the Lunar New Year holiday traditional to the Vietnamese, the communist forces started an unexpected all-out offensive. They invaded most of the provincial capitals and parts of Saigon, and they held a portion of the ancient imperial capital, Hue, for several days. U.S. encampments and installations were attacked, causing tremendous losses of material and manpower. Moreover monsoon rains prevented effective American defensive air strikes.

In the end, the spectacular offensive was dramatically defeated although it had certainly revealed the weaknesses of the South Vietnamese and U.S. forces and driven them back temporarily. The communist goal of generating a popular uprising was a dismal failure. Nevertheless, official American claims to the contrary, the North had proven that Americans were not winning the war and that it was likely to go on for many years. For Hanoi, committed as it had been for generations to the unification of the country under its rule, that price was acceptable. For the United States, by now more interested in simply finding a way out of the costly but ultimately peripheral struggle, it was not.

## Seeking "Peace with Honor"

A desperate U.S. President Lyndon Johnson suspended the bombing of North Vietnam (except the southern provinces) in 1968 and proposed talks between the combatants. Knowing he could probably not be reelected, Johnson, as stated, declined to run again. At last, negotiations were begun, but organizational issues, such as the status of the Viet Cong and seating arrangements at the conference table, resulted in endless haggling and little progress. But events within the United States were moving faster than the negotiations.

After a divisive campaign that saw the Democratic Party almost destroy itself over the war, Richard M. Nixon, the former Republican vice president, who had once advocated American intervention at Dienbienphu, was elected president of the U.S. During the campaign, Nixon had spoken somewhat vaguely about a "secret plan" to end the war. Once in power his plans became clearer.

The newly elected president was no longer primarily interested in South Vietnam, but in ending the war in a fashion that would retain American influence in the postwar era. This would not have been accomplished by simply pulling out, as many Americans had advocated. Rather, Nixon feared, it would send shock waves through the entire American alliance system. Thus, he wanted a way to withdraw that would allow U.S. prestige to continue undiminished.

His method to accomplish these goals came to be known as "Vietnamization." What Nixon and his soon famous advisor Henry Kissinger had in mind was to transfer the bulk of the ground war to the Army of the Republic of South Vietnam. In their plan, the United States would withdraw to the relatively safer position of offering air support. The goal was to reduce the number of American casualties while building up South Vietnam's ability to defend itself. Certainly, a good idea in theory, the plan dangerously reduced American military force in Vietnam even as its prestige remained closely tied to events there.

U.S. troop withdrawals thus started in 1969. From Hanoi's perspective their chances of victory probably seemed closer than ever. In mid-1969 they proclaimed a "provisional government" for the South. 1969 also saw the death of their longtime leader Ho Chi Minh.

The Saigon government of President Thieu then turned to what it considered the most reliable elements for support: the armed forces and Catholics. Spurred by land reform in the south, the economy improved. Thieu was reelected (unopposed) in late 1971 in a contest his opponents charged was rigged. Although he made an attempt to build an effective government party, disruption came when the northern provinces of South Vietnam were struck by a massive North Vietnam invasion in March 1972.

President Nixon, who was facing a reelection contest responded by ordering the mining of Haiphong Harbor. This precipitated yet another international "crisis." The military stalemate was acutely embarrassing to Nixon as the fall elections

**South Vietnamese President Nguyen Van Thieu decorates soldiers**

**The mausoleum of Ho Chi Minh in Hanoi**

approached. Yet, for a time it seemed "that peace was at hand," as Kissinger was publicly quoted. But no formal agreement was reached before Nixon's landslide reelection victory of 1972. Once reelected, Nixon ordered a resumption of the heavy bombing of North Vietnam in an attempt to persuade Hanoi to accept terms acceptable to the Saigon government.

### The End

After the intense December 1972 bombing, the North Vietnamese verbally agreed to end the conflict. The formal agreement was signed on March 2, 1973. The U.S. had already given up its insistence on a North Vietnamese withdrawal from South Vietnam and continued its own withdrawal. In exchange, it got American prisoners back although some insist to this day that many were held against their will in violation of the promise.

Hanoi accepted a political arrangement that did not guarantee the overthrow of the Thieu government as had been previously demanded. Realistically neither North nor South Vietnam had any genuine interest in abiding by the political provisions of the January 1973 agreement, which called for a vaguely defined coalition government and general elections.

To strengthen its hand, Hanoi, with the help of military aid from the Soviet Union and China, then began to create a "third Vietnam" under the nominal control of the Viet Cong in the highlands of South Vietnam. This activity, much of which was in flagrant violation of the agreement, included road building, troop buildups, the stockpiling of weapons and other measures.

Meanwhile, Saigon's principal supporter, the United States, was sinking deeply into the Watergate scandal that eventually destroyed the Nixon administration. Deprived of American air support

by Congressional prohibitions and unwilling to commit its own air force against communist-held areas in the highlands, South Vietnam made no genuine military effort to contain their longtime foe.

In the Saigon-controlled areas, the Thieu government continued its own repressive policies. Although Thieu fired a number of corrupt military and civilian officials, there was no basic change in the style of the regime. Anti-Thieu protest movements arose in 1974 among both the Buddhists, who stressed liberalization and peace, and the Roman Catholics, who emphasized opposition to corruption. Concessions were promised to both in late 1974, but little happened. By early 1975, five major opposition newspapers were closed down.

Meanwhile, North Vietnam was developing its economy through aid from the Soviet Union and China. The military strength of Hanoi was built up as was that of the Viet Cong in the highlands of South Vietnam. A strategy of "accelerated erosion" began against Saigon's military positions in both the highlands and in the Mekong Delta. This approach was obviously inadequate to achieve Hanoi's two principal objectives: imposition of the political provisions of the January 1973 agreement and/or the downfall of Thieu. One reason for this cautious approach was probably the attitude of the Soviet Union and China, which did not want their rapprochement with the United States to be endangered by a major resurgence of fighting in Vietnam.

The North Vietnamese capture of two provincial capitals in early 1975, and another closer to Saigon, was the beginning of the end. Shocked by the loss of these towns and unquestionably worried by the refusal of the U.S. Congress to vote further large-scale military aid, Thieu simply abandoned the three provinces in March. What was perhaps meant as a retreat quickly turned into a rout as Hanoi's forces, taking advantage of the dry season and the government withdrawals, moved forward. By the end of March, the two important coastal cities of Hue and Danang had fallen to the communists. Saigon fell at the end of April in a morass of confusion as people with close contacts with the Thieu administration or the Americans desperately tried to flee in overcrowded boats and planes.

The behavior of the leadership during 1975 in South Vietnam demonstrated that their concern was mainly for their personal safety rather than for the future of South Vietnam. Thieu issued military orders that were disastrous, changed daily, and led nowhere. Many field officers deserted to seek safety for themselves and their families. Several hundred thousand

refugees fled, most ultimately to the U.S. Thieu went to Taiwan. Almost the entire leadership was able to depart with substantial wealth, in contrast to most of the refugees who had little more than the clothes they wore. Most dramatically, thousands of South Vietnamese suddenly abandoned their G.I. issued boots to avoid being recognized as former South Vietnamese soldiers.

The reasons for the loss of the war were many, but especially important was the weakness of the southern regime. Despite its access to American support, it never developed deep roots among the Vietnamese population, certainly nothing similar to what Hanoi was able to call upon from the populations under its control. When South Vietnam started to lose the support of even the Americans, its ability to maintain itself became even more problematic.

### A Unified Vietnam

If Hanoi's tenacity had allowed it finally to unify the country under its own control, actually ruling a united Vietnam would require very different skills. Unified Vietnam's new leaders had an enormous challenge ahead of them, for the country had been devastated by the years of war. Over eight million tons of bombs had been dropped. The Vietnamese had experienced some two million casualties—tremendous numbers of whom would have to be taken care of for years. The people hurt and killed by the war were not the only victims. Vietnam's land had suffered horribly.

More than 11 million gallons of the herbicide and defoliant chemical Agent Orange had been sprayed over the country by the United States in order to destroy the vegetation cover used by the communist forces. According to the United Nations, U.S. chemical warfare created "black zones" within the countryside whose ability to produce crops was radically reduced. In addition, like many American Vietnam veterans, many Vietnamese and their families would suffer from the affects of Agent Orange years after the fighting ended. Unfortunately for the nation that had already experienced so many hardships, Hanoi's post-victory policies often created even more problems, as it attempted both to centralize authority and to build a communist "command economy."

After its "liberation" from the Thieu regime, South Vietnam was run by men sent from Hanoi. Chief among them was Pham Hung who, although a southerner, was a member of the top leadership of the Vietnam Workers Party, the communist party. Imposition of communist controls on the South proceeded fairly slowly.

# Vietnam

Nevertheless, tens of thousands were executed while millions were forced into political "re-indoctrination" camps. Former employees of the Thieu regime found it difficult for years to find jobs and even food. Sadly, the ostracizing of family members often continued down into the next generation as many of their children experienced continuing prejudice.

The new regime worked to reduce the population of Saigon, now renamed Ho Chi Minh City, through forced resettlement in the countryside. Their reasoning is understandable given how much the city's population had swollen with refugees from the countryside and how little work there was once the free spending Americans left. The policies, though, caused suffering for thousands as they were forced to abandon their lives in the city for the backbreaking labor of the countryside.

The party held its Fourth Congress in late 1976, at which it renamed itself the Vietnam Communist (rather than "Workers") Party. The north's domination over the south was clear. Soviet aid to and influence on the new regime was also substantial. The Soviets also took over the huge naval base at Camranh Bay built by the U.S. In contrast, Chinese influence was considerably less than that of the Soviets. Clearly Vietnam was tilting toward Moscow as the Sino-Soviet disputes continued.

Meanwhile, Hanoi naively continued to hope for the $3.25 billion in reconstruction aid Nixon was said to have promised. But no aid was forthcoming as little progress was made on the Missing-in-Action (MIA – the search for remains of U.S. forces in Vietnam) program, and Hanoi was widely disliked within the United States.

Having finally won its long independence and unification struggle, Hanoi then moved to impose a socialist economy on the south. That effort was not well received by the southerners who passively resisted efforts to collectivize agriculture and redistribute land. When efforts to socialize the urban area brought an end to the free market system of the south, large numbers of indigenous Chinese, the backbone of the urban economy, fled the country. This created yet another wave of "boat people," who had already filled refugee camps throughout Southeast Asia.

These policies hardly helped strengthen the country, and in the late 1970s Vietnam's leadership already started looking for new solutions to the nation's problems. Hanoi then moved to integrate itself into the world economic community by joining organizations like the World Bank and the Asia Development Bank. It sought outside development funds for the exploration of natural resources such as oil. In 1977, it announced it would honor the

**My Lai Memorial Peace Park**

former South Vietnamese government's debts to both France and Japan (necessary to build future economic relations). The decision was even made in 1979 to slow down the process of collectivization of agriculture.

Unfortunately, these early examples of practical economic decision-making did not bear the fruit hoped. Other problematic relationships continued to complicate Hanoi's efforts. The Americans continued to maintain their economic embargo, and newly developing tensions with China over Vietnam's role in Cambodia were soon to complicate matters even more.

### Vietnam's Cambodia Involvement

In the late 1970s, Vietnam developed a border conflict with Cambodia, which was then controlled by the murderous and vehemently nationalist Pol Pot regime. In 1978, Vietnam launched a full-scale invasion of the country. In doing so, Hanoi claimed they were responding to frequent border provocations and to the Khmer Rouge's genocidal killing within Cambodia. Under the circumstances, many Cambodians initially viewed the invading Vietnamese and their supporters as liberators. Nevertheless, despite the general hatred of the Pol Pot regime, Vietnam's own invasion was also widely condemned. The Chinese, who had

been especially supportive of the Khmer Rouge, were outraged. They saw Hanoi's actions as an extension of their enemy's, the Soviet Union's, influence in Southeast Asia. From Beijing's perspective that was unacceptable.

In retaliation for this strike against its ally, China began to pour troops over the Vietnamese border in early 1979, occupying, despite heavy fighting, a portion of its northern territory. Beijing's efforts, though, were less successful than expected. The Chinese troops, who had not fought in a generation, were hard pressed to deal with the Vietnamese military fresh from its generation-long struggle with the United States. China's efforts to teach Hanoi a "lesson" had failed, and Chinese troops were withdrawn within a few weeks. After that Beijing directed itself more toward supporting the fallen Khmer Rouge and making life "difficult" for the Vietnamese in Cambodia.

Over the next decade, Vietnam's commitment to Cambodia and its allied government would become a major burden on the regime. Predictably, as time went on, the Vietnamese, who had initially been welcomed as liberators, were themselves seen as aggressive occupiers. Finally, in the late 1980s Hanoi began its withdrawal from Cambodia after a decade that had seen the commitment there contribute to the weakening economic conditions

**Rice paddy work in northern Vietnam**                    Courtesy of Sara Zaidspiner-Leibo

in Vietnam itself and its international isolation.

### A New Economic Path

Economically the first decade of independence was a disaster. The most productive citizens had been driven from the country, and the socialist economic planning had alienated many others. The war in Cambodia had so alienated countries, including China and the United States, that it was particularly difficult for Vietnam's economy to move meaningfully toward recovery.

The aging, largely North Vietnamese leadership and its economic policies had not helped the economy grow. The continuing isolation of the regime due to the American-led boycott had hurt. Meanwhile, the efforts of many communist states from Eastern Europe to improve ties with Beijing meant less enthusiasm for Vietnam. Hanoi's economic crisis was growing.

For example, inflation was running at around 700%. By the mid 1980s, it was clear that a new direction was required.

Not surprisingly this new thinking emerged as China, under Deng Xiaoping, was several years into a major economic reform program itself. More importantly given the Soviet Union's considerable influence in Vietnam, the actions and advice of its reforming leader, Mikhail Gorbachev, was particularly important in the decision to fashion a new economic policy.

The new direction also became more possible with the death in July 1986 of Le Duan, the longtime General Secretary of the Communist Party of Vietnam, the most powerful political office. He was succeeded by Truong Chinh, also elderly but more flexible and with a reputation for being pro-Chinese. Accordingly, at a Party Congress held in December 1986, Truong Chinh, Le Duc Tho, and Pham Van Dong "resigned" from the politburo although all continued to be "advisers." Chinh retained the presidency of the state and Dong the premiership. A new General Secretary of the party, Nguyen Van Linh, a Southerner and an economic reformer, was elected. In 1987 there were major personnel changes in the government although Chinh and Dong remained in

place; the newcomers were mostly southerners with some economic expertise. The new leadership group was clearly interested in moving more decisively away from central control of the economy.

Over the next several years, agriculture was de-collectivized and many financial reforms were put into place. State factory managers were given more authority, and a partial revival of private enterprise was permitted. By 1989, Vietnam had re-emerged as a major rice exporter and is now the world's second-largest. Private businesses, such as restaurants and shops, were opened and flourished as well.

The changes were inspired both by internal developments in Vietnam as well as by the new Gorbachev leadership in the Soviet Union. These changes came to be known as Doi Moi, or "renovation." If they are less well known than the famous glasnost and perestroika of Gorbachev, they were borne of the same problems in the socialist world. Eventually, while the initial decision to open the economy was inspired by developments within the socialist bloc, by the early 1990s the Soviet Union had collapsed, and Vietnam was forced to integrate itself more deeply into the world's newly globalized economies.

A relaxation of controls occurred in Vietnam in the late 1980s, which also paralleled developments in both the Soviet Union and the People's Republic of China. Greater press and religious freedom became possible, as well as the introduction of Western music videos. Some 6,000 political prisoners were released in 1987.

Another milestone was reached in 2007 when Vietnam achieved its goal of joining the World Trade Organization. At the beginning of the year the nation became the 150th country to join. Overall, the idea of a "new Vietnam," one that was eager for foreign contacts, was energetically promoted by the government.

The benefits of economic liberalization are clear. The World Bank has noted that between 2002 and 2018, GDP per capita has increased 2.7 times, reaching $2,700 in 2019. This has brought 45 million people out of poverty, a drop from 70% of the population to 6%, though there is still much poverty in the minority areas. Infant mortality has dropped from 32.6 per 1,000 live births to 16.7. Life expectancy increased. Even COVID-19 has had a relatively limited effect on the overall economy. GDP continued to grow in 2020, one of the few countries where it did so, although household incomes have fallen somewhat.

### Vietnamese Domestic Politics

The dramatic developments of 1989–1991 in the Soviet Union and Eastern

**Ford Plant East of Hanoi**                    Courtesy of Ed Tick

# Vietnam

Europe had a serious impact on the Vietnamese leadership. The basic reaction was one of alarm and a determination that the erosion of the ruling party's power would not be repeated in Vietnam. Particularly shocking for Vietnam's leadership was the bloody fall of the Nicolae Ceausescu regime in Romania in December 1989.

Political opposition in Vietnam had been almost non-existent. Accordingly, the regime had felt free to proceed along the same lines as in China: minimal political reform combined with some reasonably effective economic reform. However, the events of the 1989–1991 era had clearly shown how easily reform efforts in the communist world could swirl out of control. The Party had no desire to lose its mandate on power. The key appeared at least to make reasonable progress on economically improving people's lives without loosening up on political controls.

One requirement was the establishment of normal commercial relations with the industrial countries. The 1989 withdrawal from Cambodia was fundamental to that process and made improved relations with the rest of Vietnam's neighbors far more possible. Relations with the U.S. remained difficult, especially as controversies continued around the political sensitive issue of American Missing-in-Action (MIA). Thus, constrained by anti-Hanoi sentiments in the U.S., Washington continued to withhold diplomatic recognition and trade from Hanoi.

Finally, as time passed Hanoi became increasingly more cooperative on the MIA issue, and by the end of 1991 the State Department even began to authorize tour groups of Americans to visit Vietnam. The U.S. presidential election prevented rapid action, but in late 1992 President George H. W. Bush finally permitted U.S. companies to open offices in Vietnam and begin negotiations for future trade relations.

Throughout the early 1990s, many signs pointed to the continued opening of Vietnam to the outside world. Vietnamese

officials were being trained in contemporary diplomatic practice, a Fulbright program was begun, and American professors were in the country at several institutions teaching business and economic courses. Americans also visited Vietnamese military bases and government offices in search of additional information on American MIAs. Vietnamese were also being trained to aid them in the process of determining the fate of their own MIAs that far outnumber the Americans lost. Unfortunately, Vietnam has lacked the financial resources to seek out the ultimate burial places of most of their own war dead. This is an issue that is often very painful to the many Vietnamese who see so much money being spent to locate the remains of lost Americans.

In the spring of 2001 a new general secretary, Nong Duc Manh, was chosen to head the communist party. Manh had come to power as a replacement to the more conservative Le Kha Phieu. His selection was greeted enthusiastically by many. He joined in leadership Prime Minister Phan Van Khai and President Tran Duc Luong. To the disappointment of some, though, in the time after he came to power, Manh took a relatively cautious approach to reform. Nevertheless, there were some provocative new changes.

One was the government's decision to allow communist party members to be officially involved in private business activities. There has even been talk of allowing people from the private sector to join the party, a practice already allowed in the People's Republic of China.

While Vietnamese politics remain largely beyond the view of outsiders, it has become more and more obvious that the upper leadership has been torn by infighting. Information about some of this has leaked to the general public. The best known example are the accusations that members of the nation's military intelligence services fabricated information to make it appear that top Vietnamese

Communist Party officials had secretly collaborated with the American Central Intelligence Agency. Examples of intraparty struggles have become more and more publicly known. In fact, some very well-known officials have circulated documents critical oft decision making.

Problems within the ruling elite have also been manifested in more public concerns about the party. Once the respected leader of the nation's struggle to free and then unify the nation, today's Vietnamese Communist Party has been experiencing considerable public dissatisfaction over the government's record of corruption. One dramatic example of such corruption was the case of a high official of the Ministry of Transport and Communications. He was accused in 2006 of having lost $7 million in public funds betting on European soccer matches.

So serious has this loss of faith become that the party has officially committed itself not only to root out corruption, but to restore public confidence. There are plenty of reasons for them to be concerned about that loss of public confidence.

In yet another sign of differences within Vietnam's ruling classes, in 2010, the National Assembly dramatically rejected the government's proposed high-speed rail project, which would have run from Hanoi in the north to Ho Chi Minh City in the south. Only a few months later the assembly took up the issue of environmental pollution associated with local bauxite mining.

At the 11th National Party Congress that met in early 2011 to select new leaders was convened. During the congress a new long-term plan for socio-economic development was approved. A number of incumbent ministers were replaced while Nguyen Phu Trong was chosen as the new party general secretary. The changes were not insignificant. Vietnam's core leadership was hardly modified.

More and more commonly, the government has had to face peasant unrest

**Former President Tran Dai Quang**

**Prime Minister Nguyen Xuan Phuc**

**General Secretary
Nguyen Phu Trong**

**Tradition continues in Vietnam . . .**

Courtesy of Steven A. Leibo

aroused by excessive taxation and corrupt local officials. Especially significant has been tension between the government and the ethnic minorities of Vietnam's central highlands. According to reports from the region, the problems have been caused by the new arrivals' confiscation of lands owned by the ethnic minorities and pressure against their local churches. The problem has, at times, grown so explosive that many of the tribal people from the central highlands have fled into Cambodia, a development that also added to the tensions between the two nations.

In April 2004, thousands of Vietnamese ethnic minorities staged a huge demonstration that apparently clashed with security forces resulting in hundreds of injuries and perhaps a dozen deaths. Given Hanoi's control of the media, the details of the reported clashes are often sketchy, but the impression is that these disturbances have been quite serious. In early 2008, similar tensions resulted in mass demonstrations carried out by the Degar peoples in the provinces of Dak Lak and Gia Lai.

Vietnam's leaders do appear to have taken some of the tensions seriously. There have been efforts to confront corruption and to expand decision making, for example making sure that the full central committee is not overshadowed by the smaller politburo and working to ensure a younger and more professionally trained bureaucracy.

That does not mean Vietnam's security forces are backing off. In 2013, after 70 influential Vietnamese called for the end of one-party rule, the government made yet another effort to silence the voices of

the new social media outlets by instituting very significant fines, over thousands of dollars, for anyone criticizing the government online. It was not just financial losses with which critics were threatened, but time in jail if their online activities aroused the ire of the authorities. In fact, people have been told they cannot comment on anything seen as a public issue and were required to confine their online comments only to non-political personal issues.

But the party retains strong control and shows no sign of giving it up." Most seats in parliament are held by party members. Signs of dissent are quickly suppressed. Several groups have received heavy prison sentences for alleged plots to overthrow the government. All media is tightly controlled. Use of the internet is closely monitored by a special military unit established in 2017. While some of this is aimed at sexual or religious content, much more important is control over political information and comment. Prohibited areas are antigovernment or human rights' material. Prior to the Vietnam Communist Party's 13th Congress in January 2021, additional controls were introduced to prevent publication of non-official comment on the leadership.

Later in June 2021, there was a further tightening up of controls on social media. Content affecting the interests of the state was not allowed. Instead, users were encouraged to show positive accounts of the country. Bad language and other anti-social behavior was also prohibited. Journalists and others who were deemed to have infringed these rules were prosecuted.

This led to some international protests, which were ignored.

### Society and Culture

The Vietnamese have been influenced by the culture of the Chinese to a greater extent than all other nations of Southeast Asia, except Singapore, where there is a Chinese majority. Chinese characters were used to write the Vietnamese language until the French replaced them with *quoc-ngu*, a system based on the French alphabet. The Red River in North Vietnam is controlled with dikes of Chinese design.

Religiously Vietnam includes a large number of followers of Mahayana Buddhism, whose practices vary widely, and many Roman Catholics. Vietnamese Buddhism includes traditions ranging from animism and Taoism to Confucianism and Buddhism and is often simply called the Triple Religion or "Vietnamese Buddhism." Along with Korea and the Philippines, Vietnam has one of the highest percentages of Christians in Asia. There is also a considerable number who follow minority traditions like the Cao Dai and Hoa Hao sects. Compared to the situation in earlier years, Vietnam has become much more religiously tolerant.

More dramatic, however, has been the ongoing confrontation between the authorities and local Catholics over property rights. More specifically it concerns the control of church lands in Hanoi and along the central coast at Dong Hoi that have seen a series of demonstrations, arrests and a rising tone of conflict. Moreover, religious organizations that are not officially sanctioned, such as Mennonites or dissident Buddhists, regularly feel the weight of government displeasure.

Most citizens are ethnically Vietnamese with a small percentage of Chinese and a block of some 54 different smaller groups that are sometimes collectively known as Montagnards. The Vietnamese tribal communities have often experienced prejudice directed against them by the majority Vietnamese people. From time to time a significant number of demonstrations and clashes has occurred in regions of the central highlands.

Unlike China, which has committed itself to reducing population growth, Vietnamese efforts have not been nearly as dedicated. Few restrictions exist to limit the number of children a family might want. Abortion is very common, and about twenty percent of those who do have them are young people. There is also a significant rise in HIV/AIDS. As in other Asian countries, more male births are reported than female. This suggests that female fetuses are more likely to be aborted than male.

# Vietnam

The government, like that in neighboring Thailand and China, has become particularly involved in trying to limit the number of Vietnamese who smoke. Currently about half of all Vietnamese men do so. To reduce that number, the government has now banned smoking scenes in all Vietnamese films. This and other measures, including limiting smoking in indoor public areas, have had some effect, but smoking is still widespread.

Most of the population remains poor and largely rural. The real economic changes made in recent years have been significant, but they have also added to the gap between the rich and poor. This is particularly true when one looks both regionally and ethnically. Some regions, like those around Ho Chi Minh City, have grown far faster than the area around the Mekong Delta and the central highlands. Ethnic Vietnamese from the lowlands have moved into the central highlands weakening the economic circumstances of the ethnic minorities who previously predominated in those areas.

Nevertheless, considerable progress has been made. According to the World Bank, 58% of the Vietnamese population lived in poverty during 1992–1993. By 1997–1998 only 37% were officially living in poverty. Even greater progress was made in the new century the number living under the official poverty rate continued to decline significantly. The World Bank reported in April 2022 that those living in poverty had dropped from 16.8% in 2012 to 5% in 2022, despite a slight halt in progress in 2020 because of COVID. However, there was still high levels among the old and in minority areas.

However, the burdens on people have also changed as the nation's emphasis on a less state-dominated economic system has grown. Health care, for example, can be very expensive, and peasants who have members of their families needing major medical treatment can often only obtain the treatment by selling off family land.

The government has acted to remove street children from the cities by pressuring them to return to their villages or to live in charity centers. The goal is to have them living in regular charity centers, where they can be trained to do more than sell souvenirs or lottery tickets.

If the situation in Vietnam is more open today than in the past, the government is still quite willing to come down hard on those it perceives as undermining its authority. In early 2009, one of Vietnam's most prominent lawyers was arrested for challenging state power. The government claimed he had been drafting a revised constitution. Later in the year, six dissidents were arrested for hanging banners in the port city of Haiphong that

. . . even as the Internet has arrived.

demanded greater political freedoms. At least one of them was sentenced to a five-year term for subversion.

For those who avoid arousing the leadership anger, today's Vietnamese government controls people's lives far less than it once did. It still decides how much free speech and press freedoms are allowed. Outside sources of information, ranging from telephones to e-mail and faxes, are controlled. Nevertheless, one of the most obvious things one notices when traveling regularly in Vietnam is that change is coming fast. The Internet is increasingly available, and many have access to e-mail through the popular Internet cafés and international accounts such as Hotmail.

Moreover, there have been enough improvements in recent years that many Vietnamese who fled earlier are returning home. Some are even buying and building homes often in more western styles. The most dramatic example was the 2004 return by the former South Vietnamese leader Nguyen Cao Ky, who made his first visit in almost 30 years. Those who have returned either for visits or to stay are not allowed to take part in public activities.

Another obvious change that even the most casual visitors will notice is the growing gap between the generations in Vietnam. The older generation, those who grew up during Vietnam's nationalist struggle against the French and the later "American" war, has far different memories and life experiences than the new generation that has come of age in a largely peaceful Vietnam ever more deeply involved in global economic activities. Given the facts that 60% of the population is under 30 and that only 15% is over 40, it is a community with very different memories of Vietnam's modern experience than

earlier generations. It is also true that the relatively young population, like their counterparts everywhere, are increasingly developing an online presence that has already aroused the ire of the authorities.

## Vietnamese Women

As mentioned in the background section of East and Southeast Asia, Southeast Asian women have historically enjoyed more rights than their sisters in other parts of Asia. In ancient Vietnam women were especially important, and many played significant roles in Vietnam's long struggle against Chinese domination. In modern Vietnam, women often played very important roles in the nationalist struggle against both the French and later the Americans. Still, the first female did not take her place in the party's all-important politburo until the summer of 1996. Since then, women have played a larger role on the political scene, holding senior roles in the party and government. Women still represent only 21% of the managerial positions in business, and within the central committee of the Communist Party males hold 89% of the seats. Within the society at large people still prefer male babies to females although that attitude is more common among the more conservative northerners than among their southern cousins.

That said, women are nevertheless an important part of the Vietnamese workforce. In Hanoi, for example, they make up more than half of the local workforce. Still, according to international reports, Vietnamese women only make around 89% as much money as men do. One especially interesting development within Vietnam that particularly affects women has been the government's campaign to reduce the number of Vietnamese couples who live together instead of marrying. Divorce is also common, and women more often than men initiate the efforts usually for reasons that range from spousal abuse to adultery and economic conflicts.

The challenges that continue to face Vietnamese women are perhaps best revealed by the reality that thousands of them have opted to offer themselves to Taiwanese men as "male order brides." Doing so allows them to live in Taiwan earning significantly more money than is possible in Vietnam. That money can then be sent home to their families.

For visitors to Hanoi interested in women's history, one especially important visit should be to the wonderfully organized and very modern museum of Vietnamese women. Along with the Ho Chi Minh museum, it is far and away one of the best in the country.

### Foreign Relations

Looking at Vietnam's foreign relations from the broadest view, two obvious periods emerge in the years since the war ended. First, the initial decade after the war saw Vietnam increasingly dependent on the Soviet Union. Later, after its invasion of Cambodia, Vietnam found itself alienated from much of the rest of the world. Her foreign policy was particularly ideological in those years as Vietnam attempted to orient its diplomatic decision-making within the framework of the Cold War era. But that approach did not prove effective and eventually moved Vietnam's leaders to reevaluate their approach.

By the mid-1980s, as Vietnam's economic problems and diplomatic isolation proved more and more problematic, its leaders began not only their effort to renovate the economy but to open Vietnam up more to the world community. Fundamental to that effort was, of course, the withdrawal from Cambodia, a move that opened up a new era in Vietnamese foreign relations.

Having removed the foremost impediment to deepening its involvement in the world community, Vietnam during the 1990s set out in a new direction. In July 1993, President Bill Clinton ended U.S. opposition to International Monetary Fund (IMF) loans to Vietnam. Somewhat later Clinton announced that American companies could bid on infrastructure projects funded by the international lending agencies.

The next year the 19-year U.S. trade embargo was finally ended. Full diplomatic relations were announced in July 1995. More recently it has become easier for American businessmen to invest and trade with Vietnam. Vietnam has even

gone as far as paying back monies the former government of South Vietnam owed to the United States. Cooperation on a range of issues between the two wartime enemies became even more possible after former U.S. Secretary of Defense William Cohen's highly successful trip to Hanoi in early 2000 and even more dramatically after President Clinton's own extremely well received visit during the last weeks of 2000.

In July 2001, the United States and Vietnam finalized and official trade treaty and in 2006 Vietnam was finally granted "most favored nation" (more correctly, normal trading status) by the Americans. That was important because it allowed Vietnamese goods to enter the U.S. as cheaply as those from America's other trading partners.

Clearly, normalization of relations with the United States has been a major element in Hanoi's efforts to strengthen the economy. By 2004 the United States had become the Vietnam's 11th largest investor, and trade relations were growing rapidly. Vietnam's total exports to the United States went up over 127%, earning the country almost $2 billion in revenues while the Americans sold almost $600 million worth of goods to Vietnam. By 2005, Vietnamese sales to the United States had reached $8.5 billion, while in early 2006 the American company, Lockheed Martin, won the contract to launch Vietnam's first telecommunications satellite.

Overall, American firms have become deeply involved in the Vietnamese economy though some, like Nike, have come under considerable public criticism for the work conditions they established there. True, things have not always worked out as hoped. The Procter and Gamble Company's soap and shampoo-making facility was plagued by legal and supply problems, and in March 1998, it was temporarily shut down. In the early 2000s, American charges that Vietnam has been "dumping" catfish and shrimp on the American market contributed to the tensions.

The same applied to the 2004 American State Department's designation of Vietnam as a country that does not respect religious freedom. This, however only lasted until 2006. Since then, while the State Department continues to express concern about restrictions on religious freedoms in the country, it has resisted demands from the U.S government-funded but independent U.S. Commission on International Religious Freedom for Vietnam to be reinstated. The Commission has reported every year since 2002 on what it considers the severe restrictions on religion that still operate in Vietnam.

Nevertheless, the relationship in general appears quite healthy. Vietnamese

Prime Minister Phan Van Khai made a historic visit to the United States during the summer of 2005. The visit was the first by a Vietnamese leader since the end of the Vietnam War. While in the U.S., Phan Van Khai was received at the White House by President George W. Bush. Eventually, agreements were even reached on Vietnam's participation in some American military training programs. Phan's 2005 visit was followed up by Prime Minister Dung in June 2008. Since 2000, when then President Bill Clinton visited Vietnam, subsequent presidential visits have been George W. Bush in November 2006, Barack Obama in 2016, and Donald Trump in February 2019—the last was not to conduct business with Vietnam, but Hanoi was the venue for the second U.S.-North Korea summit.

Hillary Clinton, who accompanied her husband on his 2000 visit, returned to Hanoi twice in 2010 as secretary of state for the Obama administration. The first visit was to strengthen U.S.-Vietnamese relations, the second to attend an East Asia summit meeting. Vietnamese officials have even visited American aircraft carriers in both Virginia and off the coast of Vietnam. In March 2018, the carrier USS *Carl Vinson* made the first such visit to Vietnam since 1978. Meetings between American officials and their Vietnamese counterparts have become commonplace. In August 2021, Kamala Harris became the first U.S. vice-president to visit. This is another sure sign that both countries have moved beyond the painful memories of their earlier relationship. Equally important is not merely the passing of time, but the Vietnamese appreciation that better relations with the United States can be helpful during those relatively frequent periods of greater tension with Beijing.

Trade has continued to grow. While bilateral trade in 1994 was $450 million, by 2019, it was $77 billion. The balance is heavily in Vietnam's favor, which led to some sarcastic comments from then President Donald Trump.

Somewhat predictably and part of a more general trend in the region, Hanoi, even as it has sought to reduce tensions with Beijing, also signed in 2011 a memorandum on defense cooperation with the United States. In the same vein one might mention Vietnam's 2011 effort to improve diplomatic and military links to India. Given Vietnam's historic ambivalence about relations with China, it is hardly surprising that the government is also nurturing stronger ties with the United States and India in order to balance the links with Beijing.

Especially important has been Vietnam's integration with its Southeast Asian neighbors. In 1995, Vietnam became a

# Vietnam

member of ASEAN (Association of Southeast Asian Nations). It hosted the ASEAN Foreign Ministers' Meeting in 2001. In January 2010, it assumed the temporary chair of the organization while hosting a series of important regional government meetings including an unprecedented gathering of national defense ministers from throughout the Pacific Rim. It was also chair in 2020, just as the COVID pandemic began. Membership in ASEAN provides Vietnam with important economic and strategic benefits. For example, being a member of ASEAN can provide Vietnam with support in its relations with China. An example of this occurred soon after Vietnam joined, when the ASEAN states spoke out with one voice at the second ASEAN Regional (security) Forum in Brunei in 1995 on the issue of conflicting claims in the South China Sea (which Vietnamese call "East Sea"). China had insisted that these claims be addressed on a bilateral basis. Countries like Vietnam and the Philippines, who have had run-ins with the Chinese military in the sea, preferred the multilateral approach.

As is often the case, Sino-Vietnamese relations remain problematic. After almost two decades of closure, the border between them opened in 1996 for rail service. Such links continue to grow, with a new freight route added in 2022. There are frequent high-level visits at the party and government levels.

Nevertheless, many problems remain. One issue, for example, is the annual midsummer Chinese moratorium against fishing in the South China Sea, introduced in 1999. This ban comes at the very height of the Vietnamese fishing season. It regularly involves Chinese ships aggressively driving Vietnamese ships from the region. The ban was ostensibly proclaimed by Beijing as a way to preserve the vital fishing resources of the area. But it has been seen more widely as an example of China's growing assertion of their claims to the region's offshore resources. However, if today's relationship between Vietnam and China is a somewhat mixed one, it is certainly an improvement over their earlier one.

The two fought one conflict in 1979 and have come to blows over conflicting claims in the South China Sea several times. In 1994, a Vietnamese patrol boat seized three Chinese fishing vessels off Bach Long Vi, an island claimed by Hanoi and located half way between Vietnam and Hainan Island (Chinese territory). The next day a Chinese boat opened fire on another patrol, wounding two Vietnamese. As we have seen, the fishing moratorium remains a continuing source of tension while conflicting claims over potentially oil-rich islands that lie in the

waters between the two nations adds significantly to the tensions.

During the spring of 2011 emotions were once again especially high as a confrontation developed between a Chinese patrol boat and a Vietnamese survey ship. Ominously one expert even claimed the tensions were higher than at any time since the cold war era. During the following summer months the dispute grew even more heated as weeks of anti-Chinese demonstrations broke out in Vietnam. This was no doubt a reflection not only of economic rivalries, but of deeper long-term anti-Chinese sentiments that are often quite close to the surface in Vietnam.

Eventually the Vietnamese government authorities officially banned the demonstrations even as they spoke openly about the importance of protection national sovereignty. The government also took the precaution of officially announcing to its citizens the possibility of a national military mobilization if the situation grew serious enough to warrant such a move. A formal confrontation seems unlikely between China and Vietnam, or between China and any of the other regional claimants to the various island chains in the region. It is also true that the possibility of an accidental and significant confrontation remains very real given the number of naval vessels from the various interested nations that are present in the area.

However, the issue is a major problem, especially as China is increasingly expanding its naval capacity. At its core is concern about having these ocean waters linked to a particular nation, in this case China. This might give the People's Republic an advantage in the ongoing effort to reap the rewards of potential vast

undersea oil and gas riches. In 2012 the Vietnamese National Assembly officially passed legislation reasserting the long-standing Vietnamese claim to the Paracel and Spratly Islands in the South China Sea while announcing the commencement of jet fighter patrols over the same area. For its part China made it clear that it was not impressed with such efforts by offering the same area for international oil investment concessions.

There is no reason to think that competing claims over the region's offshore islands will diminish. They could get considerably more volatile. In fact, they seemed to be heating up again with an even greater level of tensions by the spring of 2014. On the more positive side at least, the two nations, rather than simply assaulting each other, took their grievances to the United Nations. They hoped for a diplomatic solution to the ongoing claims each continued to make to the off shore resources that are increasingly becoming available between the two nations.

Yet another area of potential concern regarding Beijing's activities is Vietnam's worries about Chinese dam building in the areas that feed Vietnam's all-important Mekong River. That is a concern that many have in Southeast Asia. Unfortunately in different geographical regions around the world this issue is likely to become an increasingly common source of international tensions.

Vietnam also continued to talk with Cambodian officials about the treatment of ethnic Vietnamese living along the border just inside Cambodian territory. Relations, though, are not the best and they could deteriorate easily. In fact, there was considerable tension recently between the two as Cambodia claimed that Vietnam

**Fishing in central Vietnam**

314

had actually moved the border markers between the two countries. Nor did the Cambodian government appreciate it when Hanoi, after some hesitation, followed their ASEAN colleagues' lead and temporarily halted Cambodia's entrance into ASEAN in the weeks after Hun Sen's coup. As mentioned above, relations were complicated as well when many Vietnamese ethnic-minority people fled to Cambodia after tensions over land use exploded in the Central Highlands.

Of particular interest has been Vietnam's effort to reach out to the other non-Asian developing nations. During the spring of 2003 Hanoi played host to representatives from 19 African nations who arrived to discuss issues of mutual concern. Nor has Hanoi forgotten its important relationship with France, the nation that so dominated its recent modern history. This time, though, relations are on a much more equal basis. In recent years a renewed official relationship was established between the French and Vietnamese national assemblies.

Meanwhile, Hanoi restored diplomatic relations with Chile. The two countries had broken relations after Chile's democratically elected Marxist president, Salvador Allende, was overthrown in 1973. Hanoi successfully hosted the fifth Asia-Europe summit in 2004. The meeting was almost disrupted by the European nations' reticence to deal with Myanmar's presence at the conference because of its human rights record. Vietnam has also hosted Asia–Europe ministerial meetings on several occasions.

Even official anger at the Vatican's canonization in mid-1988 of 117 Vietnamese martyrs of the 17th and 18th centuries was not allowed to derail a policy of increased toleration of religion, including Catholicism. Still, Hanoi remained suspicious of the Vatican, given the deeply anti-communist reputation of the former Polish Pope John Paul II and the Church's strong ties to the hated Diem regime. The usual tensions between Vietnam and the Catholic Church became particularly heated during 2008 because of government confiscations of lands the Church claimed in Hanoi. Public demonstrations broke out, and it was reported that government supporters attacked a peaceful march organized by Church members. A similar series of confrontations took place the following year in the city of Dong Hoi along the coast in central Vietnam.

One of the most obvious examples of Vietnam's increasing integration with the wider world community was its election as a non-permanent member of the United Nation's Security Council in late 2007.

The 31st Southeast Asian Games, scheduled to be held in Vietnam in November 2021, were postponed because of COVID.

## Economy

Vietnam for years appeared as if it were on the verge of becoming another "Asian Tiger." The term, especially common before the 1997 "Asian Economic Crash," referred to the rapidly growing economies of Asia: Singapore, Taiwan, South Korea and Hong Kong. The term is no longer used as often. However, the reality of Vietnam's transition from a centrally controlled communist economy to a much more dynamic economy remains true. Today Vietnam is more and more influenced by capitalism, and it is moving into the global market.

Beginning in the late 1980s the country experienced a real economic boom with the economic growth rate during the 1990s averaging around 7.5%. That average includes even the slowdown that took place during the Asian economic crisis of 1997–1998. The momentum has continued. Growth then hovered around 8%. It even managed a respectable 5.2% for 2009 despite the global slowdown.

These changes were initially a result of the Communist Party's policy of *doi moi*, or restructuring, which ushered in a series of market reforms. A great many restrictions on the private sector were removed and the decision to move Vietnam more deeply into the world economic system largely embraced. Nevertheless, none of those domestic changes would have

**Ho Chi Minh City**

# Vietnam

mattered much if economic globalization in the late 1990s had not created a more integrated planetary economic system of which Vietnam could take advantage. One result, for example, is that Vietnam is currently among the world's largest exporters of rice (second in world) and coffee (third in world). The results have been impressive. For most of the period 2010–2020, growth was around 7% per annum. It then dipped because of the pandemic but by December 2021, the Asian Development Bank was predicting a 6.5% growth in 2022. The figures for the early months of the year seem to be this out, at over 5% for the first three months.

If 1995, per capita income was still only about $270, or using figures adjusted for living standards, around $1,310, by the first years of the new century, Vietnam had changed even more. The per capita income had risen to $400 or $1,950 when so adjusted. By 2022, based on purchasing parity power, it was $8,200.

Still there have been plenty of impediments to further integration in the world economy. One is the government's ongoing commitment to the state firms. Hanoi may be siphoning off resources needed by the private sector to help state enterprises. For example, textiles made in state concerns are given preference for export. These companies also benefit from better access to foreign currency loans. Foreign companies are even being forced to form joint ventures with local state-owned businesses.

State-run companies still produce a significant percentage of the national GDP. In contrast to China, which apparently wants the importance of such state companies to diminish over time, Hanoi's leaders hope they will remain significant. Still not all have remained economically viable. It has also been necessary for the economy to absorb excess labor from closed state enterprises. This has been partly accomplished by creating millions of new jobs in the private sector.

Especially interesting is that Vietnam has finally developed a stock market as China its giant neighbor did some years ago. Experts were hired from Taiwan to help set one up, and in July of 2000 it opened in Ho Chi Minh City to great fanfare. Another major government goal was to join the World Trade Organization (WTO). The new economic agreement worked out in 2006 between the United States and Vietnam went a long way toward accomplishing that goal. In the fall of 2006 the WTO officially recommended that Vietnam be admitted as its 150th member.

In the early years of the new millennium a number of problems arose to challenge the Vietnamese. The September 11, 2001, terrorist attack against the United States slowed the all-important American economy. Subsequently Vietnam found itself affected as well. Moreover, tourism was deeply impacted. Later, in 2003, fears of the SARS influenza-like disease weakened many Asian economies, including Vietnam's. Fear of SARS hurt Vietnam's economic growth despite the fact that Hanoi received a great deal of positive international publicity for its quick and professional response.

Just as Vietnam and much of the rest of Asia appeared to be moving past the problem, a new medical crisis appeared on the horizon. This time it was avian flu that began to kill people in various parts of Southeast Asia, including Vietnam. Local authorities destroyed millions of chickens and other poultry to stop the outbreak. Predictably, Vietnam found countries around the world banning the import of Vietnamese chickens just as many of those same countries had earlier banned American beef after reports of a cow carrying mad cow disease were published. In the end, all the effort seemed to have been worth it. Over time the number of cases dropped dramatically. However, the onset of COVID in 2020 (see below) hit Vietnam badly. As we have seen, growth suffered.

There were plenty of other bright spots in Vietnam's economic situations. The tourist industry has generally been growing well and becoming more and more important to the country's economy. Vietnam is even attracting significant numbers of Americans interested in learning more about the country that so transformed their own, now nearly half a century ago.

Vietnam is looking forward to the future when agriculture production will not be such a fundamental part of the average Vietnamese's life. Not only has the government announced plans to build over 30 new power production plants, but ambitious plans have been announced to develop an aerospace industry that will help develop technologies associated with satellite constructions and launching facilities. Those who a generation ago saw Vietnam as only a terribly poor country of peasants would find this quite amazing. More immediately Vietnam has been working with its neighbors who also live along the great Mekong River to transform it into a true vehicle to facilitate trade along its entire route. This is an effort that will require expensive engineering projects to accomplish. But it might one day bring enormous benefits to the entire community of perhaps 250 million people who live along the river's route. It is also an effort that has aroused significant opposition from environmentalists, who fear that the development of so many new dams along the river, needed for electricity production, will negatively impact fishing, an industry the nation also requires.

As is the case elsewhere in Southeast Asia, the level of Chinese investment is becoming increasingly controversial. In 2008, enormous controversy developed over the government's decision to award a Chinese company the right to mine bauxite in the Central Highlands. The opposition included a coalition of environmental, academic and religious leaders. They were against the project on both environmental and national security grounds. Even the nation's most prominent activist war hero, General Vo Nguyen Giap, who was nearing his 99th birthday, was among the opponents. In the end, the impressive coalition managed to get the government to revise its plans somewhat.

Of course, Vietnam, like the rest of the world, had to struggle with the burden of the slowing global economy in the aftermath of the 2008 American housing meltdown. In Vietnam's case, initial hopes for growth of over 6.5% had been scaled back to about 5%. More recently the economy has managed a healthy growth rate of between 6% and 7% though for a time there was hope that the now failed Trans-Pacific Partnership negotiated with the United States and others in the region would bring in even stronger economic numbers.

## The Environment: From Local to Global Climate Change

As with most of the countries of Southeast Asia, the last few decades of economic growth and resource exploitation have taken a toll on the nation's physical environment. Air pollution is especially bad. Indeed Vietnam ranks among the top 10 nations in the low quality of its air. This is a problem that has forced the nation to spend enormous sums of money treating people with respiratory problems while polluted water sickens thousands more on a regular basis. Indeed, according to a recent World Bank report, environmental pollution negatively impacts GDP by about 5% annually.

Among the other environmental challenges is the condition of the Mekong River, which feeds a good part of the nation. Human activity along the river, from dam building to polluting, is deeply impacting the river. At least one species whose habitat lies upstream from Vietnam itself, the Mekong dolphin, is said be moving toward extinction. Similar concerns are regularly raised about Vietnam's wildlife that is said to have been devastated by poaching in the nation's many so-called nature preserves.

Meanwhile changing circumstances caused by global climate change are yet another area Vietnam has reason about which to be concerned.

The most recent "impacts" section of the International Governmental Panel on Climate Change listed Asia and Africa as being among the regions most likely to be especially impacted by growing climate instability. Vietnam is no exception to that general trend, and the nation's scientists are increasingly studying the problem. Of particular importance is the fact that much of Vietnam's 3,000-kilometer coastline is a meter or less above sea level. In large measure the population works along that coastline.

That reality makes the nation especially vulnerable not only to rising sea levels, but to the more powerful storms that rising air temperatures bring. The most obvious issue, of course, is the rising temperatures in a region already known for the significant levels of heat. Those rising temperatures carry with them the greater likelihood of more significant storms and flooding simply by virtue of the fact that warmer air can hold more water.

Two especially famous regions are particularly vulnerable—southern Vietnam's Mekong Delta and the Red River valley in the north. Both are areas where agricultural activities are at risk. Those risks are significant. Half of Vietnam's total rice production comes from the Delta alone, which is about two meters above sea level. If projected global temperatures rise as expected, it is entirely possible that significant parts of the entire Mekong Delta could disappear under the relentless pressures of the rising seas. But long before that, more temporary storm surges and intrusion of more salt into the fresh waters of the delta would probably have already done significant damage. That said, a more immediate problem is that above certain temperatures during critical moments in the growing season of rice, the plant simply cannot germinate, rendering it sterile. Clearly, given the wide variety of ways rice is vulnerable to climate change and how dependent much of Asia is on the plant, the situation has to be deemed extremely important.

The Mekong Delta is regularly subjected to heavy flooding, which can have devastating effects. Another problem is the dumping of waste materials, often toxic, in and around the river. This causes health and economic problems.

Along with most nations of the world, Vietnam signed the Kyoto and Paris Climate accords. In 2021, it agreed in the context of the Glasgow Climate conference to aim to reach zero carbon by 2050. Within its borders it is planning to confront the growing challenge of finding alternative fuels. But it is also realistically working to prepare for an era when its vulnerability

to the loss of coastal land, increased salinization of agricultural land, and greater tropical storms will largely be beyond its control. With that in mind, Vietnamese cities like Danang are especially vulnerable. They are working closely with international groups like the Rockefeller Foundation, which has funded Asian Cities Climate Change Resilience Network.

## COVID-19

Given the closeness to China, it was inevitable when COVID-19 emerged in Wuhan late in 2019 that it would soon spread to Vietnam. The first cases, reported in February 2020, confirmed this. But Vietnam also had a good record in handling SARS and took quick action. Tight controls were introduced, with bans on gatherings, social distancing and rapid testing. Unlike China, there was no attempt to cover up developments, and the reasons for the tough measures were explained. With limited exceptions, foreigners were banned from entering the country in late March. By May, there was a relaxation of controls, with no adverse effects. Numbers remained low, with only 35 deaths by the end of the year. Meanwhile, work began on a vaccine, in collaboration with the University of Bristol in England, although it was not thought likely that this would be available until mid-2021.

February 2021 saw a small spike in the numbers infected, but then in May, numbers began to rise rapidly, leading to the reimposition of tight controls. By the end of May 2021, there were some 6,900 cases, of which 3,900 were current, an indication

of how quick the surge had been. However, total deaths only reached 47. Vaccination began in March 2021 but was relatively slow. The first vaccines were the AstraZeneca and the Russian-made Sputnik. By mid-May, about one million people had received a single dose, while 28,000 had been fully vaccinated.

By the end of 2021, there had been 1.6 million cases and 31,000 deaths. As in other countries, this put health services under a severe strain and there were restrictions on meetings. Tourism stopped and international trade was affected. From November 2021, numbers affected had begun to climb upward, and a large spike occured between February and early May. Numbers then began to fall back. By mid-May, total cases since the start of the pandemic reached 10.7 million, with more than 43,000 deaths. Additional vaccine supplies came from China and the United States.

Nevertheless, government restrictions were largely lifted and it was announced that from 15 May, international travelers would no longer need to show proof of vaccination.

As noted, the economic effects on the country, while not negligible, were not as far reaching as some other Southeast Asian countries, and the economy made something of a rebound in 2021, while prospects for 2022 look even more hopeful.

### The Future

The end of the U.S. embargo, the entrance into the World Trade Organization and the arrival of significant foreign investment

**Tourists explore Vietnam's Citadel**

# Vietnam

and personnel into the country are hastening the pace of change. Not all of this will be good. The environment has already suffered significantly, and many individuals have not benefited from the initial stages of economic growth and development. Nevertheless, a new middle class is emerging, and people's lives have improved enormously over the last decade despite the more recent economic slowdown.

Perhaps most emblematic of Vietnam moving beyond its troubled modern history and participation in world culture was the recent announcement that a Vietnamese horror film, known in English as *The House in the Alley*, had been invited to several American film festivals. That a younger generation of Americans may soon have a sense of Vietnam not from war-era films but from a domestically produced Vietnamese haunted house movie certainly speaks for the new Vietnam that has emerged over the last decade.

Vietnam is gaining a reputation as an attractive place for investment that can even compare satisfactorily with the long-dominant People's Republic of China. Of course, the issue of China is never far from Vietnamese concerns. China's increasing presence, both as an investor within Vietnam and an impediment to its offshore goals, remains a constant issue and one that has grown only more volatile over the last few years. This is so much so that individual Chinese have had to be evacuated by their employers for fear of the escalating violence. Moreover, increasingly within Vietnam, tensions are emerging regarding a wide range of domestic but still Chinese-related matters.

These include the potential dangers of extensive Chinese economic power and the many Chinese laborers who have entered the country. They are said to have taken advantage of job opportunities many felt should go to the locals. When the government sponsored such immigration, it became a common focus of popular anger and made the leadership even more vulnerable to the public criticism that has so aroused official concern.

Relations with Beijing have also had broader international implications as became obvious in mid 2016 when the American President Obama visited seeking an even closer relationship between Hanoi and Washington that included an end to the arms embargo that had been in place since the war.

For now, the Communist Party still runs the country although Vietnam also has a new constitution and a National Assembly that has been given a somewhat greater voice in public affairs. It has even shown a willingness to use it when the recent controversy swirled around the idea of building a high-speed train between Hanoi and Ho Chi Minh City. More significantly, tensions within the ruling elite have begun to highlight the question of how long the party will be able to maintain its domination.

As we have seen, the broader public has, at its peril, also become more involved in openly discussing and at times criticizing the regime. Not surprisingly, government forces recently carried out a major crack-down on journalists and bloggers critical of the government. The mother of one of those detained Internet activists

dramatically set herself on fire right in front of a government office to protest her son's incarceration. While another activist, known as "Mother Mushroom" was simply released from prison and sent into exile in the United States in late 2018.

Clearly, as with many countries in the early 21st century, Vietnam is struggling to gain the advantages of being part of the digital age without the potential of social media to challenge the government's monopoly on political power.

In the near future, though, the two issues that seem likely to loom especially large are the growing challenge to the Party's domination of the nation's political life and the tensions with China. They will feed not only on current developments, but on long-term suspicions the Vietnamese have had regarding their enormous neighbor for more than a thousand years. Ironically the tensions with China have inspired the recent improvement in relations with the United States, though the U.S. backing off of the Trans-Pacific Partnership has been a significant disappointment to Vietnamese officials who had been very positive on the chance to expand trade with the enormous American market.

Indeed the failed pact had also brought hope to many of those hoping for more liberalization within Vietnam given that to take part Hanoi's leaders had had to offer significant reforms in terms of greater freedom for unions, support for private firms, and in dealing with child labor. But, of course, the failure of the pact after the American 2016 elections ended those hopes, both economic and social.

# Australia

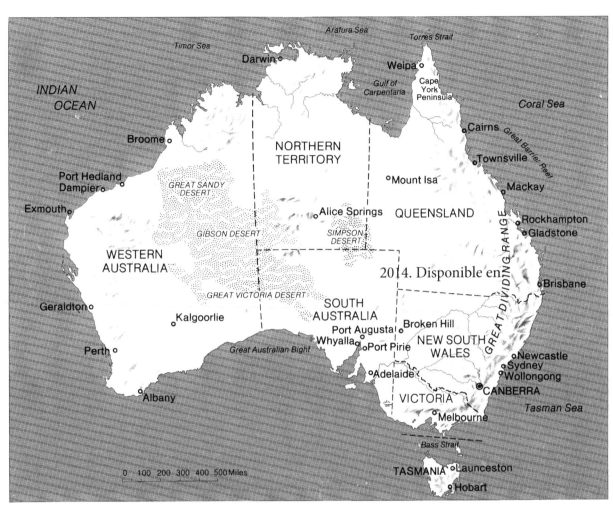

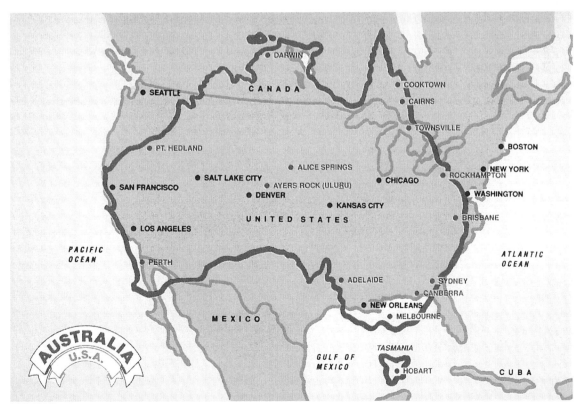

# Australia

**Area:** 2,970,000 sq. mi. (7,686,850 sq. km.)
**Population:** 26,046,051 (2022 est.)
**Capital City:** Canberra, pop. 467,000 (2022 est.)
**Climate:** Tropical to subtropical in the north, temperate in the south; the interior is highly arid
**Neighboring Countries:** Indonesia and Papua New Guinea (North); New Zealand (Southeast)
**Official Language:** English
**Ethnic Background:** Caucasian (92%), Asian (7%), aboriginal and other (1%)
**Principal Religion:** Christianity, small communities Buddhists and Muslims
**Main Exports:** (to U.S., China, S. Korea, India, U.K., New Zealand) Coal, gold, wool, meat, iron ore, aluminum ore, and transportation equipment
**Main Imports:** (from U.S. China, Japan, Germany, Singapore, U.K.) Automobiles, computers, petroleum, and telecommunication and transportation equipment
**Currency:** Australian dollar
**Former Colonial Status:** British dependency (1788–1900)
**National Day:** January 26 (anniversary of the first British settlement at Sydney in 1788)
**Head of State:** Her Majesty Queen Elizabeth II, represented by General David Hurley (since July 1, 2019)
**Head of Government:** Prime Minister Scott Morrison (since August 24, 2018)
**National Flag:** A blue field with the Union Jack in the upper left quarter, a seven-pointed star in the lower left corner, and five stars at the right side
**Per Capita GDP Income:** $51,812.15 (2021) (purchasing power parity)

The enormous island called Australia is so immense that it is classified as a continent; at 2.97 million square miles it is almost the size of the continental United

**Julia Gillard**
**Australia's first female prime minister**

States. Its 12,000 miles of coastline is relatively smooth with few harbors, but in the northeast the sandy coast is in the lee of the Great Barrier Reef, a 1,200-mile chain of coral reefs and islands extending north almost to Papua New Guinea. With its vivid coral and a profusion of other marine life, the reef is one of the world's natural wonders and a magnet for scientists and tourists.

Australia is one of the oldest of the continents and one of the flattest and driest. Its few mountains have been worn with the passage of time and the highest peak today is Mt. Kosciusko at only 7,300 feet. The largest chain of mountains is found in the east and is called the Great Dividing Range; in the southeast, they are known as the Australian Alps. They divide the narrow crescent of land along the coastline from the vast interior. It is in the fertile eastern coastal area that the great majority of Australians live and their largest cities are located.

To the west are large lowlands and plateaus that begin the vast interior region known to Australians as the Outback. This is the region containing the two-thirds of Australia classified as desert (fewer than 10 inches of rain annually) or semi-desert (fewer than 15 inches). The region's "rivers" often are chains of waterholes and flow only following infrequent rains. Most never reach the sea, but instead widen into areas called lakes which most of the time are actually mud flats encrusted with salt. By drilling to great depths, it is possible in some parts of this region to locate limited amounts of ground water, making possible the raising of livestock. However, large areas are needed to support even small numbers of animals. Some outback cattle ranches in Australia are larger than the smaller European countries. Apart from mining settlements, population is scattered and averages fewer than two persons per square mile.

Australians many years ago introduced the Royal Flying Doctor Service, utilizing two-way radio and light aircraft to bring medical services to those living in this isolated environment. Outback children also use the radio system as students of the School of the Air, working through their daily lessons with a teacher in a studio-classroom in the nearest township hundreds of miles away. Large parts of the region are not inhabited at all. An occasional thunderstorm moistens the thirsty land, and grasses and wildflowers rapidly spring up, flower, wither and die, dropping their seeds to the ground to wait many months before the next rainfall.

Apart from its dry center, Australia has a widely varied climate. It covers more than 30 parallels of latitude and more than a third of the country is in the

tropics. Normally snow falls only on the southeastern ranges during the winter as Australia's position surrounded by sea and the absence of marked physical features give a more temperate climate than other land in corresponding latitudes. Because of the low humidity in many places, the high summer temperatures are not as enervating. The north is subject to tropical cyclones (hurricanes), and the city of Darwin was almost completely destroyed by Cyclone Tracy in 1974.

Isolation from other countries by wide expanses of water has affected Australia in many ways from its plant and animal life to its contemporary culture. Australia has many wildflowers found nowhere else. The main native trees are 500 varieties of eucalyptus and 600 species of acacia (known to Australians as wattle and akin to the mimosa of North America). About half of Australia's native mammals are marsupials—animals that produce their young in embryo form which is a tiny fraction of the adult weight of the parent. The newborn offspring finds its way miraculously to the adult's pouch where it continues its development; the mammary glands on which it suckles are located within the pouch. Only when it is the equivalent of a three- to five-year-old human does it leave the pouch, returning for nourishment as needed until even more mature. Marsupials include members of the kangaroo family, the koala, the wombat, and possums. Australia is also the home of another of nature's oddities—the duck-billed platypus, a cross between bird and mammal. It lays eggs, but then nurses its young after they have hatched, yet its body is covered with fur and it lives in a water habitat. Australia's 800 bird species include the ostrich-like emu and many brightly colored parrots.

# Australia

**This painting by Algernon Talmage shows the unfurling of the British flag at Sydney Cove; Captain Arthur Phillip and his men drink to the health of King George III**
Courtesy of the Australian Information Service

### History

During the many centuries of development of the Western world, Australia was thinly populated by an estimated 300,000 aborigines, a nomadic, tribal hunting and gathering society. About 160,000 aborigines remain today, but many have embraced a largely Western lifestyle; some later racially intermixed with the European settlers. They now are a disadvantaged and increasingly assertive minority and Australian politics often revolves around questions relating to their treatment both today and in the past.

Ships of the Dutch East India Company touched on the Australian coastline in the early 17th century; the Dutch explorer Tasman circumnavigated the continent in 1642–1643. The first real penetration was by the British, led by Captain James Cook, who claimed the eastern portion of the island in 1770 in the name of the British Crown.

The principal interest of Britain in Australia was initially as a penal colony where its criminals could be exiled or held in prison. The first settlers, numbering 270 soldiers and sailors and 760 convicts, landed on the present site of the city of

Sydney in 1788 to establish the colony of New South Wales under the royally appointed Governor, Captain Arthur Phillip.

The Crown later permitted non-convict settlers to emigrate from the British Isles to Australia. Most of them became interested in raising sheep for which the island was ideally suited. A close social organization quickly emerged among these free settlers; they dominated the New South Wales Corps, which was a special military police force. They became very influential and struggled with a succession of royal governors, sometimes gaining the right to use the services of convict labor at a low wage, and to expand their sheep-raising activities. They also sought control over internal and external trade.

The notorious Captain Bligh, the former commander of HMS *Bounty*, struggled with the New South Wales Corps when he was governor in 1805 and lost. The next governor, Lachlan Macquarie, was much more respected and successful. He curbed the power of the police force, set limits on land grants and organized and permitted rapid economic development. No more convicts were sent to Australia after 1868.

The discovery of gold in 1851 gave a great boost to the Australian economy

and was accompanied by disorders in the mining camps, similar to those in the American West during the same period. In the succeeding decades, additional immigration of free settlers, exploration of the eastern and later the western parts of the continent, and general economic development took place at a steadily accelerating rate.

Six British crown colonies were successfully established in Australia from 1788 through the first half of the 19th century. All had been granted self-governing independence by the end of that century. In 1901, the colonies became the six States of an Australian Federation under the title Commonwealth of Australia. This status continues today. Like other British dominions, Australia's full independence was formally recognized by the British Parliament in the Statute of Westminster of 1931.

Although an independent, self-governing nation, Australia, along with other countries of the British Commonwealth, recognizes the British sovereign as the head of state, symbolizing historical links with Britain. The Queen is represented in Australia by a governor-general. Australia's chief executive is a prime minister

# Australia

elected by members of the majority party in the federal parliament. The parliament consists of a Senate and a House of Representatives functioning under a written constitution that borrows from both British and American experience. Cabinet officers must also be members of parliament.

Australia sent volunteer units that fought bravely on the Allied side in the Middle East and on the Western Front during World War I. The demands of the British war effort benefited the Australian economy. During the period between the two World Wars, it continued to experience growth, as well as the emergence of a powerful labor movement pressing for benefits for workers. It was gripped by the worldwide depression, with a sharp drop in trade in 1931 and the following years.

Prior to World War II, the foreign policy of Australia was one of comparative isolation from the community of nations. In spite of this, Australia responded to the outbreak of World War II by coming to the aid of the British in the European War in 1939, and after 1941 joined the Allied war effort in the Pacific. For Australia, the war was made much more complicated and dangerous because of the closeness of Japan.

Japanese troops quickly conquered most of Southeast Asia by mid-1942. Australia became the base for the headquarters of General Douglas MacArthur after the fall of the Philippines. The main concern of the Australians was that they also might be invaded next. Darwin, the northern seaport, suffered heavy Japanese bombing raids. However, Allied victories in the Pacific and fighting by Australian troops in New Guinea prevented a Japanese invasion.

The Labour Party, led by Prime Minister John Curtin, came to power in late 1941 and was responsible for major changes in Australian international thinking during World War II. After such close cooperation with the United States in achieving ultimate victory, and with the decline of Britain as a world power, Australian strategic thinking turned toward the United States after the war.

The end of World War II brought another period of growth and prosperity. Substantial immigration, encouraged by the government, resulted in a larger population, primarily Caucasian. Until 1966 Australian immigration policies discriminated against non-Europeans, and in earlier years this had been known as the "white Australia" policy. Since 1966, successive governments have removed discriminatory restrictions. However, the overall rate of immigration was reduced during the 1970s though it has picked up dramatically in recent decades. Today, the influx of newcomers has brought marked changes in Australian society, lifestyle and culture.

The country was governed by a coalition of the Liberal Party and the Country Party between 1949 and 1972, for 17 years under its leader, the colorful Sir Robert Menzies, then Harold Holt, John Gorton, and William McMahon. All maintained steady support for U.S. policies and efforts in Southeast Asia. Australian troops took part in the war in Korea, the campaign against communist terrorists in Malaya (1948–1960) and the Vietnam War.

Elections in 1972 returned the Labour Party to power. The new Prime Minister, E. Gough Whitlam, a man of strong personality and intellect, recognized the People's Republic of China and established diplomatic relations with North Vietnam, North Korea, and East Germany. He also withdrew the remaining Australian troops from South Vietnam and moved to establish closer economic relations with Japan. He then abolished the draft, lowered the defense budget, began fairer treatment of the Aborigines and introduced ambitious domestic social programs.

The world oil crisis of the early seventies affected Australia as it did other communities. Both inflation and unemployment went up. Faced with these problems, Whitlam called an election in April 1974 that reduced his majority in the House of Representatives but did enable him to continue in office.

By late 1975, the continuously poor state of the economy and controversy over various Labour Party programs prompted the Liberal and National Country parties (the latter previously known as the Country Party) opposition to press for new elections. When Whitlam refused, the opposition took the unprecedented action of using its Senate majority to block the government's budget appropriation bills, leaving it without authority to pay its creditors, including federal employees

and recipients of social security and other benefits. As the government's reserves of money ran out, the constitutional crisis intensified. It is at this point that one of the more peculiar features of Australia's government became apparent.

The governor-general, Sir John Kerr, the representative of the British Crown, stepped in, dismissed the sitting prime minister, and asked J. Malcolm Fraser to form a new Liberal government. The party, in a coalition with the National Party, won the next election. Thus, a representative of a foreign nation was able substantially to interfere in Australia's domestic political process and no doubt added to the number of Australians who were increasingly dissatisfied with their ongoing relationship with the British Crown.

Eventually the question of Australia's relationship with Britain was put before the public in 1999 in a referendum that raised the question of replacing the governor-general, the representative of Great Britain's monarch, with a president chosen by the Australian parliament. It was a struggle that revolved both around questions of Australia's continuing ties to Great Britain and whether a president chosen by the parliament rather than at large by the population was a good idea. In the end, the referendum went down to defeat when only 45% of the population voted to support it while 55% opposed the idea.

Since then, political leaders have frequently expressed their support for another referendum on the issue in due course, but, as then Prime Minister Julia Gillard put it during the 2010 election campaign, there is also widespread affection for Queen Elizabeth II. Her view was that it might be best to wait until the end of the Queen's reign before returning to the question.

**Sydney Opera House**

**Team march at lifeguard competition, Manly Beach, Sydney**

A very different sort of controversy arose in 2003 when a series of sexual misconduct charges, personal and some associated with his earlier responsibilities as an Anglican Archbishop, began swirling around Peter Hollingworth, the then governor-general. With his public support collapsing, he became only the second governor-general in Australian history to resign.

## Government

Australia is a parliamentary democracy whose political institutions and practices follow the Western democratic model, reflecting both the British and American experience. The Australian federation has a three-tier system of government: the national government consists of Parliament (House of Representatives with 150 seats and the Senate with 76 seats) and the Government. The party or parties with a majority in the lower house constitute the government, controlling all ministries; six state governments, the Capital Territory and Northern Territory (similar to states); and some 900 local governmental bodies at the city, town, municipal, and shire level. Senators in the Federal Parliament serve six-year terms (senators for the two territories serve three-year terms), and representatives serve for three years.

Australia has a written constitution that came into force on January 1, 1901, when the colonies federated to form the Commonwealth of Australia. The constitution can be amended if a majority of voters in a majority of states plus an overall majority approve the change. Proposed changes must also be passed by an absolute majority in both houses of parliament. If an amendment is passed twice by one house

but fails in the other, the governor-general may submit the amendment to the electorate.

Australia pioneered the secret ballot in parliamentary elections and has used the system since 1879. Voting is compulsory at the national level. The franchise extends to everyone over 18 years of age except criminals and the mentally incompetent. The Australian system of law resembles the British system from which it was taken. Australian law places great importance on the rights of the individual. The law provides for habeas corpus (which prevents arbitrary arrest or imprisonment without a court hearing), bail, trial by judge and jury, the presumption of innocence until proven guilty, and prevention from double jeopardy.

The High Court resembles the American Supreme Court and deals with federal and state matters. It has original jurisdiction in important areas, including interpretation of the Constitution, determination of legal disputes between the federal government and state governments, suits between state governments, and suits between citizens of different states. The Court has a chief justice and six other justices. The Federal Court is a specialized court dealing with matters such as copyrights, industrial law, trade practices, bankruptcy, and administrative law, appeals from territory supreme courts, and tribunals administering federal laws. The other specialized court is the Family Court which deals with divorce, custody of children, and associated matrimonial property disputes.

All states and territories have supreme courts and magistrates' courts, and several have intermediate district or county courts that deal mainly with

state laws, federal criminal offenses, and federal income tax. The supreme courts have the same role at the state level as the High Court does federally. Magistrates' courts deal summarily with most ordinary offenses and preliminary hearings to determine whether sufficient grounds exist in more serious offenses to be tried before a judge and jury. The capital territory and external territories of Norfolk Island, Christmas Island, and the Cocos Islands have court systems similar in general to the states. Australia has independent federal, state, and territory police.

### Contemporary Political Issues

Today the major political parties are the Australian Labour Party (ALP), the Australian Democrats (AD) and the conservative Liberal Party. The ALP controlled the government from the early 1980s through the mid-1990s. A new party, the One Nation Party, appeared on the scene in 1997 and at times gathered significant support based on its strong anti-immigration policy. Especially dramatic in 1996 was the first successful election of a representative of the Australian Green Party, founded in 1992, to the federal parliament.

From 1996 to 2007, the government was directed by John Howard of the conservatives who won a fourth term in November 2004. This resurgence of the conservative Liberal Party began in the middle of the previous decade. After John Howard was selected as the new party leader in 1996, the conservative Liberal-National coalition won a landslide victory in national elections which gave the new government a 40-seat margin in the lower house of Parliament. Two years later Howard called for elections again with a platform advocating tax code changes and was reelected.

The new coalition government, which was formed after the October 1998 election, included both Howard's Liberal Party and the National Party. Together, the two parties won 49% of the vote. In 2001 Howard's party won an unprecedented third term in office. Nevertheless, the conservative trend of those years had gone beyond the policies advocated by Howard himself.

In 1996, a newly elected political independent, a former operator of a fish and chips shop named Pauline Hanson, rose to give her maiden speech in parliament. Once standing, she proceeded to attack the Australian Asian and Aboriginal community with considerable vehemence. Hanson claimed that Asian immigration was swamping Australia. Her attacks on Australia's non-white community were nothing new. Indeed, for much of Australian

# Australia

history a largely "whites only" policy had been the norm. However, this was in late 1996, and after years of official attempts by the government and business community to improve their relationship with Asia. The storm of controversy she began has not yet let up. Indeed, early political polls showed that 10% of the population supported her racist comments and many showed support for her new political movement, the One Nation Party, which she launched during the spring of 1997.

Although he was pushed to do so for months, not until March 1997 did the conservative prime minister, John Howard, launch an official effort to discredit the racism of Hanson's rhetoric. Still, over time, the momentum of her movement seemed to slow down. By late 1999, Hanson had lost her parliamentary seat, and considerable internal dissension had broken out within her One Nation Party. For a time she even found herself in jail due to violations associated with the original registration of her party.

Nevertheless, the antipathy toward foreigners, especially non-whites that Hanson had tapped into had attracted 8% of the vote in the national elections of October 1998 and played an important role, not so much in the Hanson's fortunes but those of the conservative Liberal party. That reality was particularly apparent during the summer and fall of 2001 when a weakening Liberal Government found itself faced with the imminent arrival of a ship carrying over 400 refugees from Iran, Iraq, and Afghanistan.

Taking a strong stand against allowing the refugees to land in Australia Howard's popularity rose considerably and allowed

**The Rt. Hon. John Howard,
former prime minister**

him to win an election in November for a third term as prime minister. Eventually the Liberal government funded neighboring governments to establish temporary reception centers. Eventually some Iraqis were able to gain refugees status in Australia but those from Afghanistan were less successful. Over all, the anti-asylum policy has continued to be a mainstay of Liberal politics, and former Prime Minister Howard made it clear that refuge seekers should have no hope to establish themselves on the Australian mainland. Rather, he made sure that any who tried were arrested and sent to detention centers, such as that on Christmas Island.

As Australia neared the fall of the 2004 electoral season, the Liberal Party, under John Howard's leadership, remained relatively popular. The opposition Labour Party also seemed to be growing stronger under the direction of their new leader Mark Latham, who had taken a strong stand against Prime Minister Howard's decision to send troops to serve in the American occupation of Iraq. Nevertheless, relatively few Australians had actually taken part in the unpopular campaigns in Iraq, and the numbers who had done so had already been significantly reduced, making the issue not something that would in the end fundamentally alter the election.

When the votes were cast, domestic economic issues were clearly uppermost in the voter's minds. Prime Minister Howard's Liberal Party managed to win an unprecedented fourth term in office and significantly strengthen his party's ability to pass favored legislation. By the time the new seats were allocated, Howard's party controlled both of the legislative chambers. This was a position of influence no prime minister had had in more than 25 years.

By 2007, though, the political mood in Australia had changed dramatically. Despite the fact that the economy had continued to do well under the Liberal's, the Labour party, under the leadership of the former diplomat Kevin Rudd, not only won a significant victory in the parliamentary elections, but Mr. Howard lost his own seat.

Many issues featured in Howard's defeat, not least simply fatigue over Howard's long tenure in office; he had become the second-longest serving leader in Australian history. Certainly, the opposition to the government's long-standing commitment to the American policy in Iraq had played a part. However, that had been an issue in 2004 as well. Nevertheless, it had apparently not had a significant impact.

This time, though, there was an additional issue. Rudd proclaimed on the eve of the historic vote that dealing with

the challenge of climate change was his number-one priority and that if elected he would lead Australia's delegation to the upcoming international climate change conference in Bali. Certainly, his attitude was in clear contrast to the Liberal Party's John Howard, who had long followed a policy of dismissing the issue of global warming. He had positioned Australia as the only developed country that followed the American lead in rejecting the Kyoto Treaty on climate change. The news in Australia had in recent years been particularly dominated by problems associated with drought. Even Howard had publicly asked people to pray for rain. Thus, the question of climate change denial had become an increasingly untenable political position.

However, Rudd's tenure in office turned out to be dramatically less successful than that of his conservative rival John Howard. Originally coming into power with very strong polling numbers, Rudd soon found himself unable to carry out some of his most important legislative priorities, such as climate-change legislation, while his popularity plunged. By the spring of 2010, after two failed efforts to pass climate legislation, he gave up. He had alienated many in his own party for what were described as poor leadership skills.

Eventually, in a surprisingly quick process in late June, Rudd's premiership collapsed almost overnight. His party replaced him with Julia Gillard, who became Australia's first female prime minister. In the elections that followed, Ms. Gillard managed to carve out a hairline win that eventually saw her Labour Party form a coalition government with the help of several independent members of parliament. But while Ms. Gillard had managed to win power within her own party, the party itself was unable to retain power in the next election in 2013.

The Liberal Party, led by Tony Abbott, had returned to power. On one of the most controversial issues that separated the two parties, dealing with climate change, the effort to impose a carbon tax had apparently played a significant role in weakening the Labour Party's popularity.

Once in power, the conservatives under Abott's leadership replaced the newly installed carbon tax with a much more minor effort to encourage emission reductions. That effort might have pleased some of his supporters but overall the new government's popularity dropped dramatically as it imposed a much more austere budget that antagonized many Australians.

By the fall of 2015 the Liberal Party's Tony Abbott was replaced in leadership by Malcolm Turnbull who after an initial period of significant popularity found his own numbers dropping. And the issues

**Former Prime Minister
Malcolm Trurnbull**

that separated the two parties: topics that would be very familiar to most Americans, battles from health care and entitlements to immigration.

Once the polling took place during the summer of 2016 Trumbull's conservative managed to retain power but in a fashion that lessened their core support and made the government more dependent on the extreme right politicians like Pauline Hansen of the One Nation Party, which had gained four Senate seats.

Turnbull's premiership was beset with difficult problems. A Royal Commission report into financial institutions revealed widespread fraud and a carelessness towards money laundering. Repercussions from another Royal Commission, on child sex abuse, played out in the courts, with senior Roman Catholic clerics, including Cardinal George Pell, in the dock. Pell was convicted in November 2018 on sexual charges. (The conviction was overturned in 2020.) Right-wing politicians talked nostalgically of past British links and the days of the "White Australia" policy. Economically, there was wage stagnation and inflated house prices. The Australian dream appeared to be unravelling. By the summer of 2018, Turnbull had lost the support of many in his own party, and he was replaced by Scott Morrison, the party treasurer, in September 2018.

Morrison had a reputation as being on the right wing of the Liberal Party. He had been a tough immigration minister, whose policies had been criticized by the United Nations Human Right's Commission. He was also skeptical about climate change and attempts to ban the use of coal. Yet in May 2019, he fought and won an election, allowing the Liberal Party to govern without assistance from other parties.

Morrison was now free to pursue twin policies of economic liberalization and social conservativism. The first included a major tax cut, while the refusal to endorse a national representative forum for aborigine interests formed part of the second.

The year 2019 went out—literally—in a blaze as the regular bush fires proved more intense than usual, following prolonged dry spells in several parts of the country. Handling the fires was largely a state not a federal matter, and there was often a lack of coordination between the different services. By the time the fires burnt out in February 2020, there were 33 dead, 3000 residences had been destroyed and billions of animals, mostly native Australian species, were killed. A Royal Commission found many faults in the way the fires had been handled and recommended a greater coordinating role for the federal government in future.

By then, Australia faced a new challenge as COVID-19 struck (see below). Much of the response was a matter for the states, rather than the central government, although the latter was behind the "jobkeeper" program that helped prevent mass unemployment in various sectors, including tourism. But the major role played by the states, which are responsible for health and education, boosted the reputation of local politicians, while the relatively hands-off approach by the Commonwealth government was seen negatively. By the end of 2021, Prime Minister Morrison's popularity was in decline and he faced heavy oppositiion in parliament.

Unsurprisingly, given the situation of the aborigine community, which has long complained of police brutality and other acts of discrimination, the "Black lives matter" movement spread to Australia. Despite the ongoing pandemic, protest meetings and demonstrations attracted large numbers.

### Society and Culture

In the years after Europeans first began settling in Australia, it quickly became a society largely dominated by Westerners whose culture resembled that of North America and England. The original aboriginal peoples, like Native Americans, increasingly lost their land to the aggressive Westerners and immigration laws strongly discriminated against Asians. This "whites only" attitude was a feature of Australian society until fairly recently. Within those parameters, Australians built a society similar to many other Western societies.

Education is free and compulsory through the secondary school.

**Race riots in Australia**

# Australia

Traditionally there have been no tuition fees at the 18 government-funded universities and at many colleges offering diplomas, degrees, and postgraduate studies.

Though it has vast spaces and relatively few people, Australia is highly urbanized, perhaps because most population growth and development has taken place only over the past 75 years. More than 80% of the population lives in urban centers and more than 60% are concentrated in five major state capitals.

Two cities dominate urban life. Sydney faces the southeast coast and has a population of more than 4.5 million; Melbourne (4 million) faces the southern Bass Strait. All of the cultural entertainment and events common to Europe and America are abundant in both. Perth, with a population of around 1.5 million and lying on the southwestern coast, is caressed by a gentle climate similar to that found in the Mediterranean and Caribbean resorts of the Western world.

Australia's Federal Capital is Canberra, the basic plan for which was conceived by Chicago architect Walter Burley Griffin shortly before World War I. Today, it is a garden city with over eight million trees planted in the last half century—and it occupies the site of a former sheep station (ranch) in the foothills of the Australian Alps.

As mentioned above the world of white Australia has usually not been shared equally with that of the aboriginal community whose lot is decidedly less attractive. Aboriginal Australians can expect to live 20 years less than whites and a quarter of them are unemployed.

Of late, new controversies have entered the public arena and aroused even more tensions between the two communities. On one hand there is growing sentiment against the social welfare programs the government supplies for the aboriginal community but on the other, great anxiety about a number of recent court decisions that have authorized greater aboriginal rights to millions of acres of land now being used by Australian ranchers.

To some aboriginal leaders, these new rights should allow their people to wean themselves from government welfare programs, something whites should theoretically welcome. But since aboriginal economic empowerment is, in the case of the land, tied to competing white claims, the problems are not likely to be resolved soon.

Australia has been increasingly forced to face up to other realities of their historical treatment of Aborigines. A greater sensitivity has developed about aboriginal history. This growing consciousness had taken the form of rewriting Australian history to include aboriginal perspectives and heroes as

**Kevin Rudd, former prime minister of Australia**

well as recognizing culturally "genocidal" policies like those that had seen generations of lighter-skinned Aborigines taken from their families to be raised in the white world.

During the run-up to the successful Olympics of 2000, there was speculation that the Aborigines might demonstrate during the games. But nothing very dramatic actually happened. More recently, there has been considerable discussion within Australia over issuing a formal apology for white Australia's historic treatment of them. But, the movement toward greater sensitivity has hardly made the tensions between the majority white community and Australia's Aboriginal community a thing of the past.

In February 2004, Sydney experienced the worst outbreak of civil unrest in over a decade after the death of a young aboriginal cyclist was blamed on the police. The subsequent rioting, which lasted over nine hours, left scores of police and civilians injured and was an obvious sign of the importance of making progress on one of the most long-standing issues within Australian society.

Once in power Kevin Rudd moved quickly to address the long simmering tensions with the Aboriginal community. In February 2008, the new prime minister officially apologized to Australian's indigenous community for their treatment at the hands of Australia's European settlers. On a more practical level, Rudd committed his government to lessening the gap in life expectancy between Aboriginal and non-Aboriginal Australians and bringing

more early childhood education to their communities.

When the Liberal Party returned to office in 2013, Aborigine interests received less attention, with economic considerations tending to be seen as more important. The 2017 "Uluru Statement from the Heart," which called for a voice for Australia's first people within the national government, found little support within the party. Prime Minister Abbott rejected the idea, as did his successor in September 2018. Prime Minister Morrison argued that it would amount to a "third chamber" in parliament, a claim rejected by supporters.

One change welcomed by Aboriginal groups, was the decision by the Australian Parks' Administration to close Uluru/Ayer's Rock, long demanded by the local Aboriginal people on religious grounds. When suggested during the Turnbull premiership, the idea had been rejected as damaging to tourism, but it went ahead in 2019 without any government opposition.

That there are still issues was shown in May 2020, when the world's second largest mining company, Rio Tinto destroyed two ancient Aboriginal rock shelters in Western Australia in order to extend a mine. It also admitted that it intended to destroy other sites in order to extend the mine. The resulting protests led to the resignation of the company's global chief executive and two others, and eventually to the departure of the company's chair in March 2021. Meanwhile, a December 2020 parliamentary inquiry, which concluded that Rio Tinto knew the value of what it was destroying but went ahead anyway, ordered the rebuilding of the destroyed structures.

Relations between the larger majority community and the aboriginal peoples are not the only source of ethnic tensions that have complicated Australian life. During late 2005, an outbreak of attacks by white gangs against Middle Eastern-looking men shocked locals and gained Australia a considerable amount of unwanted international attention. Eventually then Prime Minister Howard undertook a series of efforts to try to lessen the tensions. His primary goal was to bring Australia's Muslim community more into the mainstream of national life while rooting out extremists.

## Foreign Relations

As is often the case, Australian foreign relations have revolved around its relationships with its geographic neighbors, the Asian states of the region and the Western countries whose cultures are similar to those of Australia. Historically, Australia

# Australia

tended to orient itself toward the Western communities of North America and Europe but in recent years the emphasis has been more on its regional relationships. That movement was begun by the former Australian Labour Party governments.

In early 1996, however, there were indications that the new more conservative government intended to orient the country's foreign affairs position once again to emphasize Australia's relationships with the West. There were even some tensions with China during Howard's early months in office especially when he seemed to associate himself with those Americans who were talking of "containing" China.

Indeed for a time the new government seemed to be backing away from integrating Australia more closely into Asia but that change never developed into anything significant.

Under the then new prime minister, Australia continued its growing involvement in East Asia. Kevin Rudd was a professionally trained diplomat with long experience in China and spoke Mandarin Chinese well. However, that did not mean a completely smooth relationship. In 2008, as Tibet's capital Lhasa erupted in riots against the Chinese, Australia and the United States no doubt irritated Beijing by encouraging it to open a dialogue with the Dalai Lama.

However, encouraging a dialogue with the Dalai Lama was hardly Australia's only sin in Beijing's eyes. Especially irritating was the government's unwillingness, despite the Chinese government's request, to refuse entry to Rebiya Kadeer, an ethnic Uighur whom the Chinese accused of instigating the 2009 unrest.

Overall, the country's relationship with China continues to remain controversial. Indeed in late 2017 an Australian Labour Party senator resigned amid charges that he had allowed his legislative work to be influenced by Chinese political donors.

Indeed, since then relations have deteriorated even further. Partly this was the result of close Australian-United States ties. As the latter's relationship with China grew more tense under U.S. President Donald Trump over trade, security and the South China Sea, Australia tended to follow the U.S. line. In 2018, in a move widely seen as aimed at China, then U.S. Vice President Mike Pence announced that Australia and the U.S. were to construct a joint naval basis at Lombrun in Papua-New Guinea, a former World War II naval base, to protect freedom of movement in the Pacific. The policy of closer co-operation with the United States over China has continued under President Joe Biden.

Australian criticism of China over human rights and especially events in Hong Kong and Xinjiang have been resented by China, which had invested heavily in the country. When Australia began to

**Koala munching on his favorite food, eucalyptus leaves**

question Chinese accounts of the origins of COVID-19 and banned the Huawei Company from involvement in the 5G mobile phone rollout, China accused its leaders of a "Cold War mindset." Chinese investment plunged. In 2016, there had been 111 Chinese investments, but the figure was only 20 by 2020. A 47% drop in 2019 was followed by a further 61% fall in 2020. During 2021, China reduced ministerial-level contacts with Australia, and in May 2021, suspended all economic dialogue.

Concern over growing Chinese interest in the Pacific has continued to increase. This concern was shown by efforts to try to persuade the Solomon Islands' government to draw back from an agreement under which China would be allowed to berth warships in the islands and to land military and police units. Although Japan also expressed concern, the Solomans refused to budge. Such concerns also has led Australia to invest more in that region. It has also led it to be more accommodating in settling problems.

One such example was the conclusion in 2018 of an agreement with East Timor settling their long-running dispute over maritime boundaries. An issue that has not been finally settled is the fate of would-be refugees who have tried to enter Australia but have been moved to camps in Papua New Guinea and Nauru. While

**Tom Roberts, *The Golden Fleece*, 1894**

# Australia

an agreement was reached with Papua New Guinea in October 2021 to end the arrangement, the Australian government has insisted that the Nauru arrangement would continue, despite widespread international criticism.

Australia has also become more involved with the nations of Southeast Asia and especially their regional organization, ASEAN. Australia has also been working with its Asian neighbors and the U.S. to create an Asia-Pacific Climate-control regime. But Australia's efforts to integrate itself more deeply within ASEAN were not always been appreciated. It has been more welcome in trade matters. In November 2021, it joined the Regional Comprehensive Economic Pact, whose other memebers are ASEAN, Japan, New Zealand, South Korea, and China.

It was not merely the early conservative government's policies that caused occasional strains with Asia. The overt racism of the One Nation Party obviously also caused problems. Certainly, such developments have reinforced those in the Asian community who have not welcomed Australia's recent attempts to associate itself more closely with Asia.

But it was relations with Indonesia that especially complicated Australia's international position recently. Reversing themselves after a generation of supporting Indonesia's control over East Timor, the Australians began supporting East Timorese independence aspirations. Eventually, they ended up leading the United Nations international intervention force, which included 5,000 Australians, into East Timor in the late summer of 1999. Realistically the government had little choice. Although a generation of Australia's leaders had understandably believed that Canberra's relationship with the entire country of Indonesia was more important than the East Timorese plight, the wave of violence that occurred after Jakarta agreed to the referendum in East Timor aroused the ire and sympathy of the Australian population. Within Indonesia, there was an outpouring of popular Indonesian anger over the loss of East Timor that was often directed against the Australians.

The level of tensions subsided over time, and the relationship began improving. In June 2001 Indonesia's president, Abdurrahman Wahid, visited Australia, the first such visit by a leader from Jakarta in a generation. Later when Wahid's problems within his own country forced him from office, Australia's Howard was among the first foreign leaders to visit the new president, Megawati Sukarnoputri. But that did not stop an outpouring of anger against Indonesian officials during the spring of 2005 when a young Australian woman was imprisoned in Indonesia

**Former Prime Minister Tony Abbott**

on drug charges that most Australians thought were false. Relations soured in 2013 as it was revealed that Australia's intelligence agencies had been spying on the conversations not only of the Indonesian president but of his family and principal advisers.

Understandably, developments within in Indonesia are likely to remain especially important to Australia. Instability within a neighbor as large and as close to Australia as Indonesia is something Canberra has been concerned about for a long time. During the fall of 2002, Australians found out just how deadly Indonesia frustration and anger against the West and in particular, Australia could be. For that was the year that, at a popular Bali nightclub, a horrific bombing set off by Islamic terrorists with ties to the infamous al-Qaeda killed almost 200 people, around 100 of them from Australia. It was the first time that the potentials of terrorism had been so dramatically brought home to most Australians. But it was certainly not the last. In fact, another dramatic experience with terrorism hit Australians in late December of 2014 when 17 people were taken hostage in a café by a radicalized self-proclaimed Islamic cleric. Two hostages eventually died.

Australia also, of course, took part in the American invasion of Iraq of 2003. This was a move that not only aroused unprecedented criticism within Australia but a highly publicized resignation by a senior intelligence analyst and a very public rebuke against the prime minister by the Australian Senate.

Nevertheless, the prime minister remained adamant in his support of American President George W. Bush's Iraq

policy. Although the number of Australian troops dropped from the initial 2,000 employed during the initial occupation campaign to only 850, the Australian government, despite growing public opposition to the deployment, continued to insist that their troops would remain in Iraq until the country was deemed sufficiently stabilized for the Australian contingent to be withdrawn.

As was the case around the world, Australia's role in Iraq became a central feature within the nation's internal political environment. Howard's opponent in the national elections of late 2004, then Labour Party Leader Mark Latham, came out very publicly not only against Australia's role in the Iraq occupation, but against the entire American effort there as well. Latham was, of course, unsuccessful. But Labour won the next election. Kevin Rudd, the new prime minister who had campaigned on a promise to withdraw the country's forces in Iraq, acted. By June 2008, the last of the Australian troops were home.

Australia also took part in the war in Afghanistan from 2001 until 2021. Like other Western countries, it undertook a major airlift in August 2021, as part of the overall withdrawal. It has since mounted a refugee program. A reminder of the savagery of the war came in November 2020, when an independent enquiry carried out by a Supreme Court judge found that a special forces unit had taken part in unlawful killings in Afghanistan in the early 2010s. The unit concerned was disbanded and the findings are to be investigated further for possible charges. The office charged with the investigation said in November 2021 that the process might take years to conclude.

A new stage in relations with the United States and Britain began in September 2021, when the three nations signed a security pact. Under its terms, the U.S. and Britain will supply Australia with nuclear-powered submarines, apparently as part of attempts to counter growing Chinese influence and activity in Eastern Asia. This did nothing to improve relations with China, already tense over trade issues. It also set off a furious row with France, which had a $90 billion deal with Australia to build conventional submarines. The French company that was to build the submarines said that there had been no problems with it, while France's President Macron called Australia's move "a stab in the back."

## Economy

Australia's economy has changed much in the last 50 years from one that relied heavily on primary production to a mature, diverse one with nearly two-thirds of production in the service sector. World War II and postwar immigration spurred rapid expansion of secondary industry, diversification, and overall economic growth. Large investments were made in mining and energy projects. Although the agricultural and mining sectors account for a small part of the country's production, they make a large percentage of total exports. Australia leads the world in wool production and is a major supplier of wheat, meat, and sugar. Australia is also a leading exporter of coal and a major supplier of coal, iron ore, gold, bauxite, and alumina.

The export base was diversified in the 1980s, with the fastest growth in manufactured products and in services. Tourism has also been strong. Overall Australia entered the new century with a relatively strong economy. And unlike some of its neighbors, it was not merely recovering from the regional economic downturn of previous years. Australia was not significantly affected by the Asian economic crisis that enveloped so many of its neighbors. Even at the height of the crisis in 1998 Australia kept its economy in the black with its GNP registering a respectable 3% growth rate.

Like much of the world, Australia's economy experienced the same global slowdown that much of the world encountered. Several major firms went under, most notably Ansett, Australia's second largest airline. There have been more recent concerns about a slowing of the oil production from some of the nation's older fields that have spurred recent efforts to develop new supply areas. Doing so is important because Australia is currently producing about 80% of its own

petroleum needs and has developed a growing natural gas export industry. Still, those figures were not enough to insulate Australia against rising costs as elevated prices for oil worked its way through the Australian economy.

The government has also strengthened its formal economic ties with other nations. Free-trade agreements have been signed with Thailand, and the prime minister and ex-President George W. Bush signed their own free trade pact. Overall growth rates have been relatively healthy. The year 2007 came in with a rate around 4% while 2008 was only a bit over 2.3%.

Of course, that was before the full impact of the 2008 global economic slump hit. By the time 2009 expired, the nation's growth rate, while not in the negative numbers, had plummeted to around 1.3% annual growth rate. The fact that the numbers remained out of the red was only because of the nation's trade with China, which had managed to pull itself back from the brink much faster than many of the Western world's industrial nations.

Still there was plenty to feel good about. Almost alone among the developed world, Australia had kept up its economic growth. The 2010 figures came in at a reasonably healthy 2.7% growth while 2011 paralleled much of the world's average by losing about a third of that momentum as global economic uncertainties continued. Since then, the still relatively sluggish economic figures have forced the government to cut back on social services in order to fulfill yet another promise: to pull the national budget out of the red. In the years since the economy has vacillated at a growth floating around 2.5% with the conservatives campaigning on a platform

that suggested that the carbon tax implemented by the Labour Party had been a drag on the economy. However, Australian economists, when consulted, pointed to issues that had more likely played a role in the limited slowing of the economy over the last year. Nevertheless, the Liberal government, while admitting that climate change is quite real, has been much more cautious about actually confronting the challenge with the sort of policies championed by their political opponents.

Although the Liberal government pledged "business friendly" policies, marked by a tax cut, the economy faltered in 2018. Wages stagnated as house prices rose, and growth was 2.7%. The year 2019 proved worse, with growth dropping back to 1.8%. Then came COVID-19. As international trade and tourism faltered, Australian unemployment rose, reaching 7.5% in July 2020. As growth fell, the economy was plunged into its first recession since 1991. But the picture began to brighten as the diseases seemed under control. While growth overall was expected to be down by 3.8%, the last quarter showed a bounce back to 3.1%. The IMF, which had predicted tin January 2021 that the economy would grow by 3.2% in the year, revised this figure in April to 4.5%; in the event, according to Australian government figures, it was 4.2%. 2.8% is expected in 2022. This depends on the containment of the virus and a successful vaccination program, but Australians hope for better times ahead, now that its borders were fully opened again in February 2022..

## Australia's Environmental Challenge

Like the United States, Australia signed but did not initially ratify the Kyoto Climate Change Treaty of 1997. In some ways, that was rather curious as its negotiators had worked out a particularly advantageous position for Australia within the treaty. Nevertheless, along with the United States, Australia eventually became a prominent hold-out against the protocol. Over the last few years or so, though, Australia's position on climate change has begun to change. Former American Vice President Al Gore has been running training sessions in Australia to create a cadre of local climate change educators.

Meanwhile the population has become more sensitized to environmental concerns. The core issue is that Australia has been experiencing a long-term drought in the very areas where most of the population lives. Moreover, reports have gained a lot of attention that the Great Barrier Reef, one of Australia's most famous natural coral sites, is starting to die because of coral bleaching. This is a phenomenon associated with warming waters.

# Australia

Overall, the concern about global warming was particularly obvious in March 2007 when many of the lights in Sydney were switched off to help raise consciousness about the challenge of global warming. Nevertheless, unlike the Conservative party politicians in Britain, the former Australian conservative prime minister, John Howard, was unwilling to commit the nation to taking on the transition to a less carbon-emitting society.

Still the government began to encourage the replacement of the older incandescent bulbs for more modern, energy-efficient ones. But those tentative steps were clearly not enough for the Australian population. In what may have been the first election to turn primarily on the issue of climate change, Howard's Liberal government went down in a flaming defeat in November 2007 to a resurgent Labour Party leader, Kevin Rudd, who vowed to make climate change his highest priority. He promised to take Australia into the emerging international consensus symbolized by the conferences at Kyoto and Bali.

However, as former American President Obama has himself learned, promising to make progress on moving toward a more green economy and actually passing the legislature necessary to encourage that evolution are quite different things. Rudd's efforts were, as we have seen, stalled by significant opposition from the nation's conservatives, who during their own governing years had largely refused even to recognize the problem. Rather in August and then again in December Rudd failed to win a majority on legislation to introduce carbon permits that were expected to help spur movement toward a more green energy infrastructure. Eventually, as we have seen Rudd fell from office and Tony Abbott, the new conservative prime minister has been significantly less willing to confront the challenges of a changing global climate.

But even as Australia was making progress in recognizing the importance of confronting climate change, and fighting over the legislative tools required actually to do so, its own particularly great vulnerability became especially obvious. It had long been warned by organizations like the Intergovernmental Panel on Climate Change that it was especially vulnerable to fires caused by its decade-long drought. Those predictions became painfully true in early February 2009 when horrendous fires—the worst in Australian history—broke out in areas near South Australia, Victoria, and New South Wales. The fires claimed over 180 lives and destroyed more than a thousand square miles of territory.

More recently the problem was not drought provoked by fires but horrendous flooding again of the sort associated with a warming global climate capable of holding more water within the atmosphere. In Australia's case December 2011 was said to be the wettest month in the nation's history. As a result, flash floods inundated the northern Queensland area in a fashion locals described as an inland tsunami. The region's capital, Brisbane, flooded so badly that 20,000 homes were damaged.

Unfortunately 2012 saw Australia continue its record as one of the most environmentally challenged of the developed countries. During the winter of 2012 the nation was deeply impacted by record setting and terribly demanding heat wave that saw temperatures regularly go over 48°C or 118°F and in one case rise to a scorching 121°F. What was especially unusual was how long and how widespread the heat wave was across the continent during the early summer of January 2013. Particularly poignant was the fact that adjusting to the changing circumstances the Australian meteorological service added another color, purple, to their graphic temperature charts. This represents temperatures above 50°C, a scale they had not apparently previously felt was necessary.

Because of global warming, Australia may soon find itself in a particularly unusual situation. Not only is the nation itself ironically especially vulnerable to the combination of desertification and flooding of the sort contemporary climate change makes more likely. But it has the added problem of dealing with its island neighbors, who face the question not only of drought and dramatic flooding, but the very real threat of completely losing their land. The reason, of course, is that so many of Australia's Pacific island neighbors inhabit low-lying atoll islands that are deeply at risk from rising sea waters.

Despite Australia's especially great vulnerability to the ravages of a changing global climate, legislation designed to confront the challenge has been as controversial there as elsewhere. In Australia's case, a huge battle erupted over the effort to introduce a carbon emissions tax. It did eventually pass in the nation's legislature, but not without a great deal of political bloodletting. Even more important was the news that wind energy from wind turbines are now generating energy more cheaply in Australia than energy from either coal or natural gas. This is especially good news for those committed to moving Australia and the world away from the climate destabilizing effects of burning fossil fuels. On the other hand, Australia's enormous coal exporting industry is still thriving. This is not a bad thing in itself if coal could be processed for energy more safely. But as elsewhere, dealing with climate change has been politicized in Australia, and the Liberal Party promised to repeal the new carbon tax if it came to power. That promise became a reality after the fall of 2013 when they managed to defeat the Labour Party and began a series of policies that lowered the nation's commitment to dealing with the challenge.

As it has become clearer that the problem is not going away, with Australia suffering, drought, floods, and fires, the government agree in 2021 to aim for net zero carbon emissions by 2050. But the plan remains imprecise, depending on future technological developments rather than current action.

## COVID-19

Despite tensions in government to government relations, Australia's links with China have grown enormously since the country switched diplomatic recognition from the Chinese Nationalist government on Taiwan to the People's Republic of China in 1972. Chinese tourists are regular visitors, and many Chinese study in Australia. It was not surprising therefore, that soon after COVID-19 was identified in China in late 2019, it spread to Australia. The first case was detected in 25 January, while March and April saw the first wave, largely imported by travelers. Perhaps learning from past mistakes, a deliberative effort was made at a nation-wide approach, although the states had the primary responsibility. A National Cabinet was set up, which brought all the country's prime ministers together to discuss policy. Borders were progressively closed in February and March. Other measures included lockdowns, suspension of parliamentary meetings, the closure of non-essential retail and service industries, and an injunction to work from home where possible. Schools were closed in some areas but quickly returned to normal where the infection rate was low, such as the Northern Territories. Remote learning provided some cover. As elsewhere, there was much debate about the issue, given the low rate among children, and the possible damage to their education.

The dual system of government, with the states responsible for police, hospitals, and schools, meant that there was tension between local wishes to operate tight controls, and the central government's wish to open up in order to assist the economy. Victoria, however, had the largest number of cases and the most deaths in 2020, and the state government insisted on a hard lockdown in July 2021. It worked, but once relaxed, cases again rose.

There was no doubt about the economic problems. As noted, many workers were laid off, and others furloughed. The ban on interstate and international travel had serious consequences. Unable to recruit overseas students, universities cut 10,000 jobs. By the end of 2020, the economy went into recession for the first time since 1991.

By the end of 2020, there had been 28,000 confirmed cases and 909 deaths. Victoria accounted for 70% of the total cases and 90% of the deaths. This led to a hard lockdown in Melbourne. So fierce were the measures of control that the premier, Dan Andrews, became known as "Draconian Dan." But it worked. Although the disease had a severe economic impact at first, this began to ease by the end of 2020 and a recovery was expected in 2021. Of course, COVID-19 has not gone away. Victoria saw another surge in May 2021 and a return of modified lockdown measures. By the end of May 2021, the total number of Australia-wide cases was 30,105. The number of full recoveries was 29,086, and deaths were 910.

A year later, after spikes in January and April 2022, by mid-May, the total since the start of the pandemic was 6.5 million cases, and 7,718 deaths. Hardest hit had been New South Wales and Victoria, each of which had around 3,000 deaths. A vaccination program was slow to get under way, but steadily picked up speed.

But the decision to begin opening up was adhered to, and life began to return to normal. As elsewhere, it had been decided that Australians would have to live with COVID.

## The Future

Australia faces no immediate external threats. Its growing involvement with the countries of Asia, particularly the ASEAN states of Southeast Asia, can only help to improve its regional position. But it will require a sophisticated handling of the recent resurgence of some white Australian racist sentiments. Of course, as the influence and power of China grow, that relationship will continue to be complicated given Australia and China's often divergent world views even as their economic relations grow tighter.

Economically the situation has weakened somewhat. Two decades of impressive growth started to slow and the nation was forced to confront the economic challenges that a weaker economy has begun to present to the nation's citizens. Especially significant in that regard is the growing number of citizens who having problems meeting the ever higher costs of housing as wages stagnate.

The long-term situation is also more complicated. The nation is among the most vulnerable of the developed world to the ravages of climate change. The horrific fires that periodically engulf parts of the nation are a product of years of increasing drought that parched the land. But the climate crisis that is so dramatically impacting the world carries with it the threat of not only ever drier vegetation

bursting into flames, but ever more common flooding. Beyond Australia's shores, its regional neighbors, especially those of the South Pacific Islands from Tuvalu to Kiribati, are seeing their own homes even more threatened by rising waters. Under the circumstances, Australia's people will be faced even more often than in the past with the challenge posed by increasing numbers of potential refugees. However, in the future such refugees are as likely to be the consequence of climate change as of the geopolitical struggles that had previously brought them to Australia's shores.

As we have seen, though, while Australia remains, like the Philippines, one of the countries that has shown particularly great vulnerability to a changing climate, its government, in the hands of the conservative Liberal-Nationals, if not exactly in denial, has backed off somewhat from the most proactive policies of its predecessor, the Labour Party.

However, with the departure of the Morrison coalition from office following the elections of May 2022 and the Labor Party having the largest number of seats, its leader, Anthony Albanese, has promised that climate issues will be firmly back on the agenda. Even if he does not have an outright majority, likely coalition partners, such as the Greens, will be in favor of such a policy shift.

# New Zealand

**Auckland**

**Area:** 103,000 sq. mi. (268,276 sq. km., the land surface somewhat smaller than Colorado)

**Population:** 5,084,300 (June 2020)

**Capital City:** Wellington (city area), pop. 381,000 (2021 est.)

**Climate:** Temperate, with ample rainfall; subtropical conditions at the northern tip of the North Island, with colder temperatures in the South Island

**Neighboring Countries:** Australia, about 1,200 miles to the northwest

**Official Language:** English and Maori

**Ethnic Background:** European (69.8%), Maori (7.9%), Asian (5.7%), Pacific islander (4.4%), other (0.5%), mixed (7.8%), unspecified (3.8%) (2001 census)

**Principal Religion:** Protestant Christianity (82%)

**Main Exports:** (to Australia, China, U.K., Japan, U.S.) Meat and dairy products, fish, wool, wood products, and machinery

**Main Imports:** (Australia, China, Germany, Japan, U.K., U.S.) Petroleum, cars, trucks, iron, steel, plastics, textiles, vehicles, and aircraft

**Currency:** New Zealand dollar

**Former Colonial Status:** British Colony (1839–1907)

**National Day:** February 6 is Waitangi Day, anniversary of the signing of the Treaty of Waitangi in 1840 between the British and the Maoris

**Chief of State:** Her Majesty Queen Elizabeth II, represented by Governor-General Dame Alycion Cynthia Kiro (since September 21, 2021)

**Head of Government:** Prime Minister Jacinda Ardern (since October 2017)

**National Flag:** A purple field with the Union Jack in the upper left corner and four five-pointed stars in the right half of the field

**Per Capita GDP Income:** $44,491 (World Bank 2020 est.) (purchasing power parity)

The remote islands of New Zealand are about 1,200 miles from their nearest neighbor, Australia. Prior to the advent of air transportation New Zealand was one of the world's most isolated nations. The North Island is the more habitable of the two, and, though smaller than the South Island, it has more than half the country's population. Both islands are subject to earthquakes.

In the North Island there are volcanic and thermal areas dominated by three volcanic peaks, Ruapehu, Ngauruhoe, and Tongariro. All of them are active and given to occasional eruptions of steam and ash. In the central plateau area there is activity caused by the thermal pressure from deep within the earth in the form of geysers, hot springs, steam vents, and foul-smelling deposits of sulfur. The average annual rainfall for the whole country is about 60 inches, which allows for quick growth of rich vegetation to feed the millions of sheep that abound in New Zealand.

The South Island is much more rugged and contains the Southern Alps that equal their European namesake in beauty and wildness. In this mountainous region, the climate can sometimes be sub-Arctic. In contrast to the abundant growth of the North Island, the grasses of the South Island are more suited to rearing Merino sheep, which have a fine coat to protect them from the chilly air. Most of the sheep of the North Island are crossbreeds, designed to produce both meat and wool. It is interesting for those who live in the Northern hemisphere that the reversal of warm and cold zones and of summer and winter in the Southern Hemisphere make northern New Zealand the warmer, more subtropical area while the southern region is considerably colder.

## History

Though it is known that the Maori, the original peoples of New Zealand, initially came from Eastern Polynesia, the dating of this event varies widely. Their arrival has been dated from as early as the 3rd century A.D. to as late as the 13th. An extraordinary people, they were the heirs of one of the most impressive seagoing communities the world has ever seen. Even today the descendants of those great sea voyagers live throughout much of the Pacific.

Establishing themselves in their new home must have been especially demanding given that their society had originated in the warmer climates to the north. Upon arrival the most important food was the flightless birds, the moa, which they initially found in large numbers. Over time these animals were apparently hunted to extinction. Other foodstuffs, from marine life to small-scale farming, also contributed to the diet of these early peoples.

The Maori were not a united community. Rather, they were divided along both tribal lines and the different locations of their settlements. Once the Europeans arrived in the 17th century, access to advanced Western weapons became available thus making intra-tribal warfare even more deadly. Other factors also lowered the local population. As was common throughout the colonized world, the Maori lacked the antibodies necessary to resist Western diseases which depleted their numbers.

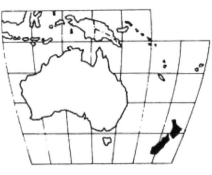

The first well documented European visit is that of Abel Janszoon Tasman, a Dutch sailor who apparently visited the islands around 1642. An account still remains of the first encounter that saw several Maori row out to the Dutch ship attempting to communicate. Unfortunately, that effort turned ugly, and only a short time later, Tasman lost three of his sailors in a clash with Maori from the southern Island. Discouraged by that first encounter, the Dutch sailed away leaving only their naming of the place, initially Nieuw Zeeland, as a contribution.

More than a century after Tasman left, the famous British seaman, Captain James Cook, arrived for an extended visit. Cook's stay included charting of the islands and a much more sophisticated contact with the Maori, whom Cook described as quite intelligent in his well-known work, *A Voyage towards the South Pole and round the World* (1777). Unfortunately for the Maori, Cook also wrote of the suitability of the islands for colonization. Over the next decades visits by various Europeans became common.

The growth of the whaling industry in the early 19th century also affected the islands. It attracted increasing European interest as whalers, especially those from Australia, created bases in New Zealand. The Maori were also drawn into the whaling economy as they supplied the Europeans with provisions and received rum and weapons from the outsiders. One Maori leader not only traveled to Australia and England, but bought weapons abroad which he later used to attack rival Maori tribes. Predictably, these bloody struggles disturbed local life enough to make settlement easier for the arriving Europeans.

Along with whalers and escaped convicts, religion also came to New Zealand via Australia. Missionaries settled in 1814 and quickly began the task of converting the Maoris to Christianity. Despite the Maori reputation for aggressiveness and cannibalism, some early missionaries were convinced that the Maori would be good candidates for conversion. Several branches of Western Christianity were active among Maori with denominations ranging from Anglicans to Catholics and Methodists. Eventually most Maori came to embrace some form of Christianity.

Over time, the islands became increasingly integrated with other British holdings in the South Pacific. Initially considered part of their Australian holdings they soon became a separate crown colony. In 1840, with the signing of the Treaty of Waitangi, Britain assumed direct control and according to the terms of the treaty was obligated not only to protect the Maori but ensure their land holdings. Not surprisingly, those promises were not

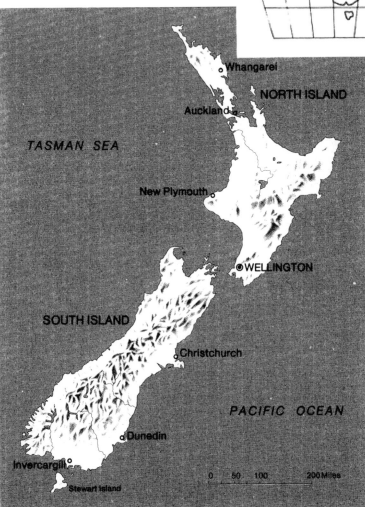

# New Zealand

**Late afternoon at Lake Hayes, South Island**

Courtesy of the New Zealand Information Service

upheld and by mid-century, the British found themselves often in open warfare with the Maori community. As was the case elsewhere, the indigenous community was unable to successfully resist the powerful Europeans and over time the Maori not only lost lands but saw their own numbers dwindle significantly. As time passed, the Maori population also underwent a gradual transformation. Many of them adopted Western dress, and began to practice agriculture and animal husbandry in the manner of the Europeans. Even for the European settlers, the economy of the islands allowed only a very difficult existence until the turn of the 20th century, when faster ships and refrigeration boosted the export of New Zealand's agricultural products.

Among the settlers the main political issue during the 19th century was the demand for greater representative government for the colony. By the mid 1850s, with the establishment of the New Zealand Constitution Act, the settler community gained more authority over domestic matters. Nevertheless, the British governors remained powerful and their clashes with elected local assemblies over their respective authority not infrequent. Yet a powerful democratic system emerged that was remarkably progressive on some issues. New Zealand, for example, in 1893 was the first country in the world to allow all women to vote in parliamentary elections. It was not until 1919, however, that women could stand for election to parliament. Three women were elected in the general election that year.

New Zealand was granted dominion status within the British Commonwealth in 1907 as a result of a new vigor imparted to the country's politics and administration by energetic Liberal leader Richard John Seddon, prime minister from 1893 to 1906. For all practical purposes, New Zealand was independent from that time on, a position officially recognized in the Statute of Wesminster in 1931. However, it was not until New Zealand ratified the Statute of Westminster in 1947 that it became officially independent.

As it entered World War I, New Zealand was governed by the Reform Party, and later by a coalition government. New Zealand fought on the allied side especially in campaigns such as Gallipoli. Though their soldiers won admiration for their fighting skills the losses were enormous. Later, New Zealand took part as an independent state in the peace settlement at Versailles. It also joined the League of Nations and was awarded a mandate over the islands of Western Samoa that had been captured from the Germans.

Adverse economic conditions from 1920–1940 created an increase in labor organization and unrest. However, by the late 1930s, prosperity began to return, aided by an ambitious program of public works and social security under a succession of Labour Party governments. New political parties emerged, the left-leaning Labour Party, which held power from 1935 to 1950, and the conservative National Party.

New Zealand took an active part in World War II. After the Pacific War began in 1941 its troops were engaged in battle not only in Europe but against imperial Japan. During the war years, both Labour and National worked together in a coalition. Once the war was over, Labour's political domination continued through the late 1940s until the more conservative National Party gained power in 1950. Since then, the two parties have alternated in power on a fairly regular basis, sometimes in coalition with smaller parties..

Despite New Zealand's ties to Great Britain, it was understood that its wartime defense depended more on the Americans than on the British. Thus, after the war, recognizing the declining influence of Great Britain and the rise of U.S. as an Asian power, New Zealand joined the ANZUS treaty (Australia, New Zealand and the U.S.) to provide security. It also joined the American led Southeast Asian Treaty Organization (SEATO) to meet the threat posed by the growth of communism in the region. During the 1960s New Zealand supplied troops for the American war in South Vietnam.

In 1972, The Labour Party came to power once again on a platform of more welfare benefits. The move to the left was reversed by late 1975 when Labour was defeated by a reinvigorated National Party that returned to power. These were the years when the country's economy suffered, buffeted by the loss of its main market when Britain joined the European Common Market. .

During the mid 1980s ties to the United States were strained when the Labour Party government announced that no nuclear-armed U.S. naval vessels would be allowed to call at New Zealand's ports. Since the U.S. refused on principle to say whether any particular vessel was nuclear-armed, this meant that no U.S. naval vessel could dock in New Zealand. As the U.S. began to apply counter-pressures, including the withholding of some intelligence information and threats to cut back on imports from New Zealand, the ANZUS alliance came under serious strain. Finally, in June 1986, at a meeting in Manila between Prime Minister David Lange and U.S. Secretary of State George Shultz, the chain broke, at least temporarily.

Good naturedly, Shultz admitted to the press that, "we part company on security matters as friends, but we part." Lange was equally gracious, but he stood by his government's policy. Eventually, the U.S. suspended its security arrangements with New Zealand until "adequate corrective measures" were taken. This ended New Zealand's military alliance with the United States.

New Zealand does maintain defense ties with Australia. The Lange government also proposed in 1987 a buildup of New Zealand's defensive forces. His stand was quite popular and contributed to Labour's reelection.

In 1987 the Labour Party won reelection with a 15-seat majority in the 120-seat parliament. In sharp contrast to previous Labour government policies Lange's administration now worked for economic liberalization and privatization that eventually weakened its support.

In 1990 the National Party, under the leadership of Jim Bolger, again returned to power. However, voters appeared to be more concerned about domestic issues, including the state of the economy than to the continuing controversy with the United States over nuclear matters. .

## Politics and Government

New Zealand is a member of the British Commonwealth with a parliamentary form of government. Differences with the British model include a unicameral House of Representatives, which until the last election held 120 seats. Today, as a result of a new proportional representation system, it includes 121 members. The prime minister's term is three years. The political system is multiparty in nature with the major parties being the National Party, Labour Party, The Maori Party, The Progressive Party, ACT New Zealand, and New Zealand First. The Queen of Great Britain is represented by a governor-general, a post currently held by Dame Alycyion Cynthia Kiro, whose presence complements the particularly important role women play in New Zealand's government and society. She is the third Maori to hold the post, the fourth woman, and the first Maori woman.

As has long been the case in neighboring Australia, there are those in New Zealand who have questioned the continuing influence of the British crown in the local affairs. That sentiment was particularly obvious in 2004 when a new supreme court, a court of last appeal, was created the replace appeals to the Privy Council in London. Even before that, New Zealand's leaders had also moved in 1975 to replace British honors with a New Zealand system. The changes were dramatic enough that the Labour Party, which then led the country, was accused by its opponents of the National Party of trying to turn New Zealand into a republic. Although there was little support for a move to a republic at that time, many politicians did favor such a move, which began to gather more widespread support in the 1990s. Supporters can be found across the political divide, and include Jacinda Arden, the current (2022) Labour Party prime minister. Many political figures have voiced support for such a move when the current British monarch, Queen Elizabeth II, dies. Yet, when the Queen's husband, Prince Philip, died in April 2021, New Zealand marked the occasion with every sign of continued loyalty to the Crown.

Other constitutional changes have included modification of the electoral laws to create a mixed-member proportional representation system. Mixed-member proportional representation (MMPR), introduced in 1996, which awards seats in a district based on the percentage of votes

**Opening day at a Christchurch prep school**

# New Zealand

**Former Prime Minister Helen Clark, leader, Labour Party**

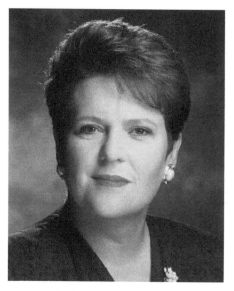

**Rt. Hon. Jenny Shipley, former prime minister**

won by a party, tends to help smaller parties and encourage a multi-party system. Six seats in parliament are specifically reserved for Maoris.

The 1990s were years of realignment among the country's political parties. The National Party under the leadership of then Prime Minister Jim Bolger maintained control, but its majority eroded and a coalition with minor parties was required to remain in office.

One significant development under the MMPR system was the growing strength of the New Zealand First Party. Long led by Winston Peters, a Maori lawyer, it has lashed out against Asian immigration that its supporters claimed had swamped the country with people who lacked a commitment to New Zealand. As we have seen in Australia, the anti-immigration campaign has attracted not only considerable attention and controversy but political support as well. Other small parties also found that the MMPR system gave them more influence in politics.

Thus, it is not surprising that Winston Peters ended up in a coalition government again headed by the National Party's Jim Bolger. Peters took the post of deputy, and treasurer. But that relationship, controversial in itself, did not work well. Over time tensions between Peters and his political colleagues fell to such an all-time low that they caused Bolger to lose his position as both head of the Nationalists and prime minister. In November 1997, Jenny Shipley, the transport minister, successfully challenged Bolger, taking over the party leadership and becoming the prime minister. If she had acted to strengthen the conservatives, it was too late, for polls had been showing that the National Party was

losing support to New Zealand's Labour Party, led by Helen Clark.

By 1999 Labour had returned to power alongside the smaller Alliance party. For Clark, a university lecturer in political science, it must have been a gratifying moment indeed. Clark had led the party since the early 1990s and had, twice before, almost become prime minister. Unfortunately for Clark, her support of various left-wing causes from Maori activism to her environmental policies alienated many moderate voters and made her first years in office quite difficult. Over time, her leadership gained more support, and she managed to win back many voters who were initially quite unhappy with some of her policies. Most notable were those associated with her effort to reimpose a level of economic regulation rejected by her predecessors. In fact, by the elections of July 2002 Clark solidified her leadership by leading her party to a significant victory (41.3% of the votes) over

**Prime Minister Jacinda Ardern**

the rival National Party's 20.9% (52 seats to the Nationals' 27).

That victory, along with Clark's ability to win allies among the 120-seat parliament, strengthened her hold on power. Still, as so often happens in politics, the population's support for the Labour Party ran its course by late 2008. In the November elections Clark's nine-year tenure in power came to an end. The resurgent National Power roared back to life with 58 seats to Labour's 43 elected to the House of Representatives.

The National Party retained its control of the government in the aftermath of the November 2011 elections by winning 59 seats in the 121-member chamber. The National Party's popularity continued to hold. Not only did Key win a third term in 2014 but the Labour Party suffered its worst showing in almost 100 years.

But as is the case often in democracies the Labour Party soon recovered and by the fall of 2017 Jacinda Ardern, its leader, had been sworn in as the nation's new prime minister, albeit in a minority coalition government with Winston Peters' New Zealand First Party, and a confidence-and-supply agreement with the Green Party. Ardern, at 37, was the world's youngest leader. Peters became the nation's Deputy Prime Minister.

The coalition government introduced a radical agenda, drawing on issues of concern to the separate parties. These included housing, welfare—this included aid with fuel payments for the elderly and the abolition of fees for first year university students—and the reactivating of the national superannuation scheme, introduced by an earlier Labour government but put on hold by the Nationalist Party when in office. New Zealand First was able to introduce a small measure of parliamentary reform, whereby MPs who switched parties were forced to resign, while the Greens concentrated on environmental issues. In another radical, if non-political, development, the prime minister took six weeks leave of absence following the birth of a daughter in June 2018—the second world leader to do so. Winston Peters took over in her absence.

The radical program faltered somewhat in 2019, with a lack of progress in many areas of reform. Citing a lack of consensus, the government abandoned a proposed capital gains' tax and admitted that its house building program was not a success. At the same time, New Zealand found that some of its widely held beliefs about what sort of society it was, were questioned. Child poverty was found to be unchanged despite government pledges to reduce it. In March 2019, a mass shooting at two mosques, which left 51 dead and 50 injured in the southern city of Christchurch, still recovering from the massive 2011 earthquake, shocked a country that had long believed it was among the safest in the world. There was little consolation in the fact that the killer was an Australian with extreme right-wing views. New stringent gun laws were brought in, to general agreement; they passed in parliament by 119 to one.

But by early 2020, the Labour government was losing popularity and it was expected that the Nationalist Party would regain lost ground and even a majority in the elections due in September. Then came the pandemic, which the government managed vigorously and successfully. (See below.) This certainly paid off in electoral terms. The elections, postponed for a month because of the pandemic, but eventually held on 17 October, proved a major triumph for Arden and her party, which secured the first absolute majority of any party since 1996. Labour took 65 of the 120 seats, up 46 from 2017. The Nationalist Party, which had suffered serious internal upheavals in May, got 33, down from 56 in 2017. The Green Party gained two seats, as did the Maori Party, while the center-right ACT gained nine. New Zealand First lost all its seats.

Despite the preoccupation with the pandemic, the new government began a program of serious reforms. Early in 2021, it announced that the Maori new year would be marked by a public holiday, to be known as Matariki, named after the star constellation known as the Pleiades. Formally proclaimed in April 2022, it was marked for the first time in June 2022. Other reforms included moves to provide more housing and limiting property speculation. A restructuring of the health service and a unit to oversee important matters, such as climate change, housing affordability, and the well-being of children, came in May. The prime minister conducted much international business via the internet.

Another terrorist incident took place in Auckland in September 2021. A Sri Lankan, already under close police observation as an ISIS supporter, stabbed seven people in a supermarket, none fatally. Police who were following him shot him dead when he charged them.

### COVID-19

As the seriousness of the virus sweeping China became apparent, New Zealand imposed a total border control and a domestic lockdown from March 26 until May 14 as the first cases were detected. Given its position far from other countries, this was highly effective but it came somewhat late as since the virus had had already arrived. From 50 detected on 25 March, numbers climbed to 71 on April 3, then fell away rapidly even after the lockdown was partially lifted in May. They rose again in August but responded to the widespread use of mask and sanitizer. Slight relaxation of the tight border controls say small numbers detected on arrival. In all, up to mid-April 2020, New Zealand had a total of 2,587 cases, of whom 2,459 fully recovered. There were 26 deaths. By then, cautious moves were in place to allow travel between Australia and New Zealand as vaccination rates increased. This was soon suspended, as the Delta variant hit Australia. The government continued a firm line. Border staff, for example, were warned that they would be moved away from front line duties if they refused to be vaccinated.

By mid-August 2021, New Zealand had a long period without community transmission. That month, however, an outbreak in Auckland led to a renewed lockdown. Schools and many businesses closed, and people were forced to stay at home. The nationwide lockdown was lifted in early September, but Auckland remained under lockdown. As in other

**Maori performer in Auckland**

parts of the world, masks were mandatory in public places. A determined vaccination program included compulsary vaccination for medical and border staff and for those working in schools, while legislation allowed companies to dismiss unvaccinated employees. Vaccination passes became essential for admission to many public places.

By December 2021, 90% of the population over 12 had been vaccinated. Deaths remained low, at 25 for the whole of 2021. This led to a relaxation of controls. The Auckland lockdown was finally lifted that month and residents who were fully vaccinated or those with a negative COVID test result were allowed to leave the city for the first time in 5 months. It was also planned to reallow quarantine-free international travel, in stages. In the event, this was postponed because of the Omicron variant, and did not begin until February 2022. It is in theory to be completed in October 2022.

But soon after the first relaxation, the Omicron variant struck, with cases rising rapidly. Most seem to have been community tranmissions. Those detected at the borders remained low. By 25 April, 56,570 cases had been reported, with five deaths. This brought the total number of deaths to around 650. But there was no lockdown and no reintroduction of vaccine pases. Masks were compulsary on transport, and people were expected to self-isolate.

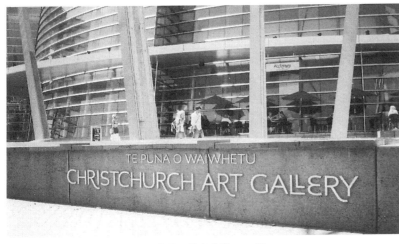

**Maori–English bilingualism**

# New Zealand

### New Zealand's Maori Community

While the evolving political landscape often attracts the most attention, other issues have played out dramatically as well. Race relations between the indigenous Maoris and the British-descended New Zealanders have been especially complicated. The problems date back to the 1840 Treaty of Waitangi which first saw the British officially establish themselves in New Zealand and, of course, the loss of so much Maori land to the new immigrants.

Today, the Maori constitute somewhere between 9% and 15% of the population (estimates vary and there are disputes about how many "pure" Maori there are), but they have shared little in the development of modern New Zealand. After public demonstrations in early 1995, both sides agreed to a multi-million-dollar settlement involving both money and the return of some Maori lands. The May 1995 deal also included an official apology for land that was confiscated as a result of conflict in the 1860s. By 1997 the government had agreed to the return of an equivalent of $450 million and some expected the eventual total to reach $750 million.

More symbolic but nevertheless important, the country's highest peak has now been renamed from Mount Cook (named after the explorer) to Aoraki which means "Cloud-Piercer" in Maori. Other place are also now known by their Maori names and the Maori name for New Zealand, *Aotearoa*, is frequently used. All these changes, like those going on in Australia, or for that matter, the United States, have been part and parcel of an attempt to

**Christchurch earthquake damage**

Courtesy of Michael Beck

make peace with the injustices of the past while not totally transforming the present.

Most New Zealanders hoped these settlements would mark the beginning of improved relations. But realistically, they are no more than partial payments on past debts. Much more will have to occur before a society emerges where the Maori share equally with the more recent New Zealanders the fruits of their society. For the moment that seems less likely. Since the 1990s, there have been Maori claims that they have rights over the fore-shore and the seabed dating back to the Treaty of Waitangi. The government ruled

against Maori demands that the national sea beds be considered Maori holding and designated the areas part of the "public domain." While then Prime Minister's Clark's party continued to support the separate Maori seats in parliament her opponents in the National Party have tried to eliminate them. The National Party's former leader, Don Brash, even went so far as to accuse the then prime minister of running a government with a "pro-Maori bias." Given the success of the Maori Party in in the 2020 elections, and the poor showing of the National Party, such sentiments are likely to be more muted for the immediate future. The issue continues to be live, with a court case in May 2021 conceding certain rights to the Maori.

### Society and Culture

Apart from the Maori community, life in New Zealand has for generations been predominantly British, more so than in any other nation of the British Commonwealth except for the British Isles. Isolated and relatively small, it has a reputation for being somewhat provincial and conservative, whereas British cultural values have rapidly changed since World War II. Thus, the old saying that New Zealanders are more British than the British has some validity today.

But the New Zealand of old has been changing rapidly. More than 200,000 Asian immigrants have established themselves in New Zealand and it is now estimated that by 2021 more than 13% of the country will be of Asian origin, a fact that has in recent years created an environment of racial tension that is unfamiliar

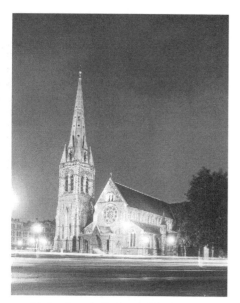

**Christchurch Cathedral before the earthquake of 2011**

**Bill English, former prime minister**

New Zealand

to many there. A recent human rights study reported that the vast majority of New Zealanders feel that the new arrivals experience a significant amount of discrimination.

Immigration is not the only way New Zealand is changing. Although it might seem somewhat quaint to Americans raised in the more challenging urban environments of the United States, the police in New Zealand in 2012 were given the right to carry weapons in their vehicles, as long as the firearms were kept in a locked box. The only police officers who regularly carry firearms are Diplomatic Protection Officers and those on duty at airports. The Police Association, the police trade union, has called for all officers to be armed. This has not happened, but officers now carry tasers.

The indigenous Maori community, though increasingly politically active, nevertheless lags behind its non-Maori neighbors in the basic social indicators such as longevity and unemployment. Most of the Maori live in urban areas having lost the bulk of their lands to the whites during the 19th century. Today there is considerable intermarriage between the Maori and the non-Maori New Zealanders. Nevertheless, as a group they are less represented in the professional classes. Unfortunately, they are over represented among prison populations, and experience a far higher unemployment record than their neighbors.

Compared to their non-Maori neighbors they are also more likely to depend on the government for employment. One bright spot since 2002 for the Maori is the brilliant feature length film *Whale Rider*, which captured the attention of a worldwide audience. The film certainly put the Maori people on the "map of world consciousness" in a way they never have been before.

One particularly interesting element of New Zealand's modern development has been the growing influence of women in political life. The country has had several female prime ministers and a woman emerged as the nation's first speaker of the House of Representatives. Indeed, Jacinda Ardern, who became prime minister in 2017 announced in early 2018 that she was pregnant took a six-week parental leave when her baby was born on June 21, 2018. Ardern returned to office on August 2, 2018.

**Foreign Policy**

Over the last few years, there has been more contact between New Zealand's leaders and those of the United States. In 1995, a significant step was taken to put New Zealand-U.S. relations back on track when Prime Minister Bolger headed for Washington for a meeting with President Bill Clinton. Leaders of the two countries had not met since former Prime Minister David Lange banned a U.S. ship suspected of carrying nuclear weapons from entering a New Zealand port. During the late 1990s Madeleine Albright made the first visit by a U.S. Secretary of State since the Tripartite ANZUS pact ended. Relations have improved even more in recent years, and the American defense secretary announced a relaxation on the ban long in place against New Zealand's naval ships visiting the U.S. ports. This was a ban that had been in place since the confrontation over U.S. nuclear ships in the 1980s.

Once the American-led War on Terrorism began, New Zealand became involved, sending her troops to serve alongside those from Australia in Afghanistan. But that improved relationship, after so many years of tension with the United States did not last long. Unlike its neighbor Australia, whose leadership committed itself deeply to the American occupation of Iraq, New Zealand's government refused to support the effort unless the United Nations sanctioned it.

When that did not occur, New Zealand refused to take part. This decision hardly improved relations with Washington. Later, however, in 2015, New Zealand Defence Forces were deployed in noncombative training in Iraq, where they remained until 2020. Meanwhile, in 2009 New Zealand's then conservative government had committed additional resources to the less controversial NATO effort in Afghanistan. Around 70 special elite military personal were sent to join the 150 non-combatants that were already serving there. Their return to New Zealand was expected after the operation's formal end in 2013, but in the event, it was not until 2020 that the majority were withdrawn. The last six remaining troops left in February 2021, a poignant conclusion to the mission that had seen ten members of the New Zealand military killed.

Since the establishment of a free trade area with Australia, the economies of the two nations have been closely intertwined though that has not always guaranteed that the two former British colonies would get along well. The two have differed, for example, on the details of the Bougainville settlement in Papua New Guinea's civil war. New Zealand, like Australia, has also attempted, over the last generation, to turn more toward Asia with its tremendous potential as an export market.

Like Australia, New Zealand, too, had been working to improve its relations with the People's Republic of China. It concluded free trade agreements with China in 2008 and with Hong Kong in 2010. Prime Minister Ardern made a one-day visit to Beijing in September 2019. Relations have become more complicated since 2020 by New Zealand's travel ban to contain COVID-19, which China has repeatedly criticized and by New Zealand's criticism of China over its South China Sea Policies, Xinjiang and Hong Kong. The Chinese government was also unhappy by a New Zealand call in May 2020 for Taiwan to be admitted to the World Health Organization. A free trade agreement with South Korea came into force in 2015. New Zealand has also taken part in anti-sanctions breaking operations against North Korea.

Again, like Australia, New Zealand became embroiled in regional politics as it also contributed to the international intervention in East Timor although its ability actually to support such an effort turned out to highlight significant deficits in the country's military equipment. In the aftermath the government made plans to spend several additional billions of dollars to modernize their military forces. In December 2021, New Zealand military and police responded to a request from the Solomon Islands' government for assistance in suppressing rioting. Earlier in 2021, New Zealand joined many other countries in condemning the military coup in Myanmar (Burma), and introduced various measures against the Myanmar military and aid restrictions.

During her tenure in office, Prime Minister Clark worked to transform New Zealand into a world leader in national sustainability. She officially declared the goal of making government services carbon neutral by 2012. This is a transformation that many other countries are likely to find themselves contemplating soon as consciousness grows about the threat of climate change.

Once New Zealand's Conservatives returned to power, though, there was initial concern about how the new government would deal with the challenge of Climate Change, given Prime Minister John Key's well known skepticism about the entire issue. Nevertheless, once in office, his government has continued down the path of building a legislative economic environment that complements the move toward a more green energy economy. This is despite the opposition the effort has raised among some members of the population and industry. The Ardern governments since 2017 have laid strong emphasis on the threat from climate change and the need to take action.

**Economy**

Agriculture, raising livestock, and dairying predominate in the New Zealand

339

# New Zealand

economy. Mining and other industries have been added in the post–World War II era which will continue gradual expansion. Over the last two decades, the economy has become much more involved in industrial production as well. The economy is also very dependent on foreign trade and this has caused some difficulty for unskilled workers. The government has taken the position, however, that this is the best course for the country in the long term. Recent governments have undertaken significant privatization efforts. The past years have seen a restructuring of the economy that makes it one of the least regulated in the world though in recent years there has been something of a reversal in that regard. Still though, New Zealand remains one of the most open economies in the world.

During the mid-1990s, the economy grew at a healthy rate of around 6%. But the economy has slowed considerably over the last few years and was stagnating even before the global recession of 2008–2009 set in. Tourism, which dropped during the Asian economic crisis of the late 1990s, has begun to show considerable improvement, although it took a severe downturn from 2020 to early 2022 because of the pandemic.

The spectacular success of the Lord of the Rings movies in the early 2000s has also played an important part in that industry's growth. The three films, all of which were filmed in New Zealand, highlighted far more than the storytelling genius of J. R. R. Tolkein, the original books' author, how extraordinarily beautiful parts of New Zealand are. This is a publicity bonanza New Zealand's tourist industry is busily taking advantage of.

Efforts to enhance New Zealand's trading relationships have picked up steam as well with progress made on establishing such ties with Singapore, South Korea, and possibly even Chile. Efforts were also begun to create a free-trade agreement with the People's Republic of China. During 2008, that effort was accomplished with the signing of a comprehensive agreement that would evolve over time and included both labor and environmental clauses. Since then the trade with China has grown significantly and the government announced plans to push total trade to around $20 billion by 2020. Unfortunately, the pandemic hit New Zealand's trade, just as it hit most other countries, but it has picked up. One new development was an agreement in principle on a free trade agreement with Britain in 2021, with details to be worked out in 2022.

Meanwhile the nation has worked to develop closer economic relations with India and the membership of the Association of Southeast Asian Nations (ASEAN).

There has even been discussion of an Asia-Pacific free-trade zone.

There is hope that such an arrangement can also be established with the United States, as Australia has already done. For the moment, though, there is little reason for significant optimism about the economy. Real growth in 2007 was only around 3%, and 2008 was much lower at −1%. More significantly, that was before the full impact of the 2008 global economic slowdown had begun. When 2008's global recession hit, it was quite significant and worse than that experienced by its near neighbor, Australia. The growth rate for 2009 was in the low negative rate of over 1.4% while the government carried out a host of measures. They included subsidizing employers who lowered the work week to encourage more hiring and funding various public works and infrastructure projects, such as a plan to build a bike network across the nation. Unfortunately, in sharp contrast to many of its regional neighbors, the economy has not shown a significant uptick since the dark days of 2009. Growth for 2010 came in at a continuingly anemic 1.5%. Since then growth has remained at around 2.5%. The COVID pandemic hit the economy overall in 2020, but it recovered in 2021. 2022 may be affected by the Omicron variant's effects but, without lockdowns, is still expected to be moderately good.

## The Environment

In Australia, as we have seen, one of the issues that divided the two major parties was their respective acceptance or rejection of the growing scientific consensus on the dangers of global warming. Under the circumstances, the defeat of the Australian conservatives made a very significant difference in that nation's goals relating to climate change. That is apparently not the case in New Zealand. John Key, the former National Party prime minister, has stated publically that he understands the threat of climate change. More importantly there were news reports in the early summer of 2009 that the government was working with the leaders of the defeated Labour Party to develop a coordinated policy on that important issue. Doing so is especially important given that New Zealand, like Australia, faces the challenge of potentially large numbers of climate refugees from the nearby Pacific Islands. On a positive note, New Zealand's relatively small population and less intense industrialization compared to some other nations makes it less environmentally damaged.

The nation does make its own special contribution to the growing density of global greenhouse gases. In this case the culprit is the nation's large sheep and

cattle herds, which emit into the atmosphere significant amounts of methane—a much more powerful greenhouse gas than CO2. This problem is recognized, and experiments are being carried out to introduce modified bacterium into the intestines of the animals that would help lessen the problem. However, according to at least one recent survey, the population is somewhat ambivalent about whether that is a good idea. The larger legislative efforts to move toward a greener energy infrastructure have also aroused opposition. But progress has been made. New Zealand and the United States just signed an agreement to cooperate on green energy development.

While energy issues often dominate national politics globally they tend to play out differently in different countries. In New Zealand's case, the big controversy last year was about the privatization of several state-owned energy companies to help deal with budgetary shortfalls. However, the plan has been delayed due to a legal battle over water rights initiated by the Maori community.

The challenges of a changing climate caused by humanity's excess burning of carbon fuels involve a relatively newly understood cost of our fossil-fuel-driven industrial society. Other problems have been understood far longer. This includes the dangers of oil spills. That is exactly what happened in 2011 when a Greek container vessel went aground spilling over 1,700 tons of heavy fuel oil and creating an environmental mess that continued for months. Eventually the ship's chief officers were sentenced to jail terms for negligence.

## The Future

The last few years certainly have had its challenges, especially the enormous earthquake damage done to the beautiful city of Christchurch. Fortunately the damage was only to property rather than the enormous loss of life both Indonesia and Japan have endured recently. But the damage was significant enough, and it will take a long time to repair all the damage. More discouraging was yet another earthquake that hit the same area some months later. The pandemic and the measures taken to cope with it were a major set back in 2020 and 2021, but now seem to have been overcome.

Still, compared to so many of its neighbors, New Zealand has plenty to be grateful for. The economy has remained reasonably stable and pulled out of the 2008 recession eventually. The pandemic has been another setback, but again recovery seems to be under way.. Some progress has been made in dealing with the injustices of the past through efforts at reconciliation with the Maori people. Plans are currently under way to attempt a settlement with the Maori over historical claims arising out of Treaty of Waitangi. The goal is finally to reconcile such claims ..

New Zealand also continues to be a social trend setter internationally. The growing strength of women throughout its political infrastructure continues unabated. As it once pioneered the role of women as voters, it more recently passed a law allowing civil union of same-sex couples. In the spring of 2013 gay marriage was legalized.

But it was, sadly, not the nation's role as a leader in gender equality and gay rights that brought New Zealand front and center in the world's concerns in 2019. Rather it was the spill-over of anti-Muslim white nationalism that reared its intolerant head as New Zealand experienced its first massacre of people peacefully praying at a mosque in March that year. While the Auckland attack in 2021 was less devastating, it was yet another sign that the country is not isolated from international trends, both positive and negative.

For a nation that has historically thought of itself as considerably more safe than many other developed nations it was quite a shock. On the other hand, like its neighbor Australia had done some years earlier in the wake of a similar horror, the nation's leaders moved decisively to outlaw military-style assault weapons. .

# Island Communities of the Western and Southern Pacific

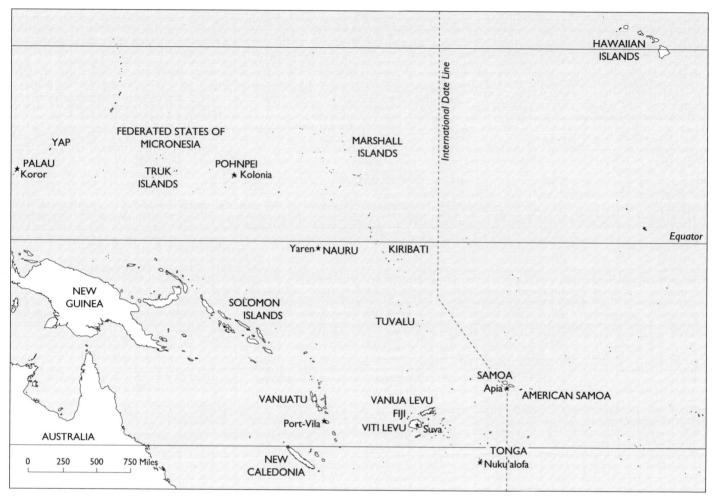

**"... the seas bring us together, they do not separate us ..."**

(From the preamble to the Constitution of the Federated States of Micronesia)

Scattered like brilliant pieces of jade across an area covering more than 3 million square miles of the Pacific Ocean lies a number of island nations. Most of them have achieved independence. They range in population from Fiji's 901,620 to Nauru's 10,878 inhabitants. Most islanders are ethnically Polynesian, Melanesian, or Micronesian, although some Asian groups, such as Indians, Chinese, and Vietnamese, have settled in the islands. Over the years these island communities have lived under the control of a range of outside countries including Britain, Germany, France, the United States, Japan, Australia, and New Zealand.

Many of the islands also bear the scars and rusted armaments left to them by the savage engagements waged throughout the region during World War II. Gentle wavelets brush the bows of hulking battleships sunk during those years, while palm trees sway in the cooling breezes that moderate the tropical climate.

Long before the Common Era, Asian peoples migrated into the area. Much later Spanish explorers combed the region for gold and spread Christianity, a belief that was often blended with the traditional religious practices. In the latter 1800s, German control was imposed over much of the region. After World War I, Japan, a wartime partner of the victorious allies, was rewarded with possession of the former German-held islands north of New Guinea.

During World War II, an island-by-island struggle by Allied troops wrested the area from the Japanese. Eventually the islands came under control of the United States, Great Britain, France, Australia, and New Zealand. Over the following decades, most of the islands achieved independence although some, like French Polynesia, remain colonial possessions.

Following World War II, the United Nations established a trusteeship over three of the primary archipelagos north of the equator: the Carolinas, the Marshalls, and the Marianas. The U.S. became the trustee, and the Department of the Interior took jurisdiction over the islands from the Navy in 1951. In 1975, the Northern

Marianas were given separate status as a commonwealth. The rest of the territory was divided into the Marshall Islands (in the East), the Federated States of Micronesia (FSM, in the South), and the Republic of Palau (in the Southwest).

In January 1986, the United States approved a Compact of Free Association for the islands. It consists of two agreements included in the same act of Congress—one between the U.S. and the Federated States of Micronesia and the other between the U.S. and the Marshall Islands. The Compact provides for extensive cooperation in numerous areas, such as law enforcement, narcotics control, economic and technical assistance, resolution of nuclear-cleanup programs, health care, fishing rights, etcetera. With the enactment of the Compact, the Trust Territory of the Pacific Islands ceased to exist. The FSM and the Marshall Islands are now independent republics and members of the United Nations. American Samoa, in contrast, is considered a territory of the United States.

The Solomon Islands, Tonga, and Vanuatu are members of the (British) Commonwealth of Nations. Nauru and Tuvalu are special members. In other words, they

# The Islands

may participate in all functional Commonwealth meetings and activities, but do not have the right to attend meetings of the Commonwealth Heads of Government. The states of this region, including Australia and New Zealand, also formed the South Pacific Forum in 1971. In 1985 they signed a South Pacific Nuclear-Free Zone Treaty barring such weapons from the region's territories, but not banning transit of its waters by nuclear-armed or nuclear-powered ships. In 1997, a subsidiary organization emerged called the Forum Economic Minister's Meeting (FEMM), which held its first meeting at Cairns, Australia. The new group, which has largely been sponsored by Australia, was partly a result of the latter's concern about the increasing economic weakness of its South Pacific Island neighbors. Other spinoffs include a Women's Forum. The Forum has not been without tensions. These came to a head in February 2021, when Palau, the Marshall Islands, the Federal States of Micronesia and Nauru left the group after a new secretary general was elected from Polynesia rather than Micronesia, whose turn it was.

## Contemporary Issues in the Region

Economically the different communities are relatively varied. Some islands are very specialized, such as Nauru with its dependence on phosphate deposits. Others produce in varying quantities basic products of a tropical climate: coconut and palm oil, fish, copra, fruits, and—in the case of Fiji—sugar and some gold. Timber is also an important export for both Fiji and the Solomon Islands. Another prime source of income is tourism including more eco-tourism which is growing in the region.

While people might consider these small communities far from the mainstream of modern international life, they have often been deeply impacted by current developments. In fact, some islands, Nauru for example, have become refugee centers for Iraqis and Afghans who had initially tried to enter Australia. Palau made international news as well in early 2009 when it agreed to take some of the prisoners the new American administration needed to relocate after its decision to close the American detention camp at Guantanamo Bay.

These may be small nations, but they can provide support on wider issues. Several states have been accused of supporting money laundering from Russia, while Nauru's recognition of the Russian occupation of Abkhazia and South Ossetia led to economic assistance, including, it is believed, financing the country's airport. Australia used Nauru and Papua-New Guinea to provide detention centers for would-be immigrants from the early 2000s. There were many domestic and

Guinea came to an end in 2021. By then, there were only 120 left there. Because of Nauru's economic decline as supplies of phosphate have ran out, the arrangement has been an important element in the country's economy. It continues but the numbers have dwindled from about a thousand in 2016 to just over a hundred by mid-2021. As they competed for diplomatic recognition China and Taiwan have provided aid to those countries which have switched sides, as the Solomon Islands and Kiribati did in 2019. Tuvalu, Nauru, the Marshall Islands and Palau continue to recognize Taiwan, so the competitions may be expected to continue.

There is some concern in both Australia and the United States about China's increased activity in the region. In April 2022, Australia made a direct appeal to the Soloman Islands not to go ahead with its pact with China. Although the details are not public, what purported to be a draft was leaked. This indicated that Chinese naval vessels would be able to dock in the Soloman Islands and that Chinese military personnel would be stationed there. The Soloman Islands' government rejected the approach, arguing that it was an attempt to infringe on the country's sovereignty. Some have seen this as a result of Australia's apparent belief that, because it was a major aid donor in the region, it would be listened to, without having to do much else to build up relations.

A number of these island communities have cashed in on the globalized economy by selling their Internet country codes to those looking for easy and readable World Wide Web addresses. Within the globalized economy, these new roles have also brought new problems. This is especially the case as some have been under considerable international pressure lately to pass laws against money laundering.

In recent years, there has been talk of expanding cooperation between the nations of the region on global political and economic issues. Those talks came to fruition when the new South Pacific Free-trade Area was created. Such a move had been felt necessary in order to have

a unified voice speak for these communities in negotiations with emerging trade blocks like the Northern American Free Trade Agreement (NAFTA) and the European Union (EU).

With such ideas in mind, several of these island nations recently joined the United Nations in order to give more voice to their concerns within the forums of the international community. The perils of not having such a voice were especially obvious during the era of nuclear testing.

In the 1950s during the Cold War, the Eniwetok and Bikini atolls in the Marshalls were the site of H-bomb tests. Such testing deeply disrupted the lives of many of the region's people. Not surprisingly there was considerable local discontent over the use of the area as a nuclear testing zone. The most recent incident arose when, in 1995, the French announced plans to resume nuclear testing. The decision resulted in an unsuccessful effort by New Zealand to use the International Court of Justice to pressure Paris not to start testing again. There was also a worldwide protest that included both government religious and anti-nuclear groups.

Finally, in January 1996, then French President Jacques Chirac announced that, having carried out six of the originally planned eight nuclear tests, the program would be discontinued. But while nuclear testing has been ended, the demands for compensation continue. In May 2005, the Marshall Islands once again unsuccessfully made their case to Congress and the Bush administration for increased compensation.

Of particular importance has been the end of the long-running civil war in Papua New Guinea. The situation was resolved after agreement was reached between many of the states in the region to provide military units for peace-keeping on Bougainville. Happily the situation has improved in recent years. Still, many of these communities have continued to experience instability. Among the best known, for example, are an uprising of armed militias in the Solomons and significant political instability in Tonga, Fiji, Nauru, and Kiribati over the last decade.

One of the most interesting challenges for the region will be the introduction of new technologies that will allow for mining the sea during the 21st century. At that point, some have speculated that the ocean floors surrounding these islands may be worth billions of dollars. Working out the legal and financial details now will facilitate harvesting the advantages in the future. On that front Fiji requested that the United Nations recognize its claim to an extended continental shelf. If accepted, that would facilitate the nation's ability to exploit those undersea resources.

Once idyllic and isolated communities, these nations are increasingly part of the globalized world community. Their new status can have an impact on a very personal level. The people of Palau, for example, were recently cited by the World Health Organization as the seventh-fattest people on the planet for the all-too-common habit of living without proper exercise "complemented" by a poor diet full of Western fast foods. Meanwhile HIV/AIDS has become increasingly common. Samoa declared a national emergency in November 2019 because of a serious outbreak of measles. Thousands were taken ill, and there were 81 deaths, mostly among children. But in many ways these island nations were not just experiencing some of the worst habits of the larger industrialized nations. They are, in fact, likely to be among the first victims of the West's development choices. On the other hand, there are certainly advantages in becoming more integrated with the world community. Nauru implemented its first national cellular and Internet service in 2009. The event was so celebrated that the nation's president declared a national holiday.

## COVID-19

COVID-19 was slow to get a grip in the Pacific Islands. Distance and small populations helped but the restrictions on tourism had a severe economic effect. Many cruise ships were quarantined. Passengers were usually repatriated but crews were often detained for months. Borders were closed and later additional measures, such as the use of masks and hand sanitizer were introduced. By June 2020, there were 305 known cases and numbers generally remained low until the autumn. The U.S. territory of Guam traced its first outbreak to a naval vessel visit in March 2020; by the end of the year, there were 120 deaths and 7000 confirmed cases. French Polynesia, which had closed its borders, reopened them in June. After 193 deaths and 16,000 cases, it closed them again. On the whole, the region escaped any serious outbreaks. Micronesia seems to have remained entirely free and began a vaccination program early in 2021. International aid, much of it from Australia, helped smaller countries cope with the extra costs, while politicians seemed quite happy to operate via video links.

## The Hunga Tonga–Hunga Ha'apai Volcanic Eruption

Toward the end of December 2021, an eruption began in the under-sea Hunga Tonga–Hunga Ha'apai volcano in the Tongan Islands, which reached its climax on 15 January 2022. This created a massive ash cloud and a series of tsunamis throughout the Pacific. There was massive destruction in Tonga, which was cut off from the rest of the world for several days. While the islands clearly needed assistance, Tonga had up to that point only one case of COVID-19 and was concerned that the virus might be introduced through aid workers. But it needed supplies of food, medicine, and drinking water, so elaborate measures were taken to try to avoid direct contact between islanders and aid workers. With international help, limited communications facilities were resumed by 20 January. Despite the elaborate precautions, two port workers in the capital, Nuk'alofa, tested positive on 2 February. Although a nationwide lockdown was imposed, by mid-April, there were 8,761 confirmed cases and 11 deaths. But although serious concerns about the virus remained, by then, there had been a significant reduction in quarantine measures, while vaccination proceded apace. On April 19, 2022, the Pfizer vaccination began to be given to children aged 5 to 11.

## The Fate of Nations: Rising Waters and Low Lying Atolls

Dwarfing all other issues is the reality that the terrain of the majority of these island communities is quite low, sometimes only a few feet above sea level. Given growing fears about global warming producing a rise in sea levels, many of the region's inhabitants are deeply concerned about their nations' long-term future.

Over the years their officials have at times spoken out forcibly, as Tuvalu's former leader did at a recent World Summit on Sustainable Development. He denounced both the United States' and Australia's "contribution" to the growing problem. Tuvalu's leaders have plenty of reason for concern. Ocean levels around the islands have been rising almost an inch a year. Some believe the Islands themselves might be submerged by 2040.

Over the last few years the realities of a changing climate and water levels have become particularly evident in Tuvalu. Most

**Fiji's Daydream Island—at risk from rising waters**

dramatically has been the contamination of local waters by seepage of sea water that is increasingly polluting the island's fresh water supplies due to the rising seas.

But rising waters were not the only challenge the people of Tuvalu have had to face recently. Especially extreme weather of course has become common place around the world. In Tuvalu's case, much of the island nation's infrastructure was devasted in early 2015 by the power of Cyclone Pam which was reported to have carried with it some of the most powerful winds ever, a storm that made homeless almost half the population.

Unfortunately, these island communities often find themselves in a difficult position politically. New Zealand's government has long been more and more conscious of the growing threat of climate change. However, Australia, their other large and influential neighbor, remained until quite recently one of the last nations on earth not to sign the Kyoto Climate Protocols. With the election of the Labour government in Australia, which campaigned on a platform committed to confronting climate change, at least that complication was removed for a time. In fact, Australia's former prime minister, Kevin Rudd, committed his government to helping the islands deal with the many challenges associated with climate change. Rudd's successor from his own Labour Party, Julia Gillard, promised to continue his climate related policies. But as we have seen, government changes in both New Zealand and Australia have brought to power some less committed to confronting the climate crisis. This is a

development that cannot be very reassuring to the citizens of these especially low-lying islands.

Politics aside, the realities of the threat continue. In 1999 two of Kiribati's uninhabited islands disappeared under the ocean. The remaining 33 islands remain at risk. The residents of Tegua, Vanuatu, were forced to abandon their island in December 2005.

It is not clear how long it will be before the permanent rising of the oceans threatens the homes of even larger numbers of people. Nevertheless, increasing numbers are already at risk during water surges brought on by stronger tropical storms, which are themselves made more powerful by the warming waters.

Rising water is not the only concern. As it happens, the coral reefs that surround these atoll nations may be among the earliest victims of global warming. These reefs are very sensitive to rising temperatures. They have long served as something akin to Holland's dikes in holding back the strongest of the ocean's surges during storms. Given that the region contains the largest collection of coral communities in the world, this issue is particularly important. The local communities depend on the coral for everything from defense against the sea, fishing, and the all-important ability to attract the money of visiting tourists.

Some Pacific Island leaders have done what they could to protect their people. The government of Tuvalu has already negotiated emigration rights for its entire citizenry to depart for New Zealand if the situation becomes critical. The emerging

climate crisis, though, is not merely the fault of outsiders far from these chains of island communities. The Solomon Islands have themselves been chastised for unsustainably logging their forests, which has a direct negative impact on global warming.

On an international level these island communities have also been quite active. In the early summer of 2009 a coalition of the islands successfully urged the United Nations General Assembly to pass a resolution encouraging the Security Council to recognize the threat climate change poses to their peoples. Meanwhile Tuvalu was particularly active at the 2009 Copenhagen Climate meeting in encouraging the international community to adopt a more serious attitude about carbon reductions. It announced its own plans to spend $20 million to employ enough renewable technologies to supply the entire country with green energy by 2020.

In theory, the peoples of the South Pacific have much to be grateful for. After all, after a generation of international negotiations, the global community finally signed the Paris Climate Accords in late 2015 which have the potential of significantly slowing down long-term global warming. The reality though is that the process of rising waters has already begun and the effort to slow that particularly devastating feature of a warming world was most probably accomplished too late for many of those who call the South Pacific Islands home. The 2021 Glasgow climate conference foresaw a grim future for Tonga, one of the most vulnerable places in the world to unchecked climate change.

# Bibliography and Additional Resources

## Podcasts

iTunes, Apple's free app which is designed to support its various audio and video Internet feeds allows one to subscribe to an enormous range of free international news services and academic think tank productions. By using this resource one can have access to an incredible range of materials available as audio podcasts. They can be most easily accessed simply by googling them or using the search feature within iTunes itself.

Among the best of them are:

Al Jazeera Listening Post
Asia Pacific Forum
BBC World Service Global News
BBC World Service Outlook
Carnegie Council
Center for Strategic and International Studies
Council on Foreign Relations Podcasts
Commonwealth Club of California
Inside Council of Foreign Relations Events
PRI America Abroad (US National Public Radio)

## Websites
### Useful General Sites
www.un.org (Website for United Nations, many links)
www.unsystem.or (Official UN website)
http://en.cop15.dk/ United Nations Climate Change Conference official site
www.oecd.org/daf/cmis/fdi/statist.htm (OECD site)
www.osce.org (Site of OSCE)
www.wto.org (World Trade Organization site)
www.worldbank.org/html/Welcome. html (World Bank news, publications with links to other financial institutions)
http://www.ncuscr.org/ (National Committee on United States-China Relations)
www.ceip.org (Carnegie Endowment for International Peace, using a fully integrated Web-database system)
www.cia.gov/index.html (Central Intelligence Agency)
http://climateprogress.org/ (Best website to follow the science & politics of climate change)
www.odci.gov/cia (Includes useful CIA publications, such as *The World Factbook* and maps)
www.state.gov/www/ind.html (U.S. Department of State, including country reports)
http://usinfo.state.gov (U.S. Department of State)
lcweb2.loc.gov/frd/cs/cshome.html (Library of Congress with coverage of over 100 countries)
www.embassy.org/embassies (A site with links to all embassy websites in Washington, DC)

www.psr.keele.ac.uk/official.htm (Collective site for governments and international organizations)
http://www.ruf.rice.edu/tnchina/ (Excellent site on various aspects of China)
http://www.crisisgroup.org/home/index.cfm? (International Crisis Group-excellent for dealing with specific contemporary issues)
https://www.lowyinstitute.org/ (The Lowy Institute is an independent, nonpartisan international policy think tank located in Sydney, Australia)
https://rusi.org/ (The Royal United Services Institute (RUSI) is the London-based world's oldest independent think tank on international defense and security)
https://www.sipri.org/ (Stockholm International Peace Research Institute—an international resource on global security)
https://www.eastasiaforum.org/ (Canberra-based East Asia Forum think tank)

## Newspapers, Journals, Television, Radio (with good coverage on international affairs)
www.chicagotribune.com (Named best overall US newspaper online service for newspapers with circulation over 100,000.)
http://foreignpolicy.com/ (*Foreign Policy*, excellent journal of Global Politics)
www.currenthistory.com (*Current History*, features monthly issues on specific areas)
www.csmonitor.com (Respected U.S. newspaper, *Christian Science Monitor*. Named best overall US newspaper online service for newspapers with circulation under 100,000)
www.economist.com (British weekly news magazine)
www.theguardian.com (British daily newspaper)
www.japantimes.co.jp (Japanese daily newspaper)
www.nytimes.com (Respected U.S. newspaper, *The New York Times*)
www.straitstimes.com (Singapore newspaper)
www.washingtonpost.com (Good international coverage)
www.foreignaffairs.org (One of best-known international affairs journal)
www.cnn.com (Latest news with external links)
www.news.BBC.co.uk (British Broadcasting Corporation site)
www.c-span.org (Includes C-SPAN International)
www.xe.com/ucc/ (Current exchange rate of currencies)

## General Books and Reports
Anderson, Benedict. *Imagined Communities.* New York: Verso, 1991.

Arifin, Evi Nurvidya, ed. *Older Persons in Southeast Asia: An Emerging Asset.* Singapore: Institute of Southeast Asian Studies, 2009.

Best, Antony, ed. *The International HIstory of East Asia, 1900–1968: Trade, Ideology and the quest for order.* Abingdon, UK, and New York: Routledge, 2010.

Borthwick, Mark. *Pacific Century: The Emergence of Modern Pacific Asia.* Boulder CO: Westview Press, 1992

Bracken, Paul. *Fire in the East: The Rise of Asian Military Power and the Second Nuclear Age.* New York: HarperCollins Publishers, 1999.

Burke, Anthony, and Matt McDonald, eds. *Critical Security in the Asia-Pacific.* Manchester, UK, and New York: Manchester University Press, 2007.

Cain, P. J., and A. G. Hopkin. *British Imperialism, 1688–2000,* Second Edition. London: Longman, 2001.

Chandler, David P., et al. eds. *End of Empire: 100 Days in 1945 That Changed Asia and the World.* Copenhagen: Nordic Institute of Asian Studies, 2016.

Clifford, Mark L., and Peter Engardio. *Meltdown: Asia's Boom, Bust, and Beyond.* Upper Saddle River, NJ: Prentice-Hall Press, 1999.

Cumings, Bruce. *Parallax Visions: Making Sense of American–East Asian Relations at the End of the Century.* Durham, NC: Duke University Press, 1999.

Das, Dilip K., ed. *Emerging Growth Pole: The Asia-Pacific Economy.* Upper Saddle River, NJ: Prentice Hall, 1997.

Dutta, Manoranjan. *Economic Regionalization in the Asia-Pacific: Challenges to Economic Cooperation.* Northampton, MA: Edward Elgar Publishing, 1999.

Eccleston, Bernard, and Michael Dawson, eds. *Asia Pacific Profile.* New York: Routledge, 1998.

Encyclopedia Britannica. *2018 Book of the Year,* Encyclopedia Britannica, Inc. Chicago, 2018. The last year published.

Europa Reginal Surveys of the World, Vol. 7: *The Far East and Australasia 2022.* London and New York: Routledge, 2021.

Fairbank, John K., et al. *East Asia: Tradition and Transformation,* Second Edition. Boston, MA: Houghton Mifflin, 1989.

Flannery, Tim. *The Weather Makers: How Man Is Changing the Climate and What It Means for Life on Earth.* New York, NY: Grove Press, 2005.

Flynn, Norman. *Miracle to Meltdown in Asia: Business, Government and Society.* New York: Oxford University Press, 2000.

Frankopan, Peter. *The Silk Roads: A New History of the World.* London and New York: Bloomsbury Publishing, 2015.

Frankopan, Peter. *The New Silk Roads: The Present and Future of the World.* London

# Bibliography and Additional Resources

and New York: Bloomsbury Publishing, 2018.

Ginsberg, Mary. *The Art of Influence: Asian propaganda*. London: British Museum, 2013.

Hobsbawm, Eric, and Terence Ranger. *The Invention of Tradition*. Cambridge: Cambridge University Press, 1983.

Ikenberry, G. John, and Inoguchi, Takashi. *Reinventing the Alliance. US–Japan Security Partnership in an Era of Change*. NY: Palgrave, 2003.

International Institute for Strategic Studies, ed. *The Military Balance 2022*. London and New York: Routledge, 2022.

Institute of Southeast Asian Studies. *Regional Outlook Southeast Asia*. Singapore: Institute of Southeast Asian Studies, annual, 2020.

Kristoff, Nicholas D., and Sheryl WuDunn. *Thunder from the East: Portrait of a Rising Asia*. New York: Alfred A. Knopf, 2000.

Lal, Rollie. *Understanding China & India: Security Implications for the United States & the World*. Westport, CT: Praeger Security International, 2006.

Lewis, D. S., and Wendy Slater, eds. *The Annual Register*. Published since 1758. Ann Arbor, MI: ProQuest, annual.

Liu, Ts-ui-jung, ed. *Asian Population History*. New York: Oxford University Press, 1999.

McArthur, Meher. *The Arts of Asia: Materials, Techniques, Styles*. London: Thames and Hudson, 2005.

Mahbubani, Kishore. *The New Asian Hemisphere: The Irresistible Shift of Global Power to the East*. New York: Public Affairs, 2008.

Marcelo, M. Suarez-Orozco, and Desiree Baolian Qin-Hilliard. *Globalization Culture and Education in the New Millennium*. Berkeley and Los Angeles: University of California Press, 2004.

Muhlhausler, Peter. *Linguistic Ecology: Language Change and Linguistic Imperialism in the Pacific Rim*. New York: Routledge, 1996.

Olds, Kris. *Globalization and the AsiaPacific: Contested Territories*. New York: Routledge, 1999.

Palgrave Macmillan, eds., *The Statesman's Yearbook*. London: Palgrave Macmillan, annual.

Pan. Lynn, general editor. *The Encyclopedia of the Overseas Chinese*. Richmond, Surrey UK: Curzon Press, 1999.

Preston, Benjamin, et al. *Climate Change in the Asia/Pacific Region: A consultancy Report Prepared for the Climate Change and Development Roundtable*, October 2006, available at www.csro.au.

Rigby, S. H. *Marxism and History: A Critical Introduction*. Manchester, UK: Manchester University Press, 1998.

Rohwer, Jim. *Re-Made in America: How Asia Is Rebuilding Its Economies American-Style*.

New York: Crown Publishing, 2001.

Simone, Vera, and Anne T. Ferara. *The Asian Pacific: Political and Economic Development in a Global Context*. White Plains, NY: Longman Publishing Group, 1999.

Tan, Gerald. *The Newly Industrializing Countries of Asia*. Portland, OR: Times Academic Press, 2000.

Terry, Edith B. *How Asia Got Rich: The Rise and Fall of Asia's Miracle Economies, What Went Wrong, and How to Fix It*. Armonk, NY: M.E. Sharpe, 2000.

Thompson, Roger C. *The Pacific Basin since 1945: A History of the Foreign Relations of the Asian, Australasian, and American Rim States and the Pacific Islands*. White Plains, NY: Longman Publishing, 1994.

*The Wilson Chronology of Asia and the Pacific*. Bronx, NY: H.W. Wilson, 1999.

The World Watch Institute. *The State of the World*, New York, NY: W. W. Norton & Company, annual, 1984–2017. .

Yomamato, Yoshinobu, ed. *Globalism, Regionalism, and Nationalism: Asia in Search of Its Role in the 21st Century*. Malden, MA: Blackwell Publishers, 1999.

**East and Southeast Asia**

Abuza, Zachary. *Militant Islam in Southeast Asia: Crucible of Terror*. Boulder, CO: Lynne Reinner, 2003.

Adams, F. Gerard, and Shinichi Ichimura, eds. *East Asian Development: Will the East Asian Growth Miracle Survive?* Westport, CT: Greenwood Publishing Group, 1998.

Athukorala, Prema-Chandra, and Chris Manning. *Structural Change and International Labour Migration in East Asia*. New York: Oxford University Press, 2000.

Balme, Richard, and Brian Bridges. *Europe-Asia Relations: Building Multilateralisms*. Basingstoke, England: Palgrave Macmillan, 2008.

Barlow, Colin, ed. *Institutions and Economic Change in Southeast Asia: The Context of Development from the 1960's to the 1990's*. Northampton, MA: Edward Elgar Publishing, 2000.

Bessho, Koro. *Identities and Security in East Asia*. New York: Oxford University Press, 1999.

Calder, Kent. *Embattled Garrisons: Comparative Base Politics and American Globalization*. Princeton NJ: Princeton University Press, 2007.

Christie, Clive J. *A Modern History of Southeast Asia: Decolonization, Nationalism, and Separatism*. New York: Tauris Academic Studies, 1996.

Cohen, Warren I. *East Asia as the Center: Four Thousand Years of Engagement with the World*. New York: Columbia University Press, 2003.

Collins, Alan. *Security and Southeast Asia: Domestic, Regional, and Global Issues*. Boulder, CO: Lynne Reinner, 2003.

Compton, Robert W., Jr. *East Asian Democratization: Impact of Globalization, Culture and Economy*. Westport, CT: Greenwood Publishing Group, 2000.

Devasahayam, Theresa W., ed. *Gender Trends in Southeast Asia*, Singapore: Institute of Southeast Asian Studies, 2009.

Dickinson, David, and Andrew W. Mullineux, eds. *Finance, Governance and Economic Performance in Pacific and South East Asia*. Northampton, MA: Edward Elgar Publishing, 2001.

Dingh, Daljit et al., eds. *Southeast Asian Affairs*. Singapore: Institute of Southeast Asian Studies, annual since 1974, 2021 edition. .

Dittmer, Lowell, et al., eds. *Informal Politics in East Asia*. New York: Cambridge University Press, 2000.

Erixon, Frederik, and Krishnan Srinivasan, eds. *Europe in Emerging Asia: Opportunities and Obstacles in Political and Economic Encounters*. London: Rowman & Littlefield, 2015.

Fogel, Joshua A. *A History of East Asia*. Upper Saddle River, NJ: Prentice Hall, 2001.

Girard-Geslan, Maud, et al., trans. J. A. Underwood. *Arts of Southeast Asia*. New York: Harry N. Abrams, Inc., 1997.

Harland, Bryce. *Collision Course: America and East Asia in the Past and in the Future*. New York: St. Martin's Press, 1996.

Hayton, Bill. *The South China Sea: The Struggle for Power in Asia*. New Haven, CONN.: Yale University Press, 2014.

Heidhues, Mary Somers. *Southeast Asia: A Concise History*. New York: Thames & Hudson, 2000.

Helgesen, Geir, and Rachel Harrison, eds. *East-West: Reflections on Demonization: North Korea Now, China Next?* Copenhagen: NIAS Press, 2020.

Hersh, Jacques. *The USA and the Rise of East Asia since 1945*. London: St Martin's Press, 1993.

Ho Khai Leong, ed. *Connecting and Distancing: Southeast Asia and China*, Singapore: Institute of Southeast Asian Studies, 2009.

Huxley, Tim, and Susan Willett. *Arming East Asia*. New York: Oxford University Press, 1999.

Ikeo, Aiko, ed. *Economic Development in Twentieth Century East Asia: The International Context*. New York: Routledge, 1997.

Keay, John. *Empire's End: A History of the Far East from High Colonialism to Hong Kong*. New York: Scribner, 1997.

Kelly, David, and Anthony Reid, eds. *Asian Freedoms: The Idea of Freedom in East and Southeast Asia*. New York: Cambridge University Press, 1998.

Kim, Samuel S. *East Asia and Globalization*. Lanham, MD: Rowman & Littlefield Publishers, 2000.

Lee Hwok Aun and Christopher Choong, eds. *Inequakity and Exclusion in Siutheast*

# Bibliography and Additional Resources

*Asia: Old Fractures, New Frontiers*. Singapore: ISEAS, 2021.

Leifer, Michael, ed. *Dictionary of the Modern Politics of South-East Asia*. New York: Routledge, 1995.

Levine, Alan J. *The United States and the Struggle for Southeast Asia, 1945–1975*. New York: Praeger, 1995.

McCloud, Donald G. *Southeast Asia: Tradition and Modernity in the Contemporary World*. Boulder, CO: Westview Press, 1995.

Mills, James H., and Patricia Barton, eds. *Drugs and Empires: Essays in Modern Imperialism and Intoxication, c.1500–c.1930*. Basingstoke, UK, and New York: Palgrave Macmillan, 2007.

Moeller, J. O. *Asia's Transformation: From Economic Globalization to Regionalization*. Singapore: ISEAS, 2020.

Montesano, Michael, J., ed. *Regional Outlook: Southeast Asia 2010–2011*, Singapore: Institute of Southeast Asian Studies, 2010.

Morley, James W. *Driven by Growth: Political Change in the Asia-Pacific Region*, Revised Edition. Armonk, NY: M. E. Sharpe, 1998.

Mulder, Niels. *Inside Southeast Asia: Religion, Everyday Life, Cultural Change*. Boston, MA: Charles E. Tuttle Company, 1997.

Murphey, Rhoads. *East Asia: A New History*. Reading, MA: Addison-Wesley Educational Publishers, 1997.

Neher, Clark D. *Southeast Asia in the New International Era*, Fourth Edition. Boulder, CO: Westview Press, 2002.

Park, Seo-hyun. *Sovereignty and Status in East Asian International Relations*. Cambridge: Cambridge University Press, 2017.

Ramesh, M., and Mukul G. Asher. *Welfare Capitalism in Southeast Asia: Social Security, Health and Education Policies*. New York: Saint Martin's Press, 2000.

Ravich, Samantha F. *Marketization and Democracy: East Asian Experiences*. New York: Cambridge University Press, 2000.

Reid, Anthony. *Southeast Asia in the Age of Commerce, 1450–1680, Volume 1: The Lands below the Winds*. New Haven, CT: Yale University Press, 1990.

Reid, Anthony. *Southeast Asia in the Age of Commerce, 1450–1680, Volume 2: Expansion and Crisis*. New Haven, CT: Yale University Press, 1993.

Rodrigo, G. Chris. *Technology, Economic Growth and Crises in East Asia*. Northampton, MA: Edward Elgar Publishing, 2000.

Rowen, Henry S. *Behind East Asian Growth: The Political and Social Foundations of Prosperity*. New York: Routledge, 1998.

Rozman, Gilbert. *Northeast Asia's Stunted Regionalism: Bilateral Distrust in the Shadow of Globalism*. Cambridge: Cambridge

University Press, 2004.

Sajise, Percy E. editor, *Moving Forward: Southeast Asian Perspectives on Climate Change and Biodiversity*, Singapore: Institute of Southeast Asian Studies, 2009.

SarDesai, D. R. *Southeast Asia. Past and Present*, Fifth Edition. Boulder, CO: Westview, 2003.

Scott, A. C. *The Theatre in Asia*. New York: Macmillan, 1973.

Shaffer, Lynda N. *Maritime Southeast Asia to 1500*. Armonk, NY: M.E. Sharpe, 1996.

Sinpeng, A., and Ross Tapsell. *From Grassroots Activisim to Disinformation: Social Media in Southeast Asia*. Singapore: ISEAS, 2021.

Sponsel, Leslie E., ed. *Endangered Peoples of Southeast and East Asia*. Westport, CT: Greenwood Publishing Group, 1999.

Sunquist, Scott W, ed. *A Dictionary of Asian Christianity*. Grand Rapids, MI.: Eardmans, 2001.

Tarling, Nicholas, ed. *The Cambridge History of Southeast Asia, Volume 1: From Early Times to c. 1800*. New York: Cambridge University Press, 1992.

Tartling, Nicholas, ed. *The Cambridge History of Southeast Asia, Volume 2: The Nineteenth and Twentieth Centuries*. New York: Cambridge University Press, 1992.

Thomson, James C. et al. *Sentimental Imperialists: The American Experience in East Asia*. New York: Harper and Row, 1981.

Tongzon, José L. *The Economies of Southeast Asia: The Growth and Development of ASEAN Economies*. Northampton, MA: Edward Elgar Publishing, 1998.

Trocki, Carl. *Gangsters, Democracy, and the State in Southeast Asia*. Ithaca, NY: Cornell University Press, 1998.

Viviano, Frank. *Dispatches from the Pacific Century*. Reading, MA: Addison-Wesley, 1993.

Westad, Odd Arne. *The Global Cold War*. Cambridge: Cambridge University Press, 2005.

Wolters, Oliver W. *History, Culture, and Region in Southeast Asian Perspectives*. Ithaca, NY: Cornell University, Southeast Asia Program Publications, 1999.

Woo-Cumings, Meredith. *Development States in East Asia*. Ithaca, NY: Cornell University Press, 1999.

World Bank Staff. *East Asia: the Road to Economic Recovery*. Washington, DC: The World Bank, 1999.

Wu, Shicun, and Keyan Zou. *Maritime Security in the South China Sea: Regional Implications and International Cooperation*. Farnham, England: Ashgate, 2009.

Yamamoto, Tadashi, ed. *Emerging Civil Society in the Asia Pacific Community: Nongovernmental Underpinnings of the Emerging Asia Regional Community*. Seattle, WA: University of Washington Press, 1995.

Zhao, Suisheng. *The Dynamics of Power Competition in East Asia: From the Old Chinese World Order to the Post-Cold War Regional Multipolarity*. New York: Saint Martin's Press, 1997.

**Australia**

Adelman, Howard, et al., eds. *Immigration and Refugee Policy: Australia and Canada Compared*. Toronto: University of Toronto Press, 1994.

Andrews, E. M. *The Anzac Illusion: Anglo-Australian Relations during World War I*. New York: Cambridge University Press, 1993.

Argy, Fred. *Australia at the Crossroads: Radical Free Market or a Progressive Liberalism?* Concord, MA: Paul & Company Publishers Consortium, 1998.

*The Australian Reference Dictionary*. New York: Oxford University Press, 1992.

Baker, Richard W., ed. *The ANZUS States and Their Region: Regional Policies of Australia, New Zealand, and the United States*. New York: Praeger, 1994.

Bassett, Jan. *The Oxford Illustrated Dictionary of Australian History*. New York: Oxford University Press, 1996.

Beilharz, Peter. *Transforming Labor: Labor Tradition and the Labor Decade in Australia*. New York: Cambridge University Press, 1994.

Bell, Stephen, ed. *The Unemployment Crisis in Australia: Which Way Out?* New York: Cambridge University Press, 2000.

Bennett, Tony, et al. *Accounting for Tastes: Australian Everyday Cultures*. New York: Cambridge University Press, 1999.

Brawley, Sean. *The White Peril: Foreign Relations and Asian Immigration to Australasia and North America, 1919–1978*. Sydney: University of New South Wales Press, 1995.

Broeze, Frank. *Mr. Brooks and the Australian Trade: Imperial Business in the Nineteenth Century*. Melbourne: Carlton University Press, 1993.

Butlin, N.G. *Forming a Colonial Economy, Australia 1810–1850*. New York: Cambridge University Press, 1994.

Castles, Stephen, et al. *Immigration and Australia*. Concord, MA: Paul & Company Publishers Consortium, 1998.

Coleman, William, ed. *Only in Australia: The History, Politics and Economics of Australian Exceptionalism*. Melbourne: Oxford University Press, 2016.

Davidson, Alastair. *From Subject to Citizen: Australian Citizenship in the Twentieth Century*. New York: Cambridge University Press, 1997.

Davidson, Alastair. *The Invisible State: The Formation of the Australian State, 1788–1901*. New York: Cambridge University Press, 1991.

Davidson, Graeme, et al., eds. *The Oxford*

# Bibliography and Additional Resources

*Companion to Australian History.* New York: Oxford University Press, 1998.

Dean, Mitchell, ed. *Governing Australia: Studies in Contemporary Rationalities of Government.* New York: Cambridge University Press, 1998.

Docherty, James C. *Historical Dictionary of Australia,* Second Edition. Lanham, MD: Scarecrow Press, 1999.

Ellis, Kate. *Sex, Lies and Question Time: Why the Successes and Struggles of Women in Australia's Parliament Matters to Us All.* Victoria: Hardie Grant, 2021.

Emy, Hugh V., ed. *Australia and New Zealand.* Brookfield, VT: Ashgate Publishing Company, 1999.

Fischer, Gerhard, and John Docker, eds. *Race, Colour and Identity in Australia and New Zealand.* Randwick, NSW: New South Wales University Press, 2000.

Garnaut, Ross. *Reset: Restoring Australia after the Great Crash of 2020.* Melbourne: La Trobe University Press, 2021.

Grey, Jeffrey. *A Military History of Australia,* Revised Edition. New York: Cambridge University Press, 2000.

Gyngell, Allan. *Fears of Abandonment: Australia in the World since 1972.* Carlton, Vic.: La Trobe University Press, 2017

Hassam, Andrew. *Sailing to Australia: Shipboard Diaries by Nineteenth-Century British Emigrants.* New York: Manchester University Press, 1994.

Heathcote, R. L. *Australia,* Second Edition. London: Longman Scientific & Technical, 1994.

Hocking, Jenny. *The Palace Letters: The Queen, the Governor General, and the Plan to Dismiss Whitlam.* Melbourne: Scribe, 2020.

Inglis, K. S. *Australian Colonists: An Exploration of Social History 1788–1870.* Carlton, Victoria: Melbourne University Press, 1993.

Inglis, K. S., and Craig S. Wilcox, eds. *Observing Australia, 1959–1999.* Carlton, Victoria: Melbourne University Press, 2000.

Irving, Helen, ed. *The Centenary Companion to Australian Federation.* New York: Cambridge University Press, 2000.

Jamrozik, Adam, et al. *Social Change and Cultural Transformation in Australia.* New York: Cambridge University Press, 1995.

Jayasuriya, Laksiri, et al., eds. *Legacies of White Australia. Race, Culture and Nation.* University of Western Australia Press, 2003.

Kenny, John. *Before the First Fleet: Europeans in Australia, 1606–1777.* Kenthurst, NSW: Kangaroo Press, 1995.

Lines, William J. *False Economy: Australia in the 20th Century.* Portland, OR: International Specialized Book Services, 1998.

Macintyre, Stuart. *A Concise History of Australia.* New York: Cambridge University

Press, 2000.

McCallum, Mungo. *The Good, the Bad and the Unlikely: Australia's Prime Ministers.* Melbourne: Black In., 2019.

McGarvie, Richard E. *Democracy: Choosing Australia's Republic.* Carlton, Victoria: Melbourne University Press, 2000.

McIntyre, W. David. *Background into the ANZUS Pact: Strategy and Diplomacy, 1945–55.* New York: Saint Martin's Press, 1995.

McKenna, Mark. *Return to Uluru: A Killing, A Hidden History, A Story That Goes to the Heart of the Nation.* Melbourne: Black Inc., 2021.

Mediansky, Fedor A., ed. *Australian Foreign Policy: Into the Next Millennium.* Concord, MA: Paul & Company Publishers Consortium, 1998.

Meredith, David, and Barrie Dyster. *Australia in the Global Economy: Continuity and Change.* New York: Cambridge University Press, 2000.

Monfries, John, ed., *Different Cultures: Shared Futures: Australia, Indonesia and the Region.* Singapore: Institute of Southeast Asian Studies, 2006

Murphy, Brian. *The Other Australia: Experiences of Migration.* New York: Cambridge University Press, 1993.

Okamoto Jiro, *Australia's Foreign Economic Policy And ASEAN.* Singapore: Institute of Southeast Asian Studies, 2010.

Painter, Martin. *Collaborative Federalism: Economic Reform in Australia in the 1990s.* New York: Cambridge University Press, 1998.

Paul, Erik. *Australia in Southeast Asia: Regionalism and Democracy.* Concord, MA: Paul & Company Consortium Publishers, 1998.

Reynolds, Henry. *Aboriginal Sovereignty: Reflections on Race, State and Nation.* New York: Paul & Company Publishers Consortium, 1997.

Robinson, Guy. *Australia and New Zealand: Economy, Society and Environment.* New York: Edward Arnold, 2000.

Rolls, Mitchell, and Murray Johnson. *Historical Dictionary of Australian Aborigines,* Second Edition. Lanham, MD: Rowman & Littlefield, 2019.

Scates, Bruce. *A New Australia: Citizenship, Radicalism and the First Republic.* New York: Cambridge University Press, 1997.

Simon, Julian L. *The Economic Consequences of Immigration.* Ann Arbor, MI: University of Michigan Press, rev. ed., 1999.

Singh, Anoop. *Australia: Benefiting from Economic Reform.* Washington, DC: International Monetary Fund, 1998.

Smith, Gary. *Australia in the World: An Introduction to Australian Foreign Policy.* New York: Oxford University Press, 1998.

Smyth, Paul, and Bettina Cass, eds.

*Contesting the Australian Way: States, Markets and Civil Society.* New York: Cambridge University Press, 1999.

Statsnay, Angélique. *Ignored Histories: The Politics of History Education and Indigenous Settler Relations in Australia and Kanaky/New Caledonia.* Honolulu, Hawai'i: University of Hawai'i Press, 2022.

Trainor, Luke. *British Imperialism and Australian Nationalism: Manipulation, Conflict and Compromise in the Late Nineteenth Century.* New York: Cambridge University Press, 1994.

Uhr, John. *Deliberative Democracy in Australia: The Changing Place of Parliament.* New York: Cambridge University Press, 1998.

van Onselen, Peter, and Wayne Errington. *How Good Is Scott Morrison?* Sydney: Hachette, 2021.

Wiseman, John. *Global Nation? Australia and the Politics of Globalisation.* New York: Cambridge University Press, 1998.

## Brunei *Darussalam*

de Venne, Marrie-Sybille. *Brunei: From the Age of Commerce to the 21st Century.* Singapore: NUS Press, 2015.

Saunders, Graham. *A History of Brunei,* Second Edition. London: Routledge, 2015.

Sidhu, Jatswam S. *Historical Dictionary of Brunei Darussalam,* Second Edition. Lanham, MD: Rowman & Littlefield, 2010.

Van der Bijl, Nicholas. *The Brunei Revolt: 1962–1963.* Barnsley, UK: Pen and Sword Military, 2012.

## Burma (Myanmar)

Carey, Peter, ed. *Burma: The Challenge of Change in a Divided Society.* New York: Saint Martin's Press, 1997.

Chao Tzang Yawnghwe, *The Shan of Burma: Memoirs of a Shan Exile.* Singapore: Institute of Southeast Asian Studies, 2010.

Cockett, Richard. *Blood, Dreams and Gold. The Changing Face of Burma.* New Haven, CN: Yale University Press, 2015.

Falco, Mathea. *Burma. Time for Change.* Washington, DC: Brookings, 2004.

Fink, Christina. *Living Silence. Burma under Military Rule.* New York: Palgrave, 2003.

Ganesan, N., and Kyaw Yin Hlang, *Myanmar: State, Society and Ethnicity.* Singapore: Institute of Southeast Asian Studies, 2007.

Herbert, Patricia M. *Burma.* Santa Barbara, CA: ABC-CLIO, 1991.

Lintner, Bertil. *Burma in Revolt: Opium and Insurgency since 1948.* Boulder, CO: Westview Press, 1994.

Montesano, M. J. et al., eds. *Praetorians, Profiteers or Professionals? Studies on the Militaries of Myanmar and Thailand.* Singapore: ISEAS, 2020.

# Bibliography and Additional Resources

Nehginpao Kipgen. Myanmar: *A Political History*. New Delhi: Oxford University Press, 2016.

Rotberg, Robert I., ed. *Burma: Prospects for a Democratic Future*. Washington, DC: Brookings Institution Press, 1998.

Seekins, Donald. *Burma and Japan since 1940: From 'Co-prosperity' to 'Quiet Dialogue.'* Copenhagen: NIAS Press, 2007.

Seekins, Donald M. *Historical Dictionary of Burma (Myanmar)*, Second Edition. Lanham, MD: Rowman & Littlefield, 2017. .

Suu Kyi, Aung S., edited by Michael Aris, foreword by Vaclav Havel. *Freedom from Fear and Other Writings*. New York: Penguin, 1991.

Suu Kyi, Aung S. *Letters from Burma*. New York: Viking Penguin, 1998.

## Cambodia

Ayers, David M. *Anatomy of a Crisis: Education, Development and the State in Cambodia, 1953–1998*. Honolulu, HI: University of Hawaii Press, 2000.

Chandler, David P. *A History of Cambodia*, Third Edition. Boulder, CO: Westview Press, 2000.

Chandler, David P. *Brother Number One: A Political Biography of Pol Pot*, Revised Edition. Thailand: Silkworm Books, 2000, originally published by Westview Press, 1999.

Chandler, David P. *Facing the Cambodian Past: Selected Essays, 1971–1994*. Seattle, WA: University of Washington Press, 1998.

Curtis, Grant. *Cambodia Reborn? The Transition to Democracy and Development*. Washington, DC: Brookings Institution Press, 1998.

Dith, Pran, and Kim DePaul, eds. *Children of Cambodia's Killing Fields: Memoirs of Survivors*. New Haven, CT: Yale University Press, 1997.

Ebihara, May M., et al., eds. *Cambodian Culture since 1975: Homeland and Exile*. Ithaca, NY: Cornell University Press, 1994.

Kamm, Henry. *Cambodia: Report from a Stricken Land*. New York: Arcade Publishing, 1998.

Kiernan, Ben, ed. *Genocide and Democracy in Cambodia: The Khmer Rouge, the United Nations and the International Community*. New Haven, CT: Yale University Southeast Asia Studies, 1993.

Kiernan, Ben. *The Pol Pot Regime: Race, Power, and Genocide in Cambodia under the Khmer Rouge, 1975–79*. New Haven, CT: Yale University Press, 1996.

Lizée, Pierre. *Peace, Power and Resistance in Cambodia: Global Governance and the Failure of International Conflict Resolution*. New York: Saint Martin's Press, 2000.

Mabbett, Ian, and David Chandler. *The Khmers*. Malden, MA: Blackwell Publishers, 1995.

Marin, Marie Alexandrine. *Cambodia: A Shattered Society*. Berkeley, CA: University of California Press, 1994.

Morris, Stephen J. *Why Vietnam Invaded Cambodia: Political Culture and the Causes of War*. Stanford, CA: Stanford University Press, 1998.

Osborne, Milton. *The Mekong: Turbulent Past, Uncertain Future*. New York: Grove/Atlantic, 2000.

Peou, Sorpong. *Cambodia: Change and Continuity in Contemporary Politics*. Brookfield, VT: Ashgate Publishing, 2000.

Strangio, Sebastian. *Cambodia from Pol Pot to Hun Sen and Beyond*. New Haven, CT, and London: Yale University Press, 2020.

Ung, Loung. *First They Killed My Father: A Daughter of Cambodia Remembers*. New York: HarperCollins Publishers, 2000.

Ung, Loung. *Lucky Child: A Daughter of Cambodia Reunites with the Sister She Left Behind*. New York: HarperCollins, 2005.

Welaratna, Usha. *Beyond the Killing Fields: Voices of the Cambodian Survivors in America*. Stanford, CA: Stanford University Press, 1993.

## China

Adshead, Samuel Adrian Miles. *China in World History*. New York: Saint Martin's Press, 2000.

Barme, Geremie R. *In the Red: Contemporary Chinese Culture*. New York: Columbia University Press, 1999.

Becker, Jasper. *The Chinese*. New York: The Free Press, 2000.

Bell, Daniel. *The China Model: Political Meritocracy and the Limits of Democracy*. Princeton, NJ: Princeton University Press, 2015.

Bennett, Terry. *History of Photography in China, 1842–1879*. 3 vols. London: Quaritch, 2009.

Bickers, Robert. *The Scramble for China: Foreign Devils in the Qing Empire, 1832–1914*. London: Allen Lane, 2011.

Bickers, Robert. *Out of China: How the Chinese Ended the Era of Western Domination*. London: Allen Lane, 2017.

Bickers, Robert. *China Bound: John Swire and Its World*, London: Bloomsbury, 2020.

Bolt, Paul J., and Albert S. Willner, eds. *China's Nuclear Future*. Boulder, CO: Lynne Rienner, 2005.

Blunden, Caroline, and Mark Elvin. *Cultural Atlas of China*, Revised Edition. New York: Facts on File, 1998.

Brook, Timothy. *Quelling the People: The Military Suppression of the Beijing Democracy Movement*. New York: Oxford University Press, 1992.

Brown, Harold, et al. *Chinese Military Power*. Washington, DC: Brookings, 2004.

Brown, Kerry. *CEO, China: The Rise of Xi Jinping*. New York: I. B. Taurus, 2016.

Brown, Kerry. *China's World*. New York: I. B. Taurus, 2017.

Brown, Kerry. *The World According to Xi: Everything You Need to Know about the New China*. New York: I. B. Taurus, 2018.

Brown, Kerry. *The Future of UK–China Relations*. Newcastle on Tyne, UK: Agenda Publishing, 2019.

Burstein, Daniel, and Arne J. De Keijzer. *Big Dragon: China's Future: What It Means for Business, the Economy, and the Global Order*. New York: Simon & Schuster, 1998.

Buruma, Ian. *Bad Elements: Chinese Rebels from Los Angeles to Beijing*, New York, NY: Vantage Books, 2006.

Clark, Douglas. *Gunboat Justice: British and American Law Courts in China and Japan (1842–1943)*. Hong Kong: Earnshaw Books, 2015.

Chan, Anita. *Transforming Asian Socialism: China and Vietnam Compared*. Lanham, MD: Rowman & Littlefield Publishers, 1999.

Chang, Jung, and Jon Halliday. *Mao: The Unknown Story*. New York, Knopf, 2005.

Chang, Tony H. *China during the Cultural Revolution, 1966–1976: A Selected Bibliography of English Language Works*. Westport, CT: Greenwood Publishing Group, 1999.

Cheng, Chu-Yuan. *Behind the Tiananmen Massacre*. Boulder, CO: Westview Press, 1990.

Clough, Ralph N. *Cooperation or Conflict in the Taiwan Strait?* Lanham, MD: Rowman & Littlefield Publishers, 1999.

Day, Kristen A. *China's Environment and the Challenge of Sustainable Development*. Armonk, NY: M.E. Sharpe, 2005.

Dikőtter, Frank, ed. *The Construction of Racial Identities in China and Japan*. London: Hurst and Co., 1997.

Dikőtter, Frank. *Things Modern: Material Culture and Everyday Life in China*. London: Hurst and Co., 2007.

Dikőtter, Frank. *The Cultural Revolution: A People's History 1962–1976*. London and New York: Bloomsbury. 2016.

Dreyer, June T. *China's Political System*. Reading, MA: Addison-Wesley Educational Publishers, 2000.

Dryer, Edward L. *China at War, 1901–1949*. White Plains, NY: Longman Publishing, 1995.

Fishman C. Ted. *China Inc. How the Rise of the Next Superpower Challenges America & the World*. New York: Scribner, 2005.

Fitzgerald, John. *Awakening China: Politics, Culture, and Class in the Nationalist Revolution*. Stanford, CA: Stanford University Press, 1996.

Foot, Rosemary. *The Practice of Power: US Relations with China since 1949*. New York: Oxford University Press, 1995.

Frayling, Christopher. *The Yellow Peril: Dr Fu Manchu and the Rise of China Phobia*.

London: Thames and Hudson, 2014.

Gamer, Robert E., ed. *Understanding Contemporary China*. Boulder, CO: Lynne Reinner, 2003.

Garrison, Jean A. *Making China Policy: From Nixon to G.W. Bush*. Boulder, CO: Lynne Rienner, 2005.

Gittings, John. *The Changing Face of China: From Mao to Market*. NY: Oxford, 2005.

Grunfeld, Thomas, ed. *The Making of Modern Tibet*, Revised Edition. Armonk, NY: M.E. Sharpe, 1996.

Goldstein, Melvyn C. *The Snow Lion and the Dragon*. Berkeley: University of California Press, 1997.

Guldin, Gregory E., ed. *Farewell to Peasant China: Rural Urbanization and Social Change in the Late Twentieth Century*. Armonk, NY: M.E. Sharpe, 1997.

Gurtov, Mel, and Byong-Moo Hwang. *China's Security: The New Role of the Military*. Boulder, CO: Lynne Rienner Publishers, 1998.

Harris, Richard B. *Wildlife Conservation in China*. Armonk, NY: M. E. Sharp, 2008.

Hayton, Bill. *The Invention of China*. New Haven, CN: Yale University Press, 2020.

He, Henry Yuhuai. *Dictionary of the Political Thought of the People's Republic of China*. Armonk, NY: M.E. Sharpe, 2000.

Henderson, Callum. *China on the Brink: The Myths and Realities of the World's Largest Market*. New York: McGraw-Hill, 1999.

Holz, Carsten, *The Role of Central Banking in China's Economic Reforms*. Ithaca, NY: Cornell University Press, 1993.

Hook, Brian, and Dennis Twitchett. *The Cambridge Encyclopedia of China*, Second Edition. New York: Cambridge University Press, 1991.

Hsieh, Chiao-Min, ed. *Changing China*. Boulder, CO: Westview Press, 2000.

Huang, Ray. *Broadening the Horizons of Chinese History: Discourses, Syntheses, and Comparisons*. Armonk, NY: M.E. Sharpe, 1999.

Hui, Wang. *China's New Order. Society, Politics, and Economy in Transition*. Cambridge, MA: Harvard University, 2003.

Hung-Mao, Tien, and Yun-Han Chu, eds. *China under Jiang Zemin*. Boulder, CO: Lynne Rienner Publishers, 2000.

Huot, Claire. *China's New Cultural Scene: A Handbook of Changes*. Durham, NC: Duke University Press, 1999.

Isaacs, Harold. *Scratches on our Minds: American Images of China and India*. New York: John Day, 1958.

Ji, You. *Armed Forces in China*. New York: I.B. Tauris & Company, 2000.

Jiaqi, Yan, and Gao Gao. Translated by D.W.K. Kwok. *Turbulent Decade: A History of the Cultural Revolution*. Honolulu, HI: University of Hawaii Press, 1996.

Joseph, William A., ed. *China Briefing: The Contradictions of Change*. Armonk, NY: M.E. Sharpe, 1997.

Kennedy, Thomas L. *The Arms of Kiangnan: Modernization in the Chinese Ordnance Industry, 1860–1895*. Boulder, CO: Westview Press, 1978.

Ke-wen, Wang, ed. *Modern China: An Encyclopedia of History, Culture, and Nationalism*. New York: Garland Publishing, 1999.

Kornberg, Judith F., and John R. Faust. *China in World Politics: Policies, Processes, Prospects*, Second Edition. Boulder, CO: Lynne Rienner, 2005.

Leibo, Steven A. *Transferring Technology to China: Prosper Giquel and the Self-Strengthening Movement*. Berkeley, CA: University of California Press, Institute of East Asian Studies, 1985.

Leung, Edwin Pak-Wah, ed. *Historical Dictionary of Revolutionary China, 1839–1976*. Westport, CT: Greenwood Press, 1992.

Levine, Marilyn Avra. *The Found Generation: Chinese Communists in Europe during the Twenties*. Seattle, WA: University of Washington Press, 1993.

Lewis, Joanna I. *Green Innovation in China: China's Wind Power Industry and the Global Transition to a Low-Carbon Economy*. New York: Columbia University Press, 2012.

Lin, Bih-Jaw, and James T. Myers. *Contemporary China and the Changing International Community*. Columbia, SC: University of South Carolina Press, 1994.

Lindsay, Hsiao Li. *Bold Plum: With the Guerrillas in China's War against Japan*. Lulu, 2007.

Lindsay, Michael. *The Unknown War: North China, 1937–1945*. London: Bergström & Boyle Books, 1977. Reissued Beijing: Foreign Languages Press, 2003.

Lo, Dic. *Market and Institutional Regulation in Chinese Industrialization, 1978–94*. New York: St. Martin's Press, 1997.

Lovell, Julia. *The Great Wall: China against the World 100 BC to 2000 AD*. New York: Atlantic Books, 2006.

MacFarquhar, Roderick, ed. *The Politics of China: The Eras of Mao and Deng*. New York: Cambridge University Press, 1997.

MacKerras, Colin, and Donald H. McMillen, eds. *Dictionary of the Politics of the People's Republic of China*. New York: Routledge, 1998.

Mair, Victor H., et al., eds. *Hawai'i Reader in Traditional Chinese Culture*. Honolulu, Hawai'i: University of Hawai'i Press, 2005.

Malik, Hafeez, ed. *Roles of the United States, Russia and China in the New World*. New York: Saint Martin's Press, 1997.

Mann, James. *The China Fantasy: How Our Leaders Explain Away Chinese Repression*. New York, NY: Penguin Group Inc., 2007.

Marks, Robert B. *China: Its Environment and History*. Lanham, MD: Rowman & Littlefield Publishers, 2012.

Marti, Michael E. *China and the Legacy of Deng Xiaoping: From Communist Revolution to Capitalist Evolution*. Washington, DC: Brassey's Inc., 2002.

Mathias, Jim, ed. *Computers, Language Reform, and Lexicography in China: A Report*. Pullman, WA: Washington State University Press, 1980.

McGiffert, Carola. *China in the American Political Imagination*. Washington: Center for Strategic and International Studies, 2003.

Meisner, Maurice. *The Deng Xiaoping Era: An Inquiry into the Fate of Chinese Socialism, 1978–1994*. New York: Hill & Wang, 1996.

Miles, James A. *The Legacy of Tiananmen: China in Disarray*. Ann Arbor, MI: University of Michigan, 1995.

Mitter, Rana. *China's War with Japan, 1937–1945: The Struggle for Survival*. London: Allen Lane, 2013.

Mok, Ka-Ho. *Intellectuals and the State in Post-Mao China*. New York: Saint Martin's Press, 1998.

Murowchick, Robert E., ed. *China: Ancient Culture, Modern Land*. Norman, OK: University of Oklahoma Press, 1994.

Nathan, Andrew J. *The Great Wall and the Empty Fortress: China's Search for Security*. New York: W.W. Norton & Company, 1997.

Nie Zeng Jifen. Translated and annotated by Thomas L. Kennedy; edited by Thomas L. Kennedy and Micki Kennedy. *Testimony of a Confucian Woman: The Autobiography of Mrs. Nie Zeng Jifen, 1852–1942*. Athens, GA: University of Georgia Press, 1993.

Pearson, Margaret M. *China's New Business Elite: The Political Consequences of Economic Reform*. Berkeley, CA: University of California Press, 1997.

Perkins, Dorothy. *The Encyclopedia of China: The Essential Reference to China, Its History and Culture*. New York: Facts on File, 1998.

Powers, John, and David Templeman. *Historical Dictionary of Tibet*, Second Edition. Lanham, MD: Rowman & Littlefield, 2020.

Ross, Robert S. *Chinese Security Policy; Structure, Power and Politics*. London: Routledge, 2009.

Rudolph, Jennifer, and Szony, Michael, eds. *The China Question Critical Insights into a Rising Power*. Cambridge, MA: Harvard University Press, 2018.

Saw Swee-Hock, ed. *Regional Economic Development in China*. Singapore: Institute of Southeast Asian Studies, 2009.

Sautman, Barry, ed. *Contemporary Tibet: Politics, Development, and Society in a Disputed Region*. Armonk, NY: M.E. Sharpe, 2006.

Schell, Orville. *Mandate of Heaven: A New Generation of Entrepreneurs, Dissidents,*

# Bibliography and Additional Resources

*Bohemians, and Technocrats Lays Claim to China's Future.* New York: Simon & Schuster, 1994.

Segal, Gerald, and Richard H. Yang, eds. *Chinese Economic Reform: The Impact on Security.* New York: Routledge, 1996.

Shakya, Tsering. *The Dragon in the Land of the Snows: A History of Modern Tibet since 1947.* New York: Columbia University Press, 1999.

Shambaugh, David. *Beautiful Imperialist: China Perceives America, 1972–1990.* Princeton, NJ: Princeton University Press, 1991.

Shambaugh, David, ed. *China's Military in Transition.* New York: Oxford University Press, 1998.

Shambaugh, David, ed. *Is China Unstable? Assessing the Factors.* Armonk, NY: M.E. Sharpe, 2000.

Shambaugh, David. *Modernizing China's Military: Progress, Problems and Prospects.* Berkeley, CA: University of California Press, 2002.

Shaoguang, Wang, and Hu Angang. *The Political Economy of Uneven Development: The Case of China.* Armonk, NY: M.E. Sharpe, 2000.

Shapiro, Judith. *China's Environmental Challenges.* Cambridge: Polity Press, 2012.

Shirk, Susan L. *China: Fragile Superpower.* New York: Oxford University Press, 2007.

Shaughnessy, Edward L., ed. *China: Empire and Civilization.* NY: Oxford University Press, 2005.

Shenkar, Oded. *The Chinese Century.* Upper Saddle River, NJ: Wharton School of Publishing, 2006.

Sidhu, Waheguru, and Jing-dong Yuan. *China and India: Cooperation or Conflict?* Boulder, CO: Lynne Reinner, 2003.

Smith, Christopher J. *China in the Post-Utopian Age.* Boulder, CO: Westview Press, 2000.

Smith, L. C., and Nigel West. *Historical Dictionary of Chinese Intelligence,* Second Edition. Lanham, MD: Rowman & Littlefield, 2021.

Sullivan, Lawrence R., and Nancy Y. Liu-Sullivan. *Historical Dictionary of Chinese Culture.* Lanham, MD: Rowman & Littlefield, 2021.

Sun, Yan. *The Chinese Reassessment of Socialism, 1976–1992.* Princeton, NJ: Princeton University Press, 1995.

Tanner, Murray Scott. *The Politics of Lawmaking in Post-Mao China: Institutions, Processes, and Democratic Prospects.* New York: Oxford University Press, 1999.

Teiwes, Frederick C., and Warren Sun. *China's Road to Disaster: Mao, Central Politicians and Provincial Leaders in the Unfolding of the Great Leap Forward, 1955–1959.* Armonk, NY: M.E. Sharpe, 1998.

Terrill, Ross. *The New Chinese Empire.*

*Bejing's Political Dilemma and What It Means for the United States.* Boulder, CO: Westview, 2003.

Tien, Hung-mao, and Yun-han Chu, eds. *China under Jiang Zemin.* Boulder, CO: Lynne Reinner, 2000.

Tyler, Patrick. *A Great Wall: Six Presidents and China.* New York: A Century Foundation Book, 1999, 2000.

Vogel, Ezra F., ed. *Living with China: U.S.–China Relations in the Twenty-First Century.* New York: W.W. Norton & Company, 1997.

Wang, Gabe T. *China's Population: Problems, Thoughts, and Policies.* Brookfield, VT: Ashgate, 1999.

Wang, Lixiong, and Tsering Shakya. *The Struggle for Tibet; Tibet's Last Stand? The Tibetan Uprising of 2008 and China's Response.* London: Verso, 2009.

Wang, Shaoguang, and Angang Hu. *The Political Economy of Uneven Development: The Case of China.* Armonk, NY: M.E. Sharpe, 1999.

Wasserstrom, Jeffrey N., and Elizabeth J. Perry, eds. *Popular Protest and Political Culture in Modern China.* Boulder, CO: Westview Press, 1994.

Waters, Harry J. *China's Economic Development Strategies for the 21st Century.* Westport, CT: Greenwood Publishing Group, 1997.

Westad, Odd Arne. *Restless Empire: China and the World since 1750.* New York: Basic Books, 2012.

Weston, Timothy B., and Lionel M. Jensen, eds. *China beyond the Headlines.* Lanham, MD: Rowman & Littlefield Publishers, 2000.

Wilbur, C. Martin. *The Nationalist Revolution in China, 1923–1928.* Cambridge: Cambridge University Press, 1985.

Winckler, Edwin A., ed. *Transition from Communism in China: Institutional and Comparative Analysis.* Boulder, CO: Lynne Rienner Publishers, 1999.

Wortzel, Larry M. *Dictionary of Contemporary Chinese Military History.* Westport, CT: Greenwood Publishing Group, 1999.

Wu, Yanrui. *China's Consumer Revolution: The Emerging Patterns of Wealth and Expenditure.* Northampton, MA: Edward Elgar Publishing, 1999.

Xu, Guoqi. *China and the Great War: China's Pursuit of a New National Identity and Internationalization.* Cambridge: Cambridge University Press, 2005.

Zhai, Qiang. *The Dragon, the Lion, and the Eagle: Chinese-British-American Relations, 1949–1958.* Kent, OH: Kent State University Press, 1994.

Zhang, Wei W. *Transforming China.* New York: St. Martin's Press, 2000.

Zhang, Xiaoguang. *China's Trade and International Comparative Advantage: Studies in the Modern Chinese Economy.* New York: Saint Martin's Press, 2000.

## Hong Kong

Butenhoff, Linda. *Social Movements and Political Reform in Hong Kong.* Westport, CT: Greenwood Publishing Group, 1999.

Callick, Rowan. *Comrades and Capitalists: Hong Kong since the Takeover.* Portland, OR: International Specialized Book Services, 1998.

Chan, Ming K., ed. *Precarious Balance: Hong Kong between China and Britain.* Armonk, NY: M.E. Sharpe, 1994.

Chan, Ming K., and Shiu-hing Lo. *Historical Dictionary of Hong Kong SAR and Macao SAR.* Lanham, MD: Scarecrow Press, 2006.

Cohen, Warren I., ed. *Hong Kong under Chinese Rule: The Economic and Political Implications of Reversion.* New York: Cambridge University Press, 1997.

Daparin, Antony. *City of Protest: A Recent History of Dissent in Hong Kong.* London: Penguin, 2017.

Hsiung, James C. *Hong Kong and the Super Paradox: Life after Return to China.* New York: St. Martin's Press, 2000.

Keay, John. *Empire's End: A History of the Far East from High Colonialism to Hong Kong.* New York: Scribner, 1997.

Ku, Agnes S. *Narratives, Politics, and the Public Sphere: Struggles over Political Reform in the Final Transitional Years in Hong Kong (1992–1994).* Brookfield, VT: Ashgate, 1999.

Lam, Waiman. *Understanding the Political Culture of Hong Kong.* Amonk, NY: M.E. Sharp, 2004.

Meyer, David R. *Hong Kong as a Global Metropolis.* New York: Cambridge University Press, 2000.

Pang-Kwong, Li. *Hong Kong from Britain to China: Political Cleavages, Electoral Dynamics and Institutional Changes.* Brookfield, VT: Ashgate Publishing, 2000.

Patten, Christopher. *East and West: The Last Governor of Hong Kong on Power, Freedom and the Future.* New York: Times Books, 1998.

Postiglione, Gerald A., and James T. H. Tang, eds. *Hong Kong's Reunion with China: The Global Dimensions.* Armonk, NY: M.E. Sharpe, 1997.

Roberti, Mark. *The Fall of Hong Kong: Britain's Betrayal and China's Triumph.* New York: John Wiley & Sons, 1994.

Roberts, Elfed Vaughan, et al. *Historical Dictionary of Hong Kong and Macao.* Lanham, MD: Scarecrow Press, 1992.

Sheridan, Michael. *The Gate to China: A New History of the People's Republic and Hong Kong.* London: William Collins, 2021.

Shipp, Steve. *Hong Kong, China: A Political History of the British Crown Colony's Transfer to Chinese Rule.* Jefferson, NC: McFarland & Company, 1995.

Thomas, Nicholas. *Democracy Denied: Identity, Civil, Society and Illiberal Democracy in Hong Kong*. Brookfield, VT: Ashgate Publishing Company, 1999.

Tsang, Steve. *Modern History of Hong Kong, 1841–1998*. London: I.B. Tauris & Company, 1998.

Van Kemendade, William. *China, Hong Kong, Taiwan, Incorporated*. New York: Alfred A. Knopf, 1997.

Yeung, Bernard. *Hong Kong's 2019–2020 Social Unrest: The Trigger, History and Lessons*. Singapore: World Scientic, 2020.

## Indonesia

Baker, Richard W. *Indonesia: The Challenge of Change*. New York: St. Martin's Press, 1999.

Bland, Ben. *Joko Widodo and the Struggle to Remake Indonesia*. Melbourne: Penguin Books, 2020.

Bresnan, John. *Managing Indonesia: The Modern Political Economy*. New York: Columbia University Press, 1993.

Cribb, Robert. *Historical Atlas of Indonesia*. Honolulu, HI: University of Hawaii Press, 1998.

Cribb, Robert, ed. *The Late Colonial State in Indonesia: Political and Economic Foundations of the Netherlands Indies, 1880–1942*. Leiden: KITLV Press, 1994.

Cribb, Robert, and Colin Brown. *Modern Indonesia: A History since 1945*. New York: Longman, 1995.

Crouch, Harold. *Political Reform in Indonesia after Soeharto*. Singapore: Institute of Southeast Asian Studies, 2010.

Emmerson, Donald K., ed. *Indonesia beyond Suharto*. Armonk, NY: M.E. Sharpe, 1998.

Frederick, William H., and Robert L. Worden, eds. *Indonesia: A Country Study*, Fifth Edition. Washington, DC: U.S. GPO, 1993.

Friend, Theodore. *Indonesian Destinies*. Cambridge, MA: Harvard University, 2003.

Gardner, Paul F. *Shared Hopes, Separate Fears: Fifty Years of U.S.—Indonesian Relations*. Westport, CT: Westview Press, 1997.

Hefner, Robert, ed. *Routledge Handbook of Contemporary Indonesia*. London: Routledge, 2018.

Hefner, Robert, W., ed. *Indonesian Pluralities: Islam, Citizenship and Democracy*. Singapore: ISEAS, 2021.

Hill, Hal. *The Indonesian Economy since 1966*. New York: Cambridge University Press, 2000.

Hilmy, Masdar. *Islamism and Democracy in Indonesia: Piety & Pragmatism*. Singapore: Institute of Southeast Asian Studies, 2010.

Kahin, Audrey. *Historical Dictionary of Indonesia*. Third Edition. Lanham, MD: Rowman & Littlefield, 2015.

Kipp, Rita Smith. *Dissociated Identities: Ethnicity, Religion, and Class in an Indonesian Society*. Ann Arbor, MI: University of Michigan Press, 1993.

Martin, Ian. *Self-Determination in East Timor: The United Nations, the Ballot, and International Intervention*. Boulder, CO: Lynne Reinner, 2001.

Platzdasch, Bernhard. *Islamism in Indonesia: Politics in the Emerging Democracy*. Singapore: Institute of Southeast Asian Studies, 2009.

Ramage, Douglas E. *Politics in Indonesia: Democracy, Islam, and the Ideology of Tolerance*. New York: Routledge, 1995.

Ricklefs, Merle Calvin. *A History of Modern Indonesia: c. 1300 to the Present*. Stanford, CA: Stanford University Press, 1993.

Robinson, Geoffrey B. *The Killing Season: A History of the Indonesian Massacres, 1965–66*. Princeton, NJ: Princeton University Press, 2019.

Schiller, Jim, and Barbara Martin-Schiller, eds. *Imagining Indonesia: Cultural Politics and Political Culture*. Athens, OH: Ohio University Press, 1997.

Schwartz, Adam. *A Nation in Waiting: Indonesia in the 1990s*. Boulder, CO: Westview Press, 1994.

Simons, G. L. *Indonesia: The Long Oppression*. New York: Saint Martin's Press, 2000.

Smith, Michael G., and Moreen Dee. *Peacekeeping in East Timor: The Path to Independence*. Boulder, CO: Lynne Reinner, 2003.

Uhlin, Anders. *Indonesia and the "Third Wave of Democratization": The Indonesian Pro-Democracy Movement in a Changing World*. New York: St. Martin's Press, 1997.

Vatikiotis, Michael R. J. *Indonesian Politics under Suharto: The Rise and Fall of the New Order*. New York: Routledge, 1999.

## Japan

Abe, Etsuo, and Robert Fitzgerald, eds. *The Origins of Japanese Industrial Power: Strategy, Institutions and the Development of Organisational Capability*. Portland, OR: Frank Cass & Company, 1995.

Alinson, Gary D., and Yasunori Sone, eds. *Political Dynamics in Contemporary Japan*. Ithaca, NY: Cornell University Press, 1993.

Aoki, Masahito, and Gary R. Saxonhouse, eds. *Finance, Governance and Competitiveness in Japan*. New York: Oxford University Press, 2000.

Aso, Noriko. *Public Properties: Museums in Imperial Japan*. Durham, NC, and London: Duke University Press, 2014.

Auslin, Michael R. *Negotiating with Imperialism: The Unequal Treaties and the Culture of Japanese Diplomacy*. Cambridge, MA: Harvard University Press, 2004.

Banno, Junji. *The Establishment of the Japanese Constitutional System*. New York: Routledge, 1995.

Beasley, W. G. *The Japanese Experience: A Short History of Japan*. Berkeley, CA: University of California Press, 1999.

Bennettt, Terry. *Photography in Japan 1853–1912*. Tokyo and Rutland, VT: Tuttle, 2006.

Bix, Herbert P. *Hirohito and the Making of Modern Japan*. New York: HarperCollins Publishers, 2000.

Breen, John, ed. *Yasukuni: The War Dead and the Struggle for Japan's Past*. London: Hurst and Co., 2007.

Browring, Richard, and Peter Kornicki, eds. *The Cambridge Encyclopedia of Japan*. New York: Cambridge University Press, 1993.

Buckley, Roger. *Japan Today*. New York: Cambridge University Press, 1999.

Carlile, Lonny E., and Mark Tilton, eds. *Is Japan Really Changing Its Ways? Regulatory Reform and the Japanese Economy*. Washington, DC: Brookings Institution Press, 1998.

Christensen, Ray. *Ending the LDP Hegemony: Party Cooperation in Japan*. Honolulu, HI: University of Hawaii Press, 2000.

Cohen, Stephen D. *An Ocean Apart: Explaining Three Decades of U.S.-Japanese Trade Frictions*. Westport, CT: Greenwood Publishing Group, 1998.

Curtis, Gerald L., ed. *Japan's Foreign Policy after the Cold War: Coping with Change*. Armonk, NY: M.E. Sharpe, 1993.

Curtis, Gerald L., ed. *Politicians and Policymaking in Japan*. Washington, DC: Brookings, 2002.

Dower, John. *War without Mercy: Race and Power in the Pacific War*. New York: W. W. Norton and Co., 1986.

Dower, John. *Embracing Defeat: Japan in the Wake of World War II*. New York: W.W. Norton & Company, 1999.

Drysdale, Peter, and Luke Gower. *The Japanese Economy*. New York: Routledge, 2000.

Edstrom, Bert. *Japan's Evolving Foreign Policy Doctrine: From Yoshida to Miyazawa*. New York: St. Martin's Press, 1999.

Eisenstadt, Samuel N. *Japanese Civilization*. Chicago: University of Chicago Press, 1998.

Fessler, Susanna. *Wandering Heart: The Work and Method of Hayashi Fumiko*. Albany: SUNY Press, 1998.

Fessler, Susanna. *Musashi in Tuscany: Japanese Overseas Travel Literature 1860–1912*. Ann Arbor, Michigan: Center for Japanese Studies, 2004.

Finn, R. B. *Winners in Peace: MacArthur, Yoshida and Post-war Japan*. Berkeley, CA: University of California Press, 1992.

Flath, David. *The Japanese Economy*. New York: Oxford University Press, 2000.

Frédéric, trans. Käthe Roth. *Japan Encyclopedia*. Cambridge, MA: Belknap Press, 2002.

Fukushima, Akiko. *Japanese Foreign Policy: The Emerging Logic of Multilateralism*. New York: St. Martin's Press, 1999.

# Bibliography and Additional Resources

Garon, Sheldon. *Molding Japanese Minds: The State in Everyday Life*. Princeton, NJ: Princeton University Press, 1997.

Giffard, Sydney. *Japan among the Powers, 1880–1990*. New Haven, CT: Yale University Press, 1994.

Gordon, Andrew, ed. *Postwar Japan as History*. Berkeley, CA: University of California Press, 1993.

Green, Michael J. *Arming Japan: Defense Production, Alliance Politics, and the Postwar Search for Autonomy*. New York: Columbia University Press, 1995.

Green, Michael J. U. *Japan's Reluctant Realism. Foreign Policy Challenges in an Era of Uncertain Power*. New York: Palgrave, 2003.

Hall, Ivan P. *Cartels of the Mind: Japan's Intellectual Closed Shop*. New York: W.W. Norton & Company, 1997.

Hall, Maximilian J. *Financial Reform in Japan: Causes and Consequences*. Northampton, MA: Edward Elgar Publishing, 1999.

Heneshall, Kenneth G. *A History of Japan: From Stone Age to Superpower*. New York: Saint Martin's Press, 1998.

Heneshall, Kenneth G. *Historical Dictionary of Japan to 1945*. Lanham, MD: Scarecrow Press, 2013.

Herbig, Paul A. *Innovation Japanese Style: A Cultural and Historical Perspective*. Westport, CT: Quorum Books, 1995.

Herzog, Peter J. *Japan's Pseudo-Democracy*. New York: New York University Press, 1993.

Holgerson, Karen M. *The Japan-U.S. Trade Friction Dilemma: The Role of Perception*. Brookfield, VT: Ashgate Publishing Company, 1998.

Hoover, William D. *Historical Dictionary of Postwar Japan*. Second Edition. Lanham, MD: Rowman & Littlefield, 2019.

Hrebenar, Ronald J. *Political Parties and Elections in Japan: The Post–1993 System*. Boulder, CO: Westview Press, 2000.

Hsu, Robert C. *The MIT Encyclopedia of the Japanese Economy*. Cambridge, MA: MIT Press, 1994.

Huber, Thomas M. *Strategic Economy in Japan*. Boulder, CO: Westview Press, 1994.

Huffman, James L. *Modern Japan: An Encyclopedia of History, Culture, and Nationalism*. New York: Garland Publishing, 1999.

Inoguchi, Takashi. *Japan's Foreign Policy Today*. New York: Saint Martin's Press, 2000.

Iriye, Akira. *Japan and the Wider World: From the Mid-Nineteenth Century to Present*. New York: Longman, 1997.

Irokawa, Daikichi. Translated by John K. Urda. *The Age of Hirohito: In Search of Modern Japan*. New York: Free Press, 1995.

Itoh, Mayumi. *Globalization of Japan: U.S. Efforts to Open Japan from Commodore Matthew Perry to Defense Secretary William Perry*. New York: St. Martin's Press, 1998.

Jansen, Marius B. *The Making of Modern Japan*. Cambridge, MA: Harvard University Press, 2000.

*Japan: An Illustrated Encyclopedia*. 2 vols. New York: Kodansha America, 1994.

Johnson, Chalmers. *Japan: Who Governs?* New York: W.W. Norton, 1995.

Johnson-Freese, Joan. *Over the Pacific: Japanese Space Policy into the Twenty-First Century*. Dubuque, IA: Kendall/Hunt Publishing, 1993.

Kersten, Rikki, and David Williams, eds. *The Left in the Shaping of Japanese Democracy: Essays in Honour of J. A. A. Stockwin*. London: Routledge, 2006.

Koppel, Bruce M., ed. *Japan's Foreign Aid: Power and Policy in a New Era*. Boulder, CO: Westview Press, 1993.

Kornicki, Peter. *Eavesdropping on the Emperor: Interrogators and Codebreakers in Britain's War with Japan*. London: Hurst and Co., 2021.

Kovner, Sarah. *Prisoners of the Empire: Inside Japanese POW Camps*. Cambridge, MA: Harvard University Press, 2020.

Kushner, Barak, and Sherzod Muminov, eds. *The Dismantling of Japan's Empire in East Asia: Deimperialization, Postwar Legitimation and Imperial Afterlife*. London: Routledge, 2018.

Large, Stephen S. *Emperor Hirohito and Showa Japan: A Political Biography*. Florence KY: Routledge, 1996.

Lincoln, Edward J. *Japan's New Global Role*. Washington, DC: Brookings Institution Press, 1993.

Luney, Percy R., Jr., and Kazuyuki Takahashi, eds. *Japanese Constitutional Law*. Tokyo: University of Tokyo Press, 1993.

Maher, John C., and Gaynor Macdonald, eds. *Diversity in Japanese Culture and Language*. New York: Kegan Paul International, 1995.

Mann, Thomas E., and Sasaki Takeshi, eds. *Governance for a New Century. Japanese Challenges, American Experience*. Washington, DC: Brookings, 2002.

McCargo, Duncan. *Contemporary Japan*. New York: St. Martin's Press, 2000.

McNeil, Frank. *Democracy in Japan: The Emerging Global Concern*. New York: Crown Publishing, 1994.

Mochizuki, Mike M. *Japan Reorients: The Quest for Wealth and Security in East Asia*. Washington, DC: Brookings Institution Press, 2001.

Morikawa, Jun. *Whaling in Japan. Power, Politics and Diplomacy*. New York: Columbia University Press, 2009.

Morris-Suzuki, Tessa. *Borderline Japan: Foreigners and Frontier Controls in the Postwar Era*. Cambridge: Cambridge University Press, 2010.

Muminov, Sherzod. *Eleven Winters of Discontent: The Siberian Internment and the Making of Modern Japan*. Cambridge, MA, and London: Harvard University Press, 2022.

Nathan, John. *Japan Unbound: A Volatile Nation's Quest for Pride and Purpose*. NY: Houghton Mifflin, 2004.

Nester, William R. *American Power, the New World Order and the Japanese Challenge*. New York: Saint Martin's Press, 1993.

Porter, Michael, et al. *Can Japan Compete?* New York: Basic Books, 2000.

Prough, Jennifer S. *Kyoto Revisited: Heritage Tourism in Contemporary Japan*. Honolulu, Hawai'i: University of Hawai'i Press, 2022.

Qinones, C. Kenneth. *Imperial Japan's Allied Prisoners of War in the South Pacific; Surviving Paradise*. Newcastle on Tyne, UK: Cambridge Scholars Publishing, 2021.

Reischauer, Edwin O., and Marius Jansen. *The Japanese Today*. Cambridge, MA: Harvard University Press, rev. ed., 1995.

Richardson, Bradley M. *Japanese Democracy: Power, Coordination, and Performance*. New Haven, CT: Yale University Press, 1997.

Sakakibara, Eisuke. *Structural Reform in Japan. Breaking the Iron Triangle*. Washington, DC: Brookings, 2003.

Saaler, Sven, and Christopher W. A. Szpilman, eds. *Routledge Handbook of Modern Japanese History*. London and New York: Routledge, 2018.

Sato, Kazuo, ed. *The Transformation of the Japanese Economy*. Armonk, NY: M.E. Sharpe, 1999.

Sato, Ryuzo. *The Chrysanthemum and the Eagle: The Future of U.S.-Japan Relations*. New York: New York University Press, 1994.

Schaller, Michael. *Altered States: The United States and Japan since Occupation*. New York: Oxford University Press, 1997.

Schoppa, Leonard J. *Bargaining with Japan: What American Pressure Can and Cannot Do*. New York: Columbia University Press, 1997.

Smith, Patrick. *Japan: A Reinterpretation*. New York: Pantheon, 1997.

Stockwin, J. A. *Governing Japan: Divided Politics in a Major Economy*. Malden, MA: Blackwell Publishers, 1998.

Sugimoto, Yoshio. *An Introduction to Japanese Society*. New York: Cambridge University Press, 1997.

Swenson-Wright, John. *Unequal Allies? United States Security and Alliance Policy towards Japan, 1945-1960*. Stanford CA: Stanford University Press, 2005.

Thorne, C. *Allies of a Kind: the United States, Britain and the War against Japan*. London: Hamish Hamilton, 1978.

Uriu, Robert M. *Troubled Industries: Confronting Economic Change in Japan*. Ithaca, NY: Cornell University Press, 1996.

Vogel, Ezra F. *China and Japan: Facing History.* Cambridge MA: The Belknap Press of Harvard University Press, 2019.

Weiner, Michael, ed. *Japan's Minorities: Illusion of Homogeneity.* New York: Routledge, 1997.

Wilson, Sandra et al. *Japanese War Criminals: The Politics of Justice after the Second World War.* New York: Columbia University Press, 2017.

Woronoff, Jon. *The Japanese Social Crisis.* New York: Saint Martin's Press, 1997.

Wicaksono, Agung. *Energy Efficiency in Japan.* Singapore: Institute of Southeast Asian Studies, 2008.

Yamazaki, Jane W. *Japanese Apologies for World War II.* New York: Routledge, 2006.

Yasutomo, Dennis T. *The New Multilateralism in Japan's Foreign Policy.* New York: Saint Martin's Press, 1995.

Zhang, Wei-Bin, and Ake E. Andersson. *Japan Versus China in the Industrial Race.* New York: Saint Martin's Press, 1998.

**Korea, North and South**

Alford, C. Fred. *Think No Evil: Korean Values in the Age of Globalization.* Ithaca, NY: Cornell University Press, 1999.

Becker, Jasper. *Rouge Regime: Kim Jong Il and the Looming Threat of North Korea.* New York: Oxford University Press, 2005.

Bedeski, Robert E. *The Transformation of South Korea: Reform and Reconstitution in the Sixth Republic under Roh Tae Woo, 1987–1992.* New York: Routledge, 1994.

Bennett, Terry. *Korea: Caught in Time.* Reading, UK: Garnett, 1997.

Buzo, Adrian. *The Making of Modern Korea. A History.* NY: Routledge, 2002.

Cha, Paul S. *Balancing Communities: Nation, State and Protestant Christianity in Korea, 1884–1942.* Honolulu, Hawai'i: University of Hawai'i Press, 2022.

Cha, Victor. *The Impossible State: North Korea Past and Future.* London: The Bodley Head, 2012.

Cherry, Judith. *Foreign Direct Investment in Post-crisis Korea: European Investors and Mismatched Globalization.* London and New York: Routledge, 2007.

Chinoy, Mike, *Meltdown: The Inside Story of the North Korean Nuclear Crisis.* New York: St. Martin's Press, 2008.

Cornell, Eric. *North Korea under Communism: Report from an Envoy in Paradise.* London: Routledge Curzon, 2002.

Cumings, Bruce. *Korea's Place in the Sun: A Modern History.* New York: W. W. Norton, 1997.

Cumings, Bruce. *North Korea: Another Country.* New York: New Press, 2004.

Demick, Barbara. *Nothing to Envy: Ordinary Lives in North Korea.* New York: Spiegel & Grau, 2009

Dong, Wonmo. *The Two Koreas and the United States: Issues of Peace, Security and Economic Cooperation.* Armonk, NY: M. E. Sharpe, 2000.

Eberstadt, Nicholas. *Korea Approaches Reunification.* Armonk, NY: M.E. Sharpe, 1995.

Fifield, Anna. *The Great Successor: The Secret Rise and Rule of Kim Jong Un.* London: John Murray, 2019.

Frank, Rüdiger, and Österreichisches Museum für Angewandte Kunst, eds. *Exploring North Korean Arts.* Nürnberg, Germany: Verlag für Moderne Kunst, 2011.

Frank, Rüdiger, and John Swenson-Wright, eds. *Korea and East Asia: The Stony Road to Collective Security.* Leiden: Brill, 2013.

Funabashi, Yoichi. *The Peninsula Question: A Chronicle of the Second Korean Nuclear Crisis.* Washington, DC: Brookings Institute Press, 2007.

Gray, Kevin, and Lee Jong-Woon. *North Korea and the Geopolitics of Development.* Cambridge: Cambridge University Press, 2021.

Harden, Blaine. *Escape from Camp 14: One Man's Remarkable Odyssey From North Korea to Freedom in the West.* London, Viking Penguin, 2012.

Hamm, Taik-Young. *Arming the Two Koreas: State, Capital, and Military Power.* New York: Routledge, 1999.

Hassig, Ralph, and Kongdan Oh. *The Hidden People of North Korea: Everyday Life in the Hermit Kingdom.* Lanham, MD: Rowman & Littlefield, 2009.

Helgensen, Geir. *Democracy and Authority in Korea.* New York: Saint Martin's Press, 1998.

Henderson, Gregory. *The Politics of the Vortex.* Cambridge MA: Harvard University Press, 1968.

Hoare, J. E. *Critical Readings on North and South Korea,* 3 vols. Leiden, Netherlands, and Boston, MA: Brill, 2013.

Hoare, James E. *Historical Dictionary of the Democratic People's Republic of Korea.* Second Edition. Lanham, MD: Rowman & Littlefield, 2019.

Hoare, James E. *Historical Dictionary of the Republic of Korea.* Fourth Edition. Lanham, MD: Rowman & Littlefield, 2020.

Howard, Keith. *Songs for Great Leaders: Ideology and Creativity in North Korean Music and Dance.* Oxford: Oxford University Press, 2020.

Hulbert, Homer B. *History of Korea.* Honolulu, HI: University of Hawaii Press, 1998.

Hunter, Helen-Louise. *Kim Il-Sung's North Korea.* Westport, CT: Greenwood Publishing Group, 1999.

Jackson, Andrew David, et al. eds. *Invented Traditions in North and South Korea.* Honolulu, Hawai'i: University of Hawai'i Press, 2021.

Jung, Walter, and Xiao-Bing Li, eds. *Korea and Regional Geopolitics.* Lanham, MD: University Press of America, 1998.

Kihl, Young Whan. *Korea and the World: Beyond the Cold War.* Boulder, CO: Westview Press, 1994.

Kim Byung-kook, and Ezra F. Vogel, eds. *The Park Chung Hee Era: The Transformation of South Korea.* Cambridge MA: Harvard University Press, 2013.

Kim, Dae Jung. *Mass Participatory Economy: Korea's Road to World Economic Power.* Lanham, MD: University Press of America, 1996.

Kim, Eun M. *Big Business, Strong State: Collusion and Conflict in South Korean Development, 1960–1990.* Albany, NY: State University of New York Press, 1997.

Kim, Gye-Dong. *Foreign Intervention in Korea.* Brookfield, VT: Dartmouth Publishing Company, 1993.

Kim, Hakjoon. *Korea's Relations with Her Neighbors in a Changing World.* Elizabeth, NJ: Hollym International, 1993.

Kim, Samuel S., ed. *Korea's Globalization.* New York: Cambridge University Press, 2000.

Kim, Samuel S., ed. *The North Korean System in the Post-Cold War Era.* New York: Palgrave, 2003.

Kim, Samuel S. *The Two Koreas and the Great Powers.* Cambridge: Cambridge University Press, 2006.

Ku Daeyeol. *Korea 1905–1945: From Japanese Colonialism to Liberation and Independence.* Folkestone, England: Renaissance Books, 2021.

Kwon, Heonik, and Byung-Ho Chung. *North Korea: Beyond Charismatic Politics.* Lanham, MD: Rowman & Littlefield, 2012.

Kwon, Heonik. *After the Korean War: An Intimate History.* Cambridge: Cambridge University Press, 2020.

Lancaster, Lewis R., et al. *Religion and Society in Contemporary Korea.* Berkeley, CA: Institute of East Asian Studies, 1998.

Lankov, Andrei. *From Stalin to Kim Il Sung: The Foundation of North Korea.* London: Hurst and Co., 2002.

Lankov, Andrei. *The Real North Korea: Life and Politics in the Failed Stalinist Utopia.* Oxford: Oxford University Press, 2013.

Lee, Chae-Jin. *China and Korea: Dynamic Relations.* Stanford, CA: Hoover Institution Press, 1996.

Lee, Hyang-jin. *Contemporary Korean Cinema. Identity, Culture, Politics.* Manchester, UK: Manchester University Press, 2003.

Lee, Hyung-Koo. *The Korean Economy: Perspectives for the Twenty-First Century.* Albany, NY: State University of New York Press, 1996.

Lee, Kenneth B. *Korea and East Asia: The Story of a Phoenix.* Westport, CT: Greenwood Publishing Group, 1997.

# Bibliography and Additional Resources

Lee, Peter H., ed. *Sourcebook of Korean Civilization, vol. 1: From Early Times to the Sixteenth Century*. New York: Columbia University Press, 1993.

Lee, Peter H., ed. *Sourcebook of Korean Civilization, vol. 2: From the Seventeenth Century to the Modern Period*. New York: Columbia University Press, 1996.

Lee, Yoon-kyung. *Between the Streets and the Assembly: Social Movements, Political Parties and Democracy in Korea*. Honolulu, Hawai'i: University of Hawai'i Press, 2022.

Lee, Yur-Bok, and Wayne Patterson, eds. *Korean-American Relations, 1866–1997*. Albany, NY: State University of New York Press, 1998.

Lie, John. *The Political Economy of South Korea*. Stanford, CA: Stanford University Press, 1998.

Macdonald, Donald Stone. *The Koreans: Contemporary Politics and Society*, Third Edition. Bouder, CO: Westview Press, 1996.

Martin, Bradley. *Under the Loving Care of the Fatherly Leader, North Korea and the Kim Dynasty*. New York: St. Martin's Press, 2004.

Mazarr, Michael J. *North Korea and the Bomb: A Case Study in Nonproliferation*. New York: St. Martin's Press, 1995.

McNamara, Dennis L. *Trade and Transformation in Korea, 1876–1945*. Boulder, CO: Westview Press, 1996.

Myers, B. R. *The Cleanest Race: How the North Koreans See Themselves and —Why It Matters*. Brooklyn, New York: Melvilee House, 2010.

Natsios, Andrew S. *The Great North Korean Famine*. Herndon, VA: U.S. Institute of Peace Press, 2002.

Noland, Marcus. *Avoiding the Apocalypse: The Future of the Two Koreas*. Washington, DC: Institute for International Economics, 2000.

Oberdorfer, Don, and Robert Carlin. *The Two Koreas: A Contemporary History*, Third Edition. New York: Basic Books, 2014.

Oh, John K. *Korean Democracy on Trial*. Ithaca, NY: Cornell University Press, 1968.

Oh, John K. *Korean Politics: The Quest for Democratization and Economic Development*. Ithaca, NY: Cornell University Press, 1999.

Oh, Kongdan, ed. *Korea Briefing, 1997–1999: Challenges and Change at the Turn of the Century*. Armonk, NY: M.E. Sharpe, 2000.

Oh, Kongdan, and Ralph C. Hassig. *North Korea through the Looking Glass*. Washington, DC: Brookings, 2000.

O'Hanlon, Michael, and Mochizuki, Mike. *Crisis on the Korean Peninsula. How to Deal with a Nuclear North Korea*. Washington, DC: Brookings, 2003.

Oliver, Robert T. *A History of the Korean People in Modern Times: 1800 to the Present*. Cranbury, NJ: University of Delaware Press, 1993.

Pai, Hyung Il. *Constructing "Korean" Origins: A Critical Review of Archaeolgy, Historiography, and Racial Myth in Korean State-Formation Theories*. Cambridge, MA, and London: Harvard University Asia Center, 2000.

Pak, Jung H. *Becoming Kim Jong Il: Understanding North Korea's Young Dictator*. New York: Ballentine Books, 2020.

Pratt, Keith et al. *Korea: A Historical and Cultural Dictionary*. Richmond, Surrey, UK: Curzon Press, 1999.

Ra Jong-il, trans. Jinna Park. *Inside North Korea's Theocracy: The Rise and Sudden Fall of Jang Song-Thaek*. New York. SUNY Press, 2019.

SaKong, Il. *Korea in the World Economy*. Washington, DC: Institute for International Economics, 1993.

Savada, Andrea Matles, ed. *North Korea: A Country Study*, Fourth Edition. Washington, DC: U.S. GPO, 1994.

Savada, Andrea Matles, and William R. Shaw, eds. *South Korea: A Country Study*, Fourth Edition. Washington, DC: U.S. GPO, 1992.

Shin, Gi-Wook, and Michael Robinson, eds., *Colonial Modernity in Korea*. Cambridge, MA, and London: Harvard University Asia Center, 1999.

Shin, Gi-wook, and Paul Chang, eds. *South Korean Social Movements: From Democracy to Civil Society*. London and New York: Routledge, 2011.

Sigel, Leon V. *Disarming Strangers: Nuclear Diplomacy with North Korea*. Princeton, NJ: Princeton University Press, 1998.

Simons, Geoff. *Korea: The Search for Sovereignty*. New York: Saint Martin's Press, 1995.

Smith, Hazel. *North Korea: Markets and Military Rule*. Cambridge: Cambridge University Press, 2015.

Suh, Dae-sook. *Kim Il Sung: The North Korean Leader*. New York: Columbia University Press, 1988.

Sun, De-Soon, ed. *North Korea after Kim Il Sung*. Boulder, CO: Lynne Rienner Publishers, 1998.

Swartout, Robert R. *Mandarins, Gunboats, and Power Politics: Owen Nickerson and the International Rivalries in Korea*. Honolulu, HI: Asian Studies Program, University of Hawaii, 1980.

Westad, Odd Arne. *Empire & Righteous Nation: 600 Years of China-Korea Relations*. Cambridge, MA: The Belknap Press, 2021.

Wit, Joel S., et al., *Going Critical: The First Korean Nuclear Crisis*. Washington, DC: Brookings Institute Press, 2004.

## Laos

Bourdet, Yves. *The Economics of Transition in Laos: From Socialism to ASEAN Integration*. Northampton, MA: Edward Elgar Publishing, 2000.

Castle, Timothy N. *At War in the Shadow of Vietnam: U.S. Military Aid to the Royal Lao Government, 1955–1975*. New York: Columbia University Press, 1993.

Cordell, Helen. *Laos*. Santa Barbara, CA: ABC-CLIO, 1991.

High, Holly. *Projectland: Life in a Lao Socialist Model Village*. Honolulu, Hawai'i: University of Hawai'i Press, 2021.

Pholsena, Vatthana. *Post-War Laos: The Politics of Culture, History and Identity*. Singapore: Institute of Southeast Asian Studies, 2006.

Savada, Andrea Matles. *Laos: A Country Study*, Third Edition. Washington, DC: U.S. GPO, 1995.

Stuart-Fox, Martin. *A History of Laos*. New York: Cambridge University Press, 1997.

Stuart-Fox, Martin. *Historical Dictionary of Laos*. Lanham, MD: Scarecrow Press, 1992.

Than, Mya, and Joseph L.H. Tan, eds. *Laos' Dilemmas and Options: The Challenge of Economic Transition in the 1990s*. New York: St. Martin's Press, 1997.

## Macao

Chan, Ming K., and Shiu-hing Lo. *Historical Dictionary of the Hong Kong SAR and Macao SAR*. Lanham, MD: Scarecrow Press, 1996.

Cheng, Christina M. *Macao: A Cultural Janus*. Hong Kong: Hong Kong University Press, 1999.

Hao, Zhidong. *Macao: History and Society*. Hong Kong: Hong Kong University Press, 2011.

Pons, Phillipe, trans Sarah Adams. *Macao*. London: Reaktion Books, 2003.

Porter, Jonathan. *Macao, the Imaginary City: Culture and Society, 1557 to the Present*. Boulder, CO: Westview Press, 1996.

Shipp, Steve. *Macao, China: A Political History of the Portuguese Colony's Transition to Chinese Rule*. Jefferson, NC: McFarland & Company, 1997.

Wordie, Jason. *Macao: People and Places, Past and Present*. Hong Kong: Angsana Ltd., 2013.

## Malaysia

Beng, Oui Kee. *Era of Transition: Malaysia after Mahathir*. Singapore: Institute of Southeast Asian Studies, 2006.

Bruton, Henry J. *Sri Lanka and Malaysia*. New York: Oxford University Press, 1992.

Drabble, John H. *An Economic History of Malaysia, C. 1800–1990: The Transition to Modern Economic Growth*. New York: St. Martin's Press, 2000.

# Bibliography and Additional Resources

Gomez, Edmund T. *Malaysia's Political Economy: Politics, Patronage and Profits.* New York: Cambridge University Press, 1997.

Kaur, Amarjit. *Historical Dictionary of Malaysia.* Lanham, MD: Scarecrow Press, 1993.

Kaur, Amarjit, and Ian Metcalfe, eds. *The Shaping of Malaysia.* New York: St. Martin's Press, 1999.

Lemière, Sophie, ed. *Illusions of Democracy: Malaysian Politics and People.* Amsterdam: Amsterdam University Press, 2019.

Lucas, Robert E. *Restructuring the Malaysian Economy: Development and Human Resources.* New York: St. Martin's Press, 1999.

Milne, R. S. *Politics under Mahathir.* New York: Routledge, 1999.

Munro-Kua, Anne. *Authoritarian Populism in Malaysia.* New York: St. Martin's Press, 1997.

Ooi, Keat Gin. *Historical Dictionary of Malaysia.* Lanham MD: Rowman & Littlefield, 2009.

Tomaru, J. *The Post-war Rapprochment of Malaysia and Japan: The Roles of Britain and Japan in South-East Asia.* New York: St Martin's Press, 2000.

## Mongolia

Buell, Paul D., and Francesca Fiarchetti. *Historical Dictionary of the Mongol World Empire.* Lanham, MD: Rowman & Littlefield, 2018.

Kotkin, Stephen, ed. *Mongolia in the Twentieth Century.* Armonk, NY: M.E. Sharpe, 2000.

Morgan, David O. *The Mongols,* Second Edition. Malden, MA: Blackwell Publishing, 2007.

Nordby, Judith. *Mongolia.* Santa Barbara, CA: ABC-CLIO, 1993.

Rossabi, Morris. *Modern Mongolia: Descendants of Khubilai Khan in Transition.* Berkeley, CA: University of California Press, 2005.

Sanders, Alan J. K. *Historical Dictionary of Mongolia,* Third Edition. Lanham, MD: Scarecrow Press, 2010.

Worden, Robert L., and Andrea Matles Savada, eds. *Mongolia: A Country Study,* Second Edition. Washington, DC: U.S. GPO, 1991.

## New Zealand

Alves, Dora, ed. *The Maori and the Crown: An Indigenous People's Struggle for Self-Determination.* Westport, CT: Greenwood Publishing Group, 1999.

Barretta-Herman, Angela. *Welfare State to Welfare Society: Restructuring New Zealand Social Services.* New York: Garland Publishing, 1994.

Boston, Jonathan, et al., eds. *Redesigning the Welfare State in New Zealand: Problems, Policies, Prospects.* New York: Oxford University Press, 1999.

Clements, Kevin P. *Breaking Nuclear Ties: New Zealand's Nuclear-Free Course.* Boulder, CO: Westview Press, 2000.

Emy, Hugh V., ed. *Australia and New Zealand.* Brookfield, VT: Ashgate Publishing Company, 1999.

Fischer, Gerhard, and John Docker, eds. *Race, Colour and Identity in Australia and New Zealand.* Randwick, NSW: New South Wales University Press, 2000.

Hayward, Janine, and Richard Shaw. *Historical Dictionary of New Zealand,* Third Edition. Lanham, MD: Rowman & Littlefield, 2016.

Keenan, Danny. *Wars without End: Ngā pakamga whenua O Mua: New Zealand's Land Wars from a Maori Perspective.* Auckland: Penguin Books, 2021.

King, Michael. T*he Penguin History of New Zealand.* Auckland, New Zealand: Benguin New Zealand, 2012.

Maddock, Shirley. *A Pictorial History of New Zealand.* Auckland, New Zealand: Heinemann Reid, 1988.

McKinnon, Malcolm. *Independence and Foreign Policy: New Zealand in the World since 1935.* Auckland: Auckland University Press, 1993.

McLeay, Elizabeth. *The Cabinet and Political Power in New Zealand.* New York: Oxford University Press, 1995.

Miller, Raymond, *New Zealand Government and Politics.* New York: Oxford University Press, 2006.

Miller, Raymond. *Democracy in New Zealand.* Auckland: Auckland University Press, 2015.

Rice, Geoffrey W., ed. *The Oxford History of New Zealand,* Second Edition. New York: Oxford University Press, 1992.

Robinson, Guy. *Australia and New Zealand: Economy, Society and Environment.* New York: Edward Arnold, 2000.

Rudd, Chris, ed. *The Political Economy of New Zealand.* New York: Oxford University Press, 1997.

Sharp, Andrew, ed. *Leap into the Dark: The Changing Role of the State in New Zealand since 1984.* Auckland: Auckland University Press, 1994.

Sinclair, Keith, ed. *The Oxford Illustrated History of New Zealand, Second Edition.* New York: Oxford University Press, 1996.

Wood, G. A., and Rudd, Christ. *Politics and Government of New Zealand.* University of Otago Press, 2003.

## Papua New Guinea

Dinnen, Sinclair. *Law and Order in a Weak State: Crime and Politics in Papua New Guinea.* Honolulu, HI: University of Hawaii Press, 2000.

Gewertz, Deborah B., and Frederick K. Errington. *Emerging Class in Papua New Guinea: The Telling of Difference.* New York: Cambridge University Press, 1999.

Rannells, Jackson. *PNG: A Fact Book on Modern Papua New Guinea,* Second Edition. New York: Oxford University Press, 1995.

Turner, Ann. *Historical Dictionary of Papua New Guinea,* Second Edition. Lanham, MD: Scarecrow Press, 2001..

Waiko, John Dadeno. *A Short History of Papaua-New Guinea,* Second Edition. Melbourne, Australia: Oxford University Press, 2014.

Webb-Gannon, Camellia. *The Politics of Decolonization in West Papua.* Honolulu, Hawai'i: University of Hawai'i Press, 2021.

## The Philippines

Aboitiz, Nicole CuUnjiang, *Asian Place, Filipino Nation: A Global Intellectual History of the Philippine Revolution, 1887–1912.* New York: Columbia University Press, 2020.

Broad, Robin. *Plundering Paradise: The Struggle for the Environment in the Philippines.* Berkeley, CA: University of California Press, 1993.

Canoy, Jose Raymund. *An Illustrated History of the Philippines.* Oxford: John Beaufoy Publishing, 2019.

Corpuz, O. D. *An Economic History of the Philippines.* Honolulu, HI: University of Hawaii Press, 1999.

Cullather, Nick. *Illusions of Influence: The Political Economy of United States-Philippines Relations, 1942–1960.* Stanford, CA: Stanford University Press, 1994.

Francia, Luis H. *History of the Philiippines: From Indos Bravos to Filipinos.* New York: Harry H Abrams, 2010.

Guillermo, Artemio R. *Historical Dictionary of the Philippines,* Third Edition. Lanham, MD: Scarecrow Press, 2011. .

Karnow, Stanley. *In Our Image: America's Empire in the Philippines.* New York: Ballantine Publishing Group, 1989.

Kwiatkowski, Lynn M. *Struggling with Development: The Politics of Hunger and Gender in the Philippines.* Westport, CT: Westview Press, 1998.

Reid, Robert H., and Eileen Guerrero. *Corazon Aquino and the Brushfire Revolution.* Baton Rouge, LA: Louisiana State University Press, 1995.

Steinberg, David. *The Philippines,* Fourth Edition. Boulder, Co: Westview, 2000.

## Singapore

Clammer, John. *Race and State in Independent Singapore: The Cultural Politics of Pluralism in a Multiethnic Society.* Brookfield, VT: Ashgate Publishing Company, 1998.

# Bibliography and Additional Resources

Frost, Mark R., and Yu-Mei Balsingham-chow. *Singapore: A Biography.* Singapore: Editions Didier Millet Pte. Ltd., 2013.

George, Cherian. *Singapore Incomplete: Reflections on a First World Nation's Arrested Development.* Singapore: Woodsville News, 2017.

Gopinathan, S., et al., eds. *Language, Society and Education in Singapore: Issues and Trends.* Portland, OR: International Specialized Book Services, 1998.

Haas, Michael, ed. *The Singapore Puzzle.* Westport, CT: Greenwood Publishing Group, 1999.

Hill, Michael, and Lian Kwen Fee. *The Politics of Nation Building and Citizenship in Singapore.* New York: Routledge, 1995.

Huff, W. G. *The Economic Growth of Singapore: Trade and Development in the Twentieth Century.* New York: Cambridge University Press, 1994.

Kong, Lily. *Singapore: A Developmental City State.* New York: John Wiley & Sons, 1997.

Lee, Kuan Yew. *From Third World to First: The Singapore Story, 1965–2000.* New York: HarperCollins Publishers, 2000.

Leifer, Michael. *Singapore's Foreign Policy: Coping with Vulnerability.* New York: Routledge, 2000.

Leong, Ho Khai. *Shared Responsibilities, Unshared Power. The Politics of Policy-making in Singapore.* Cheney, WA: Eastern Universities Press, 2003.

Ling, Qui G. *The City and the State: Singapore's Built Environment Revisited.* New York: Oxford University Press, 1997.

Mauzy, Diane K., and R. S. Milne. *Singapore Politics under the People's Action Party.* New York: Routledge, 2002.

Mulliner, K., and Lian The-Mulliner. *Historical Dictionary of Singapore.* Lanham, MD: Scarecrow Press, 1991.

Rodan, Garry, ed. *Singapore Changes Guard: Social, Political and Economic Directions in the 1990s.* New York: St. Martin's Press, 1993.

Von Alten, Florian. *The Role of Government in the Singapore Economy.* New York: Peter Lang Publishing, 1995.

## Taiwan

Bullard, Monte. *The Soldier and the Citizen: The Role of the Military in Taiwan's Development.* Armonk, NY: M. E. Sharpe, 1997.

Chao, Linda. *The First Chinese Democracy: Political Life in the Republic of China on Taiwan.* Baltimore, MD: Johns Hopkins University Press, 1997.

Clough, Ralph. *Cooperation or Conflict in the Taiwan Strait?* Lanham, MD: Rowman & Littlefield Publishers, 1999.

Copper, John F. *Taiwan. Nation-State or Province?* Boulder, CO: Westview, 2003.

Copper, John F. *Historical Dictionary of Taiwan,* Second Edition. Lanham, MD: Scarecrow Press, 2000.

Finkelstein, David Michael. *Washington's Dilemma, 1949–1950: From Abandonment to Salvation.* Fairfax, VA: George Mason University Press, 1993.

Garver, John W. *The Sino-American Alliance: Nationalist China and American Cold War Strategy in Asia.* Armonk, NY: M. E. Sharpe, 1997.

Hickey, Dennis Van Vranken. *United States Taiwan Security Ties: From Cold War to Beyond Containment.* New York: Praeger, 1994.

Hood, Steven J. *The Kuomintang and the Democratization of Taiwan.* Boulder, CO: Westview Press, 1997.

Hughes, Christopher. *Taiwan and Chinese Nationalism: National Identity and Status in International Society.* New York: Routledge, 1997.

Hui, Kalley, Wu Tzu, and Kerry Brown. *The Trouble with Taiwan: History, the United States and a Rising China.* London: Zed Books, 2019.

Lasater, Martin L. *U.S. Interests in the New Taiwan.* Boulder, CO: Westview Press, 1993.

Lee, Bernice. *The Security Implications of the New Taiwan.* New York: Oxford University Press, 2000.

Maguire, Keith. *The Rise of Modern Taiwan.* Brookfield, VT: Ashgate Publishing Company, 1998.

McBeath, Gerald A. *Wealth and Freedom: Taiwan's New Political Economy.* Brookfield, VT: Ashgate Publishing Company, 1998.

Rawnsley, Gary D. *Taiwan's Informal Diplomacy and Propaganda.* New York: St. Martin's Press, 2000.

Rubinstein, Murray A., ed. *Taiwan: A New History,* Expanded Edition. Armonk, NY: M. E. Sharpe, 2007.

Schive, Chi. *Taiwan's Economic Role in East Asia.* Washington, DC: Center for Strategic and International Studies, 1995.

Shambaugh, David, ed. *Contemporary Taiwan.* New York: Oxford University Press, 1998.

Skoggard, Ian A. *The Indigenous Dynamic in Taiwan's Postwar Development: The Religious and Historical Roots of Entrepreneurship.* Armonk, NY: M.E. Sharpe, 1996.

Sutter, Robert G., and William R. Johnson, eds. *Taiwan in World Affairs.* Boulder, CO: Westview Press, 1994.

Tsang, Steve, and Hung-mao Tien. *Democratization in Taiwan: Implications for China.* New York: St. Martin's Press, 1999.

Tsang, Steve, ed. *In the Shadow of China: Political Developments in Taiwan since 1949.* Honolulu, HI: University of Hawaii Press, 1993.

Wachman, Alan M. *Taiwan: National Identity and Democratization.* Armonk, NY: M. E. Sharpe, 1994.

Wu, Jaushieh Joseph. *Taiwan's Democratization: Forces behind the New Momentum.*

New York: Oxford University Press, 1995.

Zhao, Suisheng. *Power by Design: Constitution-Making in Nationalist China.* Honolulu, HI: University of Hawaii Press, 1996.

## Thailand

Campbell, Burnham O., et al., eds. *The Economic Impact of Demographic Change in Thailand, 1980–2015.* Honolulu, HI: University of Hawaii Press, 1993.

Chachavalpongpun, Pavin, ed. *Reinventing Thailand: Thaksin and His Foreign Policy.* Singapore: Institute of Southeast Asian Studies, 2010.

Dixon, Chris. *The Thai Economy: Uneven Development and Internationalism.* New York: Routledge, 1999.

Funston, John. *Southern Thailand: The Dynamics of Conflict.* Singapore: Institute of Southeast Asian Studies, 2008.

Hall, Denise. *Business Prospects in Thailand.* Upper Saddle River, NJ: Prentice Hall, 1997.

Jansen, Karel. *External Finance in Thailand's Development: An Interpretation of Thailand's Growth Boom.* New York: St. Martin's Press, 1997.

Krongkaew, Medhi, ed. *Thailand's Industrialization and Its Consequences.* New York: Saint Martin's Press, 1995.

Mills, Mary Beth. *Thai Women in the Global Labor Force: Consuming Desires, Contested Selves.* New Brunswick, NY: Rutgers University Press, 1999.

Mulder, Niels. *Inside Thai Society: An Interpretation of Everyday Life.* Boston, MA: Charles E. Tuttle, 1997.

Muscat, Robert J. *The Fifth Tiger: A Study of Thai Development Policy.* Armonk, NY: M. E. Sharpe, 1994.

Phongpaichit, Pasuk and Sungsidh Piriyarangsan. *Corruption and Democracy in Thailand.* Seattle, WA: University of Washington Press, 1998.

Phongpaichit, Pasuk, and Chris Baker. *Thaksin.* Chiang Mai: Silkworm Books, 2009.

Skagner, Kerbo. *Modern Thailand.* New York: McGraw-Hill, 1999.

Strate, Shane. *The Lost Territories: Thailand's History of National Humiliation.* Honolulu, Hawai'i: University of Hawai'i Press, 2015.

## Vietnam

Anderson, David L. *Facing My Lai: Moving beyond the Massacre.* Lawrence, KS: University Press of Kansas, 2000.

Arkadie, Brian, and Mallon, Raymond. *Viet Nam: A Transition Tiger?* Acton, Australia: Asia Pacific Press, 2003.

Ashwill, Mark A. *Vietnam Today: A Guide to a Nation at a Crossroads.* Yarmouth, ME,:Intercultural Press, 2005.

Chan, Anita. *Transforming Asian Socialism: China and Vietnam Compared.* Lanham,

MD: Rowman & Littlefield, 1999.

Chapuis, Oscar M. *A History of Vietnam: From Hong Bang to Tu Duc*. Westport, CT: Greenwood Press, 1995.

Cima, Ronald J., ed. *Vietnam: A Country Study*. Washington, DC: U.S. GPO, 1989.

Clodfelter, Michael. *Vietnam in Military Statistics: A History of the Indochina Wars, 1772–1991*. Jefferson, NC: McFarland & Company, 1995.

Davidson, Phillip B. *Vietnam at War: The History, 1946–1975*. New York: Oxford University Press, 1991.

Duiker, William J. *Historical Dictionary of Vietnam*. Lanham, MD: Scarecrow Press, 1997.

Duiker, William J. *Ho Chi Minh: A Life*. New York: Hyperion, 2000.

Elliott, David. *The Vietnamese War: Revolution and Social Change in the Mekong Delta*. Armonk, NY: M. E. Sharpe, 2001.

Harvie, Charles, and Tran Van Hoa. *Vietnam's Reforms and Economic Growth*. New York: St. Martin's Press, 1997.

Hayton, Bill. *Vietnam: Rising Dragon*, New Edition. New Haven, CT: Yale University Press, 2020.

Hunt, Michael H. *Lyndon Johnson's War: America's Cold War Crusade in Vietnam, 1945–1968*. New York: Hill & Wang, 1996.

Jamieson, Neil L. *Understanding Vietnam*. Berkeley, CA: University of California Press, 1993.

Kamm, Henry. *Dragon Ascending: Vietnam and the Vietnamese*. New York: Arcade Publishing, 1996.

Kerkvliet, Benedict J. Tria, and Doug J. Porter, eds. *Vietnam's Rural Transformation*. Boulder, CO: Westview Press, 1995.

Lamb, David. *Vietnam Now*. Boulder, CO: Westview, 2002.

Langguth, A. J. *Our Vietnam: A History of the War, 1954–1975*. New York: Simon & Schuster, 2000.

Lomperis, Timothy J. *From People's War to People's Rule: Insurgency, Intervention, and the Lessons of Vietnam*. Chapel Hill, NC: University of North Carolina Press, 1996.

Luong, Hy V. *Post War Vietnam: Dynamics of a Transforming Society*. Singapore: Institute of Southeast Asian Studies and Rowman & Littlefield Publishers, 2003.

McNamara, Robert T. *Argument without End: In Search of Answers to the Vietnam Tragedy*. New York: Public Affairs, 1999.

Morley, James W., and Masashi Nishihara, eds. *Vietnam Joins the World*. Armonk, NY: M. E. Sharpe, 1997.

Moses, George D. *Vietnam: An American Ordeal*. Upper Saddle River, NJ: Prentice-Hall, 1994.

Murray, Geoffrey. *Vietnam: Dawn of a New Market*. New York: St. Martin's Press, 1997.

Nguyen Vu Tung. *Flying Blind: Vietnam's Decision to join ASEAN*. Singapore: ISEAS, 2021.

Osborne, Milton. *The Mekong: Turbulent Past, Uncertain Future*. New York: Grove/Atlantic, 2000.

Rotter, Andrew J., ed. *Light at the End of the Tunnel: A Vietnam War Anthology*. Wilmington, DE: Scholarly Resources, 1999.

SarDesai, D. R. *Vietnam: Past and Present*. Boulder, CO: Westview Press, 1998.

Schulzinger, Robert D. *A Time for War: The United States and Vietnam, 1941–1975*. New York: Oxford University Press, 1997.

Stern, Lewis M. *Imprisoned or Missing in Vietnam: Policies of the Vietnames Government Concerning Captured and Unaccounted for United States Soldiers, 1969–1994*. Jefferson, NC: McFarland & Company, 1995.

Tucker, Spencer C. *Vietnam*. Lexington, KY: University Press of Kentucky, 1999.

Vandemark, Brian. *Into the Quagmire: Lyndon Johnson and the Escalation of the Vietnam War*. New York: Oxford University Press, 1991.

Wolff, Peter. *Vietnam: The Complete Transformation*. Portland, OR: Frank Cass Publishers, 1999.

## Pacific Islands

Craig, Robert D. et al., eds. *Historical Dictionary of Oceania*. Westport, CT: Greenwood Press, 1981.

Gorman, G. E., and J. J. Mills. *Fiji*. Santa Barbara, CA: ABC-CLIO, 1994.

Hanlon, David L. *Remaking Micronesia: Discourses over Development in a Pacific Territory*. Honolulu, HI: University of Hawaii Press, 1998.

Hill, Hal, and João M. Saldanha, eds. *East Timor. Development Challenges for the World's Newest Nation*. NY: Palgrave, 2003.

Lal, Brij V. *Broken Waves: A History of the Fiji Islands in the Twentieth Century*. Honolulu, HI: University of Hawaii Press, 1992.

Leibowitz, Arnold H. *Embattled Island: Palau's Struggle for Independence*. New York: Praeger, 1996.

Levy, Neil M. *Micronesia Handbook*, Fourth Edition. Chico, CA: Moon Publications, 1997.

Sahlins, Marshall D. *Islands of History*. Chicago: University of Chicago Press, 1987.

Stanley, David. *South Pacific Handbook*, Sixth Edition. Chico, CA: Moon Publications, 1996.

Wuerch, William L. and Dirk Anthony Ballendorf. *Historical Dictionary of Guam and Micronesia*. Lanham, MD: Scarecrow Press, 1994.

# Hanging Gardens

## INDOORS & OUTDOORS
### BY ELVIN McDONALD

GROSSET
GOOD LIFE
BOOKS

PUBLISHERS · GROSSET & DUNLAP · NEW YORK
A FILMWAYS COMPANY

# Acknowledgments

Cover photograph by Mort Engel

The author wishes to express his appreciation to the following for permission to use their illustrations in this book:

Antonelli Brothers, p. 6, 58; Black & Decker, p. 36; Bodger Seeds, Ltd., p. 75; Burpee Seeds, p. 50, 51, 64, 82, 83; Desert Botanical Garden, p. 37; Hort-Pix, p. 27, 33, 67, 81, 87; House Plant Corner, Ltd., p. 36; Jackson & Perkins, p. 16, 18; Leaf Nurseries, 37, 52, 53, 88; Bob Lopez, 45; Elvin McDonald, 6, 8, 12, 13, 18, 20, 21, 37–41, 44, 49, 54, 56, 60, 61, 63, 68, 71, 72, 74, 76, 78, 80, 81, 84, 88; Rod McLellan Co., 37, 42, 45, 48, 54, 55, 62, 79, 85; Merry Gardens, 50–52, 56, 57, 64–67, 69, 76–80; Bill Mulligan, 7, 9 (Horticultural Designer, Linda Trinkle Wolf), 14, 15, 17 (Horticultural Designer, Linda Trinkle Wolf), 19, 20, 22, 23, 32, 34, 40, 47; Pan-American Seed Co., 72; George W. Park Seed Co., Inc., 21, 44, 49, 57, 63, 64, 68, 69, 70, 83, 86; Maynard Parker, 24, 26; Paul J. Peart, 84; Phillips Products, 18; Redwood Domes Greenhouses, 30; Stokes Seeds, 46, 66; Max Tatch, 28; USDA, 86; Verilux TruBloom, 10; Western Wood Products, 29; Window Shade Manufacturers Association, 17.

# Contents

# 1
# Hanging Gardens
# of Fable and Fact

Four thousand years ago, 60 miles south of Baghdad, the fabled hanging gardens of Babylon grew near the banks of the Euphrates River. Today the site lies in ruins outside of Al Hillah, Iraq, but in the years 1800–1500 B.C. it was so spectacular as to be considered in Hellenistic times as one of the Seven Wonders of the World. Fact and fable blur as to exactly what the hanging gardens were. They may have grown from the terraces of a vaulted substructure to help cool the interior, or they may have been the trees and vines that grew on various levels of the ziggurat (pyramidal temple towers).

In either case, the words "hanging gardens of Babylon" were all I heard the day we studied the ancient kingdom of Babylonia in sixth grade. Since my parents and I lived on a barren, windswept hillside in western Oklahoma, I immediately began to plan its transformation. There would be lush green and flower-covered plants growing all over our hill, considered already something of a Local Wonder because of the peculiar way it rose from flat land all around. Grandaddy King said this meant there was a pool of oil underneath, and whether or not one had anything to do with the other, he was right. But to get back to my story, I went home that night with a new vision of our hill—which Mamma promptly erased by reminding me of our impossibly dry climate. But as I munched jam-filled cookies still warm from the oven and gulped a couple of glasses of cold milk, she suggested I could grow a hanging garden in the little lean-to greenhouse I had built the summer before. In an instant I was off and running.

By night there was a shelf on the wall of the building to which the greenhouse was attached, with pots of every dangling or trailing plant I could find lining the edge. Cup hooks in the roof, spirited from Mamma's kitchen cabinets, held pots of petunias hurriedly dug from the garden and suspended by even more hurriedly knotted twine—which I had found in Daddy's tool box. To me the effect was absolutely breathtaking and, probably more important to my parents, I was so happy that neither of them scolded me about the missing hooks or twine.

Obviously, hanging plants or the dream of them will always inspire romantic fantasies which are based on fact. And in our time we have seen hanging plants make a major contribution to the greening of America.

*Cascade tuberous begonias in California lath house.*

*Hybrid tuberous begonias in window boxes grow well along a north-facing wall in warm weather.*

My oasis in the desert can be yours, too, no matter where you live, your level of green thumbery or wallet credentials. As a matter of fact, Master Charge—and other major cards —will buy you an instant hanging garden in an increasing number of nurseries nationwide. As a people we have finally accepted flowers and plants as necessities of life, not luxuries. If the idea of having a beautiful plant makes you feel wonderful, then you deserve it. And if you don't have the cash, that plant is as chargeable as anything—food, clothing, perfume, travel—in our society.

What makes that plant vital is that it is real. It is a living, breathing creature which undoubtedly has its own sophisticated communications system. Plants and people belong together. Plan your hanging garden accordingly. Whether indoors or outdoors, it will live—or die—in the environment you provide. If first you evaluate that environment in terms of sun or shade, hot or cold, moist or dry, then you'll at least know half of what it takes to select a plant most likely to thrive in the conditions you have. The other half lies in knowing the environmental needs of specific plants. Since gardening is an inexact science, no expert has the last word on all of these matters. One gardens by practice—and there is always room for another practitioner.

Having been distracted from that history lesson, I seem to have learned something anyway, and hanging plants and gardens have been a fascination for me ever since. When I moved to New York City in 1958, there were almost no hanging plants except in public conservatories and in a few home greenhouses belonging to the adventuresome. But already in the mid-America from which I came the gardening buffs were discovering ways to make hanging basket tuberous begonias and fuchsias thrive outdoors in summers that were either muggy and hot or dry and windy. Part of this interest began in the Forties as progeny of the

*In the author's south-facing living room in a high-rise apartment, hanging plants serve as living draperies. Kinds include various cissus, Charm begonia, orchids, spider plant, lipstick vine, fittonia and asparagus-fern. A building across the street cuts off direct sun in early afternoon.*

*Boston ferns thrive in this north-facing window with Tahitian bridal veil above and a begonia on the sill. One fluorescent supplements daylight.*

*Grapes of Wrath* folk shared the Eden they had found in California with the family and friends who stayed back home.

Then came the mobility and affluence of the Fifties and everybody could fly and drive around seeing for themselves the fabled hanging begonias and fuchsias of the West Coast from San Diego to British Columbia.

Meanwhile, back on the Island of Manhattan, a new breed of restaurant had begun to spring up for what we know today as the Sixties swinging singles. Places like Maxwell's Plum became glamorous in part because there were real flowers on the tables and real foliage plants hanging overhead. The naturally chic, the trendy, and the would-be, all felt better drinking, dining, and meeting in a surround of living plants. And, if living plants were that effective in public, wouldn't they make home a nicer place to be?

In the years since, all plants—not just hanging types alone—have become an important part of the lives of people in general, not just the gardeners. Indoors, living draperies are replacing fabrics. Hanging plants and potted trees may divide spaces, indoors or outdoors. And each may be cultivated with tender, loving care simply for its uniqueness.

Another way we get into plants today is by an active or appreciative interest in the beauties of hand-crafted macramé hangers or hand-thrown pottery.

Plants in hanging containers also soften the reality of not having space for them on the floor or sill, it being understood that plants are a necessity, and therefore just as important in the environment as a chair or table—maybe more so. Depending on your personality, and the space, a single hanging plant may be what you want, or a whole row of mixed or matched baskets hung all at the same level or all at different levels. One nice thing about plants suspended in the air is that you can move them up or down easily to create an entirely different effect. And containers of hanging plants may be used to frame a beautiful view or to block a bad one.

Another appeal of hanging plants is that they swing and move about with relative freedom. Even trailers spilling from a container placed on a pedestal or shelf, or in a window

*Ordinary hanging plants become extraordinary when well grown, perfectly groomed and thoughtfully displayed.*

box or strawberry jar, gently sway leaves and flowers in the breezes. Like theater-in-the-round, a hanging garden offers an enlightening and presumably delightful perspective.

There are only a few absolute rules to follow if you want your hanging garden to be delightful. Most important is never to let the soil in which a hanging plant is growing dry out completely, even if you are growing a cactus or other succulent from the desert. Before you hang a plant, look up its needs in a book (specific recipes for success are given for approximately 200 different selections in Chapter 6). Try to give your plant what it needs from the beginning. Almost any plant can be suspended in the air—provided you have the space and inclination. And kinds that neither trail nor climb such as ponytail, agave, or screw-pine may look all the better given the opportunity to fly in a magnificent hanging container.

Look for hanging plants at local nurseries, garden centers, and plant shops. Not all that hangs may be worth growing, and vice versa. But if you see any plant you like especially, whether it is airborne or earthbound, envision it hung in your hanging garden. This consideration has to be visual as well as practical: Will its beauty and the environment be mutually complementary? If you're not sure of a good match, ask a plant person for advice. And don't be afraid to experiment a little; that's part of what makes gardening fun.

Besides, not everything hung in the air has to live forever. For an experience in ephemeral beauty, try hanging pots of crocus, cyclamen, daffodil, tulip, or hyacinth at the moment the flowerbuds begin to show color. In a properly cool, moist, airy and bright environment, the cyclamen may bloom for months, but the others will be gone in a few days—at most a week or so—and then they'll have to be replaced by something else. Maybe chives, basil, parsley, and rosemary to bask in the sunny warmth of summer. Or cherry tomatoes, peppers, cucumbers and squash.

All of these and countless other plants for foliage, flowers, and ornamental or edible fruit may be nurtured in hanging gardens. How-to details, what to grow and where to buy it, are covered in the pages that follow.

*A fluorescent fixture with two 40-watt tubes supplements natural light in this north-facing window garden. The fluorescents are burned 8 to 12 hours daily, up to 16 in cloudy, dark weather.*

# 2
# Hanging Gardens Indoors

Were it not for the necessity of light, hanging plants might be enjoyed indoors anywhere—suspended in a high-ceilinged but dimly lighted entryway, over the tub in a bathroom with one small, stained-glass window facing north, or hung in the corner of a windowless basement den. In the 1960s, plastic plants were often used in places like these. The growing awareness of ecology made us realize it wasn't right to kill plants by putting them in the wrong environment, but it took the Seventies for us to realize that scarce by-products of the petroleum industry go into the manufacture of plastic plants, and that these very petrochemicals are in fact needed for products necessary to human survival. In the jargon of the Seventies, people who have their heads together either grow real hanging plants where the light and other conditions are naturally right and arrange the rest of the room's furnishings accordingly, or else they provide suitable artificial light, having first spent some time studying the situation to determine how it could be made hospitable for living plants.

If living plants are truly important to you, either of these approaches can be made to work in almost any situation. Even where no natural light reaches, as in many interior offices, 10 to 16 hours of illumination daily from ceiling fluorescents will sustain plants hung 12 to 24 inches from ordinary Cool White or Warm White tubes (one of each in the fixture is preferable for well-balanced plant growth).

## Best Hanging Plants for Ceiling Fluorescent Light

| Latin Name | Common Name |
| --- | --- |
| *Aechmea* | Bromeliad |
| *Aeschynanthus* | Lipstick vine |
| *Aglaonema* | Chinese evergreen |
| *Asparagus* | Asparagus-fern |
| *Asplenium bulbiferum* | Mother fern |
| *Begonia* | (Rexes and canes) |
| *Billbergia* | Queen's tears |

| | |
|---|---|
| *Bowiea* | Climbing onion |
| *Chlorophytum* | Spider plant |
| *Cissus* | Grape-ivy; kangaroo vine |
| *Columnea* | Gesneriad |
| *Cyanotis* | Teddy-bear plant |
| *Cymbalaria* | Kenilworth-ivy |
| *Davallia* | Rabbit's-foot fern |
| *Episcia* | Flame violet |
| *Ficus* | Creeping fig |
| *Fittonia* | Nerve plant |
| *Gibasis* | Tahitian bridal veil |
| *Gynura* | Purple passion |
| *Hedera* | English ivy |
| *Helxine* | Baby's-tears |
| *Hoya* | Wax plant |
| *Maranta* | Prayer plant |
| *Nephrolepis* | Boston fern; Fluffy Ruffles fern |
| *Oxalis regnellii* | Oxalis |
| *Pellionia* | Pellionia |
| *Peperomia* | Peperomia |
| *Philodendron* | Philodendron |
| *Pilea* | Pilea |
| *Plectranthus* | Swedish-ivy |
| *Polypodium* | Bear's-paw fern |
| *Saintpaulia* | African violet |
| *Saxifraga* | Strawberry-begonia |
| *Scindapsus* | Pothos |
| *Senecio* | String of pearls |
| *Tolmiea* | Piggyback |
| *Tradescantia* | Wandering jew |
| *Zebrina* | Wandering jew |

ABOVE: *Hanging bubble bowl holds a dwarf palm, hoya and young plants of echeveria.*

BELOW: Aeschynanthus marmoratus, *a form of lipstick vine, grows near an east-facing kitchen window.*

If you want to grow hanging plants in natural light, first evaluate how much direct sun they will receive, if any. Lack of direct sun, at least in the morning or afternoon, cuts down the list of suitable plants; but if the light is bright enough in the daytime for you to read by, there are a surprising number of possibilities.

## Best Hanging Plants for Bright Natural Light

| Latin Name | Common Name |
|---|---|
| *Aeschynanthus* | Lipstick vine |
| *Aglaonema* | Chinese evergreen |
| *Asparagus* | Asparagus-fern |
| *Asplenium bulbiferum* | Mother fern |
| *Chlorophytum* | Spider plant |
| *Cissus* | Grape-ivy; kangaroo vine |
| *Cymbalaria* | Kenilworth-ivy |
| *Davallia* | Rabbit's-foot fern |
| *Ficus* | Creeping fig |
| *Hedera* | English ivy |
| *Helxine* | Baby's-tears |
| *Hoya* | Wax plant |
| *Maranta* | Prayer plant |
| *Pellionia* | Pellionia |
| *Philodendron* | Philodendron |
| *Plectranthus* | Swedish-ivy |
| *Polypodium* | Bear's-paw fern |

ABOVE: *Heartleaf philodendron makes a pretty hanging plant near a north-facing window.*

BELOW: *Shelf placed high up in a west window provides space for numerous hanging plants.*

*Adjustable floodlights may be used to supplement weak natural light. The pedestal holds a Boston fern.*

| | |
|---|---|
| *Saxifraga* | Strawberry-begonia |
| *Scindapsus* | Pothos |
| *Tolmiea* | Piggyback |
| *Tradescantia* | Wandering jew |

In Chapter 6 the light needs of plants are indicated as full sun, half-sun, part shade, full shade, or any combination of these. Applied to naturally lighted indoor gardens these terms mean:

*Full sun:* unobstructed, south-facing window
*Half sun:* unobstructed, east- or west-facing window
*Part shade:* direct sun less than one-fourth of the day
*Shade:* little or no direct sun, but bright light

Hanging plants placed outdoors in the summer, but kept indoors during cold weather, almost always need more sun in the winter than they do in the open. And obviously a plant hung six feet back from an unobstructed south-facing window may in reality be receiving only part shade; and if a plant is hung on the wall opposite the window, possibly 18 feet away, the daylight there may not even qualify as shade. This is the place to use supplementary lighting, probably from one or more incandescent floodlights, but possibly from fluorescents.

Select incandescent floods with built-in reflectors; kinds such as General Electric's Cool Beam, Sylvania's Cool Lux and Duro-Lite's Plant Lite are available generally in sizes from 75 to 150 watts. Use these in fixtures with ceramic sockets, placing them two to three feet away from the plants so as not to burn the leaves. As a supplement to weak natural light, burn 1 or 2 floods 6 to 8 hours daily over each hanging basket—probably in the evening so that you can enjoy the dramatic effect of your artificially lighted plants.

If incandescent floods are the sole source of light for a hanging garden, burn them 14 to 16 hours out of every 24. Fixtures and suggested arrangements for artificially lighted hanging plants are shown in the accompanying illustrations.

Although fluorescents for lighting a hanging

ABOVE: *Lipstick vine in macramé holder grows in author's south-facing living-room window.*

BELOW: *This floodlight fixture is designed specifically for lighting a hanging plant.*

ABOVE: *A decorative ceramic pedestal holds asparagus-fern in this garden room.*

BELOW: *A bamboo plant stand lifts this Boston fern so that the fronds can cascade freely.*

garden may be hung at almost any level, their shape and appearance drastically reduce the number of places where they can be used, both in terms of practicality and aesthetics.

With proper light, either natural or artificial, you can now proceed to hang plants from the ceiling or from wall brackets, or display them on pedestals of varied heights that allow trailing growth to cascade freely. Hanging plants are especially pleasing to the eye when used in the company of paintings, sculpture or objets d'art.

The care of hanging plants in general is detailed in Chapter 5, but other than light, the main concerns indoors are temperature, humidity, and soil moisture. Hanging gardens, which are in reality only a specialized form of container gardening, tend to require watering more often to maintain an evenly moist growing medium. And if the container hangs so high that you cannot see the soil, you will have to reach up with your fingers or climb a stepstool to determine if it is wet, moist, or dry. Baskets hung near the ceiling during the winter heating season have to endure more warmth than those closer to the floor, and will therefore dry out more quickly. Perhaps most vulnerable of all is the plant hung directly over a radiator or other type of heating unit. The plants suggested in Chapter 6 for low humidity and temperatures between 62 and 75 degrees F. during the winter heating season are the most likely to tolerate such a situation.

Pedestals intended for plant display may be purchased, or you can make your own using half-inch plywood or quarter-inch Plexiglas. Usually an 8- to 14-inch width works well, and height can vary from 12 to 48 inches; obviously, the taller the pedestal, the greater the width has to be for stability. Found objects that cost little or nothing also may be turned into holders for hanging plants. Clay flue tiles and concrete conduit can be used to advantage in some situations. Empty cannisters available from ice-cream stores may be used singly or stacked and joined together in twos, threes or fours; cover the exteriors with fabric, wallpaper, or a peel-and-stick product such as silver mylar. To show off small hanging plants, you can simply invert stacks of clean, empty

*Spider plant (left) and kangaroo-vine cissus (right) placed on either side of window away from radiator.*

*An unusual bromeliad, Acanthostachys strobila-ceae, grows in a bright, east-facing window; the pot is attached to the frame by means of a metal clip.*

**NEAR RIGHT:** *This metal plant stand provides an excellent means for growing and displaying both upright and hanging plants. Kinds (from the top) include pothos, African violet, peperomia and Boston fern.*

**FAR RIGHT:** *This yard urn and pedestal may look as if it were centuries old. In reality it is an inexpensive copy made of high density polyethylene; may be used indoors or outdoors.*

**18    Hanging Gardens**

*This rex begonia thrives on a glass shelf installed on wood brackets in a bright living-room window.*

flowerpots all of the same size. And there are always stepladders and wicker stools of various heights that can be used for giving hanging plants a lift.

Many of the plants included in Chapter 6 are suggested for growing on a shelf. Glass shelves installed in front of a window make a great place to grow and show off a variety of plants, some trailing in habit, some upright. Bookshelves facing or at right-angles to a bright window may also receive enough light or sun to nurture some hanging plants. Although plants placed among books require extreme caution at watering time, the combination is a winner aesthetically.

Besides the plants suggested in Chapter 6 for hanging indoors, you can also suspend terrariums, tropical trees and shrubs trained as bonsai, and moss-filled wire or metal topiary forms covered with small-leaved English ivy, creeping fig, baby's-tears, or creeping Charlie pilea. All of these may be equally effective when displayed on a pedestal of appropriate size, height, and color.

## How to Hang Containers

Installing either hook or eye screws where wood in the ceiling is exposed—beams, for example—is relatively easy. Some woods are soft enough to allow installing a screw without drilling a pilot hole first. Exposed wood on walls or around windows also simplifies the installation of brackets to hold hanging plants.

If you have plaster- or gypsum-board ceilings or walls, locate a wood ceiling joist or wall stud in which to anchor long screws. To find a joist or stud, measure 14½ inches from a corner; thereafter joists or studs usually will be found every 16 inches, but sometimes they have 20- or 24-inch spacing. After you find a joist or stud in approximately the right place, drill a pilot hole, then install a screw hook, an eye, or a bracket screw long enough to extend well into the wood.

If you cannot locate a wood ceiling joist or wall stud in plaster- or gypsum-board ceilings or walls, you may be able to solve the problem by using split-wing toggle bolts, expansion

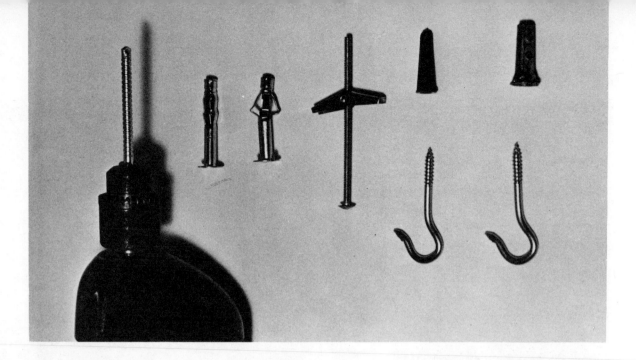

bolts or expansion plugs, provided the plant to be hung is relatively lightweight. Since expansion bolts come with a machine bolt, it will be necessary to replace this with a long machine-threaded hook or an eye bolt for ceiling installations.

Where walls and ceilings are brick, concrete or masonry, first make a hole with a carbide bit and electric drill, then lightly hammer into the hole a lead anchor plug, or sleeve, into which you can screw a hook or an eye. Some hardware stores have only plastic or fiber anchor plugs, and I have used both successfully in the concrete ceilings of my high-rise apartment.

Kitchen cup hooks are nice to use indoors for fairly lightweight hanging plants. Standard hook and eye screws come in a variety of finishes in a wide range of sizes; the larger the number, the smaller the size. For large, heavy plantings you might use a 00, 0, 1, or 2 hook or eye, while a 4, 6, or 8 might be used for medium to small containers. Wall brackets which may be used for hanging plants are available in hardware and dime stores, garden centers, lumber yards, and discount chains.

Once you have hooks, eyes or brackets installed in satisfactory light, selecting the containers is easy, primarily a matter of personal taste and budget. The words "hanging basket" referred originally to wire baskets shaped either as half spheres for hanging or quarter spheres for mounting against a wall, with the addition of a thick lining of unmilled sphagnum moss or florist's sheet moss. These are available today in both wire and open-mesh plastic and they are excellent outdoors where excess water dripping from them is of no consequence. But indoors, every time you water one of them, it has to be taken to a sink or tub, soaked, allowed to drain, and then returned to the growing area. If you're careful not to apply too much all at once, most hanging containers available today don't have to be moved at watering time. Choose from clay, plastic, wood, and ceramic.

The more porous the container, the more water it will require and the greater is the danger of excess spilling on the floor, especially moss-lined wire or plastic and unlined wood baskets. If you water carefully, excess drainage should not be a problem with nonporous plas-

ABOVE: *For installing hooks or eyes for holding hanging plants from the top: carbide-tipped bit and electric drill; expansion bolts before and after expanding; split-wing toggle bolt; two kinds of anchor plugs or sleeves.*
BELOW: *Columnea in a moss-lined wire basket.*

BELOW: *Cherry tomato in redwood wall planter.*
BELOW RIGHT: *Swedish-ivy in utilitarian white plastic container with wire hanger.*

ABOVE: *Rhipsalis in a redwood slat basket.*
ABOVE RIGHT: *Fuchsia in a moss-lined plastic hanging container.*

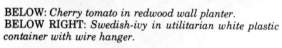

*Wall-mounted bracket holds ivyleaf geranium.*

*Moss-lined wood box holds a thriving orchid.*

tic, glazed clay and metal- or plastic-lined containers. Unglazed clay fitted with a saucer underneath offers no particular excess drainage problem, but since moisture evaporates through the walls of the pot, more water will be required to keep the plant's roots properly moist.

A vast majority of hanging plants sold come planted already in a white, green or terra-cotta colored plastic container with a wire hanger attached to holes in the rim. If the appearance of these is too utilitarian, you can cover them with attractive woven baskets just slightly wider and deeper. Or you can remove the wire hangers and slip the utilitarian plastic basket down inside a more decorative hanging container, perhaps hand-thrown pottery, or wood-shaped as a box, inverted pyramid, or cradle. If the plant hides the plastic pot, you can replace the wire hanger with lengths of chain purchased at a hardware store. Besides three or four equal lengths of chain, which comes in several finishes and sizes (a #14 or #16 works well for most baskets indoors), you'll need an S hook to join them together at the top plus three or four S hooks to insert in the rim of the container.

Clay and ceramic pots are available with and without drainage holes, and with and without

*Metal clip attaches to pot rim; hang on wall.*

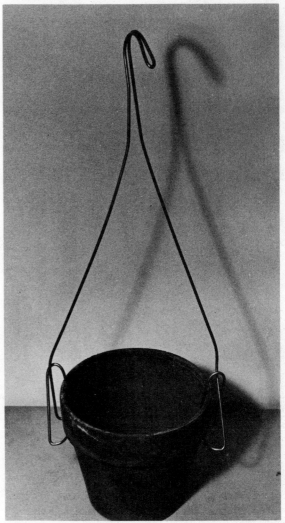

*Wire hanger with clips to suspend a clay pot.*

holes in the rim for hangers. Usually a pot with holes in the rim comes with a hanger designed to be used with it. You can also buy or make hangers of macramé, monofilament nylon fishing line, wire and chain, leather, and rope. Wire hangers which clip over the edges of clay pots are available from orchid specialists; one kind is for hanging from above, the other for wall mounting.

The use of swivel hangers makes it easy to rotate containers a quarter turn every few days so that all sides of the plant receive an equal share of light. Some containers come equipped with swivel hangers, but if not, you can pur-

chase swivel joints at a hardware or store that sells fishing equipment and install them yourself between the hook and the point at which strands of the hanger join at the top.

Besides baskets and pedestals, another way to display hanging plants indoors is to plant a selection of fairly small-growing danglers and creepers in the pockets of a strawberry jar. If large and heavy, you may want to set it on a wheeled platform or dolly to facilitate rotation for equal light on all sides. There are also smaller hanging strawberry jars available. Plants suited to growing in a strawberry jar indoors are indicated in Chapter 6.

*Ivyleaf, scented and zonal geraniums cascade from this balcony and down the steps to a patio.*

# 3
# Hanging Gardens Outdoors

The *ground* is only one of the places in which to garden outdoors. If you take advantage of your air rights, you can have another world in which to grow beautiful plants. Since some of them are fragrant at night, you and your family or guests can dine in an outdoor surround as inviting as that of a flower-filled greenhouse while snow lies in drifts on the other side of the glass. What you need on which to hang a container outdoors is essentially the same as indoors: a support overhead, or on a wall strong enough to hold the total weight of the plant—which increases gradually as the season progresses and sharply when the soil is saturated with water. If stormy winds are usual where you live, additional strength may be needed by the support.

You can hang a plant outdoors from a strong tree limb, the overhang of a roof, a post, fence or a wall with brackets, an arbor, gazebo or lath house, from the eaves of an entryway, or all along a porch front. Pedestals, so long as they are weatherproof, can be as effective for hanging gardens outdoors as inside, not to mention the infinite possibilities of window boxes, raised urns, and the tops of columns, posts, and thick stone or brick walls. A shelf or ledge, 6 inches wide or more, placed fairly high up on a wall or fence, also makes a perfect place to grow hanging plants.

Since a certain amount of water is likely to drip from any plant hanging outdoors, it is best not to position one over a stainable surface such as outdoor carpeting. Roof overhangs need to be wide enough for the plant to hang freely—and strong enough to carry its weight; installing hooks in roof joists instead of the subroofing assures the necessary strength. Where several hanging plants are used together, they can be all the same variety in matching containers hung at the same level or different levels; or a mix of different plants in any combination of heights and containers that pleases you. Matching all containers and all plants is an easy way to achieve a stylish, formal effect; mixing everything gives a casual effect which can be equally charming, depending on the situation. Hanging plants well placed can be used to enhance a beautiful view, to create one—or to screen out ugliness.

The amount of sun or shade received by a hanging plant outdoors affects its choice just as it does indoors. The light requirements of approximately 200

*This lath house shelters fuchsias, begonias and other hanging shade plants in warm weather.*

different hanging plants are included in Chapter 6, indicated as follows:

> *Full sun:* direct sun most of the day
> *Half sun:* direct sun for half of the day
> *Part shade:* direct sun 2 to 4 hours daily
> *Full shade:* little or no direct sun

Plants that can take full sun in a climate where the summers are cool and moist may need half sun to part shade in hot, dry, windy climates. Plants that need warm temperatures during the winter heating season should not be put outdoors in the spring until all danger of frost has passed, and night temperatures stay generally above 60 degrees F. Plants that prefer coolness or actual cold during the winter heating season can be put outdoors in the spring as soon as danger of hard freezing is past. But in either case it is vitally important not to overexpose any plant taken from indoors into the open. For the first few days keep the plant in less light or sun than it requires normally and be sure to provide protection from strong winds. This period of adjustment from one environment to another is as much needed by plants as by our own winter-pale bodies which need gradual exposure to the sun in order to tan instead of burn.

Some of the plants included in Chapter 6 can be left outdoors all year, even where freezing temperatures occur in the winter. Where this happens be sure the soil in the hanging container is well moistened at the time of the winter freeze-up. If you want baskets of annual flowers in the summer, but hate the bare appearance left when they have to be taken down at frost time in autumn, try this: Cut off the frosted plants and discard them; moisten the soil well, then insert enough stems pruned from needle evergreens to give each basket a lush, full appearance before rehanging. These can be left until the first warm days of spring, at which time you can discard the branches and old soil, and replant for the new season.

Hanging mechanisms and containers for outdoors are virtually the same as those discussed for indoors in Chapter 2. Use eye screws or hooks in tree branches, not rubber pads and wires wrappd around them. Outdoors it is bet-

*The donkey's- or burro's-tail plant,* Sedum morganianum, *thrives hanging from this east-facing balcony in warm weather.*

*Wood framing makes a small window appear larger and provides a convenient place to display variegated ivies.*

*Sturdy wood trellis added in this entry area holds an assortment of flowering and foliage hanging plants.*

ter to use containers with drainage holes; otherwise heavy rains may suffocate the roots or add too much weight. The day-to-day care of hanging plants outdoors is detailed in Chapter 5, but one thing worth stressing twice is that in hot summer weather, containers may need to be watered well once a day, if not twice, morning and evening. Obviously, a hose that reaches every plant in your hanging garden will save you a lot of trouble.

Wherever you may hang plants outdoors, try to keep them in clear view and away from places where you will constantly brush against them while walking along a path. Also watch out for placement where you or someone else might inadvertently walk into a hanging plant, especially one with sharp-pointed leaves, or where you might rise up under a container and bump your head.

Hanging gardens outdoors offer great freedom to experiment with all kinds of plants, either mixed or matched, at any time of the year when the weather is mild enough for you to enjoy being in the open air. Primroses and forget-me-nots in spring may be followed by petunias and lobelias in summer, followed by cascade chrysanthemums and dwarf asters in autumn, followed by branches of cut evergreens and bright-berried holly or pyracantha in winter. As soon as you begin to think of a hanging container outdoors as a little space in which to garden, instead of a place merely to grow one plant, you will be well on your way to discovering infinite pleasures.

Cascade tuberous begonias have been brought into early bloom in this geodesic dome greenhouse.

# 4
# How to Plant
# a Hanging Basket

With the exception of wire, plastic-mesh and open wood-slat baskets, hanging gardens generally require the same planting techniques as container gardens. After deciding on the containers and the plants you want to grow in them, select a suitable growing medium. Since airborne gardens need to be as lightweight as possible and they tend to dry out quickly, mix soil ingredients to produce a medium that is light and spongy, yet holds moisture well.

You can mix the all-purpose soil recommended for most of the plants included in Chapter 6 by combining equal parts of garden loam (or packaged potting soil), perlite, vermiculite, and sphagnum peat moss. The addition to the mix of a wetting agent such as Viterra, following directions on the container, will help hanging gardens outdoors stay moist for longer periods of time. If you are a weekend gardener, this can be a lifesaver for your plants from Sunday to Friday evenings.

In recent years the soil-less mixes have also become popular for hanging-basket plantings. They are lightweight and conveniently packaged, ready to use, sold under such trade names as Jiffy-Mix, Redi-Earth, Supersoil, and Vita-Bark University Mix. The only drawback to these is that plants growing in them need to be fed a little with almost every watering and this can get to be time-consuming and expensive if you have a lot of plants.

If you have selected a porous basket, for example, a container constructed of wire, openwork plastic, or wooden slats, line it completely with unmilled sphagnum moss or florist's sheet moss before you add potting soil. If the wooden slats fit fairly tightly together before planting, only a single layer of moss will be needed since wood swells when moistened. Open wire, plastic and wood-slat containers need a 2- to 3-inch lining of moss before adding potting soil.

Lining and planting a rounded basket will be easier if you first place the bottom in the top of a large clay pot, or small pail, to hold it steady and upright as you work. Soak the moss in water for a half-hour or so, then squeeze out the excess as you begin to place pieces in the basket, overlapping them shingle-fashion until they are 2 to 3 inches thick all over. Allow a little extra at the top to cushion the edges and give a pleasing finish.

If you want an almost instant effect from hanging-basket plants, you may

Use unmilled sphagnum moss to line wire mesh baskets. Soak the moss in water, then squeeze out the excess.

BELOW: *Large clay pot holds basket steady.*

BELOW: *Extra moss at top cushions edges.*

prefer to buy established specimens. However, many of the ones sold locally have reached peak growth and will be difficult to keep in good condition. Generally, the better way is to grow your own hanging gardens, starting from seeds, established seedlings, rooted cuttings, bulbs, or healthy divisions.

Large plants with a multitude of trailing stems are the most difficult to plant in a hanging container. To do so, first remove the hangers from both the old and the new pots, then you will be much less likely to bruise leaves and break stems in the transfer. If you work with the new container resting on the top of some kind of pedestal so that the stems can trail freely, there will be even less likelihood of damaging growth.

When you want to combine several different kinds of plants in one hanging container, be sure they are all compatible as to requirements of light, temperature, moisture, humidity, and growing medium. Foliages that contrast in color, texture, or growth habit make pretty hanging gardens as well as combinations of foliage and flowering or upright and cascading plants.

After the plants are in place and the soil firmed about them, water well. Moss-lined baskets need to be immersed in a pail, sink, or tub of water for a good soaking; then remove and allow to drain before hanging in the growing place. If a hanging basket of this type is never allowed to dry out severely, you will not need to remove it for soaking. However, if such a basket dries out severely, remove it, soak in a container of water, allow to drain, and then hang it back up.

If the roots of newly planted hanging plants have been badly disturbed in the process, condition them out of full sun for a few days. As soon as the leaves show no signs of wilting, it should be safe to move the container to its intended position.

RIGHT: *This pottery planter suspended from a tree limb holds an assortment of succulent plants, all of which require similar growing conditions. When combining different kinds of plants in one hanging planter, remember the cultural needs of each, especially light and soil moisture requirements.*

*The author is shown pinching out tip growth on a Swedish-ivy in order to promote maximum branching.*

# 5
# How to Care for Hanging Gardens

The care of a hanging garden is very much the same as for any plant cultivated in any kind of container. The chief differences lie in quantities and frequency of watering, and in pinching or pruning techniques aimed at encouraging a graceful, pendant habit of growth.

The placement of hanging plants in satisfactory light or sun is discussed for the indoors in Chapter 2, for the outdoors in Chapter 3. Symptoms of too much direct sun include unnaturally yellowish green leaves; malformed or stunted growth; stems, leaves and flowers wilted in the heat of the day even when the soil is well moistened; yellow, tan, brown, or black spots literally burned in the leaves. Plants receiving insufficient light have unnaturally pale green leaves; stems elongated to the point of appearing spindly and smaller than usual; flower buds fail to form or fall off before opening; leaves turn pale or yellow and fall even though soil moisture, temperature, and humidity are satisfactory.

In order for a hanging basket or pedestal plant indoors to develop properly all around, it needs to be rotated toward the light every few days. This is easy for a plant placed on a pedestal, since the pot can be given a quarter turn without any trouble. For a plant suspended in the air, this is not so easily done unless a swivel hanger (Chapter 2) is used. However, all of the hanging plants in my apartment do nicely on one full half turn weekly which means that once every week as I happen to be watering them, I lift each basket off its hook and turn it around so that the hook is inserted in the ceiling eye bolt facing the opposite direction. Outdoors the turning of hanging plants is less important since light intensities are generally far greater than they are indoors.

Other than light, the single most important factor about hanging gardens is watering. Soil moisture needs are described in Chapter 6 either as wet, moist, or on the dry side. *Wet* is equivalent roughly to a sponge so saturated with water that when you pick it up, excess drains freely without squeezing the sponge. *Moist* may be likened to a sponge containing enough water to drain some excess when it is squeezed. *On the dry side* is like a sponge that feels damp but from which no drops of water can be squeezed.

No plant—not even a cactus or other succulent from the desert—can exist for long in soil that is completely dry. The only way to tell for sure whether or not a hanging plant needs water is to reach into the container and squeeze some of

ABOVE: *Bulb and siphon gadget for watering high up.*
BELOW: *Use battery-powered unit for misting baskets.*

the soil between your fingers. If you think about the sponge equivalencies suggested in the preceding paragraph, you should have no trouble deciding if the soil feels wet, moist, or on the dry side. Hanging plants tend to need the most water indoors during coldest weather when maximum artificial heating is required; and outdoors in summer during hot, dry weather.

Adding water to a container suspended high in the air requires certain care; otherwise you're likely to wind up splashing more water on the floor or ground—or yourself—than in the container itself. Most hanging plants are hung within a height range so that water can be applied directly to the soil from the spout of a watering can while you stand on the floor, on a sturdy chair, or a stepstool. If the situation dictates hanging plants high overhead, you can use one of the bulb-and-siphon gadgets available for this purpose, or else suspend the containers by means of a pulley and nylon cord arrangement so that each can be lowered to convenient height for watering and other routine attentions such as pinching and grooming.

Hanging plants are fertilized in much the same way as container gardens. If the plant is cultivated primarily for its foliage, feed with an all-purpose house-plant food, following directions on the label. If the plant is grown mostly for flowers, feed with a blossom-booster type fertilizer, usually labeled as being for African violets or for flowering house plants. Most liquid, granular, and powdered fertilizer concentrates are diluted in water, then applied to the soil of the plants. Apply fertilizer only to soil which is nicely moist, never when the soil is dry.

Frequency varies according to the product, but most are formulated to be used once every 2 weeks through the active growing season. There are also pelletized, time-release fertilizers, available in formulations both for foliage and flowering plants, which need to be applied to the surface of the soil only once every 3 months.

If you are growing in one of the soil-less mixes described in Chapter 4, mix and apply fertilizer at the strength and frequency rec-

ABOVE: *Take care not to overwater drainless pot.*
BELOW: *Underwatering causes dead spider plant leaves.*

ABOVE: *Soak staghorn fern in sink twice each week.*
BELOW: *Water piggyback heavily; never allow to dry.*

*How to Care for Hanging Gardens* 37

*Pinch back wandering jew frequently for full growth.*    *Episcia grows compactly without any pinching.*

ommended on the label for plants growing without soil or in a soil-less medium; if the label does not include this information, mix the fertilizer at one-fourth to one-fifth the normal strength, and apply nearly every time you have to water the plant.

Pinching and pruning play an important role in directing the growth habit and shape of hanging plants. Some grow naturally into perfect fountains or cascades of foliage and flowers without any pinching or pruning; for example, lipstick vine, episcia, and spider plant. Others, notably Swedish-ivy and wandering jew, need to be planted in the hanging container as short, young, rooted cuttings, and then to have the growing tips pinched out following approximately every 2 inches of new growth in order to

assure formation of the maximum number of branches.

If you have a hanging plant such as Swedish-ivy or wandering jew, which has only a few woody stems that emerge mostly bare from the hanging container but form a mass of leaves underneath, the way to have foliage higher up is to add 2 or 3 rooted cuttings in the soil, and keep them pinched back regularly as described in the preceding paragraph; meanwhile maintain regular pinching on the older, lower growth.

Sometimes it is better when you have such a plant simply to take tip cuttings, root them separately in pots of moist vermiculite, then discard the old plant, clean the container in which it has been growing, add fresh soil, and

*Pinching helps Cyclone impatiens grow compactly.*

*Coleus also needs frequent pinching to keep full.*

replant with the rooted cuttings. This is especially true of relatively fast-growing plants such as coleus, Swedish-ivy, wandering jew, and piggyback.

To keep hanging plants looking their best, pinch or cut off yellowed or dead leaves and flowers as soon as you notice them. Indoor hanging plants will look better and enjoy greater health if at least once a month you take them to the sink or tub and give the leaves a cleansing shower of tepid water; allow to drain, then rehang.

Regular and frequent showering with water helps discourage insect infestations on hanging plants, but eventually you may encounter problems with aphids, mealybugs, red spider-mites, white flies, scale, and thrips the same as

with any other plants. Synthetic pyrethrins or malathion may be sprayed to control all excepting red spider-mites and they will require the use of a miticide such as Kelthane or Dimite. For hanging plants indoors, the placement of a Shell No-Pest Strip within the same room is reported by many growers to be highly effective, especially in a home greenhouse. Strictly organic controls include the regular showering or bathing of the plants in water to which Ced-o-flora or Dr. Bronner's Peppermint Soap has been added according to directions on the label. Mealybugs and red spider-mites are the most serious problems indoors, and a bad infestation of either requires considerable vigilance to clear up completely. The presence of red spider-mites indicates an atmosphere that is

ABOVE: *Making a rhizome cutting of davallia fern.*

ABOVE: *Planting davallia cutting in pot of soil.*

BELOW: *Rooting yarnlike stolon of Boston fern.*

BELOW: *Secure davallia rhizome cutting in soil.*

hot, dry and stale, and no amount of spraying with a miticide is likely to be completely effective unless the environmental conditions are improved simultaneously.

Plants for hanging gardens may be started from seeds, cuttings or bulbs, or by division of plants which have several stems or crowns of leaves that emerge from the soil. Purchased plants of all sizes may be used as the basis for starting a hanging garden. Smaller, younger plants in general adapt more readily to a change in environment—as from the grower's greenhouse to the atmosphere of your house or apartment—than older, more mature specimens. Although nearly countless plants for hanging gardens are available at local nurseries, plant shops, and garden centers, more unusual types may be available only by mail from one of the specialists listed in Appendix A. Each of these specialists has been assigned a number in order to give specific sources for unusual plants included in Chapter 6.

Although a majority of the house plants in Chapter 6 stay in active growth most or all of the year, there are others which grow outdoors during frost-free weather but need to be wintered-over in a cool, but frost-free place. During this semidormant resting period such plants need no fertilizer, and soil that is on the dry side, but never completely dry. Such plants may be stored on the floor in a cool basement, frost-free garage, attic, or coldframe, or possibly in a cool sun porch, or mostly unused room that does not need the usual amount of winter heat.

The most common problem with hanging plants is allowing the soil to dry out too much between waterings. If growth actually wilts from lack of moisture, the tips of leaves will die back (spider plant often shows this sign of stress), flower buds may fail to develop, and older leaves will dry up and die prematurely. If a hanging container with no provision for draining excess moisture is watered carelessly, the roots may rot eventually for lack of air, and when this happens, the only thing to do is to make tip cuttings of healthy growth, root them and start over; discard the old roots and soil, clean the container, and replant, using fresh soil and newly rooted cuttings.

ABOVE: *Young senecios ready for basket planting.*

BELOW: *Sanvitalia seedlings, ready to plant out.*

*Left to right: Small-leaved* Hedera helix *(English ivy), tolmiea (piggyback) and Boston fern.*

# 6
# Plants for
# Hanging Gardens

In this chapter the growth habits, suggested uses, cultural needs and sources for approximately 200 different hanging plants are given. Any perennial or shrub, whether tender (not able to withstand freezing) or hardy (able to withstand freezing) should live over year after year. Annuals and tender perennials often treated as annuals (impatiens, for example) are usually started from seeds each year; seedlings mature, bear flowers, may form new seeds, and usually die at the end of the season when frost occurs in autumn.

Growth habits, indicated as trailing, cascading, creeping, fountain-form, dangling, climbing or clambering are more or less self-explanatory although admittedly assigned arbitrarily. A number of plants have been included which are primarily low, upright bushes, but experience has proven that they grow well and look beautiful when suspended in the air, and that in time the growth may spread out and billow downward over the edge of the container—exacum, for example.

If the branches of any plant grow more upright in a hanging container than you would like, weight the ends of each with a lead fishing-line sinker or a few metal washers tied together. This will pull down the branch tips, encouraging them to grow into a graceful, arching curve; at the same time, this change in direction may cause some plants to set more flower buds along the branches and may also cause more secondary branches to form, the net result being a prettier habit for a plant that is better branched and more flower-covered.

Suggested uses include indoors, outdoors, or outdoors in frost-free weather. Most of the plants have indoor/outdoor mobility, meaning that they may be cultivated all year indoors, or indoors in freezing weather and outdoors in warm, frost-free weather. In either situation, hanging plants may be enjoyed in baskets (meaning planted in any container suspended in the air), displayed on a pedestal which allows the stems to cascade freely, grown on a shelf or window box where growth can spill off the edge, or in the pockets of a strawberry jar.

The cultural needs outlined for each plant include when and how to start, optimum light, temperature, humidity, soil and soil moisture. Noteworthy traits, good and bad, are listed as *Notes* for any plant where appropriate. The numbers listed under *Sources* correspond to numbers preceding the names and

ABOVE: Achimenes *Tarantella*.

BELOW: Adiantum hispidulum, *maidenhair fern*.

addresses of nurseries listed in Appendix A.

For the sake of clarity, all plants are listed by Latin names. If you don't find what you're looking for, check the index; all common or popular names are cross-referenced to the proper Latin. For example, if you look up tomato in the Index, you will find that it is listed under its true name, *Lycopersicon;* geranium will be found under *Pelargonium*, African violet under *Saintpaulia*, and so on.

*Abelia grandiflora prostrata*. Hardy shrub. Fountain-form. Leaves bronzy green. Flowers white, summer–autumn. *Uses:* Outdoors. Basket. Pedestal. Window box. *Start:* Summer–fall from cuttings. *Light:* Full sun to part shade. *Air:* 40–60 degrees F. if kept indoors in winter (recommended where winter temperatures dip below 15 degrees F.). *Humidity:* Medium. *Soil:* All-purpose. *Moisture:* Moist. *Sources:* Local nurseries.

*Abutilon megapotamicum*. Flowering maple; Chinese bellflower. Tender shrub. Cascading. Leaves medium green or green and yellow (variety *variegatum*). Flowers yellow with red calyx, summer–autumn or intermittently all year. *Uses:* Indoors. Outdoors in frost-free weather. Basket. Pedestal. Shelf. Window box. *Start:* Winter–spring from cuttings. *Light:* Full sun (cool, moist climates) to part shade. *Air:* 50–70 degrees F. during winter heating season. *Humidity:* Medium. *Soil:* All-purpose. *Moisture:* Moist. *Notes:* One of the showiest flowering basket plants, but indoors in winter a sunny, moist, airy atmosphere is needed. *Sources:* 55, 60, 84.

*Achimenes*. Cupid's bower; magic flower. Tender perennial. Trailing. Leaves medium to olive-green or green and burgundy. Flowers blue, lavender, orange, pink, purple, red, rose, white, often marked with contrasting color in summer–autumn. *Uses:* Indoors; outdoors in frost-free weather. Basket, pedestal, shelf, window box, strawberry jar. *Start:* Winter–spring from scaly rhizome planted ½ inch deep. *Light:* Half sun to full shade. *Air:* Warm. *Humidity:* Medium to high; mist often. *Soil:* All-purpose. *Moisture:* Wet to moist in growing season; nearly dry during winter dormancy. *Sources:* 4, 9, 21, 22, 50, 54, 68.

*Adiantum*. Maidenhair fern. Tender peren-

Aeschynanthus, *lipstick vine.*

*Silver King* Aechmea, *a bromeliad.*

nial. Fountain-form. Leaves fresh green. *Uses:* Indoors. Outdoors in frost-free weather. Basket. Pedestal. Shelf. Window box. *Start:* Spring–summer by division. *Light:* Part to full shade. *Air:* 50–70 degrees F. during winter heating season. *Humidity:* Medium to high. Mist often. *Soil:* All-purpose. *Moisture:* Moist. *Sources:* 4, 50, 55, 60, 67, 68, 84.

*Aechmea.* Bromeliad. Tender perennial. Fountain-form. Leaves green and burgundy or silver-green. Flowers blue, pink, red, rose, on mature plants. *Uses:* Indoors. Outdoors in frost-free weather. Basket. Pedestal. Shelf. *Start:* Any time by division. *Light:* Half sun to part shade. *Air:* 62–75 degrees F. during winter heating season. *Humidity:* Medium to high. Mist often. *Soil:* Equal parts all-purpose and shredded fir bark. *Moisture:* Moist to on the dry side; keep cups formed by leaves filled with water. *Notes:* Many aechmeas and other bromeliads make superb plants for hanging gardens. *Sources:* 3, and local plant shops.

*Aeschynanthus.* Lipstick plant. Tender perennial. Trailing. Leaves medium green. Flowers red intermittently all year. *Uses:* Indoors.

Outdoors in frost-free weather. Basket. Pedestal. Shelf. Window box. *Start:* Any time from cuttings. *Light:* Half sun to part shade. *Air:* 62–75 degrees F. during winter heating season. *Humidity:* Medium to high. Mist often. *Soil:* All-purpose. *Moisture:* Moist. *Notes:* In good light indoors, aeschynanthus makes a beautiful hanging foliage plant all year even if conditions are not conducive to flowering. *Sources:* 9, 16, 21, 22, 28, 50, 54, 56, 86.

*Aglaonema.* Chinese evergreen. Tender perennial. Mostly upright, but in time spreading. Leaves dark green, green and white, or green and yellow. Occasional flowers white, followed by long lasting red berries. *Uses:* Indoors. Outdoors in frost-free weather. Basket. Pedestal. Shelf. Window box. *Start:* Any time from cuttings. *Light:* Part to full shade. *Air:* 62–75 degrees F. during winter heating season. *Humidity:* Low to high. Mist often, ideally. *Soil:* All-purpose. *Moisture:* Wet to moist. *Sources:* Local plant shops; also 3.

*Allium schoenoprasum.* Chives. Hardy perennial. Fountain-form. Leaves medium green. Flowers lavender in spring. *Uses:* Indoors.

Aeschynanthus marmoratus, *lipstick vine.*

Meyeri *asparagus-fern.*

Outdoors. Basket. Pedestal. Shelf. Window box. Strawberry jar. *Start:* Seeds indoors 12 weeks before frost-free weather outdoors; by division in spring. *Light:* Full sun. *Air:* 50–70 degrees F. during winter heating season. *Humidity:* Medium. *Soil:* All-purpose. *Moisture:* Moist. *Notes:* Unless frozen for a period of 1 to 3 months annually, chives cultivated as a house plant tends to go into decline. Trim off leaves as needed for seasoning. *Sources:* Local nurseries; also 60, 84.

*Aloe. A. ciliaris* is known as climbing or firecracker aloe. Tender perennial succulent. Sprawling. Leaves dark green. Flowers red in spring–summer. *Uses:* Indoors. Outdoors in frost-free weather. Basket. Pedestal. Shelf. Window box. *Start:* Spring–summer from cuttings or by division. *Light:* Full sun. *Air:* 62–75 degrees F. during winter heating season. *Humidity:* Low. *Soil:* All-purpose. *Moisture:* On the dry side. *Sources:* 1, 13, 18, 25, 35, 38, 39, 51, 62, 63, 79, 80.

*Amaracus dictamnus.* Crete dittany. Hardy perennial. Fountain-form. Leaves gray-green. Flowers pink, purple, summer–autumn. *Uses:*

Outdoors. Basket. Pedestal. Shelf. *Start:* Spring–summer from cuttings. *Light:* Full sun to part shade. *Air:* 40–50 degrees F. if wintered-over indoors. *Humidity:* Low to medium. *Soil:* All-purpose. *Moisture:* Moist. *Sources:* 40, 84.

*Antigonon leptopus.* Coral vine. Tender perennial. Cascading. Climbing. Leaves light green. Flowers pink to rose in summer–autumn. *Uses:* Outdoors in frost-free weather. Basket. Pedestal. Shelf. *Start:* Spring from seeds, tuber divisions, cuttings. *Light:* Full sun. *Air:* Warm. *Humidity:* Medium. *Soil:* All-purpose. *Moisture:* Wet to moist; store tubers nearly dry in winter. *Notes:* Prune back frequently to size; overfeeding reduces flower crop. *Sources:* 68.

*Aporocactus.* Rat-tail cactus. Tender perennial. Dangling. Leaves medium green in spring–summer. *Uses:* Indoors. Outdoors in frost-free weather. Basket. Pedestal. Shelf. *Start:* Spring–summer from cuttings. *Light:* Full sun. *Air:* 50–70 degrees F. during winter heating season. *Humidity:* Low. *Soil:* All-purpose. *Moisture:* On the dry side. *Sources:* 1,

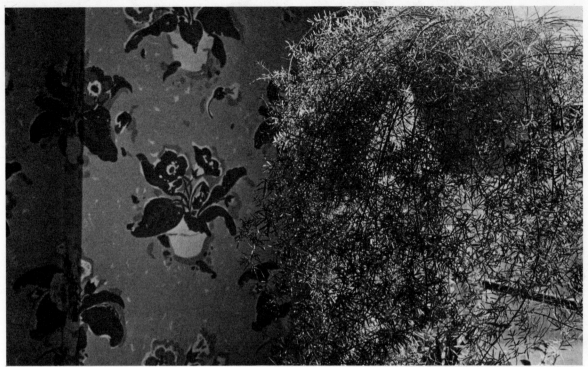

Sprengeri *asparagus-fern*.

13, 18, 25, 35, 38, 39, 51, 62, 63, 79, 80.

*Arabis caucasica variegata*. Wall rockcress. Hardy perennial. Creeping. Leaves gray with white margins. Flowers pink (in selected forms) or white (species) in spring. *Uses:* Outdoors. Basket. Pedestal. Shelf. Window box. *Start:* Spring–summer from seeds or cuttings. *Light:* Full to half sun. *Air:* 35–45 degrees F. if wintered-over indoors. *Humidity:* Low to medium. *Soil:* All-purpose. *Moisture:* Moist, except on the dry side if wintered-over indoors. *Sources:* Local nurseries; also 68.

*Arenaria montana*. Sandwort. Hardy perennial. Trailing. Leaves medium green. Flowers white in spring–summer. *Uses:* Outdoors. Basket. Pedestal. Shelf. Window box. *Start:* Spring from seeds or by division. *Light:* Part shade. *Air:* 35–50 degrees F. if wintered-over indoors. *Humidity:* Low to medium. *Soil:* All-purpose. *Moisture:* Moist, except on the dry side if wintered-over indoors. *Sources:* Local nurseries; also 68.

*Artemisia schmidtiana*. Silver Mound. Hardy perennial. Bushy or fountain-form. Leaves silvery-white. *Uses:* Outdoors. Basket.

Pedestal. Shelf. Window box. *Start:* Spring by division. *Light:* Full sun. *Air:* 35–50 degrees F. if wintered-over indoors. *Humidity:* Low to medium. *Soil:* All-purpose. *Moisture:* Moist to on the dry side. *Notes:* An ideal plant to combine in a basket with a trailing, flowering type. *Sources:* Local nurseries; also 68.

*Asparagus*. Asparagus-fern. Tender perennial. Cascading or fountain-form. Leaves medium green. Flowers white, followed by red berries. *Uses:* Indoors. Outdoors in frost-free weather. Basket. Pedestal. Shelf. Window box. *Start:* Any time from seeds or by division. *Light:* Full sun to part shade. *Air:* 50–70 degrees F. during winter heating season. *Humidity:* Medium. Mist often. *Soil:* All-purpose. *Moisture:* Moist. *Notes:* Avoid drafts of hot, dry air in winter. *Sources:* Most local nurseries and plant shops.

*Asplenium*. *A. bulbiferum* is the mother fern; *A. nidus* is the bird's-nest fern. Tender perennial. Fountain-form. Leaves fresh green. *Uses:* Indoors. Outdoors in frost-free weather. Basket. Pedestal. Window box. *Start:* Any time by division. *Light:* Part to full shade. *Air:* 62–75

*BEGONIAS: top, Little Sweetheart; left, Red Reuben; right, Babylon Lace.*

degrees F. during winter heating season. *Humidity:* Medium to high. Mist often. *Soil:* All-purpose. *Moisture:* Moist. *Sources:* 4, 50, 55, 60, 67, 68, 84.

*Aubrieta deltoidea.* Purple rockcress. Creeping. Leaves medium green. Flowers lavender, purple, red in spring–summer. *Uses:* Outdoors. Basket. Pedestal. Shelf. Window box. *Start:* Spring–summer from seeds or cuttings. *Light:* Full sun. *Air:* 35–50 degrees F. if wintered-over indoors. *Humidity:* Low to medium. *Soil:* All-purpose. *Moisture:* Moist except on the dry side if wintered-over indoors. *Sources:* Local nurseries; also 68.

*Aurinia saxatilis* (Alyssum saxatile). Basket-of-gold. Hardy perennial. Trailing. Leaves medium green. Flowers yellow in spring–summer. *Uses:* Outdoors. Basket. Pedestal. Shelf. Window box. *Start:* Spring from seeds. *Light:* Full sun. *Air:* 35–50 degrees F. if wintered-over indoors in severely cold climates. *Humidity:* Medium. *Soil:* All-purpose. *Moisture:* Moist, except on the dry side if wintered-over indoors. *Sources:* Most local nurseries.

*Begonia.* Tender perennial. Trailing. Cascading. Leaves light to dark green; often silver-spotted in angel-wing or cane types; red, purple or silver with various greens in the rex varieties. Flowers orange, pink, red, rose, white intermittently all year. *Uses:* Indoors. Outdoors in frost-free weather. Basket. Pedestal. Shelf. *Start:* Any time from seeds or cuttings. *Light:* Half sun to part shade. *Air:* 62–75 degrees F. during winter heating season. *Humidity:* Medium to high. *Soil:* All-purpose. *Moisture:* Moist. *Notes:* Wax or semperflorens are excellent basket plants outdoors in warm weather; provided the soil is constantly moist, they can take all but hottest midday sun. *Sources:* 50, 54, 55, 60, 84, 89.

*Begonia tuberhybrida, pendula* types. Tuberous-rooted, hanging basket begonia. Tender perennial bulb. Cascading. Leaves light green. Flowers orange, pink, red, rose, white, yellow in summer–autumn. *Uses:* Outdoors in frost-free weather. Basket. Pedestal. Shelf. Window box. *Start:* Bulb indoors 8 weeks before frost-free weather outdoors. *Light:* Part to full shade. *Air:* 62–75 degrees F. indoors; avoid ex-

posure to hot, dry winds outdoors in summer. *Humidity:* Medium to high. *Soil:* All-purpose. *Moisture:* Moist; store nearly dry in a cool but frost-free place from late fall to planting time the following late winter or early spring. *Notes:* Among the most spectacular of all flowering hanging plants. *Sources:* 4, 10, 11, 20, 68, 85.

*Beloperone guttata.* Shrimp plant. Tender perennial. Fountain-form. Leaves light green. Flowers white, spotted purple, in showy bracts of yellow-green or coppery orange intermittently all year. *Uses:* Indoors. Outdoors in frost-free weather. Basket. Pedestal. Shelf. Window box. *Start:* Any time from cuttings. *Light:* Full sun to part shade. *Air:* 50–70 degrees F. during winter heating season. *Humidity:* Medium. *Soil:* All-purpose. *Moisture:* Moist. *Sources:* 3, 55, 60, 68, 84.

*Billbergia nutans.* Queen's tears; a bromeliad. Leaves silver-bronze. Flowers green, rose, violet when plant is mature. *Uses:* Indoors. Outdoors in frost-free weather. Basket. Pedestal. Shelf. *Start:* Any time by division. *Light:* Half sun to part shade. *Air:* 62–75 degrees F. during winter heating season. *Humidity:* Medium to high. Mist often. *Soil:* Mix equal parts all-purpose with shredded fir bark. *Moisture:* Moist to on the dry side. *Sources:* 3 and local plant shops.

*Bougainvillea.* Paper flower. Tender shrub. Clambering; requires pruning after flowering and training to hanging form. Leaves medium green. Flowers lavender, orange, pink, purple, red, rose, white, yellow, winter–spring. *Uses:* Indoors. Outdoors in frost-free weather. Basket. Pedestal. Shelf. *Start:* Summer from cuttings or purchase plant. *Light:* Full sun. *Air:* 50–70 degrees F. during winter heating season. *Humidity:* Medium. *Soil:* All-purpose. *Moisture:* Moist to on the dry side. *Sources:* 55, 60, 68.

*Bouvardia longiflora* 'Albatross.' Tender shrub. Clambering. Leaves fresh green. Flowers fragrant white in autumn–winter. *Uses:* Indoors. Outdoors in frost-free weather. Basket. Pedestal. Shelf. *Start:* Spring–summer from cuttings. *Light:* Full sun to part shade. *Air:* 50–70 degrees F. during winter heating season. *Humidity:* Medium to high. *Soil:* All-purpose. *Moisture:* Moist. *Sources:* 19, 68.

ABOVE: *Rieger begonia.*
BELOW: Bougainvillea *Barbara Karst.*

Bowiea volubilis, *sea onion.*

Browallia speciosa major.

*Bowiea.* Climbing or sea onion. Tender bulb; a succulent. Trailing. Leaves light green. *Uses:* Indoors. Outdoors in frost-free weather. Basket. Pedestal. *Start:* In fall from bulb. *Light:* Full to half sun. *Air:* 62–75 degrees F. during winter heating season. *Humidity:* Low. *Soil:* All-purpose. *Moisture:* Moist. *Sources:* 1, 13, 18, 25, 35, 38, 39, 51, 62, 63, 79, 80.

*Browallia.* Amethyst flower. Tender perennial treated as an annual. Cascading. Leaves light to medium green. Flowers blue, white, all year. *Uses:* Indoors. Outdoors in frost-free weather. Basket. Pedestal. Shelf. Window box. *Start:* Seeds in summer for winter flowers; in winter for summer flowers. *Light:* Half sun to part shade. *Air:* 50–70 degrees F. during winter heating season. *Humidity:* Medium to high. Mist often. *Soil:* All-purpose. *Moisture:* Moist. *Sources:* 68.

*Calceolaria integrifolia.* Pocketbook plant. Tender perennial. Bushy or fountain-form. Leaves medium green. Flowers orange, red, yellow. *Uses:* Indoors. Outdoors in frost-free weather. Basket. Pedestal. Shelf. Window box. *Start:* Spring–summer from seeds or cuttings.

*Light:* Full sun to part shade. *Air:* 40–60 degrees F. during winter heating season. *Humidity:* Medium to high. *Soil:* All-purpose. *Moisture:* Moist to on the dry side. *Notes:* Difficult to keep over summer in hot, dry climates. *Sources:* 68.

*Callisia.* Setcreasea or spironema; wandering jew family. Tender perennial. Creeping. Leaves green and white *(C. elegans)* or purplish green. Flowers white and fragrant in *C. fragrans* intermittently. *Uses:* Indoors. Outdoors in frost-free weather. Basket. Pedestal. Shelf. Window box. *Start:* Any time from cuttings. *Light:* Full sun to part shade. *Air:* 62–75 degrees F. during winter heating season. *Humidity:* Medium. Mist often. *Soil:* All-purpose. *Moisture:* Moist. *Sources:* 55, 60, 84.

*Camellia.* Hanging-basket camellia. Half-hardy shrub. Trailing or fountain-form. Leaves dark green. Flowers pink, red, rose, white in autumn, winter or spring. *Uses:* Outdoors in mild weather. Basket. Pedestal. Shelf. Window box. *Start:* Any time from purchased plant. *Light:* Half sun to part shade. *Air:* 50–60 degrees F. during winter heating season. *Humid-*

*ity:* Medium. Mist often. *Soil:* All-purpose; feed with acid-type fertilizer. *Moisture:* Moist. *Notes:* New types of camellia are available for hanging gardens. *Sources:* 2; also Nuccio's Nurseries, 3555 Chaney Trail, Altadena, California 91001 and Orinda Nursery, Bridgeville, Delaware 19933.

*Campanula isophylla.* Star-of-Bethlehem. Tender perennial. Trailing. Leaves light to medium green. Flowers blue or white in summer–autumn. *Uses:* Indoors. Outdoors in frost-free weather. Basket. Pedestal. Shelf. Window box. Strawberry jar. *Start:* Winter–spring from cuttings. *Light:* Full to half sun. *Air:* 50–70 degrees F. during winter heating season. *Humidity:* Medium. *Soil:* All-purpose. *Moisture:* Moist in spring–summer; moist to on the dry side in fall–winter. *Notes:* Needs alkaline soil. *Sources:* 55, 60.

*Capsicum.* Pepper, sweet and hot. Tender perennial usually treated as an annual. Bushy, spreading. Leaves medium green. Flowers white followed by fruits that mature to brilliant red or yellow in summer–autumn. *Uses:* Indoors. Outdoors in frost-free weather. Basket. Pedestal. Shelf. Window box. *Start:* Seeds indoors 8–10 weeks before frost-free weather outdoors; or purchase started plants. *Light:* Full sun. *Air:* 62–75 degrees F. during winter heating season. *Humidity:* Medium. *Soil:* All-purpose. *Moisture:* Moist; dry soil causes leaf and flower drop. *Notes:* Edible peppers make attractive plants for a hanging garden in warmth and sun, not to mention the harvest they produce. *Sources:* Local nurseries; also 68.

*Carissa grandiflora horizontalis.* Natal plum. Tender shrub. Trailing. Leaves medium green. Flowers fragrant white intermittently all year. *Uses:* Indoors. Outdoors in frost-free weather. Basket. Pedestal. Shelf. Window box. *Start:* Winter–spring from cuttings. *Light:* Full sun to part shade. *Air:* 50–70 degrees F. during winter heating season. *Humidity:* Medium. *Soil:* All-purpose. *Moisture:* Moist. *Notes:* Varieties 'Green Carpet' and *C. g. minima* are also hanging-garden candidates. *Sources:* 3.

*Catharanthus roseus* (Vinca rosea). Madagascar periwinkle. Tender perennial treated as an annual. Leaves medium green. Flowers pink, rose, white, summer–autumn. *Uses:* Out-

ABOVE: Campanula.

BELOW: Catharanthus roseus *(vinca).*

ABOVE: Ceropegia *species, rosary vine.*

BELOW: Chlorophytum comosum, *spider plant.*

doors in frost-free weather. Basket. Pedestal. Shelf. Window box. *Start:* Winter–spring from seeds. *Light:* Full sun to part shade. *Air:* 62–72 degrees F. during winter heating season. *Humidity:* Medium. *Soil:* All-purpose. *Moisture:* Moist. *Sources:* 11, 68.

*Ceropegia.* Rosary vine; hearts entangled. Tender perennial. Dangling. Leaves light to dark green, sometimes silver-variegated. Flowers greenish, lavender, purple, in spring, summer, autumn. *Uses:* Indoors. Outdoors in frost-free weather. Basket. Pedestal. Shelf. *Start:* Spring–summer from cuttings. *Light:* Full to half sun. *Air:* 62–75 degrees F. during winter heating season. *Humidity:* Low to medium. *Soil:* All-purpose. *Moisture:* Moist to on the dry side. *Sources:* 55, 60, 84.

*Cestrum nocturnum.* Night-blooming jasmine. Tender shrub. Fountain-form or clambering. Leaves light green. Flowers white, intensely fragrant, intermittently all year. *Uses:* Indoors. Outdoors in frost-free weather. Basket. Pedestal. Shelf. Window box. *Start:* Spring from cuttings. *Light:* Full to half sun. *Air:* 50–70 degrees F. during winter heating season. *Humidity:* Medium. Mist often. *Soil:* All-purpose. *Moisture:* Moist. *Notes:* Pinch or prune to encourage compact growth. *Sources:* 55, 60.

*Chlorophytum.* Airplane or spider plant. Tender perennial. Fountain-form. Leaves medium green or green and white. Flowers white in season. *Uses:* Indoors. Outdoors in frost-free weather. Basket. Pedestal. Shelf. Window box. *Start:* Any time from cuttings or by division. *Light:* Half sun to part shade. *Air:* 62–75 degrees F. during winter heating season. *Humidity:* Medium. Mist often. *Soil:* All-purpose. *Moisture:* Moist. *Notes:* More likely to flower and produce baby plants if slightly cramped in the pot. *Sources:* Most local nurseries and plant shops.

*Chrysanthemum,* cascade varieties. Hardy perennial. Cascading. Leaves medium green. Flowers lavender, pink, rose, white, yellow, in autumn. *Uses:* Outdoors in frost-free weather. Basket. Pedestal. Shelf. Window box. *Start:* Spring from cuttings or purchased plants. *Light:* Full sun. *Air:* 40–60 degrees F. if brought indoors for bloom continuing into

winter. *Humidity:* Medium. *Soil:* All-purpose. *Moisture:* Moist while in active growth; on the dry side in winter if kept indoors in a cool place during dormancy. *Notes:* For best effect, provide a lightweight wire framework on which to tie and train the branches into a cascade effect; begin pinching and training in the spring, but stop pinching by August. *Sources:* Sunnyslope Gardens, 8638 Huntington Drive, San Gabriel, California 91775.

*Cissus.* Grape-ivy is *C. rhombifolia;* kangaroo-vine is *C. antarctica;* rex-begonia vine is *C. discolor.* Tender perennial. Trailing or cascading. Leaves medium or olive-green; *C. discolor* is variegated silver and burgundy. *Uses:* Indoors. Outdoors in frost-free weather. Basket. Pedestal. Shelf. Window box. *Start:* Any time from cuttings. *Light:* Half sun to part shade. *Air:* 50–70 degrees F. during winter heating season. *Humidity:* Low to medium, except medium to high for *C. discolor;* mist often. *Soil:* All-purpose. *Moisture:* Moist. *Notes: C. striata* is a miniature form of grape-ivy; *C. adenopodus* resembles grape-ivy but has hairy leaves that are olive-green and reddish purple. *Sources:* 55, 60, 84, 89.

*Clerodendrum thomsoniae.* Bleeding-heart vine. Tender shrub. Clambering. Leaves medium green. Flowers red and white in spring–summer. *Uses:* Indoors. Outdoors in frost-free weather. Basket. Pedestal. Shelf. Window box. *Start:* Winter–spring from cuttings. *Light:* Full sun in winter. Half sun to part shade in summer. *Air:* 50–70 degrees F. during winter heating season. *Humidity:* Medium to high. Mist often. *Soil:* All-purpose. *Moisture:* Wet to moist. *Sources:* 55, 60.

*Clianthus. C. dampieri* is called glory or desert pea; *C. puniceus* is called parrot's beak or lobster claw. Tender perennial. Trailing. Creeping. Leaves green or silver-gray. Flowers pink, red, white in spring–summer. *Uses:* Indoors. Outdoors in frost-free weather. Basket. Pedestal. Shelf. Window box. *Start:* Winter–spring from seeds or cuttings. *Light:* Full sun. *Air:* 50–70 degrees F. during winter heating season. *Humidity:* Medium. *Soil:* All-purpose. *Moisture:* Wet to moist, but less in fall–winter. *Sources:* 68.

*Codonanthe crassifolia.* Gesneriad. Tender

ABOVE: Cissus antarctica, *kangaroo vine.*

BELOW: Cissus rhombifolia, *grape-ivy.*

Cissus discolor, *rex-begonia vine.*

Columneas.

perennial. Trailing. Leaves bright green, red-dotted underneath. Flowers white with red spots intermittently all year. *Uses:* Indoors. Outdoors in frost-free weather. Basket. Pedestal. Shelf. *Start:* Any time from cuttings. *Light:* Half sun to part shade. *Air:* 62–75 degrees F. during winter heating season. *Humidity:* Medium to high. Mist often. *Soil:* All-purpose. *Moisture:* Moist to on the dry side. *Notes:* Grows well in a fluorescent-light garden displayed on an inverted flowerpot so the stems can trail. *Sources:* 9, 16, 21, 22, 28, 50, 54, 56, 86.

*Coleus.* Tender perennial. Trailing. Leaves green, yellow, red, burgundy, pink, rose—many highly variegated. Flowers blue, but insignificant; pinch off the buds before much developed. *Uses:* Indoors. Outdoors in frost-free weather. Basket. Pedestal. Shelf. Window box. *Start:* Any time from seeds or cuttings. *Light:* Half sun to part shade. *Air:* 62–75 degrees F. during winter heating season. *Humidity:* Low to medium. *Soil:* All-purpose. *Moisture:* Moist. *Notes: C. rehneltianus* is the trailing coleus, but the hybrids of *C. blumei,* common coleus,

have more spectacular coloring; either kind makes a good hanging plant only if several seedlings or cuttings are planted in the container and growing tips kept pinched regularly to encourage bushy, compact growth. *Sources:* Local nurseries; also 11, 68.

*Columnea.* Gesneriad. Tender perennial. Trailing or fountain-form. Leaves medium olive or bronzy green. Flowers orange, red, rose, yellow, intermittently all year. *Uses:* Indoors. Outdoors in frost-free weather. Basket. Pedestal. Shelf. *Start:* Any time from cuttings. *Light:* Half sun to part shade. *Air:* 62–75 degrees F. during winter heating season. *Humidity:* Medium to high. *Soil:* All-purpose. *Moisture:* Moist to on the dry side. *Notes:* The more upright hybrids grow well in a fluorescent-light garden. *Sources:* 9, 16, 21, 22, 28, 50, 54, 56, 86.

*Convolvulus mauritanicus.* A morning-glory relative. Tender perennial. Trailing. Leaves medium green. Flowers blue, spring, summer, autumn. *Uses:* Indoors. Outdoors in frost-free weather. Basket. Pedestal. Shelf. *Start:* Winter–spring from seeds or cuttings. *Light:*

Full sun. *Air:* 50–70 degrees F. during winter heating season. *Humidity:* Medium. *Soil:* All-purpose. *Moisture:* Moist. *Sources:* 68.

*Convolvulus tricolor.* Dwarf morning-glory. Annual. Sprawling or half climbing. Leaves medium green. Flowers blue marked with white and yellow, summer–autumn. *Uses:* Indoors. Outdoors in frost-free weather. Basket. Pedestal. Shelf. Window box. *Start:* Spring from seeds first soaked overnight in water; sow in peat pots so roots will not have to be disturbed at transplanting time. *Light:* Full sun. *Air:* 62–75 degrees F. during winter heating season. *Humidity:* Medium. *Soil:* All-purpose. *Moisture:* Moist. *Sources:* 11, 19, 68, 85.

*Cotoneaster.* Hardy shrub. Trailing. Leaves medium to dark green, evergreen in *C. dammeri*, deciduous in *C. adpressa*. Flowers pink *(C. adpressa)* or white *(C. dammeri)* in spring followed by colorful fruit summer–autumn. *Uses:* Outdoors. Basket. Pedestal. Shelf. Window box. *Start:* Winter–spring from cuttings. *Light:* Full sun. *Air:* 35–45 degrees F. if wintered-over indoors. *Humidity:* Medium. *Soil:* All-purpose. *Moisture:* Moist. *Sources:* Local nurseries.

*Crassula.* Tender perennial succulent. Trailing. Dangling. Leaves medium green. Flowers pink, white in spring–summer. *Uses:* Indoors. Outdoors in frost-free weather. Basket. Pedestal. Shelf. Window box. Strawberry jar. *Start:* Spring–summer from seeds, cuttings. *Light:* Full to half sun. *Air:* 62–75 degrees F. during winter heating season. *Humidity:* Low. *Soil:* All-purpose. *Moisture:* Moist to on the dry side. *Notes:* Recommended for hanging gardens: *C. marginalis, C. perforata, C. pseudolycopodioides, C. rupestris. Sources:* 1, 13, 18, 25, 35, 38, 39, 51, 62, 63, 79, 80.

*Cucumis sativa.* Cucumber. Annual. Trailing or climbing. Leaves medium green. Flowers yellow followed by cucumbers in summer. *Uses:* Outdoors in frost-free weather. Basket. Pedestal. Shelf. Window box. *Start:* Seeds indoors 8 weeks before frost-free weather outdoors; or purchase plants. *Light:* Full sun. *Air:* 62–75 degrees F. during winter heating season. *Humidity:* Low to medium. *Soil:* All-purpose. *Moisture:* Moist. *Notes:* Relatively small-growing varieties such as 'Patio Pik' are

*Columnea.*

Cymbalaria muralis, *Kenilworth-ivy*.

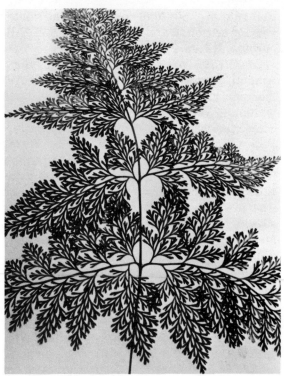

Davallia, *rabbit's-foot fern*.

best for hanging gardens. *Sources:* 11, 68.

*Cucurbita.* Squash; zucchini. Annual. Spreading to umbrellalike. Leaves medium green. Flowers yellow followed by the green or yellow fruit in summer–autumn. *Uses:* Outdoors in frost-free weather. Basket. Pedestal. *Start:* Seeds indoors 6–8 weeks before frost-free weather outdoors; or purchase plants. *Light:* Full sun. *Air:* 62–75 degrees F. during winter heating season. *Humidity:* Medium. *Soil:* All-purpose. *Moisture:* Moist; never allow to dry out. *Notes:* These grow into huge hanging plants in a short time if never allowed to dry out and the soil is well fertilized. *Sources:* Local nurseries; also 11, 68.

*Cyanotis.* Teddy-bear plant is *C. kewensis;* pussy ears is *C. somaliensis.* Tender perennial. Trailing. Leaves brown and hairy *(C. kewensis);* bright green with white hairs *(C. somaliensis).* Flowers pale blue *(C. kewensis)* intermittently. *Uses:* Indoors. Outdoors in frost-free weather. Basket. Pedestal. Shelf. *Start:* Any time from cuttings. *Light:* Full sun to part shade. *Air:* 62–75 degrees F. during winter heating season. *Humidity:* Medium.

*Soil:* All-purpose. *Moisture:* Moist. *Sources:* 55, 60, 67, 84.

*Cymbalaria muralis.* Kenilworth-ivy. Hardy perennial usually treated as a house plant. Trailing. Creeping. Leaves light green. Flowers blue intermittently. *Uses:* Indoors. Outdoors in frost-free weather. Basket. Pedestal. Shelf. Window box. Strawberry jar. *Start:* Summer–fall from cuttings. *Light:* Full sun to part shade. *Air:* 50–70 degrees F. during winter heating season. *Humidity:* Medium. Mist often. *Soil:* All-purpose. *Moisture:* Moist. *Sources:* 55, 60, 84.

*Davallia.* Rabbit's-foot fern. Tender perennial. Trailing. Fountain-form. Leaves light to medium green. *Uses:* Indoors. Outdoors in frost-free weather. Basket. Pedestal. *Start:* Any time from rhizome cuttings or by division. *Light:* Part to full shade. *Air:* 62–75 degrees F. during winter heating season. *Humidity:* Medium to high. Mist often. *Soil:* All-purpose. *Moisture:* Moist. *Sources:* 4, 50, 55, 60, 67, 68, 84.

*Diosma reevesi.* Breath of heaven. Tender shrub. Fountain-form. Leaves green, needle-

Episcia dianthiflora.

*Assorted episcias, flame-violets.*

like and pine-scented. Flowers white in spring–summer. *Uses:* Indoors. Outdoors in frost-free weather. Basket. Pedestal. Shelf. Window box. *Start:* Spring from cuttings. *Light:* Full sun. *Air:* 50–70 degrees F. during winter heating season. *Humidity:* Medium. *Soil:* All-purpose. *Moisture:* Moist to on the dry side. *Sources:* 60, 68.

*Epiphyllum.* Orchid cactus. Tender perennial succulent. Trailing. Leaves medium green. Flowers lavender, pink, red, rose, white, yellow in spring–summer. *Uses:* Indoors. Outdoors in frost-free weather. Basket. Pedestal. Shelf. *Start:* Spring–summer from cuttings. *Light:* Half sun to part shade. *Air:* 50–70 degrees F. during winter heating season. *Humidity:* Low to medium. Mist often. *Soil:* All-purpose. *Moisture:* Moist to on the dry side; keep drier in fall and winter, but mist leaves to prevent shriveling. *Sources:* 1, 13, 18, 25, 35, 38, 39, 51, 62, 63, 79, 80.

*Episcia.* Flame violet; peacock plant. Tender perennial. Trailing. Cascading. Leaves light, medium or dark green; also olive or bronze, sometimes variegated with silver, pink or white. Flowers blue, pink, red, rose, white, yellow in spring–summer. *Uses:* Indoors. Outdoors in frost-free weather. Basket. Pedestal. Shelf. Window box. Strawberry jar. *Start:* Any time from cuttings. *Light:* Half sun to part shade. *Air:* 62–75 degrees F. during winter heating season; suffers below 55 degrees F. *Humidity:* Medium to high. *Soil:* All-purpose. *Moisture:* Moist. *Notes:* One of the most beautiful of all indoor plants for hanging. *Sources:* 7, 9, 16, 21, 22, 28, 50, 54, 56, 86.

*Erigeron karvinskianus.* Bonytip fleabane. Hardy perennial. Trailing. Leaves medium green. Flowers pink, white in spring–summer. *Uses:* Outdoors in frost-free weather. Basket. Pedestal. Shelf. Window box. *Start:* Winter–spring from seeds; by division in spring. *Light:* Full sun to part shade. *Air:* 35–45 degrees F. if wintered-over indoors. *Humidity:* Medium. *Soil:* All-purpose. *Moisture:* Moist except on the dry side if wintered-over indoors. *Sources:* 68, 85.

*Euonymus.* Hardy shrub. *E. fortunei gracilis* is trailing. Leaves dark green and white. *Uses:* Outdoors. Basket. Pedestal. Shelf. Window

*A close-up of hybrid fuchsia flowers.*

box. *Start:* Winter–spring from cuttings or by division. *Light:* Full sun to part shade. *Air:* 35–50 degrees F. if wintered-over indoors. *Humidity:* Medium. *Soil:* All-purpose. *Moisture:* Moist. *Sources:* Local nurseries.

*Euphorbia myrsinites.* Hardy perennial. Fountain-form. Leaves blue-gray. Flowers yellow in spring–summer. *Uses:* Outdoors. Basket. Pedestal. Shelf. Window box. *Start:* Spring by division. *Light:* Full sun to part shade. *Air:* Preferably not over 45 degrees F. in winter. *Humidity:* Medium. *Soil:* All-purpose. *Moisture:* Moist to on the dry side. *Sources:* 68, 85.

*Exacum.* Annual. Bushy or trailing. Fountain-form. Leaves medium green. Flowers blue, white in almost any season. *Uses:* Indoors. Outdoors in frost-free weather. Basket. Pedestal. Shelf. Window box. *Start:* Any time from seeds. *Light:* Half sun to part shade. *Air:* 62–75 degrees F. during winter heating season. *Humidity:* Medium. *Soil:* All-purpose. *Moisture:* Moist. *Notes:* When well grown, exacum makes a spectacular hanging plant; discard after flowering ceases. *Sources:* 68, 85.

*Felicia amelloides.* Blue marguerite. Tender perennial. Cascading. Leaves medium green. Flowers blue in summer or winter. *Uses:* Indoors. Outdoors in frost-free weather. Basket. Pedestal. Shelf. Window box. Strawberry jar. *Start:* Spring–summer from seeds or cuttings. *Light:* Full sun. *Air:* 50–60 degrees F. during winter heating season. *Humidity:* Medium. *Moisture:* Moist to on the dry side. *Notes:* A great winter-flowering hanging plant for a sunny home greenhouse kept cool, moist and airy in winter. *Sources:* 60, 68, 85.

*Ficus.* Creeping fig. Somewhat hardy perennial, usually treated as a house plant. Creeping. Leaves medium green in *F. pumila;* green and white in *F. radicans variegata. Uses:* Indoors. Outdoors in frost-free weather. Basket. Pedestal. Shelf. Window box. Strawberry jar. *Start:* Any time from cuttings. *Light:* Half sun to part shade. *Air:* 50–70 degrees F. during winter heating season. *Humidity:* Medium. Mist often. *Soil:* All-purpose. *Moisture:* Moist. *Notes:* Nice to grow in a moss-lined basket with a larger, more upright plant such as rex begonia; the ficus will carpet the ground and root into the sides of the basket. *Sources:* Local nur-

series; also 55, 60, 84.

*Fittonia.* Nerve plant. Tender perennial. Trailing. Leaves green and white or green and rose-pink. Flowers white, but insignificant. *Uses:* Indoors. Outdoors in frost-free weather. Basket. Pedestal. Shelf. Window box. Strawberry jar. *Start:* Any time from cuttings. *Light:* Half sun to part shade. *Air:* 62–75 degrees F. during winter heating season. *Humidity:* Medium to high. Mist often. *Soil:* All-purpose. *Moisture:* Moist. *Sources:* Most local plant shops; also 3, 55, 60, 84.

*Fragaria.* Strawberry. Hardy perennial. Fountain-form, dangling. Leaves medium green. Flowers white followed by red fruit in spring–summer (if variety is everbearing). *Uses:* Indoors. Outdoors. Basket. Pedestal. Shelf. Window box. Strawberry jar. *Start:* Spring by division or purchased plants. *Light:* Full sun. *Air:* 50–60 degrees F. if kept indoors during winter heating season. *Humidity:* Medium. *Soil:* All-purpose. *Moisture:* Wet to moist. *Notes:* Varieties available at your local nursery should, theoretically, be suited to the climate in which you live. *Sources:* Local nurseries; also 10, 27, 36, 85.

*Fuchsia.* Tender shrub. Trailing. Cascading. Dangling. Leaves light to dark green, green and white in some. Flowers blue, lavender, pink, purple, red, rose, white, often two or more colors in combination; spring to autumn. Honeysuckle fuchsia (Gartenmeister Bohnstedt) tends to be everblooming and is a superb plant for a home greenhouse. *Uses:* Outdoors in frost-free weather. Basket. Pedestal. Shelf. Window box. *Start:* Winter–spring from cuttings. *Light:* Half sun to part shade. *Air:* 50–70 degrees F. during winter heating season. *Humidity:* Medium. Mist often. *Soil:* All-purpose. *Moisture:* Moist. *Notes:* Cut back and keep cool (but frost-free) and on the dry side in winter indoors. *Sources:* 55, 60, 84.

*Gardenia jasminoides radicans.* Gardenia. Tender shrub. Fountain-form. Leaves dark green. Flowers white and fragrant in spring–summer. *Uses:* Indoors. Outdoors in frost-free weather. Basket. Pedestal. Shelf. Window box. *Start:* Spring–summer from cuttings. *Light:* Full sun (cool, moist climates) to part shade. *Air:* 50–70 degrees F. during winter heating

Gibasis, *Tahitian bridal veil*.

Hedera helix, *English ivy*.

season. *Humidity:* Medium. *Soil:* Equal parts all-purpose and acid peat moss. *Moisture:* Wet to moist; never allow a hanging gardenia to dry out severely. *Sources:* 55, 60.

*Gazania*. African daisy. Tender perennial. Trailing. Leaves green with silvery reverses. Flowers in spring–summer, sometimes intermittently all year. *Uses:* Indoors. Outdoors in frost-free weather. Basket. Pedestal. Shelf. Window box. *Start:* Winter–spring from seeds; from cuttings in autumn. *Light:* Full sun to part shade. *Air:* 50–70 degrees F. during winter heating season. *Humidity:* Medium. *Soil:* All-purpose. *Moisture:* Moist. *Notes:* Trailing gazanias such as *G. leucolaena* and *G. uniflora* are best for hanging gardens. *Sources:* 68, 85.

*Gibasis*. Tahitian bridal veil; miniature wandering jew. Tender perennial. Cascading. Creeping. Leaves olive-green and burgundy. Flowers white intermittently. *Uses:* Indoors. Outdoors in frost-free weather. Basket. Pedestal. Shelf. Window box. *Start:* Any time from cuttings. *Light:* Full sun to part shade. *Air:* 62–75 degrees F. during winter heating season.

*Humidity:* Medium. Mist often. *Soil:* All-purpose. *Moisture:* Moist. *Notes:* Pinch out growing tips on young plants frequently to encourage compact, dense growth. *Sources:* Many local nurseries and plant shops; also 55, 60, 84.

*Gynura*. Purple passion; velvet plant. Tender perennial. Trailing. Leaves green and reddish purple. Flowers yellow, but of no consequence; pinch off buds. *Uses:* Indoors. Outdoors in frost-free weather. Basket. Pedestal. Shelf. Window box. *Start:* Any time from cuttings. *Light:* Half sun to part shade. *Air:* 62–75 degrees F. during winter heating season. *Humidity:* Medium. *Soil:* All-purpose. *Moisture:* Moist. *Notes:* Pinch out growing tips regularly to encourage dense, well-branched growth. *Sources:* Local plant shops; also 55, 60, 84.

*Harrisia*. Night-blooming cereus. Tender perennial succulent. Trailing. Leaves medium green. Flowers white in spring–summer. *Uses:* Indoors. Outdoors in frost-free weather. Basket. Pedestal. Shelf. *Start:* Spring–summer from cuttings. *Light:* Full to half sun. *Air:* 50–70 degrees F. during winter heating season. *Humidity:* Low to medium. *Soil:* All-purpose.

*Variegated* Hoya carnosa, *wax plant.*

*Moisture:* Moist to on the dry side. *Sources:* 1, 13, 18, 25, 35, 38, 39, 51, 62, 63, 79, 80.

*Hatiora.* Drunkard's dream. Tender perennial succulent. Trailing or cascading. Leaves light to medium green. *Uses:* Outdoors in frost-free weather. Basket. Pedestal. Shelf. *Start:* Spring–summer from cuttings. *Light:* Half sun to part shade. *Air:* 50–70 degrees F. during winter heating season. *Humidity:* Low to medium. Mist often. *Soil:* All-purpose. *Moisture:* Moist to on the dry side. *Sources:* 1, 13, 18, 25, 35, 38, 39, 51, 62, 63, 79, 80.

*Hedera helix.* English ivy. Hardy perennial, but many smaller-leaved named varieties are best protected from severe winter cold. Trailing. Cascading. Leaves all shades of green, sometimes variegated white or yellow. *Uses:* Indoors. Outdoors in frost-free weather. Basket. Pedestal. Shelf. Window box. Strawberry jar. *Start:* Any time from cuttings. *Light:* Half sun to part shade. *Air:* 50–70 degrees F. during winter heating season. *Humidity:* Medium. Mist often. *Soil:* All-purpose. *Moisture:* Moist. *Notes:* Never allow English ivy to dry out; do not hang in draft of hot, dry air. *Sources:* Local

nurseries; also 60.

*Helichrysum petiolatum.* Licorice plant. Tender perennial treated as an annual. Trailing. Leaves medium green, densely coated with white hair. *Uses:* Outdoors in frost-free weather. Basket. Pedestal. Shelf. Window box. *Start:* From seeds in winter–spring; from cuttings in autumn. *Light:* Full sun. *Air:* Warm. *Humidity:* Low to medium. *Soil:* All-purpose. *Moisture:* Moist. *Notes:* Nice to combine with bright-flowered annuals such as petunia or marigold. *Sources:* 60, 84.

*Helxine soleirolii.* Baby's-tears. Tender perennial. Trailing. Creeping. Leaves medium green or yellow-green, depending on variety. *Uses:* Indoors. Outdoors in frost-free weather. Basket. Pedestal. Shelf. Strawberry jar. *Start:* Any time from cuttings. *Light:* Half sun to part shade. *Air:* 62–75 degrees F. during winter heating season. *Humidity:* Medium. Mist often. *Soil:* All-purpose. *Moisture:* Moist. *Sources:* Local plant shops.

*Hemigraphis colorata.* Flame or red ivy. Tender perennial. Creeping. Leaves green and burgundy, sometimes with silver. Flowers

*Left,* Senecio, *string of pearls; center,* Hoya bella *miniature wax plant;* *Right:* Selaginella

white but insignificant. *Uses:* Indoors. Outdoors in frost-free weather. Basket. Pedestal. Shelf. Window box. *Start:* Any time from cuttings. *Light:* Full to half sun. *Air:* 62–75 degrees F. during winter heating season. *Humidity:* Medium to high. Mist often. *Soil:* All-purpose. *Moisture:* Moist. *Notes:* Avoid drafts of hot, dry air; be careful about overfeeding. *Sources:* Local plant shops; also 55, 60.

*Hoya.* Wax plant. Tender perennial. Trailing. Fountain-form. Dangling. Climbing. Leaves medium green, green and white, sometimes with pink. Flowers white, fragrant, in spring–summer. *Uses:* Indoors. Outdoors in frost-free weather. Basket. Pedestal. Shelf. Strawberry jar. *Start:* Spring cuttings in warmth. *Light:* Full to half sun. *Air:* 62–75 degrees F. during winter heating season. *Humidity:* Medium. Mist often (except when buds or flowers are present). *Soil:* All-purpose. *Moisture:* Moist in spring and summer; on the dry side in fall and winter. *Sources:* 55, 60, 84.

*Impatiens.* Tender perennial. Bushy or clambering. Leaves light to dark green; highly variegated in the New Guinea hybrids. Flowers lavender, orange, pink, purple, red, rose, white; everblooming. *Uses:* Indoors. Outdoors in frost-free weather. Basket. Pedestal. Shelf. Window box. Strawberry jar. *Start:* Any time from seeds or cuttings. *Light:* Half sun (indoors) to full shade (outdoors). *Air:* 50–70 degrees F. during winter heating season. *Humidity:* Medium to high; fresh air is important during winter heating season. *Soil:* All-purpose. *Moisture:* Wet to moist. *Sources:* Seeds available by mail from most seed firms (see Appendix A); plants available by mail, or at local garden centers.

*Ipomoea batatas.* Sweet potato. Tender perennial. Trailing. Leaves medium green. *Uses:* Indoors. Outdoors in frost-free weather. Basket. Pedestal. Shelf. Window box. *Start:* Any time from sweet potato tuber that has not been heat-treated (which prevents sprouting); plant

Impatiens *Shady Lady*.

Ipomoea, *sweet potato vine*.

upright in pot of soil or grow in a container of water with the tip exposed to air. *Light:* Full to half sun. *Air:* 62–75 degrees F. during winter heating season. *Humidity:* Low to medium. *Soil:* All-purpose. *Moisture:* On the dry side until roots form in soil and growth begins, then always moist. *Notes:* Frequent pinching out of the growth tips encourages a bushy, dense shape.

*Juniperus.* Juniper. Best for hanging gardens: *J. conferta* and *J. horizontalis wiltonii*. Hardy shrub. Fountain-form. Leaves medium green or blue-green. *Uses:* Outdoors. Basket. Pedestal. Shelf. Window box. *Start:* Fall–winter from cuttings. *Light:* Full sun (in cool, moist climate) to part shade. *Air:* Cool and moist if brought indoors during winter heating season. *Humidity:* Medium. *Soil:* All-purpose. *Moisture:* Moist; never allow a hanging juniper to dry out. *Notes:* If hanging junipers are subject to severe cold, be sure the soil is well moistened before freeze-up. *Sources:* Local

nurseries have a variety of junipers.

*Kalanchoe uniflora.* Kitchingia. Tender perennial succulent. Creeping. Dangling. Leaves fresh green. Flowers rose in spring. *Uses:* Indoors. Outdoors in frost-free weather. Basket. Pedestal. Shelf. Window box. Strawberry jar. *Start:* Any time from cuttings. *Light:* Full to half sun. *Air:* 62–75 degrees F. during winter heating season. *Humidity:* Low. *Soil:* All-purpose. *Moisture:* Moist to on the dry side. *Sources:* 1, 13, 18, 25, 35, 38, 39, 51, 62, 63, 79, 80.

*Kleinia.* Tender perennial succulent. Trailing. Creeping. Leaves light green. Flowers orange (*K. tomentosa*), red (*K. pendula*), white (*K. herreianus, K. radicans*), in spring–summer. *Uses:* Indoors. Outdoors in frost-free weather. Basket. Pedestal. Shelf. Strawberry jar. *Start:* Spring–summer from cuttings. *Light:* Full to half sun. *Air:* 50–70 degrees F. during winter heating season. *Humidity:* Low. *Soil:* All-purpose. *Moisture:* Moist to on the dry

*Variegated* Lantana.

ABOVE: Lathyrus, *Bijou sweet pea.*
BELOW: Lobelia.

side. *Sources:* 1, 13, 18, 25, 35, 38, 39, 51, 62, 63, 79, 80.

*Lantana montevidensis.* Trailing lantana. Tender perennial. Trailing. Cascading. Leaves medium green. Flowers lavender, pink, red, white, yellow; almost everblooming. *Uses:* Indoors. Outdoors in frost-free weather. Basket. Pedestal. Shelf. Window box. *Start:* Spring or summer; fall from cuttings. *Light:* Full sun. *Air:* 62–75 degrees F. during winter heating season. *Humidity:* Medium to high. *Soil:* All-purpose. *Moisture:* Moist. *Notes:* White flies are notoriously attracted to lantana. Prune back old plants to 6 inches in the spring and replant in fresh soil. *Sources:* 55, 60, 84.

*Lathyrus odoratus.* Sweet pea. Best for hanging gardens are Bijou, Knee-Hi, and other bushy hybrids. Annual. Trailing. Leaves medium green. Flowers fragrant in blue, lavender, pink, purple, red, rose, white in winter, spring, summer. *Uses:* Outdoors in frost-free weather. Basket. Pedestal. Shelf. Window box. *Start:* Winter–spring from seeds. *Light:* Full sun. *Air:* 50–65 degrees F. during winter heating season. *Humidity:* Medium. *Soil:* All-purpose. *Moisture:* Wet to moist; never allow the soil to dry out severely. *Notes:* Give an early start indoors in cold climates inclined to short springs that abruptly turn to hot weather; hot weather is not to the liking of sweet peas. *Sources:* Most seed catalogs and local seed racks.

*Lobelia erinus.* Lobelia. Tender perennial treated as an annual. Trailing. Leaves light green. Flowers blue, rose, white in spring–summer (from winter-sown seeds), autumn–winter (from summer-sown seeds). *Uses:* Indoors. Outdoors in frost-free weather. Basket. Pedestal. Shelf. Window box. Strawberry jar. *Start:* Indoors from seeds 12 weeks before frost-free weather; sow seeds or cuttings in August for winter flowers indoors. *Light:* Full to half sun. *Air:* 50–70 degrees F. during winter heating season. *Humidity:* Medium. Mist often. *Soil:* All-purpose. *Moisture:* Moist. *Sources:* Commonly listed in seed catalogs; select varieties indicated as trailing in habit.

*Lobularia maritima.* Sweet alyssum. Tender perennial treated as an annual. Trailing. Leaves light green. Flowers lavender, pink,

purple, white, over a long period of time beginning 8 weeks after sowing seeds. *Uses:* Indoors. Outdoors in frost-free weather. Basket. Pedestal. Shelf. Window box. Strawberry jar. *Start:* Any time, 8 weeks before flowers are wanted, from seeds. *Light:* Full sun. *Air:* 50–70 degrees F. during winter heating season. *Humidity:* Medium. *Soil:* All-purpose. *Moisture:* Moist. *Notes:* Shear back seedheads and other old growth after a period of heavy flowering; this will encourage compact new stems and more flowers. *Sources:* Most seed catalogs and local seed racks.

*Loropetalum chinense.* Tender shrub (hardy to 20 degrees F.). Fountain-form. Leaves light green; some turn attractively red or yellow. Flowers white in spring. *Uses:* Indoors. Outdoors in frost-free weather. Basket. Pedestal. Shelf. Window box. *Start:* Winter–spring from seeds. *Light:* Full sun to part shade. *Air:* 50–70 degrees F. during winter heating season. *Humidity:* Medium. *Soil:* Equal parts all-purpose, sand, and peat moss. *Moisture:* Wet to moist. *Sources:* 55, 60, 68.

*Lotus bertheloti.* Winged pea. Tender perennial. Trailing. Leaves silver-green. Flowers red in spring–summer. *Uses:* Indoors. Outdoors in frost-free weather. Basket. Pedestal. Shelf. Window box. *Start:* Winter–spring from cuttings. *Light:* Full to half sun. *Air:* 50–70 degrees F. during winter heating season. *Humidity:* High. Mist often. *Soil:* All-purpose. *Moisture:* Moist to on the dry side. *Notes:* Cut back large lotus plants in autumn. *Sources:* 55, 60, 84.

*Lycopersicon esculentum.* Tomato. Annual. Cascading. Leaves medium green. Flowers yellow followed by red or yellow fruit, usually in summer, but possible in other seasons. *Uses:* Indoors. Outdoors in frost-free weather. Basket. Pedestal. Shelf. Window box. *Start:* Indoors 8 weeks before frost-free weather; outdoors from seeds or purchased plants after the weather is warm. *Light:* Full sun to part shade. *Air:* 62–75 degrees F. during winter heating season. *Humidity:* Medium. *Soil:* All-purpose. *Moisture:* Wet to moist; never allow to dry out severely. *Notes:* Tomatoes such as 'Tiny Tim,'

Lobularia maritima.

Lotus bertheloti.

ABOVE: Lycopersicon, *Tumblin' Tom tomato*.

BELOW: Mikania.

'Sugar Lump,' 'Yellow Plum,' 'Red Pear' and 'Tumblin' Tom' are best for hanging gardens. *Sources:* Local nurseries; also 11, 68, 85.

*Lysimachia nummularia.* Moneywort, Creeping Charlie (or Jennie). Hardy perennial, usually brought indoors for winter when cultivated in a container. Creeping. Leaves light green. Flowers yellow in summer. *Uses:* Indoors. Outdoors in frost-free weather. Basket. Pedestal. Shelf. Window box. *Start:* Any time from cuttings. *Light:* Half sun to part shade. *Air:* 50–70 degrees F. during winter heating season. *Humidity:* Medium. Mist often. *Soil:* All-purpose. *Moisture:* Wet to moist. *Sources:* Local nurseries; also 55, 60, 84.

*Mahernia verticillata.* Honey bells. Tender shrub. Cascading. Leaves green, needlelike. Flowers yellow and fragrant in winter–spring. *Uses:* Indoors. Outdoors in frost-free weather. Basket. Pedestal. Shelf. Window box. *Start:* Summer from cuttings or by root division. *Light:* Full to half sun. *Air:* 50–70 degrees F. during winter heating season. *Humidity:* Medium. *Soil:* All-purpose. *Moisture:* Wet to moist. *Sources:* 55, 60, 84.

*Malvastrum coccineum.* Prairie mallow. Hardy perennial. Cascading. Leaves silver-haired, medium green. Flowers orange-pink in summer. *Uses:* Indoors. Outdoors in frost-free weather. Basket. Pedestal. Shelf. Window box. *Start:* Indoors from seeds 12 weeks before frost-free weather outdoors; also from cuttings or by division. *Light:* Full sun. *Air:* 50–70 degrees F. during winter heating season. *Humidity:* Medium. *Soil:* All-purpose. *Moisture:* Moist. *Sources:* 68, 85.

*Mandevilla* (sometimes listed as Dipladenia). Tender shrub. Trailing or climbing. Leaves dark green. Flowers fragrant pink or white in summer. *Uses:* Indoors. Outdoors in frost-free weather. Basket. Pedestal. Shelf. Window box. *Start:* Winter–spring from cuttings. *Light:* Full sun to part shade. *Air:* 62–75 degrees F. during winter heating season. *Humidity:* Medium to high. *Soil:* All-purpose. *Moisture:* Moist. *Sources:* 55, 60, 84.

*Maranta.* Prayer plant. Tender perennial. Trailing. Leaves bright green with reddish brown markings *(M. leuconeura)* or rose-pink veins *(M. l. massangeana).* Flowers white but

insignificant. *Uses:* Indoors. Outdoors in frost-free weather. Basket. Pedestal. Shelf. Window box. *Start:* Any time by division. *Light:* Part to full shade. *Air:* 62–75 degrees F. during winter heating season. *Humidity:* Medium to high. Mist often. *Soil:* All-purpose. *Moisture:* Moist; allowing soil to dry out causes leaf tips to die. *Sources:* 55, 60, 84.

*Mesembryanthemum.* Ice plant; livingstone daisy. Tender perennial succulent treated as an annual. Trailing. Leaves light green. Flowers pink, purple, rose, white, yellow in summer. *Uses:* Outdoors in frost-free weather. Basket. Pedestal. Shelf. Window box. Strawberry jar. *Start:* Indoors 12 weeks before frost-free weather; sow seeds outdoors in warm weather. *Light:* Full sun. *Air:* Warm. *Humidity:* Low. *Soil:* All-purpose. *Moisture:* Moist to on the dry side. *Sources:* 68, 85.

*Mikania scandens.* Tender perennial. Trailing. Leaves olive-green and burgundy. Flowers pink, white in autumn. *Uses:* Indoors. Outdoors in frost-free weather. Basket. Pedestal. Shelf. Window box. *Start:* Winter–spring from cuttings. *Light:* Half sun to part shade. *Air:* 62–75 degrees F. during winter heating season. *Humidity:* Medium. *Soil:* All-purpose. *Moisture:* Moist. *Sources:* 55, 60.

*Mimulus moschatus.* Monkey flower. Tender perennial. Dangling. Leaves light green. Flowers yellow in spring–summer. *Uses:* Indoors. Outdoors in frost-free weather. Basket. Pedestal. Shelf. Window box. *Start:* Winter–spring from seeds or cuttings. *Light:* Full to half sun. *Air:* 50–70 degrees F. during winter heating season. *Humidity:* Medium. *Soil:* All-purpose. *Moisture:* Wet to moist. *Sources:* 55, 60, 68, 84.

*Muehlenbeckia complexa.* Wire vine. Hardy perennial often treated as a house plant. Cascading. Leaves light green. Flowers white followed by white berries in spring–summer. *Uses:* Indoors. Outdoors in frost-free weather. Basket. Pedestal. Shelf. *Start:* Any time from seeds; cuttings in late summer. *Light:* Full sun to part shade. *Air:* 50–70 degrees F. during winter heating season. *Humidity:* Medium. *Soil:* All-purpose. *Moisture:* Moist. *Sources:* 55, 60.

*Myoporum parvifolium.* Tender shrub. Low and spreading. Leaves fresh green. Flowers

ABOVE: Muehlenbeckia complexa.
BELOW: Mesembryanthemum, *ice plant.*

Oplismenus, *basket or ribbon grass.*

Nierembergia, *dwarf cup flower.*

white followed by purple berries in summer. *Uses:* Outdoors in frost-free weather. Basket. Pedestal. Shelf. Window box. *Start:* Winter–spring from cuttings. *Light:* Half sun to part shade. *Air:* 50–70 degrees F. during winter heating season. *Humidity:* Medium. *Soil:* All-purpose. *Moisture:* Moist. *Sources:* 55, 60, 68.

*Nepeta hederacea variegata.* Ground ivy; gill-over-the-ground. Hardy perennial. Creeping. Leaves green and white. Flowers rarely; they are blue. *Uses:* Indoors. Outdoors in frost-free weather. Basket. Pedestal. Shelf. Window box. *Start:* Any time from seeds or cuttings. *Light:* Half sun to part shade. *Air:* 50–70 degrees F. during winter heating season. *Humidity:* Medium. *Soil:* All-purpose. *Moisture:* Moist. *Sources:* 55, 60, 84.

*Nephrolepis.* Boston fern; Fluffy Ruffles fern. Tender perennial. Fountain-form. Leaves light green. *Uses:* Indoors. Outdoors in frost-free weather. Basket. Pedestal. Shelf. Window box. *Start:* Any time by division or rooting yarnlike runners that form on mature plants. *Light:* Half sun to part shade. *Air:* 50–70 degrees F. during winter heating season. *Humidity:*

Medium to high. Mist often. *Soil:* All-purpose. *Moisture:* Moist. *Sources:* Local plant shops; also 4, 50, 55, 60, 67, 68, 84.

*Nierembergia hippomanica caerulea.* Dwarf cup flower. Tender perennial. Trailing. Flowers blue, lavender in summer. *Uses:* Indoors. Outdoors in frost-free weather. Basket. Pedestal. Shelf. Window box. *Start:* 12 weeks before frost-free weather outdoors. *Light:* Full sun to part shade. *Air:* 50–70 degrees F. during winter heating season. *Humidity:* Medium. *Soil:* All-purpose. *Moisture:* Moist. *Sources:* 68, 85.

*Nolana atriplicifolia.* Tender perennial. Trailing. Creeping. Leaves medium green. Flowers blue with white throat, summer–autumn. *Uses:* Outdoors in frost-free weather. Basket. Pedestal. Shelf. Window box. *Start:* Seeds indoors 12 weeks before frost-free weather; sow seeds outdoors in warm weather. *Light:* Full to half sun. *Air:* 50–70 degrees F. during winter heating season. *Humidity:* Medium. *Soil:* All-purpose. *Moisture:* Moist to on the dry side. *Notes:* Keep cool and on the dry side indoors in winter. *Sources:* 68.

Oxalis *Bermuda Buttercup.*

Oxalis siliquosa.

*Ocimum basilicum.* Sweet basil. Bushy to trailing. Leaves light green; dark purple in variety 'Dark Opal.' Flowers white but insignificant; keep the buds pinched off. *Uses:* Indoors. Outdoors in frost-free weather. Basket. Pedestal. Shelf. Window box. *Start:* Any time from seeds. *Light:* Full to half sun. *Air:* 62–75 degrees F. during winter heating season. *Humidity:* Medium. *Soil:* All-purpose. *Moisture:* Moist. *Notes:* Pinch back often to encourage bushy, compact growth; parts pinched off may be used for seasoning. May be combined with a cascade plant such as petunia in the same container. *Sources:* 11, 68, 85.

*Oplismenus hirtellus variegatus.* Basket or ribbon grass. Tender perennial. Leaves green and white with pink or red variegation in sun. Flowers purple in summer. *Uses:* Indoors. Outdoors in frost-free weather. Basket. Pedestal. Shelf. Window box. *Start:* Any time from cuttings. *Light:* Half sun to part shade. *Air:* 50–70 degrees F. during winter heating season. *Humidity:* Medium. *Soil:* All-purpose. *Moisture:* Wet to moist. *Sources:* 55, 60, 84.

*Ornithogalum caudatum.* Pregnant onion;

false sea onion. Tender perennial bulb. Fountain-form. Leaves fresh green. Flowers small, white in summer. *Uses:* Indoors. Outdoors in frost-free weather. Basket. Pedestal. Shelf. *Start:* Any time by removing baby bulbs which form on the surface of the parent. *Light:* Full to half sun. *Air:* 62–75 degrees F. during winter heating season. *Humidity:* Low. *Soil:* All-purpose. *Moisture:* Moist to on the dry side. *Notes:* Leaves may die down in summer, followed by the long stalk of flowers. Easy to grow and fascinating to watch in various stages. *Sources:* 55, 60.

*Oscularia deltoides.* Ice plant. Tender perennial succulent. Trailing. Leaves blue-green. Flowers rose in spring–summer. *Uses:* Indoors. Outdoors in frost-free weather. Basket. Pedestal. Shelf. Window box. Strawberry jar. *Start:* Spring–summer from cuttings. *Light:* Full sun. *Air:* 50–70 degrees F. during winter heating season. *Humidity:* Low. *Soil:* All-purpose. *Moisture:* Moist to on the dry side. *Sources:* 1, 13, 18, 25, 35, 38, 39, 51, 62, 63, 79, 80.

*Othonna crassifolia.* Pickle plant. Tender perennial succulent. Dangling. Leaves light

ABOVE: Passiflora, *passion flower.*

BELOW: Pelargonium, *miniature ivy geranium.*

green, shaped as little pickles. Flowers yellow in spring–summer. *Uses:* Indoors. Outdoors in frost-free weather. Basket. Pedestal. Shelf. Window box. *Start:* Spring–summer from cuttings. *Light:* Full sun. *Air:* 50–70 degrees F. during winter heating season. *Humidity:* Low. *Soil:* All-purpose. *Moisture:* Moist except on the dry side in winter. *Sources:* 1, 13, 18, 25, 35, 38, 39, 51, 62, 63, 79, 80.

*Oxalis.* Tender perennial bulbous or tuberous plants. Fountain-form. Leaves light to medium green. Flowers pink, purple, rose, white, yellow intermittently all year, depending on species. *Uses:* Indoors. Outdoors in frost-free weather. Basket. Pedestal. Shelf. Window box. *Start:* Any time from bulbs or by division of tuberous types *(O. rubra* and *O. regnellii). Light:* Full to half sun. *Air:* 50–70 degrees F. during winter heating season. *Humidity:* Medium. *Soil:* All-purpose. *Moisture:* Moist, except bulbous types need to be kept dry and dormant for 2–3 months after flowering stops. *Notes: O. rubra* (crassipes) and *O. regnellii* are both tuberous-rooted and tend to be everblooming. Bulbous types *O. bowieana, O. cernua* (Bermuda buttercup), are excellent for hanging gardens. *Sources:* 55, 60, 84.

*Parochetus communis.* Shamrock pea; blue oxalis. Tender perennial. Trailing. Leaves green and cloverlike with brown marking. Flowers blue and pink almost everblooming. *Uses:* Indoors. Outdoors in frost-free weather. Basket. Pedestal. Shelf. Window box. *Start:* Winter–spring from seeds, cuttings or by division. *Light:* Half sun to part shade. *Air:* 50–70 degrees F. during winter heating season. *Humidity:* Medium. *Soil:* All-purpose. *Moisture:* Moist in summer, on the dry side in winter. *Sources:* 55, 60, 68.

*Passiflora.* Passion flower. Tender to hardy vines. Climbing but may be pruned and trained for a hanging garden. Leaves medium green. Flowers blue, pink, purple, red, intermittently all year. *Uses:* Indoors. Outdoors in frost-free weather. Basket. Pedestal. Shelf. Window box. *Start:* Winter–spring from seeds or cuttings. *Light:* Full to half sun. *Air:* 62–75 degrees F. during winter heating season. *Humidity:* Medium to high. *Soil:* All-purpose. *Moisture:*

Moist. *Notes:* The hybrid *P. alato-caerulea* has the showiest flowers. The white-and-purple flowers of *P. edulis* are followed by three-inch edible fruits. *P. coccinea* has red flowers. *Sources:* 55, 60, 84.

*Pelargonium peltatum.* Ivyleaf geranium. Tender perennial. Cascading. Leaves light green, green and white or green and yellow. Flowers lavender, pink, purple, red, rose, white intermittently. *Uses:* Indoors. Outdoors in frost-free weather. Basket. Pedestal. Shelf. Window box. *Start:* Any time from cuttings. *Light:* Full sun. *Air:* 50–70 degrees F. during winter heating season. *Humidity:* Medium. *Soil:* All-purpose. *Moisture:* Moist to on the dry side. *Notes:* The only way to have winter bloom is to provide full sun in an atmosphere that is cool, moist and airy—as in a greenhouse. Of the scented-leaf geraniums, Apple, Nutmeg and Coconut make fine hanging-basket subjects. *Sources:* 17, 60, 89.

*Pellaea rotundifolia.* Roundleaf fern. Tender perennial (withstands light frosts). Trailing. Leaves dark green. *Uses:* Indoors. Outdoors in frost-free weather. Basket. Pedestal. Shelf. Window box. Strawberry jar. *Start:* Spring by division. *Light:* Part shade. *Air:* 50–70 degrees F. during winter heating season. *Humidity:* Medium. *Soil:* All-purpose. *Moisture:* Moist. *Sources:* 4, 50, 55, 60, 67, 68, 84.

*Pellionia.* Tender perennial. Creeping. Dangling. Leaves blue-gray with black veins (*P. daveauana*) or bronzy green (*P. pulchra*). *Uses:* Indoors. Outdoors in frost-free weather. Basket. Pedestal. Shelf. Window box. Strawberry jar. *Start:* Any time from cuttings. *Light:* Part to full shade. *Air:* 62–75 degrees F. during winter heating season. *Humidity:* Medium to high. Mist often. *Soil:* All-purpose. *Moisture:* Wet to moist. *Sources:* 3, 55, 60, 84.

*Peperomia.* Tender perennial. Trailing. Leaves green, gray-green, green and white, green and yellow, or bronzy green. *Uses:* Indoors. Outdoors in frost-free weather. Basket. Pedestal. Shelf. Window box. *Start:* Any time from cuttings. *Light:* Half sun to part shade. *Air:* 62–75 degrees F. during winter heating season. *Humidity:* Low to medium. *Soil:* All-purpose. *Moisture:* Moist to on the dry side. *Sources:* 3, 55, 60, 84.

ABOVE: Pelargonium, *variegated ivy geranium.*

BELOW: Pellionia daveauana.

Peperomia columella.

Champagne petunia.

*Pernettya mucronata.* Hardy shrub. Bushy, spreading. Leaves dark green. Flowers pink, white in spring–summer. *Uses:* Outdoors. Basket. Pedestal. Shelf. Window box. *Start:* Summer from cuttings or by layering. *Light:* Full to half sun. *Air:* Cool and moist if wintered-over indoors in severely cold climates. *Humidity:* Medium. *Soil:* Equal parts all-purpose and acid peat moss. *Moisture:* Moist. *Sources:* 68.

*Petroselinum crispum.* Parsley. Hardy biennial often treated as an annual. Fountain-form. Leaves medium green. *Uses:* Indoors. Outdoors in frost-free weather. Basket. Pedestal. Shelf. Window box. Strawberry jar. *Start:* Any time from seeds or purchase plants. *Light:* Full to half sun. *Air:* 50–70 degrees F. during winter heating season. *Humidity:* Medium. *Soil:* All-purpose. *Moisture:* Moist; never allow to dry out. *Notes:* Parsley suffers indoors if placed in draft of hot, dry air. *Sources:* Local nurseries; also 60, 84.

*Petunia.* Tender perennial usually treated as an annual. Cascading. Leaves light to medium green. Flowers blue, lavender, pink, purple, red, rose, white, yellow, often marked with contrasting color; everblooming. *Uses:* Indoors. Outdoors in frost-free weather. Basket. Pedestal. Shelf. Window box. *Start:* Seeds indoors 12 weeks before frost-free weather; sow seeds outdoors in warm weather or purchase started plants. *Light:* Full to half sun. *Air:* 62–72 degrees F. during winter heating season. *Humidity:* Low to medium. *Soil:* All-purpose. *Moisture:* Moist. *Notes:* Outdoor petunias cut back to three or four inches in autumn and brought indoors before frost will begin to flower again in a few weeks. *Sources:* Local nurseries; also 11, 68, 85.

*Philodendron.* Tender perennial. Climbing. Leaves light to medium green *(P. scandens,* sometimes called cordatum or oxycardium) and silver-marked green *(P. sodiroi). Uses:* Indoors. Outdoors in frost-free weather. Basket. Pedestal. Shelf. *Start:* Any time from cuttings. *Light:* Half sun to full shade. *Air:* 62–75 degrees F. during winter heating season. *Humidity:* Low

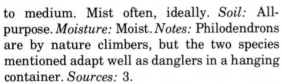

Pilea *on pedestal of clay pots.*

Platycerium, *staghorn fern.*

to medium. Mist often, ideally. *Soil:* All-purpose. *Moisture:* Moist. *Notes:* Philodendrons are by nature climbers, but the two species mentioned adapt well as danglers in a hanging container. *Sources:* 3.

*Phlox.* Hardy perennial *(P. nivalis* and *P. subulata);* annual *(P. drummondii).* Trailing. Creeping. Leaves medium green. Flowers blue, lavender, pink, purple, red, rose, white, yellow in spring–summer. *Uses:* Outdoors; annual phlox only in frost-free weather. Basket. Pedestal. Shelf. Window box. Strawberry jar. *Start:* Annual phlox indoors 8–12 weeks before frost-free weather outdoors from seeds; perennials in spring by division. *Light:* Full sun. *Air:* 60–72 degrees F. for seedlings started early indoors. *Humidity:* Medium. *Soil:* All-purpose. *Moisture:* Moist. *Notes:* Beauty and Twinkle, both hybrid strains of *P. drummondii,* are excellent for hanging gardens. *Sources:* Local nurseries; also 6, 68, 85.

*Pilea.* Tender perennial. Trailing. Creeping. Leaves fresh green *(P. depressa* and *P. num-*

*mulariifolia),* silver and blue-green *(P. pubescens)* and brown *(P. repens). Uses:* Indoors. Outdoors in frost-free weather. Basket. Pedestal. Shelf. Window box. *Start:* Any time from cuttings. *Light:* Half sun to full shade. *Air:* 62–75 degrees F. during winter heating season. *Humidity:* Low to medium. *Soil:* All-purpose. *Moisture:* Moist. *Sources:* 55, 60, 84.

*Piper betle.* Betel leaf. Tender perennial. Trailing. Leaves dark green. *Uses:* Indoors. Outdoors in frost-free weather. Basket. Pedestal. Shelf. *Start:* Spring–summer from cuttings. *Light:* Half sun to part shade. *Air:* 62–75 degrees F. during winter heating season. *Humidity:* Medium to high. Mist often. *Soil:* All-purpose. *Moisture:* Wet to moist. *Sources:* 55, 60, 68.

*Platycerium.* Staghorn fern. Tender perennial. Fountain-form or dangling. Leaves light green. *Uses:* Indoors. Outdoors in frost-free weather. Basket, shelf or mounted on slab of bark and hung on a wall. *Start:* Any time by division. *Light:* Part to full shade. *Air:* 62–75

ABOVE: *Variegated* Plectranthus, *Swedish-ivy.*

BELOW: Polypodium, *bear's-paw fern.*

degrees F. during winter heating season. *Humidity:* Medium to high. Mist often. *Soil:* Osmunda fiber mounted on slab of bark or piece of wood. *Moisture:* Moist to on the dry side. *Notes:* Avoid hanging in drafts of hot, dry air. Remove from hanger and soak roots at least once a week. *Sources:* 4, 50, 55, 60, 67, 68, 84.

*Plectranthus.* Swedish-ivy is *P. australis.* Tender perennial. Trailing. Cascading. Leaves light to dark green; green and white in variegated form of *P. australis;* bronzy green with silver and purple *(P. oertendahlii).* Flowers white, but insignificant; buds are best pinched off. *Uses:* Indoors. Outdoors in frost-free weather. Basket. Pedestal. Shelf. Window box. *Start:* Any time from cuttings. *Light:* Half sun to part shade. *Air:* 62–75 degrees F. during winter heating season. *Humidity:* Low to medium. Mist often, ideally. *Soil:* All-purpose. *Moisture:* Moist. *Notes:* Pinch out growing tips often to encourage dense, compact habit. *Sources:* Local plant shops; also 55, 60, 84.

*Plumbago capensis.* Tender perennial. Clambering. Leaves light green. Flowers blue or white on new growth in any season. *Uses:* Indoors. Outdoors in frost-free weather. Basket. Pedestal. Shelf. Window box. *Start:* Spring or fall from cuttings. Plant seeds indoors 12 weeks before frost-free weather outdoors. *Light:* Full to half sun. *Air:* 50–70 degrees F. during winter heating season. *Humidity:* Medium to high. *Soil:* All-purpose. *Moisture:* Moist. *Notes:* Prune back in spring for summer flowers; in autumn for winter bloom. *Sources:* 68.

*Polygonum capitatum.* Tender perennial. Trailing. Leaves copper-green with black **V** mark. Flowers pink intermittently. *Uses:* Indoors. Outdoors in frost-free weather. Basket. Pedestal. Shelf. Window box. *Start:* Any time from seeds or cuttings. *Light:* Full to half sun. *Air:* 50–70 degrees F. during winter heating season. *Humidity:* Low to medium. *Soil:* All-purpose. *Moisture:* Moist. *Notes:* Shear back scraggly old plant to an inch or 2 from the soil; new growth will appear. *Sources:* 68.

*Polypodium.* Bear's-paw fern. Tender perennial. Creeping. Fountain-form. Leaves light green or bluish. *Uses:* Indoors. Outdoors in

frost-free weather. Basket. Pedestal. *Start:* Spring–summer from rhizome cuttings or by division. *Light:* Half sun to full shade. *Air:* 50–70 degrees F. during winter heating season. *Humidity:* Medium to high. Mist often. *Soil:* All-purpose. *Moisture:* Moist. *Notes:* May grow to 2 feet or more in diameter. *Sources:* 4, 50, 55, 60, 67, 68, 84.

*Portulaca.* Rose-moss. Annual. Trailing. Leaves medium green and succulent. Flowers lavender, orange, pink, purple, red, rose, white, yellow in spring–summer. *Uses:* Outdoors in frost-free weather. Basket. Pedestal. Shelf. Window box. Strawberry jar. *Start:* Seeds indoors 8 weeks before frost-free weather outdoors. *Light:* Full sun. *Air:* Warm. *Humidity:* Low. *Soil:* All-purpose. *Moisture:* Moist to on the dry side. *Notes:* Superb flowering basket plants for hot, dry climate. *Sources:* Seeds and started plants at local nurseries; seeds also from 11, 68, 85.

*Primula.* Primrose. Tender and hardy perennial. Low rosettes of leaves surrounding flowers, nosegay-fashion. Leaves medium green. Flowers blue, lavender, orange, pink, purple, red, rose, white, yellow, often marked with contrasting color, winter–spring. *Uses:* Indoors. Outdoors. Basket. Pedestal. Shelf. Window box. Strawberry jar. *Start:* Spring–summer from seeds; by division summer–autumn. *Light:* Half sun to part shade. *Air:* 40–55 degrees F. during winter heating season. *Humidity:* Medium to high. *Soil:* All-purpose. *Moisture:* Moist. *Notes:* Tender primroses include *P. malacoides, P. obconica* and *P. sinensis,* all 3 usually started from seeds annually in spring–summer for flowers the following winter–spring. *P. polyantha,* the hardy English primrose will live over year after year where summers are not too hot and dry. *Sources:* 11, 68, 85.

*Quamoclit sloteri.* Cardinal climber. Annual. Climbing; pinch back frequently to encourage branching. Leaves medium green. Flowers red in summer. *Uses:* Outdoors in frost-free weather. Basket. Pedestal. Shelf. Window box. *Start:* Indoors 8 weeks before frost-free weather outdoors from seeds planted in peat pots (to avoid disturbing roots at transplanting time). *Light:* Full sun. *Air:* 62–75 degrees F.

Portulaca, *rose-moss.*

Saxifraga, *strawberry-geranium.*

ABOVE: Rhoeo spathacea, *Moses-in-the-cradle.*
BELOW: Russelia, *fountain plant.*

during winter heating season. *Humidity:* Medium. *Soil:* All-purpose. *Moisture:* Moist. *Sources:* 68, 85.

*Rhipsalis.* Mistletoe cactus. Tender perennial succulent. Trailing or cascading. Leaves light to medium green. *Uses:* Outdoors in frost-free weather. Basket. Pedestal. Shelf. *Start:* Spring–summer from cuttings. *Light:* Half sun to part shade. *Air:* 50–70 degrees F. during winter heating season. *Humidity:* Low to medium. Mist often. *Soil:* All-purpose. *Moisture:* On the dry side. *Sources:* 1, 13, 18, 25, 35, 38, 39, 51, 62, 63, 79, 80.

*Rhododendron.* Azalea. Tender or hardy shrub. Fountain-form. Leaves medium green. Flowers lavender, pink, purple, red, rose, white in winter–spring. *Uses:* Outdoors mostly in frost-free weather. Basket. Pedestal. Shelf. Window box. *Start:* Summer–fall from cuttings. *Light:* Half sun to part shade. *Air:* 40–60 degrees F. if brought indoors during winter heating season. *Humidity:* Medium to high. *Soil:* Mix equal parts all-purpose with acid peat moss. *Moisture:* Wet to moist; never allow to dry out. *Notes:* Hardiness varies considerably; a good local nursery will have suitable azaleas for hanging gardens—provided azaleas are cultivated in your climate. *Sources:* Local nurseries.

*Rhoeo spathacea.* Moses-in-the-cradle. Tender perennial. Fountain-form. Leaves purple and dark green; *R. s. vittata* leaves are green with red and yellow stripes. Flowers white in

boat-shaped bracts intermittently all year. *Uses:* Indoors. Outdoors in frost-free weather. Basket. Pedestal. Shelf. Window box. *Start:* Any time from cuttings or by division. *Light:* Full sun to part shade. *Air:* 62–75 degrees F. during winter heating season. *Humidity:* Medium. *Soil:* All-purpose. *Moisture:* Moist; allowing the soil to dry out severely will cause the leaf tips to turn brown. *Sources:* 55, 60, 84.

*Rhoicissus capensis* (Cissus capensis). Evergreen grape. Tender perennial. Trailing. Leaves medium green and scalloped. *Uses:* Indoors. Outdoors in frost-free weather. Basket. Pedestal. Shelf. *Start:* Any time from cuttings. *Light:* Full sun to part shade. *Air:* 50–70 degrees F. during winter heating season. *Humidity:* Medium. Mist often. *Soil:* All-purpose. *Moisture:* Moist. *Sources:* 55, 60, 84.

*Rosa.* Rose, miniature. Hardy shrub. Fountain-form. Leaves medium green. Flowers pink, red, rose, white, yellow in spring, summer–autumn. *Uses:* Outdoors in frost-free weather. Basket. Pedestal. Shelf. Window box. Strawberry jar. *Start:* Spring, from purchased plant. *Light:* Full to half sun. *Air:* 30–40 degrees F. during winter heating season. *Humidity:* Medium. *Soil:* All-purpose. *Moisture:* Moist. *Notes:* New varieties of miniature roses are available in hanging-basket types. *Sources:* 61, 74, 81.

*Rosmarinus officinalis.* Rosemary. Hardy perennial (to about 10 degrees F.). Bushy or trailing. Leaves dark to grayish green. Flowers blue-lavender in spring. *Uses:* Indoors. Outdoors. Basket. Pedestal. Shelf. Window box. Strawberry jar. *Start:* Summer–fall from cuttings; in winter–spring from seeds. *Light:* Half sun to part shade. *Air:* 40–60 degrees F. during winter heating season. *Humidity:* Medium. *Soil:* All-purpose. *Moisture:* Moist to on the dry side, but be sure the soil never dries out severely. *Notes:* Varieties *R. o. prostratus* and 'Lockwood de Forest' are recommended for hanging gardens. *Sources:* 60, 84.

*Ruellia makoyana.* Trailing velvet plant. Tender perennial. Trailing. Leaves dark green with silver veins and purple underneath. Flowers rose in spring–summer. *Uses:* Indoors. Outdoors in frost-free weather. Basket. Pedestal. Shelf. Window box. *Start:* Any time from

seeds, cuttings or by division. *Light:* Half sun to part shade. *Air:* 50–70 degrees F. during winter heating season. *Humidity:* Medium to high. Mist often. *Soil:* All-purpose. *Moisture:* Wet to moist. *Sources:* 55, 60, 84.

*Russelia sarmentosa.* Fountain plant. Tender shrub. Trailing. Leaves medium green and scale-like. Flowers red in summer or intermittently all year. *Uses:* Indoors. Outdoors in frost-free weather. Basket. Pedestal. *Start:* Summer–fall from cuttings. *Light:* Full to half sun. *Air:* 62–75 degrees F. during winter heating season. *Humidity:* Medium. *Soil:* All-purpose. *Moisture:* Moist to on the dry side. *Sources:* 55, 60.

*Saintpaulia.* African violet. Tender peren-

Rhoicissus capensis, *evergreen grape.*

ABOVE: Saxifraga stolonifera *Maroon Beauty*.

BELOW: Schlumbergera, *Christmas cactus*.

nial. Trailing. Leaves medium green. Flowers blue, lavender, pink, purple, red, rose, white; everblooming. *Uses:* Indoors. Basket. Pedestal. Shelf. *Start:* Any time from seeds, cuttings or by division. *Light:* Half sun to part shade. *Air:* 62–75 degrees F. during winter heating season. *Humidity:* Medium to high. *Soil:* All-purpose. *Moisture:* Moist. *Notes:* Select varieties listed as trailing from catalogs of specialists; many miniatures fit in this category and make delightful small hanging plants. *Sources:* 5, 7, 9, 11, 12, 14, 15, 16, 21, 26, 28, 42, 50, 52, 54, 56, 57, 72, 86, 88, 91.

*Sansevieria parva.* Related to snake plant. Tender perennial. Dangling. Leaves light and dark green. *Uses:* Indoors. Outdoors in frost-free weather. Basket. Pedestal. Shelf. *Start:* Any time by division. *Light:* Half sun to part shade. *Air:* 62–75 degrees F. during winter heating season. *Humidity:* Low. *Soil:* All-purpose. *Moisture:* Moist to on the dry side. *Notes:* A tough basket plant and a good choice for an apartment. *Sources:* 1, 13, 18, 25, 35, 38, 39, 51, 62, 63, 79, 80.

*Sanvitalia procumbens.* Creeping zinnia. Annual. Trailing. Leaves medium green. Flowers yellow in summer–autumn. *Uses:* Outdoors in frost-free weather. Basket. Pedestal. Shelf. Window box. *Start:* Seeds indoors 8 weeks before frost-free weather outdoors. *Light:* Full sun. *Air:* Warm. *Humidity:* Low to medium. *Soil:* All-purpose. *Moisture:* Moist. *Notes:* Good choice for a flowering basket plant in a hot, dry climate. *Sources:* 68, 85.

*Saxifraga stolonifera.* Strawberry-begonia; strawberry-geranium. Hardy perennial usually treated as a house plant. Dangling. Leaves medium green with silver veins and burgundy reverses or green-white-and-pink variegated. Flowers white in spring–summer. *Uses:* Indoors. Outdoors in frost-free weather. Basket. Pedestal. Shelf. Window box. Strawberry jar. *Start:* Any time from offsets or by division. *Light:* Full to half sun in winter; half sun to part shade in summer. *Air:* 50–70 degrees F. during winter heating season. *Humidity:* Medium to high. *Soil:* All-purpose. *Moisture:* Moist to on the dry side. *Sources:* 55, 60, 84.

*Schizanthus pinnatus.* Poor man's orchid. Annual. Flowers lavender, pink, purple, rose,

white, winter–spring and early summer. *Uses:* Indoors. Outdoors in frost-free weather. Basket. Pedestal. Shelf. Window box. *Start:* Fall–winter from seeds. *Light:* Half sun to part shade. *Air:* 40–55 degrees F. during winter heating season. *Humidity:* Medium. *Soil:* All-purpose. *Moisture:* Moist. *Notes:* Ideal for winter flowers in mild-climate gardens, or in a home greenhouse kept cool, moist and airy. *Sources:* Started plants at many local nurseries; also seeds from 68, 85.

*Schizocentron elegans.* Spanish shawl. Tender perennial. Creeping. Leaves medium green on red stems. Flowers rose-purple in spring–summer. *Uses:* Indoors. Outdoors in frost-free weather. Basket. Pedestal. Shelf. Window box. Strawberry jar. *Start:* Any time from cuttings. *Light:* Half sun to part shade. *Air:* 50–70 degrees F. during winter heating season. *Humidity:* Medium to high. Mist often. *Soil:* All-purpose. *Moisture:* Moist. *Notes:* Cut back in summer after flowering. *Sources:* 55, 60, 68, 84.

*Schlumbergera.* Thanksgiving–Christmas cactus. Tender perennial succulent. Fountainform. Leaves medium green. Flowers lavender, orange, pink, red, rose, white, autumn–winter. *Uses:* Indoors. Outdoors in frost-free weather. Basket. Pedestal. Shelf. *Start:* Spring–summer from cuttings. *Light:* Full to half sun. *Air:* 50–70 degrees F. during winter heating season. *Humidity:* Low to medium. Mist often. *Soil:* All-purpose. *Moisture:* Moist to on the dry side. *Notes:* To initiate flowering, withhold fertilizer and keep on the dry side in autumn; allow no artificial light to strike plant from sundown to sunup during this period. *Sources:* 1, 13, 18, 25, 35, 38, 39, 51, 62, 63, 79, 80.

*Scindapsus.* Pothos; devil's-ivy. Tender perennial. Dangling. Climbing. Leaves green and white, green and yellow or green and silver. *Uses:* Outdoors in frost-free weather. Basket. Pedestal. Shelf. *Start:* Any time from cuttings. *Light:* Half sun to part shade. *Air:* 62–75 degrees F. during winter heating season. *Humidity:* Low to medium. *Soil:* All-purpose. *Moisture:* Moist to on the dry side. *Notes:* *S. pictus argyraeus* has silver-and-green leaves and needs more humidity than the more common pothos. *Sources:* 3, 55, 60, 84.

*Sedum morganianum.* Burro's- or donkey's-

ABOVE: *Schizocentron elegans, Spanish shawl.*
BELOW: Scindapsus, *pothos.*

ABOVE: *Burro's-tail or* Sedum morganianum.

BELOW: *Orange browallia,* Streptosolen.

tail. Tender perennial succulent. Trailing. Leaves silvery blue-green. *Uses:* Indoors. Outdoors in frost-free weather. Basket. Pedestal. Shelf. *Start:* Spring–summer from cuttings. *Light:* Full to half sun. *Air:* 50–70 degrees F. during winter heating season. *Humidity:* Low to medium. *Soil:* All-purpose. *Moisture:* Moist to on the dry side. *Notes:* Many other sedums make delightful, easy-care plants for hanging gardens; check descriptions in catalogs from specialists in cacti and other succulents. *Sources:* 1, 13, 18, 25, 35, 38, 39, 51, 62, 63, 79, 80.

*Selenicereus macdonaldiae.* Queen-of-the-night. Tender perennial cactus. Trailing. Leaves dark green. Flowers white night-blooming, in summer. *Uses:* Indoors. Outdoors in frost-free weather. Basket. Pedestal. Shelf. *Start:* Spring–summer from cuttings. *Light:* Half sun to part shade. *Air:* 50–70 degrees F. during winter heating season. *Humidity:* Low to medium. *Soil:* All-purpose. *Moisture:* Moist, except on the dry side in winter. *Sources:* 1, 13, 18, 25, 35, 38, 39, 51, 62, 63, 79, 80.

*Senecio rowleyanus.* String-of-pearls. Tender perennial succulent. Dangling. Leaves light green and beadlike. Flowers white, lightly clove-scented in spring–summer. *Uses:* Indoors. Outdoors in frost-free weather. Basket. Pedestal. Shelf. *Start:* Spring–summer from cuttings. *Light:* Half sun to part shade. *Air:* 50–70 degrees F. during winter heating season. *Humidity:* Low to medium. *Soil:* All-purpose. *Moisture:* Moist, except on the dry side in winter. *Sources:* 1, 13, 18, 25, 35, 38, 39, 51, 62, 63, 79, 80, 84.

*Sollya fusiformis.* Australian bluebell creeper. Tender shrub. Cascading. Leaves medium green. Flowers blue in summer. *Uses:* Indoors. Outdoors in frost-free weather. Basket. Pedestal. Shelf. *Start:* Winter–spring from seeds or cuttings. *Light:* Full sun to part shade. *Air:* 40–60 degrees F. during winter heating season. *Humidity:* Medium. *Soil:* All-purpose. *Moisture:* Moist. *Sources:* 55, 60, 68.

*Stapelia.* Carrion or starfish flower. Tender perennial succulent. Trailing. Leaves dull to gray-green. Flowers bizarre, star-shaped and often foul-smelling; yellow, brown or purple in summer. *Uses:* Indoors. Outdoors in frost-free

ABOVE: *Variegated* Senecio *vine.*

RIGHT: Senecio rowleyanus, *string of pearls.*

weather. Basket. Pedestal. Shelf. *Start:* Spring–summer from cuttings. *Light:* Full to half sun. *Air:* 62–75 degrees F. during winter heating season. *Humidity:* Low. *Soil:* All-purpose. *Moisture:* Moist in spring and summer; on the dry side in fall and winter. *Notes:* S. *variegata* is probably the best choice as a house or apartment plant. *Sources:* 1, 13, 18, 25, 35, 38, 39, 51, 62, 63, 79, 80.

*Stenotaphrum secundatum variegatum.* Variegated St. Augustine grass. Tender perennial. Creeping. Leaves green and white. *Uses:* Indoors. Outdoors in frost-free weather. Basket. Pedestal. Shelf. Window box. *Start:* Winter–spring by division. *Light:* Full to half sun. *Air:*

50–70 degrees F. during winter heating season. *Humidity:* Medium. *Soil:* All-purpose. *Moisture:* Moist to on the dry side. *Sources:* 60.

*Stephanotis floribunda.* Madagascar jasmine. Tender perennial. Trailing or climbing. Leaves fresh green. Flowers white, fragrant, spring–summer. *Uses:* Indoors. Outdoors in frost-free weather. Basket. Pedestal. Shelf. Window box. *Start:* Summer–fall from cuttings. *Light:* Half sun to part shade. *Air:* 62–72 degrees F. during winter heating season. *Humidity:* Medium to high. *Soil:* All-purpose. *Moisture:* Moist. *Sources:* 55, 60.

*Streptocarpus saxorum.* Gesneriad. Tender perennial. Trailing. Leaves medium green.

ABOVE: Tagetes, *Red Seven Star marigold.*

BELOW: Tetragonia, *New Zealand spinach.*

Flowers lavender-blue intermittently all year. *Uses:* Indoors. Outdoors in frost-free weather. Basket. Pedestal. Shelf. Window box. *Start:* Any time from cuttings. *Light:* Half sun to part shade. *Air:* 62–75 degrees F. during winter heating season. *Humidity:* High. *Soil:* All-purpose. *Moisture:* Moist to on the dry side. *Sources:* 9, 16, 21, 22, 28, 50, 54, 56, 86.

*Streptosolen jamesonii.* Orange browallia. Tender shrub. Trailing. Leaves medium green. Flowers orange in winter–spring. *Uses:* Indoors. Outdoors in frost-free weather. Basket. Pedestal. Shelf. Window box. *Start:* Spring from cuttings. *Light:* Half sun to part shade. *Air:* 55–70 degrees F. during winter heating season. *Humidity:* Medium. *Soil:* All-purpose. *Moisture:* Moist. *Notes:* Pinch out tips of young plants often to encourage bushy, dense growth. *Sources:* 55, 60, 68, 84.

*Tagetes.* Marigold. Annual. Bushy to trailing. Leaves medium green. Flowers orange, red, yellow in summer–autumn. *Uses:* Outdoors in frost-free weather. Basket. Pedestal. Shelf. Window box. *Start:* Seeds indoors 8–10 weeks before frost-free weather outdoors, or purchase plants. *Light:* Full sun. *Air:* 50–70 degrees F. during winter heating season. *Humidity:* Low to medium. *Soil:* All-purpose. *Moisture:* Moist. *Notes:* The small-flowered, dwarf French hybrid marigolds are excellent plants for hanging gardens in a warm, sunny environment. *Sources:* Local nurseries; seeds also from 11, 68, 85.

*Tetragonia expansa.* New Zealand spinach. Annual. Trailing. Leaves medium green, a hot-weather replacement for spinach. *Uses:* Outdoors in frost-free weather. Basket. Pedestal. Shelf. Window box. *Start:* Seeds indoors 8 weeks before frost-free weather outdoors; soak seeds 24–48 hours in water before planting in peat pots. *Light:* Full to half sun. *Air:* 62–75 degrees F. during winter heating season. *Humidity:* Low to medium. *Soil:* All-purpose. *Moisture:* Moist. *Notes:* Begin harvesting New Zealand spinach about 70 days after planting. It tastes especially good combined with Swiss chard. *Sources:* 11, 68, 85.

*Tetrastigma.* Giant grape-ivy. Tender perennial. Cascading. Leaves olive-green. *Uses:* Indoors, outdoors in frost-free weather. Basket.

Pedestal. Shelf. *Start:* Spring–summer from cuttings. *Light:* Half sun to part shade. *Air:* 50–70 degrees F. during winter heating season. *Humidity:* Medium. *Soil:* All-purpose. *Moisture:* Moist. *Notes:* Avoid hot, dry drafts of air in winter. *Sources:* 55, 60.

*Thunbergia alata.* Black-eyed Susan vine. Tender perennial treated as an annual. Trailing or climbing. Leaves medium green. Flowers orange, white, yellow in summer. *Uses:* Outdoors in frost-free weather. Basket. Pedestal. Shelf. Window box. *Start:* Seeds indoors 8–10 weeks before frost-free weather outdoors. *Light:* Full sun. *Air:* 62–75 degrees F. during winter heating season. *Humidity:* Medium. *Soil:* All-purpose. *Moisture:* Moist. *Notes:* Highly susceptible to red spider-mites in hot, dry, stale air. *Sources:* 11, 68, 85.

*Thymophylla.* Dahlberg daisy. Annual. Bushy to trailing. Leaves light green and fernlike. Flowers yellow, summer–autumn. *Uses:* Outdoors in frost-free weather. Basket. Pedestal. Shelf. Window box. Strawberry jar. *Start:* Seeds indoors 8–10 weeks before frost-free weather outdoors. *Light:* Full sun. *Air:* 62–75 degrees F. during winter heating season. *Humidity:* Low to medium. *Soil:* All-purpose. *Moisture:* Moist. *Notes:* A fine-textured plant that becomes covered with little yellow daisies in early summer and continues until frost. Plants outdoors may be brought into a home greenhouse before frost for more flowering; shear back to encourage additional blooms. *Sources:* 68.

*Thymus.* Thyme. Hardy perennial. Trailing. Creeping. Leaves golden green, dark green, gray, green and white, or green and yellow. Flowers in spring–summer. *Uses:* Indoors. Outdoors. Basket. Pedestal. Shelf. Window box. Strawberry jar. *Start:* Winter–spring from seeds or by division. *Light:* Full to half sun. *Air:* 50–70 degrees F. during winter heating season. *Humidity:* Medium. *Soil:* All-purpose. *Moisture:* Moist to on the dry side. *Notes:* Pick off fresh leaves as you need them for seasoning. *Sources:* 60.

*Tolmiea.* Piggyback or pickaback. Hardy perennial treated as a house plant. Fountain-form. Leaves medium green. No flowers. *Uses:* Indoors; outdoors in frost-free weather. Basket.

ABOVE: Thunbergia alata, *black-eyed-Susan vine.*

BELOW: Thunbergia *White Wings.*

ABOVE: Tropaeolum, *Gleam nasturtium.*

BELOW: Trachelospermum jasminoides, *star jasmine.*

Pedestal. Shelf. Window box. Strawberry jar. *Start:* Any time from leaf cuttings. *Light:* Part to full shade. *Air:* 50–70 degrees F. during winter heating season. *Humidity:* Medium. Mist often. *Soil:* All-purpose. *Moisture:* Wet to moist. *Sources:* 55, 60, 84.

*Torenia fournieri.* Wishbone flower. Annual. Bushy or trailing. Leaves light green. Flowers blue and yellow, or white, spring, summer, and autumn. *Uses:* Indoors. Outdoors in frost-free weather. Basket. Pedestal. Shelf. Window box. *Start:* Seeds indoors 8–10 weeks before frost-free weather outdoors. *Light:* Half sun to part shade. *Air:* 62–72 degrees F. during winter heating season. *Humidity:* Medium. *Soil:* All-purpose. *Moisture:* Moist. *Sources:* 68, 85.

*Trachelospermum jasminoides.* Star jasmine. Tender shrub. Fountain-form or climbing. Leaves dark green. Flowers fragrant white in summer. *Uses:* Indoors. Outdoors in frost-free weather. Basket. Pedestal. Shelf. *Start:* Spring–summer from cuttings. *Light:* Half sun to part shade. *Air:* 62–75 degrees F. during winter heating season. *Humidity:* Medium. Mist often. *Soil:* All-purpose. *Moisture:* Moist. *Notes:* Pinch and prune regularly to encourage a hanging instead of a climbing habit. *Sources:* Local nurseries in mild climates; also 55, 60.

*Tradescantia.* Wandering jew. Tender perennial. Cascading. Creeping. Leaves green, green and white, green and burgundy, olive-green, silver variegated in some. Flowers white intermittently. *Uses:* Indoors. Basket. Pedestal. Shelf. Window box. *Start:* Any time from cuttings. *Light:* Full sun to part shade. *Air:* 62–75 degrees F. during winter heating season. *Humidity:* Medium. *Soil:* All-purpose. *Moisture:* Moist. *Notes:* Pinch out growing tips after every few inches growth to encourage compact, dense growth. *Sources:* Local plant shops; also 55, 60, 84.

*Tropaeolum.* Nasturtium. Tender perennial treated as an annual. Trailing. Leaves light green. Flowers orange, pink, red, rose, white, yellow in spring–summer. *Uses:* Indoors. Outdoors in frost-free weather. Basket. Pedestal. Shelf. Window box. *Start:* Seeds indoors 8 weeks before frost-free weather outdoors; plant seeds indoors in winter for spring bloom indoors. *Light:* Full sun. *Air:* 50–70 degrees F.

*Left to right: Tricolor tradescantia, plain green tradescantia, and green-and-white tradescantia.*

ABOVE: *Pansy (Viola) hybrids in basket.*

RIGHT: *Red-and-white verbena flowers.*

during winter heating season. *Humidity:* Medium. *Soil:* All-purpose. *Moisture:* Moist. *Notes:* Aphids are notorious for attacking nasturtiums; spraying with synthetic pyrethrin may be necessary. Read catalog descriptions; order hanging or climbing varieties. *Sources:* 19, 68, 85.

*Verbena.* Tender perennial usually treated as an annual. Trailing. Leaves medium green. Flowers lavender, pink, purple, red, rose, white in spring, summer and autumn. *Uses:* Indoors. Outdoors in frost-free weather. Basket. Pedestal. Shelf. Window box. *Start:* Seeds indoors 12 weeks before frost-free weather outdoors; root cuttings of favorite plants in early fall to save over winter indoors. *Light:* Full sun. *Air:* 50–70 degrees F. during winter heating season. *Humidity:* Medium. *Soil:* All-purpose. *Moisture:* Moist. *Notes:* Large basket-grown verbenas may be cut back in autumn and wintered-over indoors in a cool, but frost-free place; keep soil barely moist, but never bone dry. Select seeds labeled "trailing verbena." *Sources:* Most seed catalogs.

*Vinca major variegata.* Periwinkle. Hardy perennial usually treated as a tender plant when cultivated in a container. Trailing. Leaves green and white. Flowers blue in spring. *Uses:* Indoors. Outdoors in frost-free weather. Basket. Pedestal. Shelf. Window box. *Start:* Any time from cuttings. *Light:* Full sun to part shade. *Air:* 50–70 degrees F. during winter heating season. *Humidity:* Medium. *Soil:* All-purpose. *Moisture:* Wet to moist. *Notes:* Great trailer to use around the edge of a hanging container in which you want to grow a bushy, upright, flowering plant such as geranium or dwarf marigold. *Sources:* Most local nurseries.

*Viola.* Pansy or viola. Perennials usually treated as annuals. Trailing. Leaves medium green. Flowers blue, lavender, orange, pink, purple, rose, white, yellow, often marked with contrasting color, in winter–spring. *Uses:* Indoors. Outdoors. Basket. Pedestal. Shelf. Window box. Strawberry jar. *Start:* Summer–fall from seeds or purchase plants. *Light:* Half sun to part shade. *Air:* 40–60 degrees F. during winter heating season. *Humidity:* Medium. *Soil:* All-purpose. *Moisture:* Moist. *Notes:* Re-

Vinca major *in split wood hanger.*

moving withered flowers before seeds form keeps pansies and violas blooming for a much longer season. *Sources:* Local nurseries; also 11, 68, 85.

*Wedelia trilobata.* Tender shrub. Trailing. Leaves fresh green. Flowers yellow in spring–summer. *Uses:* Indoors. Outdoors in frost-free weather. Basket. Pedestal. Shelf. Window box. *Start:* Any time from cuttings. *Light:* Half sun to part shade. *Air:* 62–75 degrees F. during winter heating season. *Humidity:* Medium. *Soil:* All-purpose. *Moisture:* Wet to moist. *Sources:* 55, 60.

*Zebrina.* Wandering jew. Tender perennial. Cascading. Creeping. Leaves green, pink, burgundy, silver and white. Flowers purple intermittently. *Uses:* Indoors. Outdoors in frost-free weather. Basket. Pedestal. Shelf. Window box. *Start:* Any time from cuttings. *Light:* Full sun to part shade. *Air:* 62–75 degrees F. during winter heating season. *Humidity:* Medium. Mist often. *Soil:* All-purpose. *Moisture:* Moist. *Notes:* Pinch out growing tips frequently to encourage compact, dense growth. *Sources:* 55, 60, 84.

*Zinnia linearis.* Annual. Trailing. Leaves medium green. Flowers yellow in summer–autumn. *Uses:* Outdoors in frost-free weather. Basket. Pedestal. Shelf. *Start:* Seeds indoors 8 weeks before frost-free weather outdoors. *Light:* Full sun. *Air:* 62–75 degrees F. during winter heating season. *Humidity:* Low to medium. *Soil:* All-purpose. *Moisture:* Moist. *Notes:* Great hanging plant in hot, dry climates. *Sources:* 19, 68, 85.

*Zygocactus.* Christmas cactus. Tender perennial succulent. Fountain-form. Leaves medium green. Flowers orange, pink, red, rose, white in winter. *Uses:* Indoors. Outdoors in frost-free weather. Basket. Pedestal. *Start:* Spring–summer from cuttings. *Light:* Full to half sun. *Air:* 50–70 degrees F. during winter heating season. *Humidity:* Low to medium. Mist often. *Soil:* All-purpose. *Moisture:* Moist to on the dry side. *Notes:* To initiate flowering, withhold fertilizer and keep on the dry side in autumn; allow no artificial light to strike plant from sundown to sunup during this period. *Sources:* 1, 13, 18, 25, 35, 38, 39, 51, 62, 63, 79, 80.

ABOVE: *Tricolor* Zebrina, *wandering jew.*

BELOW: Zygocactus *in clay tile pedestal.*

# Appendix A

## By-Mail Sources for Hanging Plants and Supplies

(The number preceding each firm name corresponds to the source numbers included for the plants in Chapter 6.)

(1) *Abbey Garden,* 176 Toro Canyon Rd., Carpinteria, Calif. 93013—Complete listing of cacti and other succulents; catalog 50¢.

(2) *Abbot's Nursery,* Route 4, Box 482, Mobile, Ala. 36609—Camellias.

(3) *Alberts & Merkel Bros., Inc.,* 2210 S. Federal Highway, Boynton Beach, Fla. 33435—Orchids, plus an amazing array of tropical foliage and flowering house plants; 25¢ for list.

(4) *Antonelli Bros.,* 2545 Capitola Rd., Santa Cruz, Calif. 95060—Tuberous begonias, gloxinias, achimenes.

(5) *Louise Barnaby,* 12178 Highview St., Vicksburg, Mich. 49097—African violets; send stamp for list.

(6) *Bluestone Perennials,* 3500 Jackson St., Mentor, Ohio 44060—Started plants of hardy perennial flowers.

(7) *Mrs. Mary V. Boose,* 9 Turney Place, Trumbull, Conn. 06611—African violets and episcias; 15¢ for list.

(8) *John Brudy's Rare Plant House,* P.O. Box 1348, Cocoa Beach, Fla. 32931—Unusual seeds and plants; catalog $1.

(9) *Buell's Greenhouses,* Weeks Road, Eastford, Conn. 06242—Complete listing of gloxinias, African violets and other gesneriads; send $1 for catalog.

(10) *Burgess Seed & Plant Co.,* 67 E. Battle Creek, Galesburg, Mich. 49053—House plants, vegetables, herbs, bulbs.

(11) *W. Atlee Burpee Co.,* 300 Park Ave., Warminster, Pa. 18974—Seeds, bulbs, supplies and equipment for container gardening.

(12) *David Buttram,* P.O. Box 193, Independence, Mo. 64051—African violets; send stamp for list.

(13) *Cactus Gem Nursery,* 10092 Mann Dr., Cupertino, Calif. (visit Thurs.-Sun.); by mail, write P.O. Box 327, Aromas, Calif. 95004.

(14) *Castle Violets,* 614 Castle Rd., Colorado Springs, Colo. 80904—African violets.

(15) *Champion's African Violets,* 8848 Van Hoesen Rd., Clay, N.Y. 13041—African violets; send stamp for list.

(16) *Victor Constantinov,* 3321 21st St., Apt. 7, San Francisco, Calif. 94110—African violets, columneas and episcias; send stamp for list.

(17) *Cook's Geranium Nursery,* 714 N. Grand, Lyons, Kans. 67544—Geraniums; send 25¢ for catalog.

(18) *Davis Cactus Garden,* 1522 Jefferson St., Kerrville, Tex. 78028—Send 25¢ for catalog.

(19) *DeGiorgi Bros., Inc.,* Council Bluffs, Iowa—Seeds of all kinds for container gardens.

(20) *P. de Jager and Sons,* 188 Asbury St., South Hamilton, Mass. 01982—Bulbs for indoors and outdoors.

(21) *L. Easterbrook Greenhouses,* 10 Craig St., Butler, Ohio 44822—African violets, other gesneriads, terrarium plants and supplies; complete catalog 75¢.

(22) *Electric Farm,* 104 B Lee Rd., Oak Hill, N.Y. 12460—Gesneriads; send self-addressed stamped envelope for list.

(23) *Farmer Seed and Nursery Co.,* Faribault, Minn. 55021—Flowers, bulbs, vegetables, herbs, fruit for container gardens.

(24) *Fennell Orchid Co., Inc.,* 26715 S.W. 157th Ave., Homestead, Fla. 33030.

(25) *Fernwood Plants,* 1311 Fernwood Pacific Dr., Topanga, Calf. 90290—Rare and unusual cacti.

(26) *Ffoulkes,* 610 Bryan St., Jacksonville, Fla. 32202—African violets; send 25¢ for list.

(27) *Henry Field Seed & Nursery Co.,* 407 Sycamore, Shenandoah, Iowa 51601—Flowers, bulbs, vegetables, herbs, fruit for container gardens.

(28) *Fischer Greenhouses,* Linwood, N.J. 08221—African violets and other gesneriads; send 20¢ for catalog.

(29) *Floralite Co.,* 4124 E. Oakwood Rd., Oak Creek, Wis. 53154—Fluorescent-light gardening equipment and supplies.

(30) *Fox Orchids,* 6615 W. Markham, Little Rock, Ark. 72205—Orchids and supplies for growing them at home.

(31) *Arthur Freed Orchids, Inc.,* 5731 S. Bonsall Dr., Malibu, Calif. 90265—Orchids and supplies for growing them.

(32) *Howard French,* P.O. Box 87, Center Rutland, Vt. 05736—Bulbs for forcing.

(33) *Girard Nurseries,* P.O. Box 428, Geneva, Ohio 44041—Bonsai materials.

(34) *The Greenhouse,* 9515 Flower St., Bellflower, Calif. 90706—Fluorescent-light gardening equipment.

(35) *Grigsby Cactus Gardens,* 2354 Bella Vista Dr., Vista, Calif. 92083—Catalog 50¢.

(36) *Gurney Seed and Nursery Co.,* Yankton, S. Dak. 57078—House plants, flowers, vegetables, herbs, fruits for container gardens.

(37) *Orchids by Hausermann, Inc.,* P.O. Box 363, Elmhurst, Ill. 60126—Complete array of orchids and supplies for growing them.

(38) *Helen's Cactus,* 2205 Mirasol, Brownsville, Tex. 78520—Send stamp for list.

(39) *Henrietta's Nursery,* 1345 N. Brawley Ave., Fresno, Calif. 93705—Cacti and other succulents; catalog 20¢.

(40) *Hilltop Farm,* Route 3, Box 216, Cleveland, Tex. 77327—Geraniums and herbs.

(41) *Sim T. Holmes,* 100 Tustarawas Rd., Beaver, Pa. 15009—African violets, miniature and regular; all grown under fluorescent lights.

(42) *The House of Violets,* 936 Garland St. S.W., Camden, Ark. 71701—Self-watering African violet planters.

(43) *House Plant Corner,* Box 5000, Cambridge, Md. 21613—Supplies and equipment for growing house plants; send 20¢ for catalog.

(44) *Spencer M. Howard Orchid Imports,* 11802 Huston St., N. Hollywood, Calif. 91607—Species and unusual orchids; free list.

(45) *Gordon M. Hoyt Orchids,* Seattle Heights, Wash. 98036—Complete listing of interesting orchids for the home grower.

(46) *Hydroponic Chemical Co.,* Copley, Ohio 44321—Special fertilizers for container gardening.

(47) *Margaret Ilgenfritz Orchids,* Blossom Lane, P.O. Box 1114, Monroe, Mich. 48161—Catalog $1.

(48) *Indoor Gardening Supplies,* P.O. Box 40551, Detroit, Mich. 48240—Fluorescent-light gardening equipment.

(49) *Jones and Scully,* 2200 N.W. 33rd Ave., Miami, Fla. 33142—Remarkable catalog of orchids and supplies for growing them; $3.50 per copy.

(50) *Kartuz Greenhouses,* 92 Chestnut St., Wilmington, Mass. 01887—Begonias, gesneriads, wide range of other plants for container gardening; catalog 25¢.

(51) *Kirkpatrick's,* 27785 De Anza St., Barstow, Calif. 92311—Cacti/succulents;

send stamp for list.

(52) *Kolb's Greenhouses,* 725 Belvidere Rd., Phillipsburg, N.J. 08865—African violets; send stamp for list.

(53) *J & D Lamps,* 245 S. Broadway, Yonkers, N.Y. 10705—Fluorescent-light gardening equipment.

(54) *Lauray,* Undermountain Rd., Rt. 41, Salisbury, Conn. 06068—Gesneriads, cacti/succulents, begonias; send 50¢ for catalog.

(55) *Logee's Greenhouses,* 55 North St., Danielson, Conn. 06239—Complete selection of rare and unusual plants for container gardening; catalog $1.

(56) *Lyndon Lyon,* 14 Mutchler St., Dolgeville, N.Y. 13329—African violets and other gesneriads.

(57) *Mary's African Violets,* 19788 San Juan, Detroit, Mich. 48221—Supplies and lighting equipment.

(58) *Earl May Seed & Nursery Co.,* Shenandoah, Iowa 51603—Flowers, vegetables, herbs, trees, shrubs, fruit to grow in containers.

(59) *Rod McLellan Co.,* 1450 El Camino Real, S. San Francisco, Calif. 94080—Orchids and supplies for growing them at home.

(60) *Merry Gardens,* Camden, Maine 04843 —House plants, herbs, unusual plants for container gardens; catalog $1.

(61) *Mini-Roses,* P.O. Box 245, Station A., Dallas, Tex. 75208—Miniature roses for container gardens.

(62) *Modlin's Cactus Gardens,* Rt. 4, Box 3035, Vista, Calif. 92083—Catalog 25¢.

(63) *Cactus by Mueller,* 10411 Rosedale Highway, Bakersfield, Calif. 93308—send stamp for list.

(64) *Nature's Way Products,* 3505 Mozart Ave., Cincinnati, Ohio 45211—Perlite, other soil conditioners, fertilizer, potting soils; send stamp for list.

(65) *Nichols Garden Nursery,* 1190 N. Pacific Highway, Albany, Ore. 97321—Unusual vegetables; herbs.

(66) *Walter F. Nicke,* Hudson, N.Y. 12534—Useful as well as unusual gardening supplies and equipment, much of it made in England.

(67) *Norvell Greenhouses,* 318 S. Greenacres Rd., Greenacres, Wash. 99016—House plants.

(68) *George W. Park Seed Co., Inc.,* Greenwood, S.C. 29646—Seeds, bulbs, fluorescent-light gardening supplies and equipment; very large, complete catalog, free for the asking.

(69) *Penn Valley Orchids,* 239 Old Gulph Rd., Wynnewood, Pa. 19096—Orchids.

(70) *Robert B. Peters Co., Inc.,* 2833 Pennsylvania St., Allentown, Pa.—Peters fertilizers, available in several formulations designed for specific growth responses.

(71) *Ra-Pid-Gro Corp.,* 88 Ossian, Dansville, N.Y. 14437—Manufacturers of Ra-Pid-Gro, root and foliar fertilizer.

(72) *Schmelling's African Violets,* 5133 Peck Hill Rd., Jamesville, N.Y. 13078—African violets; catalog 20¢.

(73) *Schultz Co.,* 11730 Northline, St. Louis, Mo. 63043—Manufacturers of excellent container garden fertilizer.

(74) *Sequoia Nursery,* 2519 E. Noble, Visalia, Calif. 93277—Miniature roses.

(75) *Shaffer's Tropical Gardens, Inc.,* 1220 41st Ave., Capitola, Calif. 95010—Orchids.

(76) *P. R. Sharp,* 104 N. Chapel Ave., #3, Alhambra, Calif. 91801—South American and Mexican cacti.

(77) *Shoplite Co., Inc.,* 566 Franklin Ave., Nutley, N.J. 07110—Fluorescent-light gardening equipment; catalog 25¢.

(78) *R. H. Shumway Seedsman,* Rockford, Ill. 61101—Flowers, vegetables, herbs, bulbs, fruit, trees, shrubs for container gardening.

(79) *Singers' Growing Things,* 6385 Enfield Ave., Reseda, Calif. 91335—Succulents for container gardens.

(80) *Smith's Cactus Garden,* P.O. Box 871, Paramount, Calif. 90723—Send 30¢ for list.

(81) *Star Roses,* Box 203, West Grove, Pa. 19390—Miniature roses, other woody plants for container gardening.

(82) *Fred A. Stewart, Inc., Orchids,* 1212 E. Las Tunas Dr., San Gabriel, Calif.

91778—Orchids.

(83) *Ed Storms,* 4223 Pershing, Ft. Worth, Tex. 76107—Lithops and other succulents.

(84) *Sunnybrook Farms,* 9448 Mayfield Rd., Chesterland, Ohio 44026—Herbs; scented geraniums; source for *Aloe vera,* the "unguentine plant."

(85) *Thompson & Morgan, Ltd.,* P.O. Box 24, Somerdale, N.J. 08083—Many unusual seeds of plants for container gardens.

(86) *Tinari Greenhouses,* Box 190, 2325 Valley Rd., Huntingdon Valley, Pa. 19006—African violets, gesneriads, supplies and equipment; catalog 25¢.

(87) *Tube Craft, Inc.,* 1311 W. 80th St., Cleveland, Ohio 44102—Fluorescent-light gardening equipment.

(88) *Volkmann Bros. Greenhouses,* 2714 Minert St., Dallas, Tex. 75219—Send stamped, self-addressed long envelope for catalog of African violets and supplies; Reservoir Wick Pot.

(89) *Wilson Brothers,* Roachdale, Ind. 47121 —Geraniums, begonias, many other flowering plants for container gardens.

(90) *H. E. Wise,* 3710 June St., San Bernardino, Calif. 92405—Cacti; send stamp for list.

(91) *Mrs. Ernie Wurster,* Route 1, Box 156, Elizabeth, Ill. 61028—African violets; send 15¢ for list.

# Appendix B

## Plant Societies and Periodicals

*African Violet Magazine,* bimonthly publication of the African Violet Society of America, Inc., Box 1326, Knoxville, Tenn. 37901.

*American Fern Journal,* quarterly publication of the American Fern Society, Biological Sciences Group, University of Connecticut, Storrs, Conn. 06268.

*American Horticulturist,* bimonthly publication of the American Horticultural Society, Mount Vernon, Va. 22121.

*American Ivy Society Bulletin,* periodical of the American Ivy Society, 128 W. 58th St., New York, N.Y. 10019.

*American Orchid Society Bulletin,* monthly publication of the American Orchid Society, Inc., Botanical Museum of Harvard University, Cambridge, Mass. 02138.

*The Begonian,* monthly of the American Begonia Society, Inc., 139 N. Ledoux Rd., Beverly Hills, Calif. 90211.

*Bonsai* (quarterly) and *Abstracts* (monthly newsletter), publications of the American Bonsai Society, 953 S. Shore Dr., Lake Waukomis, Parksville, Mo. 64151.

*Bonsai Magazine,* ten times a year, publication of Bonsai Clubs International, 445 Blake St., Menlo Park, Calif. 94025.

*The Bromeliad Journal,* bimonthly publication of the Bromeliad Society, Inc., P.O. Box 3279, Santa Monica, Calif. 90403.

*Cactus and Succulent Journal,* bimonthly publication of the Cactus and Succulent Society of America, Inc., Box 167, Reseda, Calif. 91335.

*The Camellia Journal,* quarterly publication of the American Camellia Society, Box 212, Fort Valley, Ga. 31030.

*Cymbidium Society News,* monthly publication

of the Cymbidium Society of America, Inc., 6787 Worsham Dr., Whittier, Calif. 90602.

*Epiphyllum Bulletin,* publication of the Epiphyllum Society of America, Inc., 218 E. Greystone Ave., Monrovia, Calif. 91016.

*Geraniums Around the World,* quarterly publication of the International Geranium Society, 11960 Pascal Ave., Colton, Calif. 92324.

*Gesneriad Saintpaulia News,* bimonthly publication of the American Gesneriad Society, 11983 Darlington Ave., Los Angeles, Calif. 90049.

*Gesneriad Saintpaulia News,* bimonthly publication of Saintpaulia International, P.O. Box 10604, Knoxville, Tenn. 37919.

*The Gloxinian,* bimonthly publication of the American Gloxinia/Gesneriad Society, Inc., P.O. Box 174, New Milford, Conn. 06776.

*Light Garden,* bimonthly publication of the Indoor Light Gardening Society of America, Inc., 128 W. 58th St., New York, N.Y. 10019.

*Monthly Fern Lessons,* with newsletter and annual magazine, publications of the Los Angeles International Fern Society, 2423 Burritt Ave., Redondo Beach, Calif. 90278.

*The National Fuchsia Fan,* monthly publication of the National Fuchsia Society, 10934 E. Flory St., Whittier, Calif. 90606.

*The Orchid Digest,* 25 Ash Ave., Corte Madera, Calif. 94925.

*Plantlife-Amaryllis Yearbook,* bulletin of the American Plant Life Society, Box 150, La Jolla, Calif. 92037.

*Plants Alive,* monthly magazine about indoor gardening, 1255 Portland Place, Boulder, Colo. 80302.

*Popular Gardening Indoors,* quarterly periodical, published by CBS Publications/Popular Magazine Group, 383 Madison Avenue, New York, N.Y. 10017.

*Princepes,* quarterly publication of the Palm Society, 1320 S. Venetian Way, Miami, Fla. 33139.

*Seed Pod,* quarterly publication of the American Hibiscus Society, Box 98, Eagle Lake, Fla. 33139.

*Terrarium Topics,* published by The Terrarium Association, 57 Wolfpit Ave., Norwalk, Conn. 06851.

*Under Glass,* bimonthly devoted to home greenhouse growing; c/o Lord and Burnham, Irvington, N.Y. 10533.

# Index